Fundamentals of
Corporate Finance

Second
Edition

Fundamentals of Corporate Finance

Stephen A. Ross
Yale University

Randolph W. Westerfield
University of Southern California

Bradford D. Jordan
University of Missouri-Columbia

IRWIN

Burr Ridge, Illinois
Boston, Massachusetts
Sydney, Australia

Executive editor: Michael W. Junior
Sponsoring editor: Joanne Dorff
Marketing manager: Ron Bloecher
Project editor: Gladys True
Production manager: Bette K. Ittersagen
Cover and interior design: Jeanne Calabrese
Cover, part, and chapter illustrations: Thomas Hennessy
Art manager: Kim Meriwether
Compositor: Beacon Graphics Corp.
Typeface: 10/12 Times Roman
Printer: Von Hoffmann Press

Library of Congress Cataloging-in-Publication Data

Ross, Stephen A.
  Fundamentals of corporate finance/Stephen A. Ross, Randolph W.
Westerfield, Bradford D. Jordan—2nd. ed.
    p.   cm.—(The Irwin series in finance)
  Includes index.
  ISBN 0-256-11113-8.—ISBN 0-256-12873-1 (International ed.) ISBN 0-7863-18591-3 (Special ed.)
  1. Corporations—Finance. I. Westerfield, Randolph. II. Jordan,
Bradford D. III. Title. IV. Series
  HG4026.R677 1993
  658.15—dc20

92–28101

Printed in the United States of America
  2 3 4 5 6 7 8 9 0 VH 9 8 7 6 5 4

To our families and friends with love and gratitude.

S. A. R.
R. W. W.
B. D. J.

Irwin Series in Finance

The Irwin Series in Finance
Consulting Editor Stephen A. Ross
Sterling Professor of Economics and Finance
Yale University

FINANCIAL MANAGEMENT

Block and Hirt
Foundations of Financial Management
Sixth Edition

Brooks
PC FinGame
First Edition

Brooks
FinGame: The Financial Management Decision Game
Third Edition

Bruner
Case Studies in Finance: Managing for Corporate Value Creation
First Edition

Fruhan, Kester, Mason, Piper, and Ruback
Case Problems in Finance
Tenth Edition

Harrington
Corporate Financial Analysis: Decisions in a Global Environment
Fourth Edition

Helfert
Techniques of Financial Analysis
Seventh Edition

Higgins
Analysis for Financial Management
Third Edition

Jones
Introduction to Financial Management
First Edition

Ross, Westerfield, and Jordan
Fundamentals of Corporate Finance
Second Edition

Ross, Westerfield, and Jaffe
Corporate Finance
Third Edition

Schary
Cases in Financial Management
First Edition

Stonehill and Eiteman
Finance: An International Perspective
First Edition

INVESTMENTS

Bodie, Kane, and Marcus
Essentials of Investments
First Edition

Bodie, Kane, and Marcus
Investments
Second Edition

Cohen, Zinbarg, Zeikel
Investment Analysis and Portfolio Management
Fifth Edition

Hirt and Block
Fundamentals of Investment Management
Fourth Edition

Lorie, Dodd, and Kimpton
The Stock Market: Theories & Evidence
Second Edition

FINANCIAL INSTITUTIONS AND MARKETS

Rose
Readings on Financial Institutions and Markets
Fourth Edition

Rose
Money and Capital Markets: The Financial System in an Increasingly Global Economy
Fifth Edition

Rose
Commercial Bank Management: Producing and Selling Financial Services
Second Edition

Rose, Kolari, and Fraser
Financial Institutions: Understanding & Managing Financial Services
Fourth Edition

REAL ESTATE

Berston
California Real Estate Practice
Fifth Edition

Berston
California Real Estate Principles
Sixth Edition

Brueggeman and Fisher
Real Estate Finance
Ninth Edition

Smith and Corgel
Real Estate Perspectives: An Introduction to Real Estate
Second Edition

Shenkel
Real Estate Finance
First Edition

FINANCIAL PLANNING AND INSURANCE

Allen, Melone, Rosenbloom, and VanDerhei
Pension Planning: Pensions, Profit-Sharing, and Other Deferred Compensation Plans
Seventh Edition

Crawford and Beadles
Law and the Life Insurance Contract
Sixth Edition

Hirsch and Donaldson
Casualty Claims Practice
Fifth Edition

Kapoor, Dlabay, and Hughes
Personal Finance
Second Edition

Kellison
Theory of Interest
Second Edition

Rokes
Human Relations in Handling Insurance Claims
Revised Edition

About the Authors

Stephen A. Ross, *Yale University*

Stephen Ross has held the position of Sterling Professor of Economics and Finance at Yale University since 1985. One of the most widely published authors in finance and economics, Professor Ross is recognized for his work in developing the Arbitrage Pricing Theory. He has also made substantial contributions to the discipline through his research in signalling, agency theory, options, and the theory of the term structure of interest rates. Previously the president of the American Finance Association, he serves as an associate editor of the *Journal of Finance* and the *Journal of Economic Theory*. He is co-chairman of Roll and Ross Asset Management Corporation.

Randolph W. Westerfield, *University of Southern California*

Randolph Westerfield is Chairman of the Finance and Business Economics Department and Charles B. Thornton Professor of Finance at the University of Southern California.

Dr. Westerfield came to USC from the Wharton School, University of Pennsylvania, where he was Chairman of the Finance Department and Senior Research Associate at the Rodney L. White Center for Financial Research. For three consecutive years, the Wharton Student Committee on Undergraduate Teaching Evaluation awarded him the highest score for teaching undergraduate finance.

His research interests are in corporate financial policy, investment management and analysis, mergers and acquisitions, and pension fund management. Dr. Westerfield has served as a member of the Continental Bank (Philadelphia) trust committee. He has also been a consultant to a number of corporations, including AT&T, Mobil Oil Corp., and Westinghouse, as well as to the United Nations and the U.S. Departments of Justice and Labor. Dr. Westerfield is the author of more than 30 monographs and articles.

Bradford D. Jordan, *University of Missouri–Columbia*

Bradford Jordan is Associate Professor of Finance at the University of Missouri. He has a longstanding interest in both applied and theoretical issues in corporate finance, and he has extensive experience teaching all levels of corporate finance and financial management policy. Professor Jordan has published numerous articles on issues such as cost of capital, capital structure, and the behavior of security prices. He currently is a director of the Southern Finance Association, and he is Ph.D. Coordinator for the Finance Department at the University of Missouri.

"Statistics are no substitute for judgment."
Henry Clay

I wanted to be a manager, but I never wanted to be a financial manager. After all, I was going to be an editor. Let someone else worry about the numbers.

When I took this course, the book I used only served to reinforce these opinions. It dragged me through an endless, detached set of equations and computations, never linking the various components together. I had no chance to discover what I know today: finance is an intriguing subject that influences virtually every business decision made by all managers—even editors.

By selecting *Fundamentals of Corporate Finance,* your professor has demonstrated a genuine interest in your future as a manager. The topics covered in this book are linked to one another and to the other subject areas you are studying. Instructors worldwide have recognized the benefit of assigning this text. It not only provides you with the underlying principles and how they fit together; it supplies a basic logic for financial decision making.

Although there are many factors contributing to the popularity of *Fundamentals of Corporate Finance,* the considerable emphasis placed on managerial judgment has been frequently proclaimed a favorite. The authors continually reinforce the message that as decision makers we must make informed judgments, not simply calculate solutions by filling in missing variables in distinct and unrelated formulas. Few real-world finance issues have tailor-made equations where plug and chug is the only job at hand.

The formulas and equations found in this book are extremely valuable in helping a manager make correct decisions; however, it is you, the manager, who must determine the inputs that make these techniques invaluable. After studying *Fundamentals of Corporate Finance,* you will be prepared to face dynamic managerial challenges as you strive to make the best decisions.

Michael W. Junior

In the 1990s, the challenge of financial management is greater than ever. The previous decade brought fundamental changes in financial markets and instruments, and the practice of corporate finance continues to evolve rapidly. Often, what was yesterday's state of the art is commonplace today, and it is essential that our finance courses and finance texts do not get left behind. *Fundamentals of Corporate Finance* provides what we believe is a modern, unified treatment of financial management that is suitable for beginning students.

The Underlying Philosophy

Rapid and extensive changes place new burdens on the teaching of corporate finance. On the one hand, it is much more difficult to keep materials up to date. On the other, the permanent must be distinguished from the temporary to avoid following what is merely the latest fad. Our solution is to stress the modern fundamentals of finance and to make the subject come alive with contemporary examples. As we emphasize throughout this book, we view the subject of corporate finance as the working of a small number of integrated and very powerful intuitions.

From our survey of existing introductory textbooks, including the ones we have used, this commonsense approach seems to be the exception rather than the rule. All too often, the beginning student views corporate finance as a collection of unrelated topics which are unified by virtue of being bound together between the covers of one book. In many cases, this perception is only natural because the subject is treated in a way that is both topic oriented and procedural. Commonly, emphasis is placed on detailed and specific "solutions" to certain narrowly posed problems. How often have we heard students exclaim that they could solve a particular problem if only they knew which formula to use?

We think this approach misses the forest for the trees. As time passes, the details fade, and what remains, if we are successful, is a sound grasp of the underlying principles. This is why our overriding concern, from the first page to the last, is with the basic logic of financial decision making.

Distinctive Features

Our general philosophy is apparent in the following ways:

An Emphasis on Intuition   We are always careful to separate and explain the principles at work on an intuitive level before launching into any specifics. The underlying ideas are discussed first in very general terms and then by way of examples that illustrate in more concrete terms how a financial manager might proceed in a given situation.

A Unified Valuation Approach   Many texts pay only lip service to net present value (NPV) as the basic concept of corporate finance and stop short of consistently integrating this important principle. The most basic notion, that NPV represents the excess of market value over cost, tends to get lost in an overly mechanical approach to NPV that emphasizes computation at the expense of understanding. Every subject covered in *Fundamentals of Corporate Finance* is firmly rooted in valuation, and care is taken throughout to explain how particular decisions have valuation effects.

A Managerial Focus   Students won't lose sight of the fact that financial management concerns *management*. Throughout the text, the role of the financial manager as decision maker is emphasized, and the need for managerial input and judgment is stressed. "Black box" approaches to finance are consciously avoided.

In *Fundamentals of Corporate Finance,* these three themes work together to provide consistent treatment, a sound foundation, and a practical, workable understanding of how to evaluate financial decisions.

Intended Audience

This text is designed and developed explicitly for a first course in business or corporate finance. The typical student will not have previously taken a course in finance, and no previous knowledge of finance is assumed. Since this course is frequently part of a common business core, the text is intended for majors and nonmajors alike. In terms of background or prerequisites, the book is nearly self-contained. Some familiarity with basic accounting principles is assumed, but even these are reviewed very early on. The only other tool the student needs is basic algebra. As a result, students with very different backgrounds will find the text very accessible.

Coverage

From the start, *Fundamentals of Corporate Finance* contains innovative coverage on a wide variety of subjects. For example, Chapter 4, on long-term financial planning, contains a thorough discussion of the sustainable growth rate as a planning tool. Chapter 9, on project analysis and evaluation, contains an extensive discussion of how to evaluate NPV estimates. Chapter 10, on capital market history, discusses in detail the famous Ibbotson-Sinquefield study and the nature of capital market risks and returns. Chapter 13, on selling securities to the public, contains a modern, up-to-date discussion of IPOs and the costs of going public.

This is just a sampling. Because *Fundamentals of Corporate Finance* is not a "me-too" book, we have taken a very close look at what is likely to be relevant in the 1990s, and we have taken a fresh, modern approach to many traditional subjects. In doing so, we eliminated topics of dubious relevance, downplayed purely theoretical issues, and minimized the use of extensive and elaborate computations to illustrate points that are either intuitively obvious or of limited practical use.

Unlike virtually any other introductory text, *Fundamentals of Corporate Finance* provides extensive real-world practical advice and guidance. We try to go beyond just presenting dry, standard textbook material to show how to actually *use* the tools discussed in the text. When necessary, the approximate, pragmatic nature of some types of financial analysis is made explicit, possible pitfalls are described, and limitations are outlined.

Attention to Pedagogy

In addition to illustrating pertinent concepts and presenting up-to-date coverage, *Fundamentals of Corporate Finance* strives to present the material in a way that makes it coherent and easy to understand. To meet the varied needs of its intended audience, *Fundamentals of Corporate Finance* is rich in valuable learning tools, including:

Extensive Examples, Questions, and Problems

1. *Examples.* Every chapter contains a variety of detailed, worked-out examples. These examples are found both in the main body of the text and separately as numbered examples that correspond to the main text. Based on our classroom testing, these examples are among the most useful learnings aids because they provide both detail and explanation.

2. *Concept Questions.* Chapter sections are kept relatively short and are followed by a series of concept questions that provide a quick check concerning the material just covered. Because they highlight key concepts, we have found that students rely heavily on them when reviewing chapter material.

3. *Self-Test Questions.* At the end of each chapter, comprehensive self-test questions appear. They are followed by detailed solutions (with final answers shown in green) and comments on the solutions. These frequently combine topics covered in the chapter to illustrate how they fit together.

4. *End-of-Chapter Problems.* Finally, we have found that students learn better when they have plenty of opportunity for practice. We therefore provide extensive end-of-chapter questions and problems. For the most part, there are at least 20, and as many as 63, problems for each chapter. This greatly exceeds what is typical in an introductory textbook.

   The questions and problems range in difficulty from relatively easy practice problems to thought-provoking "challenge" problems designed to intrigue enthusiastic students. All problems are fully annotated so that students and instructors can readily identify particular types. Throughout the text, we have worked to supply interesting problems that illustrate real-world applications of chapter material.

Boxed Essays   A unique series of brief essays entitled "In Their Own Words" is written by distinguished scholars and practitioners on key topics in the text. To name just a few, these include essays by Merton Miller on capital structure, Richard Roll on security prices, and Fischer Black on dividends. In all cases, the essays are enlightening, informative, and entertaining.

Other Chapter Features   Other features, designed to promote learning, include:

1. *Key Terms.* Within each chapter, key terms are highlighted in **boldface** type the first time they appear. Key terms are defined in the text, and there is a running glossary in the margins of the text for quick reminders. For reference there is a comprehensive list of key terms at the end of each chapter.

2. *Key Concept Call-Outs.* Throughout the text, key concepts are broken out separately from the main body of the text and set in color for special emphasis.

3. *Key Result Summary Tables.* Most chapters contain at least one table that succinctly summarizes key principles, results, and equations.

4. *Formula Appendix.* For ease of reference (and formula-sheet preparation), an appendix contains a chapter-by-chapter annotated listing of all the important formulas in the text.

5. *Chapter Reviews.* Each chapter ends with a summary that enumerates the key points and provides an overall perspective on the chapter material.

6. *Suggested Readings.* A short, annotated list of books and articles to which the interested reader may refer for additional information follows each chapter.

7. *Writing Style.* To better engage the reader, the writing style in *Fundamentals of Corporate Finance* is informal. Throughout, we try to convey our considerable enthusiasm for the subject. Students consistently find the relaxed style approachable and likable.

New in the Second Edition

Our new, four-color format is the most obvious change from the first edition. In going this route, we concentrated on using color in ways that made pedagogical sense, rather than using it in a merely decorative way. We use color as a learning tool in a variety of ways—to tie together text, tables, and figures; to highlight key results and equations; to distinguish important terms and concepts; and to draw attention to central calculations and figure elements. A more detailed discussion of color usage can be found inside the back cover of the text. We highly recommend that you refer to this discussion throughout the course; as you begin each chapter, check to see if color will be playing a particular role.

We are especially pleased with the new in-text acetate contained in Chapter 15. Here we combined a detailed color scheme with a series of transparent overlays to illustrate the basics of capital structure and cost of capital as tax and bankruptcy effects are brought into play. The result is a visually effective, building-block approach to optimal capital structure.

We've also added two completely new chapters. First, in response to requests from some of our first edition adopters, Chapter 23 covers leasing in an approachable, straightforward way that is suitable for a principles class. Second, we think that corporate risk management and financial engineering are only going to become more important, so Chapter 24 provides a survey of this rapidly growing area. To our knowledge, no other text contains similar material. We placed these two new chapters at the end of the text to minimize changes in course material for our existing users, but, based on user feedback, we will move them into the section on long-term financing in future editions.

Our working capital chapters have been extensively revised. Chapter 18, our cash management chapter, contains a fully up-to-date discussion of modern practice. We've added to and improved our credit management discussion in Chapter 19, and based on user requests, we've added completely new coverage of inventory management.

Beyond these major changes, we made a very large number of very small changes to update and fine tune our coverage. We simplified our discussion in various places to keep the level of presentation completely consistent, we beefed up international examples throughout, and we made our discussion as current as possible.

Organization of the Text

We have found that the phrase "so much to do, so little time" accurately describes an introductory finance course. For this reason, we designed *Fundamentals of Corporate Finance* to be as flexible and modular as possible. There are a total of nine parts, and, in broad terms, the instructor is free to decide the particular sequence. Further, within each part, the first chapter generally contains an overview and survey. Thus, when time is limited, subsequent chapters can be omitted. Finally, the sections placed early in each chapter are generally the most important, and later sections frequently can be omitted without loss of continuity. For these reasons, the instructor has great control over the topics covered, the sequence in which they are covered, and the depth of coverage.

Part One of the text contains two chapters. Chapter 1 considers the goal of the corporation, the corporate form of organization, the agency problem, and, briefly, financial markets. Chapter 2 succinctly discusses cash flow versus accounting income, market value versus book value, and taxes. It also provides a useful review of financial statements.

After Part One, either Part Two, on financial statements analysis, long-range planning, and corporate growth, or Part Three, on time value and stock and bond valuation, follows naturally. Part Two can be omitted entirely if desired. After Part Three, most instructors will probably want to move directly into Part Four, which covers net present value, discounted cash flow valuation, and capital budgeting.

Part Five contains two chapters on risk and return. The first one, on market history, is designed to give students a feel for typical rates of return on risky assets. The second one discusses the expected return/risk tradeoff, and it develops the security market line in a highly intuitive way that bypasses much of the usual portfolio theory and statistics.

The first chapter of Part Six introduces long-term financing by discussing the essential features of debt and equity instruments. Important elements of bankruptcy and reorganization are covered briefly as well. The second chapter in Part Six covers selling securities to the public with an emphasis on the role of the investment banker and the costs of going public. Because both chapters contain a fair amount of descriptive material, they can easily be assigned as out-of-class reading as time constraints dictate.

Cost of capital, capital structure, and dividend policy are covered in the three consecutive chapters of Part Seven. The chapter on dividends can be covered independently, if desired, and the chapter on capital structure can be omitted without creating loss of continuity.

Part Eight covers issues in short-term financial management. The first of the three chapters is a general survey of short-term management, which is very useful when time does not permit a more in-depth treatment. The next two chapters provide greater detail on cash, credit, and inventory management.

Last, Part Nine covers five important topics: options and optionlike securities, mergers, international finance, leasing, and financial engineering. These chapters contain somewhat greater depth of coverage than the basic text chapters and may be covered partially in courses where time is constrained or completely in courses that give special emphasis to these topics.

Acknowledgments

To borrow a phrase, writing an introductory finance textbook is easy; all you do is sit down at a word processor and open a vein. We never would have completed this book without the incredible amount of help and support we received from literally dozens of our colleagues, editors, family members, and friends. We would like to thank, without implicating, all of you.

Clearly, our greatest debt is to our many colleagues who took the plunge and used the first edition. Needless to say, without this support, there never would have been a second edition!

A great many of our colleagues read the original drafts of our first edition. The fact that this book has so little in common with those drafts is a reflection of the value we placed on the many comments and suggestions that we received. Our second edition reviewers continued this tradition and kept us working to improve the content, organization, and exposition of our text. To the following reviewers, then, we are grateful for their many contributions:

Scott Besley: *University of South Florida*

Ray Brooks: *University of Missouri-Columbia*

Charles C. Bown: *Eastern Washington University*

Charles M. Cox: *Brigham Young University*

Michael Dunn: *California State University, Northridge*

Adrian C. Edwards: *Western Michigan University*

Thomas H. Eyssell: *University of Missouri, St. Louis*

Deborah Ann Ford: *University of Baltimore*

Darryl E. J. Gurley: *Northeastern University*

John M. Harris, Jr.: *Clemson University*

Delvin D. Hawley: *University of Mississippi*

Robert C. Higgins: *University of Washington, Seattle*

Steve Isberg: *University of Baltimore*

James M. Johnson: *Northern Illinois University*

Jarl G. Kallberg: *New York University*

David N. Ketcher: *Drake University*

Morris A. Lamberson: *University of Central Arkansas*

Dubos J. Masson: *University of Denver*

Richard R. Mendenhall: *University of Notre Dame*

Lalatendu Misra: *University of Texas, San Antonio*

Michael J. Murray: *Winona State University (Minnesota)*

Gladys E. Perry: *Roosevelt University (Illinois)*

Pamela P. Peterson: *Florida State University*

George A. Racette: *University of Oregon*

Ron Reiber: *Canisius College*

Jay R. Ritter: *University of Illinois at Urbana-Champaign*

Ricardo J. Rodriguez: *University of Miami*

Martha A. Schary: *Boston University*

Roger Severns: *Mankato State University*

Dilip K. Shome: *Virginia Polytechnic Institute and State University*

Neil W. Sicherman: *University of South Carolina*

George S. Swales, Jr.: *Southwest Missouri State University*

Rolf K. Tedefalk: *University of New Haven*

John G. Thatcher: *Marquette University*

Harry Thiewes: *Mankato State University*

Michael R. Vetsuypens: *Southern Methodist University*

David J. Wright: *University of Notre Dame*

Steve B. Wyatt: *University of Cincinnati*

J. Kenton Zumwalt: *Colorado State University*

Several of our most respected colleagues contributed original essays, which are entitled "In Their Own Words" and appear in selected chapters. To these individuals we extend a special thanks:

Edward I. Altman: *New York University*

Fischer Black: *Goldman Sachs & Co.*

Robert C. Higgins: *University of Washington*

Roger Ibbotson: *Yale University, Ibbotson Associates*

Michael C. Jensen: *Harvard University*

Jarl Kallberg: *New York University*

Richard M. Levich: *New York University*

Robert C. Merton: *Harvard University*

Merton H. Miller: *University of Chicago*

Jay R. Ritter: *University of Illinois at Urbana-Champaign*

Richard Roll: *University of California at Los Angeles*

Charles W. Smithson: *The Chase Manhattan Bank, N.A.*

Stender E. Sweeney: *Times Mirror Company*

Samuel C. Weaver: *Hershey Foods Corporation*

We owe a particular debt to those instructors who risked their teacher evaluations by classroom testing our text in its different incarnations. Of this group, we especially thank Wayne Mikkelson, Megan Partch, and Gordon Melms of the University of Oregon, who offered unsolicited feedback while teaching from the text. And, to the hundreds of students at various universities who suffered through classroom testing of this text, our special thanks.

The following University of Missouri doctoral students did outstanding work for the first and second editions of *Fundamentals:* Susan Chiou, Cheri Etling, Randy Jorgensen, Tie Su, Paul Weise, and Michael Young. To them fell the unenviable task of technical proofreading and, in particular, of carefully checking calculations throughout the text. David Ketcher of Drake University provided especially valuable help in checking answers to our end-of-chapter problems.

Finally, in every phase of this project, we have been privileged to have had the complete and unwavering support of a great organization: Richard D. Irwin, Inc. We are deeply grateful to the select group of professionals that served as our development team. They are: Ron Bloecher, Joanne Dorff, Lew Gossage, Bette Ittersagen, Mike Junior, Rita McMullen, Ann Sass, Gladys True, and Michael Warrell.

Of this group, two deserve particular mention. First, with charm, grace, and tenaciousness, Ann Sass, our longtime and long-suffering developmental editor, coordinated all of the people involved on a day-to-day basis, made sure that the authors kept their promises about deadlines, and generally kept track of thousands of details. Second, Mike Junior, the executive editor, worked with us on this book from conception to completion. As only he can attest, this was no easy task. For his unflagging enthusiasm and support, then, our special appreciation. Others at Irwin, too numerous to list here, have improved this book in countless ways.

Throughout the development of this edition, we have taken great care to discover and eliminate errors. Our goal is to provide the best textbook available on the subject. We want to ensure that future editions are error free, and, to that end, we will gladly offer $10 per arithmetic error to the first individual reporting it as a modest token of our appreciation. More than this, we would like to hear from instructors and students alike. Please write and tell us how to make this a better text. Forward your comments to: Professor Randolph W. Westerfield, School of Business Administration, University of Southern California, University Park, Los Angeles, CA 90089-1421.

Stephen A. Ross
Randolph W. Westerfield
Bradford D. Jordan

Brief Contents

Contents

List of *In Their Own Words* Boxes

Fundamentals of Corporate Finance

Chapter 1

Introduction to Corporate Finance

To begin our study of modern corporate finance and financial management, we need to address two central issues. First, what is corporate finance and what is the role of the financial manager in the corporation? Second, what is the goal of financial management? To describe the financial management environment, we consider the corporate form of organization and discuss some conflicts that can arise within the corporation. We also take a brief look at financial markets in the United States.

CORPORATE FINANCE AND THE FINANCIAL MANAGER | 1.1

In this section, we discuss where the financial manager fits in the corporation. We start by defining corporate finance and the financial manager's job.

What Is Corporate Finance?

Imagine that you were to start your own business. No matter what type you started, you would have to answer the following three questions in some form or another:

1. What long-term investments should you take on? That is, what lines of business will you be in and what sorts of buildings, machinery, and equipment will you need?
2. Where will you get the long-term financing to pay for your investment? Will you bring in other owners or will you borrow the money?

3. How will you manage your everyday financial activities such as collecting from customers and paying suppliers?

These are not the only questions by any means, but they are among the most important. Corporate finance, broadly speaking, is the study of ways to answer these three questions. Accordingly, we'll be looking at each of them in the chapters ahead.

The Financial Manager

A striking feature of large corporations is that the owners (the stockholders) are usually not directly involved in making business decisions, particularly on a day-to-day basis. Instead, the corporation employs managers to represent the owners' interests and make decisions on their behalf. In a large corporation, the financial manager would be in charge of answering the three questions we raised above.

The financial management function is usually associated with a top officer of the firm, such as a vice president of finance or some other chief financial officer (CFO). Figure 1.1 is a simplified organizational chart that highlights the finance activity in a large firm. As shown, the vice president of finance coordinates the activities of the treasurer and the controller. The controller's office handles cost and financial accounting, tax payments, and management information systems. The treasurer's office is responsible for managing the firm's cash and credit, its financial planning, and its capital expenditures. These treasury activities are all related to the three general questions raised above, and the chapters ahead deal primarily with these issues. Our study thus bears mostly on activities usually associated with the treasurer's office.

Financial Management Decisions

As our discussion above suggests, the financial manager must be concerned with three basic types of questions. We consider these in greater detail next.

capital budgeting

The process of planning and managing a firm's long-term investments.

Capital Budgeting   The first question concerns the firm's long-term investments. The process of planning and managing a firm's long-term investments is called **capital budgeting**. In capital budgeting, the financial manager tries to identify investment opportunities that are worth more to the firm than they cost to acquire. Loosely speaking, this means that the value of the cash flow generated by an asset exceeds the cost of that asset.

Financial managers must be concerned with not only how much cash they expect to receive, but also with when they expect to receive it and how likely they are to receive it. Evaluating the *size, timing,* and *risk* of future cash flows is the essence of capital budgeting. How to do so is discussed in detail in the chapters ahead.

capital structure

The mixture of debt and equity maintained by a firm.

Capital Structure   The second question for the financial manager concerns how the firm obtains and manages the long-term financing it needs to support its long-term investments. A firm's **capital structure** (or financial structure) refers to the specific mixture of long-term debt and equity the firm

Figure 1.1

A simplified organizational chart. The exact titles and organization differ from company to company.

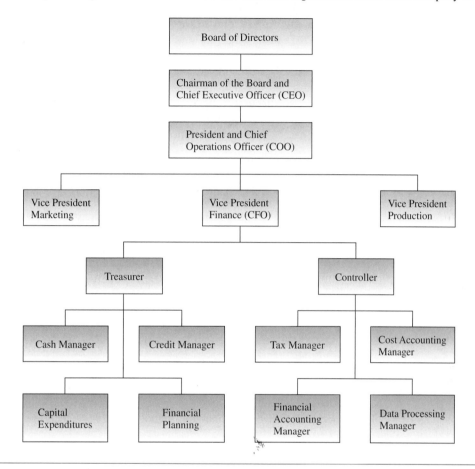

uses to finance its operations. The financial manager has two concerns in this area. First, how much should the firm borrow; that is, what mixture of debt and equity is best? The mixture chosen will affect both the risk and value of the firm. Second, what are the least expensive sources of funds for the firm?

If we picture the firm as a pie, then the firm's capital structure determines how that pie is sliced. In other words, what percentage of the firm's cash flow goes to creditors and what percentage goes to shareholders? Firms have a great deal of flexibility in choosing a financial structure. Whether one structure is better than any other for a particular firm is the heart of the capital structure issue.

In addition to deciding on the financing mix, the financial manager has to decide exactly how and where to raise the money. The expenses associated with raising long-term financing can be considerable, so different possibilities must be carefully evaluated. Also, corporations borrow money from a variety of lenders in a number of different, and sometimes exotic, ways. Choosing among lenders and among loan types is another of the jobs handled by the financial manager.

working capital

A firm's short-term assets and liabilities.

Working Capital Management   The third question concerns **working capital** management. The phrase *working capital* refers to a firm's short-term assets, such as inventory, and its short-term liabilities, such as money owed to suppliers. Managing the firm's working capital is a day-to-day activity that ensures the firm has sufficient resources to continue its operations and avoid costly interruptions. This involves a number of activities all related to the firm's receipt and disbursement of cash.

Some of the questions about working capital that must be answered are: (1) How much cash and inventory should we keep on hand? (2) Should we sell on credit? If so, what terms will we offer, and to whom will we extend them? (3) How will we obtain any needed short-term financing? Will we purchase on credit or will we borrow short-term and pay cash? If we borrow short-term, how and where should we do it? This is just a small sample of the issues that arise in managing a firm's working capital.

The three areas of corporate financial management we have described — capital budgeting, capital structure, and working capital management — are very broad categories. Each includes a rich variety of topics, and we have indicated only a few of the questions that arise in the different areas. The chapters ahead contain greater detail.

⌐CONCEPT QUESTIONS

1.1a What is the capital budgeting decision?

1.1b What do you call the specific mixture of long-term debt and equity that a firm chooses to use?

1.1c Into what category of financial management does cash management fall?

1.2 | THE CORPORATE FORM OF BUSINESS ORGANIZATION

Large firms in the United States, such as IBM and Exxon, are almost all organized as corporations. We examine the three different legal forms of business organization — sole proprietorship, partnership, and corporation — to see why this is so. Each of the three forms has distinct advantages and disadvantages in terms of the life of the business, the ability of the business to raise cash, and taxes. A key observation is that, as a firm grows, the advantages of the corporate form may come to outweigh the disadvantages.

Sole Proprietorship

sole proprietorship

A business owned by a single individual.

A **sole proprietorship** is a business owned by one person. This is the simplest type of business to start and is the least regulated form of organization. Depending on where you live, you can start up a proprietorship by doing little more than getting a business license and opening your doors. For this reason, many businesses that later become large corporations start out as small proprietorships, and there are more proprietorships than any other type of business.

The owner of a sole proprietorship keeps all the profits. That's the good news. The bad news is that the owner has *unlimited liability* for business debts. This means that creditors can look beyond business assets to the proprietor's personal assets for payment. Similarly, there is no distinction between personal and business income, so all business income is taxed as personal income.

The life of a sole proprietorship is limited to the owner's life span, and, importantly, the amount of equity that can be raised is limited to the proprietor's personal wealth. This limitation often means that the business cannot exploit new opportunities because of insufficient capital. Ownership of a sole proprietorship may be difficult to transfer since this requires the sale of the entire business to a new owner.

Partnership

A **partnership** is similar to a proprietorship, except that there are two or more owners (partners). In a *general partnership,* all the partners share in gains or losses, and all have unlimited liability for *all* partnership debts, not just some particular share. The way partnership gains (and losses) are divided is described in the *partnership agreement.* This agreement can be an informal oral agreement, such as "let's start a lawn mowing business," or a lengthy, formal written document.

In a *limited partnership,* one or more *general partners* will run the business and have unlimited liability, but there will be one or more *limited partners* who will not actively participate in the business. A limited partner's liability for business debts is limited to the amount that she contributes to the partnership. This form of organization is common in real estate ventures, for example.

The advantages and disadvantages of a partnership are basically the same as those for a proprietorship. Partnerships based on a relatively informal agreement are easy and inexpensive to form. General partners have unlimited liability for partnership debts, and the partnership terminates when a general partner wishes to sell out or dies. All income is taxed as personal income to the partners, and the amount of equity that can be raised is limited to the partners' combined wealth. Ownership by a general partner is not easily transferred because a new partnership must be formed. A limited partner's interest can be sold without dissolving the partnership, but finding a buyer may be difficult.

Based on our discussion, the primary disadvantages of sole proprietorships and partnerships as forms of business organization are (1) unlimited liability for business debts on the part of the owners, (2) limited life of the business, and (3) difficulty of transferring ownership. These three disadvantages add up to a single, central problem: the ability of such businesses to grow can be seriously limited by an inability to raise cash for investment.

partnership
A business formed by two or more individuals or entities.

Corporation

The **corporation** is the most important form (in terms of size) of business organization in the United States. A corporation is a legal "person" separate and distinct from its owners, and it has many of the rights, duties, and privileges of an actual person. Corporations can borrow money and own property, can sue

corporation
A business created as a distinct legal entity composed of one or more individuals or entities.

and be sued, and can enter into contracts. A corporation can even be a general partner or a limited partner in a partnership, and a corporation can own stock in another corporation.

Not surprisingly, starting a corporation is somewhat more complicated than starting the other forms of business organization, but not greatly so for a small business. Forming a corporation involves preparing *articles of incorporation* (or a charter) and a set of *bylaws*. The articles of incorporation must contain a number of things, including the corporation's name, its intended life (which can be forever), its business purpose, and the number of shares that can be issued. This information must normally be supplied to the state in which the firm will be incorporated. For most legal purposes, the corporation is a "resident" of that state.

The bylaws are rules describing how the corporation regulates its own existence. For example, the bylaws describe how directors are elected. These bylaws may be a very simple statement of a few rules and procedures, or they may be quite extensive for a large corporation. The bylaws may be amended or extended from time to time by the stockholders.

In a large corporation, the stockholders and the managers are usually separate groups. The stockholders elect the board of directors, who then select the managers. Management is charged with running the corporation's affairs in the stockholders' interest. In principle, stockholders control the corporation because they elect the directors.

As a result of the separation of ownership and management, the corporate form has several advantages. Ownership (represented by shares of stock) can be readily transferred, and the life of the corporation is therefore not limited. The corporation borrows money in its own name. As a result, the stockholders in a corporation have limited liability for corporate debts. The most they can lose is what they have invested.

The relative ease of transferring ownership, the limited liability for business debts, and the unlimited life of the business are the reasons why the corporate form is superior when it comes to raising cash. If a corporation needs new equity, for example, it can sell new shares of stock and attract new investors. The number of owners can be huge; larger corporations have many thousands or even millions of stockholders. At the end of 1988, for example, AT&T had 2.7 million stockholders and General Motors had about 1.7 million. In such cases, ownership can change continuously without affecting the continuity of the business.

The corporate form has a significant disadvantage. Since a corporation is a legal "person," it must pay taxes. Moreover, money paid out to stockholders in the form of dividends is taxed again as income to those stockholders. This is *double taxation,* meaning that corporate profits are taxed twice: at the corporate level when they are earned and again at the personal level when they are paid out.[1]

As the discussion in this section illustrates, the need of large businesses for outside investors and creditors is such that the corporate form will gener-

---

[1] An "S" Corporation is a special type of small corporation that is essentially taxed like a partnership and thus avoids double taxation.

Table 1.1

International corporations

Company	Country of Origin	Type of Company	Translation
Porsche AG	Germany	Aktiengesellschaft	Corporation
Bayerische Moteren Werke (BMW) AG	Germany	Aktiengesellschaft	Corporation
Dornier GmBH	Germany	Gesellshaft mit Beschraenkter Haftung	Cooperative with limited liability
Rolls-Royce PLC	United Kingdom	Public limited company	Public limited company
Shell UK LTD	United Kingdom	Limited	Corporation
Unilever N V	Netherlands	Naamloze Vennootschap	Limited liability company
Fiat SpA	Italy	Societa per Azioni	Public limited company
Volvo AB	Sweden	Aktiebolag	Joint stock company
Peugeot SA	France	Sociedad Anonima	Joint stock company

ally be the best for such firms. We focus on corporations in the chapters ahead because of the importance of the corporate form in the United States and world economies. Also, a few important financial management issues, such as dividend policy, are unique to corporations. However, businesses of all types and sizes need financial management, so the majority of the subjects we discuss bear on any form of business.

A Corporation by Another Name . . .

The corporate form of organization has many variations around the world. The exact laws and regulations differ from country to country, of course, but the essential features of public ownership and limited liability remain. These firms are often called *joint stock companies, public limited companies,* or *limited liability companies,* depending on the specific nature of the firm and the country of origin.

Table 1.1 gives the names of a few well-known international corporations, their country of origin, and a translation of the abbreviation that follows the company name.

⌐CONCEPT QUESTIONS

1.2a What are the three forms of business organization?

1.2b What are the primary advantages and disadvantages of a sole proprietorship or partnership?

1.2c What is the difference between a general and a limited partnership?

1.2d Why is the corporate form superior when it comes to raising cash?

1.3 | THE GOAL OF FINANCIAL MANAGEMENT

Assuming that we restrict ourselves to for-profit businesses, the goal of financial management is to make money or add value for the owners. This goal is a little vague, of course, so we examine some different ways of formulating it in order to come up with a more precise definition. Such a definition is important because it leads to an objective basis for making and evaluating financial decisions.

Possible Goals

If we were to consider possible financial goals, we might come up with some ideas like the following:

> Survive.
>
> Avoid financial distress and bankruptcy.
>
> Beat the competition.
>
> Maximize sales or market share.
>
> Minimize costs.
>
> Maximize profits.
>
> Maintain steady earnings growth.

These are only a few of the goals we could list. Furthermore, each of these possibilities presents problems as a goal for the financial manager.

For example, it's easy to increase market share or unit sales; all we have to do is lower our prices or relax our credit terms. Similarly, we can always cut costs simply by doing away with things such as research and development. We can avoid bankruptcy by never borrowing any money or never taking any risks, and so on. It's not clear that any of these actions are in the stockholders' best interests.

Profit maximization would probably be the most commonly cited goal, but even this is not a very precise objective. Do we mean profits this year? If so, then actions such as deferring maintenance, letting inventories run down, and other short-run cost-cutting measures will tend to increase profits now, but these activities aren't necessarily desirable.

The goal of maximizing profits may refer to some sort of "long-run" or "average" profits, but it's still unclear exactly what this means. First, do we mean something like accounting net income or earnings per share? As we will see in more detail in the next chapter, these accounting numbers may have little to do with what is good or bad for the firm. Second, what do we mean by the long run? As a famous economist once remarked, in the long run, we're all dead! More to the point, this goal doesn't tell us what the appropriate trade-off is between current and future profits.

The goals we've listed above are all different, but they do tend to fall into two classes. The first of these relates to profitability. The goals involving sales, market share, and cost control all relate, at least potentially, to different ways of earning or increasing profits. The second group, involving bankruptcy avoidance, stability, and safety, relates in some way to controlling risk. Unfortunately, these two types of goals are somewhat contradictory. The pursuit of profit normally involves some element of risk, so it isn't really possible to maximize both safety and profit. What we need, therefore, is a goal that encompasses both these factors.

The Goal of Financial Management

The financial manager in a corporation makes decisions for the stockholders of the firm. Given this, instead of listing possible goals for the financial manager, we really need to answer a more fundamental question: From the stockholders' point of view, what is a good financial management decision?

If we assume that stockholders buy stock because they seek to gain financially, then the answer is obvious: Good decisions increase the value of the stock, and poor decisions decrease it.

Given our observations, it follows that the financial manager acts in the shareholders' best interests by making decisions that increase the value of the stock. The appropriate goal for the financial manager can thus be stated quite easily:

> The goal of financial management is to maximize the current value per share of the existing stock.

The goal of maximizing the value of the stock avoids the problems associated with the different goals we listed above. There is no ambiguity in the criterion, and there is no short-run versus long-run issue. We explicitly mean that our goal is to maximize the *current* stock value.

Since the goal of financial management is to maximize the value of the stock, we need to learn how to identify those investments and financing arrangements that favorably impact the value of the stock. This is precisely what we will be studying. In fact, we could have defined corporate finance as the study of the relationship between business decisions and the value of the stock in the business.

A More General Goal

Given our goal as stated above (maximize the value of the stock), an obvious question comes up: What is the appropriate goal when the firm has no traded stock? Corporations are certainly not the only type of business, and the stock in many corporations rarely changes hands, so it's difficult to say what the value per share is at any given time.

As long as we are dealing with for-profit businesses, only a slight modification is needed. The total value of the stock in a corporation is simply equal to the value of the owners' equity. Therefore, a more general way of stating our goal is: Maximize the market value of the owners' equity.

With this in mind, it doesn't matter whether the business is a proprietorship, a partnership, or a corporation. For each of these, good financial decisions increase the market value of the owners' equity and poor financial decisions decrease it. In fact, although we choose to focus on corporations in the chapters ahead, the principles we develop apply to all forms of business. Many of them even apply to the not-for-profit sector.

Finally, our goal does not imply that the financial manager should take illegal or unethical actions in the hope of increasing the value of the equity in the firm. What we mean is that the financial manager best serves the owners of the business by identifying goods and services that add value to the firm because they are desired and valued in the free marketplace.

⌐ CONCEPT QUESTIONS

1.3a What is the goal of financial management?

1.3b What are some shortcomings of the goal of profit maximization?

1.3c Can you give a definition of corporate finance?

1.4 | THE AGENCY PROBLEM AND CONTROL OF THE CORPORATION

We've seen that the financial manager acts in the best interests of the stockholders by taking actions that increase the value of the stock. However, we've also seen that in large corporations ownership can be spread over a huge number of stockholders. This dispersion of ownership arguably means that management effectively controls the firm. In this case, will management necessarily act in the best interests of the stockholders? Put another way, might not management pursue its own goals at the stockholders' expense? We briefly consider some of the arguments below.

Agency Relationships

The relationship between stockholders and management is called an *agency relationship*. Such a relationship exists whenever someone (the principal) hires another (the agent) to represent her interests. For example, you might hire someone (an agent) to sell a car that you own while you are away at school. In all such relationships, there is a possibility of conflicts of interest between the principal and the agent. Such a conflict is called an **agency problem.**

agency problem

The possibility of conflicts of interest between the stockholders and management of a firm.

Suppose that you do hire someone to sell your car and that you agree to pay her a flat fee when the car sells. The agent's incentive in this case is to make the sale, not necessarily to get you the best price. If you paid a commission of, say, 10 percent of the sales price instead of a flat fee, then this problem might not exist. This example illustrates that the way an agent is compensated is one factor that affects agency problems.

Management Goals

To see how management and stockholder interests might differ, imagine that the firm has a new investment under consideration. The new investment is expected to favorably impact the share value, but it is also a relatively risky venture. The owners of the firm will wish to take the investment (because the stock value will rise), but management may not because there is the possibility that things will turn out badly and management jobs will be lost. If management does not take the investment, then the stockholders may have lost a valuable opportunity. This is one example of an *agency cost.*

In Their Own Words...
Stender E. Sweeney on Shareholder Wealth: Management's Primary Responsibility

The role of the financial manager and the management team's responsibility is serving the shareholders' interests. It sounds pretty simple and straightforward, but in the real world there are many reasons why it rarely works out that easily!

Shareholder wealth is the key focus of the corporation, and management's primary responsibility is to maximize shareholder wealth. While there are many reasons why management should and might pursue the shareholders' best interests, many management teams fail to do so, simply because the relationships between traditional accounting measures (like earnings per share) and stock prices aren't clearly understood by most operating executives.

Unfortunately, not nearly enough managers correctly understand how their operating and financial decisions affect shareholder value. All too many managers are in hot pursuit of maximizing reported earnings to the detriment of cash on cash returns. And too often when management does focus on cash flows, they ignore the importance of discounting the value of future years' results to the present.

Gradually, companies are coming to the realization that maximizing shareholder wealth is not the same as maximizing reported earnings. Nevertheless, many Fortune 500 companies are still equating earnings growth with growth in shareholder value. It is true that managers are motivated to seek maximization of shareholder wealth because their compensation and their professional progress are dependent upon it, but the linkages to cash flow are often not clearly enough articulated.

A considerable volume of literature has been developed on the subject in recent years, and while the methodology may vary somewhat from source to source, the message from academics, consultants, investment bankers, and investors is clear: "Ignore the time value of money and the overriding importance of cash flow at your own great peril!"

Stender E. Sweeney is Vice-President, Finance of The Times Mirror Company. Over the last 10 years, he has been responsible for operating and capital budgeting. He heads The Times Mirror Companies' customized approach to shareholder wealth maximization.

More generally, *agency costs* refer to the costs of the conflict of interests between stockholders and management. These costs can be indirect or direct. An indirect agency cost is a lost opportunity such as the one we have just described.

Direct agency costs come in two forms. The first type is a corporate expenditure that benefits management but costs the stockholders. Perhaps the purchase of a luxurious and unneeded corporate jet would fall under this heading. The second type of direct agency cost is an expense that arises from the need to monitor management actions. Paying outside auditors to assess the accuracy of financial statement information could be one example.

It is sometimes argued that, left to themselves, managers would tend to maximize the amount of resources over which they have control or, more generally, corporate power or wealth. This goal could lead to an overemphasis on corporate size or growth. For example, cases where management is accused of overpaying to buy up another company just to increase the size of the business or to demonstrate corporate power are not uncommon. Obviously, if overpayment does take place, such a purchase does not benefit the stockholders of the purchasing company.

Our discussion indicates that management may tend to overemphasize organizational survival to protect job security. Also, management may dislike outside interference, so independence and corporate self-sufficiency may be important goals.

Do Managers Act in the Stockholders' Interests?

Whether managers will, in fact, act in the best interests of stockholders depends on two factors. First, how closely are management goals aligned with stockholder goals? This question relates to the way managers are compensated. Second, can management be replaced if they do not pursue stockholder goals? This issue relates to control of the firm. As we will discuss, there are a number of reasons to think that, even in the largest of firms, management has a significant incentive to act in the interests of stockholders.

Managerial Compensation   Management will frequently have a significant economic incentive to increase share value for two reasons. First, managerial compensation, particularly at the top, is usually tied to financial performance in general and oftentimes to share value in particular. For example, managers are frequently given the option to buy stock at a bargain price. The more the stock is worth, the more valuable is this option. The second incentive managers have relates to job prospects. Better performers within the firm will tend to get promoted. More generally, those managers who are successful in pursuing stockholder goals will be in greater demand in the labor market and thus command higher salaries.

Control of the Firm   Control of the firm ultimately rests with stockholders. They elect the board of directors, who, in turn, hire and fire management. The mechanism by which unhappy stockholders can act to replace existing management is called a *proxy fight*. A proxy is the authority to vote someone else's stock. A proxy fight develops when a group solicits proxies in order to replace the existing board, and thereby replace existing management.

Another way that management can be replaced is by takeover. Those firms that are poorly managed are more attractive as acquisitions than well-managed firms because a greater profit potential exists. Thus, avoiding a takeover by another firm gives management another incentive to act in the stockholders' interest.

The available theory and evidence are consistent with the view that stockholders control the firm and that stockholder wealth maximization is the relevant goal of the corporation. Even so, there will undoubtedly be times where management goals are pursued at the expense of the stockholders, at least temporarily.

stakeholder

Someone other than a stockholder or creditor who potentially has a claim on a firm.

Stakeholders   Our discussion thus far implies that management and stockholders are the only parties with an interest in the firm's decisions. This is an oversimplification, of course. Employees, customers, suppliers, and even the government all have a financial interest in the firm.

Taken together, these various groups are called **stakeholders** in the firm. In general, a stakeholder is someone other than a stockholder or creditor who potentially has a claim on the cash flows of the firm. Such groups will also attempt to exert control over the firm, perhaps to the detriment of the owners.

⌐ **CONCEPT QUESTIONS**

1.4a What is an agency relationship?

1.4b What are agency problems and how do they come about? What are agency costs?

1.4c What incentives do managers in large corporations have to maximize share value?

FINANCIAL MARKETS AND THE CORPORATION ⌐ **1.5**

We've seen that the primary advantages of the corporate form of organization are that ownership can be transferred more quickly and easily than with other forms and that money can be raised more readily. Both of these advantages are significantly enhanced by the existence of financial markets, and financial markets play an extremely important role in corporate finance.

Cash Flows to and from the Firm

The interplay between the corporation and the financial markets is illustrated in Figure 1.2. The arrows in Figure 1.2 trace the passage of cash from the financial markets to the firm and from the firm back to the financial markets.

Suppose we start with the firm selling shares of stock and borrowing money to raise cash. Cash flows to the firm from the financial markets (A). The firm invests the cash in current and fixed assets (B). These assets generate some cash (C), some of which goes to pay corporate taxes (D). After taxes are paid, some of this cash flow is reinvested in the firm (E). The rest goes back to the financial markets as cash paid to creditors and shareholders (F).

A financial market, like any market, is just a way of bringing buyers and sellers together. In financial markets, it is debt and equity securities that are bought and sold. Financial markets differ in detail, however. The most important differences concern the types of securities that are traded, how trading is conducted, and who the buyers and sellers are. Some of these differences are discussed below.

Primary versus Secondary Markets

Financial markets function as both primary and secondary markets for debt and equity securities. The term *primary market* refers to the original sale of securities by governments and corporations. The *secondary markets* are where these securities are bought and sold after the original sale. Equities are, of course, issued solely by corporations. Debt securities are issued by both governments and corporations. In the discussion below, we focus on corporate securities only.

Figure 1.2

Cash flows between the firm and the financial markets.

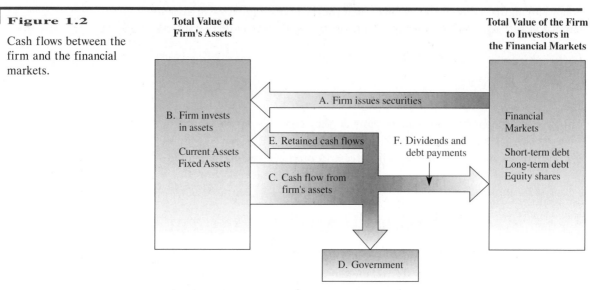

A. Firm issues securities to raise cash. B. Firm invests in assets. C. Firm's operations generate cash flow. D. Cash is paid to government as taxes. E. Retained cash flows are reinvested in firm. F. Cash is paid out to investors in the form of interest and dividends.

Primary Markets   In a primary market transaction, the corporation is the seller, and the transaction raises money for the corporation. Corporations engage in two types of primary market transactions: public offerings and private placements. A public offering, as the name suggests, involves selling securities to the general public, while a private placement is a negotiated sale involving a specific buyer.

By law, public offerings of debt and equity must be registered with the Securities and Exchange Commission (SEC). Registration requires the firm to disclose a great deal of information before selling any securities. The accounting, legal, and selling costs of public offerings can be considerable.

Partly to avoid the various regulatory requirements and the expense of public offerings, debt and equity are often sold privately to large financial institutions such as life insurance companies or mutual funds. Such private placements do not have to be registered with the SEC and do not require the involvement of underwriters (investment banks that specialize in selling securities to the public).

Secondary Markets   A secondary market transaction involves one owner or creditor selling to another. It is therefore the secondary markets that provide the means for transferring ownership of corporate securities. There are two kinds of secondary markets: *auction* markets and *dealer* markets.

Generally speaking, dealers buy and sell for themselves, at their own risk. A car dealer, for example, buys and sells automobiles. In contrast, brokers and agents match buyers and sellers, but they do not actually own the commodity that is bought or sold. A real estate agent, for example, does not normally buy and sell houses.

Dealer markets in stocks and long-term debt are called *over-the-counter* (OTC) markets. Most trading in debt securities takes place over the counter. The expression *over-the-counter* refers to days of old when securities were literally bought and sold at counters in offices around the country. Today, a significant fraction of the market for stocks and almost all of the market for long-term debt have no central location; the many dealers are connected electronically.

Auction markets differ from dealer markets in two ways. First, an auction market or exchange has a physical location (like Wall Street). Second, in a dealer market, most of the buying and selling is done by the dealer. The primary purpose of an auction market, on the other hand, is to match those who wish to sell with those who wish to buy. Dealers play a limited role.

The equity shares of most of the large firms in the United States trade in organized auction markets. The largest such market is the New York Stock Exchange (NYSE, pronounced "ny-see") which accounts for more than 85 percent of all the shares traded in auction markets. Other auction exchanges include the American Stock Exchange (AMEX) and regional exchanges such as the Midwest Stock Exchange.

In addition to the stock exchanges, there is a large OTC market for stocks. In 1971, the National Association of Securities Dealers (NASD) made available to dealers and brokers an electronic quotation system called NASDAQ (NASD Automated Quotation system, pronounced "naz-dak"). There are roughly three times as many companies on NASDAQ as there are on NYSE, but they tend to be much smaller in size and trade less actively. There are exceptions, of course. Both Apple Computer and MCI trade OTC, for example. Nonetheless, the total value of NASDAQ stocks is only about 20 percent of the total value of NYSE stocks.

Listing   Stocks that trade on an organized exchange are said to be *listed* on that exchange. In order to be listed, firms must meet certain minimum criteria concerning, for example, asset size and number of shareholders. These criteria differ for different exchanges.

NYSE has the most stringent requirements of the exchanges in the United States. For example, to be listed on NYSE, a company is expected to have a market value for its publicly held shares of at least $18 million and a total of at least 2,000 shareholders with at least 100 shares each. There are additional minimums on earnings, assets, and number of shares outstanding.

CONCEPT QUESTIONS

1.5a What is a dealer market? How do dealer and auction markets differ?

1.5b What is the largest auction market in the United States?

1.5c What does OTC stand for? What is the large OTC market for stocks called?

1.6 | OUTLINE OF THE TEXT

Now that we've completed a quick tour through the concerns of corporate finance, we can take a closer look at the organization of this book. The text is organized into the following nine parts:

Part One:	Overview of Corporate Finance
Part Two:	Financial Statements and Long-Term Financial Planning
Part Three:	Valuation of Future Cash Flows
Part Four:	Capital Budgeting
Part Five:	Risk and Return
Part Six:	Long-Term Financing
Part Seven:	Cost of Capital and Long-Term Financial Policy
Part Eight:	Short-Term Financial Planning and Management
Part Nine:	Topics in Corporate Finance

Part One of the text contains some introductory material (this chapter) and goes on to explain the relationship between accounting income and cash flow. Part Two explores financial statements and how they are used in finance in greater depth.

Parts Three and Four contain our core discussion on valuation. In Part Three, we develop the basic procedures for valuing future cash flows with particular emphasis on stocks and bonds. Part Four draws on this material and deals with capital budgeting and the effect of long-term investment decisions on the firm.

In Part Five, we develop some tools for evaluating risk. We then discuss how to evaluate the risks associated with long-term investments by the firm. The emphasis in this section is on coming up with a benchmark for making investment decisions.

Parts Six and Seven deal with the related issues of long-term financing, dividend policy, and capital structure. We discuss corporate securities in some detail and describe the procedures used to raise capital and sell securities to the public. We also introduce and describe the important concept of the cost of capital. We go on to examine dividends and dividend policy and important considerations in determining a capital structure.

The working capital question is addressed in Part Eight. The subjects of short-term financial planning, cash management, credit management, and inventory management are covered.

The final part, Part Nine, contains some important special topics. There are chapters on the subject of options and optionlike securities, mergers and acquisitions, international aspects of corporate finance, leasing, and financial engineering.

1.7 | SUMMARY AND CONCLUSIONS

This chapter has introduced you to some of the basic ideas in corporate finance. In it, we saw that:

1. Corporate finance has three main areas of concern:
    a. Capital budgeting. What long-term investments should the firm take?
    b. Capital structure. Where will the firm get the long-term financing to pay for its investments? In other words, what mixture of debt and equity should we use to fund our operations?
    c. Working capital management. How should the firm manage its everyday financial activities?

2. The goal of financial management in a for-profit business is to make decisions that increase the value of the stock or, more generally, increase the market value of the equity.

3. The corporate form of organization is superior to other forms when it comes to raising money and transferring ownership interests, but it has the significant disadvantage of double taxation.

4. There is the possibility of conflicts between stockholders and management in a large corporation. We called these conflicts agency problems and discussed how they might be controlled and reduced.

5. The advantages of the corporate form are enhanced by the existence of financial markets. Financial markets function as both primary and secondary markets for corporate securities and can be organized as either dealer or auction markets.

Of the topics we've discussed thus far, the most important is the goal of financial management: maximizing the value of the stock. Throughout the text, we will be analyzing financial decisions, but we always ask the same question: How does a decision under consideration affect the value of the stock?

Key Terms

capital budgeting 6
capital structure 6
working capital 8
sole proprietorship 8

partnership 9
corporation 9
agency problem 14
stakeholder 16

Questions and Problems

1. Not-for-Profit Firm Goals   Suppose you were the financial manager of a not-for-profit business (a not-for-profit hospital, perhaps). What kinds of goals do you think would be appropriate?

2. Firm Goals and Stock Value   Evaluate the following statement: "Managers should not focus on the current stock value because doing so will lead to an overemphasis on short-term profits at the expense of long-term profits."

3. Firm Goals and Ethics   Can our goal of maximizing the value of the stock conflict with other goals such as avoiding unethical or illegal behavior? In particular, do you think subjects like customer and employee safety, the environment, and the general good of society fit in this framework, or are they essentially ignored? Try to think of some specific scenarios to illustrate your answer.

4.   **Firm Goals and Multinational Firms**   Would our goal of maximizing the value of the stock be different if we were thinking about financial management in a foreign country? Why or why not?

5.   **Agency Issues and International Finance**   The following table gives a breakdown of corporate ownership in the United States and other major countries. Based on these figures, do you think that agency problems are likely to be more or less severe in other countries? Why?

Corporate Ownership in Major Countries

	United States (1988)	Japan (1989)	West Germany (1989)	United Kingdom (1989)
Individual	58.3%	20.5%	17.6%	28.0%
Nonfinancial institutions	—	29.5	41.1	10.1
Bank	0.3	21.3	9.3	4.3
Other financial institutions	35.1	24.2	11.1	48.5
Government	—	0.3	5.8	2.6
Other	6.3	4.2	15.1	6.5

Source: "The World Economic White Paper in 1990" edited by Japanese Economic Planning Agency; Daiwa Securities. Reproduced from *Trade and Investment in Japan: The Current Environment* by A.T. Kearney, June 1991.
Note: Figures are based on market values. Figures for U.S.A. may be larger than actual because exact number of nonfinancial institutions is not available.

Chapter 2

Financial Statements, Taxes, and Cash Flow

In this chapter, we examine financial statements, taxes, and cash flow. Our emphasis is not on preparing financial statements. Instead, we recognize that financial statements are frequently a key source of information for financial decisions, so our goal is to briefly examine such statements and point out some of their more relevant features. We pay special attention to some of the practical details of cash flow.

As you read, pay particular attention to two important differences: (1) the difference between accounting value and market value, and (2) the difference between accounting income and cash flow. These distinctions will be important throughout the book.

THE BALANCE SHEET | 2.1

The **balance sheet** is a snapshot of the firm. It is a convenient means of organizing and summarizing what a firm owns (its *assets*), what a firm owes (its *liabilities*), and the difference between the two (the firm's *equity*) at a given point in time. Figure 2.1 illustrates how the balance sheet is constructed. As shown, the left-hand side lists the assets of the firm, and the right-hand side lists the liabilities and equity.

balance sheet
Financial statement showing a firm's accounting value on a particular date.

Assets: The Left-Hand Side

Assets are classified as either *current* or *fixed*. A fixed asset is one that has a relatively long life. Fixed assets can either be *tangible,* such as a truck or a

Figure 2.1

The balance sheet. Left side, total value of assets. Right side, total value of liabilities and shareholders' equity.

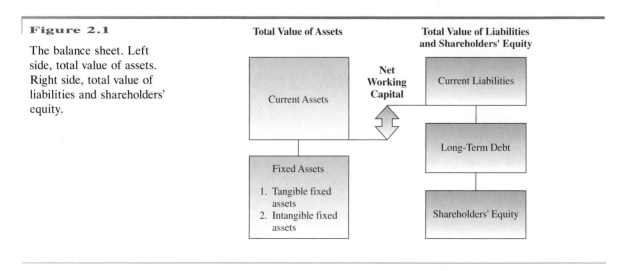

computer, or *intangible,* such as a trademark or patent. A current asset has a life of less than one year. This means that the asset will convert to cash within 12 months. For example, inventory would normally be purchased and sold within a year and is thus classified as a current asset. Obviously, cash itself is a current asset. Accounts receivable (money owed to the firm by its customers) is also a current asset.

Liabilities and Owners' Equity: The Right-Hand Side

The firm's liabilities are the first thing listed on the right-hand side of the balance sheet. These are classified as either *current* or *long-term*. Current liabilities, like current assets, have a life of less than one year (meaning they must be paid within the year) and are listed before long-term liabilities. Accounts payable (money the firm owes to its suppliers) is one example of a current liability.

A debt that is not due in the coming year is classified as a long-term liability. A loan that the firm will pay off in five years is one such long-term debt. Firms borrow long term from a variety of sources. We will tend to use the terms *bond* and *bondholders* generically to refer to long-term debt and long-term creditors, respectively.

Finally, by definition, the difference between the total value of the assets (current and fixed) and the total value of the liabilities (current and long-term) is the *shareholders' equity,* also called *common equity* or *owners' equity*. This feature of the balance sheet is intended to reflect the fact that, if the firm were to sell all of its assets and use the money to pay off its debts, then whatever residual value remains belongs to the shareholders. So, the balance sheet "balances" because the value of the left-hand side always equals the value of the right-hand side. That is, the value of the firm's assets is equal to the sum of its liabilities and shareholders' equity:[1]

$$\text{Assets} = \text{Liabilities} + \text{Shareholders' equity} \qquad [2.1]$$

This is the balance sheet identity or equation, and it always holds because shareholders' equity is defined as the difference between assets and liabilities.

Net Working Capital

As shown in Figure 2.1, the difference between a firm's current assets and its current liabilities is called **net working capital**. Net working capital is positive when current assets exceed current liabilities. Based on the definitions of current assets and current liabilities, this means that the cash that will become available over the next 12 months exceeds the cash that must be paid over that same period. For this reason, net working capital is usually positive in a healthy firm.

net working capital
Current assets less current liabilities.

Example 2.1   Building the Balance Sheet
A firm has current assets of $100, net fixed assets of $500, short-term debt of $70, and long-term debt of $200. What does the balance sheet look like? What is shareholders' equity? What is net working capital?

In this case, total assets are $100 + 500 = $600 and total liabilities are $70 + 200 = $270, so shareholders' equity is the difference: $600 − 270 = $330. The balance sheet would thus look like:

Assets		Liabilities and Shareholders' Equity	
Current assets	$100	Current liabilities	$ 70
Net fixed assets	500	Long-term debt	200
		Shareholders' equity	330
Total assets	$600	Total liabilities and shareholders' equity	$600

Net working capital is the difference between current assets and current liabilities, or $100 − 70 = $30. ∎

Table 2.1 shows a simplified balance sheet for the fictitious U.S. Corporation. The assets in the balance sheet are listed in order of the length of time it takes for them to convert to cash in the normal course of business. Similarly, the liabilities are listed in the order in which they would normally be paid.

The structure of the assets for a particular firm reflects the line of business that the firm is in and also managerial decisions about how much cash and inventory to have and about credit policy, fixed asset acquisition, and so on.

---

[1]The terms *owners' equity, shareholders' equity,* and *stockholders' equity* are used interchangeably to refer to the equity in a corporation. The term *net worth* is also used. Variations exist in addition to these.

Table 2.1

U.S. CORPORATION
Balance Sheets as of December 31, 1991 and 1992
($ in millions)

	1991	1992		1991	1992
Assets			*Liabilities and Owners' Equity*		
Current assets			Current liabilities		
Cash	$ 104	$ 160	Accounts payable	$ 232	$ 266
Accounts receivable	455	688	Notes payable	196	123
Inventory	553	555	Total	$ 428	$ 389
Total	$1,112	$1,403			
Fixed assets					
Net plant and equipment	$1,644	$1,709	Long-term debt	$ 408	$ 454
			Owners' equity		
			Common stock and paid-in surplus	600	640
			Retained earnings	1,320	1,629
			Total	$1,920	$2,269
Total assets	$2,756	$3,112	Total liabilities and owners' equity	$2,756	$3,112

The liabilities side of the balance sheet primarily reflects managerial decisions about capital structure and the use of short-term debt. For example, in 1992, total long-term debt for U.S. was $454 and total equity was $640 + 1,629 = $2,269, so total long-term financing was $454 + 2,269 = $2,723. Of this amount, $454/2,723 = 16.67% was long-term debt. This percentage reflects capital structure decisions made in the past by the management of U.S.

There are three particularly important things to keep in mind when examining a balance sheet: liquidity, debt versus equity, and market value versus book value.

Liquidity

Liquidity refers to the speed and ease with which an asset can be converted to cash. Gold is a relatively liquid asset; a custom manufacturing facility is not. Liquidity really has two dimensions: ease of conversion versus loss of value. Any asset can be converted to cash quickly if we cut the price enough. A highly liquid asset is therefore one that can be quickly sold without significant loss of value. An illiquid asset is one that cannot be quickly converted to cash without a substantial price reduction.

Assets are normally listed on the balance sheet in order of decreasing liquidity, meaning that the most liquid assets are listed first. Current assets are relatively liquid and include cash and those assets that we expect to convert to cash over the next 12 months. Accounts receivable, for example, represents amounts not yet collected from customers on sales already made. Naturally, we hope these will convert to cash in the near future. Inventory is probably the least liquid of the current assets, at least for many businesses.

Fixed assets are, for the most part, relatively illiquid. These consist of tangible things such as buildings and equipment that don't convert to cash at all in normal business activity. Intangible assets, such as a trademark, have no physical existence but can be very valuable. Like tangible fixed assets, they won't ordinarily convert to cash and are generally considered illiquid.

Liquidity is valuable. The more liquid a business is, the less likely it is to experience financial distress (that is, difficulty in paying debts or buying needed assets). Unfortunately, liquid assets are generally less profitable to hold. For example, cash holdings are the most liquid of all investments, but they sometimes earn no return at all — they just sit there. There is therefore a trade-off between the advantages of liquidity and forgone potential profits.

Debt versus Equity

To the extent that a firm borrows money, it usually gives first claim to the firm's cash flow to creditors. Equity holders are only entitled to the residual value, the portion left after creditors are paid. The value of this residual portion is the shareholders' equity in the firm and is just the asset value less the value of the firm's liabilities:

Shareholders' equity = Assets − Liabilities

This is true in an accounting sense because shareholders' equity is defined as this residual portion. More importantly, it is true in an economic sense: If the firm sells its assets and pays its debts, whatever cash is left belongs to the shareholders.

The use of debt in a firm's capital structure is called *financial leverage*. The more debt a firm has (as a percentage of assets), the greater is its degree of financial leverage. As we discuss in later chapters, debt acts like a lever in the sense that using it can greatly magnify both gains and losses. So financial leverage increases the potential reward to shareholders, but it also increases the potential for financial distress and business failure.

Market Value versus Book Value

The values shown on the balance sheet for the firm's assets are *book values* and generally are not what the assets are actually worth. Under **Generally Accepted Accounting Principles (GAAP)**, audited financial statements in the United States show assets at *historical cost*. In other words, assets are "carried on the books" at what the firm paid for them, no matter how long ago they were purchased or how much they are worth today.

For current assets, market value and book value might be somewhat similar since current assets are bought and converted into cash over a relatively short span of time. In other circumstances, they might differ quite a bit. Moreover, for fixed assets, it would be purely a coincidence if the actual market

Generally Accepted Accounting Principles (GAAP)
The common set of standards and procedures by which audited financial statements are prepared.

value of an asset (what the asset could be sold for) were equal to its book value. For example, a railroad might own enormous tracts of land purchased a century or more ago. What the railroad paid for that land could be hundreds or thousands of times less than it is worth today. The balance sheet would nonetheless show the historical cost.

The balance sheet is potentially useful to many different parties. A supplier might look at the size of accounts payable to see how promptly the firm pays its bills. A potential creditor would examine the liquidity and degree of financial leverage. Managers within the firm can track things like the amount of cash and the amount of inventory that the firm keeps on hand. Uses such as these are discussed in more detail in Chapter 3.

Managers and investors will frequently be interested in knowing the value of the firm. This information is not on the balance sheet. The fact that balance sheet assets are listed at cost means that there is no necessary connection between the total assets shown and the value of the firm. Indeed, many of the most valuable assets that a firm might have — good management, a good reputation, talented employees — don't appear on the balance sheet at all.

Similarly, the shareholders' equity figure on the balance sheet and the true value of the stock need not be related. For financial managers, then, the accounting value of the stock is not an especially important concern; it is the market value that matters. Henceforth, whenever we speak of the value of an asset or the value of the firm, we will normally mean its *market value*. So, for example, when we say the goal of the financial manager is to increase the value of the stock, we mean the market value of the stock.

Example 2.2 Market versus Book Values

The Klingon Corporation has fixed assets with a book value of $700 and an appraised market value of about $1,000. Net working capital is $400 on the books, but approximately $600 would be realized if all the current accounts were liquidated. Klingon has $500 in long-term debt, both book value and market value. What is the book value of the equity? What is the market value?

We can construct two simplified balance sheets, one in accounting (book value) terms and one in economic (market value) terms:

KLINGON CORPORATION
Balance Sheets
Market Value versus Book Value

	Book	Market		Book	Market
Assets			*Liabilities and Shareholders' Equity*		
Net working capital	$ 400	$ 600	Long-term debt	$ 500	$ 500
Net fixed assets	700	1,000	Shareholders' equity	600	1,100
	$1,100	$1,600		$1,100	$1,600

In this example, shareholders' equity is actually worth almost twice as much as what is shown on the books. The distinction between book and market values is important precisely because book values can be so different from true economic value. ∎

⌐ CONCEPT QUESTIONS

2.1a What is the balance sheet identity?

2.1b What is liquidity? Why is it important?

2.1c What do we mean by financial leverage?

2.1d Explain the difference between accounting value and market value. Which is more important to the financial manager? Why?

THE INCOME STATEMENT | 2.2

The **income statement** measures performance over some period of time, usually a year. The income statement equation is:

$$\text{Revenues} - \text{Expenses} = \text{Income} \qquad [2.2]$$

income statement
Financial statement summarizing a firm's performance over a period of time.

If you think of the balance sheet as a snapshot, then you can think of the income statement as a video recording covering the period between a before and an after picture. Table 2.2 gives a simplified income statement for U.S. Corporation.

The first thing reported on an income statement would usually be revenue and expenses from the firm's principal operations. Subsequent parts include, among other things, financing expenses such as interest paid. Taxes paid are reported separately. The last item is *net income* (the so-called bottom line). Net income is often expressed on a per share basis and called *earnings per share (EPS)*.

As indicated, U.S. paid cash dividends of $103. The difference between net income and cash dividends, $309, is the addition to retained earnings for the year. This amount is added to the cumulative retained earnings account on the balance sheet. If you'll look back at the two balance sheets for U.S. Corporation, you'll see that retained earnings did go up by this amount, $1,320 + 309 = $1,629.

Table 2.2

U.S. CORPORATION 1992 Income Statement ($ in millions)		
Net sales		$1,509
Cost of goods sold		750
Depreciation		65
Earnings before interest and taxes		$ 694
Interest paid		70
Taxable income		$ 624
Taxes		212
Net income		$ 412
Addition to retained earnings	$309	
Dividends	103	

Example 2.3 Calculating Earnings and Dividends per Share

Suppose that U.S. had 200 million shares outstanding at the end of 1992. Based on the income statement above, what was EPS? What were dividends per share?

From the income statement, U.S. had a net income of $412 million for the year. Since 200 million shares were outstanding, EPS was $412/200 = $2.06 per share. Similarly, dividends per share were $103/200 = $0.515 per share. ■

When looking at an income statement, the financial manager needs to keep three things in mind: GAAP, cash versus noncash items, and time and costs.

GAAP and the Income Statement

An income statement prepared using GAAP will show revenue when it accrues. This is not necessarily when the cash comes in. The general rule (the realization principle) is to recognize revenue when the earnings process is virtually complete and the value of an exchange of goods or services is known or can be reliably determined. In practice, this principle usually means that revenue is recognized at the time of sale, which need not be the same as the time of collection.

Costs shown on the income statement are based on the matching principle. The basic idea here is to first determine revenues as described above and then match those revenues with the costs associated with producing them. So, if we manufacture and then sell a product on credit, the revenue is realized at the time of sale. The production and other costs associated with the sale of that product would likewise be recognized at that time. Once again, the actual cash outflows may have occurred at some very different time.

As a result of the way revenues and costs are realized, the figures shown on the income statement may not be at all representative of the actual cash inflows and outflows that occurred during a particular period.

Noncash Items

noncash items
Expenses charged against revenues that do not directly affect cash flow, such as depreciation.

A primary reason that accounting income differs from cash flow is that an income statement contains **noncash items.** The most important of these is *depreciation.* Suppose a firm purchases an asset for $5,000 and pays in cash. Obviously, the firm has a $5,000 cash outflow at the time of purchase. However, instead of deducting the $5,000 as an expense, an accountant might depreciate the asset over a five-year period.

If the depreciation is straight-line and the asset is written down to zero over that period, then $5,000/5 = $1,000 would be deducted each year as an expense.[2] The important thing to recognize is that this $1,000 deduction isn't cash — it's an accounting number. The actual cash outflow occurred when the asset was purchased.

---

[2]By "straight-line," we mean that the depreciation deduction is the same every year. By "written down to zero," we mean that the asset is assumed to have no value at the end of five years. Depreciation is discussed in more detail in Chapter 8.

The depreciation deduction is simply another application of the matching principle in accounting. The revenues associated with an asset would generally occur over some length of time. So the accountant seeks to match the expense of purchasing the asset with the benefits produced from owning it.

As we will see, for the financial manager, the actual timing of cash inflows and outflows is critical in coming up with a reasonable estimate of market value, so we need to learn how to separate the cash flows from the noncash accounting entries.

Time and Costs

It is often useful to think of the future as having two distinct parts: the short run and the long run. These are not precise time periods. The distinction has to do with whether costs are fixed or variable. In the long run, all business costs are variable. Given sufficient time, assets can be sold, debts can be paid, and so on.

If our time horizon is relatively short, however, some costs are effectively fixed — they must be paid no matter what (property taxes, for example). Other costs such as wages to laborers and payments to suppliers are still variable. As a result, even in the short run, the firm can vary its output level by varying expenditures in these areas.

The distinction between fixed and variable costs is important, at times, to the financial manager, but the way costs are reported on the income statement is not a good guide as to which costs are which. The reason is that, in practice, accountants tend to classify costs as either product costs or period costs.

Product costs include such things as raw materials, direct labor expense, and manufacturing overhead. These are reported on the income statement as costs of goods sold, but they include both fixed and variable costs. Similarly, period costs are incurred during a particular time period and are reported as selling, general, and administrative expenses. Once again, some of these period costs may be fixed and others may be variable. The company president's salary, for example, is a period cost and is probably fixed, at least in the short run.

⌐ **CONCEPT QUESTIONS**

2.2a What is the income statement equation?

2.2b What are the three things to keep in mind when looking at an income statement?

2.2c Why is accounting income not the same as cash flow? Give two reasons.

TAXES ⌐ 2.3

Taxes can be one of the largest cash outflows that a firm experiences. The size of the tax bill is determined through the tax code, an often amended and changed set of rules. In this section, we examine corporate and personal tax rates and how taxes are calculated.

If the various rules of taxation seem a little bizarre or convoluted to you, keep in mind that the tax code is the result of political, not economic, forces. As a result, there is no reason why it has to make economic sense.

Corporate and Personal Tax Rates

Corporate and personal tax rates in effect for 1991 are shown in Table 2.3. A peculiar feature of taxation instituted by the Tax Reform Act of 1986 is that corporate tax rates are not strictly increasing. As shown, corporate tax rates rise from 15 percent to 39 percent, but they drop back to 34 percent on income over $335,000. Personal rates rise to a maximum of 31 percent and stay there.

According to the originators of the current tax rules, there are only three corporate rates, 15 percent, 25 percent, and 34 percent. The 39 percent bracket arises because of a 5 percent "surcharge" applied on top of the 34 percent rate. A tax is a tax is a tax, however, so there are really four corporate tax brackets as we have shown.

Another important feature of the current tax code is evident when corporate tax rates are compared to personal tax rates: The top corporate tax rates exceed the top personal rate. Before 1986, the top personal rate always exceeded the top corporate rate.

Average versus Marginal Tax Rates

average tax rate

Total taxes paid divided by total taxable income.

marginal tax rate

Amount of tax payable on the next dollar earned.

In making financial decisions, it is frequently important to distinguish between average and marginal tax rates. Your **average tax rate** is your tax bill divided by your taxable income, in other words, the percentage of your income that goes to pay taxes. Your **marginal tax rate** is the extra tax you would pay if you earned one more dollar. The percentage tax rates shown in Table 2.3 are all marginal rates. Put another way, the tax rates in Table 2.3 apply to the part of income in the indicated range only, not all income.

The difference between average and marginal tax rates can best be illustrated with a simple example. Suppose that our corporation has a taxable income of $200,000. What is the tax bill? From Table 2.3, we can figure our tax bill as:

$$
\begin{array}{lcr}
.15(\$\ 50,000) & = & \$\ 7,500 \\
.25(\$\ 75,000 - 50,000) & = & 6,250 \\
.34(\$100,000 - 75,000) & = & 8,500 \\
.39(\$200,000 - 100,000) & = & \underline{39,000} \\
& & \$61,250
\end{array}
$$

Our total tax is thus $61,250.

In our example, what is the average tax rate? We had a taxable income of $200,000 and a tax bill of $61,250, so the average tax rate is $61,250/200,000 = 30.625\%$. What is the marginal tax rate? If we made one more dollar, the tax on that dollar would be 39 cents, so our marginal rate is 39 percent.

Corporate Tax Rates		Personal Tax Rates: Single		**Table 2.3**
Taxable Income	Tax Rate	Taxable Income	Tax Rate	Corporate and personal tax rates
$ 0– 50,000	15%	$ 0–20,350	15%	
50,001– 75,000	25	20,350–49,300	28	
75,001–100,000	34	49,300+	31	
100,001–335,000	39			
335,001+	34			

(1) Taxable Income	(2) Marginal Tax Rate	(3) Total Tax	(3)/(1) Average Tax Rate	**Table 2.4**
$ 45,000	15%	$ 6,750	15.00%	Corporate taxes and tax rates
70,000	25	12,500	17.86	
95,000	34	20,550	21.63	
120,000	39	30,050	25.04	
250,000	39	80,750	32.30	
500,000	34	170,000	34.00	
1,000,000	34	340,000	34.00	

Example 2.4   Deep in the Heart of Taxes

Algernon, Inc., has a taxable income of $85,000. What is its tax bill? What is its average tax rate? Its marginal tax rate?

From Table 2.3 above, the tax rate applied to the first $50,000 is 15 percent; the rate applied to the next $25,000 is 25 percent, and the rate applied after that up to $100,000 is 34 percent. So Algernon must pay $.15 \times \$50,000 + .25 \times \$25,000 + .34 \times (\$85,000 - 75,000) = \$17,150$. The average tax rate is thus $\$17,150/85,000 = 20.18\%$. The marginal rate is 34 percent since Algernon's taxes would rise by 34 cents if it had another dollar in taxable income. ∎

Table 2.4 summarizes some different taxable incomes, marginal tax rates, and average tax rates for corporations. Notice how the average and marginal tax rates come together at 34 percent.

With a *flat rate* tax, there is only one tax rate, and this rate is the same for all income levels. With such a tax, the marginal tax rate is always the same as the average tax rate. As it stands now, corporate taxation in the United States is a modified flat rate tax, becoming a true flat rate for the highest incomes.

In looking at Table 2.4, notice that the more a corporation makes, the greater is the percentage of taxable income paid in taxes. Put another way, under current tax law, the average tax rate never goes down, even though the marginal tax rate does. As illustrated, for corporations, average tax rates begin at 15 percent and rise to a maximum of 34 percent.

It will normally be the marginal tax rate that is relevant for financial decision making. The reason is that any new cash flows will be taxed at that marginal rate. Since financial decisions usually involve new cash flows or changes in existing ones, this rate will tell us the marginal effect on our tax bill.

There is one last thing to notice about the tax code as it affects corporations. It's easy to verify that the corporate tax bill is just a flat 34 percent of taxable income if our taxable income is more than $335,000. Since we will normally be talking about large corporations, you can assume that the average and marginal tax rates are 34 percent unless we explicitly say otherwise.

CONCEPT QUESTIONS

2.3a What is the difference between a marginal and an average tax rate?

2.3b Do the wealthiest corporations receive a tax break in terms of a lower tax rate? Explain.

2.4 | CASH FLOW

At this point, we are ready to discuss perhaps one of the most important pieces of financial information that can be gleaned from financial statements: *cash flow.* By cash flow, we simply mean the difference between the number of dollars that came in and the number that went out. For example, if you were the owner of a business, you might be very interested in how much cash you actually took out of your business in a given year. How to determine this amount is one of the things we discuss next.

There is no standard financial statement that presents this information in the way that we wish. We will therefore discuss how to calculate cash flow for U.S. Corporation and point out how the result differs from standard financial statement calculations. There is a standard financial accounting statement called the *statement of cash flows,* but it is concerned with a somewhat different issue and should not be confused with what is discussed in this section. The accounting statement of cash flows is discussed in Chapter 3.

From the balance sheet identity, we know that the value of a firm's assets is equal to the value of its liabilities plus the value of its equity. Similarly, the cash flow from the firm's assets must equal the sum of the cash flow to creditors plus the cash flow to stockholders (or owners):

$$\text{Cash flow from assets} = \text{Cash flow to creditors} \\ + \text{Cash flow to stockholders} \qquad [2.3]$$

This is the cash flow identity. It says that the cash flow from the firm's assets is equal to the cash flow paid to suppliers of capital to the firm. What it reflects is the fact that a firm generates cash through its various activities, and that cash is either used to pay creditors or else it is paid out to the owners of the firm. We discuss the various things that make up these cash flows next.

Cash Flow from Assets

Cash flow from assets involves three components: operating cash flow, capital spending, and additions to net working capital. **Operating cash flow** refers to the cash flow that results from the firm's day-to-day activities of producing and selling. Expenses associated with the firm's financing of its assets are not included since they are not operating expenses.

As we discussed in Chapter 1, some portion of the firm's cash flow is reinvested in the firm. *Capital spending* refers to the net spending on fixed assets (purchases of fixed assets less sales of fixed assets). Finally, *additions to net working capital* is the amount spent on net working capital. It is measured as the change in net working capital over the period being examined and represents the net increase in current assets over current liabilities. The three components of cash flow are examined in more detail below.

Operating Cash Flow   To calculate operating cash flow, we want to calculate revenues minus costs, but we don't want to include depreciation since it's not a cash outflow, and we don't want to include interest because it's a financing expense. We do want to include taxes, because taxes are, unfortunately, paid in cash.

If we look at U.S. Corporation's income statement (Table 2.2), earnings before interest and taxes (EBIT) are $694. This is almost what we want since it doesn't include interest paid. We need to make two adjustments. First, recall that depreciation is a noncash expense. To get cash flow, we first add back the $65 in depreciation since it wasn't a cash deduction. The other adjustment is to subtract the $212 in taxes since these were paid in cash. The result is operating cash flow:

U.S. CORPORATION
1992 Operating Cash Flow

Earnings before interest and taxes	$694
+ Depreciation	65
− Taxes	212
Operating cash flow	$547

U.S. Corporation thus had a 1992 operating cash flow of $547.

There is an unpleasant possibility for confusion when we speak of operating cash flow. In accounting practice, operating cash flow is often defined as net income plus depreciation. For U.S. Corporation, this would amount to $412 + 65 = $477.

The accounting definition of operating cash flow differs from ours in one important way: Interest is deducted when net income is computed. Notice that the difference between the $547 operating cash flow we calculated and this $477 is $70, the amount of interest paid for the year.

This definition of cash flow thus considers interest paid to be an operating expense. Our definition treats it properly as a financing expense. If there were no interest expense, the two definitions would be the same.

cash flow from assets
The total of cash flow to creditors and cash flow to stockholders, consisting of the following: operating cash flow, capital spending, and additions to net working capital.

operating cash flow
Cash generated from a firm's normal business activities.

To finish our calculation of cash flow from assets for U.S. Corporation, we need to consider how much of the $547 operating cash flow was reinvested in the firm. We consider spending on fixed assets first.

Capital Spending   Net capital spending is just money spent on fixed assets less money received from the sale of fixed assets. At the end of 1991, net fixed assets for U.S. Corporation (Table 2.1) were $1,644. During the year, we wrote off (depreciated) $65 worth of fixed assets on the income statement. So, if we didn't purchase any new fixed assets, net fixed assets would have been $1,644 − 65 = $1,579 at year's end. The 1992 balance sheet shows $1,709 in net fixed assets, so we must have spent a total of $1,709 − 1,579 = $130 on fixed assets during the year:

Ending net fixed assets	$1,709
− Beginning net fixed assets	1,644
+ Depreciation	65
Net investment in fixed assets	$ 130

This $130 is our net capital spending for 1992.

Could net capital spending be negative? The answer is yes. This would happen if the firm sold off more assets than it purchased. The *net* here refers to purchases of fixed assets net of any sales of fixed assets.

Additions to Net Working Capital   In addition to investing in fixed assets, a firm will also invest in current assets. For example, going back to the balance sheet in Table 2.1, we see that, at the end of 1992, U.S. had current assets of $1,403. At the end of 1991, current assets were $1,112, so, during the year, U.S. invested $1,403 − 1,112 = $291 in current assets.

As the firm changes its investment in current assets, its current liabilities will usually change as well. To determine the additions to net working capital, the easiest approach is just to take the difference between the beginning and ending net working capital (NWC) figures. Net working capital at the end of 1992 was $1,403 − 389 = $1,014. Similarly, at the end of 1991, net working capital was $1,112 − 428 = $684. So, given these figures, we have:

Ending NWC	$1,014
− Beginning NWC	684
Additions to NWC	$ 330

Net working capital thus increased by $330. Put another way, U.S. Corporation had a net investment of $330 in NWC for the year.

Cash Flow from Assets   Given the figures we've come up with, we're ready to calculate cash flow from assets. The total cash flow from assets is given by operating cash flow less the amounts invested in fixed assets and net working capital. So, for U.S., we have:

U.S. CORPORATION
1992 Cash Flow from Assets

Operating cash flow	$547
− Net capital spending	130
− Additions to NWC	330
Cash flow from assets	$ 87

From the cash flow identity above, this $87 cash flow from assets equals the sum of the firm's cash flow to creditors and cash flow to stockholders. We consider these next.

It wouldn't be at all unusual for a growing corporation to have a negative cash flow. As we see next, a negative cash flow means that the firm raised more money by borrowing and selling stock than it paid out to creditors and stockholders that year.

Cash Flow to Creditors and Stockholders

The cash flows to creditors and stockholders represent the net payments to creditors and owners during the year. They are calculated in a similar way. **Cash flow to creditors** is interest paid less net new borrowing; **cash flow to stockholders** is dividends paid less net new equity raised.

cash flow to creditors
A firm's interest payments to creditors less net new borrowings.

cash flow to stockholders
Dividends paid out by a firm less net new equity raised.

Cash Flow to Creditors   Looking at the income statement in Table 2.2, U.S. paid $70 in interest to creditors. From the balance sheets in Table 2.1, long-term debt rose by $454 − 408 = $46. So, U.S. Corporation paid out $70 in interest, but it borrowed an additional $46. Net cash flow to creditors is thus:

U.S. CORPORATION
1992 Cash Flow to Creditors

Interest paid	$70
− Net new borrowing	46
Cash flow to creditors	$24

Cash flow to creditors is sometimes called *cash flow to "bondholders";* we will use these terms interchangeably.

Cash Flow to Stockholders   From the income statement, dividends paid to stockholders amount to $103. To get net new equity raised, we need to look at the common stock and paid-in surplus account. This account tells us how

Table 2.5	I.	The cash flow identity

Cash Flow Summary

Cash flow from assets = Cash flow to creditors (bondholders)
+ Cash flow to stockholders (owners)

II. Cash flow from assets

Cash flow from assets = Operating cash flow
− Net capital spending
− Additions to net working capital (NWC)

where:

Operating cash flow = Earnings before interest and taxes (EBIT)
+ Depreciation − Taxes

Net capital spending = Ending net fixed assets − Beginning net fixed assets
+ Depreciation

Additions to NWC = Ending NWC − Beginning NWC

III. Cash flow to creditors (bondholders)

Cash flow to creditors = Interest paid − Net new borrowing

IV. Cash flow to stockholders (owners)

Cash flow to stockholders = Dividends paid − Net new equity raised

---

much stock the company has sold. During the year, this account rose by $40, so $40 in net new equity was raised. Given this, we have:

U.S. CORPORATION
1992 Cash Flow to Stockholders

Dividends paid	$103
− Net new equity raised	40
Cash flow to stockholders	$ 63

The cash flow to stockholders for 1992 was thus $63.

The last thing that we need to do is to check that the cash flow identity holds to be sure that we didn't make any mistakes. From above, cash flow from assets is $87. Cash flow to creditors and stockholders is $24 + 63 = $87, so everything checks out. Table 2.5 contains a summary of the various cash flow calculations for future reference.

As our discussion indicates, it is essential that a firm keep an eye on its cash flow. The following serves as an excellent reminder of why doing so is a good idea, unless the firm's owners wish to end up in the "Poe" house.

Quoth the Banker, "Watch Cash Flow"

Once upon a midnight dreary as I pondered weak and weary
Over many a quaint and curious volume of accounting lore,

Seeking gimmicks (without scruple) to squeeze through
    some new tax loophole,
Suddenly I heard a knock upon my door,
       Only this, and nothing more.

Then I felt a queasy tingling and I heard the cash a-jingling
As a fearsome banker entered whom I'd often seen before.
His face was money-green and in his eyes there could be seen
Dollar-signs that seemed to glitter as he reckoned up the score.
       "Cash flow," the banker said, and nothing more.

I had always thought it fine to show a jet black bottom line.
But the banker sounded a resounding, "No.
Your receivables are high, mounting upward toward the sky;
Write-offs loom. What matters is cash flow."
       He repeated, "Watch cash flow."

Then I tried to tell the story of our lovely inventory
Which, though large, is full of most delightful stuff.
But the banker saw its growth, and with a mighty oath
He waved his arms and shouted, "Stop! Enough!
       Pay the interest, and don't give me any guff!"

Next I looked for noncash items which could add ad infinitum
To replace the ever-outward flow of cash,
But to keep my statement black I'd held depreciation back,
And my banker said that I'd done something rash.
       He quivered, and his teeth began to gnash.

When I asked him for a loan, he responded, with a groan,
That the interest rate would be just prime plus eight,
And to guarantee my purity he'd insist on some security—
All my assets plus the scalp upon my pate.
       Only this, a standard rate.

Though my bottom line is black, I am flat upon my back,
My cash flows out and customers pay slow.
The growth of my receivables is almost unbelievable:
The result is certain—unremitting woe!
And I hear the banker utter an ominous low mutter,
       "Watch cash flow."

Herbert S. Bailey, Jr.

Reprinted from the January 13, 1975, issue of *Publishers Weekly,* published by
R. R. Bowker, a Xerox company. Copyright © 1975 by the Xerox Corporation.

To which we can only add: "Amen."

An Example: Cash Flows for Dole Cola

This extended example covers the various cash flow calculations discussed in
the chapter. It also illustrates a few variations that may arise.

Operating Cash Flow   During the year, Dole Cola, Inc., had sales and costs of goods sold of $600 and $300, respectively. Depreciation was $150 and interest paid was $30. Taxes were calculated at a straight 34 percent. Dividends were $30. (All figures are in millions of dollars.) What was operating cash flow for Dole? Why is this different from net income?

The easiest thing to do here is to go ahead and create an income statement. We can then pick up the numbers we need. Dole Cola's income statement is given below.

DOLE COLA
1992 Income Statement
($ in millions)

Net sales	$600
Cost of goods sold	300
Depreciation	150
Earnings before interest and taxes	$150
Interest paid	30
Taxable income	$120
Taxes	41
Net income	$ 79

Addition to retained earnings	$49	
Dividends	30	

Net income for Dole was thus $79. We now have all the numbers we need. Referring back to the U.S. Corporation example and Table 2.5, we have:

DOLE COLA
1992 Operating Cash Flow

Earnings before interest and taxes	$150
+ Depreciation	150
− Taxes	41
Operating cash flow	$259

As this example illustrates, operating cash flow is not the same as net income, because depreciation and interest are subtracted out when net income is calculated. If you recall our earlier discussion, we don't subtract these out in computing operating cash flow because depreciation is not a cash expense and interest paid is a financing expense, not an operating expense.

Net Capital Spending   Suppose that beginning net fixed assets were $500 and ending net fixed assets were $750. What was the net capital spending for the year?

From the income statement for Dole, depreciation for the year was $150. Net fixed assets rose by $250. Dole thus spent $250 along with an additional $150, for a total of $400.

Change in NWC and Cash Flow from Assets   Suppose that Dole Cola started the year with $2,130 in current assets and $1,620 in current liabilities. The corresponding ending figures were $2,260 and $1,710. What was the addition to NWC during the year? What was cash flow from assets? How does this compare to net income?

Net working capital started out as $2,130 − 1,620 = $510 and ended up at $2,260 − 1,710 = $550. The addition to NWC was thus $550 − 510 = $40. Putting together all the information for Dole we have:

DOLE COLA
1992 Cash Flow from Assets

Operating cash flow	$259
− Net capital spending	400
− Additions to NWC	40
Cash flow from assets	−$181

Dole had a cash flow from assets of negative $181. Net income was positive at $79. Is the fact that cash flow from assets was negative a cause for alarm? Not necessarily. The cash flow here is negative primarily because of a large investment in fixed assets. If these are good investments, then the resulting negative cash flow is not a worry.

Cash Flow to Creditors and Stockholders   We saw that Dole Cola had cash flow from assets of −$181. The fact that this is negative means that Dole raised more money in the form of new debt and equity than it paid out for the year. For example, suppose we know that Dole didn't sell any new equity for the year. What was cash flow to stockholders? To creditors?

Since it didn't raise any new equity, Dole's cash flow to stockholders is just equal to the cash dividend paid:

DOLE COLA
1992 Cash Flow to Stockholders

Dividends paid	$30
− Net new equity	0
Cash flow to stockholders	$30

Now, from the cash flow identity the total cash paid to creditors and stockholders was −$181. Cash flow to stockholders is $30, so cash flow to creditors must be equal to −$181 − $30 = −$211:

Cash flow to creditors + Cash flow to stockholders = −$181
Cash flow to creditors + $30   = −$181
Cash flow to creditors   = −$211

Since cash flow to creditors is −$211 and interest paid is $30 (from the income statement), we can now determine net new borrowing. Dole must have borrowed $241 during the year to help finance the fixed asset expansion:

DOLE COLA
1992 Cash Flow to Creditors

Interest paid	$ 30
− Net new borrowing	− 241
Cash flow to creditors	−$211

⌐CONCEPT QUESTIONS

2.4a What is the cash flow identity? Explain what it says.

2.4b What are the components of operating cash flow?

2.4c Why is interest paid not a component of operating cash flow?

2.5 | SUMMARY AND CONCLUSIONS

This chapter has introduced you to some of the basics of financial statements, taxes, and cash flow. In it we saw that:

1. The book values on an accounting balance sheet can be very different from market values. The goal of financial management is to maximize the market value of the stock, not its book value.

2. Net income as it is computed on the income statement is not cash flow. A primary reason is that depreciation, a noncash expense, is deducted when net income is computed.

3. Marginal and average tax rates can be different, and it is the marginal tax rate that is relevant for most financial decisions.

4. Corporate tax rates in the United States generally exceed personal tax rates. The marginal tax rate paid by the corporations with the largest incomes is 34 percent.

5. There is a cash flow identity much like the balance sheet identity. It says that cash flow from assets equals cash flow to creditors and stockholders.

The calculation of cash flow from financial statements isn't difficult. Care must be taken in handling noncash expenses, such as depreciation, and in not confusing operating costs with financing costs. Most of all, it is important not to confuse book values with market values and accounting income with cash flow.

Key Terms

balance sheet 23	average tax rate 32
net working capital 25	marginal tax rate 32
Generally Accepted Accounting	cash flow from assets 35
Principles (GAAP) 27	operating cash flow 35
income statement 29	cash flow to creditors 37
noncash items 30	cash flow to stockholders 37

Chapter Review Problem and Self-Test

2.1 Cash Flow for Rasputin Corporation   This problem will give you some practice working with financial statements and figuring cash flow. Based on the following information for Rasputin Corporation, prepare an income statement for 1992 and balance sheets for 1991 and 1992. Next, following our U.S. Corporation examples in the chapter, calculate cash flow from assets for Rasputin, cash flow to creditors, and cash flow to stockholders for 1992. Use a 34 percent tax rate throughout. You can check your answers below.

	1991	1992
Sales	$3,790	$3,990
Cost of goods sold	2,043	2,137
Depreciation	975	1,018
Interest	225	267
Dividends	200	225
Current assets	2,140	2,346
Net fixed assets	6,770	7,087
Current liabilities	994	1,126
Long-term debt	2,869	2,956

Answer to Self-Test Problem

2.1   In preparing the balance sheets, remember that shareholders' equity is the residual. With this in mind, Rasputin's balance sheets are as follows:

RASPUTIN CORPORATION
Balance Sheets as of December 31, 1991 and 1992

	1991	1992		1991	1992
Current assets	$2,140	$2,346	Current liabilities	$ 994	$1,126
Net fixed assets	6,770	7,087	Long-term debt	2,869	2,956
			Equity	5,047	5,351
Total assets	$8,910	$9,433	Total liabilities and shareholders' equity	$8,910	$9,433

The income statement is straightforward:

RASPUTIN CORPORATION
1992 Income Statement

Sales		$3,990
Cost of goods sold		2,137
Depreciation		1,018
Earnings before interest and taxes		$ 835
Interest paid		267
Taxable income		$ 568
Taxes (34%)		193
Net income		$ 375
Addition to retained earnings	$150	
Dividends	225	

Notice that we've used a flat 34 percent tax rate. Also notice that the addition to retained earnings is just net income less cash dividends.

We can now pick up the figures we need to get operating cash flow:

RASPUTIN CORPORATION
1992 Operating Cash Flow

Earnings before interest and taxes	$ 835
+ Depreciation	1,018
− Current taxes	193
Operating cash flow	$1,660

Next, we get the capital spending for the year by looking at the change in fixed assets, remembering to account for the depreciation:

Ending fixed assets	$7,087
− Beginning fixed assets	6,770
+ Depreciation	1,018
Net investment in fixed assets	$1,335

After calculating beginning and ending NWC, we take the difference to get the additions to NWC:

Ending NWC	$1,220
− Beginning NWC	1,146
Additions to NWC	$ 74

We now combine operating cash flow, net capital spending, and the additions to net working capital to get the total cash flow from assets:

RASPUTIN CORPORATION
1992 Cash Flow from Assets

Operating cash flow	$1,660
− Net capital spending	1,335
− Additions to NWC	74
Cash flow from assets	$ 251

To get cash flow to creditors, notice that long-term borrowing increased by $87 during the year and that interest paid was $267, so:

RASPUTIN CORPORATION
1992 Cash Flow to Creditors

Interest paid	$267
− Net new borrowing	87
Cash flow to creditors	$180

Finally, dividends paid were $225. To get net new equity, we have to do some extra calculating. Total equity was up by $5,351 − 5,047 = $304. Of this increase, $150 was from additions to retained earnings, so $154 in new equity was raised during the year. Cash flow to stockholders was thus:

RASPUTIN CORPORATION
1992 Cash Flow to Stockholders

Dividends paid	$225
− Net new equity	154
Cash flow to stockholders	$ 71

As a check, notice that cash flow from assets ($251) does equal cash flow to creditors plus cash flow to stockholders ($180 + 71 = $251).

Questions and Problems

1. Preparing an Income Statement   Prepare an income statement from the following information: sales, $500,000; cost of goods sold, $200,000; administrative expenses, $100,000; interest paid, $50,000. The tax rate is 34 percent.

2. Income Statements   The Dorff Company had sales of $2,500, cost of goods sold of $900, depreciation of $650, and interest paid of $550. If the tax rate is 34 percent and all taxes are paid currently, what is net income?

3. Calculating OCF   Based on the information in Problem 2, what is Dorff's operating cash flow?

4. OCF versus Net Income   What is the difference between net income and operating cash flow? Could operating cash flow be positive if net income is negative?

5. OCF versus Net Income   The Flying Lion Corporation reported the following income statement data:

	19X2	19X3
Net sales	$1,000	$800
Cost of goods sold	560	320
Operating expenses	75	56
Depreciation	300	200

The tax rate is 34 percent.
a. Prepare an income statement for both years.
b. Determine operating cash flow for both years.
c. Comment on the difference between accounting profit and cash flow for Flying Lion.

6. OCF and Net Income   During 1991, the Senbet Discount Tire Company had gross sales of $1 million. Its cost of goods sold and selling expenses were $300,000 and $200,000, respectively. Senbet also has notes payable of $1 million. The interest rate is 10 percent. Depreciation was $100,000. The tax rate is 34 percent.
a. What are Senbet's earnings before interest and taxes?
b. What is its net income?
c. What is its cash flow from operations?

7.   Liquidity   What is liquidity? Explain why we say that liquidity has two dimensions.

8.   Preparing a Balance Sheet   Prepare a balance sheet for the Junior Corp. as of December 31 based on the following information: cash, $4,000; patents, $82,000; accounts payable, $6,000; accounts receivable, $8,000; machinery and other tangible net fixed assets, $40,000; long-term debt, $70,000; accumulated retained earnings, $38,000. (Hint: remember that Assets = Liabilities + Equity.)

9.   Balance Sheet Calculations   Following are the long-term liabilities and stockholders' equity of the Data Control Company's balance sheet on December 31, 1991. During 1992, Data Control issues $10 million of new common stock, but no additional debt. Data Control generates $5 million of net income and pays out $3 million in dividends. Complete the account balances shown for December 31, 1992.

	December 31, 1991	December 31, 1992
Long-term debt	$ 50,000,000	
Common stock	100,000,000	
Retained earnings	20,000,000	
Total	$170,000,000	

10. Tax Rates   The Stowe Co. had a taxable income of $140,000 in 1992. Based on Table 2.3 in the chapter, calculate the actual tax bill for the year. What is the average tax rate? The marginal tax rate?

11. Tax Rates   In Problem 10, what would the answers be if taxable income were $640,000?

12. Capital Spending   The Patel Co. began the year with $50,000 in net fixed assets. Depreciation for the year was $17,000. Ending net fixed assets were $60,000. What was Patel's net capital spending for the year?

13. Calculating Changes in NWC   Hamm Co.'s beginning current assets were $400. Ending current assets were $530. Current liabilities rose from $225 to $390. What was Hamm's NWC at the beginning and the end of the year? How much did Hamm invest in NWC for the year?

14. Depreciation and Capital Spending   MaxModem, Inc., invested $65,000 total in capital equipment for the year. Beginning net fixed assets were $147,000 and ending net fixed assets were $133,000. What was depreciation for the year?

15. Market Value versus Book Value   Explain the difference between market value and book value. Which is more relevant? Why?

16. Computing Cash Flows   Consider the following financial statement information for RTE Corporation:

RTE CORPORATION
Partial Balance Sheets as of December 31, 1991 and 1992

Assets	1991	1992	Liabilities and Owners' Equity	1991	1992
Current assets	$176	$208	Current liabilities	$ 98	$116
Net fixed assets	770	881	Long-term debt	569	576

RTE CORPORATION
1992 Income Statement

Sales	$1,995
Costs	647
Depreciation	228
Interest	116

a. What is owners' equity for 1991 and 1992?

b. What is net working capital for 1991 and 1992? What is the addition to NWC for 1992?

c. What is net income for 1992? What is operating cash flow? Assume a 34 percent tax rate.

d. In 1992, RTE purchased $500 in new fixed assets. How much in fixed assets did RTE sell? What is cash flow from assets for the year?

e. During the year 1992, RTE raised $50 in new long-term debt. How much must RTE have paid off during the year? What is the net cash flow to bondholders (creditors) for the year?

Use the following information for NearPerfect Co. to work Problems 17 and 18:

	1991	1992
Sales	$1,145	$1,200
Depreciation	128	128
Cost of goods sold	450	537
Other expenses	110	98
Interest	85	96
Cash	640	735
Receivables	912	967
Short-term notes payable	122	103
Long-term debt	2,349	2,666
Net fixed assets	5,556	5,637
Accounts payable	664	659
Inventory	1,440	1,489
Dividends	100	110

17. Financial Statements   Draw up an income statement and a balance sheet for NearPerfect for 1991 and 1992. The tax rate is 34 percent.

18. Computing Cash Flow   (This one's a little harder.) For 1992, calculate NearPerfect's cash flow from assets, cash flow to creditors, and cash flow to stockholders. The tax rate is 34 percent.

Suggested Reading

There are many excellent textbooks on accounting and financial statements. One that we have found helpful is:

Welsch, G. A., and C.T. Zlatkovich. *Intermediate Accounting.* 8th ed. Homewood, Ill.: Richard D. Irwin, 1989.

Part Two

Financial Statements and Long-Term Financial Planning

CHAPTER 3
Working with Financial Statements

This chapter discusses different aspects of financial statements, including how the statement of cash flows is constructed, how to standardize financial statements, and how to determine and interpret some common financial ratios.

CHAPTER 4
Long-Term Financial Planning and Growth

Chapter 4 examines the basic elements of financial planning. It introduces the concept of sustainable growth, which can be a very useful tool in financial planning.

Chapter 3

Working with Financial Statements

In Chapter 2, we discussed some of the essential concepts of financial statements and cash flows. Part Two, this chapter and the next, continues where our earlier discussion left off. Our goal here is to expand your understanding of the uses (and abuses) of financial statement information.

Financial statement information will crop up in various places in the remainder of our book. Part Two is not essential for understanding this material, but it will help give you an overall perspective on the role of financial statement information in corporate finance.

A good working knowledge of financial statements is desirable simply because such statements, and numbers derived from those statements, are the primary means of communicating financial information both within the firm and outside the firm. In short, much of the language of corporate finance is rooted in the ideas we discuss in this chapter.

Furthermore, as we shall see, there are many different ways of using financial statement information and many different types of users. This diversity reflects the fact that financial statement information plays an important part in many types of decisions.

In the best of all worlds, the financial manager has full market value information about all of the firm's assets. This will rarely (if ever) happen. So the reason that we rely on accounting figures for much of our financial information is that we almost always cannot obtain all (or even part) of the market information that we want. The only meaningful yardstick for evaluating business decisions is whether or not they create economic value (see Chapter 1). However, in many important situations, it will not be possible to make this judgment directly because we can't see the market value effects.

We recognize that accounting numbers are often just pale reflections of economic reality, but they frequently are the best available information. For privately held corporations, not-for-profit businesses, and smaller firms, for example, very little direct market value information exists at all. The accountant's reporting function is crucial in these circumstances.

Clearly, one important goal of the accountant is to report financial information to the user in a form that is useful for decision making. Ironically, the information frequently does not come to the user in such a form. In other words, financial statements don't come with a user's guide. This chapter and the next are first steps in filling this gap.

3.1 | CASH FLOW AND FINANCIAL STATEMENTS: A CLOSER LOOK

At the most fundamental level, firms do two different things: They generate cash and they spend it. Cash is generated by selling a product, an asset, or a security. Selling a security involves either borrowing or selling an equity interest (i.e., shares of stock) in the firm. Cash is spent by paying for materials and labor to produce a product and by purchasing assets. Payments to creditors and owners also require spending cash.

In Chapter 2, we saw that the cash activities of a firm could be summarized by a simple identity:

Cash flow from assets = Cash flow to creditors + Cash flow to owners

This cash flow identity summarizes the total cash result of all of the transactions that the firm engaged in during the year. In this section, we return to the subject of cash flows by taking a closer look at the cash events during the year that lead to these total figures.

Sources and Uses of Cash

sources of cash

A firm's activities that generate cash.

uses of cash

A firm's activities in which cash is spent. Also applications of cash.

Those activities that bring in cash are called **sources of cash.** Those activities that involve spending cash are called **uses** (or applications) **of cash.** What we need to do is to trace the changes in the firm's balance sheet to see how the firm obtained its cash and how the firm spent its cash during some time period.

To get started, consider the balance sheets for the Prufrock Corporation in Table 3.1. Notice that we have calculated the changes in each of the items on the balance sheet.

Looking over the balance sheets for Prufrock, we see that quite a few things changed during the year. For example, Prufrock increased its net fixed assets by $149 million and its inventory by $29 million. Where did the money come from? To answer this and related questions, we need to first identify those changes that used up cash (uses) and those that brought cash in (sources).

A little common sense is useful here. A firm uses cash by either buying assets or making payments. So, loosely speaking, an increase in an asset ac-

PRUFROCK CORPORATION Balance Sheets as of December 31, 1991 and 1992 ($ in millions)			
	1991	1992	Change
Assets			
Current assets			
Cash	$ 84	$ 98	+$ 14
Accounts receivable	165	188	+ 23
Inventory	393	422	+ 29
Total	$ 642	$ 708	+$ 66
Fixed assets			
Net plant and equipment	$2,731	$2,880	+$149
Total assets	$3,373	$3,588	+$215
Liabilities and Owners' Equity			
Current liabilities			
Accounts payable	$ 312	$ 344	+$ 32
Notes payable	231	196	− 35
Total	$ 543	$ 540	−$ 3
Long-term debt	$ 531	$ 457	−$ 74
Owners' equity			
Common stock and paid-in surplus	$ 500	$ 550	+$ 50
Retained earnings	1,799	2,041	+ 242
Total	$2,299	$2,591	+$292
Total liabilities and owners' equity	$3,373	$3,588	+$215

Table 3.1

count means that the firm, on a net basis, bought some assets, a use of cash. If an asset account went down, then, on a net basis, the firm sold some assets. This would be a net source. Similarly, if a liability account goes down, then the firm has made a net payment, a use of cash.

Given this reasoning, there is a simple, albeit mechanical, definition that you may find useful. An increase in a left-hand side (asset) account or a decrease in a right-hand side (liability or equity) account is a use of cash. Likewise, a decrease in an asset account or an increase in a liability (or equity) account is a source of cash.

Looking back at Prufrock, we see that inventory rose by $29. This is a net use since Prufrock effectively paid out $29 to increase inventories. Accounts payable rose by $32. This is a source of cash since Prufrock effectively has borrowed an additional $32 by the end of the year. Notes payable, on the other hand, went down by $35, so Prufrock effectively paid off $35 worth of short-term debt—a use of cash.

Based on our discussion, we can summarize the sources and uses from the balance sheet as follows:

Sources of cash:	
Increase in accounts payable	$ 32
Increase in common stock	50
Increase in retained earnings	242
Total sources	$324
Uses of cash:	
Increase in accounts receivable	$ 23
Increase in inventory	29
Decrease in notes payable	35
Decrease in long-term debt	74
Net fixed asset acquisitions	149
Total uses	$310
Net addition to cash	$ 14

The net addition to cash is just the difference between sources and uses, and our $14 result here agrees with the $14 change shown on the balance sheet.

This simple statement tells us much of what happened during the year, but it doesn't tell the whole story. For example, the increase in retained earnings is net income (a source of funds) less dividends (a use of funds). It would be more enlightening to have these reported separately so we could see the breakdown. Also, we have only considered net fixed asset acquisitions. Total or gross spending would be more interesting to know.

To further trace the flow of cash through the firm during the year, we need an income statement. For Prufrock, the results for the year are shown in Table 3.2.

Table 3.2	PRUFROCK CORPORATION 1992 Income Statement ($ in millions)

Sales	$2,311
Cost of goods sold	1,344
Depreciation	276
Earnings before interest and taxes	$ 691
Interest paid	141
Taxable income	$ 550
Taxes (34%)	187
Net income	$ 363

Addition to retained earnings	$242
Dividends	121

Notice here that the $242 addition to retained earnings we calculated from the balance sheet is just the difference between the net income of $363 and the dividend of $121.

The Statement of Cash Flows

There is some flexibility in summarizing the sources and uses of cash in the form of a financial statement. However it is presented, the result is called the **statement of cash flows.** Historically, this statement was called the *statement of changes in financial position* and it was presented in terms of the changes in net working capital rather than cash flows. We will work with the newer cash format.

We present a particular format in Table 3.3 for this statement. The basic idea is to group all the changes into one of three categories: operating activities, financing activities, and investment activities. The exact form differs in detail from one preparer to the next.

Don't be surprised if you come across different arrangements. The types of information presented will be very similar; the exact order can differ. The key thing to remember in this case is that we started out with $84 in cash and

statement of cash flows
A firm's financial statement that summarizes its sources and uses of cash over a specified period.

Table 3.3

PRUFROCK CORPORATION
1992 Statement of Cash Flows
($ in millions)

Cash, beginning of year	$ 84
Operating activity	
Net income	363
Plus:	
Depreciation	276
Increase in accounts payable	32
Less:	
Increase in accounts receivable	− 23
Increase in inventory	− 29
Net cash from operating activity	$619
Investment activity	
Fixed asset acquisitions	−$425
Net cash from investment activity	−$425
Financing activity	
Decrease in notes payable	−$ 35
Decrease in long-term debt	− 74
Dividends paid	− 121
Increase in common stock	50
Net cash from financing activity	−$180
Net increase in cash	$ 14
Cash, end of year	$ 98

ended up with $98, for a net increase of $14. We're just trying to see what events led to this change.

Going back to Chapter 2, there is a slight conceptual problem here. Interest paid should really go under financing activities, but, unfortunately, that's not the way the accounting is handled. The reason, you may recall, is that interest is deducted as an expense when net income is computed. Also, as shown, notice that our net purchase of fixed assets was $149. Since we wrote off $276 worth (the depreciation), we must have actually spent a total of $149 + 276 = $425 on fixed assets.

Once we have this statement, it might seem appropriate to express the change in cash on a per share basis, much as we did for net income. Ironically, despite the interest that we might have in some measure of cash flow per share, standard accounting practice expressly prohibits reporting this information. The reason is that accountants feel that cash flow (or some component of cash flow) is not an alternative to accounting income, so only earnings per share are to be reported.

As shown in Table 3.4, it is sometimes useful to present the same information a bit differently. We will call this the "sources and uses of cash" state-

Table 3.4	PRUFROCK CORPORATION 1992 Sources and Uses of Cash ($ in millions)	
	Cash, beginning of year	$ 84
	Sources of cash	
	Operations:	
	Net income	363
	Depreciation	276
		$639
	Working capital:	
	Increase in accounts payable	$ 32
	Long-term financing:	
	Increase in common stock	50
	Total sources of cash	$721
	Uses of cash	
	Working capital:	
	Increase in accounts receivable	$ 23
	Increase in inventory	29
	Decrease in notes payable	35
	Long-term financing:	
	Decrease in long-term debt	74
	Fixed asset acquisitions	425
	Dividends paid	121
	Total uses of cash	$707
	Net addition to cash	$ 14
	Cash, end of year	$ 98

ment. There is no such statement in financial accounting, but this arrangement resembles one that was used many years ago. As we discuss below, this form can come in handy, but we emphasize again that it is not the way this information is normally presented.

Now that we have the various cash pieces in place, we can get a good idea of what happened during the year. Prufrock's major cash outlays were fixed asset acquisitions and cash dividends. They paid for these activities primarily with cash generated from operations.

Prufrock also retired some long-term debt and increased current assets. Finally, current liabilities were virtually unchanged, and a relatively small amount of new equity was sold. Altogether, this short sketch captures Prufrock's major sources and uses of cash for the year.

CONCEPT QUESTIONS

3.1a What is a source of cash? Give three examples.
3.1b What is a use or application of cash? Give three examples.

STANDARDIZED FINANCIAL STATEMENTS | 3.2

The next thing we might want to do with Prufrock's financial statements is to compare them to those of other, similar companies. We would immediately have a problem, however. It's almost impossible to directly compare the financial statements for two companies because of differences in size.

For example, Ford and GM are obviously serious rivals in the auto market, but GM is much larger (in terms of assets), so it is difficult to compare them directly. For that matter, it's difficult to even compare financial statements from different points in time for the same company if the company's size has changed. The size problem is compounded if we try to compare GM and, say, Toyota. If Toyota's financial statements are denominated in yen, then we have a size *and* a currency difference.

To start making comparisons, one obvious thing we might try to do is to somehow standardize the financial statements. One very common and useful way of doing this is to work with percentages instead of total dollars. In this section, we describe two different ways of standardizing financial statements along these lines.

Common-Size Statements

To get started, a useful way of standardizing financial statements is to express the balance sheet as a percentage of assets and to express the income statement as a percentage of sales. Such financial statements are called **common-size statements.** We consider these next.

Common-Size Balance Sheets   One way, but not the only way, to construct a common-size balance sheet is to express each item as a percentage of total assets. Prufrock's 1991 and 1992 common-size balance sheets are shown in Table 3.5.

common-size statement
A standardized financial statement presenting all items in percentage terms. Balance sheets are shown as a percentage of assets and income statements as a percentage of sales.

Table 3.5

PRUFROCK CORPORATION
Common-Size Balance Sheets
December 31, 1991 and 1992

	1991	1992	Change
Assets			
Current assets			
Cash	2.5%	2.7%	+ .2%
Accounts receivable	4.9	5.2	+ .3
Inventory	11.7	11.8	+ .1
Total	19.1	19.7	+ .6
Fixed assets			
Net plant and equipment	80.9	80.3	− .6
Total assets	100.0%	100.0%	0
Liabilities and Owners' Equity			
Current liabilities			
Accounts payable	9.2%	9.6%	+ .4%
Notes payable	6.8	5.5	−1.3
Total	16.0	15.1	− .9
Long-term debt	15.7	12.7	−3.0
Owners' equity			
Common stock and paid-in surplus	14.8	15.3	+ .5
Retained earnings	53.3	56.9	+3.6
Total	68.1	72.2	+4.1
Total liabilities and owners' equity	100.0%	100.0%	0

Notice that some of the totals don't check exactly because of rounding errors. Also, notice that the total change has to be zero since the beginning and ending numbers must add up to 100 percent.

In this form, financial statements are relatively easy to read and compare. For example, just looking at the two balance sheets for Prufrock, we see that current assets were 19.7 percent of total assets in 1992, up from 19.1 percent in 1991. Current liabilities declined from 16.0 percent to 15.1 percent of total liabilities and equity over that same time. Similarly, total equity rose from 68.1 percent of total liabilities and equity to 72.2 percent.

Overall, Prufrock's liquidity, as measured by current assets compared to current liabilities, increased over the year. Simultaneously, Prufrock's indebtedness diminished as a percentage of total assets. We might be tempted to conclude that the balance sheet has grown "stronger." We will say more about this later.

Common-Size Income Statements   A useful way of standardizing the income statement is to express each item as a percentage of total sales, as illustrated for Prufrock in Table 3.6.

PRUFROCK CORPORATION Common-Size Income Statement 1992		Table 3.6
Sales	100.0%	
Cost of goods sold	58.2	
Depreciation	11.9	
Earnings before interest and taxes	29.9	
Interest paid	6.1	
Taxable income	23.8	
Taxes (34%)	8.1	
Net income	15.7%	
Addition to retained earnings	10.5%	
Dividends	5.2	

This income statement tells us what happens to each dollar in sales. For Prufrock, interest expense eats up $.061 out of every sales dollar and taxes take another $.081. When all is said and done, $.157 of each dollar flows through to the bottom line (net income), and that amount is split into $.105 retained in the business and $.052 paid out in dividends.

These percentages are very useful in comparisons. For example, a very relevant figure is the cost percentage. For Prufrock, $.582 of each $1.00 in sales goes to pay for goods sold. It would be interesting to compute the same percentage for Prufrock's main competitors to see how Prufrock stacks up in terms of cost control.

Although we have not presented it here, it is also possible and useful to prepare a common-size statement of cash flows. Unfortunately, with the current statement of cash flows, there is no obvious denominator such as total assets or total sales. However, if the information is arranged in a way similar to Table 3.4, then each item can be expressed as a percentage of total sources (or total uses). The results can then be interpreted as the percentage of total sources of cash supplied or as the percentage of total uses of cash for a particular item.

Common-Base-Year Financial Statements: Trend Analysis

Imagine that we were given balance sheets for the last 10 years for some company and we were trying to investigate trends in the firm's pattern of operations. Does the firm use more or less debt? Has the firm grown more or less liquid? A useful way of standardizing financial statements in this case is to choose a base year and then express each item relative to the base amount. We will call such statements **common-base-year statements.**

For example, Prufrock's inventory rose from $393 to $422. If we pick 1991 as our base year, then we would set inventory equal to 1.00 for that year. For the next year, we would calculate inventory relative to the base year as $422/$393 = 1.07. In this case, we could say that inventory grew by about 7 percent during the year. If we had multiple years, we would just divide each

common-base-year statement

A standardized financial statement presenting all items relative to a certain base-year amount.

Table 3.7	PRUFROCK CORPORATION Summary of Standardized Balance Sheets (Asset side only)					

	Assets ($ in millions)		Common-Size Assets		Common-Base- Year Assets 1992	Combined Common-Size and Base-Year Assets 1992
	1991	1992	1991	1992		
Current assets						
Cash	$ 84	$ 98	2.5%	2.7%	1.17	1.08
Accounts receivable	165	188	4.9	5.2	1.14	1.06
Inventory	393	422	11.7	11.8	1.07	1.01
Total current assets	$ 642	$ 708	19.1	19.7	1.10	1.03
Fixed assets						
Net plant and equipment	$2,731	$2,880	80.9	80.3	1.05	0.99
Total assets	$3,373	$3,588	100.0%	100.0%	1.06	1.00

The common-size numbers are calculated by dividing each item by total assets for that year. For example, the 1991 common-size cash amount is $84/$3,373 = 2.5%. The common-base-year numbers are calculated by dividing each 1992 item by the base-year (1991) dollar amount. The common-base cash is thus $98/$84 = 1.17, representing a 17 percent increase. The combined common-size and base-year figures are calculated by dividing each common-size amount by the base-year (1991) common-size amount. The cash figure is therefore 2.7%/2.5% = 1.08, representing an 8 percent increase in cash holdings as a percentage of total assets. Columns may not total precisely due to rounding.

one by $393. The resulting series is very easy to plot, and it is then very easy to compare two or more different companies. Table 3.7 summarizes these calculations for the asset side of the balance sheet.

Combined Common-Size and Base-Year Analysis   The trend analysis we have been discussing can be combined with the common-size analysis discussed above. The reason for doing this is that as total assets grow, most of the other accounts must grow as well. By first forming the common-size statements, we eliminate the effect of this overall growth.

For example, looking at Table 3.7, Prufrock's accounts receivable were $165, or 4.9 percent of total assets in 1991. In 1992, they had risen to $188, which is 5.2 percent of total assets. If we do our analysis in terms of dollars, then the 1992 figure would be $188/$165 = 1.14, a 14 percent increase in receivables. However, if we work with the common-size statements, then the 1992 figure would be 5.2%/4.9% = 1.06. This tells us that accounts receivable, as a percentage of total assets, grew by 6 percent. Roughly speaking, what we see is that of the 14 percent total increase, about 8 percent (14% − 6%) is attributable simply to growth in total assets.

CONCEPT QUESTIONS

3.2a Why is it often necessary to standardize financial statements?

3.2b Name two types of standardized statements and describe how each is formed.

RATIO ANALYSIS | 3.3

Another way of avoiding the problem of comparing companies of different sizes is to calculate and compare **financial ratios.** Such ratios are ways of comparing and investigating the relationships between different pieces of financial information. Using ratios eliminates the size problem since the size effectively divides out. We're then left with percentages, multiples, or time periods.

financial ratios
Relationships determined from a firm's financial information and used for comparison purposes.

There is a problem in discussing financial ratios. Since a ratio is simply one number divided by another, and since there is a substantial quantity of accounting numbers out there, there are a huge number of possible ratios we could examine. Everybody has their favorite. We will restrict ourselves to a representative sampling.

In this section, we only want to introduce you to some commonly used financial ratios. We don't choose the ones we think are necessarily the best. In fact, some of the definitions may strike you as illogical or not as useful as some alternatives. If they do, don't be concerned. As a financial analyst, you can always decide how to compute your own ratios.

What you do need to worry about is the fact that different people and different sources frequently don't compute these ratios in exactly the same way, and this leads to much confusion. The specific definitions we use here may or may not be the same as ones you have seen or will see elsewhere. If you are ever using ratios as a tool for analysis, you should be careful to document how you calculate each one.

We will defer much of our discussion of how ratios are used and some problems that come up with using them to the next section. For now, for each of the ratios we discuss, several questions come to mind:

1. How is it computed?
2. What is it intended to measure, and why might we be interested?
3. What is the unit of measurement?
4. What might a high or low value be telling us? How might such values be misleading?
5. How could this measure be improved?

Financial ratios are traditionally grouped into the following categories:

1. Short-term solvency or liquidity ratios
2. Long-term solvency or financial leverage ratios
3. Asset management or turnover ratios
4. Profitability ratios
5. Market value ratios

We will consider each of these in turn. In calculating these numbers for Prufrock, we will use the ending balance sheet (1992) figures unless we explicitly say otherwise. Also, notice that the various ratios are color-keyed to indicate which numbers come from the income statement and which come from the balance sheet.

Short-Term Solvency or Liquidity Measures

As the name suggests, short-term solvency ratios as a group are intended to provide information about a firm's liquidity, and these ratios are sometimes called *liquidity measures*. The primary concern is the firm's ability to pay its bills over the short run without undue stress. Consequently, these ratios focus on current assets and current liabilities.

For obvious reasons, liquidity ratios are particularly interesting to short-term creditors. Since financial managers are constantly working with banks and other short-term lenders, an understanding of these ratios is essential.

One advantage of looking at current assets and liabilities is that their book values and market values are likely to be similar. Often (but not always), these assets and liabilities just don't live long enough for the two to get seriously out of step. On the other hand, like any type of near-cash, current assets and liabilities can and do change fairly rapidly, so today's amounts may not be a reliable guide to the future.

Current Ratio   One of the best known and most widely used ratios is the *current ratio*. As you might guess, the current ratio is defined as:

$$\text{Current ratio} = \frac{\text{Current assets}}{\text{Current liabilities}} \qquad [3.1]$$

For Prufrock, the 1992 current ratio is:

$$\text{Current ratio} = \frac{\$708}{\$540} = 1.31 \text{ times}$$

Because current assets and liabilities are, in principle, converted to cash over the following 12 months, the current ratio is a measure of short-term liquidity. The unit of measurement is either dollars or times. So, we could say that Prufrock has $1.31 in current assets for every $1 in current liabilities, or we could say that Prufrock has its current liabilities covered 1.31 times over.

To a creditor, particularly a short-term creditor such as a supplier, the higher the current ratio, the better. To the firm, a high current ratio indicates liquidity, but it also may indicate an inefficient use of cash and other short-term assets. Absent some extraordinary circumstances, we would expect to see a current ratio of at least 1, because a current ratio of less than 1 would mean that net working capital (current assets less current liabilities) is negative. This would be unusual in a healthy firm, at least for most types of business.

The current ratio, like any ratio, is affected by various types of transactions. For example, suppose the firm borrows long term to raise money. The short-run effect would be an increase in cash from the issue proceeds and an increase in long-term debt. Current liabilities would not be affected, so the current ratio would rise.

Finally, note that an apparently low current ratio may not be a bad sign for a company with a large reserve of untapped borrowing power.

Example 3.1 Current Events
Suppose a firm were to pay off some of its suppliers and short-term creditors. What would happen to the current ratio? Suppose a firm buys some inventory. What happens in this case? What happens if a firm sells some merchandise?

The first case is a trick question. What happens is that the current ratio moves away from 1. If it is greater than 1 (the usual case), it will get bigger, but if it is less than one, it will get smaller. To see this, suppose the firm has $4 in current assets and $2 in current liabilities for a current ratio of 2. If we use $1 in cash to reduce current liabilities, then the new current ratio is ($4 − $1)/($2 − $1) = 3. If we reverse this to $2 in current assets and $4 in current liabilities, the current ratio would fall to 1/3 from 1/2.

The second case is not quite as tricky. Nothing happens to the current ratio because cash goes down while inventory goes up—total current assets are unaffected.

In the third case, the current ratio would usually rise because inventory is normally shown at cost and the sale would normally be at something greater than cost (the difference is the markup). The increase in either cash or receivables is therefore greater than the decrease in inventory. This increases current assets, and the current ratio rises. ■

The Quick (or Acid-Test) Ratio   Inventory is often the least liquid current asset. It's also the one for which the book values are least reliable as measures of market value, since the quality of the inventory isn't considered. Some of it may be damaged, obsolete, or lost.

More to the point, relatively large inventories are often a sign of short-term trouble. The firm may have overestimated sales and overbought or overproduced as a result. In this case, the firm may have a substantial portion of its liquidity tied up in slow-moving inventory.

To further evaluate liquidity, the *quick* or *acid-test ratio* is computed just like the current ratio, except inventory is omitted:

$$\text{Quick ratio} = \frac{\text{Current assets} - \text{Inventory}}{\text{Current liabilities}} \qquad [3.2]$$

Notice that using cash to buy inventory does not affect the current ratio, but it reduces the quick ratio. Again, the idea is that inventory is relatively illiquid compared to cash.

For Prufrock, this ratio in 1992 was:

$$\text{Quick ratio} = \frac{\$708 - 422}{\$540} = .53 \text{ times}$$

The quick ratio here tells a somewhat different story than the current ratio, because inventory accounts for more than half of Prufrock's current assets. To exaggerate the point, if this inventory consisted of, say, unsold nuclear power plants, then this is a cause for concern.

Other Liquidity Ratios   We briefly mention three other measures of liquidity. A very short-term creditor might be interested in the *cash ratio:*

$$\text{Cash ratio} = \frac{\text{Cash}}{\text{Current liabilities}} \qquad [3.3]$$

You can verify that this works out to be .18 times for Prufrock.

Since net working capital (NWC) is frequently viewed as the amount of short-term liquidity a firm has, we can measure the ratio of *NWC to total assets:*

$$\text{Net working capital to total assets} = \frac{\text{Net working capital}}{\text{Total assets}} \qquad [3.4]$$

A relatively low value might indicate relatively low levels of liquidity. Here, this ratio works out to be ($708 − 540)/$3,588 = 4.7%.

Finally, imagine that Prufrock was facing a strike and cash inflows will begin to dry up. How long could the business keep running? One answer is given by the *interval measure:*

$$\text{Interval measure} = \frac{\text{Current assets}}{\text{Average daily operating costs}} \qquad [3.5]$$

Total costs for the year, excluding depreciation and interest, were $1,344. The average daily cost was $1,344/365 = $3.68 per day.[1] The interval measure is thus $708/$3.68 = 192 days. Based on this, Prufrock could hang on for six months or so.[2]

Long-Term Solvency Measures

This group of ratios is intended to address the firm's long-run ability to meet its obligations or, more generally, its financial leverage. These are sometimes called *financial leverage ratios* or just *leverage ratios*. We consider three commonly used measures and some variations.

Total Debt Ratio   The *total debt ratio* takes into account all debts of all maturities to all creditors. It can be defined in several ways, the easiest of which is:

$$\text{Total debt ratio} = \frac{\text{Total assets} − \text{Total equity}}{\text{Total assets}} \qquad [3.6]$$

$$= \frac{\$3,588 − 2,591}{\$3,588} = .28 \text{ times}$$

In this case, an analyst might say that Prufrock uses 28 percent debt.[3] Whether this is high or low or whether it even makes any difference depends on whether or not capital structure matters, a subject we discuss in Part Seven.

---

[1] In many of these ratios that involve average daily amounts, a 360-day year is often used in practice. This so-called "banker's year" has exactly 4 quarters of 90 days each and was computationally convenient in the days before pocket calculators. We'll use 365 days.

[2] Sometimes depreciation and/or interest is included in calculating average daily costs. Depreciation isn't a cash expense, so this doesn't make a lot of sense. Interest is a financing cost, so we excluded it by definition (we only looked at operating costs). We could, of course, define a different ratio that included interest expense.

[3] Total equity here includes preferred stock (discussed in Chapter 12 and elsewhere), if there is any. An equivalent numerator in this ratio would be (Current liabilities + Long-term debt).

Prufrock has $.28 in debt for every $1 in assets. Therefore, there is $.72 in equity ($1 − $.28) for every $.28 in debt. With this in mind, we can define two useful variations on the total debt ratio, the *debt/equity ratio* and the *equity multiplier:*

$$\text{Debt/equity ratio} = \text{Total debt/Total equity} \qquad [3.7]$$

$$= \$.28/\$.72 = .39 \text{ times}$$

$$\text{Equity multiplier} = \text{Total assets/Total equity} \qquad [3.8]$$

$$= \$1/\$.72 = 1.39 \text{ times}$$

The fact that the equity multiplier is 1 plus the debt/equity ratio is not a coincidence:

$$\text{Equity multiplier} = \text{Total assets/Total equity} = \$1/\$.72 = 1.39$$

$$= (\text{Total equity} + \text{Total debt})/\text{Total equity}$$

$$= 1 + \text{Debt/Equity ratio} = 1.39 \text{ times}$$

The thing to notice here is that given any one of these three ratios, you can immediately calculate the other two, so they all say exactly the same thing.

A Brief Digression: Total Capitalization versus Total Assets   Frequently, financial analysts are more concerned with the firm's long-term debt than its short-term debt, since the short-term debt will constantly be changing. Also, a firm's accounts payable may be more of a reflection of trade practice than debt management policy. For these reasons, the *long-term debt ratio* is often calculated as:

$$\text{Long-term debt ratio} = \frac{\text{Long-term debt}}{\text{Long-term debt} + \text{Total equity}} \qquad [3.9]$$

$$= \frac{\$457}{\$457 + 2,591} = \frac{\$457}{\$3,048} = .15 \text{ times}$$

The $3,048 in total long-term debt and equity is sometimes called the firm's *total capitalization,* and the financial manager will frequently focus on this quantity rather than total assets.

To complicate matters, different people (and different books) mean different things by the term *debt ratio.* Some mean total debt, and some mean long-term debt only, and, unfortunately, a substantial number are simply vague about which one they mean.

This is a source of confusion, so we choose to give two separate names to the two measures. The same problem comes up in discussing the debt/equity ratio. Financial analysts frequently calculate this ratio using only long-term debt.

Times Interest Earned Another common measure of long-term solvency is the *times interest earned* (TIE) *ratio*. Once again, there are several possible (and common) definitions, but we'll stick with the most traditional:

$$\text{Times interest earned ratio} = \frac{\text{EBIT}}{\text{Interest}} \qquad [3.10]$$

$$= \frac{\$691}{\$141} = 4.9 \text{ times}$$

As the name suggests, this ratio measures how well a company has its interest obligations covered. For Prufrock, the interest bill is covered 4.9 times over.

Cash Coverage A problem with the TIE ratio is that it is based on EBIT, which is not really a measure of cash available to pay interest. The reason is that depreciation, a noncash expense, has been deducted out. Since interest is most definitely a cash outflow (to creditors), one way to define the *cash coverage ratio* is:

$$\text{Cash coverage ratio} = \frac{\text{EBIT} + \text{Depreciation}}{\text{Interest}} \qquad [3.11]$$

$$= \frac{\$691 + 276}{\$141} = \frac{\$967}{\$141} = 6.9 \text{ times}$$

The numerator here, EBIT plus depreciation, is often abbreviated EBDIT (earnings before depreciation, interest, and taxes). It is a basic measure of the firm's ability to generate cash from operations, and it is frequently used as a measure of cash flow available to meet financial obligations.

Asset Management or Turnover Measures

We next turn our attention to the efficiency with which Prufrock uses its assets. The measures in this section are sometimes called *asset utilization ratios*. The specific ratios we discuss can all be interpreted as measures of turnover. What they are intended to describe is how efficiently or intensively a firm uses its assets to generate sales. We first look at two important current assets, inventory and receivables.

Inventory Turnover and Days' Sales in Inventory During the year, Prufrock had a cost of goods sold of $1,344. Inventory at the end of the year was $422. With these numbers, *inventory turnover* can be calculated as:

$$\text{Inventory turnover} = \frac{\text{Cost of goods sold}}{\text{Inventory}} \qquad [3.12]$$

$$= \frac{\$1,344}{\$422} = 3.2 \text{ times}$$

In a sense, we sold off or turned over the entire inventory 3.2 times.[4] As long as we are not running out of stock and thereby forgoing sales, the higher this ratio is, the more efficiently we are managing inventory.

If we turned our inventory over 3.2 times during the year, then we can immediately figure out how long it took us to turn it over on average. The result is the average *days' sales in inventory:*

$$\text{Days' sales in inventory} = \frac{365 \text{ days}}{\text{Inventory turnover}} \qquad [3.13]$$

$$= \frac{365}{3.2} = 114 \text{ days}$$

This tells us that, roughly speaking, inventory sits 114 days on average before it is sold. Alternatively, assuming we used the most recent inventory and cost figures, it will take about 114 days to work off our current inventory.

For example, we frequently hear things like "Majestic Motors has a 60 days' supply of cars. Thirty days is considered normal." This means that, at current daily sales, it would take 60 days to deplete the available inventory. We could also say that we have 60 days of sales in inventory.

It might make more sense to use the average inventory in calculating turnover. Inventory turnover would then be $\$1,344/[(\$393 + \$422)/2] = 3.3$ times.[5] It really depends on the purpose of the calculation. If we are interested in how long it will take us to sell our current inventory, then using the ending figure (as we did initially) is probably better.

In many of the ratios we discuss below, average figures could just as well be used. Again, it really depends on whether we are worried about the past, in which case averages are appropriate, or the future, in which case ending figures might be better. Also, using ending figures is very common in reporting industry averages; so, for comparison purposes, ending figures should be used in this case. In any event, using ending figures is definitely less work, so we'll continue to use them.

Receivables Turnover and Days' Sales in Receivables   Our inventory measures give some indication of how fast we can sell product. We now look at how fast we collect on those sales. The *receivables turnover* is defined in the same way as inventory turnover:

$$\text{Receivables turnover} = \frac{\text{Sales}}{\text{Accounts receivable}} \qquad [3.14]$$

$$= \frac{\$2,311}{\$188} = 12.3 \text{ times}$$

---

[4]Notice that we used cost of goods sold in the top of this ratio. For some purposes, it might be more useful to use sales instead of costs. For example, if we wanted to know the amount of sales generated per dollar of inventory, then we could just replace the cost of goods sold with sales.

[5]Notice that we calculated the average as (Beginning value + Ending value)/2.

Loosely speaking, we collected our outstanding credit accounts and reloaned the money 12.3 times during the year.[6]

This ratio makes more sense if we convert it to days, so the *days' sales in receivables* is:

$$\text{Days' sales in receivables} = \frac{365 \text{ days}}{\text{Receivables turnover}} \qquad [3.15]$$

$$= \frac{365}{12.3} = 30 \text{ days}$$

Therefore, on average, we collect on our credit sales in 30 days. For this reason, this ratio is very frequently called the *average collection period (ACP)*.

Also, note that if we are using the most recent figures, we could also say that we have 30 days' worth of sales that are currently uncollected. We will learn more about this subject when we study credit policy in Chapter 19.

Example 3.2 Payables Turnover

Here is a variation on the receivables collection period. How long, on average, does it take for Prufrock Corporation to pay its bills? To answer, we need to calculate the accounts payable turnover rate using cost of goods sold. We will assume that Prufrock purchases everything on credit.

The cost of goods sold is $1,344, and accounts payable are $344. The turnover is therefore $1,344/$344 = 3.9 times. So payables turned over about every 365/3.9 = 94 days. On average, then, Prufrock takes 94 days to pay. As a potential creditor, we might take note of this fact. ∎

Asset Turnover Ratios   Moving away from specific accounts like inventory or receivables, we can consider several "big picture" ratios. For example, *NWC turnover* is:

$$\text{NWC turnover} = \frac{\text{Sales}}{\text{NWC}} \qquad [3.16]$$

$$= \frac{\$2,311}{\$708 - 540} = 13.8 \text{ times}$$

This ratio measures how much "work" we get out of our working capital. Once again, assuming that we aren't missing out on sales, a high value is preferred (why?).

Similarly, *fixed asset turnover* is:

$$\text{Fixed asset turnover} = \frac{\text{Sales}}{\text{Net fixed assets}} \qquad [3.17]$$

$$= \frac{\$2,311}{\$2,880} = .80 \text{ times}$$

With this ratio, it probably makes more sense to say that, for every dollar in fixed assets, we generated $.80 in sales.

---

[6]Here we have implicitly assumed that all sales are credit sales. If they are not, then we would simply use total credit sales in these calculations, not total sales.

Our final asset management ratio, the *total asset turnover*, comes up quite a bit. We will see it later in this chapter and in the next chapter. As the name suggests, the total asset turnover is:

$$\text{Total asset turnover} = \frac{\text{Sales}}{\text{Total assets}} \qquad [3.18]$$

$$= \frac{\$2,311}{\$3,588} = .64 \text{ times}$$

In other words, for every dollar in assets, we generated $.64 in sales.

Example 3.3   More Turnover

Suppose you find that a particular company generates $.40 in sales for every dollar in total assets. How often does this company turn over its total assets?

The total asset turnover here is .40 times per year. It takes 1/.40 = 2.5 years to turn them over completely. ∎

Profitability Measures

The three measures we discuss in this section are probably the best known and most widely used of all financial ratios. In one form or another, they are intended to measure how efficiently the firm uses its assets and how efficiently the firm manages its operations. The focus in this group is on the bottom line, net income.

Profit Margin   Companies pay a great deal of attention to their *profit margin:*

$$\text{Profit margin} = \frac{\text{Net income}}{\text{Sales}} \qquad [3.19]$$

$$= \frac{\$363}{\$2,311} = 15.7\%$$

This tells us that Prufrock, in an accounting sense, generates a little less than 16 cents in profit for every dollar in sales.

All other things being equal, a relatively high profit margin is obviously desirable. This situation corresponds to low expense ratios relative to sales. However, we hasten to add that other things are often not equal.

For example, lowering our sales price will normally increase unit volume, but profit margins will normally shrink. Total profit (or more importantly, operating cash flow) may go up or down; so the fact that margins are smaller isn't necessarily bad. After all, isn't it possible that, as the saying goes, "Our prices are so low that we lose money on everything we sell, but we make it up in volume!"?[7]

---

[7]No, it's not.

Return on Assets *Return on assets* (ROA) is a measure of profit per dollar of assets. It can be defined several ways, but the most common is:

$$\text{Return on assets} = \frac{\text{Net income}}{\text{Total assets}} \qquad [3.20]$$

$$= \frac{\$363}{\$3,588} = 10.12\%$$

Return on Equity *Return on equity* (ROE) is a measure of how the stockholders fared during the year. Since benefiting shareholders is our goal, ROE is, in an accounting sense, the true bottom-line measure of performance. ROE is usually measured as:

$$\text{Return on equity} = \frac{\text{Net income}}{\text{Total equity}} \qquad [3.21]$$

$$= \frac{\$363}{\$2,591} = 14\%$$

For every dollar in equity, therefore, Prufrock generated 14 cents in profit, but, again, this is only correct in accounting terms.

Because ROA and ROE are such commonly cited numbers, we stress that it is important to remember that they are accounting rates of return. For this reason, these measures should properly be called *return on book assets* and *return on book equity*. In fact, ROE is sometimes called *return on net worth*. Whatever it's called, it would be inappropriate to compare the result to, for example, an interest rate observed in the financial markets. We will have more to say about accounting rates of return in later chapters.

The fact that ROE exceeds ROA reflects Prufrock's use of financial leverage. We will examine the relationship between these two measures in more detail below.

Example 3.4 ROE and ROA
Since ROE and ROA are usually intended to measure performance over a prior period, it makes a certain amount of sense to base them on average equity and average assets, respectively. For Prufrock, how would you calculate these?

We first need to calculate average assets and average equity:

Average assets = ($3,373 + $3,588)/2 = $3,481

Average equity = ($2,299 + $2,591)/2 = $2,445

With these averages, we can recalculate ROA and ROE as follows:

$$\text{ROA} = \frac{\$363}{\$3,481} = 10.43\%$$

$$\text{ROE} = \frac{\$363}{\$2,445} = 14.85\%$$

These are slightly higher than our previous calculations because assets grew during the year, with the result that the average is below the ending value. ∎

Market Value Measures

Our final group of measures is based, in part, on information that is not necessarily contained in financial statements—the market price per share of the stock. Obviously, these measures can only be calculated directly for publicly traded companies.

We assume that Prufrock has 33 million shares outstanding and the stock sold for $88 per share at the end of the year. If we recall Prufrock's net income was $363 million, then its earnings per share (EPS) were:

$$\text{EPS} = \frac{\text{Net income}}{\text{Shares outstanding}} = \frac{\$363}{33} = \$11$$

Price/Earnings Ratio   The first of our market value measures, the *price/ earnings (P/E) ratio* (or multiple), is defined as:

$$\text{P/E ratio} = \frac{\text{Price per share}}{\text{Earnings per share}} \qquad [3.22]$$

$$= \frac{\$88}{\$11} = 8 \text{ times}$$

In the vernacular, we would say that Prufrock shares sell for 8 times earnings, or we might say that Prufrock shares have or "carry" a P/E multiple of 8.

Since the P/E ratio measures how much investors are willing to pay per dollar of current earnings, higher P/Es are often taken to mean that the firm has significant prospects for future growth. Of course, if a firm had no or almost no earnings, its P/E would probably be quite large; so, as always, care is needed in interpreting this ratio.

Market-to-Book Ratio   A second commonly quoted measure is the *market-to-book ratio:*

$$\text{Market-to-book ratio} = \frac{\text{Market value per share}}{\text{Book value per share}} \qquad [3.23]$$

$$= \frac{\$88}{(\$2{,}591/33)} = \frac{\$88}{\$78.5} = 1.12 \text{ times}$$

Notice that book value per share is total equity (not just common stock) divided by the number of shares outstanding.

Since book value per share is an accounting number, it reflects historical costs. In a loose sense, the market-to-book ratio therefore compares the market value of the firm's investments to their cost. A value less than 1 could mean that the firm has not been successful overall in creating value for its stockholders.

This completes our definitions of some common ratios. We could tell you about more of them, but these are enough for now. We'll leave it here and go

Table 3.8

Common financial ratios

I. Short-Term Solvency or Liquidity Ratios

$$\text{Current ratio} = \frac{\text{Current assets}}{\text{Current liabilities}}$$

$$\text{Quick ratio} = \frac{\text{Current assets} - \text{Inventory}}{\text{Current liabilities}}$$

$$\text{Cash ratio} = \frac{\text{Cash}}{\text{Current liabilities}}$$

$$\text{Net working capital to total assets} = \frac{\text{Net working capital}}{\text{Total assets}}$$

$$\text{Interval measure} = \frac{\text{Current assets}}{\text{Average daily operating costs}}$$

III. Asset Utilization or Turnover Ratios

$$\text{Inventory turnover} = \frac{\text{Cost of goods sold}}{\text{Inventory}}$$

$$\text{Days' sales in inventory} = \frac{365 \text{ days}}{\text{Inventory turnover}}$$

$$\text{Receivables turnover} = \frac{\text{Sales}}{\text{Accounts receivable}}$$

$$\text{Days' sales in receivables} = \frac{365 \text{ days}}{\text{Receivables turnover}}$$

$$\text{NWC turnover} = \frac{\text{Sales}}{\text{NWC}}$$

$$\text{Fixed asset turnover} = \frac{\text{Sales}}{\text{Net fixed assets}}$$

$$\text{Total asset turnover} = \frac{\text{Sales}}{\text{Total assets}}$$

II. Long-Term Solvency or Financial Leverage Ratios

$$\text{Total debt ratio} = \frac{\text{Total assets} - \text{Total equity}}{\text{Total assets}}$$

$$\text{Debt/equity ratio} = \text{Total debt/Total equity}$$

$$\text{Equity multiplier} = \text{Total assets/Total equity}$$

$$\text{Long-term debt ratio} = \frac{\text{Long-term debt}}{\text{Long-term debt} + \text{Total equity}}$$

$$\text{Times interest earned ratio} = \frac{\text{EBIT}}{\text{Interest}}$$

$$\text{Cash coverage ratio} = \frac{\text{EBIT} + \text{Depreciation}}{\text{Interest}}$$

IV. Profitability Ratios

$$\text{Profit margin} = \frac{\text{Net income}}{\text{Sales}}$$

$$\text{Return on assets (ROA)} = \frac{\text{Net income}}{\text{Total assets}}$$

$$\text{Return on equity (ROE)} = \frac{\text{Net income}}{\text{Total equity}}$$

$$\text{ROE} = \frac{\text{Net income}}{\text{Sales}} \times \frac{\text{Sales}}{\text{Assets}} \times \frac{\text{Assets}}{\text{Equity}}$$

V. Market Value Ratios

$$\text{Price/earnings ratio} = \frac{\text{Price per share}}{\text{Earnings per share}}$$

$$\text{Market-to-book ratio} = \frac{\text{Market value per share}}{\text{Book value per share}}$$

on to discuss some ways of using these ratios instead of just how to calculate them. Table 3.8 summarizes the ratios that we've discussed.

CONCEPT QUESTIONS

3.3a What are the five groups of ratios? Give two or three examples of each kind.

3.3b Turnover ratios all have one of two figures as numerators. What are they? What do these ratios measure? How do you interpret the results?

3.3c Profitability ratios all have the same figure in the numerator. What is it? What do these ratios measure? How do you interpret the results?

THE DU PONT IDENTITY | 3.4

As we mentioned in discussing ROA and ROE, the difference between these two profitability measures is a reflection of the use of debt financing or financial leverage. We illustrate the relationship between these measures in this section by investigating a famous way of decomposing ROE into its component parts.

To begin, let's recall the definition of ROE:

$$\text{Return on equity} = \frac{\text{Net income}}{\text{Total equity}}$$

If we were so inclined, we could multiply this ratio by Assets/Assets without changing anything:

$$\text{Return on equity} = \frac{\text{Net income}}{\text{Total equity}} = \frac{\text{Net income}}{\text{Total equity}} \times \frac{\text{Assets}}{\text{Assets}}$$

$$= \frac{\text{Net income}}{\text{Assets}} \times \frac{\text{Assets}}{\text{Equity}}$$

Notice that we have expressed the return on equity as the product of two other ratios — return on assets and the equity multiplier:

$$\text{ROE} = \text{ROA} \times \text{Equity multiplier} = \text{ROA} \times (1 + \text{Debt/Equity ratio})$$

Looking back at Prufrock, for example, the debt/equity ratio was .39 and ROA was 10.12 percent. Our work here implies that Prufrock's return on equity, as we previously calculated, is:

$$\text{ROE} = 10.12\% \times 1.39 = 14\%$$

We can further decompose ROE by multiplying the top and bottom by total sales:

$$\text{ROE} = \frac{\text{Sales}}{\text{Sales}} \times \frac{\text{Net income}}{\text{Assets}} \times \frac{\text{Assets}}{\text{Equity}}$$

If we rearrange things a bit, ROE is:

$$\text{ROE} = \underbrace{\frac{\text{Net income}}{\text{Sales}} \times \frac{\text{Sales}}{\text{Assets}}}_{\text{Return on assets}} \times \frac{\text{Assets}}{\text{Equity}} \qquad [3.24]$$

= Profit margin × Total asset turnover × Equity multiplier

Du Pont identity

Popular expression breaking ROE into three parts: operating efficiency, asset use efficiency, and financial leverage.

What we have now done is to partition the return on assets into its two component parts, profit margin and total asset turnover. This last expression is called the **Du Pont identity,** after the Du Pont Corporation, which popularized its use.

We can check this relationship for Prufrock by noting that the profit margin was 15.7 percent and the total asset turnover was .64. ROE should thus be:

ROE = Profit margin × Total asset turnover × Equity multiplier
    =   15.7%   ×   .64   ×   1.39
    =   14%

This 14 percent ROE is exactly what we had before.

The Du Pont identity tells us that ROE is affected by three things:

1. Operating efficiency (as measured by profit margin).
2. Asset use efficiency (as measured by total asset turnover).
3. Financial leverage (as measured by the equity multiplier).

Weakness in either operating or asset use efficiency (or both) will show up in a diminished return on assets, which will translate into a lower ROE.

Considering the Du Pont identity, it appears that the ROE could be leveraged up by increasing the amount of debt in the firm. It turns out that this will only happen if the firm's ROA exceeds the interest rate on the debt. More importantly, the use of debt financing has a number of other effects, and, as we discuss at some length in Part Seven, the amount of leverage a firm uses is governed by its capital structure policy.

The decomposition of ROE we've discussed in this section is a convenient way of systematically approaching financial statement analysis. If ROE is unsatisfactory by some measure, then the Du Pont identity tells you where to start looking for the reasons.

CONCEPT QUESTIONS

3.4a Return on assets (ROA) can be expressed as the product of two ratios. Which two?

3.4b Return on equity (ROE) can be expressed as the product of three ratios. Which three?

USING FINANCIAL STATEMENT INFORMATION | 3.5

Our last task in this chapter is to discuss in more detail some practical aspects of financial statements analysis. In particular, we will look at reasons for doing financial statements analysis, how to go about getting benchmark information, and some of the problems that come up in the process.

Why Evaluate Financial Statements?

As we have discussed, the primary reason for looking at accounting information is that we don't have, and can't reasonably expect to get, market value information. It is important to emphasize that, whenever we have market information, we would use it instead of accounting data. Also, if there is a conflict between accounting and market data, market data should be given precedence.

Financial statements analysis is essentially an application of "management by exception." In many cases, such analysis will boil down to comparing ratios for one business with some kind of average or representative ratios. Those ratios that seem to differ the most from the averages are tagged for further study.

Internal Uses   Financial statement information has a variety of uses within a firm. Among the most important of these is performance evaluation. For example, managers are frequently evaluated and compensated on the basis of accounting measures of performance such as profit margin and return on equity. Also, firms with multiple divisions frequently compare the performance of those divisions using financial statement information.

Another important internal use that we will explore in the next chapter is planning for the future. As we will see, historical financial statement information is very useful for generating projections about the future and for checking the realism of assumptions made in those projections.

External Uses   Financial statements are useful to parties outside the firm, including short-term and long-term creditors and potential investors. For example, we would find such information quite useful in deciding whether or not to grant credit to a new customer.

We would also find such information useful in evaluating our main competitors. We might be thinking of launching a new product. A prime concern would be whether the competition would jump in shortly thereafter. In this case, we would be interested in our competitors' financial strength to see if they can afford the necessary development.

Finally, we might be thinking of acquiring another firm. Financial statement information would be essential in identifying potential targets and deciding what to offer.

Choosing a Benchmark

Given that we want to evaluate a division or a firm based on its financial statements, a basic problem immediately comes up. How do we choose a benchmark or a standard of comparison? We describe some ways of getting started in this section.

Time-Trend Analysis   One standard we could use is history. Suppose we found that the current ratio for a particular firm is 2.4 based on the most recent financial statement information. Looking back over the last 10 years, we might find that this ratio has declined fairly steadily over that period.

Based on this, we might wonder if the liquidity position of the firm has deteriorated. It could be, of course, that the firm has made changes that allow it to more efficiently use its current assets, the nature of the firm's business has changed, or business practices have changed. If we investigate, these are all possible explanations. This is an example of what we mean by management by exception — a deteriorating time trend may not be bad, but it does merit investigation.

Peer Group Analysis   The second means of establishing a benchmark is to identify firms that are similar in the sense that they compete in the same markets, have similar assets, and operate in similar ways. In other words, we need to identify a *peer group*. There are obvious problems with doing this since no two companies are identical. Ultimately, the choice of which companies to use as a basis for comparison is subjective.

Standard Industry Classification (SIC) code

U.S. government code used to classify a firm by its type of business operations.

One common way of identifying potential peers is based on **Standard Industry Classification (SIC) codes**. These are four-digit codes established by the U.S. government for statistical reporting purposes. Firms with the same SIC code are frequently assumed to be similar.

The first digit in an SIC code establishes the general type of business. For example, firms engaged in finance, insurance, and real estate have SIC codes beginning with 6. Each additional digit narrows down the industry. So, companies with SIC codes beginning with 60 are mostly banks and banklike businesses, those beginning with 602 are mostly commercial banks, and SIC code 6025 is assigned to national banks that are members of the Federal Reserve system. Table 3.9 is a list of selected two-digit codes (the first two digits of the four-digit SIC codes) and the industries they represent.

SIC codes are far from perfect. For example, suppose you were examining financial statements for Wal-Mart, the largest retailer in the United States. The relevant SIC code is 5310, Department Stores. After a quick scan of the nearest financial database, you would find about 20 large, publicly owned corporations with this same SIC code, but you might not be too comfortable with some of them. Kmart would seem to be a reasonable peer, but Neiman-Marcus also carries the same industry code. Are Wal-Mart and Neiman-Marcus really comparable?

With this caveat about SIC codes in mind, we can now take a look at a specific industry. Suppose that we are a small manufacturer of plastic materials. Table 3.10 contains some condensed common-size financial statements for this industry from Robert Morris Associates, one of many sources of such information. Table 3.11 contains selected ratios from the same source.

There is a large amount of information here, most of which is self-explanatory. On the right in Table 3.10, we have current information reported for different groups based on sales. Within each sales group, common-size information is reported. For example, firms with sales in the $10 million to

Agriculture, Forestry, and Fishing

   01   Agriculture production — crops

   08   Forestry

   09   Fishing, hunting, and trapping

Mining

   10   Metal mining

   12   Bituminous coal and lignite mining

   13   Oil and gas extraction

Construction

   15   Building construction

   16   Construction other than building

   17   Construction — special trade contractors

Manufacturing

   28   Chemicals and allied products

   29   Petroleum refining and related industries

   35   Machinery, except electrical

   37   Transportation equipment

Transportation, Communication, Electric, Gas, and Sanitary Service

   40   Railroad transportation

   45   Transportation by air

   49   Electric, gas, and sanitary services

Wholesale Trade

   50   Wholesale trade — durable goods

   51   Wholesale trade — nondurable goods

Retail Trade

   54   Food stores

   55   Automobile dealers and gas stations

   58   Eating and drinking places

Finance, Insurance, and Real Estate

   60   Banking

   63   Insurance

   65   Real estate

Services

   78   Motion pictures

   80   Health services

   82   Educational services

Table 3.9

Selected two-digit SIC codes

$25 million range have Cash & Equivalents equal to 4.6 percent of total assets. There are 23 companies in this group out of 127 in all.

On the left, we have three years' worth of summary historical information for the entire group. For example, operating expenses fell from 20.2 percent of sales to 19.6 percent over that time.

Table 3.11 contains some selected ratios, again reported by sales groups on the right and time period on the left. To see how we might use this information, suppose our firm has a current ratio of 2. Based on these ratios, is this value unusual?

Looking at the current ratio for the overall group (third column from the left), three numbers are reported. The one in the middle, 1.5, is the median, meaning that half of the 127 firms had current ratios that were lower and half had bigger current ratios. The other two numbers are the upper and lower quartiles. So, 25 percent of the firms had a current ratio larger than 2.2 and 25 percent had a current ratio smaller than 1.1. Our value of 2 falls comfortably within these bounds, so it doesn't appear too unusual. This comparison illustrates how knowledge of the range of ratios is important in addition to knowledge of the average. Notice how stable the current ratio has been for the last three years.

Table 3.10   Selected financial statement information

MANUFACTURERS - PLASTIC MATERIALS, SYNTHETIC RESINS & NONVULCANIZABLE ELASTOMERS   SIC# 2821

Comparative Historical Data			Type of Statement	Current Data Sorted by Sales					
60	41	45	Unqualified	2	2	3	5	10	23
5	2	4	Qualified		2		1	1	
24	33	37	Reviewed	2	9	6	11	8	1
18	27	19	Compiled	3	9	3	2	2	
23	28	22	Other	3	5	4	2	2	6
6/30/87-	6/30/88-	6/30/89-		44(6/30-9/30/89)			83(10/1/89-3/31/90)		
3/31/88	3/31/89	3/31/90							
ALL	ALL	ALL		0-1MM	1-3MM	3-5MM	5-10MM	10-25MM	25MM & OVER
130	131	127	**NUMBER OF STATEMENTS**	10	27	16	21	23	30
%	%	%	**ASSETS**	%	%	%	%	%	%
6.5	4.7	6.2	Cash & Equivalents	11.5	8.4	5.7	4.5	4.6	5.1
27.8	30.3	27.9	Trade Receivables (net)	24.3	30.9	26.7	30.5	28.0	25.1
21.7	23.5	21.6	Inventory	18.6	22.6	20.7	19.9	25.5	20.2
2.2	1.3	1.5	All Other Current	1.0	1.6	2.3	.4	.7	2.3
58.2	59.8	57.1	Total Current	55.4	63.5	55.4	55.4	58.9	52.6
34.7	33.0	35.2	Fixed Assets (net)	38.0	30.1	38.0	40.0	32.5	36.1
.9	1.3	2.3	Intangibles (net)	1.6	.4	.1	.4	3.1	6.1
6.3	6.0	5.4	All Other Non-Current	5.0	6.0	6.5	4.3	5.5	5.1
100.0	100.0	100.0	Total	100.0	100.0	100.0	100.0	100.0	100.0
			LIABILITIES						
7.7	11.0	9.2	Notes Payable-Short Term	4.7	9.2	13.0	12.7	8.3	7.0
5.0	4.4	4.4	Cur. Mat.-L/T/D	2.3	6.2	4.7	3.7	3.8	4.3
18.2	22.0	17.9	Trade Payables	8.0	18.6	16.3	22.6	20.9	15.8
1.1	1.0	.4	Income Taxes Payable	.6	.5	.0	.3	.5	.2
8.9	6.5	7.8	All Other Current	5.6	8.3	12.0	6.1	6.4	8.1
40.8	44.8	39.7	Total Current	21.2	42.9	46.1	45.4	40.0	35.4
17.2	17.7	19.8	Long Term Debt	19.9	16.0	23.9	20.3	17.7	22.2
1.4	1.1	1.4	Deferred Taxes	1.4	.7	.3	1.0	1.2	2.9
1.6	1.8	2.9	All Other Non-Current	1.4	2.0	3.9	4.0	1.7	3.7
38.9	34.6	36.3	Net Worth	56.1	38.4	25.8	29.3	39.5	35.9
100.0	100.0	100.0	Total Liabilities & Net Worth	100.0	100.0	100.0	100.0	100.0	100.0
			INCOME DATA						
100.0	100.0	100.0	Net Sales	100.0	100.0	100.0	100.0	100.0	100.0
25.9	25.3	25.7	Gross Profit	40.0	27.5	31.7	23.6	20.8	21.4
20.2	20.8	19.6	Operating Expenses	26.9	22.3	26.6	17.4	16.5	15.0
5.7	4.5	6.1	Operating Profit	13.1	5.2	5.2	6.1	4.3	6.3
1.5	1.4	2.3	All Other Expenses (net)	3.9	1.6	1.7	3.4	1.7	2.3
4.3	3.1	3.8	Profit Before Taxes	9.2	3.6	3.5	2.8	2.5	4.0
3062731M	1780650M	3509831M	Net Sales ($)	7613M	55793M	63330M	144254M	353265M	2885576M
1616658M	838206M	1880209M	Total Assets ($)	4946M	25731M	31179M	66906M	161818M	1589629M

© Robert Morris Associates 1990   M = $thousand   MM = $million
See Pages 1 through 15 for Explanation of Ratios and Data

Interpretation of Statement Studies Figures: Robert Morris Associates cautions that the studies be regarded only as a general guideline and not as an absolute industry norm. This is due to limited samples within categories, the categorization of companies by their primary Standard Industrial Classification (SIC) number only, and different methods of operations by companies within the same industry. For these reasons, RMA recommends that the figures be used only as general guidelines in addition to other methods of financial analysis.

Selected ratios **Table 3.11**

MANUFACTURERS - PLASTIC MATERIALS, SYNTHETIC RESINS & NONVULCANIZABLE ELASTOMERS   SIC# 2821

Comparative Historical Data			Type of Statement	Current Data Sorted By Sales					
60	41	45	Unqualified	2	2	3	5	10	23
5	2	4	Qualified		2		1	1	
24	33	37	Reviewed	2	9	6	11	8	1
18	27	19	Compiled	3	9	3	2	2	
23	28	22	Other	3	5	4	2	2	6
6/30/87-3/31/88 ALL 130	6/30/88-3/31/89 ALL 131	6/30/89-3/31/90 ALL 127		44(6/30-9/30/89)			83(10/1/89-3/31/90)		
				0-1MM 10	1-3MM 27	3-5MM 16	5-10MM 21	10-25MM 23	25MM & OVER 30
130	131	127	**NUMBER OF STATEMENTS**	10	27	16	21	23	30
			RATIOS						
2.1	1.8	2.2		4.5	2.2	1.6	2.1	2.0	2.2
1.6	1.4	1.5	Current	2.7	1.5	1.3	1.3	1.5	1.5
1.1	1.1	1.1		1.8	1.2	1.0	1.0	1.2	1.2
1.2	1.1	1.2		3.5	1.2	1.0	1.2	1.2	1.1
.8	.8	.8	Quick	2.0	1.0	.7	.8	.7	.9
.6	.6	.6		1.0	.6	.6	.6	.6	.7
38 9.5	37 9.9	37 9.9		34 10.6	35 10.3	32 11.5	40 9.1	31 11.6	40 9.1
49 7.5	47 7.8	46 8.0	Sales/Receivables	49 7.5	46 8.0	45 8.1	44 8.3	40 9.2	48 7.6
57 6.4	59 6.2	54 6.8		69 5.3	59 6.2	55 6.6	51 7.1	49 7.4	54 6.7
33 11.1	30 12.3	32 11.5		29 12.7	24 15.1	31 11.6	29 12.4	29 12.5	34 10.7
47 7.7	51 7.2	45 8.1	Cost of Sales/Inventory	60 6.1	51 7.2	50 7.3	38 9.5	51 7.1	46 8.0
74 4.9	66 5.5	64 5.7		85 4.3	66 5.5	56 6.5	45 8.1	73 5.0	68 5.4
27 13.5	29 12.4	26 13.9		14 25.3	18 20.2	19 19.6	31 11.9	31 11.8	28 13.1
40 9.2	43 8.5	35 10.3	Cost of Sales/Payables	23 15.8	31 11.6	33 10.9	31 9.5	34 10.0	34 10.6
54 6.7	59 6.2	48 7.6		57 6.4	50 7.3	51 7.2	48 7.6	45 8.1	43 8.5
6.8	8.6	7.2		3.7	5.7	10.2	8.6	8.3	7.0
10.9	15.2	14.3	Sales/Working Capital	5.1	18.6	16.6	20.4	18.7	12.3
52.9	95.3	35.2		9.1	32.3	313.0	NM	39.6	32.7
9.3	6.7	5.3			5.4	6.6	3.8	8.1	5.1
(110) 4.0	(117) 2.5	(117) 2.6	EBIT/Interest	(26) 2.2	3.2	(20) 2.2	(21) 3.3	(28) 2.4	2.4
1.6	1.4	1.4			1.5	1.2	1.5	1.3	1.4
7.3	6.1	4.9			4.5		5.7	6.7	5.8
(76) 2.7	(78) 2.5	(78) 3.0	Net Profit + Depr., Dep., Amort./Cur. Mat. L/T/D	(16) 1.7		(17) 2.9	(11) 3.6	(24) 2.9	2.9
1.1	1.5	1.2			.5		1.3	2.6	1.1
.5	.5	.6		.3	.5	.6	.6	.4	.8
1.0	.9	1.1	Fixed/Worth	.7	.9	1.2	1.5	1.2	1.1
1.7	1.9	2.0		2.3	1.6	2.8	2.8	1.4	2.2
.8	1.0	.9		.2	.8	1.6	.9	1.1	1.1
1.8	1.8	1.9	Debt/Worth	.5	1.6	2.2	2.6	1.8	2.3
3.0	4.2	4.3		2.8	4.8	7.1	4.2	2.4	7.1
42.2	42.2	33.3		39.8	33.6	54.8	30.0	44.1	30.5
(123) 24.5	(119) 20.3	(122) 19.6	% Profit Before Taxes/Tangible Net Worth	27.7	19.1	(15) 25.2	(20) 18.7	(22) 17.2	(28) 18.8
8.6	4.2	8.3		11.3	6.8	2.3	10.3	6.7	8.9
15.5	15.2	14.0		26.6	14.0	16.0	10.6	13.4	12.3
7.8	6.6	6.5	% Profit Before Taxes/Total Assets	18.2	5.6	9.4	4.6	7.0	7.0
2.9	1.2	2.2		3.4	1.7	.4	2.6	2.4	1.7
10.8	13.5	12.5		14.6	18.2	13.5	12.5	13.8	6.7
6.8	7.0	6.2	Sales/Net Fixed Assets	4.7	6.6	8.6	7.8	6.3	4.6
3.9	4.5	3.4		2.1	5.4	3.3	2.9	3.5	3.2
2.7	2.9	2.9		2.5	2.9	3.3	3.3	3.3	2.2
2.1	2.3	2.2	Sales/Total Assets	1.6	2.5	2.4	2.7	2.2	1.8
1.5	1.8	1.6		1.1	1.9	1.6	1.7	1.7	1.3
1.5	1.6	1.7			1.3	.6	1.5	1.7	2.3
(117) 2.6	(118) 2.7	(112) 2.8	% Depr., Dep., Amort./Sales	(26) 2.8	(14) 1.8	1.9	(19) 3.0	(25) 3.0	3.0
3.5	3.9	4.0			5.4	3.5	3.3	4.6	3.8
1.8	2.2	2.1			3.3		2.0		
(29) 3.1	(46) 3.4	(53) 2.9	$ Officers' Comp/Sales	(19) 4.5		(11) 2.4			
6.4	6.4	5.9			7.2		4.6		
3062731M	1780650M	3509831M	Net Sales ($)	7613M	55793M	63330M	144254M	353265M	2885576M
1616658M	838206M	1880209M	Total Assets ($)	4946M	25731M	31179M	66906M	161818M	1589629M

© Robert Morris Associates 1990

M = $thousand   MM = $million

See Pages 1 through 15 for Explanation of Ratios and Data

Example 3.5 More Ratios

Take a look at the numbers reported for Sales/Receivables and EBIT/Interest in Table 3.11. What are the overall median values? What are these ratios?

If you look back at our discussion, these are the receivables turnover and the times interest earned (TIE) ratios. The median value for receivables turnover for the entire group is 8.0 times. So, the days in receivables is 365/8 = 46, which is the bold-faced number reported. The median for the TIE is 2.6 times. The number in parentheses indicates that the calculation is meaningful for, and therefore based on, only 117 of the 127 companies. In this case, the reason is probably that only 117 companies paid any significant amount of interest. ■

Problems with Financial Statements Analysis

We close out our chapter on financial statements by discussing some additional problems that can arise in using financial statements. In one way or another, the basic problem with financial statements analysis is that there is no underlying theory to help us identify which quantities to look at and to guide us in establishing benchmarks.

As we discuss in other chapters, there are many cases where financial theory and economic logic provide guidance to making judgments about value and risk. Very little such help exists with financial statements. This is why we can't say which ratios matter the most and what a high or low value might be.

One particularly severe problem is that many firms are conglomerates, owning more or less unrelated lines of business. The consolidated financial statements for such firms don't really fit any neat industry category. Going back to department stores, for example, Sears has an SIC code of 6710 (Holding Offices) because of its diverse financial and retailing operations. More generally, the kind of peer group analysis that we have been describing is going to work best when the firms are strictly in the same line of business, the industry is competitive, and there is only one way of operating.

Even companies that are clearly in the same line of business may not be comparable. For example, electric utilities engaged primarily in power generation are all classified in the same group (SIC 4911). This group is often thought to be relatively homogeneous. However, utilities generally operate as regulated monopolies, so they don't compete with each other. Many have stockholders, and many are organized as cooperatives with no stockholders. There are several different ways of generating power, ranging from hydroelectric to nuclear, so their operating activities can differ quite a bit. Finally, profitability is strongly affected by regulatory environment, so utilities in different locations can be very similar but show very different profits.

Several other general problems frequently crop up. First, different firms use different accounting procedures for inventory, for example. This makes it difficult to compare statements. Second, different firms end their fiscal years at different times. For firms in seasonal businesses (such as a retailer with a large Christmas season), this can lead to difficulties in comparing balance sheets because of fluctuations in accounts during the year. Finally, for any particular firm, unusual or transient events, such as a one-time profit from an asset sale, may affect financial performance. In comparing firms, such events can give misleading signals.

⌐CONCEPT QUESTIONS

3.5a What are some uses for financial statements analysis?

3.5b What are SIC codes and how might they be useful?

3.5c Why do we say that financial statements analysis is "management by exception?"

3.5d What are some of the problems that can come up with financial statements analysis?

SUMMARY AND CONCLUSIONS ⌐3.6

This chapter has discussed aspects of financial statements analysis:

1. Sources and uses of cash. We discussed how to identify the ways that businesses obtain and use cash, and we described how to trace the flow of cash through the business over the course of the year. We briefly looked at the statement of cash flows.

2. Standardized financial statements. We explained that differences in size make it difficult to compare financial statements, and we discussed how to form common-size and common-base-period statements to make comparisons easier.

3. Ratio analysis. Evaluating ratios of accounting numbers is another way of comparing financial statement information. We therefore defined and discussed a number of the most commonly reported and used financial ratios. We also discussed the famous Du Pont identity as a way of analyzing financial performance.

4. Using financial statements. We described how to establish benchmarks for comparison purposes and discussed some of the types of information that are available. We then examined some of the potential problems that can arise.

After you study this chapter, we hope that you will have some perspective on the uses and abuses of financial statements. You should also find that your vocabulary of business and financial terms has grown substantially.

Key Terms

sources of cash 52
uses of cash 52
statement of cash flows 55
common-size statement 57
common-base-year statement 59

financial ratios (see Table 3.8) 61
Du Pont identity 74
Standard Industry Classification
(SIC) code 76

Chapter Review Problems and Self-Test

3.1   Sources and Uses of Cash   Consider the following balance sheets for the Wildhack Corporation. Calculate the changes in the various accounts and, where applicable, identify the change as a source or use of cash. What were the major sources and uses of cash? Did the company become more or less liquid during the year? What happened to cash during the year?

WILDHACK CORPORATION
Balance Sheets as of December 31, 1991 and 1992
($ in millions)

	1991	1992
Assets		
Current assets		
Cash	$ 120	$ 88
Accounts receivable	224	192
Inventory	424	368
Total	$ 768	$ 648
Fixed assets		
Net plant and equipment	$5,228	$5,354
Total assets	$5,996	$6,002
Liabilities and Owners' Equity		
Current liabilities		
Accounts payable	$ 124	$ 144
Notes payable	1,412	1,039
Total	$1,536	$1,183
Long-term debt	$1,804	$2,077
Owners' equity		
Common stock and paid-in surplus	300	300
Retained earnings	2,356	2,442
Total	$2,656	$2,742
Total liabilities and owners' equity	$5,996	$6,002

3.2   **Common-Size Statements**   Below is the most recent income statement for Wildhack. Prepare a common-size income statement based on this information. How do you interpret the standardized net income? What percentage of sales goes to cost of goods sold?

WILDHACK CORPORATION
1992 Income Statement
($ in millions)

Sales	$3,756
Cost of goods sold	2,453
Depreciation	490
Earnings before interest and taxes	$ 813
Interest paid	613
Taxable income	$ 200
Taxes (34%)	68
Net income	$ 132

Addition to retained earnings	$86
Dividends	46

3.3   **Financial Ratios**   Based on the balance sheets and income statement in the previous two problems, calculate the following ratios for 1992:

Current ratio _____
Quick ratio _____
Cash ratio _____
Inventory turnover _____
Receivables turnover _____
Days' sales in inventory _____
Days' sales in receivables _____
Total debt ratio _____
Long-term debt ratio _____
Times interest earned ratio _____
Cash coverage ratio _____

3.4   **ROE and the Du Pont Identity**
Calculate the 1992 ROE for the Wildhack Corporation and then break down your answer into its component parts using the Du Pont identity.

Answers to Self-Test Problems

3.1   We've filled in the answers below. Remember, increases in assets and decreases in liabilities indicate that we spent some cash. Decreases in assets and increases in liabilities are ways of getting cash.

WILDHACK CORPORATION
Balance Sheets as of December 31, 1991 and 1992
($ in millions)

	1991	1992	Change	Source/Use of cash
Assets				
Current assets				
Cash	$ 120	$ 88	−$ 32	
Accounts receivable	224	192	− 32	Source
Inventory	424	368	− 56	Source
Total	$ 768	$ 648	−$120	
Fixed assets				
Net plant and equipment	$5,228	$5,354	+$126	Use
Total assets	$5,996	$6,002	+$ 6	
Liabilities and owners' equity				
Current liabilities				
Accounts payable	$ 124	$ 144	+$ 20	Source
Notes payable	1,412	1,039	− 373	Use
Total	$1,536	$1,183	−$353	
Long-term debt	$1,804	$2,077	+$273	Source

Owners' equity

Common stock and paid-in surplus	300	300	+ 0	—
Retained earnings	2,356	2,442	+ 86	Source
Total	$2,656	$2,742	+$ 86	
Total liabilities and owners' equity	$5,996	$6,002	+$ 6	

Wildhack used its cash primarily to purchase fixed assets and to pay off short-term debt. The major sources of cash to do this were additional long-term borrowing, and, to a larger extent, reductions in current assets and additions to retained earnings.

The current ratio went from $768/$1,536 = .5 to $648/$1,183 = .55; so the firm's liquidity appears to have improved somewhat, primarily because of the large reduction in short-term debt. Overall, however, the amount of cash on hand declined by $32.

3.2   We've calculated the common-size income statement below. Remember that we simply divide each item by total sales.

WILDHACK CORPORATION
1992 Common-Size Income Statement

Sales	100.0%
Cost of goods sold	65.3
Depreciation	13.0
Earnings before interest and taxes	21.6
Interest paid	16.3
Taxable income	5.3
Taxes (34%)	1.8
Net income	3.5%
Addition to retained earnings	2.3%
Dividends	1.2

Net income is 3.5 percent of sales. Since this is the percentage of each sales dollar that makes its way to the bottom line, the standardized net income is the firm's profit margin. Cost of goods sold is 65.3 percent of sales.

3.3   We've calculated the ratios below based on the ending figures. If you don't remember a definition, refer back to Table 3.8.

Current ratio	$648/$1,183	= .55 times
Quick ratio	$280/$1,183	= .24 times
Cash ratio	$88/$1,183	= .07 times
Inventory turnover	$2,453/$368	= 6.7 times
Receivables turnover	$3,756/$192	= 19.6 times
Days' sales in inventory	365/6.7	= 54.5 days
Days' sales in receivables	365/19.6	= 18.6 days

Total debt ratio $3,260/$6,002 = 54.3%
Long-term debt ratio $2,077/$4,819 = 43.1%
Times interest earned ratio $813/$613   = 1.33 times
Cash coverage ratio $1,303/$613   = 2.13 times

3.4   The return on equity is the ratio of net income to total equity. For Wildhack, this is $132/$2,742 = 4.8%, which is not outstanding.

Given the Du Pont identity, ROE can be written as:

$$\text{ROE} = \text{Profit margin} \times \text{Total asset turnover} \times \text{Equity multiplier}$$

$$= \$132/\$3,756 \quad \times \quad \$3,756/\$6,002 \quad \times \quad \$6,002/\$2,742$$

$$= \quad 3.5\% \quad \times \quad .626 \quad \times \quad 2.19$$

$$= \quad 4.8\%$$

Notice that return on assets, ROA, is $3.5\% \times .626 = 2.2\%$.

Questions and Problems

1.   Changes in the Current Ratio   What effect would the following actions have on a firm's current ratio? Assume that net working capital is positive.
     a. Inventory is purchased.
     b. A supplier is paid.
     c. A short-term bank loan is repaid.
     d. A long-term debt matures and is paid.
     e. A customer pays off an account.
     f. Inventory is sold.

2.   Liquidity and Ratios   In recent years, Yankee Co. has greatly increased its current ratio. At the same time, the quick ratio has fallen. What has happened? Has the liquidity of the company improved?

3.   Calculating the Equity Multiplier   A firm has a total debt ratio of .40. What is its debt/equity ratio? Its equity multiplier?

4.   ROA and ROE   If a company reports a 5 percent profit margin, a total asset turnover of 2, and a total debt ratio of .50, what is its ROA? Its ROE?

5.   Calculating the Quick Ratio   The Xenon Co. has a current ratio of 3. Its current inventory is $12,000. If current liabilities are $30,000, what is the quick ratio?

6.   Cash Flow and Asset Expenditure   For the year just completed, the Akella Co. shows an increase in net fixed assets of $130. The depreciation for the year was $80. How much did Akella spend on fixed assets? Is this a source or use of cash?

7.   Common Size Statements   The Montana Dental Floss Company reports the following balance sheet information. Prepare a common-size and common-base-year balance sheet for 1992. What is the long-term debt ratio in 1992?

MONTANA DENTAL FLOSS CORPORATION
Balance Sheets as of December 31, 1991 and 1992
($ in millions)

	1991	1992
Assets		
Current assets		
Cash	$ 1,482	$ 1,553
Accounts receivable	3,446	4,229
Inventory	8,402	8,430
Total	$13,330	$14,212
Fixed assets		
Net plant and equipment	$53,408	$56,354
Total assets	$66,738	$70,566
Liabilities and Owners' Equity		
Current liabilities		
Accounts payable	$ 8,885	$ 9,003
Notes payable	7,633	8,355
Total	$16,518	$17,358
Long-term debt	$ 6,764	$ 4,356
Owners' equity		
Common stock and paid-in surplus	9,000	9,000
Retained earnings	34,456	39,852
Total	$43,456	$48,852
Total liabilities and owners' equity	$66,738	$70,566

8. **Source and Uses of Cash**   Based on the balance sheets in the previous question, what was the largest use of cash? The largest source?

9. **Calculating Ratios**   Based on the balance sheets in Question 7, calculate the following ratios for both years.
    a. Current ratio.
    b. Quick ratio.
    c. NWC/Total assets.
    d. Total debt ratio, debt/equity ratio, and equity multiplier.
    e. Long-term debt ratio.

10. **Calculating the Average Collection Period**   Dorigan's Deli has receivables of $4,388. Credit sales for the year just ended were $24,890. What is the receivables turnover? The days' sales in receivables? The average collection period?

11. **Calculating Inventory Turnover**   The Celany Group, Inc., has inventory totalling $10,980. Cost of goods sold last year was $74,882. What is the inventory turnover for the year? The days' sales in inventory?

12. **Calculating Collection and Payables Periods**   Consider the following information for the PVI Corporation:

Credit sales $5,885
Cost of goods sold   4,021

Accounts receivable   880

Accounts payable   642

How long does it take PVI to collect on its sales? How long does PVI take to pay its suppliers?

13. Calculating COGS   The Nonest Co. has about 60 days' sales in inventory. What is its inventory turnover? If inventories are currently $5,000, what is the cost of goods sold?

14. Calculating ROA   The Stansfield Corporation's net income for the most recent year was $3,299 on sales of $80,320. Total assets were $120,655. What was ROA for Stansfield?

15. More Sources and Uses   Based only on the following information for the Hydraphonics Corp., did cash go up or down? By how much? Classify each event as a source or a use of cash.

Decrease in inventory $100

Decrease in accounts payable   200

Decrease in notes payable   300

Increase in accounts receivable   500

16. Calculating TIE Ratios   The Semipole Group's net income for the most recent year was $1,200. The tax rate was 34 percent. Total interest paid was $4,000. What was the times interest earned ratio?

17. ROE and the Equity Multiplier   The Harris Pontoon Company has a debt/equity ratio of 1. The return on assets is 10 percent and total equity is $5 million. What is net income? What is ROE? The equity multiplier?

18. Ratios and Foreign Companies   Toyota Motor Company's 1989 net income was ¥346,262 on sales of ¥8,021,042 (both in millions of yen). What was its profit margin? Does the fact that these figures are quoted in yen make any difference? Why? In thousands of dollars, sales were $55,701,681. What was net income in dollars?

Some recent financial statement information for Stowe Enterprises is listed below. Use this information to work Problems 19–23.

STOWE ENTERPRISES
Income Statement and Abbreviated Balance Sheets

Sales	$1,400
Cost of goods sold	700
Depreciation	200
Earnings before interest and taxes	$ 500
Interest paid	150
Taxable income	$ 350
Taxes	119
Net income	$ 231

Addition to retained earnings	$ 62
Dividends	169

	1991	1992		1991	1992
Assets			*Liabilities and Owners' Equity*		
Current assets			Current liabilities		
Cash	$ 200	$ 503	Accounts payable	$ 500	$ 530
Accounts receivable	650	688	Notes payable	543	460
			Other	214	183
Inventory	1,045	700	Long-term debt	1,097	1,184
Fixed assets			Owners' equity		
Net plant and equipment	1,490	1,689	Common stock	190	240
			Capital surplus	400	480
			Accumulated retained earnings	441	503
Total assets	$3,385	$3,580	Total liabilities and owners' equity	$3,385	$3,580

19.   Ratios   Compute the following ratios for Stowe Enterprises:

Short-term solvency ratios

Current ratio   _____

Quick ratio   _____

Cash ratio   _____

Asset management ratios

Total asset turnover   _____

Inventory turnover   _____

Receivables turnover   _____

Long-term solvency ratios

Debt ratio   _____

Debt-to-equity ratio   _____

Equity multiplier   _____

Times interest earned ratio   _____

Cash coverage ratio   _____

Profitability ratios

Profit margin   _____

Return on assets   _____

Return on equity   _____

20.   Du Pont Identity   Construct the Du Pont identity for Stowe Enterprises.

21.   Preparing a Statement of Cash Flows   Prepare a statement of cash flows for Stowe.

22.   Calculating the Interval Measure   For how many days could Stowe continue to operate if its operations were suspended?

23.   Calculating P/E   Stowe has 60 shares outstanding. The price per share is $40. What is the P/E ratio? The market-to-book ratio?

24.   Ratios and Net Income   A firm has sales of $1,000, assets of $500, and a debt/equity ratio of 1.00. If its return on equity is 20 percent, what is its net income?

25.   **Ratios and Fixed Assets**   A firm has a long-term debt ratio of .50 and a current ratio of 2.00. Current liabilities are $200, sales are $1,000, the profit margin is 5 percent, and ROE is 20 percent. What are its net fixed assets?

26.   **Ratios and ROE**   The Mordor Corp. has a net income of $14,000. There are currently about 10 days' sales in receivables. Total assets are $100,000, total receivables are $4,000, and the debt/equity ratio is .40. What is Mordor's profit margin? Its total asset turnover? Its ROE?

27.   **Profit Margin**   In response to complaints about high prices, a grocery chain runs the following advertising campaign: "If you pay your child 25 cents to go buy $10 worth of groceries, then your child makes twice as much on the trip as we do." You've collected the following information from the grocery chain's financial statements:

Sales	$114 million
Net income	1.42 million
Total assets	8 million
Total debt	3 million

Evaluate the claim. What is the basis for the statement? Is this claim misleading? Why or why not?

Suggested Reading

There are many excellent textbooks on financial statements analysis. One that we have found helpful is:

Gibson, C. H., and P. A. Frishkoff. *Financial Statement Analysis.* Boston: Kent Publishing, 1986.

Chapter 4

Long-Term Financial Planning and Growth

A lack of effective long-range planning is a commonly cited reason for financial distress and failure. As we will develop in this chapter, long-range planning is a means of systematically thinking about the future and anticipating possible problems before they arrive. There are no magic mirrors, of course, so the best we can hope for is a logical and organized procedure for exploring the unknown. As one member of GM's board was heard to say, "Planning is a process that at best helps the firm avoid stumbling into the future backwards."

Financial planning establishes guidelines for change and growth in a firm. It normally focuses on the "big picture." This means that it is concerned with the major elements of a firm's financial and investment policies without examining the individual components of those policies in detail.

Our primary goal in this chapter is to discuss financial planning and to illustrate the interrelatedness of the various investment and financing decisions that a firm makes. In the chapters ahead, we will examine in much more detail how these decisions are made.

We first describe what is usually meant by financial planning. For the most part, we talk about long-term planning. Short-term financial planning is discussed in Chapter 17. We examine what the firm can accomplish by developing a long-term financial plan. To do this, we develop a simple, but very useful, long-range planning technique: the percentage of sales approach. We describe how to apply this approach in some simple cases, and we discuss some extensions.

To develop an explicit financial plan, management must establish certain elements of the firm's financial policy. These basic policy elements of financial planning are:

1. The firm's needed investment in new assets. This will arise from the investment opportunities that the firm chooses to undertake, and it is the result of the firm's capital budgeting decisions.

2. The degree of financial leverage the firm chooses to employ. This will determine the amount of borrowing the firm will use to finance its investments in real assets. This is the firm's capital structure policy.

3. The amount of cash the firm thinks is necessary and appropriate to pay shareholders. This is the firm's dividend policy.

4. The amount of liquidity and working capital the firm needs on an ongoing basis. This is the firm's net working capital decision.

As we will see, the decisions that a firm makes in these four areas will directly affect its future profitability, need for external financing, and opportunities for growth.

A key lesson from this chapter is that the firm's investment and financing policies interact and thus cannot truly be considered in isolation from one another. The types and amounts of assets that the firm plans on purchasing must be considered along with the firm's ability to raise the necessary capital to fund those investments.

Financial planning forces the corporation to think about goals. A goal frequently espoused by corporations is growth, and almost all firms use an explicit, companywide growth rate as a major component of their long-run financial planning. In the mid-1980s IBM's stated growth goal had been simple but typical (and overoptimistic): to match the growth of the computer industry, which it projected would be 15 percent per year through 1995.

There are direct connections between the growth that a company can achieve and its financial policy. In the sections below, we show how financial planning models can be used to better understand how growth is achieved. We also show how such models can be used to establish the limits on possible growth.

WHAT IS FINANCIAL PLANNING? | 4.1

Financial planning formulates the way financial goals are to be achieved. A financial plan is thus a statement of what is to be done in the future. Most decisions have long lead times, which means they take a long time to implement. In an uncertain world, this requires that decisions be made far in advance of their implementation. If a firm wants to build a factory in 1997, for example, it might have to begin lining up contractors and financing in 1995, or even earlier.

Growth as a Financial Management Goal

Because the subject of growth will be discussed in various places in this chapter, we need to start out with an important warning: Growth, by itself, is *not* an appropriate goal for the financial manager. As we discuss in Chapter 1, the appropriate goal is increasing the market value of the owners' equity. Of course, if a firm is successful in doing this, then growth will usually result.

Growth may thus be a desirable consequence of good decision making, but it is not an end unto itself. We discuss growth simply because growth rates are so commonly used in the planning process. As we will see, growth is a convenient means of summarizing various aspects of a firm's financial and investment policies. Also, if we think of growth as growth in the market value of the equity in the firm, then goals of growth and increasing the market value of the equity in the firm are not all that different.

Dimensions of Financial Planning

planning horizon
The long-range time period the financial planning process focuses on, usually the next two to five years.

It is often useful for planning purposes to think of the future as having a short run and a long run. The short run, in practice, is usually the coming 12 months. We focus our attention on financial planning over the long run, which is usually taken to be the coming two to five years. This is called the **planning horizon,** and it is the first dimension of the planning process that must be established.

aggregation
Process by which smaller investment proposals of each of a firm's operational units are added up and treated as one big project.

In drawing up a financial plan, all of the individual projects and investments that the firm will undertake are combined to determine the total needed investment. In effect, the smaller investment proposals of each operational unit are added up and treated as one big project. This process is called **aggregation**. This is the second dimension of the planning process.

Once the planning horizon and level of aggregation are established, a financial plan would need inputs in the form of alternative sets of assumptions about important variables. For example, suppose a company has two separate divisions: one for consumer products and one for gas turbine engines. The financial planning process might require each division to prepare three alternative business plans for the next three years:

1. A worst case. This plan would require making the worst possible assumptions about the company's products and the state of the economy. This kind of disaster planning would emphasize a division's ability to withstand significant economic adversity, and it would require details concerning cost cutting, and even divestiture and liquidation.

2. A normal case. This plan would require making most likely assumptions about the company and the economy.

3. A best case. Each division would be required to work out a case based on the most optimistic assumptions. It could involve new products and expansion and then would detail the financing needed to fund the expansion.

In this example, business activities are aggregated along divisional lines and the planning horizon is three years.

What Can Planning Accomplish?

Because the company is likely to spend a lot of time examining the different scenarios that will become the basis for the company's financial plan, it seems reasonable to ask what the planning process will accomplish.

Interactions   As we discuss in greater detail below, the financial plan must make explicit the linkages between investment proposals for the different operating activities of the firm and the financing choices available to the firm. In other words, if the firm is planning on expanding and undertaking new investments and projects, where will the financing be obtained to pay for this activity?

Options   The financial plan provides the opportunity for the firm to develop, analyze, and compare many different scenarios in a consistent way. Various investment and financing options can be explored, and their impact on the firm's shareholders can be evaluated. Questions concerning the firm's future lines of business and questions of what financing arrangements are optimal are addressed. Options such as marketing new products or closing plants might be evaluated.

Avoiding Surprises   Financial planning should identify what may happen to the firm if different events take place. In particular, it should address what actions the firm will take if things go seriously wrong or, more generally, if assumptions made today about the future are seriously in error. Thus, one of the purposes of financial planning is to avoid surprises and develop contingency plans.

Feasibility and Internal Consistency   Beyond a general goal of creating value, a firm will normally have many specific goals. Such goals might be couched in terms of market share, return on equity, financial leverage, and so on. At times, the linkages between different goals and different aspects of a firm's business are difficult to see. Not only does a financial plan make explicit these linkages, but it also imposes a unified structure for reconciling differing goals and objectives. In other words, financial planning is a way of checking that the goals and plans made with regard to specific areas of a firm's operations are feasible and internally consistent. Conflicting goals will often exist. To generate a coherent plan, goals and objectives will therefore have to be modified, and priorities will have to be established.

For example, one goal a firm might have is 12 percent growth in unit sales per year. Another goal might be to reduce the firm's total debt ratio from 40 percent to 20 percent. Are these two goals compatible? Can they be accomplished simultaneously? Maybe yes, maybe no. As we discuss below, financial planning is a way of finding out just what is possible, and, by implication, what is not possible.

The fact that planning forces management to think about goals and to establish priorities is probably the most important result of the process. In fact, conventional business wisdom holds that financial plans don't work, but financial planning does. The future is inherently unknown. What we can do is establish the direction that we want to travel and take some educated guesses at what we will find along the way. If we do a good job, then we won't be caught off guard when the future rolls around.

⌐ CONCEPT QUESTIONS

4.1a What are the two dimensions of the financial planning process?

4.1b Why should firms draw up financial plans?

4.2 | FINANCIAL PLANNING MODELS: A FIRST LOOK

Just as companies differ in size and products, the financial planning process will differ from firm to firm. In this section, we discuss some common elements in financial plans and develop a basic model to illustrate these elements.

A Financial Planning Model: The Ingredients

Most financial planning models require the user to specify some assumptions about the future. Based on those assumptions, the model generates predicted values for a large number of other variables. Models can vary quite a bit in terms of their complexity, but almost all will have the elements that we discuss next.

Sales Forecast   Almost all financial plans require an externally supplied sales forecast. In our models below, for example, the sales forecast will be the "driver," meaning that the user of the planning model will supply this value and most other values will be calculated based on it. This arrangement would be common for many types of business; planning will focus on projected future sales and the assets and financing needed to support those sales.

Frequently, the sales forecast will be given as the growth rate in sales rather than as an explicit sales figure. These two approaches are essentially the same since we can calculate projected sales once we know the growth rate. Perfect sales forecasts are not possible, of course, because sales depend on the uncertain future state of the economy. To help a firm come up with such projections, some businesses specialize in macroeconomic and industry projections.

As we discuss above, we frequently will be interested in evaluating alternative scenarios, so it isn't necessarily crucial that the sales forecast be accurate. In such cases, our goal is to examine the interplay between investment and financing needs at different possible sales levels, not to pinpoint what we expect to happen.

Pro Forma Statements   A financial plan will have a forecasted balance sheet, an income statement, and a statement of cash flows. These are called *pro forma statements,* or *pro formas* for short. The phrase *pro forma* literally means "as a matter of form." In our case, this means that the financial statements are the form we use to summarize the different events that are projected for the future. At a minimum, a financial planning model will generate these statements based on projections of key items such as sales.

In the planning models we describe below, the pro formas are the output from the financial planning model. The user will supply a sales figure, and the model will generate the resulting income statement and balance sheet.

Asset Requirements   The plan will describe projected capital spending. At a minimum, the projected balance sheet will contain changes in total fixed assets and net working capital. These changes are effectively the firm's total capital budget. Proposed capital spending in different areas must thus be reconciled with the overall increases contained in the long-range plan.

Financial Requirements   The plan will include a section on the financing arrangements that are necessary. This part of the plan should discuss dividend policy and debt policy. Sometimes firms will expect to raise cash by selling new shares of stock or by borrowing. In this case, the plan will have to consider what kinds of securities have to be sold and what methods of issuance are most appropriate. These are subjects we consider in Parts Six and Seven of our book when we discuss long-term financing, capital structure, and dividend policy.

The "Plug"   After the firm has a sales forecast and an estimate of the required spending on assets, some amount of new financing will often be necessary because projected total assets will exceed projected total liabilities and equity. In other words, the balance sheet will no longer balance.

Since new financing may be necessary to cover all of the projected capital spending, a financial "plug" variable must be selected. The plug is the designated source or sources of external financing needed to deal with any shortfall (or surplus) in financing and thereby bring the balance sheet into balance.

For example, a firm with a great number of investment opportunities and limited cash flow may have to raise new equity. Other firms with few growth opportunities and ample cash flow will have a surplus and thus might pay an extra dividend. In the first case, external equity is the plug variable. In the second, the dividend is used.

Economic Assumptions   The plan will have to state explicitly the economic environment in which the firm expects to reside over the life of the plan. Among the more important economic assumptions that will have to be made are the level of interest rates and the firm's tax rate.

A Simple Financial Planning Model

We can begin our discussion of long-term planning models with a relatively simple example. The Computerfield Corporation's financial statements from the most recent year are as follows:

COMPUTERFIELD CORPORATION
Financial Statements

Income Statement		Balance Sheet			
Sales	$1,000	Assets	$500	Debt	$250
Costs	800			Equity	250
Net income	$ 200	Total	$500	Total	$500

Unless otherwise stated, the financial planners at Computerfield assume that all variables are tied directly to sales and that current relationships are optimal. This means that all items will grow at exactly the same rate as sales. This is obviously oversimplified; we use this assumption only to make a point.

Suppose that sales increase by 20 percent, rising from $1,000 to $1,200. Planners would then also forecast a 20 percent increase in costs, from $800 to $800 × 1.2 = $960. The pro forma income statement would thus be:

Pro Forma
Income Statement

Sales	$1,200
Costs	960
Net income	$ 240

The assumption that all variables will grow by 20 percent will enable us to easily construct the pro forma balance sheet as well:

Pro Forma Balance Sheet

Assets	$600 (+100)	Debt	$300 (+ 50)
		Equity	300 (+ 50)
Total	$600 (+100)	Total	$600 (+100)

Notice that we have simply increased every item by 20 percent. The numbers in parentheses are the dollar changes for the different items.

Now we have to reconcile these two pro formas. How, for example, can net income be equal to $240 and equity increase by only $50? The answer is that Computerfield must have paid out the difference of $240 − 50 = $190, possibly as a cash dividend. In this case, dividends are the plug variable.

Suppose Computerfield does not pay out the $190. In this case, the addition to retained earnings is the full $240. Computerfield's equity will thus grow to $250 (the starting amount) + $240 (net income) = $490, and debt must be retired to keep total assets equal to $600.

With $600 in total assets and $490 in equity, debt will have to be $600 − 490 = $110. Since we started with $250 in debt, Computerfield will have to retire $250 − 110 = $140 in debt. The resulting pro forma balance sheet would look like this:

Pro Forma Balance Sheet

Assets	$600 (+100)	Debt	$110 (−140)
		Equity	490 (+240)
Total	$600 (+100)	Total	$600 (+100)

In this case, debt is the plug variable used to balance out projected total assets and liabilities.

This example shows the interaction between sales growth and financial policy. As sales increase, so do total assets. This occurs because the firm must invest in net working capital and fixed assets to support higher sales levels. Since assets are growing, total liabilities and equity, the right-hand side of the balance sheet, will grow as well.

The thing to notice from our simple example is that the way the liabilities and owners' equity change depends on the firm's financing policy and its dividend policy. The growth in assets requires that the firm decide on how to finance that growth. This is strictly a managerial decision. Also, in our example the firm needed no outside funds. This won't usually be the case, so we explore a more detailed situation in the next section.

CONCEPT QUESTIONS

4.2a What are the basic components of a financial plan?

4.2b Why is it necessary to designate a plug in a financial planning model?

THE PERCENTAGE OF SALES APPROACH | 4.3

In the previous section, we described a simple planning model in which every item increased at the same rate as sales. This may be a reasonable assumption for some elements. For others, such as long-term borrowing, it probably is not, because the amount of long-term borrowing is something set by management, and it does not necessarily relate directly to the level of sales.

In this section, we describe an extended version of our simple model above. The basic idea is to separate the income statement and balance sheet accounts into two groups, those that do vary directly with sales and those that do not. Given a sales forecast, we will then be able to calculate how much financing the firm will need to support the predicted sales level.

An Illustration of the Percentage of Sales Approach

The financial planning model we describe next is based on the **percentage of sales approach.** Our goal here is to develop a quick and practical way of generating pro forma statements. We defer discussion of some "bells and whistles" to a later section.

percentage of sales approach
Financial planning method in which accounts are varied depending on a firm's predicted sales level.

The Income Statement   We start out with the most recent income statement for the Rosengarten Corporation, as shown in Table 4.1. Notice that we

---

	ROSENGARTEN CORPORATION Income Statement		**Table 4.1**
Sales		$1,000	
Costs		800	
Taxable income		$ 200	
Taxes (34%)		68	
Net income		$ 132	
Addition to retained earnings	$88		
Dividends	44		

Table 4.2

ROSENGARTEN CORPORATION
Pro Forma Income Statement

Sales (projected)	$1,250
Costs (80% of sales)	1,000
Taxable income	$ 250
Taxes (34%)	85
Net income	$ 165

have still simplified things by including costs, depreciation, and interest in a single cost figure. We separate these out in a later section.

Rosengarten has projected a 25 percent increase in sales for the coming year, so we are anticipating sales of $1,000 × 1.25 = $1,250. To generate a pro forma income statement, we assume that total costs will continue to run at $800/$1,000 = 80% of sales. With this assumption, Rosengarten's pro forma income statement is as shown in Table 4.2. The effect here of assuming that costs are a constant percentage of sales is to assume that the profit margin is constant. To check this, notice that the profit margin was $132/$1,000 = 13.2%. In our pro forma, the profit margin is $165/$1,250 = 13.2%; so it is unchanged.

Next, we need to project the dividend payment. This amount is up to Rosengarten's management. We will assume that Rosengarten has a policy of paying out a constant fraction of net income in the form of a cash dividend. From the most recent year, the **dividend payout ratio** was:

dividend payout ratio

Amount of cash paid out to shareholders divided by net income.

$$\text{Dividend payout ratio} = \text{Cash dividends/Net income} \qquad [4.1]$$

$$= \$44/\$132 = 33\ 1/3\%$$

We can also calculate the ratio of the addition to retained earnings to net income as:

$$\text{Addition to retained earnings/Net income} = \$88/\$132 = 66\ 2/3\%.$$

retention ratio

Addition to retained earnings divided by net income. Also called the *plowback ratio*.

This ratio is called the **retention ratio** or **plowback ratio,** and it is equal to 1 minus the dividend payout ratio because everything not paid out is retained. Assuming that the payout and retention ratios are constant, the projected dividends and addition to retained earnings will be:

Projected addition to retained earnings = $165 × 2/3 = $110
Projected dividends paid to shareholders = $165 × 1/3 =   55
                                                        $165

The Balance Sheet   To generate a pro forma balance sheet, we start with the most recent statement, as shown in Table 4.3.

	($)	(%)		($)	(%)	
						Table 4.3
Assets			*Liabilities and Owners' Equity*			
Current assets			Current liabilities			
Cash	$ 160	16%	Accounts payable	$ 300	30%	
Accounts receivable	440	44	Notes payable	100	n/a	
Inventory	600	60	Total	$ 400	n/a	
Total	$1,200	120%				
			Long-term debt	$ 800	n/a	
Fixed assets			Owners' equity			
Net plant and equipment	$1,800	180%	Common stock and paid-in surplus	$ 800	n/a	
			Retained earnings	1,000	n/a	
			Total	$1,800	n/a	
Total assets	$3,000	300%	Total liabilities and owners' equity	$3,000	n/a	

ROSENGARTEN CORPORATION — Balance Sheet

On our balance sheet, we assume that some of the items vary directly with sales while others do not. For those items that do vary with sales, we express each as a percentage of sales for the year just completed. When an item does not vary directly with sales, we write "n/a" for "not applicable."

For example, on the asset side, inventory is equal to 60 percent of sales ($600/$1,000) for the year just ended. We assume that this percentage applies to the coming year, so for each $1 increase in sales, inventory will rise by $.60. More generally, the ratio of total assets to sales for the year just ended is $3,000/$1,000 = 3, or 300%.

This ratio of total assets to sales is sometimes called the **capital intensity ratio.** It tells us the assets needed to generate $1 in sales; so the higher the ratio is, the more capital intensive is the firm. Notice also that this ratio is just the reciprocal of the total asset turnover ratio we defined in the last chapter.

For Rosengarten, assuming this ratio is constant, it takes $3 in total assets to generate $1 in sales (apparently Rosengarten is in a relatively capital intensive business). Therefore, if sales are to increase by $100, then Rosengarten will have to increase total assets by three times this amount, or $300.

On the liability side of the balance sheet, we show accounts payable varying with sales. The reason is that we expect to place more orders with our suppliers as sales volume increases, so payables will change "spontaneously" with sales. Notes payable, on the other hand, represent short-term debt such as bank borrowing. These will not vary unless we take specific actions to change the amount, so we mark them as "n/a."

Similarly, we use "n/a" for long-term debt because it won't automatically change with sales. The same is true for common stock and paid-in surplus. The last item on the right-hand side, retained earnings, will vary with sales, but it

capital intensity ratio
A firm's total assets divided by its sales, or the amount of assets needed to generate $1 in sales.

Table 4.4			ROSENGARTEN CORPORATION		
			Partial Pro Forma Balance Sheet		
	Present Year	Change from Previous Year		Present Year	Change from Previous Year
Assets			*Liabilities and Owners' Equity*		
Current assets			Current liabilities		
Cash	$ 200	$ 40	Accounts payable	$ 375	$ 75
Accounts receivable	550	110	Notes payable	100	0
			Total	$ 475	$ 75
Inventory	750	150			
Total	$1,500	$300	Long-term debt	$ 800	$ 0
Fixed assets			Owners' equity		
Net plant and equipment	$2,250	$450	Common stock and paid-in surplus	800	0
			Retained earnings	1,110	110
			Total	$1,910	$110
			Total liabilities and owners' equity	$3,185	$185
Total assets	$3,750	$750	External financing needed	$ 565	$565

won't be a simple percentage of sales. Instead, we will explicitly calculate the change in retained earnings based on our projected net income and dividends.

We can now construct a partial pro forma balance sheet for Rosengarten. We do this by using the percentages we calculated above wherever possible to calculate the projected amounts. For example, net fixed assets are 180 percent of sales; so, with a new sales level of $1,250, the net fixed asset amount will be $1.80 \times \$1,250 = \$2,250$, an increase of $2,250 - 1,800 = \$450$ in plant and equipment. Importantly, for those items that don't vary directly with sales, we initially assume no change and simply write in the original amounts. The result is shown in Table 4.4. Notice that the change in retained earnings is equal to the $110 addition to retained earnings that we calculated above.

Inspecting our pro forma balance sheet, we notice that assets are projected to increase by $750. However, without additional financing, liabilities and equity will only increase by $185, leaving a shortfall of $750 - 185 = \$565$. We label this amount *external financing needed* (EFN).

A Particular Scenario   Our financial planning model now reminds us of one of those good news/bad news jokes. The good news is that we're projecting a 25 percent increase in sales. The bad news is that this isn't going to happen unless we can somehow raise $565 in new financing.

This is a good example of how the planning process can point out problems and potential conflicts. If, for example, Rosengarten had a goal of not borrowing any additional funds and not selling any new equity, then a 25 percent increase in sales is probably not feasible.

| | ROSENGARTEN CORPORATION | | | | **Table 4.5** |
| | Pro Forma Balance Sheet | | | | |
	Present Year	Change from Previous Year		Present Year	Change from Previous Year
Assets			*Liabilities and Owners' Equity*		
Current assets			Current liabilities		
Cash	$ 200	$ 40	Accounts payable	$ 375	$ 75
Accounts receivable	550	110	Notes payable	325	225
			Total	$ 700	$300
Inventory	750	150	Long-term debt	$1,140	$340
Total	$1,500	$300	Owners' equity		
Fixed assets			Common stock and paid-in surplus	800	0
Net plant and equipment	$2,250	$450	Retained earnings	1,110	110
			Total	$1,910	$110
Total assets	$3,750	$750	Total liabilities and owners' equity	$3,750	$750

If we take the need for $565 in new financing as given, Rosengarten has three possible sources: short-term borrowing, long-term borrowing, and new equity. The choice of a combination among these three is up to management; we will illustrate only one of the many possibilities.

Suppose that Rosengarten decides to borrow the needed funds. In this case, they might choose to borrow some short-term and some long-term. For example, current assets increased by $300 while current liabilities rose by only $75. Rosengarten could borrow $300 − 75 = $225 in short-term notes payable and leave total net working capital unchanged. With $565 needed, the remaining $565 − 225 = $340 would have to come from long-term debt. Table 4.5 shows the completed pro forma balance sheet for Rosengarten.

We have used a combination of short- and long-term debt as the plug here, but we emphasize that this is just one possible strategy; it is not necessarily the best one by any means. There are many other scenarios that we could (and should) investigate.

Now that we have finished our balance sheet, we have all of the projected sources and uses of cash. We could finish off our pro formas by drawing up the projected statement of cash flows along the lines discussed in Chapter 3. We will leave this as an exercise and instead investigate an important alternative scenario.

An Alternative Scenario   The assumption that assets are a fixed percentage of sales is convenient, but it may not be suitable in many cases. For example, we effectively assumed that Rosengarten was using its fixed assets at 100 percent of capacity because any increase in sales led to an increase in fixed assets. For most businesses, there would be some slack or excess capacity, and production could be increased by, perhaps, running an extra shift.

If we assume that Rosengarten is only operating at 70 percent of capacity, then the need for external funds will be quite different. When we say "70 percent of capacity," we mean that the current sales level is 70 percent of the full capacity sales level:

Current sales = $1,000 = .70 × Full capacity sales

Full capacity sales = $1,000/.70 = $1,429

This tells us that sales could increase by almost 43 percent—from $1,000 to $1,429—before any new fixed assets were needed.

In our previous scenario, we assumed that it would be necessary to add $450 in net fixed assets. In the current scenario, no spending on net fixed assets is needed, because sales are projected to rise to $1,250, which is substantially less than the $1,429 full capacity level.

As a result, our original estimate of $565 in external funds needed is too high. We estimated that $450 in net new fixed assets would be needed. Instead, no spending on new net fixed assets is necessary. Thus, if we are currently operating at 70 percent capacity, then we only need $565 − 450 = $115 in external funds. The excess capacity thus makes a considerable difference in our projections.

Example 4.1 EFN and Capacity Usage

Suppose that Rosengarten were operating at 90 percent capacity. What would sales be at full capacity? What is the capital intensity ratio at full capacity? What is EFN in this case?

Full capacity sales would be $1,000/.90 = $1,111. From Table 4.3, fixed assets are $1,800. At full capacity, the ratio of fixed assets to sales is thus:

Fixed assets/Full capacity sales = $1,800/$1,111 = 1.62

This tells us that we need $1.62 in fixed assets for every $1 in sales once we reach full capacity. At the projected sales level of $1,250, then, we need $1,250 × 1.62 = $2,025 in fixed assets. Compared to the $2,250 we originally projected, this is $225 less, so EFN is $565 − 225 = $340.

Current assets would still be $1,500, so total assets would be $1,500 + 2,025 = $3,525. The capital intensity ratio would thus be $3,525/$1,250 = 2.82, less than our original value of 3 because of the excess capacity. ∎

These alternative scenarios illustrate that it is inappropriate to blindly manipulate financial statement information in the planning process. The results depend critically on the assumptions made about the relationships between sales and asset needs. We return to this point below.

⌐CONCEPT QUESTIONS

4.3a What is the basic idea behind the percentage of sales approach?

4.3b Unless it is modified, what does the percentage of sales approach assume about fixed asset capacity usage?

EXTERNAL FINANCING AND GROWTH | 4.4

External financing needed and growth are obviously related. All other things the same, the higher the rate of growth in sales or assets, the greater will be the need for external financing. In the previous section, we took a growth rate as given, and then we determined the amount of external financing needed to support that growth. In this section, we turn things around a bit. We will take the firm's financial policy as given and then examine the relationship between that financial policy and the firm's ability to finance new investments and thereby grow.

Once again, we emphasize that we are focusing on growth not because growth is an appropriate goal; instead, for our purposes, growth is simply a convenient means of examining the interactions between investment and financing decisions. In effect, we assume that the use of growth as a basis for planning is just a reflection of the very high level of aggregation used in the planning process.

EFN and Growth

The first thing we need to do is establish the relationship between EFN and growth. To do this, we introduce the simplified income statement and balance sheet for the Hoffman Company in Table 4.6. Notice that we have simplified the balance sheet by combining short-term and long-term debt into a single total debt figure. Effectively, we are assuming that none of the current liabilities vary spontaneously with sales. This assumption isn't as restrictive as it

Table 4.6

HOFFMAN COMPANY
Income Statement and Balance Sheet

Income Statement

Sales	$500
Costs	400
Taxable income	$100
Taxes (34%)	34
Net income	$ 66

Addition to retained earnings	$44
Dividends	22

Balance Sheet

	($)	(% of sales)		($)	(% of sales)
Assets			*Liabilities and Owners' Equity*		
Current assets	$200	40%	Total debt	$250	n/a
Net fixed assets	300	60	Owners' equity	250	n/a
Total assets	$500	100%	Total liabilities and owners' equity	$500	n/a

Table 4.7

HOFFMAN COMPANY
Pro Forma Income Statement and Balance Sheet

Income Statement

Sales	$600.0
Costs (80% of sales)	480.0
Taxable income	$120.0
Taxes (34%)	40.8
Net income	$ 79.2

Addition to retained earnings	$52.8
Dividends	26.4

Balance Sheet

	($)	(% of sales)		($)	(% of sales)
Assets			*Liabilities and Owners' Equity*		
Current assets	$240.0	40%	Total debt	$250.0	n/a
Net fixed assets	360.0	60	Owners' equity	302.8	n/a
Total assets	$600.0	100%	Total liabilities and owners' equity	$552.8	n/a
			External financing needed	$ 47.2	

sounds. If any current liabilities (such as accounts payable) vary with sales, we can assume that they have been netted out in current assets. Also, we continue to combine depreciation, interest, and costs on the income statement.

Suppose the Hoffman Company is forecasting next year's sales level at $600, a $100 increase. Notice that the percentage increase in sales is $100/$500 = 20%. Using the percentage of sales approach and the figures in Table 4.6, we can prepare a pro forma income statement and balance sheet as in Table 4.7. As Table 4.7 illustrates, at a 20 percent growth rate, Hoffman needs $100 in new assets (assuming full capacity). The projected addition to retained earnings is $52.8, so the external financing needed (EFN) is $100 − 52.8 = $47.2.

Notice that the debt/equity ratio for Hoffman was originally (from Table 4.6) equal to $250/$250 = 1.0. We will assume that the Hoffman Corporation does not wish to sell new equity. In this case, the $47.2 in EFN will have to be borrowed. What will the new debt/equity ratio be? From Table 4.7, total owners' equity is projected at $302.8. The new total debt will be the original $250 plus $47.2 in new borrowing, or $297.2 total. The debt/equity ratio thus falls slightly from 1.0 to $297.2/$302.8 = .98.

Table 4.8 shows EFN for several different growth rates. The projected addition to retained earnings and the projected debt/equity ratio for each scenario are also given (you should probably calculate a few of these for practice). In determining the debt/equity ratios, we assumed that any needed funds were borrowed, and we also assumed that any surplus funds were used to pay off debt. Thus, for the zero growth case, the debt falls by $44, from

Projected Sales Growth	Increase in Assets Required	Addition to Retained Earnings	External Financing Needed (EFN)	Projected Debt/Equity Ratio	**Table 4.8**
0%	$ 0	$44.0	−$44.0	.70	Growth and projected EFN for the Hoffman Company
5	25	46.2	− 21.2	.77	
10	50	48.4	1.6	.84	
15	75	50.6	24.4	.91	
20	100	52.8	47.2	.98	
25	125	55.0	70.0	1.05	

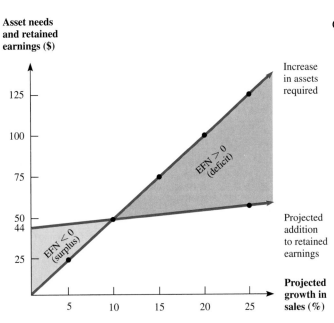

Figure 4.1

Growth and financing needed for the Hoffman Company

$250 to $206. In Table 4.8, notice that the increase in assets required is simply equal to the original assets of $500 multiplied by the growth rate. Similarly, the addition to retained earnings is equal to the original $44 plus $44 times the growth rate.

Table 4.8 shows that for relatively low growth rates, Hoffman will run a surplus, and its debt/equity ratio will decline. Once the growth rate increases to about 10 percent, however, the surplus becomes a deficit. Furthermore, as the growth rate exceeds approximately 20 percent, the debt/equity ratio passes its original value of 1.0.

Figure 4.1 illustrates the connection between growth in sales and external financing needed in more detail by plotting asset needs and additions to retained earnings from Table 4.8 against the growth rates. As shown, the need for new assets grows at a much faster rate than the addition to retained earnings, so the internal financing provided by the addition to retained earnings rapidly disappears.

Financial Policy and Growth

Based on our discussion just above, there is a direct link between growth and external financing. In this section, we discuss two growth rates that are particularly useful in long-range planning.

internal growth rate

The maximum growth rate a firm can achieve without external financing of any kind.

The Internal Growth Rate   The first growth rate of interest is the maximum growth rate that can be achieved with no external financing of any kind. We will call this the **internal growth rate** because this is the rate the firm can maintain with internal financing only. In Figure 4.1, this internal growth rate is the point where the two lines cross. At this point, the required increase in assets is exactly equal to the addition to retained earnings, and EFN is therefore zero. We have seen that this happens when the growth rate is slightly less than 10 percent. With a little algebra (see Problem 30 at the end of the chapter), we find this growth rate more precisely as:

$$\text{Internal growth rate} = \frac{ROA \times b}{1 - ROA \times b} \qquad [4.2]$$

where ROA is the return on assets we discussed in Chapter 3, and b is the plowback or retention ratio defined earlier in this chapter.

For the Hoffman Company, net income was $66 and total assets were $500. ROA is thus $66/$500 = 13.2 percent. Of the $66 net income, $44 was retained, so the plowback ratio, b, is $44/$66 = 2/3. With these numbers, we can calculate the internal growth rate as:

$$\text{Internal growth rate} = \frac{ROA \times b}{1 - ROA \times b}$$

$$= \frac{.132 \times (2/3)}{1 - .132 \times (2/3)}$$

$$= 9.65\%$$

Thus, the Hoffman Company can expand at a maximum rate of 9.65 percent per year without external financing.

The Sustainable Growth Rate   We have seen that if the Hoffman Company wishes to grow more rapidly than 9.65 percent per year, then external financing must be arranged. The second growth rate of interest is the maximum growth rate that a firm can achieve with no external *equity* financing while it maintains a constant debt/equity ratio. This rate is commonly called the

sustainable growth rate because it is the maximum rate of growth a firm can maintain without increasing its financial leverage.

There are various reasons why a firm might wish to avoid equity sales. For example, as we discuss in Chapter 13, new equity sales can be very expensive. Alternatively, the current owners may not wish to bring in new owners or contribute additional equity. Why a firm might view a particular debt/equity ratio as optimal is discussed in Chapters 14 and 15; for now, we will take it as given.

Based on Table 4.8, the sustainable growth rate for Hoffman is approximately 20 percent because the debt/equity is near 1.0 at that growth rate. The precise value can be calculated as (see Problem 30 at the end of the chapter):

$$\text{Sustainable growth rate} = \frac{ROE \times b}{1 - ROE \times b} \qquad [4.3]$$

sustainable growth rate
The maximum growth rate a firm can achieve without external equity financing while maintaining a constant debt/equity ratio.

This is identical to the internal growth rate except ROE (return on equity) is used instead of ROA.

For the Hoffman Company, net income was $66 and total equity was $250; ROE is thus $66/$250 = 26.4 percent. The plowback ratio, b, is still 2/3, so we can calculate the sustainable growth rate as:

$$
\begin{aligned}
\text{Sustainable growth rate} &= \frac{ROE \times b}{1 - ROE \times b} \\[2mm]
&= \frac{.264 \times (2/3)}{1 - .264 \times (2/3)} \\[2mm]
&= 21.36\%
\end{aligned}
$$

Thus, the Hoffman Company can expand at a maximum rate of 21.36 percent per year without external equity financing.

Example 4.2 Sustainable Growth

Suppose that Hoffman grows at exactly the sustainable growth rate of 21.36 percent. What will the pro forma statements look like?

At a 21.36 percent growth rate, sales will rise from $500 to $606.8. The pro forma income statement will look like this:

HOFFMAN COMPANY
Pro Forma Income Statement

Sales		$606.8
Costs (80% of sales)		485.4
Taxable income		$121.4
Taxes (34%)		41.3
Net income		$ 80.1
Addition to retained earnings	$53.4	
Dividends	26.7	

We construct the balance sheet just as we did above. Notice that, in this case, owners' equity will rise from $250 to $303.4 because the addition to retained earnings is $53.4.

HOFFMAN COMPANY
Pro Forma Balance Sheet

	($)	(% of sales)		($)	(% of sales)
Assets			*Liabilities and Owners' Equity*		
Current assets	$242.7	40%	Total debt	$250.0	n/a
Net fixed assets	364.1	60	Owners' equity	303.4	n/a
Total assets	$606.8	100%	Total liabilities and owners' equity	$553.4	n/a
			External funds needed	$ 53.4	

As illustrated, EFN is $53.4. If Hoffman borrows this amount, then total debt will rise to $303.4, and the debt/equity ratio will be exactly 1.0, thereby verifying our earlier calculation. At any other growth rate, something would have to change. ■

Determinants of Growth   In the last chapter, we saw that the return on equity (ROE) could be decomposed into its various components using the Du Pont identity. Since ROE appears so prominently in the determination of the sustainable growth rate, the factors that are important in determining ROE are also important determinants of growth.

From Chapter 3, we know that ROE can be written as the product of three factors:

$$ROE = \text{Profit margin} \times \text{Total asset turnover} \times \text{Equity multiplier}$$

If we examine our expression for the sustainable growth rate, anything that increases ROE will increase the sustainable growth rate by making the top bigger and the bottom smaller. Increasing the plowback ratio will have the same effect.

Putting it all together, what we have is that a firm's ability to sustain growth depends explicitly on the following four factors:

1. Profit margin. An increase in profit margin will increase the firm's ability to generate funds internally and thereby increase its sustainable growth.
2. Dividend policy. A decrease in the percentage of net income paid out as dividends will increase the retention ratio. This increases internally generated equity and thus increases sustainable growth.
3. Financial policy. An increase in the debt/equity ratio increases the firm's financial leverage. Since this makes additional debt financing available, it increases the sustainable growth rate.
4. Total asset turnover. An increase in the firm's total asset turnover increases the sales generated for each dollar in assets. This decreases the firm's need for new assets as sales grow and thereby increases the sustainable growth rate. Notice that increasing total asset turnover is the same thing as decreasing capital intensity.

In Their Own Words . . .
Robert C. Higgins on Sustainable Growth

Most financial officers know intuitively that it takes money to make money. Rapid sales growth requires increased assets in the form of accounts receivable, inventory, and fixed plant, which, in turn, require money to pay for assets. They also know that if their company does not have the money when needed, it can literally "grow broke." The sustainable growth equation states these intuitive truths explicitly.

To illustrate, sustainable growth is often used by bankers and other external analysts to assess a company's credit worthiness. They are aided in this exercise by several sophisticated computer software packages that provide detailed analyses of the company's past financial performance, including its annual sustainable growth rate.

Bankers use this information in several ways. Quick comparison of a company's actual growth rate to its sustainable rate tells the banker what issues will be at the top of management's financial agenda. If actual growth consistently exceeds sustainable growth, management's problem will be where to get the cash to finance growth, and the banker can anticipate interest in loan products. Conversely, if sustainable growth consistently exceeds actual, the banker had best be prepared to talk about investment products, because management's problem will be what to do with all the cash that keeps piling up in the till.

Bankers also find the sustainable growth equation useful for explaining to financially inexperienced small business owners and overly optimistic entrepreneurs that, for the long-run viability of their business, it is necessary to keep growth and profitability in proper balance.

Finally, comparison of actual to sustainable growth rates helps a banker understand why a loan applicant needs money and for how long the need might continue. In one instance, a loan applicant requested $100,000 to pay off several insistent suppliers and promised to repay in a few months when he collected some accounts receivable that were coming due. A sustainable growth analysis revealed that the firm had been growing at four to six times its sustainable growth rate and that this pattern was likely to continue in the foreseeable future. This alerted the banker that impatient suppliers were only a symptom of the much more fundamental disease of overly rapid growth, and that a $100,000 loan would likely prove to be only the down payment on a much larger, multiyear commitment.

Robert C. Higgins is Professor of Finance at the University of Washington. He pioneered the use of sustainable growth as a tool for financial analysis.

The sustainable growth rate is a very useful planning number. What it illustrates is the explicit relationship between the firm's four major areas of concern: its operating efficiency as measured by profit margin, its asset use efficiency as measured by total asset turnover, its dividend policy as measured by the retention ratio, and its financial policy as measured by the debt/equity ratio.

Given values for all four of these, there is only one growth rate that can be achieved. This is an important point, so it bears restating:

> If a firm does not wish to sell new equity and its profit margin, dividend policy, financial policy, and total asset turnover (or capital intensity) are all fixed, then there is only one possible growth rate.

As we described early in this chapter, one of the primary benefits of financial planning is to ensure internal consistency among the firm's various goals. The sustainable growth rate captures this element nicely. Also, we now see how a financial planning model can be used to test the feasibility of a planned growth rate. If sales are to grow at a rate higher than the sustainable growth rate, the firm must increase profit margins, increase total asset turnover, increase financial leverage, increase earnings retention, or sell new shares.

The two growth rates, internal and sustainable, are summarized in Table 4.9.

Example 4.3 Profit Margins and Sustainable Growth

The Sandar Co. has a debt/equity ratio of .5, a profit margin of 3 percent, a dividend payout of 40 percent, and a capital intensity ratio of 1. What is its sustainable growth rate? If Sandar desires a 10 percent sustainable growth rate and plans to achieve this goal by improving profit margins, what would you think?

ROE is $.03 \times 1 \times 1.5 = 4.5$ percent. The retention ratio is $1 - .40 = .60$. Sustainable growth is thus $.045(.60)/[1 - .045(.60)] = 2.77$ percent.

To achieve a 10 percent growth rate, the profit margin will have to rise. To see this, assume that sustainable growth is equal to 10 percent and then solve for profit margin, PM:

$$.10 = PM(1.5)(.6)/[1 - PM(1.5)(.6)]$$

$$PM = .1/.99 = 10.1\%$$

For the plan to succeed, the necessary increase in profit margin is substantial, from 3 percent to about 10 percent. This may not be feasible. ∎

⌐CONCEPT QUESTIONS

4.4a What are the determinants of growth?

4.4b How is a firm's sustainable growth related to its accounting return on equity (ROE)?

4.5 │ SOME CAVEATS OF FINANCIAL PLANNING MODELS

Financial planning models do not always ask the right questions. A primary reason is that they tend to rely on accounting relationships and not financial relationships. In particular, the three basic elements of firm value tend to get left out, namely, cash flow size, risk, and timing.

Because of this, financial planning models sometimes do not produce output that gives the user many meaningful clues about what strategies will lead to increases in value. Instead, they divert the user's attention to questions concerning the association of, say, the debt/equity ratio and firm growth.

The financial model we used for the Hoffman Company was simple, in fact, too simple. Our model, like many in use today, is really an accounting statement generator at heart. Such models are useful for pointing out inconsistencies and reminding us of financial needs, but they offer very little guidance concerning what to do about these problems.

In closing our discussion, we should add that financial planning is an iterative process. Plans are created, examined, and modified over and over. The final plan will be a negotiated result between all the different parties to the process. In fact, long-term financial planning in most corporations relies

I.   Internal Growth Rate

$$\text{Internal growth rate} = \frac{\text{ROA} \times b}{1 - \text{ROA} \times b}$$

Table 4.9

Summary of internal and
sustainable growth rates

where

ROA = Return on assets = Net income/Total assets

b = Plowback (retention) ratio

= Addition to retained earnings/Net income

The internal growth rate is the maximum growth rate than can be achieved with
no external financing of any kind.

II.   Sustainable Growth Rate

$$\text{Sustainable growth rate} = \frac{\text{ROE} \times b}{1 - \text{ROE} \times b}$$

where

ROE = Return on equity = Net income/Total equity

b = Plowback (retention) ratio

= Addition to retained earnings/Net income

The sustainable growth rate is the maximum growth rate than can be achieved
with no external equity financing while maintaining a constant debt/equity ratio.

on what might be called the Procrustes approach.[1] Upper-level management
has a goal in mind, and it is up to the planning staff to rework and ultimately
deliver a feasible plan that meets that goal.

The final plan will therefore implicitly contain different goals in different
areas and also satisfy many constraints. For this reason, such a plan need not
be a dispassionate assessment of what we think the future will bring; it may
instead be a means of reconciling the planned activities of different groups and
a way of setting common goals for the future.

⌐ CONCEPT QUESTIONS

4.5a   What are some important elements that are often missing in financial
        planning models?

4.5b   Why do we say that planning is an iterative process?

---

[1]In Greek mythology, Procrustes is a giant who seizes travelers and ties them to an iron bed.
He stretches them or cuts off their legs as needed to make them fit the bed.

4.6 | SUMMARY AND CONCLUSIONS

Financial planning forces the firm to think about the future. We have examined a number of features of the planning process. We describe what financial planning can accomplish and the components of a financial model. We go on to develop the relationship between growth and financing needs, and we discuss how a financial planning model is useful in exploring that relationship.

Corporate financial planning should not become a purely mechanical activity. If it does, it will probably focus on the wrong things. In particular, plans all too often are formulated in terms of a growth target with no explicit linkage to value creation, and they frequently are overly concerned with accounting statements. Nevertheless, the alternative to financial planning is "stumbling into the future."

Key Terms

planning horizon 92
aggregation 92
percentage of sales approach 97
dividend payout ratio 98

retention ratio or plowback ratio 98
capital intensity ratio 99
internal growth rate 106
sustainable growth rate 107

Chapter Review Problems and Self-Test

4.1 **Calculating EFN**   Based on the following information for the Corwin Company, what is EFN if sales are predicted to grow by 20 percent? Use the percentage of sales approach and assume full capacity. The payout ratio is constant.

CORWIN COMPANY
Financial Statements

Income Statement		Balance Sheet			
Sales	$2,750	Current assets	$ 600	Long-term debt	$ 200
Cost of sales	2,400	Net fixed assets	800	Equity	1,200
Tax (34%)	119	Total	$1,400	Total	$1,400
Net income	$ 231				
Dividends	$ 77				

4.2 **EFN and Capacity Use**   Based on the information in Problem 4.1, what is EFN, assuming 75 percent capacity usage for net fixed assets? 90 percent capacity?

4.3 **Sustainable Growth**   Based on the information in Problem 4.1, what growth rate can Corwin maintain if no external financing is used? What is the sustainable growth rate?

Answers to Self-Test Problems

4.1   We can calculate EFN by preparing the pro forma statements using the percentage of sales approach. Note that sales are forecast to be $2,750 × 1.2 = $3,300.

CORWIN COMPANY
Financial Statements

Income Statement

Sales	$3,300.0	forecast
Cost of sales	2,880.0	87.27% of sales
Tax (34%)	142.8	
Net income	$ 277.2	
Dividends	$ 92.4	33.33% of net income

Balance Sheet

Current assets	$ 720	21.81% of sales	Long-term debt	$ 200.0
Net fixed assets	· 960	29.09% of sales	Equity	1,384.8
Total	$1,680	50.90% of sales	Total	$1,584.8
			EFN	$ 95.2

4.2   Full capacity sales are equal to current sales divided by the capacity utilization. At 75 percent of capacity:

$2,750 = .75 × Full capacity sales

$3,667 = Full capacity sales

With a sales level of $3,300, no net new fixed assets will be needed, so our earlier estimate is too high. We estimated an increase in fixed assets of $960 − 800 = $160. The new EFN would thus be $95.2 − 160 = −$64.8, a surplus. No external financing is needed in this case.

At 90 percent capacity, full capacity sales are $3,056. The ratio of fixed assets to full capacity sales is thus $800/$3,056 = .262. At a sales level of $3,300, we will thus need $3,300 × .262 = $864 in net fixed assets, an increase of $64. This is $160 − 64 = $96 less than we originally predicted, so the EFN is now $95.2 − 96 = −$.80, a small surplus. No additional financing is needed.

4.3   Corwin retains $b = (1 − .33) = .67$ of net income. Return on assets is $231/$1,400 = 16.5\%$. The internal growth rate is

$$\frac{(ROA \times b)}{(1 - ROA \times b)}$$

$$= \frac{(.165 \times .67)}{(1 - .165 \times .67)}$$

$$= 12.36\%$$

Return on equity for Corwin is $231/$1,200 = 19.25\%$, so we can calculate the sustainable growth rate as

$$\frac{(ROE \times b)}{(1 - ROE \times b)}$$

$$= \frac{(.1925 \times .67)}{(1 - .1925 \times .67)}$$

$$= 14.81\%$$

Questions and Problems

1.   **Pro Forma Statements**   Consider the following simplified financial statements for the Goldfinch Corporation:

Income Statement			Balance Sheet			
Sales	$1,000		Assets	$500	Debt	$250
Costs	900				Equity	250
Net income	$ 100		Total	$500	Total	$500

Goldfinch has predicted a sales increase of 25 percent. It has also predicted that every item on the balance sheet will increase by 25 percent as well. Create the pro forma statements and reconcile them. What is the plug variable here?

2.   **Pro Forma Statements and EFN**   In the previous question, assume that Goldfinch pays out half of net income in the form of a cash dividend. Costs and assets vary with sales, but debt and equity do not. Prepare the pro forma statements and determine the external financing needed.

3.   **Calculating EFN**   The most recent financial statements for Gletglen Co. are shown below.

Income Statement			Balance Sheet			
Sales	$500		Assets	$1,300	Debt	$ 800
Costs	200				Equity	500
Net income	$300		Total	$1,300	Total	$1,300

Assets and costs are proportional to sales. Debt is not. No dividends are paid. Next year's sales are projected to be $550. What is external financing needed (EFN)?

4.   **EFN**   The most recent financial statements for REM Co. are shown below.

Income Statement		Balance Sheet			
Sales	$800	Assets	$2,400	Debt	$1,500
Costs	200			Equity	900
EBIT	$600	Total	$2,400	Total	$2,400
Taxes	50				
Net income	$550				

Assets and costs are proportional to sales. Debt is not. A dividend of $341 was paid, and REM wishes to maintain a constant payout. Next year's sales are projected to be $920. What is external financing needed (EFN)?

5.   **EFN**   The most recent financial statements for Aprostate Co. are shown below.

Income Statement

Sales	$500
Costs	440
Taxes	30
Net income	$ 30

Balance Sheet

Current assets	$ 400	Current liabilities	$ 200
Fixed assets	800	Long-term debt	200
		Equity	800
Total	$1,200	Total	$1,200

Assets, costs, and current liabilities are proportional to sales. Long-term debt is not. Aprostate maintains a constant 70 percent dividend payout. Next year's sales are projected to be $640. What is external financing needed (EFN)?

6.   **Calculating Sustainable Growth**   The most recent financial statements for Piltdown Co. are shown below.

Income Statement

Sales	$262
Costs	142
Taxes	30
Net income	$ 90

Balance Sheet

Current assets	$ 100	Debt	$ 830
Fixed assets	1,230	Equity	500
Total	$1,330	Total	$1,330

Assets and costs are proportional to sales. Debt is not. Piltdown maintains a constant 20 percent dividend payout. No equity external financing is possible. What is the sustainable growth rate?

7.   Growth as a Firm Goal   Explain why growth by itself is not an appropriate goal for financial management. In particular, describe a scenario under which the goals of growth and owner wealth maximization could be in conflict.

8.   Sales and Growth   The most recent financial statements for Fiddich Co. are shown below.

Income Statement

Sales	$490
Costs	400
Taxes	40
Net income	$ 50

Balance Sheet

Net working capital	$ 532	Long-term debt	$1,300
Fixed assets	1,998	Equity	1,230
Total	$2,530	Total	$2,530

Assets and costs are proportional to sales. Fiddich maintains a constant 30 percent dividend payout and a constant debt-to-equity ratio. What is the maximum increase in sales that can be sustained assuming no new equity is issued?

9.   Calculating Retained Earnings from Pro Forma Income   Consider the following income statement for the Gerald Corporation:

GERALD CORPORATION
Income Statement

Sales		$4,000
Costs		3,000
Taxable income		$1,000
Taxes (34%)		340
Net income		$ 660
Dividends	$110	

A 10 percent growth rate is projected. Prepare a pro forma income statement assuming that costs vary with sales and the dividend payout ratio is constant. What is the projected addition to retained earnings?

10.   Applying Percentage of Sales   The balance sheet for the Gerald Corporation is shown below. Based on this information and the income statement in the previous problem, supply the missing information using the percentage of sales approach. Assume that accounts payable vary with sales while notes payable do not. Put "n/a" where needed.

GERALD CORPORATION
Balance Sheet

	($)	(%)		($)	(%)
Assets			*Liabilities and Owners' Equity*		
Current assets			Current liabilities		
Cash	$ 500	___	Accounts payable	$2,000	___
Accounts receivable	1,000	___	Notes payable	1,000	___
Inventory	1,000	___	Total	$3,000	___
Total	$2,500	___	Long-term debt	$1,000	___
Fixed assets			Owners' equity		
Net plant and equipment	$3,000	___	Common stock and paid-in surplus	500	___
			Retained earnings	1,000	___
			Total	$1,500	___
Total assets	$5,500		Total liabilities and owners' equity	$5,500	

11.   EFN and Sales   From the previous two questions, prepare a partial pro forma balance sheet showing EFN assuming a 10 percent increase in sales.

12.   Calculating ROE   From the previous question, assuming that long-term debt is the plug, prepare the completed pro forma balance sheet. What is the projected ROE?

13.   Determinants of Growth   Assuming a firm does not wish to sell new equity, what are the four determinants of growth? Explain how an increase in each of these affects the firm's growth rate. If these four elements are taken as fixed and no new equity will be issued, then what must be true?

14.   Using Accounting Statements   Evaluate the following statement: "There is no finance in financial planning models."

15.   EFN   Tempis Fugit, Inc., has $5,000 in total assets. The retention ratio is .50, the debt/equity ratio is 1, and the profit margin is 5 percent. Sales for the year just ended were $2,000. If sales are to rise by 10 percent, what is EFN?

16.   EFN and Sales   In the previous question, what is the general relationship between growth in sales and EFN? Illustrate your answer graphically. What growth rate can be supported with no external financing? What would happen if growth were zero? How do you interpret this?

17.   Calculating Sustainable Growth   In the previous question, what is the sustainable growth rate?

18. **Sustainable Growth**   If a firm has a 20 percent ROE and a 40 percent payout ratio, what is its sustainable growth rate?

19. **Percentage of Sales Issues**   What are the advantages and disadvantages of the percentage of sales approach? In particular, is the assumption that many of the firm's costs and assets are directly proportional to sales a reasonable assumption? Does your answer depend on the time horizon being considered?

20. **Sustainable Growth**   Based on the following information, calculate the sustainable growth rate:

Profit margin = 4%

Capital intensity ratio = 2

Debt/equity ratio = .5

Net income = $1,000

Dividends = $300

What is the ROE here?

21. **Sustainable Growth**   Assuming the following ratios are constant, what is the sustainable growth rate?

Total assets/sales = 1.0

Net income/sales = .05

Debt/equity = .5

Dividends/net income = .6

22. **Sustainable Growth**   Assuming the following ratios are constant, what is the sustainable growth rate?

Sales/total assets = .6

Net income/sales = .1

Debt/total assets = .5

Retained earnings/net income = .8

23. **Growth and Profit Margin**   A firm wishes to maintain a growth rate of 5 percent per year, a debt-to-equity ratio of .5, and a dividend payout of 60 percent. The ratio of total assets to sales is constant at 2. What profit margin must it achieve?

24. **Growth and D/E**   A firm wishes to maintain a growth rate of 10 percent per year and a dividend payout of 20 percent. The ratio of total assets to sales is constant at 2, and profit margin is 10 percent. What must the debt/equity ratio be?

25. Growth and Assets   A firm wishes to maintain a growth rate of 4 percent per year, a debt-to-equity ratio of .5, and a dividend payout of 80 percent. If the profit margin is 8 percent and next year's sales are projected at $1,500, what is the total asset projection?

26. Sustainable Growth   Based on the following information, calculate the sustainable growth rate:

    Profit margin = 4%

    Total asset turnover = 2

    Total debt ratio = .5

    Payout ratio = 60%

    What is ROA here?

27. Sustainable Growth and Outside Financing   You've collected the following information about the Wutzup Corporation:

    Sales = $4,000

    Net income = $200

    Dividends = $50

    Total debt = $5,000

    Total equity = $10,000

    What is the sustainable growth rate for Wutzup? If they do grow at this rate, how much borrowing will take place in the coming year? What rate could be supported with no outside financing at all?

28. Constraints on Growth   A firm wishes to maintain a growth rate of 8 percent per year and a debt-to-equity ratio of .25. Profit margin is 4 percent, and the ratio of total assets to sales is constant at 2. Is the growth rate possible? To answer, determine what the dividend payout must be. How do you interpret the result?

29. EFN   Define the following:

    S = Previous year's sales

    A = Total assets

    D = Total debt

    E = Total equity

    g = Projected growth in sales

    PM = Profit margin

    b = Retention (plowback) ratio

Show that EFN can be written as:

$$EFN = -PM(S)b + (A - PM(S)b) \times g$$

Hint: Asset needs will equal $A \times g$. The addition to retained earnings will equal $PM(S)b \times (1 + g)$.

Challenge Problem   30.   **Growth Rates**   Based on the result in Problem 29, show that the internal and sustainable growth rates are as given in the chapter. Hint: For the internal growth rate, set EFN equal to zero and solve for g.

Suggested Readings

Approaches to building a financial planning model are contained in:

Carleton, W.T.; D. H. Downes; and C. L. Dick, Jr. "Financial Policy Models: Theory and Practice." *Journal of Financial and Quantitative Analysis* 8, 1973.

Francis, J. C., and D. R. Rowell. "A Simultaneous-Equation Model of the Firm for Financial Analysis and Planning." *Financial Management* 7, Spring 1978.

Myers, S. C., and G. A. Pogue. "A Programming Approach to Corporate Financial Management." *Journal of Finance* 29, May 1974.

Warren, J. M., and J. R. Shelton. "A Simultaneous-Equation Approach to Financial Planning." *Journal of Finance* 26, December 1971.

The most extensive textbook treatment of financial planning is:

Lee, C. F. *Financial Analysis and Planning: Theory and Application.* Reading, Mass.: Addison-Wesley, 1985.

Sustainable growth is discussed in:

Higgins, R. C. "Sustainable Growth Under Inflation." *Financial Management* 10, Autumn 1981.

For a critical discussion of sustainable growth, see:

Rappaport, A. *Creating Shareholder Value: The New Standard for Business Performance.* New York: The Free Press, 1986.

Appendix 4A   A FINANCIAL PLANNING MODEL FOR THE ROBERTS COMPANY*

In this appendix, we discuss how to get started with building a financial planning model in somewhat greater detail. Our goal is to build a simple model for the Roberts Company that incorporates some features commonly found in

---

*This appendix draws, in part, from R. A. Brealey and S. C. Myers, *Principles of Corporate Finance,* 3rd ed. (New York: McGraw-Hill, 1988), Chapter 28.

ROBERTS COMPANY
Income Statement and Balance Sheet

Income Statement

Sales	(S)	$500
Costs	(C)	235
Depreciation	(DEP)	120
Interest	(INT)	45
Taxable income	(TI)	$100
Taxes (34%)	(T)	34
Net income	(NI)	$ 66
Addition to retained earnings	(ARE)	$ 22
Dividends	(DIV)	$ 44

Balance Sheet

($)			($)		
Assets			*Liabilities and Owners' Equity*		
Current assets	(CA)	$ 400	Total debt	(D)	$ 450
Net fixed assets	(FA)	600	Owners' equity	(E)	550
Total assets	(TA)	$1,000	Total liabilities and owners' equity	(L)	$1,000

planning models. This model will include our earlier percentage of sales approach as a special case, but it will be more flexible and a little more realistic. It is by no means complete, but it should give you a good idea of how to proceed.

Table 4A.1 shows the financial statements for the Roberts Company in slightly more detail than the financial statements shown earlier in the chapter. Primarily, we have separated out depreciation and interest. We have also included some abbreviations that we will use to refer to the various items on these statements.

As we have discussed, it is necessary to designate a plug. We will use new borrowing as the plug in our model, and we will assume that Roberts does not issue new equity. This means that our model will allow the debt/equity ratio to change if needed. Our model will take a sales forecast as its input and supply the pro forma financial statements as its output.

To create our model, we take the financial statements and replace the numbers with formulas describing their relationships. In addition to the symbols above, we will use E_0 to stand for the beginning equity. With this in mind, Table 4A.2 contains the resulting model.

In Table 4A.2, the symbols a_1 through a_7 are called the *model parameters*. These describe the relationships among the variables. For example, a_7 is the

Table 4A.2

ROBERTS COMPANY
Long-Term Financial Planning Model
Income Statement

Sales	S = Input by user
Costs	$C = a_1 \times S$
Depreciation	$DEP = a_2 \times FA$
Interest	$INT = a_3 \times D$
Taxable income	$TI = S - C - DEP - INT$
Taxes	$T = a_4 \times TI$
Net income	$NI = TI - T$
Addition to retained earnings	$ARE = NI - DIV$
Dividends	$DIV = a_5 \times NI$

Balance Sheet

Assets		*Liabilities and Owners' Equity*	
Current assets	$CA = TA - FA$	Total debt	$D = TA - E$
Net fixed assets	$FA = a_6 \times TA$	Owners' equity	$E = E_0 + ARE$
Total assets	$TA = a_7 \times S$	Total liabilities and owners' equity	$L = TA$

relationship between sales and total assets, and it can be interpreted as the capital intensity ratio:

$$TA = a_7 \times S$$

$$a_7 = TA/S = \text{Capital intensity ratio}$$

Similarly, a_3 is the relationship between total debt and interest paid, so a_3 can be interpreted as an overall interest rate. The tax rate is given by a_4, and a_5 is the dividend payout ratio.

This model uses new borrowing as the plug by first setting total liabilities and owners' equity equal to total assets. Next, the ending amount for owners' equity is calculated as the beginning amount, E_0, plus the addition to retained earnings, ARE. The difference between these amounts, $TA - E$, is the new total debt needed to balance the balance sheet.

The primary difference between this model and our earlier EFN approach is that we have separated out depreciation and interest. Notice that a_2 expresses depreciation as a fraction of beginning fixed assets. This, along with the assumption that the interest paid depends on total debt, is a more realistic approach than we used earlier. However, since interest and depreciation now do not necessarily vary directly with sales, we no longer have a constant profit margin.

The model parameters a_1–a_7 can be based on a simple percentage of sales approach, or they can be determined by any other means that the model builder wishes. For example, they might be based on average values for the last several years, industry standards, subjective estimates, or even company targets. Alternatively, sophisticated statistical techniques can be used to estimate them.

We will finish this discussion by estimating the model parameters for Roberts using simple percentages and then generating pro forma statements for a $600 predicted sales level. We estimate the parameters as:

$a_1 = \$235/\$500 = .47 = $ Cost percentage

$a_2 = \$120/\$600 = .20 = $ Depreciation rate

$a_3 = \$\ 45/\$450 = .10 = $ Interest rate

$a_4 = \$\ 34/\$100 = .34 = $ Tax rate

$a_5 = \$\ 44/\$66 = 2/3 = $ Payout ratio

$a_6 = \$600/\$1,000 = .60 = $ Fixed assets/Total assets

$a_7 = \$1,000/\$500 = 2 = $ Capital intensity ratio

With these parameters and a sales forecast of $600, our pro forma financial statements are shown in Table 4A.3.[2]

What our model is now telling us is that a sales increase of $100 will require $200 in net new assets (since the capital intensity ratio is 2). To finance this, we will use $24 in internally generated funds. The balance of $200 − 24 = $176 will have to be borrowed. This amount is the increase in total debt on the balance sheet: $626 − 450 = $176. If we pursue this plan, our profit margin will decline somewhat and the debt/equity ratio will rise.

---

[2]If you put this model in a standard computer spreadsheet (as we did to generate the numbers), the software may "complain" that a "circular" reference exists, because the amount of new borrowing depends on the addition to retained earnings, the addition to retained earnings depends on the interest paid, the interest paid depends on the borrowing, and so on. This isn't really a problem; we can have the spreadsheet recalculate a few times until the numbers stop changing.

There really is no circular problem with this model because there is only one unknown, the ending total debt, which we can solve for explicitly. This will usually be the case as long as there is a single plug variable. The algebra can get to be somewhat tedious, however. See the problems at the end of this appendix for more information.

Table 4A.3

ROBERTS COMPANY
Pro Forma Financial Statements

Income Statement

Sales	(S)	$600 = Input
Cost of sales	(C)	282 = .47 × $600
Depreciation	(DEP)	144 = .20 × $720
Interest	(INT)	63 = .10 × $626
Taxable income	(TI)	$111 = $600 − 282 − 144 − 63
Taxes (34%)	(T)	38 = .34 × $111
Net income	(NI)	$ 73 = $111 − 38
Addition to retained earnings	(ARE)	$ 24 = $73 − 49
Dividends	(DIV)	49 = .67 × $73

Balance Sheet

Assets			Liabilities and Owners' Equity		
Current assets	(CA)	$ 480 = $1,200 − 720	Total debt	(D)	$ 626 = $1,200 − 574
Net fixed assets	(FA)	720 = .6 × $1,200	Owners' equity	(E)	574 = $550 + 24
Total assets	(TA)	$1,200 = 2.0 × $600	Total liabilities and owners' equity	(L)	$1,200 = $1,200

Appendix Questions and Problems

A.1   Pro Forma Statements from a Model   Consider the following simplified financial statements from the Dotsa Lot Company.

DOTSA LOT COMPANY
Income Statement and Balance Sheet

Income Statement

Sales	$500
Costs	400
Taxable income	$100
Taxes (34%)	34
Net income	$ 66

Addition to retained earnings	$22
Dividends	44

Balance Sheet

	($)		($)
Assets		*Liabilities and Owners' Equity*	
Current assets	$ 400	Total debt	$ 450
Net fixed assets	600	Owners' equity	550
Total assets	$1,000	Total liabilities and owners' equity	$1,000

Prepare a financial planning model along the lines of our model for the Roberts Company. Estimate the values for the model parameters using percentages calculated from these statements. Prepare the pro forma statements by recalculating the model by hand three or four times.

A.2   A Modification   Modify the model in the previous question so that borrowing doesn't change and new equity sales are the plug.

A.3   A Further Modification   How would you modify the model for the Roberts Company if you wanted to maintain a constant debt/equity ratio?   Challenge Question

A.4   Borrowing and the Financial Model   In our financial planning model for Roberts, show that it is possible to solve algebraically for the amount of new borrowing. Can you interpret the resulting expression?   Challenge Question

Chapter 5

First Principles of Valuation: The Time Value of Money

One of the basic problems faced by the financial manager is how to determine the value today of cash flows that are expected in the future. For example, the jackpot in a Florida state lottery drawing was $54 million. Does this mean that the winning ticket was worth $54 million? The answer is no because the jackpot was actually going to pay out over a 20-year period at a rate of $2.7 million per year. How much is the ticket worth then? The answer depends on the time value of money, the subject of this chapter.

In the most general sense, the phrase *time value of money* refers to the fact that a dollar in hand today is worth more than a dollar promised at some time in the future. On a practical level, one reason for this is that you could earn interest while you waited; so a dollar today would grow to more than a dollar later. The trade-off between money now and money later thus depends on, among other things, the rate you can earn by investing. Our goal in this chapter is to explicitly evaluate this trade-off between dollars today and dollars at some future time.

In this chapter, we look at the basic mechanics of common financial calculations. When you finish this chapter, you should have some very practical skills. For example, you will know how to calculate your own car payments or student loan payments. You will also be able to determine how long it will take to pay off a credit card if you make the minimum payment each month (a practice we do not recommend). We will show you how to compare interest rates to determine which are the highest and which are the lowest, and we will also show you how interest rates can be quoted in different, and at times deceptive, ways.

A thorough understanding of the material in this chapter is critical to understanding material in subsequent chapters, so you should study it with particular care. We will present a large number of examples in this chapter. In many problems, your answer may differ from ours slightly. This can happen because of rounding and is not a cause for concern.

5.1 | FUTURE VALUE AND COMPOUNDING

future value (FV)

The amount an investment is worth after one or more periods. Also *compound value*.

The first thing we will study is future value. **Future value (FV)** refers to the amount of money an investment will grow to over some length of time at some given interest rate. Put another way, future value is the cash value of an investment sometime in the future. We start out by considering the simplest case, a single period investment.

Investing for a Single Period

Suppose you were to invest $100 in a savings account that pays 10 percent interest per year. How much will you have in one year? You would have $110. This $110 is equal to your original *principal* of $100 plus $10 in interest that you earn. We say that $110 is the future value of $100 invested for one year at 10 percent, and we simply mean that $100 today is worth $110 in one year, given that 10 percent is the interest rate.

In general, if you invest for one period at an interest rate of r, your investment will grow to $(1 + r)$ per dollar invested. In our example, r is 10 percent, so your investment grows to $(1 + .10) = 1.1$ dollars per dollar invested. You invested $100 in this case, so you ended up with $100 \times (1.10) = $110.

You might wonder if the single period in this example has to be a year. The answer is no. For example, if the interest rate were 2 percent per quarter, your $100 would grow to $100 \times (1 + .02) = $102 by the end of the quarter. You might also wonder if 2 percent every quarter is the same as 8 percent per year. The answer is again no, but we'll explain why a little later.

Investing for More than One Period

Going back to our $100 investment, what will you have after two years, assuming that the interest rate doesn't change? If you leave the entire $110 in the bank, you will earn $110 \times .10 = $11 in interest during the second year, so you will have a total of $110 + 11 = $121. This $121 is the future value of $100 in two years at 10 percent. Another way of looking at it is that one year from now you are effectively investing $110 at 10 percent for a year. This is a single period problem, so you'll end up with $1.1 for every dollar invested or $110 \times 1.1 = $121 total.

This $121 has four parts. The first part is the $100 original principal. The second part is the $10 in interest you earned in the first year along with another $10 (the third part) you earn in the second year, for a total of $120. The last $1 you end up with (the fourth part) is interest you earn in the second year on the interest paid in the first year: $10 \times .10 = $1.

This process of leaving your money and any accumulated interest in an investment for more than one period, thereby *reinvesting* the interest, is called

compounding. Compounding the interest means earning **interest on interest,** so we call the result **compound interest.** With **simple interest,** the interest is not reinvested, so interest is earned each period only on the original principal.

Example 5.1 Interest on Interest

Suppose you locate a two-year investment that pays 14 percent per year. If you invest $325, how much will you have at the end of the two years? How much of this is simple interest? How much is compound interest?

At the end of the first year, you will have $325 × (1 + .14) = $370.50. If you reinvest this entire amount and thereby compound the interest, you will have $370.50 × 1.14 = $422.37 at the end of the second year. The total interest you earn is thus $422.37 − 325 = $97.37. Your $325 original principal earns $325 × .14 = $45.50 in interest each year, for a two-year total of $91 in simple interest. The remaining $97.37 − 91 = $6.37 results from compounding. You can check this by noting that the interest earned in the first year is $45.50. The interest on interest earned in the second year thus amounts to $45.50 × .14 = $6.37, as we calculated. ∎

We now take a closer look at how we calculated the $121 future value. We multiplied $110 by 1.1 to get $121. The $110, however, was $100 also multiplied by 1.1. In other words:

$$
\begin{aligned}
\$121 &= \$110 \times 1.1 \\
&= (\$100 \times 1.1) \times 1.1 \\
&= \$100 \times (1.1 \times 1.1) \\
&= \$100 \times 1.1^2 \\
&= \$100 \times 1.21
\end{aligned}
$$

At the risk of belaboring the obvious, let's ask: How much would our $100 grow to after three years? Once again, in two years, we'll be investing $121 for one period at 10 percent. We'll end up with $1.1 for every dollar we invest, or $121 × 1.1 = $133.1 total. This $133.1 is thus:

$$
\begin{aligned}
\$133.1 &= \$121 \times 1.1 \\
&= (\$110 \times 1.1) \times 1.1 \\
&= (\$100 \times 1.1) \times 1.1 \times 1.1 \\
&= \$100 \times (1.1 \times 1.1 \times 1.1) \\
&= \$100 \times 1.1^3 \\
&= \$100 \times 1.331
\end{aligned}
$$

---

compounding

The process of accumulating interest in an investment over time to earn more interest.

interest on interest

Interest earned on the reinvestment of previous interest payments.

compound interest

Interest earned on both the initial principal and the interest reinvested from prior periods.

simple interest

Interest earned only on the original principal amount invested.

You're probably noticing a pattern to these calculations, so we can now go ahead and state the general result. As our examples suggest, the future value of $1 invested for t periods at a rate of r per period is:

$$\text{Future value} = \$1 \times (1 + r)^t \qquad [5.1]$$

The expression $(1 + r)^t$ is sometimes called the *future value interest factor* (or just *future value factor*) for $1 invested at r percent for t periods and can be abbreviated as FVIF(r, t).

In our example, what would your $100 be worth after five years? We can first compute the relevant future value factor as:

$$(1 + r)^t = (1 + .10)^5 = 1.1^5 = 1.6105$$

Your $100 will thus grow to:

$$\$100 \times 1.6105 = \$161.05$$

The growth of your $100 each year is illustrated in Table 5.1. As shown, the interest earned in each year is equal to the beginning amount multiplied by the interest rate of 10 percent.

In Table 5.1, notice that the total interest you earn is $61.05. Over the five-year span of this investment, the simple interest is $100 \times .10 = $10 per year, so you accumulate $50 this way. The other $11.05 is from compounding.

Figure 5.1 illustrates the growth of the compound interest in Table 5.1. Notice how the simple interest is constant each year, but the compound interest you earn gets bigger every year. The size of the compound interest keeps increasing because more and more interest builds up and there is thus more to compound.

Future values depend critically on the assumed interest rate, particularly for long-lived investments. Figure 5.2 illustrates this relationship by plotting the growth of $1 for different rates and lengths of time. Notice that the future value of $1 after 10 years is about $6.20 at a 20 percent rate, but it is only about

Table 5.1	Year	Beginning Amount	Interest Earned	Ending Amount
Future value of $100 at 10 percent	1	$100.00	$10.00	$110.00
	2	110.00	11.00	121.00
	3	121.00	12.10	133.10
	4	133.10	13.31	146.41
	5	146.41	14.64	161.05
			Total interest $61.05	

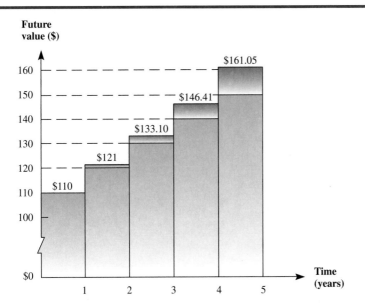

Figure 5.1

Future value, simple interest, and compound interest

Growth of $100 original amount at 10% per year. Green shaded area represents the portion of the total that results from compounding of interest.

$2.60 at 10 percent. In this case, doubling the interest rate more than doubles the future value.

To solve future value problems, we need to come up with the relevant future value factors. There are several different ways of doing this. In our example, we could have multiplied 1.1 by itself 5 times. This will work just fine, but it would get to be very tedious for, say, a 30-year investment.

Fortunately, there are several easier ways to get future value factors. Most calculators have a key labeled "y^x." You can usually just enter 1.1, press this key, enter 5, and press the "=" key to get the answer. This is an easy way to calculate future value factors because it's quick and accurate.

Alternatively, you can use a table that contains future value factors for some common interest rates and time periods. Table 5.2 contains some of these factors. Table A.1 in the Appendix at the end of the book contains a much larger set. To use the table, find the column that corresponds to 10 percent. Then look down the rows until you come to five periods. You should find the factor that we calculated, 1.6105.

Tables such as 5.2 are not as common as they once were because they predate inexpensive calculators and are only available for a relatively small number of rates. Interest rates are often quoted to three or four decimal points, so the size of tables needed to deal with these accurately would be quite large. As a result, the "real world" has moved away from using them. We will emphasize the use of a calculator in this chapter.

Figure 5.2

Future value of $1 for different periods and rates

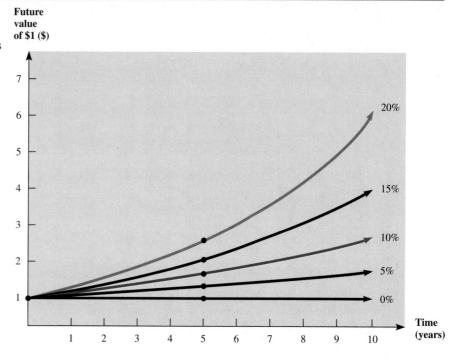

Number of Periods	Interest Rate			
	5%	10%	15%	20%
1	1.0500	1.1000	1.1500	1.2000
2	1.1025	1.2100	1.3225	1.4400
3	1.1576	1.3310	1.5209	1.7280
4	1.2155	1.4641	1.7490	2.0736
5	1.2763	1.6105	2.0114	2.4883

Table 5.2

Future value interest factors

These tables still serve a useful purpose. To make sure that you are doing the calculations correctly, pick a factor from the table and then calculate it yourself to see that you get the same answer. There are plenty of numbers to choose from.

Example 5.2 Compound Interest

You've located an investment that pays 12 percent. That rate sounds good to you, so you invest $400. How much will you have in three years? How much will you have in seven years? At the end of seven years, how much interest have you earned? How much of that interest results from compounding?

Based on our discussion, we can calculate the future value factor for 12 percent and three years as:

$$(1 + r)^t = 1.12^3 = 1.4049$$

Your $400 thus grows to:

$$\$400 \times 1.4049 = \$561.97$$

After seven years, you would have:

$$\$400 \times 1.12^7 = \$400 \times 2.2107 = \$884.27$$

Thus, you will more than double your money over seven years.

Since you invested $400, the interest in the $884.27 future value is $884.27 − 400 = $484.27. At 12 percent, your $400 investment earns $400 × .12 = $48 in simple interest every year. Over seven years, the simple interest thus totals 7 × $48 = $336. The other $484.27 − 336 = $148.27 is from compounding. ∎

The effect of compounding is not great over short time periods, but it really starts to add up as the horizon grows. To take an extreme case, suppose one of your more frugal ancestors had invested $5 for you at a 6 percent interest rate 200 years ago, how much would you have today? The future value factor is a substantial $(1.06)^{200} = 115,125.91$ (you won't find this one in a table), so you would have $5 × 115,125.91 = $575,629.53 today. Notice that the simple interest is just $5 × .06 = $.30 per year. After 200 years, this amounts to $60. The rest is from reinvesting. Such is the power of compound interest!

Example 5.3   How Much for That Island?

To further illustrate the effect of compounding for long horizons, consider the case of Peter Minuit and the Indians. In 1626, Minuit bought all of Manhattan Island for about $24 in goods and trinkets. This sounds cheap, but the Indians may have gotten the better end of the deal. To see why, suppose that the Indians had sold the goods and invested the $24 at 10 percent. How much would it be worth today?

Roughly 365 years have passed since the transaction. At 10 percent, $24 will grow by quite a bit over that time. How much? The future value factor is approximately:

$$(1 + r)^t = 1.1^{365} \approx 1,300,000,000,000,000$$

That is, 13 followed by 14 zeroes. The future value is thus on the order of 24 × 1.3 quadrillion or about 31.2 *quadrillion* dollars (give or take a few hundreds of trillions).

Well, $31.2 quadrillion is a lot of money. How much? If you had it, you could buy the United States. All of it. Cash. With money left over to buy Canada, Mexico, and the rest of the world, for that matter.

This example is something of an exaggeration, of course. In 1626, it would not have been easy to locate an investment that would pay 10 percent every year without fail for the next 365 years. ∎

A Note on Compound Growth

If you are considering depositing money in an interest-bearing account, then the interest rate on that account is just the rate at which your money grows, assuming you don't remove any of it. If that rate is 10 percent, then each year you simply have 10 percent more money than you had the year before. In this case, the interest rate is just an example of a compound growth rate.

The way we calculated future values is actually quite general and lets you answer some other types of questions related to growth. For example, your company currently has 10,000 employees. You've estimated that the number of employees grows by 3 percent per year. How many employees will there be in five years? Here, we start with 10,000 people instead of dollars, and we don't think of the growth rate as an interest rate, but the calculation is exactly the same:

$$10,000 \times (1.03)^5 = 10,000 \times 1.1593 = 11,593 \text{ employees}$$

There will be about 1,593 net new hires over the coming five years.

Example 5.4   Dividend Growth

The TICO Corporation currently pays a cash dividend of $5 per share. You believe that the dividend will be increased by 4 percent each year indefinitely. How big will the dividend be in eight years?

Here we have a cash dividend growing because it is being increased by management, but, once again, the calculation is the same:

$$\text{Future value} = \$5 \times (1.04)^8 = \$5 \times (1.3686) = \$6.84$$

The dividend will grow by $1.84 over that period. Dividend growth is a subject we will return to in a later chapter. ∎

⌐CONCEPT QUESTIONS

5.1a What do we mean by the future value of an investment?

5.1b What does it mean to compound interest? How does compound interest differ from simple interest?

5.1c In general, what is the future value of $1 invested at r per period for t periods?

PRESENT VALUE AND DISCOUNTING | 5.2

When we discuss future value, we are thinking of questions like "What will my $2,000 investment grow to if it earns a 6.5 percent return every year for the next six years?" The answer to this question is what we called the future value of $2,000 invested at 6.5 percent for six years (check that the answer is about $2,918).

There is another type of question that comes up even more often in financial management and is obviously related to future value. Suppose you need to have $10,000 in 10 years, and you can earn 6.5 percent on your money. How much do you have to invest today to reach your goal? You can verify that the answer is $5,327.26. How do we know this? Read on.

The Single Period Case

We've seen that the future value of $1 invested for one year at 10 percent is $1.10. We now ask a slightly different question: How much do we have to invest today at 10 percent to get $1 in one year? In other words, we know the future value here is $1, but what is the **present value (PV)**? The answer isn't too hard to figure out. Whatever we invest today will be 1.1 times bigger at the end of the year. Since we need $1 at the end of the year:

present value (PV)
The current value of future cash flows discounted at the appropriate discount rate.

Present value × 1.1 = $1

Or:

Present value = $1/1.1 = $.909

In this case, the present value is the answer to the following question: "What amount, invested today, will grow to $1 in one year if the interest rate is 10 percent?" Present value is thus just the reverse of future value. Instead of compounding the money forward into the future, we **discount** it back to the present.

discount
Calculate the present value of some future amount.

Example 5.5 Single Period PV
Suppose you need $400 to buy textbooks next year. You can earn 7 percent on your money. How much do you have to put up today?

We need to know the PV of $400 in one year at 7 percent. Proceeding as above:

Present value × 1.07 = $400

We can now solve for the present value:

Present value = $400 × [1/1.07] = $373.83

Thus, $373.83 is the present value. Again, this just means that investing this amount for one year at 7 percent will result in your having a future value of $400. ∎

From our examples, the present value of $1 to be received in one period is generally given as:

$$PV = \$1 \times [1/(1 + r)]$$

We next examine how to get the present value of an amount to be paid in two or more periods into the future.

Present Values for Multiple Periods

Suppose you needed to have $1,000 in two years. If you can earn 7 percent, how much do you have to invest to make sure that you have the $1,000 when you need it? In other words, what is the present value of $1,000 in two years if the relevant rate is 7 percent?

Based on your knowledge of future values, you know that the amount invested must grow to $1,000 over the two years. In other words, it must be the case that:

$$\$1,000 = PV \times 1.07 \times 1.07$$
$$= PV \times 1.07^2$$
$$= PV \times 1.1449$$

Given this, we can solve for the present value:

$$\text{Present value} = \$1,000/1.1449 = \$873.44$$

Therefore, $873.44 is the amount you must invest in order to achieve your goal.

Example 5.6 Saving Up
You would like to buy a new automobile. You have about $50,000 or so, but the car costs $68,500. If you can earn 9 percent, how much do you have to invest today to buy the car in two years? Do you have enough? Assume the price will stay the same.

What we need to know is the present value of $68,500 to be paid in two years, assuming a 9 percent rate. Based on our discussion, this is:

$$PV = \$68,500/1.09^2 = \$68,500/1.1881 = \$57,655.08$$

You're still about $7,655 short, even if you're willing to wait two years. ∎

As you have probably recognized by now, calculating present values is quite similar to calculating future values, and the general result looks much the same. The present value of $1 to be received t periods in the future at a discount rate of r is:

$$PV = \$1 \times [1/(1 + r)^t] = \$1/(1 + r)^t \qquad [5.2]$$

Number of Periods	Interest Rate				Table 5.3
	5%	10%	15%	20%	Present value interest factors
1	.9524	.9091	.8696	.8333	
2	.9070	.8264	.7561	.6944	
3	.8638	.7513	.6575	.5787	
4	.8227	.6830	.5718	.4823	
5	.7835	.6209	.4972	.4019	

The quantity in brackets, $1/(1 + r)^t$, goes by several different names. Since it's used to discount a future cash flow, it is often called a *discount factor.* With this name, it is not surprising that the rate used in the calculation is often called the **discount rate.** We will tend to call it this in talking about present values. The quantity in brackets is also called the *present value interest factor* for $1 at r percent for t periods and is sometimes abbreviated as PVIF(r, t). Finally, calculating the present value of a future cash flow to determine its worth today is commonly called *discounted cash flow (DCF)* valuation.

discount rate
The rate used to calculate the present value of future cash flows.

To illustrate, suppose you need $1,000 in three years. You can earn 15 percent on your money. How much do you have to invest today? To find out, we have to determine the present value of $1,000 in three years at 15 percent. We do this by discounting $1,000 back three periods at 15 percent. With these numbers, the discount factor is:

$$1/(1 + .15)^3 = 1/1.5209 = .6575$$

The amount you must invest is thus:

$$\$1,000 \times .6575 = \$657.50$$

We say that $657.50 is the present or discounted value of $1,000 to be received in three years at 15 percent.

There are tables for present value factors just as there are tables for future value factors, and you use them in the same way (if you use them at all). Table 5.3 contains a small set. A much larger set can be found in Table A.2 in the book's Appendix.

In Table 5.3, the discount factor we just calculated (.6575) can be found by looking down the column labelled 15% until you come to the third row.

Example 5.7   Deceptive Advertising?
Recently, some businesses have been advertising things like "Come try our product. If you do, we'll give you $100 just for coming by!" If you read the fine print, what you find out is that they will give you a savings certificate that will pay you $100 in 25 years or so. If the going interest rate on such certificates is 10 percent per year, how much are they really giving you today?

What you're actually getting is the present value of $100 to be paid in 25 years. If the discount rate is 10 percent per year, then the discount factor is:

$$1/1.1^{25} = 1/10.8347 = .0923$$

This tells you that a dollar in 25 years is worth a little more than nine cents today, assuming a 10 percent discount rate. Given this, the promotion is actually paying you about $.0923 \times \$100 = \$9.23$. Maybe this is enough to draw customers, but it's not $100. ∎

As the length of time until payment grows, present values decline. As Example 5.7 illustrates, present values tend to become small as the time horizon grows. If you look out far enough, they will always get close to zero. Also, for a given length of time, the higher the discount rate is, the lower is the pres-ent value. Put another way, present values and discount rates are inversely related. Increasing the discount rate decreases the PV and vice versa.

The relationship between time, discount rates, and present values is illustrated in Figure 5.3. Notice that by the time we get to 10 years, the present values are all substantially smaller than the future amounts.

Figure 5.3

Present value of $1 for different periods and rates

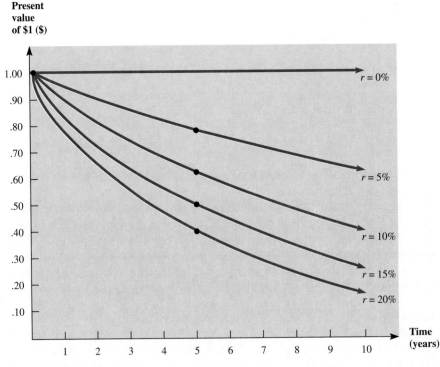

5.2a What do we mean by the present value of an investment?
5.2b The process of discounting a future amount back to the present is the opposite of doing what?
5.2c What do we mean by discounted cash flow or DCF valuation?

MORE ON PRESENT AND FUTURE VALUES | 5.3

If you look back at the expressions that we came up with for present and future values, you will see that there is a very simple relationship between the two. We explore this relationship and some related issues in this section.

Present versus Future Value

What we called the present value factor is just the reciprocal of (that is, 1 divided by) the future value factor:

$$\text{Future value factor} = (1 + r)^t$$

$$\text{Present value factor} = 1/(1 + r)^t$$

In fact, the easy way to calculate a present value factor on many calculators is to first calculate the future value factor and then press the "1/x" key to flip it over.

If we let FV_t stand for the future value after t periods, then the relationship between future value and present value can be written very simply as one of the following:

$$PV \times (1 + r)^t = FV_t \qquad\qquad [5.3]$$

$$PV = FV_t/(1 + r)^t = FV_t \times [1/(1 + r)^t]$$

This last result we will call the *basic present value equation*. We will use it throughout the text. There are a number of variations that come up, but this simple equation underlies many of the most important ideas in corporate finance.

Example 5.8 Evaluating Investments

To give you an idea of how we will be using present and future values, consider the following simple investment. Your company proposes to buy an asset for $335. This investment is very safe. You will sell off the asset in three years for $400. You know that you could invest the $335 elsewhere at 10 percent with very little risk. What do you think of the proposed investment?

This is not a good investment. Why not? Because you can invest the $335 elsewhere at 10 percent. If you do, after three years it will grow to:

$$\$335 \times (1 + r)^t = \$335 \times 1.1^3$$
$$= \$335 \times 1.331$$
$$= \$445.89$$

Since the proposed investment only pays out $400, it is not as good as other alternatives that we have. Another way of saying the same thing is to notice that the present value of $400 in three years at 10 percent is:

$$\$400 \times [1/(1 + r)^t] = \$400/1.1^3 = \$400/1.331 = \$300.53$$

This tells us that we only have to invest about $300 to get $400 in three years, not $335. We will return to this type of analysis later on. ∎

Determining the Discount Rate

It will turn out that we will frequently need to determine what discount rate is implicit in an investment. We can do this by looking at the basic present value equation:

$$PV = FV_t/(1 + r)^t$$

There are only four parts to this equation: the present value (PV), the future value (FV_t), the discount rate (r), and the life of the investment (t). Given any three of these, we can always find the fourth.

Example 5.9   Finding r for a Single Period Investment

You are considering a one year investment. If you put up $1,250, you will get back $1,350. What rate is this investment paying?

First of all, in this single period case, the answer is fairly obvious. You are getting a total of $100 in addition to your $1,250. The implicit rate on this investment is thus $100/1,250 = 8$ percent.

More formally, from the basic present value equation, the present value (the amount you must put up today) is $1,250. The future value (what the present value grows to) is $1,350. The time involved is one period, so we have:

$$\$1,250 = \$1,350/(1 + r)^1$$
$$(1 + r) = \$1,350/1,250 = 1.08$$
$$r = 8\%$$

In this simple case, of course, there was no need to go through this calculation, but, as we describe below, it gets a little harder when there is more than one period. ∎

To illustrate what happens with multiple periods, we might be offered an investment that costs us $100 and will double our money in eight years. To compare this to other investments, we would like to know what discount rate is implicit in these numbers. This discount rate is called the *rate of return* or sometimes just *return* on the investment. In this case, we have a present value of $100, a future value of $200 (double our money), and an eight-year life. To calculate the return, we can write the basic present value equation as:

$$PV = FV_t/(1 + r)^t$$

$$\$100 = \$200/(1 + r)^8$$

It could also be written as:

$$(1 + r)^8 = 200/100 = 2$$

We now need to solve for *r*. There are three ways we could do it:

1. Use a financial calculator.
2. Solve the equation for $1 + r$ by taking the eighth root of both sides. Since this is the same thing as raising both sides to the power of ⅛ or .125, this is actually easy to do with the "y^x" key on a calculator. Just enter 2, then press "y^x," enter .125, and press the " = " key. The eighth root should be about 1.09, which implies that *r* is 9 percent.
3. Use a future value table. The future value factor after eight years is equal to 2. If you look across the row corresponding to eight periods in Table A.1, you will see that a future value factor of 2 corresponds to the 9 percent column, again implying that the return here is 9 percent.

Actually, in this particular example, there is a useful "back of the envelope" means of solving for *r* — the Rule of 72. For reasonable rates of return, the time it takes to double your money is given approximately by $72/r\%$. In our example, this is $72/r\% = 8$ years, implying that *r* is 9 percent as we calculated. This rule is fairly accurate for discount rates in the 5 percent to 20 percent range.

A slightly more extreme example involves money bequeathed by Benjamin Franklin, who died on April 17, 1790. In his will, he gave 1,000 pounds sterling to Massachusetts and the city of Boston. He gave a like amount to Pennsylvania and the city of Philadelphia. The money was paid to Franklin when he held political office, but he believed that politicians should not be paid for their service!

Franklin originally specified that the money should be paid out 100 years after his death and used to train young people. Later, however, after some legal wrangling, it was agreed that the money would be paid out in 1990, 200 years after Franklin's death. By that time, the Pennsylvania bequest had grown to about $2 million; the Massachusetts bequest had grown to $4.5 million. The money was used to fund the Franklin Institutes in Boston and Philadelphia. Assuming that 1,000 pounds sterling was equivalent to 1,000 dollars, what rate of return did the two states earn (the dollar did not become the official U.S. currency until 1792)?

For Pennsylvania, the future value is $2 million and the present value is $1,000. There are 200 years involved, so we need to solve for r in the following:

$$\$1000 = \$2 \text{ million}/(1 + r)^{200}$$

$$(1 + r)^{200} = 2,000$$

Solving for r, the Pennsylvania money grew at about 3.87 percent per year. The Massachusetts money did better; check that the rate of return in this case was 4.3 percent. Small differences can add up!

Example 5.10 Double Your Fun

You have been offered an investment that promises to double your money every 10 years. What is the approximate rate of return on the investment?

From the Rule of 72, the rate of return is approximately $72/r\% = 10$, so the rate is approximately $72/10 = 7.2\%$. Check that the exact answer is 7.177 percent. ∎

Example 5.11 Saving for College

You estimate that you will need about $80,000 to send your child to college in eight years. You have about $35,000 now. If you can earn 20 percent per year, will you make it? At what rate will you just reach your goal?

If you can earn 20 percent, the future value of your $35,000 in eight years will be:

$$FV = \$35,000 \times (1.20)^8 = \$35,000 \times 4.2998 = \$150,493.59$$

So you will make it easily. The minimum rate is the unknown r in the following:

$$FV = \$35,000 \times (1 + r)^8 = \$80,000$$

$$(1 + r)^8 = \$80,000/35,000 = 2.2857$$

Therefore, the future value factor is 2.2857. Looking at the row in Table A.1 that corresponds to eight periods, our future value factor is roughly halfway between the ones shown for 10 percent (2.1436) and 12 percent (2.4760), so you will just reach your goal if you earn approximately 11 percent. To get the exact answer, we could use a financial calculator or we can solve for r:

$$(1 + r)^8 = \$80,000/35,000 = 2.2857$$

$$(1 + r) = 2.2857^{(1/8)} = 2.2857^{.125} = 1.1089$$

$$r = 10.89\% \quad ∎$$

Example 5.12 Only 18,262.5 Days to Retirement

You would like to retire in 50 years as a millionaire. If you have $10,000 today, what rate of return do you need to earn to achieve your goal?

The future value is $1,000,000. The present value is $10,000, and there are 50 years until payment. We need to calculate the unknown discount rate in the following:

$$\$10,000 = \$1,000,000/(1 + r)^{50}$$

$$(1 + r)^{50} = 100$$

The future value factor is thus 100. You can verify that the implicit rate is about 9.65 percent. ∎

Finding the Number of Periods

Suppose we were interested in purchasing an asset that costs $50,000. We currently have $25,000. If we can earn 12 percent on this $25,000, how long until we have the $50,000? The answer involves solving for the last variable in the basic present value equation, the number of periods. You already know how to get an approximate answer to this particular problem. Notice that we need to double our money. From the Rule of 72, this will take about $72/12 = 6$ years at 12 percent.

To come up with the exact answer, we can again manipulate the basic present value equation. The present value is $25,000, and the future value is $50,000. With a 12 percent discount rate, the basic equation takes one of the following forms:

$$\$25,000 = \$50,000/(1.12)^{t}$$

$$\$50,000/25,000 = (1.12)^{t} = 2$$

We thus have a future value factor of 2 for a 12 percent rate. We now need to solve for t. If you look down the column in Table A.1 that corresponds to 12 percent, you will see that a future value factor of 1.9738 occurs at six periods. It will thus take about six years as we calculated. To get the exact answer, we have to explicitly solve for t (or use a financial calculator). If you do this, the answer is 6.1163 years, so our approximation was quite close in this case.[1]

---

[1]To solve for t, we have to take the logarithm of both sides of the equation:

$$1.12^{t} = 2$$

$$\log 1.12^{t} = \log 2$$

$$t \log 1.12 = \log 2$$

We can then solve for t explicitly:

$$t = \log 2/\log 1.12$$

$$= 6.1163$$

Almost all calculators can determine a logarithm; look for a key labeled "log" or "ln." If both are present, use either one.

Example 5.13 Waiting for Godot

You've been saving up to buy the Godot Company. The total cost will be $10 million. You currently have about $2.3 million. If you can earn 5 percent on your money, how long will you have to wait? At 16 percent, how long must you wait?

At 5 percent, you'll have to wait a long time. From the basic present value equation:

$$\$2.3 = 10/(1.05)^t$$

$$1.05^t = 4.35$$

$$t = 30 \text{ years}$$

At 16 percent, things are a little better. Check for yourself that it will take about 10 years. ∎

CONCEPT QUESTIONS

5.3a What is the basic present value equation?

5.3b What is the Rule of 72?

5.3c In general, what is the present value of $1 to be received in t periods, assuming a discount rate of r per period?

5.4 | PRESENT AND FUTURE VALUES OF MULTIPLE CASH FLOWS

Thus far, we have restricted our attention to either the future value of a lump-sum present amount or the present value of some single future cash flow. In this section, we extend these basic results to handle any number of cash flows. We start with future value.

Future Value with Multiple Cash Flows

Suppose you deposit $100 today in an account paying 8 percent. In one year, you will deposit another $100. How much will you have in two years? This particular problem is relatively easy. At the end of the first year, you will have $108 plus the second $100 you deposit for a total of $208. You leave this $208 on deposit at 8 percent for another year. At the end of this second year, it is worth:

$$\$208 \times 1.08 = \$224.64$$

Figure 5.4 is a *time line* that illustrates the process of calculating the future value of these two $100 deposits. Figures such as this one are very useful for solving complicated problems. Anytime you are having trouble with a present or future value problem, drawing a time line will usually help you to see what is happening.

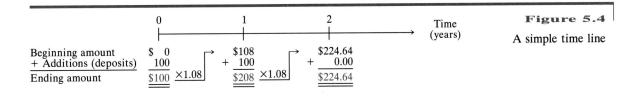

Figure 5.4

A simple time line

Example 5.14 Saving Up Revisited

You think that you will be able to deposit $4,000 at the end of each of the next three years in a bank account paying 8 percent interest. You currently have $7,000 in the account. How much will you have in three years? In four years?

At the end of the first year, you will have:

$$\$7,000 \times (1.08) + \$4,000 = \$11,560$$

At the end of the second year, you will have:

$$\$11,560 \times (1.08) + \$4,000 = \$16,484.80$$

Repeating this for the third year gives:

$$\$16,484.8 \times (1.08) + \$4,000 = \$21,803.58$$

Therefore, you will have $21,803.58 in three years. If you leave this on deposit for one more year (and don't add to it), at the end of the fourth year you'll have:

$$\$21,803.58 \times (1.08) = \$23,547.87 \quad \blacksquare$$

When we calculated the future value of the two $100 deposits, we simply calculated the balance as of the beginning of each year and then rolled that amount forward to the next year. We could have done it another, quicker way. The first $100 was on deposit for two years at 8 percent, so its future value is:

$$\$100 \times (1.08)^2 = \$100 \times 1.1664 = \$116.64$$

The second $100 was on deposit for one year at 8 percent, and its future value is thus:

$$\$100 \times 1.08 = \$108.00$$

The total future value, as we previously calculated, is equal to the sum of these two future values:

$$\$116.64 + 108 = \$224.64$$

Based on this example, there are two ways to calculate future values for multiple cash flows: (1) Compound the accumulated balance forward one year at a time or (2) calculate the future value of each cash flow first and then add them up. These give the same answer, so you can do it either way.

To illustrate the two different ways of calculating future values, consider the future value of $2,000 invested at the end of each of the next five years. The current balance is zero, and the rate is 10 percent. We first draw a time line in Figure 5.5.

On the time line, notice that nothing happens until the end of the first year when we make the first $2,000 investment. This first $2,000 earns interest for the next four (not five) years. Also notice that the last $2,000 is invested at the end of the fifth year, so it earns no interest at all.

Figure 5.6 illustrates the calculations involved if we compound the investment one period at a time. As illustrated, the future value is $12,210.20.

Figure 5.7 goes through the same calculations, but the second technique is used. Naturally, the answer is the same.

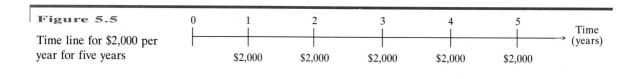

Figure 5.5

Time line for $2,000 per year for five years

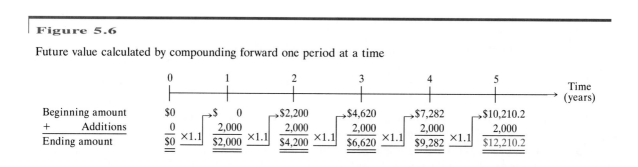

Figure 5.6

Future value calculated by compounding forward one period at a time

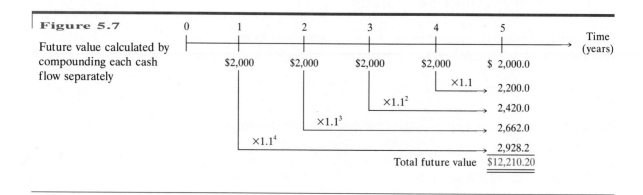

Figure 5.7

Future value calculated by compounding each cash flow separately

Example 5.15 Saving Up Once Again

If you deposit $100 in one year, $200 in two years, and $300 in three years, how much will you have in three years? How much of this is interest? How much will you have in five years if you don't add additional amounts? Assume a 7 percent interest rate throughout.

We will calculate the future value of each amount in three years. Notice that the $100 earns interest for two years, and the $200 earns interest for one year. The final $300 earns no interest. The future values are thus:

$$\$100 \times 1.07^2 = \$114.49$$
$$\$200 \times 1.07\ \ = \ \ 214.00$$
$$+\ \$300 \qquad\ \ = \ \ \underline{300.00}$$
$$\text{Total future value} = \underline{\underline{\$628.49}}$$

The future value is thus $628.49. The total interest is:

$$\$628.49 - (\$100 + 200 + 300) = \$28.49$$

How much will you have in five years? We know that you will have $628.49 in three years. If you leave that in for two more years, it will grow to:

$$\$628.49 \times (1.07)^2 = \$628.49 \times 1.1449 = \$719.56$$

Notice that we could have calculated the future value of each amount separately. Once again, be careful about the lengths of time. As we previously calculated, the first $100 earns interest for only four years, the second deposit earns three years' interest, and the last earns two years' interest:

$$\$100 \times (1.07)^4 = \$100 \times 1.3108 = \$131.08$$
$$\$200 \times (1.07)^3 = \$200 \times 1.2250 = \ \ 245.01$$
$$+\ \$300 \times (1.07)^2 = \$300 \times 1.1449 = \ \ \underline{343.47}$$
$$\text{Total future value} \qquad \underline{\underline{\$719.56}}\ \blacksquare$$

Present Value with Multiple Cash Flows

It will turn out that we will very often need to determine the present value of a series of future cash flows. As with future values, there are two ways we can do it. We can either discount back one period at a time, or we can just calculate the present values individually and add them up.

Suppose that you needed $1,000 in one year and $2,000 more in two years. If you can earn 9 percent on your money, how much do you have to put up today to exactly cover these amounts in the future? In other words, what is the present value of the two cash flows at 9 percent?

The present value of $2,000 in two years at 9 percent is:

$2,000/1.09^2 = $1,683.36

The present value of $1,000 in one year is:

$1,000/1.09 = $917.43

Therefore, the total present value is:

$1,683.36 + 917.43 = $2,600.79

To see why $2,600.79 is the right answer, we can check to see that after the $2,000 is paid out in two years, there is no money left. If we invest $2,600.79 for one year at 9 percent, we will have:

$2,600.79 × 1.09 = $2,834.86

We take out $1,000, leaving $1,834.86. This amount earns 9 percent for another year, leaving us with:

$1,834.86 × 1.09 = $2,000

This is just as we planned. As this example illustrates, the present value of a series of future cash flows is simply the amount that you would need today in order to exactly duplicate those future cash flows (for a given discount rate).

An alternative way of calculating present values for multiple future cash flows is to discount back to the present one period at a time. To illustrate, suppose we had an investment that was going to pay $1,000 at the end of every year for the next five years. To find the present value, we could discount each $1,000 back to the present separately and then add them up. Figure 5.8 illustrates this approach for a 6 percent discount rate.

As Figure 5.8 shows, the answer is $4,212.37 (ignoring a small rounding error).

Alternatively, we could discount the last cash flow back one period and add it to the next-to-the-last cash flow:

$1,000/1.06 + 1,000 = $943.40 + 1,000 = $1,943.40

We could then discount this amount back one period and add it to the year three cash flow:

$1,943.40/1.06 + 1,000 = $1,833.39 + 1,000 = $2,833.40

This process could be repeated as necessary. Figure 5.9 illustrates this approach and the remaining calculations.

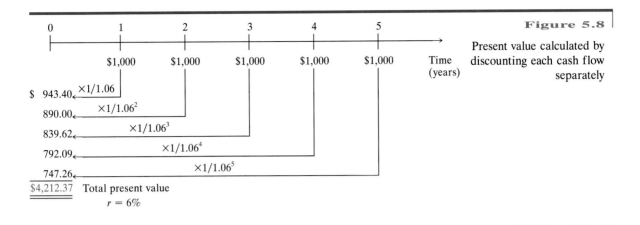

Figure 5.8

Present value calculated by discounting each cash flow separately

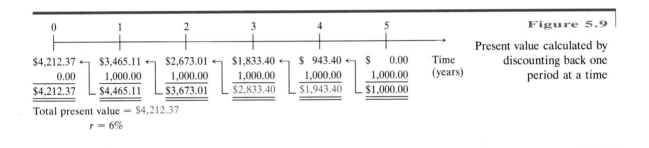

Figure 5.9

Present value calculated by discounting back one period at a time

Example 5.16 How Much Is It Worth?

You are offered an investment that will pay you $200 in one year, $400 the next year, $600 the next year, and $800 at end of the last year. You can earn 12 percent on very similar investments. What is the most you should pay for this one?

We need to calculate the present value of these cash flows at 12 percent. Taking them one at a time gives:

$$\$200 \times 1/1.12^1 = \$200/1.1200 = \$\ \ 178.57$$

$$\$400 \times 1/1.12^2 = \$400/1.2544 = \ \ \ 318.88$$

$$\$600 \times 1/1.12^3 = \$600/1.4049 = \ \ \ 427.07$$

$$+ \ \$800 \times 1/1.12^4 = \$800/1.5735 = \ \ \ \underline{508.41}$$

$$\text{Total present value} \qquad\qquad \underline{\$1,432.93}$$

If you can earn 12 percent on your money, then you can duplicate this investment's cash flows for $1,432.93, so this is the most you should be willing to pay. ∎

Example 5.17 How Much Is It Worth? Part 2

You are offered an investment that will make three $5,000 payments. The first payment will occur four years from today. The second will occur in five years, the third will follow in six years. If you can earn 11 percent, what is the most this investment is worth today? What is the future value of the cash flows?

We will answer the questions in reverse order to illustrate a point. The future value of the cash flows in six years is:

$$\$5,000 \times (1.11)^2 + 5,000 \times (1.11) + 5,000 = \$6,160.50 + 5,550 + 5,000$$

$$= \$16,710.50$$

The present value must be:

$$\$16,710.50/1.11^6 = \$8,934.12$$

Let's check this. Taking them one at a time, the PV of the cash flows is:

$$\$5,000 \times (1/1.11^6) = \$5,000/1.8704 = \$2,673.20$$

$$\$5,000 \times (1/1.11^5) = \$5,000/1.6851 = \$2,967.26$$

$$+ \$5,000 \times (1/1.11^4) = \$5,000/1.5181 = \underline{\$3,293.65}$$

Total present value $\underline{\underline{\$8,934.12}}$

This is as we previously calculated. The point we want to make is that we can calculate present and future values in any order and convert between them using whatever way seems most convenient. The answers will always be the same as long as we stick with the same discount rate and are careful to keep track of the right number of periods. ∎

⌐ CONCEPT QUESTIONS

5.4a Describe how to calculate the present value of a series of cash flows.

5.4b Describe how to calculate the future value of a series of cash flows.

5.5 | VALUING LEVEL CASH FLOWS: ANNUITIES AND PERPETUITIES

We will frequently encounter situations where we have multiple cash flows that are all the same amount. For example, a very common type of loan repayment plan calls for the borrower to repay the loan by making a series of equal payments for some length of time. Almost all consumer loans (such as car loans) and home mortgages feature equal payments, usually made each month.

annuity

A level stream of cash flows for a fixed period of time.

More generally, a series of constant or level cash flows that occurs at the end of each period for some fixed number of periods is called an ordinary **annuity**, or, more correctly, the cash flows are said to be in ordinary *annuity form*. Annuities appear very frequently in financial arrangements, and there are some useful shortcuts for determining their values. We consider these next.

Present Value for Annuity Cash Flows

Suppose we were examining an asset that promised to pay $500 at the end of each of the next three years. The cash flows from this asset are in the form of a three-year, $500 annuity. If we wanted to earn 10 percent on our money, how much would we offer for this annuity?

From the previous section, we can discount each of these $500 payments back to the present at 10 percent to determine the total present value:

$$\text{Present value} = \$500/1.1^1 + 500/1.1^2 + 500/1.1^3$$

$$= \$500/1.10 + 500/1.21 + 500/1.331$$

$$= \$454.55 + 413.22 + 375.66$$

$$= \$1,243.43$$

This approach works just fine. However, we will often encounter situations where the number of cash flows is quite large. For example, a typical home mortgage calls for monthly payments over 30 years, for a total of 360 payments. If we were trying to determine the present value of those payments, it would be useful to have a shortcut.

Since the cash flows on an annuity are all the same, we can come up with a very useful variation on the basic present value equation. It turns out that the present value of an annuity of C dollars per period for t periods when the rate of return or interest rate is r is given by:

$$\text{Annuity present value} = C \times \left[\frac{1 - \text{Present value factor}}{r} \right] \qquad [5.4]$$

$$= C \times \left[\frac{1 - \{1/(1 + r)^t\}}{r} \right]$$

The term in square brackets is sometimes called the present value interest factor for annuities and abbreviated PVIFA(r, t).

The expression for the annuity present value may look a little complicated, but it isn't difficult to use. Notice that the term in curly braces, $\{1/(1 + r)^t\}$, is the same present value factor we've been calculating. In our example just above, the interest rate is 10 percent and there are three years involved. The usual present value factor is thus:

$$\text{Present value factor} = 1/1.1^3 = 1/1.331 = .75131$$

To calculate the annuity present value factor, we just plug this in:

$$\text{Annuity present value factor} = (1 - \text{Present value factor})/r$$

$$= (1 - .75131)/.10$$

$$= .248685/.10 = 2.48685$$

Just as we calculated before, the present value of our $500 annuity is then:[2]

Annuity present value = $500 × 2.48685 = $1,243.43

Example 5.18   How Much Can You Afford?

After carefully going over your budget, you have determined you can afford to pay $632 per month towards a new sports car. You call up your local bank and find out that the going rate is 1 percent per month for 48 months. How much can you borrow?

To determine how much you can borrow, we need to calculate the present value of $632 per month for 48 months at 1 percent per month. The loan payments are in ordinary annuity form, so the annuity present value factor is:

$$\text{Annuity PV factor} = (1 - \text{Present value factor})/r$$

$$= [1 - (1/(1.01)^{48})]/.01$$

$$= (1 - .6203)/.01 = 37.9740$$

With this factor, we can calculate the present value of the 48 payments of $632 each as:

Present value = $632 × 37.9740 = $24,000

Therefore, $24,000 is what you can afford to borrow and repay. ∎

Annuity Tables   Just as there are tables for ordinary present value factors, there are tables for annuity factors as well. Table 5.4 contains a few such factors; Table A.3 in the Appendix to the book contains a larger set. To find the annuity present value factor we just calculated, look for the row corresponding to three periods and then find the column for 10 percent. The number you see at that intersection should be 2.4869 (rounded to 4 decimal places), as we calculated. Once again, try calculating a few of these factors yourself and compare your answers to the ones in the table to make sure you know how to do it. If you are using a financial calculator, just enter $1 as the payment and calculate the present value; the result should be the annuity present value factor.

---

[2]To solve this problem on a common type of financial calculator, you would need to do the following:

1. Enter the "payment" of C = $500 and press "PMT."
2. Enter the "interest rate" of r = 10 percent as 10 (not .10) and press "i."
3. Enter the number of periods as 3 and press "n."
4. Ask the calculator for the PV by pressing the "compute" or "solve" key and then pressing PV.

Here is a useful tip: Many financial calculators have the feature of "constant memory." As a practical matter, what this can mean is that the calculator will remember your mistakes, even if you turn it off. You need to be sure and press the appropriate key(s) to clear out the calculator's memory before you begin. If you make a mistake, it is usually better to clear the memory and start over. Otherwise, you may learn the hard way what "GIGO" stands for (it stands for "garbage in, garbage out").

Number of Periods	Interest Rate				Table 5.4
	5%	10%	15%	20%	Annuity present value interest factors
1	.9524	.9091	.8696	.8333	
2	1.8594	1.7355	1.6257	1.5278	
3	2.7232	2.4869	2.2832	2.1065	
4	3.5460	3.1699	2.8550	2.5887	
5	4.3295	3.7908	3.3522	2.9906	

Finding the Payment   Suppose you wished to start up a new business that specializes in the latest of health food trends, frozen yak milk. To produce and market your product, the Yakkee Doodle Dandy, you need to borrow $100,000. Because it strikes you as unlikely that this particular fad will be long-lived, you propose to pay off the loan quickly by making five equal annual payments. If the interest rate is 18 percent, what will the payment be?

In this case, we know the present value is $100,000. The interest rate is 18 percent, and there are five years. The payments are all equal, so we need to find the relevant annuity factor and solve for the unknown cash flow:

$$\text{Annuity present value} = \$100,000 = C \times (1 - \text{Present value factor})/r$$

$$\$100,000 = C \times (1 - 1/1.18^5)/.18$$

$$= C \times (1 - .4371)/.18$$

$$= C \times (3.1272)$$

$$C = \$100,000/3.1272 = \$31,977$$

Therefore, you'll make five payments of just under $32,000 each.

Example 5.19   Finding the Number of Payments
You ran a little short on your spring break vacation, so you put $1,000 on your credit card. You can only afford to make the minimum payment of $20 per month. The interest rate on the credit card is 1.5 percent per month. How long will you need to pay off the $1,000?

What we have here is an annuity of $20 per month at 1.5 percent per month for some unknown length of time. The present value is $1,000 (the amount you owe today). We need to do a little algebra:

$$\$1,000 = \$20 \times (1 - \text{Present value factor})/.015$$

$$(\$1,000/20) \times .015 = 1 - \text{Present value factor}$$

$$\text{Present value factor} = .25 = 1/(1 + r)^t$$

$$(1.015)^t = 1/.25 = 4$$

At this point, the problem boils down to asking the question "How long does it take for your money to quadruple at 1.5 percent per month?" Based on the previous sections (see Example 5.13) the answer is about 93 months:

$$1.015^{93} = 3.99 \approx 4$$

It will take you about 93/12 = 7.75 years at this rate. ▪

Finding the Rate   The last question we might want to ask concerns the interest rate implicit in an annuity. For example, an insurance company offers to pay you $1,000 per year for 10 years if you will pay $6,710 up front. What rate is implicit in this 10-year annuity?

In this case, we know the present value ($6,710), we know the cash flows ($1,000 per year), and we know the life of the investment (10 years). What we don't know is the discount rate:

$$\$6{,}710 = \$1{,}000 \times (1 - \text{Present value factor})/r$$

$$\$6{,}710/1{,}000 = 6.71 = [1 - \{1/(1 + r)^{10}\}]/r$$

So, the annuity factor for 10 periods is equal to 6.71, and we need to solve this equation for the unknown value of r. Unfortunately, this is mathematically impossible to do directly. The only way to do it is to use a table or trial and error to find a value for r.[3]

If you look across the row corresponding to 10 periods in Table A.3, you will see a factor of 6.7101 for 8 percent, so we see right away that the insurance company is offering just about 8 percent. Alternatively, we could just start trying different values until we get very close to the answer. Using this trial-and-error approach can be a little tedious, but, fortunately, machines are good at that sort of thing.

To illustrate how to find the answer by trial and error, suppose a relative of yours wants to borrow $3,000. She offers to repay you $1,000 every year for four years. What interest rate are you being offered?

The cash flows here have the form of a four-year $1,000 annuity. The present value is $3,000. We need to find the discount rate, r. Our goal in doing so is primarily to give you a feel for the relationship between annuity values and discount rates.

We need to start somewhere, so 10 percent is probably as good a place as any to begin. At 10 percent, the annuity factor is:

$$\text{Annuity present value factor} = (1 - 1/1.10^4)/.10 = 3.1699$$

---

[3]Financial calculators rely on trial and error to find the answer. That's why they sometimes appear to be "thinking" before coming up with the answer. Actually, it is possible to directly solve for r if there are less than five periods, but it's usually not worth the trouble.

The present value of the cash flows at 10 percent is thus:

Present value = $1,000 × 3.1699 = $3,169.90

You can see that we're already in the right ballpark.

Is 10 percent too high or too low? Recall that present values and discount rates move in opposite directions: Increasing the discount rate lowers the PV and vice versa. Our present value here is too high, so the discount rate is too low. If we try 12 percent:

Present value = $1,000 × (1 − 1/1.12^4)/.12 = $3,037.35

Now we're almost there. We are still a little low on the discount rate (because the PV is a little high), so we'll try 13 percent:

Present value = $1,000 × (1 − 1/1.13^4)/.13 = $2,974.47

This is less than $3,000, so we now know that the answer is between 12 percent and 13 percent, and it looks to be about 12.5 percent. For practice, work at it for a while longer and see if you find that the answer is about 12.59 percent.

Future Value for Annuities

On occasion, it's also handy to know a shortcut for calculating the future value of an annuity. For example, suppose you plan to contribute $2,000 every year into a retirement account paying 8 percent. If you retire in 30 years, how much will you have?

One way to answer this particular problem is to calculate the present value of a $2,000, 30-year annuity at 8 percent to convert it to a lump sum, and then calculate the future value of that lump sum:

$$\text{Annuity present value} = \$2,000 \times (1 - 1/1.08^{30})/.08$$
$$= \$2,000 \times 11.2578$$
$$= \$22,515.57$$

The future value of this amount in 30 years is:

Future value = $22,515.57 × 1.08^{30} = $22,515.57 × 10.0627 = $226,566.4

We could have done this calculation in one step:

$$\text{Annuity future value} = \text{Annuity present value} \times (1.08)^{30}$$
$$= \$2,000 \times (1 - 1/1.08^{30})/.08 \times (1.08)^{30}$$
$$= \$2,000 \times (1.08^{30} - 1)/.08$$
$$= \$2,000 \times (10.0627 - 1)/.08$$
$$= \$2,000 \times 113.2832 = \$226,566.4$$

As this example illustrates, there are future value factors for annuities as well as present value factors. In general, the future value factor for an annuity is given by:

$$\text{Annuity FV factor} = (\text{Future value factor} - 1)/r \qquad [5.5]$$

$$= [\{(1 + r)^t\} - 1]/r$$

For example, you think that you will need to have a total of $50,000 in six years to pay for your graduate education. If you put $7,000 in an 8 percent account at the end of each of the next six years, will you make it?

In this case, the annuity future value factor is given by:

$$\text{Annuity FV factor} = (\text{Future value factor} - 1)/r$$

$$= (1.08^6 - 1)/.08$$

$$= (1.5869 - 1)/.08$$

$$= 7.336$$

The future value of this six-year, $7,000 annuity is thus:

$$\text{Annuity future value} = \$7,000 \times 7.336$$

$$= \$51,352$$

Thus you'll make it with $1,352 to spare.

In our example, notice that the first deposit occurs in one year and the last in six years. As we discussed earlier, the first deposit earns five years' interest; the last deposit earns none.

Perpetuities

We've seen that a series of level cash flows can be valued by treating those cash flows as an annuity. An important special case of an annuity arises when the level stream of cash flows continues forever. Such an asset is called a **perpetuity** since the cash flows are perpetual. Perpetuities are also called **consols**.

Since a perpetuity has an infinite number of cash flows, we obviously can't compute its value by discounting each one. Fortunately, valuing a perpetuity turns out to be the easiest possible case. Consider a perpetuity that costs $1,000 and offers a 12 percent rate of return. The cash flow each year must be $1,000 \times .12 = $120 in this case. More generally, the present value of a perpetuity (PV = $1,000) multiplied by the rate (r = 12%) must equal the cash flow (C = $120):

$$\text{Perpetuity present value} \times \text{Rate} = \text{Cash flow}$$

$$PV \times r = C$$

Therefore, given a cash flow and a rate of return, we can compute the present value very easily:

$$\text{PV for a perpetuity} = C/r = C \times (1/r) \qquad [5.6]$$

perpetuity

An annuity in which the cash flows continue forever.

consol

A type of perpetuity.

For example, an investment offers a perpetual cash flow of $500 every year. The return you require on such an investment is 8 percent. What is the value of this investment? The value of this perpetuity is:

Perpetuity PV $= C/r =$ $500/.08 = $6,250

Another way of seeing why a perpetuity's value is so easy to determine is to take a look at the expression for an annuity present value factor:

Annuity present value factor $= (1 -$ Present value factor$)/r$

$$= (1/r) \times (1 - \text{Present value factor})$$

As we have seen, when the number of periods involved gets very large, the present value factor gets very small. As a result, the annuity factor gets closer and closer to $1/r$. At 10 percent, for example, the annuity present value factor for 100 years is:

Annuity present value factor $= (1/.10) \times (1 - 1/1.10^{100})$

$$= (1/.10) \times (1 - .000073)$$

$$\approx (1/.10)$$

This concludes our discussion of the basics of the time value of money. For future reference, Table 5.5 contains a summary of the five basic calculations we described.

Example 5.20   Preferred Stock

Preferred stock (or preference stock) is an important example of a perpetuity. When a corporation sells preferred stock, the buyer is promised a fixed cash dividend every period (usually every quarter) forever. This dividend must be paid before any dividend can be paid to regular stockholders, hence the term *preferred*.

Suppose the Fillini Co. wants to sell preferred stock at $100 per share. A very similar issue of preferred stock already outstanding has a price of $40 per share and offers a dividend of $1 every quarter. What dividend will Fillini have to offer if the preferred stock is going to sell?

The issue that is already out has a present value of $40 and a cash flow of $1 every quarter forever. Since this is a perpetuity:

Present value $=$ $40 $=$ $1 $\times$ $(1/r)$

$r = 2.5\%$

To be competitive, the new Fellini issue will also have to offer 2.5 percent *per quarter;* so, if the present value is to be $100, the dividend must be such that:

Present value $=$ $100 $= C \times (1/.025)$

$C =$ $2.5 (per quarter)   ∎

Table 5.5	I. Symbols:
Summary of time value calculations	PV = Present value, what future cash flows are worth today

I. Symbols:

PV = Present value, what future cash flows are worth today

FV_t = Future value, what cash flows are worth in the future

r = Interest rate, rate of return, or discount rate per period — typically, but not always, one year

t = Number of periods — typically, but not always, the number of years

C = Cash amount

II. Future value of C invested at r percent per period for t periods:

$$FV_t = C \times (1 + r)^t$$

The term $(1 + r)^t$ is called the *future value factor.*

III. Present value of C to be received in t periods at r percent per period:

$$PV = C/(1 + r)^t$$

The term $1/(1 + r)^t$ is called the *present value factor.*

IV. Future value of C per period for t periods at r percent per period:

$$FV_t = C \times [(1 + r)^t - 1]/r$$

A series of identical cash flows is called an *annuity,* and the term $[(1 + r)^t - 1]/r$ is called the *annuity future value factor.*

V. Present value of C per period for t periods at r percent per period:

$$PV = C \times [1 - \{1/(1 + r)^t\}]/r$$

The term $[1 - \{1/(1 + r)\}^t]/r$ is called the *annuity present value factor.*

VI. Present value of a perpetuity of C per period:

$$PV = C/r$$

A perpetuity has the same cash flow every year forever.

CONCEPT QUESTIONS

5.5a In general, what is the present value of an annuity of C dollars per period at a discount rate of r per period? The future value?

5.5b In general, what is the present value of a perpetuity?

COMPARING RATES: THE EFFECT OF COMPOUNDING PERIODS | 5.6

The last issue we need to discuss has to do with the way interest rates are quoted. This subject causes a fair amount of confusion because rates are quoted in many different ways. Sometimes the way a rate is quoted is the result of tradition, and sometimes it's the result of legislation. Unfortunately, at times, rates are quoted in deliberately deceptive ways to mislead borrowers and investors. We will discuss these topics in this section.

Effective Annual Rates and Compounding

If a rate were quoted as 10 percent compounded semiannually, then what this means is that the investment actually pays 5 percent every six months. A natural question then arises: Is 5 percent every six months the same thing as 10 percent per year? It's easy to see that it is not. If you invest $1 at 10 percent per year, you will have $1.10 at the end of the year. If you invest at 5 percent every six months, then you'll have the future value of $1 at 5 percent for two periods, or:

$$\$1 \times (1.05)^2 = \$1.1025$$

This is .0025 more. The reason is very simple. What has occurred is that your account is credited with $1 \times .05 = 5$ cents in interest after 6 months. In the following six months, you earned 5 percent on that nickel, for an extra $5 \times .05 = .25$ cents.

As our example illustrates, 10 percent compounded semiannually is actually equivalent to 10.25 percent per year. Put another way, we would be indifferent between 10 percent compounded semiannually and 10.25 percent compounded annually. Anytime we have compounding during the year, we need to be concerned about what the rate really is.

In our example, the 10 percent is called a **stated** or **quoted interest rate**. Other names are used as well. The 10.25 percent, which is actually the rate that you will earn, is called the **effective annual rate (EAR)**. To compare different investments or interest rates, we will always need to convert to effective rates. Some general procedures for doing this are discussed next.

stated interest rate
The interest rate expressed in terms of the interest payment made each period. Also *quoted interest rate*.

effective annual rate (EAR)
The interest rate expressed as if it were compounded once per year.

Calculating and Comparing Effective Annual Rates

To see why it is important to work only with effective rates, suppose that you've shopped around and come up with the following three rates:

Bank A: 15%, compounded daily
Bank B: 15.5%, compounded quarterly
Bank C: 16%, compounded annually

Which of these is the best if you are thinking of opening a savings account? Which of these is best if they represent loan rates?

To begin, Bank C is offering 16 percent per year. Since there is no compounding during the year, this is the effective rate. Bank B is actually paying .155/4 = .03875 or 3.875 percent per quarter. At this rate, an investment of $1 for four quarters would grow to:

$$\$1 \times (1.03875)^4 = \$1.1642$$

The EAR, therefore, is 16.42 percent. For a saver, this is much better than the 16 percent rate Bank C is offering; for a borrower, it's worse.

Bank A is compounding every day. This may seem a little extreme, but it is very common to calculate interest daily. In this case, the daily interest rate is actually:

$$.15/365 = .000411$$

This is .0411 percent per day. At this rate, an investment of $1 for 365 periods would grow to:

$$\$1 \times (1.000411)^{365} = \$1.1618$$

The EAR is 16.18 percent. This is not as good as Bank B's 16.42 percent for a saver, and not as good as Bank A's 16 percent for a borrower.

This example illustrates two things. First, the highest quoted rate is not necessarily the best. Second, the compounding during the year can lead to a significant difference between the quoted rate and the effective rate. Remember that the *effective* rate is what you get or what you pay.

If you look at our examples, we computed the EARs in three steps. We first divided the quoted rate by the number of times that the interest is compounded. We then added 1 to the result and raised it to the power of the number of times the interest is compounded. Finally, we subtracted the 1. If we let *m* be the number of times the interest is compounded during the year, these steps can be summarized simply as:

$$\text{EAR} = [1 + (\text{Quoted rate})/m]^m - 1 \qquad [5.7]$$

For example, suppose you were offered 12 percent compounded monthly. In this case, the interest is compounded 12 times a year; so *m* is 12. You can calculate the effective rate as:

$$
\begin{aligned}
\text{EAR} &= [1 + (\text{Quoted rate})/m]^m - 1 \\
&= [1 + .12/12]^{12} - 1 \\
&= 1.01^{12} - 1 \\
&= 1.126825 - 1 \\
&= 12.6825\%
\end{aligned}
$$

Example 5.21   What's the EAR?

A bank is offering 12 percent compounded quarterly. If you put $100 in an account, how much will you have at the end of one year? What's the EAR? How much will you have at the end of two years?

The bank is effectively offering 12%/4 = 3% every quarter. If you invest $100 for four periods at 3 percent per period, the future value is:

$$\text{Future value} = \$100 \times (1.03)^4$$
$$= \$100 \times 1.1255$$
$$= \$112.55$$

The EAR is 12.55 percent [$100 × (1 + .1255) = $112.55].

We can determine what you would have at the end of two years in two different ways. One way is to recognize that two years is the same as eight quarters. At 3 percent per quarter, after eight quarters, you would have:

$$\$100 \times (1.03)^8 = \$100 \times 1.2668 = \$126.68$$

Alternatively, we could determine the value after two years by using an EAR of 12.55 percent; so after two years you would have:

$$\$100 \times (1.1255)^2 = \$100 \times 1.2688 = \$126.68$$

Thus, the two calculations produce the same answer. This illustrates an important point. Anytime we do a present or future value calculation, the rate we use must be an actual or effective rate. In this case, the actual rate is 3 percent per quarter. The effective annual rate is 12.55 percent. It doesn't matter which one we use once we know the EAR. ∎

Example 5.22   Quoting a Rate

Now that you know how to convert a quoted rate to an EAR, consider going the other way. As a lender, you know that you want to actually earn 18 percent on a particular loan. You want to quote a rate that features monthly compounding. What rate do you quote?

In this case, we know the EAR is 18 percent, and we know that this is the result of monthly compounding. Let q stand for the quoted rate. We thus have:

$$\text{EAR} = [1 + (\text{Quoted rate})/m]^m - 1$$
$$.18 = [1 + q/12]^{12} - 1$$
$$1.18 = [1 + q/12]^{12}$$

We need to solve this equation for the quoted rate. This calculation is the same as the ones we did to find an unknown interest rate in Section 5.3 above:

$$1.18^{(1/12)} = (1 + q/12)$$
$$1.18^{.08333} = 1 + q/12$$
$$1.0139 = 1 + q/12$$
$$q = .0139 \times 12$$
$$= 16.68\%$$

Therefore, the rate you would quote is 16.68 percent, compounded monthly. ∎

EARs and APRs

Sometimes it's not altogether clear whether a rate is an effective annual rate or not. A case in point concerns what is called the **annual percentage rate** or **APR** on a loan. Truth-in-lending laws in the United States require that lenders disclose an APR on virtually all consumer loans. This rate must be displayed on a loan document in a prominent and unambiguous way.

Given that an APR must be calculated and displayed, an obvious question arises: Is an APR an effective annual rate? Put another way, if a bank quotes a car loan at 12 percent APR, is the consumer actually paying 12 percent interest? Surprisingly, the answer is no. There is some confusion over this point, which we discuss next.

The confusion over APRs arises because lenders are required by law to compute the APR in a particular way. By law, the APR is simply equal to the interest rate per period multiplied by the number of periods in a year. For example, if a bank is charging 1.2 percent per month on car loans, then the APR that must be reported is 1.2% × 12 = 14.4%. So, an APR is in fact a quoted or stated rate in the sense we've been discussing. For example, an APR of 12 percent on a loan calling for monthly payments is really 1 percent per month. The EAR on such a loan is thus:

$$EAR = (1 + APR/12)^{12} - 1$$

$$= 1.01^{12} - 1 = 12.6825\%$$

Example 5.23   What Rate Are You Paying?
Depending on the issuer, a typical credit card agreement quotes an interest rate of 18 percent APR. Monthly payments are required. What is the actual interest rate you pay on such a credit card?

Based on our discussion, an APR of 18 percent with monthly payments is really .18/12 = .015 or 1.5 percent per month. The EAR is thus:

$$EAR = (1 + .18/12)^{12} - 1$$

$$= 1.015^{12} - 1$$

$$= 1.1956 - 1$$

$$= 19.56\%$$

This is the rate you actually pay. ∎

The difference between an APR and an EAR probably won't be all that great, but it is somewhat ironic that truth-in-lending laws sometimes require lenders to be *un*truthful about the actual rate on a loan.

Taking It to the Limit: A Note on Continuous Compounding

If you made a deposit in a savings account, how often could your money be compounded during the year? If you think about it, there isn't really any upper

Compounding Period	Number of Times Compounded	Effective Annual Rate	**Table 5.6**
Year	1	10.00000%	Compounding frequency and
Quarter	4	10.38129	effective annual rates
Month	12	10.47131	
Week	52	10.50648	
Day	365	10.51558	
Hour	8,760	10.51703	
Minute	525,600	10.51709	

limit. We've seen that daily compounding, for example, isn't a problem. There is no reason to stop here, however. We could compound every hour or minute or second. How high would the EAR get in this case? Table 5.6 illustrates the EARs that would result as 10 percent is compounded at shorter and shorter intervals. Notice that the EARs do keep getting larger, but the differences get very small.

As the numbers in Table 5.6 seem to suggest, there is an upper limit to the EAR. If we let q stand for the quoted rate, then, as the number of times the interest is compounded gets extremely large, the EAR approaches:

$$EAR = e^q - 1 \qquad\qquad [5.8]$$

where e is the number 2.71828 (look for a key labeled "e^x" on your calculator). For example, with our 10 percent rate, the highest possible EAR is:

$$EAR = e^q - 1$$
$$= 2.71828^{.10} - 1$$
$$= 1.1051709 - 1$$
$$= 10.51709\%$$

In this case, we say that the money is continuously or instantaneously compounded. What is happening is that interest is credited the instant it is earned, so the amount of interest grows continuously.

Example 5.24   What's the Law?
In the not-too-distant past, commercial banks and savings and loan associations (S&Ls) were restricted in the interest rates they could offer on savings accounts. Under what was known as Regulation Q, S&Ls were allowed to pay at most 5.5 percent and banks were not allowed to pay more than 5.25 percent (the idea was to give the S&Ls a competitive advantage; it didn't work). The law did not say how often these rates could be compounded, however. Under Regulation Q, then, what were the maximum allowed interest rates?

The maximum allowed rates occurred with continuous or instantaneous compounding. For the commercial banks, 5.25 percent compounded continuously is:

$$\text{EAR} = e^{.0525} - 1$$

$$= 2.71828^{.0525} - 1$$

$$= 1.0539026 - 1$$

$$= 5.39026\%$$

This is actually what banks could pay. Check for yourself that S&Ls could effectively pay 5.65406 percent. ∎

CONCEPT QUESTIONS

5.6a If an interest rate is given as 12 percent, compounded daily, what do we call this rate?

5.6b What is an APR? What is an EAR? Are they the same thing?

5.6c In general, what is the relationship between a stated interest rate and an effective interest rate? Which is more relevant for financial decisions?

5.6d What does continuous compounding mean?

5.7 | SUMMARY AND CONCLUSIONS

This chapter has introduced you to the basic principles of present value and discounted cash flow valuation. In it, we explain a number of things about the time value of money, including:

1. For a given rate of return, the value at some point in the future of an investment made today can be determined by calculating the future value of that investment.

2. The current worth of a future cash flow or series of cash flows can be determined for a given rate of return by calculating the present value of the cash flow(s) involved.

3. The relationship between present value (PV) and future value (FV) for a given rate r and time t is given by the basic present value equation:

$$\text{PV} = \text{FV}_t / (1 + r)^t$$

As we have shown, it is possible to find any one of the four components $(\text{PV}, \text{FV}_t, r, t)$ given the other three.

4. A series of constant cash flows that arrive or are paid at the end of each period is called an ordinary annuity, and we describe some useful shortcuts for determining the present and future values of annuities.

5. Interest rates can be quoted in a variety of ways. For financial decisions, it is important that any rates being compared be first converted to effective rates. The relationship between a quoted rate, such as an annual percentage rate (APR), and an effective annual rate (EAR) is given by:

$$\text{EAR} = (1 + \text{Quoted rate}/m)^m - 1$$

where m is the number of times during the year the money is compounded or, equivalently, the number of payments during the year.

The principles developed in this chapter will figure prominently in the chapters to come. The reason for this is that most investments, whether they involve real assets or financial assets, can be analyzed using the discounted cash flow (DCF) approach. As a result, the DCF approach is broadly applicable and widely used in practice. For example, the next chapter shows how to value bonds and stocks using an extension of the techniques presented in this chapter. Before going on, however, you might want to do some of the problems below.

Key Terms

future value (FV) 130
compounding 131
interest on interest 131
compound interest 131
simple interest 131
present value (PV) 137
discount 137

discount rate 139
annuity 152
perpetuity 158
consol 158
stated or quoted interest rate 161
effective annual rate (EAR) 161
annual percentage rate (APR) 164

Chapter Review Problems and Self-Test

5.1 Calculating Future Values   Assume that you deposit $1,000 today in an account that pays 8 percent interest. How much will you have in four years? How much will you have if the 8 percent is compounded quarterly? How much will you have in 4½ years in this case?

5.2 Calculating Present Values   Suppose that you have just celebrated your 19th birthday. A rich uncle set up a trust fund for you that will pay you $100,000 when you turn 25. If the relevant discount rate is 11 percent, how much is this fund worth today?

5.3 Present Values with Multiple Cash Flows   A first-round draft choice quarterback has been signed to a three-year, $10 million contract. The details provide for an immediate cash bonus of $1 million. The player is to receive $2 million in salary at the end of the first year, $3 million the next, and $4 million at the end of the last year. Assuming a 10 percent discount rate, is this package worth $10 million? How much is it worth?

5.4 Future Value with Multiple Cash Flows   You plan to make a series of deposits in an interest-bearing account. You will deposit $1,000 today, $2,000 in two years, and $8,000 in five years. If you withdraw $3,000 in three years and $5,000 in seven years, how much will you have after eight years if the interest rate is 9 percent? What is the present value of these cash flows?

5.5 Annuity Present Value   You are looking into an investment that will pay you $12,000 per year for the next 10 years. If you require a 15 percent return, what is the most you would pay for this investment?

5.6 APR versus EAR   The going rate on student loans is quoted as 9 percent APR. The terms of the loan call for monthly payments. What is the effective annual rate (EAR) on such a student loan?

Answers to Self-Test Problems

5.1 We need to calculate the future value of $1,000 at 8 percent for four years. The future value factor is:

$$1.08^4 = 1.3605$$

The future value is thus $1,000 × 1.3605 = $1,360.50. If the 8 percent is compounded quarterly, then the rate is actually 2 percent per quarter. In four years, there are 16 quarters; so the future value factor is now:

$$1.02^{16} = 1.3728$$

The future value of your $1,000 is thus $1,372.80 in this case, which is a little more than before because of the extra compounding. Notice that we could have calculated the EAR first:

$$\text{EAR} = (1 + .08/4)^4 - 1 = 8.24322\%$$

The future value factor would then be:

$$1.0824322^4 = 1.3728$$

This is just as we calculated. To find the future value after 4½ years, we could either use the actual quarterly rate with 18 quarters or the effective annual rate with 4.5 years. We'll do both:

$$\text{Future value} = \$1,000 \times (1.02)^{18} = \$1,000 \times 1.42825 = \$1,428.25$$

Or:

$$\text{Future value} = \$1,000 \times (1.0824322)^{4.5} = \$1,000 \times 1.42825$$
$$= \$1,428.25$$

5.2   We need the present value of $100,000 to be paid in six years at 11 percent. The discount factor is:

$$1/1.11^6 = 1/1.8704 = .5346$$

The present value is thus about $53,460.

5.3   Obviously, the package is not worth $10 million because the payments are spread out over three years. The bonus is paid today, so it's worth $1 million. The present values for the three subsequent salary payments are:

$$\$2/1.1 + 3/1.1^2 + 4/1.1^3 = \$2/1.1 + 3/1.21 + 4/1.3310$$

$$= \$7.3028$$

The package is worth a total of $8.3028 million.

5.4   We will calculate the future values for each of the cash flows separately and then add them up. Notice that we treat the withdrawals as negative cash flows:

$$\$1,000 \times 1.09^8 = \quad \$1,000 \times 1.9926 = \quad \$\ 1,992.60$$

$$\$2,000 \times 1.09^6 = \quad \$2,000 \times 1.6771 = \quad \$\ 3,354.20$$

$$-\$3,000 \times 1.09^5 = -\$3,000 \times 1.5386 = -\$\ 4,615.87$$

$$\$8,000 \times 1.09^3 = \quad \$8,000 \times 1.2950 = \quad \$10,360.23$$

$$-\$5,000 \times 1.09^1 = -\$5,000 \times 1.0900 = -\$\ 5,450.00$$

Total future value $ 5,641.12

This value includes a small rounding error.

To calculate the present value, we could discount each cash flow back to the present or we could discount back a single year at a time. However, since we already know that the future value in eight years is $5,641.12, the easy way to get the PV is just to discount this amount back eight years:

$$\text{Present value} = \$5,641.12/1.09^8 = \$5,641.12/1.9926 = \$2,831.03$$

We again ignore a small rounding error. For practice, you can verify that this is what you get if you discount each cash flow back separately.

5.5   The most you would be willing to pay is the present value of $12,000 per year for 10 years at a 15 percent discount rate. The cash flows here are in ordinary annuity form, so the relevant present value factor is:

$$\text{Annuity present value factor} = [1 - (1/1.15^{10})]/.15$$

$$= [1 - .2472]/.15$$

$$= 5.0188$$

The present value of the 10 cash flows is thus:

Present value = $12,000 × 5.0188

= $60,225

This is the most you would pay.

5.6   A rate of 9 percent APR with monthly payments is actually 9%/12 = .75% per month. The EAR is thus:

$$EAR = (1 + .09/12)^{12} - 1 = 9.38\%$$

Questions and Problems

1.   **Calculating Present Values**   For each of the following, compute the present value:

Future Value	Years	Interest Rate	Present Value
$ 498	7	13%	
1,033	13	6	
14,784	23	4	
898,156	4	31	

2.   **Calculating Future Values**   For each of the following, compute the future value:

Present Value	Years	Interest Rate	Future Value
$ 123	13	13%	
4,555	8	8	
74,484	5	10	
167,332	9	1	

3.   **Calculating Interest Rates**   Assume that the cost of a college education will be $20,000 when your child enters college in 12 years. You presently have $10,000 to invest. What rate of interest must be earned on your investment to cover the cost of a college education 12 years from now?

4.   **Present Value with Multiple Cash Flows**   An investment has the following cash flows. If the discount rate is 8 percent, what is the present value of these flows? What is the present value at 12 percent?

Year	Cash Flow
1	$100
2	200
3	700

5.   Calculating Future Values   What is the future value of $5,000 in 12 years assuming a rate of 10 percent compounded quarterly?

6.   Calculating Future Values   A local bank is offering 9 percent compounded monthly on savings accounts. If you deposit $700 today, how much will you have in two years? How much will you have in 2.5 years?

7.   Present Value with Multiple Cash Flows   You've just joined the investment banking firm of Godel, Esher, and Bock. They've offered you two different salary arrangements. You can have $40,000 per year for the next two years or $20,000 per year for the next two years, along with a $30,000 signing bonus today. If the interest rate is 16 percent compounded quarterly, which do you prefer?

8.   Calculating EAR   Find the EAR in each of the cases below:

Stated Rate (APR)	Number of Times Compounded	Effective Rate (EAR)
4%	Semiannually	
6	Quarterly	
18	Daily	
22	Infinite	

9.   Calculating APR   Find the APR or stated rate in each of the cases below:

Stated Rate (APR)	Number of Times Compounded	Effective Rate (EAR)
	Semiannually	6%
	Quarterly	8
	Daily	12
	Infinite	14

10.   Calculating EAR   First National Bank charges 10 percent, compounded quarterly, on its personal loans. First Federal Bank charges 10.5 percent, compounded semiannually. As a potential borrower, which do you prefer?

11.   Present Value with Multiple Cash Flows   Investment A pays $100 per year for three years. Investment B pays $80 per year for four years. Which of these cash flow streams has the higher PV if the discount rate is 10 percent? If the discount rate is 25 percent?

12.   Calculating the Number of Periods   At 12 percent interest, how long does it take for your money to double? To triple?

13.   Calculating Present Value   An investment will pay $55,000 in three years. If the appropriate discount rate is 8 percent, continuously compounded, what is the PV?

14.   Calculating Future Value and Number of Periods   The population of Lower East Country is growing at 4 percent per year. The current population is 500 million. What will the population be in eight years? How long until the population exceeds 1 billion?

15. **Calculating Interest Rates**   You are offered an investment that requires you to put up $1,000 today in exchange for $2,500 in 10 years.
What is the rate of return on this investment?

16. **Calculating Interest Rates**   You are comparing two investments.
Both require a $5,000 initial investment. Investment A returns $9,400
in eight years. Investment B pays $11,300 in 12 years. Which of these
investments has the higher return?

17. **Calculating the Number of Periods**   Solve for the unknown number
of years in each of the following:

Present Value	Future Value	Interest Rate	Time (years)
$ 100	$ 350	12%	
123	251	10	
4,100	8,523	5	
10,543	26,783	6	

18. **EAR versus APR**   A typical rate at a pawn shop would be
20 percent per month. Pawnbrokers are legally required to report an
APR. What rate should they report? What is the effective annual rate?

19. **Calculating Present Value**   An investment offers $500 per year for
10 years. If the required return is 10 percent, what is the value of the
investment? What would the value be if the term were 30 years?
50 years? Forever?

20. **Calculating Annuity Cash Flows**   If you put up $100,000 today in ex-
change for a 12 percent, 6-year annuity, what will the annual cash
flow be?

21. **Calculating Interest Rates**   Solve for the unknown interest rate in
each of the following:

Present Value	Future Value	Interest Rate	Time (years)
$ 100	$ 305		5
123	218		6
4,100	8,523		7
10,543	21,215		12

22. **Calculating Annuity Values**   You have determined that your company can afford a $15,000 annual payment for the next 10 years. A
new computer system costs $100,000 total. If you can borrow the
money at 12 percent, can you afford the new system?

23. **Present Value and Interest Rates**   What is the relationship between
the value of an annuity and the level of the interest rate? What would
happen to the value of an annuity if the interest rate were to suddenly
increase? Illustrate your answer by calculating the present value of a
10-year annuity of $100 per year at 5 percent, 10 percent, and
15 percent.

24.   Loan Payments and EAR   If you borrow $12,000 at 14 percent APR for 60 months, what will your monthly payment be? What is the effective interest rate on this loan?

25.   EAR versus APR   You have just concluded the purchase of a new warehouse. To finance the purchase, you've arranged for a 20-year mortgage for 80 percent of the $400,000 purchase price. The monthly payment will be $3,000. What is the APR on the loan? The effective annual rate?

26.   Calculating Number of Periods   One of your customers is having trouble paying her bills. You agree to a repayment schedule of $112 per month. You charge 0.8 percent per month interest on late accounts. If the current account balance is $5,000, how long will it take until the debt is fully paid?

27.   Annuity Values   If you deposit $2,000 at the end of each of the next eight years in an account paying 11 percent interest, how much will you have in eight years? How much will you have in 10 years?

28.   Annuity Values   This one's a little harder. In Problem 27 suppose you made the first deposit today. If you make 10 deposits in all, how much would you have in 10 years?

29.   Calculating EAR   A local loan shark offers "four for five on payday." This means you get $4 today and you must repay $5 in six days when you get your next paycheck. What's the effective annual interest rate on this loan?

30.   Calculating Number of Periods   You think that the value of a piece of real estate you just purchased will increase by 14 percent per year. You paid $850,000 for the property and plan to sell when you can make a $200,000 profit. How long will you wait if the value does increase by 14 percent per year?

31.   EAR versus APR   If a loan has an APR of 16 percent, what is the EAR assuming the loan calls for semiannual payments? If the loan calls for monthly payments?

32.   Calculating EAR   You are looking at an investment that has an effective annual rate of 14 percent. What is the effective semiannual return? The effective quarterly return? The effective monthly return?

33.   Calculating Present Value   It is estimated that a firm has a pension liability of $1 million to be paid in 24 years. To assess the value of the firm's stock, financial analysts want to discount this liability back to the present. If the discount rate is 6 percent, what is the present value of this liability?

34.   Calculating PV and Break-Even Interest   Consider a firm with a contract to sell an asset for $70,000. Payment is to be received at the end of two years. The asset costs $60,000 to produce. Given that the relevant interest rate is 10 percent, did the firm make a profit on this item? What is the rate at which the firm breaks even?

35.   Present Value and Interest Rates   You have won the Florida state lottery. Lottery officials offer you the choice of the following alternative payouts:

Alternative 1: $10,000 one year from now
Alternative 2: $20,000 five years from now

Which should you choose if the discount rate is:
a. 0 percent?
b. 10 percent?
c. 20 percent?

36.   Present Value and Annuity Cash Flow   With a 10 percent interest rate, calculate the present value of the following streams of *beginning-of-year* payments:
a. $1,000 per year forever.
b. $500 per year forever, with the first payment two years from today.
c. $2,420 per year forever, with the first payment three years from today.

37.   Present Value and Multiple Cash Flows   What is the present value of end-of-year cash flows of $2,000 per year, with the first cash flow received 3 years from today and the last one 22 years from today (a total of $40,000)? Use an 8 percent interest rate.

38.   Present Value of a Perpetuity   Given an interest rate of 8 percent per year, what is the value at date $t = 7$ of a perpetual stream of $100 payments coming at dates $t = 12, 13, 14\ldots$?

39.   Present Value and Aftertax Cash Flows   You have recently won the super jackpot in the Illinois state lottery, with a payoff of $4,960,000. On reading the fine print, you discover that you have the following two options:
a. You could receive $160,000 per year for 31 years at the beginning of each year. The income would be taxed at an average rate of 28 percent. Assuming that the appropriate interest rate for you is 10 percent, what is the present value of the after-tax cash flows? (Taxes are withheld when the checks are mailed.)
b. You could receive $1,750,000 now. Once again using a 28 percent tax rate, what is the aftertax value of the payoff under this scenario?
Which option would you take?

40.   Present Value and Nonconstant Interest Rates   What is the value of a 10-year annuity that pays $300 a year (at year-end) if the annuity's first cash flow starts at the end of Year 6 and the interest rate is 15 percent for Years 1 through 5 and 10 percent thereafter?

41.   Calculating EAR with Discount Interest   This question illustrates what is known as *discount interest*. Imagine that you are discussing a loan with a somewhat unscrupulous lender. You want to borrow $10,000 for a year. The interest rate is 15 percent. You and the lender agree that the interest on the $10,000 will be $.15 \times \$10,000 = \$1,500$. So the lender deducts this amount from the loan and gives you $8,500. You repay the $10,000 in a year, thereby paying the $1,500 interest as agreed. In this case, we say that the discount is $1,500. What's wrong here?

42.   Calculating EAR with Discount Interest   You are considering a one-year loan of $100,000. The interest rate is quoted on a discount basis (see the previous problem) as 14 percent. What is the effective annual interest rate?

43. Calculating EAR with Points   You are looking at a one-year loan of $100. The interest rate is quoted as 10 percent plus two points. A *point* on a loan is simply 1 percent (one percentage point) of the loan amount. Quotes similar to this one are very common with home mortgages. The interest rate quotation in this example requires that the borrower pay two points to the lender up front and repay the loan later with 10 percent interest. What rate would you actually be paying here?

44. Calculating EAR with Points   The interest rate on a one-year loan is quoted as 16 percent plus three points (see the previous problem). What is the EAR? Is your answer affected by the loan amount?

45. Calculating EAR with Add-On Interest   This problem illustrates a deceptive way of quoting interest rates called *add-on interest*. Imagine that you see an advertisement for Ripov Retailing that reads something like: "$1,000 Instant Credit! 12% Simple Interest! Three Years to Pay! Low, Low Monthly Payments!" You're not exactly sure what all this means and somebody spilled ink over the APR on the loan contract, so you ask for clarification.

    Roger Ripov explains that if you borrow $1,000 for three years at 12 percent interest, in three years you will owe:

    $$\$1,000 \times 1.12^3 = \$1,000 \times 1.405 = \$1,405$$

    Now Roger recognizes that coming up with $1,405 all at once might be a strain; so, he lets you make "low, low monthly payments" of $1,405/36 = $39 per month, even though this is extra bookkeeping work for him.

    Is this a 12 percent loan? Why or why not? What is the APR on this loan? What is the EAR? Why do you think this is called "add-on" interest?

46. Calculating EAR   A local finance company quotes a 20 percent interest rate on one-year loans. So, if you borrow $10,000, the interest for the year will be $2,000. Since you will pay a total of $12,000, the finance company requires you to pay $1,000 per month over the next 12 months. Is this a 20 percent loan? What rate would legally have to be quoted? What is the effective annual rate?

47. Calculating Annuity Payments   This is a classic "retirement" problem. A time line will help in solving it. Your friend is celebrating his 35th birthday today and wants to start saving for his anticipated retirement at age 65. He wants to be able to withdraw $10,000 from his savings account on each birthday for 10 years following his retirement; the first withdrawal will be on his 66th birthday. Your friend intends to invest his money in the local savings and loan, which offers 8 percent interest per year. He wants to make equal, annual payments on each birthday in a new savings account he will establish for his retirement fund.

    a. If he starts making these deposits on his 36th birthday and continues to make deposits until he is 65 (the last deposit will be on his 65th birthday), what amount must he deposit annually to be able to make the desired withdrawals on retirement?

b. Suppose your friend has just inherited a large sum of money. Rather than making equal payments, he has decided to make one lump-sum payment on his 36th birthday to cover his retirement needs. What amount would he have to deposit?

Challenge Problem   48.   **Present Value with Multiple Cash Flows**   In January 1984, Richard "Goose" Gossage signed a contract to play for the San Diego Padres that guaranteed him a minimum of $9,955,000. The guaranteed payments were $875,000 for 1984, $650,000 for 1985, $800,000 in 1986, $1 million in 1987, $1 million in 1988, and $300,000 in 1989. In addition, the contract called for $5,330,000 in deferred money payable at the rate of $240,000 per year from 1990 through 2006 and then $125,000 a year from 2007 through 2016. If the relevant rate of interest is 9 percent and all payments are made on July 1 of each year, what would the present value of these guaranteed payments be on January 1, 1984? If he were to receive an equal annual salary at the end of each of the five years from 1984 through 1988, what would his equivalent annual salary be? Ignore taxes throughout this problem.

Challenge Problem   49.   **Future Value and Multiple Cash Flows**   A well-known insurance company offers a policy known as the "estate creator six pay." Typically, the policy is bought by a parent or grandparent for a child at the child's birth. The details of the policy are as follows: The purchaser (say, the parent) makes the following six payments to the insurance company:

1st birthday	$730	4th birthday	$855
2nd birthday	$730	5th birthday	$855
3rd birthday	$730	6th birthday	$855

After the child's sixth birthday, no more payments are made. When the child reaches age 65, he or she receives $143,723. If the relevant interest rate is 6 percent for the first six years and 7 percent for all subsequent years, is the policy worth buying?

Challenge Problem   50.   **Calculating Interest Rates**   A financial planning service offers a college savings program. The plan calls for you to pay six annual payments of $1,000 each. The first payment occurs today, on your child's 12th birthday. Beginning on your child's 18th birthday, the plan will provide $3,000 per year for four years. What return is the investment offering?

Challenge Problem   51.   **Present Value of a Perpetuity**   What is the value of an investment that pays $100 every other year forever with the first cash flow occurring in one year? What would the value be if the first cash flow occurs in two years? The discount rate is 16 percent per year.

Challenge Problem   52.   **Ordinary Annuity versus Annuity Due**   As we discussed in the chapter, an ordinary annuity has cash flows that occur at the end of each period and the first cash flow occurs in exactly one period. For an *annuity due,* things are slightly different. With this arrangement, we still have a fixed number of equal payments, but the first payment occurs today, not one period from now. The cash flows associated with a real estate lease, for example, are usually in the form of an annuity due because you have to pay the first month's rent up front.

a. Suppose you are comparing two annuities. Both offer five payments of $6,000. The interest rate in both cases is 6 percent. One of these is an ordinary annuity and the other is an annuity due. What is the difference in their values?

b. What is the general relationship between the value of annuity due and the value of an ordinary annuity?

Suggested Readings

One of the best places to learn more about the mathematics of present value is the owner's manual that comes with a financial calculator. One of the best is the one that comes with the Hewlett-Packard 12C calculator:

Hewlett-Packard HP-12C. *Owner's Handbook and Problem Solving Guide,* April 1986.

Hewlett-Packard HP-12C. *Solutions Handbook,* October 1984.

Another useful reference is:

Texas Instruments. *Business Analyst™ Guidebook,* 1982.

LOAN TYPES AND LOAN AMORTIZATION   Appendix 5A

Whenever a lender extends a loan, some provision will be made for repayment of the principal (the original loan amount). A loan might be repaid in equal installments, for example, or it might be repaid in a single lump sum. Because the way that the principal and interest are paid is up to the parties involved, there is actually an unlimited number of possibilities.

As we describe in this appendix, there are a few forms of repayment that come up quite often, and more complicated forms can usually be built up from these. The three basic types are: pure discount loans, interest-only loans, and amortized loans. As we will see, working with these loans is a very straightforward application of the present value principles that we have already developed.

PURE DISCOUNT LOANS | 5A.1

The *pure discount loan* is the simplest form. With such a loan, the borrower receives money today and repays a single lump sum at some time in the future. A one-year, 10 percent pure discount loan, for example, would require the borrower to repay $1.1 in one year for every dollar borrowed today.

Because a pure discount loan is so simple, we already know how to value one. Suppose that a borrower was able to repay $25,000 in five years. If we, acting as the lender, wanted a 12 percent interest rate on the loan, how much would we be willing to lend? Put another way, what value would we assign today to that $25,000 to be repaid in five years? Based on our work in this chapter, we know that the answer is just the present value of $25,000 at 12 percent for five years:

$$\text{Present value} = \$25,000/1.12^5$$

$$= \$25,000/1.7623$$

$$= \$14,186$$

Pure discount loans are very common when the loan term is short, say, a year or less. In recent years, they have become increasingly common for much longer periods.

Example 5A.1   Treasury Bills

When the U.S. government borrows money on a short-term basis (a year or less), it does so by selling what are called *Treasury bills* or *T-bills* for short. A T-bill is a promise by the government to repay a fixed amount at some time in the future, for example, 3 months or 12 months.

Treasury bills are pure discount loans. If a T-bill promises to repay $10,000 in 12 months, and the market interest rate is 7 percent, how much will the bill sell for in the market?

Since the going rate is 7 percent, the T-bill will sell for the present value of $10,000 to be paid in one year at 7 percent, or:

$$\text{Present value} = \$10,000/1.07 = \$9,345.79$$

For historical reasons, the interest rate on a T-bill is actually quoted in discount form (see Problems 41 and 42 at the end of the chapter). In this case, the discount is $10,000 - 9,345.79 = \$654.21$. The interest rate would thus be quoted as $\$654.21/10,000 = 6.5421\%$, even though the T-bill is really paying 7 percent. ∎

5A.2 | INTEREST-ONLY LOANS

A second type of loan repayment plan calls for the borrower to pay interest each period and to repay the entire principal (the original loan amount) at some point in the future. Such loans are called *interest-only loans*. Notice that if there is just one period, a pure discount loan and an interest-only loan are the same thing.

For example, with a three-year, 10 percent, interest-only loan of $1,000, the borrower would pay $1,000 \times .10 = \$100$ in interest at the end of the first and second years. At the end of the third year, the borrower would return the $1,000 along with another $100 in interest for that year. Similarly, a 50-year interest-only loan would call for the borrower to pay interest every year for the next 50 years and then repay the principal. In the extreme, the borrower pays the interest every period forever and never repays any principal. As we discussed in the chapter, the result is a perpetuity.

Most corporate bonds have the general form of an interest-only loan. Because we will be considering bonds in some detail in the next chapter, we will defer a further discussion of them for now.

AMORTIZED LOANS | 5A.3

With a pure discount or interest-only loan, the principal is repaid all at once. An alternative is an *amortized loan* where the lender may require the borrower to repay parts of the loan amount over time. The process of paying off a loan by making regular principal reductions is called *amortizing* the loan.

A simple way of amortizing a loan is to have the borrower pay the interest each period plus some fixed amount. This approach is common with medium-term business loans. For example, suppose a business takes out a $5,000, five-year loan at 9 percent. The loan agreement calls for the borrower to pay the interest on the loan balance each year and to reduce the loan balance each year by $1,000. Since the loan amount declines by $1,000 each year, it is fully paid in five years.

In the case we are considering, notice that the total payment each year will decline. The reason is that the loan balance goes down, resulting in a lower interest charge each year, while the $1,000 principal reduction is constant. For example, the interest in the first year will be $5,000 × .09 = $450. The total payment will be $1,000 + 450 = $1,450. In the second year, the loan balance is $4,000, so the interest is $4,000 × .09 = $360, and the total payment is $1,360. We can calculate the total payment in each of the remaining years by preparing a simple *amortization schedule* as follows:

Year	Beginning Balance	Total Payment	Interest Paid	Principal Paid	Ending Balance
1	$5,000	$1,450	$ 450	$1,000	$4,000
2	4,000	1,360	360	1,000	3,000
3	3,000	1,270	270	1,000	2,000
4	2,000	1,180	180	1,000	1,000
5	1,000	1,090	90	1,000	0
Totals		$6,350	$1,350	$5,000	

Notice that, in each year, the interest paid is just given by the beginning balance multiplied by the interest rate. Also notice that the beginning balance is given by the ending balance from the previous year.

Probably the most common way of amortizing a loan is for the borrower to make a single, fixed payment every period. Almost all consumer loans (such as car loans) and mortgages work this way. For example, suppose our five-year, 9 percent, $5,000 loan was amortized this way. How would the amortization schedule look?

We first need to determine the payment. From our discussion in the chapter, we know that the loan's cash flows are in the form of an ordinary annuity in this case, so we can solve for the payment as follows:

$$\$5,000 = C \times (1 - 1/1.09^5)/.09$$

$$= C \times (1 - .6499)/.09$$

This gives us:

$$C = \$5,000/3.8897$$

$$= \$1,285.46$$

The borrower will therefore make five equal payments of $1,285.46. Will this pay off the loan? We will check by filling in an amortization schedule.

In our previous example, we knew the principal reduction each year. We then calculated the interest owed to get the total payment. In this example, we know the total payment. We will thus calculate the interest and then subtract it from the total payment to calculate the principal portion in each payment.

In the first year, the interest is $450 as we calculated before. Since the total payment is $1,285.46, the principal paid in the first year must be:

$$\text{Principal paid} = \$1,285.46 - 450 = \$835.46$$

The ending loan balance is thus:

$$\text{Ending balance} = \$5,000 - 835.46 = \$4,164.54$$

The interest in the second year is $4,164.54 \times .09 = \$374.81$, and the loan balance declines by $1,285.46 - 374.81 = \$910.65$. We can summarize all of the relevant calculations in the following schedule:

Year	Beginning Balance	Total Payment	Interest Paid	Principal Paid	Ending Balance
1	$5,000.00	$1,285.46	$ 450.00	$ 835.46	$4,164.54
2	4,164.54	1,285.46	374.81	910.65	3,253.88
3	3,253.88	1,285.46	292.85	992.61	2,261.27
4	2,261.27	1,285.46	203.51	1,081.95	1,179.32
5	1,179.32	1,285.46	106.14	1,179.32	0.00
Totals		$6,427.30	$1,427.31	$5,000.00	

Since the loan balance declines to zero, the five equal payments do pay off the loan. Notice that the interest paid declines each period. This isn't surprising since the loan balance is going down. Given that the total payment is fixed, the principal paid must be rising each period.

If you compare the two loan amortizations in this section, you will see that the total interest is greater for the equal total payment case, $1,427.31 versus $1,350. The reason for this is that the loan is repaid more slowly early on, so the interest is somewhat higher. This doesn't mean that one loan is better than the other; it simply means that one is effectively paid off faster than the other. For example, the principal reduction in the first year is $835.46 in the equal total payment case compared to $1,000 in the first case.

Example 5A.2 Partial Amortization or "Bite the Bullet"

A common arrangement in real estate lending might call for a 5-year loan with, say, a 15-year amortization. What this means is that the borrower makes a payment every month of a fixed amount based on a 15-year amortization. However, after 60 months, the borrower makes a single, much larger payment called a "balloon" or "bullet" to pay off the loan. Because the monthly payments don't fully pay off the loan, the loan is said to be partially amortized.

Suppose we have a $100,000 commercial mortgage with a 12 percent APR and a 20-year (240-month) amortization. Further suppose that the mortgage has a five-year balloon. What will the monthly payment be? How big will the balloon payment be?

The monthly payment can be calculated based on an ordinary annuity with a present value of $100,000. There are 240 payments, and the interest rate is 1 percent per month. The payment is:

$$\$100,000 = C \times (1 - 1/1.01^{240})/.01$$

$$= C \times 90.8194$$

$$C = \$1,101.09$$

Now, there is an easy way and a hard way to determine the balloon payment. The hard way is to actually amortize the loan for 60 months to see what the balance is at that time. The easy way is to recognize that after 60 months, we have a $240 - 60 = 180$-month loan. The payment is still $1,101.09 per month, and the interest rate is still 1 percent per month. The loan balance is thus the present value of the remaining payments:

$$\text{Loan balance} = \$1,101.09 \times (1 - 1/1.01^{180})/.01$$

$$= \$1,101.09 \times 83.3217$$

$$= \$91,744.69$$

The balloon payment is a substantial $91,744. Why is it so large? To get an idea, consider the first payment on the mortgage. The interest in the first month is $100,000 \times .01 = \$1,000$. Your payment is $1,101.09, so the loan balance declines by only $101.09. Since the loan balance declines so slowly, the cumulative "pay down" over five years is not great. ∎

Appendix Review Problems and Self-Test

A.1 **It's the Principal that Matters** Suppose you borrow $10,000. You are going to repay the loan by making equal annual payments for five years. The interest rate on the loan is 14 percent per year. Prepare an amortization schedule for the loan. How much interest will you pay over the life of the loan?

A.2   Just a Little Bit Each Month   You've recently finished your MBA at
the Darnit School. Naturally, you must purchase a new BMW
immediately. The car costs about $21,000. The bank quotes an
interest rate of 15 percent APR for a 72-month loan with a 10 percent
down payment. You plan on trading the car in for a new one in two
years. What will your monthly payment be? What is the effective
interest rate on the loan? What will the loan balance be when you
trade the car in?

Answers to Self-Test Problems

A.1   We first need to calculate the annual payment. With a present value
of $10,000, an interest rate of 14 percent, and a term of five years, the
payment can be determined from:

$$\$10,000 = \text{Payment} \times (1 - 1/1.14^5)/.14$$

$$= \text{Payment} \times 3.4331$$

Therefore, the payment is $10,000/3.4331 = $2,912.84 (actually, it's
$2,912.8355; this will create some small rounding errors in the
schedule below). We can now prepare the amortization schedule
as follows:

Year	Beginning Balance	Total Payment	Interest Paid	Principal Paid	Ending Balance
1	$10,000.00	$ 2,912.84	$1,400.00	$ 1,512.84	$8,487.16
2	8,487.16	2,912.84	1,188.20	1,724.63	6,762.53
3	6,762.53	2,912.84	946.75	1,966.08	4,796.45
4	4,796.45	2,912.84	671.50	2,241.33	2,555.12
5	2,555.12	2,912.84	357.72	2,555.12	0.00
Totals		$14,564.17	$4,564.17	$10,000.00	

A.2   The cash flows on the car loan are in annuity form, so we only need
to find the payment. The interest rate is 15%/12 = 1.25% per month,
and there are 72 months. The first thing we need is the annuity factor
for 72 periods at 1.25 percent per period:

$$\text{Annuity present value factor} = (1 - \text{Present value factor})/r$$

$$= [1 - (1/1.0125^{72})]/.0125$$

$$= [1 - (1/2.4459)]/.0125$$

$$= (1 - .4088)/.0125$$

$$= 47.2925$$

The present value is the amount we finance. With a 10 percent down payment, we will be borrowing 90 percent of $21,000, or $18,900. So, to find the payment, we need to solve for C in the following:

$$\$18,900 = C \times \text{Annuity present value factor}$$
$$= C \times 47.2925$$

Rearranging things a bit, we have:

$$C = \$18,900 \times (1/47.2925)$$
$$= \$18,900 \times .02115$$
$$= \$399.64$$

Your payment is just under $400 per month.

The actual interest rate on this loan is 1.25 percent per month. Based on our work in the chapter, we can calculate the effective annual rate as:

$$\text{EAR} = (1.0125)^{12} - 1 = 16.08\%$$

The effective rate is about one point higher than the quoted rate.

To determine the loan balance in two years, we could amortize the loan out to see what the balance is at that time. This would be fairly tedious to do by hand. Going back to Example 5A.2, we can instead simply calculate the present value of the remaining payments. After two years, we have made 24 payments, so there are $72 - 24 = 48$ payments left. What is the present value of 48 monthly payments of $399.64 at 1.25 percent per month? The relevant annuity factor is:

$$\text{Annuity present value factor} = (1 - \text{Present value factor})/r$$
$$= [1 - (1/1.0125^{48})]/.0125$$
$$= [1 - (1/1.8154)]/.0125$$
$$= (1 - .5509)/.0125$$
$$= 35.9315$$

The present value is thus:

$$\text{Present value} = \$399.64 \times 35.9315 = \$14,359.66$$

You will owe about $14,360 on the loan in two years.

Appendix Questions and Problems

1. Amortization with Equal Payments   Prepare an amortization sched-
    ule for a three-year loan of $6,000. The interest rate is 16 percent per
    year and the loan calls for equal annual payments. How much interest
    is paid in the third year? How much total interest is paid over the life
    of the loan?

2. Amortization with Equal Principal Payments   Rework Appendix
    Problem 1 assuming that the loan agreement calls for a principal re-
    duction of $2,000 every year instead of equal annual payments.

3. Calculating a Balloon Payment   You have just arranged for a
    $100,000 mortgage to finance the purchase of a large tract of land.
    The mortgage has a 12 percent APR, and it calls for monthly
    payments over the next 10 years. However, the loan has a three-year
    balloon payment, meaning that the loan must be paid off then. How
    big will the balloon payment be?

Chapter 6

Valuing Stocks and Bonds

In our previous chapter, we introduced you to the basic procedures used to value future cash flows. In this chapter, we show you how to use those procedures to value stocks and bonds. Along the way, we introduce you to some of the terminology that commonly appears in these areas, and we also describe how the prices for these assets are reported in the financial press.

Throughout this and the next several chapters, we will generally assume that we know the appropriate discount rate. The question of what determines this discount rate and how we might go about measuring it is sufficiently important that we will devote several chapters to it later on in the text. For now, we focus on the relevant cash flows from financial assets and how to value them, given a suitable discount rate.

BONDS AND BOND VALUATION | 6.1

When a corporation (or government) wishes to borrow money from the public on a long-term basis, it usually does so by issuing or selling debt securities that are generically called *bonds*. In this section, we describe the various features of corporate bonds and some of the terminology associated with bonds. These subjects are discussed in greater detail in Parts Six and Seven when we examine long-term financing and capital structure; we examine only the essentials in this chapter. We then discuss the cash flows associated with a bond and how bonds can be valued using our discounted cash flow procedure. We conclude this section with a discussion of how bond prices are quoted in the financial press.

Bond Features and Prices

A bond is normally an interest-only loan, meaning that the borrower will pay the interest every period, but none of the principal will be repaid until the end of the loan.[1] For example, suppose the TBA Corporation wants to borrow $1,000 for 30 years. The interest rate on similar debt issued by similar corporations is 12 percent. TBA will thus pay .12 × $1,000 = $120 in interest every year for 30 years. At the end of 30 years, TBA will repay the $1,000. As this example suggests, a bond is a fairly simple financing arrangement. There is, however, a rich jargon associated with bonds, so we will use this example to define some of the more important terms.

In our example, the $120 regular interest payments that TBA promises to make are called the bond's **coupons**. Because the coupon is constant and paid every year, the type of bond we are describing is sometimes called a *level coupon bond*. The amount that will be repaid at the end of the loan is called the bond's **face value** or **par value**. As in our example, this par value is usually $1,000 for corporate bonds, and a bond that sells for its par value is called a *par value bond*. Government bonds frequently have much larger face or par values. Finally, the annual coupon divided by the face value is called the **coupon rate** on the bond, which, in this case, is $120/1,000 = 12\%$; so the bond has a 12 percent coupon rate.

The number of years until the face value is paid is called the bond's time to **maturity**. A corporate bond will frequently have a maturity of 30 years when it is originally issued, but this varies. Once the bond has been issued, the number of years to maturity declines as time goes by.

coupon

The stated interest payments made on a bond.

face value

The principal amount of a bond that is repaid at the end of the term. Also *par value*.

coupon rate

The annual coupon divided by the face value of a bond.

maturity

Specified date at which the principal amount of a bond is paid.

Bond Values and Yields

As time passes, interest rates change in the marketplace. The cash flows from a bond, however, stay the same. As a result, the value of the bond will fluctuate. When interest rates rise, the present value of the bond's remaining cash flows declines, and the bond is worth less. When interest rates fall, the bond is worth more.

To determine the value of a bond at a particular point in time, we need to know the number of periods remaining until maturity, the face value, the coupon, and the market interest rate for bonds with similar features. This interest rate required in the market on a bond is called the bond's **yield to maturity (YTM)**. This rate is sometimes called the bond's *yield* for short. Given this information, we can calculate the present value of the cash flows as an estimate of the bond's current market value.

For example, suppose the Xanth (pronounced "zanth") Co. were to issue a bond with 10 years to maturity. The Xanth bond has an annual coupon of $80. Similar bonds have a yield to maturity of 8 percent. Based on our discussion above, the Xanth bond will pay $80 per year for the next 10 years in coupon interest. In 10 years, Xanth will pay $1,000 to the owner of the bond. The cash flows from the bond are shown in Figure 6.1. What would this bond sell for?

yield to maturity (YTM)

The rate required in the market on a bond.

---

[1]See the appendix to Chapter 5 for more detail on basic loan types.

Figure 6.1

Cash flows for Xanth Co. bond.

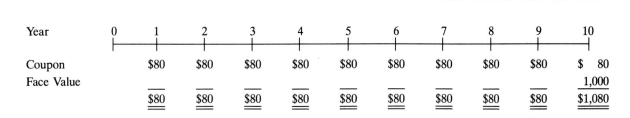

Year	0	1	2	3	4	5	6	7	8	9	10
Coupon		$80	$80	$80	$80	$80	$80	$80	$80	$80	$ 80
Face Value											1,000
		$80	$80	$80	$80	$80	$80	$80	$80	$80	$1,080

As shown, the Xanth bond has an annual coupon of $80 and a face or par value of $1,000 paid at maturity in 10 years.

As illustrated in Figure 6.1, the Xanth bond's cash flows have an annuity component (the coupons) and a lump sum (the face value paid at maturity). We thus estimate the market value of the bond by calculating the present value of these two components separately and adding the results together. First, at the going rate of 8 percent, the present value of the $1,000 paid in 10 years is:

$$\text{Present value} = \$1,000/1.08^{10} = \$1,000/2.1589 = \$463.19$$

Second, the bond offers $80 per year for 10 years, so the present value of this annuity stream is:

$$
\begin{aligned}
\text{Annuity present value} &= \$80 \times (1 - 1/1.08^{10})/.08 \\
&= \$80 \times (1 - 1/2.1589)/.08 \\
&= \$80 \times 6.7101 \\
&= \$536.81
\end{aligned}
$$

We can now add the values for the two parts together to get the bond's value:

$$\text{Total bond value} = \$463.19 + 536.81 = \$1,000.00$$

This bond sells exactly for its face value. This is not a coincidence. The going interest rate in the market is 8 percent. Considered as an interest-only loan, what interest rate does this bond have? With an $80 coupon, this bond pays exactly 8 percent interest only when it sells for $1,000.

To illustrate what happens as interest rates change, suppose that a year has gone by. The Xanth bond now has nine years to maturity. If the interest rate in the market had risen to 10 percent, what would the bond be worth? To find out, we repeat the present value calculations above with 9 years instead of 10, and a 10 percent yield instead of an 8 percent yield. First, the present value of the $1,000 paid in nine years at 10 percent is:

$$\text{Present value} = \$1,000/1.10^{9} = \$1,000/2.3579 = \$424.10$$

Second, the bond now offers $80 per year for nine years, so the present value of this annuity stream at 10 percent is:

$$\text{Annuity present value} = \$80 \times (1 - 1/1.10^9)/.10$$

$$= \$80 \times (1 - 1/2.3579)/.10$$

$$= \$80 \times 5.7590$$

$$= \$460.72$$

We can now add the values for the two parts together to get the bond's value:

$$\text{Total bond value} = \$424.10 + 460.72 = \$884.82$$

Therefore, the bond should sell for about $885. In the vernacular, we say that this bond, with its 8 percent coupon, is priced to yield 10 percent at $885.

The Xanth Co. bond now sells for less than its $1,000 face value. Why? The market interest rate is 10 percent. Considered as an interest-only loan of $1,000, this bond only pays 8 percent, its coupon rate. Since this bond pays less than the going rate, investors are only willing to lend something less than the $1,000 promised repayment. Since the bond sells for less than face value, it is said to be a *discount bond*.

The only way to get the interest rate up to 10 percent is for the price to be less than $1,000 so that the purchaser, in effect, has a built-in gain. For the Xanth bond, the price of $885 is $115 less than the face value, so an investor who purchased and kept the bond would get $80 per year and would have a $115 gain at maturity as well. This gain compensates the lender for the below-market coupon rate.

Another way to see why the bond is discounted by $115 is to note that the $80 coupon is $20 below the coupon on a newly issued par value bond, based on current market conditions. By this we mean that the bond would be worth $1,000 only if it had a coupon of $100 per year. In a sense, an investor who buys and keeps the bond gives up $20 per year for nine years. At 10 percent, this annuity stream is worth:

$$\text{Annuity present value} = \$20 \times (1 - 1/1.10^9)/.10$$

$$= \$20 \times 5.7590$$

$$= \$115.18$$

This is just the amount of the discount.

What would the Xanth bond sell for if interest rates had dropped by 2 percent instead of rising by 2 percent? As you might guess, the bond will sell for more than $1,000. Such a bond is said to sell at a *premium* and is called a *premium bond*.

This case is just the opposite of a discount bond. The Xanth bond now has a coupon rate of 8 percent when the market rate is only 6 percent. Investors are willing to pay a premium to get this extra coupon. In this case, the relevant discount rate is 6 percent, and there are nine years remaining. The present value of the $1,000 face amount is:

Present value $= \$1,000/1.06^9 = \$1,000/1.6895 = \$591.89$

The present value of the coupon stream is:

$$
\begin{aligned}
\text{Annuity present value} &= \$80 \times (1 - 1/1.06^9)/.06 \\
&= \$80 \times (1 - 1/1.6895)/.06 \\
&= \$80 \times 6.8017 \\
&= \$544.14
\end{aligned}
$$

We can now add the values for the two parts together to get the bond's value:

Total bond value $= \$591.89 + 544.14 = \$1,136.03$

Total bond value is therefore about $136 in excess of par value. Once again, we can verify this amount by noting that the coupon is now $20 too high, based on current market conditions. The present value of $20 per year for nine years at 6 percent is:

$$
\begin{aligned}
\text{Annuity present value} &= \$20 \times (1 - 1/1.06^9)/.06 \\
&= \$20 \times 6.8017 \\
&= \$136.03
\end{aligned}
$$

This is just as we calculated.

Based on our examples, we can now write the general expression for the value of a bond. If a bond has (1) a face value of F paid at maturity, (2) a coupon of C paid per period, (3) t periods to maturity, and (4) a yield of r per period, its value is:

Bond value $= C \times [1 - 1/(1 + r)^t]/r + \quad F/(1 + r)^t$ [6.1]

$$
\text{Bond value} = \begin{array}{c} \text{Present value} \\ \text{of the coupons} \end{array} + \begin{array}{c} \text{Present value} \\ \text{of the face amount} \end{array}
$$

Example 6.1   Semiannual Coupons

In practice, bonds issued in the United States usually make coupon payments twice a year. So, if an ordinary bond has a coupon rate of 14 percent, then the owner will get a total of $140 per year, but this $140 will come in two payments of $70 each. Suppose we were examining such a bond. The yield to maturity is quoted at 16 percent.

Bond yields are quoted like APRs; the quoted rate is equal to the actual rate per period multiplied by the number of periods. In this case, with a

16 percent quoted yield and semiannual payments, the true yield is 8 percent per six months. The bond matures in seven years. What is the bond's price? What is the effective annual yield on this bond?

Based on our discussion, we know the bond will sell at a discount because it has a coupon rate of 7 percent every six months when the market requires 8 percent every six months. So, if our answer exceeds $1,000, we know that we made a mistake.

To get the exact price, we first calculate the present value of the bond's face value of $1,000 paid in seven years. This seven years has 14 periods of six months each. At 8 percent per period, the value is:

$$\text{Present value} = \$1,000/1.08^{14} = \$1,000/2.9372 = \$340.46$$

The coupons can be viewed as a 14-period annuity of $70 per period. At an 8 percent discount rate, the present value of such an annuity is:

$$\text{Annuity present value} = \$70 \times (1 - 1/1.08^{14})/.08$$
$$= \$70 \times (1 - .3405)/.08$$
$$= \$70 \times 8.2442$$
$$= \$577.10$$

The total present value gives us what the bond should sell for:

$$\text{Total present value} = \$340.46 + 577.10 = \$917.56$$

To calculate the effective yield on this bond, note that 8 percent every six months is equivalent to:

$$\text{Effective annual rate} = (1 + .08)^2 - 1 = 16.64\%$$

The effective yield, therefore, is 16.64 percent. ■

As we have illustrated in this section, bond prices and interest rates always move in opposite directions. When interest rates rise, a bond's value, like any other present value, will decline. Similarly, when interest rates fall, bond values rise. Even if we are considering a bond that is riskless in the sense that the borrower is certain to make all the payments, there is still risk in owning a bond. We discuss this next.

Interest Rate Risk

The risk that arises for bond owners from fluctuating interest rates is called *interest rate risk*. How much interest rate risk a bond has depends on how sensitive its price is to interest rate changes. This sensitivity directly depends on two things: the time to maturity and the coupon rate. As we will see momentarily, you should keep the following in mind when looking at a bond:

1. All other things being equal, the longer the time to maturity, the greater the interest rate risk.

2. All other things being equal, the lower the coupon rate, the greater the interest rate risk.

We illustrate the first of these two points in Figure 6.2. As shown, we compute and plot prices under different interest rate scenarios for 10 percent coupon bonds with maturities of 1 year and 30 years. Notice how the slope of the line connecting the prices is much steeper for the 30-year maturity than it

Figure 6.2

Interest rate risk and time to maturity

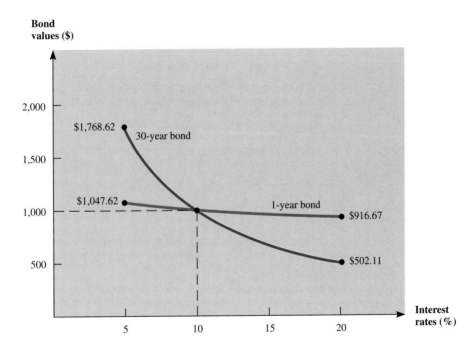

Value of a Bond with a 10% Coupon Rate for Different Interest Rates and Maturities

	Time to Maturity	
Interest Rate	1 Year	30 Years
5%	$1,047.62	$1,768.62
10	1,000.00	1,000.00
15	956.52	671.70
20	916.67	502.11

is for the 1-year maturity. This tells us that a relatively small change in interest rates could lead to a substantial change in the bond's value. In comparison, the 1-year bond's price is relatively insensitive to interest rate changes.

Intuitively, the reason that longer-term bonds have greater interest rate sensitivity is that a large portion of a bond's value comes from the $1,000 face amount. The present value of this amount isn't greatly affected by a small change in interest rates if it is to be received in one year. If it is to be received in 30 years, however, even a small change in the interest rate can have a significant effect once it is compounded for 30 years. The present value of the face amount will be much more volatile with a longer-term bond as a result.

The reason that bonds with lower coupons have greater interest rate risk is essentially the same. As we discussed above, the value of a bond depends on the present value of its coupons and the present value of the face amount. If two bonds with different coupon rates have the same maturity, then the value of the one with the lower coupon is proportionately more dependent on the face amount to be received at maturity. As a result, all other things being equal, its value will fluctuate more as interest rates change. Put another way, the bond with the higher coupon has a larger cash flow early in its life, so its value is less sensitive to changes in the discount rate.

Finding the Yield to Maturity: More Trial and Error

Frequently, we will know a bond's price, coupon rate, and maturity date, but not its yield to maturity. For example, suppose we were interested in a six-year, 8 percent coupon bond. A broker quotes a price of $955.14. What is the yield on this bond?

We've seen that the price of a bond can be written as the sum of its annuity and lump-sum components. With an $80 coupon for six years and a $1,000 face value, this price is:

$$\$955.14 = \$80 \times [1 - 1/(1 + r)^6]/r + \$1,000/(1 + r)^6$$

where r is the unknown discount rate or yield to maturity. We have one equation here and one unknown, but we cannot solve it for r explicitly. The only way to find the answer is to use trial and error.

This problem is essentially identical to the one we examined in the last chapter when we tried to find the unknown interest rate on an annuity. However, finding the rate (or yield) on a bond is even more complicated because of the $1,000 face amount.

We can speed up the trial-and-error process by using what we know about bond prices and yields. In this case, the bond has an $80 coupon and is selling at a discount. We thus know that the yield is greater than 8 percent. If we compute the price at 10 percent:

$$\text{Bond value} = \$80 \times (1 - 1/1.10^6)/.10 + \$1,000/1.10^6$$

$$= \$80 \times (4.3553) + \$1,000/1.7716$$

$$= \$912.89$$

At 10 percent, the value we calculate is lower than the actual price, so 10 percent is too high. The true yield must be somewhere between 8 percent and

I. Finding the Value of a Bond

Table 6.1
Summary of bond valuation

Bond value $= C \times [1 - 1/(1 + r)^t]/r + F/(1 + r)^t$

where

C = Coupon paid each period

r = Rate per period

t = Number of periods

F = Bond's face value

II. Finding the Yield on a Bond

Given a bond value, coupon, time to maturity, and face value, it is possible to find the implicit discount rate or yield to maturity by trial and error only. To do this, try different discount rates until the calculated bond value equals the given value. Remember that increasing the rate *decreases* the bond value.

---

10 percent. At this point, it's "plug and chug" to find the answer. You would probably want to try 9 percent next. If you do, you will see that this is in fact the bond's yield to maturity.[2]

Our discussion of bond valuation is summarized in Table 6.1.

Example 6.2   Bond Yields

You're looking at two bonds that are identical in every way except for their coupons and, of course, their prices. Both have 12 years to maturity. The first bond has a 10 percent coupon rate and sells for $935.08. The second has a 12 percent coupon rate. What do you think it would sell for?

Since the two bonds are very similar, they will be priced to yield about the same rate. We first need to calculate the yield on the 10 percent coupon bond. Proceeding as before, the yield must be greater than 10 percent since the bond is selling at a discount. The bond has a fairly long maturity of 12 years. We've seen that long-term bond prices are relatively sensitive to interest rate changes, so the yield is probably close to 10 percent. A little trial and error reveals that the yield is actually 11 percent:

Bond value $= \$100 \times (1 - 1/1.11^{12})/.11 + \$1,000/1.11^{12}$

$= \$100 \times 6.4924 + \$1,000/3.4985$

$= \$649.24 + 285.84$

$= \$935.08$

---

[2]Most financial calculators will find a bond's yield to maturity. A common procedure would involve entering $80 (the coupon) as the payment (PMT), 6 as the number of periods (n), $955.14 (the current price) as the present value (PV), and $1,000 (the face value) as the future value (FV). If you solve for the interest rate (i), the answer should be 9 percent. On some calculators, either the future value or the payment must be entered with a negative sign.

With an 11 percent yield, the second bond will sell at a premium because of its $120 coupon. Its value is:

$$\text{Bond value} = \$120 \times (1 - 1/1.11^{12})/.11 + \$1,000/1.11^{12}$$

$$= \$120 \times 6.4924 + \$1,000/3.4985$$

$$= \$779.08 + 285.84$$

$$= \$1,064.92 \;\blacksquare$$

Bond Price Reporting

If you were to look in *The Wall Street Journal* (or similar financial newspaper), you would see information on various bonds issued by large corporations. Figure 6.3 reproduces a small section of the bond page from August 21, 1991. If you look down the list, you will come to an entry marked "ATT 7s01." This tells us that the bond was issued by ATT, and it will mature in '01, meaning the year 2001. The 7 is the bond's coupon rate, so the coupon is 7% of the face value. Assuming the face value is $1,000, the annual coupon on this bond is .07 × $1,000 = $70. The small "s" doesn't mean anything important.

The column marked "Close" gives us the last available price on the bond at close of business the day before. As with the coupon, the price is quoted as a percentage of face value; so, again assuming a face value of $1,000, this bond last sold for 91.50 percent of $1,000 or $915.00. Since this bond is selling for about 92 percent of its par value, it is trading at a discount. The last column, marked "Net Chg.," indicates that yesterday's closing price was ½ of 1 percent higher than the previous day's closing price.

current yield

A bond's coupon payment divided by its price.

The bond's **current yield** (abbreviated as "Cur Yld") is given in the first column. The current yield is equal to the coupon payment divided by the bond's closing price. For this bond, assuming a face value of $1,000, this works out to be $70/$915 = 7.65%, or 7.7% rounded off to one decimal point. Notice that this is not equal to the bond's yield to maturity (unless the bond sells for par). Finally, the volume for the day (the number of bonds that were bought and sold) is reported in the second column ("Vol"). For this particular issue, 119 bonds changed hands during the day (in this market).

Example 6.3 Current Yields

Below are several bond quotations for the Albanon Corporation. Assuming these are from *The Wall Street Journal*, supply the missing information for each.

Albanon 8s98	?.?	8	84.5	+½
Albanon ?s06	9.4	8	74.5	+⅛
Albanon 8s10	9.0	8	??.?	+¼

In each case, we need to recall that the current yield is equal to the *annual* coupon divided by the price (even if the bond makes semiannual payments). Also, remember that the price is expressed as a percentage of par. In the first

Figure 6.3

Sample *Wall Street Journal* bond quotation

NEW YORK EXCHANGE BONDS

Quotations as of 4 p.m. Eastern Time
Wednesday, August 21, 1991

CORPORATION BONDS
Volume, $41,580,000

Bonds	Cur Yld	Vol	Close	Net Chg.
AMR zr06	...	125	40 1/2 +	1/4
Ala P 9s2000	8.9	7	101 1/4 +	1/4
Ala P 8 7/8 s03	8.8	3	100 3/4	...
Ala P 9 3/4 s04	9.3	10	104 1/2	...
Ala P 9 1/4 07	9.1	28	101 3/8 −	3/8
Ala P 9 5/8 08	9.2	10	105 +	2
AlskAr 6 7/8 14	CV	45	88 +	1
AlskAr zr06	...	10	33 1/2 +	1/2
AlldC zr98	...	5	54 +	5/8
AlldC zr92	...	66	92 1/2	...
AlldC zr2000	...	4	45 −	1/2
AlldC zr95	...	80	73 1/4 +	1/2
AlldC zr99	...	15	49 1/2	...
AlldC zr01	...	20	42 1/8 −	3/4
AlldC zr09	...	145	18 3/4 −	1/8
Alcoa 6s92	6.1	4	98 3/4	...
AMAX 8 1/2 96	8.7	5	97 1/4 −	1 1/4
AMAX 9.23s95	9.3	35	99 1/2	...
ATT 5 5/8 95	6.0	18	94 3/8 −	1/8
ATT 5 1/2 97	6.2	2	89 −	1
ATT 6s00	7.0	70	86	...
ATT 5 1/8 01	6.5	50	79 1/4 +	5/8
→ ATT 7s01	7.7	119	91 1/2 +	1/2
ATT 7 1/8 03	7.9	140	90 3/8 +	1/8
ATT 8.80s05	8.6	94	101 3/4 −	1/8
ATT 8 5/8 s07	8.6	71	100 3/4 +	1/4
ATT 8 3/4 00	8.6	127	102 1/4	...
ATT 8 5/8 26	8.8	105	97 7/8 −	1/8
vjAmes 7 1/2 14f	CV	24	12 1/4 −	1/8
Amoco 6s98	6.6	5	90 1/4 −	1/4
Amoco 8 3/8 05	8.3	30	100 7/8 +	1 1/8
Amoco 8 5/8 16	8.7	42	99 5/8 −	1/4
AmocoCda 7 3/8 13	6.7	146	110 −	1
Ancp 13 7/8 02f	CV	40	90	...
Andarko 6 1/4 14	6.6	20	94 1/2 +	1/2
Anhr 9.20s05	9.0	25	102 1/2 +	5/8

Source: Reprinted by permission of *The Wall Street Journal,* © 1991 Dow Jones & Company, Inc., August 21, 1991. All Rights Reserved Worldwide.

case, the coupon rate is 8 percent and the price is 84.5, so the current yield must be 8/84.5 or 9.5 percent. In the second case, the current yield is 9.4 percent, so the coupon rate must be such that:

$$\text{Coupon rate}/74.5\% = 9.4\%$$

Therefore, the coupon rate must be about 7 percent. Finally, in the third case, the price must be such that:

$$8\%/\text{Price} = 9\%$$

Therefore, the price is 8/9 or 88.9% of par value. ■

⌐ CONCEPT QUESTIONS

6.1a What are the cash flows associated with a bond?

6.1b What is the general expression for the value of a bond?

6.1c Is it true that the only risk associated with owning a bond is that the issuer will not make all the payments? Explain.

6.2 | COMMON STOCK VALUATION

A share of common stock is more difficult to value in practice than a bond for at least three reasons. First, not even the promised cash flows are known in advance. Second, the life of the investment is essentially forever since common stock has no maturity. Third, there is no way to easily observe the rate of return that the market requires. Nonetheless, as we will see, there are cases under which we can come up with the present value of the future cash flows for a share of stock and thus determine its value.

Common Stock Cash Flows

Imagine that you were to buy a share of stock today. You plan to sell the stock in one year. You somehow know that the stock will be worth $70 at that time. You predict that the stock will also pay a $10 per share dividend at the end of the year. If you require a 25 percent return on your investment, what is the most you would pay for the stock? In other words, what is the present value of the $10 dividend along with the $70 ending value at 25 percent?

If you buy the stock today and sell it at the end of the year, you will have a total of $80 in cash. At 25 percent:

Present value = ($10 + 70)/1.25 = $64

Therefore, $64 is the value you would assign to the stock today.

More generally, let P_0 be the current price of the stock, and define P_1 to be the price in one period. If D_1 is the cash dividend paid at the end of the period, then:

$$P_0 = (D_1 + P_1)/(1 + r) \qquad [6.2]$$

where r is the required return in the market on this investment.

Notice that we really haven't said much so far. If we wanted to determine the value of a share of stock today (P_0), we would first have to come up with the value in one year (P_1). This is even harder to do, so we've only made the problem more complicated.

What is the price in one period, P_1? We don't know in general. Instead, suppose that we somehow knew the price in two periods, P_2. Given a predicted dividend in two periods, D_2, the stock price in one period would be:

$$P_1 = (D_2 + P_2)/(1 + r)$$

If we were to substitute this expression for P_1 into our expression for P_0, we would have:

$$P_0 = \frac{D_1 + P_1}{1 + r} = \frac{D_1 + \dfrac{D_2 + P_2}{1 + r}}{1 + r}$$

$$= \frac{D_1}{(1 + r)^1} + \frac{D_2}{(1 + r)^2} + \frac{P_2}{(1 + r)^2}$$

Now we need to get a price in two periods. We don't know this either, so we can procrastinate again and write:

$$P_2 = (D_3 + P_3)/(1 + r)$$

If we substitute this back in for P_2, we would have:

$$P_0 = \frac{D_1}{(1 + r)^1} + \frac{D_2}{(1 + r)^2} + \frac{P_2}{(1 + r)^2}$$

$$= \frac{D_1}{(1 + r)^1} + \frac{D_2}{(1 + r)^2} + \frac{\dfrac{D_3 + P_3}{1 + r}}{(1 + r)^2}$$

$$= \frac{D_1}{(1 + r)^1} + \frac{D_2}{(1 + r)^2} + \frac{D_3}{(1 + r)^3} + \frac{P_3}{(1 + r)^3}$$

You should start to notice that we can push the problem of coming up with the stock price off into the future forever. Importantly, no matter what the stock price is, the present value is essentially zero if we push it far enough away.[3] What we would be left with is the result that the current price of the stock can be written as the present value of the dividends beginning in one period and extending out forever:

$$P_0 = \frac{D_1}{(1 + r)^1} + \frac{D_2}{(1 + r)^2} + \frac{D_3}{(1 + r)^3} + \frac{D_4}{(1 + r)^4} + \frac{D_5}{(1 + r)^5} + \cdots$$

We have illustrated here that the price of the stock today is equal to the present value of all of the future dividends. How many future dividends are there? In principle, there can be an infinite number. This means that we still can't compute a value for the stock because we would have to forecast an infinite number of dividends and then discount them all. In the next section, we consider some special cases where we can get around this problem.

---

[3] The only assumption we make about the stock price is that it is a finite number no matter how far away we push it. It can be extremely large, just not infinitely so. Since no one has ever observed an infinite stock price, this assumption is plausible.

Example 6.4 Growth Stocks

You might be wondering about shares of stock in companies that currently pay
no dividends. Small, growing companies frequently plow back everything and
thus pay no dividends. Are such shares worth nothing? It depends. When we
say that the value of the stock is equal to the present value of the future dividends, we don't rule out the possibility that some number of those dividends
are zero. They just can't *all* be zero.

Imagine a company that had a provision in its corporate charter that prohibited the paying of dividends now or ever. The corporation never borrows
any money, never pays out any money to stockholders in any form whatsoever,
and never sells any assets. Such a corporation couldn't really exist because
the IRS wouldn't like it, and the stockholders could always vote to amend
the charter if they wanted to. If it did exist, however, what would the stock
be worth?

The stock is worth absolutely nothing. Such a company is a financial "black
hole." Money goes in, but nothing valuable ever comes out. Since nobody would
ever get any return on this investment, the investment has no value. This example is a little absurd, but it illustrates that when we speak of companies that
don't pay dividends, what we really mean is that they are not *currently* paying
dividends. ∎

Common Stock Valuation: Some Special Cases

There are a few very useful special circumstances where we can come up with
a value for the stock. What we have to do is make some simplifying assumptions about the pattern of future dividends. The three cases we consider are:
(1) the dividend has a zero growth rate, (2) the dividend grows at a constant
rate, and (3) the dividend grows at a constant rate after some length of time.
We consider each of these separately.

Zero Growth   The case of zero growth is one we've already seen. A share
of common stock in a company with a constant dividend is much like a share
of preferred stock. From the previous chapter (Example 5.20), we know that
the dividend on a share of preferred stock has zero growth and thus is constant
through time. For a zero growth share of common stock, this implies that:

$$D_1 = D_2 = D_3 = D = \text{constant}$$

So, the value of the stock is:

$$P_0 = \frac{D}{(1 + r)^1} + \frac{D}{(1 + r)^2} + \frac{D}{(1 + r)^3} + \frac{D}{(1 + r)^4} + \frac{D}{(1 + r)^5} + \cdots$$

Since the dividend is always the same, the stock can be viewed as an ordinary
perpetuity with a cash flow equal to D every period. The per share value is
thus given by:

$$P_0 = D/r \qquad\qquad [6.3]$$

where r is the required return.

For example, suppose the Paradise Prototyping Company has a policy of paying a $10 per share dividend every year. If this policy is to be continued indefinitely, what is the value of a share of stock if the required return is 20 percent? The stock in this case amounts to an ordinary perpetuity, so the stock is worth $10/.20 = $50 per share.

Constant Growth   Suppose we know that the dividend for some company always grows at a steady rate. Call this growth rate g. If we let D_0 be the dividend just paid, then the next dividend, D_1, is:

$$D_1 = D_0 \times (1 + g)$$

The dividend in two periods is:

$$D_2 = D_1 \times (1 + g)$$
$$= [D_0 \times (1 + g)] \times (1 + g)$$
$$= D_0 \times (1 + g)^2$$

We could repeat this process to come up with the dividend at any point in the future. In general, from our discussion of compound growth in the previous chapter, we know that the dividend t periods in the future, D_t, is given by:

$$D_t = D_0 \times (1 + g)^t$$

An asset with cash flows that grow at a constant rate forever is called a *growing perpetuity.* As we will see momentarily, there is a simple expression for determining the value of such an asset.

The assumption of steady dividend growth might strike you as peculiar. Why would the dividend grow at a constant rate? The reason is that, for many companies, steady growth in dividends is an explicit goal. This subject falls under the general heading of dividend policy, so we will defer further discussion of it to Chapter 16.

Example 6.5 Dividend Growth

The Hedless Corporation has just paid a dividend of $3 per share. The dividend grows at a steady rate of 8 percent per year. Based on this information, what will the dividend be in five years?

Here we have a $3 current amount that grows at 8 percent per year for five years. The future amount is thus:

$$\$3 \times (1.08)^5 = \$3 \times 1.4693 = \$4.41$$

The dividend will therefore increase by $1.41 over the coming five years. ∎

If the dividend grows at a steady rate, then we have replaced the problem of forecasting an infinite number of future dividends with the problem of coming up with a single growth rate, a considerable simplification. In this case, if we take D_0 to be the dividend just paid and g to be the constant growth rate, the value of a share of stock can be written as:

$$P_0 = \frac{D_1}{(1 + r)^1} + \frac{D_2}{(1 + r)^2} + \frac{D_3}{(1 + r)^3} + \cdots$$

$$= \frac{D_0(1 + g)^1}{(1 + r)^1} + \frac{D_0(1 + g)^2}{(1 + r)^2} + \frac{D_0(1 + g)^3}{(1 + r)^3} + \cdots$$

As long as the growth rate, g, is less than the discount rate, r, the present value of this series of cash flows can be written very simply as:

$$P_0 = \frac{D_0 \times (1 + g)}{r - g} = \frac{D_1}{r - g} \qquad [6.4]$$

dividend growth model

Model that determines the current price of a stock as its dividend next period divided by the discount rate less the dividend growth rate.

This elegant result goes by a lot of different names. We will call it the **dividend growth model.** By any name, it is very easy to use. To illustrate, suppose that D_0 is $2.30, r is 13 percent, and g is 5 percent. The price per share in this case is:

$$P_0 = D_0 \times (1 + g)/(r - g)$$

$$= \$2.30 \times (1.05)/(.13 - .05)$$

$$= \$2.415/(.08)$$

$$= \$30.19$$

We can actually use the dividend growth model to get the stock price at any point in time, not just today. In general, the price of the stock as of time t is:

$$P_t = \frac{D_t \times (1 + g)}{r - g} = \frac{D_{t+1}}{r - g} \qquad [6.5]$$

In our example, suppose we were interested in the price of the stock in five years, P_5. We first need the dividend at time 5, D_5. Since the dividend just paid is $2.30 and the growth rate is 5 percent per year, D_5 is:

$$D_5 = \$2.30 \times (1.05)^5 = \$2.30 \times 1.2763 = \$2.935$$

From the dividend growth model, the price of stock in five years is:

$$P_5 = \frac{D_5 \times (1 + g)}{r - g} = \frac{\$2.935 \times (1.05)}{.13 - .05} = \frac{\$3.0822}{.08} = \$38.53$$

Example 6.6   Gordon Growth Company

The next dividend for the Gordon Growth Company will be $4.00 per share. Investors require a 16 percent return on companies such as Gordon. Gordon's dividend increases by 6 percent every year. Based on the dividend growth model, what is the value of Gordon's stock today? What is the value in four years?

The only tricky thing here is that the next dividend, D_1, is given as $4.00, so we won't multiply this by $(1 + g)$. With this in mind, the price per share is given by:

$$P_0 = D_1/(r - g)$$
$$= \$4.00/(.16 - .06)$$
$$= \$4.00/(.10)$$
$$= \$40.00$$

Since we already have the dividend in one year, the dividend in four years is equal to $D_1 \times (1 + g)^3 = \$4.00 \times (1.06)^3 = \$4.764$. The price in four years is therefore:

$$P_4 = [D_4 \times (1 + g)]/(r - g)$$
$$= [\$4.764 \times 1.06]/(.16 - .06)$$
$$= \$5.05/(.10)$$
$$= \$50.50$$

Notice in this example that P_4 is equal to $P_0 \times (1 + g)^4$.

$$P_4 = \$50.50 = \$40.00 \times (1.06)^4 = P_0 \times (1 + g)^4$$

To see why this is so, notice first that:

$$P_4 = D_5/(r - g)$$

However, D_5 is just equal to $D_1 \times (1 + g)^4$, so we can write P_4 as:

$$P_4 = D_1 \times (1 + g)^4/(r - g)$$
$$= [D_1/(r - g)] \times (1 + g)^4$$
$$= P_0 \times (1 + g)^4$$

This last example illustrates that the dividend growth model has the implicit assumption that the stock price will grow at the same constant rate as the dividend. This really isn't too surprising. What it tells us is that if the cash flows on an investment grow at a constant rate through time, so does the value of that investment. ■

You might wonder what would happen with the dividend growth model if the growth rate, g, were greater than the discount rate, r. It looks like we would get a negative stock price because $r - g$ would be less than zero. This is not what would happen.

Instead, if the constant growth rate exceeds the discount rate, then the stock price is infinitely large. Why? If the growth rate is bigger than the discount rate, then the present value of the dividends keeps on getting bigger and bigger. Essentially, the same is true if the growth rate and the discount rate are equal. In both cases, the simplification that allows us to replace the infinite stream of dividends with the dividend growth model is "illegal," so the answers we get from the dividend growth model are nonsense unless the growth rate is less than the discount rate.

Finally, the expression we came up with for the constant growth case will work for any growing perpetuity, not just dividends on common stock. If C_1 is the next cash flow on a growing perpetuity, then the present value of the cash flows is given by:

$$\text{Present value} = C_1/(r - g) = C_0(1 + g)/(r - g)$$

Notice that this expression looks like the result for an ordinary perpetuity except that we have $r - g$ on the bottom instead of just r.

Nonconstant Growth   The last case we consider is nonconstant growth. The main reason to consider this case is to allow for "supernormal" growth rates over some finite length of time. As we discussed above, the growth rate cannot exceed the required return indefinitely, but it certainly could do so for some number of years. To avoid the problem of having to forecast and discount an infinite number of dividends, we will require that the dividends start growing at a constant rate sometime in the future.

To give a simple example of nonconstant growth, consider the case of a company that is not currently paying dividends. You predict that in five years, the company will pay a dividend for the first time. The dividend will be $.50 per share. You expect that this dividend will then grow at 10 percent indefinitely. The required return on companies such as this one is 20 percent. What is the price of the stock today?

To see what the stock is worth today, we first find out what it will be worth once dividends are paid. We can then calculate the present value of that future price to get today's price. The first dividend will be paid in five years, and the dividend will grow steadily from then on. Using the dividend growth model, the price in four years will be:

$$P_4 = D_4 \times (1 + g)/(r - g)$$
$$= D_5/(r - g)$$
$$= \$.50/(.20 - .10)$$
$$= \$5.00$$

If the stock will be worth $5.00 in four years, then we can get the current value by discounting this back four years at 20 percent:

$$P_0 = \$5.00/(1.20)^4 = \$5.00/2.0736 = \$2.41$$

The stock is therefore worth $2.41 today.

The problem of nonconstant growth is only slightly more complicated if the dividends are not zero for the first several years. For example, suppose that you have come up with the following dividend forecasts for the next three years:

Year	Expected Dividend
1	$1.00
2	2.00
3	2.50

After the third year, the dividend will grow at a constant rate of 5 percent per year. The required return is 10 percent. What is the value of the stock today?

As always, the value of the stock is the present value of all the future dividends. To calculate this present value, we first have to compute the present value of the stock price three years down the road just as we did above. We then have to add in the present value of the dividends that will be paid between now and then. So, the price in three years is:

$$P_3 = D_3 \times (1 + g)/(r - g)$$

$$= \$2.50 \times (1.05)/(.10 - .05)$$

$$= \$52.50$$

We can now calculate the total value of the stock as the present value of the first three dividends plus the present value of the price at time 3, P_3:

$$P_0 = \frac{D_1}{(1 + r)^1} + \frac{D_2}{(1 + r)^2} + \frac{D_3}{(1 + r)^3} + \frac{P_3}{(1 + r)^3}$$

$$= \frac{\$1.00}{1.10} + \frac{\$2.00}{1.10^2} + \frac{\$2.50}{1.10^3} + \frac{\$52.50}{1.10^3}$$

$$= \$0.91 + 1.65 + 1.88 + 39.44$$

$$= \$43.88$$

The value of the stock today is thus $43.88.

Example 6.7 Supernormal Growth

Chain Reaction, Inc., has been growing at a phenomenal rate of 30 percent per year because of its rapid expansion and explosive sales. You believe that this growth rate will last for three more years and then drop to 10 percent per year. If the growth rate then remains at 10 percent indefinitely, what is the total value of the stock? Total dividends just paid were $5 million, and the required return is 20 percent.

Chain Reaction is an example of supernormal growth. It is unlikely that a 30 percent growth can be sustained for any extended length of time. To value the equity in this company, we first need to calculate the total dividends over the supernormal growth period:

Year	Total Dividends (in millions)
1	$5.00 × (1.3) = $ 6.500
2	$6.50 × (1.3) = $ 8.450
3	$8.45 × (1.3) = $10.985

The price at time 3 can be calculated as:

$$P_3 = D_3 \times (1 + g)/(r - g)$$

where g is the long-run growth rate. So we have:

$$P_3 = \$10.985 \times (1.10)/(.20 - .10) = \$120.835$$

To determine the value today, we need the present value of this amount plus the present value of the total dividends:

$$P_0 = \frac{D_1}{(1 + r)^1} + \frac{D_2}{(1 + r)^2} + \frac{D_3}{(1 + r)^3} + \frac{P_3}{(1 + r)^3}$$

$$= \frac{\$6.50}{1.20} + \frac{\$8.45}{1.20^2} + \frac{\$10.985}{1.20^3} + \frac{\$120.835}{1.20^3}$$

$$= \$5.42 + 5.87 + 6.36 + 69.93$$

$$= \$87.58$$

The total value of the stock today is thus $87.58 million. If there were, for example, 20 million shares, then the stock would be worth $87.58/20 = $4.38 per share. ∎

Components of the Required Return

Thus far, we have taken the required return or discount rate, r, as given. We will have quite a bit to say on this subject in Chapters 10 and 11. For now, we want to examine the implications of the dividend growth model for this required return. Earlier, we calculated P_0 as:

$$P_0 = D_1/(r - g)$$

If we rearrange this to solve for r, we get:

$$(r - g) = D_1/P_0 \qquad\qquad [6.6]$$

$$r = D_1/P_0 + g$$

This tells us that the total return, r, has two components. The first of these, D_1/P_0, is called the **dividend yield**. Since this is calculated as the cash dividend divided by the current price, it is conceptually similar to the current yield on a bond.

dividend yield
A stock's cash dividend divided by its current price.

The second part of the total return is the growth rate, g. We know that the dividend growth rate is also the rate at which the stock price grows (see Example 6.6). Thus, this growth rate can be interpreted as the **capital gains yield**, that is, the rate at which the value of the investment grows.[4]

capital gains yield
The dividend growth rate or the rate at which the value of an investment grows.

To illustrate the components of the required return, suppose we observe a stock selling for $20 per share. The next dividend will be $1 per share. You think that the dividend will grow by 10 percent more or less indefinitely. What return does this stock offer you if this is correct?

The dividend growth model calculates total return as:

$$r = \text{Dividend yield} + \text{Capital gains yield}$$

$$r = \quad D_1/P_0 \quad + \quad g$$

In this case, total return works out to be:

$$r = \$1/\$20 + 10\%$$

$$= 5\% + 10\%$$

$$= 15\%$$

This stock, therefore, has a return of 15 percent.

We can verify this answer by calculating the price in one year, P_1, using 15 percent as the required return. Based on the dividend growth model, this price is:

$$P_1 = D_1 \times (1 + g)/(r - g)$$

$$= \$1 \times (1.10)/(.15 - .10)$$

$$= \$1.1/.05$$

$$= \$22$$

Notice that this $22 is $20 × (1.1), so the stock price has grown by 10 percent as it should. If you pay $20 for the stock today, you will get a $1 dividend at the end of the year, and you will have a $22 − 20 = $2 gain. Your dividend yield is thus $1/$20 = 5%. Your capital gains yield is $2/$20 = 10%, so your total return would be 5% + 10% = 15%.

Our discussion of stock valuation is summarized in Table 6.2.

---

[4]Here and elsewhere, we use the term *capital gain* a little loosely. For the record, a capital gain (or loss) is, strictly speaking, something defined by the IRS. For our purposes, it would be more accurate (but less common) to use the term *price appreciation* instead of *capital gain*.

Table 6.2	I. The General Case

Summary of stock valuation

I. The General Case

In general, the price today of a share of stock, P_0, is the present value of all of its future dividends, $D_1, D_2, D_3, \ldots$:

$$P_0 = \frac{D_1}{(1 + r)^1} + \frac{D_2}{(1 + r)^2} + \frac{D_3}{(1 + r)^3} \cdots$$

where r is the required return.

II. Constant Growth Case

If the dividend grows at a steady rate, g, then the price can be written as:

$$P_0 = \frac{D_1}{(r - g)}$$

This result is called the *dividend growth model*.

III. Supernormal Growth

If the dividend grows steadily after t periods, then the price can be written as:

$$P_0 = \frac{D_1}{(1 + r)^1} + \frac{D_2}{(1 + r)^2} + \cdots + \frac{D_t}{(1 + r)^t} + \frac{P_t}{(1 + r)^t}$$

where

$$P_t = \frac{D_t \times (1 + g)}{(r - g)}$$

IV. The Required Return

The required return, r, can be written as the sum of two things:

$$r = D_1/P_0 + g$$

where D_1/P_0 is the *dividend yield* and g is the *capital gains yield* (which is the same thing as the growth rate in dividends for the steady-growth case).

Stock Market Reporting

If you look through the pages of *The Wall Street Journal* (or other financial newspaper), you will find information on a large number of stocks in several different markets. Figure 6.4 reproduces a small section of the stock page for the New York Stock Exchange (NYSE) from August 21, 1991. In Figure 6.4, locate the line for IBM. With the column headings, the line reads:

52 Weeks					Yld		Vol				Net
Hi	Lo	Stock	Sym	Div	%	PE	100s	Hi	Lo	Close	Chg
139¾	92	IBM	IBM	4.84	5.1	13	28281	96⅜	94	95⅝	−⅛

Figure 6.4

Sample stock quotation
from *The Wall Street
Journal*

NEW YORK STOCK EXCHANGE COMPOSITE TRANSACTIONS

Quotations as of 5 p.m. Eastern Time
Wednesday, August 21, 1991

| 52 Weeks | | | | | Yld | | Vol | | | | Net |
Hi	Lo	Stock	Sym	Div	%	PE	100s	Hi	Lo	Close	Chg.
13 1/2	5 3/8	Intellicall	ICL		...	6	754	6 5/8	6 3/8	6 3/8	+ 1/8
12 3/4	4 7/8	IntrRgnlFnl	IFG			13	97	12 1/4	12	12 1/4	+ 1/4
21	16 3/4	IntcapSec	ICB	1.98	9.9	...	92	20	19 7/8	20	+ 1/4
n 15 1/4	14 1/2	IntcapMnBd	IMB			...	49	15	14 7/8	15	...
13/16	1/16	vjInterco	ISS		...	...	544	9/32	1/4	9/32	...
6 3/4	2 3/4	Intlake	IK		...	11	62	3 7/8	3 3/8	3 3/4	+ 3/8
30	18 7/8	IntAlum	IAL	1.00	4.0	17	9	24 3/4	24 1/2	24 3/4	+ 1/4
139 3/4	92	IBM	IBM	4.84	5.1	13	28281	96 3/8	94	95 5/8	− 1/8
87 3/8	61 1/4	IntFlavor	IFF	2.40	2.9	19	1605	83 5/8	82	82	+ 1/4
s 56 5/8	9	IntGameTech	IGT		...	33	943	56 1/2	55 1/2	55 1/2	+ 3/4
28 5/8	4 1/2	IntGameTech wi			...	...	67	28 1/2	28 1/4	28 1/4	+ 1/4
s 31 1/2	18 1/2	IntMultfood	IMC	.80	2.8	16	271	28 7/8	28 5/8	28 7/8	+ 5/8
74 1/2	42 3/4	IntPaper	IP	1.68	2.5	17	5426	66 3/4	65	66 3/4	+ 2 1/4
19 3/4	10 3/4	IntRecvry	INT		...	14	69	15 1/2	15 1/4	15 3/8	...
25 1/4	4 1/4	IntRect	IRF		...	14	3026	18 3/8	17 1/4	18 1/4	+ 1 1/2
n 17 7/8	14	IntSpcPdt	ISP		...	...	503	16 5/8	16 1/4	16 5/8	+ 3/4
11 3/8	6 3/4	IntTech	ITX		...	18	3728	8 1/8	7 7/8	8 1/8	+ 1/4
48 3/4	29 1/4	IntpubGp	IPG	.84	1.8	20	739	48	46 7/8	48	+ 1 1/4
4 5/8	1 5/8	IntstJhnsn	IS		...	...	2	3 1/8	3 1/8	3 1/8	− 1/8
31	23	IntstPwr	IPW	2.04	6.7	10	33	30 1/4	30	30 1/4	+ 3/8
28 7/8	15 1/2	IntertanInc	ITN		...	22	159	22 3/4	22	22 5/8	+ 7/8
47 1/2	24	Ionics	ION		...	37	44	47	46 1/2	46 5/8	+ 1/4
▲ 24 3/8	18 3/4	IowaIllGas	IWG	1.71	7.0	11	590	24 1/2	24 1/4	24 3/8	...

Source: Reprinted by permission of *The Wall Street Journal,* © 1991 Dow Jones & Company, Inc., August 21, 1991. All Rights Reserved Worldwide.

The first two numbers, 139¾ and 92, are the high and low price for the last 52 weeks. The 4.84 is the annual dividend. Since IBM, like most companies, pays dividends quarterly, this $4.84 is actually the last quarterly dividend multiplied by 4. So, the last cash dividend paid was $4.84/4 = $1.21.

Jumping ahead just a bit, the Hi(gh), Lo(w), and Close figures are the high, low, and closing prices during the day. The "Net Chg" of −⅛ tells us that the closing price of $95⅝ per share is ⅛ or $.125 lower than the closing price the day before; so we say that IBM was down ⅛ for the day.

The column marked "Yld %" gives the dividend yield based on the current dividend and the closing price. For IBM, this is $4.84/95⅝ = 5.1% as shown. The next column, labelled PE (short for price/earnings or P/E ratio), is the closing price of $95⅝ divided by annual earnings per share (based on the most recent four quarters). In the jargon of Wall Street, we might say that IBM "sells for 13 times earnings."

The remaining column, marked "Vol 100s," tells us how many shares traded during the day (in hundreds). For example, the 28281 for IBM tells us that 2,828,100 or almost 3 million shares changed hands on this day alone. If the average price during the day was $95 or so, then the dollar volume of transactions was on the order of $95 × 3 million = $285 million worth of IBM stock alone. This was a relatively active day of trading in IBM shares, so this amount is somewhat larger than is typical, but it serves to illustrate how active the market can be.

⌐ CONCEPT QUESTIONS

6.2a What are the relevant cash flows for valuing a share of common stock?

6.2b Does the value of a share of stock depend on how long you expect to keep it?

6.2c What is the value of a share of stock when the dividend grows at a constant rate?

6.3 │ SUMMARY AND CONCLUSIONS

This chapter has shown you how to extend the basic present value results of Chapter 5 in some important ways. In our discussion of bonds and stocks, we saw that:

1. Bonds are long-term corporate debts. We examined the cash flows from a corporate bond and found that the present value of the cash flows and, hence, the bond's value can be readily determined. We also introduced some of the terminology associated with bonds, and we discussed how bond prices are reported in the financial press.

2. The cash flows from owning a share of stock come in the form of future dividends. We saw that in certain special cases it is possible to calculate the present value of all the future dividends and thus come up with a value for the stock. We discussed some of the terms that are associated with common stock, and we also examined how stock price information is reported.

This chapter completes Part Three of our book. By now, you should have a good grasp of what we mean by present value. You should also be familiar with how to calculate present values, loan payments, and so on. In Part Four, we cover capital budgeting decisions. As you will see, the techniques you learned in Chapters 5 and 6 form the basis for our approach to evaluating business investment decisions.

Key Terms

coupons 186	yield to maturity (YTM) 186
face value 186	current yield 194
par value 186	dividend growth model 200
coupon rate 186	dividend yield 205
maturity 186	capital gains yield 205

Chapter Review Problems and Self-Test

6.1   Bond Values   A Cowles Industries bond has a 10 percent coupon rate and a $1,000 face value. Interest is paid semiannually, and the bond has 20 years to maturity. If investors require a 12 percent yield, what is the bond's value? What is the effective annual yield on the bond?

6.2   Bond Yields   A Macrohard Corp. bond carries an 8 percent coupon, paid semiannually. The par value is $1,000, and the bond matures in six years. If the bond currently sells for $911.37, what is its yield to maturity? What is the effective annual yield?

6.3   Dividend Growth and Stock Valuation   The Brigapenski Co. has just paid a cash dividend of $2 per share. Investors require a 16 percent return from investments such as this. If the dividend is expected to grow at a steady 8 percent per year, what is the current value of the stock? What will the stock be worth in five years?

6.4   More Dividend Growth and Stock Valuation   In Self-Test Problem 6.3, what would the stock sell for today if the dividend is expected to grow at 20 percent for the next three years and then settle down to 8 percent per year?

Answers to Self-Test Problems

6.1   Since the bond has a 10 percent coupon yield while investors require a 12 percent return, we know that the bond must sell at a discount. Notice that, since the bond pays interest semiannually, the coupons amount to $100/2 = $50 every six months. The required yield is 12%/2 = 6% every six months. Finally, the bond matures in 20 years, so there are a total of 40 six-month periods.

The bond's value is thus equal to the present value of $50 every six months for the next 40 six-month periods plus the present value of the $1,000 face amount:

$$\text{Bond value} = \$50 \times [1 - 1/(1.06)^{40}]/.06 + \$1,000/(1.06)^{40}$$

$$= \$50 \times 15.04630 + \$1,000/10.2857$$

$$= \$849.54$$

Notice that we discounted the $1,000 back 40 periods at 6 percent per period, rather than 20 years at 12 percent. The reason is that the effective annual yield on the bond is $1.06^2 - 1 = 12.36\%$, not 12%. We thus could have used 12.36 percent per year for 20 years when we calculated the present value of the $1,000 face amount, and the answer would have been the same.

6.2   The present value of the bond's cash flows is its current price, $911.37. The coupon is $40 every 6 months for 12 periods. The face value is $1,000, so the bond's yield is the unknown discount rate in the following:

$$\$911.37 = \$40 \times [1 - 1/(1 + r)^{12}]/r + \$1,000/(1 + r)^{12}$$

The bond sells at a discount. Since the coupon rate is 8 percent, the yield must be something in excess of that.

If we were to solve this by trial and error, we might try 12 percent (or 6 percent per six months):

$$\text{Bond value} = \$40 \times [1 - 1/1.06^{12}]/.06 + \$1,000/1.06^{12}$$

$$= \$832.32$$

This is less than the actual value, so our discount rate is too high. We now know that the yield is somewhere between 8 percent and 12 percent. With further trial and error (or a little machine assistance), the yield works out to be 10 percent, or 5 percent every six months.

By convention, the bond's yield to maturity would be quoted as $2 \times 5\% = 10\%$. The effective yield is thus $1.05^2 - 1 = 10.25\%$.

6.3   The last dividend, D_0, was $2. The dividend is expected to grow steadily at 8 percent. The required return is 16 percent. Based on the dividend growth model, the current price is:

$$P_0 = D_1/(r - g) = D_0 \times (1 + g)/(r - g)$$

$$= \$2 \times (1.08)/(.16 - .08)$$

$$= \$2.16/(.08)$$

$$= \$27$$

We could calculate the price in five years by calculating the dividend in five years and then using the growth model again. Alternatively, we could recognize that the stock price will increase by 8 percent per year and calculate the future price directly. We'll do both. First, the dividend in five years will be:

$$D_5 = D_0 \times (1 + g)^5$$

$$= \$2 \times 1.08^5$$

$$= \$2.9387$$

The price in five years would therefore be:

$$P_5 = D_5 \times (1 + g)/(r - g)$$

$$= \$2.9387 \times (1.08)/.08$$

$$= \$3.1738/.08$$

$$= \$39.67$$

Once we understand the dividend model, however, it's easier to notice that:

$$P_5 = P_0 \times (1 + g)^5$$

$$= \$27 \times 1.08^5$$

$$= \$27 \times 1.4693$$

$$= \$39.67$$

Notice that both approaches yield the same price in five years.

6.4   In this scenario, we have supernormal growth for the next three years. We'll need to calculate the dividends during the rapid growth period and the stock price in three years. The dividends are:

$$D_1 = \$2.00 \times 1.20 = \$2.400$$

$$D_2 = \$2.40 \times 1.20 = \$2.880$$

$$D_3 = \$2.88 \times 1.20 = \$3.456$$

After three years, the growth rate falls to 8 percent indefinitely. The price at that time, P_3, is thus:

$$P_3 = D_3 \times (1 + g)/(r - g)$$

$$= \$3.456 \times 1.08/(.16 - .08)$$

$$= \$3.7325/.08$$

$$= \$46.656$$

To complete the calculation of the stock's present value, we have to determine the present value of the three dividends and the future price:

$$P_0 = \frac{D_1}{(1 + r)^1} + \frac{D_2}{(1 + r)^2} + \frac{D_3}{(1 + r)^3} + \frac{P_3}{(1 + r)^3}$$

$$= \frac{\$2.40}{1.16} + \frac{\$2.88}{1.16^2} + \frac{\$3.456}{1.16^3} + \frac{\$46.656}{1.16^3}$$

$$= \$2.07 + 2.14 + 2.21 + 29.89$$

$$= \$36.31$$

Questions and Problems

1.   **Bond Values**   Oklahoma Instruments has a bond issue outstanding that pays $100 annually. It has a face value of $1,000, and it will mature in eight years. Similar bonds are priced to yield 14 percent. What would you expect this bond to sell for?

2.   **Bond Values with Semiannual Coupons**   In Problem 1, what would the bond be worth if it paid $50 every six months? Assume the rate is 7 percent per six months. Why is this value different from the value in Problem 1?

3.   **Semiannual Coupons**   Paladin Palaver bonds have a coupon rate of 11 percent and mature in 15 years. Assuming semiannual coupons, what is the value of this bond? Similar bonds yield 12 percent.

4.   **Calculating Yields**   In Problem 3, what is the current yield on the bond?

5.   **Bond Values and Yields**   You have just purchased a newly issued $1,000 five-year Vanguard Company bond at par. This bond (Bond A) pays $60 in interest semiannually ($120 per year). You are also negotiating the purchase of a $1,000 six-year Vanguard bond that pays $30 semiannually and has five years to maturity (Bond B).
   a. What is the rate required in the market (the yield) on bonds issued by the Vanguard Company?
   b. What should you be willing to pay (at most) for Bond B?
   c. How will your answer to part b change if Bond A pays $40 (instead of $60) in semiannual interest but still sells for $1,000?

6.   **Prices versus Interest Rates**   What is the relationship between changes in interest rates and bond values? How is this relationship affected by the time to maturity? By the coupon rate?

7.   **Bond Values and Yields**   A particular bond is observed to have a coupon rate of 12 percent and a yield to maturity that is also 12 percent. What do you know about the value of the bond? What would you know if the yield to maturity were 10 percent? 14 percent?

8.   **Interest Rate Risk**   The Footfall Corporation has two bonds outstanding, both of which have a 9 percent coupon rate (with annual coupons) and sell for their $1,000 par value. The first bond, Bond A, has four years to maturity. The second bond, Bond B, has eight years to maturity. If market interest rates were to rise by 2 percent, which bond would have the larger price change? Calculate the new prices to illustrate your answer.

9.   **Bond Values and Coupons**   Your firm is contemplating selling some 10-year bonds to raise funds for a planned expansion. The firm currently has an issue outstanding with a $60 annual coupon, paid semiannually. These bonds currently sell for $900, a discount relative to their $1,000 face value, and they have 10 years remaining to maturity. What coupon rate must the new issue have if it is to sell at par when it is issued?

10.   **Bond Values**   Shaky Position, Inc., has suffered some financial reversals recently and is unable to meet its next several coupon payments. The bonds in question will mature in six years and have a 16 percent coupon rate. Coupons are paid annually. By arrangement with its creditors, Shaky will skip the next three coupons. The skipped coupons will be repaid at maturity without interest. Not surprisingly, investors view these bonds as risky and require a 25 percent return. What price would we expect to see on the bonds?

11. Bond Yields   Bonds issued by the Etling Corporation have a price of $850 and a coupon rate of 10 percent. The bonds will mature in 12 years. What is the current yield? The yield to maturity?

12. Coupon Rates   The Jorgenson Corporation has an outstanding debt issue that is currently selling for $945. The yield to maturity is 12 percent, and the bonds mature in eight years. Assuming that the face value is $1,000, what is the coupon rate?

13. Stock Values and Growth   BEV Corp. has experienced a steady growth of 8 percent per year in its annual dividend. This growth is expected to continue indefinitely. The last dividend paid was $1.10 per share. Investors require a 14 percent return on similar companies. What is the current price of BEV Corp. stock? What will the price be in four years?

14. Stock Values   Silistuff Technologies anticipates a dividend growth rate of 12 percent forever. The market-required return is 20 percent on similar securities. The next dividend is predicted to be $1.52 per share. What is the current price per share?

15. Stock Values and Yields   In Problem 13, what is the dividend yield on BEV stock? What is the capital gains yield?

16. Calculating Required Return   Sasha Husky Co. stock currently sells for $50 per share. The last dividend was $2 per share. The dividend is expected to grow at 10 percent. What is the required return on Sasha stock? The dividend yield?

17. Required Returns   Suppose that a shareholder has just paid $50 per share for XYZ Company stock. The stock will pay a $2 per share dividend in the coming year, and this dividend is expected to grow at an annual rate of 10 percent indefinitely. The shareholder felt that the price she paid was an appropriate price, given her assessment of XYZ's risks. What is the annual required rate of return of this shareholder?

18. Nonconstant Growth   Sicker-Mann Co. has just paid a $5 dividend. The dividend is expected to grow at 16 percent for the next four years. After that, the growth rate will be 5 percent indefinitely. If the required return is 18 percent, what is the current value of the stock today?

19. Nonconstant Growth   The Price-Bubble Corporation does not currently pay dividends. You predict that dividend payments will begin in four years and that the first cash dividend will be $4. The dividend will grow at 12 percent thereafter. If the required return is 25 percent, what is the value of the stock?

20. Perpetuities   What is the value of an asset that pays $2 per year forever? Assume a 20 percent required return. How would your answer change if the cash flow grows at a rate of 5 percent per year forever? Assume that $2 was the most recent payment.

21. Calculating Growth   Stock in Lockwood Corporation is selling for $60 per share. Lockwood has paid a dividend of $4 per share, and the required return on similar stocks is 12 percent. Assuming that Lockwood's dividend will grow at a constant rate in the future, what will that growth rate be?

22. **Calculating Dividends**   The Pickard Corporation's dividend growth rate is projected to be 6 percent indefinitely. The stock currently sells for $82 per share. Assuming that the market requires a 14 percent return, what is the projected dividend for the coming year?

23. **Nonconstant Growth**   Whizzkids, Inc., is experiencing a period of rapid growth. Earnings and dividends are expected to grow at a rate of 18 percent during the next two years, 15 percent in the third year, and then at a constant rate of 6 percent thereafter. Whizzkids' last dividend, which has just been paid, was $1.15. If the required return on the stock is 12 percent, what is the price of the stock today?

24. **Negative Growth**   Calamity Mining Company's ore reserves are being depleted, and its costs of recovering a declining quantity of ore are rising each year. As a result the company's earnings and dividends are declining at a rate of 10 percent per year. If the dividend, which was just paid, was $5 and the required return is 14 percent, what is the value of the stock?

25. **Required Returns**   Ribald, Inc., recently suspended its dividend payments. Management anticipates that a dividend of $2.50 per share will be restored in five years and that the dividend will be increased at a rate of 6 percent per year thereafter. The stock currently sells for $12 per share. What is the required return in this case?

26. **Nonconstant Growth**   The Feringi Corporation is expanding rapidly. Its dividend growth rate for the coming year is projected at 25 percent. This rate will decline by 5 percentage points per year until it reaches the industry average of 5 percent. Once it reaches 5 percent, it will stay there indefinitely. The most recent dividend was $8.50 per share, and the market requires a return of 16 percent on investments such as this one. What is the price per share for Feringi?

27. **Required Returns**   This one's a little harder. In the previous question, suppose that the price per share was $120. If the dividend projections remain unchanged, what is the required return on Feringi stock?

28. **Negative Growth**   The DK Corporation's profitability has steadily declined because of increasing competition. The most recent dividend was $2 per share, but management anticipates that the dividend will decrease at a rate of 10 percent per year indefinitely. If the required return is 20 percent, what is the stock worth?

Challenge Problem

29. **Negative Growth**   Locust Software is one of a myriad of companies selling word processor programs. Their newest and only program will cost $5 million to develop. First-year profits will be $1.2 million. However, as a result of competition, profits will fall by 4 percent each year. All cash inflows occur at year-end. If the market discount rate is 16 percent, what is the value of the company?

Challenge Problem

30. **Capital Gains versus Dividends**   You have predicted the following dividends for the next three years on Kahnland Software's stock:

Year	Projected Dividend
1	$5.00
2	6.00
3	7.00

After the third year, you project that the dividend will grow at an 8 percent rate indefinitely. The required return is 15 percent.

a. Calculate the price today for the stock.

b. Calculate the price at Years 1, 2, and 3.

c. Calculate the dividend yield and capital gains yield in each of the first four years. What do you observe?

Suggested Readings

The best place to look for additional information about valuing stocks and bonds is in an investments textbook. Some good ones are:

Bodie, Z., A. Kane, and A. J. Marcus. *Investments.* Homewood, Ill.: Richard D. Irwin, 1989.

Jacob, N. L., and R. R. Pettit. *Investments.* 2nd ed. Homewood, Ill.: Richard D. Irwin, 1988.

Radcliffe, R. C. *Investments: Concepts, Analysis, and Strategy.* Glenview: Ill.: Scott, Foresman, 1986.

Part Four

Capital Budgeting

CHAPTER 7
Net Present Value and Other Investment Criteria

The most important subject in this chapter is net present value. Chapter 7 compares and contrasts net present value with other methods for selecting among alternative investment proposals.

CHAPTER 8
Making Capital Investment Decisions

This chapter describes how to actually do a net present value and discounted cash flow analysis. The primary aim of the chapter is to describe how to identify a project's incremental cash flows. Chapter 8 also discusses how to handle such issues as sunk costs, opportunity costs, financing costs, net working capital, and erosion.

CHAPTER 9
Project Analysis and Evaluation

This chapter discusses problems regarding the reliability of net present value estimates. It also describes some important tools for project analysis, such as break-even analysis, operating leverage, and sensitivity analysis.

Chapter 7

Net Present Value and Other Investment Criteria

Ⅰn Chapter 1, we identified the three key areas of concern to the financial manager. The first of these was: "What fixed assets should we buy?" We called this the *capital budgeting decision*. In this chapter, we begin to deal with the issues that arise in answering this question.

The process of allocating or budgeting capital is usually more involved than just deciding on whether or not to buy a particular fixed asset. We will frequently face broader issues like whether or not we should launch a new product or enter a new market. Decisions such as these will determine the nature of a firm's operations and products for years to come, primarily because fixed asset investments are generally long-lived and not easily reversed once they are made.

The most fundamental decision that a business must make concerns its product line. What services will we offer or what will we sell? In what markets will we compete? What new products will we introduce? The answer to any of these questions will require that the firm commit its scarce and valuable capital to certain types of assets. As a result, all of these strategic issues fall under the general heading of capital budgeting. The process of capital budgeting could thus be given a more descriptive (not to mention impressive) name: *strategic asset allocation*.

For the reasons we have discussed, the capital budgeting question is probably the most important issue in corporate finance. How a firm chooses to finance its operations (the capital structure question) and how a firm manages its short-term operating activities (the working capital question) are certainly issues of concern, but it is the fixed assets that define the business of the firm. Airlines, for example, are airlines because they operate airplanes, regardless of how they finance them.

Any firm possesses a huge number of possible investments. Each of these possible investments is an option available to the firm. Some of these options are valuable and some are not. The essence of successful financial management, of course, is learning to identify which are which. With this in mind, our goal in this chapter is to introduce you to the techniques used to analyze potential business ventures to decide which are worth undertaking.

We present and compare a number of different procedures that are used in practice. Our primary goal is to acquaint you with the advantages and disadvantages of the various approaches. As we shall see, the most important concept in this area is the idea of net present value. We consider this next.

7.1 | NET PRESENT VALUE

In Chapter 1, we argued that the goal of financial management is to create value for the stockholders. The financial manager must thus examine a potential investment in light of its likely effect on the price of the firm's shares. In this section, we describe a widely used procedure for doing this, the net present value approach.

The Basic Idea

An investment is worth undertaking if it creates value for its owners. In the most general sense, we create value by identifying an investment that is worth more in the marketplace than it costs us to acquire. How can something be worth more than it costs? It's a case of the whole being worth more than the cost of the parts.

For example, suppose you buy a run-down house for $25,000 and spend another $25,000 on painters, plumbers, and so on to get it fixed up. Your total investment is $50,000. When the work is completed, you place the house back on the market and find that it's worth $60,000. The market value ($60,000) exceeds the cost ($50,000) by $10,000. What you have done here is to act as a manager and bring together some fixed assets (a house), some labor (plumbers, carpenters, and others), and some materials (carpeting, paint, and so on). The net result is that you have created $10,000 in value. Put another way, this $10,000 is the *value added* by management.

With our house example, it turned out *after the fact* that $10,000 in value was created. Things thus worked out very nicely. The real challenge, of course, was to somehow identify *ahead of time* whether or not investing the necessary $50,000 was a good idea in the first place. This is what capital budgeting is all about, namely, trying to determine whether a proposed investment or project will be worth more than it costs once it is in place.

net present value (NPV)
The difference between an investment's market value and its cost.

For reasons that will be obvious in a moment, the difference between an investment's market value and its cost is called the **net present value** of the investment, abbreviated NPV. In other words, net present value is a measure of how much value is created or added today by undertaking an investment. Given our goal of creating value for the stockholders, the capital budgeting process can be viewed as a search for investments with positive net present values.

With our run-down house, you can probably imagine how we would go about making the capital budgeting decision. We would first look at what comparable, fixed-up properties were selling for in the market. We would then get estimates of the cost of buying a particular property and bringing it to market. At this point, we have an estimated total cost and an estimated market value. If the difference is positive, then this investment is worth undertaking because it has a positive estimated net present value. There is risk, of course, because there is no guarantee that our estimates will turn out to be correct.

As our example illustrates, investment decisions are greatly simplified when there is a market for assets similar to the investment we are considering. Capital budgeting becomes much more difficult when we cannot observe the market price for at least roughly comparable investments. The reason is that we are then faced with the problem of estimating the value of an investment using only indirect market information. Unfortunately, this is precisely the situation that the financial manager usually encounters. We examine this issue next.

Estimating Net Present Value

Imagine that we are thinking of starting a business to produce and sell a new product, say, organic fertilizer. We can estimate the start-up costs with reasonable accuracy because we know what we will need to buy to begin production. Would this be a good investment? Based on our discussion, you know that the answer depends on whether or not the value of the new business exceeds the cost of starting it. In other words, does this investment have a positive NPV?

This problem is much more difficult than our "fixer-upper" house example, because entire fertilizer companies are not routinely bought and sold in the marketplace; so it is essentially impossible to observe the market value of a similar investment. As a result, we must somehow estimate this value by other means.

Based on our work in Chapters 5 and 6, you may be able to guess how we will go about estimating the value of our fertilizer business. We will first try to estimate the future cash flows that we expect the new business to produce. We will then apply our basic discounted cash flow procedure to estimate the present value of those cash flows. Once we have this estimate, we then estimate NPV as the difference between the present value of the future cash flows and the cost of the investment. As we mentioned in Chapter 5, this procedure is often called **discounted cash flow (DCF) valuation.**

discounted cash flow (DCF) valuation

The process of valuing an investment by discounting its future cash flows.

To see how we might go about estimating NPV, suppose we believe that the cash revenues from our fertilizer business will be $20,000 per year, assuming that everything goes as expected. Cash costs (including taxes) will be $14,000 per year. We will wind down the business in eight years. The plant, property, and equipment will be worth $2,000 as salvage at that time. The project costs $30,000 to launch. We use a 15 percent discount rate on new projects such as this one. Is this a good investment? If there are 1,000 shares of stock outstanding, what will be the effect on the price per share from taking it?

From a purely mechanical perspective, we need to calculate the present value of the future cash flows at 15 percent. The net cash inflow will be $20,000 cash income less $14,000 in costs per year for eight years. These cash

Figure 7.1	Time (years)	0	1	2	3	4	5	6	7	8
Project cash flows (000)										
	Initial cost	−$30								
	Inflows		$20	$20	$20	$20	$20	$20	$20	$20
	Outflows		− 14	− 14	− 14	− 14	− 14	− 14	− 14	− 14
	Net inflow		$ 6	$ 6	$ 6	$ 6	$ 6	$ 6	$ 6	$ 6
	Salvage									2
	Net cash flow	−$30	$ 6	$ 6	$ 6	$ 6	$ 6	$ 6	$ 6	$ 8

flows are illustrated in Figure 7.1. As Figure 7.1 suggests, we effectively have an eight-year annuity of $20,000 − 14,000 = $6,000 per year along with a single lump-sum inflow of $2,000 in eight years. Calculating the present value of the future cash flows thus comes down to the same type of problem we considered in Chapter 5. The total present value is:

$$\text{Present value} = \$6,000 \times (1 - 1/1.15^8)/.15 + \$2,000/1.15^8$$

$$= \$6,000 \times 4.4873 + 2,000/3.0590$$

$$= \$26,924 + 654$$

$$= \$27,578$$

When we compare this to the $30,000 estimated cost, the NPV is:

$$\text{NPV} = -\$30,000 + 27,578 = -\$2,422$$

Therefore, this is *not* a good investment. Based on our estimates, taking it would *decrease* the total value of the stock by $2,422. With 1,000 shares outstanding, our best estimate of the impact of taking this project is a loss of value of $2,422/1,000 = $2.422 per share.

Our fertilizer example illustrates how NPV estimates can be used to determine whether or not an investment is desirable. From our example, notice that, if the NPV is negative, the effect on share value will be unfavorable. If the NPV were positive, the effect would be favorable. As a consequence, all we need to know about a particular proposal for the purpose of making an accept/reject decision is whether the NPV is positive or negative.

Given that the goal of financial management is to increase share value, our discussion in this section leads us to the *net present value rule:*

An investment should be accepted if the net present value is positive and rejected if it is negative.

In the unlikely event that the net present value turned out to be exactly zero, we would be indifferent to taking the investment or not taking it.

Two comments about our example are in order. First and foremost, it is not the rather mechanical process of discounting the cash flows that is important. Once we have the cash flows and the appropriate discount rate, the required calculations are fairly straightforward. The task of coming up with the cash flows and the discount rate in the first place is much more challenging. We will have much more to say about this in the next several chapters. For the remainder of this chapter, we take it as given that we have estimates of the cash revenues and costs and, where needed, an appropriate discount rate.

The second thing to keep in mind about our example is that the $-\$2,422$ NPV is an estimate. Like any estimate, it can be high or low. The only way to find out the true NPV would be to place the investment up for sale and see what we could get for it. We generally won't be doing this, so it is important that our estimates be reliable. Once again, we will have more to say about this later. For the rest of this chapter, we will assume the estimates are accurate.

Example 7.1   Using the NPV Rule

Suppose we are asked to decide whether or not a new consumer product should be launched. Based on projected sales and costs, we expect that the cash flows over the five-year life of the project will be $2,000 in the first two years, $4,000 in the next two, and $5,000 in the last year. It will cost about $10,000 to begin production. We use a 10 percent discount rate to evaluate new products. What should we do here?

Given the cash flows and discount rate, we can calculate the total value of the product by discounting the cash flows back to the present:

$$
\begin{aligned}
\text{Present value} &= \$2,000/1.1 + 2,000/1.1^2 + 4,000/1.1^3 + 4,000/1.1^4 \\
&\quad + 5,000/1.1^5 \\
&= \$1,818 + 1,653 + 3,005 + 2,732 + 3,105 \\
&= \$12,313
\end{aligned}
$$

The present value of the expected cash flows is $12,313, but the cost of getting those cash flows is only $10,000, so the NPV is $12,313 - 10,000 = $2,313. This is positive; so, based on the net present value rule, we should take on the project. ∎

As we have seen in this section, estimating NPV is one way of assessing the profitability of a proposed investment. It is certainly not the only way that profitability is assessed, and we now turn to some alternatives. As we will see, when compared to NPV, each of the ways of assessing profitability that we examine is flawed in some key way; so NPV is the preferred approach in principle, if not always in practice.

CONCEPT QUESTIONS

7.1a What is the net present value rule?

7.1b If we say that an investment has an NPV of $1,000, what exactly do we mean?

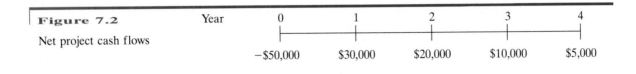

Figure 7.2

Net project cash flows

Year	0	1	2	3	4
	−$50,000	$30,000	$20,000	$10,000	$5,000

7.2 | THE PAYBACK RULE

It is very common in practice to talk of the payback on a proposed investment. Loosely, the *payback* is the length of time it takes to recover our initial investment or "get our bait back." Because this idea is widely understood and used, we will examine it in some detail.

Defining the Rule

payback period

The amount of time required for an investment to generate cash flows to recover its initial cost.

We can illustrate how to calculate a payback with an example. Figure 7.2 shows the cash flows from a proposed investment. How many years do we have to wait until the accumulated cash flows from this investment equal or exceed the cost of the investment? As Figure 7.2 indicates, the initial investment is $50,000. After the first year, the firm has recovered $30,000, leaving $20,000. The cash flow in the second year is exactly $20,000, so this investment "pays for itself" in exactly two years. Put another way, the **payback period** is two years. If we require a payback of, say, three years or less, then this investment is acceptable. This illustrates the *payback period rule:*

> Based on the payback rule, an investment is acceptable if its calculated payback period is less than some prespecified number of years.

In our example, the payback works out to be exactly two years. This won't usually happen, of course. When the numbers don't work out exactly, it is customary to work with fractional years. For example, suppose the initial investment is $60,000, and the cash flows are $20,000 in the first year and $90,000 in the second. The cash flows over the first two years are $110,000, so the project obviously pays back sometime in the second year. After the first year, the project has paid back $20,000, leaving $40,000 to be recovered. To figure out the fractional year, note that this $40,000 is $40,000/$90,000 = 4/9 of the second year's cash flow. Assuming that the $90,000 cash flow is paid uniformly throughout the year, the payback would thus be 1⁴⁄₉ years.

Example 7.2   Calculating Payback

The projected cash flows from a proposed investment are:

Year	Cash Flow
1	$100
2	200
3	500

This project costs $500. What is the payback period for this investment?

The initial cost is $500. After the first two years, the cash flows total $300. After the third year, the total cash flow is $800, so the project pays back sometime between the end of Year 2 and the end of Year 3. Since the accumulated cash flows for the first two years are $300, we need to recover $200 in the third year. The third year cash flow is $500, so we will have to wait $200/500 = .40 of the year to do this. The payback period is thus 2.4 years, or about two years and five months. ∎

Now that we know how to calculate the payback period on an investment, using the payback period rule for making decisions is straightforward. A particular cutoff time is selected, say, two years, and all investment projects that have payback periods of two years or less are accepted, and all of those that pay off in more than two years are rejected.

Table 7.1 illustrates cash flows for five different projects. The figures shown as the Year 0 cash flows are the cost of the investment. We examine these to indicate some peculiarities that can, in principle, arise with payback periods.

The payback for the first project, A, is easily calculated. The sum of the cash flows for the first two years is $70, leaving us with $100 − 70 = $30 to go. Since the cash flow in the third year is $50, the payback occurs sometime in that year. When we compare the $30 we need to the $50 that will be coming in, we get $30/50 = .60; so, payback will occur 60 percent of the way into the year. The payback period is thus 2.6 years.

Project B's payback is also easy to calculate: It *never* pays back because the cash flows never total up to the original investment. Project C has a payback of exactly four years because it supplies the $130 that B is missing in Year 4. Project D is a little strange. Because of the negative cash flow in Year 3, you can easily verify that it has two different payback periods, two years and four years. Which of these is correct? Both of them; the way the payback period is calculated doesn't guarantee a single answer. Finally, Project E is obviously unrealistic, but it does pay back in six months, thereby illustrating the point that a rapid payback does not guarantee a good investment.

Analyzing the Payback Period Rule

When compared to the NPV rule, the payback period rule has some rather severe shortcomings. First of all, the payback period is calculated by simply adding up the future cash flows. There is no discounting involved, so the time value of money is completely ignored. The payback rule also does not consider

Year	A	B	C	D	E	
0	−$100	−$200	−$200	−$200	$ −50	**Table 7.1**
1	30	40	40	100	100	Expected cash flows for Projects A through E
2	40	20	20	100	−50,000,000	
3	50	10	10	−200		
4	60		130	200		

Table 7.2	Year	Long	Short
	1	$100	$100
Investment projected cash flows	2	100	200
	3	100	0
	4	100	0

risk differences at all. The payback would be calculated the same way for both very risky and very safe projects.

Perhaps the biggest problem with the payback period rule is coming up with the right cutoff period, because we don't really have an objective basis for choosing a particular number. Put another way, there is no economic rationale for looking at payback in the first place, so we have no guide as to how to pick the cutoff. As a result, we end up using a number that is arbitrarily chosen.

Suppose we have somehow decided on an appropriate payback period, say two years or less. As we have seen, the payback period rule ignores the time value of money for the first two years. More seriously, cash flows after the second year are ignored entirely. To see this, consider the two investments, Long and Short, in Table 7.2. Both projects cost $250. Based on our discussion, the payback on Long is $2 + \$50/100 = 2.5$ years, and the payback on Short is $1 + \$150/200 = 1.75$ years. With a cutoff of two years, Short is acceptable and Long is not.

Is the payback period rule giving us the right decisions? Maybe not. Suppose again that we require a 15 percent return on this type of investment. We can calculate the NPV for these two investments as:

$$\text{NPV(Short)} = -\$250 + 100/1.15 + 200/1.15^2 = -\$11.81$$

$$\text{NPV(Long)} = -\$250 + 100 \times (1 - 1/1.15^4)/.15 = \$35.50$$

Now we have a problem. The NPV of the shorter-term investment is actually negative, meaning that taking it diminishes the value of the shareholders' equity. The opposite is true for the longer-term investment—it increases share value.

Our example illustrates two primary shortcomings of the payback period rule. First, by ignoring time value, we may be led to take investments (like Short) that actually are worth less than they cost. Second, by ignoring cash flows beyond the cutoff, we may be led to reject profitable long-term investments (like Long). More generally, using a payback period rule will tend to bias us towards shorter-term investments.

Redeeming Qualities

Despite its shortcomings, the payback period rule is often used by large and sophisticated companies when making relatively minor decisions. There are several reasons for this. The primary reason is that many decisions simply do not warrant detailed analysis because the cost of the analysis would exceed the possible loss from a mistake. As a practical matter, an investment that pays back rapidly and has benefits extending beyond the cutoff period probably has a positive NPV.

Small investment decisions are made by the hundreds every day in large organizations. Moreover, they are made at all levels. As a result, it would not be uncommon for a corporation to require, for example, a two-year payback on all investments of less than $10,000. Investments larger than this are subjected to greater scrutiny. The requirement of a two-year payback is not perfect for reasons we have seen, but it does exercise some control over expenditures and thus has the effect of limiting possible losses.

In addition to its simplicity, the payback rule has two other positive features. First, because it is biased toward short-term projects, it is biased toward liquidity. In other words, a payback rule tends to favor investments that free up cash for other uses more quickly. This could be very important for a small business; it would be less so for a large corporation. Second, the cash flows that are expected to occur later in a project's life are probably more uncertain. Arguably, a payback period rule adjusts for the extra riskiness of later cash flows, but it does so in a rather Draconian fashion—by ignoring them altogether.

We should note here that some of the apparent simplicity of the payback rule is an illusion. The reason is that we still must come up with the cash flows first, and, as we discuss above, this is not at all easy to do. Thus, it would probably be more accurate to say that the *concept* of a payback period is both intuitive and easy to understand.

Summary of the Payback Period Rule

To summarize, the payback period is a kind of "break-even" measure. Because time value is ignored, you can think of the payback period as the length of time it takes to break even in an accounting sense, but not in an economic sense. The biggest drawback to the payback period rule is that it doesn't ask the right question. The relevant issue is the impact an investment will have on the value of our stock, not how long it takes to recover the initial investment.

Nevertheless, because it is so simple, companies often use it as a screen for dealing with the myriad of minor investment decisions they have to make. There is certainly nothing wrong with this practice. Like any simple rule of thumb, there will be some errors in using it, but it wouldn't have survived all this time if it weren't useful. Now that you understand the rule, you can be on the alert for those circumstances under which it might lead to problems. To help you remember, the following table lists the pros and cons of the payback period rule.

Advantages and Disadvantages of the Payback Period Rule

Advantages	Disadvantages
1. Easy to understand.	1. Ignores the time value of money.
2. Adjusts for uncertainty of later cash flows.	2. Requires an arbitrary cutoff point.
3. Biased toward liquidity.	3. Ignores cash flows beyond the cutoff date.
	4. Biased against long-term projects, such as research and development, and new projects.

7.2a In words, what is the payback period? The payback period rule?
7.2b Why do we say that the payback period is, in a sense, an accounting break-even?

7.3 │ THE DISCOUNTED PAYBACK RULE

discounted payback period

The length of time required for an investment's discounted cash flows to equal its initial cost.

We saw that one of the shortcomings of the payback period rule was that it ignored time value. There is a variation of the payback period, the discounted payback period, that fixes this particular problem. The **discounted payback period** is the length of time until the sum of the discounted cash flows is equal to the initial investment. The *discounted payback rule* would be:

Based on the discounted payback rule, an investment is acceptable if its discounted payback is less than some prespecified number of years.

To see how we might calculate the discounted payback period, suppose that we require a 12.5 percent return on new investments. We have an investment that costs $300 and has cash flows of $100 per year for five years. To get the discounted payback, we have to discount each cash flow at 12.5 percent and then start adding them. We do this in Table 7.3. In Table 7.3, we have both the discounted and the undiscounted cash flows. Looking at the accumulated cash flows, the regular payback is exactly three years (look for the highlighted figure in Year 3). The discounted cash flows total $300 only after four years, however, so the discounted payback is four years as shown.[1]

How do we interpret the discounted payback? Recall that the ordinary payback is the time it takes to break even in an accounting sense. Since it includes the time value of money, the discounted payback is the time it takes to break even in an economic or financial sense. Loosely speaking, in our example, we get our money back along with the interest we could have earned elsewhere in four years.

Figure 7.3 illustrates this idea by comparing the *future* value at 12.5 percent of the $300 investment versus the *future* value of the $100 annual cash flows at 12.5 percent. Notice that the two lines cross at exactly four years. This

---

[1] In this case, the discounted payback is an even number of years. This won't ordinarily happen, of course. However, calculating a fractional year for the discounted payback period is more involved than it is for the ordinary payback, and it is not commonly done.

Table 7.3		Cash Flow		Accumulated Cash Flow	
Ordinary and discounted payback	Year	Undiscounted	Discounted	Undiscounted	Discounted
	1	$100	$89	$100	$ 89
	2	100	79	200	168
	3	100	70	300	238
	4	100	62	400	300
	5	100	55	500	355

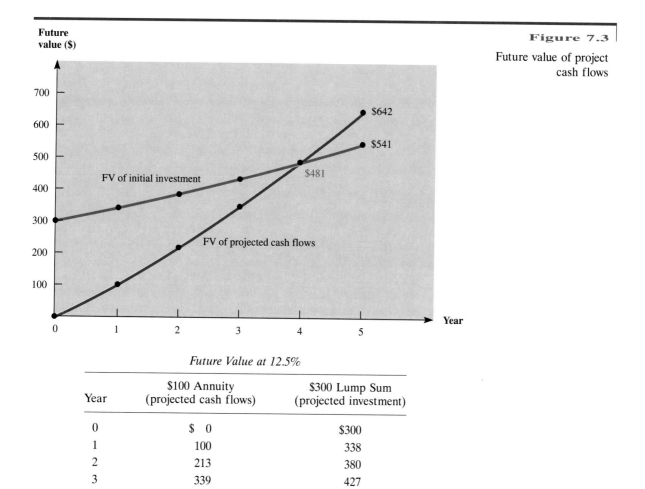

Figure 7.3

Future value of project cash flows

Future Value at 12.5%

Year	$100 Annuity (projected cash flows)	$300 Lump Sum (projected investment)
0	$ 0	$300
1	100	338
2	213	380
3	339	427
4	481	481
5	642	541

tells us that the value of the project's cash flows catches up and then passes the original investment in four years.

Table 7.3 and Figure 7.3 illustrate another interesting feature of the discounted payback period. If a project ever pays back on a discounted basis, then it must have a positive NPV.[2] This is true because, by definition, the NPV is zero when the sum of the discounted cash flows equals the initial investment. For example, the present value of all the cash flows in Table 7.3 is $355. The cost of the project was $300, so the NPV is obviously $55. This $55 is the value of the cash flow that occurs *after* the discounted payback (see the last line in Table 7.3). In general, if we use a discounted payback rule, we won't accidentally take any projects with a negative estimated NPV.

---

[2]This argument assumes the cash flows other than the first are all positive. If they are not, then these statements are not necessarily correct. Also, there may be more than one discounted payback.

Based on our example, the discounted payback would seem to have much to recommend it. You may be surprised to find out that it is rarely used in practice. Why? Probably because it really isn't any simpler than NPV. To calculate a discounted payback, you have to discount cash flows, add them up, and compare them to the cost, just as you do with NPV. So, unlike an ordinary payback, the discounted payback is not especially simple to calculate.

A discounted payback period rule still has a couple of significant drawbacks. The biggest one is that the cutoff still has to be arbitrarily set and cash flows beyond that point are ignored.[3] As a result, a project with a positive NPV may not be acceptable because the cutoff is too short. Also, just because one project has a shorter discounted payback than another does not mean it has a larger NPV.

All things considered, the discounted payback is a compromise between a regular payback and NPV that lacks the simplicity of the first and the conceptual rigor of the second. Nonetheless, if we need to assess the time it will take to recover the investment required by a project, then the discounted payback is better than the ordinary payback because it considers time value. In other words, the discounted payback recognizes that we could have invested the money elsewhere and earned a return on it. The ordinary payback does not take this into account. The advantages and disadvantages of the discounted payback rule are summarized in the table below.

Advantages and Disadvantages of the Discounted Payback Period Rule

Advantages	Disadvantages
1. Includes time value of money.	1. May reject positive NPV investments.
2. Easy to understand.	2. Requires an arbitrary cutoff point.
3. Does not accept negative estimated NPV investments.	3. Ignores cash flows beyond the cutoff date.
4. Biased toward liquidity.	4. Biased against long-term projects, such as research and development, and new projects.

Example 7.3   Calculating Discounted Payback
Consider an investment that costs $400 and pays $100 per year forever. We use a 20 percent discount rate on this type of investment. What is the ordinary payback? What is the discounted payback? What is the NPV?

The NPV and ordinary payback are easy to calculate in this case because the investment is a perpetuity. The present value of the cash flows is $100/.20 = $500, so the NPV is $500 − 400 = $100. The ordinary payback is obviously four years.

To get the discounted payback, we need to find the number of years such that a $100 annuity has a present value of $400 at 20 percent. In other words, the present value annuity factor is $400/100 = 4, and the interest rate is 20 percent per period; so what's the number of periods? If we solve for number of periods, we find that the answer is a little less than nine years, so this is the discounted payback. ■

----

[3]If the cutoff were forever, then the discounted payback rule would be the same as the NPV rule. It would also be the same as the profitability index rule considered in a later section.

7.3a In words, what is the discounted payback period? Why do we say it is, in a sense, a financial or economic break-even measure?

7.3b What advantage(s) does the discounted payback have over the ordinary payback?

THE AVERAGE ACCOUNTING RETURN ⌐7.4

Another attractive, but flawed, approach to making capital budgeting decisions is the **average accounting return (AAR)**. There are many different definitions of the AAR. However, in one form or another, the AAR is always defined as:

$$\frac{\text{Some measure of average accounting profit}}{\text{Some measure of average accounting value}}$$

The specific definition we will use is:

$$\frac{\text{Average net income}}{\text{Average book value}}$$

average accounting return (AAR)

An investment's average net income divided by its average book value.

To see how we might calculate this number, suppose we are deciding whether or not to open a store in a new shopping mall. The required investment in improvements is $500,000. The store would have a five-year life because everything reverts to the mall owners after that time. The required investment would be 100 percent depreciated (straight-line) over five years, so the depreciation would be $500,000/5 = $100,000 per year. The tax rate is 25 percent. Table 7.4 contains the projected revenues and expenses. Based on these figures, net income in each year is also shown.

	Year 1	Year 2	Year 3	Year 4	Year 5
Revenue	$433,333	$450,000	$266,667	$200,000	$133,333
Expenses	200,000	150,000	100,000	100,000	100,000
Earnings before depreciation	$233,333	$300,000	$166,667	$100,000	$ 33,333
Depreciation	100,000	100,000	100,000	100,000	100,000
Earnings before taxes	$133,333	$200,000	$ 66,667	$ 0	−$ 66,667
Taxes ($T_c = 0.25$)	33,333	50,000	16,667	0	−16,667
Net income	$100,000	$150,000	$ 50,000	$ 0	−$ 50,000

Table 7.4

Projected yearly revenue and costs for average accounting return

$$\text{Average net income} = \frac{(\$100{,}000 + 150{,}000 + 50{,}000 + 0 - 50{,}000)}{5} = \$50{,}000$$

$$\text{Average book value} = \frac{\$500{,}000 + 0}{2} = \$250{,}000$$

To calculate the average book value for this investment, we note that we started out with a book value of $500,000 (the initial cost) and ended up at $0. The average book value during the life of the investment is thus ($500,000 + 0)/2 = $250,000. As long as we use straight-line depreciation, the average investment will always be one half of the initial investment.[4]

Looking at Table 7.4, net income is $100,000 in the first year, $150,000 in the second year, $50,000 in the third year, $0 in Year 4, and −$50,000 in Year 5. The average net income, then, is:

$$[\$100,000 + 150,000 + 50,000 + 0 + (-50,000)]/5 = \$50,000$$

The average accounting return is:

$$\text{AAR} = \frac{\text{Average net income}}{\text{Average book value}} = \frac{\$50,000}{\$250,000} = 20\%$$

If the firm has a target AAR less than 20 percent, then this investment is acceptable; otherwise not. The *average accounting return rule* is thus:

> Based on the average accounting return rule, a project is acceptable if its average accounting return exceeds a target average accounting return.

As we will see in the next section, this rule has a number of problems.

Analyzing the Average Accounting Return Method

You recognize the chief drawback to the AAR immediately. Above all else, the AAR is not a rate of return in any meaningful economic sense. Instead, it is the ratio of two accounting numbers, and it is not comparable to the returns offered, for example, in financial markets.[5]

One of the reasons that the AAR is not a true rate of return is that it ignores time value. When we average figures that occur at different times, we are treating the near future and the more distant future the same way. There was no discounting involved when we computed the average net income, for example.

The second problem with the AAR is similar to the problem we had with the payback period rule concerning the lack of an objective cutoff period. Since a calculated AAR is really not comparable to a market return, the target AAR must somehow be specified. There is no generally agreed upon way to do this. One way of doing it is to calculate the AAR for the firm as a whole and use this for a benchmark, but there are lots of other ways as well.

The third, and perhaps worst, flaw in the AAR is that it doesn't even look at the right things. Instead of cash flow and market value, it uses net income and book value. These are both poor substitutes. As a result, an AAR doesn't

---

[4]We could of course calculate the average of the six book values directly. In thousands, we would have ($500 + 400 + 300 + 200 + 100 + 0)/6 = $250.

[5]The AAR is closely related to the return on assets (ROA) discussed in Chapter 3. In practice, the AAR is sometimes computed by first calculating the ROA for each year, and then averaging the results. This produces a number that is similar, but not identical, to the one we computed.

tell us what the effect on share price will be from taking an investment, so it doesn't tell us what we really want to know.

Does the AAR have any redeeming features? About the only one is that it almost always can be computed. The reason is that accounting information will almost always be available, both for the project under consideration and for the firm as a whole. We hasten to add that once the accounting information is available, we can always convert it to cash flows, so even this is not a particularly important fact. The AAR is summarized in the table below.

Advantages and Disadvantages of the Average Accounting Return

Advantages	Disadvantages
1. Easy to calculate.	1. Not a true rate of return; time value of money is ignored.
2. Needed information will usually be available.	2. Uses an arbitrary benchmark cutoff rate.
	3. Based on accounting (book) values, not cash flows and market values.

CONCEPT QUESTIONS

7.4a What is an average accounting rate of return (AAR)?

7.4b What are the weaknesses of the AAR rule?

THE INTERNAL RATE OF RETURN | 7.5

We now come to the most important alternative to NPV, the **internal rate of return,** universally known as the IRR. As we will see, the IRR is closely related to NPV. With the IRR, we try to find a single rate of return that summarizes the merits of a project. Furthermore, we want this rate to be an "internal" rate in the sense that it only depends on the cash flows of a particular investment, not on rates offered elsewhere.

To illustrate the idea behind the IRR, consider a project that costs $100 today and pays $110 in one year. Suppose you were asked "What is the return on this investment?" What would you say? It seems both natural and obvious to say that the return is 10 percent because, for every dollar we put in, we get $1.10 back. In fact, as we will see in a moment, 10 percent is the internal rate of return or IRR on this investment.

Is this project with its 10 percent IRR a good investment? Once again, it would seem apparent that this is a good investment only if our required return is less than 10 percent. This intuition is also correct and illustrates the *IRR rule:*

> Based on the IRR rule, an investment is acceptable if the IRR exceeds the required return. It should be rejected otherwise.

Imagine that we wanted to calculate the NPV for our simple investment. At a discount rate of *r*, the NPV is:

$$NPV = -\$100 + 110/(1 + r)$$

internal rate of return (IRR)

The discount rate that makes the NPV of an investment zero.

Now, suppose we didn't know the discount rate. This presents a problem, but we could still ask how high the discount rate would have to be before this project was unacceptable. We know that we are indifferent to taking or not taking this investment when its NPV is just equal to zero. In other words, this investment is *economically* a break-even proposition when the NPV is zero because value is neither created nor destroyed. To find the break-even discount rate, we set NPV equal to zero and solve for r:

$$\text{NPV} = 0 = -\$100 + 110/(1 + r)$$

$$\$100 = \$110/(1 + r)$$

$$1 + r = \$110/100 = 1.10$$

$$r = 10\%$$

This 10 percent is what we already have called the return on this investment. What we have now illustrated is that the internal rate of return on an investment (or just "return" for short) is the discount rate that makes the NPV equal to zero. This is an important observation, so it bears repeating:

> The IRR on an investment is the required return that results in a zero NPV when it is used as the discount rate.

The fact that the IRR is simply the discount rate that makes the NPV equal to zero is important because it tells us how to calculate the returns on more complicated investments. As we have seen, finding the IRR turns out to be relatively easy for a single period investment. However, suppose you were now looking at an investment with the cash flows shown in Figure 7.4. As illustrated, this investment costs $100 and has a cash flow of $60 per year for two years, so it's only slightly more complicated than our single period example. However, if you were asked for the return on this investment, what would you say? There doesn't seem to be any obvious answer (at least to us). However, based on what we now know, we can set the NPV equal to zero and solve for the discount rate:

$$\text{NPV} = 0 = -\$100 + 60/(1 + \text{IRR}) + 60/(1 + \text{IRR})^2$$

Unfortunately, the only way to find the IRR in general is by trial and error, either by hand or by calculator. This is precisely the same problem that came up in Chapter 5 when we found the unknown rate for an annuity and in Chapter 6 when we found the yield to maturity on a bond. In fact, we now see that, in both of those cases, we were finding an IRR.

In this particular case, the cash flows form a two-period, $60 annuity. To find the unknown rate, we can try some different rates until we get the

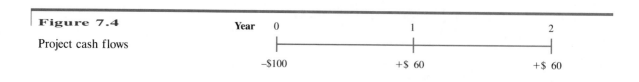

Figure 7.4

Project cash flows

Year	0	1	2
	−$100	+$ 60	+$ 60

Discount Rate	NPV
0%	$20.00
5	11.56
10	4.13
15	−2.46
20	−8.33

Table 7.5

NPV at different discount rates

answer. If we were to start with a 0 percent rate, the NPV would obviously be $120 − 100 = $20. At a 10 percent discount rate, we would have:

$$NPV = -\$100 + 60/1.1 + 60/(1.1)^2 = \$4.13$$

Now, we're getting close. We can summarize these and some other possibilities as shown in Table 7.5. From our calculations, the NPV appears to be zero between 10 percent and 15 percent, so the IRR is somewhere in that range. With a little more effort, we can find that the IRR is about 13.1 percent.[6] So, if our required return is less than 13.1 percent, we would take this investment. If our required return exceeds 13.1 percent, we would reject it.

By now, you have probably noticed that the IRR rule and the NPV rule appear to be quite similar. In fact, the IRR is sometimes simply called the *discounted cash flow* or *DCF return*. The easiest way to illustrate the relationship between NPV and IRR is to plot the numbers we calculated in Table 7.5. We put the different NPVs on the vertical or y-axis and the discount rates on the horizontal or x-axis. If we had a very large number of points, the resulting picture would be a smooth curve called a **net present value profile**. Figure 7.5 illustrates the NPV profile for this project. Beginning with a 0 percent discount rate, we have $20 plotted directly on the y-axis. As the discount rate increases, the NPV declines smoothly. Where will the curve cut through the x-axis? This will occur where the NPV is just equal to zero, so it will happen right at the IRR of 13.1 percent.

net present value profile
A graphical representation of the relationship between an investment's NPVs and various discount rates.

In our example, the NPV rule and the IRR rule lead to identical accept/reject decisions. We will accept an investment using the IRR rule if the required return is less than 13.1 percent. As Figure 7.5 illustrates, however, the NPV is positive at any discount rate less than 13.1 percent, so we would accept the investment using the NPV rule as well. The two rules are equivalent in this case.

Example 7.4   Calculating the IRR
A project has a total up-front cost of $435.44. The cash flows are $100 in the first year, $200 in the second year, and $300 in the third year. What's the IRR? If we require an 18 percent return, should we take this investment?

---

[6]With a lot more effort (or a personal computer), we can find that the IRR is approximately (to 13 decimal points) 13.0662386291808 percent, not that anybody would ever want this many decimal points.

Figure 7.5

An NPV profile

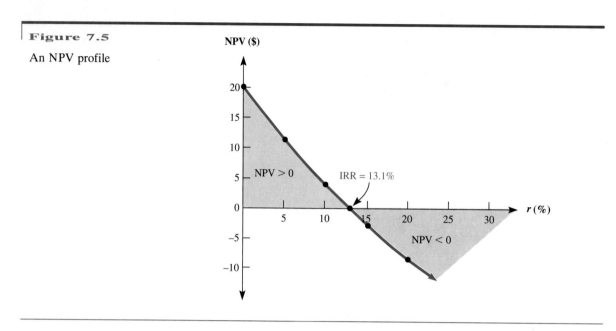

We'll describe the NPV profile and find the IRR by calculating some NPVs at different discount rates. You should check our answers for practice. Beginning with 0 percent, we have:

Discount Rate	NPV
0%	$164.56
5	100.36
10	46.15
15	0.00
20	−39.61

The NPV is zero at 15 percent, so 15 percent is the IRR. If we require an 18 percent return, then we should not take the investment. The reason is that the NPV is negative at 18 percent (check that it is −$24.47). The IRR rule tells us the same thing in this case. We shouldn't take this investment because its 15 percent return is below our required 18 percent return.

At this point, you may be wondering whether the IRR and the NPV rules always lead to identical decisions. The answer is yes as long as two very important conditions are met. First, the project's cash flows must be *conventional,* meaning that the first cash flow (the initial investment) is negative and all the rest are positive. Second, the project must be *independent,* meaning that the decision to accept or reject this project does not affect the decision to accept or reject any other. The first of these conditions is typically met, but the second often is not. In any case, when one or both of these conditions are not met, problems can arise. We discuss some of these next.

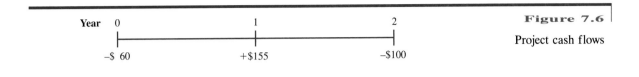

Figure 7.6

Project cash flows

Year	0	1	2
	−$ 60	+$155	−$100

Problems with the IRR

The problems with the IRR come about when the cash flows are not conventional or when we are trying to compare two or more investments to see which is best. In the first case, surprisingly, the simple question "What's the return?" can become very difficult to answer. In the second case, the IRR can be a misleading guide.

Nonconventional Cash Flows   Suppose we have a strip-mining project that requires a $60 investment. Our cash flow in the first year will be $155. In the second year, the mine is depleted, but we have to spend $100 to restore the terrain. As Figure 7.6 illustrates, both the first and third cash flows are negative.

To find the IRR on this project, we can calculate the NPV at various rates:

Discount Rate	NPV
0%	−$5.00
10	−1.74
20	−0.28
30	0.06
40	−0.31

The NPV appears to be behaving in a very peculiar fashion here. First, as the discount rate increases from 0 percent to 30 percent, the NPV starts out negative and becomes positive. This seems backwards because the NPV is rising as the discount rate rises. It then starts getting smaller and becomes negative again. What's the IRR? To find out, we draw the NPV profile in Figure 7.7.

In Figure 7.7, notice that the NPV is zero when the discount rate is 25 percent, so this is the IRR. Or is it? The NPV is also zero at 33⅓ percent. Which of these is correct? The answer is both or neither; more precisely, there is no unambiguously correct answer. This is the **multiple rates of return** problem. Many financial computer packages (including the best seller for personal computers) aren't aware of this problem and just report the first IRR that is found. Others report only the smallest positive IRR, even though this answer is no better than any other.

In our current example, the IRR rule breaks down completely. Suppose our required return were 10 percent. Should we take this investment? Both IRRs are greater than 10 percent, so, by the IRR rule, maybe we should. However, as Figure 7.7 shows, the NPV is negative at any discount rate less than 25 percent, so this is not a good investment. When should we take it? Looking

multiple rates of return
The possibility that more than one discount rate makes the NPV of an investment zero.

Figure 7.7

NPV profile

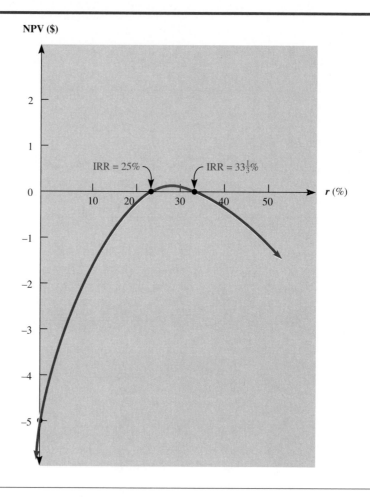

at Figure 7.7 one last time, the NPV is positive only if our required return is between 25 percent and 33⅓ percent.

The moral of the story is that when the cash flows aren't conventional, strange things can start to happen to the IRR. This is not anything to get upset about, however, because the NPV rule, as always, works just fine. This illustrates that, oddly enough, the obvious question — What's the rate of return? — may not always have a good answer.

Example 7.5   What's the IRR?

You are looking at an investment that requires you to invest $51 today. You'll get $100 in one year, but you must pay out $50 in two years. What is the IRR on this investment?

You're on the alert now to the nonconventional cash flow problem, so you probably wouldn't be surprised to see more than one IRR. However, if you start looking for an IRR by trial and error, it will take you a long time. The reason is that there is no IRR. The NPV is negative at every discount rate, so we shouldn't take this investment under any circumstances. What's the return on this investment? Your guess is as good as ours. ∎

Example 7.6   "I Think; Therefore, I Know How Many IRRs There Can Be."

We've seen that it's possible to get more than one IRR. If you wanted to make sure that you had found all of the possible IRRs, how could you tell? The answer comes from the great mathematician, philosopher, and financial analyst Descartes (of "I think; therefore I am" fame). Descartes's Rule of Sign says that the maximum number of IRRs that there can be is equal to the number of times that the cash flows change sign from positive to negative and/or negative to positive.[7]

In our example with the 25 percent and 33⅓ percent IRRs, could there be yet another IRR? The cash flows flip from negative to positive, then back to negative for a total of two sign changes. As a result, the maximum number of IRRs is two, and, from Descartes's rule, we don't need to look for any more. Note that the actual number of IRRs can be less than the maximum (see Example 7.5). ∎

Mutually Exclusive Investments   Even if there is a single IRR, another problem can arise concerning **mutually exclusive investment decisions.** If two investments, X and Y, are mutually exclusive, then taking one of them means that we cannot take the other. For example, if we own one corner lot, then we can build a gas station or an apartment building, but not both. These are mutually exclusive alternatives.

mutually exclusive investment decisions
A situation where taking one investment prevents the taking of another.

Thus far, we have asked whether or not a given investment is worth undertaking. There is a related question, however, that comes up very often: Given two or more mutually exclusive investments, which one is the best? The answer is simple enough: The best one is the one with the largest NPV. Can we also say that the best one has the highest return? As we show, the answer is no.

To illustrate the problem with the IRR rule and mutually exclusive investments, consider the cash flows from the following two mutually exclusive investments:

Year	Investment A	Investment B
0	−$100	−$100
1	50	20
2	40	40
3	40	50
4	30	60
IRR	24%	21%

Since these investments are mutually exclusive, we can only take one of them. Simple intuition suggests that Investment A is better because of its higher return. Unfortunately, simple intuition is not always correct.

---

[7]To be more precise, the number of IRRs that are bigger than −100 percent is equal to the number of sign changes, or it differs from the number of sign changes by an even number. Thus, for example, if there are five sign changes, there are either five, three, or one IRRs. If there are two sign changes, there are either two IRRs or no IRRs.

To see why Investment A is not necessarily the better of the two investments, we've calculated the NPV of these investments for different required returns:

Discount Rate	NPV(A)	NPV(B)
0%	$60.00	$70.00
5	43.13	47.88
10	29.06	29.79
15	17.18	14.82
20	7.06	2.31
25	−1.63	−8.22

The IRR for A (24%) is larger than the IRR for B (21%). However, if you compare the NPVs, you'll see that which investment has the higher NPV depends on our required return. B has greater total cash flow, but it pays back more slowly than A. As a result, it has a higher NPV at lower discount rates.

In our example, the NPV and IRR rankings conflict for some discount rates. If our required return is 10 percent, for instance, then B has the higher NPV and is thus the better of the two even though A has the higher return. If our required return is 15 percent, then there is no ranking conflict: A is better.

The conflict between the IRR and NPV for mutually exclusive investments can be illustrated by plotting their NPV profiles as we have done in Figure 7.8. In Figure 7.8, notice that the NPV profiles cross at about 11 per-

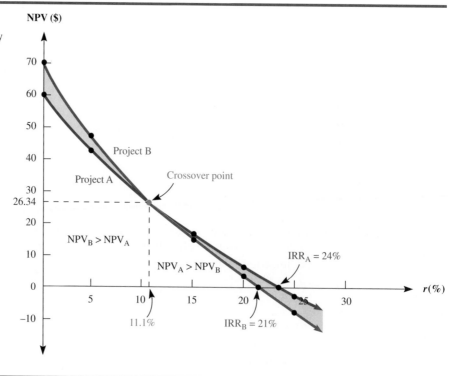

Figure 7.8

NPV profiles for mutually exclusive investments

cent. Notice also that at any discount rate less than 11 percent, the NPV for B is higher. In this range, taking B benefits us more than taking A, even though A's IRR is higher. At any rate greater that 11 percent, Project A has the greater NPV.

What this example illustrates is that whenever we have mutually exclusive projects, we shouldn't rank them based on their returns. More generally, anytime we are comparing investments to determine which is best, IRRs can be misleading. Instead, we need to look at the relative NPVs to avoid the possibility of choosing incorrectly. Remember, we're ultimately interested in creating value for the shareholders, so the option with the higher NPV is preferred, regardless of the relative returns.

If this seems counterintuitive, think of it this way. Suppose you have two investments. One has a 10 percent return and makes you $100 richer immediately. The other has a 20 percent return and makes you $50 richer immediately. Which one do you like better? We would rather have $100 than $50, regardless of the returns, so we like the first one better.

Example 7.7   Calculating the Crossover Rate

In Figure 7.8, the NPV profiles cross at about 11 percent. How can we determine just what this crossover point is? The *crossover rate,* by definition, is the discount rate that makes the NPVs of two projects equal. To illustrate, suppose we have the following two mutually exclusive investments:

Year	Investment A	Investment B
0	−$400	−$500
1	250	320
2	280	340

What's the crossover rate?

To find the crossover, first consider moving out of Investment A and into Investment B. If you make the move, you'll have to invest an extra $100 ($500 − 400). For this $100 investment, you'll get an extra $70 ($320 − 250) in the first year and an extra $60 ($340 − 280) in the second year. Is this a good move? In other words, is it worth investing the extra $100?

Based on our discussion, the NPV of the switch, NPV(B − A) is:

$$NPV(B − A) = −100 + \$70/(1 + r) + \$60/(1 + r)^2$$

We can calculate the return on this investment by setting the NPV equal to zero and solving for the IRR:

$$NPV(B − A) = 0 = −100 + \$70/(1 + r) + \$60/(1 + r)^2$$

If you go through this calculation, you will find the IRR is exactly 20 percent. What this tells us is that at a 20 percent discount rate, we are indifferent between the two investments because the NPV of the difference in their cash flows is zero. As a consequence, the two investments have the same value, so this 20 percent is the crossover rate. Check that the NPV at 20 percent is $2.78 for both.

In general, you can find the crossover rate by taking the difference in the cash flows and calculating the IRR using the differences. It doesn't make any difference which one you subtract from which. To see this, find the IRR for (A − B); you'll see it's the same number. Also, for practice, you might want to find the exact crossover in Figure 7.8 (hint: it's 11.0704%). ∎

Redeeming Qualities of the IRR

Despite its flaws, the IRR is very popular in practice, more so than even NPV. It probably survives because it fills a need that the NPV does not. In analyzing investments, people in general, and financial analysts in particular, seem to prefer talking about rates of return rather than dollar values.

In a similar vein, the IRR also appears to provide a simple way of communicating information about a proposal. One manager might say to another: "Remodeling the clerical wing has a 20 percent return." This may somehow be simpler than saying: "At a 10 percent discount rate, the net present value is $4,000."

Finally, under certain circumstances, the IRR may have a practical advantage over NPV. We can't estimate the NPV unless we know the appropriate discount rate, but we can still estimate the IRR. Suppose we didn't know the required return on an investment, but we found, for example, that it had a 40 percent return. We would probably be inclined to take it since it is very unlikely that the required return is that high. The advantages and disadvantages of the IRR are summarized below.

Advantages and Disadvantages of the Internal Rate of Return

Advantages	Disadvantages
1. Closely related to NPV, often leading to identical decisions.	1. May result in multiple answers or not deal with nonconventional cash flows.
2. Easy to understand and communicate.	2. May lead to incorrect decisions in comparisons of mutually exclusive investments.

⌐ CONCEPT QUESTIONS

7.5a Under what circumstances will the IRR and NPV rules lead to the same accept/reject decisions? When might they conflict?

7.5b Is it generally true that an advantage of the IRR rule over the NPV rule is that we don't need to know the required return to use the IRR rule?

7.6 | THE PROFITABILITY INDEX

profitability index

The present value of an investment's future cash flows divided by its initial cost. Also *benefit/cost ratio.*

Another method used to evaluate projects is called the **profitability index** (PI) or benefit/cost ratio. This index is defined as the present value of the future cash flows divided by the initial investment. So, if a project costs $200 and the present value of its future cash flows is $220, the profitability index value would be $220/200 = 1.10. Notice that the NPV for this investment is $20, so it is a desirable investment.

More generally, if a project has a positive NPV, then the present value of the future cash flows must be bigger than the initial investment. The profitability index would thus be bigger than 1.00 for a positive NPV investment and less than 1.00 for a negative NPV investment.

How do we interpret the profitability index? In our example, the PI was 1.10. This tells us that, per dollar invested, $1.10 in value or $.10 in NPV results. The profitability index thus measures "bang for the buck," that is, the value created per dollar invested. For this reason, it is often proposed as a measure of performance for government or other not-for-profit investments. Also, when capital is scarce, it may make sense to allocate it to those projects with the highest PIs. We will return to this issue in a later chapter.

The PI is obviously very similar to the NPV. However, consider an investment that costs $5 and has a $10 present value and an investment that costs $100 with a $150 present value. The first of these investments has an NPV of $5 and a PI of 2. The second has an NPV of $50 and a PI of 1.50. If these were mutually exclusive investments, then the second one is preferred even though it has a lower PI. This ranking problem is very similar to the IRR ranking problem we saw in the previous section. In all, there seems to be little reason to rely on the PI instead of the NPV. Our discussion of the PI is summarized below.

Advantages and Disadvantages of the Profitability Index

Advantages	Disadvantages
1. Closely related to NPV, generally leading to identical decisions.	1. May lead to incorrect decisions in comparisons of mutually exclusive investments.
2. Easy to understand and communicate.	
3. May be useful when available investment funds are limited.	

CONCEPT QUESTIONS

7.6a What does the profitability index measure?

7.6b How would you state the profitability index rule?

THE PRACTICE OF CAPITAL BUDGETING | 7.7

Given that NPV seems to be telling us directly what we want to know, you might be wondering why there are so many other procedures and why alternative procedures are commonly used. Recall that we are trying to make an investment decision and that we are frequently operating under considerable uncertainty about the future. We can only *estimate* the NPV of an investment in this case. The resulting estimate can be very "soft," meaning that the true NPV might be quite different.

Because the true NPV is unknown, the astute financial manager seeks clues to assess whether the estimated NPV is reliable. For this reason, firms would typically use multiple criteria for evaluating a proposal. For example,

Table 7.6

Percentage of responding firms using different types of capital budgeting methods*

Discounted Cash Flow	Payback Period	Average Accounting Return	Other (including no response)	Percentage of Firms Using Methods
Yes	Yes	Yes		28%
Yes		Yes		8
Yes	Yes			16
Yes				28
	Yes	Yes		4
	Yes			2
		Yes		2
			Yes	12
				100%

*The number of responding firms is 50. From M. Blume, E. Friend, and R. Westerfield: Rodney L. White Center for Financial Research monograph (Philadelphia: The Wharton School, University of Pennsylvania, 1980).

suppose we have an investment with a positive estimated NPV. Based on our experience with other projects, this one appears to have a short payback and a very high AAR. In this case, the different indicators seem to agree that it's "all systems go." Put another way, the payback and the AAR are consistent with the conclusion that the NPV is positive.

On the other hand, suppose we had a positive estimated NPV, a long payback, and a low AAR. This could still be a good investment, but it looks like we need to be much more careful in making the decision since we are getting conflicting signals. If the estimated NPV is based on projections in which we have little confidence, then further analysis is probably in order. We will consider how to go about this analysis in more detail in the next two chapters.

There have been a number of surveys conducted asking large firms what types of investment criteria they actually use. Table 7.6 presents the results of one such survey. Based on the results, the most frequently used capital budgeting technique is some form of discounted cash flow (such as NPV or IRR). Some 80 percent of the firms use it, but only 28 percent use it exclusively.

In practice, the payback period is the second most popular tool; about 50 percent of the responding firms use it, with only 2 percent using it exclusively. Other surveys are consistent with these results. The most common practice is to look at NPV or IRR along with nondiscounted cash flow criteria such as payback and AAR. Given our discussion, this is sound practice. For future reference, the various criteria are summarized in Table 7.7.

CONCEPT QUESTIONS

7.7a What are the most commonly used capital budgeting procedures?

7.7b Since NPV is conceptually the best procedure for capital budgeting, why do you think that multiple measures are used in practice?

I. Discounted Cash Flow Criteria

Table 7.7

Summary of investment criteria

A. *Net present value (NPV)*. The NPV of an investment is the difference between its market value and its cost. The NPV rule is to take a project if its NPV is positive. NPV is frequently estimated by calculating the present value of the future cash flows (to estimate market value) and then subtracting the cost. NPV has no serious flaws; it is the preferred decision criterion.

B. *Internal rate of return (IRR)*. The IRR is the discount rate that makes the estimated NPV of an investment equal to zero; it is sometimes called the *discounted cash flow (DCF) return*. The IRR rule is to take a project when its IRR exceeds the required return. IRR is closely related to NPV, and it leads to exactly the same decisions as NPV for conventional, independent projects. When project cash flows are not conventional, there may be no IRR or there may be more than one. More seriously, the IRR cannot be used to rank mutually exclusive projects; the project with the highest IRR is not necessarily the preferred investment.

C. *Profitability index (PI)*. The profitability index, also called the *benefit/cost ratio,* is the ratio of present value to cost. The profitability index rule is to take an investment if the index exceeds 1. The profitability index measures the present value of an investment per dollar invested. It is quite similar to NPV, but, like IRR, it cannot be used to rank mutually exclusive projects. However, it is sometimes used to rank projects when a firm has more positive NPV investments than it can currently finance.

II. Payback Criteria

A. *Payback period*. The payback period is the length of time until the sum of an investment's cash flows equals its cost. The payback period rule is to take a project if its payback is *less* than some cutoff. The payback period is a flawed criterion primarily because it ignores risk, the time value of money, and cash flows beyond the cutoff point.

B. *Discounted payback period*. The discounted payback period is the length of time until the sum of an investment's discounted cash flows equals its cost. The discounted payback period rule is to take an investment if the discounted payback is *less* than some cutoff. The discounted payback rule is flawed primarily because it ignores cash flows after the cutoff.

III. Accounting Criteria

A. *Average accounting return (AAR)*. The AAR is a measure of accounting profit relative to book value. It is *not* related to the IRR, but it is similar to the accounting return on assets (ROA) measure in Chapter 3. The AAR rule is to take an investment if its AAR exceeds a benchmark AAR. The AAR is seriously flawed for a variety of reasons, and it has little to recommend it.

SUMMARY AND CONCLUSIONS | 7.8

This chapter has covered the different criteria used to evaluate proposed investments. The six criteria, in the order we discussed them, are:

1. Net Present Value (NPV)
2. Payback Period
3. Discounted Payback Period
4. Average Accounting Return (AAR)
5. Internal Rate of Return (IRR)
6. Profitability Index (PI)

We illustrated how to calculate each of these and discussed the interpretation of the results. We also described the advantages and disadvantages of each of them.

The most important concept in this chapter is net present value (NPV). We will return to this idea repeatedly in the chapters to come. We defined NPV as the difference between the market value of an asset or project and its cost. We saw that the financial manager acts in the best interest of the shareholders by identifying and undertaking positive NPV investments.

Finally, we noted that NPVs can't normally be observed in the market; instead, they must be estimated. Because there is always the possibility of a poor estimate, financial managers use multiple criteria for examining projects. These other criteria provide additional information about whether a project truly has a positive NPV.

Key Terms

net present value (NPV) 220
discounted cash flow valuation (DCF) 221
payback period 224
discounted payback period 228
average accounting return (AAR) 231

internal rate of return (IRR) 233
net present value profile 235
multiple rates of return 237
mutually exclusive investment decisions 239
profitability index 242

Chapter Review Problems and Self-Test

7.1   Investment Criteria   This problem will give you some practice calculating NPVs and paybacks. A proposed overseas expansion has the following cash flows:

Year	Cash Flow
0	−$100
1	50
2	40
3	40
4	15

Calculate the payback, the discounted payback, and the NPV at a required return of 15 percent.

7.2   Mutually Exclusive Investments   Consider the following two mutually exclusive investments. Calculate the IRR for each and the crossover rate. Under what circumstances will the IRR and NPV criteria rank the two projects differently?

Year	Investment A	Investment B
0	−$100	−$100
1	50	70
2	70	75
3	40	10

7.3 Average Accounting Return   You are looking at a three-year project with a projected net income of $1,000 in Year 1, $2,000 in Year 2, and $4,000 in Year 3. The cost is $9,000 which will be depreciated straight-line to zero over the three-year life of the project. What is the average accounting return (AAR)?

Answers to Self-Test Problems

7.1 In the table below, we have listed the cash flows, cumulative cash flows, discounted cash flows (at 15%), and cumulative discounted cash flows.

Cash Flows and Accumulated Cash Flows

	Cash Flow		Accumulated Cash Flow	
Year	Undiscounted	Discounted	Undiscounted	Discounted
1	$50	$43.5	$ 50	$ 43.5
2	40	30.2	90	73.7
3	40	26.3	130	100.0
4	15	8.6	145	108.6

Recall that the initial investment is $100. When we compare this to accumulated undiscounted cash flows, we see that payback occurs between Years 2 and 3. The cash flows for the first two years are $90 total, so, going into the third year, we are short by $10. The total cash flow in Year 3 is $40, so the payback is 2 + $10/40 = 2.25 years.

Looking at the accumulated discounted cash flows, we see that the discounted payback occurs right at three years. The sum of the discounted cash flows is $108.6, so the NPV is $8.60. Notice that this is the present value of the cash flows that occur after the discounted payback.

7.2 To calculate the IRR, we might try some guesses as in the following table:

Discount Rate	NPV(A)	NPV(B)
0%	$60.00	$55.00
10	33.36	33.13
20	13.43	16.20
30	−1.91	2.78
40	−14.01	−8.09

Several things are immediately apparent from our guesses. First, the IRR on A must be just a little less than 30 percent (why?). With some more effort, we find that it's 28.61 percent. For B, the IRR must be a little more than 30 percent (again, why?); it works out to be 32.37 percent. Also, notice that at 10 percent, the NPVs are very close, indicating that the crossover is in that vicinity.

To find the crossover exactly, we can compute the IRR on the difference in the cash flows. If we take the cash flows from A minus the cash flows from B, the resulting cash flows are:

Year	A − B
0	$ 0
1	−20
2	−5
3	30

These cash flows look a little odd, but the sign only changes once, so we can find an IRR. With some trial and error, you'll see that the NPV is zero at a discount rate of 10.61 percent, so this is the crossover rate.

Now, the IRR for B is always higher. As we've seen, A has the larger NPV for any discount rate less than 10.61 percent, so the NPV and IRR rankings will conflict in that range. Remember, if there's a conflict, we will go with the higher NPV. Our decision rule is thus very simple: Take A if the required return is less than 10.61 percent, take B if the required return is between 10.61 percent and 32.37 percent (the IRR on B), and take neither if the required return is more than 32.37 percent.

7.3   Here we need to calculate the ratio of average net income to average book value to get the AAR. Average net income is:

Average net income = ($1,000 + 2,000 + 4,000)/3 = $2,333.33

Average book value is:

Average book value = $9,000/2 = $4,500

So the average accounting return is:

AAR = $2,333.33/4,500 = 51.85%

This is an impressive return. Remember, however, that it isn't really a rate of return like an interest rate or an IRR, so the size doesn't tell us a lot. In particular, our money is probably not going to grow at 51.85 percent per year, sorry to say.

Questions and Problems

1.   **Calculate Payback**   An investment offers $200 per year for 10 years. What is the payback if the investment costs $1,000? If it costs $1,500? If it costs $2,500?

2. **Calculate Payback**   Consider the following cash flows for two investments:

Year	Investment A	Investment B
0	−$100	−$100
1	52	41
2	63	55
3	77	110

What are the paybacks on the two investments? If we require a two-year payback to take an investment, which of these two is acceptable? Is it necessarily the best investment? Explain.

3. **Calculate NPV**   In the previous question, which of the two investments is better if we require a 5 percent return?

4. **Calculate IRR**   Compute the internal rate of return on a project with cash flows of:

Time	Cash Flow
0	−$100.0
1	72.0
2	57.6

5. **Payback**   Suppose an investment pays $100 per year and costs $600. How many years does it take to pay back? If the discount rate is 5 percent, what is the discounted payback? If the discount rate is 20 percent? Is the payback period affected by the different discount rates?

6. **Payback Intuition**   If a project has conventional cash flows, is the discounted payback always less than the regular payback? Explain.

7. **Payback Intuition**   If a project has conventional cash flows and a discounted payback that is less than the project's life, what do you know about its NPV? Explain.

8. **Budgeting Techniques and Their Relationships**   If a project has conventional cash flows and a positive NPV, what do you know about its payback? Its discounted payback? Its benefit/cost ratio? Its IRR? Explain.

9. **IRR**   Compute the internal rate of return on a project with the following cash flows:

Time	Cash Flow
0	−$1,200
1	1,100
2	242

10.   IRR versus NPV   Consider the following cash flows for two mutually exclusive investments:

	C_0	C_1	C_2
Project A	-$100	$80	$ 90
Project B	-100	70	102

For what range of discount rates is Project A better? Illustrate your answer with an NPV profile.

11.   Problems with IRR   Compute the internal rates of return (via trial and error) for the following sequences of cash flows:

Year	Sequence A	Sequence B
0	-$100	-$100
1	100	0
2	200	100
3	-100	200

12.   IRR versus NPV   Mr. Polly Femus, the president of Monocle Enterprises, is evaluating the following two mutually exclusive investments:

	Cash Flows		
	C_0	C_1	C_2
Project A	-$400	$241	$293
Project B	-200	131	172

Determine the IRR for each. If Mr. Femus chooses the project with the higher IRR, under what circumstances will his choice be incorrect? At what discount rate would Mr. Femus be indifferent between the two projects?

13.   Problems with IRR   Compute the internal rate of return (via trial and error) for the following cash flows:

Time	Cash Flows	
	A	B
0	-$200	-$150
1	200	50
2	800	100
3	-800	100

14.   Calculate AAR   You are evaluating a four-year project with a projected net income of $2,133 in Year 1, $2,455 in Year 2, $3,241 in Year 3, and $3,566 in Year 4. The $10,000 cost will be depreciated straight-line to zero over the four-year life of the project. What is the average accounting return (AAR)?

15. **AAR** Consider the following abbreviated financial statement information projected for a proposed new project:

	Year 0	Year 1	Year 2	Year 3	Year 4
Gross book value	$160				
Less: Accumulated depreciation	0				
Net book value	$160	$	$	$	$ 0
Sales		74	67	91	90
Costs		50	43	45	49
Depreciation					
Taxes (34%)					
Net Income		$	$	$	$

Supply the missing information assuming that the investment is depreciated to zero on a straight-line basis. Assume that a tax credit is generated when taxable income is negative. What is the average accounting return (AAR)? How do you interpret this number?

16. NPV versus the Discount Rate   An investment has a total installed cost of $5,346. The cash flows over the four-year life of the investment are projected to be $1,459, $2,012, $2,234, and $1,005. If the discount rate is zero, what is the NPV? If the discount rate is infinity, what is the NPV? What is the IRR on the investment? Based on these three points, sketch the NPV profile.

17. Payback Calculations   You are examining the following three-year investment:

Year	Cash Flow
0	−$100
1	50
2	40
3	60

Complete the following table assuming a 12 percent required return:

Year	Cash Flow Undiscounted	Cash Flow Discounted	Accumulated Cash Flow Undiscounted	Accumulated Cash Flow Discounted
1	$	$	$	$
2				
3				

a. What is the payback rounded up to the next whole year? What is the payback if we use fractional years? What are we assuming about the cash flows when we calculate the fractional year?

b. What is the discounted payback? Don't calculate the fractional year.

c. What is the NPV of this investment if the required return is 14 percent?

18.   Calculating NPV and IRR   Consider the following cash flows on two investments:

Year	Investment A	Investment B
0	−$100	−$100
1	44	69
2	56	51
3	65	32

a. The required return is 15 percent. The investments are not mutually exclusive. Calculate the NPV and IRR on both. Are they desirable?

b. Now suppose you wanted to combine the two investments into a single Investment C. Calculate the combined cash flows. What is the NPV of C? How does this NPV relate to the NPVs for A and B considered separately? Based on your answer, is there an obvious shortcut that we could have used to calculate the NPV of C?

c. Based on the combined cash flows, calculate the IRR for C. How does your answer relate to the IRRs for A and B? Is there an obvious shortcut that we could have used?

19.   Project Choice Using Several Techniques   Consider the following cash flows on two mutually exclusive investments:

Year	Investment A	Investment B
0	−$100	−$100
1	40	60
2	60	60
3	90	60

a. Based on the payback periods, which of these might you prefer?

b. Sketch the NPV profiles for both investments. Over what range is Investment A preferred?

c. Find the IRR for the two investments and indicate them on the graph.

d. Find the exact crossover point and indicate it on the graph.

e. Suppose the required return is 8 percent. Which of these investments do you prefer?

20.   Applications of Various Techniques   The Voltar Co. owns 140 acres of prime oceanfront property. It is considering several different development options. One option is a hotel and resort complex (Option A). Also under consideration is a more expensive multihotel/amusement park development (Option B). The cash flows (in millions of dollars) for the two options are projected to be:

Year	Option A	Option B
0	-$ 600	-$ 800
1	-40	-60
2	95	175
3	203	210
4	245	270
5	290	375
6	1,240	1,510

a. What is the payback of Option A? For Option B?

b. Assuming a required return of 20 percent, what are the profitability indices or benefit/cost ratios for the projects? How do you interpret these?

c. Do the profitability index and NPV criteria always rank projects the same way? Why or why not? Which of these two projects is preferable, again assuming a 20 percent discount rate?

21. **NPV Intuition** Projects A and B have the same cost, and both have conventional cash flows. The total cash inflows from A (undiscounted) are $400. The total for B is $360. The IRR for A is 20 percent; the IRR for B is 18 percent. What can you deduce about the NPVs for Projects A and B? What do you know about the crossover rate?

22. **Problems with IRR** Consider the following cash flows. What is the IRR? If our required return is 30 percent, should we take this investment? What is the NPV at 30 percent? What's going on here? Sketch the NPV profile. When should we take this investment? Interpret your answer.

Year	Cash Flow
0	$100
1	-50
2	-50
3	-50

23. **Payback and IRR** A project has perpetual cash flows of $C per period, a cost of $I, and a required return of r. What is the relationship between its payback and its IRR? What implications does your answer have for long-lived projects with relatively constant cash flows?

24. **NPV and the Profitability Index** If we define the NPV index as the ratio of NPV to cost, what is the relationship between this index and the profitability index?

25. **Payback and NPV** This is a challenge problem. An investment under consideration has a payback of five years and a cost of $1,200. If the required return is 20 percent, what is the worst-case NPV? Explain.

26.   Multiple IRRs   This is a challenge problem that is also useful for testing computer software. Consider the following cash flows. How many IRRs can there be? How many are there (hint: search between 20 percent and 70 percent)? When should we take this project?

Year	Cash Flow
0	−$ 252
1	1,431
2	−3,035
3	2,850
4	−1,000

Suggested Readings

For a discussion of the capital budgeting techniques used by large firms, see:

Bierman, Harold. *Implementing Capital Budgeting Techniques*. Rev. ed. The Institutional Investor Series in Finance and Financial Management Association Survey and Synthesis Series. Cambridge, Mass.: Ballinger Publishing Company, 1988.

Schall, L., and C. Sundem. "Capital Budgeting Methods and Risk: A Further Analysis." *Financial Management* 9, Spring 1980, pp. 7–11.

Chapter 8

Making Capital Investment Decisions

So far, we've covered various parts of the capital budgeting decision. Our task in this chapter is to start bringing these pieces together. In particular, we will show you how to "spread the numbers" for a proposed investment or project and, based on those numbers, make an initial assessment about whether or not the project should be undertaken.

In the discussion that follows, we focus on the process of setting up a discounted cash flow analysis. From the last chapter, we know that the projected future cash flows are the key element in such an evaluation. Accordingly, we emphasize working with financial and accounting information to come up with these figures.

In evaluating a proposed investment, we pay special attention to deciding what information is relevant to the decision at hand and what information is not. As we shall see, it is easy to overlook important pieces of the capital budgeting puzzle.

We will wait until the next chapter to describe in detail how to go about evaluating the results of our discounted cash flow analysis. Also, where needed, we will assume that we know the relevant required return or discount rate. We continue to defer discussion of this subject to Part Five.

PROJECT CASH FLOWS: A FIRST LOOK | 8.1

The effect of taking a project is to change the firm's overall cash flows today and in the future. To evaluate a proposed investment, we must consider these changes in the firm's cash flows and then decide whether or not they add

255

value to the firm. The first (and most important) step, therefore, is to decide which cash flows are relevant and which are not.

Relevant Cash Flows

incremental cash flows
The difference between a firm's future cash flows with a project or without the project.

What is a relevant cash flow for a project? The general principle is simple enough: A relevant cash flow for a project is a change in the firm's overall future cash flow that comes about as a direct consequence of the decision to take that project. Because the relevant cash flows are defined in terms of changes in or increments to the firm's existing cash flow, they are called the **incremental cash flows** associated with the project.

The concept of incremental cash flow is central to our analysis, so we will state a general definition and refer back to it as needed:

> The incremental cash flows for project evaluation consist of *any and all* changes in the firm's future cash flows that are a direct consequence of taking the project.

This definition of incremental cash flows has an obvious and important corollary: Any cash flow that exists regardless of whether or not a project is undertaken is *not* relevant.

The Stand-Alone Principle

stand-alone principle
Evaluation of a project based on the project's incremental cash flows.

In practice, it would be very cumbersome to actually calculate the future total cash flows to the firm with and without a project, especially for a large firm. Fortunately, it is not really necessary to do so. Once we identify the effect of undertaking the proposed project on the firm's cash flows, we need only focus on the project's resulting incremental cash flows. This is called the **stand-alone principle.**

What the stand-alone principle says is that, once we have determined the incremental cash flows from undertaking a project, we can view that project as a kind of "minifirm" with its own future revenues and costs, its own assets, and, of course, its own cash flows. We will then be primarily interested in comparing the cash flows from this minifirm to the cost of acquiring it. An important consequence of this approach is that we will be evaluating the proposed project purely on its own merits, in isolation from any other activities or projects.

⌐ **CONCEPT QUESTIONS**
8.1a What are the relevant incremental cash flows for project evaluation?
8.1b What is the stand-alone principle?

8.2 | INCREMENTAL CASH FLOWS

We are concerned here only with those cash flows that are incremental to a project. Looking back at our general definition, it seems easy enough to decide whether a cash flow is incremental or not. Even so, there are a few situations when mistakes are easy to make. In this section, we describe some of these common pitfalls and how to avoid them.

Sunk Costs

A **sunk cost,** by definition, is a cost we have already paid or have already incurred the liability to pay. Such a cost cannot be changed by the decision today to accept or reject a project. Put another way, the firm will have to pay this cost no matter what. Based on our general definition of incremental cash flow, such a cost is clearly not relevant to the decision at hand. So, we will always be careful to exclude sunk costs from our analysis.

That a sunk cost is not relevant seems obvious given our discussion. Nonetheless, it's easy to fall prey to the sunk cost fallacy. For example, suppose General Milk Company hires a financial consultant to help evaluate whether or not a line of chocolate milk should be launched. When the consultant turns in the report, General Milk objects to the analysis because the consultant did not include the hefty consulting fee as a cost to the chocolate milk project.

Who is correct? By now, we know that the consulting fee is a sunk cost, because the consulting fee must be paid whether or not the chocolate milk line is actually launched (this is an attractive feature of the consulting business).

sunk cost

A cost that has already been incurred and cannot be removed and therefore should not be considered in an investment decision.

Opportunity Costs

When we think of costs, we normally think of out-of-pocket costs, namely, those that require us to actually spend some amount of cash. An **opportunity cost** is slightly different; it requires us to give up a benefit. A common situation arises where a firm already owns some of the assets that a proposed project will be using. For example, we might be thinking of converting an old rustic cotton mill that we bought years ago for $100,000 into "upmarket" condominiums.

If we undertake this project, there will be no direct cash outflow associated with buying the old mill since we already own it. For purposes of evaluating the condo project, should we then treat the mill as "free?" The answer is no. The mill is a valuable resource used by the project. If we didn't use it here, we could do something else with it. Like what? The obvious answer is that, at a minimum, we could sell it. Using the mill for the condo complex thus has an opportunity cost: We give up the valuable opportunity to do something else with it.[1]

There is another issue here. Once we agree that the use of the mill has an opportunity cost, how much should the condo project be charged? Given that we paid $100,000, it might seem that we should charge this amount to the condo project. Is this correct? The answer is no, and the reason is based on our discussion concerning sunk costs.

The fact that we paid $100,000 some years ago is irrelevant. It's sunk. At a minimum, the opportunity cost that we charge the project is what the mill

opportunity cost

The most valuable alternative that is given up if a particular investment is undertaken.

---

[1]Economists sometimes use the acronym "TANSTAAFL," which is short for "There ain't no such thing as a free lunch," to describe the fact that only very rarely is something truly free.

would sell for today (net of any selling costs) because this is the amount that we give up by using it instead of selling it.[2]

Side Effects

Remember that the incremental cash flows for a project include all the changes in the *firm's* future cash flows. It would not be unusual for a project to have side or spillover effects, both good and bad. For example, if the Innovative Motors Company (IMC) introduces a new car, some of the sales might come at the expense of other IMC cars. This is called **erosion**, and the same general problem could occur for any multiline consumer producer or seller.[3] In this case, the cash flows from the new line should be adjusted downward to reflect lost profits on other lines.

In accounting for erosion, it is important to recognize that any sales lost as a result of our launching a new product might be lost anyway because of future competition. Erosion is only relevant when the sales would not otherwise be lost.

erosion

The cash flows of a new project that come at the expense of a firm's existing projects.

Net Working Capital

Normally, a project will require that the firm invest in net working capital in addition to long-term assets. For example, a project will generally need some amount of cash on hand to pay any expenses that arise. In addition, a project will need an initial investment in inventories and accounts receivable (to cover credit sales). Some of this financing will be in the form of amounts owed to suppliers (accounts payable), but the firm will have to supply the balance. This balance represents the investment in net working capital.

It's easy to overlook an important feature of net working capital in capital budgeting. As a project winds down, inventories are sold, receivables are collected, bills are paid, and cash balances can be drawn down. These activities free up the net working capital originally invested. So, the firm's investment in project net working capital closely resembles a loan. The firm supplies working capital at the beginning and recovers it towards the end.

Financing Costs

In analyzing a proposed investment, we will *not* include interest paid or any other financing costs such as dividends or principal repaid, because we are interested in the cash flow generated by the assets of the project. As we mentioned in Chapter 2, interest paid, for example, is a component of cash flow to creditors, not cash flow from assets.

---

[2]If the asset in question is unique, then the opportunity cost might be higher because there might be other valuable projects we could undertake that would use it. However, if the asset in question is of a type that is routinely bought and sold (a used car, perhaps), then the opportunity cost is always the going price in the market because that is the cost of buying another one.

[3]More colorfully, erosion is sometimes called *piracy* or *cannibalism*.

More generally, our goal in project evaluation is to compare the cash flow from a project to the cost of acquiring that project in order to estimate NPV. The particular mixture of debt and equity that a firm actually chooses to use in financing a project is a managerial variable and primarily determines how project cash flow is divided between owners and creditors. This is not to say that financing arrangements are unimportant. They are just something to be analyzed separately. We will cover this in later chapters.

Other Issues

There are some other things to watch out for. First, we are only interested in measuring cash flow. Moreover, we are interested in measuring it when it actually occurs, not when it accrues in an accounting sense. Second, we are always interested in *aftertax* cash flow since taxes are definitely a cash outflow. In fact, whenever we write *incremental cash flows,* we mean aftertax incremental cash flows. Remember, however, that aftertax cash flow and accounting profit or net income are entirely different things.

⌐CONCEPT QUESTIONS
8.2a What is a sunk cost? An opportunity cost?
8.2b Explain what erosion is and why it is relevant.
8.2c Explain why interest paid is not a relevant cash flow for project evaluation.

PRO FORMA FINANCIAL STATEMENTS AND ⌐8.3 PROJECT CASH FLOWS

The first thing we need when we begin evaluating a proposed investment is a set of pro forma or projected financial statements. Given these, we can develop the projected cash flows from the project. Once we have the cash flows, we can estimate the value of the project using the techniques we described in the previous chapter.

Getting Started: Pro Forma Financial Statements

Pro forma financial statements are a convenient and easily understood means of summarizing much of the relevant information for a project. To prepare these statements, we will need estimates of quantities such as unit sales, the selling price per unit, the variable cost per unit, and total fixed costs. We will also need to know the total investment required, including any investment in net working capital.

To illustrate, suppose we think we can sell 50,000 cans of shark attractant per year at a price of $4.00 per can. It costs us about $2.50 per can to make the attractant, and a new product such as this one typically has only a three-year life (perhaps because the customer base dwindles rapidly). We require a 20 percent return on new products.

pro forma financial statements
Financial statements projecting future years' operations.

Table 8.1

Projected income statement, shark attractant project

Sales (50,000 units at $4.00/unit)	$200,000
Variable costs ($2.50/unit)	125,000
	$ 75,000
Fixed costs	$ 12,000
Depreciation ($90,000/3)	30,000
EBIT	$ 33,000
Taxes (34%)	11,220
Net income	$ 21,780

Table 8.2

Projected capital requirements, shark attractant project

	Year			
	0	1	2	3
Net working capital	$ 20,000	$20,000	$20,000	$20,000
Net fixed assets	90,000	60,000	30,000	0
Total investment	$110,000	$80,000	$50,000	$20,000

Fixed costs for the project, including such things as rent on the production facility, will run $12,000 per year.[4] Further, we will need to invest a total of $90,000 in manufacturing equipment. For simplicity, we will assume that this $90,000 will be 100 percent depreciated over the three-year life of the project.[5] Furthermore, the cost of removing the equipment will roughly equal its actual value in three years, so it will be essentially worthless on a market value basis as well. Finally, the project will require an initial $20,000 investment in net working capital. As usual, the tax rate is 34 percent.

In Table 8.1, we organize these initial projections by first preparing the pro forma income statement. Once again, notice that we have *not* deducted any interest expense. This will always be so. As we described earlier, interest paid is a financing expense, not a component of operating cash flow.

We can also prepare a series of abbreviated balance sheets that show the capital requirements for the project as we've done in Table 8.2. Here we have net working capital of $20,000 in each year. Fixed assets are $90,000 at the start of the project's life (Year 0), and they decline by the $30,000 in depreciation each year, ending up at zero. Notice that the total investment given here for future years is the total book or accounting value, not market value.

At this point, we need to start converting this accounting information into cash flows. We consider how to do this next.

---

[4]By fixed cost, we literally mean a cash outflow that will occur regardless of the level of sales. This should not be confused with some sort of accounting period charge.

[5]We will also assume that a full year's depreciation can be taken in the first year.

Sales	$200,000	
Variable costs	125,000	
Fixed costs	12,000	
Depreciation	30,000	
Earnings before interest and taxes (EBIT)	$ 33,000	
Taxes (34%)	$ 11,220	
Net income	$ 21,780	

Table 8.3

Projected income statement, shark attractant project

Project Cash Flows

To develop the cash flows from a project, we need to recall (from Chapter 2) that cash flow from assets has three components: operating cash flow, capital spending, and additions to net working capital. To evaluate a project or minifirm, we need to arrive at estimates for each of these.

Once we have estimates of the components of cash flow, we will calculate cash flow for our minifirm just as we did in Chapter 2 for an entire firm:

Project cash flow = Project operating cash flow

− Project additions to net working capital

− Project capital spending

We consider these components next.

Project Operating Cash Flow   To determine the operating cash flow associated with a project, we first need to recall the definition of operating cash flow:

Operating cash flow = Earnings before interest and taxes (EBIT)

+ Depreciation

− Taxes

To illustrate the calculation of operating cash flow, we will use the projected information from the shark attractant project. For ease of reference, Table 8.3 repeats the income statement.

Given the income statement in Table 8.3, calculating the operating cash flow is very straightforward. As we see in Table 8.4, projected operating cash flow for the shark attractant project is $51,780.

Project Net Working Capital and Capital Spending   We next need to take care of the fixed asset and net working capital requirements. Based on our balance sheets above, the firm must spend $90,000 up front for fixed assets

Table 8.4		
Projected operating cash flow, shark attractant project	EBIT	$ 33,000
	Depreciation	+30,000
	Taxes	−11,220
	Operating cash flow	$ 51,780

Table 8.5		Year			
Projected total cash flows, shark attractant project		0	1	2	3
	Operating cash flow		$51,780	$51,780	$51,780
	Additions to NWC	−$ 20,000			+ 20,000
	Capital spending	− 90,000			
	Total project cash flow	−$110,000	$51,780	$51,780	$71,780

and invest an additional $20,000 in net working capital. The immediate out-flow is thus $110,000. At the end of the project's life, the fixed assets are worthless, but the firm will recover the $20,000 that was tied up in working capital.[6] This will lead to a $20,000 *inflow* in the last year.

On a purely mechanical level, notice that whenever we have an investment in net working capital, that same investment has to be recovered; in other words, the same number needs to appear with the opposite sign.

Projected Total Cash Flow and Value

Given the information we've accumulated, we can finish the preliminary cash flow analysis as illustrated in Table 8.5.

Now that we have cash flow projections, we are ready to apply the various criteria we discussed in the last chapter. First, the NPV at the 20 percent required return is:

$$NPV = -\$110,000 + \$51,780/1.2 + \$51,780/1.2^2 + \$71,780/1.2^3$$

$$= \$10,648$$

So, based on these projections, the project creates over $10,000 in value and should be accepted. Also, the return on this investment obviously exceeds 20 percent (since the NPV is positive at 20 percent). After some trial and error, we find that the IRR works out to be about 25.8 percent.

---

[6]In reality, the firm would probably recover something less than 100 percent of this amount because of bad debts, inventory loss, and so on. If we wanted to, we could just assume that, for example, only 90 percent was recovered and proceed from there.

In addition, if required, we could go ahead and calculate the payback and the average accounting return (AAR). Inspection of the cash flows shows that the payback on this project is just a little over two years (check that it's about 2.1 years).[7]

From the last chapter, the AAR is average net income divided by average book value. The net income each year is $21,780. The average (in thousands) of the four book values (from Table 8.2) for total investment is ($110 + 80 + 50 + 20)/4 = $65, so the AAR is $21,780/65,000 = 33.51 percent.[8] We've already seen that the return on this investment (the IRR) is about 26 percent. The fact that the AAR is larger illustrates again why the AAR cannot be meaningfully interpreted as the return on a project.

⌐ CONCEPT QUESTIONS

8.3a What is the definition of project operating cash flow? How does this differ from net income?

8.3b In the shark attractant project, why did we add back the firm's net working capital investment in the final year?

MORE ON PROJECT CASH FLOW ⌐ 8.4

In this section, we take a closer look at some aspects of project cash flow. In particular, we discuss project net working capital in more detail. We then examine current tax laws regarding depreciation. Finally, we work through a more involved example of the capital investment decision.

A Closer Look at Net Working Capital

In calculating operating cash flow, we did not explicitly consider the fact that some of our sales might be on credit. Also, we may not have actually paid some of the costs shown. In either case, the cash flow has not yet occurred. We show here that these possibilities are not a problem as long as we don't forget to include additions to net working capital in our analysis. This discussion thus emphasizes the importance and the effect of doing so.

Suppose that during a particular year of a project we have the following simplified income statement:

Sales	$500
Costs	310
Net income	$190

---

[7]We're guilty of a minor inconsistency here. When we calculated the NPV and the IRR, we assumed that all the cash flows occurred at end of year. When we calculated the payback, we assumed that the cash flow occurred uniformly throughout the year.

[8]Notice that the average total book value is not the initial total of $110,000 divided by 2. The reason is that the $20,000 in working capital doesn't "depreciate."

In Their Own Words . . .

Samuel Weaver on Capital Budgeting at Hershey Foods Corporation

The capital program at Hershey Foods Corporation and most Fortune 500/1,000 companies involves a three-phase approach: planning/budgeting, evaluation, and post-completion reviews.

The first phase involves identification of likely projects at strategic planning time. These are selected to support the strategic objectives of the corporation. This identification is generally broad in scope with minimal financial evaluation attached. As the planning process focuses more closely on the short-term plans, major capital expenditures are scrutinized more rigorously. Project costs are more closely honed, and specific projects may be reconsidered.

Each project is then individually reviewed and authorized. Planning, developing, and refining cash flows underlie the capital program at Hershey Foods. Once the cash flows have been determined, the application of capital evaluation techniques such as net present value, internal rate of return, and payback period is routine. Presentation of the results is enhanced using sensitivity analysis, which plays a major role for management in assessing the critical assumptions and resulting impact.

The final phase relates to post-completion reviews in which the original forecasts of the project's performance are compared to actual results and/or revised expectations.

Capital expenditure analysis is only as good as the assumptions that underlie the project. The old cliché of "GIGO" (Garbage In, Garbage Out) applies in this case. Incremental cash flows primarily result from incremental sales or margin improvements (cost savings). For the most part, a range of incremental cash flows can be identified from marketing research or engineering studies. However, for a number of projects, correctly discerning the implications and the relevant cash flows is analytically challenging. For example, when a new product is introduced and is expected to generate millions of dollars worth of sales, the appropriate analysis focuses only on the incremental sales after accounting for cannibalization of existing products.

One of the problems that we face at Hershey Foods deals with the application of net present value (NPV) versus internal rate of return (IRR). NPV offers the correct investment indication when dealing with mutually exclusive alternatives. However, decision makers at all levels sometimes find it difficult to comprehend the result. Specifically, an NPV of, say, $535,000 needs to be interpreted. It is not enough to know that the NPV is positive or even more positive than an alternative. Decision makers seek a level of "comfort" of how profitable the investment is by relating it to other standards.

Although the IRR may provide a misleading indication of which project to select, the result is provided in a way that can be interpreted by all parties. The resulting IRR can be mentally compared to expected inflation, current borrowing rates, the cost of capital, an equity portfolio's return, and so on. An IRR of, say, 18 percent is readily interpretable by management. Perhaps this ease of understanding is why surveys indicate that most Fortune 500 or Fortune 1,000 companies use the IRR method as a primary evaluation technique.

In addition to the NPV versus IRR problem, there are a limited number of projects for which traditional and capital expenditure analysis is difficult to apply because the cash flows can't be determined. When new computer equipment is purchased, an office building is renovated, or a parking lot is repaved, it is essentially impossible to identify the cash flows, so the use of traditional evaluation techniques is limited. These types of "capital expenditure" decisions are made using other techniques that hinge on management's judgment.

Samuel Weaver, Ph.D., is Manager of Corporate Financial Analysis for the Hershey Foods Corporation. He is a certified management accountant, and he currently serves on the board of directors of the Financial Management Association. His current position combines the theoretical with the pragmatic and involves the analysis of many different facets of finance in addition to capital expenditure analysis.

Depreciation and taxes are zero. No fixed assets are purchased during the year. Also, to illustrate a point, we assume that the only components of net working capital are accounts receivable and payable. The beginning and ending amounts for these accounts are:

	Beginning of Year	End of Year	Change
Accounts receivable	$880	$910	+$30
Accounts payable	550	605	+ 55
Net working capital	$330	$305	−$25

Based on this information, what is total cash flow for the year? We can first just mechanically apply what we have been discussing to come up with the answer. Operating cash flow in this particular case is the same as EBIT since there are no taxes or depreciation and thus equals $190. Also, notice that net working capital actually *declined* by $25, so the "addition" to net working capital is negative. This just means that $25 was freed up during the year. There was no capital spending, so the total cash flow for the year is:

$$\text{Total cash flow} = \text{Operating cash flow} - \text{Additions to NWC}$$
$$- \text{Capital spending}$$
$$= \$190 - (-\$25) - \$0$$
$$= \$215$$

Now, we know that this $215 total cash flow has to be "dollars in" less "dollars out" for the year. We could therefore ask a different question: What were cash revenues for the year? Also, what were cash costs?

To determine cash revenues, we need to look more closely at net working capital. During the year, we had sales of $500. However, accounts receivable rose by $30 over the same time period. What does this mean? The $30 increase tells us that sales exceeded collections by $30. In other words, we haven't yet received the cash from $30 of the $500 in sales. As a result, our cash inflow is $500 − 30 = $470. In general, cash income is sales minus the increase in accounts receivable.

Cash outflows can be similarly determined. We show costs of $310 on the income statement, but accounts payable increased by $55 during the year. This means that we have not yet paid $55 of the $310, so cash costs for the period are just $310 − 55 = $255. In other words, in this case, cash costs equal costs less the increase in accounts payable.[9]

Putting this information together, cash inflows less cash outflows is $470 − 255 = $215, just as we had before. Notice that:

$$\text{Cash flow} = \text{Cash inflow} - \text{Cash outflow}$$
$$= (\$500 - 30) - (\$310 - 55)$$
$$= (\$500 - \$310) - (30 - 55)$$

---

[9] If there were other accounts, we might have to make some further adjustments. For example, a net increase in inventory would be a cash outflow.

$$= \text{Operating cash flow} - \text{Change in NWC}$$

$$= \$190 - (-25)$$

$$= \$215$$

More generally, this example illustrates that including net working capital changes in our calculations has the effect of adjusting for the discrepancy between accounting sales and costs and actual cash receipts and payments.

Example 8.1   Cash Collections and Costs

For the year just completed, the Combat Wombat Telestat Co. (CWT) reports sales of $998 and costs of $734. You have collected the following beginning and ending balance sheet information:

	Beginning	Ending
Accounts receivable	$100	$110
Inventory	100	80
Accounts payable	100	70
Net working capital	$100	$120

Based on these figures, what are cash inflows? Cash outflows? What happened to each account? What is net cash flow?

Sales were $998, but receivables rose by $10. So cash collections were $10 less than sales, or $988. Costs were $734, but inventories fell by $20. This means that we didn't replace $20 worth of inventory, so costs are actually overstated by this amount. Also, payables fell by $30. This means that, on a net basis, we actually paid our suppliers $30 more than we received from them, resulting in a $30 understatement of costs. Adjusting for these events, cash costs are $734 − 20 + 30 = $744. Net cash flow is $988 − 744 = $244.

Finally, notice that net working capital increased by $20 overall. We can check our answer by noting that the original accounting sales less costs of $998 − 734 is $264. In addition, CWT spent $20 on net working capital, so the net result is a cash flow of $264 − 20 = $244, as we calculated. ■

Depreciation

As we note elsewhere, accounting depreciation is a noncash deduction. As a result, depreciation has cash flow consequences only because it influences the tax bill. The way that depreciation is computed for tax purposes is thus the relevant method for capital investment decisions. Not surprisingly, the procedures are governed by tax law. We now discuss some specifics of the depreciation system enacted by the Tax Reform Act of 1986. This system is a modification of the **Accelerated Cost Recovery System (ACRS)** instituted in 1981.

Modified ACRS Depreciation   Calculating depreciation is normally very mechanical. While there are a number of ifs, ands, and buts involved, the basic

Accelerated Cost Recovery System (ACRS)

Depreciation method under U.S. tax law allowing for the accelerated write-off of property under various classifications.

Class	Examples	
3-year	Equipment used in research	
5-year	Autos, computers	
7-year	Most industrial equipment	

Table 8.6

Modified ACRS
property classes

	Property Class			
Year	3-Year	5-Year	7-Year	
1	33.33%	20.00%	14.29%	
2	44.44	32.00	24.49	
3	14.82	19.20	17.49	
4	7.41	11.52	12.49	
5		11.52	8.93	
6		5.76	8.93	
7			8.93	
8			4.45	

Table 8.7

Modified ACRS
depreciation allowances

idea is that every asset is assigned to a particular class. An asset's class establishes its life for tax purposes. Once an asset's tax life is determined, the depreciation for each year is computed by multiplying the cost of the asset by a fixed percentage.[10] The expected salvage value (what we think the asset will be worth when we dispose of it) and the actual expected economic life (how long we expect the asset to be in service) are not explicitly considered in the calculation of depreciation.

Some typical depreciation classes are described in Table 8.6, and associated percentages (rounded to two decimal places) are shown in Table 8.7.[11]

A nonresidential real property, such as an office building, is depreciated over 31.5 years using straight-line depreciation. A residential real property, such as an apartment building, is depreciated straight-line over 27.5 years. Remember that land cannot be depreciated.[12]

---

[10]Under certain circumstances, the cost of the asset may be adjusted before computing depreciation. The result is called the *depreciable basis,* and depreciation is calculated using this number instead of the actual cost.

[11]For the curious, these depreciation percentages are derived from a 200 percent double-declining balance scheme with a switch to straight-line when it becomes advantageous to do so. Further, there is a half-year convention, meaning that all assets are assumed to be placed in service midway through the tax year. This convention is maintained unless more than 40 percent of an asset's cost is incurred in the final quarter. In this case, a midquarter convention is used.

[12]There are, however, depletion allowances for firms in extraction-type lines of business (e.g., mining). These are similar to depreciation allowances.

To illustrate how depreciation is calculated, we consider an automobile costing $12,000. Autos are normally five-year property. Looking at Table 8.7, the relevant figure for the first year of a five-year asset is 20 percent.[13] The depreciation in the first year is thus $12,000 × .20 = $2,400. The relevant percentage in the second year is 32 percent, so the depreciation in the second year is $12,000 × .32 = $3,840, and so on. We can summarize these calculations as follows:

Year	ACRS Percentage	Depreciation
1	20.00%	.2000 × $12,000 = $ 2,400.00
2	32.00	.3200 × 12,000 = 3,840.00
3	19.20	.1920 × 12,000 = 2,304.00
4	11.52	.1152 × 12,000 = 1,382.40
5	11.52	.1152 × 12,000 = 1,382.40
6	5.76	.0576 × 12,000 = 691.20
	100.00%	$12,000.00

Notice that the ACRS percentages sum up to 100 percent. As a result, we write off 100 percent of the cost of the asset, or $12,000 in this case.

Book Value versus Market Value   In calculating depreciation under current tax law, the economic life and future market value of the asset are not an issue. As a result, the book value of an asset can differ substantially from its actual market value. For example, with our $12,000 car, book value after the first year is $12,000 less the first year's depreciation of $2,400, or $9,600. The remaining book values are summarized in Table 8.8. After six years, the book value of the car is zero.

Suppose that we wanted to sell the car after five years. Based on historical averages, it will be worth, say, 25 percent of the purchase price or .25 × $12,000 = $3,000. If we actually sold it for this, then we would have to pay taxes at the ordinary income tax rate on the difference between the sale price of $3,000 and the book value of $691.20. For a corporation in the 34 percent bracket, the tax liability is .34 × $2,308.80 = $784.99.[14]

The reason that taxes must be paid in this case is that the difference in market value and book value is "excess" depreciation, and it must be "recaptured" when the asset is sold. What this means is that, as it turns out, we overdepreciated the asset by $3,000 − 691.20 = $2,308.80. Since we deducted $2,308.80 too much in depreciation, we paid $784.99 too little in taxes, and we simply have to make up the difference.

---

[13]It may appear odd that five-year property is depreciated over six years. As described elsewhere, the accounting reason is that it is assumed that we only have the asset for six months in the first year and, consequently, six months in the last year. As a result, there are five 12-month periods, but we have some depreciation in six different tax years.

[14]As this is written, with real property, the rules are different and more complicated. Essentially, only the difference between the actual book value and the book value that would have existed if straight-line depreciation were used is recaptured. Anything above the straight-line book value is considered a capital gain.

Year	Beginning Book Value	Depreciation	Ending Book Value
1	$12,000.00	$2,400.00	$9,600.00
2	9,600.00	3,840.00	5,760.00
3	5,760.00	2,304.00	3,456.00
4	3,456.00	1,382.40	2,073.60
5	2,073.60	1,382.40	691.20
6	691.20	691.20	0.00

Table 8.8

ACRS book values

Notice that this is *not* a tax on a capital gain. As a general (albeit rough) rule, a capital gain only occurs if the market price exceeds the original cost. However, what is and what is not a capital gain is ultimately up to taxing authorities, and the specific rules can be very complex. We will ignore capital gains taxes for the most part.

Finally, if the book value exceeds the market value, then the difference is treated as a loss for tax purposes. For example, if we sell the car after two years for $4,000, then the book value exceeds the market value by $1,760. In this case, a tax *saving* of .34 × $1,760 = $598.40 occurs.

Example 8.2   ACRS Depreciation

The Staple Supply Co. has just purchased a new computerized information system with an installed cost of $160,000. The computer is treated as five-year property. What are the yearly depreciation allowances? Based on historical experience, we think that the system will be worth only $10,000 when we get rid of it in four years. What are the tax consequences of the sale? What is the total aftertax cash flow from the sale?

The yearly depreciation allowances are calculated by just multiplying $160,000 by the five-year percentages in Table 8.7 above:

Year	ACRS Percentage	Depreciation	Ending Book Value
1	20.00%	.2000 × $160,000 = $ 32,000	$128,000
2	32.00	.3200 × 160,000 = 51,200	76,800
3	19.20	.1920 × 160,000 = 30,720	46,080
4	11.52	.1152 × 160,000 = 18,432	27,648
5	11.52	.1152 × 160,000 = 18,432	9,216
6	5.76	.0576 × 160,000 = 9,216	0
	100.00%	$160,000	

Notice that we have also computed the book value of the system as of the end of each year. The book value at the end of Year 4 is $27,648. If we sell it for $10,000 at that time, we will have a loss of $17,648 (the difference) for tax purposes. This loss, of course, is like depreciation because it isn't a cash expense.

What really happens? Two things. First, we get $10,000 from the buyer. Second, we save .34 × $17,648 = $6,000 in taxes. So the total aftertax cash flow from the sale is a $16,000 cash inflow. ∎

An Example: The Majestic Mulch and Compost Company (MMCC)

At this point, we want to go through a somewhat more involved capital budgeting analysis. Keep in mind as you read that the basic approach here is exactly the same as that in the shark attractant example above. We have only added on some more "real-world" detail (and a lot more numbers).

MMCC is investigating the feasibility of a new line of power mulching tools aimed at the growing number of home composters. Based on exploratory conversations with buyers for large garden shops, we project unit sales as follows:

Year	Unit Sales
1	3,000
2	5,000
3	6,000
4	6,500
5	6,000
6	5,000
7	4,000
8	3,000

The new power mulcher will be priced to sell at $120 per unit to start. When the competition catches up after three years, however, we anticipate that the price will drop to $110.

The power mulcher project will require $20,000 in net working capital at the start. Subsequently, total net working capital at the end of each year will be about 15 percent of sales for that year. The variable cost per unit is $60, and total fixed costs are $25,000 per year.

It will cost about $800,000 to buy the equipment necessary to begin production. This investment is primarily in industrial equipment and thus qualifies as seven-year ACRS property. The equipment will actually be worth about 20 percent of its cost in eight years, or .20 × $800,000 = $160,000. The relevant tax rate is 34 percent, and the required return is 15 percent. Based on this information, should MMCC proceed?

Operating Cash Flows   There is a lot of information here that we need to organize. The first thing we can do is calculate projected sales. Sales in the first year are projected at 3,000 units at $120 apiece, or $360,000 total. The remaining figures are shown in Table 8.9.

Next, we compute the depreciation on the $800,000 investment in Table 8.10.

With this information, we can prepare the pro forma income statements, as shown in Table 8.11 (on page 272).

From here, computing the operating cash flows is straightforward. The results are illustrated in the first part of Table 8.12 (on page 273).

Additions to NWC   Now that we have the operating cash flows, we need to determine the additions to NWC. By assumption, net working capital re-

Year	Unit Price	Unit Sales	Revenues	**Table 8.9**
1	$120	3,000	$360,000	Projected revenues, power mulcher project
2	120	5,000	600,000	
3	120	6,000	720,000	
4	110	6,500	715,000	
5	110	6,000	660,000	
6	110	5,000	550,000	
7	110	4,000	440,000	
8	110	3,000	330,000	

Year	ACRS Percentage	Depreciation	Ending Book Value	**Table 8.10**
1	14.29%	.1429 × $800,000 = $114,320	$685,680	Annual depreciation, power mulcher project
2	24.49	.2449 × 800,000 = 195,920	489,760	
3	17.49	.1749 × 800,000 = 139,920	349,840	
4	12.49	.1249 × 800,000 = 99,920	249,920	
5	8.93	.0893 × 800,000 = 71,440	178,480	
6	8.93	.0893 × 800,000 = 71,440	107,040	
7	8.93	.0893 × 800,000 = 71,440	35,600	
8	4.45	.0445 × 800,000 = 35,600	0	
	100.00%	$800,000		

quirements change as sales change. In each year, we will generally either add to or recover some of our project net working capital. Recalling that NWC starts out at $20,000 and then rises to 15 percent of sales, we can calculate the amount of NWC for each year as illustrated in Table 8.13 (on page 274).

As illustrated, during the first year, net working capital grows from $20,000 to .15 × 360,000 = $54,000. The increase in net working capital for the year is thus $54,000 − 20,000 = $34,000. The remaining figures are calculated the same way.

Remember that an increase in net working capital is a cash outflow, so a negative sign in this table represents net working capital returning to the firm. Thus, for example, $16,500 in NWC flows back to the firm in Year 6. Over the project's life, net working capital builds to a peak of $108,000 and declines from there as sales begin to drop off.

We show the result for additions to net working capital in the second part of Table 8.12. Notice that at the end of the project's life there is $49,500 in net working capital still to be recovered. Therefore, in the last year, the project returns $16,500 of NWC during the year and then returns the remaining $49,500 for a total of $66,000 (the "addition" to NWC is −$66,000).

Finally, we have to account for the long-term capital invested in the project. In this case, we invest $800,000 at Time 0. By assumption, this equipment

Table 8.11

Projected income statements, power mulcher project

					Year			
	1	2	3	4	5	6	7	8
Unit price	$ 120	$ 120	$ 120	$ 110	$ 110	$ 110	$ 110	$ 110
Unit sales	3,000	5,000	6,000	6,500	6,000	5,000	4,000	3,000
Revenues	$360,000	$600,000	$720,000	$715,000	$660,000	$550,000	$440,000	$330,000
Variable costs	180,000	300,000	360,000	390,000	360,000	300,000	240,000	180,000
Fixed costs	25,000	25,000	25,000	25,000	25,000	25,000	25,000	25,000
Depreciation	114,320	195,920	139,920	99,920	71,440	71,440	71,440	35,600
EBIT	$ 40,680	$ 79,080	$195,080	$200,080	$203,560	$153,560	$103,560	$ 89,400
Taxes	13,831	26,887	66,327	68,027	69,210	52,210	35,210	30,396
Net income	$ 26,849	$ 52,193	$128,753	$132,053	$134,350	$101,350	$ 68,350	$ 59,004

Table 8.12

Projected cash flows, power mulcher project

		Year							
	0	1	2	3	4	5	6	7	8
I. Operating Cash Flow									
EBIT		$40,680	$79,080	$195,080	$200,080	$203,560	$153,560	$103,560	$89,400
Depreciation		114,320	195,920	139,920	99,920	71,440	71,440	71,440	35,600
Taxes		$-$ 13,831	$-$ 26,887	$-$ 66,327	$-$ 68,027	$-$ 69,210	$-$ 52,210	$-$ 35,210	$-$ 30,396
Operating cash flow		$141,169	$248,113	$268,673	$231,973	$205,790	$172,790	$139,790	$94,604
II. Net Working Capital									
Initial NWC	$20,000								
Increases in NWC		$34,000	$36,000	$18,000	$-$ 750	$-$ 8,250	$-$ 16,500	$-$ 16,500	$-$ 16,500
NWC recovery									49,500
Additions to NWC	$20,000	$34,000	$36,000	$18,000	$-$ 750	$-$ 8,250	$-$ 16,500	$-$ 16,500	$-$ 66,000
III. Capital Spending									
Initial outlay	$800,000								
Aftertax salvage									$-$105,600
Capital spending	$800,000								$-$105,600

273

Table 8.13	Year	Revenues	Net Working Capital	Increase
Additions to net working capital, power mulcher project	0		$ 20,000	
	1	$360,000	54,000	$34,000
	2	600,000	90,000	36,000
	3	720,000	108,000	18,000
	4	715,000	107,250	− 750
	5	660,000	99,000	− 8,250
	6	550,000	82,500	− 16,500
	7	440,000	66,000	− 16,500
	8	330,000	49,500	− 16,500

will be worth $160,000 at the end of the project. It will have a book value of zero at that time. As we discussed above, this $160,000 excess of market value over book value is taxable, so the aftertax proceeds will be $160,000 × (1 − .34) = $105,600. These figures are shown in the third part of Table 8.12.

Total Cash Flow and Value   We now have all the cash flow pieces, and we put them together in Table 8.14. In addition to the total project cash flows, we have calculated the cumulative cash flows and the discounted cash flows. At this point, it's essentially "plug and chug" to calculate the net present value, internal rate of return, and payback.

If we sum the discounted flows and the initial investment, the net present value (at 15 percent) works out to be $65,488. This is positive, so, based on these preliminary projections, the power mulcher project is acceptable. The internal or DCF rate of return is greater than 15 percent since the NPV is positive. It works out to be 17.24 percent, again indicating that the project is acceptable.

Looking at the cumulative cash flows, we see that the project has almost paid back after four years since the cumulative cash flow is almost zero at that time. As indicated, the fractional year works out to be 17,322/214,040 = .09, so the payback is 4.09 years. We can't say whether or not this is good since we don't have a benchmark for MMCC. This is the usual problem with payback periods.

This completes our preliminary DCF analysis. Where do we go from here? If we have a great deal of confidence in our projections, then there is no further analysis to be done. We should begin production and marketing immediately. It is unlikely that this will be the case. It is important to remember that the result of our analysis is an *estimate* of NPV, and we will usually have less than complete confidence in our projections. This means we have more work to do. In particular, we will almost surely want to spend some time evaluating the quality of our estimates. We will take up this subject in the next chapter. For now, we take a look at some alternative definitions of operating cash flow, and we illustrate some different cases that arise in capital budgeting.

Table 8.14

Projected total cash flow, power mulcher project

					Year				
	0	1	2	3	4	5	6	7	8
Operating cash flow		$141,169	$248,113	$268,673	$231,973	$205,790	$172,790	$139,790	$ 94,604
Additions to NWC	–$ 20,000	– 34,000	– 36,000	– 18,000	750	8,250	16,500	16,500	66,000
Capital spending	– 800,000								105,600
Total project cash flow	–$820,000	$107,169	$212,113	$250,673	$232,723	$214,040	$189,290	$156,290	$266,204
Cumulative cash flow	–$820,000	–$712,831	–$500,718	–$250,045	–$ 17,322	$196,718	$386,008	$542,298	$808,502
Discounted cash flow @ 15%	– 820,000	93,190	160,388	164,821	133,060	106,416	81,835	58,755	87,023

Net present value (15%) = $65,488
Internal rate of return = 17.24%
Payback   = 4.09 years

275

⌐CONCEPT QUESTIONS

8.4a Why is it important to consider additions to net working capital in developing cash flows? What is the effect of doing so?

8.4b How is depreciation calculated for fixed assets under current tax law? What effect do expected salvage value and estimated economic life have on the calculated depreciation deduction?

8.5 │ ALTERNATIVE DEFINITIONS OF OPERATING CASH FLOW

The analysis we have been through in the previous section is quite general and can be adapted to just about any capital investment problem. In the next section, we illustrate some particularly useful variations. Before we do so, we need to discuss the fact that there are different definitions of project operating cash flow that are commonly used, both in practice and in finance texts.

As we will see, the different approaches to operating cash flow that exist all measure the same thing. If they are used correctly, they all produce the same answer, and one is not necessarily any better or more useful than another. Unfortunately, the fact that alternative definitions are used does sometimes lead to confusion. For this reason, we examine several of these variations next to see how they are related.

In the discussion below, keep in mind that when we speak of cash flow, we literally mean dollars in less dollars out. This is all that we are concerned with. Different definitions of operating cash flow simply amount to different ways of manipulating basic information about sales, costs, depreciation, and taxes to get at cash flow.

For a particular project and year under consideration, suppose we have the following estimates:

Sales = $1,500

Costs = $700

Depreciation = $600

With these definitions, notice that EBIT is:

$$EBIT = Sales - Costs - Depreciation$$
$$= \$1,500 - 700 - 600$$
$$= \$200$$

Once again, we assume that no interest is paid, so the tax bill is:

$$Taxes = EBIT \times T_c$$
$$= \$200 \times .34 = \$68$$

where T_c, the corporate tax rate, is 34 percent.

When we put all of this together, project operating cash flow (OCF) is:

OCF = EBIT + Depreciation − Taxes

    = $200 + 600 − 68 = $732

It turns out that there are some other ways to determine OCF that could be (and are) used. We consider these next.

The Bottom-Up Approach

Since we are ignoring any financing expenses such as interest in our calculations of project OCF, we can write project net income as:

Project net income = EBIT − Taxes

                  = $200 − 68

                  = $132

If we simply add the depreciation to both sides, we arrive at a slightly different and very common expression for OCF:

OCF = Net income + Depreciation   [8.1]

    = $132 + 600

    = $732

This is the *bottom-up* approach. Here we start with the accountant's bottom line (net income) and add back any noncash deductions such as depreciation. It is crucial to remember that this definition of operating cash flow as net income plus depreciation is correct only if there is no interest expense subtracted in the calculation of net income.

For the shark attractant project, net income was $21,780 and depreciation was $30,000, so the bottom-up calculation is:

OCF = $21,780 + 30,000 = $51,780

This is exactly the same OCF we had previously.

The Top-Down Approach

Perhaps the most obvious way to calculate OCF is:

OCF = Sales − Costs − Taxes   [8.2]

    = $1,500 − 700 − 68 = $732

This is the *top-down* approach, the second variation of the basic OCF definition. Here we start at the top of the income statement with sales and work our way down to net cash flow by subtracting costs, taxes, and other expenses. Along the way, we simply leave out any strictly noncash items such as depreciation.

For the shark attractant project, the top-down cash flow can be readily calculated. With sales of $200,000, total costs (fixed plus variable) of $137,000, and a tax bill of $11,220, the OCF is:

$$OCF = \$200,000 - 137,000 - 11,220 = \$51,780$$

This is just as we had before.

The Tax Shield Approach

The third variation on our basic definition of OCF is the *tax shield* approach. This approach will be very useful for some problems we consider in the next section. The tax shield definition of OCF is:

$$OCF = (Sales - Costs) \times (1 - T_c) + Depreciation \times T_c \qquad [8.3]$$

where T_c is again the corporate tax rate. Assuming that $T_c = 34\%$, the OCF works out to be:

$$= (\$1,500 - 700) \times .66 + \$600 \times .34$$

$$= \$528 + 204$$

$$= \$732$$

This is just as we had before.

This approach views OCF as having two components. The first part is what the project's cash flow would be if there were no depreciation expense. In this case, this would-have-been cash flow is $528.

The second part of OCF in this case is the depreciation deduction multiplied by the tax rate. This is called the **depreciation tax shield**. We know that depreciation is a noncash expense. The only cash flow effect from deducting depreciation is to reduce our taxes, a benefit to us. At the current 34 percent corporate tax rate, every dollar in depreciation expense saves us 34 cents in taxes. So, in our example, the $600 depreciation deduction saves us $600 × .34 = $204 in taxes.

depreciation tax shield

Tax saving that results from the depreciation deduction, calculated as depreciation multiplied by the corporate tax rate.

For the shark attractant project we considered earlier in the chapter, the depreciation tax shield would be $30,000 × .34 = $10,200. The aftertax value for sales less costs would be ($200,000 − 137,000) × (1 − .34) = $41,580. Adding these together yields the right answer:

$$OCF = \$41,580 + 10,200 = \$51,780$$

This calculation verifies that the tax shield approach is completely equivalent to the approach we used before.

Now that we've seen that all of these approaches are the same, you're probably wondering why everybody doesn't just agree on one of them. One reason, as we will see in the next section, is that different approaches are useful in different circumstances. The best one to use is whichever happens to be the most convenient for the problem at hand.

⌐ CONCEPT QUESTIONS

8.5a What are the top-down and bottom-up definitions of operating cash flow?

8.5b What is meant by the term *depreciation tax shield?*

SOME SPECIAL CASES OF DISCOUNTED CASH FLOW ANALYSIS | 8.6

To finish our chapter, we look at three common cases involving discounted cash flow analysis. The first case involves investments that are primarily aimed at improving efficiency and thereby cutting costs. The second case we consider comes up when a firm is involved in submitting competitive bids. The third and final case arises in choosing between equipment with different economic lives.

There are many other special cases that we could consider, but these three are particularly important because problems similar to these are so common. Also, they illustrate some very diverse applications of cash flow analysis and DCF valuation.

Evaluating Cost-Cutting Proposals

One decision we frequently face is whether or not to upgrade existing facilities to make them more cost-effective. The issue is whether or not the cost savings are large enough to justify the necessary capital expenditure.

For example, suppose we are considering automating some part of an existing production process. The necessary equipment costs $80,000 to buy and install. It will save $22,000 per year (pretax) by reducing labor and material costs. For simplicity, assume that the equipment has a five-year life and is depreciated to zero on a straight-line basis over that period. It will actually be worth $20,000 in five years. Should we do it? The tax rate is 34 percent, and the discount rate is 10 percent.

As always, the first step in making this decision is to identify the relevant incremental cash flows. First, determining the relevant capital spending is easy enough. The initial cost is $80,000. The aftertax salvage value is $20,000 × (1 − .34) = $13,200 since the book value will be zero in five years. Second, there are no working capital consequences here, so we don't need to worry about additions to net working capital.

Operating cash flows are the third component. Buying the new equipment affects our operating cash flows in two ways. First, we save $22,000 pretax every year. In other words, the firm's operating income increases by $22,000, so this is the relevant incremental project operating income.

Second, and it's easy to overlook this, we have an additional depreciation deduction. In this case, the depreciation is $80,000/5 = $16,000 per year.

Since the project has an operating income of $22,000 (the annual pretax cost saving) and a depreciation deduction of $16,000, taking the project will increase the firm's EBIT by $22,000 − 16,000 = $6,000, so this is the project's EBIT.

Finally, since EBIT is rising for the firm, taxes will increase. This increase in taxes will be $6,000 × .34 = $2,040. With this information, we can compute operating cash flow in the usual way:

EBIT	$ 6,000
+ Depreciation	16,000
− Taxes	2,040
Operating cash flow	$19,960

So our aftertax operating cash flow is $19,960.

It might be somewhat more enlightening to calculate operating cash flow using a different approach. What is actually going on here is very simple. First of all, the cost savings increase our pretax income by $22,000. We have to pay taxes on this amount, so our tax bill increases by .34 × $22,000 = $7,480. In other words, the $22,000 pretax saving amounts to $22,000 × (1 − .34) = $14,520 after taxes.

Second, the extra $16,000 in depreciation isn't really a cash outflow, but it does reduce our taxes by $16,000 × .34 = $5,440. The sum of these two components is $14,520 + 5,440 = $19,960, just as we had before. Notice that the $5,440 is the depreciation tax shield we discussed above, and we have effectively used the tax shield approach here.

We can now finish off our analysis. Based on our discussion, the relevant cash flows are:

	Year					
	0	1	2	3	4	5
Operating cash flow		$19,960	$19,960	$19,960	$19,960	$19,960
Capital spending	−$80,000					13,200
Total cash flow	−$80,000	$19,960	$19,960	$19,960	$19,960	$33,160

At 10 percent, it's straightforward to verify that the NPV here is $3,860, so we should go ahead and automate.

Example 8.3 To Buy or Not to Buy

We are considering the purchase of a $200,000 computer-based inventory management system. It will be depreciated straight-line to zero over its four-year life. It will be worth $30,000 at that time. The system would save us $60,000 pretax in inventory-related costs. The relevant tax rate is 39 percent. Because the new setup is more efficient than our existing one, we will be able to carry less total inventory and thus free up $45,000 in net working capital. What is the NPV at 16 percent? What is the DCF return (the IRR) on this investment?

We can first calculate the operating cash flow. The aftertax cost savings are $60,000 × (1 − .39) = $36,600. The depreciation is $200,000/4 = $50,000 per year, so the depreciation tax shield is $50,000 × .39 = $19,500. Operating cash flow is thus $36,600 + 19,500 = $56,100 per year.

The capital spending involves $200,000 up front to buy the system. The aftertax salvage is $30,000 × (1 − .39) = $18,300. Finally, and this is the somewhat tricky part, the initial investment in net working capital is a $45,000 *inflow* because the system frees up working capital. Furthermore, we will have to put this back in at the end of the project's life. What this really means is simple: While the system is in operation, we have $45,000 to use elsewhere.

To finish our analysis, we can compute the total cash flows:

		Year			
	0	1	2	3	4
Operating cash flow		$56,100	$56,100	$56,100	$56,100
Additions to NWC	$ 45,000				− 45,000
Capital spending	− 200,000				18,300
Total cash flow	−$155,000	$56,100	$56,100	$56,100	$29,400

At 16 percent, the NPV is −$12,768, so the investment is not attractive. After some trial and error, we find that the NPV is zero when the discount rate is 11.48 percent, so the IRR on this investment is about 11.5 percent. ■

Setting the Bid Price

Early on, we used discounted cash flow to evaluate a proposed new product. A somewhat different (and very common) scenario arises when we must submit a competitive bid to win a job. Under such circumstances, the winner is whoever submits the lowest bid.

There is an old saw concerning this process: The low bidder is whoever makes the biggest mistake. This is called the winner's curse. In other words, if you win, there is a good chance that you underbid. In this section, we look at how to go about setting the bid price to avoid the winner's curse. The procedure we describe is useful anytime we have to set a price on a product or service.

To illustrate how to go about setting a bid price, imagine that we are in the business of buying stripped-down truck platforms and then modifying them to customer specifications for resale. A local distributor has requested bids for five specially modified trucks each year for the next four years, for a total of 20 trucks in all.

We need to decide what price per truck to bid. The goal of our analysis is to determine the lowest price we can profitably charge. This maximizes our chances of being awarded the contract while guarding against the winner's curse.

Suppose we can buy the truck platforms for $10,000 each. The facilities we need can be leased for $24,000 per year. The labor and material cost to do the modification works out to be about $4,000 per truck. Total cost per year will thus be $24,000 + 5 × ($10,000 + 4,000) = $94,000.

We will need to invest $60,000 in new equipment. This equipment will be depreciated straight-line to a zero salvage value over the four years. It will be worth about $5,000 at that time. We will also need to invest $40,000 in raw materials inventory and other working capital items. The relevant tax rate is 39 percent. What price per truck should we bid if we require a 20 percent return on our investment?

We start out by looking at the capital spending and net working capital investment. We have to spend $60,000 today for new equipment. The aftertax salvage value is $5,000 × (1 − .39) = $3,050. Furthermore, we have to invest $40,000 today in working capital. We will get this back in four years.

We can't determine the operating cash flow just yet because we don't know the sales price. Thus, if we draw a time line, here is what we have so far:

		Year			
	0	1	2	3	4
Operating cash flow		+OCF	+OCF	+OCF	+OCF
Additions to NWC	−$ 40,000				$40,000
Capital spending	− 60,000				3,050
Total cash flow	−$100,000	+OCF	+OCF	+OCF	+OCF + 43,050

With this in mind, here is the key observation: The lowest possible price we can profitably charge will result in a zero NPV at 20 percent. The reason is that at that price, we earn exactly 20 percent on our investment.

Given this observation, we first need to determine what the operating cash flow must be for the NPV to be equal to zero. To do this, we calculate the present value of the $43,050 nonoperating cash flow from the last year and subtract it from the $100,000 initial investment:

$$\$100,000 - \$43,050/1.20^4 = \$100,000 - 20,761 = \$79,239$$

Once we do this, our time line is as follows:

		Year			
	0	1	2	3	4
Total cash flow	−$79,239	+OCF	+OCF	+OCF	+OCF

As the time line suggests, the operating cash flow is now an unknown ordinary annuity amount. The four-year annuity factor for 20 percent is 2.58873, so we have:

$$NPV = 0 = -\$79,239 + OCF \times 2.58873$$

This implies that:

$$OCF = \$79,239/2.58873 = \$30,609$$

So the operating cash flow needs to be $30,609 each year.

We're not quite done. The final problem is to find out what sales price results in an operating cash flow of $30,609. The easiest way to do this is to recall that operating cash flow can be written as net income plus depreciation, the bottom-up definition. The depreciation here is $60,000/4 = $15,000. Given this, we can determine what net income must be:

$$\text{Operating cash flow} = \text{Net income} + \text{Depreciation}$$

$$\$30,609 = \text{Net income} + 15,000$$

$$\text{Net income} = \$15,609$$

From here, we work our way backwards up the income statement. If net income is $15,609, then our income statement is as follows:

Sales	?
Costs	$94,000
Depreciation	15,000
Taxes (39%)	?
Net income	$15,609

So we can solve for sales by noting that:

$$\text{Net income} = (\text{Sales} - \text{Costs} - \text{Depreciation}) \times (1 - T_c)$$

$$\$15,609 = (\text{Sales} - \$94,000 - 15,000) \times (1 - .39)$$

$$\text{Sales} = \$15,609/.61 + \$94,000 + \$15,000$$

$$= \$134,589$$

Sales per year must be $134,589. Since the contract calls for five trucks per year, the sales price has to be $134,589/5 = $26,918. If we round this up a bit, it looks like we need to bid about $27,000 per truck. At this price, were we to get the contract, our return would be just over 20 percent.

Evaluating Equipment with Different Lives

The final problem we consider involves choosing among different possible systems, equipment, or procedures. Our goal is to choose the most cost-effective. The approach we consider here is only necessary when two special circumstances exist. First, the possibilities under evaluation have different economic lives. Second, and just as important, we need whatever we buy more or less indefinitely. As a result, when it wears out, we will buy another one.

We can illustrate this problem with a simple example. Imagine that we are in the business of manufacturing stamped metal subassemblies. Whenever a stamping mechanism wears out, we have to replace it with a new one to stay in business. We are considering which of two stamping mechanisms to buy.

Machine A costs $100 to buy and $10 per year to operate. It wears out and must be replaced every two years. Machine B costs $140 to buy and $8 per year to operate. It lasts for three years and must then be replaced. Ignoring taxes, which one should we go with if we use a 10 percent discount rate?

In comparing the two machines, we notice that the first is cheaper to buy, but it costs more to operate and it wears out quicker. How can we evaluate these trade-offs? We can start by computing the present value of the costs for each:

$$\text{Machine A: PV} = -\$100 + -\$10/1.1 + -\$10/1.1^2 = -\$117.36$$

$$\text{Machine B: PV} = -\$140 + -\$8/1.1 + -\$8/1.1^2 + -\$8/1.1^3$$

$$= -\$159.89$$

Notice that *all* the numbers here are costs, so they all have negative signs. If we stopped here, it might appear that A is the more attractive since the PV of the costs is less. However, all we have really discovered so far is that A effectively provides two years' worth of stamping service for $117.36 while B effectively provides three years' worth for $159.89. These are not directly comparable because of the difference in service periods.

We need to somehow work out a cost per year for these two alternatives. To do this, we ask the question "What amount, paid each year over the life of the machine, has the same PV of costs?" This amount is called the **equivalent annual cost (EAC)**.

equivalent annual cost (EAC)

The present value of a project's costs calculated on an annual basis.

Calculating the EAC involves finding an unknown payment amount. For example, for Machine A, we need to find a two-year ordinary annuity with a PV of −$117.36 at 10 percent. Going back to Chapter 4, the two-year annuity factor is:

$$\text{Annuity factor} = (1 - 1/1.10^2)/.10 = 1.7355$$

For Machine A, then, we have:

$$\text{PV of costs} = -\$117.36 = \text{EAC} \times 1.7355$$

$$\text{EAC} = -\$117.36/1.7355$$

$$= -\$67.62$$

For Machine B, the life is three years, so we first need the three-year annuity factor:

$$\text{Annuity factor} = (1 - 1/1.10^3)/.10 = 2.4869$$

We calculate the EAC for B just as we did for A:

$$\text{PV of costs} = -\$159.89 = \text{EAC} \times 2.4869$$

$$\text{EAC} = -\$159.89/2.4869$$

$$= -\$64.29$$

Based on this analysis, we should purchase B because it effectively costs $64.29 per year versus $67.62 for A. In other words, all things considered, B is cheaper. In this case, the longer life and lower operating cost is more than enough to offset the higher initial purchase price.

Example 8.4   Equivalent Annual Costs

This extended example illustrates what happens to the EAC when we consider taxes. You are evaluating two different pollution control options. A filtration system will cost $1.1 million to install and $60,000 pretax annually to operate. It will have to be completely replaced every five years. A precipitation system will cost $1.9 million to install, but only $10,000 per year to operate. The precipitation equipment has an effective operating life of eight years. Straight-line depreciation is used throughout, and neither system has any salvage value. Which method should we select if we use a 12 percent discount rate? The tax rate is 34 percent.

We need to consider the EACs for the two approaches because they have different service lives, and they will be replaced as they wear out. The relevant information can be summarized as:

	Filtration System	Precipitation System
Aftertax operating cost	−$ 39,600	−$ 6,600
Depreciation tax shield	74,800	80,750
Operating cash flow	$ 35,200	$ 74,150
Economic life	5 years	8 years
Annuity factor (12%)	3.6048	4.9676
Present value of operating cash flow	$ 126,888	$ 368,350
Capital spending	− 1,100,000	− 1,900,000
Total PV of costs	−$ 973,112	−$1,531,650

Notice that the operating cash flow is actually positive in both cases because of the large depreciation tax shields. This can occur whenever the operating cost is small relative to the purchase price.

To decide which system to purchase, we compute the EACs for both using the appropriate annuity factors:

Filtration system: −$973,112 = EAC × 3.6048

EAC = −$269,949 per year

Precipitation system: −$1,531,650 = EAC × 4.9676

EAC = −$308,328 per year

The filtration system is the cheaper of the two, so we select it. In this case, the longer life and smaller operating cost of the precipitation system are not sufficient to offset its higher initial cost. ∎

⌐CONCEPT QUESTIONS

8.6a Under what circumstances do we have to worry about unequal economic lives? How do you interpret the EAC?

8.6b In setting a bid price, we used a zero NPV as our benchmark. Explain why this is appropriate.

8.7 | SUMMARY AND CONCLUSIONS

This chapter describes how to go about putting together a discounted cash flow analysis. In it, we covered:

1. The identification of relevant project cash flows. We discussed project cash flows and described how to handle some issues that often come up, including sunk costs, opportunity costs, financing costs, net working capital, and erosion.

2. Preparing and using pro forma or projected financial statements. We showed how such financial statement information is useful in coming up with projected cash flows, and we also looked at some alternative definitions of operating cash flow.

3. The role of net working capital and depreciation in project cash flows. We saw that including the additions to net working capital was important because it adjusted for the discrepancy between accounting revenues and costs and cash revenues and costs. We also went over the calculation of depreciation expense under current tax law.

4. Some special cases in using discounted cash flow analysis. Here we looked at three special issues: cost-cutting investments, how to go about setting a bid price, and the unequal lives problem.

The discounted cash flow analysis we've covered here is a standard tool in the business world. It is a very powerful tool, so care should be taken in its use. The most important thing is to get the cash flows identified in a way that makes economic sense. This chapter gives you a good start on learning to do this.

Key Terms

incremental cash flows 256	pro forma financial statements 259
stand-alone principle 256	Accelerated Cost Recovery System
sunk cost 257	(ACRS) 266
opportunity cost 257	depreciation tax shield 278
erosion 258	equivalent annual cost (EAC) 284

Chapter Review Problems and Self-Test

These problems will give you some practice with discounted cash flow analysis. The answers appear below.

8.1   Capital Budgeting for Project X   Based on the following
        information for Project X, should we undertake the venture? To
        answer, first prepare a pro forma income statement for each year.
        Next, calculate operating cash flow. Finish the problem by
        determining total cash flow and then calculating NPV assuming a
        20 percent required return. Use a 34 percent tax rate throughout. For
        help, look back at our shark attractant and power mulcher examples.
             Project X is a new type of audiophile-grade stereo amplifier. We
        think we can sell 500 units per year at a price of $10,000 each.
        Variable costs per amplifier will run about $5,000 per unit, and the
        product should have a four-year life.
             Fixed costs for the project will run $610,000 per year. Further, we
        will need to invest a total of $1,100,000 in manufacturing equipment.
        This equipment is seven-year ACRS property for tax purposes. In
        four years, the equipment will be worth about half of what we paid
        for it. We will have to invest $900,000 in net working capital at the start.
        After that, net working capital requirements will be 30 percent of sales.

8.2   Calculating Operating Cash Flow   Mater Pasta, Inc., has projected
        a sales volume of $1,432 for the second year of a proposed expansion
        project. Costs normally run 70 percent of sales, or about $1,002 in
        this case. The depreciation expense will be $80, and the tax rate is
        34 percent. What is the operating cash flow? Calculate your answer
        using all of the approaches (including the top-down, bottom-up, and
        tax shield approaches) described in the chapter.

8.3   Spending Money to Save Money?   For help on this one, refer back
        to the computerized inventory management system in Example 8.3.
        Here, we're contemplating a new, mechanized welding system to
        replace our current manual system. It will cost $600,000 to get the
        new system. The cost will be depreciated straight-line to zero over its
        four-year expected life. The system will actually be worth $100,000 at
        the end of four years.
             We think the new system will save us $180,000 per year pretax in
        labor costs. The tax rate is 34 percent. What are the NPV and return
        on buying the new system? The required return is 15 percent.

Answers to Self-Test Problems

8.1   To develop the pro forma income statements, we need to calculate the
        depreciation for each of the four years. The relevant ACRS
        percentages, depreciation allowances, and book values for the first
        four years are:

Year	ACRS Percentage	Depreciation	Ending Book Value
1	14.29%	.1429 × $1,100,000 = $157,190	$942,810
2	24.49	.2449 × 1,100,000 = 269,390	673,420
3	17.49	.1749 × 1,100,000 = 192,390	481,030
4	12.49	.1249 × 1,100,000 = 137,390	343,640

The projected income statements, therefore, are as follows:

	Year			
	1	2	3	4
Sales	$5,000,000	$5,000,000	$5,000,000	$5,000,000
Variable costs	2,500,000	2,500,000	2,500,000	2,500,000
Fixed costs	610,000	610,000	610,000	610,000
Depreciation	157,190	269,390	192,390	137,390
EBIT	$1,732,810	$1,620,610	$1,697,610	$1,752,610
Taxes (34%)	589,155	551,007	577,187	595,887
Net income	$1,143,655	$1,069,603	$1,120,423	$1,156,723

Based on this information, the operating cash flows are:

	Year			
	1	2	3	4
EBIT	$1,732,810	$1,620,610	$1,697,610	$1,752,610
Depreciation	157,190	269,390	192,390	137,390
Taxes	− 589,155	− 551,007	− 577,187	− 595,887
Operating cash flow	$1,300,845	$1,338,993	$1,312,813	$1,294,113

We now have to worry about the nonoperating cash flows. Net working capital starts out at $900,000 and then rises to 30 percent of sales, or $1,500,000. This is a $600,000 addition to net working capital.

Finally, we have to invest $1,100,000 to get started. In four years, the book value of this investment will be $343,640 compared to an estimated market value of $550,000 (half of the cost). The aftertax salvage is thus $550,000 − .34 × ($550,000 − 343,640) = $479,838.

When we combine all this information, the projected cash flows for Project X are:

	Year				
	0	1	2	3	4
Operating cash flow		$1,300,845	$1,338,993	$1,312,813	$1,294,113
Additions to NWC	−$ 900,000	− 600,000			1,500,000
Capital spending	− 1,100,000				479,838
Total cash flow	−$2,000,000	$ 700,845	$1,338,993	$1,312,813	$3,273,951

With these cash flows, the NPV at 20 percent is:

$$NPV = -\$2,000,000 + 700,845/1.2 + 1,338,993/1.2^2$$
$$+ 1,312,813/1.2^3 + 3,273,951/1.2^4$$
$$= \$1,852,496$$

So this project appears quite profitable.

8.2   First, we can calculate the project's EBIT, its tax bill, and its net income.

$$EBIT = \$1,432 - 1,002 - 80 = \$350$$
$$Taxes = \$350 \times .34 = \$119$$
$$Net\ income = \$350 - 119 = \$231$$

With these numbers, operating cash flow is:

$$OCF = EBIT + Depreciation - Taxes$$
$$= \$350 + 80 - 119$$
$$= \$311$$

Using the other OCF definitions, we have:

$$Bottom\text{-}up\ OCF = Net\ income + Depreciation$$
$$= \$231 + 80$$
$$= \$311$$
$$Top\text{-}down\ OCF = Sales - Costs - Taxes$$
$$= \$1,432 - 1,002 - 119$$
$$= \$311$$
$$Tax\ shield\ OCF = (Sales - Costs) \times (1 - .34) + Depreciation \times .34$$
$$= (\$1,432 - 1,002) \times .66 + 80 \times .34$$
$$= \$311$$

As expected, all of these definitions produce exactly the same answer.

8.3   The $180,000 pretax saving amounts to $(1 - .34) \times \$180,000 = \$118,800$ after taxes. The annual depreciation of $\$600,000/4 = \$150,000$ generates a tax shield of $.34 \times \$150,000 = \$51,000$ each year. Taking these together, the operating cash flow is $\$118,800 + 51,000 = \$169,800$. Since the book value is zero in four years, the aftertax salvage value is $(1 - .34) \times \$100,000 = \$66,000$. There are no working capital consequences, so the cash flows are:

	Year				
	0	1	2	3	4
Operating cash flow		$169,800	$169,800	$169,800	$169,800
Capital spending	−$600,000				66,000
Total cash flow	−$600,000	$169,800	$169,800	$169,800	$235,800

You can verify that the NPV is −$77,489, and the return on the new welding system is only about 8.8 percent. The project does not appear to be profitable.

Questions and Problems

1. Calculating Net Income   A proposed new investment has projected sales in Year 4 of $125,000. Variable costs are 50 percent of sales, and fixed costs are $20,000. Depreciation for the year will be $15,000. Prepare a projected income statement assuming a 34 percent tax rate.

2. Calculating OCF   Consider the following income statement:

Sales	$144,600
Cost	84,780
Depreciation	15,000
Taxes (39%)	?
Net income	?

Fill in the missing numbers and then calculate the operating cash flow. What is the depreciation tax shield?

3. OCF from Several Approaches   A proposed new product has projected sales of $11,996, costs of $8,443, and depreciation of $3,210. The tax rate is 34 percent. Calculate operating cash flow using the four different approaches described in the chapter and verify that the answer is the same in each case.

4. Calculating Depreciation   A piece of newly purchased industrial equipment costs $168,000. It is classified as seven-year property under modified ACRS. Calculate the annual depreciation allowances and end-of-year book values.

5. Depreciation   Our new computer system cost us $80,000. We will outgrow it in three years. When we sell it, we will probably only get 20 percent of the purchase price. The computer will be depreciated as five-year ACRS property. Calculate the depreciation and book values for the three years. What will be the aftertax proceeds from the sale? Assume a 34 percent tax rate.

6. NPV Application   A new electronic process monitor costs $140,000. This cost will be depreciated straight-line to zero over five years. The

monitor will actually be worthless in five years. The new monitor would save us $50,000 per year before taxes in operating costs. If we require a 10 percent return, what is the NPV of the purchase? Assume a tax rate of 34 percent.

7. NPV and NWC Requirements   In the previous question, suppose that the new monitor also requires us to increase net working capital by $10,000 when we buy it. Further suppose that the monitor will actually be worth $20,000 in five years. What is the new NPV?

8. NPV and ACRS   In the previous question, suppose the monitor was classified as three-year ACRS property. All the other facts are the same. Will the NPV be larger or smaller? Why? Calculate the new NPV to verify your answer.

9. Identifying Relevant Costs   Rick Bardles and Ed James are considering building a new bottling plant to meet expected future demand for their new line of tropical coolers. They are considering putting it on a plot of land they have owned for three years. They are in the process of analyzing the idea and comparing it to some others. Bardles says, "Ed, when we do this analysis, we should put in an amount for the cost of the land equal to what we paid for it. After all, it did cost us a pretty penny." James retorts, "No, I don't care how much it cost—we have already paid for it. It is what they call a sunk cost. The cost of the land shouldn't be considered." What would you say to Bardles and James?

10. NPV Applications   We believe we can sell 10,000 home security devices per year at $30 apiece. They cost $20 each to manufacture (variable cost). Fixed production costs will run $30,000 per year. The necessary equipment costs $150,000 to buy and will be depreciated straight-line to a zero salvage value over the five-year life of the project. The actual value will be essentially zero in five years. We will need to invest $40,000 in net working capital up front, but no additional net working capital investment will be necessary. The discount rate is 14 percent, and the tax rate is 34 percent. What do you think of the proposal?

11. Identifying Cash Flows   Suppose a company has $500 in sales during a quarter. Over the quarter, accounts receivable increased by $60. What were cash collections?

12. Cash Flows   Last year, the Presto-Chango Paint Company reported sales of $15,778 and costs of $10,554. The following information was also reported for the same period:

	Beginning	Ending
Accounts receivable	$2,100	$1,910
Inventory	3,400	3,667
Accounts payable	6,100	6,604

Based on this information, what are cash inflows? Cash outflows? What happened to each? What is net cash flow?

13. **Cash Flows and IRR**   We are contemplating the purchase of a $900,000 computer-based customer order management system. The system will be depreciated straight-line to zero over its five-year life. It will be worth $330,000 at that time. We would save $500,000 before taxes per year in order processing costs, and we will be able to reduce working capital by $220,000 (this is a one-time reduction). What is the DCF return on this investment? The relevant tax rate is 34 percent.

14. **Calculating EAC**   You are evaluating two different sound mixers. The Jazzmaster costs $45,000, has a three-year life, and costs $5,000 per year to operate. The Discomaster costs $65,000, has a five-year life, and costs $4,000 per year to operate. The relevant discount rate is 12 percent. Ignoring depreciation and taxes, compute the EAC for both. Which do you prefer?

15. **EAC**   In the previous question, assume that straight-line depreciation is used for both. Furthermore, each has a salvage value of $10,000. The relevant tax rate is 34 percent. Compute the EAC for both. Which is preferred now?

16. **Calculating a Bid Price**   A large retailer has requested a bid for a new point-of-sale credit checking system. The system would be phased in at a rate of 20 stores per year for three years. We can purchase the relevant hardware for $25,000 per installation. The labor and material cost to put the system together and install it is about $10,000 per site. We will need to purchase $250,000 worth of specialized equipment. This will be depreciated straight-line to a zero salvage value over five years. We will sell it in three years, at which time it should be worth about half of what we paid for it. Finally, we will need to invest $60,000 in net working capital. The relevant tax rate is 39 percent. What price per system should we bid if we require a 16 percent return on our investment?

17. **EAC**   Olivaw is a leading manufacturer of positronic brains, a key component in robots. The company is considering two alternative production methods. The costs and lives associated with each are:

Year	Method 1	Method 2
0	$900	$800
1	20	80
2	20	80
3	20	80
4		80

Assuming that Olivaw will *not* replace the equipment when it wears out, which should it buy? If it is going to replace it, which should it buy ($r = 10\%$)? Ignore depreciation and taxes in answering.

18. **Calculating Cash Flows and EAC**   In the previous question, suppose that all the costs are before taxes and the tax rate is 34 percent. The equipment used in Method 1 will be worth $120 in salvage in three

years. Both will be depreciated straight-line to zero over their respective lives. Method 2 will generate a $160 salvage value. What are the EACs in this case? Which is the preferred method?

19. **Cash Flows and NPV**   We project unit sales for a new household-use laser-guided cockroach search and destroy system as follows:

Year	Unit Sales
1	53,000
2	65,000
3	76,000
4	86,000
5	46,000

The new system will be priced to sell at $95 each.

The cockroach eradicator project will require $585,000 in net working capital to start, and total net working capital will rise to 30 percent of sales. The variable cost per unit is $60, and total fixed costs are $25,000 per year. The equipment necessary to begin production will cost a total of $6,500,000. This equipment is mostly industrial machinery and thus qualifies as seven-year ACRS property. In five years, this equipment will actually be worth about 30 percent of its cost. The relevant tax rate is 34 percent, and the required return is 20 percent. Based on these preliminary estimates, what is the NPV of the project?

20. **Replacement Decisions**   Suppose we are thinking about replacing an old computer with a new one. The old one cost us $50,000; the new one will cost $35,000. The new machine will be depreciated straight-line to zero over its five-year life. It will probably be worth about $5,000 after five years.

    Challenge Problem

The old computer is being depreciated at a rate of $10,000 per year. It will be completely written off in three years. If we don't replace it now, we will have to replace it in two years. We can sell it now for $12,000. In two years, it will probably be worth half that. The new machine will save us $5,000 per year in cooling costs. The tax rate is 34 percent, and the discount rate is 10 percent.

a. Suppose that we only consider whether or not we should replace the old computer now without worrying about what's going to happen in two years. What are the relevant cash flows? Should we replace it or not? Hint: Consider the net change in the firm's aftertax cash flows if we do the replacement.

b. Suppose now that we recognize that, if we don't replace now, we will be replacing in two years. Should we replace now or should we wait? Hint: What we effectively have here is a decision to either "invest" in the old computer (by not selling it) or invest in the new one. Notice that the two investments have unequal lives.

21. **Calculating Required Savings**   This is a challenge problem. A proposed cost-saving device has an installed cost of $59,400. It is

classified as three-year ACRS property. It will actually function for five years, at which time it will have no value. There are no working capital consequences from the investment, and the tax rate is 34 percent.

a. What must the pretax cost savings be for us to favor the investment? We require a 10 percent return. Hint: This one is a variation on the problem of setting a bid price.

b. Suppose the device will be worth $11,000 in salvage (before taxes). How does this change your answer?

Challenge Problem

22.   **Cash Flows and Capital Budgeting Choices**   Klaatu Co. has recently completed a $400,000, two-year marketing study. Based on the results, Klaatu has estimated that 10,000 of its new RUR-class robots could be sold annually over the next eight years at a price of $9,615 each. Variable costs per robot are $7,400, and fixed costs total $12 million per year.

Start-up costs include $40 million to build production facilities, $2.4 million in land, and $8 million in net working capital. The $40 million facility will be straight-line depreciated to zero over the project's life. At the end of the project's life, the facilities (including the land) will be sold for an estimated $8.4 million. The value of the land is not expected to change.

Finally, start-up would also entail fully deductible expenses of $1.4 million at year zero. Klaatu is an ongoing, profitable business and pays taxes at a 34 percent rate on all income and gains. Klaatu uses a 10 percent discount rate on projects such as this one. Should Klaatu produce the RUR-class robots?

Suggested Reading

For more on the capital budgeting decision, see:

Bierman, H., and S. Smidt. *The Capital Budgeting Decision*, 6th ed. New York: Macmillan, 1984.

Chapter 9

Project Analysis and Evaluation

In our previous chapter, we discussed how to identify and organize the relevant cash flows for capital investment decisions. Our primary interest there was in coming up with a preliminary estimate of the net present value for a proposed project. In this chapter, we focus on assessing the reliability of such an estimate and on some additional considerations in project analysis.

We begin by discussing the need for an evaluation of cash flow and NPV estimates. We go on to develop some tools that are useful for doing so. We also examine some additional complications and concerns that can arise in project evaluation.

EVALUATING NPV ESTIMATES | 9.1

As we discussed in Chapter 7, an investment has a positive net present value if its market value exceeds its cost. Such an investment is desirable because it creates value for its owner. The primary problem in identifying such opportunities is that most of the time we can't actually observe the relevant market value. Instead, we estimate it. Having done so, it is only natural to wonder whether or not our estimates are at least close to the true values. We consider this question next.

The Basic Problem

Suppose we are working on a preliminary DCF analysis along the lines we described in the previous chapter. We carefully identify the relevant cash flows, avoiding such things as sunk costs, and we remember to consider working capital requirements. We add back any depreciation; we account for possible erosion; and we pay attention to opportunity costs. Finally, we double-check our calculations, and, when all is said and done, the bottom line is that the estimated NPV is positive.

Now what? Do we stop here and move on to the next proposal? Probably not. The fact that the estimated NPV is positive is definitely a good sign, but, more than anything, this tells us that we need to take a closer look.

If you think about it, there are two circumstances under which a discounted cash flow analysis could lead us to conclude that a project has a positive NPV. The first possibility is that the project really does have a positive NPV. That's the good news. The bad news is the second possibility: A project may appear to have a positive NPV because our estimate is inaccurate.

Notice that we could also err in the opposite way. If we conclude that a project has a negative NPV when the true NPV is positive, then we lose a valuable opportunity.

Projected versus Actual Cash Flows

There is a somewhat subtle point we need to make here. When we say something like: "The projected cash flow in Year 4 is $700," what exactly do we mean? Does this mean that we think the cash flow will actually be $700? Not really. It could happen, of course, but we would be surprised to see it turn out exactly that way. The reason is that the $700 projection is based only on what we know today. Almost anything could happen between now and then to change that cash flow.

Loosely speaking, we really mean that, if we took all the possible cash flows that could occur in four years and averaged them, the result would be $700. So, we don't really expect a projected cash flow to be exactly right in any one case. What we do expect is that, if we evaluate a large number of projects, our projections are right on the average.

Forecasting Risk

The key inputs into a DCF analysis are projected future cash flows. If these projections are seriously in error, then we have a classic GIGO (garbage-in, garbage-out) system. In this case, no matter how carefully we arrange the numbers and manipulate them, the resulting answer can still be grossly misleading. This is the danger in using a relatively sophisticated technique like DCF. It is sometimes easy to get caught up in number crunching and forget the underlying nuts-and-bolts economic reality.

forecasting risk

The possibility that errors in projected cash flows lead to incorrect decisions.

The possibility that we make a bad decision because of errors in the projected cash flows is called **forecasting risk** (or *estimation risk*). Because of forecasting risk, there is the danger that we think a project has a positive NPV when it really does not. How is this possible? It happens if we are overly optimistic about the future and, as a result, our projected cash flows don't realistically reflect the possible future cash flows.

So far, we have not explicitly considered what to do about the possibility of errors in our forecasts, so one of our goals in this chapter is to develop some tools that are useful in identifying areas where potential errors exist and where they might be especially damaging. In one form or another, we will be trying to assess the economic "reasonableness" of our estimates. We will also be wondering how much damage will be done by errors in those estimates.

Sources of Value

The first line of defense against forecasting risk is simply to ask: "What is it about this investment that leads to a positive NPV?" We should be able to point to something specific as the source of value. For example, if the proposal under consideration involved a new product, then we might ask questions such as: "Are we certain that our new product is significantly better than that of the competition? Can we truly manufacture at lower cost, or distribute more effectively, or identify undeveloped market niches, or gain control of a market?"

These are just a few of the potential sources of value. There are many others. A key factor to keep in mind is the degree of competition in the market. It is a basic principle of economics that positive NPV investments will be rare in a highly competitive environment. Therefore, proposals that appear to show significant value in the face of stiff competition are particularly troublesome, and the likely reaction of the competition to any innovations must be closely examined.

The point to remember is that positive NPV investments are probably not all that common, and the number of positive NPV projects is almost certainly limited for any given firm. If we can't articulate some sound economic basis for thinking ahead of time that we have found something special, then the conclusion that our project has a positive NPV should be viewed with some suspicion.

⌐ CONCEPT QUESTIONS

9.1a What is forecasting risk? Why is it a concern for the financial
      manager?

9.1b What are some potential sources of value in a new project?

SCENARIO AND OTHER "WHAT IF" ANALYSES ⌐ 9.2

Our basic approach to evaluating cash flow and NPV estimates involves asking "what if" questions. Accordingly, we discuss some organized ways of going about a what-if analysis. Our goal in doing so is to assess the degree of forecasting risk and to identify those components that are the most critical to the success or failure of an investment.

Getting Started

We are investigating a new project. Naturally, the first thing we do is estimate NPV based on our projected cash flows. We will call this the *base case*. Now, however, we recognize the possibility of error in those cash flow projections. After completing the base case, we thus wish to investigate the impact of different assumptions about the future on our estimates.

One way to organize this investigation is to put an upper and lower bound on the various components of the project. For example, suppose we forecast sales at 100 units per year. We know this estimate may be high or low, but we are relatively certain that it is not off by more than 10 units in either direction. We would thus pick a lower bound of 90 and an upper bound of 110. We go on to assign such bounds to any other cash flow components that we are unsure about.

When we pick these upper and lower bounds, we are not ruling out the possibility that the actual values could be outside this range. What we are saying, again loosely speaking, is that it is unlikely that the true average (as opposed to our estimated average) of the possible values is outside this range.

An example is useful to illustrate the idea here. The project under consideration costs $200,000, has a five-year life, and no salvage value. Depreciation is straight-line to zero. The required return is 12 percent, and the tax rate is 34 percent. In addition, we have compiled the following information:

	Base Case	Lower Bound	Upper Bound
Unit sales	6,000	5,500	6,500
Price per unit	$80	$75	$85
Variable costs per unit	$60	$58	$62
Fixed costs per year	$50,000	$45,000	$55,000

With this information, we can calculate the base-case NPV by first calculating net income:

Sales	$480,000
Variable costs	360,000
Fixed costs	50,000
Depreciation	40,000
EBIT	$ 30,000
Taxes (34%)	10,200
Net income	$ 19,800

Operating cash flow is thus $30,000 + 40,000 − 10,200 = $59,800 per year. At 12 percent, the five-year annuity factor is 3.6048, so the base-case NPV is:

$$\text{Base-case NPV} = -\$200,000 + \$59,800 \times 3.6048$$

$$= \$15,567$$

Thus, the project looks good so far.

Scenario Analysis

scenario analysis

The determination of what happens to NPV estimates when we ask what-if questions.

The basic form of what-if analysis is called **scenario analysis.** What we do is investigate the changes in our NPV estimates that result from asking questions like "What if unit sales realistically should be projected at 5,500 units instead of 6,000?"

Once we start looking at alternative scenarios, we might find that most of the plausible ones result in positive NPVs. In this case, we have some confidence in proceeding with the project. If a substantial percentage of the scenarios look bad, then the degree of forecasting risk is high and further investigation is in order.

There are a number of possible scenarios we could consider. A good place to start is the worst-case scenario. This will tell us the minimum NPV of the project. If this were positive, we would be in good shape. While we are at it, we will go ahead and determine the other extreme, the best case. This puts an upper bound on our NPV.

To get the worst case, we assign the least favorable value to each item. This means *low* values for items like units sold and price per unit and *high* values for costs. We do the reverse for the best case. For our project, these values would be:

	Worst Case	Best Case
Unit sales	5,500	6,500
Price per unit	$75	$85
Variable costs per unit	$62	$58
Fixed costs	$55,000	$45,000

With this information, we can calculate the net income and cash flows under each scenario (check these for yourself):

Scenario	Net Income	Cash Flow	Net Present Value	IRR
Base case	$19,800	$59,800	$ 15,567	15.1%
Worst case*	− 15,510	24,490	− 111,719	−14.4
Best case	59,730	99,730	159,504	40.9

*We assume a tax credit is created in our worst case scenario.

What we learn is that under the worst scenario, the cash flow is still positive at $24,490. That's good news. The bad news is that the return is −14.4 percent in this case, and the NPV is −$111,719. Since the project costs $200,000, we stand to lose a little more than half of the original investment under the worst possible scenario. The best case offers an attractive 41 percent return.

As we have mentioned, there is an unlimited number of different scenarios that we could examine. At a minimum, we might want to investigate two intermediate cases by going halfway between the base amounts and the extreme amounts. This would give us five scenarios in all, including the base case.

Beyond this point, it is hard to know when to stop. As we generate more and more possibilities, we run the risk of "paralysis of analysis." The difficulty is that no matter how many scenarios we run, all we can learn are possibilities, some good and some bad. Beyond that, we don't get any guidance as to what to do. Scenario analysis is thus useful in telling us what can happen and in helping us gauge the potential for disaster, but it does not tell us whether or not to take the project.

Sensitivity Analysis

Sensitivity analysis is a variation on scenario analysis that is useful in pinpointing the areas where forecasting risk is especially severe. The basic idea with a sensitivity analysis is to freeze all of the variables except one and then

sensitivity analysis
Investigation of what happens to NPV when only one variable is changed.

see how sensitive our estimate of NPV is to changes in that one variable. If our NPV estimate turns out to be very sensitive to relatively small changes in the projected value of some component of project cash flow, then the forecasting risk associated with that variable is high.

To illustrate how sensitivity analysis works, we go back to our base case for every item except unit sales. We can then calculate cash flow and NPV using the largest and smallest unit sales figures.

Scenario	Unit Sales	Cash Flow	Net Present Value	IRR
Base case	6,000	$59,800	$15,567	15.1%
Worst case	5,500	53,200	− 8,226	10.3
Best case	6,500	66,400	39,357	19.7

By way of comparison, we now freeze everything except fixed costs and repeat the analysis:

Scenario	Fixed Costs	Cash Flow	Net Present Value	IRR
Base case	$50,000	$59,800	$15,567	15.1%
Worst case	55,000	56,500	3,670	12.7
Best case	45,000	63,100	27,461	17.4

What we see here is that, given our ranges, the estimated NPV of this project is more sensitive to projected unit sales than it is to projected fixed costs. In fact, under the worst case for fixed costs, the NPV is still positive.

The results of our sensitivity analysis for unit sales can be illustrated graphically as in Figure 9.1. Here we place NPV on the vertical axis and unit sales on the horizontal axis. When we plot the combinations of unit sales versus NPV, we see that all possible combinations fall on a straight line. The steeper the resulting line is, the greater the sensitivity of the estimated NPV to the projected value of the variable being investigated.

As we have illustrated, sensitivity analysis is useful in pinpointing those variables that deserve the most attention. If we find that our estimated NPV is especially sensitive to a variable that is difficult to forecast (such as unit sales), then the degree of forecasting risk is high. We might decide that further market research would be a good idea in this case.

Because sensitivity analysis is a form of scenario analysis, it suffers from the same drawbacks. Sensitivity analysis is useful for pointing out where forecasting errors will do the most damage, but it does not tell us what to do about possible errors.

Simulation Analysis

simulation analysis

A combination of scenario and sensitivity analyses.

Scenario analysis and sensitivity analysis are widely used. With scenario analysis, we let all the different variables change, but we only let them take on a small number of values. With sensitivity analysis, we only let one variable change, but we let it take on a large number of values. If we combine the two approaches, the result is a crude form of **simulation analysis.**

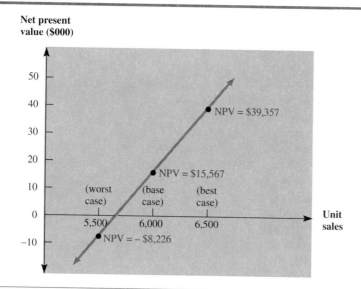

Figure 9.1

Sensitivity analysis for unit sales

If we want to let all the items vary at the same time, we have to consider a very large number of scenarios, and computer assistance is almost certainly needed. In the simplest case, we start with unit sales and assume that any value in our 5,500 to 6,500 range is equally likely. We start by randomly picking one value (or by instructing a computer to do so). We then randomly pick a price, a variable cost, and so on.

Once we have values for all the relevant components, we calculate an NPV. We repeat this sequence as much as we desire, probably several thousand times. The result is a large number of NPV estimates that we summarize by calculating the average value and some measure of how spread out the different possibilities are. For example, it would be of some interest to know what percentage of the possible scenarios result in negative estimated NPVs.

Since simulation is an extended form of scenario analysis, it has the same problems. Once we have the results, there is no simple decision rule that tells us what to do. Also, we have described a relatively simple form of simulation. To really do it right, we would have to consider the interrelationships between the different cash flow components. Furthermore, we assumed that the possible values were equally likely to occur. It is probably more realistic to assume that values near the base case are more likely than extreme values, but coming up with the probabilities is difficult, to say the least.

For these reasons, the use of simulation is somewhat limited in practice. However, recent advances in computer software and hardware (and user sophistication) lead us to believe that it may become more common in the future, particularly for large-scale projects.

⌐ CONCEPT QUESTIONS

9.2a What are scenario, sensitivity, and simulation analyses?

9.2b What are the drawbacks to the various types of what-if analyses?

9.3 | BREAK-EVEN ANALYSIS

It will frequently turn out that the crucial variable for a project will be sales volume. If we are thinking of a new product or entering a new market, for example, the hardest thing to forecast accurately is how much we can sell. For this reason, sales volume is usually analyzed more closely than other variables.

Break-even analysis is a popular and commonly used tool for analyzing the relationship between sales volume and profitability. There are a variety of different break-even measures, and we have already seen several types. For example, we discussed (in Chapter 7) how the payback period can be interpreted as the length of time until a project breaks even, ignoring time value.

All break-even measures have a similar goal. Loosely speaking, we will always be asking: "How bad do sales have to get before we actually begin to lose money?" Implicitly, we will also be asking: "Is it likely that things will get that bad?" To get started on this subject, we first discuss fixed and variable costs.

Fixed and Variable Costs

In discussing break-even, the difference between fixed and variable costs becomes very important. As a result, we need to be a little more explicit about the difference than we have been so far.

variable costs

Costs that change when the quantity of output changes.

Variable Costs   By definition, **variable costs** change as the quantity of output changes, and they are zero when production is zero. For example, direct labor costs and raw material costs are usually considered variable. This makes sense because, if we shut down operations tomorrow, there will be no future costs for labor or raw materials.

We will assume that variable costs are a constant amount per unit of output. This simply means that total variable cost is equal to the cost per unit multiplied by the number of units. In other words, the relationship between total variable cost (VC), cost per unit of output (v), and total quantity of output (Q) can be written simply as:

Total variable cost = Total quantity of output × Cost per unit of output

$$VC = Q \times v$$

For example, suppose that variable costs (v) are \$2 per unit. If total output (Q) is 1,000 units, what will total variable costs (VC) be?

$$VC = Q \times v$$
$$= 1,000 \times \$2$$
$$= \$2,000$$

Similarly, if Q is 5,000 units, then VC will be $5,000 \times \$2 = \$10,000$. Figure 9.2 illustrates the relationship between output level and variable costs in this case. In Figure 9.2, notice that increasing output by one unit results in variable costs rising by \$2, so the "rise over the run" (the slope of the line) is given by \$2/1 = \$2.

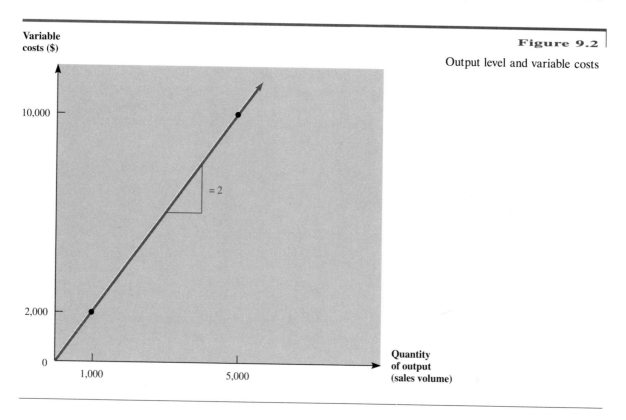

Variable costs ($)

Figure 9.2

Output level and variable costs

Example 9.1   Variable Costs

The Blume Corporation is a manufacturer of pencils. It has received an order for 5,000 pencils, and the company has to decide whether or not to accept the order. From recent experience, the company knows that each pencil requires 5 cents in raw materials and 50 cents in direct labor costs. These variable costs are expected to continue in the future. What will Blume's total variable costs be if it accepts the order?

In this case, the cost per unit is 50 cents in labor plus 5 cents in material for a total of 55 cents per unit. At 5,000 units of output, we have:

$$VC = Q \times v$$

$$= 5,000 \times \$.55$$

$$= \$2,750$$

Therefore, total variable costs will be $2,750. ■

Fixed Costs   **Fixed costs**, by definition, do not change during a specified time period. So, unlike variable costs, they do not depend on the amount of goods or services produced during a period (at least within some range of production). For example, the lease payment on a production facility and the company president's salary are fixed costs, at least over some period.

Naturally, fixed costs are not fixed forever. They are only fixed during some particular time, say a quarter or a year. Beyond that time, leases can be

fixed costs

Costs that do not change when the quantity of output changes during a particular time period.

terminated and executives "retired." More to the point, any fixed cost can be modified or eliminated given enough time; so, in the long run, all costs are variable.

Notice that during the time that a cost is fixed, that cost is effectively a sunk cost because we are going to have to pay it no matter what.

Total Costs   Total costs (TC) for a given level of output are the sum of variable costs (VC) and fixed costs (FC):

$$TC = VC + FC$$

$$TC = v \times Q + FC$$

So, for example, if we have a variable cost of $3 per unit and fixed costs of $8,000 per year, our total cost is:

$$TC = \$3 \times Q + \$8,000$$

If we produce 6,000 units, our total production cost would be $3 × 6,000 + $8,000 = $26,000. At other production levels, we have:

Quantity Produced	Total Variable Cost	Fixed Costs	Total Cost
0	$ 0	$8,000	$ 8,000
1,000	3,000	8,000	11,000
5,000	15,000	8,000	23,000
10,000	30,000	8,000	38,000

By plotting these points in Figure 9.3, we see that the relationship between quantity produced and total cost is given by a straight line. In Figure 9.3 notice that total costs are equal to fixed costs when sales are zero. Beyond that point, every one-unit increase in production leads to a $3 increase in total costs, so the slope of the line is 3. In other words, the **marginal** or **incremental cost** of producing one more unit is $3.

marginal or incremental cost

The change in costs that occurs when there is a small change in output.

Example 9.2   Average Cost versus Marginal Cost

Suppose the Blume Corporation has a variable cost per pencil of 55 cents. The lease payment on the production facility runs $5,000 per month. If Blume produces 100,000 pencils per year, what are the total costs of production? What is the average cost per pencil?

The fixed costs are $5,000 per month or $60,000 per year. The variable cost is $.55 per pencil, so the total cost for the year, assuming that we produce 100,000 pencils, is:

$$
\begin{aligned}
\text{Total cost} &= v \times Q + FC \\
&= \$.55 \times 100,000 + \$60,000 \\
&= \$115,000
\end{aligned}
$$

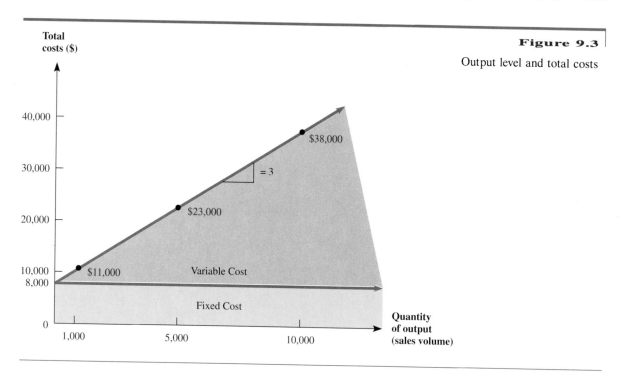

Figure 9.3

Output level and total costs

The average cost per pencil is $115,000/100,000 = $1.15.

Now suppose that Blume has received a special, one-shot order for 5,000 pencils. Blume has sufficient capacity to manufacture the 5,000 pencils on top of the 100,000 already produced, so no additional fixed costs will be incurred. Also, there will be no effect on existing orders. If Blume can get 75 cents per pencil for this order, should the order be accepted?

What this boils down to is a very simple proposition. It costs 55 cents to make another pencil. Anything we can get for this pencil in excess of our 55 cents incremental cost contributes in a positive way toward covering our fixed costs. The 75-cent **marginal** or **incremental revenue** exceeds the 55-cent marginal cost, so Blume should take the order.

The fixed cost of $60,000 is not relevant to this decision because it is effectively sunk, at least for the current period. For the same reason, the fact that the average cost was $1.15 is irrelevant because this average reflects the fixed cost. As long as producing the extra 5,000 pencils truly does not cost anything beyond the 55 cents per pencil, then Blume should accept anything over that 55 cents. ■

marginal or incremental revenue

The change in revenue that occurs when there is a small change in output.

Accounting Break-Even

The most widely used measure of break-even is **accounting break-even.** The accounting break-even point is simply the sales level that results in a zero project net income.

To determine a project's accounting break-even, we start off with some common sense. Suppose that we retail computer diskettes for $5 apiece. We

accounting break-even

The sales level that results in zero project net income.

can buy diskettes from a wholesale supplier for $3 apiece. We have accounting expenses of $600 in fixed costs and $300 in depreciation. How many diskettes do we have to sell to break even, that is, for net income to be zero?

For every diskette we sell, we pick up $5 − 3 = $2 toward covering our other expenses. We have to cover a total of $600 + 300 = $900 in accounting expenses, so we obviously need to sell $900/$2 = 450 diskettes. We can check this by noting that, at a sales level of 450 units, our revenues are $5 × 450 = $2,250 and our variable costs are $3 × 450 = $1,350. The income statement is thus:

Sales	$2,250
Variable costs	1,350
Fixed costs	600
Depreciation	300
EBIT	$ 0
Taxes	0
Net income	$ 0

Remember, since we are discussing a proposed new project, we do not consider any interest expense in calculating net income or cash flow from the project. Also, notice that we include depreciation in calculating expenses here, even though depreciation is not a cash outflow. That is why we call it accounting break-even. Finally, notice that when net income is zero, so are pretax income and, of course, taxes. In accounting terms, our revenues are equal to our costs, so there is no profit to tax.

Figure 9.4 is another way to see what is happening. This figure looks like Figure 9.3 except that we add a line for revenues. As indicated, total revenues are zero when output is zero. Beyond that, each unit sold brings in another $5, so the slope of the revenue line is 5.

From our discussion above, we break even when revenues are equal to total costs. The line for revenues and the line for total costs cross right where output is 450 units. As illustrated, at any level below 450, our accounting profit is negative and, at any level above 450, we have a positive net income.

Accounting Break-Even: A Closer Look

In our numerical example, notice that the break-even level is equal to the sum of fixed costs and depreciation, divided by price per unit less variable costs per unit. This is always true. To see why, we recall the following set of abbreviations for the different variables:

P = Selling price per unit

v = Variable cost per unit

Q = Total units sold

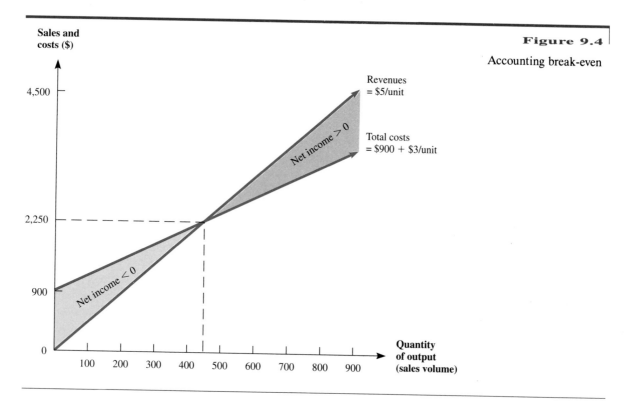

Sales and costs ($)

Figure 9.4

Accounting break-even

Revenues = $5/unit

Net income > 0

Total costs = $900 + $3/unit

Net income < 0

Quantity of output (sales volume)

FC = Fixed costs

D = Depreciation

T = Tax rate

Project net income is given by:

Net income = (Sales − Variable costs − Fixed costs − Depreciation)

$$\times (1 - T)$$

$$= (S - \text{VC} - \text{FC} - D) \times (1 - T)$$

From here, it is not difficult to calculate the break-even point. If we set this net income equal to zero, we get:

$$\text{Net income} \overset{\text{set}}{=} 0 = (S - \text{VC} - \text{FC} - D) \times (1 - T)$$

Divide both sides by $(1 - T)$ to get:

$$S - \text{VC} - \text{FC} - D = 0$$

As we have seen, this says that, when net income is zero, so is pretax income. If we recall that $S = P \times Q$ and $VC = v \times Q$, then we can rearrange this to solve for the break-even level:

$$S - VC = FC + D$$

$$P \times Q - v \times Q = FC + D$$

$$(P - v) \times Q = FC + D$$

$$Q = (FC + D)/(P - v) \qquad [9.1]$$

This is the same result we described above.

Uses for the Accounting Break-Even

Why would anyone be interested in knowing the accounting break-even point? To illustrate how it can be useful, suppose that we are a small specialty ice cream manufacturer with a strictly local distribution. We are thinking about expanding into new markets. Based on the estimated cash flows, we find that the expansion has a positive NPV.

Going back to our discussion of forecasting risk, it is likely that what will make or break our expansion is sales volume. The reason is that, in this case at least, we probably have a fairly good idea of what we can charge for the ice cream. Further, we know relevant production and distribution costs with a fair degree of accuracy since we are already in the business. What we do not know with any real precision is how much ice cream we can sell.

Given the costs and selling price, however, we can immediately calculate the break-even point. Once we have done so, we might find that we need to get 30 percent of the market just to break even. If we think that this is unlikely to occur because, for example, we only have 10 percent of our current market, then we know that our forecast is questionable and there is a real possibility that the true NPV is negative. On the other hand, we might find that we already have firm commitments from buyers for about the break-even amount, so we are almost certain that we can sell more. In this case, the forecasting risk is much lower and we have greater confidence in our estimates.

There are several other reasons why knowing the accounting break-even can be useful. First, as we discuss in more detail below, accounting break-even and payback period are very similar measures. Like payback period, accounting break-even is relatively easy to calculate and explain.

Second, managers are often concerned with the contribution a project will make to the firm's total accounting earnings. A project that does not break even in an accounting sense actually reduces total earnings.

Third, a project that just breaks even on an accounting basis loses money in a financial or opportunity cost sense. This is true because we could have earned more by investing elsewhere. Such a project does not lose money in an out-of-pocket sense. As described below, we get back exactly what we put in. For noneconomic reasons, such opportunity losses may be easier to live with than out-of-pocket losses.

⌐ CONCEPT QUESTIONS

9.3a How are fixed costs similar to sunk costs?

9.3b What is net income at the accounting break-even point? What about taxes?

9.3c Why might a financial manager be interested in the accounting break-even point?

OPERATING CASH FLOW, SALES VOLUME, AND BREAK-EVEN ⌐ 9.4

Accounting break-even is one tool that is useful for project analysis. Ultimately, however, we are more interested in cash flow than accounting income. So, for example, if sales volume is the critical variable, then we need to know more about the relationship between sales volume and cash flow than just the accounting break-even.

Our goal in this section is to illustrate the relationship between operating cash flow and sales volume. We also discuss some other break-even measures. To simplify matters somewhat, we will ignore the effect of taxes. We start off by looking at the relationship between accounting break-even and cash flow.

Accounting Break-Even and Cash Flow

Now that we know how to find the accounting break-even, it is natural to wonder what happens with cash flow. To illustrate, suppose that the Wettway Sailboat Corporation is considering whether or not to launch its new Margo-class sailboat. The selling price will be $40,000 per boat. The variable costs will be about half that, or $20,000 per boat, and fixed costs will be $500,000 per year.

The Base Case   The total investment needed to undertake the project is $3,500,000. This amount will be depreciated straight-line to zero over the five-year life of the equipment. The salvage value is zero, and there are no working capital consequences. Wettway has a 20 percent required return on new projects.

Based on market surveys and historical experience, Wettway projects total sales for the five years at 425 boats, or about 85 boats per year. Ignoring taxes, should this project be launched?

To begin, ignoring taxes, the operating cash flow at 85 boats per year is:

$$\text{Operating cash flow} = \text{EBIT} + \text{Depreciation} - \text{Taxes}$$

$$= (S - \text{VC} - \text{FC} - D) + D - 0$$

$$= 85 \times (\$40,000 - 20,000) - \$500,000$$

$$= \$1,200,000 \text{ per year}$$

At 20 percent, the five-year annuity factor is 2.9906, so the NPV is:

$$\text{NPV} = -\$3,500,000 + 1,200,000 \times 2.9906$$

$$= -\$3,500,000 + 3,588,720$$

$$= \$88,720$$

In the absence of additional information, the project should be launched.

Calculating the Break-Even Level   To begin looking a little closer at this project, you might ask a series of questions. For example, how many new boats does Wettway need to sell for the project to break even on an accounting basis? If Wettway does break even, what will be the annual cash flow from the project? What will be the return on the investment in this case?

Before fixed costs and depreciation are considered, Wettway generates $40,000 - 20,000 = $20,000 per boat (this is revenue less variable cost). Depreciation is $3,500,000/5 = $700,000 per year. Fixed costs and depreciation together total $1.2 million, so Wettway needs to sell $(FC + D)/(P - v) =$ $1.2 million/$20,000 = 60 boats per year to break even on an accounting basis. This is 25 boats less than projected sales; so, assuming that Wettway is confident that its projection is accurate to within, say, 15 boats, it appears unlikely that the new investment will fail to at least break even on an accounting basis.

To calculate Wettway's cash flow in this case, we note that, if 60 boats are sold, net income will be exactly zero. Recalling from the previous chapter that operating cash flow for a project can be written as net income plus depreciation (the bottom-up definition), the operating cash flow is obviously equal to the depreciation, or $700,000 in this case. The internal rate of return would be exactly zero (why?).

Payback and Break-Even   As our example illustrates, whenever a project breaks even on an accounting basis, the cash flow for that period will be equal to the depreciation. This result makes perfect accounting sense. For example, suppose we invest $100,000 in a five-year project. The depreciation is straight-line to a zero salvage, or $20,000 per year. If the project exactly breaks even every period, then the cash flow will be $20,000 per period.

The sum of the cash flows for the life of this project is 5 × $20,000 = $100,000, the original investment. What this shows is that a project's payback period is exactly equal to its life if the project breaks even every period. Similarly, a project that does better than break even has a payback that is shorter than the life of the project and has a positive rate of return.

The bad news is that a project that just breaks even on an accounting basis has a negative NPV and a zero return. For our sailboat project, the fact that we will almost surely break even on an accounting basis is partially comforting since our "downside" risk (our potential loss) is limited, but we still don't know if the project is truly profitable. More work is needed.

Sales Volume and Operating Cash Flow

At this point, we can generalize our example and introduce some other break-even measures. From our discussion just above, we know that, ignoring taxes, a project's operating cash flow (OCF) can be written simply as EBIT plus depreciation:

$$\text{OCF} = [(P - v) \times Q - \text{FC} - D] + D \qquad [9.2]$$

$$= (P - v) \times Q - \text{FC}$$

For the Wettway sailboat project, the general relationship (in thousands of dollars) between operating cash flow and sales volume is thus:

$$OCF = (P - v) \times Q - FC$$
$$= (\$40 - 20) \times Q - \$500$$
$$= -\$500 + \$20 \times Q$$

What this tells us is that the relationship between operating cash flow and sales volume is given by a straight line with a slope of $20 and a y-intercept of −$500. If we calculate some different values, we get:

Quantity Sold	Operating Cash Flow
0	−$ 500
15	−200
30	100
50	500
75	1,000

These points are plotted in Figure 9.5. In Figure 9.5, we have indicated three different break-even points. We discuss these next.

Cash Flow, Accounting, and Financial Break-Even Points

We know from the discussion above that the relationship between operating cash flow and sales volume (ignoring taxes) is:

$$OCF = (P - v) \times Q - FC$$

If we rearrange this and solve it for Q, we get:

$$Q = (FC + OCF)/(P - v) \qquad [9.3]$$

This tells us what sales volume (Q) is necessary to achieve any given OCF, so this result is more general than the accounting break-even. We use it to find the various break-even points in Figure 9.5.

Accounting Break-Even Revisited   Looking at Figure 9.5, suppose operating cash flow was equal to depreciation (D). Recall that this corresponds to our break-even point on an accounting basis. To find the sales volume, we substitute the $700 depreciation amount for OCF in our general expression:

$$Q = (FC + OCF)/(P - v)$$
$$= (\$500 + 700)/(\$20)$$
$$= 60$$

This is the same quantity we had before.

Figure 9.5

Operating cash flow and sales volume

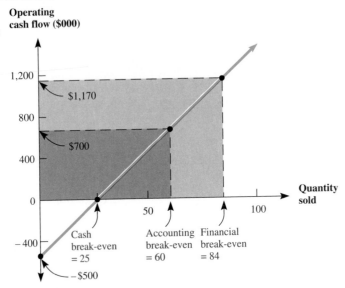

Cash Break-Even   We have seen that a project that breaks even on an accounting basis has a net income of zero, but it still has a positive cash flow. At some sales level below the accounting break-even, the operating cash flow actually goes negative. This is a particularly unpleasant occurrence. If it happens, we actually have to supply additional cash to the project just to keep it afloat.

cash break-even

The sales level that results in a zero NPV.

To calculate the **cash break-even** (the point where operating cash flow is equal to zero), we put in a zero for OCF:

$$Q = (FC + 0)/(P - v)$$

$$= \$500/\$20$$

$$= 25$$

Wettway must therefore sell 25 boats to cover the $500 in fixed costs. As we show in Figure 9.5, this point occurs right where the operating cash flow line crosses the horizontal axis.

Notice that a project that just breaks even on a cash flow basis can cover its own fixed operating costs, but that is all. It never pays back anything, so the original investment is a complete loss (the IRR is −100 percent).

financial break-even

The sales level that results in a zero NPV.

Financial Break-Even   The last case we consider is **financial break-even,** the sales level that results in a zero NPV. To the financial manager, this is the most interesting case. What we do is first determine what operating cash flow has to be for the NPV to be zero. We then use this amount to determine the sales volume.

To illustrate, recall that Wettway requires a 20 percent return on its $3,500 (in thousands) investment. How many sailboats does Wettway have to sell to break even once we account for the 20 percent per year opportunity cost?

The sailboat project has a five-year life. The project has a zero NPV when the present value of the operating cash flows equals the $3,500 investment. Since the cash flow is the same each year, we can solve for the unknown amount by viewing it as an ordinary annuity. The five-year annuity factor at 20 percent is 2.9906, and the OCF can be determined as follows:

$$\$3,500 = OCF \times 2.9906$$

$$OCF = \$3,500/2.9906$$

$$= \$1,170$$

Wettway thus needs an operating cash flow of $1,170 each year to break even. We can now plug this OCF into the equation for sales volume:

$$Q = (\$500 + \$1,170)/\$20$$

$$= 83.5$$

So Wettway needs to sell about 84 boats per year. This is not good news.

As indicated in Figure 9.5, the financial break-even is substantially higher than the accounting break-even point. This will often be the case. Moreover, what we have discovered is that the sailboat project has a substantial degree of forecasting risk. We project sales of 85 boats per year, but it takes 84 just to earn our required return.

Overall, it seems unlikely that the Wettway sailboat project would fail to break even on an accounting basis. However, there appears to be a very good chance that the true NPV is negative. This illustrates the danger in just looking at the accounting break-even.

What should Wettway do? Is the new project all wet? The decision at this point is essentially a managerial issue—a judgment call. The crucial questions are:

1. How much confidence do we have in our projections?
2. How important is the project to the future of the company?
3. How badly will the company be hurt if sales do turn out low? What options are available to the company in this case?

We will consider questions such as these in a later section. For future reference, our discussion of the different break-even measures is summarized in Table 9.1.

CONCEPT QUESTIONS

9.4a If a project breaks even on an accounting basis, what is its operating cash flow?

9.4b If a project breaks even on a cash basis, what is its operating cash flow?

9.4c If a project breaks even on a financial basis, what do you know about its *discounted* payback?

Table 9.1

Summary of break-even measures

I. The General Expression

Ignoring taxes, the relation between operating cash flow (OCF) and quantity of output or sales volume (Q) is:

$$Q = \frac{FC + OCF}{P - v}$$

where

$$FC = \text{Total fixed costs}$$

$$P = \text{Price per unit}$$

$$v = \text{variable cost per unit}$$

As shown next, this relation can be used to determine the accounting, cash, and financial break-even points.

II. The Accounting Break-Even Point

Accounting break-even occurs when net income is zero. Operating cash flow (OCF) is equal to depreciation when net income is zero, so the accounting break-even point is:

$$Q = \frac{FC + D}{P - v}$$

A project that always just breaks even on an accounting basis has a payback exactly equal to its life, a negative NPV, and an IRR of zero.

III. The Cash Break-Even Point

Cash break-even occurs when operating cash flow (OCF) is zero. The cash break-even point is thus:

$$Q = \frac{FC}{P - v}$$

A project that always just breaks even on a cash basis never pays back, its NPV is negative and equal to the initial outlay, and the IRR is -100 percent.

IV. The Financial Break-Even Point

Financial break-even occurs when the NPV of the project is zero. The financial break-even point is thus:

$$Q = \frac{FC + OCF^*}{P - v}$$

where OCF^* is the level of OCF that results in a zero NPV. A project that breaks even on a financial basis has a discounted payback equal to its life, a zero NPV, and an IRR just equal to the required return.

OPERATING LEVERAGE | 9.5

We have discussed how to calculate and interpret various measures of break-even for a proposed project. What we have not explicitly discussed is what determines these points and how they might be changed. We now turn to this subject.

The Basic Idea

Operating leverage is the degree to which a project or firm is committed to fixed production costs. A firm with low operating leverage will have low fixed costs compared to a firm with high operating leverage. Generally speaking, projects with a relatively heavy investment in plant and equipment will have a relatively high degree of operating leverage. Such projects are said to be *capital intensive.*

Any time we are thinking about a new venture, there will normally be alternative ways of producing and delivering the product. For example, Wettway Corporation can purchase the necessary equipment and build all of the components for its sailboats in-house. Alternatively, some of the work could be farmed out to other firms. The first option involves a greater investment in plant and equipment, greater fixed costs and depreciation, and, as a result, a higher degree of operating leverage.

operating leverage
The degree to which a firm or project relies on fixed costs.

Implications of Operating Leverage

Regardless of how it is measured, operating leverage has important implications for project evaluation. Fixed costs act like a lever in the sense that a small percentage change in operating revenue can be magnified into a large percentage change in operating cash flow and NPV. This explains why we call it operating "leverage."

The higher the degree of operating leverage, the greater is the potential danger from forecasting risk. The reason is that relatively small errors in forecasting sales volume can get magnified or "levered up" into large errors in cash flow projections.

From a managerial perspective, one way of coping with highly uncertain projects is to keep the degree of operating leverage as low as possible. This will generally have the effect of keeping the break-even point (however measured) at its minimum level. We will illustrate this point below, but first we need to discuss how to measure operating leverage.

Measuring Operating Leverage

One way of measuring operating leverage is to ask: "If quantity sold rises by 5 percent, what will be the percentage change in operating cash flow?" In other words, the **degree of operating leverage** (DOL) is defined such that

$$\text{Percentage change in OCF} = \text{DOL} \times \text{Percentage change in } Q$$

degree of operating leverage
The percentage change in operating cash flow relative to the percentage change in quantity sold.

Based on the relationship between OCF and Q, DOL can be written as:[1]

$$DOL = 1 + FC/OCF \qquad [9.4]$$

The ratio FC/OCF simply measures fixed costs as a percentage of total operating cash flow. Notice that zero fixed costs would result in a DOL of 1, implying that percentage changes in quantity sold would show up one for one in operating cash flow. In other words, no magnification or leverage effect would exist.

To illustrate this measure of operating leverage, we go back to the Wettway sailboat project. Fixed costs were $500 and $(P - v)$ was $20, so OCF was:

$$OCF = -\$500 + 20 \times Q$$

Suppose Q is currently 50 boats. At this level of output, OCF is $-\$500 + 1,000 = \$500$.

If Q rises by 1 unit to 51, then the percentage change in Q is $(51 - 50)/50 = .02$, or 2%. OCF rises to $520, a change of $(P - v) = \$20$. The percentage change in OCF is $(\$520 - 500)/500 = .04$, or 4%. So a 2 percent increase in the number of boats sold leads to a 4 percent increase in operating cash flow. The degree of operating leverage must be exactly 2.00. We can check this by noting that:

$$DOL = 1 + FC/OCF$$

$$= 1 + \$500/\$500$$

$$= 2$$

This verifies our calculations above.

Our formulation of DOL depends on the current output level, Q. However, it can handle changes from the current level of any size, not just one unit. For

---

[1]To see this, note that, if Q goes up by 1 unit, OCF will go up by $(P - v)$. In this case, the percentage change in Q is $1/Q$, and the percentage change in OCF is $(P - v)/OCF$. Given this, we have:

$$Percentage\ change\ in\ OCF = DOL \times Percentage\ change\ in\ Q$$

$$(P - v)/OCF = DOL \times 1/Q$$

$$DOL = (P - v) \times Q/OCF$$

Also, based on our definition of OCF:

$$OCF + FC = (P - v) \times Q$$

Thus, DOL can be written as:

$$DOL = (OCF + FC)/OCF$$

$$= 1 + FC/OCF$$

example, suppose Q rises from 50 to 75, a 50 percent increase. With DOL equal to 2, operating cash flow should increase by 100 percent, or exactly double. Does it? The answer is yes, because, at a Q of 75, OCF is:

$$OCF = -\$500 + \$20 \times 75 = \$1,000$$

Notice that operating leverage declines as output (Q) rises. For example, at an output level of 75, we have:

$$DOL = 1 + \$500/1,000$$

$$= 1.50$$

The reason DOL declines is that fixed costs, considered as a percentage of operating cash flow, get smaller and smaller, so the leverage effect diminishes.

Example 9.3 Operating Leverage

The Sasha Corp. currently sells gourmet dog food for $1.20 per can. The variable cost is 80 cents per can, and the packaging and marketing operation has fixed costs of $360,000 per year. Depreciation is $60,000 per year. What is the accounting break-even? Ignoring taxes, what will be the increase in operating cash flow if the quantity sold rises to 10 percent above the break-even point?

The accounting break-even is $420,000/.40 = 1,050,000 cans. As we know, the operating cash flow is equal to the $60,000 depreciation at this level of production, so the degree of operating leverage is:

$$DOL = 1 + FC/OCF$$

$$= 1 + \$360,000/\$60,000$$

$$= 7$$

Given this, a 10 percent increase in the number of cans of dog food sold will increase operating cash flow by a substantial 70 percent.

To check this answer, we note that if sales rise by 10 percent, then the quantity sold will rise to 1,050,000 $\times$ 1.1 = 1,155,000. Ignoring taxes, the operating cash flow is 1,155,000 $\times$ \$.40 − $360,000 = $102,000. Compared to the $60,000 cash flow we had, this is exactly 70 percent more: $102,000/60,000 = 1.70. ∎

Operating Leverage and Break-Even

We illustrate why operating leverage is an important consideration by examining the Wettway sailboat project under an alternative scenario. At a Q of 85 boats, the degree of operating leverage for the sailboat project under the original scenario is:

$$DOL = 1 + FC/OCF$$

$$= 1 + \$500/1,200$$

$$= 1.42$$

Also, recall that the NPV at a sales level of 85 boats was $88,720, and that the accounting break-even was 60 boats.

An option available to Wettway is to subcontract production of the boat hull assemblies. If they do, the necessary investment falls to $3,200,000, and the fixed operating costs fall to $180,000. However, variable costs will rise to $25,000 per boat since subcontracting is more expensive than doing it in-house. Ignoring taxes, evaluate this option.

For practice, see if you don't agree with the following:

$$\text{NPV at } 20\% \text{ (85 units)} = \$74,720$$

$$\text{Accounting break-even} = 55 \text{ boats}$$

$$\text{Degree of operating leverage} = 1.16$$

What has happened? This option results in a slightly lower estimated net present value, and the accounting break-even point falls to 55 boats from 60 boats.

Given that this alternative has the lower NPV, is there any reason to consider it further? Maybe there is. The degree of operating leverage is substantially lower in the second case. If we are worried about the possibility of an overly optimistic projection, then we might prefer to subcontract.

There is another reason why we might consider the second arrangement. If sales turned out better than expected, we always have the option of going ahead and starting to produce in-house at a later date. As a practical matter, it is much easier to increase operating leverage (by purchasing equipment) than to decrease it (by selling off equipment). As we discuss below, one of the drawbacks to discounted cash flow analysis is that it is difficult to explicitly include options of this sort, even though they may be quite important.

⌈ CONCEPT QUESTIONS

9.5a What is operating leverage?

9.5b How is operating leverage measured?

9.5c What are the implications of operating leverage for the financial manager?

9.6 | ADDITIONAL CONSIDERATIONS IN CAPITAL BUDGETING

Our final task for this chapter is a brief discussion of two additional considerations in capital budgeting: managerial options and capital rationing. Both of these can be very important in practice, but, as we will see, explicitly dealing with either of them is difficult.

Managerial Options and Capital Budgeting

In our capital budgeting analysis thus far, we have more or less ignored the possibility of future managerial actions. Implicitly, we assumed that once a project is launched, its basic features cannot be changed. For this reason, we say that our analysis is *static* (as opposed to dynamic).

In reality, depending on what actually happens in the future, there will always be ways to modify a project. We will call these opportunities **managerial options.** There are a great number of these options. The way a product is priced, manufactured, advertised, and produced can all be changed, and these are just a few of the possibilities. We discuss some of the most important ones in the next few sections.

managerial options

Opportunities that managers can exploit if certain things happen in the future.

Contingency Planning   The various what-if procedures, particularly the break-even measures, in this chapter have another use. We can also view them as primitive ways of exploring the dynamics of a project and investigating managerial options. What we think about in this case are some of the possible futures that could come about and what actions we might take if they do.

For example, we might find that a project fails to break even when sales drop below 10,000 units. This is a fact that is interesting to know, but the more important thing is to then go on and ask: "What actions are we going to take if this actually occurs?" This is called **contingency planning,** and it amounts to an investigation of some of the managerial options implicit in a project.

There is no limit to the number of possible futures or contingencies that we could investigate. However, there are some broad classes, and we consider these next.

contingency planning

Taking into account the managerial options that are implicit in a project.

The Option to Expand   One particularly important option that we have not explicitly addressed is the option to expand. If we truly find a positive NPV project, then there is an obvious consideration. Can we expand the project or repeat it to get an even larger NPV? Our static analysis implicitly assumes that the scale of the project is fixed.

For example, if the sales demand for a particular product were to greatly exceed expectations, we might investigate increasing production. If this is not feasible for some reason, then we could always increase cash flow by raising the price. Either way, the potential cash flow is higher than we have indicated because we have implicitly assumed that no expansion or price increase is possible. Overall, because we ignore the option to expand in our analysis, we *underestimate* NPV (all other things being equal).

The Option to Abandon   At the other extreme, the option to scale back or even abandon a project is also quite valuable. For example, if a project does not break even on a cash flow basis, then it can't even cover its own expenses. We would be better off if we just abandoned it. Our DCF analysis implicitly assumes that we would keep operating even in this case.

In reality, if sales demand were significantly below expectations, we might be able to sell off some capacity or put it to another use. Maybe the product or service could be redesigned or otherwise improved. Regardless of the specifics, we once again *underestimate* NPV if we assume that the project must last for some fixed number of years, no matter what happens in the future.

The Option to Wait   Implicitly, we have treated proposed investments as if they were "go or no-go" decisions. Actually, there is a third possibility. The project can be postponed, perhaps in hope of more favorable conditions. We call this the option to wait.

For example, suppose an investment costs $120 and has a perpetual cash flow of $10 per year. If the discount rate is 10 percent, then the NPV is $10/.10 − 120 = −$20, so the project should not be undertaken now. However, this does not mean that we should forget about the project forever, because in the next period, the appropriate discount rate could be different. If it fell to, say, 5 percent, then the NPV would be $10/.05 − 120 = $80, and we would take the project.

More generally, as long as there is some possible future scenario under which a project has a positive NPV, then the option to wait is valuable.

Options in Capital Budgeting: An Example   Suppose we are examining a new project. To keep things relatively simple, we expect to sell 100 units per year at $1 net cash flow apiece into perpetuity. We thus expect the cash flow will be $100 per year.

In one year, we will know more about the project. In particular, we will have a better idea of whether it is successful or not. If it looks like a long-run success, the expected sales will be revised upwards to 150 units per year. If it does not, the expected sales will be revised downward to 50 units per year.

Success and failure are equally likely. Notice that, since there is an even chance of selling 50 or 150 units, the expected sales are still 100 units as we originally projected.

The cost is $550, and the discount rate is 20 percent. The project can be dismantled and sold in one year for $400, if we decide to abandon it. Should we take it?

A standard DCF analysis is not difficult. The expected cash flow is $100 per year forever and the discount rate is 20 percent. The PV of the cash flows is $100/.20 = $500, so the NPV is $500 − 550 = −$50. We shouldn't take it.

This analysis is static, however. In one year, we can sell out for $400. How can we account for this? What we have to do is to decide what we are going to do one year from now. In this simple case, there are only two contingencies that we need to evaluate, an upward revision and a downward revision, so the extra work is not great.

In one year, if the expected cash flows are revised to $50, then the PV of the cash flows is revised downward to $50/.20 = $250. We get $400 by abandoning the project, so that is what we will do (the NPV of keeping the project in one year is $250 − 400 = −$150).

If the demand is revised upward, then the PV of the future cash flows at year one is $150/.20 = $750. This exceeds the $400 abandonment value, so we will keep the project.

We now have a project that costs $550 today. In one year, we expect a cash flow of $100 from the project. In addition, this project will either be worth $400 (if we abandon it because it is a failure) or $750 (if we keep it because it succeeds). These outcomes are equally likely, so we expect it to be worth ($400 + 750)/2, or $575.

Summing up, in one year, we expect to have $100 in cash plus a project worth $575, or $675 total. At a 20 percent discount rate, this $675 is worth $562.50 today, so the NPV is $562.50 − 550 = $12.50. We should take it.

The NPV of our project has increased by $62.50. Where did this come from? Our original analysis implicitly assumed we would keep the project even if it was a failure. At Year 1, however, we saw that we were $150 better off

($400 versus $250) if we abandoned. There was a 50 percent chance of this happening, so the expected gain from abandoning is $75. The PV of this amount is the value of the option to abandon, $75/1.20 = $62.50.

Strategic Options   Companies sometimes undertake new projects just to explore possibilities and evaluate potential future business strategies. This is a little like testing the water by sticking a toe in before diving. Such projects are difficult to analyze using conventional DCF because most of the benefits come in the form of **strategic options,** that is, options for future, related business moves. Projects that create such options may be very valuable, but that value is difficult to measure. Research and development, for example, is an important and valuable activity for many firms precisely because it creates options for new products and procedures.

strategic options
Options for future, related business products or strategies.

To give another example, a large manufacturer might decide to open a retail outlet as a pilot study. The primary goal is to gain some market insight. Because of the high start-up costs, this one operation won't break even. However, based on the sales experience from the pilot, we can then evaluate whether or not to open more outlets, to change the product mix, to enter new markets, and so on. The information gained and the resulting options for actions are all valuable, but coming up with a reliable dollar figure is probably not feasible.

We have seen that incorporating options into capital budgeting analysis is not easy. What can we do about them in practice? The answer is that we can only keep them in the back of our minds as we work with the projected cash flows. We will tend to underestimate NPV by ignoring options. The damage might be small for a highly structured, very specific proposal, but it might be great for an exploratory one.

Capital Rationing

Capital rationing is said to exist when we have profitable (positive NPV) investments available but we can't get the needed funds to undertake them. For example, as division managers for a large corporation, we might identify $5 million in excellent projects, but find that, for whatever reason, we can spend only $2 million. Now what? Unfortunately, for reasons we will discuss, there may be no truly satisfactory answer.

capital rationing
The situation that exists if a firm has positive NPV projects but cannot find the necessary financing.

Soft Rationing   The situation we have just described is **soft rationing.** This occurs when, for example, different units in a business are allocated some fixed amount of money each year for capital spending. Such an allocation is primarily a means of controlling and keeping track of overall spending. The important thing about soft rationing is that the corporation as a whole isn't short of capital; more can be raised on ordinary terms if management so desires.

soft rationing
The situation that occurs when units in a business are allocated a certain amount of financing for capital budgeting.

If we face soft rationing, the first thing to do is try and get a larger allocation. Failing that, then one common suggestion is to generate as large a net present value as possible within the existing budget. This amounts to choosing those projects with the largest benefit/cost ratio (profitability index).

Strictly speaking, this is the correct thing to do only if the soft rationing is a one-time event; that is, it won't exist next year. If the soft rationing is a chronic problem, then something is amiss. The reason goes all the way back to

Chapter 1. Ongoing soft rationing means that we are constantly by-passing positive NPV investments. This contradicts our goal of the firm. If we are not trying to maximize value, then the question of which projects to take becomes ambiguous because we no longer have an objective goal in the first place.

hard rationing

The situation that occurs when a business cannot raise financing for a project under any circumstances.

Hard Rationing   With **hard rationing,** a business cannot raise capital for a project under any circumstances. For large, healthy corporations, this situation probably does not occur very often. This is fortunate because with hard rationing our DCF analysis breaks down, and the best course of action is ambiguous.

The reason that DCF analysis breaks down has to do with the required return. Suppose we say our required return is 20 percent. Implicitly, we are saying that we will take a project with a return that exceeds this. However, if we face hard rationing, then we are not going to take a new project no matter what the return on that project is, so the whole concept of a required return is ambiguous. About the only interpretation we can give this situation is that the required return is so large that no project has a positive NPV in the first place.

Hard rationing can occur when a company experiences financial distress, meaning that bankruptcy is a possibility. Also, a firm may not be able to raise capital without violating a preexisting contractual agreement. We discuss these situations in greater detail in a later chapter.

⌐CONCEPT QUESTIONS

9.6a Why do we say that our standard discounted cash flow analysis is static?

9.6b What are managerial options in capital budgeting? Give some examples.

9.6c What is capital rationing? What types are there? What problems does it create for discounted cash flow analysis?

9.7 | SUMMARY AND CONCLUSIONS

In this chapter, we looked at some ways of evaluating the results of a discounted cash flow analysis. We also touched on some of the problems that can come up in practice. We saw that:

1. Net present value estimates depend on projected future cash flows. If there are errors in those projections, then our estimated NPVs can be misleading. We called this *forecasting risk.*

2. Scenario and sensitivity analyses are useful tools for identifying which variables are critical to a project and where forecasting problems can do the most damage.

3. Break-even analysis in its various forms is a particularly common type of scenario analysis that is useful for identifying critical levels of sales.

4. Operating leverage is a key determinant of break-even levels. It reflects the degree to which a project or a firm is committed to fixed costs. The degree of operating leverage tells us the sensitivity of operating cash flow to changes in sales volume.

5. Projects usually have future managerial options associated with them. These options may be very important, but standard discounted cash flow analysis tends to ignore them.

6. Capital rationing occurs when apparently profitable projects cannot be funded. Standard discounted cash flow analysis is troublesome in this case because NPV is not necessarily the appropriate criterion anymore.

The most important thing to carry away from reading this chapter is that estimated NPVs or returns should not be taken at face value. They depend critically on projected cash flows. If there is room for significant disagreement about those projected cash flows, the results from the analysis have to be taken with a grain of salt.

Despite the problems we have discussed, discounted cash flow is still *the* way of attacking problems, because it forces us to ask the right questions. What we learn in this chapter is that knowing the questions to ask does not guarantee that we will get all the answers.

Key Terms

forecasting risk 296
scenario analysis 298
sensitivity analysis 299
simulation analysis 300
variable costs 302
fixed costs 303
marginal or incremental cost 304
marginal or incremental revenue 305
accounting break-even 305
cash break-even 312

financial break-even 312
operating leverage 315
degree of operating leverage 315
managerial options 319
contingency planning 319
strategic options 321
capital rationing 321
soft rationing 321
hard rationing 322

Chapter Review Problems and Self-Test

Use the following base-case information to work the self-test problems. You can check your answers just below.

A project under consideration costs $500,000, has a five-year life, and has no salvage value. Depreciation is straight-line to zero. The required return is 15 percent, and the tax rate is 34 percent. Sales are projected at 400 units per year. Price per unit is $3,000, variable cost per unit is $1,900, and fixed costs are $250,000 per year.

9.1 Scenario Analysis   Suppose you think that the unit sales price, variable cost, and fixed cost projections above are accurate to within 5 percent. What are the upper and lower bounds for these projections? What is the base-case NPV? What are the best- and worst-case scenario NPVs?

9.2 Break-Even Analysis   Given the base-case projections in the previous problem, what are the cash, accounting, and financial break-even sales levels for this project? Ignore taxes in answering.

Answers to Self-Test Problems

9.1 We can summarize the relevant information as follows:

	Base Case	Lower Bound	Upper Bound
Unit sales	400	380	420
Price per unit	$3,000	$2,850	$3,150
Variable costs per unit	$1,900	$1,805	$1,995
Fixed costs	$250,000	$237,500	$262,500

The depreciation is $100,000 per year, so we can calculate the cash flows under each scenario. Remember that we assign high costs and low prices and volume under the worst case and just the opposite for the best case.

Scenario	Unit Sales	Price	Variable Cost	Fixed Costs	Cash Flow
Base	400	$3,000	$1,900	$250,000	$159,400
Best	420	3,150	1,805	237,500	250,084
Worst	380	2,850	1,995	262,500	75,184

At 15 percent, the five-year annuity factor is 3.35216, so the NPVs are:

$$\text{Base-case NPV} = -\$500,000 + 3.35216 \times \$159,400 = \$34,334$$

$$\text{Best-case NPV} = -\$500,000 + 3.35216 \times \$250,084 = \$338,320$$

$$\text{Worst-case NPV} = -\$500,000 + 3.35216 \times \$75,184 = -\$247,972$$

9.2 In this case, we have $250,000 in cash fixed costs to cover. Each unit contributes $3,000 − 1,900 = $1,100 toward doing so. The cash break-even is thus $250,000/1,100 = 227 units. We have another $100,000 in depreciation, so the accounting break-even is ($250,000 + $100,000)/1,100 = 318 units.

To get the financial break-even, we need to find the OCF such that the project has a zero NPV. As we have seen, the five-year annuity factor is 3.35216 and the project costs $500,000, so the OCF must be such that:

$$\$500,000 = \text{OCF} \times 3.35216$$

So, to break even on a financial basis, the project's cash flow must be $500,000/3.35216, or $149,158 per year. If we add this to the $250,000 in cash fixed costs, we get a total of $399,158 that we have to cover. At $1,100 per unit, we need to sell $399,158/$1,100 = 363 units.

Questions and Problems

1. **Calculating Costs and Break-Even**   NoNox manufactures gasoline additives. The variable materials cost is $1.15 per pint and the variable labor cost is $2.60 per pint.
   a. What is the variable cost per unit?
   b. Suppose NoNox incurs fixed costs of $320,000 during a year when total production is 280,000 pints. What are the total costs for the year?
   c. If the selling price is $5.30 per unit, does NoNox break even on a cash basis? If depreciation is $130,000 per year, what is the accounting break-even point?

2. **Calculating Break-Even**   In each of the following cases, calculate the accounting break-even and the cash break-even points. Ignore tax effects in calculating the cash break-even and explain any large discrepancies between the two points.

Unit Price	Unit Variable Cost	Fixed Costs	Depreciation
$ 2	$ 1	$ 100	$ 200
25	14	14,000	75,000
20,000	15,000	40,000,000	25,130,000

3. **Scenario Analysis**   We are evaluating a project that costs $70,000, has a seven-year life, and no salvage value. Assume that depreciation is straight-line to a zero salvage over the seven years. We require a return of 10 percent on such projects. The tax rate is 34 percent. Sales are projected at 15,000 units per year. Price per unit is $5.95, variable cost per unit is $2.63, and fixed costs are $25,000 per year.
   a. Calculate the accounting break-even point. What is the degree of operating leverage at the accounting break-even point?
   b. Calculate the base-case cash flow and NPV. Suppose you think that the sales projection is accurate only to within 25 percent. Evaluate the sensitivity of NPV to changes in that projection.
   c. Suppose the projections given are all accurate to within 5 percent except for sales volume, which is only accurate to within 15 percent. Calculate the NPV under the best and worst cases.

4. **Calculating Operating Leverage**   At an output level of 10,000 units, you calculate that the degree of operating leverage is 4. If output rises to 12,000 units, what will the percentage change in operating cash flow be? Will the new level of operating leverage be higher or lower? Explain.

5. **Leverage**   In the previous question, suppose that fixed costs are $50,000. What is the operating cash flow at 12,000 units? The degree of operating leverage?

6. **Computing Average Cost**   Gnosis, Inc., can manufacture gnoses for $2.30 in variable raw materials cost and $24 in variable direct labor expense. Gnoses sell for $36 each. Last year, production was

40,000 gnoses. Fixed costs were $360,000. What were total production costs? What is the marginal cost per gnose? What is the average cost? If Gnosis is considering a one-shot order for an extra 1,000 gnoses, what is the minimum acceptable total revenue from the order? Explain.

7. **Break-Even Intuition**   A co-worker claims that looking at all this marginal this and incremental that is just a bunch of nonsense, and states: "Listen, if our average revenue doesn't exceed our average cost, then we will have a negative cash flow, and we will go broke!" How do you respond?

8. **Degree of Operating Leverage and Break-Even Intuition**   If a project just breaks even on an accounting basis, show that the degree of operating leverage is:

    $$DOL = 1 + (Fixed\ costs/Depreciation)$$

9. **Break-Even Intuition**   If a project just breaks even on an accounting basis, what is its cash flow? Its payback? Its return? Explain. Suppose a project just breaks even on a financial basis. What is its discounted payback? What is its return? What is the return on a project that just breaks even on a cash basis?

10. **Break-Even and Fixed Costs**   A project is projected to break even on an accounting basis in its third year. Sales for the third year are projected at 12,000 units. Depreciation at that time will be $130,000. The price per unit less variable cost per unit is $15. What are the fixed costs?

11. **Break-Even and Variable Costs**   In the previous question, suppose fixed costs are $80,000 and the price per unit is $48. What is the variable cost per unit?

12. **Operating Cash Flow and Leverage**   A proposed project has fixed costs of $50,000 per year. The operating cash flow at 3,000 units is $125,000. What is the degree of operating leverage? If units sold rise from 3,000 to 4,000, what will the increase in operating cash flow be (ignore taxes)? What is the new degree of operating leverage?

13. **Forecasting Risk**   What is forecasting risk? In general, would the degree of forecasting risk be greatest for a new product or a cost-cutting proposal? Why?

14. **Options and NPV**   What is the option to abandon? The option to expand? Explain why we tend to underestimate NPV when we ignore these options.

15. **Cash Flow and Leverage**   At an output level of 2,000 units, you have calculated that the degree of operating leverage is 2. The cash flow is $4,500 in this case. What will the cash flow be if output rises to 2,500 units? If output falls to 1,500?

16. **Leverage**   In the previous question, what will the new degree of operating leverage be in each case? (Hint: What are fixed costs?)

17. **Project Analysis**   You are considering a new product. It will cost $945,000 to launch, have a three-year life, and have no salvage value. Depreciation is straight-line to a zero salvage. The required return is 20 percent, and the tax rate is 34 percent. Sales are projected at 80 units per year. Price per unit will be $35,000, variable cost per unit is $21,900, and fixed costs are $500,000 per year.

    a. Based on your experience, you think that the unit sales, variable cost, and fixed cost projections above are probably accurate to within 10 percent. What are the upper and lower bounds for these projections? What is the base-case NPV? What are the best- and worst-case scenarios?

    b. Evaluate the sensitivity of your base-case NPV to changes in fixed costs.

    c. What is the cash break-even for this project?

    d. What is the accounting break-even for this project? What is the degree of operating leverage at the accounting break-even point? How do you interpret this number?

18. **Break-Even and Taxes**   If you were to include the effect of taxes in break-even analysis, what do you think happens to the cash, accounting, and financial break-even points?

19. **Abandonment Value**   We are examining a new project. We expect to sell 500 units per year at $20 net cash flow apiece for the next 10 years. In other words, the annual operating cash flow is projected to be $20 × 500 = $10,000 per year. The relevant discount rate is 20 percent, and the initial investment is $55,000.

    a. What is the base-case NPV?

    b. After the first year, the project can be dismantled and sold for $40,000. If expected sales are revised based on the first year's performance, when would it make sense to abandon the investment? In other words, at what level of expected sales would it make sense to abandon the project?

    c. Explain how the $40,000 abandonment value can be viewed as the opportunity cost of keeping the project in one year.

20. **Abandonment**   In the previous question, suppose you think it is likely that expected sales will be revised up to 750 if the first year is a success and revised downward to 250 if the first year is not a success.

    a. If success and failure are equally likely, what is the NPV of the project? Consider the possibility of abandonment in answering.

    b. What is the value of the option to abandon?

21. **Abandonment and Expansion**   In the previous question, suppose that the scale of the project can be doubled in one year in the sense that twice as many units can be produced and sold. Naturally, expansion would only be desirable if the project is a success. This implies that if the project is a success, projected sales after expansion will be 1,500. Again assuming that success and failure are equally likely, what is the NPV of the project? Note that abandonment is still an option if the project is a failure. What is the value of the option to expand here?

22.   Break-Even and Taxes   It concerns the effect of taxes on the various break-even measures.

a. Show that, when we consider taxes, the general relationship between operating cash flow (OCF) and sales volume (Q) can be written as:

$$Q = \frac{FC + \dfrac{(OCF - T \times D)}{(1 - T)}}{(P - v)}$$

b. Use the expression in part a to find the cash, accounting, and financial break-even points for the Wettway sailboat example in the chapter. Assume a 34 percent tax rate.

c. In part b, the accounting break-even should be the same. Why? Verify this algebraically.

23.   Operating Leverage and Taxes   Show that if we consider the effect of taxes, the degree of operating leverage can be written as:

$$DOL = 1 + [FC \times (1 - T) - D \times T]/OCF$$

Notice that this reduces to our previous result if $T = 0$. Can you interpret this in words?

24.   Break-Even   This question uses the results from the previous two questions. The Trichermann and Sifts Company is thinking of importing and selling a line of gourmet cookware. The order and processing cost per set is $120, and the selling price will be $210 per set. Fixed costs will be $400,000 per year, and the depreciation expense will be $250,000. The tax rate is 34 percent. What are the accounting and cash break-even points if we consider taxes? Which is smaller? Why? What is the degree of operating leverage here?

Suggested Readings

For an interesting application of break-even analysis, see:

Reinhardt, U. E. "Break-Even Analysis for Lockheed's TriStar: An Application of Financial Theory." *Journal of Finance* 28, September 1973, pp. 821–38.

The following articles are "classics" on the subject of risk analysis in investment decisions:

Hertz, D. B. "Risk Analysis in Capital Investment." *Harvard Business Review* 42, January–February 1964, pp. 95–106.

————. "Investment Policies that Pay Off." *Harvard Business Review* 46, January–February 1968, pp. 96–108.

Part Five   *Risk and Return*

CHAPTER 10
Some Lessons from Capital Market History

This chapter begins with a description of investors' historical experiences in U.S. capital markets since 1926. It describes the lessons that financial managers can learn from studying capital market history and introduces the important concept of an efficient capital market.

CHAPTER 11
Return, Risk, and the Security Market Line

This chapter describes the nature of the risk-return trade-off facing investors and firms. It shows how to use the risk-return trade-off to determine the required return on an investment.

Chapter 10

Some Lessons from Capital Market History

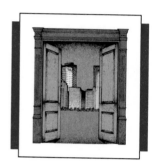

Thus far, we haven't had much to say about what determines the required return on an investment. In one sense, the answer is very simple: The required return depends on the risk of the investment. The greater the risk is, the greater is the required return.

Having said this, we are left with a somewhat more difficult problem. How can we measure the amount of risk present in an investment? Put another way, what does it mean to say that one investment is riskier than another? Obviously, we need to define what we mean by risk if we are going to answer these questions. This is our task in the next two chapters.

From the last several chapters, we know that one of the responsibilities of the financial manager is to assess the value of proposed real asset investments. In doing this, it is important that we first look at what financial investments have to offer. At a minimum, the return we require from a proposed nonfinancial investment must be greater than what we can get from buying financial assets of similar risk.

Our goal in this chapter is to provide a perspective on what capital market history can tell us about risk and return. The most important thing to get out of this chapter is a feel for the numbers. What is a high return? What is a low one? More generally, what returns should we expect from financial assets and what are the risks from such investments? This perspective is essential for understanding how to analyze and value risky investment projects.

We start our discussion of risk and return by describing the historical experience of investors in U.S. financial markets. In 1931, for example, the stock market lost 43 percent of its value. Just two years later, the stock market gained 54 percent. In more recent memory, the market lost about 25 percent of its value on October 19, 1987, alone. What lessons, if any, can financial managers learn from such shifts in the stock market? We will explore the last half-century (and then some) of market history to find out.

Not everyone agrees on the value of studying history. On the one hand, there is philosopher George Santayana's famous comment, "Those who do not remember the past are condemned to repeat it." On the other hand, there is industrialist Henry Ford's equally famous comment, "History is more or less bunk." Nonetheless, based on recent history, perhaps everyone would agree with Mark Twain when he observed, "October. This is one of the peculiarly dangerous months to speculate in stocks in. The others are July, January, September, April, November, May, March, June, December, August, and February."

There are two central lessons that emerge from our study of market history. First, there is a reward for bearing risk. Second, the greater the potential reward, the greater is the risk. To understand these facts about market returns, we devote much of this chapter to reporting the statistics and numbers that make up the modern capital market history of the United States. In the next chapter, these facts provide the foundation for our study of how financial markets put a price on risk.

10.1 | RETURNS

We wish to discuss historical returns on different types of financial assets. The first thing we need to do, then, is to briefly discuss how to calculate the return from investing.

Dollar Returns

If you buy an asset of any sort, your gain (or loss) from that investment is called the *return on your investment*. This return will usually have two components. First, you may receive some cash directly while you own the investment. This is called the *income component* of your return. Second, the value of the asset you purchase will often change. In this case, you have a capital gain or capital loss on your investment.[1]

To illustrate, suppose the Video Concept Company has several thousand shares of stock outstanding. You purchased some of these shares of stock in the company at the beginning of the year. It is now year-end, and you want to determine how well you have done on your investment.

First, over the year, a company may pay cash dividends to its shareholders. As a stockholder in Video Concept Company, you are a part owner of the company. If the company is profitable, it may choose to distribute some of its profits to shareholders (we discuss the details of dividend policy in Chapter 16). So, as the owner of some stock, you will receive some cash. This cash is the income component from owning the stock.

---

[1]As we mentioned in an earlier chapter, strictly speaking, what is and what is not a capital gain (or loss) is determined by the IRS. We thus use the terms loosely.

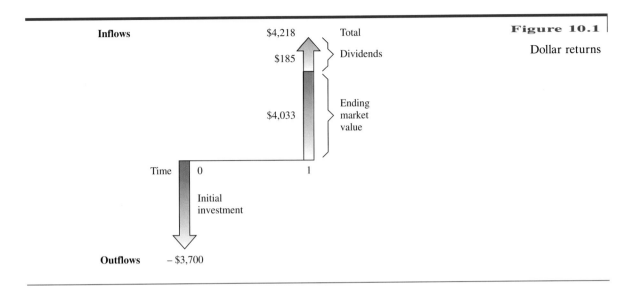

Figure 10.1

Dollar returns

In addition to the dividend, the other part of your return is the capital gain or capital loss on the stock. This part arises from changes in the value of your investment. For example, consider the cash flows illustrated in Figure 10.1. The stock is selling for $37 per share. If you buy 100 shares, you have a total outlay of $3,700. Suppose that, over the year, the stock paid a dividend of $1.85 per share. By the end of the year, then, you would have received income of:

Dividend = $1.85 × 100 = $185

Also, the value of the stock rises to $40.33 per share by the end of the year. Your 100 shares are worth $4,033, so you have a capital gain of:

Capital gain = ($40.33 − 37) × 100 = $333

On the other hand, if the price had dropped to, say, $34.78, you would have a capital loss of:

Capital loss = ($34.78 − 37) × 100 = −$222

Notice that a capital loss is the same thing as a negative capital gain.

The total dollar return on your investment is the sum of the dividend and the capital gain:

Total dollar return = Dividend income + Capital gain (or loss)   [10.1]

In our first example, the total dollar return is thus given by:

Total dollar return = $185 + 333 = $518

Notice that, if you sold the stock at the end of the year, the total amount of cash you would have would be your initial investment plus the total return. In the preceding example, then:

$$\text{Total cash if stock is sold} = \text{Initial investment} + \text{Total return} \quad [10.2]$$

$$= \$3,700 + 518$$

$$= \$4,218$$

As a check, notice that this is the same as the proceeds from the sale of the stock plus the dividends:

$$\text{Proceeds from stock sale} + \text{Dividends} = \$40.33 \times 100 + \$185$$

$$= \$4,033 + 185$$

$$= \$4,218$$

Suppose you hold on to your Video Concept stock and don't sell it at the end of the year. Should you still consider the capital gain as part of your return? Isn't this only a "paper" gain and not really a cash flow if you don't sell it?

The answer to the first question is a strong yes, and the answer to the second is an equally strong no. The capital gain is every bit as much a part of your return as the dividend, and you should certainly count it as part of your return. That you actually decided to keep the stock and not sell (you don't "realize" the gain) is irrelevant because you could have converted it to cash if you wanted to. Whether you choose to do so or not is up to you.

After all, if you insisted on converting your gain to cash, you could always sell the stock at year-end and immediately reinvest by buying the stock back. There is no net difference between doing this and just not selling (assuming, of course, that there are no tax consequences from selling the stock). Again, the point is that whether you actually cash out and buy sodas (or whatever) or reinvest by not selling doesn't affect the return you earn.

Percentage Returns

It is usually more convenient to summarize information about returns in percentage terms, rather than dollar terms, because that way your return doesn't depend on how much you actually invest. The question we want to answer is: How much do we get for each dollar we invest?

To answer this question, let P_t be the price of the stock at the beginning of the year and let D_{t+1} be the dividend paid on the stock during the year. Consider the cash flows in Figure 10.2. These are the same as those in Figure 10.1, except that we have now expressed everything on a per share basis.

In our example, the price at the beginning of the year was $37 per share and the dividend paid during the year on each share was $1.85. As we discussed in Chapter 6, expressing the dividend as a percentage of the beginning stock price results in the dividend yield:

$$\text{Dividend yield} = D_{t+1}/P_t$$

$$= \$1.85/\$37 = .05 = 5\%$$

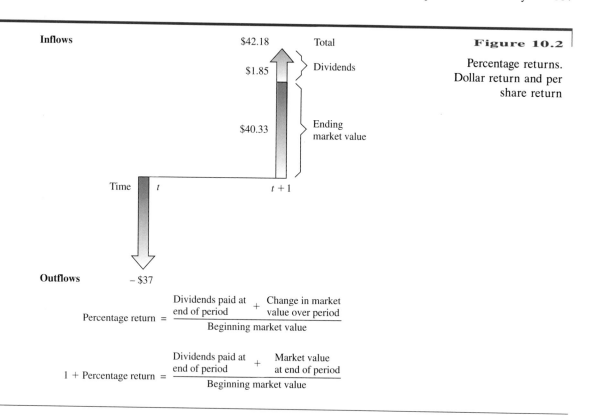

Inflows

$42.18   Total

$1.85   Dividends

$40.33   Ending market value

Time t $t+1$

Outflows   – $37

$$\text{Percentage return} = \frac{\substack{\text{Dividends paid at} \\ \text{end of period}} + \substack{\text{Change in market} \\ \text{value over period}}}{\text{Beginning market value}}$$

$$1 + \text{Percentage return} = \frac{\substack{\text{Dividends paid at} \\ \text{end of period}} + \substack{\text{Market value} \\ \text{at end of period}}}{\text{Beginning market value}}$$

Figure 10.2

Percentage returns. Dollar return and per share return

This says that, for each dollar we invest, we get 5 cents in dividends.

The second component of our percentage return is the capital gains yield. Recall (from Chapter 6) that this is calculated as the change in the price during the year (the capital gain) divided by the beginning price:

$$\text{Capital gains yield} = (P_{t+1} - P_t)/P_t$$

$$= (\$40.33 - 37)/\$37$$

$$= \$3.33/\$37$$

$$= 9\%$$

So, per dollar invested, we get 9 cents in capital gains.

Putting it together, per dollar invested, we get 5 cents in dividends and 9 cents in capital gains; so we get a total of 14 cents. Our percentage return is 14 cents on the dollar, or 14 percent.

To check this, notice that we invested $3,700 and ended up with $4,218. By what percentage did our $3,700 increase? As we saw, we picked up $4,218 − 3,700 = $518. This is a $518/$3,700 = 14% increase.

Example 10.1   Calculating Returns

Suppose you buy some stock for $25 per share. At the end of the year, the price is $35 per share. During the year, you got a $2 dividend per share. This

Figure 10.3

Cash flow—an investment
example

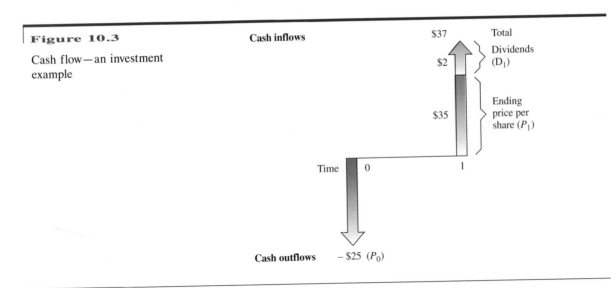

is the situation illustrated in Figure 10.3. What is the dividend yield? The capital gains yield? The percentage return? If your total investment was $1,000, how much do you have at the end of the year?

Your $2 dividend per share works out to a dividend yield of:

Dividend yield = D_{t+1}/P_t

$$= \$2/\$25 = .08 = 8\%$$

The per share capital gain is $10, so the capital gains yield is:

Capital gains yield = $(P_{t+1} - P_t)/P_t$

$$= (\$35 - 25)/\$25$$

$$= \$10/\$25$$

$$= 40\%$$

The total percentage return is thus 48 percent.

If you had invested $1,000, you would have $1,480 at the end of the year, a 48 percent increase. To check this, note that your $1,000 would have bought you $1,000/25 = 40 shares. Your 40 shares would then have paid you a total of 40 × $2 = $80 in cash dividends. Your $10 per share gain would give you a total capital gain of $10 × 40 = $400. Add these together, and you get the $480. ■

CONCEPT QUESTIONS

10.1a What are the two parts of total return?

10.1b Why are unrealized capital gains or losses included in the calculation of returns?

10.1c What is the difference between a dollar return and a percentage return? Why are percentage returns more convenient?

INFLATION AND RETURNS | 10.2

So far, we haven't worried about inflation in calculating returns. Since this is an important consideration, we consider the impact of inflation next.

Real versus Nominal Returns

The returns we calculated in the previous section are called **nominal returns** because they weren't adjusted for inflation. Returns that have been adjusted to reflect inflation are called **real returns.**

To see the effect of inflation on returns, suppose that prices are currently rising by 5 percent per year. In other words, the inflation rate is 5 percent. We are considering an investment that will be worth $115.50 in one year. It costs $100 today.

We start by calculating the percentage return. In this case, there is no income component, so the return is the capital gains yield of ($115.50 − 100)/$100 = 15.50%. Once again, we've ignored the effect of inflation, so this 15.50 percent is the nominal return.

What is the impact of inflation here? To answer, suppose pizzas cost $5 apiece at the beginning of the year. With $100, we can buy 20 pizzas. Since the inflation rate is 5 percent, pizzas will cost 5 percent more, or $5.25, at the end of the year. If we take the investment, how many pizzas can we buy at the end of the year? Measured in pizzas instead of dollars, what is our return?

Our $115.50 from the investment will buy us $115.50/$5.25 = 22 pizzas. This is up from 20 pizzas, so our pizza return is (22 − 20)/20 = 10%. What this illustrates is that even though the nominal return on our investment is 15.5 percent, our buying power has only gone up by 10 percent because of inflation. Put another way, we are really only 10 percent richer. In this case, we say that the real return is 10 percent.

Alternatively, with 5 percent inflation, each of the $115.50 nominal dollars we get is worth 5 percent less in real terms, so the real dollar value of our investment in a year is:

$$\$115.50/1.05 = \$110$$

What we have done is to *deflate* the $115.50 by 5 percent. Since we give up $100 in current buying power to get the equivalent of $110, our real return is again 10 percent. Because we have removed the effect of future inflation here, this $110 is said to be measured in current dollars.

The difference between nominal and real returns is important and bears repeating:

> Your nominal return on an investment is the percentage change in the number of dollars you have.

> Your real return on an investment is the percentage change in how much you can buy with your dollars, in other words, the percentage change in your buying power.

nominal return
Return on an investment not adjusted for inflation.

real return
Return adjusted for the effects of inflation.

The Fisher Effect

Fisher effect

Relationship between nominal
returns, real returns, and inflation.

Our discussion of real and nominal returns illustrates a relationship often called the **Fisher effect**. Since investors are ultimately concerned with what they can buy with their money, they require compensation for inflation. Let R stand for the nominal return and r stand for the real return. The Fisher effect tells us that the relationship between nominal returns, real returns, and inflation can be written as:

$$(1 + R) = (1 + r) \times (1 + h) \qquad [10.3]$$

where h is the inflation rate.

From the example above, the nominal return was 15.50 percent and the inflation rate was 5 percent. What was the real return? We can determine it by plugging in these numbers:

$$(1 + .1550) = (1 + r) \times (1 + .05)$$

$$(1 + r) = (1.1550)/(1.05) = 1.10$$

$$r = 10\%$$

This real return is the same as we had before. If we take another look at the Fisher effect, we can rearrange things a little as follows:

$$(1 + R) = (1 + r) \times (1 + h) \qquad [10.4]$$

$$R = r + h + r \times h$$

What this tells us is that the nominal return has three components. First, there is the real return on the investment, r. Next, there is the compensation for the decrease in the value of the money originally invested because of inflation, h. The third component represents compensation for the fact that the dollars earned on the investment are also worth less because of the inflation.

This third component is usually small, so it is often dropped. The nominal rate is then approximately equal to the real rate plus the inflation rate:

$$R \approx r + h \qquad [10.5]$$

Example 10.2 The Fisher Effect

If investors require a 10 percent real return, and the inflation rate is 8 percent, what must be the approximate nominal rate? The exact nominal rate?

First of all, the nominal rate is approximately equal to the sum of the real rate and the inflation rate: $10\% + 8\% = 18\%$. From the Fisher effect, we have:

$$(1 + R) = (1 + r) \times (1 + h)$$

$$= (1.10) \times (1.08)$$

$$= 1.1880$$

Therefore, the nominal rate will actually be closer to 19 percent. ∎

It is important to note that financial rates, such as interest rates, discount rates, and rates of return, are almost always quoted in nominal terms. To remind you of this, we will henceforth use the symbol R instead of r in most of our subsequent discussions about such rates.

CONCEPT QUESTIONS

10.2a What is the difference between a nominal and a real return? Which is more important to a typical investor?

10.2b What is the Fisher effect?

THE HISTORICAL RECORD | 10.3

Roger Ibbotson and Rex Sinquefield conducted a famous set of studies dealing with rates of return in U.S. financial markets.[2] They presented year-to-year historical rates of return on five important types of financial investments. The returns can be interpreted as what you would have earned if you held portfolios of the following:

1. Common stocks. The common stock portfolio is based on 500 of the largest companies (in terms of total market value of outstanding stock) in the United States.

2. Small stocks. This is a portfolio composed of the smallest 20 percent of the companies listed on the New York Stock Exchange, again as measured by market value of outstanding stock.

3. Long-term corporate bonds. This is a portfolio of high-quality bonds with 20 years to maturity.

4. Long-term U.S. government bonds. This is a portfolio of U.S. government bonds with 20 years to maturity.

5. U.S. Treasury bills. This a portfolio of Treasury bills (T-bills for short) with a three-month maturity.

These returns are not adjusted for inflation or taxes; thus, they are nominal, pretax returns.

In addition to the year-to-year returns on these financial instruments, the year-to-year percentage change in the Consumer Price Index (CPI) is also computed. This is a commonly used measure of inflation, so we can calculate real returns using this as the inflation rate.

A First Look

Before looking closely at the different portfolio returns, we take a look at the "big picture." Figure 10.4 shows what happened to $1 invested in these different portfolios at the beginning of 1926. The growth in value for each of the different portfolios over the 65-year period ending in 1990 is given separately

---

[2]R. G. Ibbotson and R. A. Sinquefield, *Stocks, Bonds, Bills, and Inflation* [SBBI] (Charlottesville, Va.: Financial Analysis Research Foundation, 1982).

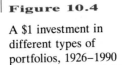

Figure 10.4

A $1 investment in different types of portfolios, 1926–1990 (Year-end 1925 = $1)*

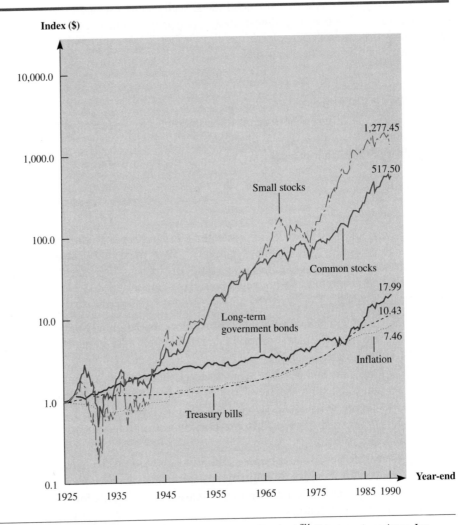

(the long-term corporate bonds are omitted). Notice that, to get everything on a single graph, some modification in scaling is used. As is commonly done with financial series, the vertical axis is scaled such that equal distances measure equal percentage (as opposed to dollar) changes in values.[3]

Looking at Figure 10.4, we see that the "small cap" (short for small capitalization) investment did the best overall. Every dollar invested grew to a remarkable $1,277.45 over the 65 years. The larger common stock portfolio did less well; a dollar invested in it grew to $517.50.

At the other end, the T-bill portfolio grew to only $10.43. This is even less impressive when we consider the inflation over this period. As illustrated, the

---

[3]In other words, the scale is logarithmic.

In Their Own Words...
Roger Ibbotson on Capital Market History

The financial markets are perhaps the most carefully documented human phenomena in history. Every day, approximately 2,000 NYSE stocks are traded, and at least 5,000 more are traded on other exchanges and in over-the-counter markets. Bonds, commodities, futures, and options also provide a wealth of data. These data daily fill a dozen pages of *The Wall Street Journal* (and numerous other newspapers), and these pages are only summaries of the day's transactions. A record actually exists of every transaction, providing not only a real-time database, but a historical record extending back, in many cases, more than a century.

The global market adds another dimension to this wealth of data. The Japanese stock market trades a billion shares on active days, and the London exchange reports trades on over 10,000 domestic and foreign issues a day.

The data generated by these transactions are quantifiable, quickly analyzed and disseminated, and made easily accessible by computer. Because of this, finance has increasingly come to resemble one of the exact sciences. The use of financial market data ranges from the simple, such as using the S&P 500 to measure the performance of a portfolio, to the incredibly complex. For example, only a generation ago, the bond market was the staidest province on Wall Street. Today, it attracts swarms of traders seeking to exploit arbitrage opportunities — small temporary mispricings — using real-time data and supercomputers to analyze them.

Financial market data are the foundation for the extensive empirical understanding we now have of the financial markets. The following is a list of some of the principal findings of such research:

- Risky securities, such as stocks, have higher average returns than riskless securities such as Treasury bills.
- Stocks of small companies have higher average returns than those of larger companies.
- Long-term bonds have higher average yields and returns than short-term bonds.
- The cost of capital for a company, project, or division can be predicted using data from the markets.

Because phenomena in the financial markets are so well measured, finance is the most readily quantifiable branch of economics. Researchers are able to do more extensive empirical research than in any other economic field, and the research can be quickly translated into action in the marketplace.

Roger Ibbotson is Professor in the Practice of Management at the Yale School of Management. He is the founder and president of Ibbotson Associates, a major supplier of financial databases to the financial services industry. An outstanding scholar, he is best known for his original estimates of the historical rates of return realized by investors in different markets and for his research on new issues.

increase in the price level was such that $7.46 is needed just to replace the original $1.

Given the historical record, why would anybody buy anything other than small cap stocks? If you look closely at Figure 10.4, you will probably see the answer. The T-bill portfolio and the long-term government bond portfolio grew more slowly than did the stock portfolios, but they also grew much more steadily. The small stocks ended up on top, but as you can see, they grew quite erratically at times. For example, the small stocks were the worst performers for about the first 10 years and had a smaller return than long-term government bonds for almost 20 years.

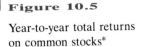

Figure 10.5

Year-to-year total returns
on common stocks*

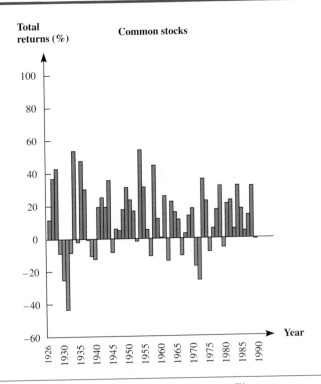

A Closer Look

To illustrate the variability of the different investments, Figures 10.5 through
10.8 (on pages 344–47) plot the year-to-year percentage returns in the form of
vertical bars drawn from the horizontal axis. The height of the bar tells us the
return for the particular year. For example, looking at the long-term government bonds (Fig-ure 10.7), we see the largest historical return (40.35 percent)
occurred not so long ago (in 1982). This was a good year for bonds. In comparing these charts, notice the differences in the vertical axis scales. With this in
mind, you can see how predictably the Treasury bills (Figure 10.7) behaved
compared to the small stocks (Figure 10.6).

The actual year-to-year returns used to draw these bar graphs are displayed in Table 10.1 (on pages 348–49). Looking at this table, we see, for example, that the largest single-year return is a remarkable 142.87 percent for
the small cap stocks in 1933. In the same year, the large stocks (common
stocks) "only" returned 53.99 percent. In contrast, the largest Treasury bill return was 14.71 percent (in 1981).

CONCEPT QUESTIONS

10.3a With 20-20 hindsight, what was the best investment for the period
       1926–35?

10.3b Why doesn't everyone just buy small stocks as investments?

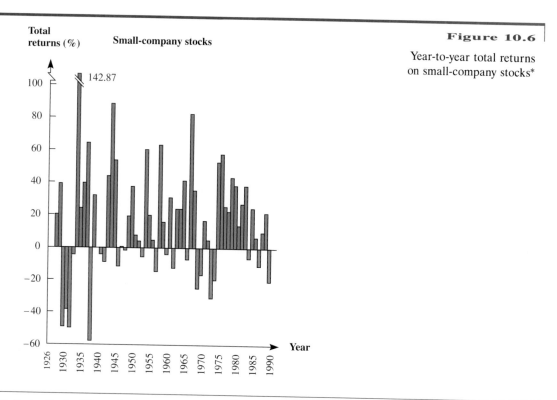

Figure 10.6

Year-to-year total returns on small-company stocks*

10.3c What was the smallest return observed over the 65 years for each of these investments? When did it occur?

10.3d How many times did large stocks (common stocks) return more than 30 percent? How many times did they return less than −20 percent?

10.3e What was the longest "winning streak" (years without a negative return) for large stocks? For long-term government bonds?

10.3f How often did the T-bill portfolio have a negative return?

AVERAGE RETURNS: THE FIRST LESSON | 10.4

As you've probably begun to notice, the history of capital market returns is too complicated to be of much use in its undigested form. We need to begin summarizing all these numbers. Accordingly, we discuss how to go about condensing the detailed data. We start out by calculating average returns.

Calculating Average Returns

The obvious way to calculate the average returns on the different investments in Table 10.1 is simply to add up the yearly returns and divide by 65. The result is the historical average of the individual values.

Figure 10.7

Year-to-year total returns on bonds and bills*

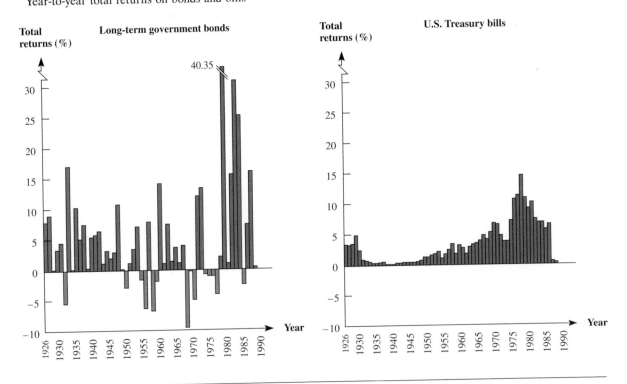

For example, if you add up the returns for the common stocks for the 65 years, you will get about 7.865. The average annual return is thus 7.865/65 = 12.1%. You interpret this 12.1 percent just like any other average. If you picked a year at random from the 65-year history and you had to guess what the return in that year was, the best guess is 12.1 percent.

Average Returns: The Historical Record

Table 10.2 shows the average returns computed from Table 10.1. As shown, in a typical year, the small stocks increased in value by 17.1 percent. Notice also how much larger the stock returns are than the bond returns.

These averages are, of course, nominal since we haven't worried about inflation. Notice that the average inflation rate was 3.2 percent per year over this 65-year span. The nominal return on U.S. Treasury bills was 3.7 percent per year. The average real return on Treasury bills was thus approximately .5 percent per year; so the real return on T-bills has been quite low historically.

At the other extreme, small stocks had an average real return of about 17.1% − 3.1% = 14.0%, which is relatively large. If you remember the Rule of

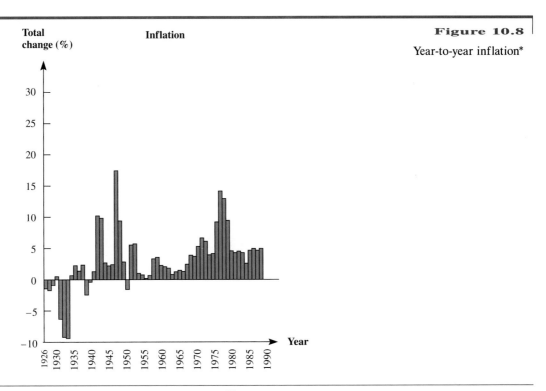

Figure 10.8

Year-to-year inflation*

Total change (%)

Inflation

Year

72 (Chapter 5), then a quick "back of the envelope" calculation tells us that 14 percent real growth doubles your buying power about every five years. Notice also that the real value of the common stock portfolio increased by 9 percent in a typical year.

Risk Premiums

Now that we have computed some average returns, it seems logical to see how they compare with each other. Based on our discussion above, one such comparison involves government-issued securities. These are free of much of the variability we see in, for example, the stock market.

The government borrows money by issuing bonds. These bonds come in different forms. The ones we will focus on are the Treasury bills. These have the shortest time to maturity of the different government bonds. Because the government can always raise taxes to pay its bills, this debt is virtually free of any default risk over its short life. Thus, we will call the rate of return on such debt the *risk-free return,* and we will use it as a kind of benchmark.

A particularly interesting comparison involves the virtually risk-free return on T-bills and the very risky return on common stocks. The difference between these two returns can be interpreted as a measure of the *excess return* on the average risky asset (assuming that the stock of a large U.S. corporation has about average risk compared to all risky assets).

Table 10.1

Year-to-year total returns, 1926–1990

Year	Common Stocks	Small Stocks	Long-Term Corporate Bonds	Long-Term Government Bonds	U.S. Treasury Bills	Consumer Price Index
1926	0.1162	0.0028	0.0737	0.0777	0.0327	−0.0149
1927	0.3749	0.2210	0.0744	0.0893	0.0312	−0.0208
1928	0.4361	0.3969	0.0284	0.0010	0.0324	−0.0097
1929	−0.0840	−0.5136	0.0327	0.0342	0.0475	0.0019
1930	−0.2490	−0.3815	0.0798	0.0466	0.0241	−0.0603
1931	−0.4334	−0.4975	−0.0185	−0.0531	0.0107	−0.0952
1932	−0.0819	−0.0539	0.1082	0.1684	0.0096	−0.1030
1933	0.5399	1.4287	0.1038	−0.0008	0.0030	0.0051
1934	−0.0144	0.2422	0.1384	0.1002	0.0016	0.0203
1935	0.4767	0.4019	0.0961	0.0498	0.0017	0.0299
1936	0.3392	0.6480	0.0674	0.0751	0.0018	0.0121
1937	−0.3503	−0.5801	0.0275	0.0023	0.0031	0.0310
1938	0.3112	0.3280	0.0613	0.0553	−0.0002	−0.0278
1939	−0.0041	0.0035	0.0397	0.0594	0.0002	−0.0048
1940	−0.0978	−0.0516	0.0339	0.0609	0.0000	0.0096
1941	−0.1159	−0.0900	0.0273	0.0093	0.0006	0.0972
1942	0.2034	0.4451	0.0260	0.0322	0.0027	0.0929
1943	0.2590	0.8837	0.0283	0.0208	0.0035	0.0316
1944	0.1975	0.5372	0.0473	0.0281	0.0033	0.0211
1945	0.3644	0.7361	0.0408	0.1073	0.0033	0.0225
1946	−0.0807	−0.1163	0.0172	−0.0010	0.0035	0.1817
1947	0.0571	0.0092	−0.0234	−0.0263	0.0050	0.0901
1948	0.0550	−0.0211	0.0414	0.0340	0.0081	0.0271
1949	0.1879	0.1975	0.0331	0.0645	0.0110	−0.0180
1950	0.3171	0.3875	0.0212	0.0006	0.0120	0.0579
1951	0.2402	0.0780	−0.0269	−0.0394	0.0149	0.0587
1952	0.1837	0.0303	0.0352	0.0116	0.0166	0.0088
1953	−0.0099	−0.0649	0.0341	0.0363	0.0182	0.0062
1954	0.5262	0.6058	0.0539	0.0719	0.0086	−0.0050
1955	0.3156	0.2044	0.0048	−0.0130	0.0157	0.0037
1956	0.0656	0.0428	−0.0681	−0.0559	0.0246	0.0286
1957	−0.1078	−0.1457	0.0871	0.0745	0.0314	0.0302
1958	0.4336	0.6489	−0.0222	−0.0610	0.0154	0.0176
1959	0.1195	0.1640	−0.0097	−0.0226	0.0295	0.0150

Table 10.1

(concluded)

Year	Common Stocks	Small Stocks	Long-Term Corporate Bonds	Long-Term Government Bonds	U.S. Treasury Bills	Consumer Price Index
1960	0.0047	−0.0329	0.0907	0.1378	0.0266	0.0148
1961	0.2689	0.3209	0.0482	0.0097	0.0213	0.0067
1962	−0.0873	−0.1190	0.0795	0.0689	0.0273	0.0122
1963	0.2280	0.2357	0.0219	0.0121	0.0312	0.0165
1964	0.1648	0.2352	0.0477	0.0351	0.0354	0.0119
1965	0.1245	0.4175	−0.0046	0.0071	0.0393	0.0192
1966	−0.1006	−0.0701	0.0020	0.0365	0.0476	0.0335
1967	0.2398	0.8357	−0.0495	−0.0919	0.0421	0.0304
1968	0.1106	0.3597	0.0257	−0.0026	0.0521	0.0472
1969	−0.0850	−0.2505	−0.0809	−0.0508	0.0658	0.0611
1970	0.0401	−0.1743	0.1837	0.1210	0.0653	0.0549
1971	0.1431	0.1650	0.1101	0.1323	0.0439	0.0336
1972	0.1898	0.0443	0.0726	0.0568	0.0384	0.0341
1973	−0.1466	−0.3090	0.0114	−0.0111	0.0693	0.0880
1974	−0.2647	−0.1995	−0.0306	0.0435	0.0800	0.1220
1975	0.3720	0.5282	0.1464	0.0919	0.0580	0.0701
1976	0.2384	0.5738	0.1865	0.1675	0.0508	0.0481
1977	−0.0718	0.2538	0.0171	−0.0067	0.0512	0.0677
1978	0.0656	0.2346	−0.0007	−0.0116	0.0718	0.0903
1979	0.1844	0.4346	−0.0418	−0.0122	0.1038	0.1331
1980	0.3242	0.3988	−0.0262	−0.0395	0.1124	0.1240
1981	−0.0491	0.1388	−0.0096	0.0185	0.1471	0.0894
1982	0.2141	0.2801	0.4379	0.4035	0.1054	0.0387
1983	0.2251	0.3967	0.0470	0.0068	0.0880	0.0380
1984	0.0627	−0.0667	0.1639	0.1543	0.0985	0.0395
1985	0.3216	0.2466	0.3090	0.3097	0.0772	0.0377
1986	0.1847	0.0685	0.1985	0.2444	0.0616	0.0113
1987	0.0523	−0.0930	−0.0027	−0.0269	0.0547	0.0441
1988	0.1681	0.2287	0.1070	0.0967	0.0635	0.0447
1989	0.3149	0.1018	0.1623	0.1811	0.0837	0.0465
1990	−0.0317	−0.2156	0.0678	0.0618	0.0781	0.0611

Table 10.2

Average annual returns: 1926–1990

Investment	Average Return
Common stocks	12.1%
Small stocks	17.1
Long-term corporate bonds	5.5
Long-term government bonds	4.9
U.S. Treasury bills	3.7
Inflation	3.2

Table 10.3

Average annual returns and risk premiums: 1926–1990

Investment	Average Return	Risk Premium
Common stocks	12.1%	8.4%
Small stocks	17.1	13.4
Long-term corporate bonds	5.5	1.8
Long-term government bonds	4.5	0.8
U.S. Treasury bills	3.7	0.0

risk premium

The excess return required from an investment in a risky asset over a risk-free investment.

We call this the "excess" return since it is the additional return we earn by moving from a relatively risk-free investment to a risky one. Because it can be interpreted as a reward for bearing risk, we will call it a **risk premium.**

From Table 10.2, we can calculate the risk premiums for the different investments. We report only the nominal risk premium in Table 10.3 because there is only a slight difference between the historical nominal and real risk premiums.

The risk premium on T-bills is shown as zero in the table because we have assumed that they are riskless.

The First Lesson

Looking at Table 10.3, we see that the average risk premium earned by a typical large common stock is 12.1% − 3.7% = 8.4%. This is a significant reward. The fact that it exists historically is an important observation, and it is the basis for our first lesson: Risky assets, on average, earn a risk premium. Put another way, there is a reward for bearing risk.

Why is this so? Why, for example, is the risk premium for small stocks so much larger than the risk premium for large stocks? More generally, what determines the relative sizes of the risk premiums for the different assets? The answers to these questions are at the heart of modern finance, and the next chapter is devoted to them. For now, part of the answer can be found by looking at the historical variability of the returns of these different investments. So, to get started, we now turn our attention to measuring variability in returns.

CONCEPT QUESTIONS

10.4a What do we mean by excess return and risk premium?

10.4b What was the real (as opposed to nominal) risk premium on the common stock portfolio?

10.4c What was the nominal risk premium on corporate bonds? The real risk premium?

10.4d What is the first lesson from capital market history?

THE VARIABILITY OF RETURNS: THE SECOND LESSON | 10.5

We have already seen that the year-to-year returns on common stocks tend to be more volatile than the returns on, say, long-term government bonds. We now discuss measuring this variability so we can begin examining the subject of risk.

Frequency Distributions and Variability

To get started, we can draw a *frequency distribution* for the common stock returns like the one in Figure 10.9. What we have done here is to count up the number of times that the annual return on the common stock portfolio falls within each 10 percent range. For example, in Figure 10.9, the height of 11 in the range 5 percent to 15 percent means that 11 of the 65 annual returns were in that range. Notice also that the most frequent return is in the 15 percent to 25 percent range. The common stock portfolio had a return in this range 15 times in 65 years.

What we need to do now is to actually measure the spread in returns. We know, for example, that the return on small stocks in a typical year was 17.1 percent. We now want to know how far the actual return deviates from this average in a typical year. In other words, we need a measure of how volatile the return is. The **variance** and its square root, the **standard deviation,** are the most commonly used measures of volatility. We describe how to calculate them next.

The Historical Variance and Standard Deviation

The variance essentially measures the average squared difference between the actual returns and the average return. The bigger this number is, the more the actual returns tend to differ from the average return. Also, the larger the variance or standard deviation is, the more spread out the returns will be.

The way that we will calculate the variance and standard deviation depends on the specific situation. In this chapter, we are looking at historical returns; so the procedure we describe here is the correct one for calculating the *historical* variance and standard deviation. If we were examining projected future returns, then the procedure would be different. We describe this procedure in the next chapter.

To illustrate how we calculate the historical variance, suppose a particular investment had returns of 10 percent, 12 percent, 3 percent, and −9 percent

variance
The average squared difference between the actual return and the average return.

standard deviation
The positive square root of the variance.

Figure 10.9

Frequency distribution of returns on common stocks, 1926–1990*

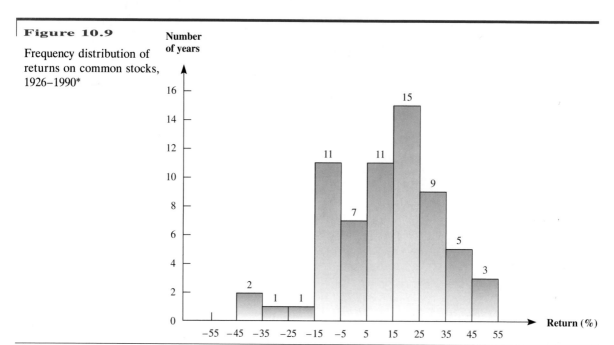

over the last four years. The average return is $(.10 + .12 + .03 - .09)/4 = 4\%$. Notice that the return is never actually equal to 4 percent. Instead, the first return deviates from the average by $.10 - .04 = .06$, the second return deviates from the average by $.12 - .04 = .08$, and so on. To compute the variance, we square each of these deviations, add them up, and divide the result by the number of returns less one, or three in this case. This information is summarized in the table below.

	(1) Actual Return	(2) Average Return	(3) Deviation (1) − (2)	(4) Squared Deviation
	.10	.04	.06	.0036
	.12	.04	.08	.0064
	.03	.04	−.01	.0001
	−.09	.04	−.13	.0169
Totals	.16		.00	.0270

In the first column, we write down the four actual returns. In the third column, we calculate the difference between the actual returns and the average by subtracting out 4 percent. Finally, in the fourth column, we square the numbers in column 3 to get the squared deviations from the average.

The variance can now be calculated by dividing .0270, the sum of the squared deviations, by the number of returns less one. Let Var(R) or σ^2 (read this as "sigma squared") stand for the variance of the return:

$$\text{Var}(R) = \sigma^2 = .027/(4 - 1) = .009$$

The standard deviation is the square root of the variance. So, if SD(R) or σ stands for the standard deviation of return:

$$SD(R) = \sigma = \sqrt{.009} = .09487$$

The square root of the variance is used because the variance is measured in "squared" percentages and thus is hard to interpret. The standard deviation is an ordinary percentage, so the answer here could be written as 9.487 percent.

In the table above, notice that the sum of the deviations is equal to zero. This will always be the case, and it provides a good way to check your work. In general, if we have T historical returns, where T is some number, we can write the historical variance as:

$$Var(R) = \frac{1}{T-1}[(R_1 - \bar{R})^2 + \cdots + (R_T - \bar{R})^2] \qquad [10.6]$$

This formula tells us to do just what we did above: Take each of the T individual returns ($R_1, R_2, \ldots$) and subtract the average return, $\bar{R}$; square the results, and add them all up; finally, divide this total by the number of returns less one ($T - 1$). The standard deviation is always the square root of Var(R).

Example 10.3   Calculating the Variance and Standard Deviation

Suppose the Supertech Company and the Hyperdrive Company have experienced the following returns in the last four years:

Year	Supertech Returns	Hyperdrive Returns
1989	−.20	.05
1990	.50	.09
1991	.30	−.12
1992	.10	.20

What are the average returns? The variances? The standard deviations? Which investment was more volatile?

To calculate the average returns, we add up the returns and divide by four. The results are:

Supertech average return = $\bar{R}$ = .70/4 = .175

Hyperdrive average return = $\bar{R}$ = .22/4 = .055

To calculate the variance for Supertech, we can summarize the relevant calculations as follows:

Year	(1) Actual Return	(2) Average Return	(3) Deviation (1) − (2)	(4) Squared Deviation
1989	−.20	.175	−.375	.140625
1990	.50	.175	.325	.105625
1991	.30	.175	.125	.015625
1992	.10	.175	−.075	.005625
Totals	.70		.00	.267500

Since there are four years of returns, we calculate the variances by dividing .2675 by $(4 - 1) = 3$:

	Supertech	Hyperdrive
Variance (σ^2)	$.2675/3 = .0892$	$.0529/3 = .0176$
Standard deviation (σ)	$\sqrt{.0892} = .2987$	$\sqrt{.0176} = .1327$

For practice, check that you get the same answer as we do for Hyperdrive. Notice that the standard deviation for Supertech, 29.87 percent, is a little more than twice Hyperdrive's 13.27 percent; Supertech is thus the more volatile investment. ∎

The Historical Record

Figure 10.10 summarizes much of our discussion of capital market history so far. It displays average returns, standard deviations, and frequency distributions of annual returns on a common scale. In Figure 10.10, notice, for example, that the standard deviation for the small stock portfolio (35.4 percent per year) is more than 10 times larger than the T-bill portfolio's standard deviation (3.4 percent per year). We will return to these figures momentarily.

Figure 10.10

Historical returns, standard deviations, and frequency distributions*

Series	Average Annual Return	Standard Deviation	Distribution
Common stocks	12.1%	20.8%	
Small stocks	17.1	35.4	
Long-term corporate bonds	5.5	8.4	
Long-term government bonds	4.9	8.5	
U.S. Treasury bills	3.7	3.4	
Inflation	3.2	4.7	

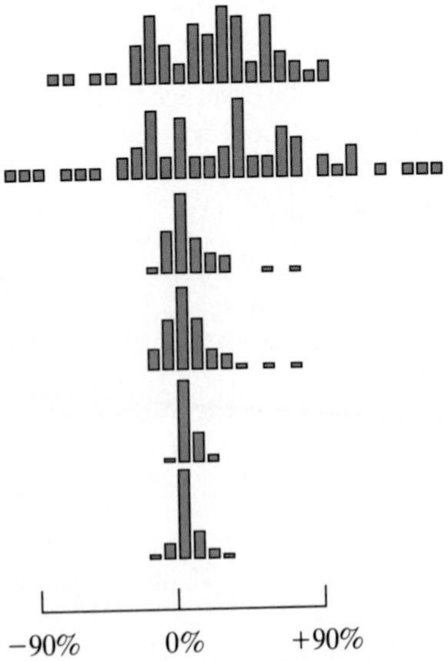

−90%   0%   +90%

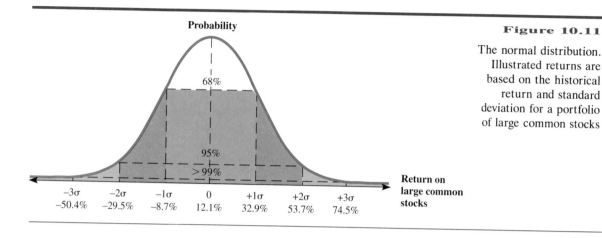

Figure 10.11

The normal distribution. Illustrated returns are based on the historical return and standard deviation for a portfolio of large common stocks

Normal Distribution

For many different random events in nature, a particular frequency distribution, the **normal distribution** (or *bell curve*), is useful for describing the probability of ending up in a given range. For example, the idea behind "grading on a curve" comes from the fact that exam scores often resemble a bell curve.

Figure 10.11 illustrates a normal distribution and its distinctive bell shape. As you can see, this distribution has a much cleaner appearance than the actual return distributions illustrated in Figure 10.10. Even so, like the normal distribution, the actual distributions do appear to be at least roughly mound-shaped and symmetrical. When this is true, the normal distribution is often a very good approximation.

Also, keep in mind that the distributions in Figure 10.10 are based on only 65 yearly observations while Figure 10.11 is, in principle, based on an infinite number. So, if we had been able to observe returns for, say, 1,000 years, we might have filled in a lot of the irregularities and ended up with a much smoother picture. For our purposes, it is enough to observe that the returns are at least roughly normally distributed.

The usefulness of the normal distribution stems from the fact that it is completely described by the average and the standard deviation. If you have these two numbers, then there is nothing else to know. For example, with a normal distribution, the probability that we end up within one standard deviation of the average is about 2/3. The probability that we end up within two standard deviations is about 95 percent. Finally, the probability of being more than three standard deviations away from the average is less than 1 percent. These ranges and the probabilities are illustrated in Figure 10.11.

To see why this is useful, recall from Figure 10.10 that the standard deviation of returns on the large common stocks is 20.8 percent. The average return is 12.1 percent. So, assuming that the frequency distribution is at least approximately normal, the probability that the return in a given year is in the range −8.7 percent to 32.9 percent (12.1 percent plus or minus one standard deviation, 20.8 percent) is about 2/3. This range is illustrated in Figure 10.11. In other words, there is about one chance in three that the return will be

normal distribution

A symmetric, bell-shaped frequency distribution that is completely defined by its mean and standard deviation.

outside this range. This literally tells you that, if you buy stocks in large companies, you should expect to be outside this range in one year out of every three. This reinforces our earlier observations about stock market volatility. However, there is only a 5 percent chance (approximately) that we would end up outside the range −29.5 percent to 53.7 percent (12.1 percent plus or minus 2 × 20.8%). These points are also illustrated in Figure 10.11.

The Second Lesson

Our observations concerning the year-to-year variability in returns are the basis for our second lesson from capital market history. On average, bearing risk is handsomely rewarded, but in a given year, there is a significant chance of a dramatic change in value. Thus, our second lesson is: The greater the potential reward, the greater is the risk.

Using Capital Market History

Based on the discussion in this section, you should begin to have an idea of the risks and rewards from investing. For example, in 1992 Treasury bills were paying about 4 percent. Suppose we had an investment that we thought had about the same risk as a portfolio of large-firm common stocks. At a minimum, what return would this investment have to offer for us to be interested?

From Table 10.3, the risk premium on larger common stocks has been 8.4 percent historically, so a reasonable estimate of our required return would be this premium plus the T-bill rate, 4% + 8.4% = 12.4%. This may strike you as high, but, if we were thinking of starting a new business, then the risks of doing so might resemble investing in small-company stocks. In this case, the risk premium is 13.4 percent, so we might require as much as 17.4 percent from such an investment at a minimum.

We will discuss the relationship between risk and required return in more detail in the next chapter. For now, you should notice that a projected internal rate of return (IRR) on a risky investment in the 15 percent to 25 percent range isn't particularly outstanding. It depends on how much risk there is. This, too, is an important lesson from capital market history.

Example 10.4 Investing in Growth Stocks
The phrase *growth stock* is frequently a euphemism for small-company stock. Are such investments suitable for "widows and orphans"? Before answering, you should consider the historical volatility. For example, from the historical record, what is the approximate probability that you will actually lose 18 percent or more of your money in a single year if you buy a portfolio of such companies?

Looking back at Figure 10.10, the average return on small stocks is 17.1 percent and the standard deviation is 35.4 percent. Assuming that the returns are approximately normal, then there is about a 1/3 probability that you will experience a return outside the range −18.3 percent to 52.5 percent (17.1% ±35.4%).

Because the normal distribution is symmetric, the odds of being above or below this range are equal. There is thus a 1/6 chance (half of 1/3) that you will lose more than 18.3 percent. So you should expect this to happen once in every six years, on average. Such investments can thus be *very* volatile, and they are not well-suited for those who cannot afford the risk. ∎

CONCEPT QUESTIONS

10.5a In words, how do we calculate a variance? A standard deviation?

10.5b With a normal distribution, what is the probability of ending up more than one standard deviation below the average?

10.5c Assuming that long-term corporate bonds have an approximately normal distribution, what is the approximate probability of earning 13.4 percent or more in a given year? With T-bills, approximately what is this probability?

10.5d What is the first lesson from capital market history? The second?

CAPITAL MARKET EFFICIENCY | 10.6

Capital market history suggests that the market values of stocks and bonds can fluctuate widely from year to year. Why does this occur? At least part of the answer is that prices change because new information arrives, and investors reassess asset values based on that information.

The behavior of market prices has been extensively studied. A question that has received particular attention is whether prices adjust quickly and correctly when new information arrives. A market is said to be "efficient" if this is the case. To be more precise, in an **efficient capital market**, current market prices fully reflect available information. By this we simply mean that, based on available information, there is no reason to believe that the current price is too low or too high.

efficient capital market
Market in which security prices reflect available information.

The concept of market efficiency is a rich one, and much has been written about it. A full discussion of the subject goes beyond the scope of our study of corporate finance. However, because the concept figures so prominently in studies of market history, we briefly describe the key points here.

Price Behavior in an Efficient Market

To illustrate how prices behave in an efficient market, suppose the F-Stop Camera Corporation (FCC) has, through years of secret research and development, developed a camera that will double the speed of the autofocusing systems that are now available. FCC's capital budgeting analysis suggests that launching the new camera is a highly profitable move; in other words, the NPV appears to be positive and substantial. The key assumption thus far is that FCC has not released any information about the new system; so, the fact of its existence is "inside" information only.

Now consider a share of stock in FCC. In an efficient market, its price reflects what is known about FCC's current operations and profitability, and it reflects market opinion about FCC's potential for future growth and profits. The value of the new autofocusing system is not reflected, however, because the market is unaware of its existence.

If the market agrees with FCC's assessment of the value of the new project, FCC's stock price will rise when the decision to launch is made public. For example, assume that the announcement is made in a press release on Wednesday morning. In an efficient market, the price of shares in FCC will adjust quickly to this new information. Investors should not be able to buy the stock on Wednesday afternoon and make a profit on Thursday. This would imply that it took the stock market a full day to realize the implication of the FCC

Figure 10.12

Reaction of stock price to new information in efficient and inefficient markets

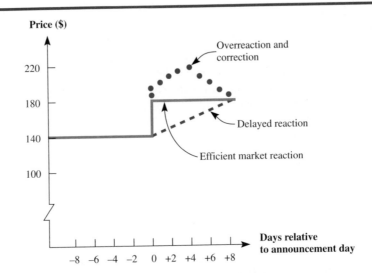

Efficient market reaction: The price instantaneously adjusts to and fully reflects new information; there is no tendency for subsequent increases and decreases.
Delayed reaction: The price partially adjusts to the new information; 8 days elapse before the price completely reflects the new information.
Overreaction: The price overadjusts to the new information; it "overshoots" the new price and subsequently corrects.

press release. If the market is efficient, the price of shares of FCC stock on Wednesday afternoon will already reflect the information contained in the Wednesday morning press release.

Figure 10.12 presents three possible stock price adjustments for FCC. In Figure 10.12, Day 0 represents the announcement day. As illustrated, before the announcement, FCC's stock sells for $140 per share. The NPV per share of the new system is, say, $40, so the new price will be $180 once the value of the new project is fully reflected.

The solid line in Figure 10.12 represents the path taken by the stock price in an efficient market. In this case, the price adjusts immediately to the new information and no further changes in the price of the stock take place. The broken line in Figure 10.12 depicts a delayed reaction. Here it takes the market eight days or so to fully absorb the information. Finally, the dotted line illustrates an overreaction and subsequent adjustment to the correct price.

The broken line and the dotted line in Figure 10.12 illustrate paths that the stock price might take in an inefficient market. If, for example, stock prices don't adjust immediately to new information (the broken line), then buying stock immediately following the release of new information and then selling it several days later would be a positive NPV activity because the price is too low for several days after the announcement.

efficient markets hypothesis (EMH)
The hypothesis is that actual capital markets, such as the NYSE, are efficient.

The Efficient Markets Hypothesis

The **efficient markets hypothesis (EMH)** asserts that well-organized capital markets, such as the NYSE, are efficient markets, at least as a practical

In Their Own Words...
Richard Roll on Market Efficiency

The concept of an efficient market is a special application of the "no free lunch" principle. In an efficient financial market, costless trading policies will not generate "excess" returns. After adjusting for the riskiness of the policy, the trader's return will be no larger than the return of a randomly selected portfolio, at least on average.

This is often thought to imply something about the amount of "information" reflected in asset prices. However, it really doesn't mean that prices reflect all information nor even that they reflect publicly available information. Instead, it means that the connection between unreflected information and prices is too subtle and tenuous to be easily or costlessly detected.

Relevant information is difficult and expensive to uncover and evaluate. Thus, if costless trading policies are ineffective, there must exist some traders who make a living by "beating the market." They cover their costs (including the opportunity cost of their time) by trading. The existence of such traders

is actually a necessary precondition for markets to become efficient. Without such professional traders, prices would fail to reflect everything that is cheap and easy to evaluate.

Efficient market prices should approximate a random walk, meaning that they will appear to fluctuate more or less randomly. Prices can fluctuate nonrandomly to the extent that their departure from randomness is expensive to discern. Also, observed price series can depart from apparent randomness due to changes in preferences and expectations, but this is really a technicality and does not imply a "free lunch" relative to current investor sentiments.

Richard Roll is Allstate Professor of Finance at UCLA. He is a preeminent financial researcher, and he has written extensively in almost every area of modern finance. He is particularly well known for his insightful analyses and great creativity in understanding empirical phenomena.

matter. In other words, an advocate of the EMH might argue that while inefficiencies may exist, they are relatively small and not common.

If a market is efficient, then there is a very important implication for market participants: All investments in an efficient market are *zero* NPV investments. The reason is not complicated. If prices are neither too low nor too high, then the difference between the market value of an investment and its cost is zero; hence, the NPV is zero. As a result, in an efficient market, investors get exactly what they pay for when they buy securities, and firms receive exactly what their stocks and bonds are worth when they sell them.

What makes a market efficient is competition among investors. Many individuals spend their entire lives trying to find mispriced stocks. For any given stock, they study what has happened in the past to the stock price and its dividends. They learn, to the extent possible, what a company's earnings have been, how much it owes to creditors, what taxes it pays, what businesses it is in, what new investments are planned, how sensitive it is to changes in the economy, and so on.

Not only is there a great deal to know about any particular company, there is a powerful incentive for knowing it, namely, the profit motive. If you know more about some company than other investors in the marketplace, you can profit from that knowledge by investing in the company's stock if you have good news and selling it if you have bad news.

The logical consequence of all this information being gathered and analyzed is that mispriced stocks will become fewer and fewer. In other words, because of competition among investors, the market will become increasingly efficient. A kind of equilibrium comes into being where there is just enough mispricing around for those who are best at identifying it to make a living at it. For most other investors, the activity of information gathering and analysis will not pay.[4]

Some Common Misconceptions about the EMH

No idea in finance has attracted as much attention as that of efficient markets, and not all of the attention has been flattering. Rather than rehash the arguments here, we will be content to observe that some markets are more efficient than others. For example, financial markets on the whole are probably much more efficient than real asset markets.

Having said this, it is the case that much of the criticism of the EMH is misguided because it is based on a misunderstanding of what the hypothesis says and what it doesn't say. For example, when the notion of market efficiency was first publicized and debated in the popular financial press, it was often characterized by words to the effect that: "throwing darts at the financial page will produce a portfolio that can be expected to do as well as any managed by professional security analysts."[5]

Confusion over statements of this sort has often led to a failure to understand the implications of market efficiency. For example, sometimes it is wrongly argued that market efficiency means it doesn't matter how you invest your money because the efficiency of the market will protect you from making a mistake. However, a random dart thrower might wind up with all of the darts sticking into one or two high-risk stocks that deal in genetic engineering. Would you really want all of your money in two such stocks?

What efficiency does imply is that the price that a firm will obtain when it sells a share of its stock is a "fair" price in the sense that it reflects the value of that stock given the information that is available about the firm. Shareholders do not have to worry that they are paying too much for a stock with a low dividend or some other sort of characteristic because the market has already incorporated that characteristic into the price. We sometimes say that the information has been "priced out."

The concept of efficient markets can be explained further by replying to a frequent objection. It is sometimes argued that the market cannot be efficient because stock prices fluctuate from day to day. If the prices are right, the argument goes, then why do they change so much and so often? From our discussion above, these price movements are in no way inconsistent with efficiency. Investors are bombarded with information every day. The fact that prices fluc-

---

[4]The idea behind the EMH can be illustrated by the following short story: A student was walking down the hall with her finance professor when they both saw a $20 bill on the ground. As the student bent down to pick it up, the professor shook his head slowly and, with a look of disappointment on his face, said patiently to the student, "Don't bother. If it were really there, someone else would have picked it up already." The moral of the story reflects the logic of the efficient markets hypothesis: If you think you have found a pattern in stock prices or a simple device for picking winners, you probably have not.

[5]B. G. Malkiel, *A Random Walk Down Wall Street,* 2nd college ed. (New York: Norton, 1981).

tuate is, at least in part, a reflection of that information flow. In fact, the absence of price movements in a world that changes as rapidly as ours would suggest inefficiency.

The Forms of Market Efficiency

It is common to distinguish between three forms of market efficiency. Depending on the degree of efficiency, we say that markets are either *weak form efficient, semistrong form efficient,* or *strong form efficient.* The difference between these forms relates to what information is reflected in prices.

We start with the extreme case. If the market is strong form efficient, then *all* information of *every* kind is reflected in stock prices. In such a market, there is no such thing as inside information. Therefore, in our FCC example just above, we apparently were assuming that the market was not strong form efficient.

Casual observation, particularly in recent years, suggests that inside information does exist and it can be valuable to possess. Whether it is lawful or ethical to use that information is another issue. In any event, we conclude that private information about a particular stock may exist that is not currently reflected in the price of the stock. For example, prior knowledge of a takeover attempt could be very valuable.

The second form of efficiency, semistrong efficiency, is the most controversial. If a market is semistrong form efficient, then all *public* information is reflected in the stock price. The reason that this form is controversial is that it implies that a security analyst who tries to identify mispriced stocks using, for example, financial statement information is wasting his time because that information is already reflected in the current price.

The third form of efficiency, weak form efficiency, suggests that, at a minimum, the current price of a stock reflects its own past prices. In other words, studying past prices in an attempt to identify mispriced securities is futile if the market is weak form efficient. While this form of efficiency might seem rather mild, it implies that searching for patterns in historical prices that are useful in identifying mispriced stocks will not work (this practice is quite common).

What does capital market history say about market efficiency? Here again, there is great controversy. At the risk of going out on a limb, the evidence does seem to tell us three things. First, prices do appear to respond very rapidly to new information, and the response is at least not grossly different from what we would expect in an efficient market. Second, the future of market prices, particularly in the short run, is very difficult to predict based on publicly available information. Third, if mispriced stocks do exist, then there is no obvious means of identifying them. Put another way, simple-minded schemes based on public information will probably not be successful.

⌐ **CONCEPT QUESTIONS**

10.6a What is an efficient market?

10.6b What are the forms of market efficiency?

10.7 | SUMMARY AND CONCLUSIONS

This chapter explores the subject of capital market history. Such history is useful because it tells us what to expect in the way of returns from risky assets. We summed up our study of market history with two key lessons:

1. Risky assets, on average, earn a risk premium. There is a reward for bearing risk.
2. The greater the potential reward from a risky investment, the greater is the risk.

These lessons have significant implications for the financial manager. We will be considering these implications in the chapters ahead.

We also discussed the concept of market efficiency. In an efficient market, prices adjust quickly and correctly to new information. Consequently, asset prices in efficient markets are rarely too high or too low. How efficient capital markets (such as the NYSE) are is a matter of debate, but, at a minimum, they are probably much more efficient than most real asset markets.

Key Terms

nominal returns 339
real returns 339
Fisher effect 340
risk premium 350
variance 351

standard deviation 351
normal distribution 355
efficient capital market 357
efficient markets hypothesis (EMH) 358

Chapter Review Problems and Self-Test

10.1 **Recent Return History**   Use Table 10.1 to calculate the average return over the last five years for common stocks, small stocks, and Treasury bills.

10.2 **More Recent Return History**   Calculate the standard deviations using information from Problem 10.1. Which of the investments was the most volatile over this period?

Answers to Self-Test Problems

10.1 We calculate the averages as follows:

| Year | Actual Returns and Averages | | |
	Common Stocks	Small Stocks	Treasury Bills
1986	0.1847	0.0685	0.0616
1987	0.0523	−0.0930	0.0547
1988	0.1681	0.2287	0.0635
1989	0.3149	0.1018	0.0837
1990	−0.0317	−0.2156	0.0781
Average:	0.1377	0.0181	0.0683

10.2   We first need to calculate the deviations from the average returns. Using the averages from Problem 10.1, we get:

Deviations from Average Returns

Year	Common Stocks	Small Stocks	Treasury Bills
1986	0.04704	0.05042	−0.00672
1987	−0.08536	−0.11108	−0.01362
1988	0.03044	0.21062	−0.00482
1989	0.17724	0.08372	0.01538
1990	−0.16936	−0.23368	0.00978
Total	0.00000	0.00000	0.00000

We square these deviations and calculate the variances and standard deviations:

Squared Deviations from Average Returns

Year	Common Stocks	Small Stocks	Treasury Bills
1986	0.00221	0.00254	0.00005
1987	0.00729	0.01234	0.00019
1988	0.00093	0.04436	0.00002
1989	0.03141	0.00701	0.00024
1990	0.02868	0.05461	0.00010
Variance:	0.01763	0.03021	0.00015
Standard deviation:	0.13278	0.17382	0.01210

To calculate the variances we added up the squared deviations and divided by four, the number of returns less one. Notice that the small stocks had substantially greater volatility with a smaller average return. Once again, such investments are risky, particularly over short periods of time.

Questions and Problems

1.   **Calculating Returns**   Suppose a stock had an initial price of $42 per share, paid a dividend of $2.40 per share during the year, and had an ending price of $31 per share. Compute the percentage return.

2.   **Calculating Yields**   In Problem 1, what was the dividend yield? The capital gains yield?

3.   **Return Calculations**   Rework Problems 1 and 2 assuming that the ending price is $60 per share.

4.   **Calculating Real Rates of Return**   If Treasury bills are currently paying 9 percent and the inflation rate is 5 percent, what is the approximate real rate? The exact real rate?

5. **Inflation and Nominal Returns**   Suppose the real rate is 3 percent and the inflation rate is 12 percent. What rate would you expect to see on a Treasury bill?

6. **Nominal and Real Returns**   An investment offers a 20 percent return. You think that the real return will only be 12 percent. What inflation rate is implicit in your calculation?

7. **Nominal versus Real Returns**   What was the average annual return on U.S. common stocks from 1926 through 1990?
   a. In nominal terms?
   b. In real terms?

8. **Bond Returns**   What is the historical real return on long-term government bonds? On long-term corporate bonds?

9. **Using Return Distributions**   Suppose that the return on long-term government bonds is normally distributed. Based on the historical record, what is the approximate probability that your return will be less than -4 percent in a given year? What range of returns would you expect to see 95 percent of the time? 99 percent of the time?

10. **Negative Rates**   Is a negative real rate of interest possible ahead of time? After the fact? A negative inflation rate? Explain.

11. **Using Return Distributions**   Assuming that the return from holding small-company stocks is normally distributed, what is the approximate probability that your money will double in value in a single year?

12. **Distributions**   In Problem 11, what is the probability that the return is less than -100 percent (think)? What are the implications for the distribution of returns?

13. **Calculating Returns and Deviations**   Using the following returns, calculate the average returns and the standard deviations for X and Y.

		Returns
Year	X	Y
1	15%	18%
2	4	-3
3	-9	-10
4	8	12
5	9	5

14. **Risk Premiums**   Consider the following common stock and T-bill returns from Table 10.1 for the period 1980–86.

Year	Common Stocks	T-Bills	Risk Premium
1980	32.4%	11.2%	
1981	-4.9	14.7	
1982	21.4	10.5	
1983	22.5	8.8	
1984	6.3	9.9	
1985	32.2	7.7	
1986	18.5	6.2	

     a. Calculate the observed risk premium in each year for the common stocks versus the T-bills.

     b. Calculate the average returns and the average risk premium over this period.

     c. Calculate the standard deviation of the returns and the risk premium.

     d. Is it possible that the observed risk premium can be negative? Explain how this can happen and what it means.

15.   Effects of Inflation   Look at Table 10.1 (and Figure 10.7). When were T-bill rates at their highest over the period 1926–90? Why do you think they were so high during this period? What relationship underlies your answer?

16.   Intuition and EMH   If a market is semistrong form efficient, is it also weak form efficient? Explain.

17.   EMH   A stock market analyst is able to identify mispriced stocks by comparing the average price for the last five days to the average price for the last 20 days. If this is true, what do you know about the market?

18.   EMH   What are the implications of the efficient markets hypothesis for investors who buy and sell stocks in an attempt to "beat the market"?

19.   EMH and NPV   Explain why a characteristic of an efficient market is that investments in that market have zero NPV.

20.   EMH and Speculation   Critically evaluate the following statement: "Playing the stock market is like gambling. Such speculative investing has no social value, other than the pleasure people get from this form of gambling."

21.   Nominal versus Real Risk Premiums   What is the exact relationship between the nominal risk premium and the real risk premium on an investment?

                                                                       Challenge Question

Suggested Reading

An important record of the performance of financial investments in U.S. capital markets can be found in:

    © *Stock, Bonds, Bills, and Inflation 1991 Yearbook*™, Ibbotson Associates, Inc., Chicago (annually updates work by Roger G. Ibbotson and Rex A. Sinquefield). All rights reserved.

Chapter 11

Return, Risk, and the Security Market Line

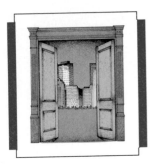

In our last chapter, we learned some important lessons from capital market history. Most importantly, there is a reward, on average, for bearing risk. We called this reward a *risk premium*. The second lesson is that this risk premium is larger for riskier investments. The principle that higher returns can be earned only by taking greater risks appeals to our moral sense that we cannot have something for nothing. This chapter explores the economic and managerial implications of this basic idea.

Thus far, we have concentrated mainly on the return behavior of a few large portfolios. We need to expand our consideration to include individual assets. Accordingly, the purpose of this chapter is to provide the background necessary for learning how the risk premium is determined for individual assets.

When we examine the risks associated with individual assets, we find that there are two types of risk: systematic and unsystematic. This distinction is crucial because, as we will see, systematic risks affect almost all assets in the economy, at least to some degree, while an unsystematic risk affects at most a small number of assets. We then develop the principle of diversification, which shows that highly diversified portfolios will tend to have almost no unsystematic risk.

The principle of diversification has an important implication: To a diversified investor, only systematic risk matters. It follows that in deciding whether or not to buy a particular individual asset, a diversified investor will only be concerned with that asset's systematic risk. This is a key observation, and it allows us to say a great deal about the risks and returns on individual assets. In particular, it is the basis for a famous relationship between risk and return called the *security market line,* or *SML.* To develop the SML, we introduce the equally famous "beta" coefficient, one of the centerpieces of modern finance.

Beta and the SML are key concepts because they supply us with at least part of the answer to the question of how to go about determining the required return on an investment.

EXPECTED RETURNS AND VARIANCES | 11.1

In our previous chapter, we discussed how to calculate average returns and variances using historical data. We now begin to discuss how to analyze returns and variances when the information we have concerns future possible returns and their probabilities.

Expected Return

We start with a straightforward case. Consider a single period of time, say, a year. We have two stocks, L and U, which have the following characteristics: Stock L is expected to have a return of 25 percent in the coming year. Stock U is expected to have a return of 20 percent for the same period.

In a situation like this, if all investors agreed on the expected returns, why would anyone want to hold Stock U? After all, why invest in one stock when the expectation is that another will do better? Clearly, the answer must depend on the risk of the two investments. The return on Stock L, although it is *expected* to be 25 percent, could actually turn out to be higher or lower.

For example, suppose the economy booms. In this case, we think Stock L will have a 70 percent return. If the economy enters a recession, we think the return will be −20 percent. In this case, we say that there are two *states of the economy,* which means that these are the only two possible situations. This setup is oversimplified, of course, but it allows us to illustrate some key ideas without a lot of computation.

Suppose we think that a boom and a recession are equally likely to happen, a 50–50 chance of each. Table 11.1 illustrates the basic information we have described and some additional information about Stock U. Notice that Stock U earns 30 percent if there is a recession and 10 percent if there is a boom.

Obviously, if you buy one of these stocks, say Stock U, what you earn in any particular year depends on what the economy does during that year. However, suppose that the probabilities stay the same through time. If you hold U

State of the Economy	Probability of State of the Economy	Security Returns if State Occurs	
		L	
Recession	0.5	−20%	30%
Boom	0.5	70	10
	1.0		

Table 11.1

States of the economy and stock returns

			Stock L		Stock U	
			(3) Rate of		(5) Rate of	
(1) State of Economy	(2) Probability of State of Economy		Return if State Occurs	(4) Product (2) × (3)	Return if State Occurs	(6) Product (2) × (5)
Recession	0.5		−.20	−.10	.30	.15
Boom	0.5		.70	.35	.10	.05
	1.0			$E(R_L) = 25\%$		$E(R_U) = 20\%$

Table 11.2

Calculation of expected return

expected return

Return on a risky asset expected in the future.

for a number of years, you'll earn 30 percent about half the time and 10 percent the other half. In this case, we say that your **expected return** on Stock U, $E(R_U)$, is 20 percent:

$$E(R_U) = .50 \times 30\% + .50 \times 10\% = 20\%$$

In other words, you should expect to earn 20 percent from this stock, on average.

For Stock L, the probabilities are the same, but the possible returns are different. Here we lose 20 percent half the time, and we gain 70 percent the other half. The expected return on L, $E(R_L)$, is thus 25 percent:

$$E(R_L) = .50 \times -20\% + .50 \times 70\% = 25\%$$

Table 11.2 illustrates these calculations.

In our previous chapter, we defined the risk premium as the difference between the return on a risky investment and a risk-free investment, and we calculated the historical risk premiums on some different investments. Using our projected returns, we can calculate the *projected* or *expected risk premium* as the difference between the expected return on a risky investment and the certain return on a risk-free investment.

For example, suppose that risk-free investments are currently offering 8 percent. We will say that the risk-free rate, which we label as R_f, is 8 percent. Given this, what is the projected risk premium on Stock U? On Stock L? Since the expected return on Stock U, $E(R_U)$, is 20 percent, the projected risk premium is:

$$\text{Risk premium} = \text{Expected return} - \text{Risk-free rate} \qquad [11.1]$$

$$= E(R_U) - R_f$$

$$= 20\% - 8\%$$

$$= 12\%$$

Similarly, the risk premium on Stock L is $25\% - 8\% = 17\%$.

(1) State of Economy	(2) Probability of State of Economy	*Stock L*		*Stock U*		**Table 11.3**
		(3) Rate of Return if State Occurs	(4) Product (2) × (3)	(5) Rate of Return if State Occurs	(6) Product (2) × (5)	Calculation of expected return
Recession	.80	−.20	−.16	.30	.24	
Boom	.20	.70	.14	.10	.02	
			$E(R_L) = -2\%$		$E(R_U) = 26\%$	

In general, the expected return on a security or other asset is simply equal to the sum of the possible returns multiplied by their probabilities. So, if we have 100 possible returns, we would multiply each one by its probability and then add the results up. The result would be the expected return. The risk premium would then be the difference between this expected return and the risk-free rate.

Example 11.1   Unequal Probabilities
Look again at Tables 11.1 and 11.2. Suppose you thought that a boom would only occur 20 percent of the time instead of 50 percent. What are the expected returns on Stocks U and L in this case? If the risk-free rate is 10 percent, what are the risk premiums?

The first thing to notice is that a recession must occur 80 percent of the time $(1 - .20 = .80)$ since there are only two possibilities. With this in mind, Stock U has a 30 percent return in 80 percent of the years and a 10 percent return in 20 percent of the years. To calculate the expected return, we again just multiply the possibilities by the probabilities and add up the results:

$$E(R_U) = .80 \times 30\% + .20 \times 10\% = 26\%$$

Table 11.3 summarizes the calculations for both stocks. Notice that the expected return on L is −2 percent.

The risk premium for Stock U is $26\% - 10\% = 16\%$ in this case. The risk premium for Stock L is negative: $-2\% - 10\% = -12\%$. This is a little odd, but it is not impossible. ■

Calculating the Variance

To calculate the variances of the returns on our two stocks, we first determine the squared deviations from the expected return. We then multiply each possible squared deviation by its probability. We add these up, and the result is the variance. The standard deviation, as always, is the square root of the variance.

To illustrate, Stock U above has an expected return of $E(R_U) = 20\%$. In a given year, it will actually return either 30 percent or 10 percent. The possible deviations are thus 30% − 20% = 10% or 10% − 20% = −10%. In this case, the variance is:

$$\text{Variance} = \sigma^2 = .50 \times (10\%)^2 + .50 \times (-10\%)^2 = .01$$

The standard deviation is the square root of this:

$$\text{Standard deviation} = \sigma = \sqrt{.01} = .10 = 10\%$$

Table 11.4 summarizes these calculations for both stocks. Notice that Stock L has a much larger variance.

When we put the expected return and variability information for our two stocks together, we have:

	Stock L	Stock U
Expected return, $E(R)$	25%	20%
Variance, σ^2	.2025	.0100
Standard deviation, σ	45%	10%

Stock L has a higher expected return, but U has less risk. You could get a 70 percent return on your investment in L, but you could also lose 20 percent. Notice that an investment in U will always pay at least 10 percent.

Which of these two stocks should you buy? We can't really say; it depends on your personal preferences. We can be reasonably sure, however, that some investors would prefer L to U and some would prefer U to L.

You've probably noticed that the way we calculated expected returns and variances here is somewhat different from the way we did it in the last chapter. The reason is that, in Chapter 10, we were examining actual historical returns, so we estimated the average return and the variance based on some actual events. Here, we have projected *future* returns and their associated probabilities, so this is the information with which we must work.

Table 11.4 Calculation of variance	(1) State of Economy	(2) Probability of State of Economy	(3) Return Deviation from Expected Return	(4) Squared Return Deviation from Expected Return	(5) Product (2) × (4)
Stock L					
Recession	0.5	−.20 − .25 = −.45	$(-.45)^2 = .2025$	.10125
Boom	0.5	.70 − .25 = .45	$(.45)^2 = .2025$	.10125
					$\sigma_L^2 = .2025$
Stock U					
Recession	0.5	.30 − .20 = .10	$(.10)^2 = .01$	.005
Boom	0.5	.10 − .20 = −.10	$(-.10)^2 = .01$	.005
					$\sigma_U^2 = .010$

Example 11.2 More Unequal Probabilities

Going back to Example 11.1, what are the variances on the two stocks once we have unequal probabilities? The standard deviations?

We can summarize the needed calculations as follows:

(1) State of Economy	(2) Probability of State of Economy	(3) Return Deviation from Expected Return	(4) Squared Return Deviation from Expected Return	(5) Product (2) × (4)
Stock L				
Recession	.80	$-.20 - (-.02) = -.18$	.0324	.02592
Boom	.20	$.70 - (-.02) = .72$	.5184	.10368
				$\sigma_L^2 = .12960$
Stock U				
Recession	.80	$.30 - .26 = .04$	.0016	.00128
Boom	.20	$.10 - .26 = -.16$	.0256	.00512
				$\sigma_U^2 = .00640$

Based on these calculations, the standard deviation for L is $\sigma_L = \sqrt{.1296} = 36\%$. The standard deviation for U is much smaller, $\sigma_U = \sqrt{.0064} = .08$ or 8%. ■

⌐ CONCEPT QUESTIONS

11.1a How do we calculate the expected return on a security?

11.1b In words, how do we calculate the variance of the expected return?

PORTFOLIOS ⌐ 11.2

Thus far in this chapter, we have concentrated on individual assets considered separately. However, most investors actually hold a **portfolio** of assets. All we mean by this is that investors tend to own more than just a single stock, bond, or other asset. Given that this is so, portfolio return and portfolio risk are of obvious relevance. Accordingly, we now discuss portfolio expected returns and variances.

portfolio
Group of assets such as stocks and bonds held by an investor.

Portfolio Weights

There are many equivalent ways of describing a portfolio. The most convenient approach is to list the percentages of the total portfolio's value that are invested in each portfolio asset. We call these percentages the **portfolio weights.**

For example, if we have $50 in one asset and $150 in another, then our total portfolio is worth $200. The percentage of our portfolio in the first asset is $50/$200 = .25. The percentage of our portfolio in the second asset is

portfolio weight
Percentage of a portfolio's total value in a particular asset.

$150/$200, or .75. Our portfolio weights are thus .25 and .75. Notice that the weights have to add up to 1.00 since all of our money is invested somewhere.[1]

Portfolio Expected Returns

Let's go back to Stocks L and U. You put half your money in each. The portfolio weights are obviously .50 and .50. What is the pattern of returns on this portfolio? The expected return?

To answer these questions, suppose the economy actually enters a recession. In this case, half your money (the half in L) loses 20 percent. The other half (the half in U) gains 30 percent. Your portfolio return, R_P, in a recession will thus be:

$$R_P = .50 \times (-20\%) + .50 \times 30\% = 5\%$$

Table 11.5 summarizes the remaining calculations. Notice that when a boom occurs, your portfolio would return 40 percent:

$$R_P = .50 \times 70\% + .50 \times 10\% = 40\%$$

As indicated in Table 11.5, the expected return on your portfolio, $E(R_P)$, is 22.5 percent.

We can save ourselves some work by calculating the expected return more directly. Given these portfolio weights, we could have reasoned that we expect half of our money to earn 25 percent (the half in L) and half of our money to earn 20 percent (the half in U). Our portfolio expected return is thus:

$$E(R_P) = .50 \times E(R_L) + .50 \times E(R_U)$$

$$= .50 \times 25\% + .50 \times 20\%$$

$$= 22.5\%$$

This is the same portfolio expected return we had before.

---

[1]Some of it could be in cash, of course, but we would then just consider the cash to be one of the portfolio assets.

Table 11.5 Expected return on an equally weighted portfolio of Stock L and Stock U	(1) State of Economy	(2) Probability of State of Economy	(3) Portfolio Return if State Occurs	(4) Product (2) × (3)
	Recession	.50	$.50 \times (-20\%) + .50 \times (30\%) = 5\%$	.025
	Boom	.50	$.50 \times (70\%) + .50 \times (10\%) = 40\%$	.20
				$E(R_P) = 22.5\%$

This method of calculating the expected return on a portfolio works no matter how many assets there are in the portfolio. Suppose we had n assets in our portfolio, where n is any number. If we let x_i stand for the percentage of our money in Asset i, then the expected return is:

$$E(R_P) = x_1 \times E(R_1) + x_2 \times E(R_2) + \ldots + x_n \times E(R_n) \qquad [11.2]$$

This says that the expected return on a portfolio is a straightforward combination of the expected returns on the assets in that portfolio. This seems somewhat obvious, but, as we will examine next, the obvious approach is not always the right one.

Example 11.3   Portfolio Expected Return

Suppose we have the following projections on three stocks:

State of Economy	Probability of State	Returns		
		Stock A	Stock B	Stock C
Boom	.40	10%	15%	20%
Bust	.60	8	4	0

What would be the expected return on a portfolio with equal amounts invested in each of the three stocks? What would the expected return be if half of the portfolio were in A, with the remainder equally divided between B and C?

From our earlier discussions, the expected returns on the individual stocks are (check these for practice):

$$E(R_A) = 8.8\%$$

$$E(R_B) = 8.4\%$$

$$E(R_C) = 8.0\%$$

If a portfolio has equal investments in each asset, the portfolio weights are all the same. Such a portfolio is said to be *equally weighted*. Since there are three stocks in this case, the weights are all equal to ⅓. The portfolio expected return is thus:

$$E(R_P) = (1/3) \times 8.8\% + (1/3) \times 8.4\% + (1/3) \times 8.0\% = 8.4\%$$

In the second case, check that the portfolio expected return is 8.5 percent. ∎

Portfolio Variance

From our discussion above, the expected return on a portfolio that contains equal investment in Stocks U and L is 22.5 percent. What is the standard deviation of return on this portfolio? Simple intuition might suggest that half of the money has a standard deviation of 45 percent and the other half has a standard deviation of 10 percent, so the portfolio's standard deviation might be calculated as:

$$\sigma_P = .50 \times 45\% + .50 \times 10\% = 27.5\%$$

Unfortunately, this approach is completely incorrect.

Let's see what the standard deviation really is. Table 11.6 summarizes the relevant calculations. As we see, the portfolio's variance is about .031, and its standard deviation is less than we thought—it's only 17.5 percent. What is illustrated here is that the variance on a portfolio is not generally a simple combination of the variances of the assets in the portfolio.

We can illustrate this point a little more dramatically by considering a slightly different set of portfolio weights. Suppose we put 2/11 (about 18 percent) in L and the other 9/11 (about 82 percent) in U. If a recession occurs, this portfolio will have a return of:

$$R_P = (2/11) \times (-20\%) + (9/11) \times (30\%) = 20.91\%$$

If a boom occurs, this portfolio will have a return of:

$$R_P = (2/11) \times (70\%) + (9/11) \times (10\%) = 20.91\%$$

Notice that the return is the same no matter what happens. No further calculations are needed: This portfolio has a zero variance. Apparently, combining assets into portfolios can substantially alter the risks faced by the investor. This is a crucial observation, and we explore its implications in the next section.

Example 11.4 Portfolio Variance and Standard Deviation

In Example 11.3, what are the standard deviations on the two portfolios? To answer, we first have to calculate the portfolio returns in the two states. We will work with the second portfolio, which has 50 percent in Stock A and 25 percent in each of Stocks B and C. The relevant calculations can be summarized as follows:

State of Economy	Probability of State	Returns			
		Stock A	Stock B	Stock C	Portfolio
Boom	.40	10%	15%	20%	13.75%
Bust	.60	8	4	0	5.00

The portfolio return when the economy booms is calculated as:

$$.50 \times 10\% + .25 \times 15\% + .25 \times 20\% = 13.75\%$$

(1) State of Economy	(2) Probability of State of Economy	(3) Portfolio Return if State Occurs	(4) Squared Deviation from Expected Return	(5) Product (2) × (4)
Recession	.50	5%	$(.05 - .225)^2 = .030625$	.0153125
Boom	.50	40	$(.40 - .225)^2 = .030625$	.0153125
				$\sigma_P^2 = .030625$
			$\sigma_P = \sqrt{.030625} = 17.5\%$	

Table 11.6

Variance on an equally weighted portfolio of Stock L and Stock U

The return when the economy goes bust is calculated the same way. The expected return on the portfolio is 8.5 percent. The variance is thus:

$$\sigma^2 = .40 \times (.1375 - .085)^2 + .60 \times (.05 - .085)^2$$

$$= .0018375$$

The standard deviation is thus about 4.3 percent. For our equally weighted portfolio, check that the standard deviation is about 5.4 percent. ∎

CONCEPT QUESTIONS

11.2a   What is a portfolio weight?

11.2b   How do we calculate the expected return on a portfolio?

11.2c   Is there a simple relationship between the standard deviation on a portfolio and the standard deviations of the assets in the portfolio?

ANNOUNCEMENTS, SURPRISES, AND EXPECTED RETURNS 11.3

Now that we know how to construct portfolios and evaluate their returns, we begin to describe more carefully the risks and returns associated with individual securities. Thus far, we have measured volatility by looking at the differences between the actual returns on an asset or portfolio, R, and the expected return, $E(R)$. We now look at why those deviations exist.

Expected and Unexpected Returns

To begin, for concreteness, we consider the return on the stock of a company called Flyers. What will determine this stock's return in, say, the coming year?

The return on any stock traded in a financial market is composed of two parts. First, the normal or expected return from the stock is the part of the return that shareholders in the market predict or expect. This return depends on the information shareholders have that bears on the stock, and it is based on the market's understanding today of the important factors that will influence the stock in the coming year.

The second part of the return on the stock is the uncertain or risky part. This is the portion that comes from unexpected information that is revealed within the year. A list of all possible sources of such information is endless, but here are a few examples:

News about Flyers' research.
Government figures released on gross national product (GNP).
The results from the latest arms control talks.
The news that Flyers' sales figures are higher than expected.
A sudden, unexpected drop in interest rates.

Based on this discussion, one way to write the return on Flyers' stock in the coming year would be:

$$\text{Total return} = \text{Expected return} + \text{Unexpected return} \qquad [11.3]$$
$$R = E(R) + U$$

where R stands for the actual total return in the year, $E(R)$ stands for the expected part of the return, and U stands for the unexpected part of the return. What this says is that the actual return, R, differs from the expected return, $E(R)$, because of surprises that occur during the year.

Announcements and News

We need to be careful when we talk about the effect of news items on the return. For example, suppose that Flyers' business is such that the company prospers when GNP (gross national product) grows at a relatively high rate and suffers when GNP is relatively stagnant. In this case, in deciding what return to expect this year from owning stock in Flyers, shareholders either implicitly or explicitly must think about what GNP is likely to be for the year.

When the government actually announces GNP figures for the year, what will happen to the value of Flyers' stock? Obviously, the answer depends on what figure is released. More to the point, however, the impact depends on how much of that figure is *new* information.

At the beginning of the year, market participants will have some idea or forecast of what the yearly GNP will be. To the extent that shareholders had predicted GNP, that prediction will already be factored into the expected part of the return on the stock, $E(R)$. On the other hand, if the announced GNP is a surprise, then the effect will be part of U, the unanticipated portion of the return.

As an example, suppose shareholders in the market had forecast that the GNP increase this year would be 0.5 percent. If the actual announcement this year is exactly 0.5 percent, the same as the forecast, then the shareholders didn't really learn anything, and the announcement isn't news. There would be no impact on the stock price as a result. This is like receiving confirmation of something that you suspected all along; it doesn't reveal anything new.

A common way of saying that an announcement isn't news is to say that the market has already "discounted" the announcement. The use of the word *discount* here is different from the use of the term in computing present values, but the spirit is the same. When we discount a dollar in the future, we say it is worth less to us because of the time value of money. When we discount an announcement or a news item, we mean that it has less of an impact on the market because the market already knew much of it.

For example, going back to Flyers, suppose the government announced that the actual GNP increase during the year was 1.5 percent. Now shareholders have learned something, namely, that the increase is 1 percentage point higher than they had forecast. This difference between the actual result and the forecast, 1 percentage point in this example, is sometimes called the *innovation* or the *surprise*.

An announcement, then, can be broken into two parts, the anticipated or expected part and the surprise or innovation:

$$\text{Announcement} = \text{Expected part} + \text{Surprise} \qquad [11.4]$$

The expected part of any announcement is part of the information that the market uses to form the expectation, $E(R)$, of the return on the stock. The surprise is the news that influences the unanticipated return on the stock, U.

To take another example, if shareholders knew in January that the president of the firm was going to resign, the official announcement in February would be fully expected and would be discounted by the market. Because the announcement was expected before February, its influence on the stock would have taken place before February. The announcement itself will contain no surprise, and the stock's price shouldn't change at all when it is actually made.

Our discussion of market efficiency in the previous chapter bears on this discussion. We are assuming that relevant information that is known today is already reflected in the expected return. This is identical to saying that the current price reflects relevant publicly available information. We are thus implicitly assuming that markets are at least reasonably efficient in the semistrong form sense.

Henceforth, when we speak of news, we will mean the surprise part of an announcement and not the portion that the market has expected and therefore already discounted.

CONCEPT QUESTIONS

11.3a What are the two basic parts of a return?

11.3b Under what conditions will an announcement have no effect on common stock prices?

RISK: SYSTEMATIC AND UNSYSTEMATIC | 11.4

The unanticipated part of the return, that portion resulting from surprises, is the true risk of any investment. After all, if we always receive exactly what we expect, then the investment is perfectly predictable and, by definition, risk-free. In other words, the risk of owning an asset comes from surprises—unanticipated events.

There are important differences, though, among various sources of risk. Look back at our previous list of news stories. Some of these stories are directed specifically at Flyers, and some are more general. Which of the news items are of specific importance to Flyers?

Announcements about interest rates or GNP are clearly important for nearly all companies, whereas the news about Flyers' president, its research, or its sales are of specific interest to Flyers. We will distinguish between these two types of events, because, as we shall see, they have very different implications.

Systematic and Unsystematic Risk

systematic risk

A risk that influences a large number of assets. Also *market risk*.

unsystematic risk

A risk that affects at most a small number of assets. Also *unique* or *asset-specific risks*.

The first type of surprise, the one that affects a large number of assets, we will label **systematic risk.** A systematic risk is one that influences a large number of assets, each to a greater or lesser extent. Because systematic risks are marketwide effects, they are sometimes called *market risks*.

The second type of surprise we will call **unsystematic risk.** An unsystematic risk is one that affects a single asset or a small group of assets. Because these risks are unique to individual companies or assets, they are sometimes called *unique* or *asset-specific risks.* We will use these terms interchangeably.

As we have seen, uncertainties about general economic conditions, such as GNP, interest rates, or inflation, are examples of systematic risks. These conditions affect nearly all companies to some degree. An unanticipated increase or surprise in inflation, for example, affects wages and the costs of the supplies that companies buy; it affects the value of the assets that companies own; and it affects the prices at which companies sell their products. Forces such as these, to which all companies are susceptible, are the essence of systematic risk.

In contrast, the announcement of an oil strike by a company will primarily affect that company and, perhaps, a few others (such as primary competitors and suppliers). It is unlikely to have much of an effect on the world oil market, however, or on the affairs of companies that are not in the oil business, so this is an unsystematic event.

Systematic and Unsystematic Components of Return

The distinction between a systematic risk and an unsystematic risk is never really as exact as we make it out to be. Even the most narrow and peculiar bit of news about a company ripples through the economy. This is true because every enterprise, no matter how tiny, is a part of the economy. It's like the tale of a kingdom that was lost because one horse lost a shoe. This is mostly hairsplitting, however. Some risks are clearly much more general than others. We'll see some evidence on this point in just a moment.

The distinction between the types of risk allows us to break down the surprise portion, U, of the return on Flyers' stock into two parts. From before, we had the actual return broken down into its expected and surprise components:

$$R = \mathrm{E}(R) + U$$

We now recognize that the total surprise for Flyers, U, has a systematic and an unsystematic component, so:

$$R = E(R) + \text{Systematic portion} + \text{Unsystematic portion} \qquad [11.5]$$

Because it is traditional, we will use the Greek letter epsilon, ε, to stand for the unsystematic portion. Since systematic risks are often called market risks, we will use the letter m to stand for the systematic part of the surprise. With these symbols, we can rewrite the total return:

$$R = E(R) + U$$
$$ = E(R) + m + \varepsilon$$

The important thing about the way we have broken down the total surprise, U, is that the unsystematic portion, ε, is more or less unique to Flyers. For this reason, it is unrelated to the unsystematic portion of return on most other assets. To see why this is important, we need to return to the subject of portfolio risk.

CONCEPT QUESTIONS

11.4a What are the two basic types of risk?

11.4b What is the distinction between the two types of risk?

DIVERSIFICATION AND PORTFOLIO RISK | 11.5

We've seen earlier that portfolio risks can, in principle, be quite different from the risks of the assets that make up the portfolio. We now look more closely at the riskiness of an individual asset versus the risk of a portfolio of many different assets. We will once again examine some market history to get an idea of what happens with actual investments in U.S. capital markets.

The Effect of Diversification: Another Lesson from Market History

In our previous chapter, we saw that the standard deviation of the annual return on a portfolio of 500 large common stocks has historically been about 21 percent per year (see Figure 10.10, for example). Does this mean that the standard deviation of the annual return on a typical stock in that group of 500 is about 21 percent? As you might suspect by now, the answer is *no*. This is an extremely important observation.

To examine the relationship between portfolio size and portfolio risk, Table 11.7 illustrates typical average annual standard deviations for equally weighted portfolios that contain different numbers of randomly selected NYSE securities.

Table 11.7 Standard deviations of annual portfolio returns	(1) Number of Stocks in Portfolio	(2) Average Standard Deviation of Annual Portfolio Returns	(3) Ratio of Portfolio Standard Deviation to Standard Deviation of a Single Stock
	1	49.24%	1.00
	2	37.36	0.76
	4	29.69	0.60
	6	26.64	0.54
	8	24.98	0.51
	10	23.93	0.49
	20	21.68	0.44
	30	20.87	0.42
	40	20.46	0.42
	50	20.20	0.41
	100	19.69	0.40
	200	19.42	0.39
	300	19.34	0.39
	400	19.29	0.39
	500	19.27	0.39
	1,000	19.21	0.39

These figures are from Table 1 in Meir Statman, "How Many Stocks Make a Diversified Portfolio?" *Journal of Financial and Quantitative Analysis* 22 (September 1987), pp. 353–64. They were derived from E. J. Elton and M. J. Gruber, "Risk Reduction and Portfolio Size: An Analytic Solution," *Journal of Business* 50 (October 1977), pp. 415–37.

In Column 2 of Table 11.7, we see that the standard deviation for a "portfolio" of one security is about 49 percent. What this means is that, if you randomly selected a single NYSE stock and put all your money into it, your standard deviation of return would typically have been a substantial 49 percent per year. If you were to randomly select two stocks and invest half your money in each, your standard deviation would have been about 37 percent on average, and so on.

The important thing to notice in Table 11.7 is that the standard deviation declines as the number of securities is increased. By the time we have 100 randomly chosen stocks, the portfolio's standard deviation has declined by about 60 percent, from 49 percent to about 20 percent. With 500 securities, the standard deviation is 19.27 percent, similar to the 21 percent we saw in our previous chapter for the large common stock portfolio. The small difference exists because the portfolio securities and time periods examined are not identical.

The Principle of Diversification

Figure 11.1 illustrates the point we've been discussing. What we have plotted is the standard deviation of return versus the number of stocks in the portfolio. Notice in Figure 11.1 that the benefit in terms of risk reduction from adding

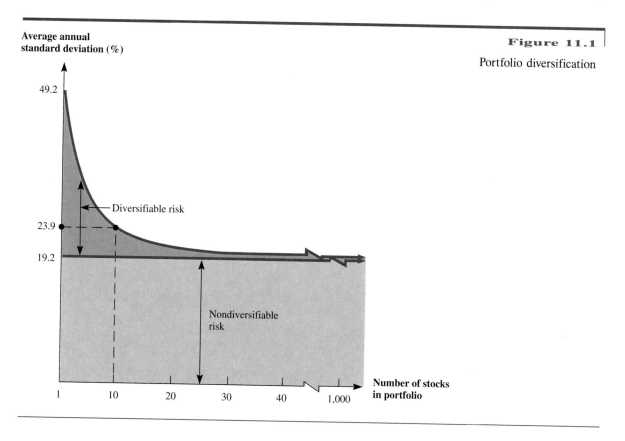

Figure 11.1

Portfolio diversification

securities drops off as we add more and more. By the time we have 10 securities, most of the effect is already realized, and by the time we get to 30 or so, there is very little remaining benefit.

Figure 11.1 illustrates two key points. First of all, some of the riskiness associated with individual assets can be eliminated by forming portfolios. The process of spreading an investment across assets (and thereby forming a portfolio) is called *diversification*. The **principle of diversification** tells us that spreading an investment across many assets will eliminate some of the risk. The green shaded area in Figure 11.1, labeled "diversifiable risk," is the part that can be eliminated by diversification.

The second point is equally important. There is a minimum level of risk that cannot be eliminated simply by diversifying. This minimum level is labeled "nondiversifiable risk" in Figure 11.1. Taken together, these two points are another important lesson from capital market history: Diversification reduces risk, but only up to a point. Put another way, some risk is diversifiable and some is not.

principle of diversification

Spreading an investment across a number of assets will eliminate some, but not all, of the risk.

Diversification and Unsystematic Risk

From our discussion of portfolio risk, we know that some of the risk associated with individual assets can be diversified away and some cannot. We are left with an obvious question: Why is this so? It turns out that the answer hinges on the distinction we made earlier between systematic and unsystematic risk.

By definition, an unsystematic risk is one that is particular to a single asset or, at most, a small group. For example, if the asset under consideration is stock in a single company, the discovery of positive NPV projects such as successful new products and innovative cost savings will tend to increase the value of the stock. Unanticipated lawsuits, industrial accidents, strikes, and similar events will tend to decrease future cash flows and thereby reduce share values.

Here is the important observation: If we only held a single stock, then the value of our investment would fluctuate because of company-specific events. If we held a large portfolio, on the other hand, some of the stocks in the portfolio will go up in value because of positive company-specific events and some will go down in value because of negative events. The net effect on the overall value of the portfolio will be relatively small, however, as these effects will tend to cancel each other out.

Now we see why some of the variability associated with individual assets is eliminated by diversification. By combining assets into portfolios, the unique or unsystematic events—both positive and negative—tend to "wash out" once we have more than just a few assets.

This is an important point that bears repeating:

> Unsystematic risk is essentially eliminated by diversification, so a relatively large portfolio has almost no unsystematic risk.

In fact, the terms *diversifiable risk* and *unsystematic risk* are often used interchangeably.

Diversification and Systematic Risk

We've seen that unsystematic risk can be eliminated by diversifying. What about systematic risk? Can it also be eliminated by diversification? The answer is no because, by definition, a systematic risk affects almost all assets to some degree. As a result, no matter how many assets we put into a portfolio, the systematic risk doesn't go away. Thus, for obvious reasons, the terms *systematic risk* and *nondiversifiable risk* are used interchangeably.

Because we have introduced so many different terms, it is useful to summarize our discussion before moving on. What we have seen is that the total risk of an investment, as measured by the standard deviation of its return, can be written as:

$$\text{Total risk} = \text{Systematic risk} + \text{Unsystematic risk} \qquad [11.6]$$

Systematic risk is also called *nondiversifiable risk* or *market risk*. Unsystematic risk is also called *diversifiable risk, unique risk,* or *asset-specific risk*. For a well-diversified portfolio, the unsystematic risk is negligible. For such a portfolio, essentially all of the risk is systematic.

⌐**CONCEPT QUESTIONS**

11.5a What happens to the standard deviation of return for a portfolio if we increase the number of securities in the portfolio?

11.5b What is the principle of diversification?

11.5c Why is some risk diversifiable? Why is some risk not diversifiable?

11.5d Why can't systematic risk be diversified away?

SYSTEMATIC RISK AND BETA | 11.6

The question that we now begin to address is: What determines the size of the risk premium on a risky asset? Put another way, why do some assets have a larger risk premium than other assets? The answer to these questions, as we discuss next, is also based on the distinction between systematic and unsystematic risk.

The Systematic Risk Principle

Thus far, we've seen that the total risk associated with an asset can be decomposed into two components: systematic and unsystematic risk. We have also seen that unsystematic risk can be essentially eliminated by diversification. The systematic risk present in an asset, on the other hand, cannot be eliminated by diversification.

Based on our study of capital market history, we know that there is a reward, on average, for bearing risk. However, we now need to be more precise about what we mean by risk. The **systematic risk principle** states that the reward for bearing risk depends only on the systematic risk of an investment. The underlying rationale for this principle is straightforward: Since unsystematic risk can be eliminated at virtually no cost (by diversifying), there is no reward for bearing it. Put another way, the market does not reward risks that are born unnecessarily.

The systematic risk principle has a remarkable and very important implication:

> The expected return on an asset depends only on that asset's systematic risk.

There is an obvious corollary to this principle: No matter how much total risk an asset has, only the systematic portion is relevant in determining the expected return (and the risk premium) on that asset.

systematic risk principle
The expected return on a risky asset depends only on that asset's systematic risk.

Measuring Systematic Risk

Since systematic risk is the crucial determinant of an asset's expected return, we need some way of measuring the level of systematic risk for different investments. The specific measure that we will use is called the **beta coefficient,** for which we will use the Greek symbol β. A beta coefficient, or beta for short, tells us how much systematic risk a particular asset has relative to an average asset. By definition, an average asset has a beta of 1.0 relative to itself. An asset with a beta of .50, therefore, has half as much systematic risk as an average asset; an asset with a beta of 2.0 has twice as much.

Table 11.8 contains the estimated beta coefficients for the stocks of some well-known companies. (This particular source rounds numbers to the nearest 0.05.) The range of betas in Table 11.8 is typical for stocks of large U.S. corporations. Betas outside this range occur, but they are less common.

beta coefficient
Amount of systematic risk present in a particular risky asset relative to an average risky asset.

Table 11.8		Beta Coefficient (β_i)
Beta coefficients for selected companies		
	IBM	0.95
	Exxon	0.75
	General Electric	1.10
	AT&T	0.85
	General Motors	1.05
	Wal-Mart	1.25
	Microsoft	1.35
	Harley-Davidson	1.60

Source: From Value Line *Investment Survey,* January 3, 1992.

The important thing to remember is that the expected return, and thus the risk premium, on an asset depends only on its systematic risk. Since assets with larger betas have greater systematic risks, they will have greater expected returns. Thus, in Table 11.8, an investor who buys stock in Exxon, with a beta of .75, should expect to earn less, on average, than an investor who buys stock in General Motors, with a beta of about 1.05.

Example 11.5   Total Risk versus Beta
Consider the following information on two securities. Which has greater total risk? Which has greater systematic risk? Greater unsystematic risk? Which asset will have a higher risk premium?

	Standard Deviation	Beta
Security A	40%	.50
Security B	20	1.50

From our discussion in this section, Security A has greater total risk, but it has substantially less systematic risk. Since total risk is the sum of systematic and unsystematic risk, Security A must have greater unsystematic risk. Finally, from the systematic risk principle, Security B will have a higher risk premium and a greater expected return, despite the fact that it has less total risk. ∎

Portfolio Betas

Earlier, we saw that the riskiness of a portfolio has no simple relationship to the risks of the assets in the portfolio. A portfolio beta, however, can be calculated just like a portfolio expected return. For example, looking back at Table 11.8, suppose you put half of your money in AT&T and half in General Electric. What would the beta of this combination be? Since AT&T has a beta of 0.85 and General Electric has a beta of 1.10, the portfolio's beta, β_P, would be:

$$\beta_P = .50 \times \beta_{AT\&T} + .50 \times \beta_{GE}$$

$$= .50 \times .85 + .50 \times 1.10$$

$$= .975$$

In general, if we had a large number of assets in a portfolio, we would multiply each asset's beta by its portfolio weight and then add the results up to get the portfolio's beta.

Example 11.6 Portfolio Betas

Suppose we had the following investments:

Security	Amount Invested	Expected Return	Beta
Stock A	$1,000	8%	.80
Stock B	2,000	12	.95
Stock C	3,000	15	1.10
Stock D	4,000	18	1.40

What is the expected return on this portfolio? What is the beta of this portfolio? Does this portfolio have more or less systematic risk than an average asset?

To answer, we first have to calculate the portfolio weights. Notice that the total amount invested is $10,000. Of this, $1,000/$10,000 = 10% is invested in Stock A. Similarly, 20 percent is invested in Stock B, 30 percent is invested in Stock C, and 40 percent is invested in Stock D. The expected return, $E(R_P)$, is thus:

$$E(R_P) = .10 \times E(R_A) + .20 \times E(R_B) + .30 \times E(R_C) + .40 \times E(R_D)$$
$$= .10 \times 8\% + .20 \times 12\% + .30 \times 15\% + .40 \times 18\%$$
$$= 14.9\%$$

Similarly, the portfolio beta, β_P, is:

$$\beta_P = .10 \times \beta_A + .20 \times \beta_B + .30 \times \beta_C + .40 \times \beta_D$$
$$= .10 \times .80 + .20 \times .95 + .30 \times 1.10 + .40 \times 1.40$$
$$= 1.16$$

This portfolio thus has an expected return of 14.9 percent and a beta of 1.16. Since the beta is larger than 1.0, this portfolio has greater systematic risk than an average asset. ∎

CONCEPT QUESTIONS

11.6a What is the systematic risk principle?

11.6b What does a beta coefficient measure?

11.6c How do you calculate a portfolio beta?

11.6d True or false: The expected return on a risky asset depends on that asset's total risk. Explain.

THE SECURITY MARKET LINE | 11.7

We're now in a position to see how risk is rewarded in the marketplace. To begin, suppose that Asset A has an expected return of $E(R_A) = 20\%$ and a beta of $\beta_A = 1.6$. Furthermore, the risk-free rate is $R_f = 8\%$. Notice that a risk-free asset, by definition, has no systematic risk (or unsystematic risk), so a risk-free asset has a beta of 0.

Beta and the Risk Premium

Consider a portfolio made up of Asset A and a risk-free asset. We can calculate some different possible portfolio expected returns and betas by varying the percentages invested in these two assets. For example, if 25 percent of the portfolio is invested in Asset A, then the expected return is:

$$E(R_P) = .25 \times E(R_A) + (1 - .25) \times R_f$$
$$= .25 \times 20\% + .75 \times 8\%$$
$$= 11.0\%$$

Similarly, the beta on the portfolio, β_P, would be:

$$\beta_P = .25 \times \beta_A + (1 - .25) \times 0$$
$$= .25 \times 1.6$$
$$= .40$$

Notice that, since the weights have to add up to 1, the percentage invested in the risk-free asset is equal to 1 minus the percentage invested in Asset A.

One thing that you might wonder about is whether it is possible for the percentage invested in Asset A to exceed 100 percent. The answer is yes. The way this can happen is for the investor to borrow at the risk-free rate. For example, suppose an investor has $100 and borrows an additional $50 at 8 percent, the risk-free rate. The total investment in Asset A would be $150, or 150 percent of the investor's wealth. The expected return in this case would be:

$$E(R_P) = 1.50 \times E(R_A) + (1 - 1.50) \times R_f$$
$$= 1.50 \times 20\% - .50 \times 8\%$$
$$= 26.0\%$$

The beta on the portfolio would be:

$$\beta_P = 1.50 \times \beta_A + (1 - 1.50) \times 0$$
$$= 1.50 \times 1.6$$
$$= 2.4$$

We can calculate some other possibilities as follows:

Percentage of Portfolio in Asset A	Portfolio Expected Return	Portfolio Beta
0%	8%	0.0
25	11	0.4
50	14	0.8
75	17	1.2
100	20	1.6
125	23	2.0
150	26	2.4

Figure 11.2A

Portfolio expected returns and betas for Asset A

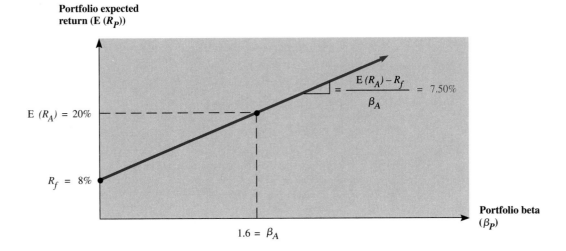

In Figure 11.2A, these portfolio expected returns are plotted against the portfolio betas. Notice that all the combinations fall on a straight line.

The Reward-to-Risk Ratio   What is the slope of the straight line in Figure 11.2A? As always, the slope of a straight line is equal to the "rise over the run." In this case, as we move out of the risk-free asset into Asset A, the beta increases from zero to 1.6 (a "run" of 1.6). At the same time, the expected return goes from 8 percent to 20 percent, a "rise" of 12 percent. The slope of the line is thus $12\%/1.6 = 7.50\%$.

Notice that the slope of our line is just the risk premium on Asset A, $E(R_A) - R_f$, divided by Asset A's beta, β_A:

$$\text{Slope} = \frac{E(R_A) - R_f}{\beta_A}$$

$$= \frac{20\% - 8\%}{1.6} = 7.50\%$$

What this tells us is that Asset A offers a *reward-to-risk ratio* of 7.50 percent.[2] In other words, Asset A has a risk premium of 7.50 percent per "unit" of systematic risk.

The Basic Argument   Now suppose we consider a second asset, Asset B. This asset has a beta of 1.2 and an expected return of 16 percent. Which investment is better, Asset A or Asset B? You might think that, once again, we really cannot say. Some investors might prefer A; some investors might prefer

---

[2]This ratio is sometimes called the *Treynor index,* after one of its originators.

B. Actually, however, we can say: A is better because, as we shall demonstrate, B offers inadequate compensation for its level of systematic risk, at least relative to A.

To begin, we calculate different combinations of expected returns and betas for portfolios of Asset B and a risk-free asset just as we did for Asset A. For example, if we put 25 percent in Asset B and the remaining 75 percent in the risk-free asset, the portfolio's expected return would be:

$$E(R_P) = .25 \times E(R_B) + (1 - .25) \times R_f$$

$$= .25 \times 16\% + .75 \times 8\%$$

$$= 10.0\%$$

Similarly, the beta on the portfolio, β_P, would be:

$$\beta_P = .25 \times \beta_B + (1 - .25) \times 0$$

$$= .25 \times 1.2$$

$$= .30$$

Some other possibilities are as follows:

Percentage of Portfolio in Asset B	Portfolio Expected Return	Portfolio Beta
0%	8%	0.0
25	10	0.3
50	12	0.6
75	14	0.9
100	16	1.2
125	18	1.5
150	20	1.8

When we plot these combinations of portfolio expected returns and portfolio betas in Figure 11.2B, we get a straight line just as we did for Asset A.

The key thing to notice is that when we compare the results for Assets A and B, as in Figure 11.2C, the line describing the combinations of expected returns and betas for Asset A is higher than the one for Asset B. What this tells us is that for any given level of systematic risk (as measured by β), some combination of Asset A and the risk-free asset always offers a larger return. This is why we were able to state that Asset A is a better investment than Asset B.

Another way of seeing that A offers a superior return for its level of risk is to note that the slope of our line for Asset B is:

$$\text{Slope} = \frac{E(R_B) - R_f}{\beta_B}$$

$$= \frac{16\% - 8\%}{1.2} = 6.67\%$$

Figure 11.2B

Portfolio expected returns and betas for Asset B

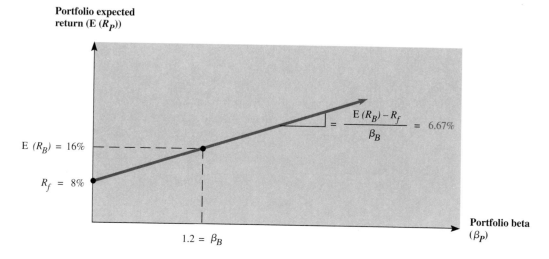

Figure 11.2C

Portfolio expected
returns and betas for
both assets

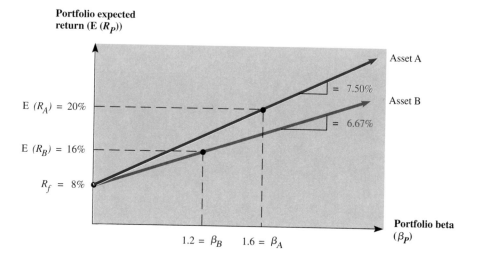

Thus, Asset B has a reward-to-risk ratio of 6.67 percent, which is less than the
7.5 percent offered by Asset A.

The Fundamental Result   The situation we have described for Assets A
and B cannot persist in a well-organized, active market, because investors
would be attracted to Asset A and away from Asset B. As a result, Asset A's
price would rise and Asset B's price would fall. Since prices and returns move

in opposite directions, the result is that A's expected return would decline and B's would rise.

This buying and selling would continue until the two assets plotted on exactly the same line, which means they offer the same reward for bearing risk. In other words, in an active, competitive market, we must have that:

$$\frac{E(R_A) - R_f}{\beta_A} = \frac{E(R_B) - R_f}{\beta_B}$$

This is the fundamental relationship between risk and return.

Our basic argument can be extended to more than just two assets. In fact, no matter how many assets we had, we would always reach the same conclusion:

The reward-to-risk ratio must be the same for all the assets in the market.

This result is really not so surprising. What it says, for example, is that, if one asset has twice as much systematic risk as another asset, its risk premium will simply be twice as large.

Since all of the assets in the market must have the same reward-to-risk ratio, they all must plot on the same line. This argument is illustrated in Figure 11.3. As shown, Assets A and B plot directly on the line and thus have the same reward-to-risk ratio. If an asset plotted above the line, such as C in Figure 11.3, its price would rise, and its expected return would fall until it

Figure 11.3

Expected returns and systematic risk

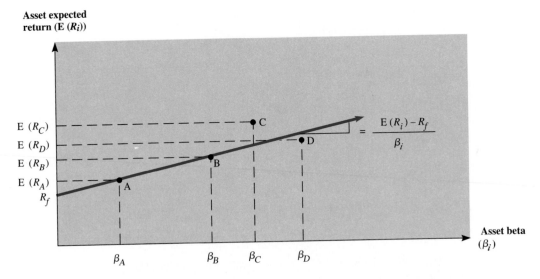

The fundamental relationship between beta and expected return is that all assets must have the same reward-to-risk ratio, $[E(R_i) - R_f]/\beta_i$. This means that they would all plot on the same straight line. Assets A and B are examples of this behavior. Asset C's expected return is too high; asset D's is too low.

plotted exactly on the line. Similarly, if an asset plotted below the line, such as D in Figure 11.3, its expected return would rise until it too plotted directly on the line.

The arguments we have presented apply to active, competitive, well-functioning markets. The financial markets, such as the NYSE, best meet these criteria. Other markets, such as real asset markets, may or may not. For this reason, these concepts are most useful in examining financial markets. We will thus focus on such markets here. However, as we discuss in a later section, the information about risk and return gleaned from financial markets is crucial in evaluating the investments that a corporation makes in real assets.

Example 11.7   Buy Low, Sell High

An asset is said to be *overvalued* if its price is too high given its expected return and risk. Suppose you observe the following situation:

Security	Beta	Expected Return
SWMS Co.	1.3	14%
Insec Co.	.8	10

The risk-free rate is currently 6 percent. Is one of the two securities above overvalued relative to the other?

To answer, we compute the reward-to-risk ratio for both. For SWMS, this ratio is $(14\% - 6\%)/1.3 = 6.15\%$. For Insec, this ratio is 5 percent. What we conclude is that Insec offers an insufficient expected return for its level of risk, at least relative to SWMS. Since its expected return is too low, its price is too high. In other words, Insec is overvalued relative to SWMS, and we would expect to see its price fall relative to SWMS's. Notice that we could also say that SWMS is *undervalued* relative to Insec. ∎

The Security Market Line

The line that results when we plot expected returns and beta coefficients is obviously of some importance, so it's time we gave it a name. This line, which we use to describe the relationship between systematic risk and expected return in financial markets, is usually called the **security market line (SML)**. After NPV, the SML is arguably the most important concept in modern finance.

security market line (SML)

Positively sloped straight line displaying the relationship between expected return and beta.

Market Portfolios   It will be very useful to know the equation of the SML. There are many different ways that we could write it, but one way is particularly common. Suppose we were to consider a portfolio made up of all of the assets in the market. Such a portfolio is called a market portfolio, and we will write the expected return on this market portfolio as $E(R_M)$.

Since all the assets in the market must plot on the SML, so must a market portfolio made of those assets. To determine where it plots on the SML, we need to know the beta of the market portfolio, β_M. Since this portfolio is representative of all of the assets in the market, it must have average systematic risk. In other words, it has a beta of one. We could therefore write the slope of the SML as:

$$\text{SML slope} = \frac{E(R_M) - R_f}{\beta_M} = \frac{E(R_M) - R_f}{1} = E(R_M) - R_f$$

market risk premium

Slope of the SML, the difference between the expected return on a market portfolio and the risk-free rate.

The term $E(R_M) - R_f$ is often called the **market risk premium** since it is the risk premium on a market portfolio.

The Capital Asset Pricing Model   To finish up, if we let $E(R_i)$ and β_i stand for the expected return and beta, respectively, on any asset in the market, then we know that it must plot on the SML. As a result, we know that its reward-to-risk ratio is the same as the overall market's:

$$\frac{E(R_i) - R_f}{\beta_i} = E(R_M) - R_f$$

If we rearrange this, then we can write the equation for the SML as:

$$E(R_i) = R_f + [E(R_M) - R_f] \times \beta_i \qquad [11.7]$$

capital asset pricing model (CAPM)

Equation of the SML showing relationship between expected return and beta.

This result is identical to the famous **capital asset pricing model (CAPM)**.[3]

What the CAPM shows is that the expected return for a particular asset depends on three things:

1. *The pure time value of money.* As measured by the risk-free rate, R_f, this is the reward for merely waiting for your money, without taking any risk.
2. *The reward for bearing systematic risk.* As measured by the market risk premium, $[E(R_M) - R_f]$, this component is the reward the market offers for bearing an average amount of systematic risk in addition to waiting.
3. *The amount of systematic risk.* As measured by β_i, this is the amount of systematic risk present in a particular asset, relative to an average asset.

Figure 11.4 summarizes our discussion of the SML and the CAPM. As before, we plot expected return against beta. Now we recognize that, based on the CAPM, the slope of the SML is equal to the market risk premium, $[E(R_M) - R_f]$.

This concludes our presentation of concepts related to the risk-return trade-off. For future reference, Table 11.9 (p. 394) summarizes the various concepts in the order we discussed them.

---

[3]Our discussion leading up to the CAPM is actually much more closely related to a more recently developed theory, known as the arbitrage pricing theory (APT). The theory underlying the CAPM is a great deal more complex than we have indicated here, and the CAPM has a number of other implications that go beyond the scope of this discussion. As we present it here, the CAPM and the APT have essentially identical implications, so we don't distinguish between them.

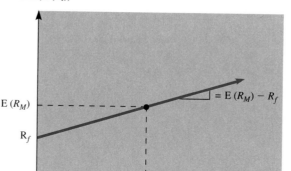

Figure 11.4

The security market
line (SML)

The slope of the security market line is equal to the market risk premium; i.e.,
the reward for bearing an average amount of systematic risk. The equation
describing the SML can be written:

$$E(R_i) = R_f + \beta_i \times [E(R_M) - R_f]$$

which is the capital asset pricing model (CAPM).

Example 11.8   Risk and Return

Suppose the risk-free rate is 4 percent, the market risk premium is 8.6 percent,
and a particular stock has a beta of 1.3. Based on the CAPM, what is the expected return on this stock? What would the expected return be if the beta
were to double?

   With a beta of 1.3, the risk premium for the stock would be $1.3 \times 8.6\%$,
or 11.18 percent. The risk-free rate is 4 percent, so the expected return is
15.18 percent. If the beta doubles to 2.6, the risk premium would double to
22.36 percent, so the expected return would be 26.36 percent. ∎

CONCEPT QUESTIONS

11.7a What is the fundamental relationship between risk and return in well-
       functioning markets?
11.7b What is the security market line? Why must all assets plot directly on it
       in a well-functioning market?
11.7c What is the capital asset pricing model (CAPM)? What does it tell us
       about the required return on a risky investment?

THE SML AND THE COST OF CAPITAL: A PREVIEW | 11.8

Our goal in studying risk and return is twofold. First, risk is an extremely
important consideration in almost all business decisions, so we want to discuss just what risk is and how it is rewarded in the market. Our second purpose is to learn what determines the appropriate discount rate for future cash

| **Table 11.9**

Summary of risk
and return | I. Total Risk
The *total risk* of an investment is measured by the variance or, more commonly, the standard deviation of its return.

II. Total Return
The *total return* on an investment has two components: the expected return and the unexpected return. The unexpected return comes about because of unanticipated events. The risk from investing stems from the possibility of an unanticipated event.

III. Systematic and Unsystematic Risks
Systematic risks (also called *market risks*) are unanticipated events that affect almost all assets to some degree because the effects are economywide. *Unsystematic risks* are unanticipated events that affect single assets or small groups of assets. Unsystematic risks are also called *unique* or *asset-specific risks.*

IV. The Effect of Diversification
Some, but not all, of the risk associated with a risky investment can be eliminated by diversification. The reason is that unsystematic risks, which are unique to individual assets, tend to wash out in a large portfolio, but systematic risks, which affect all of the assets in a portfolio to some extent, do not.

V. The Systematic Risk Principle and Beta
Because unsystematic risk can be freely eliminated by diversification, the *systematic risk principle* states that the reward for bearing risk depends only on the level of systematic risk. The level of systematic risk in a particular asset, relative to average, is given by the *beta* of that asset.

VI. The Reward-to-Risk Ratio and the Security Market Line
The *reward-to-risk ratio* for Asset *i* is the ratio of its risk premium, $E(R_i) - R_f$, to its beta, β_i:

$$\frac{E(R_i) - R_f}{\beta_i}$$

In a well-functioning market, this ratio is the same for every asset. As a result, when asset expected returns are plotted against asset betas, all assets plot on the same straight line, called the *security market line* (SML).

VII. The Capital Asset Pricing Model
From the SML, the expected return on Asset *i* can be written:

$$E(R_i) = R_f + [E(R_M) - R_f] \times \beta_i$$

This is the *capital asset pricing model* (CAPM). The expected return on a risky asset thus has three components. The first is the pure time value of money (R_f), the second is the market risk premium, $[E(R_M) - R_f]$, and the third is the beta for that asset, β_i. |

flows. We briefly discuss this second subject now; we discuss it in more detail in Chapter 14.

The Basic Idea

The security market line tells us the reward for bearing risk in financial markets. At an absolute minimum, any new investment that our firm undertakes must offer an expected return that is no worse than what the financial markets offer for the same risk. The reason for this is simply that our shareholders can always invest for themselves in the financial markets.

The only way we benefit our shareholders is by finding investments with expected returns that are superior to what the financial markets offer for the same risk. Such an investment will have a positive NPV. So, if we ask "What is the appropriate discount rate?" the answer is that we should use the expected return offered in financial markets on investments with the same systematic risk.

In other words, to determine whether or not an investment has a positive NPV, we essentially compare the expected return on that new investment to what the financial market offers on an investment with the same beta. This is why the SML is so important; it tells us the "going rate" for bearing risk in the economy.

The Cost of Capital

The appropriate discount rate on a new project is the minimum expected rate of return an investment must offer to be attractive. This minimum required return is very often called the **cost of capital** associated with the investment. It is called this because the required return is what the firm must earn on its capital investment in a project just to break even. It can thus be interpreted as the opportunity cost associated with the firm's capital investment.

cost of capital
The minimum required return on a new investment.

Notice that when we say an investment is attractive if its expected return exceeds what is offered in financial markets for investments of the same risk, we are effectively using the internal rate of return (IRR) criterion that we developed and discussed in Chapter 7. The only difference is that now we have a much better idea of what determines the required return on an investment. This understanding will be critical when we discuss cost of capital and capital structure in Part Seven of our book.

CONCEPT QUESTIONS

11.8a If an investment has a positive NPV, would it plot above or below the SML? Why?

11.8b What is meant by the term *cost of capital*?

SUMMARY AND CONCLUSIONS | 11.9

This chapter covers the essentials of risk. Along the way, we introduce a number of definitions and concepts. The most important of these is the security market line, or SML. The SML is important because it tells us the reward offered in financial markets for bearing risk. Once we know this, we have a benchmark against which we compare the returns expected from real asset investments to determine if they are desirable.

Because we cover quite a bit of ground, it's useful to summarize the basic economic logic underlying the SML as follows:

1. Based on capital market history, there is a reward for bearing risk. This reward is the risk premium on an asset.

2. The total risk associated with an asset has two parts: systematic risk and unsystematic risk. Unsystematic risk can be freely eliminated by diversification (this is the principle of diversification), so only systematic risk is

rewarded. As a result, the risk premium on an asset is determined by its systematic risk. This is the systematic risk principle.

3. An asset's systematic risk, relative to average, can be measured by its beta coefficient, β_i. The risk premium on an asset is then given by its beta coefficient multiplied by the market risk premium, $[E(R_M) - R_f] \times \beta_i$.

4. The expected return on an asset, $E(R_i)$, is equal to the risk-free rate, R_f, plus the risk premium:

$$E(R_i) = R_f + [E(R_M) - R_f] \times \beta_i$$

This is the equation of the SML, and it is often called the *capital asset pricing model* (CAPM).

This chapter completes our discussion of risk and return and concludes Part Five of our book. Now that we have a better understanding of what determines a firm's cost of capital for an investment, the next several chapters examine more closely how firms raise the long-term capital needed for investment.

Key Terms

expected return 368
portfolio 371
portfolio weight 371
systematic risk 378
unsystematic risk 378
principle of diversification 381
systematic risk principle 383

beta coefficient 383
security market line (SML) 391
market risk premium 392
capital asset pricing model (CAPM) 392
cost of capital 395

Chapter Review Problems and Self-Test

11.1   Expected Return and Standard Deviation   This problem will give you some practice calculating measures of prospective portfolio performance. There are two assets and three states of the economy:

(1) State of Economy	(2) Probability of State of Economy	(3) Stock A Rate of Return if State Occurs	(4) Stock B Rate of Return if State Occurs
Recession	.10	−.20	.30
Normal	.60	.10	.20
Boom	.30	.70	.50

What are the expected returns and standard deviations for these two stocks?

11.2   Portfolio Risk and Return   In the previous problem, suppose you have $20,000 total. If you put $6,000 in Stock A and the remainder in

Stock B, what will be the expected return and standard deviation on your portfolio?

11.3   Risk and Return   Suppose you observe the following situation:

Security	Beta	Expected Return
Cooley, Inc.	1.6	19%
Moyer Co.	1.2	16

If the risk-free rate is 8 percent, are these securities correctly priced? What would the risk-free rate have to be if they are correctly priced?

11.4   CAPM   Suppose the risk-free rate is 8 percent. The expected return on the market is 14 percent. If a particular stock has a beta of .60, what is its expected return based on the CAPM? If another stock has an expected return of 20 percent, what must its beta be?

Answers to Self-Test Problems

11.1   The expected returns are just the possible returns multiplied by the associated probabilities:

$$E(R_A) = .10 \times (-.20) + .60 \times (.10) + .30 \times (.70) = 25\%$$

$$E(R_B) = .10 \times (.30) + .60 \times (.20) + .30 \times (.50) = 30\%$$

The variances are given by the sums of the squared deviations from the expected returns multiplied by their probabilities:

$$\sigma_A^2 = .10 \times (-.20 - .25)^2 + .60 \times (.10 - .25)^2$$
$$+ .30 \times (.70 - .25)^2$$

$$= .10 \times (-.45)^2 + .60 \times (-.15)^2 + .30 \times (.45)^2$$

$$= .10 \times .2025 + .60 \times .0225 + .30 \times .2025$$

$$= .0945$$

$$\sigma_B^2 = .10 \times (.30 - .30)^2 + .60 \times (.20 - .30)^2 + .30 \times (.50 - .30)^2$$

$$= .10 \times (.00)^2 + .60 \times (-.10)^2 + .30 \times (.20)^2$$

$$= .10 \times .00 + .60 \times .01 + .30 \times .04$$

$$= .0180$$

The standard deviations are thus:

$$\sigma_A = \sqrt{.0945} = 30.74\%$$

$$\sigma_B = \sqrt{.0180} = 13.42\%$$

11.2   The portfolio weights are $6,000/20,000 = .30$ and $14,000/20,000 = .70$. The expected return is thus:

$$E(R_P) = .30 \times E(R_A) + .70 \times E(R_B)$$

$$= .30 \times 25\% + .70 \times 30\%$$

$$= 28.50\%$$

Alternatively, we could calculate the portfolio's return in each of the states:

(1) State of Economy	(2) Probability of State of Economy	(3) Portfolio Return if State Occurs
Recession	.10	$.30 \times (-.20) + .70 \times (.30) = .15$
Normal	.60	$.30 \times (.10) + .70 \times (.20) = .17$
Boom	.30	$.30 \times (.70) + .70 \times (.50) = .56$

The portfolio's expected return is:

$$E(R_P) = .10 \times (.15) + .60 \times (.17) + .30 \times (.56) = 28.50\%$$

This is the same as we had before.
   The portfolio's variance is:

$$\sigma_P^2 = .10 \times (.15 - .285)^2 + .60 \times (.17 - .285)^2 + .30$$

$$\times (.56 - .285)^2$$

$$= .03245$$

So the standard deviation is $\sqrt{.03245} = 18.01\%$.

11.3   If we compute the reward-to-risk ratios, we get $(19\% - 8\%)/1.6 = 6.875\%$ for Cooley versus 6.67 percent for Moyer. Relative to Cooley, Moyer's expected return is too low, so its price is too high.
   If they are correctly priced, then they must offer the same reward-to-risk ratio. The risk-free rate would have to be such that:

$$(19\% - R_f)/1.6 = (16\% - R_f)/1.2$$

With a little algebra, we find that the risk-free rate must be 7 percent:

$$(19\% - R_f) = (16\% - R_f)(1.6/1.2)$$

$$19\% - 16\% \times (4/3) = R_f - R_f \times (4/3)$$

$$R_f = 7\%$$

11.4   Since the expected return on the market is 14 percent, the market
risk premium is $14\% - 8\% = 6\%$ (the risk-free rate is 8 percent).
The first stock has a beta of .60, so its expected return is
$8\% + .60 \times 6\% = 11.6\%$.

For the second stock, notice that the risk premium is $20\% -
8\% = 12\%$. Since this is twice as large as the market risk premium,
the beta must be exactly equal to 2. We can verify this using the
CAPM:

$$E(R_i) = R_f + [E(R_M) - R_f] \times \beta_i$$

$$20\% = 8\% + (14\% - 8\%) \times \beta_i$$

$$\beta_i = 12\%/6\%$$

$$= 2.0$$

Questions and Problems

1.   Calculating Expected Return   Based on the following information,
calculate the expected return on the security.

(1) State of Economy	(2) Probability of State of Economy	(3) Rate of Return if State Occurs
Recession	.50	.12
Boom	.50	.18

2.   Calculating Expected Return   Based on the following information,
calculate the expected return on the security.

(1) State of Economy	(2) Probability of State of Economy	(3) Rate of Return if State Occurs
Recession	.20	.12
Boom	.80	.18

3.   Determining Portfolio Weights   What are the portfolio weights for a
portfolio that has 20 shares of a stock that sells for $50 per share and
30 shares of a stock that sells for $20 per share?

4.   Expected Portfolio Returns   If a portfolio has a positive investment
in every asset, can the expected return on the portfolio be greater
than that on every asset in the portfolio? Can it be less than that on
every asset in the portfolio? If you answer yes to one or both of these
questions, give an example to support your answer.

5.   Calculating Returns and Deviations   Based on the following information, calculate the expected returns and standard deviations for the two stocks.

(1) State of Economy	(2) Probability of State of Economy	(3) Stock A Rate of Return if State Occurs	(4) Stock B Rate of Return if State Occurs
Recession	.20	.10	.55
Normal	.40	.24	.20
Boom	.40	.44	.10

6.   Individual Asset Variance and Diversification   True or false: The most important characteristic in determining the variance of a well-diversified portfolio is the variances of the individual assets in the portfolio. Explain.

7.   Returns and Deviations   Consider the following information:

State of Economy	Probability of State	Returns		
		Stock A	Stock B	Stock C
Boom	.40	10%	15%	20%
Bust	.60	8	4	0

a. What are the expected returns on the three stocks? The standard deviations?

b. What is the expected return on an equally weighted portfolio of the three stocks?

8.   Portfolio Returns and Deviations   Consider the following information:

State of Economy	Probability of State	Return on A	Return on B
Boom	.10	25%	18%
Growth	.20	10	20
Normal	.50	15	4
Recession	.20	−12	0

a. What is the expected return for A? For B?

b. What is the standard deviation for A? For B?

c. What is the expected return on a portfolio of A and B that is 20 percent invested in A?

d. What is the variance of a portfolio that is 60 percent invested in A?

9.   Portfolio Risk   If a portfolio has a positive investment in every asset, can the standard deviation on the portfolio be less than that on every asset in the portfolio? What about the portfolio beta?

10.   Types of Risk   In broad terms, why is some risk diversifiable? Why are some risks nondiversifiable? Does it follow that an investor can control the level of unsystematic risk in a portfolio, but not the level of systematic risk?

11.   Announcements and Security Prices   Suppose that the government announces that, based on a just-completed survey, the growth rate in the economy is likely to be 4 percent in the coming year, as compared to 6 percent for the year just completed. Would security prices increase, decrease, or stay the same following this announcement?

12.   Unsystematic Risk   Evaluate the following statement: "The only truly unsystematic events are earthquakes, volcanoes, and supernovas."

13.   Systematic versus Unsystematic Risk   Classify the following events as mostly systematic or mostly unsystematic. Is the distinction clear in every case?
   a.   Short-term interest rates increase unexpectedly.
   b.   The interest rate a company pays on its short-term borrowing is increased by its bank.
   c.   Oil prices unexpectedly decline.
   d.   An oil tanker ruptures creating a large oil spill.
   e.   A manufacturer loses a multimillion dollar product liability suit.
   f.   A Supreme Court decision substantially broadens producer liability for injuries suffered by product users.

14.   Analyzing a Portfolio   Suppose we had the following investments:

Security	Amount Invested	Expected Return	Beta
Stock A	$5,000	9%	.80
Stock B	5,000	10	1.00
Stock C	6,000	11	1.20
Stock D	4,000	12	1.40

   a.   What are the portfolio weights?
   b.   What is the expected return on the portfolio?
   c.   What is the portfolio beta?

15.   Using CAPM   The risk-free asset currently earns 9 percent. A stock has a beta of .70 and an expected return of 12 percent.
   a.   What is the expected return on a portfolio that is equally invested in the two assets?
   b.   If a portfolio of the two assets has a beta of .50, what are the portfolio weights?
   c.   If a portfolio of the two assets has an expected return of 10 percent, what is its beta?
   d.   If a portfolio of the two assets has a beta of 1.50, what are the portfolio weights? How do we interpret the weight for the risk-free asset?

16.   Using the SML   Asset A has an expected return of 18 percent and a beta of 1.4. If the risk-free rate is 8 percent, complete the following table for portfolios of Asset A and the risk-free asset. Illustrate the relationship between portfolio expected return and portfolio beta by

plotting the expected returns against the betas. What is the slope of the line that results?

Percentage of Portfolio in Asset A	Portfolio Expected Return	Portfolio Beta
0%		
25		
50		
75		
100		
125		
150		

17. **Portfolio Returns**   Using information from the previous chapter on capital market history, what was the return on a portfolio that was equally invested in common stocks and long-term corporate bonds? What was the return on a portfolio that was equally invested in small stocks and Treasury bills?

18. **Using the SML**   Suppose the risk-free rate is 8 percent and the expected return on the overall market is 14 percent. If a particular stock has a beta of .60, what is its expected return based on the CAPM? If another stock has an expected return of 20 percent, what must its beta be?

19. **Reward-to-Risk Ratios**   Suppose you observe the following situation:

Security	Beta	Expected Return
Chen, Inc.	.80	10%
Kim Co.	.60	8

If the risk-free rate is 6 percent, are these securities correctly priced? What would the risk-free rate have to be if they are correctly priced?

20. **Using the SML**   The beta for the Snow-Me Corporation is .80. Its expected return is 12 percent, and the risk-free rate is 8 percent. If Snow-Me plots on the SML, what is the market risk premium?

21. **SML**   Suppose the expected return on the market is 10 percent. A security has a beta of 1.80 and an expected return of 14 percent. If this security plots on the SML, what is the risk-free rate? What is the slope of the SML?

22. **CAPM**   Using the CAPM, show that the ratio of the risk premiums on two assets is equal to the ratio of their betas.

Challenge Question

23. **SML**   Suppose you observe the following situation:

Security	Beta	Expected Return
Smith Co.	1.25	19%
MBI Co.	.75	15

Assume these securities are correctly priced. Based on the CAPM, what is the expected return on the market? What is the risk-free rate?

24.   Beta Coefficients   Is it possible that a risky asset could have a beta of zero? Explain. From the CAPM, what is the expected return on such an asset? Is it possible that a risky asset could have a negative beta? What does the CAPM predict about the expected return on such an asset? Can you give an explanation for your answer?

Challenge Question

Suggested Reading

For greater detail on the subject of risk and return, see Chapters 9, 10, and 11 of:

Ross, S. A.; R.W. Westerfield; and J. J. Jaffe. *Corporate Finance.* 3rd ed. Homewood, Ill.: Richard D. Irwin, 1993.

Part Six

Long-Term Financing

CHAPTER 12
Long-Term Financing: An Introduction

This chapter describes the main features of long-term financing and corporate securities. It begins with a discussion of long-term debt, preferred stock, and common stock and then covers the historical patterns of long-term financing.

CHAPTER 13
Issuing Securities to the Public

This chapter describes how securities are issued and discusses the different underwriting methods. Chapter 13 also discusses the direct and indirect costs associated with issuing securities.

Chapter 12

Long-Term Financing

An Introduction

Corporate securities such as stocks and bonds can be a perplexing subject. Frequently, the concepts are simple and logical, but the language is unfamiliar and rich in jargon. Many of the terms and ideas we describe in this chapter and the next have appeared elsewhere in our book. Our task here and in the next several chapters is to assemble these pieces into a reasonably complete picture of long-term corporate financing.

In this chapter, we describe the main features of long-term financing and corporate securities. We begin with a look at long-term debt, preferred stock, and common stock. We go on to briefly consider patterns of the different kinds of long-term financing. We defer to a later chapter our discussion of the institutional, legal, and regulatory complexities involved in selling securities to the public.

One consequence of debt financing is the possibility of bankruptcy. Events preceding bankruptcy are referred to as *financial distress*. Because the prospect of bankruptcy is an important consideration in long-term financing, we conclude this chapter with a brief discussion of financial distress, bankruptcy, and reorganization.

CORPORATE LONG-TERM DEBT | 12.1

In this section, we begin our discussion of corporate debt by describing in some detail the basic terms and features that make up a typical long-term corporate debt. We discuss additional issues associated with long-term debt in subsequent sections.

Securities issued by corporations may be classified roughly as *equity securities* and *debt securities*. At its crudest level, a debt represents something that must be repaid; it is the result of borrowing money. When corporations borrow, they promise to make regularly scheduled interest payments and to repay the original amount borrowed (that is, the principal). The person or firm making the loan is called the *creditor* or *lender*. The corporation borrowing the money is called the *debtor* or *borrower*.

From a financial point of view, the main differences between debt and equity are the following:

1. Debt is not an ownership interest in the firm. Creditors generally do not have voting power.
2. The corporation's payment of interest on debt is considered a cost of doing business and is fully tax deductible.
3. Unpaid debt is a liability of the firm. If it is not paid, the creditors can legally claim the assets of the firm. This action can result in liquidation or reorganization, two of the possible consequences of bankruptcy. Thus, one of the costs of issuing debt is the possibility of financial failure. This possibility does not arise when equity is issued.

Is It Debt or Equity?

Sometimes it is not clear if a particular security is debt or equity. For example, suppose a corporation issues a perpetual bond with interest payable solely from corporate income if and only if earned. Whether this is really a debt or not is hard to say and is primarily a legal and semantic issue. Courts and taxing authorities would have the final say.

Corporations are very adept at creating exotic, hybrid securities that have many features of equity but are treated as debt. Obviously, the distinction between debt and equity is very important for tax purposes. So one reason that corporations try to create a debt security that is really equity is to obtain the tax benefits of debt and the bankruptcy benefits of equity.

As a general rule, equity represents an ownership interest, and it is a residual claim. This means that equity holders are paid after debt holders. As a result of this, the risks and benefits associated with owning debt and equity are different. To give just one example, the maximum reward for owning a debt security is ultimately fixed by the amount of the loan, whereas there is no necessary upper limit to the potential reward from owning an equity interest.

Long-Term Debt: The Basics

Ultimately, all long-term debt securities are promises by the issuing firm to pay principal when due and to make timely interest payments on the unpaid balance. Beyond this, there are a number of features that distinguish these securities from one another. We discuss some of these features next.

The maturity of a long-term debt instrument refers to the length of time the debt remains outstanding with some unpaid balance. Debt securities can be short-term (maturities of one year or less) or long-term (maturities of more than 1 year).[1] Short-term debt is sometimes referred to as *unfunded debt.*[2]

Debt securities are typically called *notes, debentures,* or *bonds.* Strictly speaking, a bond is a secured debt. However, in common usage, the word *bond* refers to all kinds of secured and unsecured debt. We will therefore use the term generically to refer to long-term debt.

The two major forms of long-term debt are public issue and privately placed. We concentrate on public-issue bonds. Most of what we say about them holds true for private-issue, long-term debt as well. The main difference between public-issue and privately placed debt is that the latter is directly placed with a lender and not offered to the public. Since this is a private transaction, the specific terms are up to the parties involved.

There are many other dimensions to long-term debt, including such things as security, call features, sinking funds, ratings, and protective covenants. The following table illustrates these features for a hypothetical bond. If some of these terms are unfamiliar, have no fear. We discuss them all below.

Features of a Hypothetical Bond

Terms		Explanations
Amount of issue	$100 million	The company will issue $100 million of bonds.
Date of issue	10/21/87	The bonds will be sold on 10/21/87.
Maturity	10/21/17	The principal will be paid in 30 years.
Face value	$1,000	The denomination of the bonds is $1,000.
Annual coupon	10.50	Each bondholder will receive $105 per bond per year (10.50% of face value).
Offer price	100	The offer price will be 100% of the $1,000 face value per bond.
Yield to maturity	10.50%	If the bond is held to maturity, bondholders will receive a stated annual rate of return equal to 10.50%.
Coupon payment dates	12/31, 6/30	Coupons of $105/2 = $52.50 will be paid on these dates.
Security	None	The bonds are debentures.
Sinking fund	Annual	The firm will make annual payments toward the sinking fund.
Call provision	Not callable before 12/31/97	The bonds have a deferred call feature.
Call price	$1,100	After 12/31/97, the company can buy back the bonds for $1,100 per bond.
Rating	Moody's Aaa	This is Moody's highest rating. The bonds have the lowest probability of default.

Many of these features will be detailed in the bond indenture, so we discuss this first.

---

[1] There is no universally agreed-upon distinction between short-term and long-term debt. In addition, people often refer to intermediate-term debt, which has a maturity of more than 1 year and less than 3 to 5, or even 10, years.

[2] The word *funding* is part of the jargon of finance. It generally means long-term. Thus a firm planning to "fund" its debt requirements may be replacing short-term debt with long-term debt.

The Indenture

indenture

Written agreement between the corporation and the lender detailing the terms of the debt issue.

The **indenture** is the written agreement between the corporation (the borrower) and its creditors. It is sometimes referred to as the *deed of trust*.[3] Usually, a trustee (a bank, perhaps) is appointed by the corporation to represent the bondholders. The trust company must (1) make sure the terms of the indenture are obeyed, (2) manage the sinking fund (described below), and (3) represent the bondholders in default, that is, if the company defaults on its payments to them.

The bond indenture is a legal document. It can run several hundred pages and generally makes for very tedious reading. It is an important document, however, because it generally includes the following provisions:

1. The basic terms of the bonds.
2. The total amount of bonds issued.
3. A description of property used as security.
4. The repayment arrangements.
5. The call provisions.
6. Details of the protective covenants.

We discuss these features next.

Terms of a Bond   Corporate bonds usually have a face value (that is, a denomination) of $1,000. This is called the *principal value* and it is stated on the bond certificate. So, if a corporation wanted to borrow $1 million, 1,000 bonds would have to be sold. The par value (that is, initial accounting value) of a bond is almost always the same as the face value, and the terms are used interchangeably in practice.

registered form

Registrar of company records ownership of each bond; payment is made directly to the owner of record.

Corporate bonds are usually in **registered form.** For example, the indenture might read as follows:

Interest is payable semiannually on July 1 and January 1 of each year to the person in whose name the bond is registered at the close of business on June 15 or December 15, respectively.

This means that the company has a registrar who will record the ownership of each bond and record any changes in ownership. The company will pay the interest and principal by check mailed directly to the address of the owner of record. A corporate bond may be registered and have attached "coupons." To obtain an interest payment, the owner must separate a coupon from the bond certificate and send it to the company registrar (the paying agent).

bearer form

Bond issued without record of the owner's name; payment is made to whoever holds the bond.

Alternatively, the bond could be in **bearer form.** This means that the certificate is the basic evidence of ownership, and the corporation will "pay the bearer." Ownership is not otherwise recorded, and, as with a registered bond with attached coupons, the holder of the bond certificate detaches the coupons and sends them to the company to receive payment.

---

[3]The words *loan agreement* or *loan contract* are usually used for privately placed debt and term loans.

There are two drawbacks to bearer bonds. First, they are difficult to recover if they are lost or stolen. Second, because the company does not know who owns its bonds, it cannot notify bondholders of important events.

Security   Debt securities are classified according to the collateral and mortgages used to protect the bondholder.

Collateral is a general term that, strictly speaking, means securities (for example, bonds and stocks) that are pledged as security for payment of debt. For example, collateral trust bonds often involve a pledge of common stock held by the corporation. However, the term *collateral* often is used much more loosely to refer to any form of security.

Mortgage securities are secured by a mortgage on the real property of the borrower. The property involved is usually real estate, for example, land or buildings. The legal document that describes the mortgage is called a *mortgage trust indenture* or *trust deed.*

Sometimes mortgages are on specific property, for example, a railroad car. More often, blanket mortgages are used. A blanket mortgage pledges all the real property owned by the company.[4]

Bonds frequently represent unsecured obligations of the company. A **debenture** is an unsecured bond, where no specific pledge of property is made. The term **note** is generally used for such instruments if the maturity of the unsecured bond is less than 10 or so years when it is originally issued. Debenture holders only have a claim on property not otherwise pledged; in other words, the property that remains after mortgages and collateral trusts are taken into account.

debenture
Unsecured debt, usually with a maturity of 10 years or more.

note
Unsecured debt, usually with a maturity under 10 years.

Here and elsewhere in this chapter, our terminology is standard in the United States. Outside the United States, these same terms can have different meanings. For example, bonds issued by the British government ("gilts") are called Treasury "stock." Also, in the United Kingdom, a debenture is a *secured* obligation.

At the current time, almost all public bonds issued in the United States by industrial and financial companies are debentures. However, most utility and railroad bonds are secured by a pledge of assets.

Seniority   In general terms, *seniority* indicates preference in position over other lenders, and debts are sometimes labeled as *senior* or *junior* to indicate seniority. Some debt is *subordinated,* as in, for example, a subordinated debenture.

In the event of default, holders of subordinated debt must give preference to other specified creditors. Usually, this means that the subordinated lenders will be paid off only after the specified creditors have been compensated. However, debt cannot be subordinated to equity.

Repayment   Bonds can be repaid at maturity, at which time the bondholder will receive the stated or face value of the bond, or they may be repaid in part or in entirety before maturity. Early repayment in some form is more typical and is often handled through a sinking fund.

---

[4]Real property includes land and things "affixed thereto." It does not include cash or inventories.

sinking fund

Account managed by the bond trustee for early bond redemption.

A **sinking fund** is an account managed by the bond trustee for the purpose of repaying the bonds. The company makes annual payments to the trustee, who then uses the funds to retire a portion of the debt. The trustee does this by either buying up some of the bonds in the market or calling in a fraction of the outstanding bonds. This second option is discussed below.

There are many different kinds of sinking fund arrangements, and the details would be spelled out in the indenture. For example:

1. Some sinking funds start about 10 years after the initial issuance.
2. Some sinking funds establish equal payments over the life of the bond.
3. Some high-quality bond issues establish payments to the sinking fund that are not sufficient to redeem the entire issue. As a consequence, there is the possibility of a large "balloon payment" at maturity.

call provision

Agreement giving the corporation the option to repurchase the bond at a specified price prior to maturity.

call premium

Amount by which the call price exceeds the par value of the bond.

The Call Provision   A **call provision** allows the company to repurchase or "call" part or all of the bond issue at stated prices over a specific period. Corporate bonds are usually callable.

Generally, the call price is above the bond's stated value (that is, the par value). The difference between the call price and the stated value is the **call premium.** The amount of the call premium usually becomes smaller over time. One arrangement is to initially set the call premium equal to the annual coupon payment and then make it decline to zero the closer the call date is to maturity.

Call provisions are not usually operative during the first part of a bond's life. This makes the call provision less of a worry for bondholders in the bond's early years. For example, a company might be prohibited from calling its bonds for the first 10 years. This is a **deferred call.** During this period, the bond is said to be **call protected.**

deferred call

Call provision prohibiting the company from redeeming the bond prior to a certain date.

call protected

Bond during period in which it cannot be redeemed by the issuer.

protective covenant

Part of the indenture limiting certain actions that can be taken during the term of the loan, usually to protect the lender's interest.

Protective Covenants   A **protective covenant** is that part of the indenture or loan agreement that limits certain actions a company might otherwise wish to take during the term of the loan. Protective covenants can be classified into two types: negative covenants and positive (or affirmative) covenants.

A *negative covenant* is a "thou shalt not." It limits or prohibits actions that the company may take. Here are some typical examples:

1. The firm must limit the amount of dividends it pays according to some formula.
2. The firm cannot pledge any assets to other lenders.
3. The firm cannot merge with another firm.
4. The firm cannot sell or lease any major assets without approval by the lender.
5. The firm cannot issue additional long-term debt.

A *positive covenant* is a "thou shalt." It specifies an action that the company agrees to take or a condition the company must abide by. Here are some examples:

1. The company must maintain its working capital at or above some specified minimum level.
2. The company must periodically furnish audited financial statements to the lender.
3. The firm must maintain any collateral or security in good condition.

This is only a partial list of covenants; a particular indenture may feature many different ones.

⌈ CONCEPT QUESTIONS

12.1a What are the distinguishing features of debt as compared to equity?

12.1b What is the indenture? What are protective covenants? Give some examples.

12.1c What is a sinking fund?

BOND RATINGS ⌈ 12.2

Firms frequently pay to have their debt rated. The two leading bond rating firms are Moody's and Standard & Poor's (S&P). The debt ratings are an assessment of the creditworthiness of the corporate issuer. The definitions of creditworthiness used by Moody's and S&P are based on how likely the firm is to default and the protection creditors have in the event of a default.

It is important to recognize that bond ratings *only* concern the possibility of default. In Chapter 6, we discussed interest rate risk, which we defined as the risk of a change in the value of a bond from a change in interest rates. Bond ratings do not address this issue. As a result, the price of a highly rated bond can still be quite volatile.

Bond ratings are constructed from information supplied by the corporation. The rating classes and some information concerning them are shown in the table below.

	Investment-Quality Bond Ratings				Low Quality, Speculative, and/or "Junk"					
	High Grade		Medium Grade		Low Grade		Very Low Grade			
Standard & Poor's	AAA	AA	A	BBB	BB	B	CCC	CC	C	D
Moody's	Aaa	Aa	A	Baa	Ba	B	Caa	Ca	C	D

Moody's	S&P	
Aaa	AAA	Debt rated Aaa and AAA has the highest rating. Capacity to pay interest and principal is extremely strong.
Aa	AA	Debt rated Aa and AA has a very strong capacity to pay interest and repay principal. Together with the highest rating, this group comprises the high-grade bond class.
A	A	Debt rated A has a strong capacity to pay interest and repay principal, although it is somewhat more susceptible to the adverse effects of changes in circumstances and economic conditions than debt in high-rated categories.
Baa	BBB	Debt rated Baa and BBB is regarded as having an adequate capacity to pay interest and repay principal. Whereas it normally exhibits adequate protection parameters, adverse economic conditions or changing circumstances are more likely to lead to a weakened capacity to pay interest and repay principal for debt in this category than in higher rated categories. These bonds are medium-grade obligations.
Ba, B Caa Ca	BB, B CCC CC	Debt rated in these categories is regarded, on balance, as predominantly speculative with respect to capacity to pay interest and repay principal in accordance with the terms of the obligation. BB and Ba indicate the lowest degree of speculation, and CC and Ca the highest degree of speculation. Although such debt will likely have some quality and protective characteristics, these are outweighed by large uncertainties or major risk exposures to adverse conditions. Some issues may be in default.
C	C	This rating is reserved for income bonds on which no interest is being paid.
D	D	Debt rated D is in default, and payment of interest and/or repayment of principal is in arrears.

At times, both Moody's and S&P use adjustments to these ratings. S&P uses plus and minus signs: A+ is the strongest A rating and A− the weakest. Moody's uses a 1, 2, or 3 designation, with 1 being the highest.

The highest rating a firm can have is AAA or Aaa, and such debt is judged to be the best quality and to have the lowest degree of risk. This rating is not awarded very often; AA or Aa ratings indicate very good quality debt and are much more common. The lowest rating is D, for debt that is in default.

Beginning in the 1980s, a growing part of corporate borrowing has taken the form of low-grade, or "junk," bonds. If they are rated at all, such low-grade bonds are corporate bonds rated below investment grade by the major rating agencies. Investment-grade bonds are bonds rated at least BBB by S&P or Baa by Moody's.

CONCEPT QUESTIONS

12.2a What is a junk bond?

12.2b What does a bond rating say about the risk of fluctuations in a bond's value from interest rate changes?

12.3 | SOME DIFFERENT TYPES OF BONDS

Thus far, we have considered "plain vanilla" bonds. In this section, we look at some more unusual types: zero coupon bonds, floating-rate bonds, and others.

Zero Coupon Bonds

zero coupon bond

A bond that makes no coupon payments, thus initially priced at a deep discount.

A bond that pays no coupons at all must be offered at a price that is much lower than its stated value. Such bonds are called **zero coupon bonds,** or just *zeroes.*[5]

Suppose the DDB Company issues a $1,000 face value five-year zero coupon bond. The initial price is set at $497. It is straightforward to check that, at this price, the bond yields 15 percent to maturity. The total interest paid over the life of the bond is $1,000 − 497 = $503.

For tax purposes, the issuer of a zero coupon bond deducts interest every year even though no interest is actually paid. Similarly, the owner must pay taxes on interest accrued every year as well, even though no interest is actually received.

The way the yearly interest on a zero coupon bond is calculated is governed by tax law. Before 1982, corporations could calculate the interest deduction on a straight-line basis. For DDB, the annual interest deduction would have been $503/5 = $100.6 per year.

Under current tax law, the implicit interest is determined by amortizing the loan. We do this by first calculating the bond's value at the beginning of each year. For example, in one year, the bond has four years until maturity, so it will be worth $1,000/1.15^4 = $572; the value in two years will be $1,000/1.15^3 = $658, and so on. The implicit interest each year is simply the change in the bond's value for the year. The values and interest expenses for the DDB bond are listed in Table 12.1.

---

[5]A bond issued with a very low coupon rate (as opposed to a zero coupon rate) is an original-issue discount (OID) bond.

In Their Own Words . . .
Edward I. Altman on Junk Bonds

One of the most important developments in corporate finance over the last decade has been the reemergence of publicly owned and traded low-rated corporate debt. Originally offered to the public in the early 1900s to help finance some of our emerging growth industries, these high-yield/high-risk bonds virtually disappeared after the rash of bond defaults during the Depression. In the last 12 years, however, the junk bond market has been catapulted from an insignificant element in the corporate fixed income market to one of the fastest growing and most controversial types of financing mechanisms.

The term *junk* emanates from the dominant type of low-rated bond issues outstanding prior to 1977 when the "market" consisted almost exclusively of original-issue investment-grade bonds that fell from their lofty status to a higher default risk, speculative-grade level. These so-called "fallen angels" amounted to about $8.5 billion in 1977. At the beginning of 1990, fallen angels comprised about 20 percent of the $200 billion publicly owned junk bond market.

Beginning in 1977, issuers began to go directly to the public to raise capital for growth purposes. Early users of junk bonds were energy-related firms, cable TV companies, airlines, and assorted other industrial companies. This type of financing is a form of securitization of what heretofore was the sole province of private placements financed by banks and insurance companies. The emerging growth company rationale coupled with relatively high returns to early investors helped legitimize this sector. Most investment banks ignored junk bonds until 1983–1984, when their merits and profit potential became more evident.

Synonymous with the market's growth was the emergence of the investment banking firm, Drexel Burnham Lambert, and its junk bond wizard, Michael Milken. Drexel established a potent network of issuers and investors and rode the wave of new financing and the consequent surge in secondary trading to become one of the powerful investment banks in the late 1980s. The incredible rise in power of this firm was followed by an equally incredible fall resulting first in government civil and criminal convictions and huge fines for various misdealings and finally the firm's total collapse and bankruptcy in February 1990.

By far the most important and controversial aspect of junk bond financing was its role in the corporate restructuring movement from 1985–1989. High-leverage transactions and acquisitions, such as leveraged buyouts (LBOs), which occur when a firm is taken private, and leveraged recapitalizations (debt for equity swaps) transformed the face of corporate America leading to a heated debate as to the economic and social consequences of firms being transformed from public to private enterprises with debt/equity ratios of at least 6:1.

These transactions involved increasingly large companies, and the multibillion dollar takeover became fairly common, finally capped by the huge $25+ billion RJR Nabisco LBO in 1989. LBOs were typically financed with about 60 percent senior bank debt, about 25–30 percent subordinated public debt (junk bonds), and 10–15 percent equity. The junk bond segment is sometimes referred to as "mezzanine" financing because it lies between the "balcony" senior debt and the "basement" equity.

These restructurings resulted in huge fees to advisors and underwriters and huge premiums to the old shareholders who were bought out, and they continued as long as the market was willing to buy these new debt offerings at what appeared to be a favorable risk/return trade-off. The bottom fell out of the market in the last six months of 1989 due to a number of factors including a marked increase in defaults, government regulation against S&Ls holding junk bonds, fears of higher interest rates and a recession, and, finally, the growing realization of the leverage excesses of certain ill-conceived restructurings.

The default rate rose dramatically to 4 percent in 1989 and then skyrocketed in 1990 and 1991 to 8.7 percent and 9.0 percent respectively, with about $19 billion of defaults in 1991. By the end of 1990, the pendulum of growth in new junk bond issues and returns to investors swung dramatically downward as prices plummeted and the new issue market all but dried up. The year 1991 was a pivotal year in that despite record defaults, bond prices and new issues rebounded strongly as the prospects for the future brightened.

Will the junk bond market survive? Yes, it will, but the growth will almost certainly slow, and the new offerings will revert back to more soundly financed capital structures. Restructurings will also continue with the mezzanine debt increasingly of the private placement variety and with lower debt ratios than we observed in the 1980s.

Edward I. Altman is Max L. Heine Professor of Finance at the Stern School of Business of New York University. He is widely recognized as one of the country's experts on bankruptcy and the credit analysis associated with high-yield or "junk" bonds.

Table 12.1

Zero coupon bonds

Year	Beginning Value	Ending Value	Implicit Interest Expense	Straight-Line Interest Expense
1	$497	$ 572	$ 75	$100.6
2	572	658	86	100.6
3	658	756	98	100.6
4	756	870	114	100.6
5	870	1,000	130	100.6
Total			$503	$503.0

Notice that, under the old rules, zero coupon bonds were more attractive because the deductions for interest expense were larger in the early years (compare the implicit interest expense with the straight-line expense).

Under current tax law, DDB could deduct $75 in interest paid the first year and the owner of the bond would pay taxes on $75 in taxable income (even though no interest was actually received). This second tax feature makes taxable zero coupon bonds less attractive to individuals. However, they are still a very attractive investment for tax-exempt investors with long-term dollar-denominated liabilities, such as pension funds, because the future dollar value is known with relative certainty.

Floating-Rate Bonds

The conventional bonds we have talked about in this chapter have fixed-dollar obligations because the coupon rate is set as a fixed percentage of the par value. Similarly, the principal is set equal to the par value. Under these circumstances, the coupon payment and principal are completely fixed.

With *floating-rate bonds (floaters),* the coupon payments are adjustable. The adjustments are tied to an interest rate index such as the Treasury bill interest rate or the 30-year Treasury bond rate. For example, in 1974, Citibank issued $850 million of floating-rate notes. The coupon rate was set at 1 percent above the 90-day Treasury bill rate and adjusted semiannually.

The value of a floating-rate bond depends on exactly how the coupon payment adjustments are defined. In most cases, the coupon adjusts with a lag to some base rate. For example, suppose a coupon-rate adjustment is made on June 1. The adjustment might be based on the simple average of Treasury bond yields during the previous three months. In addition, the majority of floaters have the following features:

1. The holder has the right to redeem his or her note at par on the coupon payment date after some specified amount of time. This is called a *put* provision, and it is discussed below.
2. The coupon rate has a floor and a ceiling, meaning that the coupon is subject to a minimum and a maximum. In this case, the coupon rate is said to be "capped," and the upper and lower rates are sometimes called the *collar.*

Other Types of Bonds

Since bonds are financial contracts, the possible features are only limited by the imagination of the parties involved. As a result, bonds can be fairly exotic, particularly some more recent issues. We discuss a few of the more common features and types next.

Income bonds are similar to conventional bonds, except that coupon payments are dependent on company income. Specifically, coupons are paid to bondholders only if the firm's income is sufficient. This would appear to be an attractive feature, but income bonds are not very common.

A *convertible bond* can be swapped for a fixed number of shares of stock anytime before maturity at the holder's option. Convertibles are relatively common, but the number has been decreasing in recent years.

A *put bond* allows the *holder* to force the issuer to buy the bond back at a stated price. The put feature is therefore just the reverse of the call provision and is a relatively new development. We discuss convertible bonds, call provisions, and put provisions in more detail in Chapter 20.

A given bond may have many unusual features. To give just one example, Merrill Lynch created a very popular bond called a *liquid yield option note,* or LYON ("lion"). A LYON is the "kitchen sink" of bonds: a callable, puttable, convertible, zero coupon, subordinated note. Valuing a bond of this sort can be quite complex.

CONCEPT QUESTIONS

12.3a Why might an income bond be attractive to a corporation with volatile cash flows? Can you think of a reason why income bonds are not more popular?

12.3b What do you think would be the effect of a put feature on a bond's coupon? How about a convertibility feature? Why?

PREFERRED STOCK | 12.4

Preferred stock differs from common stock because it has preference over common stock in the payment of dividends and in the distribution of corporation assets in the event of liquidation. *Preference* means only that the holders of the preferred shares must receive a dividend (in the case of an ongoing firm) before holders of common shares are entitled to anything.

Preferred stock is a form of equity from a legal and tax standpoint. Importantly, however, holders of preferred stock sometimes have no voting privileges.

preferred stock

Stock with dividend priority over common stock, normally with a fixed dividend rate, sometimes without voting rights.

Stated Value

Preferred shares have a stated liquidating value, usually $100 per share. The cash dividend is described in terms of dollars per share. For example, General Motors "$5 preferred" translates easily into a dividend yield of 5 percent of stated value.

Cumulative and Noncumulative Dividends

A preferred dividend is *not* like interest on a bond. The board of directors may decide not to pay the dividends on preferred shares, and their decision may have nothing to do with the current net income of the corporation.

Dividends payable on preferred stock are either *cumulative* or *noncumulative;* most are cumulative. If preferred dividends are cumulative and are not paid in a particular year, they will be carried forward as an *arrearage.* Usually both the accumulated (past) preferred dividends plus the current preferred dividends must be paid before the common shareholders can receive anything.

Unpaid preferred dividends are *not* debts of the firm. Directors elected by the common shareholders can defer preferred dividends indefinitely. However, in such cases:

1. Common shareholders must also forgo dividends.
2. Holders of preferred shares are often granted voting and other rights if preferred dividends have not been paid for some time.

Because preferred stockholders receive no interest on the accumulated dividends, some have argued that firms have an incentive to delay paying preferred dividends.

Is Preferred Stock Really Debt?

A good case can be made that preferred stock is really debt in disguise, a kind of equity bond. Preferred shareholders receive a stated dividend only, and, if the corporation is liquidated, preferred shareholders get a stated value. Often, preferreds carry credit ratings much like bonds. Furthermore, preferred stock is sometimes convertible into common stock, and preferred stocks are often callable.

In addition, in recent years, many new issues of preferred stock have had obligatory sinking funds. Such a sinking fund effectively creates a final maturity since the entire issue will ultimately be retired. For example, if a sinking fund required that 2 percent of the original issue be retired each year, the issue would be completely retired in 50 years.

On top of all of this, preferred stocks with adjustable dividends have been offered in recent years. For example, a "CARP" is a cumulative, adjustable-rate, preferred. There are various types of floating-rate preferreds, some of which are quite innovative in the way that the dividend is determined.

For all these reasons, preferred stock seems to be a lot like debt. Unlike debt, however, preferred stock dividends cannot be deducted as interest expense when determining taxable corporate income. From the individual investor's standpoint, preferred dividends received are ordinary income for tax purposes. For corporate investors, however, 70 percent of the dividend amounts they receive from preferred stock are exempt from income taxes.[6]

The yields on preferred stock can appear very low. For example, General Motors actually has a preferred stock with a $5 stated dividend. In January

---

[6]As discussed later in the chapter, this exclusion depends on the amount of equity held; 70 percent is actually the minimum exclusion.

1992, the market price of the $5 General Motors preferred was $59.50. This is a $5/$59.50 = 8.4% yield, less than the yield on GM's debt.

Despite the apparently low yields, corporate investors have an incentive to hold the preferred or common stock issued by other corporations over holding their debt since a portion of the dividends they receive are exempt from income taxes. Because individual investors do not receive this tax break, most preferred stock in the United States is owned by corporate investors. Corporate investors pay a premium for preferred stock because of the tax exclusion on dividends; as a consequence, the yields are low.

Overall, there are thus two offsetting (at least partially) tax effects to consider in evaluating preferred stock:

1. Unlike interest paid, dividends paid on preferred stock are not deducted from corporate income in computing corporate taxes. This is a significant disadvantage.

2. When preferred stock is held as an asset, 70 percent of dividends received are exempt from corporate taxation. With interest received, all of it is fully taxable. This is a significant advantage.

The Preferred Stock Puzzle

Even with these offsets, however, a net tax disadvantage to the issuance of preferred stock still exists. In addition, preferred stock requires a regular dividend payment and thus lacks the flexibility of common stock. For these reasons, some have argued that preferred stock should not exist.

Why then do firms issue preferred stock? For most industrial firms, the fact that dividends are not an allowable deduction from taxable corporate income is the most serious obstacle to issuing preferred stock, but there are several reasons why preferred stock is issued.

We can start by discussing some supply factors. First, regulated public utilities can pass the tax disadvantage of issuing preferred stock on to their customers because of the way pricing formulas are set up in regulatory environments. Consequently, a substantial amount of straight preferred stock is issued by utilities.

Second, firms issuing preferred stock can avoid the threat of bankruptcy that might otherwise exist if debt were relied on. Unpaid preferred dividends are not debts of a corporation, and preferred shareholders cannot force a corporation into bankruptcy because of unpaid dividends. Further, the tax advantage to interest and the disadvantage to dividends only exist for corporations with significant tax liabilities, so preferred stock is sometimes issued by corporations with large accumulated tax losses. This is particularly true when the firm essentially cannot borrow on a long-term basis.

A third reason for issuing preferred stock concerns control of the firm. Since preferred shareholders often cannot vote, preferred stock may be a means of raising equity without surrendering control.

On the demand side, most preferred stock is owned by corporations. As we discuss elsewhere, corporate income from preferred (and common) stock dividends enjoys a 70 percent tax exemption, which can substantially lessen the tax disadvantage of preferred stock. Some of the new types of adjustable-rate preferred stocks are highly suited for corporations needing short-term investments for temporarily idle cash.

Also, in addition to the general dividend tax exemption for corporations, property and casualty insurance companies have a significant incentive to purchase preferreds because of some specific regulatory features of that industry.

⌐ CONCEPT QUESTIONS

12.4a What is preferred stock?

12.4b Why is it arguably more like debt than equity?

12.4c What are two reasons why preferred stock is issued?

12.5 │ COMMON STOCK

common stock

Equity without priority for dividends or in bankruptcy.

The term **common stock** means different things to different people, but it is usually applied to stock that has no special preference either in dividends or in bankruptcy. A description of the common stock of Anheuser-Busch in 1986 is presented in the table below.

The Shareholders' Equity of Anheuser-Busch — 1986
($ in millions)

Common stock and other shareholders' equity	
Common stock, $1 par value, authorized 400,000,000 shares in 1986; issued 295,264,924 shares	$ 295.3
Capital in excess of par value	6.1
Retained earnings	2,472.2
	$2,773.6
Less 26,399,740 shares of treasury stock	460.8
Total	$2,312.8

Par and No Par Stock

shareholders or stockholders

Owners of equity in a corporation.

Owners of common stock in a corporation are referred to as **shareholders** or **stockholders.** They receive stock certificates for the shares they own. Figure 12.1 contains a reproduction of a stock certificate. There is often a stated value on each stock certificate called the *par value*. The par value of each share of the common stock of Anheuser-Busch is $1.

dedicated capital

Total par value of all shares outstanding.

The total par value is the number of shares issued multiplied by the par value of each share and is sometimes referred to as the **dedicated capital** of a corporation. The dedicated capital of Anheuser-Busch, for example, is $1 × 295.3 million shares = $295.3 million.

It would not be unusual for a corporation to have *no par* stock. This means that there is no particular par value assigned to the stock.

Authorized versus Issued Common Stock

Shares of common stock are the fundamental ownership units of the corporation. The articles of incorporation of a new corporation must state the number of shares of common stock the corporation is authorized to issue.

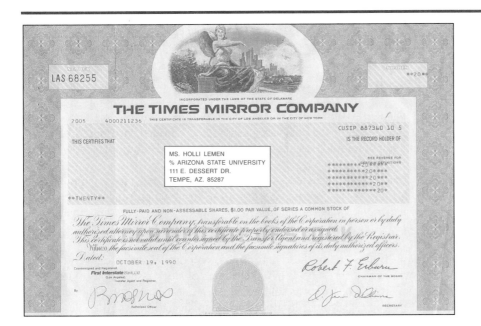

Figure 12.1

A stock certificate

The board of directors of the corporation, after a vote of the shareholders, can amend the articles of incorporation to increase the number of shares authorized; there is no legal limit to the number of shares that can be authorized this way. In 1986, Anheuser-Busch had authorized 400 million shares and had actually issued 295.3 million shares. There is no requirement that all of the authorized shares ever be issued.

Although there are no legal limits to authorizing shares of stock, some practical considerations may exist:

1. Some states impose taxes based on the number of authorized shares.
2. Authorizing a large number of shares may create concern on the part of investors, because, once they are authorized, shares can be issued later with the approval of the board of directors but *without* a vote of the shareholders.

Capital in Excess of Par Value

Capital in excess of par value (often called *capital surplus* or *additional paid-in capital*) usually refers to amounts of directly contributed equity capital in excess of par value. For example, suppose 100 shares of common stock with a par value of $1 each are sold to shareholders for $10 per share. The sale brings in a total of $10 \times 100 = \$1,000$. Of this $1,000, the total par value would be $1 \times 100 = \$100$. The capital surplus would then be $(\$10 - 1) \times 100 = \$9 \times 100 = \$900$.

What difference does it make if the total capital contribution is reported as par value or capital surplus? About the only difference is that in most states the par value is "locked in" and cannot be distributed to stockholders except upon the liquidation of the corporation.

capital in excess of par value

Directly contributed equity in excess of par. Also *capital surplus* or *additional paid-in capital.*

The capital surplus of Anheuser-Busch is $6.1 million. This figure indicates that the price of new shares issued by Anheuser-Busch has exceeded the par value and the difference has been entered as capital in excess of par value.

Retained Earnings

retained earnings

Corporate earnings not paid out as dividends.

book value

Accounting value of firm's equity. Also *net worth*.

Usually, Anheuser-Busch pays out less than half of its net income as dividends; the rest is retained in the business and is called **retained earnings**. The cumulative amount of retained earnings (since original incorporation) is $2,472.2 million in 1986.

The sum of the par value, capital in excess of par, and accumulated retained earnings is the *common equity* of the firm, which is usually referred to as the firm's **book value** (or *net worth*). The book value represents the amount contributed directly and indirectly to the corporation by equity investors (in an accounting sense).

To illustrate some of these definitions, suppose Western Redwood Corporation was formed in 1906 with 10,000 shares of stock issued and sold at its $1 par value. Since the stock was sold for $1, the first balance sheet showed a zero amount for capital surplus. By 1987, the company had been profitable and had retained profits of $100,000. The stockholders' equity of Western Redwood Corporation in 1987 is as follows:

Western Redwood Corporation Equity Accounts: 1987

Common stock (10,000 shares outstanding, $1 par)	$ 10,000
Capital surplus	0
Retained earnings	100,000
Total stockholders' equity	$110,000

$$\text{Book value per share} = \frac{\$110,000}{10,000} = \$11$$

Now suppose the company has profitable investment opportunities and decides to sell 10,000 shares of new stock to raise the necessary financing. The current market price is $20 per share. The table below shows the effects of the sale of stock on the balance sheet.

Western Redwood Corporation: 1987 (after sale of stock)

Common stock (20,000 shares outstanding, $1 par)	$ 20,000
Capital surplus ($20 − 1) × 10,000 shares	190,000
Retained earnings	100,000
Total stockholders' equity	$310,000

$$\text{Book value per share} = \frac{\$310,000}{20,000} = \$15.5$$

What happened?

1. Since 10,000 shares of new stock were issued with a par value of $1, a total of $10,000 was added to the par value.

2. The total amount raised by the new issue was $20 \times 10,000 = \$200,000$. This exceeded the par value by $19 \times 10,000 = \$190,000$, so $190,000 was entered into capital surplus.

3. The book value per share increased because the market price of the new stock was higher than the old book value.

Market Values versus Book Values

The total book value of Anheuser-Busch in 1986 was $2,312.8 million. The company had issued 295,264,924 shares and bought back 26,399,740 shares, so that the total number of outstanding shares was $295,264,924 - 26,399,740 = 268,865,184$. The shares bought back are called **treasury stock**. These are shown at cost, in other words, what the company actually paid for them.

The book value per share was thus equal to:

$$\frac{\text{Total common shareholders' equity}}{\text{Shares outstanding}} = \frac{\$2,312.8 \text{ million}}{268.9 \text{ million}} = \$8.6$$

treasury stock
Stock issued and then later repurchased by a company.

Anheuser-Busch is a publicly owned company. Its common stock trades on the New York Stock Exchange (NYSE), and thousands of shares change hands every day. The market prices of Anheuser-Busch stock were between $25 and $30 per share during 1986. Thus, the market prices were well above the book value.

Shareholders' Rights

The conceptual structure of the corporation assumes that shareholders elect directors who, in turn, hire management to carry out their directives. Shareholders, therefore, control the corporation through the right to elect the directors. Generally, only shareholders have this right.

Directors are elected each year at an annual meeting. Although there are exceptions (discussed below), the general idea is "one share, one vote" (*not* one share*holder,* one vote). Corporate democracy is thus very different from our political democracy. With corporate democracy, the "golden rule" prevails absolutely.[7]

Directors are elected at an annual shareholders' meeting by a vote of the holders of a majority of shares who are present and entitled to vote. However, the exact mechanism for electing directors differs across companies. The most important difference is whether shares must be voted cumulatively or must be voted straight.

To illustrate the two different voting procedures, imagine that a corporation has two shareholders: Smith with 20 shares and Jones with 80 shares. Both want to be a director. Jones does not want Smith, however. We assume that there are a total of four directors to be elected.

---

[7]The golden rule: Whosoever has the gold makes the rules.

cumulative voting

Procedure where a shareholder may cast all votes for one member of the board of directors.

Cumulative Voting   The effect of **cumulative voting** is to permit minority participation.[8] If cumulative voting is permitted, the total number of votes that each shareholder may cast is determined first. This is usually calculated as the number of shares (owned or controlled) multiplied by the number of directors to be elected.

With cumulative voting, the directors are elected all at once. In our example, this means that the top four vote getters will be the new directors. A shareholder can distribute votes however he or she wishes.

Will Smith get a seat on the board? If we ignore the possibility of a five-way tie, then the answer is yes. Smith will cast $20 \times 4 = 80$ votes, and Jones will cast $80 \times 4 = 320$ votes. If Smith gives all his votes to himself, he is assured of a directorship. The reason is that Jones can't divide 320 votes among four candidates in such a way as to give all of them more than 80 votes, so Smith will finish fourth at worst.

In general, if there are N directors up for election, then $1/(N + 1)$ percent of the stock (plus one share) will guarantee you a seat. In our current example, this is $1/(4 + 1) = 20\%$. So the more seats that are up for election at one time, the easier (and cheaper) it is to win one.

straight voting

Procedure where a shareholder may cast all votes for each member of the board of directors.

Straight Voting   With **straight voting**, the directors are elected one at a time. Each time, Smith can cast 20 votes and Jones can cast 80. As a consequence, Jones will elect all of the candidates. The only way to guarantee a seat is to own 50 percent plus one share. This also guarantees that you will win *every* seat, so it's really all or nothing.

Example 12.1 Buying the Election

Stock in JRJ Corporation sells for $20 per share and features cumulative voting. There are 10,000 shares outstanding. If three directors are up for election, how much does it cost to ensure yourself a seat on the board?

The question here is how many shares of stock will it take to get a seat. The answer is 2,501, so the cost is $2,501 \times \$20 = \$50,020$. Why 2,501? Because there is no way the remaining 7,499 votes can be divided among three people to give all of them more than 2,501 votes. For example, suppose two people receive 2,502 votes and the first two seats. A third person can receive at most $10,000 - 2,502 - 2,502 - 2,501 = 2,495$, so the third seat is yours. ∎

As we've illustrated, straight voting can "freeze out" minority shareholders; that is the reason many states have mandatory cumulative voting. In states where cumulative voting is mandatory, devices have been worked out to minimize its impact.

One such device is to stagger the voting for the board of directors. With staggered elections, only a fraction of the directorships are up for election at a particular time. Thus, if only two directors are up for election at any one time, it will take $1/(2 + 1) = 33.33\%$ of the stock to guarantee a seat.

---

[8]By minority participation, we mean participation by shareholders with relatively small amounts of stock.

Overall, staggering has two basic effects:

1. Staggering makes it more difficult for a minority to elect a director when there is cumulative voting because there are fewer to be elected at one time.

2. Staggering makes takeover attempts less likely to be successful because it is more difficult to vote in a majority of new directors.

We should note that staggering may serve a beneficial purpose. It provides "institutional memory," that is, continuity on the board of directors. This may be important for corporations with significant long-range plans and projects.

Proxy Voting   A **proxy** is the grant of authority by a shareholder to someone else to vote his or her shares. For convenience, much of the voting in large public corporations is actually done by proxy.

proxy
Grant of authority by shareholder allowing for another individual to vote his or her shares.

As we have seen, with straight voting, each share of stock has one vote. The owner of 10,000 shares has 10,000 votes. Many companies, such as Anheuser-Busch, have hundreds of thousands or even millions of shareholders. Shareholders can come to the annual meeting and vote in person, or they can transfer their right to vote to another party.

Obviously, management always tries to get as many proxies transferred to it as possible. However, if shareholders are not satisfied with management, an "outside" group of shareholders can try to obtain votes via proxy. They can vote by proxy to replace management by electing enough directors. This is called a *proxy fight.*

Other Rights   The value of a share of common stock in a corporation is directly related to the general rights of shareholders. In addition to the right to vote for directors, shareholders usually have the following rights:

1. The right to share proportionally in dividends paid.
2. The right to share proportionally in assets remaining after liabilities have been paid in a liquidation.
3. The right to vote on stockholder matters of great importance, such as a merger, usually done at the annual meeting or a special meeting.

In addition, stockholders sometimes have the right to share proportionally in any new stock sold. This is called the *preemptive right,* and we will discuss it in some detail in the next chapter.

Essentially, a preemptive right means that a company that wishes to sell stock must first offer it to the existing stockholders before offering it to the general public. The purpose is to give a stockholder the opportunity to protect his or her proportionate ownership in the corporation.

Dividends

A distinctive feature of corporations is that they have shares of stock on which they are authorized by law to pay dividends to their shareholders. **Dividends** paid to shareholders represent a return on the capital directly or indirectly contributed to the corporation by the shareholders. The payment of dividends is at the discretion of the board of directors.

dividends
Payment by corporation to shareholders, made in either cash or stock.

Some important characteristics of dividends include the following:

1. Unless a dividend is declared by the board of directors of a corporation, it is not a liability of the corporation. A corporation cannot default on an undeclared dividend. As a consequence, corporations cannot become bankrupt because of nonpayment of dividends. The amount of the dividend and even whether it is paid are decisions based on the business judgment of the board of directors.[9]

2. The payment of dividends by the corporation is not a business expense. Dividends are not deductible for corporate tax purposes. In short, dividends are paid out of the corporation's aftertax profits.

3. Dividends received by individual shareholders are for the most part considered ordinary income by the IRS and are fully taxable. However, corporations that own stock in other corporations are permitted to exclude 70 percent of the dividend amounts they receive and are taxed only on the remaining 30 percent.[10]

Classes of Stock

Some firms have more than one class of common stock. Often, the classes are created with unequal voting rights. The Ford Motor Company, for example, has Class B common stock, which is not publicly traded (it is held by Ford family interests and trusts). This class has about 40 percent of the voting power. However, these shares comprise only about 15 percent of the total outstanding stock.

There are many other cases of corporations with different classes of stock. For example, there is the interesting case of Citizens' Utility (traded OTC), which only pays cash dividends on its Class A shares and only pays stock dividends on its Class B shares.[11] In another example, General Motors has its "GM Classic" shares (the original) and two more recently created classes, Class E ("GME") and Class H ("GMH"). These classes were created to help pay for two large acquisitions, Electronic Data Systems and Hughes Aircraft.

In principle, the New York Stock Exchange does not allow companies to create classes of publicly traded common stock with unequal voting rights. Exceptions (e.g., Ford) appear to have been made. In addition, many non-NYSE companies have dual classes of common stock.

A primary reason for creating dual or multiple classes of stock has to do with control of the firm. If such stock exists, management of a firm can raise

---

[9]There are, however, IRS regulations regarding "improper" accumulation of retained earnings. Since dividends are taxed as income to the recipient, there is an incentive to not pay dividends. The IRS does not allow corporations to not pay dividends if the goal is merely to avoid this tax. See Chapter 16 on dividend policy for more detail.

[10]For the record, the 70 percent exclusion applies when the recipient owns less than 20 percent of the outstanding stock in a corporation. If a corporation owns more than 20 percent but less than 80 percent, the exclusion is 80 percent. If more than 80 percent is owned, the corporation can file a single "consolidated" return and the exclusion is effectively 100 percent.

[11]Cash and stock dividends are discussed in more detail when we cover dividends and dividend policy in Chapter 16.

equity capital by issuing nonvoting or limited-voting stock while maintaining control.

The subject of unequal voting rights is controversial in the United States, and the idea of one share, one vote has a strong following and a long history. Interestingly, however, shares with unequal voting rights are quite common in the United Kingdom and elsewhere around the world.

⌐CONCEPT QUESTIONS

12.5a What is a company's book value?

12.5b What rights do stockholders have?

12.5c What is a proxy?

PATTERNS OF LONG-TERM FINANCING ⌐12.6

We have looked at different types of long-term financing. We now examine the relative importance of different sources of long-term financing and how these sources are used. Table 12.2 summarizes the sources and uses of long-term financing for U.S. industrial firms from 1981 to 1990 in dollar and percentage terms.

In Table 12.2, under sources of financing, we have internally generated financing and external sources. The internal financing is defined here as net income plus depreciation less dividends, and it is a measure of the internally generated cash flow from operations that is reinvested in the firm.

The external financing consists of net new long-term borrowing, short-term borrowing, and common stock. One striking trend in recent years is the tendency for net new equity issues to be *negative,* meaning that more equity is bought back than sold. Long-term debt has become correspondingly more important as a source of financing. For example, in 1988, corporations borrowed $138.2 billion long-term. New equity sales were −$130.5 billion, meaning that repurchases of stock exceeded sales of stock by this amount.

Several other features of long-term financing are apparent in Table 12.2:

1. Internally generated cash flow has dominated as a source of funds. Between 50 percent and 85 percent of long-term financing comes from cash flow generated by operations and "plowed back." Typically, internally generated funds provide about 70 percent to 80 percent of total sources.

2. The primary use of long-term financing is capital spending, which regularly accounts for about 70 percent to 80 percent of all uses. Capital spending and internally generated cash flow are thus roughly equal.

3. A financial "deficit" is created by the difference between uses of long-term financing and internally generated sources, and corporations have been net issuers of securities. For example, in 1982, 80 percent of long-term financing came from internal cash flow, leaving a deficit of 20 percent. In this particular year, the shortfall was financed mostly with short-term debt (15 percent).

Table 12.2

Patterns of corporate financing: 1981–1990

Billions of Dollars

	1981	1982	1983	1984	1985	1986	1987	1988	1989	1990
Uses of funds:										
Capital spending	$269.4	$269.1	$261.5	$308.4	$329.1	$318.2	$318.4	$350.9	$364.5	$372.4
Short-term uses										
Inventory	$ 35.9	–$ 10.8	$ 11.5	$ 57.5	$ 8.0	–$ 3.3	$ 45.9	$ 51.3	$ 37.0	$ 4.0
Liquid assets	23.9	46.3	35.1	24.1	27.6	75.7	7.7	35.0	15.0	23.7
Accounts receivable	25.1	–15.1	55.5	50.1	43.4	16.3	68.8	19.2	26.0	25.5
Other	52.9	23.6	39.2	38.7	16.5	34.5	31.9	42.0	67.6	67.1
	$137.8	$ 44.0	$141.3	$170.4	$ 95.5	$123.2	$154.3	$147.5	$145.6	$120.3
Total uses	$407.2	$313.1	$402.8	$478.8	$424.6	$441.4	$472.7	$498.4	$510.1	$492.7
Sources of funds										
Internally generated funds*	$263.7	$252.7	$296.6	$342.1	$354.0	$338.1	$371.5	$397.6	$401.7	$381.3
External financing										
New equity sales	–$ 11.5	$ 6.4	$ 23.5	–$ 74.5	–$ 81.5	–$ 80.8	–$ 76.5	–$130.5	–$124.2	–$ 63.0
Other equity	25.3	13.8	11.5	25.6	20.5	36.1	47.3	57.6	69.7	34.3
Long-term debt	36.9	–8.2	21.0	65.3	78.5	139.7	114.6	138.2	79.1	62.0
Short-term debt	56.3	48.2	31.5	89.9	55.1	51.5	28.9	59.4	67.8	18.7
Accounts payable	28.6	4.9	37.0	33.7	34.0	3.1	18.0	3.2	27.8	30.2
Other financing	2.2	–4.5	8.9	18.6	–1.5	16.2	1.3	8.1	12.4	20.5
	$137.8	$ 60.6	$133.4	$156.8	$105.1	$165.8	$133.6	$136.0	$132.6	$102.7
Discrepancy†	5.7	–0.2	–27.2	–21.9	–34.5	–62.5	–32.4	–35.2	–24.2	8.7
Total sources	$407.2	$313.1	$402.8	$478.8	$424.6	$441.4	$472.7	$498.4	$510.1	$492.7

Percentage of Total Uses

	1981	1982	1983	1984	1985	1986	1987	1988	1989	1990
Uses of funds:										
Capital spending	0.66	0.86	0.65	0.64	0.78	0.72	0.67	0.70	.71	.76
Short-term uses										
Inventory	0.09	−0.03	0.03	0.12	0.02	−0.01	0.10	0.10	.07	.01
Liquid assets	0.06	0.15	0.09	0.05	0.07	0.17	0.02	0.07	.03	.05
Accounts receivable	0.06	−0.05	0.14	0.10	0.10	0.04	0.15	0.04	.05	.05
Other	0.13	0.07	0.10	0.08	0.04	0.08	0.07	0.09	.13	.14
	0.34	0.14	0.35	0.36	0.22	0.28	0.33	0.30	.29	.24
Total uses	1.00	1.00	1.00	1.00	1.00	1.00	1.00	1.00	1.00	1.00
Sources of funds										
Internally generated funds*	0.65	0.80	0.74	0.71	0.83	0.77	0.79	0.80	.79	.77
External financing										
New equity sales	−0.03	0.02	0.06	−0.16	−0.19	−0.18	−0.16	−0.26	−.24	−.13
Other equity	0.06	0.04	0.03	0.05	0.05	0.08	0.10	0.12	.14	.07
Long-term debt	0.09	−0.03	0.05	0.14	0.18	0.32	0.24	0.28	.16	.13
Short-term debt	0.14	0.15	0.08	0.19	0.13	0.12	0.06	0.12	.13	.04
Accounts payable	0.07	0.02	0.09	0.07	0.08	0.01	0.04	0.01	.05	.06
Other financing	0.01	−0.01	0.02	0.04	−0.00	0.04	0.01	0.02	.02	.04
	0.34	0.19	0.33	0.33	0.25	0.38	0.28	0.27	.26	.21
Discrepancy†	0.01	−0.00	−0.07	−0.05	−0.08	−0.14	−0.08	−0.07	−.05	.02
Total sources	1.00	1.00	1.00	1.00	1.00	1.00	1.00	1.00	1.00	1.00

Note: Column totals may be inexact because of rounding errors.
*Internally generated funds is net income plus depreciation less dividends.
†Discrepancy refers to the statistical error in the flow of funds accounts.
Source: Derived from various issues of Board of Governors of the Federal Reserve System, *Flow of Funds Accounts.*

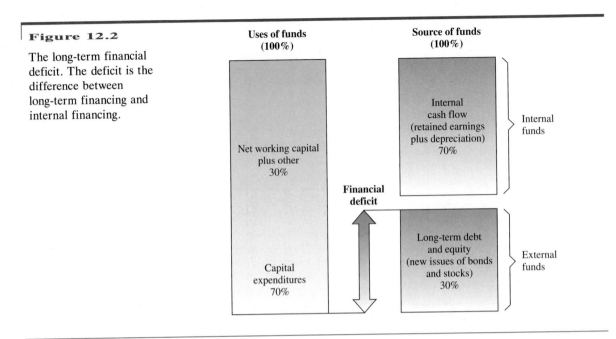

Figure 12.2

The long-term financial deficit. The deficit is the difference between long-term financing and internal financing.

As Figure 12.2 indicates, the financial deficit averages about 30 percent. In general, the deficit is covered by borrowing and new equity. However, as we have seen, one of the most prominent aspects of external financing is that new issues of equity seem to be less and less important, at least in aggregate.

CONCEPT QUESTIONS

12.6a What is the difference between internal financing and external financing?

12.6b What are the major sources of corporate financing? What trends have emerged in recent years?

12.7 | LONG-TERM FINANCING UNDER FINANCIAL DISTRESS AND BANKRUPTCY

One of the consequences of using debt is the possibility of financial distress, which can be defined in several ways:

1. *Business failure.* This is a term usually used to refer to a situation where a business has terminated with a loss to creditors, but even an all-equity firm can fail.

2. *Legal bankruptcy.* Firms bring petitions to a federal court for bankruptcy. **Bankruptcy** is a legal proceeding for liquidating or reorganizing a business.

bankruptcy

A legal proceeding for liquidating or reorganizing a business. Also, the transfer of some or all of a firm's assets to its creditors.

3. *Technical insolvency.* Technical insolvency occurs when a firm defaults on a legal obligation; for example, it does not pay a bill.
4. *Accounting insolvency.* Firms with negative net worth are insolvent on the books. This happens when the total book liabilities exceed the book value of the total assets.

For future reference, we will define *bankruptcy* as the transfer of some or all of the firm's assets to creditors. We now very briefly discuss some of the terms and more relevant issues associated with bankruptcy and financial distress.

Liquidation and Reorganization

Firms that cannot or choose not to make contractually required payments to creditors have two basic options: liquidation or reorganization. **Liquidation** means termination of the firm as a going concern, and it involves selling off the assets of the firm. The proceeds, net of selling costs, are distributed to creditors in order of established priority. **Reorganization** is the option of keeping the firm a going concern; it often involves issuing new securities to replace old securities. Liquidation or reorganization is the result of a bankruptcy proceeding. Which occurs depends on whether the firm is worth more "dead or alive."

liquidation
Termination of the firm as a going concern.

reorganization
Financial restructuring of a failing firm to attempt to continue operations as a going concern.

Bankruptcy Liquidation   Chapter 7 of the Federal Bankruptcy Reform Act of 1978 deals with "straight" liquidation. The following sequence of events is typical:

1. A petition is filed in a federal court. Corporations may file a voluntary petition, or involuntary petitions may be filed against the corporation by one or more of its creditors.
2. A trustee-in-bankruptcy is elected by the creditors to take over the assets of the debtor corporation. The trustee will attempt to liquidate the assets.
3. When the assets are liquidated, after payment of the bankruptcy administration costs, the proceeds are distributed among the creditors.
4. If any proceeds remain, after expenses and payments to creditors, they are distributed to the shareholders.

The distribution of the proceeds of the liquidation occurs according to the following priority. The higher a claim is on this list, the more likely it is to be paid. In many of these categories, there are various limitations and qualifications that we omit for the sake of brevity.

1. Administrative expenses associated with the bankruptcy.
2. Other expenses arising after the filing of an involuntary bankruptcy petition but before the appointment of a trustee.
3. Wages, salaries, and commissions.

4. Contributions to employee benefit plans.
5. Consumer claims.
6. Government tax claims.
7. Unsecured creditors.
8. Preferred stockholders.
9. Common stockholders.

absolute priority rule (APR)

Rule establishing priority of claims in liquidation.

This priority rule in liquidation is called the **absolute priority rule (APR)**.

Two qualifications to this list are in order. The first concerns secured creditors. Such creditors are entitled to the proceeds from the sale of the security and are outside this ordering. However, if the secured property is liquidated and provides cash insufficient to cover the amount owed, the secured creditors join with unsecured creditors in dividing the remaining liquidated value. In contrast, if the secured property is liquidated for proceeds greater than the secured claim, the net proceeds are used to pay unsecured creditors and others. The second qualification to the APR is that, in reality, courts have a great deal of freedom in deciding what actually happens and who actually gets what in the event of bankruptcy, and, as a result, the APR is not always followed.

Bankruptcy Reorganization   Corporate reorganization takes place under Chapter 11 of the Federal Bankruptcy Reform Act of 1978. The general objective of a proceeding under Chapter 11 is to plan to restructure the corporation with some provision for repayment of creditors. A typical sequence of events follows:

1. A voluntary petition can be filed by the corporation, or an involuntary petition can be filed by creditors.
2. A federal judge either approves or denies the petition. If the petition is approved, a time for filing proofs of claims is set.
3. In most cases, the corporation (the "debtor in possession") continues to run the business.
4. The corporation is required to submit a reorganization plan.
5. Creditors and shareholders are divided into classes. A class of creditors accepts the plan if a majority of the class agrees to the plan.
6. After acceptance by creditors, the plan is confirmed by the court.
7. Payments in cash, property, and securities are made to creditors and shareholders. The plan may provide for the issuance of new securities.

The corporation may wish to allow the old stockholders to retain some participation in the firm. Needless to say, this may involve some protest by the holders of unsecured debt.

So-called prepackaged bankruptcies are a relatively new phenomenon. What happens is that the corporation secures the necessary approval of a bankruptcy plan by a majority of its creditors first, and then it files for bankruptcy. As a result, the company enters bankruptcy and reemerges almost immediately. In some cases, the bankruptcy procedure is needed to invoke the "cram down" power of the bankruptcy court. Under certain circumstances, a class of creditors can be forced to accept a bankruptcy plan even if they vote not to approve it, hence the remarkably apt description "cram down."

Agreements to Avoid Bankruptcy

When a firm defaults on an obligation, it can avoid bankruptcy. Because the legal process of bankruptcy can be lengthy and expensive, it is often in everyone's best interest to devise a "work out" that avoids a bankruptcy filing. Much of the time creditors can work with the management of a company that has defaulted on a loan contract. Voluntary arrangements to restructure the company's debt can be and often are made. This may involve *extension,* which postpones the date of payment, or *composition,* which involves a reduced payment.

⌐ CONCEPT QUESTIONS

12.7a What is bankruptcy?

12.7b What is the difference between liquidation and reorganization?

SUMMARY AND CONCLUSIONS ⌐ 12.8

The basic sources of long-term financing are long-term debt, preferred stock, and common stock. This chapter describes the essential features of each.

1. We emphasize that common shareholders have

    a. Residual risk and return in a corporation.

    b. Voting rights.

    c. Limited liability if the corporation elects to default on its debt and must transfer some or all of the assets to the creditors.

2. Preferred stock has some features of debt and some features of common equity. Holders of preferred stock have preference in liquidation and in dividend payments compared to holders of common equity.

3. Long-term debt involves contractual obligations set out in indentures. There are many kinds of debt, but the essential feature is that debt involves a stated amount that must be repaid. If the debt is not repaid, the firm is in default and must reorganize or liquidate. Interest payments on debt are considered a business expense and are tax deductible.

4. Firms need financing for capital expenditures, working capital, and other uses. Most of the financing is provided from internally generated cash flow. Only about 20 percent of financing comes from new long-term debt and new external equity. In recent years, new external equity has actually been negative, implying that repurchases exceed new sales in aggregate.

5. The use of debt creates the possibility of financial distress. We discuss the options available to a firm and its creditors in this circumstance, and we describe the payment priority in the event of liquidation of the firm.

Key Terms

indenture 410
registered form 410
bearer form 410
debenture 411
note 411
sinking fund 412
call provision 412
call premium 412
deferred call 412
call protected 412
protective covenant 412
zero coupon bond 414
preferred stock 417
common stock 420

shareholders or stockholders 420
dedicated capital 420
capital in excess of par value 421
retained earnings 422
book value 422
treasury stock 423
cumulative voting 424
straight voting 424
proxy 425
dividends 425
bankruptcy 430
liquidation 431
reorganization 431
absolute priority rule (APR) 432

Chapter Review Problem and Self-Test

12.1   Cumulative versus Straight Voting   The Krishnamurti Corporation
has 500,000 shares outstanding. There are four directors up for
election. How many shares would you need to own to guarantee that
you will win a seat if straight voting is used? If cumulative voting is
used? Ignore possible ties.

Answer to Self-Test Problem

12.1   If there is straight voting, then you need to own half the shares, or
250,000. In this case, you could also elect the other three directors.
With cumulative voting, you need $1/(N + 1)$ percent of the shares,
where N is the number of directors up for election. With four
directors, this is 20 percent, or 100,000 shares.

Questions and Problems

1.   Equity Accounts   The Nosh Co. equity accounts in 1989 are as
follows:

Common stock (1,500 shares outstanding, $1 par value)	(1)
Capital surplus	$ 50,000
Retained earnings	100,000
Total	(2)

Supply the missing information.

2.   Changes in Equity Accounts   In the previous question, suppose the
company decides to issue 1,000 shares of new stock. The current price
is $50 per share. Show the effect on the different accounts. What is
the new market/book ratio?

3. Changes in Accounts   In the previous question, suppose the company instead *buys* 100 shares of its own stock. What is this stock called? What would happen to the accounts shown?

4. Voting   The shareholders of the Tirna-No Company need to elect four new directors. There are 1 million shares outstanding. How many shares do you need to own to be certain that you can elect at least one director:
    a. If Tirna-No has straight voting?
    b. If it has cumulative voting?

5. Preferred Stock   Which has a higher yield, preferred stock or corporate bonds? Why is there a difference? Who are the main investors in preferred stock? Why?

6. Debt versus Equity   What are the main differences between corporate debt and equity? Why do some clever firms try to issue equity in the guise of debt? Why might preferred stock be called an *equity bond*?

7. Patterns of Financing   The Babel Tower Company has $5 million of positive NPV projects that it would like to take advantage of. Based on the historical pattern of long-term financing for U.S. industrial firms, what is the likely financing strategy that Babel will use?

8. Bankruptcy   What basic options does a firm have if it cannot (or chooses not to) make a contractually required payment such as interest? Describe them.

9. Bankruptcy   A petition for the reorganization of the Dew Drop Inn Company has been filed under Chapter 11. The trustees estimate that the firm's liquidation value, after considering costs, is $50 million. Alternatively, the trustees, using the analysis of the PH Consulting firm, predict that the reorganized business will generate $8 million annual cash flows in perpetuity. The discount rate is 20 percent. Should Dew Drop be liquidated or reorganized? Why?

10. Interest on Zeroes   Hanna Co. has issued a five-year, pure discount, 10 percent bond. Assuming that the IRS allows straight-line calculation of the interest, calculate the annual interest deduction. Compare this with the true implicit interest. What is the benefit of the straight-line method?

11. Terms of Indenture   What is the effect of each of the following provisions on the coupon rate for a newly issued bond? Give a brief explanation in each case.
    a. A call provision.
    b. A convertibility provision.
    c. A put provision.
    d. A floating coupon.

Suggested Readings

The following provide some evidence on the financial structure of industrial corporations:

Kester, W. C. "Capital and Ownership Structure: A Comparison of the United States and Japanese Manufacturing Corporations." *Financial Management* 15, Spring 1986.

Taggart, R. "Secular Patterns in the Financing of U.S. Corporations." In *Corporate Capital Structure in the United States,* ed. B. Friedman. Chicago: University of Chicago Press, 1985.

Appendix 12A   CALLABLE BONDS AND BOND REFUNDING

bond refunding

The process of replacing all or part of an issue of outstanding bonds.

The process of replacing all or part of an issue of outstanding bonds is called **bond refunding.** As we have discussed, most corporate debt is callable. Typically, the first step in a bond refunding is to take advantage of this feature to call the entire issue of bonds at the call price.

Why would a firm want to refund a bond issue? One reason is obvious. Suppose a firm issues long-term debt with, say, a 12 percent coupon. Sometime after the issue, interest rates decline, and the firm finds that it could pay an 8 percent coupon and raise the same amount of money. Under such circumstances, the firm may wish to refund the debt. Notice that, in this case, refunding a bond issue is just a way of refinancing a higher-interest loan with a lower-interest one.

In the following discussion, we take a brief look at several issues concerning bond refunding and the call feature. First, what is the cost to the firm of a call provision? Second, what is the value of a call provision? Third, given that the firm has issued callable bonds, when should they be refunded?[12]

12A.1 | THE CALL PROVISION

Common sense tells us that call provisions have value. First, almost all publicly issued bonds have such a feature. Second, a call clearly works to the advantage of the issuer. If interest rates fall and bond prices go up, the issuer has an option to buy back the bond at a bargain price.

On the other hand, all other things equal, bondholders dislike call provisions. The reason is again obvious. If interest rates do fall, then the bondholder's gain is limited because of the possibility that the bond will be called away. As a result, bondholders will take the call provision into account when they buy, and they will require compensation in the form of a higher coupon rate.

---

[12]For a more in-depth discussion of the subjects discussed in this appendix, see John D. Finnerty, Andrew J. Kalotay, and Francis X. Farrell, Jr., *The Financial Manager's Guide to Evaluating Bond Refunding Opportunities,* The Institutional Investor Series in Finance and Financial Management Association Survey and Synthesis Series (Cambridge, Mass.: Ballinger Publishing Company, 1988). Our discussion is based in part on Alan Kraus, "An Analysis of Call Provisions and the Corporate Refunding Decision," *Midland Corporate Finance Journal,* Spring 1983.

This is an important observation. A call provision is not free. Instead, the firm pays a higher coupon than otherwise. Whether paying this higher coupon rate is a good idea or not is the subject we turn to next.

Cost of the Call Provision

To illustrate the effect of a call feature on a bond's coupon, suppose Kraus Intercable Company intends to issue some perpetual bonds. We will stick with perpetuities because doing so greatly simplifies some of the analysis without changing the general results.

The current interest rate on such bonds is 10 percent, and Kraus therefore sets the annual coupon at $100. Suppose that there is an equal chance that by the end of the year interest rates will either:

1. Fall to $6\frac{2}{3}$ percent. If so, the bond price will increase to $100/.067 = $1,500.

2. Increase to 20 percent. If so, the bond price will fall to $100/.20 = $500.

Notice that the bond will either sell for $500 or $1,500 with equal probability, so the expected price is $1,000. Note also that the lower interest rate is actually .0666..., not .067. We use the exact rate in all the calculations in this section.

We now consider the market price of the bond assuming that it is not callable, P_{NC}. This will simply be equal to the expected price of the bond next year plus the coupon, all discounted at the current 10 percent interest rate:

$$P_{NC} = \frac{\begin{array}{c}\text{First-year} \quad \text{Expected price} \\ \text{coupon} \; + \; \text{at the end of year}\end{array}}{1.10}$$

$$= \frac{\$100 + \$1,000}{1.10}$$

$$= \$1,000$$

Thus the bond sells at par.

Now suppose the Kraus Intercable Company decides to make the issue callable. To keep things as simple as possible, we will assume that the bonds must be called in one year or never. To call the bonds, Kraus will have to pay the $1,000 face value plus a call premium of $150 for a total of $1,150. If Kraus wants the callable bond to sell for par, what coupon, C, must be offered?

To determine the coupon, we need to calculate what the possible prices are in one year. If interest rates decline, then the bond will be called, and the bondholder will get $1,150. If interest rates rise, then the bond will not be called, and it will thus be worth $C/.20$. So the expected price in one year is $.50 \times (C/.20) + .50 \times (\$1,150)$. If the bond sells for par, then the price, P_C, is $1,000 and we have that:

$$P_C = \$1,000 = \frac{\begin{array}{c}\text{First-year} \quad \text{Expected price} \\ \text{coupon} \; + \; \text{at end of year}\end{array}}{1.10}$$

$$= \frac{\$C + [.50 \times (C/.20) + .50 \times (\$1,150)]}{1.10}$$

If we solve this for C, we find that the coupon will have to be

$$C = \$525/3.5 = \$150$$

This is substantially higher than the $100 we had before and illustrates that the call provision is not free.

What is the cost of the call provision here? To answer, we can calculate what the bond would sell for if it were not callable and had a coupon of $150:

$$P_{NC} = \frac{\text{First-year} \quad \text{Expected price}}{\text{coupon} \quad + \quad \text{at end of year}}{1.10}$$

$$= \frac{\$150 + [.50 \times (\$150/.20) + .50 \times (\$150/.067)]}{1.10}$$

$$= \$1,500$$

What we see is that the call provision effectively costs $500 per bond in this simple case because Kraus could have raised $1,500 per bond instead of $1,000 if the bonds were not callable.

Value of the Call Provision

We have seen what Kraus will have to pay to make this bond issue callable. We now need to see what the value is to Kraus from doing so. If the value is more than $500, then the call provision has a positive NPV and should be included. Otherwise, Kraus should issue noncallable bonds.

If Kraus issues a callable bond and interest rates drop to 6⅔ percent in a year, then Kraus can replace the 15 percent bond with a noncallable perpetual issue that carries a coupon of 6⅔ percent. The interest saving in this case is $150 − 66.67 = $83.33 per year every year forever (since these are perpetuities). At an interest rate of 6⅔ percent, the present value (in one year) of the interest savings is $83.33/.067 = $1,250.

To do the refunding, Kraus will have to pay a $150 premium, so the net present value of the refunding operation in one year is $1,250 − 150 = $1,100 per bond. However, there is only a 50 percent chance that the interest rate will drop, so we expect to get .50 × $1,100 = $550 from refunding in one year. The current value of this amount is $550/1.1 = $500. So we conclude that the value of the call feature to Kraus is $500.

It is *not* a coincidence that the cost and the value of the call provision are identical. All this says is that the NPV of the call feature is zero; the bondholders demand a coupon that exactly compensates them for the possibility of a call.

CONCEPT QUESTIONS

12A.1a Why might a corporation call in a bond issue? What is this action
        called?

12A.1b Explain why bondholders don't like call provisions.

THE REFUNDING ISSUE | 12A.2

In our example above, we saw that Kraus gained $1,100 per bond from the re-
funding operation if the interest rate fell. We now need to decide when, in general, a firm should refund an outstanding bond issue. The answer to this
question can get fairly complicated, so we will stick with our simplified case.
In particular, we will continue to assume that

1. The bonds in question are perpetuities.

2. There are no taxes.

3. There are no refunding costs other than the call premium.

4. The bonds must be called now or never.

Because of these assumptions, our example is unrealistic. Taxes and refunding costs, for example, are important, and the actual refunding decision is
more complicated than we indicate here. Fortunately, the first three of these
four assumptions can be eliminated without a great deal of trouble, just more
arithmetic.

The last of these assumptions cannot be easily eliminated. The problem is
that when we call a bond in, we forever destroy the option to call it in later.
Conceivably, it might be better to wait and call later in hopes of even lower interest rates.[13]

When Should Firms Refund Callable Bonds?

The following notation will be useful in analyzing the refunding issue:

c_0 = Coupon rate on the outstanding bonds

c_N = Coupon rate on the new issue, equal to the current market rate

CP = Call premium per bond

We assume that the face value is $1,000 per bond. If we replace the old issue,
then we save $(c_0 - c_N) \times \$1,000$ in interest per bond every year forever.

The current interest rate is c_N, so the present value of the interest saving is
$(c_0 - c_N)/c_N \times \$1,000$. It costs CP to call the bond, so the NPV per bond of
the refunding operation can be written simply as:

$$\text{NPV} = (c_0 - c_N)/c_N \times \$1,000 - CP \qquad [12\text{A}.1]$$

---

[13]This is the same issue that we discuss in Chapter 9 when we discuss options in capital
budgeting, in particular, the option to wait.

With our Kraus example, the bonds were originally issued with a 15 percent coupon. The going interest rate fell to $6\frac{2}{3}$ percent, and the call premium was $150. The NPV of the refunding is:

$$\text{NPV} = (c_0 - c_N)/c_N \times \$1{,}000 - CP$$

$$= (.15 - .067)/.067 \times \$1{,}000 - \$150$$

$$= 1.25 \times \$1{,}000 - \$150$$

$$= \$1{,}100 \text{ per bond}$$

This is as we had before (ignoring a slight rounding error).

Example 12A.1   Who Ya Gonna Call?

Toastdusters, Inc., has an outstanding perpetuity with a 10 percent coupon rate. This issue must be called now or never. If it is called, it will be replaced with an issue that has a coupon rate of 8 percent, equal to the current interest rate. The call premium is $200 per bond. Should refunding commence? What is the NPV of a refunding?

Assuming a $1,000 face value, the interest saving will be $100 − 80 = $20 per bond, per year, forever. The present value of this saving is $20/.08 = $250 per bond. Since the call premium is $200 per bond, refunding should commence: The NPV is $50 per bond. ■

Should Firms Issue Callable Bonds?

We have seen that the NPV of the call provision at the time a bond is issued is likely to be zero. This means that whether or not the issue is callable is a matter of indifference; we get exactly what we pay for, at least on average.

A company will prefer to issue callable bonds only if it places a higher value on the call option than do the bondholders. We consider three reasons why a company might use a call provision:

1. Superior interest rate predictions.
2. Taxes.
3. Financial flexibility for future investment opportunities.

Superior Interest Rate Forecasting   The company may prefer the call provision because it assigns a higher probability to a fall in the coupon rate it must pay than the bondholders do. For example, managers may be better informed about a potential improvement in the firm's credit rating. In this way, company insiders may know more about interest rate decreases than the bondholders.

Whether or not the companies truly know more than the creditors about future interest rates is debatable, but the point is they may *think* they do and thus prefer to issue callable bonds.

Taxes   We ignored taxes in our analysis above. Call provisions may have tax advantages to both bondholders and the company. This will be true if the bondholder is taxed at a lower rate than the company.

We have seen that callable bonds have higher rates than noncallable bonds. Because the coupons are a deductible interest expense to the corporation, if the corporate tax rate is higher than that of the individual holder, the corporation will gain more in interest savings than the bondholders will lose in extra taxes. Effectively, the government pays for a part of the call provision in reduced tax revenues.

Future Investment Opportunities   As we have seen, bond indentures contain protective covenants that restrict a company's investment opportunities. For example, protective covenants may limit the company's ability to acquire another company or to sell certain assets (for example, a division of the company). If the covenants are sufficiently restrictive, the cost to the shareholders in lost net present value can be large.

If bonds are callable, though, by paying the call premium, the company can buy back the bonds and take advantage of a superior investment opportunity.

⌐ CONCEPT QUESTIONS

12A.2a When should firms issue callable bonds?

12A.2b What is the effect on a bond's coupon rate from including a call provision? Why?

Appendix Review Problems and Self-Test

12A.1 Call Provisions and Bond Values   Timberlake Industries has decided to float a perpetual bond issue. The coupon will be 8 percent (the current interest rate). In one year, there is an even chance that interest rates will be 5 percent or 20 percent. What will the market value of the bonds be if they are noncallable? If they are callable at par plus $80?

12A.2 Call Provisions and Coupon Rates   If the Timberlake bond in Problem A.1 is callable and sells for par, what is the coupon, C? What is the cost of the call provision in this case?

Answers to Appendix Self-Test Problems

12A.1 If the bond is not callable, then, in one year, it will be worth either $80/.05 = $1,600 or $80/.2 = $400. The expected price is $1,000. The PV of the $1,000 and the first $80 coupon is $1,080/1.08 = $1,000, so the bond will sell for par.

   If the bond is callable, then either it will be called at $1,080 (if rates fall to 5 percent) or it will sell for $400. The expected value is ($1,080 + 400)/2 = $740. The PV is ($740 + 80)/1.08 = $759.26.

12A.2 In one year, the bond either will be worth $C/.20$ or it will be called for $1,080. If the bond sells for par, then:

$$\$1,000 = [C + .5(C/.20) + .5(\$1,080)]/1.08$$

$$\$540 = [C + .5(C/.20)]$$

$$= 3.5C$$

The coupon, C, must be $540/3.5 = $154.29.

If the bond had a coupon of $154.29 and was not callable, then, in one year, it would be worth either $154.29/.05 = $3,085.71 or $154.29/.20 = $771.43. There is an even chance of either of these, so we expect a value of $1,928.57. The bond would sell today for ($1,928.57 + 154.29)/1.08 = $1,928.57. The cost of the call provision is thus $928.57. This is quite a bit, but, as we shall see in a later chapter, this stems from the fact that interest rates are quite volatile in this example.

Appendix Questions and Problems

1.   NPV and Refunding   Oattoker's, Inc., has an outstanding perpetuity with a 20 percent coupon rate. This issue must be called now or never. If it is called, it will be replaced with an issue that has a coupon rate of 16 percent, equal to the current interest rate. The call premium is $200 per bond. Should refunding commence? What is the NPV of a refunding?

2.   Interest Rates and Refunding   In the previous question, what would the current rate have to be for Oattoker's to be indifferent to refunding or not refunding?

3.   Callable Bond Prices   Bummer Motor Works, Inc., has decided to float a perpetual bond issue. The current interest rate is 12 percent. In one year, there is an even chance that interest rates will be 10 percent or 15 percent. Will this issue sell for par if the coupon is $120? What would it sell for if the coupon were $150?

4.   Pricing   In the previous question, suppose the bonds are callable at $1,060. What must the coupon be for the bonds to sell at par? What is the cost of the call provision?

5.   NPV and Refunding   Horim-Ben-Levy (HBL) Co. has an outstanding bond issue with a total face value of $20 million and a coupon rate of 8 percent. The bonds are callable at par plus a premium of $80 per bond. These bonds could be reissued at 6 percent. The total issue costs of the refunding (excluding the call premium) would be $3 million. The bonds must be called now or never. What would be the NPV of this refunding? Should Horim-Ben-Levy proceed?

6.   Rates   In the previous problem, what would the current interest rate have to be for HBL Co. to be indifferent to a refunding operation?

7.   NPV and Maturity   In Problem 5, how would your answer be affected if the bonds had 20 years to maturity rather than an infinite number of years? What would the NPV of a refunding operation be?

8.   NPV, Refunding, and Taxes   This is a challenge problem. Look back at Problem 1. Suppose the firm is in a 34 percent tax bracket. The call premium is a tax-deductible expense. Interest paid on the old and new bonds is as well, of course. What is the NPV of the refunding? Note that the appropriate discount rate will be the *aftertax* borrowing rate. What is the net effect of worrying about taxes on the NPV of the refunding? Explain.

Chapter 13

Issuing Securities to the Public

In Chapter 12, we looked at the different types of corporate securities. This chapter looks at how corporations sell those securities to the investing public. The general procedures we describe apply to both debt and equity, but we place more emphasis on equity.[1]

Before securities can trade in a securities market, they must be issued to the public. A firm making a public issue must satisfy a number of requirements set out by federal regulations and statutes and enforced by the Securities and Exchange Commission (SEC). In general, investors must be given all material information in the form of a registration statement and prospectus. In the first part of this chapter, we discuss what this process entails.

A public issue of debt or equity can be sold directly to the public with the help of underwriters. This is called a *general cash offer*. Alternatively, a public equity issue can be sold to the firm's existing stockholders by what is called a *rights offer*. We examine the differences between an underwritten general cash offer and a rights offer. As we discuss, the direct costs of a rights offer appear to be significantly lower than those of a general cash offer. Even so, essentially all new equity issues in the United States are general cash offers, particularly in more recent years. This is something of a puzzle. In Europe (and elsewhere), for example, equity issues by publicly held corporations are very frequently rights offers.

---

[1] We are indebted to Jay R. Ritter of the University of Illinois for helpful comments and suggestions on this chapter.

13.1 | THE PUBLIC ISSUE

The Securities Act of 1933 sets forth the federal regulations for all new inter-state securities issues. The Securities Exchange Act of 1934 is the basis for regulating securities already outstanding. The SEC administers both acts.

The Basic Procedure for a New Issue

There is a series of steps involved in issuing securities to the public. In general terms, the basic procedure is as follows:

1. Management's first step in issuing any securities to the public is to obtain approval from the board of directors. In some cases, the number of authorized shares of common stock must be increased. This requires a vote of the shareholders.

registration statement
Registration filed with SEC that discloses all material information concerning the corporation making a public offering.

2. The firm must prepare and file a **registration statement** with the SEC. The registration statement is required for all public issues of securities with two exceptions:
   a. Loans that mature within nine months
   b. Issues that involve less than $1.5 million

Regulation A
SEC regulation that exempts public issues less than $1.5 million from most registration requirements.

The second exception is known as the *small-issues exemption.* In this case, simplified procedures are used. Under the basic small-issues exemption, issues of less than $1.5 million are governed by **Regulation A,** for which only a brief offering statement is needed. Normally, however, a registration statement contains many pages (50 or more) of financial information, including a financial history, details of the existing business, proposed financing, and plans for the future.

prospectus
Legal document describing details of the issuing corporation and the proposed offering to potential investors.

3. The SEC studies the registration statement during a waiting period. During this time, the firm may distribute copies of a preliminary **prospectus.** The prospectus contains much of the information put into the registration statement, and it is given to potential investors by the firm. The preliminary prospectus is sometimes called a **red herring,** in part because bold red letters are printed on the cover.

red herring
Preliminary prospectus distributed to prospective investors in a new issue of securities.

A registration statement becomes effective on the 20th day after its filing unless the SEC sends a *letter of comment* suggesting changes. After the changes are made, the 20-day waiting period starts again.

The registration statement does not initially contain the price of the new issue. Usually, a price amendment is filed at or near the end of the waiting period, and the registration becomes effective in an accelerated way.

4. The company cannot sell these securities during the waiting period. However, oral offers can be made.

5. On the effective date of the registration statement, a price is determined and a full-fledged selling effort gets under way. A final prospectus must accompany the delivery of securities or confirmation of sale, whichever comes first.

Tombstone advertisements are used by underwriters during and after the waiting period. An example is reproduced in Figure 13.1 (see page 452). The tombstone contains the name of the company whose securities are involved (Consolidated Rail, or Conrail, in this case). It provides some information about the issue, and it lists the investment banks (the underwriters) who are involved with selling the issue. The role of the investment banks in selling securities is discussed more fully below.

The investment banks are divided into groups called *brackets* on the tombstone, and the names of the banks are listed alphabetically within each bracket. The brackets are a kind of pecking order. In general, the higher the bracket, the greater is the underwriter's prestige.

tombstone
An advertisement announcing a public offering.

⌐ CONCEPT QUESTIONS

13.1a What are the basic procedures in selling a new issue?

13.1b What is a registration statement?

ALTERNATIVE ISSUE METHODS ⌐ 13.2

When a company decides to issue a new security, it can sell it as a public issue or a private issue. If it is a public issue, the firm is required to register the issue with the SEC. However, if the issue is sold to fewer than 35 investors, it can be done privately. If so, a registration statement is not required.[2]

There are two kinds of public issues: a **general cash offer** and a **rights offer** (or *rights offering*). With a cash offer, securities are offered to the general public on a "first come, first served" basis. With a rights offer, securities are initially offered only to existing owners. Almost all debt is sold by cash offer, but equity is sold by both cash offer and rights offer. Underwriters are used in general cash offers, but they are not always used in rights offers.

The first public equity issue that is made by a company is referred to as an **initial public offering (IPO)** or an *unseasoned new issue*. This occurs when a company decides to go public. Obviously, all initial public offerings are cash offers. If the firm's existing shareholders wanted to buy the shares, the firm wouldn't have to sell them publicly in the first place.

A **seasoned new issue** refers to a new issue for a company with securities that have been previously issued. A seasoned new issue of common stock can be made by using a cash offer or a rights offer.

These methods of issuing new securities are shown in Table 13.1. They are discussed in sections 13.3 through 13.6.

general cash offer
An issue of securities offered for sale to the general public on a cash basis.

rights offer
A public issue of securities where the securities are first offered to existing shareholders. Also a *privileged subscription*.

initial public offering (IPO)
A company's first equity issue made available to the public. Also an *unseasoned new issue*.

seasoned new issue
A new equity issue of securities by a company that has previously issued securities to the public.

---

[2]A variety of different arrangements can be made for private equity issues. Selling unregistered securities avoids the costs of complying with the Securities Exchange Act of 1934. Regulation significantly restricts the resale of unregistered equity securities. For example, the purchaser may be required to hold the securities for at least two years. Many of the restrictions were significantly eased in 1990 for very large institutional investors, however. The private placement of bonds is discussed in a later section.

Table 13.1	Method	Type	Definition
The methods of issuing new securities	Public		
	Traditional negotiated cash offer	Firm commitment cash offer	Company negotiates an agreement with an investment banker to underwrite and distribute the new stocks. A specified number of shares is bought by underwriters and sold at a higher price.
		Best efforts cash offer	Company has investment bankers sell as many of the new shares as possible at the agreed-upon price. There is no guarantee concerning how much cash will be raised.
	Privileged subscription	Direct rights offer	Company offers new stock directly to its existing shareholders.
		Standby rights offer	Like the direct rights offer, this contains a privileged subscription arrangement with existing shareholders. The net proceeds are guaranteed by the underwriters.
	Nontraditional cash offer	Shelf cash offer	Qualifying companies can authorize all shares they expect to sell over a two-year period and sell them when needed.
		Competitive firm cash offer	Company can elect to award underwriting contract through a public auction instead of negotiation.
	Private	Direct placement	Securities are sold directly to purchaser, who, at least until very recently, generally could not resell securities for at least two years.

⌐ CONCEPT QUESTIONS

13.2a Why is an initial public offering necessarily a cash offer?

13.2b What is the difference between a rights offer and a cash offer?

13.3 | THE CASH OFFER

underwriters

Investment firms that act as intermediaries between a company selling securities and the investing public.

If the public issue of securities is a cash offer, **underwriters** are usually involved. Underwriters perform services such as the following for corporate issuers:

1. Formulating the method used to issue the securities.
2. Pricing the new securities.
3. Selling the new securities.

Typically, the underwriter buys the securities for less than the offering price and accepts the risk of not being able to sell them. Because underwriting involves risk, underwriters combine to form an underwriting group called a **syndicate** to share the risk and to help sell the issue.

syndicate

A group of underwriters formed to reduce the risk and to help sell an issue.

In a syndicate, one or more managers arrange or co-manage the offering. This manager is designated as the lead manager or principal manager. The lead manager typically has the responsibility for pricing the securities. The other underwriters in the syndicate serve primarily to distribute the issue.

The difference between the underwriter's buying price and the offering price is called the **spread** or discount. It is the basic compensation received by the underwriter. Sometimes the underwriter will get noncash compensation in the form of warrants and stock in addition to the spread.[3]

Choosing an Underwriter

A firm can offer its securities to the highest bidding underwriter on a *competitive offer* basis, or it can negotiate directly with an underwriter. Except for a few large firms, new issues of debt and equity are usually done on a *negotiated offer* basis. The exception is public utility holding companies, which are essentially required to use competitive underwriting.

There is evidence that competitive underwriting is cheaper to use than negotiated underwriting, and the underlying reasons for the dominance of negotiated underwriting in the United States are the subject of ongoing debate.

Types of Underwriting

Two basic types of underwriting are involved in a cash offer: firm commitment and best efforts.

Firm Commitment Underwriting   With **firm commitment underwriting**, the issuer sells the entire issue to the underwriters, who then attempt to resell it. This is the most prevalent type of underwriting in the United States. This is really just a purchase-resale arrangement, and the underwriter's fee is the spread. For a new issue of seasoned equity, the underwriters can look at the market price to determine what the issue should sell for, and 95 percent of all such new issues are firm commitments.

If the underwriter cannot sell all of the issue at the agreed-upon offering price, it may have to lower the price on the unsold shares. Nonetheless, with firm commitment underwriting, the issuer receives the agreed-upon amount, and all the risk associated with selling the issue is transferred to the underwriter.

Because the offering price usually isn't set until the underwriters have investigated how receptive the market is to the issue, this risk is usually minimal. Also, because the offering price usually is not set until just before selling commences, the issuer doesn't know precisely what its net proceeds will be until that time.

Best Efforts Underwriting   With **best efforts underwriting**, the underwriter is legally bound to use "best efforts" to sell the securities at the agreed-upon offering price. Beyond this, the underwriter does not guarantee any particular amount of money to the issuer. This form of underwriting is more common with initial public offerings.

With best efforts underwriting, the underwriter essentially acts as an agent for the issuer and receives a commission. In practice, if the underwriter

spread
Compensation to the underwriter, determined by the difference between the underwriter's buying price and offering price.

firm commitment underwriting
Underwriter buys the entire issue, assuming full financial responsibility for any unsold shares.

best efforts underwriting
Underwriter sells as much of the issue as possible, but can return any unsold shares to the issuer without financial responsibility.

---

[3]Warrants are essentially options to buy stock at a fixed price for some fixed period of time. We discuss warrants in some detail in Chapter 20.

Table 13.2	Gross Proceeds	All Offerings	Firm Commitment	Best Efforts	Fraction Best Efforts
Initial public offerings categorized by gross proceeds: 1977–1982	$ 100,000–1,999,999	243	68	175	0.720
	2,000,000–3,999,999	311	165	146	0.469
	4,000,000–5,999,999	156	133	23	0.147
	6,000,000–9,999,999	137	122	15	0.109
	10,000,000–120,174,195	180	176	4	0.022
	All offerings	1,027	664	363	0.353

From J. R. Ritter, "The Costs of Going Public," *Journal of Financial Economics* 19 (1987) © Elsevier Science Publishers B.V. (North-Holland).

cannot sell the issue at the offer price, it is usually withdrawn. The issue might be repriced and/or reoffered at a later date.

Table 13.2 categorizes initial public offerings by size and type of underwriting. As indicated, best efforts offerings are very common with smaller issues. For issues under $2 million (which is quite small), 72 percent are best efforts. At the other end, for issues in excess of $10 million, firm commitment offerings are used almost exclusively.

The Aftermarket

The period after a new issue is initially sold to the public is referred to as the *aftermarket*. During this time, the National Association of Securities Dealers (NASD) requires that members of the underwriting syndicate not sell securities for less than the offering price until the syndicate dissolves.

The principal underwriter is permitted to buy shares if the market price falls below the offering price. The purpose would be to support the market and stabilize the price from temporary downward pressure. If the issue remains unsold after a time (for example, 30 days), members can leave the group and sell their shares at whatever price the market will allow.[4]

The Green Shoe Provision

Green Shoe provision

Contract provision giving the underwriter the option to purchase additional shares from the issuer at the offering price.

Many underwriting contracts contain a **Green Shoe provision** (sometimes called the *overallotment option*), which gives the members of the underwriting group the option to purchase additional shares from the issuer at the offering price.[5] The stated reason for the Green Shoe option is to cover excess demand and oversubscriptions. Green Shoe options usually last for about 30 days and involve no more than 15 percent of the newly issued shares.

---

[4]Occasionally, the price of a security falls dramatically when the underwriter ceases to stabilize the price. In such cases, Wall Street humorists (the ones who didn't buy any of the stock) have referred to the period following the aftermarket as the aftermath.

[5]The term *Green Shoe provision* sounds quite exotic, but the origin is relatively mundane. It comes from the Green Shoe Company, which once granted such an option.

The Green Shoe option is a benefit to the underwriting syndicate and a cost to the issuer. If the market price of the new issue goes above the offering price within 30 days, the Green Shoe option allows the underwriters to buy shares from the issuer and immediately resell the shares to the public.

The Underwriters

Underwriters are at the heart of new security issues. They provide advice, market the securities (after investigating the market's receptiveness to the issue), and provide a guarantee of the amount an issue will raise (with firm commitment underwriting).

Table 13.3, Part A, lists the largest underwriters in the United States based on the total dollars in securities offerings (debt and equity) managed in 1991. As indicated, Merrill Lynch was the leading manager of underwritten public securities offerings in 1991, with 561 issues and a total of just over $100 billion managed. In Part B of Table 13.3, we have broken out debt and equity issues separately. From our discussion in Chapter 12, it is not surprising that debt issues are much more common than equity issues.

Part C of Table 13.3 provides an international perspective by examining non-U.S. issues. Notice how the top four debt underwriters worldwide are non-U.S. investment banks, with Japanese giant Nomura leading the way. Part D of the table focuses on one domestic category that was of particular interest in the 1980s, so-called junk bonds. Drexel Burnham Lambert essentially created this market and originally dominated it. This domination ended abruptly with Drexel's spectacular collapse in 1990. Based on the 1991 figures, the junk bond market is already coming back; Merrill's $4 billion in issues is approaching Drexel's 1989 total of $10 billion.

The Offering Price and Underpricing

Determining the correct offering price is the most difficult thing an underwriter must do for an initial public offering. The issuing firm faces a potential cost if the offering price is set too high or too low. If the issue is priced too high, it may be unsuccessful and have to be withdrawn. If the issue is priced below the true market price, the issuer's existing shareholders will experience an opportunity loss when they sell their shares for less than they are worth.

Underpricing is a fairly common occurrence. It obviously helps new shareholders earn a higher return on the shares they buy. However, the existing shareholders of the issuing firm are not helped by underpricing. To them it is an indirect cost of issuing new securities.

Underpricing: The Case of Conrail   The sale on March 26, 1987, of more than 58 million shares of Conrail, the previously U.S. government–owned railroad company, was the largest new issue of stock in U.S. history. A tombstone for this issue is shown in Figure 13.1.

At the end of the first day after the Conrail offering, the shares were more than 10 percent above their initial offering price level. This is a good example

Table 13.3

Top 10 underwriters for 1991

A. United States (combined debt and equity)

Rank 1990	Rank 1991		Dollar Volume (millions)	Number of Issues
1	1	Merrill Lynch	$100,504.3	561
2	2	Goldman Sachs	69,641.5	442
8	3	Lehman Brothers	68,641.2	490
3	4	First Boston	57,984.1	310
6	5	Kidder Peabody	50,824.8	199
5	6	Morgan Stanley	48,232.9	278
4	7	Salomon Brothers	46,447.9	199
7	8	Bear Stearns	33,844.7	98
9	9	Prudential Securities	17,054.9	68
10	10	Donaldson, Lufkin & Jenrette	11,479.7	67

B. United States (debt and equity separate)

Debt Issues

Rank 1990	Rank 1991		Dollar Volume (millions)	Number of Issues
1	1	Merrill Lynch	$87,280.4	453
8	2	Lehman Brothers	63,398.8	416
2	3	Goldman Sachs	57,530.9	371
3	4	First Boston	53,296.3	262
6	5	Kidder Peabody	49,358.9	165
4	6	Salomon Brothers	42,240.6	160
5	7	Morgan Stanley	37,810.4	219
7	8	Bear Stearns	33,018.2	84
9	9	Prudential Securities	15,505.1	52
10	10	Donaldson, Lufkin & Jenrette	10,068.9	48

Equity Issues

Rank 1990	Rank 1991		Dollar Volume (millions)	Number of Issues
1	1	Merrill Lynch	$13,223.9	108
2	2	Goldman Sachs	12,110.7	71
8	3	Morgan Stanley	10,422.5	59
3	4	Alex. Brown & Sons	7,305.8	63
4	5	Lehman Brothers	5,242.4	74
9	6	First Boston	4,687.8	48
5	7	Salomon Brothers	4,207.3	39
6	8	Smith Barney, Harris Upham	2,027.4	45
7	9	PaineWebber	1,618.7	41
12	10	Prudential Securities	1,549.8	16

C. International (debt and equity separate)

Debt Issues

Rank 1990	Rank 1991		Dollar Volume (millions)	Number of Issues
1	1	Nomura International Group	$25,905.8	166
2	2	Credit Suisse/CSFB Group	21,950.4	124
5	3	Daiwa Securities	19,000.0	130
4	4	Deutsche Bank	15,603.3	91
13	5	Goldman Sachs	14,472.9	84
11	6	Paribas	12,437.6	61
12	7	Merrill Lynch	12,323.4	51
3	8	Union Bank of Switzerland	12,206.2	86
20	9	Morgan Stanley	12,188.9	29
7	10	Swiss Bank Corp.	12,140.3	89

Equity Issues

Rank 1990	Rank 1991		Dollar Volume (millions)	Number of Issues
1	1	Goldman Sachs	$4,868.6	51
8	2	S. G. Warburg Group	2,636.3	13
2	3	Credit Suisse/CSFB Group	2,009.7	37
9	4	Lehman Brothers	1,403.4	27
4	5	Merrill Lynch	1,137.1	17
16	6	Salomon Brothers	995.6	12
5	7	Morgan Stanley	976.2	16
3	8	Nomura International Group	541.1	3
12	9	Paribas	401.2	5
20	10	Daiwa Securities	353.8	3

D. United States (high-yield or junk debt)

Rank 1990	Rank 1991		Dollar Volume (millions)	Number of Issues
4	1	Merrill Lynch	$3,887.9	9
3	2	Goldman Sachs	1,723.8	9
—	3	Morgan Stanley	1,194.1	6
—	4	First Boston	634.1	5
2	5	Salomon Brothers	622.2	4
—	6	Donaldson, Lufkin & Jenrette	598.5	3
—	7	Lehman Brothers	346.9	2
—	8	Bankers Trust	299.3	2
—	9	Wasserstein Perella	200.0	1
—	10	Citicorp	175.0	1

These rankings are created by giving full credit to the lead manager. The lead manager is the investment bank with primary responsibility for the issue.
Source: *Institutional Investor*, February 1992.

Figure 13.1

An example of a tombstone advertisement

58,750,000 Shares

Consolidated Rail Corporation

Common Stock
(par value $1.00 per share)

Price $28 Per Share

The shares are being sold by the United States Government pursuant to the Conrail Privatization Act. The Company will not receive any proceeds from the sale of the shares.

Upon request a copy of the Prospectus describing these securities and the business of the Company may be obtained within any State from any Underwriter who may legally distribute it within such State. The securities are offered only by means of the Prospectus, and this announcement is neither an offer to sell nor a solicitation of any offer to buy.

52,000,000 Shares

This portion of the offering is being offered in the United States and Canada by the undersigned.

Goldman, Sachs & Co.
The First Boston Corporation
Merrill Lynch Capital Markets
Morgan Stanley & Co. Incorporated
Salomon Brothers Inc.
Shearson Lehman Brothers Inc.

Alex Brown & Sons Incorporated · Dillon, Read & Co. Inc. · Donaldson, Lufkin & Jenrette Securities Corporation · Drexel Burnham Lambert Incorporated · Hambrecht & Quist Incorporated · E. F. Hutton & Company Inc.
Kidder, Peabody & Co. Incorporated · Lazard Frères & Co. · Montgomery Securities · Prudential-Bache Capital Funding · Robertson, Colman & Stephens
L. F. Rothschild, Unterberg, Towbin, Inc. · Smith Barney, Harris Upham & Co. Incorporated · Wertheim Schroder & Co. Incorporated · Dean Witter Reynolds Inc.
William Blair & Company · J. C. Bradford & Co. Incorporated · Dain Bosworth Incorporated · A. G. Edwards & Sons, Inc. · McDonald & Company Securities Inc. · Oppenheimer & Co., Inc.
Piper, Jaffray & Hopwood Incorporated · Prescott, Ball & Turben, Inc. · Thomson McKinnon Securities Inc. · Wheat, First Securities, Inc.
Advest, Inc. · American Securities Corporation · Arnhold and S. Bleichroeder, Inc. · Robert W. Baird & Co. Incorporated · Bateman Eichler, Hill Richards Incorporated
Sanford C. Bernstein & Co., Inc. · Blunt Ellis & Loewi Incorporated · Boettcher & Company, Inc. · Burns Fry and Timmins Inc. · Butcher & Singer Inc. · Cowen & Company
Dominion Securities Corporation · Eberstadt Fleming Inc. · Eppler, Guerin & Turner, Inc. · First of Michigan Corporation · First Southwest Company
Furman Selz Mager Dietz & Birney Incorporated · Gruntal & Co., Incorporated · Howard, Weil, Labouisse, Friedrichs Incorporated · Interstate Securities Corporation
Janney Montgomery Scott Inc. · Johnson, Lane, Smith & Co., Inc. · Johnston, Lemon & Co. Incorporated · Josephthal & Co. Incorporated · Ladenburg, Thalmann & Co. Inc.
Cyrus J. Lawrence Incorporated · Legg Mason Wood Walker Incorporated · Morgan Keegan & Company, Inc. · Moseley Securities Corporation · Needham & Company, Inc.
Neuberger & Berman · The Ohio Company · Rauscher Pierce Refsnes, Inc. · The Robinson-Humphrey Company, Inc. · Rothschild Inc. · Stephens Inc.
Stifel, Nicolaus & Company Incorporated · Sutro & Co. Incorporated · Tucker, Anthony & R. L. Day, Inc. · Underwood, Neuhaus & Co. Incorporated · Wood Gundy Corp.

This special bracket of minority-owned and controlled firms assisted the Co-Lead Managers in the United States Offering pursuant to the Conrail Privatization Act:

AIBC Investment Services Corporation · **Daniels & Bell, Inc.** · **Doley Securities, Inc.**
WR Lazard Securities Corporation · **Pryor, Govan Counts & Co., Inc.** · **Muriel Siebert & Co., Inc.**

6,750,000 Shares

This portion of the offering is being offered outside the United States and Canada by the undersigned

Goldman Sachs International Corp.
First Boston International Limited
Merrill Lynch Capital Markets
Morgan Stanley International
Salomon Brothers International Limited
Shearson Lehman Brothers International

Algemene Bank Nederland N.V. · Banque Bruxelles Lambert S.A. · Banque Nationale de Paris · Cazenove & Co. · The Nikko Securities Co., (Europe) Ltd.
Nomura International Limited · N.M. Rothschild & Sons Limited · J. Henry Schroder Wagg & Co. Limited · Société Générale · S. G. Warburg Securities
ABC International Ltd. · Banque Paribas Capital Markets Limited · Caisse Nationale de Crédit Agricole · Compagnie de Banque et d'investissements, CBI
Crédit Lyonnais · Daiwa Europe Limited · IMI Capital Markets (UK) Ltd. · Joh. Berenberg, Gossier & Co. · Leu Securities Limited
Morgan Grenfell & Co. Limited · Peterbroeck, van Campenhout & Cie SCS · Swiss Volksbank · Vereins-und Westbank Aktiengesellschaft
J. Vontobel & Co Ltd · M. M. Warburg-Brinckmann, Wirtz & Co. · Westdeutsche Landesbank Girozentrale · Yamaichi International (Europe) Limited

March 27, 1987

of underpricing. Two opposing views of the sale were prominent in the press after the offering:

1. The issue was hailed as a great success by underwriters and the U.S. Congress. By selling 100 percent of the railroad company, the government achieved its largest divestiture yet of state assets.
2. Others saw the sale as the largest commercial giveaway in U.S. government history. They asked how the government could get the price so wrong.

In passing, we note that the Conrail issue raised a total of $1.65 billion. This is more than the $1.5 billion that AT&T obtained in 1983 in what had previously been the largest U.S. stock offering, but substantially less than, for example, the $4.76 billion raised when British Telecom (the British government–owned telephone company) went public in 1984. However, both of these issues pale in comparison to what NTT (Nippon Telephone and Telegraph, the Japanese telephone company) raised in 1987. In November of 1987, NTT sold 1.95 million shares at a price of 2.55 *million* yen *each*. At the then-prevailing exchange rate, this was roughly $19,000 per share. The total issue amount was thus on the order of $37 billion dollars. What is even more remarkable is that NTT had already sold 1.95 million shares in February of the same year.

The Conrail issue was apparently underpriced, but, as we discuss next, the underpricing was not atypical (in percentage terms). Even so, underpricing a $1.65 *billion* issue by 10 percent or so means that the seller misses out on almost $200 million.

Evidence on Underpricing   Figure 13.2 provides a more general illustration of the underpricing phenomenon. What is shown is the month-by-month history of underpricing for SEC–registered IPOs.[6] The period covered is 1960 through 1987. Figure 13.3 presents the number of offerings in each month for the same period.

Figure 13.2 shows that underpricing can be quite dramatic, exceeding 100 percent in some months. In such months, the average IPO more than doubled in value, sometimes in a matter of hours. Also, the degree of underpricing varies through time, and periods of severe underpricing (so-called hot issue markets) are followed by periods of little underpricing (cold issue markets). For example, in the 1960s, the average IPO was underpriced by 21.25 percent. In the 1970s, the average was much smaller (8.95 percent), and it was actually very small or even negative for much of that time. Finally, for 1980–87, IPOs were underpriced by 16.09 percent on average.

In Figure 13.3, it is apparent that the number of IPOs is also highly variable through time. Further, there are pronounced cycles in both the degree of underpricing and the number of IPOs. Comparing Figures 13.2 and 13.3, increases in the number of new offerings tend to follow periods of significant underpricing by roughly 6 to 12 months. This probably occurs because companies

---

[6]The discussion in this section draws on Roger G. Ibbotson, Jody L. Sindelar, and Jay R. Ritter, "Initial Public Offerings," *Journal of Applied Corporate Finance* 1 (Summer 1988), pp. 37–45. The degree of underpricing is calculated based on the offering price versus the price at the end of the month, less the market return for the month, over the period 1960–76. The degree of underpricing is based on the offering price and the price at the close of the first day of trading, without adjustment for the market return, for 1977–87.

Figure 13.2

Average initial returns by month for SEC–registered initial public offerings

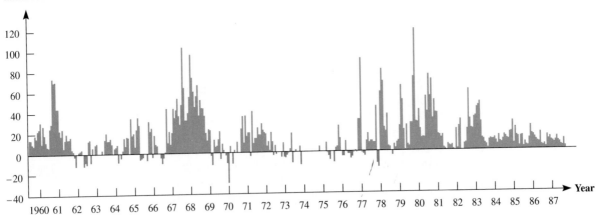

Source: Roger G. Ibbotson, Jody L. Sindelar, and Jay R. Ritter, "Initial Public Offerings," *Journal of Applied Corporate Finance* 1 (Summer 1988), pp. 37–45.

Figure 13.3

Number of offerings by month for SEC–registered initial public offerings

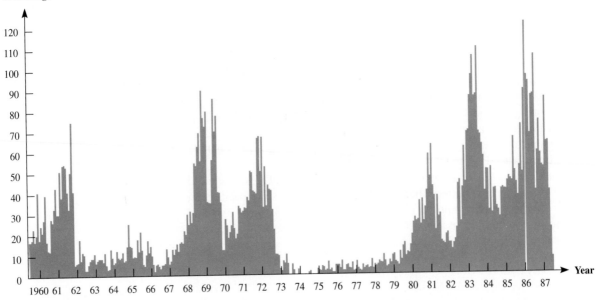

Source: Roger G. Ibbotson, Jody L. Sindelar, and Jay R. Ritter, "Initial Public Offerings," *Journal of Applied Corporate Finance* 1 (Summer 1988), pp. 37–45.

Year	Number of Offerings*	Initial Return (percent)†	Average Gross Proceeds ($ millions)‡
1960	269	17.83%	$ 553
1961	435	34.11	1,243
1962	298	−1.61	431
1963	83	3.93	246
1964	97	5.32	380
1965	146	12.75	409
1966	85	7.06	275
1967	100	37.67	641
1968	368	55.86	1,205
1969	780	12.53	2,605
1970	358	−0.67	780
1971	391	21.16	1,655
1972	562	7.51	2,724
1973	105	−17.82	330
1974	9	−6.98	51
1975	14	−1.86	264
1976	34	2.90	237
1977	40	21.02	151
1978	42	25.66	247
1979	103	24.61	429
1980	259	49.36	1,404
1981	438	16.76	3,200
1982	198	20.31	1,334
1983	848	20.79	13,168
1984	516	11.52	3,932
1985	507	12.36	10,450
1986	953	9.99	19,260
1987	630	10.39	16,380
Total	8,668	16.37	83,984

Table 13.4

Number of offerings, average initial return, and gross proceeds of initial public offerings in 1960–1987

*The number of offerings excludes Regulation A offerings (small issues, raising less than $1.5 million currently). The authors have excluded real estate investment trusts (REITs) and closed-end mutual funds.

†Initial returns are computed as the percentage return from the offering price to the end-of-the-calendar-month bid price, less the market return, for offerings in 1960–76. For 1977–87, initial returns are calculated as the percentage return from the offering price to the end-of-the-first-day bid price, without adjusting for market movements.

‡Gross proceeds data come from various issues of the *SEC Monthly Statistical Bulletin* and *Going Public: The IPO Reporter.* The gross proceeds numbers reported here have been adjusted to remove REIT and closed-end mutual fund offerings.

Source: Roger G. Ibbotson, Jody L. Sindelar, and Jay R. Ritter, "Initial Public Offerings," *Journal of Applied Corporate Finance* 1 (Summer 1988), pp. 37–45.

decide to go public when they perceive that the market is highly receptive to new issues.

Table 13.4 contains a year-by-year summary of the information presented in Figures 13.2 and 13.3. As indicated, a grand total of 8,668 companies were included in this analysis. The degree of underpricing averaged 16.37 percent overall for the 28 years examined. Securities were overpriced on average in only 5 of the 28 years; the worst was 1973 when the average decrease in value was 17.82 percent. At the other extreme, in 1968, the 368 issues were underpriced, on average, by a remarkable 55.86 percent

Why Does Underpricing Exist?   Based on the evidence we've examined, an obvious question is: Why does underpricing continue to exist? As we discuss, there are various explanations, but, to date, there is a lack of complete agreement among researchers as to which is correct.

We present some pieces of the underpricing puzzle by stressing two important caveats to our discussion above. First, the average figures we have examined tend to obscure the fact that much of the apparent underpricing is attributable to the smaller, more highly speculative issues. This point is illustrated in Table 13.5, which shows the extent of underpricing for 2,439 firms over the period 1975–84. Here, the firms are grouped based on their total sales in the 12 months prior to the IPO.

As illustrated in Table 13.5, the overall average underpricing is 20.7 percent for this sample; however, this underpricing is clearly concentrated in the firms with little to no sales in the previous year. These firms tend to have offering prices of less than $3 per share, and such *penny stocks* (as they are sometimes termed) can be very risky investments. Arguably, they must be significantly underpriced, on average, just to attract investors, and this is one explanation for the underpricing phenomenon. In fact, when the companies

Table 13.5	Annual Sales of Issuing Firm ($)*	Number of Firms[†]	Average Initial Return (percent)[‡]
Average initial returns categorized by annual sales of issuing firm, 1975–1984	0	386	42.9%
	1– 999,999	678	31.4
	1,000,000– 4,999,999	353	14.3
	5,000,000–14,999,999	347	10.7
	15,000,000–24,999,999	182	6.5
	25,000,000 and larger	493	5.3
	All	2,439	20.7

*Annual sales are measured as the 12-month revenue for the year prior to going public. No adjustments for the effects of inflation have been made.

[†]Firms included are those using S-1 or S-18 registration forms, or with Federal Home Loan Bank Board approval, and listed in *Going Public: The IPO Reporter* for 1975–84. Issues not using an investment banker are excluded.

[‡]Initial returns are calculated as the percentage return from the offering price to the first recorded closing bid price. No adjustments for market movements have been made.

Source: Roger G. Ibbotson, Jody L. Sindelar, and Jay R. Ritter, "Initial Public Offerings," *Journal of Applied Corporate Finance* 1 (Summer 1988), pp. 37–45.

considered in Table 13.5 were grouped based on price per share instead of sales, the average degree of underpricing for those companies with initial offering prices of less than $3 per share was 42.8 percent. It averaged 8.6 percent for all the others.

The second caveat is that relatively few IPO buyers will actually get the initial high average returns observed in IPOs, and many will actually lose money. Although it is true that, on average, IPOs have positive initial returns, a significant fraction of them have price drops. Furthermore, when the price is too low, the issue is often "oversubscribed." This means investors will not be able to buy all of the shares they want, and the underwriters will allocate the shares among investors.

The average investor will find it difficult to get shares in a "successful" offering (one where the price increases) because there will not be enough shares to go around. On the other hand, an investor blindly submitting orders for IPOs will find that he or she tends to get more shares in issues that go down in price.

To illustrate, consider this tale of two investors. Smith knows very accurately what the Bonanza Corporation is worth when its shares are offered. She is confident that they are underpriced. Jones knows only that prices usually rise one month after an IPO. Armed with this information, Jones decides to buy 1,000 shares of every IPO. Does he actually earn an abnormally high return on the initial offering?

The answer is no, and at least one reason is Smith. Knowing about the Bonanza Corporation, Smith invests all her money in its IPO. When the issue is oversubscribed, the underwriters have to somehow allocate the shares between Smith and Jones. The net result is that when an issue is underpriced, Jones doesn't get to buy as much of it as he wanted.

Smith also knows that the Blue Sky Corporation IPO is overpriced. In this case, she avoids its IPO altogether, and Jones ends up with a full 1,000 shares. To summarize this tale, Jones gets fewer shares when more knowledgeable investors swarm to buy an underpriced issue and gets all he wants when the smart money avoids the issue.

This is another example of a winner's curse, and it is thought to be another reason why IPOs have such a large average return. When the average investor "wins" and gets her entire allocation, it may be because those who knew better avoided the issue. The only way underwriters can counteract the winner's curse and attract the average investor is to underprice new issues (on average) so that the average investor still makes a profit.

A final reason for underpricing is that the underpricing is a kind of insurance for the investment banks. Conceivably, an investment bank could be sued successfully by angry customers if it consistently overpriced securities. Underpricing guarantees that, at least on average, customers will come out ahead.

⌐ CONCEPT QUESTIONS

13.3a What is the difference between firm commitment and best efforts underwriting?

13.3b Suppose a stockbroker calls you up out of the blue and offers to sell you "all the shares you want" of a new issue. Do you think the issue will be more or less underpriced than average?

13.4 | NEW EQUITY SALES AND THE VALUE OF THE FIRM

It seems reasonable to believe that new long-term financing is arranged by firms after positive net present value projects are put together. As a consequence, when the announcement of external financing is made, the firm's market value should go up. Interestingly, this is not what happens. Stock prices tend to decline following the announcement of a new equity issue, but they tend to not change much following a debt announcement. A number of researchers have studied this issue. Plausible reasons for this strange result include:

1. Managerial information. If management has superior information about the market value of the firm, it may know when the firm is overvalued. If it does, it will attempt to issue new shares of stock when the market value exceeds the correct value. This will benefit existing shareholders. However, the potential new shareholders are not stupid, and they will anticipate this superior information and discount it in lower market prices at the new issue date.

2. Debt usage. Issuing new equity may reveal that the company has too much debt or too little liquidity. One version of this argument is that the equity issue is a bad signal to the market. After all, if the new projects are favorable ones, why should the firm let new shareholders in on them? It could just issue debt and let the existing shareholders have all the gain.

3. Issue costs. As we discuss next, there are substantial costs associated with selling securities.

The drop in value of the existing stock following the announcement of a new issue is an example of an indirect cost of selling securities. This drop might typically be on the order of 3 percent for an industrial corporation (and somewhat smaller for a public utility), so, for a large company, it can be a substantial amount of money. We label this drop the *abnormal return* in our discussion of the costs of new issues below.

CONCEPT QUESTIONS

13.4a What are some possible reasons that the price of stock drops on the announcement of a new equity issue?

13.4b Explain why we might expect a firm with a positive NPV investment to finance it with debt instead of equity.

13.5 | THE COSTS OF ISSUING SECURITIES

Issuing securities to the public isn't free, and the costs of different methods are important determinants of which is used. These costs associated with *floating* a new issue are generically called *flotation costs*. In this section, we take a closer look at the flotation costs associated with equity sales to the public.

The costs of selling stock are classified below and fall into six categories: (1) the spread, (2) other direct expenses, (3) indirect expenses, (4) abnormal returns (discussed above), (5) underpricing, and (6) the Green Shoe option.

In Their Own Words . . .

Jay R. Ritter on IPO Underpricing around the World

The United States is not the only country in which initial public offerings of common stock (IPOs) are underpriced. The phenomenon exists in every country with a stock market, although the amount of underpricing varies from country to country.

Many countries have government regulators who force issuing companies to sell shares at a lower price than they otherwise would. Sometimes the purpose is to protect unsophisticated investors. However, in some denationalizations, or privatizations, there has been another motive for underpricing.

For example, in 1979, when Margaret Thatcher became Prime Minister of Britain amid a wave of strikes and a declining economy, there were more union members than stockholders in Britain. To give British voters a positive experience with capitalism, as the government denationalized several government-owned businesses, it intentionally sought to both underprice the shares and to allow as many voters as possible to buy them. As a result of this strategy, by the mid-1980s there were more shareholders than union members. As a by-product of the denationalizations, the British government ran a budget surplus, because of the cash raised as the asset sales continued.

The table below gives a summary of the average initial returns on IPOs in a number of countries around the world, with the figures collected from a number of studies by various authors.

Jay Ritter is professor of finance at the University of Illinois. An outstanding scholar, he is well respected for his insightful analyses of new issues and going public.

Country	Sample Size	Time Period	Average Initial Return
Australia	156	1966–85	26.8%
Brazil	62	1979–90	78.5
Canada	100	1971–83	9.3
Chile	19	1982–90	16.3
Finland	85	1984–89	9.6
France	131	1983–86	4.2
Germany	97	1977–87	21.5
Hong Kong	34	1979–85	10.5
Japan	333	1979–90	31.8
Korea	275	1984–90	79.0
Malaysia	34	1979–84	149.3
Mexico	37	1987–90	33.0
Netherlands	46	1982–87	5.1
New Zealand	149	1979–87	28.8
Singapore	66	1973–87	27.0
Sweden	55	1983–85	40.5
Switzerland	42	1983–89	35.8
Taiwan	168	1971–90	45.0
Thailand	32	1988–89	58.1
United Kingdom	297	1965–75	9.7
	632	1980–88	14.1
United States	8668	1960–87	16.4

The Costs of Issuing Securities

Spread	The spread consists of direct fees paid by the issuer to the underwriting syndicate—the difference between the price the issuer receives and the offer price.
Other direct expenses	These are direct costs, incurred by the issuer, that are not part of the compensation to underwriters. These costs include filing fees, legal fees, and taxes—all reported on the prospectus.
Indirect expenses	These costs are not reported on the prospectus and include the costs of management time spent working on the new issue.
Abnormal returns	In a seasoned issue of stock, the price drops on average by 3 percent upon the announcement of the issue.
Underpricing	For initial public offerings, losses arise from selling the stock below the correct value.
Green Shoe option	The Green Shoe option gives the underwriters the right to buy additional shares at the offer price to cover overallotments.

Table 13.6 reports the direct costs of new equity issues in 1983 for publicly traded firms. These are all seasoned offerings; the percentages in Table 13.6 are as reported in the prospectuses of the issuing companies. These costs only include the spread (underwriter discount) and other direct costs, including legal fees, accounting fees, printing costs, SEC registration costs, and taxes. Not included are indirect expenses, abnormal returns, and the Green Shoe option.

As indicated in Table 13.6, the direct costs alone can be very large, particularly for smaller (less than $10 million) issues. For this group, the direct costs, as reported by the companies, average a little over 10 percent. This means that the company, net of costs, receives 90 percent of the proceeds of the sale on average. On a $10 million issue, this is $1 million in direct expenses—a substantial cost.

Table 13.6 only tells part of the story. For IPOs, the effective costs can be much greater because of the indirect costs. Table 13.7 reports both the direct costs of going public and the degree of underpricing based on IPOs that took place during 1977–82. Issues are classified by the type of underwriting (firm commitment or best efforts) and size of the issue.

Columns (4) and (9) of Table 13.7 give some additional insight into the severity of underpricing. For example, with best efforts underwriting, the aver-

Table 13.6 Flotation costs as a percentage of gross proceeds in 1983 for underwritten new issues of equity by publicly traded firms	Gross Proceeds ($ millions)	Direct Costs Reported on Prospectus (percent)
	$ 0–10	10.10%
	10–20	7.02
	20–50	4.89
	50–100	3.99
	100–200	3.71
	200+	3.30

From Robert Hansen, "Evaluating the Costs of a New Equity Issue," *Midland Corporate Finance Journal* 4, no. 1 (Spring 1986), p. 45.

Table 13.7

Costs of going public — total transactions costs as a percentage of gross proceeds, 1977–1982

Gross Proceeds ($)	Firm Commitment Offerings					Best Efforts Offerings				
	(1) Under-writing Discount (percent)	(2) Other Expenses (percent)	(3) Total Direct Discount (percent) (1) + (2)	(4) Under-pricing (percent)	(5) Total Expenses (percent)	(6) Under-writing Discount (percent)	(7) Other Expenses (percent)	(8) Total Direct Discount (percent) (6) + (7)	(9) Under-pricing (percent)	(10) Total Expenses (percent)
1,000,000–1,999,999	9.84%	9.64%	19.48%	26.92%	31.73%	10.63%	9.52%	20.15%	39.62%	31.89%
2,000,000–3,999,999	9.83	7.60	17.43	20.70	24.93	10.00	6.21	16.21	63.41	36.28
4,000,000–5,999,999	9.10	5.67	14.77	12.57	20.90	9.86*	3.71*	13.57*	26.82*	14.49*
6,000,000–9,999,999	8.03	4.31	12.34	8.99	17.85	9.80*	3.42*	13.22*	40.79*	25.97*
10,000,000–120,174,195	7.24	2.10	9.34	10.32	16.27	8.03*	2.40*	10.43*	-5.42*	-0.17*
All offerings	8.67	5.36	14.03	14.80	21.22	10.26	7.48	17.74	47.78	31.87

The underpricing is computed as $(p - OP)/OP$, multiplied by 100 percent, where p is the closing bid price on the first day of trading and OP is the offering price. These are not annualized returns. Total costs are computed as 100 percent minus the net proceeds as a percentage of the market value of securities in the aftermarket. Consequently, total costs are not the sum of underwriting expenses and the average initial return. The underwriting discount is the commission paid by the issuing firm; this is listed on the front page of the firm's prospectus.

The other expense figure comprises accountable and nonaccountable fees of the underwriters and cash expenses of the issuing firm for legal, printing, and auditing fees and other out-of-pocket costs. These other expenses are described in footnotes on the front page of the issuing firm's prospectus. None of the expense categories includes the value of warrants granted to the underwriter, a practice that is common with best efforts offerings.

Gross proceeds categories are nominal; no price-level adjustments have been made.

Also note that the −0.17% figure for the total expenses for best efforts offerings raising $10 million or more means that, on the average, these firms received net proceeds larger than the market value of the securities after the offering. It should be mentioned that there was less than one offering per year in the category.

*Based on fewer than 25 firms.

Modified from J. R. Ritter, "The Costs of Going Public," *Journal of Financial Economics* 19 (1987) © Elsevier Science Publishers B.V. (North-Holland).

age price increase in the first full day of trading is 47.8 percent. This means that, on average, a stock offered at $10 per share sold for $14.78 at the end of the day. The underpricing was most severe for issues in the $2–3.99 million range, averaging 63.41 percent. The underpricing was much less severe with firm commitment underwriting; the worst average is 26.92 percent for the smallest offerings.

The total expenses of going public over these years averaged 21.22 percent for firm commitment and 31.87 percent for best efforts. Once again, we see that the costs of selling securities can be quite large.

Overall, five conclusions emerge from an analysis of Tables 13.6 and 13.7:

1. Substantial economies of size are evident. In percentage terms, the costs of selling securities decrease dramatically as the issue size grows.
2. The costs of selling securities are higher for best efforts offers.
3. The cost associated with underpricing can be substantial and can exceed the direct costs, particularly with smaller issues and best efforts underwriting.
4. Underpricing for best efforts offers is much greater than for firm commitment offers.
5. The issue costs are higher for an initial public offering than for a seasoned offering.

> CONCEPT QUESTIONS
>
> 13.5a What are the different costs associated with security offerings?
> 13.5b What lessons do we learn from studying issue costs?

13.6 | RIGHTS

When new shares of common stock are sold to the general public, the proportional ownership of existing shareholders will likely be reduced. However, if a preemptive right is contained in the firm's articles of incorporation, then the firm must first offer any new issue of common stock to existing shareholders. If the articles of incorporation do not include a preemptive right, the firm has a choice of offering the issue of common stock directly to existing shareholders or to the public.

An issue of common stock offered to existing stockholders is called a *rights offering* (or *offer*, for short) or a *privileged subscription*. In a rights offering, each shareholder is issued rights to buy a specified number of new shares from the firm at a specified price within a specified time, after which time the rights are said to expire. The terms of the rights offering are evidenced by certificates known as share warrants or rights. Such rights are often traded on securities exchanges or over the counter.

The Mechanics of a Rights Offering

To illustrate the various considerations a financial manager has in a rights offering, we will examine the situation faced by the National Power Company, whose abbreviated initial financial statements are given in Table 13.8.

Balance Sheet

Assets		Shareholders' Equity	
		Common stock	$ 5,000,000
Assets	$15,000,000	Retained earnings	10,000,000
Total	$15,000,000	Total	$15,000,000

Income Statement

Earnings before taxes	$ 3,030,303
Taxes (34%)	1,030,303
Net income	$ 2,000,000
Shares outstanding	1,000,000
Earnings per share	2
Market price per share	20
Total market value	$20,000,000

As indicated in Table 13.8, National Power earns $2 million after taxes and has 1 million shares outstanding. Earnings per share are thus $2, and the stock sells for $20, or 10 times earnings (that is, the price-earnings ratio is 10). To fund a planned expansion, the company intends to raise $5 million of new equity funds by a rights offering.

To execute a rights offering, the financial management of National Power will have to answer the following questions:

1. What should the price per share be for the new stock?
2. How many shares will have to be sold?
3. How many shares will each shareholder be allowed to buy?

Also management will probably want to ask:

4. What is the likely effect of the rights offering on the per-share value of the existing stock?

It turns out that the answers to these questions are highly interrelated. We will get to them in just a moment.

The early stages of a rights offering are the same as for the general cash offer. The difference between a rights offering and a general cash offer lies in how the shares are sold. With a rights offer, National Power's existing shareholders are informed that they own one right for each share of stock they own. National Power will then specify how many rights a shareholder needs to buy one additional share at a specified price.

To take advantage of the rights offering, shareholders have to exercise the rights by filling out a subscription form and sending it, along with payment, to the firm's subscription agent (the subscription agent is usually a bank). Shareholders of National Power will actually have several choices: (1) exercise and subscribe for the full number of entitled shares, (2) order all the rights sold, or (3) do nothing and let the rights expire. As we discuss below, this third course of action is inadvisable.

Number of Rights Needed to Purchase a Share

National Power wants to raise $5 million in new equity. Suppose that the subscription price is set at $10 per share. How National Power arrived at that price is something we will discuss below, but notice that the subscription price is substantially less than the current $20 per share market price.

At $10 per share, National Power will have to issue 500,000 new shares. This can be determined by dividing the total amount of funds to be raised by the subscription price:

$$\text{Number of new shares} = \frac{\text{Funds to be raised}}{\text{Subscription price}} \qquad [13.1]$$

$$= \frac{\$5,000,000}{\$10} = 500,000 \text{ shares}$$

Because stockholders always get one right for each share of stock they own, 1 million rights will be issued by National Power. To determine how many rights will be needed to buy one new share of stock, we can divide the number of existing outstanding shares of stock by the number of new shares:

$$\frac{\text{Number of rights needed}}{\text{to buy a share of stock}} = \frac{\text{Old shares}}{\text{New shares}} \qquad [13.2]$$

$$= \frac{1,000,000}{500,000} = 2 \text{ rights}$$

Thus, a shareholder will need to give up two rights plus $10 to receive a share of new stock. If all the stockholders do this, National Power will raise the required $5 million.

It should be clear that the subscription price, the number of new shares, and the number of rights needed to buy a new share of stock are interrelated. For example, National Power can lower the subscription price. If so, more new shares will have to be issued to raise $5 million in new equity. Several alternatives are worked out here:

Subscription Price	Number of New Shares	Number of Rights Needed to Buy a Share of Stock
$20	250,000	4
10	500,000	2
5	1,000,000	1

The Value of a Right

Rights clearly have value. In the case of National Power, the right to be able to buy a share of stock worth $20 for $10 is definitely worth something.

Initial Position		
Number of shares	2	
Share price	$20	
Value of holding	$40	
Terms of Offer		
Subscription price	$10	
Number of rights issued	2	
Number of rights for a new share	2	
After Offer		
Number of shares	3	
Value of holdings	$50	
Share price	$16.67	
Value of a right		
Old price − New price	$20 − 16.67 = $3.33	

Table 13.9

The value of rights: The individual shareholder

Suppose a shareholder of National Power owns two shares of stock just before the rights offering. This situation is depicted in Table 13.9. Initially, the price of National Power is $20 per share, so the shareholder's total holding is worth 2 × $20 = $40. The National Power rights offer gives shareholders with two rights the opportunity to purchase one additional share for $10. The additional share does not carry a right.

The stockholder who has two shares will receive two rights. The holding of the shareholder who exercises these rights and buys the new share would increase to three shares. The total investment would be $40 + 10 = $50 (the $40 initial value plus the $10 paid to the company).

The stockholder now holds three shares, all of which are identical because the new share does not have a right and the rights attached to the old shares have been exercised. Since the total cost of buying these three shares is $40 + 10 = $50, the price per share must end up at $50/3 = $16.67 (rounded to two decimal places).

Table 13.10 summarizes what happens to National Power's stock price. If all shareholders exercise their rights, the number of shares will increase to 1 million + .5 million = 1.5 million. The value of the firm will increase to $20 million + 5 million = $25 million. The value of each share will thus drop to $25 million/1.5 million = $16.67 after the rights offering.

The difference between the old share price of $20 and the new share price of $16.67 reflects the fact that the old shares carried rights to subscribe to the new issue. The difference must be equal to the value of one right, that is, $20 − 16.67 = $3.33.

An investor holding no shares of outstanding National Power stock who wants to subscribe to the new issue can do so by buying some rights. Suppose an outside investor buys two rights. This will cost $3.33 × 2 = $6.67 (to account for previous rounding). If the investor exercises the rights at a subscription price of $10, the total cost would be $10 + 6.67 = $16.67. In return for this expenditure, the investor will receive a share of the new stock, which, as we have seen, is worth $16.67.

Table 13.10	*Initial Position*	
National Power Company rights offering	Number of shares	1 million
	Share price	$20
	Value of firm	$20 million
	Terms of Offer	
	Subscription price	$10
	Number of rights issued	1 million
	Number of rights for a share	2
	After Offer	
	Number of shares	1.5 million
	Share price	$16.67
	Value of firm	$25 million
	Value of one right	$20 − 16.67 = $3.33

Example 13.1 Exercising Your Rights

In the National Power example, suppose the subscription price was set at $8. How many shares will have to be sold? How many rights would you need to buy a new share? What is the value of a right? What will the price per share be after the rights offer?

To raise $5 million, $5 million/$8 = 625,000 shares will need to be sold. There are 1 million shares outstanding, so it will take 1 million/625,000 = 8/5 = 1.6 rights to buy a new share of stock (you can buy 5 new shares for every 8 you own). After the rights offer, there will be 1.625 million shares, worth $25 million all together, so the per-share value is $25/1.625 = $15.38 each. The value of a right in this case is the $20 original price less the $15.38 ending price, or $4.62. ∎

ex rights

Period when stock is selling without a recently declared right, normally beginning four trading days before the holder-of-record date.

holder-of-record date

The date on which existing shareholders on company records are designated as the recipients of stock rights. Also the *date of record*.

Ex Rights

National Power's rights have a substantial value. In addition, the rights offering will have a large impact on the market price of National Power's stock. It will drop by $3.33 on the day when the shares trade **ex rights.**

The standard procedure for issuing rights involves the firm's setting a **holder-of-record date.** Following stock exchange rules, the stock typically goes ex rights four trading days before the holder-of-record date. If the stock is sold before the ex rights date—"rights on," "with rights," or "cum rights"—the new owner will receive the rights. After the ex rights date, an investor who purchases the shares will not receive the rights. This is depicted for National Power in Figure 13.4.

As illustrated, on September 30, National Power announced the terms of the rights offering, stating that the rights would be mailed on, say, November 1 to stockholders of record as of October 15. Since October 11 is the ex rights date, only those shareholders who own the stock on or before October 10 will receive the rights.

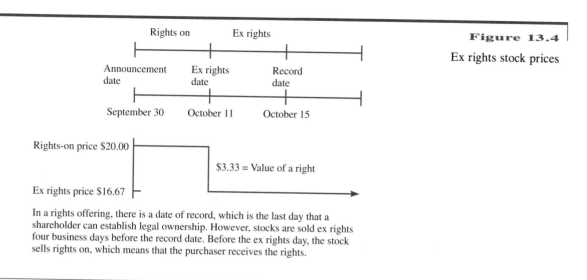

Figure 13.4

Ex rights stock prices

In a rights offering, there is a date of record, which is the last day that a shareholder can establish legal ownership. However, stocks are sold ex rights four business days before the record date. Before the ex rights day, the stock sells rights on, which means that the purchaser receives the rights.

Example 13.2   Exercising Your Rights: Part II
The Lagrange Point Co. has proposed a rights offering. The stock currently sells for $40 per share. Under the terms of the offer, stockholders will be allowed to buy one new share for every five that they own at a price of $25 per share. What is the value of a right? What is the ex rights price?

You can buy five rights on shares for 5 × $40 = $200 and then exercise the rights for another $25. Your total investment is $225, and you end up with six ex rights shares. The ex rights price per share is $225/6 = $37.50 per share. The rights are thus worth $40 − 37.50 = $2.50 apiece. ∎

Example 13.3   Right On
In Example 13.2, suppose the rights only sold for $2 instead of the $2.50 we calculated. What could you do?

You can get rich quick, because you have found a money machine. Here's the recipe: Buy five rights for $10. Exercise them and pay $25 to get a new share. Your total investment to get one ex rights share is 5 × $2 + $25 = $35. Sell the share for $37.50 and pocket the $2.50 difference. Repeat as desired. ∎

The Underwriting Arrangements

Rights offerings are typically arranged using **standby underwriting**. In standby underwriting, the issuer makes a rights offering, and the underwriter makes a firm commitment to "take up" (that is, purchase) the unsubscribed portion of the issue. The underwriter usually gets a **standby fee** and additional amounts based on the securities taken up.

Standby underwriting protects the firm against undersubscription. This can occur if investors throw away rights or if bad news causes the market price of the stock to fall below the subscription price.

standby underwriting
Agreement where the underwriter agrees to purchase the unsubscribed portion of the issue.

standby fee
Amount paid to underwriter participating in standby underwriting agreement.

In practice, a small percentage (less than 10 percent) of shareholders fail to exercise valuable rights. This can probably be attributed to ignorance or vacations. Furthermore, shareholders are usually given an **oversubscription privilege,** which enables them to purchase unsubscribed shares at the subscription price. The oversubscription privilege makes it unlikely that the corporate issuer would have to turn to its underwriter for help.

oversubscription privilege

Allows shareholders to purchase unsubscribed shares in a rights offering at the subscription price.

Rights Offers: The Case of Time-Warner

Rights offers have become less and less common in the United States. However, as media giant Time-Warner's 1991 $2.76 *billion* offer indicates, they are far from dead. The Time-Warner offer was the largest equity sale of any type in U.S. history, and it was the largest rights offer since AT&T's $1.4 billion issue in the 1970s. The offer was controversial when it was originally proposed because the subscription price varied depending on what percentage of the issue actually sold. This feature was later dropped, and the stock was sold using a straight rights offer.

In the Time-Warner deal, the stock was trading in the $90 range just before the offer became effective, and each right entitled the holder to purchase 0.6 new shares. The subscription price was $80 per share, so 34.5 million shares were sold. Approximately 56 percent of the stockholders in Time-Warner exercised their options directly and purchased stock. Another 42 percent sold their rights on the open market; these rights were subsequently exercised by the purchasers. As is typical of rights offers, about 2 percent of the rights were neither exercised nor sold, so some stockholders apparently did not act to protect their interests. Only about 586,000 shares were unsold, and subscribers sought more than five times that amount in oversubscription rights, so none of the stock went unsold.

The underwriters, led by Salomon Brothers, earned substantial fees for their services. For managing the offer and promising to buy unsold shares (of which there were none), the basic compensation was 3 percent of the amount of the issue, or $82.8 million. Furthermore, the underwriters were given the right to buy stock at a 3 percent discount on the subscription price, or $77.60 per share. By purchasing rights in the open market, exercising the rights and buying the stock at a discount, and then reselling the stock, the underwriters earned an additional profit of roughly $27.6 million. The total compensation was thus approximately $110 million, or about 4 percent of the issue proceeds. Because this is somewhat high for such a large deal, Time-Warner and its chairman Stephen Ross (no relation to the noted financial economist and textbook author of the same name) were criticized by various groups.

Outside the United States, large rights offerings are not uncommon. For example, in March of 1991, Bass PLC of Britain raised £557.9 million (about $950 million) using a rights offer. A similar amount was raised in late 1990 by Eurotunnel, the British/French consortium formed to develop the "Chunnel" (the tunnel under the English channel).

Effects on Shareholders

Shareholders can exercise their rights or sell them. In either case, the stockholder will not win or lose by the rights offering. The hypothetical holder of two shares of National Power has a portfolio worth $40. If the shareholder exercises the rights, he or she ends up with three shares worth a total of $50. In other words, by spending $10, the investor's holding increases in value by $10, which means that the shareholder is neither better nor worse off.

On the other hand, if the shareholder sells the two rights for $3.33 each, he or she would obtain $3.33 × 2 = $6.67 and end up with two shares worth $16.67 and the cash from selling the right:

$$\text{Shares held} = 2 \times \$16.67 = \$33.33$$

$$\text{Rights sold} = 2 \times \$3.33 \ = \underline{\$\ 6.67}$$

$$\text{Total} = \hspace{2.5cm} \$40.00$$

The new $33.33 market value plus $6.67 in cash is exactly the same as the original holding of $40. Thus, stockholders cannot lose or gain from exercising or selling rights.

It is obvious that after the rights offering, the new market price of the firm's stock will be lower than it was before the rights offering. As we have seen, however, stockholders have suffered no loss because of the rights offering. Thus, the stock price decline is very much like a stock split, a device that is described in Chapter 16. The lower the subscription price, the greater is the price decline of a rights offering. It is important to emphasize that because shareholders receive rights equal in value to the price drop, the rights offering does *not* hurt stockholders.

There is one last issue. How do we set the subscription price in a rights offering? If you think about it, the subscription price really does not matter. It has to be below the market price of the stock in order for the rights to have value, but, beyond this, the price is arbitrary. In principle, it could be as low as we cared to make it as long as it is not zero. In other words, it is impossible to underprice a rights offer.

The New Issues Puzzle

In the United States, firms use general cash offers much more often than rights offerings. In Table 13.11, of the 578 total issues, about 94 or 16 percent were rights offers. In the United States, this reliance on general cash offers is something of a mystery because rights offerings are usually much cheaper in terms of flotation costs.

To get an idea of the relative flotation costs, Table 13.11 shows these costs from one study expressed as a percentage of the amount raised for different issue sizes and selling procedures. Overall, general cash offers had average flotation costs equal to 6.17 percent of the amount raised. For rights offerings with standby underwriting, total costs were 6.05 percent. For pure rights offerings (those involving no underwriter), these costs were only 2.45 percent of the amount raised, a significant savings.

Overall, Table 13.11 suggests that pure rights offerings have a pronounced cost advantage. Furthermore, rights offerings protect the proportionate interest of existing shareholders. No one knows why rights offerings are not used more often, and it is an intriguing anomaly.

Table 13.11		Cash Offers			
Costs of flotation as a percentage of proceeds*	Size of Issue ($ millions)	Number	Compensation as a Percentage of Proceeds	Other Expenses as a Percentage of Proceeds	Total Cost as a Percentage of Proceeds
	Under 0.50	0	—	—	—
	0.50 to 0.99	6	6.96%	6.78%	13.74%
	1.00 to 1.99	18	10.40	4.89	15.29
	2.00 to 4.99	61	6.59	2.87	9.47
	5.00 to 9.99	66	5.50	1.53	7.03
	10.00 to 19.99	91	4.84	0.71	5.55
	20.00 to 49.99	156	4.30	0.37	4.67
	50.00 to 99.99	70	3.97	0.21	4.18
	100.00 to 500.00	16	3.81	0.14	3.95
	Total/average	484	5.02%	1.15%	6.17%

*Based on 578 common stock issues registered under the Securities Act of 1933 during 1971–75. The issues are subdivided by size of issue and method of financing: cash offers, rights with standby underwriting, and pure rights offerings.

   Issues are included only if the company's stock was listed on the NYSE, AMEX, or regional exchanges before the offering; any associated secondary distribution represents less than 10 percent of the total proceeds of the issue, and the offering contains no other types of securities. The costs reported are: (1) compensation received by investment bankers for underwriting services rendered, (2) legal fees, (3) accounting fees, (4) engineering fees, (5) trustees' fees, (6) printing and engraving expenses, (7) SEC registration fees, (8) federal reserve stamps, and (9) state taxes.

Modified from C.W. Smith, Jr. "Costs of Underwritten versus Rights Issues," *Journal of Financial Economics* 5 (December 1977), p. 277 (Table I).

Various arguments in favor of general cash offers with underwriting have been put forth:

1.   Underwriters increase the stock price. This is supposedly accomplished because of the selling effort of the underwriting group.

2.   Underwriters provide insurance against a failed offering. This is true. If the market price goes below the offer price, the firm does not lose, because the underwriter bought the shares at an agreed-upon price. However, this insurance cannot be worth much, because the offer price is not set (in most cases) until within 24 hours of the offering when the final arrangements are made and underwriters have made careful assessment of the market for the shares.

3.   Other arguments include (*a*) the proceeds of underwritten issues are available sooner than with a rights offer, (*b*) underwriters will provide a wider distribution of ownership than would be true with a rights offering, and (*c*) consulting advice from investment bankers may be beneficial.

All of the preceding arguments are pieces of the puzzle, but none seems very convincing. One recent study found that firms making underwritten rights

	Rights with Standby Underwriting			Pure Rights	
Number	Compensation as a Percentage of Proceeds	Other Expenses as a Percentage of Proceeds	Total Cost as a Percentage of Proceeds	Number	Total Cost as a Percentage of Proceeds
0	—	—	—	3	8.99%
2	3.43%	4.80%	8.24%	2	4.59
5	6.36	4.15	10.51	5	4.90
9	5.20	2.85	8.06	7	2.85
4	3.92	2.18	6.10	6	1.39
10	4.14	1.21	5.35	3	0.72
12	3.84	0.90	4.74	1	0.52
9	3.96	0.74	4.70	2	0.21
5	3.50	0.50	4.00	9	0.13
56	4.32%	1.73%	6.05%	38	2.45%

offers suffered substantially larger price drops than did firms making under-written cash offers.[7] This is a hidden cost, and it may be part of the reason that underwritten rights offers are uncommon in the United States.

CONCEPT QUESTIONS

13.6a How does a rights offering work?

13.6b What are the questions that financial management must answer in a rights offering?

13.6c How is the value of a right determined?

13.6d When does a rights offering affect the value of a company's shares?

13.6e Does a rights offer cause a share price to decrease? How are existing shareholders affected by a rights offer?

DILUTION | 13.7

A subject that comes up quite a bit in discussions involving the selling of securities is **dilution.** Dilution refers to a loss in existing shareholders' value. There are several kinds:

dilution

Loss in existing shareholders' value, in terms of either ownership, market value, book value, or EPS.

1. Dilution of percentage ownership.
2. Dilution of market value.
3. Dilution of book value and earnings per share.

[7]Robert S. Hansen, "The Demise of the Rights Issue," *The Review of Financial Studies* 1 (Fall 1988), pp. 289–309.

The differences between these three types can be a little confusing, and there are some common misconceptions about dilution, so we discuss it in this section.

Dilution of Proportionate Ownership

The first type of dilution can arise whenever a firm sells shares to the general public. For example, Joe Smith owns 5,000 shares of Merit Shoe Company. Merit Shoe currently has 50,000 shares of stock outstanding; each share gets one vote. Joe thus controls 10 percent (5,000/50,000) of the votes and gets 10 percent of the dividends.

If Merit Shoe issues 50,000 new shares of common stock to the public via a general cash offer, Joe's ownership in Merit Shoe may be diluted. If Joe does not participate in the new issue, his ownership will drop to 5 percent (5,000/100,000). Notice that the value of Joe's shares is unaffected; he just owns a smaller percentage of the firm.

Because a rights offering would ensure Joe Smith an opportunity to maintain his proportionate 10 percent share, dilution of the ownership of existing shareholders can be avoided by using a rights offering.

Dilution of Value: Book versus Market Values

We now examine dilution of value by looking at some accounting numbers. We do this to illustrate a fallacy concerning dilution; we do not mean to suggest that accounting dilution is more important than market value dilution. As we illustrate, quite the reverse is true.

Suppose Upper States Utilities (USU) wants to build a new electricity-generating plant to meet future anticipated demands. As shown in Table 13.12, USU currently has 1 million shares outstanding and no debt. Each share is selling for $5, and the company has a $5 million market value. USU's book value is $10 million total, or $10 per share.

USU has experienced a variety of difficulties in the past, including cost overruns, regulatory delays in building a nuclear-powered electricity-generating plant, and below normal profits. These difficulties are reflected in the fact that USU's market-to-book ratio is $5/$10 = .50 (successful firms rarely have market prices below book values).

Net income for USU is currently $1 million. With 1 million shares, earnings per share (EPS) are $1, and the return on equity (ROE) is $1/$10 = 10%.[8] USU thus sells for five times earnings (the price/earnings ratio is 5). USU has 200 shareholders, each of whom holds 5,000 shares. The new plant will cost $2 million, so USU will have to issue 400,000 new shares ($5 × 400,000 = $2,000,000). There will thus be 1.4 million shares outstanding after the issue.

The ROE on the new plant is expected to be the same as for the company as a whole. In other words, net income is expected to go up by .10 × $2 million =

---

[8]Return on equity (ROE) is equal to earnings per share divided by book value per share or, equivalently, net income divided by common equity. We discuss this and other financial ratios in some detail in Chapter 3.

(1) Initial		After Taking on New Project		
		(2) Dilution	(3) No dilution	
Number of shares	1,000,000	1,400,000	1,400,000	
Book value	$10,000,000	$12,000,000	$12,000,000	
Book value per share (B)	$10	$8.57	$8.57	
Market value	$5,000,000	$6,000,000	$8,000,000	
Market price (P)	$5	$4.29	$5.71	
Net income	$1,000,000	$1,200,000	$1,600,000	
Return on equity (ROE)	0.10	0.10	0.13	
Earnings per share (EPS)	$1	$0.86	$1.14	
EPS/P	0.20	0.20	0.20	
P/EPS	5	5	5	
P/B	0.5	0.5	0.67	
PROJECT				
Cost $2,000,000		NPV $= -\$1,000,000$	NPV $= \$1,000,000$	

Table 13.12

New issues and dilution:
The case of Upper States
Utilities

$200,000. Total net income will thus be $1.2 million. The following things would occur:

1. With 1.4 million shares outstanding, EPS would be $1.2/1.4 = $.857 per share, down from $1.

2. The proportionate ownership of each old shareholder drops to 5,000/ 1.4 million = .36 percent from .50 percent.

3. If the stock continues to sell for five times earnings, then the value would drop to 5 × .857 = $4.29, a loss of $.71 per share.

4. The total book value will be the old $10 million plus the new $2 million for a total of $12 million. Book value per share will fall to $12 million/1.4 million = $8.57 per share.

If we take this example at face value, then dilution of proportionate ownership, accounting dilution, and market value dilution all occur. USU's stockholders appear to suffer significant losses.

A Misconception   Our example appears to show that selling stock when the market-to-book ratio is less than 1 is detrimental to the stockholders. Some managers claim that this dilution occurs because EPS will go down whenever shares are issued where the market value is less than the book value.

When the market-to-book ratio is less than 1, increasing the number of shares does cause EPS to go down. Such a decline in EPS is accounting dilution, and accounting dilution will always occur under these circumstances.

Is it furthermore true that market value dilution will also necessarily occur? The answer is *no*. There is nothing incorrect about our example, but why the market value has decreased is not obvious. We discuss this next.

The Correct Arguments   In this example, the market price falls from $5 per share to $4.29. This is true dilution, but why does it occur? The answer has to do with the new project. USU is going to spend $2 million on the new plant. However, as shown in Table 13.12, the total market value of the company is going to rise from $5 million to $6 million, an increase of only $1 million. This simply means that the NPV of the new project is −$1 million. With 1.4 million shares, the loss per share is $1/1.4 = .71, as we calculated before.

So, true dilution takes place for the shareholders of USU because the NPV of the project is negative, not because the market-to-book ratio is less than 1. This negative NPV causes the market price to drop, and the accounting dilution has nothing to do with it.

Suppose that the new project had a positive NPV of $1 million. The total market value would rise by $2 + 1 = $3 million. As shown in Table 13.12 (third column), the price per share rises to $5.71. Notice that accounting dilution still takes place because the book value per share still falls, but there is no economic consequence to that fact. The market value of the stock rises.

The $.71 increase in share value comes about because of the $1 million NPV, which amounts to an increase in value of about $.71 per share. Also, as shown, if the ratio of price to EPS remains at 5, then EPS must rise to $5.71/5 = $1.14. Total earnings (net income) rises to $1.14 per share × 1.4 million shares = $1.6 million. Finally, ROE would rise to $1.6 million/$12 million = 13.33%.

⌐CONCEPT QUESTIONS

13.7a What are the different kinds of dilution?

13.7b Is dilution important?

13.8 | ISSUING LONG-TERM DEBT

The general procedures followed in a public issue of bonds are the same as those for stocks. The issue must be registered with the SEC, there must be a prospectus, and so on. The registration statement for a public issue of bonds, however, is different from the one for common stock. For bonds, the registration statement must indicate an indenture.

Another important difference is that more than 50 percent of all debt is issued privately. There are two basic forms of direct private long-term financing: term loans and private placement.

term loan

Direct business loans of, typically, one to five years

private placements

Loans, usually long-term in nature, provided directly by a limited number of investors.

Term loans are direct business loans. These loans have maturities of between one year and five years. Most term loans are repayable during the life of the loan. The lenders include commercial banks, insurance companies, and other lenders that specialize in corporate finance. **Private placements** are very similar to term loans except that the maturity is longer.

The important differences between direct private long-term financing and public issues of debt are:

1. A direct long-term loan avoids the cost of Securities and Exchange Commission registration.

2. Direct placement is likely to have more restrictive covenants.

3. It is easier to renegotiate a term loan or a private placement in the event of a default. It is harder to renegotiate a public issue because hundreds of holders are usually involved.

4. Life insurance companies and pension funds dominate the private-placement segment of the bond market. Commercial banks are significant participants in the term-loan market.

5. The costs of distributing bonds are lower in the private market.

The interest rates on term loans and private placements are usually higher than those on an equivalent public issue. One study found that the yield to maturity on private placements was 0.46 percent higher than on similar public issues.[9] This finding reflects the trade-off between a higher interest rate and more flexible arrangements in the event of financial distress, as well as the lower costs associated with private placements.

An additional, and very important, consideration is that the flotation costs associated with selling debt are much less than the costs associated with selling equity.

CONCEPT QUESTIONS

13.8a What is the difference between private and public bond issues?

13.8b A private placement is likely to have a higher interest rate than a public issue. Why?

SHELF REGISTRATION | 13.9

To simplify the procedures for issuing securities, in March 1982, the SEC adopted Rule 415 on a temporary basis, and it was made permanent in November 1983. Rule 415 allows shelf registration. Both debt and equity securities can be shelf registered.

Shelf registration permits a corporation to register an offering that it reasonably expects to sell within the next two years and then sell the issue whenever it wants over the next two years. Not all companies can use Rule 415. The primary qualifications are:

1. The company must be rated investment grade.

2. The firm cannot have defaulted on its debt in the past three years.

3. The aggregate market value of the firm's outstanding stock must be more than $150 million.

4. The firm must not have had a violation of the Securities Act of 1934 in the past three years.

Shelf registration allows firms to use a *dribble* method of new equity issuance.[10] With dribbling, a company registers the issue and hires an underwriter

shelf registration
SEC Rule 415 allowing a company to register all issues it expects to sell within two years at one time, with subsequent sales at any time within those two years.

---

[9]P. A. Hays, M. D. Joehnk, and R.W. Melicher, "Determinants of Risk Premiums in the Public and Private Bond Market," *Journal of Financial Research* 2 (Fall 1979).

[10]A. Hershman, "New Strategies in Equity Financing," *Dun's Business Monthly,* June 1983.

as its selling agent. The company sells shares in "dribs and drabs" from time to time directly via a stock exchange (for example, the NYSE). Companies that have used dribble programs include Middle South Utilities, Niagara Mohawk, Pacific Gas and Electric, and the Southern Company.

The rule has been very controversial. Several arguments have been constructed against shelf registration:

1. The costs of new issues might go up because underwriters may not be able to provide as much current information to potential investors as would be true otherwise, so investors will pay less. The expense of selling the issue piece by piece might therefore be higher compared to selling it all at once.
2. Some investment bankers have argued that shelf registration will cause a "market overhang" that will depress market prices. In other words, the possibility that the company could increase the supply of stock at any time will have a negative impact on the current stock price.

In a study examining these issues, the researchers found that shelf registration is less costly than conventional underwriting. There was no evidence to suggest a market overhang effect.[11] However, in recent years, relatively few eligible companies have shelf-registered new equity issues.

⌐ CONCEPT QUESTIONS

13.9a What is shelf registration?

13.9b What are the arguments against shelf registration?

13.10 │ SUMMARY AND CONCLUSIONS

This chapter looks at how corporate securities are issued. The following are the main points:

1. The costs of issuing securities can be quite large. They are much lower (as a percentage) for larger issues.
2. Firm commitment underwriting is far more prevalent for large issues than best efforts underwriting. This is probably connected to the uncertainty of smaller issues. For a given size offering, the direct expenses of best efforts underwriting and firm commitment underwriting are of the same magnitude.
3. The direct and indirect costs of going public can be substantial. However, once a firm is public it can raise additional capital with much greater ease.
4. Rights offerings are cheaper than general cash offers. Even so, most new equity issues in the United States are underwritten general cash offers.

[11]S. Bhagat, M.W. Marr, and G.R. Thompson, "The Rule 415 Experiment: Equity Markets," *Journal of Finance* 40 (December 1985).

Key Terms

registration statement 444

Regulation A 444

prospectus 444

red herring 444

tombstone 445

general cash offer 445

rights offer 445

initial public offering (IPO) 445

seasoned new issue 445

underwriters 446

syndicate 446

spread 447

firm commitment underwriting 447

best efforts underwriting 447

Green Shoe provision 448

ex rights 466

holder-of-record date 466

standby underwriting 467

standby fee 467

oversubscription privilege 468

dilution 471

term loan 474

private placements 474

shelf registration 475

Chapter Review Problems and Self-Test

13.1   Flotation Costs   The L5 Corporation is considering an equity issue to finance a new space station. A total of $10 million in new equity is needed. If the direct costs are estimated at 6 percent of the amount raised, how large does the issue need to be? What is the dollar amount of the flotation cost?

13.2   Rights Offerings   The Hadron Corporation currently has 4 million shares outstanding. The stock sells for $50 per share. To raise $30 million for a new particle accelerator, the firm is considering a rights offering at $20 per share. What is the value of a right in this case? The ex rights price?

Answers to Self-Test Problems

13.1   The firm needs to net $10 million after paying the 6 percent flotation costs. So the amount raised is given by:

Amount raised × (1 − .06) = $10 million

Amount raised = $10/.94 = $10.638 million

The total flotation cost is thus $638,000.

13.2   To raise $30 million at $20 per share, $30 million/$20 = 1.5 million shares will have to be sold. Before the offering, the firm is worth 4 million × $50 = $200 million. The issue raised $30 million and there will be 5.5 million shares outstanding. The value of an ex rights share will therefore be $230/5.5 = $41.82. The value of a right is thus $50 − 41.82 = $8.18.

Questions and Problems

1.   Underwriting versus Rights   Megabucks Industries is planning to raise fresh equity capital by selling a large new issue of common stock. Megabucks is currently a publicly traded corporation, and it is trying to choose between an underwritten cash offer and a rights offering (not underwritten) to current shareholders. Megabucks management is interested in minimizing the selling costs and has asked you for advice on the choice of issue methods. What is your recommendation and why?

2.   Rights Offerings   Jelly Beans, Inc., is proposing a rights offering. Presently there are 100,000 outstanding shares at $25 each. There will be 10,000 new shares issued at $20.
   a. What is the value of a right?
   b. What is the ex rights price?
   c. What is the new market value of the company?
   d. Why might a company have a rights offering rather than a general cash offer?

3.   Price Dilution   Suppose the Newton Company has 10,000 shares of stock. Each share is worth $40, and the company's market value of equity is $400,000. Suppose the firm issues 5,000 shares of new stock at the following prices: $40, $20, $10. What will be the effect of each of the alternative offering prices on the existing price per share?

4.   IPO Investment and Underpricing   In 1980, a certain assistant professor of finance bought 12 initial public offerings of common stock. He held each of these for approximately one month and then sold. The investment rule he followed was to submit a purchase order for every firm commitment initial public offering of oil and gas exploration companies. There were 22 of these offerings, and he submitted a purchase order for approximately $1,000 of stock for each of the companies. With 10 of these, no shares were allocated to this assistant professor. With 5 of the 12 offerings that were purchased, fewer than the requested number of shares were allocated.

   The year 1980 was very good for oil and gas exploration company owners: On average, of the 22 companies that went public, the stocks were selling for 80 percent above the offering price a month after the initial offering date. The assistant professor looked at his performance record and found the $8,400 invested in the 12 companies had grown to only $10,000, a return of only about 20 percent (commissions were negligible). Did he have bad luck, or should he have expected to do worse than the average initial public offering investor? Explain.

5.   Analysis of an IPO   The following material contains the cover page and summary of the prospectus for the initial public offering of the Pest Investigation Control Corporation (PICC), which is going public tomorrow with a firm commitment initial public offering managed by the investment banking firm of Erlanger and Ritter. Answer the following questions:
   a. Assume that you know nothing about PICC other than the information contained in the prospectus. Based on your knowledge of finance, what is your prediction for the price of PICC tomorrow? Provide a short explanation of why you think that this will occur.

b. Assume that you have several thousand dollars to invest. When you get home from class tonight, you find that your stockbroker, whom you have not talked to for weeks, has called. She has left a message that PICC is going public tomorrow and that she can get you several hundred shares at the offering price if you call her back first thing in the morning. Discuss the merits of this opportunity.

PROSPECTUS   PICC

200,000 shares

PEST INVESTIGATION CONTROL CORPORATION

Of the shares being offered hereby, all 200,000 are being sold by the Pest Investigation Control Corporation, Inc. ("the Company"). Before the offering there has been no public market for the shares of PICC, and no guarantee can be given that any market will develop.

These securities have not been approved or disapproved by the SEC nor has the commission passed upon the accuracy or adequacy of this prospectus. Any representation to the contrary is a criminal offense.

	Price to Public	Underwriting Discount	Proceeds to Company*
Per share	$11.00	$1.10	$9.90
Total	$2,200,000	$220,000	$1,980,000

*Before deducting expenses estimated at $27,000 payable by the company.

This is an initial public offering. The common shares are being offered, subject to prior sale, when, as, and if delivered to and accepted by the Underwriters and subject to approval of certain legal matters by their Counsel and by Counsel for the Company. The Underwriters reserve the right to withdraw, cancel, or modify such offer and to reject offers in whole or in part.

Erlanger and Ritter, Investment Bankers
April 12, 1992

Prospectus Summary

The Company	The Pest Investigation Control Corporation (PICC) breeds and markets toads and tree frogs as ecologically safe insect-control mechanisms.
The Offering	200,000 shares of common stock, no par value.
Listing	The Company will seek listing on NASDAQ and will trade over the counter.
Shares Outstanding	As of March 31, 1992, 400,000 shares of common stock were outstanding. After the offering, 600,000 shares of common stock will be outstanding.
Use of Proceeds	To finance expansion of inventory and receivables and general working capital, and to pay for country club memberships for certain finance professors.

(continues on next page)

Selected Financial Information
(amounts in thousands except per-share data)

Fiscal Year Ended
December 31

	1990	1991	1992
Revenues	$60.00	$120.00	$240.00
Net earnings	3.80	15.90	36.10
Earnings per share	0.01	0.04	0.09

As of March 31, 1992

	Actual	As Adjusted for This Offering
Working capital	$ 8	$1,961
Total assets	511	2,464
Stockholders' equity	423	2,376

6. **IPO Underpricing**   Analyze the following statement: Because initial public offerings of common stock are always underpriced, an investor can make money by purchasing shares in these offerings.

7. **Rights**   Superior, Inc., is a manufacturer of beta-blockers (consumers are just sick and tired of those pesky betas). Management has concluded that additional equity financing is required to increase production capacity and that these funds are best obtained through a rights offering. It has correctly concluded that as a result of the rights offering, share price will fall from $50 to $45 ($50 is the rights-on price; $45 is the ex rights price, also known as the *when-issued price*). The company is seeking $5 million in additional funds with a per-share subscription price equal to $25.

    How many shares were there before the offering? (Assume that the increment to the market value of the equity equals the gross proceeds from the offering.)

8. **Dilution**   The Radcliffe Corporation wishes to expand its manufacturing activities. Radcliffe currently has 10 million shares outstanding and no debt. The stock sells for $40 per share, but the book value per share is $60. Net income for Radcliffe is currently $20 million. The new facility will cost $60 million, and it will increase net income by $2 million.

    a. Assuming a constant price-earnings ratio, what will be the effect of taking the new investment? To answer, calculate the new book value, the new total earnings, the new EPS, the new stock price, and the new market-to-book ratio. What is going on here?

    b. What would the new net income for Radcliffe have to be for the stock price to remain unchanged?

9. Dilution   The Slide Rule Corporation wants to diversify its operations. Some recent financial information is shown below.

Stock price	$50
Number of shares	1,000
Total assets	$500,000
Total liabilities	$300,000
Net income	$10,000

Slide Rule is considering an investment that has the same P/E ratio as the firm. The cost of the investment is $50,000, and it will be financed with a new equity issue. The return on the investment will equal Slide Rule's current ROE. What will happen to the book value per share, the market value per share, and the EPS? What is the NPV of this investment?

10. Dilution   In the previous problem, what would the ROE on the investment have to be if we actually want to sell new shares for $50? What is the NPV of this investment? In this case, does accounting dilution still take place?

11. Calculating Flotation Costs   Thule Co. has just gone public. Under the firm commitment agreement, Thule received $15 for each of the 5 million shares sold. The initial offering price was $18 per share, and the stock rose to $22 per share in the first few minutes of trading. Thule paid $120,000 in direct legal and other costs. Indirect costs were $80,000. What was the flotation cost as a percentage of funds raised?

12. IPO Underpricing   The Lemon Co. and the Lime Co. have announced IPOs at $5 per share. One of these is undervalued by $1, the other is overvalued by $.50, but citrus fruits are not your specialty, so you have no way of knowing which is which. You plan on buying 100 shares of each. If an issue is underpriced, it will be rationed, and you will only get half your order. If you *could* get 100 shares in Lemon and 100 in Lime, what would your profit be? What profit do you actually expect? What principle have you illustrated?

13. Rights Offering   The Ang-Wish Corporation has announced a rights offer to raise $50 million for a new journal, the *Journal of Financial Excess*. This journal will review potential articles after the author pays a nonrefundable reviewing fee of $3,000 per page. The stock currently sells for $25 per share and there are 22 million shares outstanding. Answer the following questions.
   a. What is the maximum possible subscription price? What is the minimum?
   b. If the subscription price is set at $15 per share, how many shares must be sold? How many rights will it take to buy one share?
   c. What is the ex rights price? What is the value of a right?
   d. Show how a shareholder with 100 shares and no desire (or money) to buy additional shares is not harmed by the rights offer.

14. **Rights** This is a challenge problem. The Peter Publishing Partnership, Inc., is considering a rights offer. The company has determined that the ex rights price will be $20. The current price is $40 per share, and there are 10 million shares outstanding. The rights offer would raise a total of $40 million. What is the subscription price?

15. **Value of a Right** This is a challenge problem. Show that the value of a right can be written as

$$\text{Value of a right} = P_{RO} - P_X = (P_{RO} - P_S)/(N + 1)$$

where P_{RO}, P_S, and P_X stand for the rights-on price, the subscription price, and the ex rights price, respectively, and N is the number of rights needed to buy one new share at the subscription price.

Suggested Readings

The costs of issuing new equity are documented in:

Ritter, J. R. "The Cost of Going Public." *Journal of Financial Economics* 19, 1987.

Smith, C. W., Jr. "Alternative Methods of Raising Capital: Rights versus Underwritten Offerings." *Journal of Financial Economics* 5, 1977.

Articles that examine underpricing and investment banking include:

Booth, J., and R. Smith. "The Certification Role of the Investment Banker in New Issues Pricing." *Midland Corporate Finance Journal* 1, Spring 1986.

Ibbotson, R. G. "Price Performance of Common Stock New Issues." *Journal of Financial Economics* 2, 1975.

Muscarella, C. J., and M. R. Vetsuypens. "A Simple Test of Baron's Model of IPO Underpricing." *Journal of Financial Economics* 24, 1989.

Ritter, J. R. "The 'Hot Issue' Market of 1980." *Journal of Business* 57, 1984.

Rock, K. "Why New Issues Are Underpriced." *Journal of Financial Economics* 15, 1986.

The effect of seasoned new equity on stock prices is discussed in:

Asquith, P., and D. Mullins. "Equity Issues and Offering Dilution." *Journal of Financial Economics* 15, 1986.

Masulis, R., and A. N. Korwar. "Seasoned Equity Offerings: An Empirical Investigation." *Journal of Financial Economics* 15, 1986.

Mikkelson, W. H., and M. M. Partch. "The Valuation Effects of Security Offerings and the Issuance Process." *Journal of Financial Economics* 15, 1986.

Summaries of recent research can be found in:

Hansen, R. "Evaluating the Costs of a New Equity Issue." *Midland Corporate Finance Journal,* Spring 1986.

Ibbotson, Roger G.; Jody L. Sindelar; and Jay R. Ritter. "Initial Public Offerings." *Journal of Applied Corporate Finance* 1, Summer 1988.

Part Seven

Cost of Capital and Long-Term Financial Policy

CHAPTER 14
Cost of Capital

The discount rate used in capital budgeting is often the project's weighted average cost of capital. This chapter identifies the components to be used in a project's cost of capital, the method used to determine the cost of each component, and how the component costs are combined into a weighted average cost of capital.

CHAPTER 15
Financial Leverage and Capital Structure Policy

This chapter shows what happens when the firm's reliance on debt changes. It discusses taxes, bankruptcy costs, and capital structure decisions — those decisions concerning the extent to which a firm relies on debt.

CHAPTER 16
Dividends and Dividend Policy

To pay dividends or not to pay dividends? That is the question discussed in Chapter 16. This chapter identifies and discusses the important factors that financial managers must consider in establishing a dividend policy.

Chapter 14

Cost of Capital

Suppose you have just become the president of a large company and the first decision you face is whether to go ahead with a plan to renovate the company's warehouse distribution system. The plan will cost the company $50 million, and it is expected to save $12 million per year after taxes over the next six years.

This is a familiar problem in capital budgeting. To address it, you would determine the relevant cash flows, discount them, and, if the net present value is positive, take on the project; if the NPV is negative, you would scrap it. So far so good, but what should you use as the discount rate?

From our discussion of risk and return, you know that the correct discount rate depends on the riskiness of the warehouse distribution system. In particular, the new project will have a positive NPV only if its return exceeds what the financial markets offer on investments of similar risks. We called this minimum required return the *cost of capital* associated with the project.[1]

Thus, to make the right decision as president, you must examine what the capital markets have to offer and use this information to arrive at an estimate of the project's cost of capital. Our primary purpose in this chapter is to describe how to go about doing this. There are a variety of approaches to this task, and a number of conceptual and practical issues arise.

One of the most important concepts we develop is the weighted average cost of capital (WACC). This is the cost of capital for the firm as a whole, and it can be interpreted as the required return on the overall firm. In discussing the WACC, we will recognize the fact that a firm will normally raise capital in

---

[1] The term *cost of money* is also used.

a variety of forms and that these different forms of capital may have different costs associated with them.

We also recognize in this chapter that taxes are an important consideration in determining the required return on an investment, because we are always interested in valuing the aftertax cash flows from a project. We will therefore discuss how to incorporate taxes explicitly into our estimates of the cost of capital.

14.1 | THE COST OF CAPITAL: SOME PRELIMINARIES

In Chapter 11, we developed the security market line (SML) and used it to explore the relationship between the expected return on a security and its systematic risk. We concentrated on how the risky returns from buying securities looked from the viewpoint of, for example, a shareholder in the firm. This helped us understand more about the alternatives available to an investor in the capital markets.

In this chapter, we turn things around a bit and look more closely at the other side of the problem, which is how these returns and securities look from the viewpoint of the companies that issue them. The important fact to note is that the return an investor in a security receives is the cost of that security to the company that issued it.

Required Return versus Cost of Capital

When we say that the required return on an investment is, say, 10 percent, we usually mean that the investment will have a positive NPV only if its return exceeds 10 percent. Another way of interpreting the required return is to observe that the firm must earn 10 percent on the investment just to compensate its investors for the use of the capital needed to finance the project. This is why we could also say that 10 percent is the cost of capital associated with the investment.

To illustrate the point further, imagine that we were evaluating a risk-free project. In this case, how to determine the required return is obvious: We look at the capital markets and observe the current rate offered by risk-free investments, and we use this rate to discount the project's cash flows. Thus, the cost of capital for a risk-free investment is the risk-free rate.

If this project were risky, then, assuming that all the other information is unchanged, the required return is obviously higher. In other words, the cost of capital for this project, if it is risky, is greater than the risk-free rate, and the appropriate discount rate would exceed the risk-free rate.

We will henceforth use the terms *required return, appropriate discount rate,* and *cost of capital* more or less interchangeably because, as the discussion in this section suggests, they all mean essentially the same thing. The key fact to grasp is that the cost of capital associated with an investment depends on the risk of that investment. This is one of the most important lessons in corporate finance, so it bears repeating:

> The cost of capital depends primarily on the use of the funds, not the source.

It is a common error to forget this crucial point and fall into the trap of thinking that the cost of capital for an investment depends primarily on how and where the capital is raised.

Financial Policy and Cost of Capital

We know that the particular mixture of debt and equity that a firm chooses to employ—its capital structure—is a managerial variable. In this chapter, we will take the firm's financial policy as given. In particular, we will assume that the firm has a fixed debt/equity ratio that it maintains. This ratio reflects the firm's *target* capital structure. How a firm might choose that ratio is the subject of our next chapter.

From our discussion above, we know that a firm's overall cost of capital will reflect the required return on the firm's assets as a whole. Given that a firm uses both debt and equity capital, this overall cost of capital will be a mixture of the returns needed to compensate its creditors and its stockholders. In other words, a firm's cost of capital will reflect both its cost of debt capital and its cost of equity capital. We discuss these costs separately in the sections below.

⌐ CONCEPT QUESTIONS

14.1a What is the primary determinant of the cost of capital for an investment?

14.1b What is the relationship between the required return on an investment and the cost of capital associated with that investment?

THE COST OF EQUITY ⌐ 14.2

We begin with the most difficult question on the subject of cost of capital: What is the firm's overall **cost of equity?** The reason this is a difficult question is that there is no way of directly observing the return that the firm's equity investors require on their investment. Instead, we must somehow estimate it. This section discusses two approaches to determining the cost of equity: the dividend growth model approach and the security market line (SML) approach.

cost of equity
The return that equity investors require on their investment in the firm.

The Dividend Growth Model Approach

The easiest way to estimate the cost of equity capital is to use the dividend growth model that we developed in Chapter 6. Recall that, under the assumption that the firm's dividend will grow at a constant rate g, the price per share of the stock, P_0, can be written as:

$$P_0 = \frac{D_0 \times (1 + g)}{R_E - g} = \frac{D_1}{R_E - g}$$

where D_0 is the dividend just paid, and D_1 is the next period's projected dividend. Notice that we have used the symbol R_E (the E stands for equity) for the required return on the stock.

As we discussed in Chapter 6, we can rearrange this to solve for R_E as follows:

$$R_E = D_1/P_0 + g \qquad\qquad [14.1]$$

Since R_E is the return that the shareholders require on the stock, it can be interpreted as the firm's cost of equity capital.

Implementing the Approach   To estimate R_E using the dividend growth model approach, we obviously need three pieces of information: P_0, D_0, and g.[2] Of these, for a publicly traded, dividend-paying company, the first two can be observed directly, so they are easily obtained. Only the third component, the expected growth rate in dividends, must be estimated.

For example, suppose Greater States Public Service, a large public utility, paid a dividend of $4 per share last year. The stock currently sells for $60 per share. You estimate that the dividend will grow steadily at 6 percent per year into the indefinite future. What is the cost of equity capital for Greater States?

Using the dividend growth model, the expected dividend for the coming year, D_1, is:

$$D_1 = D_0 \times (1 + g)$$

$$= \$4 \times (1.06)$$

$$= \$4.24$$

Given this, the cost of equity, R_E, is:

$$R_E = D_1/P_0 + g$$

$$= \$4.24/\$60 + .06$$

$$= 13.07\%$$

The cost of equity is thus 13.07%.

Estimating g   To use the dividend growth model, we must come up with an estimate for g, the growth rate. There are essentially two ways of doing this: (1) use historical growth rates, or (2) use analysts' forecasts of future growth rates. Analysts' forecasts are available from a variety of sources. Naturally, different sources will have different estimates, so one approach might be to obtain multiple estimates and then average them.

Alternatively, we might observe dividends for the previous, say, five years, calculate the year-to-year growth rates, and average them. For example, suppose we observe the following for some company:

Year	Dividend
1987	$1.10
1988	1.20
1989	1.35
1990	1.40
1991	1.55

---

[2]Notice that if we have D_0 and g, we can simply calculate D_1 by multiplying D_0 by $(1 + g)$.

We can calculate the percentage changes in the dividend for each year as follows:

Year	Dividend	Dollar Change	Percentage Change
1987	$1.10	—	—
1988	1.20	$.10	9.09%
1989	1.35	.15	12.50
1990	1.40	.05	3.70
1991	1.55	.15	10.71

Notice that we calculated the change in the dividend on a year-to-year basis and then expressed the change as a percentage. Thus, in 1988 for example, the dividend rose from $1.10 to $1.20, an increase of $.10. This represents a $.10/1.10 = 9.09% increase.

If we average the four growth rates, the result is (9.09 + 12.50 + 3.70 + 10.71)/4 = 9%, so we could use this as an estimate for the expected growth rate, g. There are other, more sophisticated, statistical techniques that could be used, but they all amount to using past dividend growth to predict future dividend growth.

Advantages and Disadvantages of the Approach   The primary advantage of the dividend growth model approach is its simplicity. It is both easy to understand and easy to use. There are a number of associated practical problems and disadvantages.

First and foremost, the dividend growth model is obviously only applicable to companies that pay dividends. This means that the approach is useless in many cases. Furthermore, even for companies that do pay dividends, the key underlying assumption is that the dividend grows at a constant rate. As our example above illustrates, this will never be *exactly* the case. More generally, the model is really only applicable to cases where reasonably steady growth is likely to occur.

A second problem is that the estimated cost of equity is very sensitive to the estimated growth rate. An upward revision of g by just 1 percentage point, for example, increases the estimated cost of equity by at least a full percentage point. Since D_1 will probably be revised upwards as well, the increase will actually be somewhat larger than that.

Finally, this approach really does not explicitly consider risk. Unlike the SML approach (which we consider next), there is no direct adjustment for the riskiness of the investment. For example, there is no allowance for the degree of certainty or uncertainty surrounding the estimated growth rate in dividends. As a result, it is difficult to say whether or not the estimated return is commensurate with the level of risk.[3]

---

[3]There is an implicit adjustment for risk because the current stock price is used. All other things equal, the higher the risk, the lower is the stock price. Further, the lower the stock price, the greater is the cost of equity, again assuming all the other information is the same.

The SML Approach

In Chapter 11, we discussed the security market line (SML). Our primary conclusion was that the required or expected return on a risky investment depends on three things:

1. The risk-free rate, R_f.
2. The market risk premium, $E(R_M) - R_f$.
3. The systematic risk of the asset relative to average, which we called its beta coefficient, β.

Using the SML, the expected return on the company's equity, $E(R_E)$, can be written as:

$$E(R_E) = R_f + \beta_E \times [E(R_M) - R_f]$$

where β_E is the estimated beta for the equity. For the SML approach to be consistent with the dividend growth model, we will drop the Es denoting expectations and henceforth write the required return from the SML, R_E, as:

$$R_E = R_f + \beta_E \times [R_M - R_f] \qquad [14.2]$$

Implementing the Approach   To use the SML approach, we need a risk-free rate, R_f, an estimate of the market risk premium, $R_M - R_f$, and an estimate of the relevant beta, β_E. In Chapter 10 (Table 10.3), we saw that one estimate of the market risk premium (based on large common stocks) is 8.4 percent. U.S. Treasury bills are paying about 5 percent as this is written, so we will use this as our risk-free rate. Beta coefficients for publicly traded companies are widely available.[4]

To illustrate, in Chapter 11, we saw that IBM had an estimated beta of 0.95 (Table 11.8). We could thus estimate IBM's cost of equity as:

$$R_{IBM} = R_f + \beta_{IBM} \times [R_M - R_f]$$

$$= 5\% + .95 \times (8.4\%)$$

$$= 12.98\%$$

Thus, using the SML approach, IBM's cost of equity is about 13 percent.

Advantages and Disadvantages of the Approach   The SML approach has two primary advantages. First, it explicitly adjusts for risk. Second, it is applicable to companies other than just those with steady dividend growth. Thus, it may be useful in a wider variety of circumstances.

There are drawbacks, of course. The SML approach requires that two things be estimated, the market risk premium and the beta coefficient. To the extent that our estimates are poor, the resulting cost of equity will be inaccu-

---

[4]Beta coefficients can be estimated directly by using historical data. For a discussion of how to do this, see Chapters 9, 10, and 11 in S. A. Ross, R.W. Westerfield, and J. J. Jaffe, *Corporate Finance*, 3rd ed. (Homewood, Ill.: Richard D. Irwin, 1993).

rate. For example, our estimate of the market risk premium, 8.4 percent, is based on about 65 years of returns on a particular portfolio of stocks. Using different time periods or different stocks could result in very different estimates.

Finally, as with the dividend growth model, we essentially rely on the past to predict the future when we use the SML approach. Economic conditions can change very quickly, so, as always, the past may not be a good guide to the future. In the best of all worlds, the two approaches (dividend growth model and SML) are both applicable and both result in similar answers. If this happens, we might have some confidence in our estimates. We might also wish to compare the results to those for other, similar companies as a reality check.

Example 14.1 The Cost of Equity

Suppose that stock in Alpha Air Freight has a beta of 1.2. The market risk premium is 8 percent, and the risk-free rate is 6 percent. Alpha's last dividend was $2 per share, and the dividend is expected to grow at 8 percent indefinitely. The stock currently sells for $30. What is Alpha's cost of equity capital?

We can start off by using the SML. Doing this, we find that the expected return on the common stock of Alpha Air Freight is:

$$R_E = R_f + \beta_E \times [R_M - R_f]$$
$$= 6\% + 1.2 \times 8\%$$
$$= 15.6\%$$

This suggests that 15.6 percent is Alpha's cost of equity. We next use the dividend growth model. The projected dividend is $D_0 \times (1 + g) = \$2 \times (1.08) = \$2.16$, so the expected return using this approach is:

$$R_E = D_1/P_0 + g$$
$$= \$2.16/30 + .08$$
$$= 15.2\%$$

Our two estimates are reasonably close, so we might just average them to find that Alpha's cost of equity is approximately 15.4 percent. ∎

CONCEPT QUESTIONS

14.2a What do we mean when we say that a corporation's cost of equity capital is 16 percent?

14.2b What are two approaches to estimating the cost of equity capital?

THE COSTS OF DEBT AND PREFERRED STOCK | 14.3

In addition to ordinary equity, firms use debt and, to a lesser extent, preferred stock to finance their investments. As we discuss next, determining the costs of capital associated with these sources of financing is much easier than determining the cost of equity.

The Cost of Debt

cost of debt

The return that lenders require on the firm's debt.

The **cost of debt** is the return that the firm's creditors demand on new borrowing. In principle, we could determine the beta for the firm's debt and then use the SML to estimate the required return on debt just as we estimate the required return on equity. This isn't really necessary, however.

Unlike a firm's cost of equity, its cost of debt can normally be observed either directly or indirectly, because the cost of debt is simply the interest rate that the firm must pay on new borrowing, and we can observe interest rates in the financial markets. For example, if the firm already has bonds outstanding, then the yield to maturity on those bonds is the market-required rate on the firm's debt.

Alternatively, if we knew that the firm's bonds were rated, say, AA, then we can simply find out what the interest rate on newly issued AA-rated bonds is. Either way, there is no need to actually estimate a beta for the debt since we can directly observe the rate we want to know.

There is one thing to be careful about, though. The coupon rate on the firm's outstanding debt is irrelevant here. That just tells us roughly what the firm's cost of debt was back when the bonds were issued, not what the cost of debt is today.[5] This is why we have to look at the yield on the debt in today's marketplace. For consistency with our other notation, we will use the symbol R_D for the cost of debt.

Example 14.2 The Cost of Debt

Suppose the General Tool Company issued a 30-year, 7 percent bond eight years ago. The bond is currently selling for 96 percent of its face value, or $960. What is General Tool's cost of debt?

Going back to Chapter 6, we need to calculate the yield to maturity on this bond. Since the bond is selling at a discount, the yield is apparently greater than 7 percent, but not much greater because the discount is fairly small. You can check that the yield to maturity is about 7.37 percent, assuming annual coupons. General Tool's cost of debt, R_D, is thus 7.37 percent. ∎

The Cost of Preferred Stock

Determining the *cost of preferred stock* is quite straightforward. As we discussed in Chapters 5 and 6, preferred stock has a fixed dividend paid every period forever, so a share of preferred stock is essentially a perpetuity. The cost of preferred stock, R_P, is thus:

$$R_P = D/P_0 \qquad\qquad [14.3]$$

where D is the fixed dividend and P_0 is the current price per share of the preferred stock. Notice that the cost of preferred stock is simply equal to the dividend yield on the preferred stock. Alternatively, preferred stocks are rated in much the same way as bonds, so the cost of preferred stock can be esti-

---

[5]The firm's cost of debt based on its historic borrowing is sometimes called the *embedded debt cost.*

mated by observing the required returns on other, similarly rated shares of preferred stock.

Example 14.3 General Motors' Cost of Preferred Stock

On May 2, 1990, General Motors had two issues of preferred stock that traded on the NYSE. One issue paid $3.75 annually per share and sold for $43⅝ per share. The other paid $5.00 per share annually and sold for $57¾ per share. What is GM's cost of preferred stock?

Using the first issue, the cost of preferred stock is:

$$R_P = D/P_0$$
$$= \$3.75/43.625$$
$$= 8.60\%$$

Using the second issue, the cost is:

$$R_P = D/P_0$$
$$= \$5.00/57.75$$
$$= 8.66\%$$

So GM's cost of preferred stock appears to be in the 8.6–8.7 percent range. ■

CONCEPT QUESTIONS

14.3a How can the cost of debt be calculated?

14.3b How can the cost of preferred stock be calculated?

14.3c Why is the coupon rate a bad estimate of a firm's cost of debt?

THE WEIGHTED AVERAGE COST OF CAPITAL 14.4

Now that we have the costs associated with the main sources of capital that the firm employs, we need to worry about the specific mix. As we mentioned above, we will take this mix, which is the firm's capital structure, as given for now. Also, we will focus mostly on debt and ordinary equity in this discussion.

In Chapter 3, we mentioned that financial analysts frequently focus on a firm's total capitalization, which is the sum of its long-term debt and equity. This is particularly true in determining cost of capital; short-term liabilities are often ignored in the process. We will not explicitly distinguish between total value and total capitalization in our discussion below; however, the general approach is applicable in either case.

The Unadjusted Weighted Average Cost of Capital

We will use the symbol E (for equity) to stand for the *market* value of the firm's equity. We calculate this by taking the number of shares outstanding and multiplying it by the price per share. Similarly, we will use the symbol D (for debt) to stand for the *market* value of the firm's debt. For long-term debt, we calculate this by multiplying the market price of a single bond by the number of bonds outstanding.

If there are multiple bond issues (as there normally would be), then we repeat this calculation for each and then add up the results. If there is debt that is not publicly traded (because it is held by a life insurance company, for example), we must observe the yields on similar, publicly traded debt and then estimate the market value of the privately held debt using this yield as the discount rate. For short-term debt, the book (accounting) values and market values should be somewhat similar, so we might use the book values as estimates of the market values.

Finally, we will use the symbol V (for value) to stand for the combined market value of the debt and equity:

$$V = E + D \qquad\qquad [14.4]$$

If we divide both sides by V, we can calculate the percentages of the total capital represented by the debt and equity:

$$100\% = E/V + D/V \qquad\qquad [14.5]$$

These percentages can be interpreted just like portfolio weights, and they are often called the *capital structure weights*.

For example, if the total market value of a company's stock were calculated as $200 million and the total market value of the company's debt were calculated as $50 million, then the combined value would be $250 million. Of this total, $E/V = \$200/250 = 80\%$, so 80 percent of the firm's financing is equity and the remaining 20 percent is debt.

At this point, we have some weights (the debt and equity percentages) and some expected returns (the costs of debt and equity). We use this information to calculate the firm's overall cost of capital in the same way that we calculated a portfolio's expected return in Chapter 11: We multiply the expected returns by their weights and then add them up. In this context, the result is called the unadjusted **weighted average cost of capital (WACC)**:

weighted average cost of capital (WACC)

The weighted average of the costs of debt and equity.

$$\text{WACC (unadjusted)} = (E/V) \times R_E + (D/V) \times R_D \qquad\qquad [14.6]$$

where R_E and R_D are the required returns on (or the costs of) equity and debt, respectively.

We emphasize here that the correct way to proceed is to use the *market* values of the debt and equity. Under certain circumstances, such as a privately owned company, it may not be possible to get reliable estimates of these quantities. In this case, we might go ahead and use the accounting values for debt and equity. While this is probably better than nothing, we would have to take the answer with a grain of salt.

Taxes and the WACC

There is one final issue associated with the WACC. We called the result above the unadjusted WACC because we haven't considered taxes. Recall that we are always concerned with aftertax cash flows. If we are determining the discount rate appropriate to those cash flows, then the discount rate also needs to be expressed on an aftertax basis.

As we discussed previously in various places in this book (and as we will discuss later), the interest paid by a corporation is deductible for tax purposes. Payments to stockholders, such as dividends, are not. What this means, effectively, is that the government pays some of the interest. Thus, in determining an aftertax discount rate, we need to distinguish between the pretax and the aftertax cost of debt.

To illustrate, suppose a firm borrows $1 million at 9 percent interest. The corporate tax rate is 34 percent. What is the aftertax interest rate on this loan? The total interest bill will be $90,000 per year. This amount is tax deductible, however, so the $90,000 interest reduces our tax bill by .34 × $90,000 = $30,600. The aftertax interest bill is thus $90,000 − 30,600 = $59,400. The aftertax interest rate is thus $59,400/$1 million = 5.94%.

Notice that, in general, the aftertax interest rate is simply equal to the pretax rate multiplied by one minus the tax rate. For example, using the numbers above, we find that the aftertax interest rate is 9% × (1 − .34) = 5.94%.

If we use the symbol T_C to stand for the corporate tax rate, then the aftertax rate that we use in our WACC calculation can be written as $R_D \times (1 - T_C)$. Thus, once we consider the effect of taxes, the WACC is:

$$\text{WACC} = (E/V) \times R_E + (D/V) \times R_D \times (1 - T_C) \qquad [14.7]$$

From now on, when we speak of the WACC, this is the number that we have in mind.

This WACC has a very straightforward interpretation. It is the overall return that the firm must earn on its existing assets to maintain the value of its stock. It is also the required return on any investments by the firm that have essentially the same risks as existing operations. So, if we were evaluating the cash flows from a proposed expansion of our existing operations, this is the discount rate we would use.

Example 14.4   Calculating the WACC

The B. B. Lean Co. has 1.4 million shares of stock outstanding. The stock currently sells for $20 per share. The firm's debt is publicly traded and was recently quoted at 93 percent of face value. It has a total face value of $5 million, and it is currently priced to yield 11 percent. The risk-free rate is 8 percent, and the market risk premium is 7 percent. You've estimated that Lean has a beta of .74. If the corporate tax rate is 34 percent, what is the WACC of Lean Co.?

We can first determine the cost of equity and the cost of debt. From the SML, the cost of equity is 8% + .74 × 7% = 13.18%. The total value of the equity is 1.4 million × $20 = $28 million. The pretax cost of debt is the current yield to maturity on the outstanding debt, 11 percent. The debt sells for 93 percent of its face value, so its current market value is .93 × $5 million = $4.65 million. The total market value of the equity and debt together is $28 + 4.65 = $32.65 million.

From here, we can calculate the WACC easily enough. The percentage of equity used by Lean to finance its operations is $28/$32.65 = 85.76%. Since the weights have to add up to 1, the percentage of debt is $1 - .8576 = 14.24\%$. The WACC is thus:

$$\begin{aligned} \text{WACC} &= (E/V) \times R_E + (D/V) \times R_D \times (1 - T_C) \\ &= .8576 \times 13.18\% + .1424 \times 11\% \times (1 - .34) \\ &= 12.34\% \end{aligned}$$

B. B. Lean thus has an overall weighted average cost of capital of 12.34 percent. ∎

Solving the Warehouse Problem and Similar Capital Budgeting Problems

Now we can use the WACC to solve the warehouse problem that we posed at the beginning of the chapter. However, before we rush to discount the cash flows at the WACC to estimate NPV, we need to first make sure that we are doing the right thing.

Going back to first principles, we need to find an alternative in the financial markets that is comparable to the warehouse renovation. To be comparable, an alternative must be of the same risk as the warehouse project. Projects that have the same risk are said to be in the same risk class.

The WACC for a firm reflects the risk and the target capital structure of the firm's existing assets as a whole. As a result, strictly speaking, the firm's WACC is the appropriate discount rate only if the proposed investment is a replica of the firm's existing operating activities.

In broader terms, whether or not we can use the firm's WACC to value the warehouse project depends on whether the warehouse project is in the same risk class as the firm. We will assume that this project is an integral part of the overall business of the firm. In such cases, it is natural to think that the cost savings will be as risky as the general cash flows of the firm, and the project will thus be in the same risk class as the overall firm. More generally, projects like the warehouse renovation that are intimately related to the firm's existing operations are often viewed as being in the same risk class as the overall firm.

We can now see what the president should do. Suppose that the firm has a target debt/equity ratio of 1/3. In this case, E/V is .75 and D/V is .25. The cost of debt is 10 percent, and the cost of equity is 20 percent. Assuming a 34 percent tax rate, the WACC will be:

$$\begin{aligned} \text{WACC} &= (E/V) \times R_E + (D/V) \times R_D \times (1 - T_C) \\ &= .75 \times 20\% + .25 \times 10\% \times (1 - .34) \\ &= 16.65\% \end{aligned}$$

Recall that the warehouse project had a cost of $50 million and expected aftertax cash flows (the cost savings) of $12 million per year for six years. The NPV is thus:

$$\text{NPV} = -\$50 + \frac{\$12}{(1 + \text{WACC})^1} + \cdots + \frac{\$12}{(1 + \text{WACC})^6}$$

Since the cash flows are in the form of an ordinary annuity, we can calculate this NPV using 16.65 percent (the WACC) as the discount rate as follows:

$$NPV = -\$50 + \$12 \times \frac{1 - [1/(1 + 0.1665)^6]}{0.1665}$$

$$= -\$50 + \$12 \times 3.6222$$

$$= -\$6.53$$

Should the firm take on the warehouse renovation? The project has a negative NPV using the firm's WACC. This means that the financial markets offer superior projects in the same risk class (namely, the firm itself). The answer is clear: The project should be rejected. For future reference, our discussion of the WACC is summarized in Table 14.1.

I. The Cost of Equity, R_E

  A. Dividend growth model approach (from Chapter 6):

$$R_E = D_1/P_0 + g$$

    where D_1 is the expected dividend in one period, g is the dividend growth rate, and P_0 is the current stock price.

  B. SML approach (from Chapter 11):

$$R_E = R_f + (R_M - R_f) \times \beta_E$$

    where R_f is the risk-free rate, R_M is the expected return on the overall market, and β_E is the systematic risk of the equity.

II. The Cost of Debt, R_D

  A. For a firm with publicly held debt, the cost of debt can be measured as the yield to maturity on the outstanding debt. The coupon rate is irrelevant. Yield to maturity is covered in Chapter 6.

  B. If the firm has no publicly traded debt, then the cost of debt can be measured as the yield to maturity on similarly rated bonds (bond ratings are discussed in Chapter 12).

III. The Weighted Average Cost of Capital, WACC

  A. The firm's WACC is the overall required return on the firm as a whole. It is the appropriate discount rate to use for cash flows similar in risk to the overall firm.

  B. The WACC is calculated as

$$WACC = (E/V) \times R_E + (D/V) \times R_D \times (1 - T_C)$$

    where T_C is the corporate tax rate, E is the *market* value of the firm's equity, D is the *market* value of the firm's debt, and $V = E + D$. Note that E/V is the percentage of the firm's financing (in market value terms) that is equity, and D/V is the percentage that is debt.

Table 14.1

Summary of capital cost calculations

Example 14.5   Using the WACC

A firm is considering a project that will result in initial aftertax cash savings of $5 million at the end of the first year. These savings will grow at the rate of 5 percent per year. The firm has a debt/equity ratio of 0.5, a cost of equity of 29.2 percent, and a cost of debt of 10 percent. The cost-saving proposal is closely related to the firm's core business, so it is viewed as having the same risks as the overall firm. Should the firm take on the project?

Assuming a 34 percent tax rate, the firm should take on this project if it costs less than $30 million. To see this, first note that the PV is:

$$PV = \frac{\$5 \text{ million}}{WACC - 0.05}$$

This is an example of a growing perpetuity as discussed in Chapter 6. The WACC is:

$$
\begin{aligned}
WACC &= (E/V) \times R_E + (D/V) \times R_D \times (1 - T_C) \\
&= 2/3 \times 29.2\% + 1/3 \times 10\% \times (1 - .34) \\
&= 21.67\%
\end{aligned}
$$

The PV is thus:

$$PV = \frac{\$5 \text{ million}}{.2167 - .05} = \$30 \text{ million}$$

The NPV will be positive only if the cost is less than $30 million. ∎

⌐ CONCEPT QUESTIONS

14.4a How is the WACC calculated?

14.4b Why do we multiply the cost of debt by $(1 - T_C)$ when we compute the WACC?

14.4c Under what conditions is it correct to use the WACC to determine NPV?

14.5 ⎤ DIVISIONAL AND PROJECT COSTS OF CAPITAL

As we have seen, using the WACC as the discount rate for future cash flows is only appropriate when the proposed investment is similar to the firm's existing activities. This is not as restrictive as it sounds. If we were in the pizza business, for example, and we were thinking of opening a new location, then the WACC is the discount rate to use. The same is true of a retailer thinking of a new store, a manufacturer thinking of expanding production, or a consumer products company thinking of expanding its markets.

Nonetheless, despite the usefulness of the WACC as a benchmark, there will clearly be situations where the cash flows under consideration have risks that are distinctly different from those of the overall firm. We consider how to cope with this problem next.

The SML and the WACC

When we are evaluating investments with risks that are substantially different from the overall firm, the use of the WACC will potentially lead to poor decisions. Figure 14.1 illustrates why.

In Figure 14.1, we have plotted an SML corresponding to a risk-free rate of 7 percent and a market risk premium of 8 percent. To keep things simple, we consider an all-equity company with a beta of 1. As we have indicated, the WACC and the cost of equity are exactly equal to 15 percent for this company since there is no debt.

Suppose our firm uses its WACC to evaluate all investments. This means that any investment with a return of greater than 15 percent will be accepted and any investment with a return of less than 15 percent will be rejected. We know from our study of risk and return, however, that a desirable investment is one that plots above the SML. As Figure 14.1 illustrates, using the WACC for all types of projects can result in the firm incorrectly accepting relatively risky projects and incorrectly rejecting relatively safe ones.

For example, consider Point A. This project has a β of $\beta_A = .60$ compared to the firm's beta of 1.0. It has an expected return of 14 percent. Is this a desirable investment? The answer is yes, because its required return is only:

$$\text{Required return} = R_f + \beta \times (R_M - R_f)$$

$$= 7\% + .60 \times 8\%$$

$$= 11.8\%$$

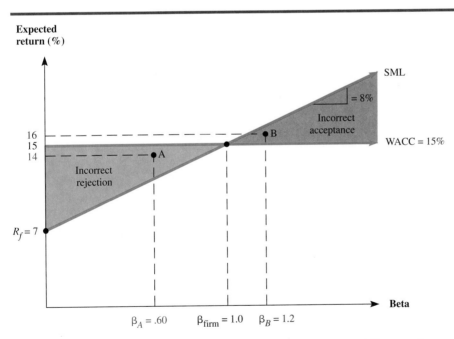

Figure 14.1

The security market line (SML) and the weighted average cost of capital (WACC)

If a firm uses its WACC to make accept/reject decisions for all types of projects, it will have a tendency toward incorrectly accepting risky projects and incorrectly rejecting less risky projects.

However, if we use the WACC as a cutoff, then this project will be rejected because its return is less than 15 percent. This example illustrates that a firm that uses its WACC as a cutoff will tend to reject profitable projects with risks less than those of the overall firm.

At the other extreme, consider Point B. This project has a β of $\beta_B = 1.2$. It offers a 16 percent return, which exceeds the firm's cost of capital. This is not a good investment, however, because, given its level of systematic risk, its return is inadequate. Nonetheless, if we use the WACC to evaluate it, it will appear to be attractive. So the second error that will arise if we use the WACC as a cutoff is that we will tend to make unprofitable investments with risks greater than the overall firm. As a consequence, through time, a firm that uses its WACC to evaluate all projects will have a tendency to both accept unprofitable investments and become increasingly risky.

Divisional Cost of Capital

The same type of problem with the WACC can arise in a corporation with more than one line of business. Imagine, for example, a corporation that has two divisions, a regulated telephone company and an electronics manufacturing operation. The first of these (the phone operation) has relatively low risk; the second has relatively high risk.

In this case, the firm's overall cost of capital is really a mixture of two different costs of capital, one for each division. If the two divisions were competing for resources, and the firm used a single WACC as a cutoff, which division would tend to be awarded greater funds for investment?

The answer is that the riskier division would tend to have greater returns (ignoring the greater risk), so it would tend to be the "winner." The less glamorous operation might have great profit potential that ends up being ignored. Large corporations in the United States are aware of this problem and many work to develop separate divisional costs of capital.

The Pure Play Approach

We've seen that using the firm's WACC inappropriately can lead to problems. How can we come up with the appropriate discount rates in such circumstances? Because we cannot observe the returns on these investments, there generally is no direct way of coming up with a beta, for example. Instead, what we must do is examine other investments outside the firm that are in the same risk class as the one we are considering and use the market-required returns on these investments as the discount rate. In other words, we will try to determine what the cost of capital is for such investments by trying to locate some similar investments in the marketplace.

For example, going back to our telephone division, suppose we wanted to come up with a discount rate to use for that division. What we can do is to identify several other phone companies that have publicly traded securities. We might find that a typical phone company has a beta of .80, AA-rated debt, and a capital structure that is about 50 percent debt and 50 percent equity. Using this information, we could develop a WACC for a typical phone company and use this as our discount rate.

Alternatively, if we are thinking of entering a new line of business, we would try to develop the appropriate cost of capital by looking at the market-required returns on companies already in that business. In the language of Wall Street, a company that focuses only on a single line of business is called a *pure play.* For example, if you wanted to bet on the price of crude oil by purchasing common stocks, you would try to identify companies that dealt exclusively with this product since they would be the most affected by changes in the price of crude oil. Such companies would be called *pure plays* on the price of crude oil.

What we try to do here is to find companies that focus as exclusively as possible on the type of project in which we are interested. Our approach, therefore, is called the **pure play approach** to estimating the required return on an investment.

In Chapter 3, we discussed the subject of identifying similar companies for comparison purposes. The same problems that we described there come up here. The most obvious one is that we may not be able to find any suitable companies. In this case, how to objectively determine a discount rate becomes a very difficult question. Even so, the important thing is to be aware of the issue so we at least reduce the possibility of the kinds of mistakes that can arise when the WACC is used as a cutoff on all investments.

pure play approach
Use of a WACC that is unique to a particular project, based on companies in similar lines of business.

The Subjective Approach

Because of the difficulties that exist in objectively establishing discount rates for individual projects, firms often adopt an approach that involves making subjective adjustments to the overall WACC. To illustrate, suppose a firm has an overall WACC of 14 percent. It places all proposed projects into four categories as follows:

Category	Examples	Adjustment Factor	Discount Rate
High risk	New products	+6%	20%
Moderate risk	Cost savings, expansion of existing lines	+0	14
Low risk	Replacement of existing equipment	−4	10
Mandatory	Pollution control equipment	n/a	n/a

n/a = Not applicable.

The effect of this crude partitioning is to assume that all projects either fall into one of three risk classes or else they are mandatory. In this last case, the cost of capital is irrelevant since the project must be taken. With the subjective approach, the firm's WACC may change through time as economic conditions change. As this happens, the discount rates for the different types of projects will also change.

Within each risk class, some projects will presumably have more risk than others, and the danger of incorrect decisions still exists. Figure 14.2 illustrates this point. Comparing Figures 14.1 and 14.2, we see that similar problems exist, but the magnitude of the potential error is less with the subjective approach. For example, the project labeled A would be accepted if the WACC

In Their Own Words...

Samuel Weaver on Cost of Capital and Hurdle Rates at Hershey Foods Corporation

At Hershey, we reevaluate our cost of capital annually or as market conditions warrant. The calculation of the cost of capital essentially involves three different issues, each with a few alternatives:

- Capital structure weighting
  Historical book value
  Target capital structure
  Market-based weights
- Cost of debt
  Historical book value
  Target capital structure
  Market-based interest rates
- Cost of equity
  Dividend growth model
  Capital asset pricing model (CAPM)

At Hershey, we calculate our cost of capital officially based upon the projected "target" capital structure at the end of our three-year intermediate planning horizon. This allows management to see the immediate impact of strategic decisions related to the planned composition of Hershey's capital pool. The cost of debt is calculated as the anticipated weighted average aftertax cost of debt in that final plan year based upon the coupon rates attached to that debt. The cost of equity is computed via the dividend growth model.

We recently conducted a survey of the 11 food processing companies that we consider our industry group competitors. The results of this survey indicated that the cost of capital for most of these companies was in the 10 to 12 percent range. Furthermore, without exception, all 11 of these companies employed the CAPM when calculating their cost of equity. Our experience has been that the dividend growth model works

better for Hershey. We do pay dividends, and we do experience steady, stable growth in our dividends. This growth is also projected within our strategic plan. Consequently, the dividend growth model is technically applicable and appealing to management since it reflects their best estimate of the future long-term growth rate.

In addition to the calculation described above, the other possible combinations and permutations are calculated as barometers. Unofficially, the cost of capital is calculated using market weights, current marginal interest rates, and the CAPM cost of equity. For the most part, and due to rounding the cost of capital to the nearest whole percentage point, these alternative calculations yield approximately the same results.

From the cost of capital, individual project hurdle rates are developed using a subjectively determined risk premium based on the characteristics of the project. Projects are grouped into separate project categories, such as cost savings, capacity expansion, product line extension, and new products. For example, in general, a new product is more risky than a cost savings product. Consequently, each project category's hurdle rate reflects the level of risk and commensurate required return as perceived by senior management. As a result, capital project hurdle rates range from a slight premium over the cost of capital to the highest hurdle rate of approximately double the cost of capital.

Samuel Weaver, Ph.D., is Manager of Corporate Financial Analysis for the Hershey Foods Corporation. He is a Certified Management Accountant, and he currently serves on the Board of Directors of the Financial Management Association. His current position combines the theoretical with the pragmatic and involves the analysis of many different facets of finance in addition to capital expenditure analysis.

were used, but it is rejected once it is classified as a high-risk investment. What this illustrates is that some risk adjustment, even if it is subjective, is probably better than no risk adjustment.

It would be better, in principle, to objectively determine the required return for each project separately. However, as a practical matter, it may not be possible to go much beyond subjective adjustments because either the neces-

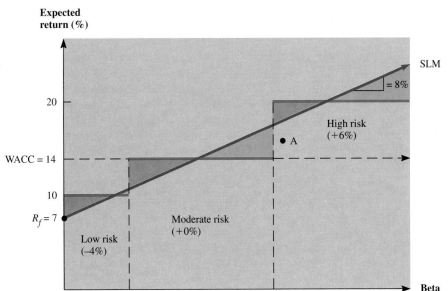

Figure 14.2

The security market line (SML) and the subjective approach

With the subjective approach, the firm places projects into one of several risk classes. The discount rate used to value the project is then determined by adding (for high risk) or subtracting (for low risk) an adjustment factor to or from the firm's WACC.

sary information is unavailable or else the cost and effort required are simply not worthwhile.

> ⌐ CONCEPT QUESTIONS
> 14.5a What are the likely consequences if a firm uses its WACC to evaluate all proposed investments?
> 14.5b What is the pure play approach to determining the appropriate discount rate? When might it be used?

FLOTATION COSTS AND THE WEIGHTED AVERAGE | 14.6
COST OF CAPITAL

So far, we have not included issue or flotation costs in our discussion of the weighted average cost of capital. If a company accepts a new project, it may be required to issue or float new bonds and stocks. This means that the firm will incur some costs, which we call *flotation costs.* The nature and magnitude of flotation costs are discussed in some detail in Chapter 13.

Sometimes it is suggested that the firm's WACC should be adjusted upward to reflect flotation costs. This is really not the best approach, because, once again, the required return on an investment depends on the risk of the investment, not the source of the funds. This is not to say that flotation costs should be ignored. Because these costs arise as a consequence of the decision to undertake a project, they are relevant cash flows. We therefore briefly discuss how to include them in a project analysis.

The Basic Approach

We start with a simple case. The Spatt Company, an all-equity firm, has a cost of equity of 20 percent. Since this firm is 100 percent equity, its WACC and its cost of equity are the same. Spatt is contemplating a large-scale $100 million expansion of its existing operations. The expansion would be funded by selling new stock.

Based on conversations with its investment banker, Spatt believes its flotation costs will run 10 percent of the amount issued. This means that Spatt's proceeds from the equity sale will only be 90 percent of the amount sold. When flotation costs are considered, what is the cost of the expansion?

As we discussed in Chapter 13, Spatt needs to sell enough equity to raise $100 million *after* covering the flotation costs. In other words:

$$\$100 \text{ million} = (1 - .10) \times \text{Amount raised}$$

$$\text{Amount raised} = \$100/.90 = \$111.11 \text{ million}$$

Spatt's flotation costs are thus $11.11 million, and the true cost of the expansion is $111.11 million once we include flotation costs.

Things are only slightly more complicated if the firm uses both debt and equity. For example, suppose that Spatt's target capital structure is 60 percent equity, 40 percent debt. The flotation costs associated with equity are still 10 percent, but the flotation costs for debt are less, say 5 percent.

Earlier, when we had different capital costs for debt and equity, we calculated a weighted average cost of capital using the target capital structure weights. Here, we will do much the same thing. We can calculate a weighted average flotation cost, f_A, by multiplying the equity flotation cost, f_E, by the percentage of equity (E/V) and the debt flotation cost, f_D, by the percentage of debt (D/V) and then adding the two together:

$$f_A = \frac{E}{V} \times f_E + \frac{D}{V} \times f_D \qquad\qquad [14.8]$$

$$= 60\% \times .10 + 40\% \times .05$$

$$= 8\%$$

The weighted average flotation cost is thus 8 percent. What this tells us is that for every dollar in outside financing needed for new projects, the firm must actually raise $1/(1 - .08) = $1.087. In our example above, the project cost is $100 million when we ignore flotation costs. If we include them, then the true cost is $100/(1 - f_A) = $100/.92 = $108.7 million.

In taking issue costs into account, the firm must be careful not to use the wrong weights. The firm should use the target weights, even if it can finance the entire cost of the project with either debt or equity. The fact that a firm can finance a specific project with debt or equity is not directly relevant. If a firm has a target debt/equity ratio of 1, for example, but chooses to finance a particular project with all debt, it will have to raise additional equity later on to maintain its target debt/equity ratio. To take this into account, the firm should always use the target weights in calculating the flotation cost.

Example 14.6 Calculating the Weighted Average Flotation Cost

The Weinstein Corporation has a target capital structure that is 80 percent equity, 20 percent debt. The flotation costs for equity issues are 20 percent of the amount raised; the flotation costs for debt issues are 6 percent. If Weinstein needs $65 million for a new manufacturing facility, what is the true cost once flotation costs are considered?

We first calculate the weighted average flotation cost, f_A:

$$f_A = \frac{E}{V} \times f_E + \frac{D}{V} \times f_D$$

$$= 80\% \times .20 + 20\% \times .06$$

$$= 17.2\%$$

The weighted average flotation cost is thus 17.2 percent. The project cost is $65 million when we ignore flotation costs. If we include them, then the true cost is $65/(1 - f_A) = \$65/.828 = \$78.5$ million, again illustrating that flotation costs can be a considerable expense. ∎

Flotation Costs and NPV

To illustrate how flotation costs can be included in an NPV analysis, suppose the Tripleday Printing Company is currently at its target debt/equity ratio of 100 percent. It is considering building a new $500,000 printing plant in Kansas. This new plant is expected to generate aftertax cash flows of $73,150 per year forever. There are two financing options:

1. A $500,000 new issue of common stock. The issuance costs of the new common stock would be about 10 percent of the amount raised. The required return on the company's new equity is 20 percent.
2. A $500,000 issue of 30-year bonds. The issuance costs of the new debt would be 2 percent of the proceeds. The company can raise new debt at 10 percent.

What is the NPV of the new printing plant?

To begin, since printing is the company's main line of business, we will use the company's weighted average cost of capital to value the new printing plant:

$$\text{WACC} = \frac{E}{V} \times R_E + \frac{D}{V} \times R_D \times (1 - T_C)$$

$$= .50 \times 20\% + .50 \times 10\% \times (1 - .34)$$

$$= 13.3\%$$

Since the cash flows are $73,150 per year forever, the PV of the cash flows at 13.3 percent per year is:

$$PV = \frac{\$73,150}{.133} = \$550,000$$

If we ignore flotation costs, the NPV is:

$$NPV = \$550,000 - 500,000 = \$50,000$$

The project generates an NPV that is greater than zero, so it should be accepted.

What about financing arrangements and issue costs? Since new financing must be raised, the flotation costs are relevant. From the information given above, we know that the flotation costs are 2 percent for debt and 10 percent for equity. Since Tripleday uses equal amounts of debt and equity, the weighted average flotation cost, f_A, is:

$$f_A = \frac{E}{V} \times f_E + \frac{D}{V} \times f_D$$

$$= .50 \times 10\% + .50 \times 2\%$$

$$= 6\%$$

Remember that the fact that Tripleday can finance the project with all debt or equity is irrelevant. Since Tripleday needs $500,000 to fund the new plant, the true cost, once we include flotation costs, is $500,000/(1 - f_A) = \$500,000/.94 = \$531,915$. Since the PV of the cash flows is $550,000, the plant has an NPV of $550,000 - 531,915 = \$18,085$, so it is still a good investment. However, its return is lower than we initially might have thought.

⌐ CONCEPT QUESTIONS

14.6a What are flotation costs?

14.6b How are flotation costs included in an NPV analysis?

14.7 | SUMMARY AND CONCLUSIONS

This chapter discussed cost of capital. The most important concept is the weighted average cost of capital (WACC), which we interpreted as the required rate of return on the overall firm. It is also the discount rate appropriate for cash flows that are similar in risk to the overall firm. We described how the WACC can be calculated, and we illustrated how it can be used in certain types of analyses.

We also pointed out situations in which it is inappropriate to use the WACC as the discount rate. To handle such cases, we described some alternative approaches to developing discount rates such as the pure play approach. We also discussed how the flotation costs associated with raising new capital can be included in an NPV analysis.

Key Terms

Chapter Review Problems and Self-Test

14.1   Calculating the Cost of Equity   Suppose that stock in Boone
Corporation has a beta of .90. The market risk premium is 7 percent,
and the risk-free rate is 8 percent. Boone's last dividend was $1.80 per
share, and the dividend is expected to grow at 7 percent indefinitely.
The stock currently sells for $25. What is Boone's cost of equity capital?

14.2   Calculating the WACC   In addition to the information in the
previous problem, suppose Boone has a target debt/equity ratio of
50 percent. Its cost of debt is 8 percent, before taxes. If the tax rate is
34 percent, what is the WACC?

14.3   Flotation Costs   Suppose that in the previous problem Boone is
seeking $40 million for a new project. The necessary funds will have
to be raised externally. Boone's flotation costs for selling debt and
equity are 3 percent and 12 percent, respectively. If flotation costs are
considered, what is the true cost of the new project?

Answers to Self-Test Problems

14.1   We start off with the SML approach. Based on the information given,
the expected return on Boone's common stock is:

$$R_E = R_f + \beta_E \times [R_M - R_f]$$

$$= 8\% + .9 \times 7\%$$

$$= 14.3\%$$

We now use the dividend growth model. The projected dividend is
$D_0 \times (1 + g) = \$1.80 \times (1.07) = \$1.926$, so the expected return
using this approach is:

$$R_E = D_1/P_0 + g$$

$$= \$1.926/25 + .07$$

$$= 14.704\%$$

Since these two estimates, 14.3 percent and 14.7 percent, are fairly
close, we will average them. Boone's cost of equity is approximately
14.5 percent.

14.2 Since the target debt/equity ratio is .50, Boone uses $.50 in debt for every $1.00 in equity. In other words, Boone's target capital structure is 1/3 debt and 2/3 equity. The WACC is thus:

$$\text{WACC} = \frac{E}{V} \times R_E + \frac{D}{V} \times R_D \times (1 - T_C)$$

$$= 2/3 \times 14.5\% + 1/3 \times 8\% \times (1 - .34)$$

$$= 11.427\%$$

14.3 Since Boone uses both debt and equity to finance its operations, we first need the weighted average flotation cost. As in the previous problem, the percentage of equity financing is 2/3, so the weighted average cost is:

$$f_A = \frac{E}{V} \times f_E + \frac{D}{V} \times f_D$$

$$= 2/3 \times 12\% + 1/3 \times 3\%$$

$$= 9\%$$

If Boone needs $40 million after flotation costs, then the true cost of the project is $40/(1 - f_A) = $40/.91 = $43.96 million.

Questions and Problems

1. **Calculating Cost of Equity** Stock in General Diversified Industries (GDI) has a beta of .80. The market risk premium is 8.6 percent, and the risk-free rate is 7.5 percent. GDI's last dividend was $4 per share, and the dividend is expected to grow at 8 percent indefinitely. The stock currently sells for $60 per share. What is GDI's cost of equity capital?

2. **Calculating Cost of Debt** Suppose Advanced Basic Enterprises (ABE) issued a 30-year, 6 percent bond five years ago. The bond is currently selling for 104 percent of its face value, or $1,040.
   a. What is ABE's pretax cost of debt?
   b. What is ABE's aftertax cost of debt? (Assume a 34 percent tax rate.)
   c. Which is more relevant, the pretax or the aftertax cost of debt? Why?

3. **Calculating WACC** The Proact Property Co. has a target capital structure of 45 percent debt, 55 percent equity. Its cost of equity is 18 percent, and its cost of debt is 9 percent. If the relevant tax rate is 34 percent, what is Proact's WACC?

4. **Taxes and WACC** The Ketcher Kennel Co. has a target debt/equity ratio of .40. Its cost of equity is 24 percent, and its cost of debt is 14 percent.
   a. What is Ketcher's unadjusted WACC?
   b. What is Ketcher's WACC assuming a tax rate of 39 percent?
   c. Which is more relevant, the WACC in part *a* or the WACC in part *b*? Why?

5.   SML and WACC   Stock in the U3 Corporation has a beta of 1.4. The market risk premium is 8.5 percent, and the risk-free rate is 6 percent. U3 has a target debt/equity ratio of 50 percent. Its cost of debt is 12 percent, before taxes. If the tax rate is 34 percent, what is the WACC?

6.   Finding Target Weights   You know that the Heisenberg Corporation's overall weighted average cost of capital is 14 percent and that Heisenberg's tax rate is 34 percent. Furthermore, Heisenberg's cost of equity is 20 percent and its cost of debt is 9 percent. What is Heisenberg's target debt/equity ratio?

7.   Capital Costs   Tom O'Bedlam, president of Bedlam Enterprises, is trying to determine Bedlam's cost of debt and cost of equity. He's not having an easy time of it.

a. First, the stock currently sells for $50 per share, and the dividend per share will probably be about $5. Tom argues, "It will cost us $5 per share to use the stockholders' money this year, so the cost of equity is equal to 10 percent ($5/$50)." What is wrong with this conclusion?

b. Second, based on the most recent financial statements, Bedlam's total liabilities are $8 million. Bedlam's total interest bill will run approximately $1 million for the coming year. Tom therefore reasons, "We owe $8 million, and we will pay $1 million interest. Our cost of debt is obviously $1 million/$8 million = 12.5%." What is wrong with this conclusion?

c. Third, based on his analysis, Tom is recommending that Bedlam increase its use of equity because "Debt costs 12.5 percent, but equity only costs 10 percent, so equity is cheaper." Ignoring all the other problems, what do you think about the conclusion that the cost of equity is less than the cost of debt?

8.   Book Value versus Market Value   The Agarwall Corporation has 3.2 million shares of stock outstanding. The most recent price per share is $46. The book value per share is $10. Agarwall also has two bond issues outstanding. The first issue has a face value of $25 million, a 10 percent coupon, and sells for 96 percent of its face value. The second issue has a face value of $14 million, an 8 percent coupon, and sells for 90 percent of its face value. The first issue matures in 10 years, the second in 16 years.

a. What are Agarwall's capital structure weights on a book value basis?

b. What are Agarwall's capital structure weights on a market value basis?

c. Which is more relevant, the book or market value weights? Why?

9.   SML and NPV   Both Dow Chemical Company, a large natural gas user, and Superior Oil, a major natural gas producer, are thinking of investing in natural gas wells near Pittsburgh. Both are all-equity companies. The well Dow is thinking of investing in is located north of Pittsburgh, while Superior Oil's would be south of Pittsburgh; otherwise the projects are identical. Both companies have analyzed their respective investments, which would involve a negative cash flow now and positive expected cash flows in the future. These cash flows would be the same for both firms. No debt would be used to finance the projects. Both companies estimate that their project would have a

net present value of $1 million at an 18 percent discount rate and a −$1.1 million NPV at a 22 percent discount rate. Dow has a beta of 1.25, and Superior Oil has a beta of 0.75. The expected risk premium on the market is 8 percent, and risk-free bonds are yielding 12 percent. Should either company proceed? Should both? Why?

10. **SML Return versus WACC**   An all-equity firm is considering the following projects:

Project	Beta	Expected Return (%)
A	0.5	12
B	0.8	13
C	1.2	18
D	1.6	19

The Treasury bill rate is 8 percent, and the expected market risk premium is 7 percent.

a. Which projects have a higher expected return than the firm's 15 percent cost of capital?

b. Which projects should be accepted?

c. Which projects would be accepted or rejected incorrectly on the basis of the firm's cost of capital as a hurdle rate?

11. **WACC**   The Gell-Mann Corporation manufactures very small particles for research purposes. Gell-Mann's debt/equity ratio is .50. Its WACC is 16 percent, and its tax rate is 39 percent.

a. Assuming that Gell-Mann's cost of equity is 22 percent, what is its pretax cost of debt?

b. Assuming that Gell-Mann can sell debt with an interest rate of 11 percent, what is its cost of equity?

12. **WACC and Preferred Stock**   Appalachia Power has a target capital structure of 35 percent equity, 10 percent preferred stock, and 55 percent debt. You have estimated that based on current market conditions, the costs of these components are 20 percent, 10 percent, and 12 percent, respectively.

a. What is Appalachia's WACC? Assume a 34 percent tax rate.

b. The company president has approached you about Appalachia's capital structure. He wants to know why Appalachia doesn't use more preferred stock since, based on your estimates, preferred stock is cheaper than debt. What would you say?

13. **Market Values and WACC**   Banquo's Banquet Supply currently has 4 million shares of stock outstanding. The stock sells for $80 per share. The firm's debt is publicly traded and was recently quoted at 86 percent of face value. It has a total face value of $15 million, and it is currently priced to yield 9 percent. The risk-free rate is 8 percent, and the market risk premium is 8 percent. You've estimated that Banquo has a beta of 1.4. If the corporate tax rate is 34 percent, what is Banquo's WACC?

14. **Calculating Cost of Preferred Stock**   On May 11, 1990, Chase Manhattan had an issue of preferred stock that traded for $80 per

share. If the face value of the issue is $100 per share and the dividend is $7.60, what is Chase Manhattan's cost of preferred stock?

15. WACC and NPV   A firm is considering a project that will result in initial cash savings of $6 million at the end of the first year, and these savings will grow at the rate of 4 percent per year indefinitely. The firm has a debt/equity ratio of 5.0, a cost of equity of 20 percent, and an aftertax cost of debt of 12 percent. The cost-saving proposal is closely related to the firm's core business, so it is viewed as having the same risks as the overall firm. Under what circumstances should the firm take on the project?

16. Calculating Flotation Costs   Crachit's Rachets needs $600,000 for a new storage facility. Crachit's target capital structure is 60 percent equity, 40 percent debt. The flotation cost for new equity is 12 percent, but the flotation cost for debt is only 3 percent. Bob Crachit, the CFO, has decided to fund the new facility by borrowing the money since the flotation cost is less and the needed amount is relatively small.
   a. What do you think about the rationale behind borrowing the entire amount?
   b. What is Crachit's weighted average flotation cost?
   c. What is the true cost of the storage facility if flotation costs are included?

17. Calculating WACC   Calculate the weighted average cost of capital for the Peach Computer Company, using the following information: The company has $10 million of debt outstanding at book value. The debt is trading in the market at 90 percent of book value. The yield to maturity at current market prices is 12 percent. The 1 million shares of Peach stock are selling at $20 each. The cost of equity is 19 percent, and the tax rate is 34 percent.

18. Flotation Costs and NPV   The Pipe Dream Corporation manufactures luxury plumbing supplies. It is currently at its target debt/equity ratio of .40. It is considering building a new $15 million manufacturing facility. This new plant is expected to generate aftertax cash flows of $3 million per year forever. There are two financing options:

   1. A new issue of common stock. The flotation costs of the new common stock would be about 12 percent of the amount raised. The required return on the company's new equity is 20 percent.
   2. A new issue of 30-year bonds. The flotation costs of the new debt would be 4 percent of the proceeds. The company can raise new debt at 10 percent.

   What is the NPV of the new plant? Assume a 34 percent tax rate.

19. Tax Shields   Recently, legislation has been proposed that would limit the deductibility of interest paid on so-called junk bonds when the bonds were issued to pay for the takeover of a corporation by another group (such bonds generally have relatively high coupon rates). What do you think is the reasoning behind the proposal?

20.   **Flotation Costs and NPV**   The National Electric Company is contemplating a $20 million expansion project in its power systems division. It has forecast aftertax cash flows for the project of $8 million per year in perpetuity. The cost of debt capital for National Electric is 10 percent, and its cost of equity capital is 20 percent. The tax rate is 34 percent. Mr. Thomas Edison, the company's chief financial officer, has come up with two financing options:

1.   A $20 million issue of 10-year debt at 10 percent interest. The issue costs would be 1 percent of the amount raised.
2.   A $20 million issue of common stock. The issue costs of the common stock would be 15 percent of the amount raised.

The target debt/equity ratio of National Electric is 2. The expansion project will have about the same risk as the existing business.

Mr. Edison has advised the company to go ahead with the new project and to use debt because debt is cheaper and the issue cost will be less with debt.

a. Is Mr. Edison correct?
b. What is the NPV of the new project?

21.   **Capital Structure Weights and WACC**   The Value Curve Company has compiled the following information on its financing costs:

Type of Financing	Book Value	Market Value	Before-Tax Cost
Long-term debt	$ 5,000,000	$ 2,000,000	10%
Short-term debt	5,000,000	5,000,000	8
Common stock	10,000,000	13,000,000	15
	$20,000,000	$20,000,000	

The Value Curve Company is in a 34 percent tax bracket and has a target debt/equity ratio of 100 percent. It wants to move its short-term debt to about the same level as its long-term debt in market value terms.

a. Calculate the weighted average cost of capital for the Value Curve Company using (*i*) book value weights, (*ii*) market value weights, and (*iii*) target weights.
b. Explain the difference in the results obtained in part *a*. What are the correct weights to use in the weighted average cost of capital?

22.   **WACC and Short-Term Debt**   This is a challenge problem. In the previous problem, suppose that the short-term debt was mostly accounts payable, that is, money owed to suppliers. Since these debts arise in the ordinary course of business, management feels that the pretax cost of capital for short-term debt is simply equal to the WACC. Using the target weights, what is Value Curve's WACC in this case?

Suggested Readings

The following article contains an excellent discussion of some of the subtleties of using the WACC for project evaluation:

Miles, J., and R. Ezzel. "The Weighted Average Cost of Capital, Perfect Capital Markets and Project Life: A Clarification." *Journal of Financial and Quantitative Analysis* 15, September 1980.

For a good discussion on how to use the SML in project evaluation, see:

Weston, J. F. "Investment Decisions Using the Capital Asset Pricing Model." *Financial Management,* Spring 1973.

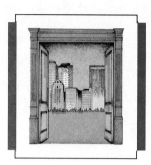

Chapter 15

Financial Leverage and Capital Structure Policy

Thus far, we have taken the firm's capital structure as given. Debt/ equity ratios don't just drop on firms from the sky, of course, so now it's time to wonder where they do come from. Going back to Chapter 1, we call decisions about a firm's debt/equity ratio *capital structure decisions.*[1]

For the most part, a firm can choose any capital structure that it wants. If management so desired, a firm could issue some bonds and use the proceeds to buy back some stock, thereby increasing the debt/equity ratio. Alternatively, it could issue stock and use the money to pay off some debt, thereby reducing the debt/equity ratio. Activities, such as these, that alter the firm's existing capital structure are called capital *restructurings.* In general, such restructurings take place whenever the firm substitutes one capital structure for another while leaving the firm's assets unchanged.

Since the assets of a firm are not directly affected by a capital restructuring, we can examine the firm's capital structure decision separately from its other activities. This means that a firm can consider capital restructuring decisions in isolation from its investment decisions. In this chapter then, we will ignore investment decisions and focus on the long-term financing, or capital structure, question.

What we will see in this chapter is that capital structure decisions can have important implications for the value of the firm and its cost of capital. We will also find that important elements of the capital structure decision are easy to identify, but precise measures of these elements are generally not obtainable. As a result, we are only able to give an incomplete answer to the

---

[1]It is conventional to refer to decisions regarding debt and equity as *capital structure decisions.* However, the term *financial structure* would be more accurate, and we use the terms interchangeably.

question of what the best capital structure might be for a particular firm at a particular time.

THE CAPITAL STRUCTURE QUESTION | 15.1

How should a firm go about choosing its debt/equity ratio? Here, as always, we assume that the guiding principle is to choose the course of action that maximizes the value of a share of stock. As we discuss next, however, when it comes to capital structure decisions, this is essentially the same thing as maximizing the value of the whole firm, and, for convenience, we will tend to frame our discussion in terms of firm value.

Firm Value and Stock Value: An Example

The following example illustrates that the capital structure that maximizes the value of the firm is the one that financial managers should choose for the shareholders, so there is no conflict in our goals. To begin, suppose the market value of the J. J. Sprint Company is $1,000. The company currently has no debt, and J. J. Sprint's 100 shares sell for $10 each. Further suppose that J. J. Sprint restructures itself by borrowing $500 and then paying out the proceeds to shareholders as an extra dividend of $500/100 = $5 per share.

This restructuring will change the capital structure of the firm with no direct effect on the firm's assets. The immediate effect will be to increase debt and decrease equity. However, what will be the final impact of the restructuring? Table 15.1 illustrates three possible outcomes in addition to the original no-debt case. Notice that, in Scenario II, the value of the firm is unchanged at $1,000. In Scenario I, firm value rises to $1,250; it falls by $250, to $750, in Scenario III. We haven't yet said what might lead to these changes. For now, we just take them as possible outcomes to illustrate a point.

Since our goal is to benefit the shareholders, we next examine, in Table 15.2, the net payoffs to the shareholders in these scenarios. We see that, if the value of the firm stays the same, then shareholders will experience a capital loss that will exactly offset the extra dividend. This is Scenario II. In Scenario I, the value of the firm increases to $1,250 and the shareholders come out ahead by $250. In other words, the restructuring has an NPV of $250 in this scenario. The NPV in Scenario III is −$250.

The key observation to make here is that the change in the value of the firm is the same as the net effect on the stockholders. Financial managers can therefore try to find the capital structure that maximizes the value of the firm. Put another way, the NPV rule applies to capital structure decisions, and the change

| | No debt | Debt plus Dividend | | |
		I	II	III
Debt	$ 0	$ 500	$ 500	$500
Equity	1,000	750	500	250
Firm value	$1,000	$1,250	$1,000	$750

Table 15.1

Possible firm values: No debt versus debt plus dividend

Table 15.2

Possible payoffs to shareholders: Debt plus dividend

	Debt plus Dividend		
	I	II	III
Equity value reduction	−$250	−$500	−$750
Dividends	500	500	500
Net effect	+$250	$ 0	−$250

in the value of the overall firm is the NPV of a restructuring. Thus, J. J. Sprint should borrow $500 if it expects Scenario I. The crucial question in determining a firm's capital structure is, of course, which scenario is likely to occur.

Capital Structure and the Cost of Capital

In Chapter 14, we discussed the concept of the firm's weighted average cost of capital (WACC). You may recall that the WACC tells us that the firm's overall cost of capital is a weighted average of the costs of the various components of the firm's capital structure. When we described the WACC, we took the firm's capital structure as given. Thus, one important issue that we will want to explore in this chapter is what happens to the cost of capital when we vary the amount of debt financing or the debt/equity ratio.

A primary reason for studying the WACC is that the value of the firm is maximized when the WACC is minimized. To see this, recall that the WACC is the discount rate that is appropriate for the firm's overall cash flows. Since values and discount rates move in opposite directions, minimizing the WACC will maximize the value of the firm's cash flows.

Thus, we will want to choose the firm's capital structure so that the WACC is minimized. For this reason, we will say that one capital structure is better than another if it results in a lower weighted average cost of capital. Further, we say that a particular debt/equity ratio represents the *optimal capital structure* if it results in the lowest possible WACC. This is sometimes called the firm's *target* capital structure as well.

CONCEPT QUESTIONS

15.1a Why should financial managers choose the capital structure that maximizes the value of the firm?

15.1b What is the relationship between the WACC and the value of the firm?

15.1c What is an optimal capital structure?

15.2 | THE EFFECT OF FINANCIAL LEVERAGE

The previous section describes why the capital structure that produces the highest firm value (or the lowest cost of capital) is the one most beneficial to stockholders. In this section, we examine the impact of financial leverage on the payoffs to stockholders. As you may recall, financial leverage refers to the extent to which a firm relies on debt. The more debt financing a firm uses in its capital structure, the more financial leverage it employs.

As we describe, financial leverage can dramatically alter the payoffs to shareholders in the firm. Remarkably, however, financial leverage may not affect the overall cost of capital. If this is true, then a firm's capital structure is irrelevant because changes in capital structure won't affect the value of the firm. We will return to this issue a little later.

The Impact of Financial Leverage

We start by illustrating how financial leverage works. For now, we ignore the impact of taxes. Also, for ease of presentation, we describe the impact of leverage in terms of its effects on earnings per share (EPS) and return on equity (ROE). These are, of course, accounting numbers, and, as such, are not our primary concern. Using cash flows instead of these accounting numbers would lead to precisely the same conclusions, but a little more work would be needed. We discuss the impact on market values in a subsequent section.

Financial Leverage, EPS, and ROE: An Example   The Trans Am Corporation currently has no debt in its capital structure. The CFO, Ms. Morris, is considering a restructuring that would involve issuing debt and using the proceeds to buy back some of the outstanding equity. Table 15.3 presents both the current and proposed capital structures. As shown, the firm's assets have a value of $8 million, and there are 400,000 shares outstanding. Because Trans Am is an all-equity firm, the price per share is $20.

The proposed debt issue would raise $4 million; the interest rate would be 10 percent. Since the stock sells for $20 per share, the $4 million in new debt would be used to purchase $4 million/$20 = 200,000 shares, leaving 200,000. After the restructuring, Trans Am would have a capital structure that was 50 percent debt, so the debt/equity ratio would be 1. Notice that, for now, we assume that the stock price will remain at $20.

To investigate the impact of the proposed restructuring, Ms. Morris has prepared Table 15.4, which compares the firm's current capital structure to the proposed capital structure under three scenarios. The scenarios reflect different assumptions about the firm's EBIT. Under the expected scenario, the EBIT is $1 million. In the recession scenario, EBIT falls to $500,000. In the expansion scenario, it rises to $1.5 million.

To illustrate some of the calculations in Table 15.4, consider the expansion case. EBIT is $1.5 million. With no debt (the current capital structure) and no taxes, net income is also $1.5 million. In this case, there are 400,000

	Current	Proposed
Assets	$8,000,000	$8,000,000
Debt	$ 0	$4,000,000
Equity	$8,000,000	$4,000,000
Debt/equity ratio	0	1
Share price	$20	$20
Shares outstanding	400,000	200,000
Interest rate	10%	10%

Table 15.3

Current and proposed capital structures for the Trans Am Corporation

Table 15.4	*Current Capital Structure: No Debt*		
Capital structure scenarios for the Trans Am Corporation		Recession	Expected	Expansion

	Recession	Expected	Expansion
EBIT	$500,000	$1,000,000	$1,500,000
Interest	0	0	0
Net income	$500,000	$1,000,000	$1,500,000
ROE	6.25%	12.50%	18.75%
EPS	$1.25	$2.50	$3.75

Proposed Capital Structure: Debt = $4 million

	Recession	Expected	Expansion
EBIT	$500,000	$1,000,000	$1,500,000
Interest	400,000	400,000	400,000
Net income	$100,000	$ 600,000	$1,100,000
ROE	2.50%	15.00%	27.50%
EPS	$.50	$3.00	$5.50

shares worth $8 million total. EPS is therefore $1.5 million/400,000 = $3.75 per share. Also, since accounting return on equity (ROE) is net income divided by total equity, ROE is $1.5 million/$8 million = 18.75%.[2]

With $4 million in debt (the proposed capital structure), things are somewhat different. Since the interest rate is 10 percent, the interest bill is $400,000. With EBIT of $1.5 million, interest of $400,000, and no taxes, net income is $1.1 million. Now there are only 200,000 shares worth $4 million total. EPS is therefore $1.1 million/200,000 = $5.5 per share versus the $3.75 per share that we calculated above. Furthermore, ROE is $1.1 million/$4 million = 27.5 percent. This is well above the 18.75 percent we calculated for the current capital structure.

EPS versus EBIT   The impact of leverage is evident when the effect of the restructuring on EPS and ROE is examined. In particular, the variability in both EPS and ROE is much larger under the proposed capital structure. This illustrates how financial leverage acts to magnify gains and losses to shareholders.

In Figure 15.1, we take a closer look at the effect of the proposed restructuring. This figure plots earnings per share (EPS) against earnings before interest and taxes (EBIT) for the current and proposed capital structures. The first line, labeled "No debt," represents the case of no leverage. This line begins at the origin, indicating that EPS would be zero if EBIT were zero. From there, every $400,000 increase in EBIT increases EPS by $1 (because there are 400,000 shares outstanding).

The second line represents the proposed capital structure. Here, EPS is negative if EBIT is zero. This follows because $400,000 of interest must be paid regardless of the firm's profits. Since there are 200,000 shares in this case, the EPS is −$2 per share as shown. Similarly, if EBIT were $400,000, EPS would be exactly zero.

The important thing to notice in Figure 15.1 is that the slope of the line in this second case is steeper. In fact, for every $400,000 increase in EBIT, EPS

---

[2]ROE is discussed in some detail in Chapter 3.

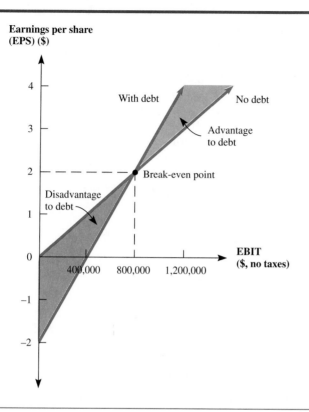

Figure 15.1

Financial leverage. EPS and EBIT for the Trans Am Corporation

rises by $2, so the line is twice as steep. This tells us that EPS is twice as sensitive to changes in EBIT because of the financial leverage employed.

Another observation to make in Figure 15.1 is that the lines intersect. At that point, EPS is exactly the same for both capital structures. To find this point, note that EPS is equal to EBIT/400,000 in the no-debt case. In the with-debt case, EPS is (EBIT − $400,000)/200,000. If we set these equal to each other, EBIT is:

$$\text{EBIT}/400{,}000 = (\text{EBIT} - \$400{,}000)/200{,}000$$

$$\text{EBIT} = 2 \times (\text{EBIT} - \$400{,}000)$$

$$\text{EBIT} = \$800{,}000$$

When EBIT is $800,000, EPS is $2 per share under either capital structure. This is labeled as the break-even point in Figure 15.1. If EBIT is above this level, leverage is beneficial; if it is below this point, it is not.

There is another, more intuitive, way of seeing why the break-even point is $800,000. Notice that, if the firm has no debt and its EBIT is $800,000, its net income is also $800,000. In this case, the ROE is 10 percent. This is precisely the same as the interest rate on the debt, so the firm earns a return that is just sufficient to pay the interest.

Example 15.1   Break-Even EBIT

The MPD Corporation has decided in favor of a capital restructuring. Currently, MPD uses no debt financing. Following the restructuring, however, debt will be $1 million. The interest rate on the debt will be 9 percent. MPD currently has 200,000 shares outstanding, and the price per share is $20. If the restructuring is expected to increase EPS, what is the minimum level for EBIT that MPD's management must be expecting? Ignore taxes in answering.

To answer, we calculate the break-even EBIT. At any EBIT above this, the increased financial leverage will increase EPS, so this will tell us the minimum level for EBIT. Under the old capital structure, EPS is simply EBIT/200,000. Under the new capital structure, the interest expense will be $1 million × .09 = $90,000. Furthermore, with the $1 million proceeds, MPD will repurchase $1 million/$20 = 50,000 shares of stock, leaving 150,000 outstanding. EPS is thus (EBIT − $90,000)/150,000.

Now that we know how to calculate EPS under both scenarios, we set them equal to each other and solve for the break-even EBIT:

$$\text{EBIT}/200,000 = (\text{EBIT} - \$90,000)/150,000$$
$$\text{EBIT} = (4/3) \times (\text{EBIT} - \$90,000)$$
$$\text{EBIT} = \$360,000$$

Check that, in either case, EPS is $1.80 when EBIT is $360,000. Management at MPD is apparently of the opinion that EPS will exceed $1.80. ∎

Corporate Borrowing and Homemade Leverage

Based on Tables 15.3 and 15.4 and Figure 15.1, Ms. Morris draws the following conclusions:

1. The effect of financial leverage depends on the company's EBIT. When EBIT is relatively high, leverage is beneficial.
2. Under the expected scenario, leverage increases the returns to shareholders, as measured by both ROE and EPS.
3. Shareholders are exposed to more risk under the proposed capital structure since the EPS and ROE are much more sensitive to changes in EBIT in this case.
4. Because of the impact that financial leverage has on both the expected return to stockholders and the riskiness of the stock, capital structure is an important consideration.

The first three of these conclusions are clearly correct. Does the last conclusion necessarily follow? Surprisingly, the answer is no. As we discuss next, the reason is that shareholders can adjust the amount of financial leverage by borrowing and lending on their own. This use of personal borrowing to alter the degree of financial leverage is called **homemade leverage**.

homemade leverage

The use of personal borrowing to change the overall amount of financial leverage to which the individual is exposed.

We will now illustrate that it actually makes no difference whether or not Trans Am adopts the proposed capital structure, because any stockholder who prefers the proposed capital structure can simply create it using homemade leverage. To begin, the first part of Table 15.5 shows what would happen to an investor who buys $2,000 worth of Trans Am stock if the proposed capital structure were adopted. This investor purchases 100 shares of stock. From Table 15.4, EPS will either be $.50, $3, or $5.50, so the total earnings for 100 shares will either be $50, $300, or $550 under the proposed capital structure.

Now, suppose that Trans Am does not adopt the proposed capital structure. In this case, EPS will be $1.25, $2.50, or $3.75. The second part of

Proposed Capital Structure			
	Recession	Expected	Expansion
EPS	$ .50	$ 3.00	$ 5.50
Earnings for 100 shares	50.00	300.00	550.00
Net cost = 100 shares at $20 = $2,000			

Original Capital Structure and Homemade Leverage			
	Recession	Expected	Expansion
EPS	$ 1.25	$ 2.50	$ 3.75
Earnings for 200 shares	250.00	500.00	750.00
Less: Interest on $2,000 at 10%	200.00	200.00	200.00
Net earnings	$ 50.00	$300.00	$550.00
Net cost = 200 shares at $20/share − Amount borrowed = $4,000 − 2,000 = $2,000			

Table 15.5 demonstrates how a stockholder who preferred the payoffs under the proposed structure can create them using personal borrowing. To do this, the stockholder borrows $2,000 at 10 percent on her own. Our investor uses this amount, along with her original $2,000, to buy 200 shares of stock. As shown, the net payoffs are exactly the same as those for the proposed capital structure.

How did we know to borrow $2,000 to create the right payoffs? We are trying to replicate Trans Am's proposed capital structure at the personal level. The proposed capital structure results in a debt/equity ratio of 1. To replicate it at the personal level, the stockholder must borrow enough to create this same debt/equity ratio. Since the stockholder has $2,000 in equity invested, borrowing another $2,000 will create a personal debt/equity ratio of 1.

This example demonstrates that investors can always increase financial leverage themselves to create a different pattern of payoffs. It thus makes no difference whether or not Trans Am chooses the proposed capital structure.

Example 15.2   Unlevering the Stock
In our Trans Am example, suppose that management adopts the proposed capital structure. Further suppose that an investor who owned 100 shares preferred the original capital structure. Show how this investor could "unlever" the stock to recreate the original payoffs.

To create leverage, investors borrow on their own. To undo leverage, investors must loan out money. For Trans Am, the corporation borrowed an amount equal to half its value. The investor can unlever the stock by simply loaning out money in the same proportion. In this case, the investor sells 50 shares for $1,000 total and then loans out the $1,000 at 10 percent. The payoffs are calculated in the table below.

	Recession	Expected	Expansion
EPS (proposed structure)	$ .50	$ 3.00	$ 5.50
Earnings for 50 shares	25.00	150.00	275.00
Plus: Interest on $1,000	100.00	100.00	100.00
Total payoff	$125.00	$250.00	$375.00

These are precisely the payoffs that the investor would have experienced under the original capital structure. ∎

15.2a What is the impact of financial leverage on stockholders?

15.2b What is homemade leverage?

15.2c Why is Trans Am's capital structure irrelevant?

15.3 │ CAPITAL STRUCTURE AND THE COST OF EQUITY CAPITAL

M&M Proposition I

The value of the firm is independent of its capital structure.

We have seen that there is nothing special about corporate borrowing because investors can borrow or lend on their own. As a result, whichever capital structure Trans Am chooses, the stock price will be the same. Trans Am's capital structure is thus irrelevant, at least in the simple world we examined.

Our Trans Am example is based on a famous argument advanced by two Nobel laureates, Franco Modigliani and Merton Miller, whom we will henceforth call M&M. What we illustrated for the Trans Am Company is a special case of **M&M Proposition I.** M&M Proposition I states that it is completely irrelevant how a firm chooses to arrange its finances.

M&M Proposition I: The Pie Model

One way to illustrate M&M Proposition I is to imagine two firms that are identical on the left-hand side of the balance sheet. Their assets and operations are exactly the same. The right-hand sides are different because the two firms finance their operations differently. In this case, we can view the capital structure question in terms of a "pie" model. Why we choose this name is apparent in Figure 15.2. Figure 15.2 gives two possible ways of cutting up this pie between the equity slice, E, and the debt slice, D: 40%–60% and 60%–40%. However, the size of the pie in Figure 15.2 is the same for both firms because the value of the assets is the same. This is precisely what M&M Proposition I states: The size of the pie doesn't depend on how it is sliced.

The Cost of Equity and Financial Leverage: M&M Proposition II

Although changing the capital structure of the firm may not change the firm's *total* value, it does cause important changes in the firm's debt and equity. We now examine what happens to a firm financed with debt and equity when the debt/equity ratio is changed. To simplify our analysis, we will continue to ignore taxes.

M&M Proposition II   In Chapter 14, we saw that, if we ignore taxes, the weighted average cost of capital, WACC, is:

$$\text{WACC} = E/V \times R_E + D/V \times R_D$$

Figure 15.2

Two pie models of capital structure

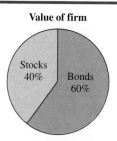

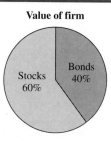

In Their Own Words . . .

Merton H. Miller on Capital Structure — M&M 30 Years Later

How difficult it is to summarize briefly the contribution of these papers was brought home to me very clearly after Franco Modigliani was awarded the Nobel Prize in Economics, in part — but, of course, only in part — for the work in finance. The television camera crews from our local stations in Chicago immediately descended upon me. "We understand," they said, "that you worked with Modigliani some years back in developing these M&M theorems, and we wonder if you could explain them briefly to our television viewers." "How briefly?" I asked. "Oh, take 10 seconds," was the reply.

Ten seconds to explain the work of a lifetime! Ten seconds to describe two carefully reasoned articles, each running to more than 30 printed pages and each with 60 or so long footnotes! When they saw the look of dismay on my face, they said: "You don't have to go into details. Just give us the main points in simple, commonsense terms."

The main point of the cost-of-capital article was, in principle at least, simple enough to make. It said that in an economist's ideal world, the total market value of all the securities issued by a firm would be governed by the earning power and risk of its underlying real assets and would be independent of how the mix of securities issued to finance it was divided between debt instruments and equity capital. Some corporate treasurers might well think that they could enhance total value by increasing the proportion of debt instruments because yields on debt instruments, given their lower risk, are, by and large, substantially below those on equity capital. But, under the ideal conditions assumed, the added risk to the shareholders from issuing more debt will raise required yields on the equity by just enough to offset the seeming gain from use of low-cost debt.

Such a summary would not only have been too long, but it relied on shorthand terms and concepts that are rich in connotations to economists, but hardly so to the general public. I thought, instead, of an analogy that we ourselves had invoked in the original paper. "Think of the firm," I said, "as a gigantic tub of whole milk. The farmer can sell the whole milk as is. Or he can separate out the cream and sell it at a considerably higher price than the whole milk would bring. (Selling cream is the analog of a firm selling low yield and hence high-priced debt securities.) But, of course, what the farmer would have left would be skim milk, with low butter-fat content and that would sell for much less than whole milk. Skim milk corresponds to the levered equity. The M&M proposition says that if there were no costs of separation (and, of course, no government dairy support programs), the cream plus the skim milk would bring the same price as the whole milk."

The television people conferred among themselves for a while. They informed me that it was still too long, too complicated, and too academic. "Have you anything simpler?" they asked. I thought for another way that the M&M proposition is presented which stresses the role of securities as devices for "partitioning" a firm's payoffs among the group of its capital suppliers. "Think of the firm," I said, "as a gigantic pizza, divided into quarters. If now, you cut each quarter in half into eighths, the M&M proposition says that you will have more pieces, but not more pizza."

Once again whispered conversation. This time, they shut the lights off. They folded up their equipment. They thanked me for my cooperation. They said they would get back to me. But I knew that I had somehow lost my chance to start a new career as a packager of economic wisdom for TV viewers in convenient 10-second sound bites. Some have the talent for it; and some just don't.

Merton H. Miller is Robert R. McCormick Distinguished Service Professor at the University of Chicago Graduate School of Business. He is famous for his path-breaking work with Franco Modigliani on corporate capital structure, cost of capital, and dividend policy. He received the Nobel Prize in Economics for his contributions shortly after this essay was prepared.

where $V = E + D$. We also saw that one way of interpreting the WACC is that it is the required return on the firm's overall assets. To remind us of this, we will use the symbol R_A to stand for the WACC and write:

$$R_A = E/V \times R_E + D/V \times R_D$$

If we rearrange this to solve for the cost of equity capital, we see that:

$$R_E = R_A + (R_A - R_D) \times (D/E) \qquad [15.1]$$

Figure 15.3

The cost of equity and the WACC. M&M Propositions I and II with no taxes

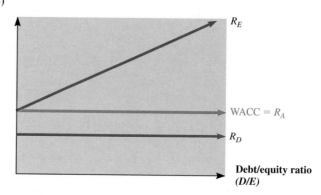

Cost of capital (%)

R_E

WACC = R_A

R_D

Debt/equity ratio (D/E)

$R_E = R_A + (R_A - R_D) \times (D/E)$ by Proposition II

$\text{WACC} = \left(\dfrac{E}{V}\right) \times R_E + \left(\dfrac{D}{V}\right) \times R_D$

$V = D + E$

M&M Proposition II

A firm's cost of equity capital is a positive linear function of its capital structure.

This is the famous **M&M Proposition II,** which tells us that the cost of equity depends on three things: the required rate of return on the firm's assets, R_A, the firm's cost of debt, R_D, and the firm's debt/equity ratio, D/E.

Figure 15.3 summarizes our discussion thus far by plotting the cost of equity capital, R_E, against the debt/equity ratio. As shown, M&M Proposition II indicates that the cost of equity, R_E, is given by a straight line with a slope of $(R_A - R_D)$. The y-intercept corresponds to a firm with a debt/equity ratio of zero, so $R_A = R_E$ in that case. Figure 15.3 shows that, as the firm raises its debt/equity ratio, the increase in leverage raises the risk of the equity and therefore the required return or cost of equity (R_E).

Notice in Figure 15.3 that the WACC doesn't depend on the debt/equity ratio; it's the same no matter what the debt/equity ratio is. This is another way of stating M&M Proposition I: The firm's overall cost of capital is unaffected by its capital structure. As illustrated, the fact that the cost of debt is lower than the cost of equity is exactly offset by the increase in the cost of equity from borrowing. In other words, the change in the capital structure weights (E/V and D/V) is exactly offset by the change in the cost of equity (R_E), so the WACC stays the same.

Example 15.3 The Cost of Equity Capital

The Ricardo Corporation has a weighted average cost of capital (unadjusted) of 12 percent. It can borrow at 8 percent. Assuming that Ricardo has a target capital structure of 80 percent equity and 20 percent debt, what is its cost of equity? What is the cost of equity if the target capital structure is 50 percent equity? Calculate the unadjusted WACC using your answers to verify that it is the same.

According to M&M Proposition II, the cost of equity, R_E, is:

$$R_E = R_A + (R_A - R_D) \times (D/E)$$

In the first case, the debt/equity ratio is $.2/.8 = .25$, so the cost of the equity is:

$$R_E = 12\% + (12\% - 8\%) \times (.25)$$

$$= 13\%$$

In the second case, check that the debt/equity ratio is 1.0, so the cost of equity is 16 percent.

We can now calculate the unadjusted WACC assuming that the percentage of equity financing is 80 percent and the cost of equity is 13 percent:

$$\text{WACC} = E/V \times R_E + D/V \times R_D$$

$$= .80 \times 13\% + .20 \times 8\%$$

$$= 12\%$$

In the second case, the percentage of equity financing is 50 percent and the cost of equity is 16 percent. The WACC is:

$$\text{WACC} = E/V \times R_E + D/V \times R_D$$

$$= .50 \times 16\% + .50 \times 8\%$$

$$= 12\%$$

As we calculated, the WACC is 12 percent in both cases. ∎

Business and Financial Risk

M&M Proposition II shows that the firm's cost of equity can be broken down into two components. The first component, R_A, is the required return on the firm's assets overall, and it depends on the nature of the firm's operating activities. The risk inherent in a firm's operations is called the **business risk** of the firm's equity. Referring back to Chapter 12, this business risk depends on the systematic risk of the firm's assets. The greater a firm's business risk, the greater R_A will be, and, all other things the same, the greater will be its cost of equity.

The second component in the cost of equity, $(R_A - R_D) \times D/E$, is determined by the firm's financial structure. For an all-equity firm, this component is zero. As the firm begins to rely on debt financing, the required return on equity rises. This occurs because the debt financing increases the risks born by the stockholders. This extra risk that arises from the use of debt financing is called the **financial risk** of the firm's equity.

The total systematic risk of the firm's equity thus has two parts: business risk and financial risk. The first part (the business risk) depends on the firm's assets and operations and is not affected by capital structure. Given the firm's business risk (and its cost of debt), the second part (the financial risk) is completely determined by financial policy. As we have illustrated, the firm's cost of equity rises when it increases its use of financial leverage because the financial risk of the equity increases while the business risk remains the same.

business risk
The equity risk that comes from the nature of the firm's operating activities.

financial risk
The equity risk that comes from the financial policy (i.e., capital structure) of the firm.

15.3a What does M&M Proposition I state?
15.3b What are the three determinants of a firm's cost of equity?
15.3c The total systematic risk of a firm's equity has two parts. What are they?

15.4 | M&M PROPOSITIONS I AND II WITH CORPORATE TAXES

Debt has two distinguishing features that we have not taken into proper account. First, as we have mentioned in a number of places, interest paid on debt is tax deductible. This is good for the firm, and it may be an added benefit to debt financing. Second, failure to meet debt obligations can result in bankruptcy. This is not good for the firm, and it may be an added cost of debt financing. Since we haven't explicitly considered either of these two features of debt, we may get a different answer about capital structure once we do. Accordingly, we consider taxes in this section and bankruptcy in the next one.

We can start by considering what happens to M&M Propositions I and II when we consider the effect of corporate taxes. To do this, we will examine two firms, Firm U (unlevered) and Firm L (levered). These two firms are identical on the left-hand side of the balance sheet, so their assets and operations are the same.

We assume that EBIT is expected to be $1,000 every year forever for both firms. The difference between them is that Firm L has issued $1,000 worth of perpetual bonds on which it pays 8 percent interest each year. The interest bill is thus $.08 \times \$1,000 = \$80$ every year forever. Also, we assume that the corporate tax rate is 30 percent.

For our two firms, U and L, we can now calculate the following:

	Firm U	Firm L
EBIT	$1,000	$1,000
Interest	0	80
Taxable income	$1,000	$ 920
Taxes (30%)	300	276
Net income	$ 700	$ 644

The Interest Tax Shield

To simplify things, we will assume that depreciation is zero. We will also assume that capital spending is zero and that there are no additions to NWC. In this case, cash flow from assets is simply equal to EBIT − Taxes. For Firms U and L we thus have:

Cash Flow from Assets	Firm U	Firm L
EBIT	$1,000	$1,000
− Taxes	300	276
Total	700	$ 724

We immediately see that capital structure is now having some effect because the cash flows from U and L are not the same even though the two firms have identical assets.

To see what's going on, we can compute the cash flow to stockholders and bondholders.

Cash Flow	Firm U	Firm L
To stockholders	$700	$644
To bondholders	0	80
Total	$700	$724

What we are seeing is that the total cash flow to L is $24 more. This occurs because L's tax bill (which is a cash outflow) is $24 less. The fact that interest is deductible for tax purposes has generated a tax saving equal to the interest payment ($80) multiplied by the corporate tax rate (30 percent): $80 \times .30 = $24. We call this tax saving the **interest tax shield.**

interest tax shield
The tax saving attained by a firm from interest expense.

Taxes and M&M Proposition I

Since the debt is perpetual, the same $24 shield will be generated every year forever. The aftertax cash flow to L will thus be the same $700 that U earns plus the $24 tax shield. Since L's cash flow is always $24 greater, Firm L is worth more than Firm U by the value of this $24 perpetuity.

Because the tax shield is generated by paying interest, it has the same risk as the debt, and 8 percent (the cost of debt) is therefore the appropriate discount rate. The value of the tax shield is thus:

$$PV = \frac{\$24}{.08} = \frac{.30 \times \$1,000 \times .08}{.08} = .30(\$1,000) = \$300$$

As our example illustrates, the present value of the interest tax shield can be written as:

$$\text{Present value of the interest tax shield} = (T_C \times R_D \times D)/R_D \qquad [15.2]$$

$$= T_C \times D$$

We have now come up with another famous result, M&M Proposition I with corporate taxes. We have seen that the value of Firm L, V_L, exceeds the value of Firm U, V_U, by the present value of the interest tax shield, $T_C \times D$. M&M Proposition I with taxes therefore states that:

$$V_L = V_U + T_C \times D \qquad [15.3]$$

The effect of borrowing in this case is illustrated in Figure 15.4. We have plotted the value of the levered firm, V_L, against the amount of debt, D. M&M Proposition I with corporate taxes implies that the relationship is given by a straight line with a slope of T_C and a y-intercept of V_U.

In Figure 15.4, we have also drawn a horizontal line representing V_U. As indicated, the distance between the two lines is $T_C \times D$, the present value of the tax shield.

Suppose that the cost of capital for Firm U is 10 percent. We will call this the **unlevered cost of capital,** and we will use the symbol R_U to represent it. We can think of R_U as the cost of capital that the firm would have if it had no debt. Firm U's cash flow is $700 every year forever, and, since U has no debt,

unlevered cost of capital
The cost of capital of a firm that has no debt.

Figure 15.4

M&M Proposition I with taxes

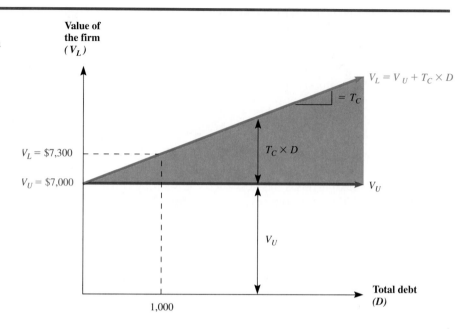

The value of the firm increases as total debt increases because of the interest tax shield. This is the basis of M&M Proposition I with taxes.

the appropriate discount rate is $R_U = 10\%$. The value of the unlevered firm, V_U, is simply:

$$V_U = \frac{\text{EBIT} \times (1 - T_C)}{R_U}$$

$$= \frac{\$700}{.10}$$

$$= \$7,000$$

The value of the levered firm, V_L, is:

$$V_L = V_U + T_C \times D$$

$$= \$7,000 + .30 \times \$1,000$$

$$= \$7,300$$

As Figure 15.4 indicates, the value of the firm goes up by $.30 for every $1 in debt. In other words, the NPV *per dollar* of debt is $.30. It is difficult to imagine why any corporation would not borrow to the absolute maximum under these circumstances.

The result of our analysis in this section is that, once we include taxes, capital structure definitely matters. However, we immediately reach the illogical conclusion that the optimal capital structure is 100 percent debt.

Taxes, the WACC, and Proposition II

The conclusion that the best capital structure is 100 percent debt also can be seen by examining the weighted average cost of capital. From our previous chapter, we know that, once we consider the effect of taxes, the WACC is:

$$\text{WACC} = E/V \times R_E + D/V \times R_D \times (1 - T_C)$$

To calculate this WACC, we need to know the cost of equity. M&M Proposition II with corporate taxes states that the cost of equity is:

$$R_E = R_U + (R_U - R_D) \times (D/E) \times (1 - T_C) \qquad [15.4]$$

To illustrate, we saw a moment ago that Firm L is worth $7,300 total. Since the debt is worth $1,000, the equity must be worth $7,300 - 1,000 = $6,300. For Firm L, the cost of equity is thus:

$$R_E = .10 + (.10 - .08) \times (\$1,000/\$6,300) \times (1 - .30)$$

$$= 10.22\%$$

The weighted average cost of capital is:

$$\text{WACC} = \$6,300/\$7,300 \times 10.22\% + \$1,000/\$7,300 \times 8\% \times (1 - .30)$$

$$= 9.6\%$$

Without debt, the WACC is 10 percent, and, with debt, it is 9.6 percent. Therefore, the firm is better off with debt.

Figure 15.5 summarizes our discussion concerning the relationship between the cost of equity, the aftertax cost of debt, and the weighted average cost of capital. For reference, we have included R_U, the unlevered cost of capital. In Figure 15.5, we have the debt/equity ratio on the horizontal axis. Notice how the WACC declines as the debt/equity ratio grows. This illustrates again that the more debt the firm uses, the lower is its WACC. Table 15.6 summarizes the key results for future reference.

Example 15.4   The Cost of Equity and the Value of the Firm

This is a comprehensive example that illustrates most of the points we have discussed thus far. You are given the following information for the Format Co.:

$$\text{EBIT} = \$151.52$$

$$T_C = .34$$

$$D = \$500$$

$$R_U = .20$$

Figure 15.5

The cost of equity and the WACC. M&M Propositions I and II with taxes

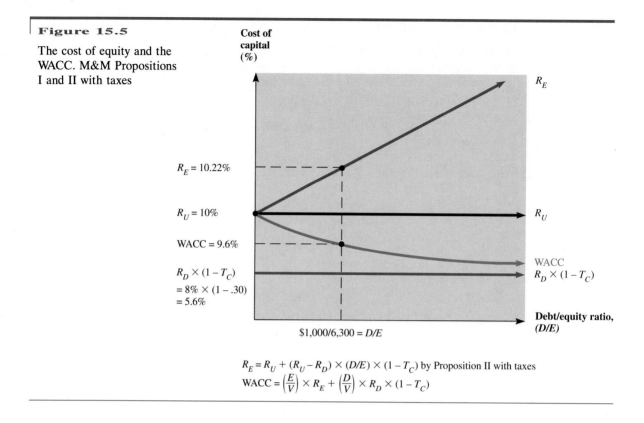

$R_E = R_U + (R_U - R_D) \times (D/E) \times (1 - T_C)$ by Proposition II with taxes

$WACC = \left(\dfrac{E}{V}\right) \times R_E + \left(\dfrac{D}{V}\right) \times R_D \times (1 - T_C)$

The cost of debt capital is 10 percent. What is the value of Format's equity? What is the cost of equity capital for Format? What is the WACC?

This one's easier than it looks. Remember that all the cash flows are perpetuities. The value of the firm if it had no debt, V_U, is:

$$V_U = \frac{EBIT - Taxes}{R_U} = \frac{EBIT \times (1 - T_C)}{R_U}$$

$$= \frac{\$100}{.20}$$

$$= \$500$$

From M&M Proposition I with taxes, we know that the value of the firm with debt is:

$$V_L = V_U + T_C \times D$$

$$= \$500 + .34 \times \$500$$

$$= \$670$$

I. The No-Tax Case

A. Proposition I: The value of the firm levered (V_L) is equal to the value of the firm unlevered (V_U):

$$V_L = V_U$$

Implications of Proposition I:

1. A firm's capital structure is irrelevant.
2. A firm's weighted average cost of capital (WACC) is the same no matter what mixture of debt and equity is used to finance the firm.

B. Proposition II: The cost of equity, R_E, is:

$$R_E = R_A + (R_A - R_D) \times D/E$$

where R_A is the WACC, R_D is the cost of debt, and D/E is the debt/equity ratio. Implications of Proposition II:

1. The cost of equity rises as the firm increases its use of debt financing.
2. The risk of the equity depends on two things: the riskiness of the firm's operations (*business risk*) and the degree of financial leverage (*financial risk*).

II. The Tax Case

A. Proposition I with taxes: The value of the firm levered (V_L) is equal to the value of the firm unlevered (V_U) plus the present value of the interest tax shield:

$$V_L = V_U + T_C \times D$$

where T_C is the corporate tax rate and D is the amount of debt. Implications of Proposition I:

1. Debt financing is highly advantageous, and, in the extreme, a firm's optimal capital structure is 100 percent debt.
2. A firm's weighted average cost of capital (WACC) decreases as the firm relies more heavily on debt financing.

B. Proposition II with taxes: The cost of equity, R_E, is:

$$R_E = R_U + (R_U - R_D) \times D/E \times (1 - T_C)$$

where R_U is the *unlevered cost of capital,* that is, the cost of capital for the firm if it had no debt. Unlike Proposition I, the general implications of Proposition II are the same whether there are taxes or not.

Table 15.6

Modigliani and Miller summary

Since the firm is worth $670 total and the debt is worth $500, the equity is worth $170:

$$E = V_L - D$$
$$= \$670 - 500$$
$$= \$170$$

Thus, from M&M Proposition II with taxes, the cost of equity is:

$$R_E = R_U + (R_U - R_D) \times (D/E) \times (1 - T_C)$$
$$= .20 + (.20 - .10) \times (\$500/\$170) \times (1 - .34)$$
$$= 39.4\%$$

Finally, the WACC is:

$$\text{WACC} = (\$170/670) \times 39.4\% + (\$500/670) \times 10\% \times (1 - .34)$$

$$= 14.92\%$$

Notice that this is substantially lower than the cost of capital for the firm with no debt ($R_U = 20\%$), so debt financing is highly advantageous. ∎

⌈ CONCEPT QUESTIONS

15.4a What is the relationship between the value of an unlevered firm and the value of a levered firm once we consider the effect of corporate taxes?

15.4b If we only consider the effect of taxes, what is the optimum capital structure?

15.5 | BANKRUPTCY COSTS

One limit to the amount of debt a firm might use comes in the form of *bankruptcy costs*. As the debt/equity ratio rises, so too does the probability that the firm will be unable to pay its bondholders what was promised to them. When this happens, ownership of the firm's assets is ultimately transferred from the stockholders to the bondholders. This was our definition of bankruptcy (in Chapter 12).

In principle, a firm is bankrupt when the value of its assets equals the value of its debt. When this occurs, the value of equity is zero and the stockholders turn over control of the firm to the bondholders. When this takes place, the bondholders hold assets whose value is exactly equal to what is owed on the debt. In a perfect world, there are no costs associated with this transfer of ownership, and the bondholders don't lose anything.

This idealized view of bankruptcy is not, of course, what happens in the real world. Ironically, it is expensive to go bankrupt. As we discuss, the costs associated with bankruptcy may eventually offset the tax-related gains from leverage.

Direct Bankruptcy Costs

When the value of a firm's assets equals the value of its debt, then the firm is economically bankrupt in the sense that the equity has no value. However, the formal means of turning over the assets to the bondholders is a *legal* process, not an economic one. There are legal and administrative costs to bankruptcy, and it has been remarked that bankruptcies are to lawyers what blood is to sharks.

direct bankruptcy costs
The costs that are directly associated with bankruptcy, such as legal and administrative expenses.

Because of the expenses associated with bankruptcy, bondholders won't get all that they are owed. Some fraction of the firm's assets will "disappear" in the legal process of going bankrupt. These are the legal and administrative expenses associated with the bankruptcy proceeding. We call these costs **direct bankruptcy costs.**

These direct bankruptcy costs are a disincentive to debt financing. If a firm goes bankrupt, then, suddenly, a piece of the firm disappears. This amounts to a bankruptcy "tax." So a firm faces a trade-off: Borrowing saves a firm money on its corporate taxes, but the more a firm borrows, the more likely it is that the firm will become bankrupt and have to pay the bankruptcy tax.

Indirect Bankruptcy Costs

Because it is expensive to go bankrupt, a firm will spend resources to avoid doing so. When a firm is having significant problems in meeting its debt obligations, we say that it is experiencing financial distress. Some financially distressed firms ultimately file for bankruptcy, but most do not because they are able to recover or otherwise survive.

The costs of avoiding a bankruptcy filing incurred by a financially distressed firm are called **indirect bankruptcy costs.** We use the term **financial distress costs** to refer generically to the direct and indirect costs associated with going bankrupt and/or avoiding a bankruptcy filing.

The problems that come up in financial distress are particularly severe, and the financial distress costs are thus larger, when the stockholders and the bondholders are different groups. Until the firm is legally bankrupt, the stockholders control it. They, of course, will take actions in their own economic interests. Since the stockholders can be wiped out in a legal bankruptcy, they have a very strong incentive to avoid a bankruptcy filing.

The bondholders, on the other hand, are primarily concerned with protecting the value of the firm's assets and will try to take control away from stockholders. They have a strong incentive to seek bankruptcy to protect their interests and keep stockholders from further dissipating the assets of the firm. The net effect of all this fighting is that a long, drawn-out, and potentially quite expensive, legal battle gets started.

Meanwhile, as the wheels of justice turn in their ponderous way, the assets of the firm lose value because management is busy trying to avoid bankruptcy instead of running the business. Normal operations are disrupted, and sales are lost. Valuable employees leave, potentially fruitful programs are dropped to preserve cash, and otherwise profitable investments are not taken.

These are all indirect bankruptcy costs, or costs of financial distress. Whether or not the firm ultimately goes bankrupt, the net effect is a loss of value because the firm chose to use debt in its capital structure. It is this possibility of loss that limits the amount of debt that a firm will choose to use.

indirect bankruptcy costs
The costs of avoiding a bankruptcy filing incurred by a financially distressed firm.

financial distress costs
The direct and indirect costs associated with going bankrupt or experiencing financial distress.

⌐CONCEPT QUESTIONS
15.5a What are direct bankruptcy costs?
15.5b What are indirect bankruptcy costs?

OPTIMAL CAPITAL STRUCTURE ⌐15.6

Our previous two sections have established the basis for an optimal capital structure. A firm will borrow because the interest tax shield is valuable. At relatively low debt levels, the probability of bankruptcy and financial distress is

Figure 15.6

The static theory of capital structure. The optimal capital structure and the value of the firm

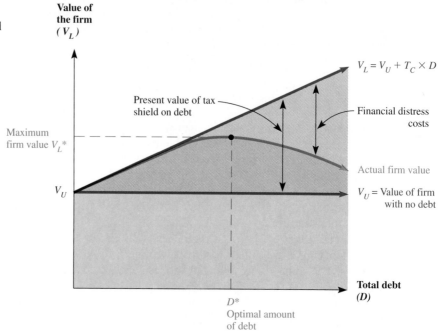

According to the static theory, the gain from the tax shield on debt is offset by financial distress costs. An optimal capital structure exists which just balances the additional gain from leverage against the added financial distress cost.

Figure 15.7

The static theory of capital structure. The optimal capital structure and the cost of capital

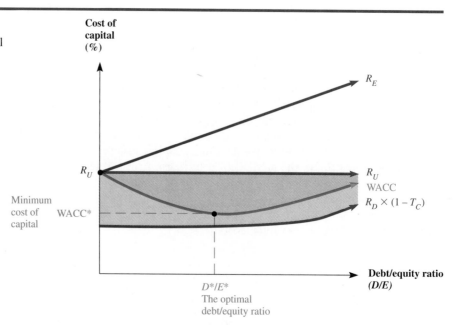

According to the static theory, the WACC falls initially because of the tax advantage to debt. Beyond the point D^*/E^*, it begins to rise because of financial distress costs.

low, and the benefit from debt outweighs the cost. At very high debt levels, the possibility of financial distress is a chronic, ongoing problem for the firm, so the benefit from debt financing may be more than offset by the financial distress costs. Based on our discussion, it would appear that an optimal capital structure exists somewhere in between these extremes.

The Static Theory of Capital Structure

The theory of capital structure that we have outlined is called the **static theory of capital structure.** It says that firms borrow up to the point where the tax benefit from an extra dollar in debt is exactly equal to the cost that comes from the increased probability of financial distress. We call this the static theory because it assumes that the firm is fixed in terms of its assets and operations and it only considers possible changes in the debt/equity ratio.

The static theory is illustrated in Figure 15.6, which plots the value of the firm, V_L, against the amount of debt, D. In Figure 15.6, we have drawn lines corresponding to three different stories. The first is M&M Proposition I with no taxes. This is the horizontal line extending from V_U, and it indicates that the value of the firm is unaffected by its capital structure. The second case, M&M Proposition I with corporate taxes, is given by the upward-sloping straight line. These two cases are exactly the same as the ones we previously illustrated in Figure 15.4.

The third case in Figure 15.6 illustrates our current discussion: The value of the firm rises to a maximum and then declines beyond that point. This is the picture that we get from our static theory. The maximum value of the firm, V_L^*, is reached at D^*, so this is the optimal amount of borrowing. Put another way, the firm's optimal capital structure is composed of D^*/V_L^* in debt and $(1 - D^*/V_L^*)$ in equity.

The final thing to notice in Figure 15.6 is that the difference between the value of the firm in our static theory and the M&M value of the firm with taxes is the loss in value from the possibility of financial distress. Also, the difference between the static theory value of the firm and the M&M value with taxes is the gain from leverage, net of distress costs.

Optimal Capital Structure and the Cost of Capital

As we discussed earlier, the capital structure that maximizes the value of the firm is also the one that minimizes the cost of capital. Figure 15.7 illustrates the static theory of capital structure in terms of the weighted average cost of capital and the costs of debt and equity. Notice in Figure 15.7 that we have plotted the various capital costs against the debt/equity ratio, D/E.

Figure 15.7 is much the same as Figure 15.5 except that we have added a new line for the WACC. This line, which corresponds to the static theory, declines at first. This occurs because the aftertax cost of debt is cheaper than equity, so, at least initially, the overall cost of capital declines.

At some point, the cost of debt begins to rise and the fact that debt is cheaper than equity is more than offset by the financial distress costs. At this point, further increases in debt actually increase the WACC. As illustrated, the minimum WACC occurs at the point D^*/E^*, just as we described above.

static theory of capital structure

Theory that a firm borrows up to the point where the tax benefit from an extra dollar in debt is exactly equal to the cost that comes from the increased probability of financial distress.

Exhibit 15.1 A
The capital structure question

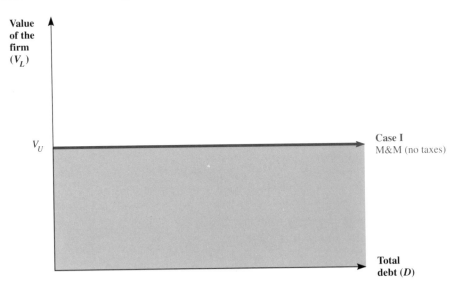

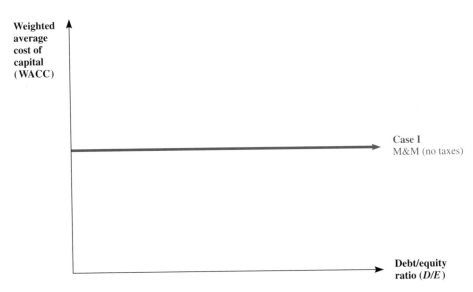

Case I
With no taxes or bankruptcy costs, the value of the firm and its weighted average cost of capital are not affected by capital structure.

Optimal Capital Structure: A Recap

With the help of Exhibit 15.1, we can recap (no pun intended) our discussion of capital structure and cost of capital. As we have noted, there are essentially three cases. We will use the simplest of the three cases as a starting point and then build up to the static theory of capital structure. Along the way, we will pay particular attention to the connection between capital structure, firm value, and cost of capital.

Exhibit 15.1A illustrates the original Modigliani and Miller (M&M) no-tax, no-bankruptcy argument. This is the most basic case. In the top part of the exhibit, we have plotted the value of the firm, V_L, against total debt, D. When there are no taxes, bankruptcy costs, or other real-world imperfections, we know that the total of the firm is not affected by its debt policy, so V_L is simply constant. The bottom part of the exhibit tells the same story in terms of the cost of capital. Here, the weighted average cost of capital, WACC, is plotted against the debt to equity ratio, D/E. As with total firm value, the overall cost of capital is not affected by debt policy in this basic case, so the WACC is constant.

To see what happens to the original M&M arguments once taxes are introduced, Exhibit 15.1B (the first transparency) is used to overlay Exhibit 15.1A. Now we see that the firm's value critically depends on its debt policy. The more the firm borrows, the more it is worth. From our earlier discussion, we know this happens because interest payments are tax deductible, and the gain in firm value is just equal to the present value of the interest tax shield.

In the bottom part of Exhibit 15.1B, notice how the WACC declines as the firm uses more and more debt financing. As the firm increases its financial leverage, the cost of equity does increase, but this increase is more than offset by the tax break associated with debt financing. As a result, the firm's overall cost of capital declines.

To finish our story, we need to consider the impact of bankruptcy or financial distress costs. When we use Exhibit 15.1C to overlay 15.1B, we see in the top part that the value of the firm will not be as large as we previously indicated. The reason is that the firm's value is reduced by the present value of the potential future bankruptcy costs. These costs grow as the firm borrows more and more, and they eventually overwhelm the tax advantage of debt financing. The optimal capital structure occurs at D^*, the point at which the tax saving from an additional dollar in debt financing is exactly balanced by the increased bankruptcy costs associated with the additional borrowing. This is the essence of the static theory of capital structure.

The bottom part of Exhibit 15.1C presents the optimal capital structure in terms of the cost of capital. Corresponding to D^*, the optimal debt level, is the optimal debt to equity ratio, D^*/E^*. At this level of debt financing, the lowest possible weighted average cost of capital, WACC*, occurs.

Capital Structure: Some Managerial Recommendations

The static model that we described is not capable of identifying a precise optimal capital structure, but it does point out two of the more relevant factors: taxes and financial distress. We can draw some limited conclusions concerning these.

Taxes   First of all, the tax benefit from leverage is obviously only important to firms that are in a tax-paying position. Firms with substantial accumulated losses will get little value from the interest tax shield. Furthermore, firms that have substantial tax shields from other sources, such as depreciation, will get less benefit from leverage.

Also, not all firms have the same tax rate. The higher the tax rate, the greater the incentive to borrow.

Financial Distress   Firms with a greater risk of experiencing financial distress will borrow less than firms with a lower risk of financial distress. For example, all other things being equal, the greater the volatility in EBIT, the less a firm should borrow.

In addition, financial distress is more costly for some firms than others. The costs of financial distress depend primarily on the firm's assets. In particular, financial distress costs will be determined by how easily ownership to those assets can be transferred.

For example, a firm with mostly tangible assets that can be sold without great loss in value will have an incentive to borrow more. For firms that rely heavily on intangibles, such as employee talent or growth opportunities, debt will be less attractive since these assets effectively cannot be sold.

┌ **CONCEPT QUESTIONS**

15.6a Can you describe the trade-off that defines the static theory of capital structure?

15.6b What are the important factors in making capital structure decisions?

15.7 | THE PIE AGAIN

Although it is comforting to know that the firm might have an optimal capital structure when we take account of such real-world matters as taxes and financial distress costs, it is disquieting to see the elegant, original M&M intuition (that is, the no-tax version) fall apart in the face of them.

Critics of the M&M theory often say that it fails to hold as soon as we add in real-world issues and that the M&M theory is really just that, a theory that doesn't have much to say about the real world that we live in. In fact, they would argue that it is the M&M theory that is irrelevant, not capital structure. As we discuss next, however, taking that view blinds critics to the real value of the M&M theory.

The Extended Pie Model

To illustrate the value of the original M&M intuition, we briefly consider an expanded version of the pie model that we introduced earlier. In the extended pie model, taxes just represent another claim on the cash flows of the firm. Since taxes are reduced as leverage is increased, the value of the government's claim (G) on the firm's cash flows decreases with leverage.

Bankruptcy costs are also a claim on the cash flows. They come into play as the firm comes close to bankruptcy and has to alter its behavior to attempt to stave off the event itself, and they become large when bankruptcy actually takes place. Thus, the value of the cash flows to this claim (B) rises with the debt/equity ratio.

The extended pie theory simply holds that all of these claims can be paid from only one source, the cash flows (CF) of the firm. Algebraically, we must have:

CF = Payments to stockholders + Payments to bondholders

+ Payments to the government

+ Payments to bankruptcy courts and lawyers

+ Payments to any and all other claimants to the cash flow of the firm

The extended pie model is illustrated in Figure 15.8. Notice that we have added a few slices for the other groups. Notice also the relative sizes of the slices as the firm's use of debt financing is increased.

With this list, we have not even begun to exhaust the potential claims to the firm's cash flows. To give an unusual example, everyone reading this book

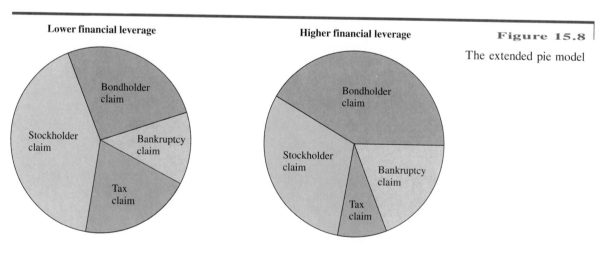

Figure 15.8

The extended pie model

In the extended pie model, the value of all the claims against the firm's cash flows is not affected by capital structure, but the relative value of claims changes as the amount of debt financing is increased.

has an economic claim to the cash flows of General Motors. After all, if you are injured in an accident, you might sue GM, and, win or lose, GM will expend some of its cash flow in dealing with the matter. For GM, or any other company, there should thus be a slice of the pie representing the potential lawsuits.

This is the essence of the M&M intuition and theory: The value of the firm depends on the total cash flow of the firm. The firm's capital structure just cuts that cash flow up into slices without altering the total. What we recognize now is that the stockholders and the bondholders may not be the only ones who can claim a slice.

Marketed Claims versus Nonmarketed Claims

With our extended pie model, there is an important distinction between claims such as those of stockholders and bondholders, on the one hand, and those of the government and potential litigants in lawsuits on the other. The first set of claims are *marketed claims,* and the second set are *nonmarketed claims.* A key difference is that the marketed claims can be bought and sold in financial markets and the nonmarketed claims cannot.

When we speak of the value of the firm, we are generally referring just to the value of the marketed claims, V_M, and not the value of the nonmarketed claims, V_N. If we write V_T for the total value of *all* the claims against a corporation's cash flows, then:

$$V_T = E + D + G + B + \cdots$$

$$= V_M + V_N$$

The essence of our extended pie model is that this total value, V_T, of all the claims to the firm's cash flows is unaltered by capital structure. However, the value of the marketed claims, V_M, may be affected by changes in the capital structure.

By the pie theory, any increase in V_M must imply an identical decrease in V_N. The optimal capital structure is thus the one that maximizes the value of the marketed claims, or, equivalently, minimizes the value of nonmarketed claims such as taxes and bankruptcy costs.

⌐ CONCEPT QUESTIONS

15.7a What are some of the claims to a firm's cash flows?

15.7b What is the difference between a marketed claim and a nonmarketed claim?

15.7c What does the extended pie model say about the value of all the claims to a firm's cash flows?

15.8 | OBSERVED CAPITAL STRUCTURES

No two firms have identical capital structures. Nonetheless, there are some regular elements that we see when we start looking at actual capital structures. We discuss a few of these next.

The most striking thing that we observe about capital structures, particularly in the United States, is that most corporations seem to have relatively low debt/equity ratios. In fact, most corporations use less debt than equity financing. This is true even though many of these corporations pay substantial taxes, and the corporate tax has been an important source of government revenue. To give one notable example, polls consistently find that Merck (a large pharmaceuticals manufacturer) is widely regarded as one of the best-run corporations in the United States, yet, Merck uses essentially no debt financing.

Table 15.7 shows several measures of debt to total value for nonfinancial corporations in the United States. The measures are in both accounting (that is, book) and market values for the years 1957 to 1978. We are more interested in the market value column. It shows that debt ratios rose until the early 1970s and then leveled off. Notice that the debt ratios are usually quite low: They range from 11.2 percent to 36.3 percent. If leases and pensions, which are

	Unadjusted Ratios		Ratios Adjusted to Number of Firms and Including Leases and Pensions	
Year	(1) Book Value	(2) Market Value	(3) Book Value	
1957	0.219	0.158	n/a	
1958	0.218	0.123	n/a	
1959	0.213	0.112	n/a	
1960	0.225	0.124	n/a	
1961	0.230	0.116	n/a	
1962	0.234	0.173	n/a	
1963	0.234	0.160	n/a	
1964	0.239	0.158	n/a	
1965	0.258	0.157	n/a	
1966	0.286	0.191	n/a	
1967	0.310	0.181	n/a	
1968	0.328	0.179	n/a	
1969	0.348	0.213	n/a	
1970	0.370	0.228	n/a	
1971	0.367	0.234	n/a	
1972	0.367	0.227	n/a	
1973	0.367	0.280	0.497	
1974	0.381	0.363	0.511	
1975	0.375	0.316	0.499	
1976	0.362	0.293	0.485	
1977	0.358	0.321	0.473	
1978	0.350	0.313	0.462	

Table 15.7

Estimated ratios of debt to total capital of nonfinancial corporations, 1957–1978

n/a = Not available.
From R. Gordon and B. Malkiel, "Corporation Finance," in *How Taxes Affect Economic Behavior*, H. Aaron and J. Pechman, eds. (Washington, D.C.: The Brookings Institute, 1981).

debtlike, are included, the averages are somewhat greater, at 45 percent to 50 percent, but they still do not indicate enormous amounts of leverage.

Although most corporations have low debt/equity ratios, they nevertheless pay substantial amounts of taxes. In 1980, for example, corporations paid $105 billion in taxes while individuals paid about $300 billion. Thus, it is clear that corporations have not issued debt up to the point that tax shelters have been completely used up, and we conclude that there must be limits to the amount of debt corporations can issue. However, there are indications that borrowing by corporations has increased in the last decade.[3]

A second regularity is apparent when we compare capital structures across industries. Table 15.8 shows debt/equity ratios in Japan and the United States by industry. As shown, there is wide variation in industry debt/equity ratios. For example, using market values, firms in the steel industry have a debt/equity ratio of 1.665 compared to .079 for firms in the pharmaceutical industry.

Because different industries have different operating characteristics in terms of, for example, EBIT volatility and asset types, there does appear to be some connection between these characteristics and capital structure. Our story involving tax savings and financial distress costs is undoubtedly part of the reason, but, to date, there is no fully satisfactory theory that explains these regularities.

⌐ CONCEPT QUESTIONS

15.8a Do U.S. corporations rely heavily on debt financing?

15.8b What regularities do we observe in capital structures?

15.9 | SUMMARY AND CONCLUSIONS

The ideal mixture of debt and equity for a firm—its optimal capital structure—is the one that maximizes the value of the firm and minimizes the overall cost of capital. If we ignore taxes, financial distress costs, and any other imperfections, we find that there is no ideal mixture. Under these circumstances, the firm's capital structure is simply irrelevant.

If we consider the effect of corporate taxes, we find that capital structure matters a great deal. This conclusion is based on the fact that interest is tax deductible and thus generates a valuable tax shield. Unfortunately, we also find that the optimal capital structure is 100 percent debt, which is not something we observe for healthy firms.

We next introduced costs associated with bankruptcy, or, more generally, financial distress. These costs reduce the attractiveness of debt financing. We concluded that an optimal capital structure exists when the net tax saving from

---

[3]For example, Ben Bernanke, "Is There Too Much Corporate Debt?" *Business Review* of the Federal Reserve Bank of Philadelphia, September–October 1989, pp. 3–13, reports that the debt of nonfinancial corporations rose 70 percent between 1983 and 1988, more than two-thirds faster than the growth in GNP.

Debt/equity ratios for different industries in the United States and Japan in 1983

Industry	Net Debt to:		Number of Companies in the Sample		
	Book Value Equity	Market Value Equity	Japan	United States	Total
Nonferrous metals	3.791	1.106	11	13	24
General chemicals	2.945	1.256	21	16	37
Steel	1.973	1.665	35	35	70
Paper	1.732	1.364	16	25	41
Paint	1.548	0.614	7	5	12
Petroleum refining	1.548	1.117	6	33	39
Audio equipment	1.539	0.631	7	10	17
Textiles	1.405	1.296	29	23	52
Cement	1.298	1.366	6	10	16
Glass	1.213	1.087	5	8	13
Soaps and detergents	1.143	0.683	6	8	14
Apparel	1.021	0.951	14	41	55
Tires and rubber	1.021	0.835	8	14	22
Motor vehicles	0.922	0.594	9	6	15
Plastics	0.843	0.792	18	25	43
Agricultural machinery	0.836	1.082	5	5	10
Electrical machinery	0.813	0.376	14	12	26
Construction machinery	0.688	0.810	6	12	18
Electronic parts	0.614	0.358	19	34	53
Motor vehicle parts	0.488	0.500	20	16	36
Machine tools	0.472	0.425	10	15	25
Photo equipment	0.468	0.222	7	7	14
Alcoholic beverages	0.427	0.284	8	10	18
Communication equipment	0.356	0.186	15	24	39
Confectionary	0.326	0.286	6	5	11
Pharmaceuticals	0.194	0.079	25	23	48
Household appliances	0.102	0.244	13	13	26

From W. C. Kester, "Capital and Ownership Structure: A Comparison of United States and Japanese Manufacturing Corporations," *Financial Management,* 15 (Spring 1986).

an additional dollar in interest just equals the increase in expected financial distress costs. This is the essence of the static theory of capital structure.

When we examine actual capital structures, we find two regularities. First, firms in the United States typically do not use great amounts of debt, but they pay substantial taxes. This suggests that there is a limit to the use of debt financing to generate tax shields. Second, firms in similar industries tend to have similar capital structures, suggesting that the nature of their assets and operations is an important determinant of capital structure.

Key Terms

Chapter Review Problems and Self-Test

15.1 **EBIT and EPS**   Suppose the GNR Corporation has decided in favor of a capital restructuring that involves increasing its existing $5 million in debt to $25 million. The interest rate on the debt is 12 percent and is not expected to change. The firm currently has 1 million shares outstanding, and the price per share is $40. If the restructuring is expected to increase the ROE, what is the minimum level for EBIT that GNR's management must be expecting? Ignore taxes in your answer.

15.2 **M&M Proposition II (no taxes)**   The Pro Bono Corporation has a WACC of 20 percent. Its cost of debt is 12 percent. If Pro Bono's debt/equity ratio is 2, what is its cost of equity capital? Ignore taxes in your answer.

15.3 **M&M Proposition I (with corporate taxes)**   The Deathstar Telecom Co. (motto: "Reach out and clutch someone") expects an EBIT of $4,000 every year forever. Deathstar can borrow at 10 percent.

Suppose that Deathstar currently has no debt and its cost of equity is 14 percent. If the corporate tax rate is 30 percent, what is the value of the firm? What will the value be if Deathstar borrows $6,000 and uses the proceeds to buy up stock?

Answers to Self-Test Problems

15.1 To answer, we can calculate the break-even EBIT. At any EBIT above this, the increased financial leverage will increase EPS. Under the old capital structure, the interest bill is $5 million × .12 = $600,000. There are 1 million shares of stock, so, ignoring taxes, EPS is (EBIT − $600,000)/1 million.

Under the new capital structure, the interest expense will be $25 million × .12 = $3 million. Furthermore, the debt rises by $20 million. This amount is sufficient to repurchase $20 million/$40 = 500,000 shares of stock, leaving 500,000 outstanding. EPS is thus (EBIT − $3 million)/500,000.

Now that we know how to calculate EPS under both scenarios, we set them equal to each other and solve for the break-even EBIT:

$$(EBIT - \$600{,}000)/1 \text{ million} = (EBIT - \$3 \text{ million})/500{,}000$$

$$(EBIT - \$600{,}000) = 2 \times (EBIT - \$3 \text{ million})$$

$$EBIT = \$5{,}400{,}000$$

Check that, in either case, EPS is $4.80 when EBIT is $5.4 million.

15.2   According to M&M Proposition II (no taxes), the cost of equity is:

$$R_E = R_A + (R_A - R_D) \times (D/E)$$

$$= 20\% + (20\% - 12\%) \times 2$$

$$= 36\%$$

15.3   With no debt, Deathstar's WACC is 14 percent. This is also the unlevered cost of capital. The aftertax cash flow is $4,000 × $(1 - .30) = \$2{,}800$, so the value is just $V_U = \$2{,}800/.14 = \$20{,}000$.

   After the debt issue, Deathstar will be worth the original $20,000 plus the present value of the tax shield. According to M&M Proposition I with taxes, the present value of the tax shield is $T_C \times D$, or $.30 \times \$6{,}000 = \$1{,}800$, so the firm is worth $20,000 + 1,800 = $21,800.

Questions and Problems

1.   Calculating Effects of Leverage   Ramrod Corp. has no debt outstanding and a total market value of $10,000. Earnings before interest and taxes (EBIT) are projected to be $1,000 if economic conditions are normal. If there is a strong expansion in the economy, then EBIT will be 20 percent higher. If there is a recession, then EBIT will be 40 percent lower. Ramrod is considering a $5,000 debt issue with a 9 percent interest rate. The proceeds will be used to buy up stock. There are currently 100 shares outstanding. Ignore taxes.
   a. Calculate earnings per share (EPS) under each of the three economic scenarios before any debt is issued. Also, calculate the percentage changes in EPS when the economy expands or enters a recession.
   b. Repeat part *a* assuming that Ramrod goes through with recapitalization. What do you observe?

2.   Leverage and Break-Even EBIT   The DuoSys Corp. is comparing two different capital structures, an all-equity plan (Plan I) and a levered plan (Plan II). Under Plan I, DuoSys would have 200 shares of stock outstanding. Under Plan II, DuoSys would have 100 shares of stock

and $5,000 in debt outstanding. The interest rate on the debt is 12 percent and there are no taxes.

a. If EBIT is $1,000, which plan will result in the higher EPS?

b. If EBIT is $2,000, which plan will result in the higher EPS?

c. What is the break-even EBIT; that is, what EBIT generates exactly the same EPS under both plans?

3. **M&M and Share Value**   In the previous question, what is the price per share of the equity under Plan I? Under Plan II? Ignore taxes. (Hint: M&M Proposition I)

4. **Capital Structure and Homemade Leverage**   The Jorgensen Corporation is debating whether to convert its current all-equity capital structure to one that is 40 percent debt. Currently, there are 100 shares outstanding and the price per share is $120. EBIT is expected to remain at $400 per year forever. The interest rate on the debt is 8 percent, and there are no taxes. Ms. Lyndi owns 10 shares.

a. What is Ms. Lyndi's cash flow under the current capital structure?

b. What will Ms. Lyndi's cash flow be under the proposed capital structure? Assume that she retains all 10 shares.

c. Suppose Jorgensen does convert, but Ms. Lyndi prefers the current capital structure. Show how she could unlever her investment to re-create the original capital structure.

d. Explain why the capital structure Jorgensen chooses is irrelevant.

5. **Homemade Leverage and WACC**   A. B. Min and T. S. Max are identical firms in every way except capital structure (Max uses perpetual debt). The EBIT for both is expected to be $10 million forever. The stock in Min is worth $100 million, and the stock in Max is worth $50 million. The interest rate on Max's debt is 8 percent, and there are no taxes. D. Draper owns $1 million of Max's stock.

a. What rate of return is D. Draper expecting?

b. Show how D. Draper could generate exactly the same cash flow and rate of return by investing in A. B. Min and using homemade leverage.

c. What is the cost of equity for T. S. Max? Compare your answer to your answer in part *a.* What do you notice? Explain.

d. What is A. B. Min's weighted average cost of capital? What is the weighted average cost of capital for Max? What principle does your answer illustrate?

6. **EPS, EBIT, and Leverage**   The Gaffee Corp. is comparing two different capital structures. The first capital structure, Plan I, would result in 1,000 shares of stock and $8,000 in debt. The second plan, Plan II, would result in 1,150 shares of stock and $5,000 in debt. The interest rate is 5 percent.

a. Ignoring taxes, compare both of these plans to an all-equity plan assuming that EBIT will be $2,000. Which has the highest EPS? The lowest? The all-equity plan would result in 1,400 shares outstanding.

b. In part *a,* what are the break-even levels of EBIT for each plan compared to an all-equity plan? Is one higher than the other? Why?

  c. Ignoring taxes, when will EPS be identical for the two plans?

  d. Answer parts *a, b,* and *c* assuming that the corporate tax rate is 40 percent. Are the break-even levels different? Why or why not?

7. **Leverage and Share Value** Ignoring taxes, in the previous question, what is the price per share of the equity under Plan I? Under Plan II? What principle is illustrated by your answer?

8. **Business and Financial Risk** Explain what is meant by business and financial risk. Suppose Firm A has greater business risk than Firm B. Is it true that Firm A also has a higher cost of equity capital? Explain.

9. **Calculating WACC** Butler Corporation has a debt/equity ratio of .50. Its WACC is 20 percent, and its cost of debt is 9 percent.

  a. Ignoring taxes, what is Butler's cost of equity?

  b. What would Butler's cost of equity be if the debt/equity ratio were 1.0?

  c. What is Butler's WACC in part *b*?

10. **WACC** McGowan Manufacturing has no debt, and its WACC is currently 12 percent. McGowan can borrow at 9 percent. The corporate tax rate is 34 percent.

  a. What is McGowan's cost of equity?

  b. If McGowan converts to 25 percent debt, what will its cost of equity be?

  c. If McGowan converts to 50 percent debt, what will its cost of equity be?

  d. What is McGowan's WACC in part *b*? In part *c*?

11. **Value and the Tax Shield** The Trius Co. expects an EBIT of $1,000 every year forever. Trius can borrow at 10 percent. Trius currently has no debt, and its cost of equity is 14 percent. If the corporate tax rate is 34 percent, what is the value of the firm? What will the value be if Trius borrows $2,000 and uses the proceeds to buy up stock?

12. **M&M** The Hilliard Hedging Corp. uses no debt. The weighted average cost of capital is 10 percent. If the current market value of the equity is $5 million and there are no taxes, what is EBIT?

13. **M&M** In the previous question, suppose the corporate tax rate is 20 percent. What is EBIT in this case?

14. **M&M and Taxes** Kau Real Estate, Inc., currently uses no debt. EBIT is expected to be $6,000 forever, and the cost of capital is currently 12 percent. The corporate tax rate is 40 percent.

  a. What is the market value of Kau Real Estate?

  b. Suppose Kau floats a $20,000 bond issue and uses the proceeds to repurchase stock. The interest rate is 8 percent. What is the new value of the business? What is the new value of the equity?

15. **Leverage and WACC** In the previous question, what is the cost of equity after the recapitalization? What is the weighted average cost of capital? What are the implications for capital structure?

16.   Risk and Capital Costs   How would you answer in the following debate?

Q: Isn't it true that the riskiness of a firm's equity will rise if it increases its use of debt financing?

A: Yes, that is the essence of M&M Proposition II.

Q: And isn't it true that, as a firm increases its borrowing, the likelihood of default increases, thereby increasing the risk of the firm's debt?

A: Yes.

Q: In other words, increased borrowing increases the risk of the equity *and* the debt?

A: That's right.

Q: Well, now, given that the firm only uses debt and equity financing, and given that the risks of both are increased by increased borrowing, does it not follow, as the night the day, that increasing debt increases the overall risk of the firm and therefore decreases the value of the firm?

A: ?

17.   Debt and Firm Value   This one's a little harder. The Corrado Corporation expects an EBIT of $5,000 every year forever. Corrado currently has no debt, and its cost of equity is 18 percent. Corrado can borrow at 10 percent. If the corporate tax rate is 34 percent, what is the value of the firm? What will the value be if Corrado converts to 100 percent debt?

Challenge Question

18.   Weighted Average Cost of Capital   Assuming a world of corporate taxes only, show that the WACC can be written as $R_U \times [1 - T_C \times (D/V)]$.

Challenge Question

19.   Cost of Equity and Leverage   Show that the cost of equity, R_E, with taxes is as given in the chapter by M&M Proposition II with corporate taxes.

Challenge Question

20.   Business and Financial Risk   Assume a firm's debt is risk-free, so that the cost of debt equals the risk-free rate, R_f. Define β_A as the firm's *asset* beta, that is, the systematic risk of the firm's assets. Define β_E to be the beta of the firm's equity. Use the capital asset pricing model along with M&M Proposition I to show that $\beta_E = \beta_A \times (1 + D/E)$, where D/E is the debt/equity ratio.

Suggested Readings

The classic articles on capital structure are:

Modigliani, F., and M. H. Miller. "The Cost of Capital, Corporate Finance, and the Theory of Investment." *American Economic Review* 48, June 1958, pp. 261–97.

———. "Corporation Income Taxes and the Cost of Capital: A Correction." *American Economic Review* 53, June 1963, pp. 433–43.

Some research on capital structure is summarized in:

Smith, C. "Raising Capital: Theory and Evidence." *Midland Corporate Finance Journal,* Spring 1986.

The text of Stewart Myers's 1984 presidential address to the American Finance Association is in the article listed below. It summarizes the academic insights on capital structure until the early 1980s and points out directions for future research:

Myers, S. "The Capital Structure Puzzle." *Midland Corporate Finance Journal,* Fall 1985.

Chapter 16

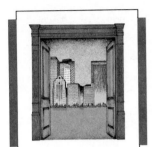

Dividends and Dividend Policy

ividend policy is an important subject in corporate finance, and dividends are a major cash outlay for many corporations. In 1990 alone, for example, New York Stock Exchange–listed firms paid out in excess of $100 billion in cash dividends. At the same time, however, about 400 of the 1,741 listed companies, or slightly less than 25 percent, paid no dividend at all.[1]

At first glance, it may seem obvious that a firm would always want to give as much as possible back to its shareholders by paying dividends. It might seem equally obvious, however, that a firm can always invest the money for its shareholders instead of paying it out. The heart of the dividend policy question is just this: Should the firm pay out money to its shareholders, or should the firm take that money and invest it for its shareholders?

It may seem surprising, but much research and economic logic suggest that dividend policy doesn't matter. In fact, it turns out that the dividend policy issue is much like the capital structure question. The important elements are not difficult to identify, but the interactions between those elements are complex and no easy answer exists.

Dividend policy is controversial. Many implausible reasons are given for why dividend policy might be important, and many of the claims made about dividend policy are economically illogical. Even so, in the real world of corporate finance, determining the most appropriate dividend policy is considered an important issue. It could be that financial managers who worry about dividend policy are wasting time, but it could also be true that we are missing something important in our discussions.

---

[1]New York Stock Exchange, *Fact Book 1991*.

In part, all discussions of dividends are plagued by the "two-handed lawyer" problem. President Truman, while discussing the legal implications of a possible presidential decision, asked his staff to set up a meeting with a lawyer. Supposedly Mr. Truman said, "But I don't want one of those two-handed lawyers." When asked what a two-handed lawyer was, he replied, "You know, a lawyer who says, 'On the one hand I recommend you do so and so because of the following reasons, but on the other hand I recommend that you don't do it because of these other reasons.'"

Unfortunately, any sensible treatment of dividend policy will appear to be written by a two-handed lawyer (or, in fairness, several two-handed financial economists). On the one hand, there are many good reasons for corporations to pay high dividends, but, on the other hand, there are also many good reasons to pay low dividends.

We will cover three broad topics that relate to dividends and dividend policy in this chapter. First, we describe the various kinds of dividends and how dividends are paid. Second, we consider an idealized case in which dividend policy doesn't matter. We then discuss the limitations of this case and present some real-world arguments for both high- and low-dividend payouts. Finally, we conclude the chapter by looking at some strategies that corporations might employ to implement a dividend policy, and we discuss share repurchases as an alternative to dividends.

CASH DIVIDENDS AND DIVIDEND PAYMENT | 16.1

The term **dividend** usually refers to cash paid out of earnings. If a payment is made from sources other than current or accumulated retained earnings, the term **distribution** rather than dividend is used. However, it is acceptable to refer to a distribution from earnings as a dividend and a distribution from capital as a liquidating dividend. More generally, any direct payment by the corporation to the shareholders may be considered a dividend or a part of dividend policy.

Dividends come in several different forms. The basic types of cash dividends are:

1. Regular cash dividends.
2. Extra dividends.
3. Special dividends.
4. Liquidating dividends.

Later in the chapter, we discuss dividends that are paid in stock instead of cash, and we also consider an alternative to cash dividends, stock repurchase.

dividend
Payment made out of a firm's earnings to its owners, either in the form of cash or stock.

distribution
Payment made by a firm to its owners from sources other than current or accumulated earnings.

Cash Dividends

The most common type of dividend is a cash dividend. Commonly, public companies pay **regular cash dividends** four times a year. As the name suggests, these are cash payments made directly to shareholders, and they are made in the regular course of business. In other words, management sees nothing unusual about the dividend and no reason why it won't be continued.

regular cash dividend
Cash payment made by a firm to its owners in the normal course of business, usually made four times a year.

Sometimes firms will pay a regular cash dividend and an *extra cash dividend*. By calling part of the payment "extra," management is indicating that it may or may not be repeated in the future. A *special dividend* is similar, but the name usually indicates that the dividend is viewed as a truly unusual or one-time event and won't be repeated. Finally, a *liquidating dividend* usually means that some or all of the business has been liquidated, that is, sold off.

However it is labeled, a cash dividend payment reduces corporate cash and retained earnings, except in the case of a liquidating dividend (where paid-in capital may be reduced).

Standard Method of Cash Dividend Payment

The decision to pay a dividend rests in the hands of the board of directors of the corporation. When a dividend has been declared, it becomes a debt of the firm and cannot be rescinded easily. Sometime after it has been declared, a dividend is distributed to all shareholders as of some specific date.

Commonly, the amount of the cash dividend is expressed in terms of the dollars per share (*dividends per share*). As we have seen in other chapters, it is also expressed as a percentage of the market price (the *dividend yield*) or as a percentage of earnings per share (the *dividend payout*).

Dividend Payment: A Chronology

The mechanics of a dividend payment can be illustrated by the example in Figure 16.1 and the following description:

declaration date

Date on which the board of directors passes a resolution to pay a dividend.

1. **Declaration date.** On January 15, the board of directors passes a resolution to pay a dividend of $1 per share on February 16 to all holders of record as of January 30.

ex-dividend date

Date four business days before the date of record, establishing those individuals entitled to a dividend.

2. **Ex-dividend date.** To make sure that dividend checks go to the right people, brokerage firms and stock exchanges establish an *ex-dividend date*. This date is four business days before the date of record (discussed next). If you buy the stock before this date, then you are entitled to the dividend. If you buy on this date or after, then the previous owner will get it.

   In Figure 16.1, Monday, January 26, is the ex-dividend date. Before this date, the stock is said to trade "with dividend" or "cum dividend." Afterwards, the stock trades "ex dividend."

   The ex-dividend date convention removes any ambiguity about who is entitled to the dividend. Since the dividend is valuable, the stock price will be affected when it goes "ex." We examine this effect below.

date of record

Date on which holders of record are designated to receive a dividend.

3. **Date of record.** Based on its records, the corporation prepares a list on January 30 of all individuals believed to be stockholders as of this date. These are the *holders of record* and January 30 is the *date of record* (or record date). The word "believed" is important here. If you buy the stock just before this date, the corporation's records may not reflect that fact because of mailing or other delays. Without some modification, some of the dividend checks will get mailed to the wrong people. This is the reason for the ex-dividend day convention.

date of payment

Date that the dividend checks are mailed.

4. **Date of payment.** The dividend checks are mailed on February 16.

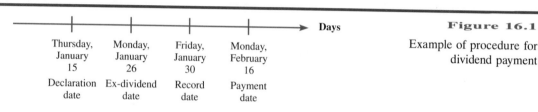

Figure 16.1

Example of procedure for dividend payment

1. *Declaration date*: The board of directors declares a payment of dividends.
2. *Ex-dividend date*: A share of stock goes ex dividend on the date the seller is entitled to keep the dividend; under NYSE rules, shares are traded ex dividend on and after the fourth business day before the record date.
3. *Record date*: The declared dividends are distributable to shareholders of record on a specific date.
4. *Payment date*: The dividend checks are mailed to shareholders of record.

More on the Ex-Dividend Date

The ex-dividend date is important and is a common source of confusion. We examine what happens to the stock when it goes ex, meaning that the ex-dividend date arrives. To illustrate, suppose we have a stock that sells for $10 per share. The board of directors declares a dividend of $1 per share, and the record date is Thursday, June 14. Based on our discussion above, we know that the ex date will be four business (not calendar) days earlier on Friday, June 8.

If you buy the stock on Thursday, June 7, right as the market closes, you'll get the $1 dividend because the stock is trading cum dividend. If you wait and buy it right as the market opens on Friday, you won't get the $1 dividend. What will happen to the value of the stock overnight?

If you think about it, the stock is obviously worth about $1 less on Friday morning, so its price will drop by this amount between close of business on Thursday and the Friday opening. In general, we expect that the value of a share of stock will go down by about the dividend amount when the stock goes ex-dividend. The key word here is *about*. Since dividends are taxed, the actual price drop might be closer to some measure of the aftertax value of the dividend. Determining this value is complicated because of the different tax rates and tax rules that apply for different buyers.

The series of events described here is illustrated in Figure 16.2.

Example 16.1 "Ex" Marks the Day

The board of directors of Divided Airlines has declared a dividend of $2.50 per share payable on Tuesday, May 30, to shareholders of record as of Tuesday, May 9. Cal Icon buys 100 shares of Divided on Tuesday, May 2, for $150 per share. What is the ex date? Describe the events that will occur with regard to the cash dividend and the stock price.

The ex date is four business days before the date of record, Tuesday, May 9, so the stock will go ex on Wednesday, May 3. Cal buys the stock on Tuesday, May 2, so Cal has purchased the stock cum dividend. In other words, Cal will get $2.50 × 100 = $250 in dividends. The check will be mailed on Tuesday, May 30. When the stock does go ex on Wednesday, its value will drop overnight by about $2.50 per share. ∎

Figure 16.2

Price behavior around ex-dividend date for a $1 cash dividend

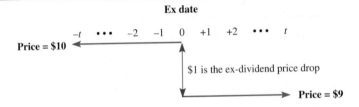

The stock price will fall by the amount of the dividend on the ex date (time 0). If the dividend is $1 per share, the price will be equal to $10 – $1 = $9 on the ex date:

	Before ex date (–1) dividend = 0	Price = $10
	Ex-date (0) dividend = $1	Price = $9

CONCEPT QUESTIONS

16.1a What are the different types of cash dividends?

16.1b What are the mechanics of the cash dividend payment?

16.1c How should the price of a stock change when it goes ex dividend?

16.2 | DOES DIVIDEND POLICY MATTER?

To decide whether or not dividend policy matters, we first have to define what we mean by dividend *policy*. All other things being the same, of course dividends matter. Dividends are paid in cash, and cash is something that everybody likes. The question we will be discussing here is whether the firm should pay out cash now or invest the cash and pay it out later. Dividend policy, therefore, is the time pattern of dividend payout. In particular, should the firm pay out a large percentage of its earnings now or a small (or even zero) percentage? This is the dividend policy question.

An Illustration of the Irrelevance of Dividend Policy

A powerful argument can be made that dividend policy does not matter. We illustrate this by considering the simple case of Wharton Corporation. Wharton is an all-equity firm that has existed for 10 years. The current financial managers plan to dissolve the firm in two years. The total cash flows that the firm will generate, including the proceeds from liquidation, are $10,000 in each of the next two years.

Current Policy: Dividends Set Equal to Cash Flow   At the present time, dividends at each date are set equal to the cash flow of $10,000. There are 100 shares outstanding, so the dividend per share will be $100. In Chapter 6, we showed that the value of the stock is equal to the present value of the future dividends. Assuming a 10 percent required return, the value of a share of stock today, P_0, is:

$$P_0 = \frac{D_1}{(1 + R)^1} + \frac{D_2}{(1 + R)^2}$$

$$= \frac{\$100}{1.10} + \frac{\$100}{1.10^2} = \$173.55$$

The firm as a whole is thus worth $100 \times \$173.55 = \$17,355$.

Several members of the board of Wharton have expressed dissatisfaction with the current dividend policy and have asked you to analyze an alternative policy.

Alternative Policy: Initial Dividend Is Greater than Cash Flow   Another policy is for the firm to pay a dividend of $110 per share on the first date, which is, of course, a total dividend of $11,000. Because the cash flow is only $10,000, an extra $1,000 must somehow be raised. One way to do it is to issue $1,000 of bonds or stock at Date 1. Assume that stock is issued. The new stockholders will desire enough cash flow at Date 2 so that they earn the required 10 percent return on their Date 1 investment.[2]

What is the value of the firm with this new dividend policy? The new stockholders invest $1,000. They require a 10 percent return, so they will demand $1,000 \times 1.10 = \$1,100$ of the Date 2 cash flow, leaving only $8,900 to the old stockholders. The dividends to the old stockholders will be:

	Date 1	Date 2
Aggregate dividends to old stockholders	$11,000	$8,900
Dividends per share	110	89

The present value of the dividends per share is therefore:

$$P_0 = \frac{\$110}{1.10} + \frac{\$89}{1.10^2} = \$173.55$$

This is the same value we had before.

The value of the stock is not affected by this switch in dividend policy even though we had to sell some new stock just to finance the dividend. In fact, no matter what pattern of dividend payout the firm chooses, the value of the stock will always be the same in this example. In other words, for the Wharton Corporation, dividend policy makes no difference. The reason is simple: Any increase in a dividend at some point in time is exactly offset by a decrease somewhere else, so the net effect, once we account for time value, is zero.

---

[2]The same results would occur after an issue of bonds, though the arguments would be less easily presented.

Homemade Dividends   There is an alternative and perhaps more intuitively appealing explanation about why dividend policy doesn't matter in our example. Suppose individual investor X prefers dividends per share of $100 at both Dates 1 and 2. Would she be disappointed when informed that the firm's management is adopting the alternative dividend policy (dividends of $110 and $89 on the two dates, respectively)? Not necessarily, because she could easily reinvest the $10 of unneeded funds received on Date 1 by buying some more Wharton stock. At 10 percent, this investment will grow to $11 at Date 2. Thus, she would receive her desired net cash flow of $110 − 10 = $100 at Date 1 and $89 + 11 = $100 at Date 2.

Conversely, imagine investor Z, preferring $110 of cash flow at Date 1 and $89 of cash flow at Date 2, finds that management will pay dividends of $100 at both Dates 1 and 2. This investor can simply sell $10 worth of stock to boost his total cash at Date 1 to $110. Because this investment returns 10 percent, investor Z gives up $11 at Date 2 ($10 × 1.1), leaving him with $100 − 11 = $89.

Our two investors are able to transform the corporation's dividend policy into a different policy by buying or selling on their own. The result is that investors are able to create **homemade dividends.** This means that dissatisfied stockholders can alter the firm's dividend policy to suit themselves. As a result, there is no particular advantage to any one dividend policy that the firm might choose.

Many corporations actually assist their stockholders in creating homemade dividend policies by offering *automatic dividend reinvestment plans* (ADRs or DRIPs). As the name suggests, with such a plan, stockholders have the option of automatically reinvesting some or all of their cash dividend in shares of stock. In some cases, they actually receive a discount on the stock, thereby making such a plan very attractive.

homemade dividend

Idea that individual investors can undo corporate dividend policy by reinvesting dividends or selling shares of stock.

A Test   Our discussion to this point can be summarized by considering the following true/false test questions:

1.   True or false: Dividends are irrelevant.
2.   True or false: Dividend policy is irrelevant.

The first statement is surely false, and the reason follows from common sense. Clearly, investors prefer higher dividends to lower dividends at any single date if the dividend level is held constant at every other date. To be more precise regarding the first question, if the dividend per share at a given date is raised while the dividend per share at every other date is held constant, the stock price will rise. The reason is that the present value of the future dividends must go up if this occurs. This action can be accomplished by management decisions that improve productivity, increase tax savings, strengthen product marketing, or otherwise improve cash flow.

The second statement is true, at least in the simple case we have been examining. Dividend policy by itself cannot raise the dividend at one date while keeping it the same at all other dates. Rather, dividend policy merely establishes the trade-off between dividends at one date and dividends at another date. Once we allow for time value, the present value of the dividend stream is unchanged. Thus, in this simple world, dividend policy does not matter, because managers choosing either to raise or to lower the current dividend do not affect the current value of their firm. However, we have ignored several real-world factors that might lead us to change our minds; we pursue some of these in subsequent sections.

⌈ CONCEPT QUESTIONS

16.2a How can an investor create a homemade dividend?

16.2b Are dividends irrelevant?

REAL-WORLD FACTORS FAVORING A LOW PAYOUT ⌐16.3

The example we used to illustrate the irrelevance of dividend policy ignored taxes and flotation costs. In this section, we will see that these factors might lead us to prefer a low-dividend payout.

Taxes

U.S. tax laws are complex, and they affect dividend policy in a number of ways. The key tax feature has to do with the taxation of dividend income and capital gains. For individual shareholders, *effective* tax rates on dividend income are higher than the tax rates on capital gains. Dividends received are taxed as ordinary income. Capital gains are taxed in much the same way, but the tax on a capital gain is deferred until the stock is sold. This makes the effective tax rate much lower because the present value of the tax is less.[3]

A firm that adopts a low-dividend payout will reinvest the money instead of paying it out. This reinvestment increases the value of the firm and of the equity. All other things being equal, the net effect is that the capital gains portion of the return will be higher in the future. So the fact that capital gains are taxed favorably may lead us to prefer this approach.

This tax disadvantage of dividends doesn't necessarily lead to a policy of paying no dividends. Suppose a firm has some excess cash after selecting all positive NPV projects (this type of excess cash is frequently referred to as *free cash flow*). It is considering two mutually exclusive uses of the excess cash: (1) pay dividends or (2) retain the excess cash for investment in the firm. The correct dividend policy will depend upon the individual tax rate and the corporate tax rate.

To see why, suppose that the Regional Electric Company has $1,000 of extra cash. It can retain the cash and invest it in Treasury bills yielding 10 percent, or it can pay the cash to shareholders as a dividend. Shareholders can also invest in Treasury bills with the same yield. The corporate tax rate is 34 percent, and the individual tax rate is 28 percent. What is the amount of cash that investors will have after five years under each policy?

---

[3]In fact, capital gains taxes can be avoided altogether. Although we do not recommend this particular tax-avoidance strategy, the capital gains tax can be avoided completely by dying. Your heirs are not considered to have a capital gain, so the tax liability dies when you do. In this instance, you can take it with you.

If dividends are paid now, shareholders will receive $1,000 before taxes, or $1,000 × (1 − .28) = $720 after taxes. This is the amount they will invest. If the rate on T-bills is 10 percent, before taxes, then the aftertax return is 10% × (1 − .28) = 7.2% per year. Thus, in five years, the shareholders will have:

$720 × (1 + 0.072)^5 = $1,019.31

If Regional Electric Company retains the cash, invests in Treasury bills, and pays out the proceeds five years from now, then $1,000 will be invested today. However, since the corporate tax rate is 34 percent, the aftertax return from the T-bills will be 10% × (1 − .34) = 6.6% per year. In five years, the investment will be worth:

$1,000 × (1 + 0.066)^5 = $1,376.53

If this amount is then paid out as a dividend, the stockholders will receive (after tax):

$1,376.53 × (1 − .28) = $991.10

In this case, dividends will be greater after taxes if the firm pays them now. The reason is that the firm simply cannot invest as profitably as the shareholders can on their own (on an aftertax basis).

This example shows that for a firm with extra cash, the dividend payout decision will depend on personal and corporate tax rates. All other things the same, when personal tax rates are higher than corporate tax rates, a firm will have an incentive to reduce dividend payouts. However, if personal tax rates are lower than corporate tax rates, a firm will have an incentive to pay out any excess cash in dividends.

Expected Return, Dividends, and Personal Taxes We illustrate the effect of personal taxes by considering an extreme situation where dividends are taxed as ordinary income and capital gains are not taxed at all. We show that a firm that provides more return in the form of dividends will have a lower value (or a higher pretax required return) than one whose return is in the form of untaxed capital gains.

Suppose every investor is in a 25 percent tax bracket and is considering the stocks of Firm G and Firm D. Firm G pays no dividend, and Firm D pays a dividend. The current price of the stock of Firm G is $100, and next year's price is expected to be $120. The shareholder in Firm G thus expects a $20 capital gain. With no dividend, the return is $20/$100 = 20%. If capital gains are not taxed, the pretax and aftertax returns must be the same.

Suppose the stock of Firm D is expected to pay a $20 dividend next year, and the ex dividend price will then be $100. If the stocks of Firm G and Firm D are equally risky, the market prices must be set so that their aftertax expected returns are equal. The aftertax return on Firm D will therefore have to be 20 percent.

What will be the price of stock in Firm D? The aftertax dividend is $20 × (1 − .25) = $15, so our investor will have a total of $115 after taxes. At a 20 percent required rate of return (after taxes), the present value of this aftertax amount is:

Present value = $115/1.20 = $95.83

The market price of the stock in Firm D thus must be $95.83.

What we see is that Firm D is worth less because of its dividend policy. Another way to see the same thing is to look at the pretax required return for Firm D:

Pretax return = ($120 − 95.83)/$95.83 = 25.2%

Firm D effectively has a higher cost of equity (25.2 percent versus 20 percent) because of its dividend policy. Shareholders demand the higher return as compensation for the extra tax liability.

Flotation Costs

In our example illustrating that dividend policy doesn't matter, we saw that the firm could sell some new stock if necessary to pay a dividend. As we mentioned in Chapter 13, selling new stock can be very expensive. If we include flotation costs in our argument, then we will find that the value of the stock decreases if we sell new stock.

More generally, imagine two firms that are identical in every way except that one pays out a greater percentage of its cash flow in the form of dividends. Since the other firm plows back more, its equity grows faster. If these two firms are to remain identical, then the one with the higher payout will have to periodically sell some stock to catch up. Since this is expensive, a firm might be inclined to have a low payout.

Dividend Restrictions

In some cases, a corporation may face restrictions on its ability to pay dividends. For example, as we discussed in Chapter 12, a common feature of a bond indenture is a covenant prohibiting dividend payments above some level. Also, a corporation may be prohibited by state law from paying dividends if the dividend amount exceeds the firm's retained earnings.

CONCEPT QUESTIONS

16.3a What are the tax benefits of low dividends?
16.3b Why do flotation costs favor a low payout?

REAL-WORLD FACTORS FAVORING A HIGH PAYOUT | 16.4

In this section, we consider reasons why a firm might pay its shareholders higher dividends even if it means that the firm must issue more shares of stock to finance the dividend payments.

In a classic textbook, Benjamin Graham, David Dodd, and Sidney Cottle have argued that firms should generally have high-dividend payouts because:

1. "The discounted value of near dividends is higher than the present worth of distant dividends."
2. Between "two companies with the same general earning power and same general position in an industry, the one paying the larger dividend will almost always sell at a higher price."[4]

Two factors favoring a high-dividend payout have been mentioned frequently by proponents of this view: the desire for current income and the resolution of uncertainty.

Desire for Current Income

It has been argued that many individuals desire current income. The classic example is the group of retired people and others living on a fixed income, the proverbial "widows and orphans." It is argued that this group is willing to pay a premium to get a higher dividend yield. If this is true, then it lends support to the second claim by Graham, Dodd, and Cottle.

It is easy to see, however, that this argument is not relevant in our simple case. An individual preferring high current cash flow but holding low-dividend securities could easily sell off shares to provide the necessary funds. Similarly, an individual desiring a low current cash flow but holding high-dividend securities can just reinvest the dividend. This is just our homemade dividend argument again. Thus, in a world of no transaction costs, a high current dividend policy would be of no value to the stockholder.

The current income argument may have relevance in the real world. Here the sale of low-dividend stocks would involve brokerage fees and other transaction costs. Such a sale might also trigger capital gains taxes. These direct cash expenses could be avoided by an investment in high-dividend securities. In addition, the expenditure of the stockholder's own time when selling securities and the natural (but not necessarily rational) fear of consuming out of principal might further lead many investors to buy high-dividend securities.

Even so, to put this argument in perspective, it should be remembered that financial intermediaries such as mutual funds can (and do) perform these "repackaging" transactions for individuals at very low cost. Such intermediaries could buy low-dividend stocks, and, by a controlled policy of realizing gains, they could pay their investors at a higher rate.

Uncertainty Resolution

We have just pointed out that investors with substantial current consumption needs will prefer high current dividends. In another classic treatment, Gordon has argued that a high-dividend policy also benefits stockholders because it resolves uncertainty.[5]

---

[4]G. Graham, D. Dodd, and S. Cottle, *Security Analysis* (New York: McGraw-Hill, 1962).

[5]M. Gordon, *The Investment, Financing and Valuation of the Corporation* (Homewood, Ill.: Richard D. Irwin, 1961).

According to Gordon, investors price a security by forecasting and discounting future dividends. Gordon then argues that forecasts of dividends to be received in the distant future have greater uncertainty than do forecasts of near-term dividends. Because investors dislike uncertainty, the stock price should be low for those companies that pay small dividends now in order to remit higher dividends at later dates.

Gordon's argument is essentially a "bird-in-hand" story. A $1 dividend in a shareholder's pocket is somehow worth more than that same $1 in a bank account held by the corporation. By now, you should see the problem with this argument. A shareholder can create a bird in hand very easily just by selling some of the stock.

Tax and Legal Benefits from High Dividends

Earlier, we saw that dividends were taxed unfavorably for individual investors. This fact is a powerful argument for a low payout. However, there are a number of other investors who do not receive unfavorable tax treatment from holding high-dividend yield, rather than low-dividend yield, securities.

Corporate Investors   A significant tax break on dividends occurs when a corporation owns stock in another corporation. A corporate stockholder receiving either common or preferred dividends is granted a 70 percent (or more) dividend exclusion. Since the 70 percent exclusion does not apply to capital gains, this group is taxed unfavorably on capital gains.

As a result of the dividend exclusion, high-dividend, low-capital-gains stocks may be more appropriate for corporations to hold. As we discuss elsewhere, this is why corporations hold a substantial percentage of the outstanding preferred stock in the economy. This tax advantage of dividends also leads some corporations to hold high-yielding stocks instead of long-term bonds because there is no similar tax exclusion of interest payments to corporate bondholders.

Tax-Exempt Investors   We have pointed out both the tax advantages and disadvantages of a low-dividend payout. Of course, this discussion is irrelevant to those in zero tax brackets. This group includes some of the largest investors in the economy, such as pension funds, endowment funds, and trust funds.

There are some legal reasons for large institutions to favor high-dividend yields. First, institutions such as pension funds and trust funds are often set up to manage money for the benefit of others. The managers of such institutions have a *fiduciary responsibility* to invest the money prudently. It has been considered imprudent in courts of law to buy stock in companies with no established dividend record.

Second, institutions such as university endowment funds and trust funds are frequently prohibited from spending any of the principal. Such institutions might therefore prefer high-dividend yield stocks so they have some ability to spend. Like widows and orphans, this group thus prefers current income. Unlike widows and orphans, this group is very large in terms of the amount of stock owned.

Overall, individual investors (for whatever reason) may have a desire for current income and may thus be willing to pay the dividend tax. In addition, some very large investors such as corporations and tax-free institutions may have a very strong preference for high-dividend payouts.

16.5 | A RESOLUTION OF REAL-WORLD FACTORS?

In the previous sections, we presented some factors that favor a low-dividend policy and others that favor a high-dividend policy. In this section, we discuss two important concepts related to dividends and dividend policy: the information content of dividends and the clientele effect. The first topic illustrates both the importance of dividends in general and the importance of distinguishing between dividends and dividend policy. The second topic suggests that, despite the many real-world considerations we have discussed, the dividend payout ratio may not be as important as we originally imagined.

Information Content of Dividends

To begin, we quickly review some of our earlier discussion. Previously, we examined three different positions on dividends:

1. Based on the homemade dividend argument, dividend policy is irrelevant.

2. Because of tax effects for individual investors and new issues costs, a low-dividend policy is the best.

3. Because of the desire for current income and related factors, a high-dividend policy is the best.

If you wanted to decide which of these positions is the right one, an obvious way to get started would be to look at what happens to stock prices when companies announce dividend changes. You would find with some consistency that stock prices rise when the current dividend is unexpectedly increased, and they generally fall when the dividend is unexpectedly decreased. What does this imply about any of the three positions just stated?

At first glance, the behavior we describe seems consistent with the third position and inconsistent with the other two. In fact, many writers have argued this. If stock prices rise on dividend increases and fall on dividend decreases, then isn't the market saying it approves of higher dividends?

Other authors have pointed out that this observation doesn't really tell us much about dividend policy. Everyone agrees that dividends are important, all other things being equal. Companies only cut dividends with great reluctance. Thus, a dividend cut is often a signal that the firm is in trouble.

More to the point, a dividend cut is usually not a voluntary, planned change in dividend policy. Instead, it usually signals that management does not think that the current dividend policy can be maintained. As a result, expectations of future dividends should generally be revised downward. The present value of expected future dividends falls and so does the stock price.

In this case, the stock price declines following a dividend cut because future dividends are generally lower, not because the firm changes the percentage of its earnings it will pay out in the form of dividends.

To give a particularly dramatic example, consider what happened to Consolidated Edison, the nation's largest public utility, in the second quarter of 1974. Faced with poor operating results and problems associated with the OPEC oil embargo, Con Ed announced after the market closed that it was omitting its regular quarterly dividend of 45 cents per share. This was somewhat surprising given Con Ed's size, prominence in the industry, and long dividend history. Also, Con Ed's earnings at that time were sufficient to pay the dividend, at least by some analysts' estimates.

The next morning was not pleasant on the NYSE. Sell orders were so heavy that a market could not be established for several hours. When trading finally got started, the stock opened at about $12 per share, down from $18 the day before. In other words, Con Ed, a very large company, lost about ⅓ of its market value overnight. As this case illustrates, shareholders can react very negatively to unanticipated cuts in dividends.

In a similar vein, an unexpected increase in the dividend signals good news. Management will raise the dividend only when future earnings, cash flow, and general prospects are expected to rise enough so that the dividend will not have to be cut later. A dividend increase is management's signal to the market that the firm is expected to do well. The stock reacts favorably because expectations of future dividends are revised upwards, not because the firm has increased its payout.

In both these cases, the stock price reacts to the dividend change. The reaction can be attributed to changes in the expected amount of future dividends, not necessarily a change in dividend payout policy. This signal is called the **information content effect** of the dividend. The fact that dividend changes convey information about the firm to the market makes it difficult to interpret the effect of the dividend policy of the firm.

information content effect

The market's reaction to a change in corporate dividend payout.

The Clientele Effect

In our earlier discussion, we saw that some groups (wealthy individuals, for example) have an incentive to pursue low-payout (or zero-payout) stocks. Other groups (corporations, for example) have an incentive to pursue high-payout stocks. Companies with high payouts will thus attract one group and low-payout companies will attract another.

These different groups are called *clienteles,* and what we have described is a **clientele effect.** The clientele effect argument states that different groups of investors desire different levels of dividends. When a firm chooses a particular dividend policy, the only effect is to attract a particular clientele. If a firm changes its dividend policy, then they just attract a different clientele.

clientele effect

Argument that stocks attract particular groups based on dividend yield and the resulting tax effects.

What we are left with is a simple supply and demand argument. Suppose that 40 percent of all investors prefer high dividends, but only 20 percent of the firms pay high dividends. Here the high-dividend firms will be in short supply;

thus, their stock prices will rise. Consequently, low-dividend firms would find it advantageous to switch policies until 40 percent of all firms have high payouts. At this point, the *dividend market* is in equilibrium. Further changes in dividend policy are pointless because all of the clienteles are satisfied. The dividend policy for any individual firm is now irrelevant.

The clientele effect on dividend policy is illustrated by the remarks made by John Childs of Kidder-Peabody (an investment bank) in the following exchange:[6]

> **Joseph T. Willet:** John, you've been around public utilities for a good many years. Why do you think that utilities have such high dividend payout ratios?
>
> **John Childs:** They're raising dividends so they can raise capital. . . . If you take the dividends out of utilities today, you'll never sell another share of stock. That's how important it is. In fact, if a few major utilities (with no special problems) cut their dividends, small investors would lose faith in the utility industry and that would finish the sales of utility stocks.
>
> **John Childs (again):** What you are trying to do with dividend policy is to enhance and strengthen the natural interest of investors in your company. The type of stockholders you attract will depend on the type of company you are. If you're Genentech, you are going to attract the type of stockholders which have absolutely no interest in dividends. In fact, you would hurt the stock if you paid dividends. On the other hand, you go over to the other extreme such as utilities and yield banks' stocks. There the stockholders are extremely interested in dividends, and these dividends have an effect on market price.

To see if you understand the clientele effect, consider the following statement: "In spite of the theoretical argument that dividend policy is irrelevant or that firms should not pay dividends, many investors like high dividends. Because of this fact, a firm can boost its share price by having a higher dividend payout ratio." True or false?

The answer is false if clienteles exist. As long as enough high-dividend firms satisfy the dividend-loving investors, a firm won't be able to boost its share price by paying high dividends. An unsatisfied clientele must exist for this to happen, and there is no evidence that this is the case.

CONCEPT QUESTIONS

16.5a How does the market react to unexpected dividend changes? What does this tell us about dividends? About dividend policy?

16.5b What is a dividend clientele? All things considered, would you expect a risky firm with significant but highly uncertain growth prospects to have a low- or high-dividend payout?

---

[6]Joseph T. Willett, moderator. "A Discussion of Corporate Policy," in *Six Roundtable Discussions of Corporate Finance with Joel Stern*, ed. D. H. Chew (Basel Blackwell, 1986). The panelists included Robert Litzenberger, Pat Hess, Bill Kealy, John Childs, and Joel Stern.

ESTABLISHING A DIVIDEND POLICY | 16.6

How do firms actually determine the level of dividends that they will pay at a particular time? As we have seen, there are good reasons for firms to pay high dividends and there are good reasons to pay low dividends.

We know some things about how dividends are paid in practice. Firms don't like to cut dividends. Consider the case of American Telephone and Telegraph Company (AT&T). It has been in business since 1885, and during that time it has never reduced or omitted a dividend. This is remarkable but not unusual. As Table 16.1 shows, one company, Chemical New York Corporation, has been paying dividends since 1827.

In the next section, we discuss a particular dividend policy strategy. In doing so, we emphasize the real-world features of dividend policy. We also analyze an increasingly important alternative to cash dividends, a stock repurchase.

Residual Dividend Approach

Earlier, we noted that firms with higher dividend payouts will have to sell stock more often. As we have seen, such sales are not very common and they can be very expensive. Consistent with this, we will assume that the firm wishes to minimize the need to sell new equity. We will also assume that the firm wishes to maintain its current capital structure.

If a firm wishes to avoid new equity sales, then it will have to rely on internally generated equity to finance new, positive NPV projects.[7] Dividends can only be paid out of what is left over. This leftover is called the *residual,* and such a dividend policy is called a **residual dividend approach.**

With a residual dividend policy, the firm's objective is to meet its investment needs and maintain its desired debt/equity ratio before paying dividends. To illustrate, imagine that a firm has $1,000 in earnings and a debt/equity ratio of .50. Notice that, since the debt/equity ratio is .50, the firm has 50 cents in

residual dividend approach

Policy under which a firm pays dividends only after meeting its investment needs while maintaining a desired debt-to-equity ratio.

---

[7]Our discussion of sustainable growth in Chapter 4 is relevant here. We assumed there that a firm has a fixed capital structure, profit margin, and capital intensity. If the firm raises no new external equity and wishes to grow at some target rate, then there is only one payout ratio consistent with these assumptions.

Stock	Year Dividend Payments Began
Chemical New York Corp.	1827
Connecticut Natural Gas Corp.	1851
Bay State Gas Co.	1852
Washington Gas Light Co.	1852
Irving Bank Corp.	1865

Table 16.1

Paying dividends

Data from the *Fact Book 1986,* published by the New York Stock Exchange.

In Their Own Words...
Fischer Black on Why Firms Pay Dividends

I think investors simply like dividends. They believe that dividends enhance stock value (given the firm's prospects), and they feel uncomfortable spending out of their capital.

We see evidence for this everywhere: Investment advisors and institutions treat a high-yield stock as both attractive and safe, financial analysts value a stock by predicting and discounting its dividends, financial economists study the relation between stock prices and actual dividends, and investors complain about dividend cuts.

What if investors were neutral toward dividends? Investment advisors would tell clients to spend indifferently from income and capital and, if taxable, to avoid income; financial analysts would ignore dividends in valuing stocks; financial economists would treat stock price and the discounted value of dividends as equal, even when stocks are mispriced; and a firm would apologize to its taxable investors when forced by an accumulated earnings tax to pay dividends. This is not what we observe of course.

Furthermore, changing dividends seems a poor way to tell the financial markets about a firm's prospects. Public statements can better detail the firm's prospects and have more impact on both the speaker's and the firm's reputations.

I predict that under current tax rules, dividends will gradually disappear.

Fischer Black is a partner at Goldman Sachs & Co., an investment banking firm. Before that he was a professor of finance at MIT. He is one of the fathers of option pricing theory, and he is widely regarded as one of the preeminent financial scholars. He is well known for his creative ideas, many of which were dismissed at first only to become part of accepted lore when others finally came to understand them.

---

debt for every $1.50 in value. The firm's capital structure is thus ⅓ debt and ⅔ equity.

The first step in implementing a residual dividend policy is to determine the amount of funds that can be generated without selling new equity. If the firm reinvests the entire $1,000 and pays no dividend, then equity will increase by $1,000. To keep the debt/equity ratio at .50, the firm must borrow an additional $500. The total amount of funds that can be generated without selling new equity is thus $1,000 + 500 = $1,500.

The second step is to decide whether or not a dividend will be paid. To do this, we compare the total amount that can be generated without selling new equity ($1,500 in this case) with planned capital spending. If funds needed exceed funds available, then no dividend is paid. In addition, the firm will have to sell new equity to raise the needed financing or else (more likely) postpone some planned capital spending.

If funds needed are less than funds generated, then a dividend will be paid. The amount of the dividend is the residual, that is, that portion of the earnings that is not needed to finance new projects. For example, suppose we have $900 in planned capital spending. To maintain the firm's capital structure, this $900 must be financed ⅔ equity and ⅓ debt. So, the firm will actually borrow ⅓ × $900 = $300. The firm will spend ⅔ × $900 = $600 of the $1,000 in equity available. There is a $1,000 − 600 = $400 residual, so the dividend will be $400.

In sum, the firm has aftertax earnings of $1,000. Dividends paid are $400. Retained earnings are $600, and new borrowing totals $300. The firm's debt/equity ratio is unchanged at .50.

Row	(1) Aftertax Earnings	(2) New Investment	(3) Additional Debt	(4) Retained Earnings	(5) Additional Stock	(6) Dividends
1	$1,000	$3,000	$1,000	$1,000	$1,000	$ 0
2	1,000	2,000	667	1,000	333	0
3	1,000	1,500	500	1,000	0	0
4	1,000	1,000	333	667	0	333
5	1,000	500	167	333	0	667
6	1,000	0	0	0	0	1,000

Table 16.2

Example of dividend policy under the residual approach

The relationship between physical investment and dividend payout is presented for six different levels of investment in Table 16.2 and illustrated in Figure 16.3. The first three rows of the table can be discussed together, because in each case no dividends are paid.

In row 1, for example, note that new investment is $3,000. Additional debt of $1,000 and equity of $2,000 must be raised to keep the debt/equity ratio constant. Since this latter figure is greater than the $1,000 of earnings, all earnings are retained. Additional stock to be raised is also $1,000. In this example, since new stock is issued, dividends are not simultaneously paid out.

In rows 2 and 3, investment drops. Additional debt needed goes down as well since it is equal to ⅓ of investment. Because the amount of new equity needed is still greater than or equal to $1,000, all earnings are retained and no dividend is paid.

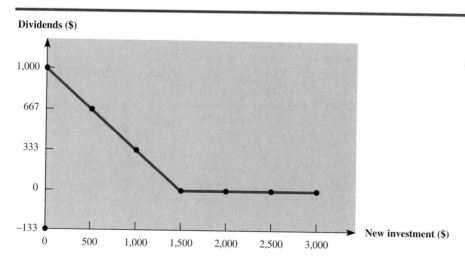

Figure 16.3

Relationship between dividends and investment in the example of residual dividend policy

This figure illustrates that a firm with many investment opportunities will pay small amounts of dividends and a firm with few investment opportunities will pay relatively large amounts of dividends.

We finally find a situation in row 4 where a dividend is paid. Here, total investment is $1,000. To keep our debt/equity ratio constant, ⅓ of this investment, or $333, is financed by debt. The remaining ⅔, or $667, comes from internal funds, implying that the residual is $1,000 − 667 = $333. The dividend is equal to this $333 residual.

In this case, note that no additional stock is issued. Since the needed investment is even lower in rows 5 and 6, new debt is reduced further, retained earnings drop, and dividends increase. Again, no additional stock is issued.

Given our discussion, we expect those firms with many investment opportunities to pay a small percentage of their earnings as dividends and other firms with fewer opportunities to pay a high percentage of their earnings as dividends. This result appears to occur in the real world. Young, fast-growing firms commonly employ a low payout ratio, whereas older, slower-growing firms in more mature industries use a higher ratio.

We see this pattern somewhat in Table 16.3. Duke Power and Philadelphia Electric are slower-growing firms with high payouts, and Capital Cities is a fast-growing firm with a pattern of low payouts. In general, notice how much steadier the dividends are than the earnings and payout ratios. For example, Delta has a relatively low payout in most of the years, but the payout exceeds 100 percent on one occasion. This illustrates that firms will adjust their payouts if needed to avoid or soften dividend cuts. We discuss this next.

Dividend Stability

The key point of the residual dividend approach is that dividends are paid only after all profitable investment opportunities are exhausted. Of course, a strict residual approach might lead to a very unstable dividend policy. If investment opportunities in one period are quite high, dividends would be low or zero. Conversely, dividends might be high in the next period if investment opportunities are considered less promising.

Consider the case of Big Department Stores, Inc., a retailer whose annual earnings are forecasted to be equal from year to year but whose quarterly earnings change throughout the year. They are low in each year's first quarter because of the post-Christmas business slump. Although earnings increase only slightly in the second and third quarters, they advance greatly in the fourth quarter as a result of the Christmas season. A graph of this firm's earnings is presented in Figure 16.4.

The firm can choose between at least two types of dividend policies. First, each quarter's dividend can be a fixed fraction of that quarter's earnings. Here, dividends will vary throughout the year. This is a cyclical dividend policy. Second, each quarter's dividend can be a fixed fraction of yearly earnings, implying that all dividend payments would be equal. This is a stable dividend policy. These two types of dividend policies are displayed in Figure 16.5.

Corporate officials generally agree that a stable policy is in the interest of the firm and its stockholders, so the stable policy would be more common. For example, looking back at Table 16.3, the dividends are much less volatile through time than the earnings.

Table 16.3

The stability of dividends

	EPS ($)	DPS ($)	Payout (%)	Yield (%)	EPS ($)	DPS ($)	Payout (%)	Yield (%)
				High Payout Firms				
			Duke Power				*Philadelphia Electric*	
1990	$ 2.75	$2.23	81%	7.4%	$ 2.16	$1.45	67%	8.4%
1989	2.76	2.15	78	7.4	2.49	2.20	88	10.2
1988	3.01	2.07	69	7.2	2.33	2.20	94	11.7
1987	3.03	1.99	66	6.9	2.33	2.20	94	10.3
1986	2.65	1.91	72	6.7	2.60	2.20	85	10.6
1985	2.40	1.83	76	8.9	2.56	2.20	86	14.3
1984	2.31	1.73	75	10.7	2.70	2.20	82	16.3
1983	2.11	1.63	77	10.9	2.40	2.12	88	12.6
1982	1.98	1.53	77	11.6	2.39	2.06	86	14.6
1981	1.77	1.43	81	12.4	2.25	1.90	84	13.2
				Average Payout Firms				
			General Motors				*IBM*	
1990	$ 4.09	$3.00	73%	7.0%	$10.51	$4.84	46%	4.4%
1989	6.33	3.00	47	6.9	9.05	4.73	52	4.2
1988	6.82	2.50	37	6.6	9.83	4.40	45	3.8
1987	5.03	2.50	50	6.5	8.72	4.40	50	3.0
1986	8.21	5.00	61	6.6	7.81	4.40	56	3.1
1985	12.28	5.00	40	6.9	10.67	4.40	41	3.4
1984	14.22	4.75	34	6.7	10.77	4.10	38	3.5
1983	11.84	2.80	24	4.1	9.04	3.71	41	3.2
1982	3.98	2.40	60	5.2	7.39	3.44	47	5.0
1981	1.07	2.40	224	5.1	5.63	3.44	61	5.9
				Low Payout Firms				
			Capital Cities				*Delta Air Lines*	
1990	$27.71	$0.20	1%	0.1%	$ 5.28	$1.70	32%	2.4%
1989	27.25	0.20	1	0.1	9.37	1.20	13	2.2
1988	22.31	0.20	1	0.1	6.30	1.20	19	2.5
1987	16.46	0.20	1	0.1	5.90	1.00	17	2.0
1986	11.20	0.20	2	0.1	1.18	1.00	85	2.3
1985	10.87	0.20	2	0.1	6.50	0.70	11	1.7
1984	10.40	0.20	2	0.1	4.42	0.60	14	1.7
1983	8.53	0.20	2	0.1	(2.18)	1.00	—	2.5
1982	7.25	0.20	3	0.1	0.52	0.95	182	3.2
1981	6.12	0.20	3	0.2	3.68	0.70	19	2.4

Note: EPS ($) is dollar amount of earnings per share; DPS ($) is dollar amount of dividends per share; payout (%) is DPS ($) divided by EPS ($); yield (%) is dividend paid out during the year divided by stock price at the end of the year.

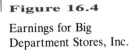

Figure 16.4

Earnings for Big Department Stores, Inc.

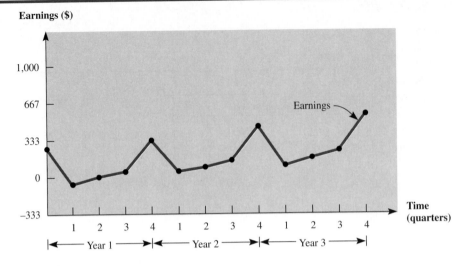

A Compromise Dividend Policy

In practice, many firms appear to follow what amounts to a compromise dividend policy. Such a policy is based on five main goals:

1. Avoid cutting back on positive NPV projects to pay a dividend.
2. Avoid dividend cuts.
3. Avoid the need to sell equity.
4. Maintain a target debt/equity ratio.
5. Maintain a target dividend payout ratio.

These goals are ranked more or less in order of their importance. In our strict residual approach, we assumed that the firm maintained a fixed debt/equity ratio. Under the compromise approach, that debt/equity ratio is viewed as a long-range goal. It is allowed to vary in the short run if necessary to avoid a dividend cut or the need to sell new equity.

In addition to a strong reluctance to cut dividends, financial managers tend to think of dividend payments in terms of a proportion of income, and they also tend to think investors are entitled to a "fair" share of corporate income. This share is the long-run **target payout ratio,** and it is the fraction of the earnings that the firm expects to pay as dividends under ordinary circumstances. Again, this is viewed as a long-range goal, so it might vary in the short run if needed. As a result, in the long run, earnings growth is followed by dividend increases, but only with a lag.

One can minimize the problems of dividend instability by creating two types of dividends: regular and extra. For companies using this approach, the regular dividend would likely be a relatively small fraction of permanent earnings, so that it could be sustained easily. Extra dividends would be granted when an increase in earnings was expected to be temporary.

target payout ratio

A firm's long-term desired dividend-to-earnings ratio.

Dollars

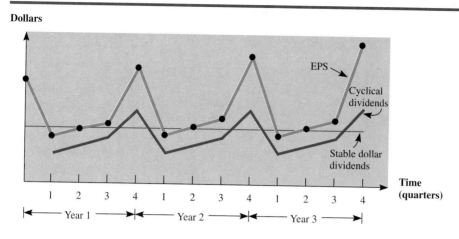

Figure 16.5

Alternative dividend
policies for Big
Department Stores, Inc.

Cyclical dividend policy: Dividends are a constant proportion of earnings at each pay date.
Stable dividend policy: Dividends are a constant proportion of earnings over an earnings cycle.

Since investors look on an extra dividend as a bonus, there is relatively little disappointment when an extra dividend is not repeated. Although the extra-dividend approach appears quite sensible, few companies use it in practice. One reason is that a share repurchase, which we discuss next, does much the same thing with some extra advantages.

CONCEPT QUESTIONS

16.6a What is a residual dividend policy?

16.6b What is the chief drawback to a strict residual policy? What do many
firms do in practice?

STOCK REPURCHASE: AN ALTERNATIVE TO CASH DIVIDENDS | 16.7

When a firm wants to pay cash to its shareholders, it normally pays a cash dividend. Another way is to **repurchase** its own stock. IBM, for example, discovered share repurchasing in 1974 when it bought back $1.4 billion of its own shares.

repurchase

Another method used to pay out a firm's earnings to its owners, which provides more preferable tax treatment than dividends.

As we discussed in Chapter 13, net equity sales in the United States have frequently been negative in recent years. This has occurred because corporations actually repurchased more stock than they sold. Stock repurchasing has thus been a major financial activity, and it appears that it will continue to be one. For example, in 1989, General Electric announced a $10 billion repurchase and IBM announced a $5 billion buy-back.

Cash Dividends versus Repurchase

Imagine an all-equity company with excess cash of $300,000. The firm pays no dividends, and its net income for the year just ended is $49,000. The market value balance sheet at the end of the year is represented below.

Market Value Balance Sheet
(before paying out excess cash)

Excess cash	$ 300,000	$ 0	Debt
Other assets	700,000	1,000,000	Equity
Total	$1,000,000	$1,000,000	

There are 100,000 shares outstanding. The total market value of the equity is $1 million, so the stock sells for $10 per share. Earnings per share (EPS) were $49,000/100,000 = $.49, and the price/earnings ratio (P/E) is $10/$.49 = 20.4.

One option the company is considering is a $300,000/100,000 = $3 per share extra cash dividend. Alternatively, the company is thinking of using the money to repurchase $300,000/$10 = 30,000 shares of stock.

If commissions, taxes, and other imperfections are ignored in our example, the stockholders shouldn't care which option is chosen. Does this seem surprising? It shouldn't, really. What is happening here is that the firm is paying out $300,000 in cash. The new balance sheet is represented below.

Market Value Balance Sheet
(after paying out excess cash)

Excess cash	$ 0	$ 0	Debt
Other assets	700,000	700,000	Equity
Total	$700,000	$700,000	

If the cash is paid out as a dividend, there are still 100,000 shares outstanding, so each is worth $7.

The fact that the per-share value fell from $10 to $7 isn't a cause for concern. Consider a stockholder who owns 100 shares. At $10 per share before the dividend, the total value is $1,000.

After the $3 dividend, this same stockholder has 100 shares worth $7 each, for a total of $700, plus 100 × $3 = $300 in cash, for a combined total of $1,000. This just illustrates what we saw early on: A cash dividend doesn't affect a stockholder's wealth if there are no imperfections. In this case, the stock price simply fell by $3 when the stock went ex dividend.

Also, since total earnings and the number of shares outstanding haven't changed, EPS is still 49 cents. The price/earnings ratio (P/E), however, falls to $7/$.490 = 14.3. Why we are looking at accounting earnings and P/E ratios will be apparent just below.

Alternatively, if the company repurchases 30,000 shares, there will be 70,000 left outstanding. The balance sheet looks the same.

Market Value Balance Sheet
(after share repurchase)

Excess cash	$ 0	$ 0	Debt
Other assets	700,000	700,000	Equity
Total	$700,000	$700,000	

The company is worth $700,000 again, so each remaining share is worth $700,000/70,000 = $10 each. Our stockholder with 100 shares is obviously unaffected. For example, if she were so inclined, she could sell 30 shares and end up with $300 in cash and $700 in stock, just as she has if the firm pays the cash dividend. This is another example of a homemade dividend.

In this second case, EPS goes up since total earnings are the same while the number of shares goes down. The new EPS will be $49,000/70,000 = $.7 per share. However, the important thing to notice is that the P/E ratio is $10/$.7 = 14.3, just as it was following the dividend.

This example illustrates the important point that, if there are no imperfections, a cash dividend and a share repurchase are essentially the same thing. This is just another illustration of dividend policy irrelevance when there are no taxes or other imperfections.

Real-World Considerations in a Repurchase

The example we have just described shows that a repurchase and a cash dividend are the same thing in a world without taxes and transaction costs. In the real world, there are some accounting differences between a share repurchase and a cash dividend, but the most important difference is in the tax treatment.

Under current tax law, a repurchase has a significant tax advantage over a cash dividend. A dividend is fully taxed as ordinary income, and a shareholder has no choice about whether or not to receive the dividend. In a repurchase, a shareholder pays taxes only if (1) the shareholder actually chooses to sell and (2) the shareholder has a capital gain on the sale.

For example, a dividend of $1 per share is taxed at ordinary rates. Investors in the 28 percent tax bracket who own 100 shares of the security would pay as much as $100 × .28 = $28 in taxes. Selling shareholders would pay far lower taxes if $100 worth of stock were repurchased. This is because taxes are paid only on the profit from a sale. Thus, the gain on a sale would be only $40 if shares sold at $100 were originally purchased at $60. The capital gains tax would be 0.28 × $40 = $11.20.

If this example strikes you as being too good to be true, you are quite likely right. The IRS does not allow a repurchase solely for the purpose of avoiding taxes. There must be some other business-related reason for doing it. Probably the most common reason is that "the stock is a good investment." The second most common is that "investing in the stock is a good use for the money" or that "the stock is undervalued," and so on.

However it is justified, some corporations have engaged in massive repurchases in recent years. Because of the tax treatment, a repurchase is a very sensible alternative to an extra dividend and executing a repurchase every once in a while provides a useful means of stabilizing cash dividends.

Share Repurchase and EPS

You may read in the popular financial press that a share repurchase is beneficial because earnings per share increase. As we have seen, this will happen. The reason is simply that a share repurchase reduces the number of shares, but it has no effect on total earnings. As a result, EPS rises.

However, the financial press may place undue emphasis on EPS figures in a repurchase agreement. In our example above, we saw that the value of the stock wasn't affected by the EPS change. In fact, the price/earnings ratio was exactly the same when we compared a cash dividend to a repurchase.

Since the increase in earnings per share is exactly tracked by the increase in the price per share, there is no net effect. Put another way, the increase in EPS is just an accounting adjustment that reflects (correctly) the change in the number of shares.

In the real world, to the extent that repurchases benefit the firm, we would argue that they do so primarily because of the tax considerations we discussed above.

⌐CONCEPT QUESTIONS

16.7a Why might a stock repurchase make more sense than an extra cash dividend?

16.7b Why don't all firms use stock repurchases instead of cash dividends?

16.8 | STOCK DIVIDENDS AND STOCK SPLITS

stock dividend
Payment made by a firm to its owners in the form of stock, diluting the value of each share outstanding.

stock split
An increase in a firm's shares outstanding without any change in owner's equity.

Another type of dividend is paid out in shares of stock. This type of dividend is called a **stock dividend.** A stock dividend is not a true dividend because it is not paid in cash. The effect of a stock dividend is to increase the number of shares that each owner holds. Since there are more shares outstanding, each is simply worth less.

A stock dividend is commonly expressed as a percentage; for example, a 20 percent stock dividend means that a shareholder receives one new share for every five currently owned (a 20 percent increase). Since every shareholder owns 20 percent more stock, the total number of shares outstanding rises by 20 percent. As we will see in a moment, the result would be that each share of stock is worth about 20 percent less.

A **stock split** is essentially the same thing as a stock dividend, except that a split is expressed as a ratio instead of a percentage. When a split is declared, each share is split up to create additional shares. For example, in a three-for-one stock split, each old share is split into three new shares.

Some Details on Stock Splits and Stock Dividends

Stock splits and stock dividends have essentially the same impacts on the corporation and the shareholder: They increase the number of shares outstanding and reduce the value per share. The accounting treatment is not the same, however, and it depends on two things: (1) whether the distribution is a stock split or a stock dividend and (2) the size of the stock dividend if it is called a dividend.

By convention, stock dividends of less than 20 to 25 percent are called *small stock dividends.* The accounting procedure for such a dividend is discussed below. A stock dividend greater than this 20 to 25 percent is called a *large stock dividend.* Large stock dividends are not uncommon. For example, in 1973, Walt Disney declared a 100 percent stock dividend, thereby doubling the number of outstanding shares. Except for some relatively minor accounting differences, this has the same effect as a two-for-one stock split.

Example of a Small Stock Dividend   The Peterson Co., a consulting firm specializing in difficult accounting problems, has 10,000 shares of stock outstanding, each selling at $66. The total market value of the equity is $66 × 10,000 = $660,000. With a 10 percent stock dividend, each stockholder receives one additional share for each 10 that she owns, and the total number of shares outstanding after the dividend is 11,000.

Before the stock dividend, the equity portion of Peterson's balance sheet might look like this:

Common stock ($1 par, 10,000 shares outstanding)	$ 10,000
Capital in excess of par value	200,000
Retained earnings	290,000
Total owners' equity	$500,000

A seemingly arbitrary accounting procedure is used to adjust the balance sheet after a small stock dividend. Since 1,000 new shares are issued, the common stock account is increased by $1,000 (1,000 shares at $1 par value each), for a total of $11,000. The market price of $66 is $65 greater than the par value, so the "excess" of $65 × 1,000 shares = $65,000 is added to the capital surplus account (capital in excess of par value), producing a total of $265,000.

Total owners' equity is unaffected by the stock dividend because no cash has come in or out, so retained earnings is reduced by the entire $66,000, leaving $224,000. The net effect of these machinations is that Peterson's equity accounts now look like this:

Common stock ($1 par, 11,000 shares outstanding)	$ 11,000
Capital in excess of par value	265,000
Retained earnings	224,000
Total owners' equity	$500,000

Example of a Stock Split   A stock split is conceptually similar to a stock dividend, but it is commonly expressed as a ratio. For example, in a three-for-two split, each shareholder receives one additional share of stock for each two held originally, so a three-for-two split amounts to a 50 percent stock dividend. Again, no cash is paid out, and the percentage of the entire firm that each shareholder owns is unaffected.

The accounting treatment of a stock split is a little different (and simpler) from that of a stock dividend. Suppose that Peterson decides to declare a two-for-one stock split. The number of shares outstanding will double to 20,000, and the par value will be halved to .50 per share. The owners' equity after the split is represented as:

Common stock ($.50 par, 20,000 shares outstanding)	$ 10,000
Capital in excess of par value	200,000
Retained earnings	290,000
Total owners' equity	$500,000

Note that, for all three of the categories, the figures on the right are completely unaffected by the split. The only change is in the par value. Since the number of shares has doubled, the par value of each is cut in half.

Example of a Large Stock Dividend   In our example above, if a 100 percent stock dividend were declared, 10,000 new shares would be distributed, so 20,000 shares will be outstanding. At a $1 par value per share, the common stock account would rise by $10,000, for a total of $20,000. The capital in excess of par account or, more commonly, the retained earnings account would be reduced by this amount. Here we reduced the retained earnings account by $10,000, leaving $280,000. The result is the following:

Common stock ($1.00 par, 20,000 shares outstanding)	$ 20,000
Capital in excess of par value	200,000
Retained earnings	280,000
Total owners' equity	$500,000

Value of Stock Splits and Stock Dividends

The laws of logic tell us that stock splits and stock dividends can (1) leave the value of the firm unaffected, (2) increase its value, or (3) decrease its value. Unfortunately, the issues are complex enough that one cannot easily determine which of the three relationships holds.

The Benchmark Case   A strong case can be made that stock dividends and splits do not change either the wealth of any shareholder or the wealth of the firm as a whole. In our example above, the equity had a total market value of $660,000. With the stock dividend, the number of shares increased to 11,000, so it seems that each would be worth $660,000/11,000 = $60.

For example, a shareholder who had 100 shares worth $66 each before the dividend would have 110 shares worth $60 each afterwards. The total value of the stock is $6,600 either way; so the stock dividend doesn't really have any economic effect.

After the stock split, there were 20,000 shares outstanding, so each should be worth $660,000/20,000 = $33. In other words, the number of shares doubles and the price halves. From these calculations, it appears that stock dividends and splits are just paper transactions.

Although these results are relatively obvious, there are reasons that are often given to suggest that there may be some benefits to these actions. The typical financial manager is aware of many real-world complexities, and, for that reason, the stock split or stock dividend decision is not treated lightly in practice.

Popular Trading Range   Proponents of stock dividends and stock splits frequently argue that a security has a proper **trading range.** When the security is priced above this level, many investors do not have the funds to buy the common trading unit of 100 shares, called a *round lot.* Although securities can be purchased in *odd-lot* form (fewer than 100 shares), the commissions are greater. Thus, firms will split the stock to keep the price in this trading range.

trading range
Price range between highest and lowest prices at which a stock is traded.

Although this argument is a popular one, its validity is questionable for a number of reasons. Mutual funds, pension funds, and other institutions have steadily increased their trading activity since World War II and now handle a sizable percentage of total trading volume (on the order of 80 percent of NYSE trading volume, for example). Because these institutions buy and sell in huge amounts, the individual share price is of little concern.

Furthermore, we sometimes observe share prices that are quite large without appearing to cause problems. To take an extreme case, the largest company in the world (in terms of the total market value of outstanding equity) is the Japanese telecommunications giant, NTT. In early 1989, NTT shares were selling for about $12,000 *each,* so a round lot would have cost a cool $1.2 million. This is fairly expensive, but the stock has sold for more than $20,000 per share. Closer to home, Berkshire-Hathaway, a widely respected company, sold for about $5,000 per share at that time.

Finally, there is evidence that stock splits may actually decrease the liquidity of the company's shares. Following a two-for-one split, the number of shares traded should more than double if liquidity is increased by the split. This doesn't appear to happen, and the reverse is sometimes observed.

Reverse Splits

A less frequently encountered financial maneuver is the **reverse split.** In a one-for-three reverse split, each investor exchanges three old shares for one new share. The par value is tripled in the process. As mentioned previously with reference to stock splits and stock dividends, a case can be made that a reverse split changes nothing substantial about the company.

reverse split
Stock split under which a firm's number of shares outstanding is reduced.

Given real-world imperfections, three related reasons are cited for reverse splits. First, transaction costs to shareholders may be less after the reverse split. Second, the liquidity and marketability of a company's stock might be improved when its price is raised to the popular trading range. Third, stocks selling below a certain level are not considered respectable, meaning that investors underestimate these firms' earnings, cash flow, growth, and stability. Some financial analysts argue that a reverse split can achieve instant respectability. As with stock splits, none of these reasons is particularly compelling, especially the third one.

There are two other reasons for reverse splits. First, stock exchanges have minimum price per share requirements. A reverse split may bring the stock price up to such a minimum. Second, companies sometimes perform reverse splits and, at the same time, buy out any stockholders who end up with less than a certain number of shares. This second tactic can be abusive if it is used to force out minority shareholders.

CONCEPT QUESTIONS

16.8a What is the effect of a stock split on stockholder wealth?

16.8b How does the accounting treatment of a stock split differ from that used with a small stock dividend?

16.9 | SUMMARY AND CONCLUSIONS

In this chapter, we discussed the types of dividends and how they are paid. We then defined dividend policy and examined whether or not dividend policy matters. Next, we illustrated how a firm might establish a dividend policy and described an important alternative to cash dividends, a share repurchase.

In covering these subjects, we saw that:

1. Dividend policy is irrelevant when there are no taxes or other imperfections because shareholders can effectively undo the firm's dividend strategy. If a shareholder receives a dividend greater than desired, he or she can reinvest the excess. Conversely, if the shareholder receives a dividend that is smaller than desired, he or she can sell off extra shares of stock.

2. Individual shareholder income taxes and new issue flotation costs are real-world considerations that favor a low-dividend payout. With taxes and new issue costs, the firm should pay out dividends only after all positive NPV projects have been fully financed.

3. There are groups in the economy that may favor a high payout. These include many large institutions such as pension plans. Recognizing that some groups prefer a high payout and some prefer a low payout, the clientele effect supports the idea that dividend policy responds to the needs of stockholders. For example, if 40 percent of the stockholders prefer low dividends and 60 percent of the stockholders prefer high dividends, approximately 40 percent of companies will have a low-dividend payout, while 60 percent will have a high payout. This sharply reduces the impact of any individual firm's dividend policy on its market price.

4. A firm wishing to pursue a strict residual dividend payout will have an unstable dividend. Dividend stability is usually viewed as highly desirable. We therefore discussed a compromise strategy that provides

for a stable dividend and appears to be quite similar to the dividend policies many firms follow in practice.

5. A stock repurchase acts much like a cash dividend, but has a significant tax advantage. Stock repurchases are therefore a very useful part of overall dividend policy.

To close out our discussion of dividends, we emphasize one last time the difference between dividends and dividend policy. Dividends are important, because the value of a share of stock is ultimately determined by the dividends that will be paid. What is less clear is whether or not the time pattern of dividends (more now versus more later) matters. This is the dividend policy question, and it is not easy to give a definitive answer to it.

Key Terms

dividend 553
distribution 553
regular cash dividends 553
declaration date 554
ex-dividend date 554
date of record 554
date of payment 554
homemade dividends 558
information content effect 565

clientele effect 565
residual dividend approach 567
target payout ratio 572
repurchase 573
stock dividend 576
stock split 576
trading range 579
reverse split 579

Chapter Review Problems and Self-Test

16.1 **Residual Dividend Policy**   The Rapscallion Corporation practices a strict residual dividend policy and maintains a capital structure of 40 percent debt, 60 percent equity. Earnings for the year are $2,500. What is the maximum amount of capital spending possible without selling new equity? Suppose that planned investment outlays for the coming year are $3,000. Will Rapscallion be paying a dividend? If so, how much?

16.2 **Repurchase versus Cash Dividend**   Trantor Corporation is deciding whether to pay out $300 in excess cash in the form of an extra dividend or a share repurchase. Current earnings are $1.50 per share and the stock sells for $15. The market value balance sheet before paying out the $300 is as follows:

Market Value Balance Sheet
(before paying out excess cash)

Excess cash	$ 300	$ 400	Debt
Other assets	1,600	1,500	Equity
Total	$1,900	$1,900	

Evaluate the two alternatives in terms of the effect on the price per share of the stock, the EPS, and the P/E ratio.

Answers to Self-Test Problems

16.1   Rapscallion has a debt/equity ratio of .40/.60 = ⅔. If the entire
$2,500 in earnings were reinvested, then $2,500 × ⅔ = $1,667 in new
borrowing would be needed to keep the debt/equity ratio unchanged.
Total new financing possible without external equity is thus $2,500 +
1,667 = $4,167.

   If planned outlays are $3,000, then this amount will be financed
with 60 percent equity. The needed equity is thus $3,000 × .60 =
$1,800. This is less than the $2,500 in earnings, so a dividend of
$2,500 − 1,800 = $700 would be paid.

16.2   The market value of the equity is $1,500. The price per share is $15, so
there are 100 shares outstanding. The cash dividend would amount to
$300/100 = $3 per share. When the stock goes ex dividend, the price
will drop by $3 per share to $12. Put another way, the total assets
decrease by $300, so the equity value goes down by this amount to
$1,200. With 100 shares, the new stock price is $12 per share. After
the dividend, EPS will be the same, $1.50, but the P/E ratio will be
$12/1.50 = 8 times.

   With a repurchase, $300/15 = 20 shares will be bought up,
leaving 80. The equity will again be worth $1,200 total. With
80 shares, this is $1,200/80 = $15 per share, so the price doesn't
change. Total earnings for Trantor must be $1.50 × 100 = $150.
After the repurchase, EPS will be higher at $150/80 = 1.875. The
P/E ratio, however, will still be $15/1.875 = 8 times.

Questions and Problems

1.   Accounting for Splits   The owners' equity accounts for the Polyanna
Co. are shown below (in millions).

Common stock ($1 par value)	$ 50
Capital surplus	500
Retained earnings	5,000
	$5,550

   a. If Polyanna stock currently sells for $50 per share and a 10 percent
stock dividend is declared, how would these accounts change?
   b. If Polyanna declared a 10-for-1 split, how would these accounts
change?

2.   Dividends and Taxes   The University of Pennsylvania pays no taxes
on its capital gains nor on its dividend income and interest income.
Would it be irrational to find low-dividend, high-growth stocks in its
portfolio? Would it be irrational to find municipal (tax-free) bonds in
its portfolio? Explain.

3.   Determining the Ex-Dividend Date   On Thursday, June 22, Nuke
Power's board of directors declares a dividend of 45 cents per share
payable on Thursday, July 20, to shareholders of record as of

Thursday, July 6. When is the ex-dividend date? If a shareholder buys stock before that date, what events will take place?

4.   Regular Dividends   The balance sheet for Peelout Corp. is shown below in market value terms. There are 100 shares outstanding.

Assets		Liabilities & Equity	
Cash	$100	Equity	$1,000
Fixed assets	900		

Peelout has declared a dividend of 50 cents per share. The stock goes ex tomorrow. What is it selling for today? What will it sell for tomorrow? Ignore taxes in answering.

5.   Stock Repurchase   In the previous question, suppose that Peelout has announced that it is going to repurchase $50 worth of stock. What will the effect of this be? Ignoring taxes, show how this is effectively the same as the cash dividend.

6.   Dividends and Taxes   Alphaxenics Co. has declared a $2 per share dividend. Suppose that capital gains are not taxed, but dividends are taxed at 28 percent. New IRS regulations require that taxes be withheld at the time the dividend is paid. Alphaxenics sells for $20 per share and the stock is about to go ex dividend. What do you think the ex-dividend price will be?

7.   Stock Dividends   The market value balance sheet for Poohbah, Inc., is shown below. Poohbah has declared a 20 percent stock dividend. The stock goes ex dividend tomorrow (the chronology for a stock dividend is similar to a cash dividend). There are 500 shares outstanding. What will the ex-dividend price be?

Assets		Liabilities & Equity	
Cash	$800	Debt	$650
Fixed assets	800	Equity	950

8.   Dividends versus Capital Gains   Piker Shoes has an expected dividend yield of 8 percent, while Rinky Shoes pays no dividends. The equity in the two firms has the same risk. The required return on Rinky is 15 percent. Capital gains are not taxed, but dividends are taxed at 28 percent. What is the required pretax return on Piker Shoes?

9.   Homemade Dividends   You own 100 shares of stock in Srinivas Submersibles. You will receive a 35 cents per share dividend in one year. In two years, Srinivas will pay a liquidating dividend of $15. The required return is 18 percent. How much is your stock worth per share (ignoring taxes)? If you would rather have equal dividends in each of the next two years, show how you can accomplish this by homemade dividends (hint: dividends will have annuity form).

10.   Homemade Dividends   In the previous question, suppose you want only $20 total in dividends the first year. What will your homemade dividend be in two years?

11.   **Residual Dividend Policy**   Okefenokee Ferns predicts that earnings in the coming year will be $10 million. There are 1 million shares outstanding, and Okefenokee Ferns maintains a total debt ratio of .50.
   a. Calculate the total funds that can be generated directly from earnings and the resultant increase in borrowing.
   b. Suppose Okefenokee Ferns uses a residual dividend policy. Planned capital expenditures total $12 million. Based on this information, what will the dividend per share amount be?
   c. In part b, how much borrowing will take place? What is the addition to retained earnings?
   d. Suppose Okefenokee plans no capital outlays for the coming year. What will the dividend be under a residual policy? What would new borrowing be?

12.   **Alternative Dividends**   Some corporations, like one British company that offers its large shareholders free crematorium use, pay dividends in kind (that is, offer their services to shareholders at below-market cost). Should mutual funds invest in stocks that pay these dividends in kind? (The fundholders do not receive these services.)

13.   **Dividend Policy**   If increases in dividends tend to be followed by (immediate) increases in share prices, how can it be said that dividend policy is irrelevant?

14.   **Changes in Dividends**   Last month, Central Virginia Power Company, which had been having trouble with cost overruns on a nuclear power plant that it had been building, announced that it was "temporarily suspending payments due to the cash flow crunch associated with its investment program." The company's stock price dropped from $28.50 to $25 when this announcement was made. How would you interpret this change in the stock price (that is, what caused it)?

15.   **Accounting for Stock Dividends**   A company, whose common equity accounts follow, has declared a 5 percent stock dividend at a time when the market value of its stock is $6 per share. What effects on the equity accounts will the distribution of the stock dividend have?

Common stock ($1 par)	$1,000,000
Excess over par (paid-in surplus)	2,000,000
Retained earnings	5,000,000
Total common equity	$8,000,000

16.   **Accounting for Stock Splits**   In the previous question, suppose that the company instead decides on a four-for-one stock split. The firm's 20-cent cash dividend on the new (split) shares represents an increase of 5 percent over last year's dividend on presplit stock. What effect does this have on the equity accounts? What was last year's dividend per share?

17.   **DRIPs**   The RWW Corporation has recently developed a dividend reinvestment plan (DRIP). The plan allows investors to reinvest cash dividends automatically in RWW in exchange for new shares of stock.

Over time, investors in RWW will be able to build their holdings by reinvesting dividends to purchase additional shares of the company.

About 1,000 companies offer dividend reinvestment plans. Most companies with dividend reinvestment plans charge no brokerage or service fees. In fact, the shares of RWW will be purchased at a 10 percent "discount" from the market price.

A consultant for RWW estimates that about 75 percent of RWW's shareholders will take part in this plan. This is somewhat higher than the average.

Evaluate RWW's dividend reinvestment plan. Will it increase shareholder wealth? Give the pros and cons.

18.   **Dividend Policy**   For initial public offerings of common stock, 1983 was a very big year, with 888 firms going public, raising over $10 billion. Except for bank stocks, hardly any of these paid cash dividends. Why do you think that most chose not to pay cash dividends?

19.   **Dividend Policy**   Consider the following article from the *Philadelphia Bulletin,* April 16, 1976:

THE DIVIDEND QUESTION AT CLARK EQUIPMENT

If you're one of the 13,000 shareholders of Clark Equipment Co., you can look forward to an increase in the $1.60 annual dividend—but don't spend the money yet.

Says Leonard M. Savoie, vice president and controller, "We'll have to raise it some day. There's a lot of pressure for an increase."

The $1.60 rate has been in effect since 1973. What with the ravages of inflation, the purchasing power of the $1.60 is considerably less than in 1973.

But an increase isn't likely soon, Bert E. Phillips, president and chief executive, strongly indicated. The two officials of the Buchanan, Michigan, maker of materials-handling and construction equipment were in town yesterday for a meeting with the Financial Analysts of Philadelphia at the Racquet Club.

Two Reasons

Clark's first-quarter earnings weren't "very good," according to Phillips, who said the first half "will likely be somewhat depressed" too. That's no time to raise the dividend.

On top of that, Phillips thinks that Clark can reinvest the money in the business at a higher return than shareholders could on their own.

That's unlikely to cut much ice with shareholders who depend on dividends. But Phillips thinks it's foolish for a company to pay a higher dividend and then have to borrow the money it needs for expansion and modernization of its plants.

In effect, he told analysts, that's borrowing to pay dividends.

Traditionally, Clark has been paying out between 45 percent and 50 percent of earnings in dividends. Phillips hopes to be able to persuade directors to let the payout ratio shrink as earnings pick up later this year and the next, as he expects.

Some directors might resist, worrying about the "little old lady in tennis shoes out in Iowa" who wants an increase in the $1.60 dividend, according to Phillips.

Said Phillips, "I think she died, but they don't know it yet."

Next year might be different, the Clark official indicated.

"We think the downturn has bottomed," Phillips said, "and that the second half (of 1976) will see improvement as the whole capital-goods sector comes back to a healthier state." Sales and earnings of capital-goods producers like Clark generally lag behind the economy by six to nine months.

Omen

Clark's shipments of forklifts and other industrial trucks declined throughout 1975. But in the past few months, according to Phillips, shipments have been "trending upward, and we expect this to continue gradually over the remainder of the year." Construction machinery, however, continues flat.

In 1975, Clark earned $46.6 million, or $3.43 a share, on sales of $1.4 billion. Some Wall Street analysts are forecasting 1976 earnings between $3.60 and $4 a share.

Evaluate "The Dividend Question at Clark Equipment" in light of what you have learned about dividend policy. In particular:

a. What do you think of the two reasons for not raising the $1.60 dividend this year?

b. What do you think of "borrowing to pay dividends?"

c. Should Clark base its dividend policy on the payout ratio? On the dividend per share?

d. Assuming that she's still alive, how much should the company worry about the little old lady in Iowa?

20.   Residual Dividend Policy   Zappit uses a residual dividend policy. A debt/equity ratio of 1 is considered optimal. Earnings for the period just ended were $100, and a dividend of $60 was declared. What were capital outlays? New borrowing?

21.   Residual Policy   Heavy Water, Inc., had declared an annual dividend of 50 cents per share. For the year just ended, earnings were $1.40 per share.

a. What is Heavy Water's payout ratio?

b. Suppose Heavy Water has 5 million shares outstanding. Borrowing for the coming year is planned at $14 million. What are planned investment outlays assuming a residual dividend policy? What target capital structure is implicit in these calculations?

22.   Residual Policy   The Grendel Corporation follows a strict residual dividend policy. Its debt/equity ratio is 1.

a. If earnings for the year are $600,000, what is the maximum amount of capital spending possible with no new equity?

b. If planned investment outlays for the coming year are $1.5 million, will Grendel pay a dividend? If so, how much?

c. Does the Grendel Corporation maintain a constant dividend payout? Why or why not?

23.   Stock Repurchase   Izberg-Kooperman Corporation is evaluating an extra dividend versus a share repurchase. In either case, $1,000 would be spent. Current earnings are $5 per share, and the stock currently sells for $100 per share. There are 20 shares outstanding. Ignore taxes and other imperfections in answering the first two questions.

a. Evaluate the two alternatives in terms of the effect on the price per share of the stock and shareholder wealth.

  b. What will be the effect on Izberg-Kooperman's EPS and P/E ratio?

  c. In the real world, which of these actions would you recommend? Why?

24.   Residual Policy versus a Compromise   What is the chief drawback to a strict residual dividend policy? Why is this a problem? How does a compromise policy work? How does it differ from a strict residual policy?

Suggested Readings

Our dividend irrelevance argument is based on a classic article:

Miller, M. H., and F. Modigliani. "Dividend Policy, Growth and the Valuation of Shares." *Journal of Business* 34, October 1961.

Higgins describes the residual dividend approach in:

Higgins, R. C. "The Corporate Dividend-Saving Decision." *Journal of Financial and Quantitative Analysis* 7, March 1972.

Part Eight

Short-Term Financial Planning and Management

CHAPTER 17
Short-Term Finance and Planning

To this point, we have described the decisions of long-term finance, including capital budgeting, capital structure, and dividend policy. This chapter introduces some aspects of short-term finance. Short-term finance is the analysis of decisions made when the relevant cash flows all occur in the near future. The focus of short-term finance is on current assets and current liabilities.

CHAPTER 18
Cash and Liquidity Management

Why do firms hold any cash? This is the question Chapter 18 attempts to answer, and it discusses some very good reasons for firms to do so. This chapter shows how firms can keep investments in cash low while still operating effectively.

CHAPTER 19
Credit and Inventory Management

This chapter looks at a firm's decision to grant credit. Granting credit can result in increased sales for the firm, but this benefit must be balanced against the extra costs of a credit sale. The chapter also discusses some important financial aspects of inventory management.

Chapter 17

Short-Term Finance and Planning

To this point, we have described many of the decisions of long-term finance, for example, capital budgeting, dividend policy, and financial structure. In this chapter, we begin to discuss short-term finance. Short-term finance is primarily concerned with the analysis of decisions that affect current assets and current liabilities.

Frequently, the term *net working capital* is associated with short-term financial decision making. As we describe in Chapter 2 and elsewhere, net working capital is the difference between current assets and current liabilities. Often, short-term financial management is called *working capital management*. These mean the same thing.

There is no universally accepted definition of short-term finance. The most important difference between short-term and long-term finance is the timing of cash flows. Short-term financial decisions typically involve cash inflows and outflows that occur within a year or less. For example, short-term financial decisions are involved when a firm orders raw materials, pays in cash, and anticipates selling finished goods in one year for cash. In contrast, long-term financial decisions are involved when a firm purchases a special machine that will reduce operating costs over, say, the next five years.

What types of questions fall under the general heading of short-term finance? To name just a very few:

1. What is a reasonable level of cash to keep on hand (in a bank) to pay bills?
2. How much should the firm borrow short-term?
3. How much credit should be extended to customers?

This chapter introduces the basic elements of short-term financial decisions. First, we discuss the short-term operating activities of the firm. We then identify some alternative short-term financial policies. Finally, we outline the basic elements in a short-term financial plan and describe short-term financing instruments.

17.1 | TRACING CASH AND NET WORKING CAPITAL

In this section, we examine the components of cash and net working capital as they change from one year to the next. We have already discussed various aspects of this subject in Chapters 2, 3, and 4. We briefly review some of that discussion as it relates to short-term financing decisions. Our goal is to describe the short-term operating activities of the firm and their impact on cash and working capital.

To begin, recall that *current assets* are cash and other assets that are expected to convert to cash within the year. Current assets are presented in the balance sheet in order of their accounting liquidity—the ease with which they can be converted to cash and the time it takes to do so. Four of the most important items found in the current asset section of a balance sheet are cash, marketable securities (or cash equivalents), accounts receivable, and inventories.

Analogous to their investment in current assets, firms use several kinds of short-term debt, called *current liabilities*. Current liabilities are obligations that are expected to require cash payment within one year (or within the operating period if it is different from one year). Three major items found as current liabilities are accounts payable, expenses payable, including accrued wages and taxes, and notes payable.

Because we want to focus on changes in cash, we start off by defining cash in terms of the other elements of the balance sheet. This lets us isolate the cash account and explore the impact on cash from the firm's operating and financing decisions. The basic balance sheet identity can be written as:

$$\text{Net working capital} + \text{Fixed assets} = \text{Long-term debt} + \text{Equity} \qquad [17.1]$$

Net working capital is cash plus other current assets, less current liabilities; that is,

$$\text{Net working capital} = (\text{Cash} + \text{Other current assets}) \qquad [17.2]$$
$$- \text{Current liabilities}$$

If we substitute this for net working capital in the basic balance sheet identity and rearrange things a bit, cash is:

$$\text{Cash} = \text{Long-term debt} + \text{Equity} + \text{Current liabilities} \qquad [17.3]$$
$$- \text{Current assets (other than cash)} - \text{Fixed assets}$$

This tells us in general terms that some activities naturally increase cash and some activities decrease it. We can list these along with an example of each as follows:

Activities that Increase Cash

> Increasing long-term debt (borrowing long-term).
>
> Increasing equity (selling some stock).
>
> Increasing current liabilities (getting a 90-day loan).
>
> Decreasing current assets other than cash (selling some inventory for cash).
>
> Decreasing fixed assets (selling some property).

Activities that Decrease Cash

> Decreasing long-term debt (paying off a long-term debt).
>
> Decreasing equity (repurchasing some stock).
>
> Decreasing current liabilities (paying off a 90-day loan).
>
> Increasing current assets other than cash (buying some inventory for cash).
>
> Increasing fixed assets (buying some property).

Notice that our two lists are exact opposites. For example, floating a long-term bond issue increases cash (at least until the money is spent). Paying off a long-term bond issue decreases cash.

As we discussed in Chapter 3, those activities that increase cash are called *sources of cash*. Those activities that decrease cash are called *uses of cash*. Looking back at our list, sources of cash always involve increasing a liability (or equity) account or decreasing an asset account. This makes sense because increasing a liability means we have raised money by borrowing it or by selling an ownership interest in the firm. A decrease in an asset means that we have sold or otherwise liquidated an asset. In either case, there is a cash inflow.

Uses of cash are just the reverse. A use of cash involves decreasing a liability by paying it off, perhaps, or increasing assets by purchasing something. Both of these activities require that the firm spend some cash.

Example 17.1 Sources and Uses

Here is a quick check of your understanding of sources and uses: If accounts payable go up by $100, is this a source or use? If accounts receivable go up by $100, is this a source or use?

Accounts payable are what we owe our suppliers. This is a short-term debt. If it rises by $100, we have effectively borrowed the money, so this is a *source* of cash. Receivables are what our customers owe to us, so an increase of $100 means that we loaned the money; this is a *use* of cash. ∎

CONCEPT QUESTIONS

17.1a What is the difference between net working capital and cash?

17.1b Will net working capital always increase when cash increases?

17.1c List five potential uses of cash.

17.1d List five potential sources of cash.

17.2 | THE OPERATING CYCLE AND THE CASH CYCLE

The primary concern in short-term finance is the firm's short-run operating and financing activities. For a typical manufacturing firm, these short-run activities might consist of the following sequence of events and decisions:

Events	Decisions
1. Buying raw materials	1. How much inventory to order?
2. Paying cash	2. Borrow or draw down cash balances?
3. Manufacturing the product	3. What choice of production technology?
4. Selling the product	4. Should credit be extended to a particular customer?
5. Collecting cash	5. How to collect?

These activities create patterns of cash inflows and cash outflows. These cash flows are both unsynchronized and uncertain. They are unsynchronized because, for example, the payment of cash for raw materials does not happen at the same time as the receipt of cash from selling the product. They are uncertain because future sales and costs cannot be precisely predicted.

Defining the Operating and Cash Cycles

We can start with a simple case. One day, call it Day 0, you purchase $1,000 worth of inventory on credit. You pay the bill 30 days later, and, after 30 more days, someone buys the $1,000 in inventory for $1,400. Your buyer does not actually pay for another 45 days. We can summarize these events chronologically as follows:

Day	Activity	Cash Effect
0	Acquire inventory	None
30	Pay for inventory	−$1,000
60	Sell inventory on credit	None
105	Collect on sale	+$1,400

operating cycle
The time period between the acquisition of inventory and the collection of cash from receivables.

inventory period
The time it takes to acquire and sell inventory.

accounts receivable period
The time between sale of inventory and collection of the receivable.

The Operating Cycle   There are several things to notice in our example. First, the entire cycle, from the time we acquire some inventory to the time we collect the cash, takes 105 days. This is called the **operating cycle.**

As we illustrate, the operating cycle is the length of time it takes to acquire inventory, sell it, and collect for it. This cycle has two distinct components. The first part is the time it takes to acquire and sell the inventory. This 60-day span in our example is called the **inventory period.** The second part is the time it takes to collect on the sale, 45 days in our example. This is called the **accounts receivable period.**

Based on our definitions, the operating cycle is obviously just the sum of the inventory and receivables periods:

$$\text{Operating cycle} = \text{Inventory period} \qquad\qquad [17.4]$$
$$+ \text{ Accounts receivable period}$$
$$105 \text{ days} = 60 \text{ days} + 45 \text{ days}$$

What the operating cycle describes is how a product moves through the current asset accounts. It begins life as inventory, it is converted to a receivable when it is sold, and it is finally converted to cash when we collect from the sale. Notice that, at each step, the asset is moving closer to cash.

The Cash Cycle   The second thing to notice is that the cash flows and other events that occur are not synchronized. For example, we didn't actually pay for the inventory until 30 days after we acquired it. This 30-day period is called the **accounts payable period.** Next, we spend cash on Day 30, but we don't collect until Day 105. Somehow or the other, we have to arrange to finance the $1,000 for $105 - 30 = 75$ days. This period is called the **cash cycle.**

The cash cycle, therefore, is the number of days that pass until we collect the cash from a sale, measured from when we actually pay for the inventory. Notice that, based on our definitions, the cash cycle is the difference between the operating cycle and the accounts payable period:

$$\text{Cash cycle} = \text{Operating cycle} - \text{Accounts payable period} \qquad [17.5]$$
$$75 \text{ days} = 105 \text{ days} - 30 \text{ days}$$

Figure 17.1 depicts the short-term operating activities and cash flows for a typical manufacturing firm by looking at the cash flow time line. As shown, the **cash flow time line** is made up of the operating cycle and the cash cycle. In Figure 17.1, the need for short-term financial management is suggested by the gap between the cash inflows and cash outflows. This is related to the length of the operating cycle and accounts payable period.

The gap between short-term inflows and outflows can be filled either by borrowing or by holding a liquidity reserve in the form of cash or marketable securities. Alternatively, the gap can be shortened by changing the inventory, receivable, and payable periods. These are all managerial options that we discuss below and in subsequent chapters.

accounts payable period
The time between receipt of inventory and payment for it.

cash cycle
The time between cash disbursement and cash collection.

cash flow time line
Graphical representation of the operating cycle and the cash cycle.

The Operating Cycle and the Firm's Organizational Chart

Before we examine the operating and cash cycles in greater detail, it is useful to take a look at the people involved in managing a firm's current assets and liabilities. As Table 17.1 illustrates, short-term financial management in a large corporation involves a number of different financial and nonfinancial

Figure 17.1

Cash flow time line and the short-term operating activities of a typical manufacturing firm

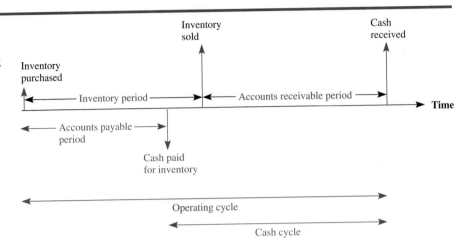

The operating cycle is the time period from inventory purchase until the receipt of cash. (Sometimes the operating cycle does not include the time from placement of the order until arrival of the stock.) The cash cycle is the time period from when cash is paid out to when cash is received.

managers.[1] Examining Table 17.1, selling on credit involves at least three different entities: the credit manager, the marketing manager, and the controller. Of these three, only two are responsible to the vice president of finance (the marketing function is usually associated with the vice president of marketing). Thus, there is the potential for conflict, particularly if different managers only concentrate on part of the picture. For example, if marketing is trying to land a new account, it may seek more liberal credit terms as an inducement. However, this may increase the firm's investment in receivables or its exposure to bad-debt risk, and conflict can result.

Calculating the Operating and Cash Cycles

In our example, the lengths of time that made up the different periods were obvious. If all we have is financial statement information, we will have to do a little more work. We illustrate these calculations next.

To begin, we need to determine various things such as how long it takes, on average, to sell inventory and how long it takes, on average, to collect. We start by gathering some balance sheet information such as the following (in thousands):

Item	Beginning	Ending	Average
Inventory	$2,000	$3,000	$2,500
Accounts receivable	1,600	2,000	1,800
Accounts payable	750	1,000	875

---

[1]The discussion draws on N. C. Hill and W. L. Sartoris, *Short-Term Financial Management* (New York: Macmillan, 1988), Chapter 1.

Table 17.1

Managers who deal with short-term financial problems

Title of manager	Duties related to short-term financial management	Assets/liabilities influenced
Cash manager	Collection, concentration, disbursement; short-term investments; short-term borrowing; banking relations	Cash, marketable securities, short-term loans
Credit manager	Monitoring and control of accounts receivable; credit policy decisions	Accounts receivable
Marketing manager	Credit policy decisions	Accounts receivable
Purchasing manager	Decisions on purchases, suppliers; may negotiate payment terms	Inventory, accounts payable
Production manager	Setting of production schedules and materials requirements	Inventory, accounts payable
Payables manager	Decisions on payment policies and on whether to take discounts	Accounts payable
Controller	Accounting information on cash flows; reconciliation of accounts payable; application of payments to accounts receivable	Accounts receivable, accounts payable

Source: Ned C. Hill and William L. Sartoris, *Short-Term Financial Management* (New York: Macmillan, 1988), p. 17.

Also, from the most recent income statement, we might have the following figures (in thousands):

Net sales	$11,500
Cost of goods sold	8,200

We now need to calculate some financial ratios. We discussed these in some detail in Chapter 3; here we just define them and use them as needed.

The Operating Cycle   First of all, we need the inventory period. We spent $8.2 million on inventory (our cost of goods sold). Our average inventory was $2.5 million. We thus turned our inventory over $8.2/2.5 times during the year:[2]

$$\text{Inventory turnover} = \frac{\text{Cost of goods sold}}{\text{Average inventory}}$$

$$= \frac{\$8.2 \text{ million}}{\$2.5 \text{ million}} = 3.28 \text{ times}$$

---

[2]Notice that we have used the cost of goods sold in calculating inventory turnover. Sales is sometimes used instead. Also, ending inventory, rather than average inventory, is often used. See Chapter 3 for some examples.

Loosely speaking, this tells us that we bought and sold off our inventory 3.28 times during the year. This means that, on average, we held our inventory for:

$$\text{Inventory period} = \frac{365 \text{ days}}{\text{Inventory turnover}}$$

$$= \frac{365}{3.28} = 111.3 \text{ days}$$

So the inventory period is about 111 days. On average, in other words, inventory sat for about 111 days before it was sold.[3]

Similarly, receivables averaged \$1.8 million, and sales were \$11.5 million Assuming that all sales were credit sales, the receivables turnover is:[4]

$$\text{Receivables turnover} = \frac{\text{Credit sales}}{\text{Average accounts receivable}}$$

$$= \frac{\$11.5 \text{ million}}{\$1.8 \text{ million}} = 6.4 \text{ times}$$

If we turn over our receivables 6.4 times, then the receivables period is:

$$\text{Receivables period} = \frac{365 \text{ days}}{\text{Receivables turnover}}$$

$$= \frac{365}{6.4} = 57 \text{ days}$$

The receivables period is also called the *days' sales in receivables* or the *average collection period*. Whatever it is called, it tells us that our customers took an average of 57 days to pay.

The operating cycle is the sum of the inventory and receivables periods:

$$\text{Operating cycle} = \text{Inventory period} + \text{Accounts receivables period}$$

$$= 111 \text{ days} + 57 \text{ days} = 168 \text{ days}$$

This tells us that, on average, 168 days elapse between the time we acquire inventory, sell it, and collect for the sale.

---

[3]This measure is conceptually identical to the days' sales in inventory we discussed in Chapter 3.

[4]If less than 100 percent of our sales are credit sales, then we would just need a little more information, namely, credit sales for the year. See Chapter 3 for more discussion of this measure.

The Cash Cycle   We now need the payables period. From the information given above, average payables were $875,000, and cost of goods sold was again $8.2 million. Our payables turnover is thus:

$$\text{Payables turnover} = \frac{\text{Cost of goods sold}}{\text{Average payables}}$$

$$= \frac{\$8.2 \text{ million}}{\$.875 \text{ million}} = 9.4 \text{ times}$$

The payables period is:

$$\text{Payables period} = \frac{365 \text{ days}}{\text{Payables turnover}}$$

$$= \frac{365}{9.4} = 39 \text{ days}$$

Thus, we took an average of 39 days to pay our bills.

Finally, the cash cycle is the difference between the operating cycle and the payables period:

$$\text{Cash cycle} = \text{Operating cycle} - \text{Accounts payable period}$$

$$= 168 \text{ days} - 39 \text{ days} = 129 \text{ days}$$

So, on average, there is a 129-day delay from the time we pay for merchandise and the time we collect on the sale.

Example 17.2   The Operating and Cash Cycles
You have collected the following information for the Slowpay Company.

Item	Beginning	Ending
Inventory	$5,000	$7,000
Accounts receivable	1,600	2,400
Accounts payable	2,700	4,800

Sales for the year just ended were $50,000, and cost of goods sold was $30,000. How long does it take Slowpay to collect on its receivables? How long does merchandise stay around before it is sold? How long does Slowpay take to pay its bills?

We can first calculate the three turnover ratios:

$$\text{Inventory turnover} = \$30,000/\$6,000 = 5 \text{ times}$$

$$\text{Receivables turnover} = \$50,000/\$2,000 = 25 \text{ times}$$

$$\text{Payables turnover} = \$30,000/\$3,750 = 8 \text{ times}$$

We use these to get the various periods:

$$\text{Inventory period} = 365/5 = 73 \text{ days}$$

$$\text{Receivables period} = 365/25 = 14.6 \text{ days}$$

$$\text{Payables period} = 365/8 = 45.6 \text{ days}$$

All told, Slowpay collects on a sale in 14.6 days, inventory sits around for 73 days, and bills get paid after about 46 days. The operating cycle here is the sum of the inventory and receivables periods: $73 + 14.6 = 87.6$ days. The cash cycle is the difference between the operating cycle and the payables period: $87.6 - 45.6 = 42$ days. ∎

Interpreting the Cash Cycle

Our examples show that the cash cycle depends on the inventory, receivables, and payables periods. Taken one at a time, the cash cycle increases as the inventory and receivables periods get longer. It decreases if the company is able to defer payment of payables and thereby lengthen the payables period.

Most firms have a positive cash cycle, and they thus require financing for inventories and receivables. The longer the cash cycle, the more financing required. Also, changes in the firm's cash cycle are often monitored as an early warning measure. A lengthening cycle can indicate that the firm is having trouble moving inventory or collecting on its receivables. Such problems can be masked, at least partially, by an increased payables cycle, so both should be monitored.

The link between the firm's cash cycle and its profitability can be easily seen by recalling that one of the basic determinants of profitability and growth for a firm is its total asset turnover, which is defined as sales/total assets. In Chapter 3, we saw that the higher this ratio is, the greater is the firm's accounting return on assets (ROA) and return on equity (ROE). Thus, all other things the same, the shorter the cash cycle is, the lower is the firm's investment in inventories and receivables. In this case, the firm's total assets are lower, and total turnover is higher as a result.

⌐ CONCEPT QUESTIONS

17.2a What does it mean to say that a firm has an inventory turnover ratio of 4?

17.2b Describe the operating cycle and cash cycle. What are the differences?

17.2c Explain the connection between a firm's accounting-based profitability and its cash cycle.

17.3 | SOME ASPECTS OF SHORT-TERM FINANCIAL POLICY

The short-term financial policy that a firm adopts will be reflected in at least two ways:

1. *The size of the firm's investment in current assets.* This is usually measured relative to the firm's level of total operating revenues. A

flexible or accommodative short-term financial policy would maintain a relatively high ratio of current assets to sales. A *restrictive* short-term financial policy would entail a low ratio of current assets to sales.[5]

2. *The financing of current assets.* This is measured as the proportion of short-term debt (that is, current liabilities) and long-term debt used to finance current assets. A restrictive short-term financial policy means a high proportion of short-term debt relative to long-term financing, and a flexible policy means less short-term debt and more long-term debt.

If we take these two areas together, a firm with a flexible policy would have a relatively large investment in current assets. It would finance this investment with relatively less in short-term debt. The net effect of a flexible policy is thus a relatively high level of net working capital. Put another way, with a flexible policy, the firm maintains a larger overall level of liquidity.

The Size of the Firm's Investment in Current Assets

Flexible short-term financial policies with regard to current assets include such actions as:

1. Keeping large balances of cash and marketable securities.
2. Making large investments in inventory.
3. Granting liberal credit terms, which results in a high level of accounts receivable.

Restrictive short-term financial policies would be just the opposite of these:

1. Keeping low cash balances and little investment in marketable securities.
2. Making small investments in inventory.
3. Allowing little or no credit sales, thereby minimizing accounts receivable.

Determining the optimal investment level in short-term assets requires an identification of the different costs of alternative short-term financing policies. The objective is to trade off the cost of a restrictive policy against the cost of a flexible one to arrive at the best compromise.

Current asset holdings are highest with a flexible short-term financial policy and lowest with a restrictive policy. So flexible short-term financial policies are costly in that they require a greater investment in cash and marketable securities, inventory, and accounts receivable. However, we expect that future cash inflows will be higher with a flexible policy. For example, sales are stimulated by the use of a credit policy that provides liberal financing to customers. A large amount of finished inventory on hand ("on the shelf") provides a quick delivery service to customers and may increase sales. Similarly, a large inventory of raw materials may result in fewer production stoppages because of inventory shortages.

A more restrictive short-term financial policy probably reduces future sales levels below those that would be achieved under flexible policies. It is also possible that higher prices can be charged to customers under flexible working

[5]Some people use the term *conservative* in place of flexible and the term *aggressive* in place of restrictive.

capital policies. Customers may be willing to pay higher prices for the quick delivery service and more liberal credit terms implicit in flexible policies.

Managing current assets can be thought of as involving a trade-off between costs that rise and costs that fall with the level of investment. Costs that rise with increases in the level of investment in current assets are called **carrying costs**. The larger the investment a firm makes in its current assets, the higher its carrying costs will be. Costs that fall with increases in the level of investment in current assets are called **shortage costs**.

In a general sense, carrying costs are the opportunity costs associated with current assets. The rate of return on current assets is very low when compared to other assets. For example, the rate of return on U.S. Treasury bills is usually less than 10 percent. This is very low compared to the rate of return firms would like to achieve overall. (U.S. Treasury bills are an important component of cash and marketable securities.)

Shortage costs are incurred when the investment in current assets is low. If a firm runs out of cash, it will be forced to sell marketable securities. Of course, if a firm runs out of cash and cannot readily sell marketable securities, it may have to borrow or default on an obligation. This situation is called a *cash out*. A firm will lose customers if it runs out of inventory (a *stock out*) or if it cannot extend credit to customers.

More generally, there are two kinds of shortage costs:

1. *Trading or order costs.* Order costs are the costs of placing an order for more cash (brokerage costs, for example) or more inventory (production set-up costs, for example).
2. *Costs related to lack of safety reserves.* These are costs of lost sales, lost customer goodwill, and disruption of production schedules.

The top part of Figure 17.2 illustrates the basic trade-off between carrying costs and shortage costs. On the vertical axis, we have costs measured in dollars and, on the horizontal axis, we have the amount of current assets. Carrying costs start out at zero when current assets are zero and then climb steadily as current assets grow. Shortage costs start out very high and then decline as we add current assets. The total costs of holding current assets is the sum of the two. Notice how the combined costs reach a minimum at CA*. This is the optimal level of current assets.

Current asset holdings are highest under a flexible policy. This policy is one in which the carrying costs are perceived to be low relative to shortage costs. This is Case A in Figure 17.2. In comparison, under restrictive current asset policies, carrying costs are perceived to be high relative to shortage costs. This is Case B in Figure 17.2

Alternative Financing Policies for Current Assets

In previous sections, we looked at the basic determinants of the level of investment in current assets, and we thus focused on the asset side of the balance sheet. Now we turn to the financing side of the question. Here we are concerned with the relative amounts of short-term and long-term debt, assuming the investment in current assets is constant.

---

carrying costs

Costs that rise with increases in the level of investment in current assets.

shortage costs

Costs that fall with increases in the level of investment in current assets.

Short-term financial policy: the optimal investment in current assets.

Figure 17.2

Carrying costs and
shortage costs

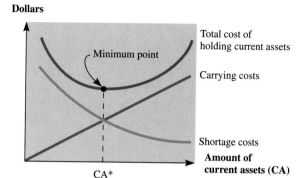

Dollars

Minimum point

Total cost of
holding current assets

Carrying costs

Shortage costs

**Amount of
current assets (CA)**

CA*

The optimal amount of current assets.
This point minimizes costs.

Carrying costs increase with the level of investment in current assets. They include the costs of maintaining economic value and opportunity costs. Shortage costs decrease with increases in the level of investment in current assets. They include trading costs and the costs related to being short of the current asset (for example, being short of cash). The firm's policy can be characterized as flexible or restrictive.

A. Flexible policy

Dollars

Minimum point

Total cost

Carrying costs
Shortage costs

**Amount of
current assets (CA)**

CA*

A flexible policy is most appropriate when carrying costs are low relative to shortage costs.

B. Restrictive policy

Dollars

Minimum point

Total cost

Carrying costs

Shortage costs

**Amount of
current assets (CA)**

CA*

A restrictive policy is most appropriate when carrying costs are high relative to shortage costs.

An Ideal Case   We start off with the simplest possible case: an "ideal" economy. In such an economy, short-term assets can always be financed with short-term debt, and long-term assets can be financed with long-term debt and equity. In this economy, net working capital is always zero.

Consider a simplified case for a grain elevator operator. Grain elevator operators buy crops after harvest, store them, and sell them during the year. They have high inventories of grain after the harvest and end up with low inventories just before the next harvest.

Bank loans with maturities of less than one year are used to finance the purchase of grain and the storage costs. These loans are paid off from the proceeds of the sale of grain.

The situation is shown in Figure 17.3. Long-term assets are assumed to grow over time, whereas current assets increase at the end of the harvest and then decline during the year. Short-term assets end up at zero just before the next harvest. Current (short-term) assets are financed by short-term debt, and long-term assets are financed with long-term debt and equity. Net working capital—current assets minus current liabilities—is always zero. Figure 17.3 displays a "sawtooth" pattern that we will see again when we get to our discussion on cash management in the next chapter. For now, we need to discuss some alternative policies for financing current assets under less idealized conditions.

Different Policies for Financing Current Assets   In the real world, it is not likely that current assets will ever drop to zero. For example, a long-term rising level of sales will result in some permanent investment in current assets. Moreover, the firm's investments in long-term assets may show a great deal of variation.

A growing firm can be thought of as having a total asset requirement consisting of the current assets and long-term assets needed to run the business efficiently. The total asset requirement may exhibit change over time for many reasons, including (1) a general growth trend, (2) seasonal variation around the

Figure 17.3

Financing policy for an "ideal" economy

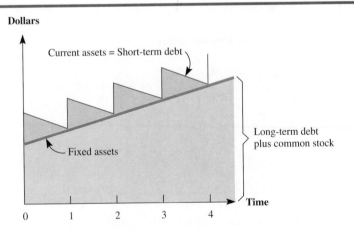

In an ideal world, net working capital is always zero because short-term assets are financed by short-term debt.

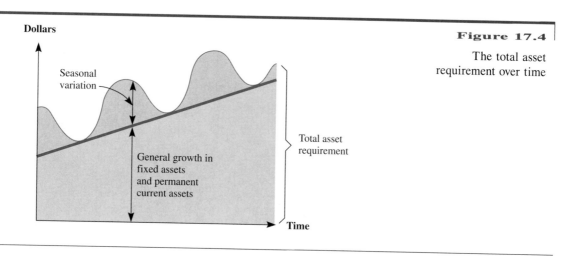

Figure 17.4

The total asset
requirement over time

trend, and (3) unpredictable day-to-day and month-to-month fluctuations. This
situation is depicted in Figure 17.4. (We have not tried to show the unpredictable day-to-day and month-to-month variations in the total asset requirement.)

When long-term financing covers more than the total asset requirements,
the firm has excess cash available for investment in marketable securities.
Policy F, the flexible policy in Figure 17.5, always implies a short-term cash
surplus and a large investment in net working capital.

When long-term financing does not cover the total asset requirement, the
firm must use short-term borrowing to make up the deficit. In Figure 17.5,
Policy R, the restrictive policy, implies a persistent need for short-term borrowing. Whenever current assets rise because of seasonal variations, the firm
borrows short-term to finance the growth. As these assets are worked off, the
firm repays the short-term debt out of the proceeds.

Which is Best?

What is the most appropriate amount of short-term borrowing? There is no definitive answer. Several considerations must be included in a proper analysis:

1. *Cash reserves.* The flexible financing policy implies surplus cash and
    little short-term borrowing. This policy reduces the probability that a
    firm will experience financial distress. Firms may not have to worry as
    much about meeting recurring, short-run obligations. However,
    investments in cash and marketable securities are zero net present value
    investments at best.

2. *Maturity hedging.* Most firms attempt to match the maturities of assets
    and liabilities. They finance inventories with short-term bank loans and
    fixed assets with long-term financing. Firms tend to avoid financing
    long-lived assets with short-term borrowing. This type of maturity
    mismatching would necessitate frequent refinancing and is inherently
    risky because short-term interest rates are more volatile than longer-term
    rates.

Figure 17.5

Alternative asset financing policies

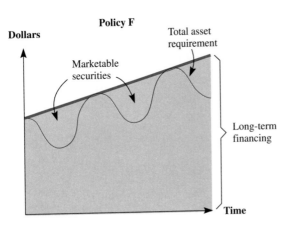

Policy F always implies a short-term cash surplus and a large investment in cash and marketable securities.

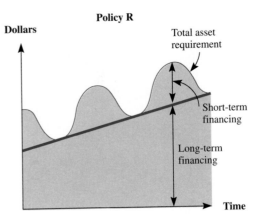

Policy R uses long-term financing for permanent asset requirements only and short-term borrowing for seasonal variations.

3. *Relative interest rates.* Short-term interest rates are usually lower than long-term rates. This implies that it is, on the average, more costly to rely on long-term borrowing as compared to short-term borrowing.

The two policies, F and R, we discuss above are, of course, extreme cases. With F, the firm never does any short-term borrowing, and, with R, the firm never has a cash reserve (an investment in marketable securities). Figure 17.6 illustrates these two policies along with a compromise, Policy C.

With this compromise approach, the firm borrows short-term to cover peak financing needs, but it maintains a cash reserve in the form of marketable securities during slow periods. As current assets build up, the firm draws down this reserve before doing any short-term borrowing. This allows for some run-up in current assets before the firm has to resort to short-term borrowing.

Current Assets and Liabilities in Practice

Short-term assets represent a significant portion of a typical firm's overall assets. For U.S. manufacturing, mining, and trade corporations, current assets were about 50 percent of total assets in the 1960s. Today, this figure is closer to 40 percent. Most of the decline is due to more efficient cash and inventory management. Over this same period, current liabilities rose from about 20 percent of total liabilities and equity to almost 30 percent. The result is that liquidity (as measured by net working capital to total assets) has declined, signaling a move to more restrictive short-term policies.

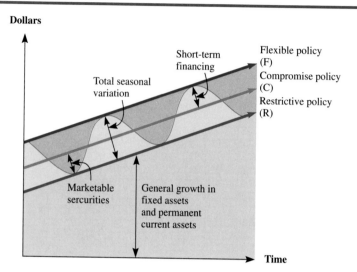

Figure 17.6

A compromise financing policy

With a compromise policy, the firm keeps a reserve of liquidity which it uses to initially finance seasonal variations in current asset needs. Short-term borrowing is used when the reserve is exhausted.

The cash cycle is longer in some industries than others because of different products and industry practices.[6] Table 17.2 illustrates this point by comparing the current asset and liability percentages for four different industries. Of the four, the aircraft and missiles industry has more than twice the investment in inventories. Does this mean that aircraft and missile producers are less efficient? Probably not; instead, it is likely that the relatively high inventory levels consist largely of aircraft under construction. Because these are expensive products that take a long time to manufacture, inventories are naturally higher.

CONCEPT QUESTIONS

17.3a What keeps the real world from being an ideal one where net working capital could always be zero?

17.3b What considerations determine the optimal size of the firm's investment in current assets?

17.3c What considerations determine the optimal compromise between flexible and restrictive net working capital policies?

---

[6]This example is drawn from Chapter 1 of N. C. Hill and W. L. Sartoris, *Short-Term Financial Management* (New York: Macmillan, 1988).

Table 17.2

Current assets and current liabilities as a percentage of total assets for selected industries, 1985

	Printing and Publishing (%)	Industrial Chemicals (%)	Iron and Steel (%)	Aircraft and Missiles (%)
Current assets				
Cash	5.2	1.1	1.3	2.2
Marketable securities	4.8	0.8	2.4	2.6
Accounts receivable	16.4	14.5	16.9	13.8
Inventory	8.4	13.0	19.8	46.8
Other current assets	4.3	3.2	1.3	1.3
Total current assets	39.1	32.6	41.7	66.7
Current liabilities				
Notes payable	2.9	4.3	5.6	4.0
Accounts payable	7.9	6.6	9.5	8.4
Accruals and other current liabilities	10.3	11.8	13.6	44.1
Total current liabilities	21.1	22.7	28.7	56.5

Source: Ned C. Hill and William L. Sartoris, *Short-Term Financial Management* (New York: Macmillan, 1988), p. 15.

17.4 | THE CASH BUDGET

cash budget

A forecast of cash receipts and disbursements for the next planning period.

The **cash budget** is a primary tool in short-run financial planning. It allows the financial manager to identify short-term financial needs and opportunities. Importantly, the cash budget will help the manager explore the need for short-term borrowing. The idea of the cash budget is simple: It records estimates of cash receipts (cash in) and disbursements (cash out). The result is an estimate of the cash surplus or deficit.

Sales and Cash Collections

We start with an example for the Fun Toys Corporation. We will prepare a quarterly cash budget. We could just as well use a monthly, weekly, or even daily basis. We choose quarters for convenience and also because a quarter is a common short-term business planning period.

All of Fun Toys' cash inflows come from the sale of toys. Cash budgeting for Fun Toys must therefore start with a sales forecast for the next year, by quarter:

	Q1	Q2	Q3	Q4
Sales (in millions)	$200	$300	$250	$400

Note that these are predicted sales, so there is forecasting risk here because actual sales could be more or less. Also, Fun Toys started the year with accounts receivable equal to $120.

Fun Toys has a 45-day receivables or average collection period. This means that half of the sales in a given quarter will be collected the following quarter. This happens because sales made during the first 45 days of a quarter will be collected in that quarter. Sales made in the second 45 days will be collected in the next quarter. Note that we are assuming that each quarter has 90 days, so the 45-day collection period is the same as a half-quarter collection period.

Based on the sales forecasts, we now need to estimate Fun Toys' projected cash collections. First, any receivables that we have at the beginning of a quarter will be collected within 45 days, so all of them will be collected sometime during the quarter. Second, as we discussed, any sales made in the first half of the quarter will be collected, so total cash collections are:

$$\text{Cash collections} = \text{Beginning accounts receivable} + 1/2 \times \text{Sales} \qquad [17.6]$$

For example, in the first quarter, cash collections would be the beginning receivables of $120 plus half of sales, $1/2 \times \$200 = \$100$, for a total of $220.

Since beginning receivables are all collected along with half of sales, ending receivables for a particular quarter would be the other half of sales. First quarter sales are projected at $200, so ending receivables will be $100. This will be the beginning receivables in the second quarter. Cash collections in the second quarter will thus be $100 plus half of the projected $300 in sales, or $250 total.

Continuing this process, we can summarize Fun Toys' projected cash collections as shown in Table 17.3.

In Table 17.3, collections are shown as the only source of cash. Of course, this need not be the case. Other sources of cash could include asset sales, investment income, and receipts from planned long-term financing.

Cash Outflows

Next, we consider the cash disbursements or payments. These come in four basic categories:

1. *Payments of accounts payable.* These are payments for goods or services rendered by suppliers, such as raw materials. Generally, these payments will be made sometime after purchases.

	Q1	Q2	Q3	Q4	**Table 17.3**
Beginning receivables	$120	$100	$150	$125	Cash collections for Fun
Sales	200	300	250	400	Toys (in millions)
Cash collections	220	250	275	325	
Ending receivables	100	150	125	200	

Notes: Collections = Beginning receivables + 1/2 × Sales

Ending receivables = Beginning receivables + Sales − Collections

= 1/2 × Sales

2. *Wages, taxes, and other expenses.* This category includes all other regular costs of doing business that require actual expenditures. Depreciation, for example, is often thought of as a regular cost of business, but it requires no cash outflow, and is not included.
3. *Capital expenditures.* These are payments of cash for long-lived assets.
4. *Long-term financing expenses.* This category, for example, includes interest payments on long-term debt outstanding and dividend payments to shareholders.

Fun Toys' purchases from suppliers (in dollars) in a quarter are equal to 60 percent of next quarter's predicted sales. Fun Toys' payments to suppliers are equal to the previous quarter's purchases, so the accounts payable period is 90 days. For example, in the quarter just ended, Fun Toys ordered .60 × $200 = $120 in supplies. This will actually be paid in the first quarter (Q1) of the coming year.

Wages, taxes, and other expenses are routinely 20 percent of sales; interest and dividends are currently $20 per quarter. In addition, Fun Toys plans a major plant expansion (a capital expenditure) of $100 in the second quarter. If we put all this information together, the cash outflows are as shown in Table 17.4.

The Cash Balance

The predicted *net cash inflow* is the difference between cash collections and cash disbursements. The net cash inflow for Fun Toys is shown in Table 17.5. What we see immediately is that there is a cash surplus in the first and third quarters and a cash deficit in the second and fourth.

We will assume that Fun Toys starts the year with a $20 cash balance. Furthermore, Fun Toys maintains a $10 minimum cash balance to guard against unforeseen contingencies and forecasting errors. So we start the first quarter

Table 17.4

Cash disbursements for Fun Toys (in millions)

	Q1	Q2	Q3	Q4
Payment of accounts (60% of sales)	$120	$180	$150	$240
Wages, taxes, other expenses	40	60	50	80
Capital expenditures	0	100	0	0
Long-term financing expenses (interest and dividends)	20	20	20	20
Total cash disbursements	$180	$360	$220	$340

Table 17.5

Net cash inflow for Fun Toys (in millions)

	Q1	Q2	Q3	Q4
Total cash collections	$220	$250	$275	$325
Total cash disbursements	180	360	220	340
Net cash inflow	$ 40	−$110	$ 55	−$ 15

with $20 in cash. This rises by $40 during the quarter, and the ending balance is $60. Of this, $10 is reserved as a minimum, so we subtract it out and find that the first quarter surplus is $60 − 10 = $50.

Fun Toys starts the second quarter with $60 in cash (the ending balance from the previous quarter). There is a net cash inflow of −$110, so the ending balance is $60 − 110 = −$50. We need another $10 as a buffer, so the total deficit is −$60. These calculations and those for the last two quarters are summarized in Table 17.6.

Beginning in the second quarter, Fun Toys has a cash shortfall of $60. This occurs because of the seasonal pattern of sales (higher toward the end of the second quarter), the delay in collections, and the planned capital expenditure.

The cash situation at Fun Toys is projected to improve to a $5 deficit in the third quarter, but, by year's end, Fun Toys still has a $20 deficit. Without some sort of financing, this deficit will carry over into the next year. We explore this subject in the next section.

For now, we can make the following general comments on Fun Toys' cash needs:

1. Fun Toys' large outflow in the second quarter is not necessarily a sign of trouble. It results from delayed collections on sales and a planned capital expenditure (presumably a worthwhile one).
2. The figures in our example are based on a forecast. Sales could be much worse (or better) than the forecast.

⌐ CONCEPT QUESTIONS

17.4a How would you do a sensitivity analysis (discussed in Chapter 9) for Fun Toys' net cash balance?

17.4b What could you learn from such an analysis?

SHORT-TERM BORROWING ⌐ 17.5

Fun Toys has a short-term financing problem. It cannot meet the forecasted cash outflows in the second quarter from internal sources. How it will finance that shortfall depends on its financial policy. With a very flexible policy, Fun Toys might seek up to $60 million in long-term debt financing.

	Q1	Q2	Q3	Q4
Beginning cash balance	$20	$ 60	−$50	$ 5
Net cash inflow	40	− 110	55	− 15
Ending cash balance	$60	−$ 50	$ 5	−$10
Minimum cash balance	− 10	− 10	− 10	− 10
Cumulative surplus (deficit)	$50	−$ 60	−$ 5	−$20

Table 17.6

Cash balance for Fun Toys (in millions)

In addition, much of the cash deficit comes from the large capital expenditure. Arguably, this is a candidate for long-term financing. Nonetheless, because we have discussed long-term financing elsewhere, we will concentrate here on two short-term borrowing options: (1) unsecured borrowing and (2) secured borrowing.

Unsecured Loans

line of credit

A formal (committed) or informal (noncommitted) prearranged, short-term bank loan.

The most common way to finance a temporary cash deficit is to arrange a short-term, unsecured bank loan. Firms that use short-term bank loans often arrange a line of credit. A **line of credit** is an agreement under which a firm is authorized to borrow up to a specified amount. To ensure that the line is used for short-term purposes, the borrower will sometimes be required to pay the line down to zero and keep it there for some period during the year, typically 60 days (called a *clean-up period*).

Short-term lines of credit are classified as either *committed* or *noncommitted*. The latter is an informal arrangement that allows firms to borrow up to a previously specified limit without going through the normal paperwork (much like a credit card). A *revolving credit arrangement* (or just *revolver*) is similar to a line of credit, but it is usually open for two or more years whereas a line of credit would usually be evaluated on an annual basis.

Committed lines of credit are more formal legal arrangements and usually involve a commitment fee paid by the firm to the bank (usually the fee is on the order of 0.25 percent of the total committed funds per year). The interest rate on the line of credit is usually set equal to the bank's prime lending rate plus an additional percentage, and the rate will usually float. A firm that pays a commitment fee for a committed line of credit is essentially buying insurance to guarantee that the bank can't back out of the agreement (absent some material change in the borrower's status).

compensating balance

Money kept by the firm with a bank in low-interest or non–interest-bearing accounts as part of a loan agreement.

Compensating Balances   As a part of a credit line or other lending arrangement, banks will sometimes require that the firm keep some amount of money on deposit. This is called a compensating balance. A **compensating balance** is some of the firm's money kept by the bank in low-interest or non–interest-bearing accounts. By leaving these funds with the bank and receiving no interest, the firm further increases the effective interest rate earned by the bank on the line of credit, thereby "compensating" the bank. A compensating balance might be on the order of 2 percent to 5 percent of the amount borrowed.

Firms also use compensating balances to pay for noncredit bank services such as cash management services. A traditionally contentious issue is whether the firm should pay for bank credit and noncredit services by fees or by compensating balances. Most major firms have now negotiated for banks to use the corporation's collected funds for compensation and use fees to cover any shortfall. Arrangements such as this one and some similar approaches discussed in the next chapter make the subject of minimum balances less of an issue than it once was.

Cost of a Compensating Balance   A compensating balance requirement has an obvious opportunity cost because the money often must be deposited in a zero or low interest rate account. For example, suppose that we have a $100,000 line of credit with a 10 percent compensating balance requirement. This means that 10 percent of the amount actually used must be left on deposit in a non–interest-bearing account.

The quoted interest rate on the credit line is 16 percent. Suppose we need $54,000 to purchase some inventory. How much do we have to borrow? What interest rate are we effectively paying?

If we need $54,000, we have to borrow enough so that $54,000 is left over after we take out the 10 percent compensating balance:

$$\$54,000 = (1 - .10) \times \text{Amount borrowed}$$

$$\$60,000 = 54,000/.90 = \text{Amount borrowed}$$

The interest on the $60,000 for one year at 16 percent is $60,000 \times .16 = $9,600. We're actually only getting $54,000 to use, so the effective interest rate is:

$$\text{Effective interest rate} = \text{Interest paid/Amount available}$$

$$= \$9,600/\$54,000$$

$$= 17.78\%$$

Notice that what effectively happens here is that we pay 16 cents in interest on every 90 cents that we borrow because we don't get to use the 10 cents that is tied up in the compensating balance. The interest rate is thus .16/.90 = 17.78% as we calculated.

Several points bear mentioning. First, compensating balances are usually computed as a monthly *average* of the daily balances. This may mean that the effective interest rate will be lower than our example illustrates. Second, it has become common for compensating balances to be based on the *unused* amount of the credit line. This amounts to an implicit commitment fee. Third, and most important, the details of any short-term business lending arrangements are highly negotiable. Banks will generally work with firms to design a package of fees and interest.

Letters of Credit   A *letter of credit* is a common arrangement in international finance. With a letter of credit, the bank issuing the letter promises to make a loan if certain conditions are met. Typically, the letter guarantees payment on a shipment of goods provided that the goods arrive as promised. A letter of credit can be revocable (subject to cancelation) or irrevocable (not subject to cancelation if the specified conditions are met).

Secured Loans

Banks and other finance companies often require security for a short-term loan just as they do for a long-term loan. Security for short-term loans usually consists of accounts receivable, inventories, or both.

accounts receivable financing

A secured short-term loan that involves either the assignment or factoring of receivables.

Accounts Receivable Financing Accounts receivable financing involves either *assigning* receivables or *factoring* receivables. Under assignment, the lender has the receivables as security, but the borrower is still responsible if a receivable can't be collected. With *conventional factoring,* the receivable is discounted and sold to the lender (the factor). Once it is sold, collection is the factor's problem, and the factor assumes the full risk of default on bad accounts. With *maturity factoring,* the factor forwards the money on an agreed-upon future date.

Example 17.3 Cost of Factoring

For the year just ended, LuLu's Pies had an average of $50,000 in accounts receivable. Credit sales were $500,000. LuLu's factors its receivables by discounting them 3 percent; in other words, by selling them for 97 cents on the dollar. What is the effective interest rate on this source of short-term financing?

To determine the interest rate, we first have to know the accounts receivable or average collection period. During the year, LuLu's turned over its receivables $500,000/$50,000 = 10 times. The average collection period is therefore 365/10 = 36.5 days.

The interest paid here is a form of discount interest (discussed in Chapter 5). In this case, LuLu's is paying 3 cents in interest on every 97 cents of financing. The interest rate per 36.5 days is thus .03/.97 = 3.09%. The APR is 10 × 3.09% = 30.9%, but the effective annual rate is:

$$EAR = (1.0309)^{10} - 1 = 35.6\%$$

The factoring is a relatively expensive source of money in this case.

We should note that if the factor takes on the risk of default by a buyer, then the factor is providing insurance as well as immediate cash. More generally, the factor essentially takes over the firm's credit operations. This can result in a significant saving. The interest rate we calculated is therefore overstated, particularly if default is a significant possibility. ∎

inventory loan

A secured short-term loan to purchase inventory.

Inventory Loans Inventory loans, short-term loans to purchase inventory, come in three basic forms: blanket inventory liens, trust receipts, and field warehouse financing:

1. *Blanket inventory lien.* A blanket lien gives the lender a lien against all the borrower's inventories (the blanket "covers" everything).
2. *Trust receipt.* A trust receipt is a device in which the borrower holds specific inventory in "trust" for the lender. Automobile dealer financing, for example, is done by trust receipts. This type of secured financing is also called *floor planning,* in reference to inventory on the showroom floor. However, it is somewhat cumbersome to use trust receipts for, say, wheat grain.
3. *Field warehouse financing.* In field warehouse financing, a public warehouse company (an independent company that specializes in inventory management) acts as a control agent to supervise the inventory for the lender.

Other Sources

There are a variety of other sources of short-term funds employed by corporations. Two of the most important are *commercial paper* and *trade credit.*

Commercial paper consists of short-term notes issued by large and highly rated firms. Typically, these notes are of short maturity, ranging up to 270 days (beyond that limit, the firm must file a registration statement with the SEC). Because the firm issues these directly and because it usually backs the issue with a special bank line of credit, the interest rate the firm obtains is often significantly below the rate a bank would charge for a direct loan.

Another option available to a firm is to increase the accounts payable period; in other words, it may take longer to pay its bills. This amounts to borrowing from suppliers in the form of trade credit. This is an extremely important form of financing for smaller businesses in particular. As we discuss in Chapter 19, a firm using trade credit may end up paying a much higher price for what it purchases, so this can be a very expensive source of financing.

⌐CONCEPT QUESTIONS

17.5a What are the two basic forms of short-term financing?

17.5b Describe two types of secured loans.

A SHORT-TERM FINANCIAL PLAN ⌐ 17.6

To illustrate a completed short-term financial plan, we will assume that Fun Toys arranges to borrow any needed funds on a short-term basis. The interest rate is 20 percent APR, and it is calculated on a quarterly basis. From Chapter 5, we know that the rate is $20\%/4 = 5\%$ per quarter. We will assume that Fun Toys starts the year with no short-term debt.

From Table 17.6, Fun Toys has a second quarter deficit of $60 million. We will have to borrow this amount. Net cash inflow in the following quarter is $55 million. We now have to pay $60 \times .05 = \$3$ million in interest out of that, leaving $52 million to reduce the borrowing.

We still owe $60 - 52 = \$8$ million at the end of the third quarter. Interest in the last quarter will thus be $8 \times .05 = \$.4$ million. In addition, net inflows in the last quarter are -$15 million, so we have to borrow a total of $15.4 million, bringing our total borrowing up to $15.4 + 8 = \$23.4$ million. Table 17.7 extends Table 17.6 to include these calculations.

Notice that the ending short-term debt is just equal to the cumulative deficit for the entire year, $20, plus the interest paid during the year, $3 + .4 = \$3.4$, for a total of $23.4.

Our plan is very simple. For example, we ignored the fact that the interest paid on the short-term debt is tax deductible. We also ignored the fact that the cash surplus in the first quarter would earn some interest (which would be taxable). We could add on a number of refinements. Even so, our plan highlights the fact that in about 90 days, Fun Toys will need to borrow $60 million or so on a short-term basis. It's time to start lining up the source of the funds.

Our plan also illustrates that financing the firm's short-term needs will cost about $3.4 million in interest (before taxes) for the year. This is a starting

Table 17.7		Q1	Q2	Q3	Q4
Short-term financial plan for Fun Toys (in millions)	Beginning cash balance	$20	$ 60	$10	$10.0
	Net cash inflow	40	− 110	55	− 15.0
	New short-term borrowing	—	60	—	15.4
	Interest on short-term borrowing	—	—	− 3	− .4
	Short-term borrowing repaid	—	—	− 52	—
	Ending cash balance	$60	$ 10	$10	$10.0
	Minimum cash balance	− 10	− 10	− 10	− 10.0
	Cumulative surplus (deficit)	$50	$ 0	$ 0	$ 0.0
	Beginning short-term borrowing	0	0	60	8.0
	Change in short-term debt	0	60	− 52	15.4
	Ending short-term debt	$ 0	$ 60	$ 8	$23.4

point for Fun Toys to begin evaluating alternatives to reduce this expense. For example, can the $100 million planned expenditure be postponed or spread out? At 5 percent per quarter, short-term credit is expensive.

Also, if Fun Toys' sales are expected to keep growing, then the $20 million plus deficit will probably also keep growing, and the need for additional financing is permanent. Fun Toys may wish to think about raising money on a long-term basis to cover this need.

17.7 | SUMMARY AND CONCLUSIONS

1. This chapter introduces the management of short-term finance. Short-term finance involves short-lived assets and liabilities. We trace and examine the short-term sources and uses of cash as they appear on the firm's financial statements. We see how current assets and current liabilities arise in the short-term operating activities and the cash cycle of the firm.

2. Managing short-term cash flows involves the minimizing of costs. The two major costs are carrying costs, the return forgone by keeping too much invested in short-term assets such as cash, and shortage costs, the cost of running out of short-term assets. The objective of managing short-term finance and doing short-term financial planning is to find the optimal trade-off between these two costs.

3. In an "ideal" economy, the firm could perfectly predict its short-term uses and sources of cash, and net working capital could be kept at zero. In the real world we live in, cash and net working capital provide a buffer that lets the firm meet its ongoing obligations. The financial manager seeks the optimal level of each of the current assets.

4. The financial manager can use the cash budget to identify short-term financial needs. The cash budget tells the manager what borrowing is required or what lending will be possible in the short run. The firm has available to it a number of possible ways of acquiring funds to meet short-term shortfalls, including unsecured and secured loans.

Key Terms

operating cycle 594
inventory period 594
accounts receivable period 594
accounts payable period 595
cash cycle 595
cash flow time line 595
carrying costs 602

shortage costs 602
cash budget 608
line of credit 612
compensating balance 612
accounts receivable financing 614
inventory loans 614

Chapter Review Problems and Self-Test

17.1 **The Operating and Cash Cycles**   Consider the following financial statement information for the Glory Road Company:

Item	Beginning	Ending
Inventory	$1,543	$1,669
Accounts receivable	4,418	3,952
Accounts payable	2,551	2,673
Net sales	$11,500	
Cost of goods sold	8,200	

Calculate the operating and cash cycles.

17.2 **Cash Balance for Masson Corporation**   The Masson Corporation has a 60-day average collection period and wishes to maintain a $5 million minimum cash balance. Based on this and the information below, complete the following cash budget. What conclusions do you draw?

MASSON CORPORATION
Cash Budget
(in millions)

	Q1	Q2	Q3	Q4
Beginning receivables	$120			
Sales	90	120	150	120
Cash collections				
Ending receivables				
Total cash collections				
Total cash disbursements	80	160	180	160
Net cash inflow				
Beginning cash balance	$ 5			
Net cash inflow				
Ending cash balance				
Minimum cash balance				
Cumulative surplus (deficit)				

Answers to Self-Test Problems

17.1 We first need the turnover ratios. Note that we use the average values for all balance sheet items and that we base the inventory and payables turnover measures on cost of goods sold.

$$\text{Inventory turnover} = \$8{,}200/[(1{,}543 + 1{,}669)/2] = 5.11 \text{ times}$$

$$\text{Receivables turnover} = \$11{,}500/[(4{,}418 + 3{,}952)/2] = 2.75 \text{ times}$$

$$\text{Payables turnover} = \$8{,}200/[(2{,}551 + 2{,}673)/2] = 3.14 \text{ times}$$

We can now calculate the various periods:

$$\text{Inventory period} = 365 \text{ days}/5.11 \text{ times} = 71.43 \text{ days}$$

$$\text{Receivables period} = 365 \text{ days}/2.75 \text{ times} = 132.73 \text{ days}$$

$$\text{Payables period} = 365 \text{ days}/3.14 \text{ times} = 116.24 \text{ days}$$

So the time it takes to acquire inventory and sell it is about 71 days. Collection takes another 133 days, and the operating cycle is thus 71 + 133 = 204 days. The cash cycle is this 204 days less the payables period, 204 − 116 = 88 days.

17.2 Since Masson has a 60-day collection period, only those sales made in the first 30 days of the quarter will be collected in the same quarter. Total cash collections in the first quarter will thus equal 30/90 = ⅓ of sales plus beginning receivables, or $120 + ⅓ × $90 = $150. Ending receivables for the first quarter (and the second quarter beginning receivables) are the other ⅔ of sales, or ⅔ × $90 = $60. The remaining calculations are straightforward, and the completed budget follows.

MASSON CORPORATION
Cash Budget
(in millions)

	Q1	Q2	Q3	Q4
Beginning receivables	$120	$ 60	$ 80	$100
Sales	90	120	150	120
Cash collections	150	100	130	140
Ending receivables	$ 60	$ 80	$100	$ 80
Total cash collections	$150	$100	$130	$140
Total cash disbursements	80	160	180	160
Net cash inflow	$ 70	−$ 60	−$ 50	−$ 20
Beginning cash balance	$ 5	$ 75	$ 15	−$ 35
Net cash inflow	70	− 60	− 50	− 20
Ending cash balance	$ 75	$ 15	−$ 35	−$ 55
Minimum cash balance	−$ 5	−$ 5	−$ 5	−$ 5
Cumulative surplus (deficit)	$ 70	$ 10	−$ 40	−$ 60

The primary conclusion from this schedule is that, beginning in the third quarter, Masson's cash surplus becomes a cash deficit. By the end of the year, Masson will need to arrange for $60 million in cash beyond what will be available.

Questions and Problems

1. Cash Equation   The Lake Heartwell Company has a book net worth of $1,500. Long-term debt is $400. Net working capital, other than cash, is $650. Fixed assets are $1,000. How much cash does the company have? If current liabilities are $600, what are current assets?

2. Sources and Uses   For the year just ended, you have gathered the following information on the Senior Corporation:
    a. Accounts payable declined by $210.
    b. A $90 dividend was paid.
    c. Inventories were decreased by $430.
    d. Long-term debt increased by $800.
    e. Fixed asset purchases were $600.
    Label each as a source or use of cash and describe its effect on the firm's cash balance.

3. Changes in the Cash Account   Indicate the impact of the following corporate actions on cash, using the letter I for an increase, D for a decrease, or N when no change occurs.
    a. Cash is paid for raw materials purchased for inventory.
    b. A dividend is paid.
    c. Merchandise is sold on credit.
    d. Common stock is issued.
    e. Raw material is purchased for inventory on credit.
    f. A piece of machinery is purchased and paid for with long-term debt.
    g. Payments for previous sales are collected.
    h. Merchandise is sold for cash.
    i. Payment is made for a previous purchase.
    j. A short-term bank loan is received.
    k. A dividend is paid with funds received from a sale of common stock.
    l. A piece of office equipment is purchased and paid for with a short-term note.
    m. Marketable securities are purchased.
    n. Last year's taxes are paid.
    o. Interest on long-term debt is paid.

4. Changes in the Operating Cycle   Indicate the effect that the following company actions will have on the operating cycle. Use the letter I to show an increase, the letter D for a decrease, and the letter N for no change.
    a. Inventory turnover goes from 10 times to 5 times.
    b. Receivables turnover goes from 10 times to 5 times.
    c. Payables turnover goes from 10 times to 5 times.
    d. Average receivables goes down.
    e. Payments to suppliers are speeded up.
    f. Credit sales are discontinued.

5. **Cost of Current Assets** The Avid Imitator Corporation has recently installed a just-in-time (JIT) inventory system. Describe the likely effect on Avid's carrying costs, shortage costs, and operating cycle.

6. **Changes in the Cycles** Indicate the impact of the following company actions on the cash cycle and the operating cycle. Use the letter I to show an increase, the letter D for a decrease, and the letter N for no change.

   a. The use of cash discounts offered by suppliers is decreased; so payments are made later.

   b. More finished goods are being produced for order instead of for inventory.

   c. A greater percentage of raw material purchases are paid for with cash.

   d. The terms of cash discounts offered to customers are made more favorable.

   e. A larger than usual amount of raw materials is purchased as a result of a price decline.

   f. An increased number of customers pay with cash instead of credit.

7. **Calculating Cycles** Consider the following financial statement information for the Flying Carpet Company:

Item	Beginning	Ending
Inventory	$2,331	$2,567
Accounts receivable	1,108	1,426
Accounts payable	4,927	5,300
Net sales	$23,750	
Cost of goods sold	13,776	

   Calculate the operating and cash cycles. How do you interpret your answer?

8. **Calculating Cash Collections** The Twaddle Company has projected the following quarterly sales amounts for the coming year:

	Q1	Q2	Q3	Q4
Sales	$120	$160	$200	$140

   Accounts receivable at the beginning of the year are $100. Twaddle has a 60-day collection period. Calculate cash collections in each of the four quarters by completing the following:

	Q1	Q2	Q3	Q4
Beginning receivables	$	$	$	$
Sales				
Cash collections				
Ending receivables				

   What would be the effect of shortening the collection period to 30 days?

9. **Calculating Payments**   Raven, Inc., has projected the following sales for the coming year:

	Q1	Q2	Q3	Q4
Projected sales	$345	$330	$263	$290

Sales in the year following this one are projected to be 20 percent greater in each quarter.

a. Calculate payments to suppliers assuming that Raven places orders during each quarter equal to 60 percent of projected sales in the next quarter. Assume that Raven pays immediately. What is the payables period in this case?

	Q1	Q2	Q3	Q4
Payment of accounts	$	$	$	$

b. Rework part a assuming a 90-day payables period:

	Q1	Q2	Q3	Q4
Payment of accounts	$	$	$	$

c. Rework part a assuming a 60-day payables period:

	Q1	Q2	Q3	Q4
Payment of accounts	$	$	$	$

10. **Calculating Payments**   The Lenore Corporation's purchases from suppliers in a quarter are equal to 80 percent of the next quarter's forecasted sales. The payables deferral period is 45 days. Wages, taxes, and other expenses are 10 percent of sales, while interest and dividends are $50 per quarter. No capital expenditures are planned. Projected quarterly sales are:

	Q1	Q2	Q3	Q4
Sales	$500	$700	$460	$420

Sales in the first quarter of the following year are projected at $550. Calculate Lenore's cash outlays by completing the following:

	Q1	Q2	Q3	Q4
Payment of accounts	$	$	$	$
Wages, taxes, other expenses				
Long-term financing expenses (interest and dividends)				
Total	$	$	$	$

622 Part Eight   Short-Term Financial Planning and Management

11. **Costs of Borrowing**   You've worked out a line of credit arrangement that allows you to borrow up to $100 million at any time. The interest rate is 3 percent per quarter. In addition, 5 percent of the amount that you borrow must be deposited in a non–interest-bearing account.
  a. What is the effective annual interest rate on this lending arrangement?
  b. Suppose you need $50 million today and you repay it in six months. How much interest will you pay?

12. **Factoring Receivables**   Your firm has an average collection period of 60 days. Current practice is to factor all receivables immediately at a 4 percent discount. What is the effective cost of borrowing in this case? Assume that default is extremely unlikely.

13. **Cycles**   Is it possible for a firm's cash cycle to be longer than its operating cycle? Explain why or why not.

14. **Calculating the Cash Budget**   Randy's Candy, Inc., has estimated sales (in millions) for the next four quarters as:

	Q1	Q2	Q3	Q4
Sales	$340	$443	$574	$522

Sales in the first quarter of the year after this one are projected at $410. Accounts receivable at the beginning of the year were $108. Randy's has a 30-day collection period.

  Randy's purchases from suppliers in a quarter are equal to 60 percent of the next quarter's forecasted sales, and suppliers are normally paid in 30 days. Wages, taxes, and other expenses run about 20 percent of sales. Interest and dividends are $40 per quarter.

  Randy's plans a major capital outlay in the third quarter of $200. Finally, Randy's started the year with a $35 cash balance and wishes to maintain a $25 minimum balance.
  a. Complete a cash budget for Randy's by filling in the following:

RANDY'S CANDY
Cash Balance
(in millions)

	Q1	Q2	Q3	Q4
Beginning cash balance	$35	$	$	$
Net cash inflow				
Ending cash balance				
Minimum cash balance	25			
Cumulative surplus (deficit)				

  b. Assume that Randy's can borrow any needed funds on a short-term basis at a rate of 3 percent per quarter. Prepare a short-term financial plan by filling in the following schedule. What is the total interest paid for the year?

RANDY'S CANDY
Short-Term Financial Plan
(in millions)

	Q1	Q2	Q3	Q4
Beginning cash balance	$35	$	$	$
Net cash inflow				
New short-term borrowing				
Interest on short-term borrowing				
Short-term borrowing repaid				
Ending cash balance				
Minimum cash balance	25			
Cumulative surplus (deficit)				
Beginning short-term borrowing				
Change in short-term debt				
Ending short-term debt				

15. **Short-Term Policy**   Cleveland Compressor and Pnew York Pneumatic are competing manufacturing firms. Use the information contained in their financial statements to answer the following questions:
   a. How are the current assets of each firm financed?
   b. Which firm has the larger investment in current assets on an absolute basis? On a relative basis? Which of these is more meaningful in determining working capital policy? Why?
   c. Which firm is more likely to incur carrying costs, and which is more likely to incur shortage costs? Why?

CLEVELAND COMPRESSOR
Balance Sheets
December 31, 19X2 and 19X1

	19X2	19X1
Assets		
Cash	$ 13,862	$ 17,339
Accounts receivable (net)	23,887	25,778
Inventory	54,867	42,287
Total current assets	$ 92,616	$ 85,404
Plant, property, and equipment	101,543	99,715
Less: accumulated depreciation	34,331	32,057
Net fixed assets	$ 67,212	$ 67,658
Prepaid expenses	1,914	1,791
Other assets	13,052	13,138
Total assets	$174,794	$167,991

Liabilities and Stockholders' Equity

Accounts payable	$ 6,494	$ 4,893
Notes payable	10,483	11,617
Payroll taxes and accrued expenses	7,422	7,227
Other taxes payable	9,924	8,460
Total current liabilities	$ 34,323	$ 32,197
Long-term debt	22,036	22,036
Total liabilities	$ 56,359	$ 54,233
Common stock	38,000	38,000
Paid-in capital	12,000	12,000
Retained earnings	68,435	63,758
Total stockholders' equity	$118,435	$113,758
Total liabilities and stockholders' equity	$174,794	$167,991

CLEVELAND COMPRESSOR
Income Statement
19X2

Sales	$162,749
Other income	1,002
Total income	$163,751
Cost of goods sold	103,570
Selling and administrative costs	26,395
Depreciation	2,274
Total operating expenses	$132,239
Interest paid	2,100
Pretax earnings	$ 29,412
Taxes	14,890
Net earnings	$ 14,522
Dividends	9,845
Retained earnings	4,677

PNEW YORK PNEUMATIC
Balance Sheet
December 31, 19X2 and 19X1

	19X2	19X1
Assets		
Cash	$ 5,794	$ 3,307
Accounts receivable (net)	26,177	22,133
Inventory	46,463	44,661
Total current assets	$78,434	$70,101
Plant, property, and equipment	31,842	31,116
Less: accumulated depreciation	19,297	18,143
Net fixed assets	$12,545	$12,973
Prepaid expenses	763	688
Other assets	1,601	1,385
Total assets	$93,343	$85,147

Liabilities and Stockholders' Equity

Accounts payable	$ 6,008	$ 5,019
Bank loans	3,722	645
Payroll taxes and accrued expenses	4,254	3,295
Other taxes payable	5,688	4,951
Total current liabilities	$19,672	$13,910
Common stock	20,576	20,576
Paid-in capital	5,624	5,624
Retained earnings	48,598	46,164
	$74,798	$72,364
Less: Treasury stock	1,127	1,127
Total stockholders' equity	$73,671	$71,237
Total liabilities and stockholders' equity	$93,343	$85,147

PNEW YORK PNEUMATIC
Income Statement
19X2

Sales	$91,374
Other income	1,067
Total income	$92,441
Costs of goods sold	59,042
Selling and administrative costs	18,068
Depreciation	1,154
Total operating expenses	$78,264
Earnings before taxes	$14,177
Taxes	6,838
Net earnings	$ 7,339
Dividends	4,905
Retained earnings	2,434

16. Calculating Cash Collections   The following is the sales budget for the Smith and Weston Company for the first quarter of 19X1:

	January	February	March
Sales budget	$90,000	$100,000	$120,000

Credit sales are collected as follows:

   30 percent in the month of sale
   40 percent in the month after sale
   30 percent in the second month after sale

The accounts receivable balance at the end of the previous quarter is $36,000 ($30,000 of which is uncollected December sales).

a. Compute the sales for December.

b. Compute the cash collections from sales for each month from January through March.

17.   Calculating the Cash Budget   Here are some important figures from the budget of the Fine Mulch Company for the second quarter of 19X5:

	April	May	June
Credit sales	$160,000	$140,000	$192,000
Credit purchases	68,000	64,000	80,000
Cash disbursements			
Wages, taxes, and expenses	8,000	7,000	8,400
Interest	3,000	3,000	3,000
Equipment purchases	50,000	0	4,000

The company predicts that 10 percent of its sales will never be collected, 50 percent of its sales will be collected in the month of the sale, and the remaining 40 percent will be collected in the following month. Credit purchases will be paid in the month following the purchase.

In March 19X5, credit sales were $180,000. Using this information, complete the following cash budget:

	April	May	June
Beginning cash balances	$200,000		
Cash receipts			
Cash collections from credit sales			
Total cash available			
Cash disbursements			
Purchases	65,000		
Wages, taxes, and expenses			
Interest			
Equipment purchases			
Total cash disbursements			
Ending cash balance			

Challenge Problem

18.   Costs of Borrowing   In exchange for a $500 million fixed commitment line of credit, your firm has agreed to do the following:
1. Pay 4 percent per quarter on any funds actually borrowed.
2. Maintain a 3 percent compensating balance on any funds actually borrowed.
3. Pay an up-front commitment fee of .20 percent of the amount of the line.

Based on this information, answer the following:
a. Ignoring the fixed commitment fee, what is the effective annual interest rate on this line of credit?
b. Suppose your firm immediately uses $40 million of the line and pays it off in a year. What is the effective annual interest rate on this $40 million loan?

Suggested Readings

Fabozzi, F., and L. N. Masonson. *Corporate Cash Management Techniques and Analysis.* Homewood, Ill.: Dow Jones-Irwin, 1985.

Gallinger, G.W., and P. B. Healey. *Liquidity Analysis and Management.* Reading, Mass.: Addison-Wesley Publishing Co., 1987.

Hill, N.C., and W. L. Sartoris. *Short-Term Financial Management.* New York: Macmillan, 1988.

Vander Weide, J., and S. F. Maier. *Managing Corporate Liquidity: An Introduction to Working Capital Management.* New York: John Wiley & Sons, 1985.

Chapter 18

Cash and Liquidity Management

T he balance sheet of Exxon showed total assets of $87.7 billion at the end of 1990. On this basis, Exxon was the largest industrial firm in the world. In addition, Exxon held $1.3 billion in "cash," which was about 1.5 percent of its assets. This cash included currency, demand deposits at commercial banks, and undeposited checks.[1]

Since cash earns no interest, why would Exxon choose to hold cash? It would seem more sensible for Exxon to put all its cash into marketable securities, such as Treasury bills, and thereby earn a return on the money. Of course, one reason Exxon holds cash is to pay for goods and services. While Exxon might prefer to pay its employees in Treasury bills, the minimum denomination of Treasury bills is $10,000. In this case, cash must be used because cash is more divisible than Treasury bills.[2]

This chapter is about how firms manage cash. The basic objective in cash management is to keep the investment in cash as low as possible while still operating the firm's activities efficiently and effectively. This goal usually reduces to the dictum: "Collect early and pay late." Accordingly, we discuss ways of accelerating collections and managing disbursements.

In addition, firms must invest temporarily idle cash in short-term marketable securities. As we discuss in various places, these securities can be bought and sold in the financial markets. As a group, they have very little default risk

---

[1] We are indebted to Jarl Kallberg of New York University and to David Wright of the University of Notre Dame for helpful comments and suggestions on this chapter.

[2] Cash is liquid. One property of liquidity is divisibility, that is, how easily an asset can be divided into parts.

and most are highly marketable. There are different types of these so-called money market securities, and we discuss a few of the most important ones.

REASONS FOR HOLDING CASH | 18.1

John Maynard Keynes, in his great work, *The General Theory of Employment, Interest, and Money,* identified three reasons why liquidity is important: the speculative motive, the precautionary motive, and the transaction motive. We discuss these next.

Speculative and Precautionary Motives

The **speculative motive** is the need to hold cash in order to be able to take advantage of, for example, bargain purchases that might arise, attractive interest rates, and (in the case of international firms) favorable exchange rate fluctuations.

speculative motive
The need to hold cash to take advantage of additional investment opportunities, such as bargain purchases.

For most firms, reserve borrowing ability and marketable securities can be used to satisfy speculative motives. Thus, for a modern firm, there might be a speculative motive for liquidity, but not necessarily for cash per se. Think of it this way: If you have a credit card with a very large credit limit, then you can probably take advantage of any unusual bargains that come along without carrying any cash.

This is also true, to a lesser extent, for precautionary motives. The **precautionary motive** is the need for a safety supply to act as a financial reserve. Once again, there probably is a precautionary motive for liquidity. However, given that the value of money market instruments is relatively certain and that instruments such as T-bills are extremely liquid, there is no real need to hold substantial amounts of cash for precautionary purposes.

precautionary motive
The need to hold cash as a safety margin to act as a financial reserve.

The Transaction Motive

Cash is needed to satisfy the **transaction motive,** the need to have cash on hand to pay bills. Transaction-related needs come from the normal disbursement and collection activities of the firm. The disbursement of cash includes the payment of wages and salaries, trade debts, taxes, and dividends.

transaction motive
The need to hold cash to satisfy normal disbursement and collection activities associated with a firm's ongoing operations.

Cash is collected from sales, the selling of assets, and new financing. The cash inflows (collections) and outflows (disbursements) are not perfectly synchronized, and some level of cash holdings is necessary to serve as a buffer. Perfect liquidity is the characteristic of cash that allows it to satisfy the transaction motive.

As electronic funds transfers and other high-speed, "paperless" payment mechanisms continue to develop, even the transaction demand for cash may all but disappear. Even if it does, however, there will still be a demand for liquidity and a need to manage it efficiently.

Compensating Balances

Compensating balances are another reason to hold cash. As we discussed in the previous chapter, cash balances are kept at commercial banks to compensate for banking services the firm receives. A minimum compensating balance requirement by banks providing credit services to the firm may impose a lower limit on the level of cash a firm holds.

Costs of Holding Cash

When a firm holds cash in excess of some necessary minimum, it incurs an opportunity cost. The opportunity cost of excess cash (held in currency or bank deposits) is the interest income that could be earned in the next best use, such as investment in marketable securities.

Given the opportunity cost of holding cash, why would a firm hold cash in excess of its compensating balance requirements? The answer is that a cash balance must be maintained to provide the liquidity necessary for transaction needs—paying bills. If the firm maintains too small a cash balance, it may run out of cash. If so, the firm may have to raise cash on a short-term basis. This could involve, for example, selling marketable securities or borrowing.

Activities such as selling marketable securities and borrowing involve various costs. As we've discussed, holding cash has an opportunity cost. To determine the appropriate cash balance, the firm must weigh the benefits of holding cash against these costs. We discuss this subject in more detail in the sections the follow.

> **CONCEPT QUESTIONS**
> 18.1a What is the transaction motive, and how does it lead firms to hold cash?
> 18.1b What is the cost to the firm of holding excess cash?

18.2 | UNDERSTANDING FLOAT

As you no doubt know, the amount of money you have according to your checkbook can be very different from the amount of money that your bank thinks you have. The reason is that some of the checks you have written haven't yet been presented to the bank for payment. The same thing is true for a business. The cash balance that a firm shows on its books is called the firm's *book* or *ledger balance*. The balance shown in its bank account as available to spend is called its *available* or *collected balance*. The difference between the available balance and the ledger balance is called the **float**, and it represents the net effect of checks in the process of *clearing* (moving through the banking system).

float

The difference between book cash and bank cash, representing the net effect of checks in the process of clearing.

Disbursement Float

Checks written by a firm generate *disbursement float*, causing a decrease in its book balance but no change in its available balance. For example, suppose General Mechanics, Inc. (GMI), currently has $100,000 on deposit with its bank. On June 8, it buys some raw materials and pays with a check for $100,000. The company's book balance is immediately reduced by $100,000 as a result.

GMI's bank, however, will not find out about this check until it is presented to GMI's bank for payment on, say, June 14. Until the check is presented, the firm's available balance is greater than its book balance by $100,000. In other words, before June 8, GMI has a zero float:

$$\text{Float} = \text{Firm's available balance} - \text{Firm's book balance}$$

$$= \$100,000 \qquad\qquad - 100,000$$

$$= \$0$$

GMI's position from June 8 to June 14 is:

$$\text{Disbursement float} = \text{Firm's available balance} - \text{Firm's book balance}$$

$$= \$100,000 \qquad\qquad - 0$$

$$= \$100,000$$

During this period of time that the check is clearing, GMI has a balance with the bank of $100,000. It can obtain the benefit of this cash while the check is clearing. For example, the available balance could be temporarily invested in marketable securities and thus earn some interest. We will return to this subject a little later.

Collection Float and Net Float

Checks received by the firm create *collection float*. Collection float increases book balances but does not immediately change available balances. For example, suppose GMI receives a check from a customer for $100,000 on October 8. Assume, as before, that the company has $100,000 deposited at its bank and a zero float. It deposits the check and increases its book balance by $100,000 to $200,000. However, the additional cash is not available to GMI until its bank has presented the check to the customer's bank and received $100,000. This will occur on, say, October 14. In the meantime, the cash position at GMI will reflect a collection float of $100,000. We can summarize these events. Before October 8, GMI's position is:

$$\text{Float} = \text{Firm's available balance} - \text{Firm's book balance}$$

$$= \$100,000 \qquad\qquad - 100,000$$

$$= \$0$$

GMI's position from October 8 to October 14 is:

$$\text{Collection float} = \text{Firm's available balance} - \text{Firm's book balance}$$

$$= \$100,000 \qquad\qquad - 200,000$$

$$= -\$100,000$$

In general, a firm's payment (disbursement) activities generate disbursement float, and its collection activities generate collection float. The net effect, that is, the sum of the total collection and disbursement floats, is the net float. The net float at a point in time is simply the overall difference between the firm's available balance and its book balance. If the net float is positive, then the firm's disbursement float exceeds its collection float and its available balance exceeds its book balance. If the available balance is less than the book balance, then the firm has a net collection float.

A firm should be concerned with its net float and available balance more than its book balance. If a financial manager knows that a check will not clear for several days, he or she will be able to keep a lower cash balance at the bank than might be true otherwise. This can generate a great deal of money.

For example, take the case of Exxon. The average daily sales of Exxon are about $248 million. If Exxon's collections could be speeded up by a single day, then Exxon could free up $248 million for investing. At a relatively modest 0.02 percent daily rate, the interest earned would be on the order of $50,000 *per day.*

Example 18.1 Staying Afloat

Suppose you have $5,000 on deposit. You write a check for $1,000 to pay for books, and you deposit $2,000. What are your disbursement, collection, and net floats?

After you write the $1,000 check, you show a balance of $4,000 on your books, but the bank shows $5,000 while the check is clearing. This is a disbursement float of $1,000.

After you deposit the $2,000 check, you show a balance of $6,000. Your available balance doesn't rise until the check clears. This is a collection float of −$2,000. Your net float is the sum of the collection and disbursement floats, or −$1,000.

Overall, you show $6,000 on your books. The bank shows a $7,000 balance, but only $5,000 is available because your deposit has not been cleared. The discrepancy between your available balance and your book balance is the net float (−$1,000), and it is bad for you. If you write another check for $5,500, there may not be sufficient available funds to cover it, and it might bounce. This is the reason that the financial manager has to be more concerned with available balances than book balances. ∎

Float Management

Float management involves controlling the collection and disbursement of cash. The objective in cash collection is to speed up collections and reduce the lag between the time customers pay their bills and the time the cash becomes available. The objective in cash disbursement is to control payments and minimize the firm's costs associated with making payments.

Total collection or disbursement times can be broken down into three parts: mailing time, processing delay, and availability delay:

1. *Mailing time* is the part of the collection and disbursement process where checks are trapped in the postal system.
2. *Processing delay* is the time it takes the receiver of a check to process the payment and deposit it in a bank for collection.

3. *Availability delay* refers to the time required to clear a check through the banking system.

Speeding up collections involves reducing one or more of these components. Slowing up disbursements involves increasing one of them. We will describe some procedures for managing collection and disbursement times below. First, we need to discuss how float is measured.

Measuring Float   The size of the float depends on both the dollars and time delay involved. For example, suppose that you mail a check for $500 to another state each month. It takes five days in the mail to reach its destination (the mailing time) and one day for the recipient to get over to the bank (the processing delay). The recipient's bank holds out-of-state checks for three days (availability delay). The total delay is $5 + 1 + 3 = 9$ days.

In this case, what is your average daily disbursement float? There are two equivalent ways of calculating the answer. First, you have a $500 float for nine days, so we say that the total float is $9 \times \$500 = \$4,500$. Assuming 30 days in the month, the average daily float is $\$4,500/30 = \$150$.

Alternatively, your disbursement float is $500 for 9 days out of the month and zero the other 21 days (again assuming 30 days in a month). Your average daily float is thus:

$$\text{Average daily float} = (9 \times \$500 + 21 \times 0)/30$$
$$= 9/30 \times \$500 + 21/30 \times 0$$
$$= \$4,500/30$$
$$= \$150$$

This means that, on an average day, your book balance is $150 less than your available balance, a $150 average disbursement float.

Things are only a little more complicated when there are multiple disbursements or receipts. To illustrate, suppose that Concepts, Inc., receives two items each month as follows:

	Amount	Processing and availability delay	Total float
Item 1:	$5,000,000	× 9	= $45,000,000
Item 2:	$3,000,000	× 5	= $15,000,000
Total	$8,000,000		$60,000,000

The average daily float is equal to:

$$\text{Average daily float} = \frac{\text{Total float}}{\text{Total days}} \qquad \text{[18.1]}$$

$$= \frac{\$60,000,000}{30} = \$2,000,000$$

So, on an average day, there is $2,000,000 that is uncollected and not available.

Another way to see this is to calculate the average daily receipts and multiply by the weighted average delay. Average daily receipts are:

$$\text{Average daily receipts} = \frac{\text{Total receipts}}{\text{Total days}} = \frac{\$8,000,000}{30} = \$266,666.67$$

Of the $8,000,000 total receipts, $5,000,000, or ⅝ of the total, is delayed for nine days. The other ⅜ is delayed for five days. The weighted average delay is thus:

$$\text{Weighted average delay} = (5/8) \times 9 \text{ days} + (3/8) \times 5 \text{ days}$$

$$= 5.625 + 1.875 = 7.50 \text{ days}$$

The average daily float is thus:

$$\text{Average daily float} = \text{Average daily receipts} \qquad [18.2]$$

$$\times \text{Weighted average delay}$$

$$= \$266,666.67 \times 7.50 \text{ days} = \$2,000,000$$

This is just as we had before.

Some Details   In measuring float, there is an important difference between collection and disbursement float. We defined float as the difference between the firm's available cash balance and its book balance. With a disbursement, the firm's book balance goes down when the check is *mailed,* so the mailing time is an important component in disbursement float. However, with a collection, the firm's book balance isn't increased until the check is *received,* so mailing time is not a component of collection float.

This doesn't mean that mailing time is not important with collections. The point is that when collection *float* is calculated, mailing time should not be considered. As we will discuss, when total collection *time* is considered, the mailing time is a crucial component.

Also, when we talk about availability delay, how long it actually takes a check to clear isn't really crucial. What matters is how long we must wait before the bank grants availability; that is, use of the funds. Banks actually have availability schedules that are used to determine how long a check is held based on time of deposit and other factors. Beyond this, availability delay can be a matter of negotiation between the bank and a customer. In a similar vein, for outgoing checks, what matters is the date our account is debited, not when the recipient is granted availability.

Cost of the Float   The basic cost of collection float to the firm is simply the opportunity cost of not being able to use the cash. At a minimum, the firm could earn interest on the cash if it were available for investing.

Suppose the Lambo Corporation has average daily receipts of $1,000 and a weighted average delay of three days. The average daily float is thus $3 \times \$1,000 = \$3,000$. This means that, on a typical day, there is $3,000 that is

	Day					
	1	2	3	4	5 ...	
Beginning float	$ 0 →	$1,000 →	$2,000 →	$3,000 →	$3,000...	
Checks received	+ 1,000	1,000	1,000	1,000	1,000...	
Checks cleared (cash available)	− 0	− 0	− 0	− 1,000	− 1,000...	
Ending float	$1,000	$2,000	$3,000	$3,000	$3,000...	

Figure 18.1

Buildup of the float

	Day			
	t	t + 1	t + 2	...
Beginning float	$3,000 →	$ 0 →	$ 0	...
Checks received	1,000	1,000	1,000	...
Checks cleared (cash available)	− 4,000	− 1,000	− 1,000	...
Ending float	$ 0	$ 0	$ 0	...

Figure 18.2

Effect of eliminating the float

not earning interest. Suppose Lambo could eliminate the float entirely. What would be the benefit? If it costs $2,000 to eliminate the float, what is the NPV of doing so?

Figure 18.1 illustrates the situation for Lambo. Suppose Lambo starts with a zero float. On a given day, Day 1, Lambo receives and deposits a check for $1,000. The cash becomes available three days later on Day 4. At the end of the day, the book balance is $1,000 more than the available balance, so the float is $1,000. On Day 2, they receive and deposit another check. They collect three days later on Day 5. Now there are two uncollected checks, and the books show a $2,000 balance. The bank, however, still shows a zero available balance; so the float is $2,000. The same sequence occurs on Day 3, and the float rises to a total of $3,000.

On Day 4, Lambo again receives and deposits a check for $1,000. How-ever, they also collect $1,000 from the Day 1 check. The change in book balance and the change in available balance are identical, +$1,000; so the float stays at $3,000. The same thing happens every day after Day 4; the float therefore stays at $3,000 forever.[3]

Figure 18.2 illustrates what happens if the float is eliminated entirely on some Day t in the future. After the float is eliminated, daily receipts are still $1,000. We collect the same day since the float is eliminated, so daily collec-tions are also still $1,000. As Figure 18.2 illustrates, the only change occurs the first day. On that day, as usual, we collect $1,000 from the sale made three

---

[3]This permanent float that exists forever is sometimes called the *steady-state float.*

days ago. Because the float is gone, we also collect on the sales made two days ago, one day ago, and today, for an additional $3,000. Total collections today are thus $4,000 instead of $1,000.

What we see is that Lambo generates an extra $3,000 today by eliminating the float. On every subsequent day, Lambo receives $1,000 in cash just as it did before the float was eliminated. If you recall our definition of relevant cash flows, the only change in the firm's cash flows from eliminating the float is this extra $3,000 that comes in immediately. No other cash flows are affected, so Lambo is $3,000 richer.

In other words, the PV of eliminating the float is simply equal to the total float. Lambo could pay this amount out as a dividend, invest it in interest-bearing assets, or do anything else with it. If it costs $2,000 to eliminate the float, then the NPV is $3,000 − 2,000 = $1,000; so Lambo should do it.

Example 18.2   Reducing the Float: Part I
Instead of eliminating the float, suppose that Lambo can reduce it to one day. What is the maximum Lambo should be willing to pay for this?

If Lambo can reduce the float from three days to one day, then the amount of the float will fall from $3,000 to $1,000. From our discussion just above, we see immediately that the PV of doing this is just equal to the $2,000 float reduction. Lambo should thus be willing to pay up to $2,000. ∎

Example 18.3   Reducing the Float: Part II
Look back at Example 18.2. Suppose that a large bank was willing to provide the float reduction service for a cost of $175 per year, payable at the end of each year. The relevant discount rate is 8 percent. Should Lambo hire the bank? What is the NPV of the investment? How do you interpret this discount rate? What is the most per year that Lambo should be willing to pay?

The PV to Lambo is still $2,000. The $175 would have to be paid out every year forever to maintain the float reduction; so the cost is perpetual, and its PV is $175/.08 = $2,187.50. The NPV is $2,000 − 2,187.50 = −$187.50; therefore, it's not a good deal.

Ignoring the possibility of bounced checks, the discount rate here corresponds most closely to the cost of short-term borrowing. The reason is that Lambo could borrow $1,000 from the bank every time a check is deposited and pay it back three days later. The cost is the interest that Lambo would have to pay.

The most Lambo would be willing to pay is whatever charge results in an NPV of zero. This occurs when the $2,000 benefit exactly equals the PV of the costs, that is, when $2,000 = C/.08, where C is the annual cost. Solving for C, we find that C = .08 × $2,000 = $160 per year. ∎

Ethical and Legal Questions   The cash manager must work with collected bank cash balances and not the firm's book balance (which reflects checks that have been deposited but not collected). If this is not done, a cash manager could be drawing on uncollected cash as a source of funds for short-term investing. Most banks charge a penalty rate for the use of uncollected funds. However, banks may not have good enough accounting and control procedures to be fully aware of the use of uncollected funds. This raises some ethical and legal questions for the firm.

For example, in May 1985, Robert Fomon, chairman of E. F. Hutton (a large investment bank), pleaded guilty to 2,000 charges of mail and wire fraud in connection with a scheme the firm had operated from 1980 to 1982. E. F. Hutton employees wrote checks totaling hundreds of millions of dollars against uncollected cash. The proceeds were then invested in short-term money market assets. This type of systematic overdrafting of accounts (or check *kiting* as it is sometimes called) is neither legal nor ethical and is apparently not a widespread practice among corporations. Also, the particular inefficiencies in the banking system that Hutton was exploiting have been largely eliminated.

For its part, E. F. Hutton paid a $2 million fine, reimbursed the government (the U.S. Department of Justice) $750,000 and reserved an additional $8 million for restitution to defrauded banks. We should note that the key issue in the case against Hutton was not its float management per se, but, rather, its practice of writing checks for no economic reason other than to exploit float.

CONCEPT QUESTIONS

18.2a Which of these would a firm be most interested in reducing: collection or disbursement float? Why?

18.2b How is daily average float calculated?

18.2c What is the benefit from reducing or eliminating float?

CASH COLLECTION AND CONCENTRATION | 18.3

From our previous discussion, collection delays work against the firm. All other things the same, then, a firm will adopt procedures to speed up collections and thereby decrease collection times. In addition, even after cash is collected, firms need procedures to funnel, or concentrate, that cash to where it can be best used. We discuss some common collection and concentration procedures next.

Components of Collection Time

Based on our discussion above, we can depict the basic parts of the cash collection process as follows: The total time in this process is made up of mailing time, check-processing delay, and the bank's availability delay.

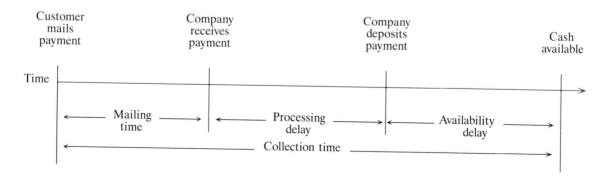

The amount of time that cash spends in each part of the cash collection process depends on where the firm's customers and banks are located and how efficient the firm is at collecting cash.

Cash Collection

How a firm collects from its customers depends in large part on the nature of the business. The simplest case would be a business such as a restaurant chain. Most of its customers will pay with cash, check, or credit card at the point of sale (this is called *over-the-counter collection*), so there is no problem with mailing delay. Normally, the funds would be deposited in a local bank, and the firm would have some means (discussed below) of gaining access to the funds.

When some or all of the payments a company receives are checks that arrive through the mail, all three components of collection time become relevant. The firm may choose to have all the checks mailed to one location, or, more commonly, the firm might have a number of different mail collection points to reduce mailing times. Also, the firm may run its collection operation itself or might hire an outside firm that specializes in cash collection. We discuss these issues in more detail below.

Other approaches to cash collection exist. One that is becoming more common is the preauthorized payment. With this arrangement, the payment amounts and payment dates are fixed in advance. When the agreed-upon date arrives, the amount is automatically transferred from the customer's bank account to the firm's bank account, sharply reducing or even eliminating collection delays. The same approach is used by firms that have "on-line" terminals, meaning that when a sale is rung up, the money is immediately transferred to the firm's accounts.

Lockboxes

lockboxes

Special post office boxes set up to intercept and speed up accounts receivable payments.

When a firm receives its payments by mail, it must decide where the checks will be mailed and how the checks will be picked up and deposited. Careful selection of the number and locations of the collection points can greatly reduce collection times. Many firms use special post office boxes called **lockboxes** to intercept payments and speed cash collection.

Figure 18.3 illustrates a lockbox system. The collection process is started by customers mailing their checks to a post office box instead of sending them to the firm. The lockbox is maintained by a local bank. A large corporation may actually maintain more than 20 lockboxes around the country.

In the typical lockbox system, the local bank collects the lockbox checks from the post office several times a day. The bank deposits the checks directly to the firm's account. Details of the operation are recorded (in some computer-usable form) and sent to the firm.

A lockbox system reduces mailing time because checks are received at a nearby post office instead of at corporate headquarters. Lockboxes also reduce the processing time because the corporation doesn't have to open the envelopes and deposit checks for collection. In all, a bank lockbox should enable a firm to get its receipts processed, deposited, and cleared faster than if it were to receive checks at its headquarters and deliver them itself to the bank for deposit and clearing.

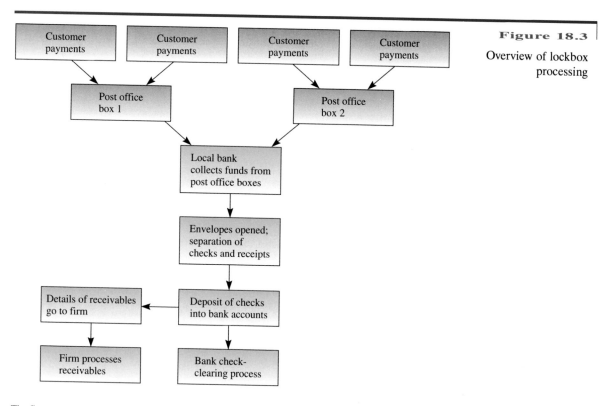

Figure 18.3

Overview of lockbox
processing

The flow starts when a corporate customer mails remittances to a post office box instead of to the corporation. Several times a day the bank collects the lockbox receipts from the post office. The checks are then put into the company bank accounts.

Cash Concentration

As we discussed earlier, a firm will typically have a number of cash collection points, and, as a result, cash collections may end up in many different banks and bank accounts. From here, the firm needs procedures to move the cash into its main accounts. This is called **cash concentration**. By routinely pooling its cash, the firm's cash management is greatly simplified because only a small number of accounts must be tracked. Also, by having a larger pool of funds available, a firm may be able to negotiate or otherwise obtain a better rate on any short-term investments.

In setting up a concentration system, firms will typically use one or more *concentration banks*. A concentration bank pools the funds obtained from local banks contained within some geographic region. Concentration systems are often used in conjunction with lockbox systems. Figure 18.4 illustrates how an integrated cash collection and cash concentration system might look. As Figure 18.4 illustrates, a key part of the cash collection and concentration process is the transfer of funds to the concentration bank. There are several options available for accomplishing this transfer. The cheapest is a *depository transfer check (DTC),* which is a preprinted check that usually needs no signature and is valid only for transferring funds between specific accounts within

cash concentration
The practice of and procedures for moving cash from multiple banks into the firm's main accounts.

Figure 18.4

Lockboxes and
concentration banks in a
cash management system

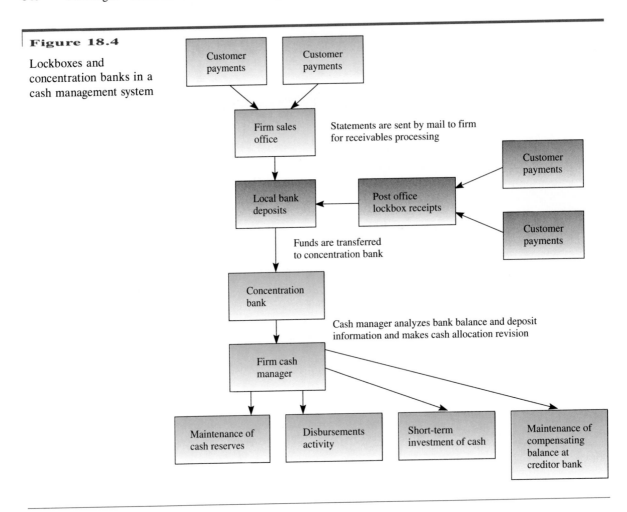

the *same* firm. The money becomes available one to two days later. *Automated Clearing House (ACH)* transfers are basically electronic versions of paper checks. These may be more expensive depending on the circumstances, but the funds are available the next day. The most expensive means of transfer is *wire transfer,* which provides same-day availability. Which approach a firm will choose depends on the number and size of payments. For example, a typical ACH transfer might be $200, whereas a typical wire transfer would be several million dollars. Firms with a large number of collection points and relatively small payments will choose the cheaper route, while firms that receive smaller numbers of relatively large payments may choose more expensive procedures.

Accelerating Collections: An Example

The decision to use a bank cash management service incorporating lockboxes and concentration banks depends on where a firm's customers are located and

In Their Own Words...

Jarl Kallberg on Increasing Automation in Cash Management

The increasing computerization of corporate America has affected all areas of working capital management. It has had far-reaching impacts on the way firms manage inventories, in many cases, helping them move closer to Japanese (just-in-time) approaches. For example, in the accounts receivable area, credit grantors have established on-line computer links with both consumer and commercial credit data providers, enabling them to make credit decisions in a totally automated environment, often in less than one minute.

Increased automation has also streamlined the cash and treasury management area, but sometimes the benefits don't accrue to all concerned. One notable example involved the automating of a major firm's cash management system. The assistant treasurer worked for two years to develop a highly automated operation. On the collection side, the firm had over 100 banks collecting deposits from local offices. The assistant treasurer developed a PC system to concentrate these deposits overnight using ACH transfers. The system used two lockbox banks, and it automatically concentrated the available balances daily using wire transfers. All of these funds were moved into a single concentration bank. All disbursements were drawn on one zero balance account, which was funded overnight, again using the ACH.

This system eventually functioned so that the assistant treasurer basically had to make no decisions. This was fine until one day his boss, the vice president of finance, finally understood how the system operated (and how little work the assistant treasurer had to do) and promptly fired him. His justification was that there really wasn't much need for an assistant treasurer anymore.

Jarl Kallberg is an associate professor of finance at New York University's Stern School of Business. From 1984 to 1991, he was editor of The Journal of Cash Management. *In 1989 and 1990, he was associate vice president at Dun & Bradstreet's, where he headed a group that developed financial models for D&B and its major clients.*

the speed of the U.S. postal system. Suppose Atlantic Corporation, located in Philadelphia, is considering a lockbox system. Its collection delay is currently eight days.

Atlantic does business in the southwestern part of the country (New Mexico, Arizona, and California). The proposed lockbox system would be located in Los Angeles and operated by Pacific Bank. Pacific Bank has analyzed Atlantic's cash-gathering system and has concluded it can decrease collection time by two days. Specifically, the bank has come up with the following information on the proposed lockbox system:

Reduction in mailing time	= 1.0 day
Reduction in clearing time	= 0.5 day
Reduction in firm processing time	= 0.5 day
TOTAL	= 2.0 days
Daily interest on Treasury bills	= 0.025%
Average number of daily payments to lockboxes	= 2,000
Average size of payment	= $600

The cash flows for the current collection operation are shown in the following cash flow time chart:

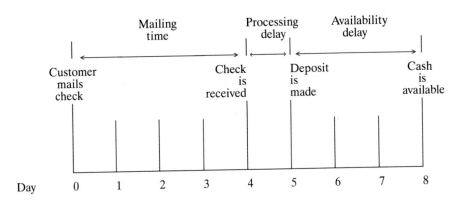

The cash flows for the lockbox collection operation will be as follows:

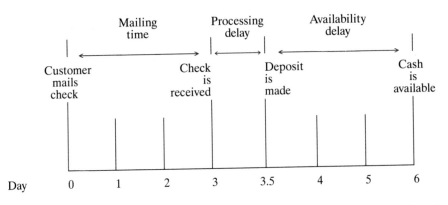

The Pacific Bank has agreed to operate this lockbox system for a fee of 25 cents per check processed. Should Atlantic give the go-ahead?

We first need to determine the benefit of the system. The average daily collections from the southwestern region are $1.2 million (2,000 × $600). The collection time will be decreased by two days, so the lockbox would increase the collected bank balance by $1.2 million × 2 = $2.4 million. In other words, the lockbox releases $2.4 million to the firm by reducing processing, mailing, and clearing time by two days. From our discussion above, this $2.4 million is the PV of the proposal.

To calculate the NPV, we need to determine the PV of the costs. There are several different ways to proceed. First, at 2,000 checks per day and $.25 per check, the daily cost is $500. This cost will be incurred every day forever. At an interest rate of .025 percent per day, the PV is therefore $500/.00025 = $2 million. The NPV is thus $2.4 million − 2 million = $400,000, and the system appears to be desirable.

Alternatively, Atlantic could invest the $2.4 million at .025 percent per day. The interest earned would be $2.4 million × .00025 = $600 per day. The cost of the system is $500 per day; so running it is obviously profitable in the amount of $100 per day. The PV of $100 per day forever is $100/.00025 = $400,000, just as we had before.

Finally, and most simply, each check is for $600 and is available two days sooner if the system is used. The interest on $600 for two days is $2 \times \$600 \times .00025 = \$.30$. The cost is 25 cents per check, so Atlantic makes a nickel ($\$.30 - .25$) on every check. With 2,000 checks per day, the profit is $\$.05 \times 2,000$ checks $= \$100$ per day as we calculated.

Example 18.4 Accelerating Collections

In our example concerning the Atlantic Corporation's proposed lockbox system, suppose that the Pacific Bank wanted a $20,000 fixed fee (paid annually) in addition to the 25 cents per check. Is the system still a good idea?

To answer, we need to calculate the PV of the fixed fee. The daily interest rate is .025 percent. The annual rate is therefore $(1.00025)^{365} - 1 = 9.553\%$. The PV of the fixed fee (which is paid each year forever) is $\$20,000/.09553 = \$209,358$. Since the NPV without the fee is $400,000, the NPV with the fee is $\$400,000 - 209,358 = \$190,642$. It's still a good idea. ■

⌐CONCEPT QUESTIONS

18.3a What is a lockbox? What purpose does it serve?

18.3b What is a concentration bank? What purpose does it serve?

MANAGING CASH DISBURSEMENTS ⌐18.4

From the firm's point of view, disbursement float is desirable, so the goal in managing disbursement float is to slow down disbursements as much as possible. To do this, the firm may develop strategies to *increase* mail float, processing float, and availability float on the checks that it writes. Beyond this, firms have developed procedures for minimizing cash held for payment purposes. We discuss the most common of these below.

Increasing Disbursement Float

As we have seen, float in terms of slowing down payments comes from mail delivery, check-processing time, and collection of funds. Disbursement float can be increased by writing a check on a geographically distant bank. For example, a New York supplier might be paid with checks drawn on a Los Angeles bank. This will increase the time required for the checks to clear through the banking system. Mailing checks from remote post offices is another way firms slow down disbursement. Figure 18.5 illustrates some of these practices.

Tactics for maximizing disbursement float are debatable on both ethical and economic grounds. First, as we discuss in some detail in the next chapter, payment terms very frequently offer a substantial discount for early payment. The discount is usually much larger than any possible savings from "playing the float game." In such cases, increasing mailing time will be of no benefit if the recipient dates payments based on the date received (as is common) as opposed to the postmark date.

Beyond this, suppliers are not likely to be fooled by attempts to slow down disbursement. The negative consequences from poor relations with suppliers

Figure 18.5

Cash disbursement

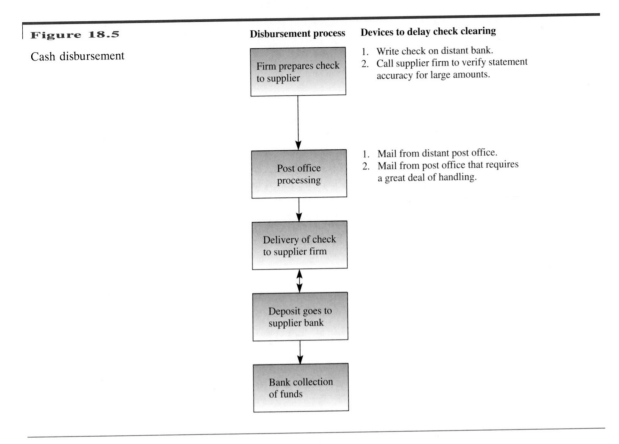

Disbursement process	Devices to delay check clearing
Firm prepares check to supplier	1. Write check on distant bank. 2. Call supplier firm to verify statement accuracy for large amounts.
Post office processing	1. Mail from distant post office. 2. Mail from post office that requires a great deal of handling.
Delivery of check to supplier firm	
Deposit goes to supplier bank	
Bank collection of funds	

can be costly. In broader terms, intentionally delaying payments by taking advantage of mailing times or unsophisticated suppliers may amount to avoiding paying bills when they are due, an unethical business procedure.

Controlling Disbursements

We have seen that maximizing disbursement float is probably poor business practice. However, a firm will still wish to tie up as little cash as possible in disbursements. Firms have therefore developed systems for efficiently managing the disbursement process. The general idea in such systems is to have no more than the minimum amount necessary to pay bills on deposit in the bank. We discuss some approaches to accomplish this goal next.

zero-balance account

A disbursement account in which the firm maintains a zero balance, transferring funds in from a master account only as needed to cover checks presented for payment.

Zero-Balance Accounts   With a **zero-balance account,** the firm, in cooperation with its bank, maintains a master account and a set of subaccounts. When a check written on one of the subaccounts must be paid, the necessary funds are transferred in from the master account. Figure 18.6 illustrates how such a system might work. In this case, the firm maintains two disbursement accounts, one for suppliers and one for payroll. As shown, if the firm does not use zero-balance accounts, then each of these accounts must have a safety

Figure 18.6

Zero-balance accounts

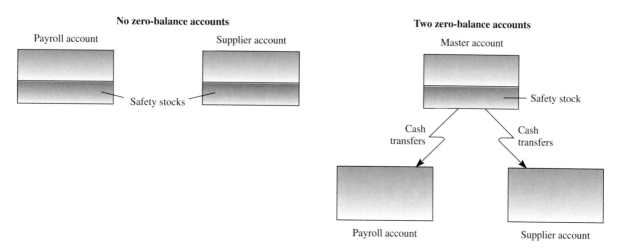

With zero-balance accounts, the firm keeps a single safety stock of cash in a master account. Funds are transferred into disbursement accounts as needed. With no zero-balance accounts, separate safety stocks must be maintained, thereby tying up cash unnecessarily.

stock of cash to meet unanticipated demands. If the firm does use zero-balance accounts, then it can keep one safety stock in a master account and transfer the funds to the two subsidiary accounts as needed. The key is that the total amount of cash held as a buffer is smaller under the zero-balance arrangement, thereby freeing up cash to be used elsewhere.

Controlled Disbursement Accounts   With a **controlled disbursement account,** almost all payments that must be made in a given day are known in the morning. The bank informs the firm of the total, and the firm transfers (usually by wire) the amount needed.

controlled disbursement account

A disbursement practice under which the firm transfers an amount to a disbursing account that is sufficient to cover demands for payment.

CONCEPT QUESTIONS

18.4a Is maximizing disbursement float a sound business practice?

18.4b What is a zero-balance account? What is the advantage of such an account?

INVESTING IDLE CASH | 18.5

If a firm has a temporary cash surplus, it can invest in short-term securities. As we have mentioned at various times, the market for short-term financial assets is called the *money market*. The maturity of short-term financial assets that trade in the money market is one year or less.

Most large firms manage their own short-term financial assets, transacting through banks and dealers. Some large firms and many small firms use money market mutual funds. These are funds that invest in short-term financial assets for a management fee. The management fee is compensation for the professional expertise and diversification provided by the fund manager.

Among the many money market mutual funds, some specialize in corporate customers. In addition, banks offer arrangements in which the bank takes all excess available funds at the close of each business day and invests them for the firm.

Temporary Cash Surpluses

Firms have temporary cash surpluses for various reasons. Two of the most important are the financing of seasonal or cyclical activities of the firm and the financing of planned or possible expenditures.

Seasonal or Cyclical Activities   Some firms have a predictable cash flow pattern. They have surplus cash flows during part of the year and deficit cash flows the rest of the year. For example, Toys "R" Us, a retail toy firm, has a seasonal cash flow pattern influenced by Christmas.

A firm such as Toys "R" Us may buy marketable securities when surplus cash flows occur and sell marketable securities when deficits occur. Of course, bank loans are another short-term financing device. The use of bank loans and marketable securities to meet temporary financing needs is illustrated in Figure 18.7. In this case, the firm is following a compromise working capital policy in the sense we discussed in the previous chapter.

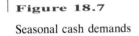

Figure 18.7

Seasonal cash demands

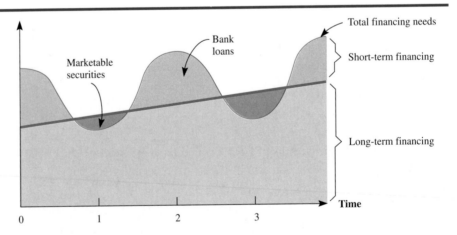

Time 1: A surplus cash flow exists. Seasonal demand for assets is low. The surplus cash flow is invested in short-term marketable securities.

Time 2: A deficit cash flow exists. Seasonal demand for assets is high. The financial deficit is financed by selling marketable securities and by bank borrowing.

Planned or Possible Expenditures   Firms frequently accumulate temporary investments in marketable securities to provide the cash for a plant construction program, dividend payment, or other large expenditures. Thus, firms may issue bonds and stocks before the cash is needed, investing the proceeds in short-term marketable securities and then selling the securities to finance the expenditures. Also, firms may face the possibility of having to make a large cash outlay. An obvious example would be the possibility of losing a large lawsuit. Firms may build up cash surpluses against such a contingency.

For example, on December 31, 1981, U.S. Steel (now USX Corporation) had $1.5 billion invested in marketable securities. This represented more than 11 percent of the total assets of U.S. Steel. This balance had been built up to finance a merger with Marathon Oil that was completed in March 1982.

Characteristics of Short-Term Securities

Given that a firm has some temporarily idle cash, there are a variety of short-term securities available for investing. The most important characteristics of these short-term marketable securities are their maturity, default risk, marketability, and taxability.

Maturity   Maturity refers to the time period over which interest and principal payments are made.

From Chapter 6, we know that for a given change in the level of interest rates, the prices of longer-maturity securities will change more than those of shorter-maturity securities. As a consequence, firms that invest in long-term securities are accepting greater risk than firms that invest in securities with short-term maturities.

We called this type of risk *interest rate risk*. Firms often limit their investments in marketable securities to those maturing in less than 90 days to avoid the risk of losses in value from changing interest rates. Of course, the expected return on securities with short-term maturities is usually less than the expected return on securities with longer maturities.

Default Risk   Default risk refers to the probability that interest and principal will not be paid in the promised amounts on the due dates (or not paid at all). In Chapter 12, we observed that various financial reporting agencies, such as Moody's Investors Service and Standard & Poor's, compile and publish ratings of various corporate and other publicly-held securities. These ratings are connected to default risk. Of course, some securities have negligible default risk, such as U.S. Treasury bills. Given the purposes of investing idle corporate cash, firms typically avoid investing in marketable securities with significant default risk.

Marketability   Marketability refers to how easy it is to convert an asset to cash; so marketability and liquidity mean much the same thing. Some money market instruments are much more marketable than others. At the top of the list are U.S. Treasury bills, which can be bought and sold very cheaply and very quickly.

Taxes   Interest earned on money market securities that are not some kind of government obligation (either federal or state) are taxable at the local, state, and federal levels. U.S. Treasury obligations such as T-bills are exempt from state taxation, but other government-backed debt is not. Municipal securities are exempt from federal taxes, but they may be taxed at the state level.

Some Different Types of Money Market Securities

Money market securities are generally highly marketable and short-term. They usually have low risk of default. They are issued by the U.S. government (for example, U.S. Treasury bills), domestic and foreign banks (for example, certificates of deposit), and business corporations (for example, commercial paper). There are many types in all, and we only illustrate a few of the most common here.

U.S. Treasury bills are obligations of the U.S. government that mature in 90, 180, 270, or 360 days. The 90-day and 180-day bills are sold by auction every week, and 270-day and 360-day bills are sold every month.

Short-term tax-exempts are short-term securities issued by states, municipalities, local housing agencies, and urban renewal agencies. Since these are all considered municipal securities, they are exempt from federal taxes. RANs, BANs, and TANs, for example, are revenue, bond, and tax anticipation notes, respectively. In other words, they represent short-term borrowing by municipalities in anticipation of cash receipts.

Short-term tax-exempts have more default risk than U.S. Treasury issues and are less marketable. Since the interest is exempt from federal income tax, the pretax yield on tax-exempts is lower than those on comparable securities such as U.S. Treasury bills. Also, corporations face some restrictions on holding tax-exempts as investments.

Commercial paper refers to short-term securities issued by finance companies, banks, and corporations. Typically, commercial paper is unsecured. Maturities range from a few weeks to 270 days.

There is no active secondary market in commercial paper. As a consequence, the marketability is low; however, firms that issue commercial paper will often repurchase it directly before maturity. The default risk of commercial paper depends on the financial strength of the issuer. Moody's and S&P publish quality ratings for commercial paper. These ratings are similar to the bond ratings we discussed in Chapter 12.

Certificates of deposit (CDs) are short-term loans to commercial banks. These are normally jumbo CDs—those in excess of $100,000. There are active markets in CDs of 3-month, 6-month, 9-month, and 12-month maturities.

Repurchase agreements (repos) are sales of government securities (for example, U.S. Treasury bills) by a bank or securities dealer with an agreement to repurchase. Typically, an investor buys some Treasury securities from a bond dealer and simultaneously agrees to sell them back at a later date at a specified higher price. Repurchase agreements are usually very short term—overnight to a few days.

Because 70 to 80 percent of the dividends received by one corporation from another are exempt from taxation, the relatively high dividend yields on preferred stock provide a strong incentive for investment. The only problem is that the dividend is fixed with ordinary preferred stock, so the price can fluctuate more than is desirable in a short-term investment. However, as we discuss in Chapter 12, money market preferred stock is a recent innovation featuring a floating dividend. The dividend is reset fairly often (usually every 49 days), so this type of preferred has much less price volatility than ordinary preferred, and it has become a popular short-term investment.

⌐ CONCEPT QUESTIONS

18.5a What are some reasons why firms find themselves with idle cash?

18.5b What are some types of money market securities?

18.5c Why are money market preferred stocks an attractive short-term investment?

SUMMARY AND CONCLUSIONS ⌐ 18.6

1. A firm holds cash to conduct transactions and to compensate banks for the various services they render.

2. The difference between a firm's available balance and its book balance is the firm's net float. The float reflects the fact that some checks have not cleared and are thus uncollected. The financial manager must always work with collected cash balances and not with the company's book balance. To do otherwise is to use the bank's cash without the bank knowing it, raising ethical and legal questions.

3. The firm can make use of a variety of procedures to manage the collection and disbursement of cash in such a way as to speed up the collection of cash and slow down the payments. Some methods to speed up the collection are lockboxes, concentration banking, and wire transfers.

4. Because of seasonal and cyclical activities, to help finance planned expenditures or as a contingency reserve, firms temporarily find themselves with a cash surplus. The money market offers a variety of possible vehicles for "parking" this idle cash.

Key Terms

speculative motive 629
precautionary motive 629
transaction motive 629
float 630

lockboxes 638
cash concentration 639
zero-balance account 644
controlled disbursement account 645

Chapter Review Problem and Self-Test

18.1 Float Measurement   On a typical business day, a firm writes checks totaling $1,000. These checks clear in 10 days on average. Simultaneously, the firm receives $1,300. The cash is available in five days on average. Calculate the disbursement float, the collection float, and the net float. How do you interpret the answer?

Answer to Self-Test Problem

18.1   The disbursement float is 10 days × $1,000 = $10,000. The collection float is 5 days × −$1,300 = −$6,500. The net float is $10,000 + (−6,500) = $3,500. In other words, at any given time, the firm typically has uncashed checks outstanding of $10,000. At the same time, it has uncollected receipts of $6,500. Thus, the firm's book balance is typically $3,500 less than its available balance, a positive $3,500 net float.

Questions and Problems

1.   Float   Which would a firm prefer: a net collection float or a net disbursement float? Why?

2.   Disbursement Float   Suppose a firm has a book balance of $1.4 million dollars. At the ATM (automatic teller machine), the cash manager finds out that the bank balance is $1.8 million. What is the situation here? If this is an ongoing situation, what ethical dilemma arises?

3.   Calculating Float   In a typical month, the Roenfeldt Company receives 20 checks totalling $35,000. These are delayed four days on average. What is the average daily float?

4.   Calculating Net Float   Each business day, on average, a company writes checks totaling $12,000 to pay its suppliers. The usual clearing time for these checks is five days. Meanwhile, the company is receiving payments from its customers each day, in the form of checks, totaling $15,000. The cash from the payments is available to the firm after three days.
   a. Calculate the company's disbursement float, collection float, and net float.
   b. How would your answer to part a change if the collected funds were available in four days instead of three?

5.   Float and Weighted Average Delay   A little old lady in Pasadena drives to the post office once a month and picks up two checks, one for $5,000 and one for $2,000. The larger check takes four days to clear after it is deposited; the smaller one takes eight days.
   a. What is the total float for the month?
   b. What is the average daily float?
   c. What are the average daily receipts and weighted average delay?

6.   Costs of Float   The Kau Audio Salon receives an average of $5,000 in checks per day. The delay in clearing is typically four days. The current interest rate is .02 percent per day.
   a. What is Kau's float?
   b. What is the total opportunity cost of the float?
   c. What is the daily opportunity cost of the float?

7.   Using Weighted Average Delay   A mail order firm processes 10,000 checks per month. Of these, 20 percent are for $30 and

80 percent are for $60. The $30 checks are delayed two days on average; the $60 checks are delayed four days on average.

a. What is the average daily collection float? How do you interpret your answer?

b. What is the weighted average delay? Use the result to calculate the average daily float.

c. How much should the firm be willing to pay to eliminate the float?

d. If the interest rate is 8 percent per year, calculate the daily cost of the float.

e. What would the firm pay to reduce the weighted average float by two days?

8. NPV of Reducing Collection Time   Your firm has an average receipt size of $10. A bank has approached you concerning a lockbox service that will decrease your total collection time by three days. You typically receive 25,000 checks per day. The daily interest rate is .02 percent. What would the annual savings be if the service is adopted?

9. Value of Lockboxes   The Rao Radiator Company is investigating a lockbox system to reduce its collection time. They have determined the following:

Average number of payments per day	100
Average value of payment	$1,000
Variable lockbox fee (per transaction)	$.75
Daily interest rate on money market securities	.03%

The total collection time would be reduced by three days if the system is adopted.

a. What is the PV of adopting the system?

b. What is the NPV of adopting the system?

c. What is the net cash flow per day from adopting? Per check?

10. Lockboxes and Collection Time   Garden Groves, Inc., a Florida-based company, has determined that a majority of its customers are located in the New York City area. It therefore is considering using a lockbox system offered by a bank located in New York. The bank has estimated that use of the system will reduce collection time by three days. Based on the following information, should the lockbox system be adopted?

Average number of payments per day	200
Average value of payment	$10,000
Variable lockbox fee (per transaction)	$.50
Annual interest rate on money market securities	7.5%

How would your answer change if there were a fixed charge of $50,000 per year in addition to the variable charge?

11. Calculating Transactions Required   A large New England lumber producer, Salisbury Stakes, Inc., is planning to use a lockbox system

to speed collections from its customers located in the midwestern United States. A Chicago area bank will provide this service for an annual fee of $15,000 plus 25 cents per transaction. The estimated reduction in collection and processing time is two days. If the average customer payment in this region is $4,500, how many customers each day, on average, are needed to make the system profitable? Treasury bills are currently yielding 6 percent per year.

12. Lockboxes and Collections   It takes the Herman Company about seven days to receive and deposit checks from customers. The top management of the Herman Company is considering a lockbox system. It is expected that the lockbox system will reduce receipt and deposit times to four days. Average daily collections are $100,000. The rate of return is 12 percent.

   a. What is the reduction in outstanding cash balances as a result of implementing the lockbox system?
   b. What is the dollar return that could be earned on these savings?
   c. What is the maximum monthly charge the Herman Company should pay for this lockbox system?

13. Value of Delay   The Walter Company disburses checks every two weeks that average $200,000 and take three days to clear. How much interest can the Walter Company earn annually if it delays transfer of funds from an interest-bearing account that pays 0.04 percent per day for these three days?

14. NPV of Reducing Float   The Miller Company has an agreement with the First National Bank whereby the bank handles $4 million in collections a day and requires a $500,000 compensating balance. Miller is contemplating canceling the agreement and dividing its eastern region so that two other banks will handle its business. Banks 1 and 2 will each handle $2 million a day of collections, and each requires a compensating balance of $300,000. Miller's financial management expects that collections will be accelerated by one day if the eastern region is divided. Should the Miller Company implement the new system? What will be the annual net savings? The T-bill rate is 7 percent.

Suggested Readings

We have benefited from the following books on short-term finance:

Hill, Ned C., and William L. Sartoris. *Short-Term Financial Management.* New York: Macmillan, 1988.

Scherr, Frederick C. *Modern Working Capital Management.* Englewood Cliffs, N.J.: Prentice Hall, 1989.

DETERMINING THE TARGET CASH BALANCE

Based on our general discussion of current assets in the previous chapter, the **target cash balance** involves a trade-off between the opportunity costs of holding too much cash (the carrying costs) and the costs of holding too little (the shortage costs, also called **adjustment costs**). The nature of these costs depends on the firm's working capital policy.

If the firm has a flexible working capital policy, then it will probably maintain a marketable securities portfolio. In this case, the adjustment or shortage costs will be the trading costs associated with buying and selling securities. If the firm has a restrictive working capital policy, it will probably borrow short-term to meet cash shortages. The costs in this case will be the interest and other expenses associated with arranging a loan.

In our discussion below, we will assume that the firm has a flexible policy. Its cash management then consists of moving money in and out of marketable securities. This is a very traditional approach to the subject, and it is a nice way of illustrating the costs and benefits of holding cash. Keep in mind, however, that the distinction between cash and money market investments is becoming increasingly blurred.

For example, how do we classify a money market fund with check-writing privileges? Such "near-cash" arrangements are becoming more and more common. It may be that the prime reason they are not universal is regulation limiting their usage. We will return to this subject at various points below.

> **target cash balance**
> A firm's desired cash level as determined by the trade-off between carrying costs and shortage costs.
>
> **adjustment costs**
> The costs associated with holding too little cash. Also *shortage costs*.

The Basic Idea

Figure 18A.1 presents the cash management problem for our flexible firm. If a firm tries to keep its cash holdings too low, it will find itself running out of cash more often than is desirable, and thus selling marketable securities (and perhaps later buying marketable securities to replace those sold) more frequently than would be true if the cash balance were higher. Thus, trading costs will be high when the size of the cash balance is low. These costs will fall as the cash balance becomes larger.

In contrast, the opportunity costs of holding cash are very low if the firm holds very little cash. These costs increase as the cash holdings rise because the firm is giving up more and more in interest that could have been earned.

At Point C^* in Figure 18A.1, the sum of the costs is given by the total cost curve. As shown, the minimum total cost occurs where the two individual cost curves cross. At this point, the opportunity costs and the trading costs are equal. This is the target cash balance, and it is the point the firm should try to find.

Figure 18A.1 is essentially the same as Figure 17.2 in the previous chapter. As we discuss next, however, we can now say more about the optimum investment in cash and the factors that influence it.

The BAT Model

The Baumol-Allais-Tobin (BAT) model is a classic means of analyzing our cash management problem. We will illustrate how this model can be used to actually establish the target cash balance. It is a straightforward model and very

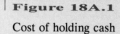

Figure 18A.1

Cost of holding cash

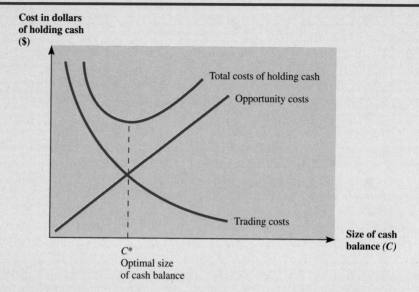

Cost in dollars
of holding cash
($)

Total costs of holding cash

Opportunity costs

Trading costs

Size of cash
balance (C)

C^*
Optimal size
of cash balance

Trading costs are increased when the firm must sell securities to establish a cash balance.
Opportunity costs are increased when there is a cash balance because there is no return to cash.

useful for illustrating the factors in cash management and, more generally, current asset management.

To develop the BAT model, suppose the Golden Socks Corporation starts off at Time 0 with a cash balance of C = $1.2 million. Each week, outflows exceed inflows by $600,000. As a result, the cash balance will drop to zero at the end of Week 2. The average cash balance will be the beginning balance ($1.2 million) plus the ending balance ($0) divided by 2, or ($1.2 million + 0)/2 = $600,000 over the two-week period. At the end of Week 2, Golden Socks replenishes its cash by depositing another $1.2 million.

As we have described, the cash management strategy for Golden Socks is very simple and boils down to depositing $1.2 million every two weeks. This policy is shown in Figure 18A.2. Notice how the cash balance declines by $600,000 per week. Since we bring the account up to $1.2 million, the balance hits zero every two weeks. This results in the "sawtooth" pattern displayed in Figure 18A.2.

Implicitly, we assume that the net cash outflow is the same every day and that it is known with certainty. These two assumptions make the model easy to handle. We will indicate what happens when they do not hold in the next section.

If C were set higher, say, at $2.4 million, cash would last four weeks before the firm would have to sell marketable securities, but the firm's average cash balance would increase to $1.2 million (from $600,000). If C were set at $600,000, cash would run out in one week and the firm would have to replenish cash more frequently, but its average cash balance would fall from $600,000 to $300,000.

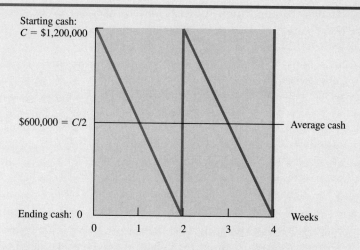

Starting cash:
$C = \$1,200,000$

$\$600,000 = C/2$ —— Average cash

Ending cash: 0

0   1   2   3   4   Weeks

The Golden Socks Corporation starts at Time 0 with cash of $1,200,000. The
balance drops to zero by the second week. The average cash balance is
$C/2 = \$1,200,000/2 = \$600,000$ over the period.

Because transactions costs must be incurred whenever cash is replenished
(for example, the brokerage costs of selling marketable securities), establishing
large initial balances will lower the trading costs connected with cash management. However, the larger the average cash balance, the greater is the opportunity cost (the return that could have been earned on marketable securities).

To determine the optimal strategy, Golden Socks needs to know the following three things:

F = The fixed cost of making a securities trade to replenish cash

T = The total amount of new cash needed for transactions purposes over
the relevant planning period, say, one year

R = The opportunity cost of holding cash. This is the interest rate on
marketable securities.

With this information, Golden Socks can determine the total costs of any
particular cash balance policy. It can then determine the optimal cash balance policy.

The Opportunity Costs   To determine the opportunity costs of holding
cash, we have to find out how much interest is forgone. Golden Socks has, on
average, $\$C/2$ in cash. This amount could be earning interest at rate R. So the
total dollar opportunity costs of cash balances are equal to the average cash
balance multiplied by the interest rate:

Opportunity costs = $(C/2) \times R$ [18A.1]

For example, the opportunity costs of various alternatives are given here assuming that the interest rate is 10 percent:

Initial Cash Balance	Average Cash Balance	Opportunity Cost ($R = 0.10$)
C	$C/2$	$(C/2) \times R$
$4,800,000	$2,400,000	$240,000
2,400,000	1,200,000	120,000
1,200,000	600,000	60,000
600,000	300,000	30,000
300,000	150,000	15,000

In our original case where the initial cash balance is $1.2 million, the average balance is $600,000. The interest we could have earned on this (at 10 percent) is $60,000, so this is what we give up with this strategy. Notice that the opportunity costs increase as the initial (and average) cash balance rises.

The Trading Costs   To determine the total trading costs for the year, we need to know how many times Golden Socks will have to sell marketable securities during the year. First of all, the total amount of cash disbursed during the year is $600,000 per week or $T = \$600,000 \times 52$ weeks $= \$31.2$ million. If the initial cash balance is set at $C = \$1.2$ mjllion, then Golden Socks will sell $1.2 million of marketable securities $T/C = \$31.2$ million/$1.2 million $= 26$ times per year. It costs F dollars each time, so trading costs are given by:

$$\frac{\$31.2 \text{ million}}{\$1.2 \text{ million}} \times F = 26 \times F$$

In general, the total trading costs will be given by:

$$\text{Trading costs} = (T/C) \times F \qquad \text{[18A.2]}$$

In this example, if F were $1,000 (an unrealistically large amount), then the trading costs would be $26,000.

We can calculate the trading costs associated with some different strategies as follows:

Total Amount of Disbursements during Relevant Period	Initial Cash Balance	Trading Costs ($F = \$1,000$)
T	C	$(T/C) \times F$
$31,200,000	$4,800,000	$ 6,500
31,200,000	2,400,000	13,000
31,200,000	1,200,000	26,000
31,200,000	600,000	52,000
31,200,000	300,000	104,000

The Total Cost   Now that we have the opportunity costs and the trading costs, we can calculate the total cost by adding them together:

$$\text{Total cost} = \text{Opportunity costs} + \text{Trading costs} \qquad [18A.3]$$
$$= (C/2) \times R + (T/C) \times F$$

Using the numbers above, we have:

Cash Balance	Opportunity Costs	+	Trading Costs	=	Total Cost
$4,800,000	$240,000		$ 6,500		$246,500
2,400,000	120,000		13,000		133,000
1,200,000	60,000		26,000		86,000
600,000	30,000		52,000		82,000
300,000	15,000		104,000		119,000

Notice how the total cost starts out at almost $250,000 and declines to about $80,000 before starting to rise again.

The Solution   We can see from the preceding schedule that a $600,000 cash balance results in the lowest total cost of the possibilities presented: $82,000. But what about $700,000 or $500,000 or other possibilities? It appears that the optimum balance is somewhere between $300,000 and $1.2 million. With this in mind, we could easily proceed by trial and error to find the optimum balance. It is not difficult to find it directly, however, so we do this next.

Take a look back at Figure 18A.1. As drawn, the optimal size of the cash balance, C^*, occurs right where the two lines cross. At this point, the opportunity costs and the trading costs are exactly equal. So, at C^*, we must have that:

$$\text{Opportunity costs} = \text{Trading costs}$$
$$C^*/2 \times R = (T/C^*) \times F$$

With a little algebra, we can write:

$$C^{*2} = (2T \times F)/R$$

To solve for C^*, we take the square root of both sides to get:

$$C^* = \sqrt{(2T \times F)/R} \qquad [18A.4]$$

This is the optimum initial cash balance.

For Golden Socks, we have $T = \$31.2$ million, $F = \$1,000$, and $R = 10\%$. We can now find the optimum cash balance as:

$$C^* = \sqrt{(2 \times \$31,200,000 \times \$1,000)/.10}$$
$$= \sqrt{\$624 \text{ billion}}$$
$$= \$789,937$$

We can verify this answer by calculating the various costs at this balance as well as a little above and a little below:

Cash Balance	Opportunity Costs	+	Trading Costs	=	Total Cost
$850,000	$42,500		$36,706		$79,206
800,000	40,000		39,000		79,000
789,937	**39,497**		**39,497**		**78,994**
750,000	37,500		41,600		79,100
700,000	35,000		44,571		79,571

The total cost at the optimum is $78,994, and it does appear to increase as we move in either direction.

Example 18A.1   The BAT Model

The Vulcan Corporation has cash outflows of $100 per day, seven days a week. The interest rate is 5 percent, and the fixed cost of replenishing cash balances is $10 per transaction. What is the optimal initial cash balance? What is the total cost?

The total cash needed for the year is 365 days × $100 = $36,500. From the BAT model, the optimal initial balance is:

$$C^* = \sqrt{(2T \times F)/R}$$

$$= \sqrt{(2 \times \$36,500 \times \$10)/.05}$$

$$= \sqrt{14.6 \text{ million}}$$

$$= \$3,821$$

The average cash balance is $3,821/2 = $1,911, so the opportunity cost is $1,911 × .05 = $96. Since we need $100 per day, the $3,821 balance will last $3,821/$100 = 38.21 days. We need to resupply the account 365/38.21 = 9.6 times, so the trading (order) cost is $96. The total cost is $192. ∎

The BAT model is possibly the simplest and most stripped-down sensible model for determining the optimal cash position. Its chief weakness is that it assumes steady, certain cash outflows. We next discuss a more involved model designed to deal with this limitation.

The Miller-Orr Model: A More General Approach

We now describe a cash management system designed to deal with cash inflows and outflows that fluctuate randomly from day to day. With this model, we again concentrate on the cash balance, but, in contrast to the BAT model, we assume that this balance fluctuates up and down randomly and that the average change is zero.

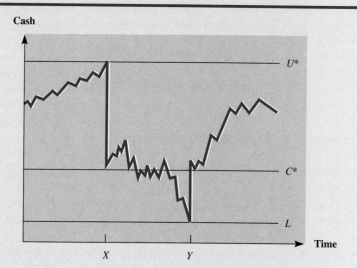

Figure 18A.3

The Miller-Orr model

U^* is the upper control limit. L is the lower control limit. The target cash balance is C^*. As long as cash is between L and U^*, no transaction is made.

The Basic Idea   Figure 18A.3 shows how the system works. It operates in terms of an upper limit to the amount of cash (U^*) and a lower limit (L), and a target cash balance (C^*). The firm allows its cash balance to wander around between the lower and upper limits. As long as the cash balance is somewhere between U^* and L, nothing happens.

When the cash balance reaches the upper limit (U^*), such as it does at Point X, the firm moves $U^* - C^*$ dollars out of the account and into marketable securities. This action moves the cash balance down to C^*. In the same way, if the cash balance falls to the lower limit (L), as it does at Point Y, the firm will sell $C^* - L$ worth of securities and deposit the cash in the account. This action takes the cash balance up to C^*.

Using the Model   To get started, management sets the lower limit (L). This limit is essentially a safety stock; so where it is set depends on how much risk of a cash shortfall the firm is willing to tolerate. Alternatively, the minimum might just equal a required compensating balance.

Like the BAT model, the optimal cash balance depends on trading costs and opportunity costs. Once again, the cost per transaction of buying and selling marketable securities, F, is assumed to be fixed. Also, the opportunity cost of holding cash is R, the interest rate per period on marketable securities.

The only extra piece of information needed is σ^2, the variance of the net cash flow per period. For our purposes, the period can be anything, a day or a week, for example, as long as the interest rate and the variance are based on the same length of time.

Given L, which is set by the firm, Miller and Orr show that the cash balance target, C^*, and the upper limit, U^*, that minimize the total costs of holding cash are:[4]

$$C^* = L + (3/4 \times F \times \sigma^2/R)^{1/3} \qquad\qquad \text{[18A.5]}$$

$$U^* = 3 \times C^* - 2 \times L \qquad\qquad \text{[18A.6]}$$

Also, the average cash balance in the Miller-Orr model is:

$$\text{Average cash balance} = (4 \times C^* - L)/3 \qquad\qquad \text{[18A.7]}$$

The derivation of these expressions is relatively complex, so we will not present it here. Fortunately, as we illustrate next, the results are not difficult to use.

For example, suppose $F = \$10$, the interest rate is 1 percent per month, and the standard deviation of the monthly net cash flows is $200. The variance of the monthly net cash flows is:

$$\sigma^2 = (\$200)^2 = \$40{,}000$$

We assume a minimum cash balance of $L = \$100$. We can calculate the cash balance target, C^*, as:

$$
\begin{aligned}
C^* &= L + (3/4 \times F \times \sigma^2/R)^{1/3} \\
&= \$100 + (3/4 \times \$10 \times \$40{,}000/.01)^{1/3} \\
&= \$100 + (30{,}000{,}000)^{1/3} \\
&= \$100 + 311 = \$411
\end{aligned}
$$

The upper limit, U^*, is thus:

$$
\begin{aligned}
U^* &= 3 \times C^* - 2 \times L \\
&= 3 \times \$411 - 2 \times \$100 \\
&= \$1{,}033
\end{aligned}
$$

Finally, the average cash balance will be:

$$
\begin{aligned}
\text{Average cash balance} &= (4 \times C^* - L)/3 \\
&= (4 \times \$411 - \$100)/3 \\
&= \$515
\end{aligned}
$$

---

[4]M. H. Miller and D. Orr, "A Model of the Demand for Money by Firms," *Quarterly Journal of Economics,* August 1966.

Implications of the BAT and Miller-Orr Models

Our two cash management models differ in complexity, but they have some similar implications. In both cases, all other things being equal, we see that:

1. The greater the interest rate, the lower is the target cash balance.
2. The greater the order cost, the higher is the target balance.

These are both fairly obvious. The advantage of the Miller-Orr model is that it improves our understanding of the problem of cash management by considering the effect of uncertainty as measured by the variation in net cash inflows.

The Miller-Orr model shows that the greater the uncertainty is (the higher σ^2 is), the greater is the difference between the target balance and the minimum balance. Similarly, the greater the uncertainty is, the higher is the upper limit and the higher is the average cash balance. These all make intuitive sense. For example, the greater the variability is, the greater is the chance that the balance will drop below the minimum. We thus keep a higher balance to guard against this happening.

Other Factors Influencing the Target Cash Balance

Before moving on, we briefly discuss two additional considerations that affect the target cash balance.

First, in our discussion of cash management, we assume that cash is invested in marketable securities such as Treasury bills. The firm obtains cash by selling these securities. Another alternative is to borrow cash. Borrowing introduces additional considerations to cash management:

1. Borrowing is likely to be more expensive than selling marketable securities because the interest rate is likely to be higher.
2. The need to borrow will depend on management's desire to hold low cash balances. A firm is more likely to have to borrow to cover an unexpected cash outflow the greater its cash flow variability and the lower its investment in marketable securities.

Second, for large firms, the trading costs of buying and selling securities are very small when compared to the opportunity costs of holding cash. For example, suppose a firm has $1 million in cash that won't be needed for 24 hours. Should the firm invest the money or leave it sitting?

Suppose the firm can invest the money at an annualized rate of 7.57 percent per year. The daily rate in this case is about two basis points (.02 percent or .0002).[5] The daily return earned on $1 million is thus $0.0002 \times \$1$ million = $200. In many cases, the order cost would be much less than this; so a large firm will buy and sell securities very often before it will leave substantial amounts of cash idle.

Large firms hold significant amounts of cash for the following reasons:

1. From the previous chapter, we know that firms may leave cash in the bank as a compensating balance in payment for banking services.

[5]A basis point is 1 percent of 1 percent. Also, the annual interest rate is calculated as $(1 + R)^{365} = 1.0757$, implying a daily rate of .02 percent.

2. Large corporations may have thousands of accounts with several dozen banks. Sometimes it makes more sense to leave cash alone than to manage each account daily and make daily transfers among them.

⌐ CONCEPT QUESTIONS

18A.1a What is a target cash balance?

18A.1b What is the basic trade-off in the BAT model?

18A.1c Describe how the Miller-Orr model works.

Key Terms

target cash balance 653
adjustment costs 653

Appendix Review Problem and Self-Test

18A.1 The BAT Model   Given the following information, calculate the target cash balance using the BAT model:

Annual interest rate	12%
Fixed order cost	$100
Total cash needed	$240,000

What are the opportunity cost of holding cash, the trading cost, and the total cost? What would these be if $15,000 were held instead? If $25,000 were held?

Answer to Appendix Self-Test Problem

18A.1 From the BAT model, the target cash balance is:

$$C^* = \sqrt{2F \times T/R}$$

$$= \sqrt{(2 \times \$100 \times \$240,000)/.12}$$

$$= \sqrt{\$400,000,000}$$

$$= \$20,000$$

The average cash balance will be $C^*/2 = \$20,000/2 = \$10,000$. The opportunity cost of holding $10,000 when the going rate is 12 percent is $\$10,000 \times .12 = \$1,200$. There will be $\$240,000/20,000 = 12$ orders during the year, so the order cost, or trading cost, is also $12 \times \$100 = \$1,200$. The total cost is thus $2,400.

If $15,000 is held, then the average balance is $7,500. Check that the opportunity, trading, and total costs in this case are $900, $1,600, and $2,500, respectively. At $25,000, these numbers are $1,500, $960, and $2,460, respectively.

Appendix Questions and Problems

1. Changes in Target Cash Balances   Indicate the likely impact of each of the following on a company's target cash balance. Use the letter I to denote an increase and D to denote a decrease. Briefly explain your reasoning in each case.

    a. Interest rates paid on money market securities rise.
    b. Commissions charged by brokers increase.
    c. The compensating balance requirement of a bank is lowered.
    d. The cost of borrowing decreases.
    e. The firm's credit rating declines.
    f. Direct fees for banking services are established.

2. Using the BAT Model   Given the following information, calculate the target cash balance using the BAT model:

Annual interest rate	9%
Fixed order cost	$5
Total cash needed	$2,250

    How do you interpret your answer?

3. Opportunity versus Trading Costs   The Big Gene Company has an average daily cash balance of $100. Total cash needed for the year is $10,000. The interest rate is 8 percent, and replenishing the cash costs $4 each time. What are the opportunity cost of holding cash, the trading cost, and the total cost? What do you think of Big Gene's strategy?

4. Costs and the BAT Model   The Perestroika Free Press Company needs a total of $5,000 in cash during the year for transactions and other purposes. Whenever cash runs low, they sell off $1,000 in securities and transfer the cash in. The interest rate is 16 percent per year, and selling off securities costs $100 per sale.

    a. What is the opportunity cost under the current policy? The trading cost? Without any further calculations, does Perestroika keep too much or too little in cash? Explain.
    b. What is the target cash balance using the BAT model?

5. Determining Optimal Cash Balances   The Casablanca Piano Company is currently holding $800,000 in cash. It projects that over the next year its cash outflows will exceed its cash inflows by $345,000 per month. How much of the current cash holding should be retained and how much should be used to increase the company's holdings of marketable securities? Each time these securities are bought or sold through a broker, the company pays a fee of $500. The annual interest rate on money market securities is 7 percent. After the initial investment of excess cash, how many times during the next 12 months will securities be sold?

6. Interpreting Miller-Orr   The Puck Corporation uses a Miller-Orr cash management approach with a lower limit of $10,000, an upper limit of $100,000, and a target balance of $30,000. Explain what each of these points represents and then explain how the system will work.

7. **Using Miller-Orr**   The Silverlock Corporation has a fixed cost associated with buying and selling marketable securities of $100. The interest rate is currently .02 percent per day, and Silverlock has estimated that the standard deviation of its daily net cash flows is $90. Management has set a lower limit of $1,000 on cash holdings. Calculate the target cash balance and upper limit using the Miller-Orr model. Describe how the system will work.

8. **Interpretation of Miller-Orr**   Based on the Miller-Orr model describe what will happen to the lower limit, the upper limit, and the spread (the distance between the two) if the variation in net cash flow grows. Give an intuitive explanation for why this happens. What happens if the variance drops to zero?

9. **Using Miller-Orr**   The variance of the daily net cash flows for the Tseneg Asian Import Company is $1.44 million. The opportunity cost to the firm of holding cash is 8 percent per year. What should be the target cash level and the upper limit if the tolerable lower limit has been established as $20,000? The fixed cost of buying and selling securities is $600 per transaction.

10. **Using BAT**   The Glasnost Vodka Company has determined that its target cash balance using the BAT model is $707. The total cash needed for the year is $10,000, and the order cost is $2. What interest rate is Glasnost using?

Chapter 19

Credit and Inventory Management

CREDIT AND RECEIVABLES | 19.1

When a firm sells goods and services, it can demand cash on or before the delivery date or it can extend credit to customers and allow some delay in payment. The next few sections provide an idea of what is involved in the firm's decision to grant credit to its customers. Granting credit is investing in a customer, an investment tied to the sale of a product or service.

Why do firms grant credit? Not all do, but the practice is extremely common. The obvious reason is that offering credit is a way of stimulating sales. The costs associated with granting credit are not trivial. First, there is the chance that the customer will not pay. Second, the firm has to bear the costs of carrying the receivables. The credit policy decision thus involves a trade-off between the benefits of increased sales versus the costs of granting credit.

From an accounting perspective, when credit is granted, an account receivable is created. These receivables include credit to other firms, called *trade credit,* and credit granted consumers, called *consumer credit.* About one sixth of all of the assets of U.S. industrial firms are in the form of accounts receivable, so receivables obviously represent a major investment of financial resources by U.S. businesses.

Furthermore, trade credit is a very important source of financing for corporations. Looking back at Table 12.2 in Chapter 12, in 1983, U.S. nonfinancial corporations collectively raised $37 billion in the form of accounts payable, more than any other single source of external financing in that year.

However we look at it, receivables and receivables management are very important aspects of a firm's short-term financial policy.

Components of Credit Policy

If a firm decides to grant credit to its customers, then it must establish procedures for extending credit and collecting. In particular, the firm will have to deal with the following components of credit policy:

1. **Terms of sale**. The terms of sale establish how the firm proposes to sell its goods and services. A basic distinction is whether the firm will

terms of sale

Conditions under which a firm sells its goods and services for cash or credit.

665

require cash or will extend credit. If the firm does grant credit to a customer, the terms of sale will specify (perhaps implicitly) the credit period, the cash discount and discount period, and the type of credit instrument.

credit analysis

The process of determining the probability that customers will or will not pay.

2. **Credit analysis.** In granting credit, a firm determines how much effort to expend trying to distinguish between customers who will pay and customers who will not pay. Firms use a number of devices and procedures to determine the probability that customers will not pay, and, put together, these are called *credit analysis*.

collection policy

Procedures followed by a firm in collecting accounts receivable.

3. **Collection policy.** After credit has been granted, the firm has the potential problem of collecting the cash when it becomes due, for which it must establish a collection policy.

In the next several sections, we will discuss these components of credit policy that collectively make up the decision to grant credit.

The Cash Flows from Granting Credit

In a previous chapter, we described the accounts receivable period as the time it takes to collect on a sale. There are several events that occur during that period. These are the cash flows associated with granting credit, and they can be illustrated with a cash flow diagram:

The Cash Flows of Granting Credit

As our time line indicates, the typical sequence of events when a firm grants credit is (1) the credit sale is made, (2) the customer sends a check to the firm, (3) the firm deposits the check, and (4) the firm's account is credited for the amount of the check.

Based on our discussion in the previous chapter, it is apparent that one of the factors influencing the receivables period is float. Thus, one way to reduce the receivables period is to speed up the check mailing, processing, and clearing. Because we cover this subject elsewhere, we will ignore float in subsequent discussion and focus on what is likely to be the major determinant of the receivables period, credit policy.

The Investment in Receivables

The investment in accounts receivable for any firm depends on the amount of credit sales and the average collection period. For example, if a firm's average collection period (ACP) is 30 days, then at any given time there will be 30 days' worth of sales outstanding. If sales run $1,000 per day, the firm's accounts receivable will then be equal to 30 days × $1,000 per day = $30,000.

As our example illustrates, a firm's receivables generally will be equal to its average daily sales multiplied by its average collection period (ACP):

$$\text{Accounts receivable} = \text{Average daily sales} \times \text{ACP} \qquad [19.1]$$

Thus, a firm's investment in accounts receivable depends on factors that influence credit sales and collections.

We have seen the average collection period in various places, including Chapter 3 and Chapter 17. Recall that we use the terms *days' sales in receivables, receivables period,* and *average collection period* interchangeably to refer to the length of time it takes for the firm to collect on a sale.

⌐ **CONCEPT QUESTIONS**

19.1a What are the basic components of credit policy?

19.1b What are the basic components of the terms of sale if a firm chooses to sell on credit?

TERMS OF THE SALE ⌐ **19.2**

As we described above, the terms of a sale are made up of three distinct elements:

1. The period for which credit is granted (the credit period).
2. The cash discount and the discount period.
3. The type of credit instrument.

Within a given industry, the terms of sale are usually fairly standard, but these terms vary quite a bit across industries. In many cases, the terms of sale are remarkably archaic and literally date to previous centuries. Organized systems of trade credit that resemble current practice can be easily traced to the great fairs of medieval Europe, and they almost surely existed long before then.

The Basic Form

The easiest way to understand the terms of sale is to consider an example. For bulk candy, terms of 2/10, net 60 are common.[1] This means that customers have 60 days from the invoice date (discussed below) to pay the full amount. However, if payment is made within 10 days, a 2 percent cash discount can be taken.

---

[1]The terms of sale cited from specific industries in this section and elsewhere are drawn from Theodore N. Beckman, *Credits and Collections: Management and Theory* (New York: McGraw-Hill, 1962).

Consider a buyer who places an order for $1,000, and assume that the terms of the sale are 2/10, net 60. The buyer has the option of paying $1,000 × (1 − .02) = $980 in 10 days, or paying the full $1,000 in 60 days. If the terms were stated as just net 30, then the customer has 30 days from the invoice date to pay the entire $1,000, and no discount is offered for early payment.

In general, credit terms are quoted in the following form:

⟨take this discount off the invoice price⟩/⟨if you pay in this many days⟩, ⟨else pay the full invoice amount in this many days⟩

Thus, 5/10, net 45 means take a 5 percent discount from the full price if you pay within 10 days, or else pay the full amount in 45 days.

The Credit Period

credit period

The length of time that credit is granted.

The **credit period** is the basic length of time that credit is granted. The credit period varies widely from industry to industry, but it is almost always between 30 and 120 days. If a cash discount is offered, then the credit period has two components: the net credit period and the cash discount period.

The net credit period is the length of time the customer has to pay. The cash discount period, as the name suggests, is the time during which the discount is available. With 2/10, net 30, for example, the net credit period is 30 days and the cash discount period is 10 days.

invoice

Bill for goods or services provided by the seller to the purchaser.

The Invoice Date   The invoice date is the beginning of the credit period. An **invoice** is a written account of merchandise shipped to the buyer. For individual items, by convention, the invoice date is usually the shipping date or the billing date, *not* the date that the buyer receives the goods or the bill.

Many other arrangements exist. For example, the terms of sale might be ROG, for "receipt of goods." In this case, the credit starts when the customer receives the order. This might be used when the customer is in a remote location.

End-of-month (EOM) terms are fairly common. With EOM dating, all sales made during a particular month are assumed to be made at the end of that month. This is useful when a buyer makes purchases throughout the month, but the seller only bills once a month.

For example, terms of 2/10th EOM tell the buyer to take a 2 percent discount if payment is made by the 10th of the month, otherwise the full amount is due after that. Confusingly, the end of the month is sometimes taken to be the 25th day of the month. MOM, for middle of month, is another variation.

Seasonal dating is sometimes used to encourage sales of seasonal products during the off-season. A product that is sold primarily in the summer (suntan oil?) can be shipped in January with credit terms of 2/10, net 30. However, the invoice might be dated May 1, so the credit period actually begins at that time. This practice encourages buyers to order early.

Length of the Credit Period   A number of factors influence the length of the credit period. One of the most important is the *buyer's* inventory period and operating cycle. All other things being equal, the shorter these are, the shorter the credit period will normally be.

Based on our discussion in Chapter 17, the operating cycle has two components: the inventory period and the receivables period. The inventory period is the time it takes the buyer to acquire inventory (from us), process it, and sell it. The receivables period is the time it then takes the buyer to collect on the sale. Note that the credit period that we offer is effectively the buyer's payables period.

By extending credit, we finance a portion of our buyer's operating cycle and thereby shorten his or her cash cycle. If our credit period exceeds the buyer's inventory period, then we are not only financing the buyer's inventory purchases, but part of the buyer's receivables as well.

Furthermore, if our credit period exceeds our buyer's operating cycle, then we are effectively providing financing for aspects of our customer's business beyond the immediate purchase and sale of our merchandise. The reason is that the buyer effectively has a loan from us even after the merchandise is resold, and the buyer can use that credit for other purposes. For this reason, the length of the buyer's operating cycle is often cited as an appropriate upper limit to the credit period.

There are a number of other factors that influence the credit period. Many of these also influence our customers' operating cycles; so, once again, these are related subjects. Among the most important are:

1. *Perishability and collateral value.* Perishable items have relatively rapid turnover and relatively low collateral value. Credit periods are thus shorter for such goods. For example, a food wholesaler selling fresh fruit and produce might use net seven days. Alternatively, jewelry might be sold for 5/30, net four months.

2. *Consumer demand.* Products that are well established generally have more rapid turnover. Newer or slow-moving products will often have longer credit periods associated with them to entice buyers. Also, as we have seen, sellers may choose to extend much longer credit periods for off-season sales (when customer demand is low).

3. *Cost, profitability, and standardization.* Relatively inexpensive goods tend to have shorter credit periods. The same is true for relatively standardized goods and raw materials. These all tend to have lower markups and higher turnover rates, both of which lead to shorter credit periods. There are exceptions. Auto dealers, for example, generally pay for cars as they are received.

4. *Credit risk.* The greater the credit risk of the buyer, the shorter the credit period is likely to be (assuming that credit is granted at all).

5. *The size of the account.* If the account is small, the credit period may be shorter because small accounts are more costly to manage, and the customers are less important.

6. *Competition.* When the seller is in a highly competitive market, longer credit periods may be offered as a way of attracting customers.

7. *Customer type.* A single seller might offer different credit terms to different buyers. A food wholesaler, for example, might supply groceries, bakeries, and restaurants. Each group would probably have different credit terms. More generally, sellers often have both wholesale and retail customers, and they frequently quote different terms to the two types.

Cash Discounts

cash discount

A discount given for a cash purchase.

As we have seen, **cash discounts** are often part of the terms of sale. The practice of granting discounts for cash purchases in the United States dates to the Civil War and is widespread today. One reason discounts are offered is to speed up the collection of receivables. This will have the effect of reducing the amount of credit being offered, and the firm must trade this off against the cost of the discount.

Notice that when a cash discount is offered, the credit is essentially free during the discount period. The buyer only pays for the credit after the discount expires. With 2/10, net 30, a rational buyer either pays in 10 days to make the greatest possible use of the free credit or pays in 30 days to get the longest possible use of the money in exchange for giving up the discount. So, by giving up the discount, the buyer effectively gets $30 - 10 = 20$ days' credit.

Another reason for cash discounts is that they are a way of charging higher prices to customers that have had credit extended to them. In this sense, cash discounts are a convenient way of charging for the credit granted to customers.

Cost of the Credit   In our examples, it might seem that the discounts are rather small. With 2/10, net 30, for example, early payment only gets the buyer a 2 percent discount. Does this provide a significant incentive for early payment? The answer is yes because the implicit interest rate is extremely high.

To see why the discount is important, we will calculate the cost to the buyer of not paying early. To do this, we will find the interest rate that the buyer is effectively paying for the trade credit. Suppose the order is for $1,000. The buyer can pay $980 in 10 days or wait another 20 days and pay $1,000. It's obvious that the buyer is effectively borrowing $980 for 20 days and that the buyer pays $20 in interest on the "loan." What's the interest rate?

This interest is ordinary discount interest, which we discussed in Chapter 5. With $20 in interest on $980 borrowed, the rate is $20/$980 = 2.0408%. This is relatively low, but remember that this is the rate per 20-day period. There are $365/20 = 18.25$ such periods in a year, so, by not taking the discount, the buyer is paying an effective annual rate (EAR) of:

$$EAR = (1.020408)^{18.25} - 1 = 44.6\%$$

From the buyer's point of view, this is an expensive source of financing!

Given that the interest rate is so high here, it is unlikely that the seller benefits from early payment. Ignoring the possibility of default by the buyer, the decision by a customer to forgo the discount almost surely works to the seller's advantage.

Example 19.1 What's the Rate?

Ordinary tiles are often sold 3/30, net 60. What effective annual rate does a buyer pay by not taking the discount? What would the APR be if one were quoted?

Here we have 3 percent discount interest on $60 - 30 = 30$ days' credit. The rate per 30 days is .03/.97 = 3.093%. There are $365/30 = 12.17$ such periods in a year, so the effective annual rate is:

$$EAR = (1.03093)^{12.17} - 1 = 44.9\%$$

The APR, as always, would be calculated by multiplying the rate per period by the number of periods:

$$APR = .03093 \times 12.17 = 37.6\%$$

An interest rate calculated like this APR is often quoted as the cost of the trade credit, and, as this example illustrates, can seriously understate the true cost. ∎

Trade Discounts   In some circumstances, the discount is not really an incentive for early payment and is instead a *trade discount,* a discount routinely given to some type of buyer. For example, with our 2/10th, EOM terms, the buyer takes a 2 percent discount if the invoice is paid by the 10th, but the bill is considered due on the 10th, and overdue after that. Thus, the credit period and the discount period are effectively the same, and there is no reward for paying before the due date.

The Cash Discount and the ACP   To the extent that a cash discount encourages customers to pay early, it will shorten the receivables period and, all other things being equal, reduce the firm's investment in receivables.

For example, suppose a firm currently has terms of net 30 and an ACP of 30 days. If it offers terms of 2/10, net 30, then perhaps 50 percent of its customers (in terms of volume of purchases) will pay in 10 days. The remaining customers will still take an average of 30 days to pay. What will the new average collection period (ACP) be? If the firm's annual sales are $15 million (before discounts), what will happen to the investment in receivables?

If half of the customers take 10 days to pay and half take 30, then the new average collection period will be:

$$New\ ACP = .50 \times 10\ days + .50 \times 30\ days = 20\ days$$

The ACP thus falls from 30 days to 20 days. Average daily sales are $15 million/365 = $41,096 per day. Receivables will thus fall by $41,096 \times 10 = $410,960.

Credit Instruments

The **credit instrument** is the basic evidence of indebtedness. Most trade credit is offered on *open account.* This means that the only formal instrument of credit is the invoice, which is sent with the shipment of goods and which the customer signs as evidence that the goods have been received. Afterward, the firm and its customers record the exchange on their books of account.

At times, the firm may require that the customer sign a *promissory note.* This is a basic IOU and might be used when the order is large, when there is no cash discount involved, or when the firm anticipates a problem in collections. Promissory notes are not common, but they can eliminate possible controversies later about the existence of debt.

One problem with promissory notes is that they are signed after delivery of the goods. One way to obtain a credit commitment from a customer before the goods are delivered is to arrange a *commercial draft.* Typically, the firm draws up a commercial draft calling for the customer to pay a specific amount by a specified date. The draft is then sent to the customer's bank with the shipping invoices.

credit instrument
The evidence of indebtedness.

If immediate payment on the draft is required, it is called a *sight draft*. If immediate payment is not required, then the draft is a *time draft*. When the draft is presented and the buyer "accepts" it, meaning that the buyer promises to pay it in the future, then it is called a *trade acceptance* and is sent back to the selling firm. The seller can then keep the acceptance or sell it to someone else. If a bank accepts the draft, meaning that the bank is guaranteeing payment, then the draft becomes a *banker's acceptance*. This arrangement is common in international trade, and banker's acceptances are actively traded in the money market.

A firm can also use a conditional sales contract as a credit instrument. This is an arrangement where the firm retains legal ownership of the goods until the customer has completed payment. Conditional sales contracts usually are paid in installments and have an interest cost built into them.

⌐ CONCEPT QUESTIONS

19.2a What considerations enter into the determination of the terms of sale?

19.2b Explain what terms of "3/45, net 90" mean. What is the implicit interest rate?

19.3 | ANALYZING CREDIT POLICY

In this section, we take a closer look at the factors that influence the decision to grant credit. Granting credit only makes sense if the NPV from doing so is positive. We thus need to look at the NPV of the decision to grant credit.

Credit Policy Effects

In evaluating credit policy, there are five basic factors to consider:

1. *Revenue effects.* If the firm grants credit, then there will be a delay in revenue collections as some customers take advantage of the credit offered and pay later. However, the firm may be able to charge a higher price if it grants credit and it may be able to increase the quantity sold. Total revenues may thus increase.

2. *Cost effects.* Although the firm may experience delayed revenues if it grants credit, it will still incur the costs of sales immediately. Whether or not the firm sells for cash or credit, it will still have to acquire or produce the merchandise (and pay for it).

3. *The cost of debt.* When the firm grants credit, it must arrange to finance the resulting receivables. As a result, the firm's cost of short-term borrowing is a factor in the decision to grant credit.[2]

---

[2]The cost of short-term debt is not necessarily the required return on receivables, although it is commonly assumed to be. As always, the required return on an investment depends on the risk of the investment, not the source of the financing. The *buyer's* cost of short-term debt is closer in spirit to the correct rate. We will maintain the implicit assumption that the seller and the buyer have the same short-term debt cost. In any case, the time periods in credit decisions are relatively short, so a relatively small error in the discount rate will not have a large effect on our estimated NPV.

4. *The probability of nonpayment.* If the firm grants credit, some percentage of the credit buyers will not pay. This can't happen, of course, if the firm sells for cash.

5. *The cash discount.* When the firm offers a cash discount as part of its credit terms, some customers will choose to pay early to take advantage of the discount.

Evaluating a Proposed Credit Policy

To illustrate how credit policy can be analyzed, we will start with a relatively simple case. Locust Software has been in existence for two years, and it is one of several successful firms that develop computer programs. Currently, Locust sells for cash only.

Locust is evaluating a request from some major customers to change its current policy to net one month (30 days). To analyze this proposal, we define the following:

P = Price per unit

v = Variable cost per unit

Q = Current quantity sold per month

Q' = Quantity sold under new policy

R = Monthly required return

For now, we ignore discounts and the possibility of default. Also, we ignore taxes because they don't affect our conclusions.

NPV of Switching Policies   To illustrate the NPV of switching credit policies, suppose we have the following for Locust:

P = $49

v = $20

Q = 100

Q' = 110

If the required return, R, is 2 percent per month, should Locust make the switch?

Currently, Locust has monthly sales of $P \times Q$ = $4,900. Variable costs each month are $v \times Q$ = $2,000, so the monthly cash flow from this activity is:

$$\text{Cash flow (old policy)} = (P - v)Q \qquad [19.2]$$

$$= (\$49 - 20) \times 100$$

$$= \$2,900$$

This is not the total cash flow for Locust, of course, but it is all that we need to look at because fixed costs and other components of cash flow are the same whether or not the switch is made.

If Locust does switch to net 30 days on sales, then the quantity sold will rise to $Q' = 110$. Monthly revenues will increase to $P \times Q'$, and costs will be $v \times Q'$. The monthly cash flow under the new policy will thus be:

$$\text{Cash flow (new policy)} = (P - v)Q' \qquad [19.3]$$

$$= (\$49 - 20) \times 110$$

$$= \$3,190$$

Going back to Chapter 8, the relevant incremental cash flow is the difference between the new and old cash flows:

$$\text{Incremental cash inflow} = (P - v)(Q' - Q)$$

$$= (\$49 - 20) \times (110 - 100)$$

$$= \$290$$

This says that the benefit each month of changing policies is equal to the gross profit per unit sold, $(P - v) = \$29$, multiplied by the increase in sales, $(Q' - Q) = 10$. The present value of the future incremental cash flows is thus:

$$PV = [(P - v)(Q' - Q)]/R \qquad [19.4]$$

For Locust, this present value works out to be:

$$PV = (\$29 \times 10)/.02 = \$14,500$$

Notice that we have treated the monthly cash flow as a perpetuity since the same benefit will be realized each month forever.

Now that we know the benefit of switching, what's the cost? There are two components to consider. First, since the quantity sold will rise from Q to Q', Locust will have to produce $Q' - Q$ more units today at a cost of $v(Q' - Q) = \$20 \times (110 - 100) = \$200$. Second, the sales that would have been collected this month under the current policy ($P \times Q = \$4,900$) will not be collected. This happens because the sales made this month won't be collected until 30 days later under the new policy. The cost of the switch is the sum of these two components:

$$\text{Cost of switching} = PQ + v(Q' - Q) \qquad [19.5]$$

For Locust, this cost would be $\$4,900 + 200 = \$5,100$.

Putting it all together, the NPV of the switch is:

$$\text{NPV of switching} = -[PQ + v(Q' - Q)] + (P - v)(Q' - Q)/R \quad [19.6]$$

For Locust, the cost of switching is $5,100. As we saw above, the benefit is $290 per month, forever. At 2 percent per month, the NPV is:

$$NPV = -\$5,100 + \$290/.02$$

$$= -\$5,100 + 14,500$$

$$= \$9,400$$

Therefore, the switch is very profitable.

Example 19.2   We'd Rather Fight than Switch
Suppose that a company is considering a switch from all cash to net 30, but the quantity sold is not expected to change. What is the NPV of the switch? Explain.

In this case, $Q' - Q$ is zero, so the NPV is just $-P \times Q$. What this says is that the effect of the switch is simply to postpone one month's collections forever, with no benefit from doing so. ∎

A Break-Even Application   Based on our discussion thus far, the key variable for Locust is $Q' - Q$, the increase in unit sales. The projected increase of 10 units is only an estimate, so there is some forecasting risk. Under the circumstances, it's natural to wonder what increase in unit sales is necessary to break even.

Earlier, the NPV of the switch was defined as:

$$NPV = -[PQ + v(Q' - Q)] + (P - v)(Q' - Q)/R$$

We can calculate the break-even point explicitly by setting the NPV equal to zero and solving for $(Q' - Q)$:

$$NPV = 0 = -[PQ + v(Q' - Q)] + (P - v)(Q' - Q)/R$$

$$Q' - Q = (PQ)/[(P - v)/R - v] \qquad\qquad [19.7]$$

For Locust, the break-even sales increase is thus:

$$Q' - Q = \$4,900/[\$29/.02 - \$20]$$

$$= 3.43 \text{ units}$$

This tells us that the switch is a good idea as long as we are confident that we can sell at least 3.43 more units per month.

CONCEPT QUESTIONS

19.3a What are the important effects to consider in a decision to offer credit?

19.3b Explain how to estimate the NPV of a credit policy switch.

19.4 | OPTIMAL CREDIT POLICY

So far, we've discussed how to compute net present values for a switch in credit policy. We have not discussed the optimal amount of credit or the optimal credit policy. In principle, the optimal amount of credit is determined where the incremental cash flows from increased sales are exactly equal to the incremental costs of carrying the increase in investment in accounts receivable.

The Total Credit Cost Curve

The trade-off between granting credit and not granting credit isn't hard to identify, but it is difficult to quantify precisely. As a result, we can only describe an optimal credit policy.

To begin, the carrying costs associated with granting credit come in three forms:

1. The required return on receivables
2. The losses from bad debts
3. The costs of managing credit and credit collections

We have already discussed the first and second of these. The third cost, the costs of managing credit, is the expenses associated with running the credit department. Firms that don't grant credit have no such department and no such expense. These three costs will all increase as credit policy is relaxed.

If a firm has a very restrictive credit policy, then all of the above costs will be low. In this case, the firm will have a "shortage" of credit, so there will be an opportunity cost. This opportunity cost is the extra potential profit from credit sales that is lost because credit is refused. This forgone benefit comes from two sources, the increase in quantity sold, Q' versus Q, and, potentially, a higher price. These costs go down as credit policy is relaxed.

credit cost curve

Graphical representation of the sum of the carrying costs and the opportunity costs of a credit policy.

The sum of the carrying costs and the opportunity costs of a particular credit policy is called the total **credit cost curve.** We have drawn such a curve in Figure 19.1. As Figure 19.1 illustrates, there is a point where the total credit cost is minimized. This point corresponds to the optimal amount of credit or, equivalently, the optimal investment in receivables.

If the firm extends more credit than this minimum, the additional net cash flow from new customers will not cover the carrying costs of the investment in receivables. If the level of receivables is below this amount, then the firm is forgoing valuable profit opportunities.

In general, the costs and benefits from extending credit will depend on characteristics of particular firms and industries. All other things being equal, for example, it is likely that firms with (1) excess capacity, (2) low variable operating costs, and (3) repeat customers will extend credit more liberally than otherwise. See if you can explain why each of these contributes to a more liberal credit policy.

CONCEPT QUESTIONS

19.4a What are the carrying costs of granting credit?

19.4b What are the opportunity costs of not granting credit?

Figure 19.1

The costs of granting
credit

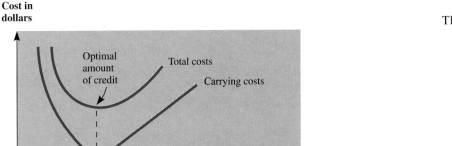

**Cost in
dollars**

Optimal
amount
of credit

Total costs

Carrying costs

Opportunity costs

**Level of credit
extended**

Carrying costs are the cash flows that must be incurred when credit is granted. They are
positively related to the amount of credit extended.

Opportunity costs are the lost sales from refusing credit. These costs go down when credit
is granted.

CREDIT ANALYSIS | 19.5

Thus far, we have focused on establishing credit terms. Once a firm decides to
grant credit to its customers, it must then establish guidelines for determining
who will and who will not be allowed to buy on credit. *Credit analysis* refers to
the process of deciding whether or not to extend credit to a particular customer. It usually involves two steps: gathering relevant information and determining creditworthiness.

When Should Credit Be Granted?

Imagine that a firm is trying to decide whether or not to grant credit to a customer. This decision can get complicated. For example, the answer depends on
what will happen if credit is refused. Will the customer simply pay cash or will
the customer not make the purchase at all? To avoid this and other difficulties,
we will use some special cases to illustrate the key points.

A One-Time Sale   We start by considering the simplest case. A new customer wishes to buy one unit on credit at a price of P per unit. If credit is refused, then the customer will not make the purchase.

Furthermore, we assume that, if credit is granted, then, in one month, the
customer will either pay up or default. The probability of the second of these
events is π. In this case, the probability (π) can be interpreted as the percentage of *new* customers who will not pay. Our business does not have repeat customers, so this is strictly a one-time sale. Finally, the required return on
receivables is R per month and the variable cost is v per unit.

The analysis here is straightforward. If the firm refuses credit, then the incremental cash flow is zero. If it grants credit, then it spends v (the variable cost) this month and expects to collect $(1 - \pi)P$ next month. The NPV of granting credit is:

$$NPV = -v + (1 - \pi)P/(1 + R) \qquad [19.8]$$

For example, for Locust Software, this NPV is:

$$NPV = -\$20 + (1 - \pi) \times \$49/(1.02)$$

With, say, a 20 percent rate of default, this works out to be:

$$NPV = -\$20 + .80 \times \$49/1.02 = \$18.43$$

Therefore, credit should be granted.

Our example illustrates an important point. In granting credit to a new customer, a firm risks its variable cost (v). It stands to gain the full price (P). For a new customer, then, credit may be granted even if the default probability is high. For example, the break-even probability in this case can be determined by setting the NPV equal to zero and solving for π:

$$NPV = 0 = -\$20 + (1 - \pi) \times \$49/(1.02)$$

$$(1 - \pi) = \$20/\$49 \times 1.02$$

$$\pi = 58.4\%$$

Locust should extend credit as long as there is at least a $1 - .584 = 41.6\%$ chance or better of collecting. This explains why firms with higher markups will tend to have looser credit terms.

This percentage (58.4%) is the maximum acceptable default probability for a *new* customer. If an old, cash-paying customer wants to switch to a credit basis, the analysis would be different, and maximum acceptable default probability would be much lower.

The important difference is that, if we extend credit to an old customer, then we risk the total sales price (P), since this is what we collect if we don't extend credit. If we extend credit to a new customer, we only risk our variable cost.

Repeat Business   A second, very important factor to keep in mind is the possibility of repeat business. We can illustrate this by extending our one-time sale example. We make one important assumption: A new customer who does not default the first time around will remain a customer forever and never default.

If the firm grants credit, it spends v this month. Next month, it either gets nothing if the customer defaults or it gets P if the customer pays. If the customer does pay, then she will buy another unit on credit and the firm will spend v again. The net cash inflow for the month is thus $P - v$. In every subsequent month, this same $P - v$ will occur as the customer pays for the previous month's order and places a new one.

It follows from our discussion that, in one month, the firm will receive $0 with probability π. With probability $(1 - \pi)$, however, the firm will have a permanent new customer. The value of a new customer is equal to the present value of $(P - v)$ every month forever:

$$PV = (P - v)/R$$

The NPV of extending credit is therefore:

$$NPV = -v + (1 - \pi)(P - v)/R \qquad [19.9]$$

For Locust, this is:

$$NPV = -\$20 + (1 - \pi) \times (\$49 - \$20)/.02$$

$$= -\$20 + (1 - \pi) \times \$1,450$$

Even if the probability of default is 90 percent, the NPV is:

$$NPV = -\$20 + .10 \times \$1,450 = \$125$$

Locust should extend credit unless default is a virtual certainty. The reason is that it only costs $20 to find out who is a good customer and who is not. A good customer is worth $1,450, however, so Locust can afford quite a few defaults.

Our repeat business example probably exaggerates the acceptable default probability, but it does illustrate that it will often turn out that the best way to do credit analysis is simply to extend credit to almost anyone. It also points out that the possibility of repeat business is a crucial consideration. In such cases, the important thing is to control the amount of credit initially offered to any one customer so that the possible loss is limited. The amount can be increased with time. Most often, the best predictor of whether or not someone will pay in the future is whether or not they have paid in the past.

Credit Information

If a firm does want credit information on customers, there are a number of sources. Information commonly used to assess creditworthiness includes the following:

1. *Financial statements.* A firm can ask a customer to supply financial statement information such as balance sheets and income statements. Minimum standards and rules of thumb based on financial ratios like the ones we discussed in Chapter 3 can then be used as a basis for extending or refusing credit.
2. *Credit reports on the customer's payment history with other firms.* Quite a few organizations sell information on the credit strength and credit history of business firms. The best known and largest firm of this type is Dun & Bradstreet, which provides subscribers with a credit reference book and credit reports on individual firms. TRW is another well-known

credit reporting firm. Ratings and information are available for a huge number of firms, including very small ones. Equifax, Transunion, and TRW are the major suppliers of consumer credit information.

3. *Banks.* Banks will generally provide some assistance to their business customers in acquiring information on the creditworthiness of other firms.

4. *The customer's payment history with the firm.* The most obvious way to obtain information about the likelihood of a customer not paying is to examine whether they have settled past obligations and how quickly they have met these obligations.

Figure 19.2 illustrates part of a Dun & Bradstreet credit report, called a payment analysis report (PAR). As you can see, quite detailed firm and industry payment information can be obtained if more basic, summary information is inadequate.

Credit Evaluation and Scoring

five Cs of credit

The five basic credit factors to be evaluated: character, capacity, capital, collateral, and conditions.

There are no magical formulas for assessing the probability that a customer will not pay. In very general terms, the classic **five Cs of credit** are the basic factors to be evaluated:

1. *Character.* The customer's willingness to meet credit obligations.
2. *Capacity.* The customer's ability to meet credit obligations out of operating cash flows.
3. *Capital.* The customer's financial reserves.
4. *Collateral.* A pledged asset in the case of default.
5. *Conditions.* General economic conditions in the customer's line of business.

credit scoring

The process of quantifying the probability of default when granting consumer credit.

Credit scoring refers to the process of calculating a numerical rating for a customer based on information collected and then granting or refusing credit based on the result. For example, a firm might rate a customer on a scale of 1 (very poor) to 10 (very good) on each of the five Cs of credit using all the information available about the customer. A credit score could then be calculated based on the total. From experience, a firm might choose to grant credit only to customers with a score above, say, 30.

Firms such as credit card issuers have developed elaborate statistical models for credit scoring. Usually, all of the legally relevant and observable characteristics of a large pool of customers are studied to find their historic relation to default rates. Based on the results, it is possible to determine the variables that best predict whether or not a customer will pay and then calculate a credit score based on those variables.

Because credit-scoring models and procedures determine who is and who is not creditworthy, it is not surprising that they have been the subject of government regulation. In particular, the kinds of background and demographic information that can be used in the credit decision are limited.

CONCEPT QUESTIONS

19.5a What is credit analysis?

19.5b What are the five Cs of credit?

A Dun & Bradstreet credit report   **Figure 19.2**

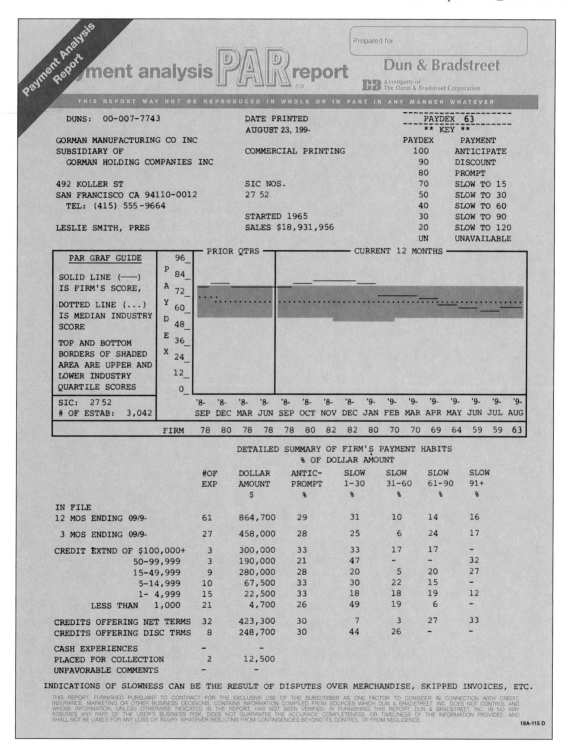

19.6 | COLLECTION POLICY

Collection policy is the final element in credit policy. Collection policy involves monitoring receivables to spot trouble and obtaining payment on past-due accounts.

Monitoring Receivables

To keep track of payments by customers, most firms will monitor outstanding accounts. First of all, a firm will normally keep track of its average collection period (ACP) through time. If a firm is in a seasonal business, the ACP will fluctuate during the year, but unexpected increases in the ACP are a cause for concern. Either customers in general are taking longer to pay, or some percentage of accounts receivable is seriously overdue.

aging schedule

A compilation of accounts receivable by the age of each account.

The **aging schedule** is a second basic tool for monitoring receivables. To prepare one, the credit department classifies accounts by age.[3] Suppose a firm has $100,000 in receivables. Some of these accounts are only a few days old, but others have been outstanding for quite some time. The following is an example of an aging schedule.

Aging Schedule

Age of Account	Amount	Percent of Total Value of Accounts Receivable
0–10 days	$ 50,000	50
11–60 days	25,000	25
61–80 days	20,000	20
Over 80 days	5,000	5
	$100,000	100

If this firm has a credit period of 60 days, then 25 percent of its accounts are late. Whether or not this is serious depends on the nature of the firm's collections and customers. It is often the case that accounts beyond a certain age are almost never collected. Monitoring the age of accounts is very important in such cases.

Firms with seasonal sales will find the percentages on the aging schedule changing during the year. For example, if sales in the current month are very high, then total receivables will also increase sharply. This means that the older accounts, as a percentage of total receivables, become smaller and might appear less important. Some firms have refined the aging schedule so that they have an idea of how it should change with peaks and valleys in their sales.

---

[3] Aging schedules are used elsewhere in business. For example, aging schedules are often prepared for inventory items.

Collection Effort

A firm usually goes through the following procedures for customers whose payments are overdue:

1. It sends out a delinquency letter informing the customer of the past-due status of the account.
2. It makes a telephone call to the customer.
3. It employs a collection agency.
4. It takes legal action against the customer.

At times, a firm may refuse to grant additional credit to customers until arrearages are cleared up. This may antagonize a normally good customer, and it points to a potential conflict of interest between the collections department and the sales department.

CONCEPT QUESTIONS

19.6a What tools can a manager use to monitor receivables?
19.6b What is an aging schedule?

INVENTORY MANAGEMENT | 19.7

Like receivables, inventories represent a significant investment for many firms. For a typical manufacturing operation, inventories will often exceed 15 percent of assets. For a retailer, inventories could represent more than 25 percent of assets. From our discussion in Chapter 17, we know that a firm's operating cycle is made up of its inventory period and its receivables period. This is one reason for considering credit and inventory policy in the same chapter. Beyond this, both credit policy and inventory policy are used to drive sales, and the two must be coordinated to ensure that the process of acquiring inventory, selling it, and collecting on the sale proceeds smoothly. For example, changes in credit policy designed to stimulate sales must be simultaneously accompanied by planning for adequate inventory.

The Financial Manager and Inventory Policy

Despite the size of a typical firm's investment in inventories, the financial manager of a firm will not normally have primary control over inventory management. Instead, other functional areas such as purchasing, production, and marketing will usually share decision-making authority. Inventory management has become an increasingly important specialty in its own right, and financial management will often only have input into the decision. For this reason, we will only survey some basics of inventory and inventory policy in the sections ahead.

Inventory Types

For a manufacturer, inventory is normally classified into one of three categories. The first category is *raw material*. This is whatever the firm uses as a starting point in its production process. Raw materials might be something as basic as iron ore for a steel manufacturer or something as sophisticated as disk drives for a computer manufacturer.

The second type of inventory is *work-in-progress,* which is just what the name suggests—unfinished product. How big this portion of inventory is depends in large part on the length of the production process. For an airframe manufacturer, for example, work-in-progress can be substantial. The third and final type of inventory is *finished goods,* that is, products ready to ship or sell.

There are three things to keep in mind concerning inventory types. First, the names for the different types can be a little misleading because one company's raw materials could be another's finished goods. For example, going back to our steel manufacturer, iron ore would be a raw material, and steel would be the final product. An auto body panel stamping operation will have steel as its raw material and auto body panels as its finished goods, and an automobile assembler will have body panels as raw materials and automobiles as finished products.

The second thing to keep in mind is that the various types of inventory can be quite different in terms of their liquidity. Raw materials that are commodity-like or relatively standardized can be easy to convert to cash. Work-in-progress, on the other hand, can be quite illiquid and have little more than scrap value. As always, the liquidity of finished goods depends on the nature of the product.

Finally, a very important distinction between finished goods and other types of inventories is that the demand for an inventory item that becomes a part of another item is usually termed *derived* or *dependent demand* because the firm's need for these inventory types depends on its need for finished items. In contrast, the firm's demand for finished goods is not derived from demand for other inventory items, so it is sometimes said to be *independent*.

Inventory Costs

As we discussed in Chapter 17, there are two basic types of costs associated with current assets in general and with inventory in particular. The first of these are *carrying costs*. Here, carrying costs represent all of the direct and opportunity costs of keeping inventory on hand. These include:

1. Storage and tracking costs.
2. Insurance and taxes.
3. Losses due to obsolescence, deterioration, or theft.
4. The opportunity cost of capital on the invested amount.

The sum of these costs can be substantial, roughly ranging from 20 to 40 percent of inventory value per year.

The other types of costs associated with inventory are *shortage costs*. These are costs associated with having inadequate inventory on hand. The two components of shortage costs are restocking costs and costs related to safety reserves. Depending on the firm's business, restocking or order costs are either the costs of placing an order with suppliers or the cost of setting up a production run. The costs related to safety reserves are opportunity losses such as lost sales and loss of customer goodwill that result from having inadequate inventory.

A basic trade-off in inventory management exists because carrying costs increase with inventory levels while shortage or restocking costs decline with inventory levels. The basic goal of inventory management is thus to minimize the sum of these two costs. We consider ways to reach this goal in the next section.

⌐ **CONCEPT QUESTIONS**

19.7a What are the different types of inventory?

19.7b What are three things to remember when examining inventory types?

19.7c What is the basic goal of inventory management?

INVENTORY MANAGEMENT TECHNIQUES ⌐ 19.8

As we described earlier, the goal of inventory management is usually framed as cost minimization. Three techniques are discussed in this section, ranging from the relatively simple to the very complex.

The ABC Approach

The ABC approach is a simple approach to inventory management where the basic idea is to divide inventory into three (or more) groups. The underlying rationale is that a small portion of inventory in terms of quantity might represent a large portion in terms of inventory value. For example, this situation would exist for a manufacturer that uses some relatively expensive, high-tech components and some relatively inexpensive basic materials in producing its products.

Figure 19.3 illustrates an ABC comparison of items in terms of the percentage of inventory value represented by each group versus the percentage of items represented. As Figure 19.3 shows, the A Group constitutes only 10 percent of inventory by item count, but it represents over half of the value of inventory. The A Group items are thus monitored closely, and inventory levels are kept relatively low. At the other end, basic inventory items, such as nuts and bolts, will also exist, but because these are crucial and inexpensive, large quantities are ordered and kept on hand. These would be C Group items. The B Group is made up of inbetween items.

The Economic Order Quantity (EOQ) Model

The economic order quantity (EOQ) model is the best-known approach to explicitly establishing an optimal inventory level. The basic idea is illustrated in Figure 19.4, which plots the various costs associated with holding inventory (on the vertical axis) against inventory levels (on the horizontal axis). As shown, inventory carrying costs rise and restocking costs decrease as inventory levels

Figure 19.3

ABC inventory analysis

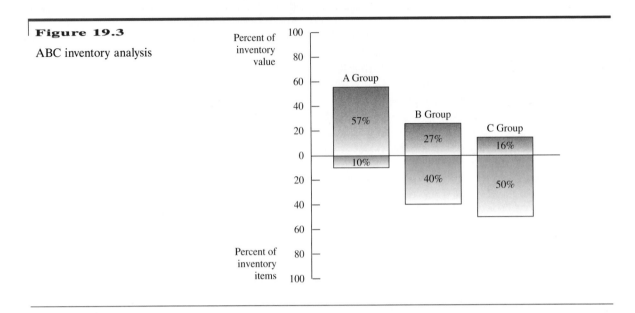

increase. From our general discussion in Chapter 17 and our discussion of the total credit cost curve in this chapter, the general shape of the total inventory cost curve is familiar. With the EOQ model, we will attempt to specifically locate the minimum total cost point, Q^*.

In our discussion below, an important point to keep in mind is that the actual cost of the inventory itself is not included. The reason is that the *total* amount of inventory the firm needs in a given year is dictated by sales. What we are analyzing here is how much the firm should have on hand at any particular time. More precisely, we are trying to determine what size order the firm should place when it restocks its inventory.

Inventory Depletion   To develop the EOQ, we will assume that the firm's inventory is sold off at a steady rate until it hits zero. At that point, the firm restocks its inventory back to some optimal level. For example, suppose the Eyssell Corporation starts out today with 3,600 units of a particular item in inventory. Annual sales of this item are 46,800 units, which is about 900 per week. If Eyssell sells off 900 units in inventory each week, then, after four weeks, all the available inventory will be sold, and Eyssell will restock by ordering (or manufacturing) another 3,600 and start over. This selling and restocking process produces a sawtooth pattern for inventory holdings; this pattern is illustrated in Figure 19.5. As the figure shows, Eyssell always starts with 3,600 units in inventory and ends up at zero. On average, then, inventory is half of 3,600, or 1,800 units.

The Carrying Costs   As Figure 19.4 illustrates, carrying costs are normally assumed to be directly proportional to inventory levels. Suppose we let Q be the quantity of inventory that Eyssell orders each time (3,600 units); we will

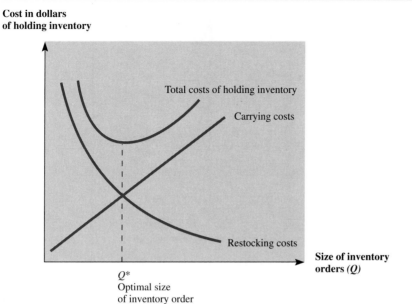

Figure 19.4

Costs of holding
inventory

Restocking costs are increased when the firm holds a small quantity of inventory. Carrying
costs are increased when there is a large quantity of inventory on hand. Total costs are the
sum of the carrying and restocking costs.

call this the restocking quantity. Average inventory would then just be $Q/2$, or
1,800 units. If we let CC be the carrying cost per unit per year, Eyssell's total
carrying costs will be:

$$\text{Total carrying costs} = \text{Average inventory} \times \text{Carrying costs per unit}$$

$$= (Q/2) \times \text{CC} \qquad\qquad [19.10]$$

In Eyssell's case, if carrying costs were \$0.75 per unit per year, then total car-
rying costs would be the average inventory of 1,800 multiplied by \$0.75, or
\$1,350 per year.

The Shortage Costs   For now, we will focus only on the restocking costs.
In essence, we will assume that the firm never actually runs short on inventory,
so that costs relating to safety reserves are not important. We will return to
this issue below.

Restocking costs are normally assumed to be fixed. In other words, every
time we place an order, there are fixed costs associated with that order (remember the cost of the inventory itself is not considered here). Suppose we let
T be the firm's total unit sales per year. If the firm orders Q units each time,
then it will need to place a total of T/Q orders. For Eyssell, annual sales were

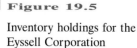

Figure 19.5

Inventory holdings for the Eyssell Corporation

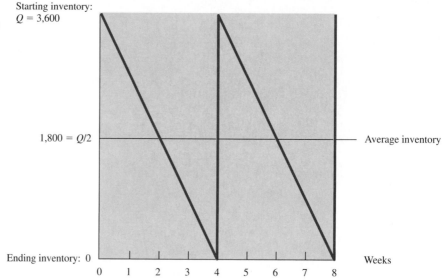

Starting inventory:
$Q = 3,600$

$1,800 = Q/2$ — Average inventory

Ending inventory: 0

Weeks

0 1 2 3 4 5 6 7 8

The Eyssell Corporation starts with inventory of 3,600 units. The quantity drops to zero by the fourth week. The average inventory is $Q/2 = 3,600/2 = 1,800$ over the period.

46,800, and the order size was 3,600. Eyssell thus places a total of 46,800/ 3,600 = 13 orders per year. If the fixed cost per order is F, the total restocking cost for the year would be:

Total restocking cost = Fixed cost per order × Number of orders

$$= F \times (T/Q) \qquad [19.11]$$

For Eyssell, order costs might be $50 per order, so the total restocking cost for 13 orders would be $50 × 13 = $650 per year.

The Total Costs   The total costs associated with holding inventory are the sum of the carrying costs and the restocking costs:

Total costs = Carrying costs + Restocking costs

$$= (Q/2) \times CC + F \times (T/Q) \qquad [19.12]$$

Our goal is to find the value of Q, the restocking quantity, that minimizes this cost. To see how we might go about this, we can calculate total costs for some different values of Q. For the Eyssell Corporation, we had carrying costs (CC) of $0.75 per unit per year, fixed costs per order (F) of $50 per order, and total unit sales (T) of 46,800 units. With these numbers, some possible total costs are (check some of these for practice):

Restocking Quantity (Q)	Total Carrying Costs ($Q/2 \times$ CC)	+	Restocking Costs ($F \times T/Q$)	=	Total Costs
500	$ 187.5		$4,680.0		$4,867.5
1,000	375.0		2,340.0		2,715.0
1,500	562.5		1,560.0		2,122.5
2,000	750.0		1,170.0		1,920.0
2,500	937.5		936.0		1,873.5
3,000	1,125.0		780.0		1,905.0
3,500	1,312.5		668.6		1,981.1

Inspecting the numbers, we see that total costs start out at almost $5,000, and they decline to just under $1,900. The cost-minimizing quantity appears to be approximately 2,500.

To find the precise cost-minimizing quantity, we can take a look back at Figure 19.4. What we notice is that the minimum point occurs right where the two lines cross. At this point, carrying costs and restocking costs are the same. For the particular types of costs we have assumed here this will always be true, so we can find the minimum point just by setting these costs equal to each other and solving for Q^*:

Carrying costs = Restocking costs

$$(Q^*/2) \times CC = F \times (T/Q^*) \qquad [19.13]$$

With a little algebra, we get:

$$Q^{*2} = \frac{2T \times F}{CC} \qquad [19.14]$$

To solve for Q^*, we take the square root of both sides to find:

$$Q^* = \sqrt{\frac{2T \times F}{CC}} \qquad [19.15]$$

This reorder quantity, which minimizes the total inventory cost, is called the **economic order quantity (EOQ).** For the Eyssell Corporation, the EOQ is:

$$
\begin{aligned}
Q^* &= \sqrt{\frac{2T \times F}{CC}} \qquad [19.16] \\
&= \sqrt{\frac{(2 \times 46,800) \times \$50}{\$.75}} \\
&= \sqrt{6,240,000} \\
&= 2,498 \text{ units}
\end{aligned}
$$

economic order quantity (EOQ)

The restocking quantity that minimizes the total inventory costs.

Thus, for Eyssell, the economic order quantity is actually 2,498 units. At this level, check that the restocking costs and carrying costs are identical (they're both $936.75).

Example 19.3 Carrying Costs

Thiewes Shoes begins each period with 100 pairs of hiking boots in stock. This stock is depleted each period and reordered. If the carrying cost per pair of boots per year is $3, what are the total carrying costs for the hiking boots?

Inventories always start at 100 items and end up at 0, so average inventory is 50 items. At an annual cost of $3 per item, total carrying costs are $150. ∎

Example 19.4 Restocking Costs

In our previous example (Example 19.3), suppose Thiewes sells a total of 600 pairs of boots in a year. How many times per year does Thiewes restock? Suppose that the restocking cost is $20 per order. What are total restocking costs?

Thiewes orders 100 items each time. Total sales are 600 items per year, so Thiewes restocks six times per year, or about every two months. The restocking costs would be 6 orders × $20 per order = $120. ∎

Example 19.5 The EOQ

Based on our previous two examples, what size orders should Thiewes place to minimize costs? How often will Thiewes restock? What are the total carrying and restocking costs? The total costs?

We have that the total number of pairs of boots ordered for the year (T) is 600. The restocking cost (F) is $20 per order, and the carrying cost (CC) is $3. We can calculate the EOQ for Thiewes as follows:

$$\text{EOQ} = \sqrt{\frac{2T \times F}{\text{CC}}}$$

$$= \sqrt{\frac{(2 \times 600) \times \$20}{\$3}}$$

$$= \sqrt{8,000}$$

$$= 89.44 \text{ units}$$

Since Thiewes sells 600 pairs per year, it will restock 600/89.44 = 6.71 times. The total restocking costs will be $20 × 6.71 = $134.16. Average inventory will be 89.44/2 = 44.72. The carrying costs will be $3 × 44.72 = $134.16, the same as the restocking costs. The total costs are thus $268.33. ∎

Extensions to the EOQ model

Thus far, we have assumed that a company will let its inventory run down to zero and then reorder. In reality, a company will wish to reorder before its inventory goes to zero for two reasons. First, by always having at least some inventory on hand, the firm minimizes the risk of a stock-out and the resulting losses of sales and customers. Second, when a firm does reorder, there will be some time lag before the inventory arrives. Thus, to finish our discussion of the EOQ, we consider two extensions, safety stocks and reordering points.

Safety Stocks   A *safety stock* refers to the minimum level of inventory that a firm keeps on hand. Inventories are reordered whenever the level of inventory falls to the safety stock level. The top of Figure 19.6 illustrates how a safety stock can be incorporated into an EOQ model. Notice that adding a safety stock simply means that the firm does not run its inventory all the way down to zero. Other than this, the situation is identical to our earlier discussion of the EOQ.

Reorder Points   To allow for delivery time, a firm will place orders before inventories reach a critical level. The *reorder points* are the times at which the firm will actually place its inventory orders. These points are illustrated in the middle of Figure 19.6. As shown, the reorder points simply occur some fixed number of days (or weeks or months) before inventories are projected to reach zero.

One of the reasons that a firm will keep a safety stock is to allow for uncertain delivery times. We can therefore combine our reorder point and safety stock discussions in the bottom part of Figure 19.6. The result is a generalized EOQ in which the firm orders in advance of anticipated needs and also keeps a safety stock of inventory to guard against unforeseen fluctuations in demand and delivery times.

Managing Derived-Demand Inventories

The third type of inventory management technique is used to manage derived-demand inventories. As we described above, demand for some inventory types is derived from or dependent on other inventory needs. A good example is an auto manufacturer where the demand for finished products depends on consumer demand, marketing programs, and other factors related to projected unit sales. The demand for inventory items such as tires, batteries, headlights, and other components is then completely determined by the number of autos planned. Materials requirements planning and just-in-time inventory management are two methods for managing demand-dependent inventories.

Materials Requirements Planning (MRP)   Production and inventory specialists have developed computer-based systems for ordering and/or scheduling production of demand-dependent type inventories. These systems fall under the general heading of **materials requirements planning (MRP).** The basic idea behind MRP is that, once finished goods inventory levels are set, it is possible to determine what levels of work-in-progress inventories must exist to meet the need for finished goods. From there, it is possible to calculate the quantity of raw materials that must be on hand. This ability to schedule backward from finished goods inventories stems from the dependent nature of work-in-progress and raw materials inventories. MRP is particularly important for complicated products where a variety of components are needed to create the finished product.

materials requirements planning (MRP)
A set of procedures used to determine inventory levels for demand-dependent inventory types such as work-in-progress and raw materials.

Figure 19.6

Safety stocks and reorder points

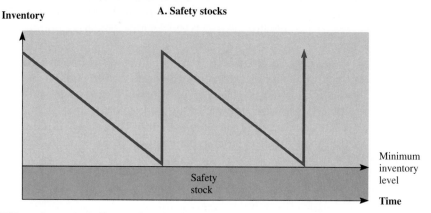

Inventory   **A. Safety stocks**

Safety
stock

Minimum
inventory
level

Time

With a safety stock, the firm reorders when inventory reaches a minimum level.

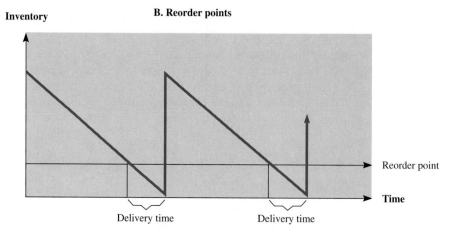

Inventory   **B. Reorder points**

Reorder point

Time

Delivery time   Delivery time

When there are lags in delivery or production times, the firm reorders when inventory reaches the reorder point.

Inventory   **C. Combined reorder points and safety stocks**

Reorder point

Minimum
inventory
level

Delivery time   Safety   Delivery time
stock

Time

By combining safety stocks and reorder points, the firm maintains a buffer against unforeseen events.

Just-in-Time Inventory   **Just-in-time (JIT) inventory** is a modern approach to managing dependent inventories. The goal of JIT is essentially to minimize such inventories, thereby maximizing turnover. The approach began in Japan, and it is a fundamental part of much of Japanese manufacturing philosophy. As the name suggests, the basic goal of JIT is to have only enough inventory on hand to meet immediate production needs.

The result of the JIT system is that inventories are reordered and restocked frequently. Making such a system work and avoiding shortages requires a high degree of cooperation among suppliers. Japanese manufacturers often have a relatively small, tightly integrated group of suppliers with whom they work closely to achieve the needed coordination. These suppliers are a part of a large manufacturer's (such as Toyota's) industrial group, or *keiretsu*. Each large manufacturer tends to have its own *keiretsu*. It also helps to have suppliers located nearby, a situation that is common in Japan.

The *kanban* is an integral part of a JIT inventory system, and JIT systems are sometimes called *kanban systems*. The literal meaning of kanban is "card" or "sign," but, broadly speaking, a kanban is a signal to a supplier to send more inventory. For example, a kanban could literally be a card attached to a bin of parts. When a worker pulls that bin, the card is detached and routed back to the supplier who then supplies a replacement bin.

A JIT inventory system is an important part of a larger production planning process. A full discussion of it would necessarily shift our focus away from finance to production and operations management, so we will leave it here. For further reading, consult the references at the end of the chapter.

just-in-time (JIT) inventory
A system for managing demand-dependent inventories that minimizes inventory holdings.

CONCEPT QUESTIONS

19.8a What does the EOQ model determine for the firm?

19.8b Which cost component of the EOQ model does JIT inventory minimize?

SUMMARY AND CONCLUSIONS | 19.9

This chapter covered the basics of credit and inventory policy. The major topics we discussed include:

1. The components of credit policy. We discussed the terms of sale, credit analysis, and collection policy. Under the general subject of terms of sale, the credit period, the cash discount and discount period, and the credit instrument were described.

2. Credit policy analysis. We developed the cash flows from the decision to grant credit and showed how the credit decision can be analyzed in an NPV setting. The NPV of granting credit depends on five factors: revenue effects, cost effects, the cost of debt, the probability of non-payment, and the cash discount.

3. Optimal credit policy. The optimal amount of credit the firm offers depends on the competitive conditions under which the firm operates. These conditions will determine the carrying costs associated with

granting credit and the opportunity costs of the lost sales from refusing to offer credit. The optimal credit policy minimizes the sum of these two costs.

4. Credit analysis. We looked at the decision to grant credit to a particular customer. We saw that two considerations are very important: the cost relative to the selling price and the possibility of repeat business.

5. Collection policy. Collection policy is the method of monitoring the age of accounts receivable and dealing with past-due accounts. We described how an aging schedule can be prepared and the procedures a firm might use to collect on past-due accounts.

6. Inventory types. We described the different inventory types and how they differ in terms of liquidity and demand.

7. Inventory costs. The two basic inventory costs are carrying and restocking costs, and we discussed how inventory management involves a trade-off between these two costs.

8. Inventory management techniques. We described the ABC approach and the EOQ model approach to inventory management. We also briefly touched on materials requirements planning (MRP) and just-in-time (JIT) inventory management.

Key Terms

terms of sale 665
credit analysis 666
collection policy 666
credit period 668
invoice 668
cash discount 670
credit instrument 671
credit cost curve 676

five Cs of credit 680
credit scoring 680
aging schedule 682
economic order quantity (EOQ) 689
materials requirements planning (MRP) 691
just-in-time (JIT) inventory 693

Chapter Review Problems and Self-Test

19.1   Credit Policy   The Cold Fusion Corp. (manufacturer of the Mr. Fusion home powerplant) is considering a new credit policy. The current policy is cash only. The new policy would involve extending credit for one period. Based on the information below, determine if a switch is advisable. The interest rate is 1.5 percent per period.

	Current Policy	New Policy
Price per unit	$150	$150
Cost per unit	$120	$120
Sales per period in units	2,000	2,200

19.2 **Credit Where Credit Is Due** You are trying to decide whether or not to extend credit to a particular customer. Your variable cost is $10 per unit; the selling price is $14. This customer wants to buy 100 units today and pay in 60 days. You think there is a 10 percent chance of default. The required return is 3 percent per 60 days. Should you extend credit? Assume that this is a one-time sale and the customer will not buy if credit is not extended.

19.3 **The EOQ** Heusen Computer Manufacturing starts each period with 4,000 CPUs in stock. This stock is depleted each month and reordered. If the carrying cost per CPU is $1, and the fixed order cost is $10, is Heusen following an economically advisable strategy?

Answers to Self-Test Problems

19.1. If the switch is made, an extra 200 units per period will be sold at a gross profit of $150 − 120 = $30 each. The total benefit is thus $30 × 200 = $6,000 per period. At 1.5 percent per period forever, the PV is $6,000/.015 = $400,000.

The cost of the switch is equal to this period's revenue of $150 × 2,000 units = $300,000 plus the cost of producing the extra 200 units, 200 × $120 = $24,000. The total cost is thus $324,000, and the NPV is $400,000 − 324,000 = $76,000. The switch should be made.

19.2 If the customer pays in 60 days, then you will collect $14 × 100 = $1,400. There's only a 90 percent chance of collecting this; so you expect to get $1,400 × .90 = $1,260 in 60 days. The present value of this is $1,260/1.03 = $1,223.3. Your cost is $10 × 100 = $1,000; so the NPV is $223.3. Credit should be extended.

19.3 We can answer by first calculating Heusen's carrying and restocking costs. The average inventory is 2,000 CPUs, and, since the carrying costs are $1 per CPU, total carrying costs are $2,000. Heusen restocks every month at a fixed order cost of $10, so the total restocking costs are $120. What we see is that carrying costs are large relative to reorder costs, so Heusen is carrying too much inventory.

To determine the optimal inventory policy, we can use the EOQ model. Because Heusen orders 4,000 CPUs 12 times per year, total needs (T) are 48,000 CPUs. The fixed order cost is $10, and the carrying cost per unit (CC) is $1. The EOQ is therefore:

$$\text{EOQ} = \sqrt{\frac{2T \times F}{\text{CC}}}$$

$$= \sqrt{\frac{(2 \times 48,000) \times \$10}{\$1}}$$

$$= \sqrt{960,000}$$

$$= 979.80 \text{ units}$$

We can check this by noting that the average inventory is about 490 CPUs, so the carrying cost is $490. Heusen will have to reorder 48,000/979.8 = 49 times. The fixed order cost is $10, so the total restocking cost is also $490.

Questions and Problems

1. **Credit Policy Components**   What are the three components of credit policy?

2. **Terms of Sale**   The conditions under which a firm proposes to grant credit are called the *terms of sale*. What are the elements that make up the terms of sale?

3. **Cash Discounts**   You place an order for 100 units of Good X at a price of $20 per unit. The supplier offers terms of 2/30, net 120.
    a. How long do you have to pay before the account is overdue? If you take the full period, how much should you remit?
    b. What is the discount being offered? How quickly must you pay to get the discount? If you do take the discount, how much should you remit?
    c. If you don't take the discount, how much interest are you paying implicitly? How many days' credit are you receiving?

4. **Credit Period Length**   What are some of the factors that determine the length of the credit period? Why is the length of the buyer's operating cycle often considered an upper bound on the length of the credit period?

5. **Credit Period Length**   In each of the following, indicate which firm would probably have a longer credit period and explain your reasoning.
    a. Firm A sells fresh fruit; Firm B sells canned fruit.
    b. Firm A sells a miracle cure for baldness; Firm B sells toupees.
    c. Firm A specializes in products for landlords; Firm B specializes in products for renters.
    d. Firm A sells and installs carpeting; Firm B sells rugs.
    e. Firm A sells to customers with an inventory turnover of 10 times; Firm B sells to customers with an inventory turnover of 20 times.

6. **Credit Instruments**   Describe each of the following:
    a. time draft
    b. promissory note
    c. sight draft
    d. trade acceptance
    e. banker's acceptance

7. **Trade Credit Forms**   In what form is trade credit most commonly offered? What is the credit instrument in this case?

8. **Credit Costs**   What are the costs associated with carrying receivables? What are the costs associated with not granting credit? What do we call the sum of the costs for different levels of receivables?

9. **Five Cs of Credit**   What are the five Cs of credit? Explain why each is important.

10. **Size of Accounts Receivable**   International Furthburner's annual credit sales are $45 million. The average collection period is 60 days. What is Furthburner's average investment in accounts receivable as shown on the balance sheet?

11. **ACP and Size of Accounts Receivable**   Macrothink, Inc., sells economic models based on the revolutionary data-free, least-squares

approach. Its credit terms are 5/10, net 60. Based on experience, 60 percent of all customers will take the discount.

a. What is the average collection period for Macrothink?

b. If Macrothink sells 200 models every month at a price of $1,400 each what is its average balance sheet amount in accounts receivable?

12. Size of Accounts Receivable   The Allen Company has monthly credit sales of $600,000, and the average collection period is 90 days. The cost of production is 70 percent of the selling price. What is the Allen Company's average accounts receivable?

13. Terms of Sale   A firm offers terms of 2/10, net 30. What effective annual interest rate does the firm earn when a customer does not take the discount? Without doing any calculations, explain what would happen to this effective rate if:

a. the discount were changed to 3 percent.

b. the credit period were extended to 60 days.

c. the discount period were extended to 15 days.

14. ACP and Receivables Turnover   The Last Mohican Corp. has an average collection period of 50 days. Its average daily investment in receivables is $3 million. What are annual credit sales? What is the receivables turnover?

15. Inventory Types   What are the different inventory types? How do the types differ? Why are some types said to have dependent demand whereas other types are said to have independent demand?

16. Evaluating Credit Policy   Macrohard Hardware supplies off-the-shelf computer components to systems rationalizers. A new customer has placed an order for 100 electronic nanocytes. The variable cost is $2 per unit, and the credit price is $3 each. Credit is extended for one period, and, based on historical experience, about 1 out of every 10 such orders is never collected. The required return is 2.5 percent per period.

a. Assuming that this is a one-time order, should it be filled? The customer will not buy if credit is not extended.

b. What is the break-even probability of default in part *a*?

c. Suppose that customers who don't default become repeat customers and place the same order every period forever. Further assume that repeat customers never default. Should the order be filled? What is the break-even probability of default?

d. Describe in general terms why credit terms will be more liberal when repeat orders are a possibility.

17. Just-in-Time Inventory   If a company moves to a JIT inventory management system, what will happen to inventory turnover? What will happen to total asset turnover? What will happen to return on equity (ROE)? (Hint: Remember the Du Pont equation from Chapter 3.)

18. Size of Accounts Receivable   Major Electronics sells 85,000 personal stereos each year at a price per unit of $55. All sales are on credit with the terms being 3/15, net 40. The discount is taken by 40 percent of the customers. What is Major's accounts receivable?

In reaction to a competitor, Major Electronics is considering changing its credit terms to 5/15, net 40 to preserve its sales level. How will this affect accounts receivable?

19.   **Size of Accounts Receivable**   The Webster's Company sells on credit terms of net 45. Its accounts are on the average 45 days past due. If annual credit sales are $5 million, what is the company's balance sheet amount in accounts receivable?

20.   **Credit Policy Evaluation**   The Tin Ear Stereo Corporation is considering changing its cash-only policy. The new terms would be net two months. Based on the information below, determine if Tin Ear should proceed or not. Describe the buildup of receivables in this case. The required return is 1 percent per period.

	Current Policy	New Policy
Price per unit	$840	$840
Cost per unit	690	690
Sales per month in units	345	390

21.   **Inventory Costs**   If a company's inventory carrying costs were $12 million per year and its fixed order costs were $20 million per year, do you think the firm keeps too much inventory on hand or too little? Why?

22.   **EOQ**   Hall Manufacturing uses 12,000 subframes per week and then reorders another 12,000. If the relevant carrying cost per subframe is $20, and the fixed order cost is $2,000, is Hall's inventory policy optimal? Why or why not?

23.   **EOQ**   The Brooks Pottery Store begins each week with 100 pots in stock. This stock is depleted each week and reordered. If the carrying cost per pot is $10 and the fixed order cost is $1,200, what is the carrying cost? What is the restocking cost? Should Brooks increase or decrease its order size? Describe an optimal inventory policy for Brooks in terms of order size and order frequency.

Challenge Problem   24.   **Credit Policy Evaluation**   Trion Clothing Co. currently has a credit policy of "in God we trust, everybody else pays cash." It is considering altering this policy by going to terms of net 30 days. Based on the following information, what do you recommend? The required return is 1 percent per month.

	Current Policy	New Policy
Price per unit	$10	$12
Cost per unit	$ 6	$ 7
Sales per month in units	40,000	40,000

Challenge Problem   25.   **Credit Policy Evaluation**   The Heavy Metal Corp. is considering changing its cash-only policy. The new terms would be net one month. Based on the information below, determine if Heavy Metal should proceed or not. The required return is 2 percent per period.

	Current Policy	New Policy
Price per unit	$20	$22
Cost per unit	$12	$12
Sales per period in units	2,000	2,150

26.   **EOQ Derivation**   Prove that when carrying costs and restocking costs are as described in the chapter, the EOQ must occur when the carrying costs and restocking costs are equal.

Challenge Problem

Suggested Readings

We have benefited from reading the following articles on short-term financial decisions:

Sartoris, W. L., and N. C. Hill. "Evaluating Credit Policy Alternatives: A Present Value Framework." *Journal of Financial Research* 4, Spring 1981.

_____. "A Generalized Cash Flow Approach to Short-Term Financial Decisions." *Journal of Finance* 38, May 1983.

For more on MRP, JIT, and related acronyms, see:

Chase, Richard B., and Nicholas J. Aquilano. *Production and Operations Management.* 6th ed. Homewood, Ill.: Richard D. Irwin, 1992.

MORE ON CREDIT POLICY ANALYSIS

This appendix takes a closer look at credit policy analysis by investigating some alternative approaches and by examining the effect of cash discounts and the possibility of nonpayment.

Two Alternative Approaches

From our chapter discussion, we know how to analyze the NPV of a proposed credit policy switch. We now discuss two alternative approaches: the "one-shot" approach and the accounts receivable approach. These are very common means of analysis; our goal is to show that these two and our NPV approach are all the same. Afterwards, we will use whichever of the three is most convenient.

The One-Shot Approach   Looking back at our example for Locust Software (in Section 19.3), if the switch is not made, Locust will have a net cash flow this month of $(P - v)Q = \$29 \times 100 = \$2,900$. If the switch is made, Locust will invest $vQ' = \$20 \times 110 = \$2,200$ this month and will receive $PQ' = \$49 \times 110 = \$5,390$ next month. Suppose we ignore all other months and cash flows and view this as a one-shot investment. Is Locust better off with $2,900 in cash this month, or should Locust invest the $2,200 to get $5,390 next month?

The present value of the $5,390 to be received next month is $5,390/ 1.02 = \$5,284.31$; the cost is $2,200, so the net benefit is $\$5,284.31 - 2,200 = \$3,084.31$. If we compare this to the net cash flow of $2,900 under the current policy, then Locust should switch. The NPV is $\$3,084.31 - 2,900 = \$184.31$.

In effect, Locust can repeat this one-shot investment every month and thereby generate an NPV of $184.31 every month (including the current one). The PV of this series of NPVs is:

Present value = $\$184.31 + \$184.31/.02 = \$9,400$

This PV is the same as our answer in Section 19.3.

The Accounts Receivable Approach   Our second approach is the one that is most commonly discussed and is very useful. By extending credit, the firm increases its cash flow through increased gross profits. However, the firm must increase its investment in receivables and bear the carrying cost of doing so. The accounts receivable approach focuses on the expense of the incremental investment in receivables compared to the increased gross profit.

As we have seen, the monthly benefit from extending credit is given by the gross profit per unit $(P - v)$ multiplied by the increase in quantity sold $(Q' - Q)$. For Locust, this benefit was $(\$49 - 20) \times (110 - 100) = \$290$ per month.

If Locust makes the switch, then receivables will rise from zero (since there are no credit sales) to PQ', so Locust must invest in receivables. The necessary investment has two components. The first part is what Locust would have collected under the old policy (PQ). Locust must carry this amount in receivables each month because collections are delayed by 30 days.

The second part is related to the increase in receivables that results from the increase in sales. Since unit sales increase from Q to Q', Locust must produce this quantity today even though it won't collect for 30 days. The actual cost to Locust of producing the extra quantity is equal to v per unit, so the investment necessary to provide the extra quantity sold is $v(Q' - Q)$.

In sum, if Locust switches, its investment in receivables is equal to the $P \times Q$ in revenues plus an additional $v(Q' - Q)$ in production costs:

$$\text{Incremental investment in receivables} = PQ + v(Q' - Q)$$

The required return on this investment (the carrying cost of the receivables) is R per month; so, for Locust, the accounts receivable carrying cost is:

$$\begin{aligned}
\text{Carrying cost} &= [PQ + v(Q' - Q)] \times R \\
&= [\$4{,}900 + 200] \times .02 \\
&= \$102 \text{ per month}
\end{aligned}$$

Since the monthly benefit is \$290 and the cost per month is only \$102, the net benefit is $\$290 - 102 = \$188$ per month. Locust earns this \$188 every month, so the PV of the switch is:

$$\begin{aligned}
\text{Present value} &= \$188/.02 \\
&= \$9{,}400
\end{aligned}$$

Again, this is the same figure we previously calculated.

One of the advantages of looking at the accounts receivable approach is that it helps us interpret our earlier NPV calculation. As we have seen, the investment in receivables necessary to make the switch is $PQ + v(Q' - Q)$. If you take a look back at our original NPV calculation, this is precisely what we had as the cost to Locust of making the switch. Our earlier NPV calculation thus amounts to a comparison of the incremental investment in receivables to the PV of the increased future cash flows.

There is one final thing to notice. The increase in accounts receivable is PQ', and this amount corresponds to the amount of receivables shown on the balance sheet. However, the incremental investment in receivables is $PQ + v(Q' - Q)$. It is straightforward to verify that this second quantity is smaller by $(P - v)(Q' - Q)$. This difference is the gross profit on the new sales, which Locust does not actually have to put up in order to switch credit policies.

Put another way, whenever we extend credit to a new customer who would not otherwise pay cash, all we risk is our cost, not the full sales price. This is the same issue that we discussed in Section 19.5.

Example 19A.1 Extra Credit

Looking back at Locust Software, determine the NPV of the switch if the quantity sold is projected to increase by only 5 units instead of 10. What will be the investment in receivables? What is the carrying cost? What is the monthly net benefit from switching?

If the switch is made, Locust gives up $P \times Q = \$4,900$ today. An extra five units have to be produced at a cost of $20 each, so the cost of switching is $\$4,900 + 5 \times \$20 = \$5,000$. The benefit of selling the extra five units each month is $5 \times (\$49 - 20) = \$145$. The NPV of the switch is $-\$5,000 + \$145/.02 = \$2,250$, so it's still profitable.

The $5,000 cost of switching can be interpreted as the investment in receivables. At 2 percent per month, the carrying cost is $.02 \times \$5,000 = \$100$. Since the benefit each month is $145, the net benefit from switching is $45 per month ($145 − 100). Notice that the PV of $45 per month forever at 2 percent is $\$45/.02 = \$2,250$ as we calculated. ∎

Discounts and Default Risk

We now take a look at cash discounts, default risk, and the relationship between the two. To get started, we define the following:

π = Percentage of credit sales that go uncollected

d = Percentage discount allowed for cash customers

P' = Credit price (the no-discount price)

Notice that the cash price (P) is equal to the credit price (P') multiplied by $(1 - d)$: $P = P'(1 - d)$ or, equivalently, $P' = P/(1 - d)$.

The situation at Locust is now a little more complicated. If a switch is made from the current policy of no credit, then the benefit to the switch will come from both the higher price (P') and, potentially, the increased quantity sold (Q').

Furthermore, in our previous case, it was reasonable to assume that all customers took the credit since it was free. Now, not all customers will take the credit because a discount is offered. In addition, of the customers who do take the credit offered, a certain percentage (π) will not pay.

To simplify the discussion below, we will assume that the quantity sold (Q) is not affected by the switch. This assumption isn't crucial, but it does cut down on the work (see Problem 5 at the end of the appendix). We will also assume that all customers take the credit terms. This assumption also isn't crucial. It actually doesn't matter what percentage of our customers take the offered credit.[4]

NPV of the Credit Decision   Currently, Locust sells Q units at a price of $P = \$49$. Locust is considering a new policy that involves 30 days' credit and an increase in price to $P' = \$50$ on credit sales. The cash price will remain

---

[4]The reason is that all customers are offered the same terms. If the NPV of offering credit is $100, assuming that all customers switch, then it will be $50 if only 50 percent of our customers switch. The hidden assumption is that the default rate is a constant percentage of credit sales.

at \$49, so Locust is effectively allowing a discount of ($50 − 49)/$50 = 2% for cash.

What is the NPV to Locust of extending credit? To answer, note that Locust is already receiving $(P - v)Q$ every month. With the new, higher price, this will rise to $(P' - v)Q$ assuming that everybody pays. However, since π percent of sales will not be collected, Locust will only collect on $(1 - \pi) \times P'Q$; so net receipts will be $[(1 - \pi)P' - v] \times Q$.

The net effect of the switch for Locust is thus the difference between the cash flows under the new policy and the old policy:

$$\text{Net incremental cash flow} = [(1 - \pi)P' - v] \times Q - (P - v) \times Q$$

Since $P = P' \times (1 - d)$, this simplifies to:[5]

$$\text{Net incremental cash flow} = P'Q \times (d - \pi) \qquad\qquad \text{[19A.1]}$$

If Locust does make the switch, then the cost in terms of the investment in receivables is just $P \times Q$ since $Q = Q'$. The NPV of the switch is thus:

$$\text{NPV} = -PQ + P'Q \times (d - \pi)/R \qquad\qquad \text{[19A.2]}$$

For example, suppose that, based on industry experience, the percentage of "deadbeats" (π) will be 1 percent. What is the NPV of changing credit terms for Locust? We can plug in the relevant numbers as follows:

$$
\begin{aligned}
\text{NPV} &= -PQ + P'Q \times (d - \pi)/R \\
&= -\$49 \times 100 + \$50 \times 100 \times (.02 - .01)/.02 \\
&= -\$2,400
\end{aligned}
$$

Since the NPV of the change is negative, Locust shouldn't switch.

In our expression for NPV, the key elements are the cash discount percentage (d) and the default rate (π). One thing we see immediately is that, if the percentage of sales that goes uncollected exceeds the discount percentage, then $d - \pi$ is negative. Obviously, the NPV of the switch would then be negative as well. More generally, our result tells us that the decision to grant credit

---

[5]To see this, note that the net incremental cash flow is:

$$
\begin{aligned}
\text{Cash flow} &= [(1 - \pi) \times P' - v] \times Q - (P - v) \times Q \\
&= [(1 - \pi) \times P' - P] \times Q
\end{aligned}
$$

Since $P = P' \times (1 - d)$, this can be written as:

$$
\begin{aligned}
\text{Net incremental cash flow} &= [(1 - \pi) \times P' - (1 - d) \times P'] \times Q \\
&= P' \times Q \times (d - \pi)
\end{aligned}
$$

here is a trade-off between getting a higher price, thereby increasing sales, versus not collecting on some fraction of those sales.

With this in mind, $P'Q \times (d - \pi)$ is the increase in sales less the portion of that increase that won't be collected. This increase is the incremental cash inflow from the switch in credit policy. If d is 5 percent and π is 2 percent, for example, then, loosely speaking, revenues are increasing by 5 percent because of the higher price, but collections only rise by 3 percent since the default rate is 2 percent. Unless $d > \pi$, we will actually have a decrease in cash inflows from the switch.

A Break-Even Application   Since the discount percentage (d) is controlled by the firm, the key unknown in this case is the default rate (π). What is the break-even default rate for Locust Software?

We can answer by finding the default rate that makes the NPV equal to zero.

$$\text{NPV} = 0 = -PQ + P'Q \times (d - \pi)/R$$

Rearranging things a bit:

$$PR = P'(d - \pi)$$

$$\pi = d - R \times (1 - d)$$

For Locust, the break-even default rate works out to be:

$$\pi = .02 - .02 \times (.98)$$

$$= .0004$$

$$= .04\%$$

This is quite small because the implicit interest rate Locust will be charging its credit customers (2 percent discount interest per month, or about $.02/.98 = 2.0408\%$) is only slightly greater than the required return of 2 percent per month. As a result, there's not much room for defaults if the switch is going to make sense.

⌈CONCEPT QUESTIONS

19A.1a What is the incremental investment that a firm must make in receivables if credit is extended?

19A.1b Describe the trade-off between the default rate and the cash discount.

Appendix Review Problems and Self-Test

19A.1 Credit Policy   Rework Self-Test Problem 19.1 using the one-shot and accounts receivable approaches. As before, the required return is

1.5 percent per period, and there will be no defaults. The basic information was:

	Current Policy	New Policy
Price per unit	$150	$150
Cost per unit	$120	$120
Sales per period in units	2,000	2,200

19A.2 **Discounts and Default Risk**   The ICU Binocular Corporation is considering a change in credit policy. The current policy is cash only, and sales per period are 5,000 units at a price of $95. If credit is offered, the new price will be $100 per unit and the credit will be extended for one period. Unit sales are not expected to change, and all customers will take the credit. ICU anticipates that 2 percent of its customers will default. If the required return is 3 percent per period, is the change a good idea? What if only half the customers take the offered credit?

Answers to Appendix Self-Test Problems

19A.1 As we saw earlier, if the switch is made, an extra 200 units per period will be sold at a gross profit of $150 − 120 = $30 each. The total benefit is thus $30 × 200 = $6,000 per period. At 1.5 percent per period forever, the PV is $6,000/.015 = $400,000.

   The cost of the switch is equal to this period's revenue of $150 × 2,000 units = $300,000 plus the cost of producing the extra 200 units, 200 × $120 = $24,000. The total cost is thus $324,000, and the NPV is $400,000 − 324,000 = $76,000. The switch should be made.

   For the accounts receivable approach, we interpret the $324,000 cost as the investment in receivables. At 1.5 percent per period, the carrying cost is $324,000 × 1.5% = $4,860 per period. The benefit per period we calculated as $6,000; so the net gain per period is $6,000 − 4,860 = $1,140. At 1.5 percent per period, the PV of this is $1,140/.015 = $76,000.

   Finally, for the one-shot approach, if credit is not granted, the firm will generate ($150 − 120) × 2,000 = $60,000 this period. If credit is extended, the firm will invest $120 × 2,200 = $264,000 today and receive $150 × 2,200 = $330,000 in one period. The NPV of this second option is $330,000/1.015 − $264,000 = $61,123.15. The firm is $61,123.15 − 60,000 = $1,123.15 better off today and in each future period by granting credit. The PV of this stream is $1,123.15 + $1,123.15/.015 = $76,000 (allowing for a rounding error).

19A.2 The costs per period are the same whether or not credit is offered; so we can ignore the production costs. The firm currently sells and collects $95 × 5,000 = $475,000 per period. If credit is offered, sales will rise to $100 × 5,000 = $500,000.

   Defaults will be 2 percent of sales, so the cash inflow under the new policy will be .98 × $500,000 = $490,000. This amounts to an extra $15,000 every period. At 3 percent per period, the PV is

$15,000/.03 = $500,000$. If the switch is made, ICU will give up this month's revenues of $475,000; so the NPV of the switch is $25,000. If only half switch, then the NPV is half as large: $12,500.

Appendix Questions and Problems

1. Evaluating Credit Policy   The Megaflops Computer Corporation is in the process of considering a change in its terms of sale. The current policy is cash only; the new policy will involve one period's credit. Sales are 1,000 units per period at a price of $15,000 per unit. If credit is offered, the new price will be $16,000. Unit sales are not expected to change, and all customers will take the credit. Megaflops estimates that 5 percent of credit sales will be uncollectible. If the required return is 2 percent per period, is the change a good idea?

2. Credit Policy Evaluation   The Running Dog Corporation sells 10,000 pairs of jogging shoes per month at a cash price of $78 per pair. Running Dog is considering a new policy that involves 30 days' credit and an increase in price to $80 per pair on credit sales. The cash price will remain at $78, and the new policy is not expected to affect the quantity sold. The discount period will be 10 days. The required return is 1 percent per month.
    a. How would the new credit terms be quoted?
    b. What is the investment in receivables required under the new policy?
    c. Explain why the variable cost of manufacturing the shoes is not relevant here.
    d. If the default rate is anticipated to be 3 percent, should the switch be made? What is the break-even credit price? The break-even cash discount?

3. Credit Analysis   Psychic Psionics Corp. (PPC) is debating whether or not to extend credit to a particular customer. PPC's product, a psionic amplifier, sells for $1,400 per unit. The variable cost is $600 per unit. The order under consideration is for five units today. Payment is promised in 90 days.
    a. If there is a 20 percent chance for a default, should PPC fill the order? The required return is 4 percent per quarter. This is a one-time sale, and the customer will not buy if credit is not extended.
    b. What is the break-even probability in part *a*?
    c. This part is a little harder. In general terms, how do you think your answer to part *a* will be affected if the customer would purchase the merchandise for cash if the credit is refused? The cash price is $1,300 per unit.

Challenge Problem   4. Credit Analysis   Consider the following information concerning two credit strategies:

	Refuse Credit	Grant Credit
Price per unit	$25	$27
Cost per unit	$15	$16
Quantity sold (per quarter)	3,000	3,300
Probability of payment	1.0	.90

The higher cost per unit reflects the expense associated with credit orders, and the higher price per unit reflects the existence of a cash discount. The credit period will be 90 days, and the cost of debt is 1 percent per month.

a. Based on this information, should credit be granted?

b. In part *a*, what does the sale price have to be to break even?

c. In part *a*, suppose we can obtain a credit report for 25 cents per customer. Assuming that each customer buys one unit and that the credit report identifies all customers who would not pay, should credit be extended?

5. NPV of Credit Policy Switch   Suppose a corporation currently sells Q units per month for a cash-only price of P. Under a new credit policy that allows one month's credit, the quantity sold will be Q' and the price per unit will be P'. Defaults will be π percent of credit sales. The variable cost is v per unit and is not expected to change. The percentage of customers who will take the credit is α, and the required return is R per month. What is the NPV of the decision to switch? Interpret the various parts of your expression.

Challenge Question

Part Nine

Topics in Corporate Finance

CHAPTER 20
Options and Corporate Securities

Options are special contractual arrangements that give the owner the right to buy or to sell an asset (usually stock) at a fixed price on or before a particular date. This chapter studies options and discusses two financing instruments — warrants and convertible bonds — which are corporate securities with explicit option features.

CHAPTER 21
Mergers and Acquisitions

This chapter describes the corporate finance of mergers and acquisitions. It shows that the acquisition of one firm by another is essentially a capital budgeting decision, and the NPV framework still applies. This chapter discusses the tax, accounting, and legal aspects of mergers and acquisitions along with recent developments in areas such as takeover defenses.

CHAPTER 22
International Corporate Finance

This chapter discusses international financial management. It describes the special factors that affect firms with significant foreign operations. The most important new factor that foreign operations introduce is foreign exchange rates. This chapter discusses how to deal with foreign exchange rates in financial management.

Chapter 20

Options and Corporate Securities

Options are a part of everyday life. "Keep your options open" is sound business advice, and "We're out of options" is a sure sign of trouble. Options are obviously valuable, but actually putting a dollar value on one is not easy. How to value options is an important topic of research, and option pricing is one of the great success stories of modern finance.

In finance, an **option** is an arrangement that gives its owner the right to buy or sell an asset at a fixed price anytime on or before a given date. The most familiar options are stock options. These are options to buy and sell shares of common stock, and we will discuss them in some detail below.

Almost all corporate securities have implicit or explicit option features. Furthermore, the use of such features is growing. As a result, understanding securities that possess option features requires a general knowledge of the factors that determine an option's value.

This chapter starts with a description of different types of options. We identify and discuss the general factors that determine option values and show how ordinary debt and equity have optionlike characteristics. We then go on to illustrate how option features are incorporated into corporate securities by discussing warrants, convertible bonds, and other optionlike securities.

option
A contract that gives its owner the right to buy or sell some asset at a fixed price on or before a given date.

OPTIONS: THE BASICS | 20.1

An option is a contract that gives its owner the right to buy or sell some asset at a fixed price on or before a given date. For example, an option on a building might give the holder of the option the right to buy the building for $1 million anytime on or before the Saturday prior to the third Wednesday in January 2010.

Options are a unique type of financial contract because they give the buyer the right, but not the obligation, to do something. The buyer uses the option only if it is profitable to do so; otherwise, the option can be thrown away.

There is a special vocabulary associated with options. Here are some important definitions:

exercising the option

The act of buying or selling the underlying asset via the option contract.

striking price

The fixed price in the option contract at which the holder can buy or sell the underlying asset. Also the *exercise price* or *strike price*.

expiration date

The last day on which an option can be exercised.

American option

An option that can be exercised at any time until its expiration date.

European option

An option that can only be exercised on the expiration date.

call option

The right to buy an asset at a fixed price during a particular period of time.

put option

The right to sell an asset at a fixed price during a particular period of time. The opposite of a call option.

1. **Exercising the option.** The act of buying or selling the underlying asset via the option contract is called *exercising the option*.

2. **Striking price or exercise price.** The fixed price specified in the option contract at which the holder can buy or sell the underlying asset is called the *striking price* or *exercise price*. The striking price is often just called the *strike price*.

3. **Expiration date.** An option usually has a limited life. The option is said to expire at the end of its life. The last day on which the option can be exercised is called the *expiration date*.

4. **American and European options.** An American option may be exercised anytime up to the expiration date. A European option can be exercised only on the expiration date.

Puts and Calls

Options come in two basic types: puts and calls. Call options are the more common of the two. A **call option** gives the owner the right to *buy* an asset at a fixed price during a particular time period. It may help you to remember that a call option gives you the right to "call in" an asset.

A **put option** is essentially the opposite of a call option. Instead of giving the holder the right to buy some asset, it gives the holder the right to *sell* that asset for a fixed exercise price. If you buy a put option, you can force the seller to buy the asset from you for a fixed price and thereby "put it to them."

What about an investor who *sells* a call option? The seller receives money up front and has the *obligation* to sell the asset at the exercise price if the option holder wants it. Similarly, an investor who *sells* a put option receives cash up front and is then obligated to buy the asset at the exercise price if the option holder demands it.[1]

The asset involved in an option could be anything. The options that are most widely bought and sold, however, are stock options. These are options to buy and sell shares of stock. Because these are the best-known types of options, we will study them first. As we discuss stock options, keep in mind that the general principles apply to options involving any asset, not just shares of stock.

Stock Option Quotations

On April 26, 1973, the Chicago Board Options Exchange (CBOE) opened and began organized trading in stock options. Put and call options involving stock in some of the best-known corporations in the United States are traded there.

---

[1]An investor who sells an option is often said to have "written" the option.

The CBOE is still the largest organized options market, but options are traded in a number of other places today, including the New York, American, and Philadelphia stock exchanges. Almost all such options are American (as opposed to European).

A simplified *Wall Street Journal* quotation for a CBOE option might look something like this:

Option & NY Close	Strike Price	Calls—Last			Puts—Last		
		June	Jul	Aug	Jun	Jul	Aug
RWJ							
100	95	6	6 $\frac{7}{8}$	8	2	2 $\frac{7}{8}$	4

The first thing to notice here is the company identifier, RWJ. This tells us that these options involve the right to buy or sell shares of stock in the RWJ Corporation. Just below the company identifier is the closing price on the stock. As of the close of business yesterday (in New York), RWJ was selling for $100 per share.

To the right of the NYSE closing price is the striking price. The RWJ options listed here have an exercise price of $95. Next, we have the option prices themselves. The first three are call option prices, and the second three are put option prices. The column headings (Jun, Jul, and Aug) are the expiration months. All CBOE options expire on the third Friday of the expiration month.

The first option listed would be described as the "RWJ June 95 call." The price for this option is $6. If you pay the $6, then you have the right anytime between now and the third Friday of June to buy one share of RWJ stock for $95. Actually, trading takes place in round lots (multiples of 100 shares), so one option *contract* costs $6 \times 100 = 600.

The other quotations are similar. For example, the July 95 put option costs 2 $\frac{7}{8}$. If you pay $2.875 \times 100 = 287.50, then you have the right to sell 100 shares of RWJ stock anytime between now and the third Friday in July at a price of $95 per share.

Table 20.1 contains a more detailed CBOE quote reproduced from *The Wall Street Journal*. From our discussion above, we know that these are IBM options and that IBM closed at 92 $\frac{1}{8}$ per share on the NYSE. Notice that there are multiple striking prices instead of just one. As shown, puts and calls with striking prices ranging from 80 up to 115 are available. The symbol *r* in the quote means that the particular contract didn't trade that day, and the symbol *s* means that the contract is not currently available.

To check your understanding of option quotes, suppose that you wanted the right to sell 100 shares of IBM for $100 anytime between now and the third Friday in April. What should you tell your broker and how much will it cost you?

Since you want the right to sell the stock for $100, you need to buy a *put* option with a $100 exercise price. So you call up your broker and place an order for one IBM April 100 put. Since the April 100 put is quoted at 8 $\frac{1}{2}$, you will have to pay $8.50 per share, or $850 in all (plus commission).

Table 20.1

A sample *Wall Street Journal* option quotation

Option & NY Close	Strike Price	CHICAGO BOARD Calls — Last			Puts — Last		
		Feb	Mar	Apr	Feb	Mar	Apr
IBM	80	r	s	r	$\frac{1}{16}$	s	$\frac{1}{2}$
92$\frac{1}{8}$	85	7$\frac{1}{4}$	8$\frac{1}{8}$	8$\frac{3}{4}$	$\frac{1}{8}$	$\frac{11}{16}$	1$\frac{5}{16}$
92$\frac{1}{8}$	90	2$\frac{7}{8}$	4$\frac{3}{8}$	5$\frac{1}{2}$	$\frac{11}{16}$	2	2$\frac{13}{16}$
92$\frac{1}{8}$	95	$\frac{3}{4}$	2$\frac{1}{16}$	3$\frac{1}{8}$	3$\frac{1}{2}$	4$\frac{3}{4}$	5$\frac{3}{8}$
92$\frac{1}{8}$	100	$\frac{1}{8}$	$\frac{3}{4}$	1$\frac{9}{16}$	r	r	8$\frac{1}{2}$
92$\frac{1}{8}$	105	r	$\frac{1}{4}$	$\frac{3}{4}$	r	r	r
92$\frac{1}{8}$	110	s	s	$\frac{3}{8}$	s	s	r
92$\frac{1}{8}$	115	s	s	$\frac{3}{16}$	s	s	r

Wednesday, February 12, 1992

Options closing prices. Sales unit usually is 100 shares

Stock close is New York or American exchange final price.

Option Payoffs

Looking back at Table 20.1, suppose you were to buy 50 April 90 call contracts. The option is quoted at $5.50, so the contracts cost $550 each. You would spend a total of 50 × $550 = $27,500. You wait a while, and the expiration date rolls around.

Now what? You have the right to buy IBM stock for $90 per share. If IBM is selling for less than $90 a share, then this option isn't worth anything, and you throw it away. In this case, we say that the option has finished "out of the money" since the stock price is less than the exercise price. Your $27,500 is, alas, a complete loss.

If IBM is selling for more than $90 per share, then you need to exercise your option. In this case, the option is "in the money" since the stock price exceeds the exercise price. Suppose that IBM rises to, say, $100 per share. Since you have the right to buy IBM at $90, you make a $10 profit on each share upon exercise. Each contract involves 100 shares, so you make $10 per share × 100 shares per contract = $1,000 per contract. Finally, you own 50 contracts, so the value of your options is a handsome $50,000. Notice that, since you invested $27,500, your net profit is $22,500.

As our example indicates, the gains and losses from buying call options can be quite large. To illustrate further, suppose you had simply purchased the stock with the $27,500 instead of buying call options. In this case, you would have about $27,500/$92.125 = 298.5 shares. We can now compare what you have when the option expires for different stock prices:

Ending Stock Price	Option Value (50 contracts)	Net Profit (loss)	Stock Value (298.5 shares)	Net Profit (loss)
$ 80	$ 0	−$27,500	$23,880.0	−$3,620.0
85	0	− 27,500	25,372.5	− 2,127.5
90	0	− 27,500	26,865.0	− 635.0
95	25,000	− 2,500	28,357.5	857.5
100	50,000	22,500	29,850.0	2,350.0
105	75,000	47,500	31,342.5	3,842.5

The option position clearly magnifies the gains and losses on the stock by a substantial amount. The reason is that the payoff on your 50 option contracts is based on $50 \times 100 = 5,000$ shares of stock instead of just 298.5.

In our example, notice that, if the stock price only changes by a small amount, then you lose all $27,500 with the option. With the stock, you still have about what you started with. Also notice that the option can never be worth less than zero because you can always just throw it away. As a result, you can never lose more than your original investment (the $27,500 in our example).

It is important to recognize that stock options are a zero sum game. By this we mean that whatever the buyer of a stock option makes, the seller loses and vice versa. To illustrate, suppose that, in our example just above, you had *sold* 50 option contracts. You would receive $27,500 up front, and you would be obligated to sell the stock for $90 if the buyer of the option wished to exercise it. In this situation, if the stock price ends up below $90, you would be $27,500 ahead. If the stock price ends up above $90, you have to sell something for less than it is worth, so you lose the difference. For example, if the stock price were $100, you would have to sell $50 \times 100 = 5,000$ shares at $90 per share, so you would be out $100 − 90 = $10 per share, or $50,000 total. Because you received $27,500 up front, your net loss is $22,500. We can summarize some other possibilities as follows:

Ending Stock Price	Net Profit to Option Seller
$ 80	+$27,500
85	+ 27,500
90	+ 27,500
95	+ 2,500
100	− 22,500
105	− 47,500

Notice that the net profits to the option buyer (calculated above) are just the opposites of these amounts.

Example 20.1   Put Payoffs

Looking at Table 20.1, suppose you buy 10 IBM February 95 put contracts. How much does this cost (ignoring commissions)? Just before the option expires, IBM is selling for $90 per share. Is this good news or bad news? What is your net profit?

The option is quoted at $3\frac{1}{2}$, so one contract costs $100 \times 3\frac{1}{2} = \$350$. Your 10 contracts total $3,500. You now have the right to sell 1,000 shares of IBM for $95 per share. If the stock is currently selling for $90 per share, then this is most definitely good news. You can buy 1,000 shares at $90 and sell them for $95. Your puts are thus worth $\$5 \times 1,000 = \$5,000$. Since you paid $3,500, your net profit is $\$5,000 - 3,500 = \$1,500$. ∎

CONCEPT QUESTIONS

20.1a What is a call option? A put option?

20.1b If you thought that a stock was going to drop sharply in value, how might you use stock options to profit from the decline?

20.2 | FUNDAMENTALS OF OPTION VALUATION

Now that we understand the basics of puts and calls, we can discuss what determines their values. We will focus on call options in the discussion below, but the same type of analysis can be applied to put options.

Value of a Call Option at Expiration

We have already described the payoffs from call options for different stock prices. To continue this discussion, the following notation will be useful:

S_1 = Stock price at expiration (in one period)

S_0 = Stock price today

C_1 = Value of the call option on the expiration date (in one period)

C_0 = Value of the call option today

E = Exercise price on the option

From our previous discussion, remember that, if the stock price (S_1) ends up below the exercise price (E) on the expiration date, then the call option (C_1) is worth zero. In other words:

$$C_1 = 0 \quad \text{if} \quad S_1 \leq E$$

Or, equivalently:

$$C_1 = 0 \quad \text{if} \quad (S_1 - E) \leq 0 \tag{20.1}$$

This is the case where the option is out of the money when it expires.

If the option finishes in the money, then $S_1 > E$, and the value of the option at expiration is equal to the difference:

$$C_1 = S_1 - E \quad \text{if} \quad S_1 > E$$

Or, equivalently:

$$C_1 = S_1 - E \quad \text{if} \quad (S_1 - E) > 0 \qquad \qquad [20.2]$$

For example, suppose we have a call option with an exercise price of $10. The option is about to expire. If the stock is selling for $8, then we have the right to pay $10 for something only worth $8. Our option is thus worth exactly zero because the stock price is less than the exercise price on the option ($S_1 \leq E$). If the stock is selling for $12, then the option has value. Since we can buy the stock for $10, it is worth $(S_1 - E) = \$12 - 10 = \$2$.

Figure 20.1 plots the value of a call option at expiration against the stock price. The result looks something like a hockey stick. Notice that for every stock price less than E, the value of the option is zero. For every stock price greater than E, the value of the call option is $(S_1 - E)$. Also, once the stock price exceeds the exercise price, the option's value goes up dollar for dollar with the stock price.

The Upper and Lower Bounds on a Call Option's Value

Now that we know how to determine C_1, the value of the call at expiration, we turn to a somewhat more challenging question: How can we determine C_0, the value sometime *before* expiration? We will be discussing this in the next several sections. For now, we will establish the upper and lower bounds for the value of a call option.

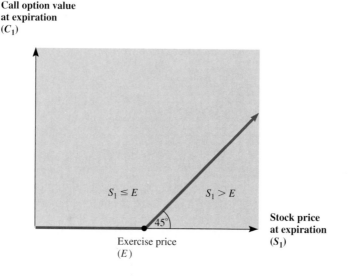

Call option value
at expiration
(C_1)

$S_1 \leq E$

$S_1 > E$

45°

Exercise price
(E)

Stock price
at expiration
(S_1)

Figure 20.1

Value of a call option at
expiration for different
stock prices

As shown, the value of a call option at expiration is equal to zero if the stock price is less than or equal to the exercise price. The value of the call is equal to the stock price minus the exercise price $(S_1 - E)$ if the stock price exceeds the exercise price. The resulting "hockey stick" shape is highlighted.

The Upper Bound   What is the most that a call option could sell for? If you think about it, the answer is obvious. A call option gives you the right to buy a share of stock, so it can never be worth more the stock itself. This tells us the upper bound on a call's value: A call option will always sell for no more than the underlying asset. So, in our notation, the upper bound is:

$$C_0 \leq S_0 \qquad\qquad\qquad [20.3]$$

The Lower Bound   What is the least a call option could sell for? The answer here is a little less obvious. First of all, the call can't sell for less than zero, so $C_0 \geq 0$. Furthermore, if the stock price is greater than the exercise price, the call option is worth at least $S_0 - E$.

To see why, suppose we had a call option selling for $4. The stock price is $10, and the exercise price is $5. Is there a profit opportunity here? The answer is yes because you could buy the call for $4 and immediately exercise it by spending an additional $5. Your total cost of acquiring the stock is $4 + 5 = $9. If you turn around and immediately sell the stock for $10, you pocket a $1 certain profit.

Opportunities for riskless profits such as this one are called *arbitrages* (say "are-bi-trazh," with the accent on the first syllable) or *arbitrage opportunities.* One who arbitrages is called an *arbitrageur.* The root for the term *arbitrage* is the same as the root for the word *arbitrate,* and an arbitrageur essentially arbitrates prices. In a well-organized market, significant arbitrages will, of course, be rare.

In the case of a call option, to prevent arbitrage, the value of the call today must be greater than the stock price less the exercise price:

$$C_0 \geq S_0 - E$$

If we put our two conditions together, we have:

$$C_0 \geq 0 \quad \text{if} \quad S_0 - E < 0 \qquad\qquad\qquad [20.4]$$

$$C_0 \geq S_0 - E \quad \text{if} \quad S_0 - E \geq 0$$

These conditions simply say that the lower bound on the call's value is either zero or $S_0 - E$, whichever is bigger.

intrinsic value

The lower bound of an option's value, or what the option would be worth if it were about to expire.

Our lower bound is called the **intrinsic value** of the option, and it is simply what the option would be worth if it were about to expire. With this definition, our discussion thus far can be restated as follows: At expiration, an option is worth its intrinsic value; it will generally be worth more than that any time before expiration.

Figure 20.2 displays the upper and lower bounds on the value of a call option. Also plotted is a curve representing typical call option values for different stock prices prior to maturity. The exact shape and location of this curve depends on a number of factors. We begin our discussion of these factors in the next section.

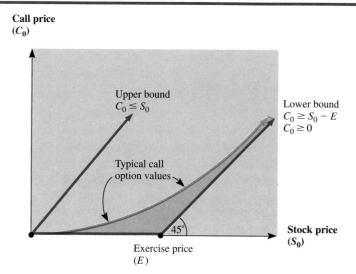

Figure 20.2

Value of a call option
before expiration for
different stock prices

As shown, the upper bound on a call's value is given by the value of the stock
($C_0 \leq S_0$). The lower bound is either $S_0 - E$ or 0, whichever is larger. The
highlighted curve illustrates the value of a call option prior to maturity for
different stock prices.

A Simple Model: Part I

Option pricing can be a complex subject. Fortunately, as is often the case,
many of the key insights can be illustrated with a simple example. Suppose
that we are looking at a call option with one year to expiration and an exercise
price of $105. The stock currently sells for $100, and the risk-free rate, R_f, is
20 percent.

The value of the stock in one year is uncertain, of course. To keep things
simple, suppose that we know that the stock price will either be $110 or $130.
Importantly, we *don't* know the odds associated with these two prices. In other
words, we know the possible values for the stock, but not the probabilities associated with those values.

Since the exercise price on the option is $105, we know that the option
will be worth either $110 − 105 = $5 or $130 − 105 = $25, but, once again,
we don't know which. We do know one thing, however: Our call option is certain to finish in the money.

The Basic Approach   Here is the crucial observation: It is possible to exactly duplicate the payoffs on the stock using a combination of the option and
the risk-free asset. How? Do the following: Buy one call option and invest
$87.50 in a risk-free asset (such as a T-bill).

What will you have in a year? Your risk-free asset will earn 20 percent, so it will be worth $87.50 \times 1.20 = $105. Your option is worth $5 or $25, so the total value is either $110 or $130, just like the stock:

Stock value		Risk-free asset value	+	Call value	=	Total value
$110	vs.	$105	+	$ 5	=	$110
130	vs.	105	+	25	=	130

As illustrated, these two strategies—buy a share of stock versus buy a call and invest in the risk-free asset—have exactly the same payoffs in the future.

Since these two strategies have the same future payoffs, they must have the same value today or else there would be an arbitrage opportunity. The stock sells for $100 today, so the value of the call option today, C_0, is:

$$\$100 = \$87.50 + C_0$$
$$C_0 = \$12.50$$

Where did we get the $87.50? This is just the present value of the exercise price on the option, calculated at the risk-free rate:

$$E/(1 + R_f) = \$105/1.20 = \$87.5$$

Given this, our example shows that the value of a call option in this simple case is given by:

$$S_0 = C_0 + E/(1 + R_f)$$
$$C_0 = S_0 - E/(1 + R_f) \tag{20.5}$$

In words, the value of the call option is equal to the stock price minus the present value of the exercise price.

A More Complicated Case Obviously, our assumption that the stock price would be either $110 or $130 is a vast oversimplification. We can now develop a more realistic model by assuming that the stock price can be *anything* greater than or equal to the exercise price. Once again, we don't know how likely the different possibilities are, but we are certain that the option will finish somewhere in the money.

We again let S_1 stand for the stock price in one year. Now consider our strategy of investing $87.50 in a riskless asset and buying one call option. The riskless asset will again be worth $105 in one year, and the option will be worth $S_1 - \$105$, depending on what the stock price is.

When we investigate the combined value of the option and the riskless asset, we observe something very interesting:

$$\text{Combined value} = \text{Riskless asset value} + \text{Option value}$$
$$= \$105 + (S_1 - \$105)$$
$$= S_1$$

Just as we had before, buying a share of stock has exactly the same payoff as buying a call option and investing the present value of the exercise price in the riskless asset.

Once again, to prevent arbitrage, these two strategies must have the same cost, so the value of the call option is equal to the stock price less the present value of the exercise price:[2]

$$C_0 = S_0 - E/(1 + R_f)$$

Our conclusion from this discussion is that determining the value of a call option is not difficult as long as we are certain that the option will finish somewhere in the money.

Four Factors Determining Option Values

If we continue to suppose that our option is certain to finish in the money, then we can readily identify four factors that determine an option's value. There is a fifth factor that comes into play if the option can finish out of the money. We will discuss this last factor in the next section.

For now, if we assume that the option expires in t periods, then the present value of the exercise price is $E/(1 + R_f)^t$, and the value of the call is:

Call option value = Stock value − Present value of the exercise price

$$C_0 = S_0 - E/(1 + R_f)^t \qquad \text{[20.6]}$$

If we take a look at this expression, the value of the call obviously depends on four things:

1. *The stock price.* The higher the stock price (S_0) is, the more the call is worth. This comes as no surprise since the option gives us the right to buy the stock at a fixed price.

2. *The exercise price.* The higher the exercise price (E) is, the less the call is worth. This is also not a surprise since the exercise price is what we have to pay to get the stock.

3. *The time to expiration.* The longer the time to expiration is (the bigger t is), the more the option is worth. Once again, this is obvious. Since the option gives us the right to buy for a fixed length of time, its value goes up as that length of time increases.

---

[2]You're probably wondering what would happen if the stock price were less than the present value of the exercise price, resulting in a negative value for the call option. This can't happen because we are certain that the stock price will be at least E in one year since we know the option will finish in the money. If the current price of the stock is less than $E/(1 + R_f)$, then the return on the stock is certain to be greater than the risk-free rate, thereby creating an arbitrage opportunity. For example, if the stock were currently selling for $80, then the *minimum* return would be ($105 − 80)/$80 = 31.25%. Since we can borrow at 20 percent, we can earn a certain minimum return of 11.25 percent per dollar borrowed. This, of course, is an arbitrage.

4. *The risk-free rate.* The higher the risk-free rate (R_f) is, the more the call is worth. This result is a little less obvious. Normally, we think of asset values going down as rates rise. In this case, the exercise price is a cash *outflow*, a liability. The current value of that liability goes down as the discount rate goes up.

⌐CONCEPT QUESTIONS

20.2a What is the value of a call option at expiration?

20.2b What are the upper and lower bounds on the value of a call option anytime before expiration?

20.2c Assuming that the stock price is certain to be greater than the exercise price on a call option, what is the value of the call? Why?

20.3 | VALUING A CALL OPTION

We now investigate the value of a call option when there is the possibility that the option will finish out of the money. We will again examine the simple case of two possible future stock prices. This case will let us identify the remaining factor that determines an option's value.

A Simple Model: Part II

From our previous example, we have a stock that currently sells for $100. It will be worth either $110 or $130 in a year, and we don't know which. The risk-free rate is 20 percent. We are now looking at a different call option, however. This one has an exercise price of $120 instead of $105. What is the value of this call option?

This case is a little harder. If the stock ends up at $110, the option is out of the money and worth nothing. If the stock ends up at $130, the option is worth $130 − 120 = $10.

Our basic approach to determining the value of the call option will be the same. We will show once again that it is possible to combine the call option and a risk-free investment in a way that exactly duplicates the payoff from holding the stock. The only complication is that it's a little harder to determine how to do it.

For example, suppose we bought one call and invested the present value of the exercise price in a riskless asset as we did before. In one year, we would have $120 from the riskless investment plus an option worth either zero or $10. The total value is either $120 or $130. This is not the same as the value of the stock ($110 or $130), so the two strategies are not comparable.

Instead, consider investing the present value of $110 (the lower stock price) in a riskless asset. This guarantees us a $110 payoff. If the stock price is $110, then any call options we own are worthless, and we have exactly $110 as desired.

When the stock is worth $130, the call option is worth $10. Our risk-free investment is worth $110, so we are $130 − 110 = $20 short. Since each call option is worth $10, we need to buy two of them to replicate the stock.

Thus, in this case, investing the present value of the lower stock price in a riskless asset and buying two call options exactly duplicates owning the stock. When the stock is worth $110, we have $110 from our risk-free investment. When the stock is worth $130, we have $110 from the risk-free investment plus two call options worth $10 each.

Since these two strategies have exactly the same value in the future, they must have the same today, or else arbitrage would be possible:

$$S_0 = \$100 = 2 \times C_0 + \$110/(1 + R_f)$$

$$2 \times C_0 = \$100 - \$110/1.20$$

$$C_0 = \$4.17$$

Each call option is thus worth $4.17.

Example 20.2 Don't Call Us, We'll Call You
We are looking at two call options on the same stock, one with an exercise price of $20 and one with an exercise price of $30. The stock currently sells for $35. Its future price will either be $25 or $50. If the risk-free rate is 10 percent, what are the values of these call options?

The first case (the $20 exercise price) is not difficult since the option is sure to finish in the money. We know that the value is equal to the stock price less the present value of the exercise price:

$$C_0 = S_0 - E/(1 + R_f)$$

$$= \$35 - \$20/1.1$$

$$= \$16.82$$

In the second case, the exercise price is $30, so the option can finish out of the money. At expiration, the option is worth $0 if the stock is worth $25. The option is worth $50 - 30 = $20 if it finishes in the money.

As before, we start by investing the present value of the lowest stock price in the risk-free asset. This costs $25/1.1 = $22.73. At expiration, we have $25 from this investment.

If the stock price is $50, then we need an additional $25 to duplicate the stock payoff. Since each option is worth $20 in this case, we need $25/$20 = 1.25 options. So, to prevent arbitrage, investing the present value of $25 in a risk-free asset and buying 1.25 call options has the same value as the stock:

$$S_0 = 1.25 \times C_0 + \$25/(1 + R_f)$$

$$\$35 = 1.25 \times C_0 + \$25/(1 + .10)$$

$$C_0 = \$9.82$$

Notice that this second option had to be worth less because it has the higher exercise price. ∎

The Fifth Factor

We now illustrate the fifth (and last) factor that determines an option's value. Suppose that everything in our example above is the same except that the stock price can be $105 or $135 instead of $110 or $130. Notice that the effect of this change is to make the stock's future price more volatile than before.

We investigate the same strategy that we used above: Invest the present value of the lowest stock price ($105 in this case) in the risk-free asset and buy two call options. If the stock price is $105, then, as before, the call options have no value and we have $105 in all.

If the stock price is $135, then each option is worth $S_1 - E = \$135 - 120 = \$15$. We have two calls, so our portfolio is worth $\$105 + 2 \times \$15 = \$135$. Once again, we have exactly replicated the value of the stock.

What has happened to the option's value? More to the point, the variance of the return on the stock has increased. Does the option's value go up or down? To find out, we need to solve for the value of the call just as we did before:

$$S_0 = \$100 = 2 \times C_0 + \$105/(1 + R_f)$$

$$2 \times C_0 = \$100 - \$105/1.20$$

$$C_0 = \$6.25$$

The value of the call option has gone up from $4.17 to $6.25.

Based on our example, the fifth and final factor that determines an option's value is the variance of the return on the underlying asset. Furthermore, the *greater* that variance is, the *more* the option is worth. This result appears a little odd at first, and it may be somewhat surprising to learn that increasing the risk (as measured by return variance) on the underlying asset increases the value of the option.

The reason that increasing the variance on the underlying asset increases the value of the option isn't hard to see in our example. Changing the lower stock price to $105 from $110 doesn't hurt a bit because the option is worth zero in either case. However, moving the upper possible price to $135 from $130 makes the option worth more when it is in the money.

More generally, increasing the variance of the possible future prices on the underlying asset doesn't affect the option's value when the option finishes out of the money. The value is always zero in this case. On the other hand, increasing that variance when the option is in the money only increases the possible payoffs, so the net effect is to increase the option's value. Put another way, since the downside risk is always limited, the only effect is to increase the upside potential.

In later discussion, we will use the usual symbol, σ^2, to stand for the variance of the return on the underlying asset.

A Closer Look

Before moving on, it will be useful to consider one last example. Suppose the stock price is $100 and it will either move up or down by 20 percent. The risk-free rate is 5 percent. What is the value of a call option with a $90 exercise price?

The stock price will either be $80 or $120. The option is worth zero when the stock is worth $80, and it's worth $120 − 90 = $30 when the stock is worth $120. We will therefore invest the present value of $80 in the risk-free asset and buy some call options.

When the stock finishes at $120, our risk-free asset pays $80, leaving us $40 short. Each option is worth $30 in this case, so we need $40/$30 = 4/3 options to match the payoff on the stock. The option's value must thus be given by:

$$S_0 = \$100 = 4/3 \times C_0 + \$80/1.05$$

$$C_0 = (3/4) \times (\$100 - \$76.19)$$

$$= \$17.86$$

To make our result a little bit more general, notice that the number of options that you need to buy to replicate the stock is always equal to $\Delta S/\Delta C$, where ΔS is the difference in the possible stock prices and ΔC is the difference in the possible option values. In our current case, for example, ΔS would be $120 − 80 = \$40$ and ΔC would be $30 − 0 = \$30$, so $\Delta S/\Delta C$ is $40/30 = 4/3$ as we calculated.

Notice also that when the stock is certain to finish in the money, $\Delta S/\Delta C$ is always exactly equal to one, so one call option is always needed. Otherwise, $\Delta S/\Delta C$ is greater than one, so more than one call option is needed.

This concludes our discussion of option valuation. The most important thing to remember is that the value of an option depends on five factors. Table 20.2 summarizes these factors and the direction of their influence for both puts and calls. In Table 20.2, the sign in parentheses indicates the direction of the influence.[3] In other words, the sign tells us whether the value of the option goes up or down when the value of a factor increases. For example, notice that increasing the exercise price reduces the value of a call option. Increasing any of the other four factors increases the value of the call. Notice also that the time to expiration and the variance act the same for puts and calls. The other three factors have opposite signs.

We have not considered how to value a call option when the option can finish out of the money and the stock price can take on more than two values. A very famous result, the Black-Scholes option pricing model, is needed in this case. We cover this subject in the chapter appendix.

⌐ CONCEPT QUESTIONS

20.3a What are the five factors that determine an option's value?

20.3b What is the effect of an increase in each of the five factors on the value of a call option? Give an intuitive explanation for your answer.

20.3c What is the effect of an increase in each of the five factors on the value of a put option? Give an intuitive explanation for your answer.

---

[3]The signs in Table 20.2 are for American options. For a European put option, the effect of increasing the time to expiration is ambiguous, and the direction of the influence can be positive or negative.

	Factor	Calls	Puts
Table 20.2	Current value of the underlying asset	(+)	(−)
Five factors that determine option values	Exercise price on the option	(−)	(+)
	Time to expiration on the option	(+)	(+)
	Risk-free rate	(+)	(−)
	Variance of return on the underlying asset	(+)	(+)

20.4 | EQUITY AS A CALL OPTION ON THE FIRM'S ASSETS

Now that we understand the basic determinants of an option's value, we turn to examining some of the many ways that options appear in corporate finance. One of the most important insights we gain from studying options is that the common stock in a leveraged firm (one that has issued debt) is effectively a call option on the assets of the firm. This is a remarkable observation, and we explore it next.

An example is the easiest way to get started. Suppose a firm has a single debt issue outstanding. The face value is $1,000, and the debt is coming due in a year. There are no coupon payments between now and then, so the debt is effectively a pure discount bond. In addition, the current market value of the firm's assets is $950, and the risk-free rate is 12.5 percent.

In a year, the stockholders will have a choice. They can pay off the debt for $1,000 and thereby acquire the assets of the firm free and clear, or they can default on the debt. If they default, the bondholders will own the assets of the firm.

In this situation, the stockholders essentially have a call option on the assets of the firm with an exercise price of $1,000. They can exercise the option by paying the $1,000, or they can not exercise the option by defaulting. Whether or not they choose to exercise obviously depends on the value of the firm's assets when the debt becomes due.

If the value of the firm's assets exceeds $1,000, then the option is in the money, and the stockholders will exercise by paying off the debt. If the value of the firm's assets is less than $1,000, then the option is out of the money, and the stockholders will optimally choose to default. What we now illustrate is that we can determine the values of the debt and equity using our option pricing results.

Case I: The Debt Is Risk-Free

Suppose that in one year the firm's assets will either be worth $1,100 or $1,200. What is the value today of the equity in the firm? The value of the debt? What is the interest rate on the debt?

To answer these questions, we first recognize that the option (the equity in the firm) is certain to finish in the money because the value of the firm's assets ($1,100 or $1,200) will always exceed the face value of the debt. In this case, from our discussion in previous sections, we know that the option value is simply the difference between the value of the underlying asset and the present value of the exercise price (calculated at the risk-free rate). The present value of $1,000 in one year at 12.5 percent is $888.89. The current value of the firm is $950, so the option (the firm's equity) is worth $950 − 888.89 = $61.11.

What we see is that the equity, which is effectively an option to purchase the firm's assets, must be worth $61.11. The debt must therefore actually be worth $888.89. In fact, we really didn't need to know about options to handle this example, because the debt is risk-free. The reason is that the bondholders are certain to receive $1,000. Since the debt is risk-free, the appropriate discount rate (and the interest rate on the debt) is the risk-free rate, and we therefore know immediately that the current value of the debt is $1,000/1.125 = $888.89. The equity is thus worth $950 − 888.89 = $61.11 as we calculated.

Case II: The Debt Is Risky

Suppose now that the value of the firm's assets in one year will be either $800 or $1,200. This case is a little more difficult because the debt is no longer risk-free. If the value of the assets turns out to be $800, then the stockholders will not exercise their option and thereby default. The stock is worth nothing in this case. If the assets are worth $1,200, then the stockholders will exercise their option to pay off the debt and enjoy a profit of $1,200 − 1,000 = $200.

What we see is that the option (the equity in the firm) will be worth either zero or $200. The assets will be worth either $1,200 or $800. Based on our discussion in previous sections, a portfolio that has the present value of $800 invested in a risk-free asset and ($1,200 − 800)/(200 − $0) = 2 call options exactly replicates the assets of the firm.

The present value of $800 at the risk-free rate of 12.5 percent is $800/1.125 = $711.11. This amount, plus the value of the two call options, is equal to $950, the current value of the firm:

$$\$950 = 2 \times C_0 + \$711.11$$

$$C_0 = \$119.44$$

Since the call option in this case is actually the firm's equity, the value of the equity is $119.44. The value of the debt is thus $950 − 119.44 = $830.56.

Finally, since the debt has a $1,000 face value and a current value of $830.55, the interest rate is ($1,000/$830.55) − 1 = 20.4%. This exceeds the risk-free rate, of course, since the debt is now risky.

Example 20.3 Equity as a Call Option

Swenson Software has a pure discount debt issue with a face value of $100. The issue is due in a year. At that time, the assets of the firm will be worth either $55 or $160, depending on the sales success of Swenson's latest product. The assets of the firm are currently worth $110. If the risk-free rate is 10 percent, what is the value of the equity in Swenson? The value of the debt? The interest rate on the debt?

To replicate the assets of the firm, we first need to invest the present value of $55 in the risk-free asset. This costs $55/1.10 = $50. If the assets turn out

In Their Own Words...

Robert C. Merton on Applications of Options Analysis

Organized markets for trading options on stocks, fixed-income securities, currencies, financial futures, and a variety of commodities are among the most successful financial innovations of the past two decades. Commercial success is not, however, the reason that option pricing analysis has become one of the cornerstones of finance theory. Instead, its central role derives from the fact that optionlike structures permeate virtually every part of the field.

From the first observation nearly 20 years ago, that leveraged equity has the same payoff structure as a call option, option pricing theory has provided an integrated approach to the pricing of corporate liabilities, including all types of debt, preferred stocks, warrants, and rights. The same methodology has been applied to the pricing of pension fund insurance, deposit insurance, and other government loan guarantees. It has also been used to evaluate various labor-contract provisions such as wage floors and guaranteed employment including tenure.

A significant and recent extension of options analysis has been to the evaluation of operating or "real" options in capital budgeting decisions. For example, a facility that can use various inputs to produce various outputs provides the firm with operating options not available from a specialized facility that uses a fixed set of inputs to produce a single type of output. Similarly, choosing among technologies with different proportions of fixed and variable costs can be viewed as evaluating alternative options to change production levels, including abandonment of the project. Research and development projects are essentially options to either establish new markets, expand market share, or reduce production costs. As these examples suggest, options analysis is especially well-suited to the task of evaluating the "flexibility" components of projects. These are precisely the components whose values are especially difficult to estimate by using traditional capital budgeting techniques.

Robert C. Merton holds the George F. Baker Chair of Finance at Harvard University. He previously held the J.C. Penney Chair of Finance at MIT. He has made major contributions to financial theory and practice through his work on pricing options and other contingent claims and through his work on risk and uncertainty.

---

to be worth $160, then the option is worth $160 − 100 = $60. Our risk-free asset will be worth $55, so we need ($160 − 55)/$60 = 1.75 call options. Since the firm is currently worth $110, we have:

$$\$110 = 1.75 \times C_0 + \$50$$

$$C_0 = \$34.29$$

The equity is thus worth $34.29; the debt is worth $110 − 34.29 = $75.71. The interest rate on the debt is about ($100/$75.71) − 1 = 32.1%. ∎

CONCEPT QUESTIONS

20.4a Why do we say that the equity in a leveraged firm is effectively a call option on the firm's assets?

20.4b All other things being the same, would the stockholders of a firm prefer to increase or decrease the volatility of the firm's return on assets? Why? What about the bondholders? Give an intuitive explanation.

A **warrant** is a corporate security that looks a lot like a call option. It gives the holder the right, but not the obligation, to buy shares of common stock directly from a company at a fixed price for a given time period. Each warrant specifies the number of shares of stock that the holder can buy, the exercise price, and the expiration date.

warrant

A security that gives the holder the right to purchase shares of stock at a fixed price over a given period of time.

The differences in contractual features between the call options that trade on the Chicago Board Options Exchange and warrants are relatively minor. Warrants usually have much longer maturity periods, however. In fact, some warrants are actually perpetual and have no fixed expiration date.

Warrants are often called *sweeteners* or *equity kickers* because they are usually issued in combination with privately placed loans or bonds.[4] Throwing in some warrants is a way of making the deal a little more attractive to the lender, and it is a very common practice. Also, warrants have been listed and traded on the NYSE since April 13, 1970. As of the end of 1990, there were 17 issues of warrants listed with a combined market value of $2.192 billion.[5]

In most cases, warrants are attached to the bonds when issued. The loan agreement will state whether the warrants are detachable from the bond. Usually, the warrant can be detached immediately and sold by the holder as a separate security.

For example, Navistar International is one of the world's largest manufacturers and marketers of diesel-powered trucks and replacement parts.[6] On April 14, 1985, Navistar raised $200 million by publicly issuing a combination of notes and warrants. Forty warrants were attached to each 13.25 percent senior note due in 1995. The holder was given the right to use each warrant to buy one share of common stock for $9 on any date up to and including December 31, 1990. Each unit, "note plus 40 warrants," sold for $1,000 when initially issued.

As is usually the case, the Navistar warrants were detachable, which means that they could be traded separately soon after the issue of notes and warrants was completed. The warrants first traded on July 8, 1985, when more than 1,000 of them changed hands. The closing price for the warrants was $3.50, and the price for Navistar common stock was $8.50.

Just as we had with call options, the lower limit on the value of a warrant is zero if Navistar's stock price is below $9 per share. If the price of Navistar's common stock rises above $9 per share, the lower limit is the stock price minus $9. The upper limit is the price of Navistar's common stock. A warrant to buy one share of common stock cannot sell at a price above the price of the underlying common stock.

The Difference between Warrants and Call Options

As we have explained, from the holder's point of view, warrants are very similar to call options on common stock. A warrant, like a call option, gives its

---

[4]Warrants are also issued with publicly distributed bonds and new issues of common stock.

[5]New York Stock Exchange, *Fact Book 1991*.

[6]Before February 1, 1986, the company was called International Harvester.

holder the right to buy common stock at a specified price. From the firm's point of view, however, a warrant is very different from a call option sold on the company's common stock.

The most important difference between call options and warrants is that call options are issued by individuals and warrants are issued by firms. When a call option is exercised, one investor buys stock from another investor. The company is not involved. When a warrant is exercised, the firm must issue new shares of stock. Each time a warrant is exercised, then, the firm receives some cash and the number of shares outstanding increases.

To illustrate, suppose the Endrun Company issues a warrant giving holders the right to buy one share of common stock at $25. Further suppose the warrant is exercised. Endrun must print one new stock certificate. In exchange for the stock certificate, it receives $25 from the holder.

In contrast, when a call option is exercised, there is no change in the number of shares outstanding. Suppose Ms. Enger purchases a call option on the common stock of the Endrun Company from Mr. Swift. The call option gives Ms. Enger the right to buy one share of common stock of the Endrun Company for $25.

If Ms. Enger chooses to exercise the call option, Mr. Swift is obligated to give her one share of Endrun's common stock in exchange for $25. If Mr. Swift does not already own a share, he must go into the stock market and buy one.

The call option amounts to a side bet between Ms. Enger and Mr. Swift on the value of the Endrun Company's common stock. When a call option is exercised, one investor gains and the other loses. The total number of shares outstanding of the Endrun Company remains constant, and no new funds are made available to the company.

Warrants and the Value of the Firm

Since the company is not involved in buying or selling options, puts and calls have no effect on the value of the firm. However, the firm is the original seller when warrants are involved, and warrants do affect the value of the firm. We compare the effect of call options and warrants in this section.

Imagine that Mr. Gould and Ms. Rockefeller are two investors who together purchase six ounces of platinum at a price of $500 per ounce. The total investment is 6 × $500 = $3,000, and each of the investors puts up half. They incorporate, print two stock certificates, and name the firm the GR Company. Each certificate represents a one-half claim to the platinum, and Mr. Gould and Ms. Rockefeller each own one certificate. The net effect of all of this is that Mr. Gould and Ms. Rockefeller have formed a company with platinum as its only asset.

The Effect of a Call Option   Suppose Mr. Gould later decides to sell a call option to Mrs. Fiske. The call option gives Mrs. Fiske the right to buy Mr. Gould's share for $1,800 in one year.

At the end of the year, platinum is selling for $700 per ounce, so the value of the GR Company is 6 × $700 = $4,200. Each share is worth $4,200/2 = $2,100. Mrs. Fiske will exercise her option, and Mr. Gould must turn over his stock certificate and receive $1,800.

How would the firm be affected by the exercise? The number of shares won't be affected. There will still be two of them, now owned by Ms. Rockefeller and Mrs. Fiske. The shares are still worth $2,100. The only thing that happens is that, when Mrs. Fiske exercises her option, she profits by $2,100 − 1,800 = $300. Mr. Gould loses by the same amount.

The Effect of a Warrant   This story changes if a warrant is issued. Suppose that Mr. Gould does not sell a call option to Mrs. Fiske. Instead, Mr. Gould and Ms. Rockefeller get together and decide to issue a warrant and sell it to Mrs. Fiske. This means that, in effect, the GR Company decides to issue a warrant.

The warrant will give Mrs. Fiske the right to receive a share of stock in the company at an exercise price of $1,800. If Mrs. Fiske decides to exercise the warrant, the firm will issue another stock certificate and give it to Mrs. Fiske in exchange for $1,800.

Suppose again that platinum rises to $700 an ounce. The firm will be worth $4,200. Further suppose that Mrs. Fiske exercises her warrant. Two things will occur:

1. Mrs. Fiske will pay $1,800 to the firm.
2. The firm will print one stock certificate and give it to Mrs. Fiske. The stock certificate will represent a one-third claim on the assets of the firm.

Mrs. Fiske's one-third share seems to be worth only $4,200/3 = $1,400. This is not correct, because we have to add the $1,800 contributed to the firm by Mrs. Fiske. The value of the firm increases by this amount, so:

New value of firm = Value of platinum + Contribution to the firm
by Mrs. Fiske

= $4,200 + 1,800

= $6,000

Because Mrs. Fiske has a one-third claim on the firm's value, her share is worth $6,000/3 = $2,000. By exercising the warrant, Mrs. Fiske gains $2,000 − 1,800 = $200. This is illustrated in Table 20.3.

When the warrant is exercised, the exercise money goes to the firm. Since Mrs. Fiske ends up owning one third of the firm, she effectively gets back one third of what she pays in. Since she really gives up only two thirds of $1,800 to buy the stock, the effective exercise price is $2/3 \times \$1,800 = \$1,200$.

Mrs. Fiske effectively pays out $1,200 to obtain a one-third interest in the assets of the firm (the platinum). This is worth $4,200/3 = $1,400. Mrs. Fiske's gain, from this perspective, is $1,400 − 1,200 = $200 (exactly what we calculated earlier).

Warrant Value and Stock Value   What is the value of the common stock of a firm that has issued warrants? Let's look at the *market* value of the GR

Table 20.3		Value of Firm if Price of Platinum per Ounce	
Effect of a call option versus a warrant on the GR Company		$700	$600
	No Warrant or Call Option		
Mr. Gould's share		$2,100	$1,800
Ms. Rockefeller's share		2,100	1,800
Firm value		$4,200	$3,600
	Call Option		
Mr. Gould's claim		$ 0	$1,800
Ms. Rockefeller's claim		2,100	1,800
Mrs. Fiske's claim		2,100	0
Firm value		$4,200	$3,600
	*Warrant**		
Mr. Gould's share		$2,000	$1,800
Ms. Rockefeller's share		2,000	1,800
Mrs. Fiske's share		2,000	0
Firm		$6,000	$3,600

*If the price of platinum is $700, the value of the firm is equal to the value of six ounces of platinum plus the excess dollars paid into the firm by Mrs. Fiske. This amount is $4,200 + 1,800 = $6,000.

Company just before and just after the exercise of Mrs. Fiske's warrant. Just after exercise, the balance sheet looks like this:

Cash	$1,800	Stock	$6,000
Platinum	4,200	(3 shares)	
Total	$6,000	Total	$6,000

As we saw above, each share of stock is worth $6,000/3 = $2,000.

Since whoever holds the warrant will profit by $200 when the warrant is exercised, the warrant is worth $200 just before expiration. The balance sheet for the GR Company just before expiration is thus:

Platinum	$4,200	Warrant	$ 200
		Stock (2 shares)	4,000
Total	$4,200	Total	$4,200

We calculate the value of the stock as the value of the assets ($4,200) less the value of the warrant ($200).

Notice that the value of each share just before expiration is $4,000/2 = $2,000 just as it is after expiration. The value of each share of stock is thus not changed by the exercise of the warrant. There is no dilution of share value from the exercise.

Earnings Dilution   Warrants and (as we shall see) convertible bonds frequently cause the number of shares to increase. This happens (1) when the warrants are exercised and (2) when the bonds are converted. As we have seen, this increase does not lower the per-share value of the stock. However, it does cause the firm's net income to be spread over a larger number of shares, and, thus, earnings per share decrease.

Firms with significant amounts of warrants and convertible issues outstanding will generally calculate and report earnings per share on a *fully diluted basis*. This means that the calculation is based on the number of shares that would be outstanding if all the warrants were exercised and all the convertibles were converted. Since this increases the number of shares, fully diluted EPS will be lower than EPS calculated only on the basis of shares actually outstanding.

⌐ **CONCEPT QUESTIONS**
20.5a What is a warrant?
20.5b Why are warrants different from call options?

CONVERTIBLE BONDS ⎮ 20.6

A **convertible bond** is similar to a bond with warrants. The most important difference is that a bond with warrants can be separated into distinct securities (a bond and some warrants), but a convertible bond cannot be. A convertible bond gives the holder the right to exchange the bond for a fixed number of shares of stock anytime up to and including the maturity date of the bond.

Preferred stock can frequently be converted into common stock. A convertible preferred stock is the same as a convertible bond except that it has an infinite maturity date.[7]

convertible bond
A bond that can be exchanged for a fixed number of shares of stock for a specified amount of time.

Features of a Convertible Bond

The basic features of a convertible bond can be illustrated by examining a particular issue. On June 24, 1986, Crazy Eddie, a New York retailer of home entertainment and consumer electronic products, issued $72 million of 6 percent convertible subordinated debentures due in 2011. It planned to use the proceeds to add new stores to its chain. In some respects, the bonds were like typical debentures. For example, they had a sinking fund and were callable after two years.

The particular feature that made the Crazy Eddie bonds interesting was that they were convertible into the common stock of Crazy Eddie anytime before the maturity at a **conversion price** of $46.25 per share. Since each bond

conversion price
The dollar amount of a bond's par value that is exchangeable for one share of stock.

---

[7]The dividends paid are, of course, not tax deductible for the corporation. Interest paid on a convertible bond is tax deductible.

had a face value of $1,000, this means that the holder of a Crazy Eddie convertible bond could exchange that bond for $1,000/$46.25 = 21.62 shares of Crazy Eddie common stock. The number of shares received for each debenture, 21.62 in this example, is called the **conversion ratio.**

conversion ratio

The number of shares per $1,000 bond received for conversion into stock.

When Crazy Eddie issued its convertible bonds, its common stock was trading at $38 per share. The conversion price of $46.25 was thus ($46.25 − 38)/$38 = 22% higher than the actual common stock price. This 22 percent is called the **conversion premium.** It reflects the fact that the conversion option in Crazy Eddie convertible bonds is out of the money. This conversion premium is typical.

conversion premium

Difference between the conversion price and the current stock price divided by the current stock price.

Value of a Convertible Bond

Even though the conversion feature of the convertible bond cannot be detached like a warrant, the value of the bond can still be decomposed into its bond value and the value of the conversion feature. We discuss how this is done next.[8]

straight bond value

The value of a convertible bond if it could not be converted into common stock.

Straight Bond Value   The **straight bond value** is what the convertible bond would sell for if it could not be converted into common stock. This value will depend on the general level of interest rates on debentures and on the default risk of the issuer.

Suppose that straight debentures issued by Crazy Eddie are rated A, and A-rated bonds are priced to yield 10 percent on June 24, 1986. The straight bond value of Crazy Eddie convertible bonds can be determined by discounting the $60 annual coupon payment and maturity value at 10 percent, just as we did in Chapter 6:

$$\text{Straight bond value} = \$60 \times (1 - 1/1.10^{25})/.10 + \$1,000/1.10^{25}$$

$$= \$544.62 + 92.30$$

$$= \$636.92$$

The straight bond value of a convertible bond is a minimum value in the sense that the bond is always worth at least this amount. As we discuss, it will usually be worth more.

conversion value

The value of a convertible bond if it was immediately converted into common stock.

Conversion Value   The **conversion value** of a convertible bond is what the bond would be worth if it were immediately converted into common stock. This value is computed by multiplying the current price of the stock by the number of shares that will be received when the bond is converted.

---

[8]Our coverage is necessarily brief. See J. C. Van Horne, *Financial Market Rates and Flows,* 2nd ed. (Englewood Cliffs, N.J.: Prentice Hall, 1987), Chapter 11 for a similar, in-depth treatment. See also R. A. Brealey and S. C. Myers, *Principles of Corporate Finance,* 3rd ed. (New York: McGraw-Hill, 1988), Chapter 22.

For example, on June 24, 1986, each Crazy Eddie convertible bond could be converted into 21.62 shares of Crazy Eddie common stock. Crazy Eddie common was selling for $38. Thus, the conversion value was 21.62 × $38 = $821.56.

A convertible cannot sell for less than its conversion value or an arbitrage exists. If Crazy Eddie's convertible sold for less than $821.56, investors would buy the bonds and convert them into common stock and sell the stock. The arbitrage profit would be the difference between the value of the stock and the bond's conversion value.

Floor Value for a Convertible   As we have seen, convertible bonds have two *floor values:* the straight bond value and the conversion value. The minimum value of a convertible bond is given by the greater of these two values. For the Crazy Eddie issue, the conversion value is $821.56 while the straight bond value is $636.92. At a minimum, this bond is thus worth $821.56.

Figure 20.3 plots the minimum value of a convertible bond against the value of the stock. The conversion value is determined by the value of the firm's underlying common stock. As the value of common stock rises and falls, the conversion value rises and falls with it. For example, if the value of Crazy Eddie's common stock increases by $1, the conversion value of its convertible bonds will increase by $21.62.

In Figure 20.3, we have implicitly assumed that the convertible bond is default-free. In this case, the straight bond value does not depend on the stock price, so it is plotted as a horizontal line. Given the straight bond value, the minimum value of the convertible depends on the value of the stock. When this is low, the minimum value of a convertible is most significantly influenced by the underlying value as straight debt. However, when the value of the firm is very high, the value of a convertible bond is mostly determined by the underlying conversion value. This is also illustrated in Figure 20.3.

Option Value   The value of a convertible bond will always exceed the straight bond value and the conversion value unless the firm is in default or the bondholders are forced to convert. The reason is that holders of convertibles do not have to convert immediately. Instead, by waiting, they can take advantage of whichever is greater in the future, the straight bond value or the conversion value.

This option to wait has value, and it raises the value of the convertible bond over its floor value. The total value of the convertible is thus equal to the sum of the floor value and the option value. This is illustrated in Figure 20.4. Notice the similarity between this picture and the representation of the value of a call option in Figure 20.2 above.

CONCEPT QUESTIONS

20.6a What are the conversion ratio, the conversion price, and the conversion premium?

20.6b What three elements make up the value of a convertible bond?

Figure 20.3

Minimum value of a
convertible bond versus
the value of the stock for
a given interest rate

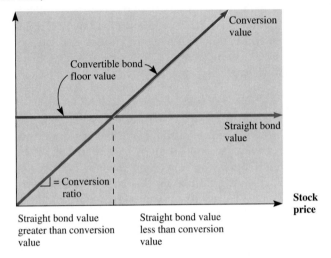

As shown, the minimum or "floor" value of a convertible bond is either its
straight bond value or its conversion value, whichever is greater.

Figure 20.4

Value of a convertible
bond versus value of the
stock for a given interest
rate

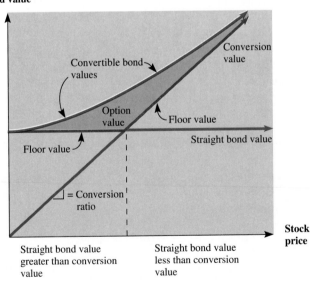

As shown, the value of a convertible bond is the sum of its floor value and its
option value (highlighted region).

REASONS FOR ISSUING WARRANTS AND CONVERTIBLES | 20.7

Until recently, bonds with warrants and convertible bonds were not well understood. Surveys of financial executives have provided the most popular "textbook" reasons for warrants and convertibles. Here are two of them:

1. They allow companies to issue "cheap" bonds by attaching sweeteners to the bonds. Sweeteners allow the coupon rate on convertibles and bonds with warrants to be set below the market rates on straight bonds.
2. They give companies the chance to issue common stock at a premium over current prices in the future. In this way, convertibles and bonds with warrants represent deferred sales of common stock at relatively high prices.

These justifications for convertibles and bonds with warrants are frequently mixed into "free lunch" explanations.

The Free Lunch Story

Suppose the RWJ Company can issue subordinated debentures at 10 percent. It can also issue convertible bonds at 6 percent with a conversion value of $800. The conversion value means that the holders can convert a convertible bond into 40 shares of common stock, which currently trades at $20.

A company treasurer who believes in free lunches might argue that convertible bonds should be issued because they represent a cheaper source of financing than *either* subordinated bonds or common stock. The treasurer will point out that, if the company does poorly and the stock price does not rise above $20, the convertible bondholders will not convert the bonds into common stock. In this case, the company will have obtained debt financing at below market rates by attaching worthless equity kickers.

On the other hand, if the firm does well, then the bondholders will convert. The company will issue 40 shares. Since the company will receive a bond with face value of $1,000 in exchange for issuing 40 shares of common stock, the conversion price is $25.

Effectively, if the bondholders convert, the company will have issued common stock at $25 per share. This is 25 percent above the current common stock price of $20, so the company gets more money per share of stock. Thus, the treasurer happily points out, regardless of whether the company does well or poorly, convertible bonds are the cheapest form of financing. RWJ can't lose.

The problem with this story is that we can turn it around and create an argument showing that issuing warrants and convertibles is always a disaster. We call this the "expensive lunch" story.

The Expensive Lunch Story

Suppose we take a closer look at the RWJ Company and its proposal to sell convertible bonds. If the company performs badly and the stock price falls, bondholders will not exercise their conversion option. This suggests the RWJ Company should have issued common stock when prices were high. By issuing convertible bonds, the company lost a valuable opportunity.

On the other hand, if the company does well and the stock price rises, bondholders will convert. Suppose the stock price rises to $40. In this case, the bondholders convert and the company is forced to sell stock worth $40 for an effective price of only $25. The new shareholders benefit. Put another way, if the company prospers, it would have been better to have issued straight debt so that the gains would not have to be shared.

Whether the convertible bonds are converted or not, the company will have done worse than with straight bonds or new common stock. Issuing convertible bonds is a terrible idea.

Which is correct: the free lunch story or the expensive lunch story?

A Reconciliation

Reconciling our two stories requires only that we remember our central goal: Increase the wealth of the existing shareholders. Thus, with 20-20 hindsight, issuing convertible bonds will turn out to be worse than issuing straight bonds and better than issuing common stock if the company prospers. The reason is that the prosperity has to be shared with bondholders after they convert.

In contrast, if a company does poorly, issuing convertible bonds will turn out to be better than issuing straight bonds and worse than issuing common stock. The reason is that the firm will have benefited from the lower coupon payments on the convertible bond.

Both of our stories thus have a grain of truth; we just need to combine them. This is done in Table 20.4. Exactly the same arguments would be used in a comparison of a straight debt issue versus a bond/warrant package.

⌐CONCEPT QUESTIONS

20.7a What is wrong with the view that it is cheaper to issue a bond with a warrant or a convertible feature because the required coupon is lower?

20.7b What is wrong with the theory that says a convertible can be a good security to issue because it can be a way to sell stock at a price that is higher than the current stock price?

Table 20.4		If Firm Does Poorly	If Firm Prospers
The case for and against convertibles		Low stock price and no conversion	High stock price and conversion
	Convertible bonds issued instead of straight bonds	Cheap financing because coupon rate is lower (good outcome)	Expensive financing because bonds are converted, which dilutes existing equity (bad outcome)
	Convertible bonds issued instead of common stock	Expensive financing because the firm could have issued common stock at high prices (bad outcome)	Cheap financing because firm issues stock at high prices when bonds are converted (good outcome)

OTHER OPTIONS | 20.8

We've discussed two of the more common optionlike securities, warrants, and convertibles. Options appear in many other places. We briefly describe a few such cases in this section.

The Call Provision on a Bond

As we discussed in Chapter 12, most corporate bonds are callable. A call provision allows a corporation to buy the bonds at a fixed price for a fixed period of time. In other words, the corporation has a call option on the bonds. The cost of the call feature to the corporation is the cost of the option.

Convertible bonds are almost always callable. This means that a convertible bond is really a package of three securities: a straight bond, a call option held by the bondholder (the conversion feature), and a call option held by the corporation (the call provision).

Put Bonds

Put bonds are a relatively new innovation. The owner of a put bond has the right to force the issuer to repurchase the bond at a fixed price for a fixed period of time. Such a bond is a combination of a straight bond and a put option, hence the name.

For example, in Chapter 12, we briefly discussed a LYON, a liquid yield option note. This is a callable, putable, convertible, pure discount bond. It is thus a package of a pure discount bond, two call options, and a put option.

The Green Shoe Provision

In Chapter 13, we mentioned that underwriters are frequently given the right to purchase additional shares of stock from a firm in an initial public offering (IPO). We called this the *Green Shoe provision*. We now recognize that this provision is simply a call option (or, more accurately, a warrant) granted to the underwriter. The value of the option is an indirect form of compensation paid to the underwriter.

Insurance and Loan Guarantees

Insurance of one kind or another is a financial feature of everyday life. Most of the time, having insurance is like having a put option. For example, suppose you have $1 million in fire insurance on an office building. One night, your building burns down, reducing its value to nothing. In this case, you would effectively exercise your put option and force the insurer to pay you $1 million for something worth very little.

Loan guarantees are a form of insurance. If you loan money to someone and they default, then, with a guaranteed loan, you can collect from someone else, often the government. For example, when you loan money to a commercial bank (by making a deposit), your loan is guaranteed (up to $100,000) by the government.

In two well-known cases of loan guarantees, Lockheed Corporation in 1971 and Chrysler Corporation in 1980 were saved from impending financial doom when the U.S. government came to the rescue by agreeing to guarantee new loans. Under the guarantees, if Lockheed or Chrysler had defaulted, the lenders could have obtained the full value of their claims from the U.S. government. From the lender's point of view, the loans were as risk-free as Treasury bonds. These guarantees enabled Lockheed and Chrysler to borrow large amounts of cash and to get through difficult times.

Loan guarantees are not cost-free. The U.S. government, with a loan guarantee, has provided a put option to the holders of risky bonds. The value of the put option is the cost of the loan guarantee. This point has been made abundantly clear by the collapse of the savings and loan industry. The final cost to U.S. taxpayers of making good on the guaranteed deposits in these institutions is still unknown as this is written, but it is a staggering amount and seems certain to exceed $200 billion by a considerable margin.

⌐CONCEPT QUESTIONS

20.8a Explain how car insurance acts like a put option.

20.8b Explain why U.S. government loan guarantees are not free.

20.9 | SUMMARY AND CONCLUSIONS

This chapter described the basics of option valuation and discussed optionlike corporate securities. In it, we saw that:

1. Options are contracts giving the right, but not the obligation, to buy and sell underlying assets at a fixed price during a specified time period.

    The most familiar options are puts and calls involving shares of stock. These options give the holder the right, but not the obligation, to sell (the put option) or buy (the call option) shares of common stock at a given price.

    As we discussed, the value of any option depends only on five factors:

    a. The price of the underlying asset.

    b. The exercise price.

    c. The expiration date.

    d. The interest rate on risk-free bonds.

    e. The volatility of the underlying asset's value.

2. A warrant gives the holder the right to buy shares of common stock directly from the company at a fixed exercise price for a given period of time. Typically, warrants are issued in a package with privately placed bonds. Afterward, they often can be detached and traded separately.

3. A convertible bond is a combination of a straight bond and a call option. The holder can give up the bond in exchange for a fixed number of shares of stock. The minimum value of a convertible bond is given by its straight bond value or its conversion value, whichever is greater.

4. Convertible bonds, warrants, and call options are similar, but important differences do exist:

    a. Warrants and convertible securities are issued by corporations. Call options are issued by and traded between individual investors.

    b. Warrants are usually issued privately and are combined with a bond. In most cases, the warrants can be detached immediately after the issue. In some cases, warrants are issued with preferred stock, with common stock, or in publicly traded bond issues.

    c. Warrants and call options are exercised for cash. The holder of a warrant gives the company cash and receives new shares of the company's stock. The holder of a call option gives another individual cash in exchange for common stock. Convertible bonds are exercised by exchange; the individual gives the company back the bond in exchange for stock.

5. Many other corporate securities have option features. Bonds with call provisions, bonds with put provisions, and bonds backed by a loan guarantee are just a few examples.

Key Terms

option 711	intrinsic value 718
exercising the option 712	warrant 729
striking price or exercise price 712	convertible bond 733
expiration date 712	conversion price 733
American options 712	conversion ratio 734
European options 712	conversion premium 734
call option 712	straight bond value 734
put option 712	conversion value 734

Chapter Review Problems and Self-Test

20.1   **Value of a Call Option**   Stock in the Barsoom Corporation is currently selling for $20 per share. In one year, the price will either be $20 or $30. T-bills with one year to maturity are paying 10 percent. What is the value of a call option with a $20 exercise price? A $24 exercise price?

20.2   **Convertible Bonds**   The Kau Corporation, publisher of *Gourmand* magazine, has a convertible bond issue that is currently selling in the market for $900. Each bond can be exchanged for 100 shares of stock at the holder's option.

The bond has a 6 percent coupon, payable annually, and it will mature in 12 years. Kau's debt is BBB-rated. Debt with this rating is priced to yield 12 percent. Stock in Kau is trading at $6 per share.

What is the conversion ratio on this bond? The conversion price? The conversion premium? What is the floor value of the bond? What is its option value?

Answers to Self-Test Problems

20.1 With a $20 exercise price, the option can't finish out of the money (it can finish "at the money" if the stock price is $20). We can replicate the stock by investing the present value of $20 in T-bills and buying one call option. Buying the T-bill will cost $20/1.1 = $18.18.

   If the stock ends up at $20, the call option will be worth zero and the T-bill will pay $20. If the stock ends up at $30, the T-bill will again pay $20, and the option will be worth $30 − 20 = $10, so the package is worth $30. Since the T-bill/call option combination exactly duplicates the payoff on the stock, it has to be worth $20 or arbitrage is possible. Using the notation from the chapter, we can calculate the value of the call option:

$$S_0 = C_0 + E/(1 + R_f)$$
$$\$20 = C_0 + \$18.18$$
$$C_0 = \$1.82$$

   With the $24 exercise price, we start by investing the present value of the lower stock price in T-bills. This guarantees us $20 when the stock price is $20. If the stock price is $30, then the option is worth $30 − 24 = $6. We have $20 from our T-bill, so we need $10 from the options in order to match the stock. Since each option is worth $6 in this case, we need to buy $10/$6 = 1.67 call options. Notice that the difference in the possible stock prices is $10 ($\Delta S$) and the difference in the possible option prices is $6 ($\Delta C$), so $\Delta S/\Delta C = 1.67$.

   To complete the calculation, the present value of the $20 plus 1.67 call options has to be $20 to prevent arbitrage, so:

$$\$20 = 1.67 \times C_0 + \$20/1.1$$
$$C_0 = \$1.82/1.67$$
$$= \$1.09$$

20.2 Since each bond can be exchanged for 100 shares, the conversion ratio is 100. The conversion price is the face value of the bond ($1,000) divided by the conversion ratio, $1,000/100 = $10. The conversion premium is the percentage difference between the current price and the conversion price, ($10 − 6)/$6 = 67%.

   The floor value of the bond is the greater of its straight bond value or its conversion value. Its conversion value is what the bond is worth if it is immediately converted: 100 × $6 = $600. The straight bond value is what the bond would be worth if it were not convertible. The annual coupon is $60, and the bond matures in 12 years. At a 12 percent required return, the straight bond value is:

$$\text{Straight bond value} = \$60 \times (1 - 1/1.12^{12})/.12 + \$1,000/1.12^{12}$$
$$= \$371.66 + 256.68$$
$$= \$628.34$$

This exceeds the conversion value, so the floor value of the bond is $628.34. Finally, the option value is the value of the convertible in excess of its floor value. Since the bond is selling for $900, the option value is:

$$\text{Option value} = \$900 - 628.34$$

$$= \$271.66$$

Questions and Problems

1. **Basic Properties of Options**   What is a call option? A put option? Under what circumstances might you want to buy each? Which one has greater *potential* profit?

2. **Calls versus Puts**   Complete the following sentence for each of these investors:
   a. A buyer of call options
   b. A buyer of put options
   c. A seller of call options
   d. A seller of put options
      "The (buyer/seller) of a (put/call) option (pays/receives) money for the (right/obligation) to (buy/sell) a specified asset at a fixed price for a fixed length of time."

3. **Arbitrage and Options**   You notice that shares of stock in the Masson Corp. are going for $80 per share. Call options with an exercise price of $60 per share are selling for $15. What's wrong here?

4. **Defining Intrinsic Value**   What is the intrinsic value of a call option? How do we interpret this value?

5. **Defining Intrinsic Value**   What is the value of a put option at maturity? Based on your answer, what is the intrinsic value of a put option?

6. **Understanding Option Quotes**   Use the following option quote to answer the questions below.

Option & NY Close	Strike Price	Calls—Last			Puts—Last		
		Jun	Jul	Aug	Jun	Jul	Aug
Dune							
50	40	8	11½	14	4	5½	8

   a. Are the call options in the money? What is the intrinsic value of a Dune Co. call option?
   b. One of the options is clearly mispriced. Which one? At a minimum, what should it sell for? Explain how you could profit from the mispricing.
   c. This is a little harder: What is the most the mispriced option should sell for? Explain.

7.   **Calculating Payoffs**   Use the following option quote to answer the questions below.

Option & NY Close	Strike Price	Calls—Last			Puts—Last		
		Jun	Jul	Aug	Jun	Jul	Aug
Besley							
80	90	2	2⅞	4	12	13⅞	16

   a. Suppose you buy 50 July 90 call contracts. How much will you pay, ignoring commissions?

   b. In part *a*, suppose that Besley is selling for $100 per share on the expiration date. What are your options worth?

   c. Suppose you buy 10 Aug put contracts. What is your maximum gain? On the expiration date, Besley is selling for $75 per share. What are your options worth?

   d. In part *c*, suppose you *sold* 10 Aug put contracts. What is your net gain or loss if Besley is selling for $75? For $100? What is the break-even price, that is, the stock price that results in a profit of zero?

8.   **Option Value and Firm Risk**   True or false: "The unsystematic risk of a share of stock is irrelevant in valuing the stock since it can be diversified away. It is also irrelevant for valuing a call option on the stock." Explain.

9.   **Calls versus Puts**   Stock in the Zinfidel Co. currently sells for $20 per share. If a put option and a call option are available with $20 exercise prices, which do you think will sell for more, the put or the call? Explain.

10.   **Option Value and Firm Risk**   If the risk of a stock increases, what is likely to happen to the price of call options on the stock? To the price of put options? Why?

11.   **Calculating Intrinsic Value**   T-bills currently yield 8 percent. Stock in the Nostradamus Corporation is currently selling for $28 per share. There is no possibility that the stock will be worth less than $20 in one year.

   a. What is the value of a call option with a $20 exercise price?

   b. What is the value of a call option with a $10 exercise price?

   c. What is the value of a put option with a $20 exercise price?

12.   **Option Value and Interest Rates**   Suppose that the interest rate on T-bills suddenly and unexpectedly rises. All other things being the same, what is the impact on call option values? On put option values?

13.   **Calculating Option Values**   The price of Schome Corp. stock will be either $60 or $80 at the end of the year. Call options are available with one year to expiration. T-bills currently yield 7 percent.

   a. Suppose the current price of Schome stock is $65. What is the value of the call option if the exercise price is $55 per share?

   b. Suppose that the exercise price is $65 in part *a* above. What would the value of the call option be?

14. **Using the Pricing Equation**   A one-year call *contract* on Dilleep Co. stock sells for $1,000. In one year, the stock will be worth $20 or $40 per share. The exercise price on the call option is $25. What is the current value of the stock if the risk-free rate is 10 percent?

15. **Equity as an Option**   The Su-Jane Company's assets are currently worth $800. In a year, they will be worth $600 or $1,000. The risk-free rate is 8 percent. Suppose that Su-Jane has an outstanding debt issue with a face value of $500.
    a. What is the value of the equity?
    b. What is the value of the debt? The interest rate on the debt?
    c. Would the value of the equity go up or down if the risk-free rate were 20 percent? Why? What does your answer illustrate?

16. **Equity as an Option**   The Wansley Corporation has a bond issue with a face value of $1,000 that is coming due in one year. The value of Wansley's assets is currently $1,200. Jimbo Wansley, the CEO, believes that the assets in the firm will be worth $800 or $1,800 in a year. The going rate on one-year T-bills is 6 percent.
    a. What is the value of the equity? The value of the debt?
    b. Suppose that Wansley can reconfigure its existing assets such that the value in a year will be $500 or $2,000. If the current value of the assets is unchanged, would the stockholders favor such a move? Why?

17. **Intuition and Option Value**   Suppose a share of stock sells for $50. The risk-free rate is 8 percent. The price of the stock in one year will be $55 or $60.
    a. What is the value of a call option with a $55 exercise price?
    b. What's wrong here? What would you do?

18. **Calculating Conversion Value**   A $1,000 par convertible debenture has a conversion price for common stock of $180 per share. With the common stock selling at $60, what is the conversion value of the bond?

19. **Convertible Bonds**   The following facts apply to a convertible bond:

Conversion price	$50/share
Coupon rate	9%
Par value	$1,000
Yield on nonconvertible debenture of same quality	10%
Maturity	10 years
Market price of stock	$52/share

    a. What is the minimum price at which the convertible should sell?
    b. What accounts for the premium of the market price of a convertible over the total market value of the common stock into which it can be converted?

20. **Calculating Values for Convertibles**   You have been hired to value a new 30-year callable, convertible bond. The bond has a 6 percent

coupon, payable annually, and its face value is $1,000. The conversion price is $100, and the stock currently sells for $50.12.

a. What is the minimum value of the bond? Comparable nonconvertible bonds are priced to yield 7 percent.

b. What is the conversion value? The conversion premium?

21. **Convertible Calculations** Better Beta, Inc., has a convertible bond issue that is currently selling in the market for $840. Each bond is exchangeable anytime for 50 shares of Better Beta's common stock.

The convertible bond has an 8 percent coupon, payable semiannually. Similar nonconvertible bonds are priced to yield 12 percent. The bond matures in eight years. Stock in Better Beta sells for $16 per share.

a. What are the conversion ratio, conversion price, and conversion premium?

b. What is the straight bond value? The conversion value?

c. In part b, what would the stock price have to be for the conversion value and straight bond value to be equal?

d. What is the option value of the bond?

22. **Intuition and Convertibles** Which of the following two sets of relationships is more typical? Why? At time of issuance of convertible bonds:

	A	B
Offering price of bond	$ 900	$1,000
Bond value (straight debt)	900	950
Conversion value	1,000	900

23. **Calculating Warrant Values** A bond with 20 detachable warrants has just been offered for sale at $1,000. The bond matures in 10 years and has an annual coupon of $80. Each warrant gives the owner the right to purchase four shares of stock at $10 per share. Ordinary bonds (no warrants) of similar quality are priced to yield 11 percent. What is the value of a warrant?

24. **Warrants and Share Value** In the previous question, what is the minimum value of the stock? What is the maximum value?

25. **Warrants and the Balance Sheet** Ringworld Co. has 5,000 shares of stock outstanding. The market value of Ringworld's assets is $700,000. The market value of outstanding debt is $200,000. Ringworld issued 100 warrants some time ago that are about to expire. Each warrant gives the owner the right to purchase 10 shares of stock at a price of $80 per share.

a. What is the price per share of Ringworld stock? What is the value of a warrant?

b. Create a market value balance sheet for just before and just after the warrants expire.

c. What is the effective exercise price on the warrants?

26. Pricing Convertibles   This is a challenge question. You have been hired to value a new 30-year callable, convertible bond. The bond has a 6 percent coupon, payable annually. The conversion price is $100, and the stock currently sells for $50.12. The stock price is expected to grow at 10 percent per year. The bond is callable at $1,100, but, based on prior experience, it won't be called unless the conversion value is $1,300. The required return on this bond is 8 percent. What value would you assign?

Suggested Readings

For a detailed discussion of options read:

Cox, J. S., and M. Rubinstein. *Option Markets.* Englewood Cliffs, N.J.: Prentice Hall, 1985. Section 7.3 analyzes corporate securities.

Our free lunch and expensive lunch stories are adapted from Michael Brennan, who examines the conventional arguments for convertible bonds and offers a new "risk synergy" rationale in:

Brennan, M. "The Case for Convertibles." In *The Revolution in Corporate Finance,* eds. J. M. Stern and D. H. Chew. New York: Basil Blackwell 1986.

Appendix 20A   THE BLACK-SCHOLES OPTION PRICING MODEL

In our discussion of call options in this chapter, we did not discuss the general case where the stock can take on any value *and* the option can finish out of the money. The general approach to valuing a call option falls under the heading of the *Black-Scholes Option Pricing Model (OPM)*, a very famous result in finance. This appendix briefly discusses the Black-Scholes model. Because the underlying development is relatively complex, we will only present the result and then focus on how to use it.

From our earlier discussion, when a t-period call option is certain to finish somewhere in the money, its value today, C_0, is equal to the value of the stock today, S_0, less the present value of the exercise price, $E/(1 + R_f)^t$:

$$C_0 = S_0 - E/(1 + R_f)^t$$

If the option can finish out of the money, then this result needs modifying. Black and Scholes show that the value of a call option in this case is given by:

$$C_0 = S_0 \times N(d_1) - E/(1 + R_f)^t \times N(d_2) \qquad [20A.1]$$

where $N(d_1)$ and $N(d_2)$ are probabilities that must be calculated. This is the Black-Scholes OPM.[9]

In the Black-Scholes model, $N(d_1)$ is the probability that a standardized, normally distributed random variable (widely known as a "z" variable) is less than or equal to d_1, and $N(d_2)$ is the probability of a value that is less than or equal to d_2. Determining these probabilities requires a table such as Table 20A.1.

To illustrate, suppose we were given the following information:

$S_0 = \$100$

$E = \$80$

$R_f = 1\%$ per month

$d_1 = 1.20$

$d_2 = .90$

$t = 9$ months

Based on this information, what is the value of the call option, C_0?

To answer, we need to determine $N(d_1)$ and $N(d_2)$. In Table 20A.1, we first find the row corresponding to a d of 1.20. The corresponding probability,

---

[9]Strictly speaking, the risk-free rate in the Black-Scholes model is the continuously compounded risk-free rate. Continuous compounding is discussed in Chapter 5.

Table 20A.1

Cumulative normal distribution

d	N(d)	d	N(d)	d	N(d)	d	N(d)	d	N(d)	d	N(d)
−3.00	.0013	−1.58	.0571	−0.76	.2236	0.06	.5239	0.86	.8051	1.66	.9515
−2.95	.0016	−1.56	.0594	−0.74	.2297	0.08	.5319	0.88	.8106	1.68	.9535
−2.90	.0019	−1.54	.0618	−0.72	.2358	0.10	.5398	0.90	.8159	1.70	.9554
−2.85	.0022	−1.52	.0643	−0.70	.2420	0.12	.5478	0.92	.8212	1.72	.9573
−2.80	.0026	−1.50	.0668	−0.68	.2483	0.14	.5557	0.94	.8264	1.74	.9591
−2.75	.0030	−1.48	.0694	−0.66	.2546	0.16	.5636	0.96	.8315	1.76	.9608
−2.70	.0035	−1.46	.0721	−0.64	.2611	0.18	.5714	0.98	.8365	1.78	.9625
−2.65	.0040	−1.44	.0749	−0.62	.2676	0.20	.5793	1.00	.8414	1.80	.9641
−2.60	.0047	−1.42	.0778	−0.60	.2743	0.22	.5871	1.02	.8461	1.82	.9656
−2.55	.0054	−1.40	.0808	−0.58	.2810	0.24	.5948	1.04	.8508	1.84	.9671
−2.50	.0062	−1.38	.0838	−0.56	.2877	0.26	.6026	1.06	.8554	1.86	.9686
−2.45	.0071	−1.36	.0869	−0.54	.2946	0.28	.6103	1.08	.8599	1.88	.9699
−2.40	.0082	−1.34	.0901	−0.52	.3015	0.30	.6179	1.10	.8643	1.90	.9713
−2.35	.0094	−1.32	.0934	−0.50	.3085	0.32	.6255	1.12	.8686	1.92	.9726
−2.30	.0107	−1.30	.0968	−0.48	.3156	0.34	.6331	1.14	.8729	1.94	.9738
−2.25	.0122	−1.28	.1003	−0.46	.3228	0.36	.6406	1.16	.8770	1.96	.9750
−2.20	.0139	−1.26	.1038	−0.44	.3300	0.38	.6480	1.18	.8810	1.98	.9761
−2.15	.0158	−1.24	.1075	−0.42	.3373	0.40	.6554	1.20	.8849	2.00	.9772
−2.10	.0179	−1.22	.1112	−0.40	.3446	0.42	.6628	1.22	.8888	2.05	.9798
−2.05	.0202	−1.20	.1151	−0.38	.3520	0.44	.6700	1.24	.8925	2.10	.9821
−2.00	.0228	−1.18	.1190	−0.36	.3594	0.46	.6773	1.26	.8962	2.15	.9842
−1.98	.0239	−1.16	.1230	−0.34	.3669	0.48	.6844	1.28	.8997	2.20	.9861
−1.96	.0250	−1.14	.1271	−0.32	.3745	0.50	.6915	1.30	.9032	2.25	.9878
−1.94	.0262	−1.12	.1314	−0.30	.3821	0.52	.6985	1.32	.9066	2.30	.9893
−1.92	.0274	−1.10	.1357	−0.28	.3897	0.54	.7054	1.34	.9099	2.35	.9906
−1.90	.0287	−1.08	.1401	−0.26	.3974	0.56	.7123	1.36	.9131	2.40	.9918
−1.88	.0301	−1.06	.1446	−0.24	.4052	0.58	.7191	1.38	.9162	2.45	.9929
−1.86	.0314	−1.04	.1492	−0.22	.4129	0.60	.7258	1.40	.9192	2.50	.9938
−1.84	.0329	−1.02	.1539	−0.20	.4207	0.62	.7324	1.42	.9222	2.55	.9946
−1.82	.0344	−1.00	.1587	−0.18	.4286	0.64	.7389	1.44	.9251	2.60	.9953
−1.80	.0359	−0.98	.1635	−0.16	.4365	0.66	.7454	1.46	.9279	2.65	.9960
−1.78	.0375	−0.96	.1685	−0.14	.4443	0.68	.7518	1.48	.9306	2.70	.9965
−1.76	.0392	−0.94	.1736	−0.12	.4523	0.70	.7580	1.50	.9332	2.75	.9970
−1.74	.0409	−0.92	.1788	−0.10	.4602	0.72	.7642	1.52	.9357	2.80	.9974
−1.72	.0427	−0.90	.1841	−0.08	.4681	0.74	.7704	1.54	.9382	2.85	.9978
−1.70	.0446	−0.88	.1894	−0.06	.4761	0.76	.7764	1.56	.9406	2.90	.9981
−1.68	.0465	−0.86	.1949	−0.04	.4841	0.78	.7823	1.58	.9429	2.95	.9984
−1.66	.0485	−0.84	.2005	−0.02	.4920	0.80	.7882	1.60	.9452	3.00	.9986
−1.64	.0505	−0.82	.2061	0.00	.5000	0.82	.7939	1.62	.9474	3.05	.9989
−1.62	.0526	−0.80	.2119	0.02	.5080	0.84	.7996	1.64	.9495		
−1.60	.0548	−0.78	.2177	0.04	.5160						

This table shows the probability [N(d)] of observing a value less than or equal to d. For example, as illustrated, if d is −.24, then N(d) is .4052.

$N(d)$, is .8849, so this is $N(d_1)$. For d_2, the associated probability $N(d_2)$ is .8159. Using the Black-Scholes OPM, the value of the call option is thus:

$$C_0 = S_0 \times N(d_1) - E/(1 + R_f)^t \times N(d_2)$$

$$= \$100 \times .8849 - \$80/1.01^9 \times .8159$$

$$= \$88.49 - 59.68$$

$$= \$28.81$$

As this example illustrates, if we are given values for d_1 and d_2 (and the table), then using the Black-Scholes model is not difficult. In general, however, we will not be given the values of d_1 and d_2, and we must calculate them instead. This requires a little extra effort. The values for d_1 and d_2 for the Black-Scholes OPM are given by:

$$d_1 = [\ln(S_0/E) + (R_f + \tfrac{1}{2} \times \sigma^2) \times t]/(\sigma \times \sqrt{t}) \qquad \text{[20A.2]}$$
$$d_2 = d_1 - \sigma \times \sqrt{t}$$

In these expressions, σ is the standard deviation of the rate of return on the underlying asset. Also, $\ln(S_0/E)$ is the natural logarithm of the current stock price divided by the exercise price (most calculators have a key labeled "ln" to perform this calculation).

The formula for d_1 looks intimidating, but using it is mostly a matter of "plug and chug" with a calculator. To illustrate, suppose we had the following:

$$S_0 = \$70$$

$$E = \$80$$

$$R_f = 1\% \text{ per month}$$

$$\sigma = 2\% \text{ per month}$$

$$t = 9 \text{ months}$$

With these numbers, d_1 is:

$$d_1 = [\ln(S_0/E) + (R_f + \tfrac{1}{2} \times \sigma^2) \times t]/(\sigma \times \sqrt{t})$$

$$= [\ln(.875) + (.01 + \tfrac{1}{2} \times .02^2) \times 9]/(.02 \times 3)$$

$$= [-.1335 + .0918]/.06$$

$$\approx -.70$$

Given this result, d_2 is:

$$d_2 = d_1 - \sigma \times \sqrt{t}$$

$$= -.70 - .02 \times 3$$

$$= -.76$$

Referring to Table 20A.1, the values for $N(d_1)$ and $N(d_2)$ are .2420 and .2236, respectively. The value of the option is thus:

$$C_0 = S_0 \times N(d_1) - E/(1 + R_f)^t \times N(d_2)$$
$$= \$70 \times .2420 - \$80/1.01^9 \times .2236$$
$$= \$.58$$

This may seem a little small, but the stock price would have to rise by \$10 before the option would even be in the money.

Notice that we quoted the risk-free rate, the standard deviation, and the time to maturity in months in this example. We could have used days, weeks, or years as long as we were consistent in quoting all three of these using the same time units.

Appendix Review Problems and Self-Test

20A.1 Black-Scholes OPM: Part I
Calculate the Black-Scholes price for a six-month option given the following:

$S_0 = \$80$

$E = \$70$

$R_f = 10\%$ (per year)

$d_1 = .82$

$d_2 = .74$

20A.2 Black-Scholes OPM: Part II
Calculate the Black-Scholes price for a nine-month option given the following:

$S_0 = \$80$

$E = \$70$

$\sigma = .30$ (per year)

$R_f = 10\%$ (per year)

Answers to Appendix Self-Test Problems

20A.1 We need to evaluate the following:

$$C_0 = 80 \times N(.82) - 70/(1.10)^{.5} \times N(.74)$$

From Table 20A.1, the values for $N(.82)$ and $N(.74)$ are .7939 and .7704, respectively. The value of the option is about \$12.09. Notice that since the interest rate is quoted on an annual basis, we used a t value of .50, representing a half year, in calculating the present value of the exercise price.

20A.2 We first calculate d_1 and d_2:

$$d_1 = [\ln(S_0/E) + (R_f + \tfrac{1}{2} \times \sigma^2) \times t]/(\sigma \times \sqrt{t})$$

$$= [\ln(80/70) + (.10 + \tfrac{1}{2} \times .30^2) \times (.75)]/(.30 \times \sqrt{.75})$$

$$= .9325$$

$$d_2 = d_1 - \sigma \times \sqrt{t}$$

$$= .9325 - .30 \times \sqrt{.75}$$

$$= .6727$$

From Table 20A.1, $N(d_1)$ appears to be roughly .825, and $N(d_2)$ is about .75. Plugging these in, we determine that the option's value is $17.12. Notice again that we used an annual t value of 9/12 = .75 in this case.

Appendix Questions and Problems

1.   Using the OPM   Calculate the Black-Scholes option prices in each of the cases below. The risk-free rate and the variance are quoted in annual terms. Notice that the variance is given, not the standard deviation. The last three may require some thought.

Stock Price	Exercise Price	Risk-Free Rate	Maturity	Variance	Call Price
$50	$60	8%	6 months	.20	
25	15	6	9 months	.30	
50	60	8	6 months	.40	
0	10	9	12 months	.65	
90	30	7	Forever	.22	
50	0	8	6 months	.44	

2.   Equity as an Option and the OPM   Anondezi Co. has a discount bank loan that matures in one year and requires the firm to pay $1,000. The current market value of the firm's assets is $1,200. The annual variance for the firm's return on assets is .30, and the annual risk-free interest rate is 6 percent. Based on the Black-Scholes model, what is the market value of the firm's debt and equity?

Challenge Problem   3.   Changes in Variance and Equity Value   From the previous problem, Anondezi is considering two mutually exclusive investments. Project A has an NPV of $100, and Project B has an NPV of $150. As a result of taking Project A, the variance of the firm's return on assets will increase to .40. If Project B is taken, the variance will fall to .25.
   a. What is the value of the firm's debt and equity if Project A is undertaken? If Project B is undertaken?
   b. Which project do the stockholders prefer? Can you reconcile your answer with the NPV rule?
   c. Suppose the stockholders and bondholders are in fact the same group of investors. Would this affect the answer to part b?
   d. What does this problem suggest about stockholder incentives?

Chapter 21

Mergers and Acquisitions

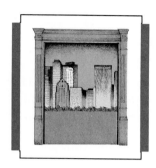

There is no more dramatic or controversial activity in corporate finance than the acquisition of one firm by another or the merger of two firms. It is the stuff of headlines in the financial press, and it is occasionally an embarrassing source of scandal.

The acquisition of one firm by another is, of course, an investment made under uncertainty, and the basic principles of valuation apply. Another firm should be acquired only if doing so generates a positive net present value to the shareholders of the acquiring firm. However, because the NPV of an acquisition candidate can be difficult to determine, mergers and acquisitions are interesting topics in their own right.

Some of the special problems that come up in this area of finance include:

1. The benefits from acquisitions can depend on such things as strategic fits. Strategic fits are difficult to define precisely, and it is not easy to estimate the value of strategic fits using discounted cash flow techniques.

2. There can be complex accounting, tax, and legal effects that must be taken into account when one firm is acquired by another.

3. Acquisitions are an important control device for shareholders. Some acquisitions are a consequence of an underlying conflict between the interests of existing managers and shareholders. Agreeing to be acquired by another firm is one way that shareholders can remove existing managers.

4. Mergers and acquisitions sometimes involve "unfriendly" transactions. In such cases, when one firm attempts to acquire another, it does not always involve quiet, genteel negotiations. The sought-after firm often resists takeover and may resort to defensive tactics with exotic names such as poison pills, greenmail, and white knights.

In Their Own Words...

Michael C. Jensen on
Mergers and Acquisitions

Economic analysis and evidence indicate that takeovers, LBOs, and corporate restructurings are playing an important role in helping the economy adjust to major competitive changes in the last two decades. The competition among alternative management teams and organizational structures for control of corporate assets has enabled vast economic resources to move more quickly to their highest-valued use. In the process, substantial benefits for the economy as a whole as well as for shareholders have been created. Overall gains to selling-firm shareholders from mergers, acquisitions, leveraged buyouts, and other corporate restructurings in the 12-year period 1977–1988 total over $500 billion in 1988 dollars. I estimate gains to buying-firm shareholders to be at least $50 billion for the same period. These gains equal 53 percent of the total cash dividends (valued in 1988 dollars) paid to investors by the entire corporate sector in the same period.

Mergers and acquisitions are a response to new technologies or market conditions which require a strategic change in a company's direction or use of resources. Compared to current management, a new owner is often better able to accomplish major change in the existing organizational structure. Alternatively, leveraged buyouts bring about organizational change by creating entrepreneurial incentives for management and by eliminating the centralized bureaucratic obstacles to maneuverability that are inherent in large public corporations.

When managers have a substantial ownership interest in the organization, the conflicts of interest between shareholders and managers over the payout of the company's free cash flow are reduced. Management's incentives are focused on maximizing the value of the enterprise, rather than building empires — often through poorly conceived diversification acquisitions — without regard to shareholder value. Finally, the required repayment of debt replaces management's discretion in paying dividends and the tendency to overretain cash. Substantial increases in efficiency are thereby created.

Michael C. Jensen is Edsel Bryant Ford Professor of Business Administration at Harvard University. An outstanding scholar and researcher, he is famous for his path-breaking analysis of the modern corporation and its relations with its stockholders.

We discuss these and other issues associated with mergers in the section below. We begin by introducing the basic legal, accounting, and tax aspects of acquisitions.

21.1 | THE LEGAL FORMS OF ACQUISITIONS

There are three basic legal procedures that one firm can use to acquire another firm:

1. Merger or consolidation.
2. Acquisition of stock.
3. Acquisition of assets.

Although these forms are different from a legal standpoint, the financial press frequently does not distinguish between them. The term *merger* is often used regardless of the actual form of the acquisition.

In our discussion, we will frequently refer to the acquiring firm as the *bidder.* This is the company that will make an offer to distribute cash or securities to obtain the stock or assets of another company. The firm that is sought (and perhaps acquired) is often called the *target firm*. The cash or securities offered to the target firm are the *consideration* in the acquisition.

Merger or Consolidation

A **merger** refers to the complete absorption of one firm by another. The acquiring firm retains its name and its identity, and it acquires all of the assets and liabilities of the acquired firm. After a merger, the acquired firm ceases to exist as a separate business entity.

A **consolidation** is the same as a merger except that an entirely new firm is created. In a consolidation, both the acquiring firm and the acquired firm terminate their previous legal existence and become part of a new firm. For this reason, the distinction between the acquiring and the acquired firm is not as important in a consolidation as it is in a merger.

The rules for mergers and consolidations are basically the same. Acquisition by merger or consolidation results in a combination of the assets and liabilities of acquired and acquiring firms; the only difference is whether or not a new firm is created. We will henceforth use the term *merger* to refer generically to both mergers and consolidations.

There are some advantages and some disadvantages to using a merger to acquire a firm:

1. A primary advantage is that a merger is legally simple and does not cost as much as other forms of acquisition. The reason is that the firms simply agree to combine their entire operations. Thus, for example, there is no need to transfer title to individual assets of the acquired firm to the acquiring firm.

2. A primary disadvantage is that a merger must be approved by a vote of the stockholders of each firm.[1] Typically, two thirds (or even more) of the share votes are required for approval. Obtaining the necessary votes can be time-consuming and difficult. Furthermore, as we discuss in greater detail below, the cooperation of the target firm's existing management is almost a necessity for a merger. This cooperation may not be easily or cheaply obtained.

Acquisition of Stock

A second way to acquire another firm is to simply purchase the firm's voting stock in exchange for cash, shares of stock, or other securities. This process will often start as a private offer from the management of one firm to another.

Regardless of how it starts, at some point the offer is taken directly to the target firm's stockholders. This can be accomplished by a tender offer. A **tender offer** is a public offer to buy shares. It is made by one firm directly to the shareholders of another firm.

merger
The complete absorption of one company by another, where the acquiring firm retains its identity and the acquired firm ceases to exist as a separate entity.

consolidation
A merger in which an entirely new firm is created and both the acquired and acquiring firms cease to exist.

tender offer
A public offer by one firm to directly buy the shares of another firm.

---

[1]Mergers between corporations require compliance with state laws. In virtually all states, the shareholders of each corporation must give their assent.

If a shareholder chooses to accept the offer, then that shareholder tenders her shares by exchanging them for cash or securities (or both), depending on the offer. A tender offer is frequently contingent on the bidder's obtaining some percentage of the total voting shares. If not enough shares are tendered, then the offer might be withdrawn or reformulated.

The tender offer is communicated to the target firm's shareholders by public announcements such as newspaper advertisements. Sometimes, a general mailing is used in a tender offer. This is not common, however, because a general mailing requires the name and addresses of the stockholders of record. Obtaining such a list without the target firm's cooperation is not easy.

The following are some factors involved in choosing between an acquisition by stock and a merger.

1. In an acquisition by stock, no shareholder meetings have to be held and no vote is required. If the shareholders of the target firm don't like the offer, they are not required to accept it and need not tender their shares.

2. In an acquisition by stock, the bidding firm can deal directly with the shareholders of the target firm by using a tender offer. The target firm's management and board of directors can be bypassed.

3. Acquisition by stock is occasionally unfriendly. In such cases, a stock acquisition is used in an effort to circumvent the target firm's management, which is usually actively resisting acquisition. Resistance by the target firm's management often makes the cost of acquisition by stock higher than the cost of a merger.

4. Frequently, a significant minority of shareholders will hold out in a tender offer. The target firm cannot be completely absorbed when this happens, and this may delay realization of the merger benefits or otherwise be costly. For example, if the bidder ends up with less than 80 percent of the target firm's shares, it must pay tax on 20 percent to 30 percent of any dividends paid by the target firm to the bidder.

5. Complete absorption of one firm by another requires a merger. Many acquisitions by stock end up with a formal merger later.

Acquisition of Assets

A firm can effectively acquire another firm by buying most or all of its assets. This accomplishes the same thing as buying the company. In this case, however, the target firm will not necessarily cease to exist; it will have just sold off its assets. The "shell" will still exist unless its stockholders choose to dissolve it.

This type of acquisition requires a formal vote of the shareholders of the selling firm. One advantage to this approach is that there is no problem with minority shareholders holding out. However, acquisition of assets may involve transferring titles to individual assets. The legal process of transferring assets can be costly.

Acquisition Classifications

Financial analysts typically classify acquisitions into three types:

1. *Horizontal acquisition.* This is acquisition of a firm in the same industry as the bidder. The firms compete with each other in their product markets.

2. *Vertical acquisition.* A vertical acquisition involves firms at different steps of the production process. The acquisition by an airline company of a travel agency would be a vertical acquisition.

3. *Conglomerate acquisition.* When the bidder and the target firm are not related to each other, the merger is called a *conglomerate acquisition.* The acquisition of a food products firm by a computer firm would be considered a conglomerate acquisition.

A Note on Takeovers

Takeover is a general and imprecise term referring to the transfer of control of a firm from one group of shareholders to another. A takeover thus occurs whenever one group takes control from another.[2] This can occur in three ways: acquisitions, proxy contests, and going-private transactions. Thus, takeovers encompass a broader set of activities than just acquisitions. These activities can be depicted as follows:

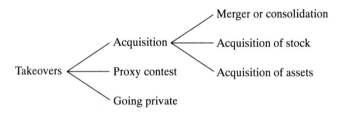

As we have mentioned above, a takeover achieved by acquisition will occur by merger, tender offer, or purchase of assets. In mergers and tender offers, the bidder buys the voting common stock of the target firm.

Takeovers can also occur with **proxy contests.** Proxy contests occur when a group attempts to gain controlling seats on the board of directors by voting in new directors. A proxy is the right to cast someone else's votes. In a proxy contest, proxies are solicited by an unhappy group of shareholders from the rest of the shareholders.

In **going-private transactions,** all of the equity shares of a public firm are purchased by a small group of investors. Usually, the group includes members of incumbent management and some outside investors. Such transactions have come to be known generically as **leveraged buyouts (LBOs)** because a large percentage of the money needed to buy up the stock is usually borrowed. Such transactions are also termed *MBOs* (management buyouts) when existing management is heavily involved. The shares of the firm are delisted from stock exchanges and no longer can be purchased in the open market.

LBOs have become increasingly common, and some recent ones have been quite large. As this is written, the largest acquisition in history (and possibly the single largest private transaction ever of any kind) is the 1989 LBO of RJR Nabisco, the tobacco and food products giant. The acquisition price in that buyout was an astonishing $30.6 billion. In that LBO, as with most of the large ones, much of the financing came from junk bond sales (see Chapter 12 for a discussion of junk bonds).

proxy contest
An attempt to gain control of a firm by soliciting a sufficient number of stockholder votes to replace existing management.

going-private transactions
All publicly owned stock in a firm is replaced with complete equity ownership by a private group.

leveraged buyouts (LBO)
Going-private transactions in which a large percentage of the money used to buy the stock is borrowed. Oftentimes, incumbent management is involved.

---

[2]*Control* may be defined as having a majority vote on the board of directors.

The 1980s saw a large number of mergers, acquisitions, and LBOs, many of them involving very familiar companies. In fact, as of December 31, 1989, the 10 largest such transactions ever had taken place in the 1980s.[3]

Ten Largest Mergers, Acquisitions, and LBOs
(as of December 31, 1989)

Companies or Groups	Cost (billions)	Year
Kohlberg Kravis Roberts/RJR Nabisco	$30.6	1989
Philip Morris/Kraft	13.4	1988
Chevron/Gulf	13.3	1984
Bristol-Myers/Squibb	12.1	1989
Texaco/Getty	10.1	1984
DuPont/Conoco	8.0	1981
Beecham/SmithKline Beckman	7.9	1989
British Petroleum/Standard Oil	7.8	1987
Time/Warner	7.0	1989
U.S. Steel/Marathon Oil	6.6	1982

Very large mergers continue to occur. For example, in 1991, AT&T acquired NCR for $7.89 billion and GTE merged with Contel for $6.24 billion.

⌐CONCEPT QUESTIONS

21.1a What is a merger? How does a merger differ from other acquisition forms?

21.1b What is a takeover?

21.2 ⌐ TAXES AND ACQUISITIONS

If one firm buys another firm, the transaction may be taxable or tax-free. In a *taxable acquisition,* the shareholders of the target firm are considered to have sold their shares, and they will have capital gains or losses that will be taxed. In a *tax-free acquisition,* the acquisition is considered an exchange instead of a sale, so no capital gain or loss occurs at that time.

Determinants of Tax Status

The general requirements for tax-free status are that the acquisition be for a business purpose, and not to avoid taxes, and that there be a continuity of equity interest. In other words, the stockholders in the target firm must retain an equity interest in the bidder.

The specific requirements for a tax-free acquisition depend on the legal form of the acquisition, but, in general, if the buying firm offers the selling firm cash for its equity, it will be a taxable acquisition. If shares of stock are offered, it will be a tax-free acquisition.

---

[3]*The Wall Street Journal*, January 2, 1990.

In a tax-free acquisition, the selling shareholders are considered to have exchanged their old shares for new ones of equal value, and no capital gains or losses are experienced.

Taxable versus Tax-Free Acquisitions

There are two factors to consider when comparing a tax-free acquisition and a taxable acquisition: the capital gains effect and the write-up effect. The *capital gains effect* refers to the fact that the target firm's shareholders may have to pay capital gains taxes in a taxable acquisition. They may demand a higher price as compensation, thereby increasing the cost of the merger. This is a cost of a taxable acquisition.

The tax status of an acquisition also affects the appraised value of the assets of the selling firm. In a taxable acquisition, the assets of the selling firm are revalued or "written up" from their historic book value to their estimated current market value. This is the *write-up effect,* and it is important because the depreciation expense on the acquired firm's assets can be increased in taxable acquisitions. Remember that an increase in depreciation is a noncash expense, but it has the desirable effect of reducing taxes.

The benefit from the write-up effect was sharply curtailed by the Tax Reform Act of 1986. The reason is that the increase in value from writing up the assets is now considered a taxable gain. Before this change, taxable mergers were much more attractive, because the write-up was not taxed.

CONCEPT QUESTIONS

21.2a What factors influence the choice between a taxable and a tax-free acquisition?

21.2b Under current tax law, why are taxable acquisitions less attractive than they once were?

ACCOUNTING FOR ACQUISITIONS | 21.3

When one firm acquires another firm, the bidder must decide whether the acquisition should be treated as a *purchase* or a *pooling of interests.* In the discussion below, a key point to remember is that the accounting method has no cash flow consequences.

The Purchase Method

The *purchase accounting method* of reporting acquisitions requires that the assets of the target firm be reported at their fair market value on the books of the bidder. With this method, an asset called *goodwill* is created for accounting purposes. Goodwill is the difference between the purchase price and the estimated fair market value of the assets acquired.

To illustrate, suppose Firm A acquires Firm B, thereby creating a new firm, AB. The balance sheets for the two firms on the date of the acquisition are shown in Table 21.1. Suppose Firm A pays $18 million in cash for Firm B. The

Table 21.1	Firm A				Firm B			
Accounting for acquisitions: Purchase (in millions)	Working capital	$ 4	Equity	$20	Working capital	$ 2	Equity	$10
	Fixed assets	16			Fixed assets	8		
	Total	$20		$20	Total	$10		$10

	Firm AB			
	Working capital	$ 6	Debt	$18
	Fixed assets	30	Equity	20
	Goodwill	2		
	Total	$38		$38

The market value of the fixed assets of Company B is $14 million. Company A pays $18 million for Company B by issuing debt.

money is raised by borrowing the full amount. The fixed assets in Firm B, which are carried on the books at $8 million, are appraised at $14 million fair market value. Since the working capital is $2 million, the balance sheet assets are worth $16 million. Firm A thus pays $2 million in excess of the estimated market value of these assets. This amount is the goodwill.[4]

The last balance sheet in Table 21.1 shows what the new firm looks like under purchase accounting. Notice that:

1. The total assets of Firm AB increase to $38 million. The fixed assets increase to $30 million. This is the sum of the fixed assets of Firm A and the revalued fixed assets of Firm B ($16 million + 14 million = $30 million). Note that the tax effect of the write-up is ignored in this example.

2. The $2 million excess of the purchase price over the fair market value is reported as goodwill on the balance sheet.[5]

Pooling of Interests

Under a pooling of interests, the assets of the acquiring and acquired firms are pooled, meaning that the balance sheets are just added together. Using our previous example, assume that Firm A buys Firm B by giving B's shareholders $18 million worth of common stock. The result is shown in Table 21.2.

The new firm is owned jointly by all the stockholders of the previously separate firms. The accounting is much simpler here; we just add the two old bal-

---

[4]Remember, there are assets such as employee talents, good customers, growth opportunities, and other intangibles that don't show up on the balance sheet. The $2 million excess pays for these.

[5]You might wonder what would happen if the purchase price were less than the estimated fair market value. Amusingly, to be consistent, it seems that the accountants would need to create a liability called *illwill!* Instead, the fair market value is revised downward to equal the purchase price.

Firm A				Firm B				**Table 21.2**
Working capital	$ 4	Equity	$20	Working capital	$ 2	Equity	$10	Accounting for acquisitions: Pooling of interests (in millions)
Fixed assets	16			Fixed assets	8			
Total	$20		$20	Total	$10		$10	

Firm AB			
Working capital	$ 6	Equity	$30
Fixed assets	24		
Total	$30		$30

ance sheets together. The total assets are unchanged by the acquisition, and no goodwill is created.

Which Is Better: Purchase or Pooling of Interests?

One important difference between purchase and pooling of interests accounting is goodwill. A firm may prefer pooling because it does not involve goodwill. Some firms do not like goodwill because the original amount must be amortized over a period of years (not to exceed 40 years).

The goodwill amortization expense must be deducted from reported income. This is a noncash deduction, of course, but, unlike depreciation, it is not tax deductible. As a result of this expense, purchase accounting will usually result in lower reported income than pooling of interests accounting. Also, purchase accounting may result in a larger book value for total assets (because of the write-up in asset values). The combination of lower reported income and larger book value from purchase accounting has an unfavorable impact on accounting-based performance measures, such as return on assets (ROA) and return on equity (ROE).

Purchase accounting does not in itself affect taxes. The tax status of a merger is determined by the Internal Revenue Service. However, purchase accounting is typically used in taxable acquisitions, because the IRS rules that determine whether an acquisition is taxable or tax-free are similar to the accounting rules that determine whether an acquisition is to be treated as a purchase or as a pooling of interests.

Because the amount of tax-deductible expense is not directly affected by the method of acquisition accounting, cash flows are not affected, and the NPV of the acquisition should be the same whether pooling or purchase accounting is used. Not surprisingly, there doesn't appear to be any evidence suggesting that acquiring firms create more value under one method than the other.

CONCEPT QUESTIONS

21.3a What is the difference between a purchase and a pooling of interests?

21.3b Why would management care about the choice if it has no effect on cash flows?

21.4 | GAINS FROM ACQUISITION

To determine the gains from an acquisition, we need to first identify the relevant incremental cash flows, or, more generally, the source of value. In the broadest sense, acquiring another firm only makes sense if there is some concrete reason to believe that the target firm will somehow be worth more in our hands than it is worth now. As we will see, there are a number of reasons why this might be so.

Synergy

Suppose Firm A is contemplating acquiring Firm B. The acquisition will be beneficial if the combined firm has value that is greater than the sum of the values of the separate firms. If we let V_{AB} stand for the value of the merged firm, then the merger makes sense only if:

$$V_{AB} > V_A + V_B$$

where V_A and V_B are the separate values. A successful merger thus requires that the value of the whole exceeds the sum of the parts.

The difference between the value of the combined firm and the sum of the values of the firms as separate entities is the incremental net gain from the acquisition:

$$\Delta V = V_{AB} - (V_A + V_B)$$

synergy
The positive incremental net gain associated with the combination of two firms through a merger or acquisition.

When ΔV is positive, the acquisition is said to generate **synergy**.

If Firm A buys Firm B, it gets a company worth V_B plus the incremental gain, ΔV. The value of Firm B to Firm A (V_B^*) is thus:

$$\text{Value of Firm B to Firm A} = V_B^* = \Delta V + V_B$$

We place a * on V_B^* to emphasize that we are referring to the value of Firm B to Firm A, not the value of Firm B as a separate entity.

V_B^* can be determined in two steps: (1) estimating V_B, and (2) estimating ΔV. If B is a public company, then its market value as an independent firm under existing management (V_B) can be observed directly. If Firm B is not publicly owned, then its value will have to be estimated based on similar companies that are. Either way, the problem of determining a value for V_B^* requires determining a value for ΔV.

To determine the incremental value of an acquisition, we need to know the incremental cash flows. These are the cash flows for the combined firm less what A and B could generate separately. In other words, the incremental cash flow for evaluating a merger is the difference between the cash flow of the combined company and the sum of the cash flows for the two companies considered separately. We will label this incremental cash flow as ΔCF.

Example 21.1 Synergy

Firms A and B are competitors with very similar assets and business risks. Both are all-equity firms with aftertax cash flows of $10 per year forever, and both have an overall cost of capital of 10 percent. Firm A is thinking of buying Firm B. The aftertax cash flow from the merged firm would be $21 per year. Does the merger generate synergy? What is V_B^*? What is ΔV?

The merger does generate synergy because the cash flow from the merged firm is $\Delta CF = \$1$ greater than the sum of the individual cash flows ($21 versus $20). Assuming that the risks stay the same, the value of the merged firm is $21/.10 = $210. Firms A and B are each worth $10/.10 = $100, for a total of $200. The incremental gain from the merger, ΔV, is thus $210 − 200 = $10. The total value of Firm B to Firm A, V_B^*, is $100 (the value of B as a separate company) + $10 (the incremental gain) = $110. ∎

From our discussions in earlier chapters, we know that the incremental cash flow, ΔCF, can be broken down into four parts:

$$\Delta CF = \Delta EBIT + \Delta Depreciation - \Delta Tax - \Delta Capital\ requirements$$

$$= \Delta Revenue - \Delta Cost - \Delta Tax - \Delta Capital\ requirements$$

where ΔRevenue is the difference in revenues, ΔCost is the difference in costs, ΔTax is the difference in taxes, and ΔCapital requirements is the change in new fixed assets and net working capital.

Based on this breakdown, the merger will only make sense if one or more of these cash flow components is beneficially affected by the merger. The possible cash flow benefits of mergers and acquisitions thus fall into four basic categories: revenue enhancement, cost reductions, lower taxes, and reductions in capital needs.

Revenue Enhancement

One important reason for an acquisition is that the combined firm may generate greater revenues than two separate firms. Increases in revenue may come from marketing gains, strategic benefits, and increases in market power.

Marketing Gains   It is frequently claimed that mergers and acquisitions can produce greater operating revenues from improved marketing. For example, improvements might be made in the following areas:

1. Previously ineffective media programming and advertising efforts.
2. A weak existing distribution network.
3. An unbalanced product mix.

Strategic Benefits   Some acquisitions promise a strategic advantage. This is an opportunity to take advantage of the competitive environment if certain things occur or, more generally, to enhance management flexibility with regard to the company's future operations. In this regard, a strategic benefit is more like an option than it is a standard investment opportunity.

For example, suppose a sewing machine manufacturer can use its technology to enter other businesses. The small-motor technology from the original business can provide opportunities to begin manufacturing small appliances and electric typewriters. Similarly, electronics expertise gained in producing typewriters can be used to manufacture electronic printers.

The word *beachhead* has been used to describe the process of entering a new industry to exploit perceived opportunities. The beachhead is used to spawn new opportunities based on "intangible" relationships. One example is Procter & Gamble's initial acquisition of the Charmin Paper Company as a beachhead that allowed Procter & Gamble to develop a highly interrelated cluster of paper products—disposable diapers, paper towels, feminine hygiene products, and bathroom tissue.[6]

Market Power   One firm may acquire another to increase its market share and market power. In such mergers, profits can be enhanced through higher prices and reduced competition for customers. Of course, mergers that substantially reduce competition in the market may be challenged by the U.S. Department of Justice or the Federal Trade Commission on antitrust grounds.

Cost Reductions

One of the most basic reasons to merge is that a combined firm may operate more efficiently than two separate firms. A firm can obtain greater operating efficiency in several different ways through a merger or an acquisition.

Economies of Scale   Economies of scale relate to the average cost per unit of producing goods and services. If the per unit cost of production falls as the level of production increases, then an economy of scale exists.

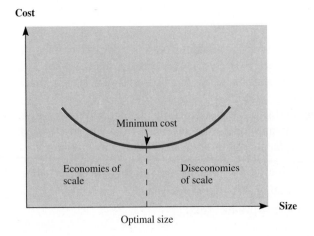

---

[6]This example comes from Michael Porter's *Competitive Advantage* (New York: Free Press, 1985).

Frequently, the phrase *spreading overhead* is used in connection with economies of scale. This expression refers to the sharing of central facilities such as corporate headquarters, top management, and computer services.

Economies of Vertical Integration   Operating economies can be gained from vertical combinations as well as from horizontal combinations. The main purpose of vertical acquisitions is to make coordinating closely related operating activities easier. Benefits from vertical integration are probably the reason that most forest product firms that cut timber also own sawmills and hauling equipment. Such economies may explain why some airline companies have purchased hotels and car rental companies.

Technology transfers are another reason for vertical integration. Consider the merger of General Motors and Hughes Aircraft in 1985. It seems natural that an automobile manufacturer might acquire an advanced electronics firm if the special technology of the electronics firm could be used to improve the quality of the automobile.

Complementary Resources   Some firms acquire others to make better use of existing resources or to provide the missing ingredient for success. Think of a ski-equipment store that could merge with a tennis-equipment store to produce more even sales over both the winter and summer seasons, and thereby better use store capacity.

Tax Gains

Tax gains often are a powerful incentive for some acquisitions. The possible tax gains from an acquisition include the following:

1. The use of tax losses.
2. The use of unused debt capacity.
3. The use of surplus funds.
4. The ability to write up the value of depreciable assets.

Net Operating Losses   Firms that lose money on a pretax basis will not pay taxes. Such firms can end up with tax losses that they cannot use. These tax losses are referred to as *NOL* (an acronym for net operating losses).

A firm with net operating losses may be an attractive merger partner for a firm with significant tax liabilities. Absent any other effects, the combined firm will have a lower tax bill than the two firms considered separately. This is a good example of how a firm can be more valuable merged than standing alone.

There are two qualifications to our NOL discussion:

1. Federal tax laws permit firms that experience periods of profit and losses to even things out through loss carry-back and carry-forward provisions. A firm that has been profitable in the past but has a loss in the current year can get refunds of income taxes paid in the three previous years.

After that, losses can be carried forward for up to 15 years. Thus, a merger to exploit unused tax shields must offer tax savings over and above what can be accomplished by firms via carry-overs.[7]

2. The IRS may disallow an acquisition if the principal purpose of the acquisition is to avoid federal tax by acquiring a deduction or credit that would not otherwise be available.

Unused Debt Capacity   Some firms do not use as much debt as they are able. This makes them potential acquisition candidates. Adding debt can provide important tax savings, and many acquisitions are financed with debt. The acquiring company can deduct interest payments on the newly created debt and reduce taxes.[8]

Surplus Funds   Another quirk in the tax laws involves surplus funds. Consider a firm that has free cash flow—cash flow available after all taxes have been paid and after all positive net present value projects have been financed. In this situation, aside from purchasing fixed income securities, the firm has several ways to spend the free cash flow, including:

1. Paying dividends.
2. Buying back its own shares.
3. Acquiring shares in another firm.

We discussed the first two options in Chapter 16. We saw that an extra dividend will increase the income tax paid by some investors. A share repurchase will reduce the taxes paid by shareholders when compared to paying dividends, but this is not a legal option if the sole purpose is to avoid taxes that would have otherwise been paid by shareholders.

To avoid these problems, the firm can buy another firm. By doing this, the tax problem associated with paying a dividend is avoided. Also, the dividends received from the purchased firm are not taxed in a merger.

Asset Write-Ups   We have previously observed that, in a taxable acquisition, the assets of the acquired firm can be revalued. If the value of the assets is increased, tax deductions for depreciation will be a benefit.

Changing Capital Requirements

All firms must make investments in working capital and fixed assets to sustain an efficient level of operating activity. A merger may reduce the combined in-

---

[7]Under the 1986 Tax Reform Act, a corporation's ability to carry forward net operating losses (and other tax credits) is limited when more than 50 percent of the stock changes hands over a three-year period.

[8]Unused debt capacity is often cited as a benefit in many mergers. An example was the proposed merger of Hospital Corporation of America and American Hospital Supply Corporation in 1985. Insiders were quoted as saying that the combined companies could borrow as much as an additional $1 billion, 10 times the usual borrowing capacity of Hospital Corporation of America alone (*The Wall Street Journal,* April 1, 1985). Even so, the merger never took place.

vestments needed by the two firms. For example, Firm A may need to expand its manufacturing facilities while Firm B has significant excess capacity. It may be much cheaper for Firm A to buy Firm B than to build from scratch.

In addition, acquiring firms may see ways of more effectively managing existing assets. This can occur with a reduction in working capital by more efficient handling of cash, accounts receivable, and inventory. Finally, the acquiring firm may also sell off certain assets that are not needed in the combined firm.

Firms will often cite a large number of reasons for merging. Typically, when firms agree to merge, they sign an *agreement of merger,* which contains, among other things, a list of the economic benefits that shareholders can expect from the merger. For example, the U.S. Steel and Marathon Oil agreement stated (emphasis added):

> U.S. Steel believes that the acquisition of Marathon provides U.S. Steel with an attractive opportunity to *diversify* into the energy business. Reasons for the merger include, but are not limited to, the facts that consummation of the merger will allow U.S. Steel to consolidate Marathon in U.S. Steel's federal *income tax return,* will also contribute to *greater efficiency,* and will enhance the *ability to manage capital* by permitting movements of cash between U.S. Steel and Marathon. Additionally, the merger will *eliminate the possibility of conflicts of interest* between the interests of minority and majority shareholders and will *enhance management flexibility.* The acquisition will provide Marathon shareholders with a substantial premium over historic market prices for their shares. However, [Marathon] shareholders will no longer continue to share in the future prospects of the company.

Avoiding Mistakes

Evaluating the benefit of a potential acquisition is more difficult than a standard capital budgeting analysis because so much of the value can come from intangible, or otherwise difficult to quantify, benefits. Consequently, there is a great deal of room for error. Here are some general rules that should be remembered:

1. *Do not ignore market values.* There is no point and little gain to estimating the value of a publicly traded firm when that value can be directly observed. The current market value represents a consensus opinion of investors concerning the firm's value (under existing management). Use this value as a starting point. If the firm is not publicly held, then the place to start is with similar firms that are publicly held.

2. *Estimate only incremental cash flows.* It is important to estimate the cash flows that are incremental to the acquisition. Only incremental cash flows from an acquisition will add value to the acquiring firm. Acquisition analysis should thus focus only on the newly created, incremental cash flows from the proposed acquisition.

3. *Use the correct discount rate.* The discount rate should be the required rate of return for the incremental cash flows associated with the acquisition. It should reflect the risk associated with the use of funds, not the source. In particular, if Firm A is acquiring Firm B, then Firm A's cost of capital is not particularly relevant. Firm B's cost of capital is a much more appropriate discount rate because it reflects the risk of Firm B's cash flows.

4. *Be aware of transactions costs.* An acquisition may involve substantial (and sometimes astounding) transactions costs. These will include fees to investment bankers, legal fees, and disclosure requirements.

A Note on Inefficient Management

There are firms whose value could be increased with a change in management. These are firms that are poorly run or otherwise do not efficiently use their assets to create shareholder value. Mergers are a means of replacing management in such cases.

Furthermore, the fact that a firm might benefit from a change in management does not necessarily mean that existing management is dishonest, incompetent, or negligent. Instead, just as some athletes are better than others, so might some management teams be better at running a business. This can be particularly true during times of technological change or other periods when innovations in business practice are occurring. In any case, to the extent that corporate "raiders" can identify poorly run firms or firms that otherwise would benefit from a change in management, corporate raiders provide a valuable service to target-firm shareholders and society in general.

⌐ CONCEPT QUESTIONS

21.4a What are the relevant incremental cash flows for evaluating a merger candidate?

21.4b What are some different sources of gain from acquisition?

21.5 │ SOME FINANCIAL SIDE EFFECTS OF ACQUISITIONS

In addition to the various possibilities we discussed above, mergers can have some purely financial side effects, that is, things that occur regardless of whether the merger makes economic sense or not. Two such effects are particularly worth mentioning: EPS growth and diversification.

EPS Growth

An acquisition can create the appearance of growth in earnings per share (EPS). This may fool investors into thinking that the firm is doing better than it really is. What happens is easiest to see with an example.

Suppose Global Resources, Ltd., acquires Regional Enterprises. The financial positions of Global and Regional before the acquisition are shown in Table 21.3. Since the merger creates no additional value, the combined firm (Global Resources after acquiring Regional) has a value that is equal to the sum of the values of the two firms before the merger.

Before the merger, both Global and Regional have 100 shares outstanding. However, Global sells for $25 per share versus $10 per share for Regional. Global therefore acquires Regional by exchanging 1 of its shares for every 2.5 Regional shares. Since there are 100 shares in Regional, it will take $100/2.5 = 40$ shares in all.

	Global Resources before Merger	Regional Enterprises before Merger	Global Resources after Merger		
			The Market Is "Smart"	The Market Is "Fooled"	**Table 21.3** Financial positions of Global Resources and Regional Enterprises
Earnings per share	$1.00	$1.00	$1.43	$1.43	
Price per share	$25.00	$10.00	$25.00	$35.71	
Price/earnings ratio	25	10	17.5	25	
Number of shares	100	100	140	140	
Total earnings	$100	$100	$200	$200	
Total value	$2,500	$1,000	$3,500	$5,000	

Exchange ratio: 1 share in Global for 2.5 shares in Regional.

After the merger, Global will have 140 shares outstanding, and several things will happen (see Column 3 of Table 21.3):

1. The market value of the combined firm is $3,500. This is equal to the sum of the values of the separate firms before the merger. If the market is "smart," it will realize that the combined firm is worth the sum of the values of the separate firms.

2. The earnings per share of the merged firm are $1.43. The acquisition enables Global to increase its earnings per share from $1 to $1.43, an increase of 43 percent.

3. Because the stock price of Global after the merger is the same as before the merger, the price/earnings ratio must fall. This is true as long as the market is smart and recognizes that the total market value has not been altered by the merger.

If the market is "fooled," it might mistake the 43 percent increase in earnings per share for true growth. In this case, the price/earnings ratio of Global may not fall after the merger. Suppose the price/earnings ratio of Global remains equal to 25. Since the combined firm has earnings of $200, the total value of the combined firm will increase to $5,000 (25 × $200). The per-share value for Global will increase to $35.71 ($5,000/140).

This is earnings growth magic. Like all good magic, it is just illusion. For it to work, the shareholders of Global and Regional must receive something for nothing. This, of course, is unlikely with so simple a trick.

Diversification

Diversification is commonly mentioned as a benefit to a merger. We previously noted that U.S. Steel included diversification as a benefit in its acquisition of Marathon Oil. The problem is that diversification per se probably does not create value.

Going back to Chapter 11, diversification reduces unsystematic risk. We also saw that the value of an asset depends on its systematic risk, and systematic risk is not directly affected by diversification. Since the unsystematic risk is not especially important, there is no particular benefit to reducing it.

An easy way to see why diversification isn't an important benefit to a merger is to consider someone who owned stock in U.S. Steel and Marathon Oil. Such a stockholder is already diversified between these two investments. The merger doesn't do anything that the stockholders can't do for themselves.

More generally, stockholders can get all the diversification they want by buying stock in different companies. As a result, they won't pay a premium for a merged company just for the benefit of diversification.

By the way, we are not saying that U.S. Steel (now USX) made a mistake. In 1982, U.S. Steel was a cash-rich company (over 20 percent of its assets were in the form of cash and marketable securities). It is not uncommon to see firms with surplus cash articulating a "need" for diversification.

⌐CONCEPT QUESTIONS

21.5a Why can a merger create the appearance of earnings growth?

21.5b Why is diversification by itself not a good reason for a merger?

21.6 | THE COST OF AN ACQUISITION

We've discussed some of the benefits of acquisition. We now need to discuss the cost of a merger.[9] We learned earlier that the net incremental gain to a merger is:

$$\Delta V = V_{AB} - (V_A + V_B)$$

Also, the total value of Firm B to Firm A, V_B^*, is:

$$V_B^* = V_B + \Delta V$$

The NPV of the merger is therefore:

$$\text{NPV} = V_B^* - \text{Cost to Firm A of the acquisition} \qquad [21.1]$$

To illustrate, suppose we have the following premerger information for Firm A and Firm B:

	Firm A	Firm B
Price per share	$20	$10
Number of shares	25	10
Total market value	$500	$100

Both of these firms are 100 percent equity. You estimate that the incremental value of the acquisition, ΔV, is $100.

---

[9]For a more complete discussion of the costs of a merger and the NPV approach, see S. C. Myers, "A Framework for Evaluating Mergers," in *Modern Developments in Financial Management,* ed. S. C. Myers (New York: Praeger Publishers, 1976).

The board of Firm B has indicated that it will agree to a sale if the price is $150, payable in cash or stock. This price for Firm B has two parts. Firm B is worth $100 as a standalone, so this is the minimum value that we could assign to Firm B. The second part, $50, is called the *merger premium,* and it represents the amount paid above the stand-alone value.

Should Firm A acquire Firm B? Should it pay in cash or stock? To answer, we need to determine the NPV of the acquisition under both alternatives. We can start by noting that the value of Firm B to Firm A is:

$$V_B^* = \Delta V + V_B$$

$$= \$100 + 100 = \$200$$

The total value received by A from buying Firm B is thus $200. The question then is: How much does Firm A have to give up? The answer depends on whether cash or stock is used as the means of payment.

Case I: Cash Acquisition

The cost of an acquisition when cash is used is just the cash itself. So, if Firm A pays $150 in cash to purchase all of the shares of Firm B, the cost of acquiring Firm B is $150. The NPV of a cash acquisition is:

$$NPV = V_B^* - Cost$$

$$= \$200 - 150 = \$50$$

The acquisition is therefore profitable.

After the merger, Firm AB will still have 25 shares outstanding. The value of Firm A after the merger is:

$$V_{AB} = V_A + (V_B^* - Cost)$$

$$= \$500 + 200 - 150$$

$$= \$550$$

This is just the premerger value of $500 plus the $50 NPV. The price per share after the merger is $550/25 = $22, a gain of $2 per share.

Case II: Stock Acquisition

Things are somewhat more complicated when stock is the means of payment. In a cash merger, the shareholders in B receive cash for their stock, and, as in the U.S. Steel/Marathon Oil example above, they no longer participate in the company. Thus, as we have seen, the cost of the acquisition in this case is the amount of cash needed to pay off B's stockholders.

In a stock merger, no cash actually changes hands. Instead, the shareholders of Firm B come in as new shareholders in the merged firm. The value of the merged firm in this case will be equal to the premerger values of Firms A and B plus the incremental gain from the merger, ΔV:

$$
\begin{aligned}
V_{AB} &= V_A + V_B + \Delta V \\
&= \$500 + 100 + 100 \\
&= \$700
\end{aligned}
$$

To give \$150 worth of stock for Firm B, Firm A will have to give up \$150/\$20 = 7.5 shares. After the merger, there will be 25 + 7.5 = 32.5 shares outstanding and the per-share value will be \$700/32.5 = \$21.54.

Notice that the per-share price after the merger is lower under the stock purchase option. The reason has to do with the fact that B's shareholders own stock in the new firm.

It appears that Firm A paid \$150 for Firm B. However, they actually paid more than that. When all is said and done, B's stockholders own 7.5 shares of stock in the merged firm. After the merger, each of these shares is worth \$21.54. The total value of the consideration received by B's stockholders is thus 7.5 $\times$ \$21.54 = \$161.55.

This \$161.55 is the true cost of the acquisition since it is what the sellers actually end up receiving. The NPV of the merger to Firm A is:

$$
\begin{aligned}
NPV &= V_B^* - \text{Cost} \\
&= \$200 - 161.55 = \$38.45
\end{aligned}
$$

We can check this by noting that A started with 25 shares worth \$20 each. The gain to A of \$38.45 works out to be \$38.45/25 = \$1.54 per share. The value of the stock increases to \$21.54 as we calculated.

When we compare the cash acquisition to the stock acquisition, we see that the cash acquisition is better in this case, because Firm A gets to keep all of the NPV if it pays in cash. If it pays in stock, Firm B's stockholders share in the NPV by becoming new stockholders in A.

Cash versus Common Stock

The distinction between cash and common stock financing in a merger is an important one. If cash is used, the cost of an acquisition is not dependent on the acquisition gains. All other things being the same, if common stock is used, the cost is higher because Firm A's shareholders must share the acquisition gains with the shareholders of Firm B. However, if the NPV of the acquisition is negative, then the loss will be shared between the two firms.

Whether to finance an acquisition by cash or by shares of stock depends on several factors, including:[10]

1. *Sharing gains.* If cash is used to finance an acquisition, the selling firm's shareholders will not participate in the potential gains of the merger. Of

---

[10]All-cash transactions are much more common than all-stock transactions. In 1985, for example, only about 10 percent of acquisitions were financed solely by stock (see *Mergers and Acquisitions,* "Almanac and Review: 1985").

course, if the acquisition is not a success, the losses will not be shared, and shareholders of the acquiring firm will be worse off than if stock were used.

2. *Taxes.* Acquisition by cash usually results in a taxable transaction. Acquisition by exchanging stock is generally tax-free.

3. *Control.* Acquisition by cash does not affect the control of the acquiring firm. Acquisition with voting shares may have implications for control of the merged firm.

⌐**CONCEPT QUESTIONS**

21.6a Why does the true cost of a stock acquisition depend on the gain from the merger?

21.6b What are some important factors in deciding whether to use stock or cash in an acquisition?

DEFENSIVE TACTICS ⌐ 21.7

Target-firm managers frequently resist takeover attempts. Resistance usually starts with press releases and mailings to shareholders that present management's viewpoint. It can eventually lead to legal action and solicitation of competing bids. Managerial action to defeat a takeover attempt may make target-firm shareholders better off if it elicits a higher offer premium from the bidding firm or another firm.

Of course, management resistance may simply reflect pursuit of self-interest at the expense of shareholders. This is a controversial subject. At times, management resistance has greatly increased the amount ultimately received by their shareholders. At other times, management resistance appears to have defeated all takeover attempts to the detriment of their shareholders.

In this section, we describe various defensive tactics that have been used by target firms' managements to resist unfriendly attempts. The law surrounding these defenses is not settled, and some of these maneuvers may ultimately be deemed illegal or otherwise unsuitable.

The Corporate Charter

The *corporate charter* refers to the articles of incorporation and corporate by-laws that establish the governance rules of the firm. The corporate charter establishes the conditions that allow for a takeover. Firms frequently amend corporate charters to make acquisitions more difficult. For example, usually two-thirds (67 percent) of the shareholders of record must approve a merger. Firms can make it more difficult to be acquired by changing this to 80 percent or so. This is called a *supermajority amendment.*

Another device is to stagger the election of the board members. This makes it more difficult to elect a new board of directors quickly. We discussed staggered elections in Chapter 12.

Repurchase/Standstill Agreements

Managers of target firms may attempt to negotiate *standstill agreements.* Standstill agreements are contracts where the bidding firm agrees to limit its holdings in the target firm. These agreements usually lead to the end of a takeover attempt.

Standstill agreements often occur at the same time that a *targeted repurchase* is arranged. In a targeted repurchase, a firm buys a certain amount of its own stock from an individual investor, usually at a substantial premium. These premiums can be thought of as payments to potential bidders to eliminate unfriendly takeover attempts. Critics of such payments view them as bribes and label them **greenmail.**

greenmail

A targeted stock repurchase where payments are made to potential bidders to eliminate unfriendly takeover attempts.

For example, on April 2, 1986, Ashland Oil, Inc., the nation's largest independent oil refiner, had 28 million shares outstanding. The company's stock price the day before was $48 per share on the New York Stock Exchange. On April 2, Ashland's board of directors made two decisions:

1. The board approved management's agreement with the Belzberg family of Canada to buy, for $51 a share, the Belzbergs' 2.6 million shares in Ashland. This was a standstill agreement that ended a takeover skirmish in which the Belzberg family offered $60 per share for all of the common stock of Ashland.
2. The board authorized the company to repurchase 7.5 million shares (27 percent of the outstanding shares) of its stock. Simultaneously, the board approved a proposal to establish an employee stock ownership plan to be funded with 5.3 million shares of Ashland stock.

The result of these actions was to eliminate a takeover threat and to make Ashland invulnerable to future unfriendly takeover attempts. Earlier, Ashland had put in place a provision that said 80 percent of the stockholders have to approve a takeover (a supermajority provision). The shares of stock placed in the employee stock ownership plan are effectively controlled by management and total more than 20 percent of the shares, so no one can get the needed 80 percent approval without management's help.

Exclusionary Self-Tenders

An *exclusionary self-tender* is the opposite of a targeted repurchase. Here the firm makes a tender offer for a given amount of its own stock while *excluding* targeted stockholders.

In one of the most celebrated cases in merger history, Unocal, a large integrated oil firm, made a tender offer for 29 percent of its shares while excluding its largest shareholder, Mesa Partners II (led by T. Boone Pickens). Unocal's self-tender was for $72 per share, which was $26 over the prevailing market price. It was designed to defeat Mesa's attempted takeover of Unocal by, in effect, transferring wealth from Mesa to Unocal's other stockholders.

At present, it appears that an exclusionary self-tender is likely to be viewed as an illegal form of discrimination against one group of stockholders.

Poison Pills and Share Rights Plans

A **poison pill** is a tactic designed to repel would-be suitors. The term comes from the world of espionage. Agents are supposed to bite a pill of cyanide rather than permit capture. Presumably, this prevents enemy interrogators from learning important secrets.

In the equally colorful world of corporate finance, a poison pill is a financial device designed to make it impossible for a firm to be acquired without management's consent—unless the buyer is willing to commit financial suicide.

In recent years, a majority of the largest firms in the United States have adopted poison pill provisions of one form or another, often calling them **share rights plans** (SRPs) or something similar. Figure 21.1 contains the body of a letter mailed by Contel Corporation (a large telecommunications firm) in late 1988 to its stockholders announcing its adoption of such a plan and sketching some of the features.[11]

SRPs differ quite a bit in detail from company to company; we will describe a kind of generic approach here. In general, when a company adopts an SRP, it distributes share rights to its existing stockholders.[12] These rights allow shareholders to buy shares of stock (or preferred stock) at some fixed price.

The rights issued with an SRP have a number of unusual features. First, the exercise or subscription price on the right is usually set high enough such that the rights are well out of the money, meaning that the purchase price is much higher than the current stock price. The rights will often be good for 10 years, and the purchase or exercise price is usually a reasonable estimate of what the stock will be worth at that time.

In addition, unlike ordinary stock rights, these rights can't be exercised immediately, and they can't be bought and sold separately from the stock. Also, they can essentially be canceled by management at any time; often, they can be redeemed (bought back) for a penny apiece, or some similarly trivial amount.

Things get interesting when, under certain circumstances, the rights are "triggered." This means that the rights become exercisable, they can be bought and sold separately from the stock, and they are not easily canceled or redeemed. Typically, the rights will be triggered when someone acquires 20 percent of the common stock or otherwise announces a tender offer.

When the rights are triggered, they can be exercised. Since they are out of the money, this fact is not especially important. Certain other features come into play, however. The most important is the *flip-over provision*.

The flip-over provision is the "poison" in the pill. In the event of a merger, the holder of a right can pay the exercise price and receive common stock in the merged firm worth twice the exercise price. In other words, holders of the right can buy stock in the merged firm at half price.[13]

poison pill
A financial device designed to make unfriendly takeover attempts unappealing, if not impossible.

share rights plans
Provisions allowing existing stockholders to purchase stock at some fixed price should an outside takeover bid take place, discouraging hostile takeover attempts.

---

[11]Contel's SRP appears to have achieved its purpose. In the summer of 1990, Contel management agreed to a friendly merger with GTE Corporation.

[12]We discuss ordinary share rights in Chapter 13.

[13]Some plans also contain "flip-in" provisions. These allow the holder to buy stock in the target company at half price when the target company is the surviving company in a merger. Simultaneously, the rights owned by the raider (the acquirer) are voided. This tactic is of questionable legality. A merger where the target is the surviving company is called a *reverse merger*.

Figure 21.1

Adoption of a share rights
plan (SRP)

CONTEL

Dear Stockholder:

In the current corporate takeover environment, Contel is concerned about certain abusive techniques that are sometimes employed during takeover attempts. The use of such tactics is increasing and often threatens the investment position of a company's stockholders. In response to the increasing use of these abusive tactics, your Board of Directors has adopted a share rights plan designed to ensure that stockholders are treated fairly by anyone who might seek to obtain control of the company. The plan consists of a preferred stock rights agreement and a dividend distribution of one preferred stock purchase right on each outstanding share of Contel common stock.

The share rights plan was not adopted because of any current effort by another party to acquire the company. In fact, we are not aware of any such effort. Rather, it is a precautionary step that will increase the Board's ability to represent effectively the interests of the company's stockholders in the event of an unsolicited takeover attempt. While the share rights plan will not prevent a takeover, it should encourage anyone seeking to acquire Contel to negotiate first with the Board of Directors. In adopting the share rights plan, the Board also considered the fact that more than 650 public companies, including many major independent telephone companies, have adopted share rights plans.

Under the share rights plan, you will receive one right for each share of Contel common stock you own. Each right will entitle you to buy one one-hundredth of a share of a new series of preferred stock at an exercise price of $120. The rights can only be exercised if a person or group acquires 20 percent or more of Contel common stock or announces a tender offer for 30 percent or more of Contel common stock.

If certain triggering events occur, each right would entitle you to receive Contel common stock or, in certain circumstances, cash, property or other Contel securities with a value equal to twice the exercise price. Triggering events include the acquisition by a person or group of 20 percent or more of Contel common stock, or a merger with a company that owns 20 percent or more of Contel common stock in which Contel is the surviving company.

If Contel were acquired in certain other mergers or business combinations, or if 50 percent of the company's assets or earning power is sold or transferred, each right would entitle you to receive common stock in the acquiring company with a value equal to twice the exercise price. Contel can redeem the rights for 1 cent each at any time prior to 10 days following the date that a person or group acquires 20 percent or more of Contel common stock. The details of the rights plan are explained in the attachment to this letter. We urge you to read it carefully.

The dividend distribution is payable to stockholders of record on December 7, 1988, and one right will attach to each new share of common stock issued after the record date and prior to the time someone acquires 20 percent or more of Contel common stock or announces a tender offer for 30 percent or more of Contel common stock. The rights will become part of your existing stock certificate and no separate rights certificates will be issued at this time.

* * * * *

Sincerely,

Charles Wohlstetter
Chairman

Donald W. Weber
President and Chief Executive Officer

The rights issued in connection with an SRP are poison pills because anyone trying to force a merger would trigger the rights. When this happens, all the target firm's stockholders can effectively buy stock in the merged firm at half price. This greatly increases the cost of the merger to the bidder because the target firm's shareholders end up with a much larger percentage of the merged firm.

Notice that the flip-over provision doesn't prevent someone from acquiring control of a firm by purchasing a majority interest. It just acts to prevent a complete merger of the two firms. Even so, this inability to combine can have serious tax and other implications for the buyer. For example, if the buyer cannot obtain 80 percent of the stock, any dividends received will be taxable.

The intention of a poison pill is to force a bidder to negotiate with management. Frequently, merger offers are made with the contingency that the rights are canceled by the target firm.

Going Private and Leveraged Buyouts

As we have previously discussed, going private refers to what happens when the publicly owned stock in a firm is replaced with complete equity ownership by a private group, which may include elements of existing management. As a consequence, the firm's stock is taken off the market (if it is an exchange-traded stock, it is delisted) and is no longer traded.

One result of going private is that takeovers via tender offer can no longer occur since there are no publicly held shares. In this sense, an LBO (or, more specifically, an MBO) can be a takeover defense. However, it's only a defense for management. From the stockholder's point of view, an LBO is a takeover because they are bought out.

Other Devices and Jargon of Corporate Takeovers

As corporate takeovers have become more common, a new vocabulary has developed. The terms are colorful, and, in no particular order, some of them are listed here:

1. *Golden parachutes.* Some target firms provide compensation to top-level management if a takeover occurs. For example, when the Scoville board endorsed a $523 million tender offer by First City Properties, it arranged for 13 top executives to get termination payments of about $5 million. Depending on your perspective and the amounts involved, this can be viewed as a payment to management to make it less concerned for its own welfare and more interested in stockholders when considering a takeover bid.

2. *Poison puts.* A poison put is a variation on the poison pill we described above. A poison put forces the firm to buy securities back at some set price.

3. *Crown jewels.* Firms often sell or threaten to sell major assets—crown jewels—when faced with a takeover threat. This is sometimes referred to as the "scorched earth" strategy. This tactic often involves a lockup, which we discuss below.

4. *White knights.* A firm facing an unfriendly merger offer might arrange to be acquired by a different, friendly firm. The firm is thereby rescued by a white knight. Alternatively, the firm may arrange for a friendly entity to acquire a large block of stock. So-called white squires or big brothers are individuals, firms, or even mutual funds involved in friendly transactions of these types. Sometimes white knights or others are granted exceptional terms or otherwise compensated. Inevitably it seems, this has recently been called *whitemail*.

5. *Lockups.* A lockup is an option granted to a friendly suitor (a white knight, perhaps) giving them the right to purchase stock or some of the assets (the crown jewels, possibly) of a target firm at a fixed price in the event of an unfriendly takeover.

6. *Shark repellent.* A shark repellent is any tactic (a poison pill, for example) designed to discourage unwanted merger offers.

⌐ CONCEPT QUESTIONS

21.7a What can a firm do to make a takeover less likely?

21.7b What is a share rights plan? Explain how the rights work.

21.8 | SOME EVIDENCE ON ACQUISITIONS

One of the most controversial issues surrounding our subject is whether mergers and acquisitions benefit shareholders. Several studies have attempted to estimate the effect of mergers and takeovers on stock prices of the bidding and target firms. These studies have examined the gains and losses in stock value around the time of merger announcements. Table 21.4 summarizes the results of numerous such studies that look at the effects of merger and tender offers on stock prices.

Table 21.4 shows that the shareholders of target companies in successful takeovers gain substantially. When the takeover is accomplished by merger, the gains are 20 percent, and, when the takeover is via tender offer, the gains are 30 percent. These gains are a reflection of the merger premium that is typically paid by the acquiring firm. These gains are excess returns, that is, the returns over and above what the shareholders would normally have earned.

Table 21.4

Stock price changes in successful corporate takeovers

Takeover Technique	Target	Bidders
Tender offer	30%	4%
Merger	20	0
Proxy contest	8	n/a

n/a = Not applicable.

Modified from Michael C. Jensen and Richard S. Ruback, "The Market for Corporate Control: The Scientific Evidence," *Journal of Financial Economics* 11 (April 1983), pp. 7, 8. © Elsevier Science Publishers B.V. (North-Holland).

The shareholders of bidding firms do not fare nearly so well. According to the studies summarized in Table 21.4, bidders experience gains of 4 percent in tender offers, but this gain is about zero in mergers. These numbers are sufficiently small to leave doubt about the precise effect on bidders.

What conclusions can be drawn from Table 21.4? First, the evidence strongly suggests that the shareholders of successful target firms achieve substantial gains as a result of takeovers. The gains appear to be larger in tender offers than in mergers. This may reflect the fact that takeovers sometimes start with a friendly merger proposal from the bidder to the management of the target firm. If management rejects the offer, the bidding firm may take the offer directly to the shareholders with a tender offer. As a consequence, tender offers are frequently unfriendly.

Also, the target firm's management may actively oppose the offer with defensive tactics. This often has the result of raising the tender offer from the bidding firm, and, on average, friendly mergers may be arranged at lower premiums than unfriendly tender offers.

The second conclusion we can draw is that the shareholders of bidding firms earn comparatively little from takeovers. They earn an average of only 4 percent from tender offers; they appear to break even on mergers. In fact, studies have found that the acquiring firms actually lose value in many mergers. These findings are a puzzle, and there are a variety of explanations:

1. Anticipated merger gains may not have been completely achieved, and shareholders thus experienced losses. This can happen if managers of bidding firms tend to overestimate the gains from acquisition.

2. The bidding firms are usually much larger than the target firms. Thus, even though the dollar gains to the bidder may be similar to the dollar gains earned by shareholders of the target firm, the percentage gains will be much lower.

3. Another possible explanation for the low returns to the shareholders of bidding firms in takeovers is simply that management may not be acting in the interest of shareholders when it attempts to acquire other firms. Perhaps it is attempting to increase the size of the firm, even if this reduces its value per share.

4. The market for takeovers may be sufficiently competitive that the NPV of acquiring is zero because the prices paid in acquisitions fully reflect the value of the acquired firms. In other words, the sellers capture all of the gain.

5. Finally, the announcement of a takeover may not convey much new information to the market about the bidding firm. This can occur because firms frequently announce intentions to engage in merger "programs" long before they announce specific acquisitions. In this case, the stock price in the bidding firm may already reflect anticipated gains from mergers.

⌐ CONCEPT QUESTIONS

21.8a What does the evidence say about the benefits of mergers and acquisitions to target-company shareholders?

21.8b What does the evidence say about the benefits of mergers and acquisitions to acquiring-company shareholders?

21.9 | SUMMARY AND CONCLUSIONS

This chapter introduced you to the extensive literature on mergers and acquisitions. We touched on a number of issues, including:

1. Forms of merger. One firm can acquire another in several different ways. The three legal forms of acquisition are merger and consolidation, acquisition of stock, and acquisition of assets.

2. Tax issues. Mergers and acquisitions can be taxable or tax-free transactions. The primary issue is whether the target firm's stockholders sell or exchange their shares. Generally, a cash purchase will be a taxable merger, while a stock exchange will not be taxable. In a taxable merger, there are capital gains effects and asset write-up effects to consider. In a stock exchange, the target firm's shareholders become shareholders in the merged firm.

3. Accounting issues. Accounting for mergers and acquisitions involves a choice between the purchase method and the pooling of interests method. The choice between these two methods does not affect the aftertax cash flows of the combined firm. However, financial managers may prefer the pooling of interests method because the net income of the combined firm is higher than is true for the purchase method.

4. Merger valuation. If Firm A is acquiring Firm B, the benefits (ΔV) from an acquisition are defined as the value of the combined firm (V_{AB}) less the value of the firms as separate entities (V_A and V_B), or:

$$\Delta V = V_{AB} - (V_A + V_B)$$

The gain to Firm A from acquiring Firm B is the increased value of the acquired firm (ΔV) plus the value of B as a separate firm. The total value of Firm B to Firm A, V_B^*, is thus:

$$V_B^* = \Delta V + V_B$$

An acquisition will benefit the shareholders of the acquiring firm if this value is greater than the cost of the acquisition.

The cost of an acquisition can be defined in general terms as the price paid to the shareholders of the acquired firm. The cost frequently includes a merger premium paid to the shareholders of the acquired firm. Moreover, the cost depends on the form of payment, that is, the choice between cash or common stock.

5. The possible benefits of an acquisition come from several possible sources, including the following:
   a. Revenue enhancement.
   b. Cost reductions.
   c. Tax benefits.
   d. Changing capital requirements.

6. Some of the most colorful language of finance comes from defensive tactics in acquisition battles. *Poison pills, golden parachutes, crown jewels,* and *greenmail* are terms that describe various antitakeover tactics.

7. Mergers and acquisitions have been extensively studied. The basic conclusions are that, on average, the shareholders of target firms do very well, while the shareholders of bidding firms do not appear to gain very much.

Key Terms

merger 755
consolidation 755
tender offer 755
proxy contests 757
going-private transactions 757

leveraged buyouts (LBOs) 757
synergy 762
greenmail 774
poison pill 775
share rights plans 775

Chapter Review Problems and Self-Test

21.1 **Merger Value and Cost** Consider the following information for two all-equity firms, A and B:

	Firm A	Firm B
Shares outstanding	100	50
Price per share	$50	$30

Firm A estimates that the value of the synergistic benefit from acquiring Firm B is $200. Firm B has indicated that it would accept a cash purchase offer of $35 per share. Should Firm A proceed?

21.2 **Stock Mergers and EPS** Consider the following information for two all-equity firms, A and B:

	Firm A	Firm B
Total earnings	$1,000	$400
Shares outstanding	100	80
Price per share	$80	$25

Firm A is acquiring Firm B by exchanging 25 of its shares for all the shares in B. What is the cost of the merger if the merged firm is worth $11,000? What will happen to Firm A's EPS? Its P/E ratio?

Answers to Self-Test Problems

21.1 The total value of Firm B to Firm A is the premerger value of B plus the $200 gain from the merger. The premerger value of B is $30 × 50 = $1,500, so the total value is $1,700. At $35 per share, A is paying $35 × 50 = $1,750; the merger therefore has a negative NPV of −$50. At $35 per share, B is not an attractive merger partner.

21.2   After the merger, the firm will have 125 shares outstanding. Since the total value is $11,000, the price per share is $11,000/125 = $88, up from $80. Since Firm B's stockholders end up with 25 shares in the merged firm, the cost of the merger is 25 × $88 = $2,200, not 25 × $80 = $2,000.

Also, the combined firm will have $1,000 + 400 = $1,400 in earnings, so EPS will be $1,400/125 = $11.2, up from $1,000/100 = $10. The old P/E ratio was $80/$10 = 8. The new one is $88/11.2 = 7.86.

Questions and Problems

1.   Calculating Synergy   Ingulf and Devourer Realty has offered $10 million cash for all of the common stock in Faullty Tower Realty. Based on recent market information, Faullty Tower is worth $8 million as an independent operation. If the merger makes economic sense for Ingulf, what is the minimum estimated value of the synergistic benefits from the merger?

2.   Cash versus Stock as Payment   Consider the following information about a bidding firm (Firm A) and a target firm (Firm B). Assume that both firms have no debt outstanding.

	Firm A	Firm B
Shares outstanding	50	20
Price per share	$10	$5

Firm A has estimated that the value of the synergistic benefits from acquiring Firm B is $40.
a. If Firm B is willing to be acquired for $6 per share, cash, what is the NPV of the merger?
b. What will the price per share of the stock be after the merger?
c. In part a, what is the merger premium?
d. Suppose Firm B is agreeable to a merger by stock exchange. If A swaps one of its shares for every two shares in B, what is the NPV of the merger?
e. What will the price per share of the stock be after the merger in part d?
f. In part d, explain why the cost that A is paying to acquire B is greater than $5 per share.

3.   Mergers and Taxes   Describe the advantages and disadvantages of a taxable merger as opposed to a tax-free exchange. What is the basic determinant of tax status in a merger? Would an LBO be taxable or nontaxable? Explain.

4.   Merger Accounting   Explain the difference between purchase and pooling of interests accounting for mergers. What is the effect on cash flows from the choice? The effect on EPS?

5.   **Effects of a Stock Exchange**   Consider the following premerger information about Firms A and B:

	Firm A	Firm B
Total earnings	$800	$200
Shares outstanding	100	40
Price per share	$160	$30

Assume that Firm A acquires Firm B via a stock exchange at a price of $40 per share for each share of B's stock. Both firms are all equity.
a. What will happen to the earnings per share for Firm A?
b. What will the price per share be in the new firm if the market is fooled by this earnings growth (meaning that the price/earnings ratio does not change)?
c. What will the price/earnings ratio be if the market is not fooled?

6.   **Constructing Balance Sheets**   Consider the following premerger information about Firms A and B:

	Firm A	Firm B
Total earnings	$6,000	$2,000
Shares outstanding	500	500
Per-share values:		
Market	$100	$20
Book	$22	$10

Assume that Firm A acquires Firm B by paying cash in the amount of $25 per share. Assuming that neither firm has any debt before or after the merger, construct the balance sheets for Firm A assuming (1) pooling of interests accounting and (2) purchase accounting.

7.   **Constructing Balance Sheets**   Assume that the following balance sheets are book values. Construct the balance sheet for Kau Co. assuming that Kau purchases Hilliard and the pooling of interest method of accounting is used.

Kau Vineyards (thousands)

Current assets	$ 100	Current liabilities	$ 60
Fixed assets	900	Long-term debt	200
		Equity	740
Total	$1,000		$1,000

Hilliard Vineyards (thousands)

Current assets	$ 200	Current liabilities	$ 140
Fixed assets	600	Long-term debt	100
		Equity	560
Total	$ 800		$ 800

8.   **Incorporating Goodwill**   In the previous question, suppose that the fair market value of Hilliard's fixed assets is $900 versus the $600 book value shown. Kau Co. pays $1,200 for Hilliard and raises the needed funds through an issue of long-term debt. Construct the balance sheet assuming that the purchase method of accounting is used.

9.   **Economies of Scale and Mergers**   What are economies of scale? Suppose that Eastern Power and Western Power are located in different time zones. Both of them operate at 60 percent of capacity except for peak periods when they operate at 100 percent of capacity. The peak periods begin at 9:00 A.M. and 5:00 P.M., local time, and last about 45 minutes. Explain why a merger might make sense.

10. **Constructing Balance Sheets**   The Lager Brewing Corporation has acquired the Philadelphia Pretzel Company in a merger. Construct the balance sheet for the new corporation if the merger is treated as a pooling of interests for accounting purposes. The balance sheets shown here represent the assets of both firms at their current book values.

Lager Brewing (thousands)

Current assets	$ 400	Current liabilities	$ 200
Other assets	100	Long-term debt	100
Net fixed assets	500	Equity	700
Total	$1,000	Total	$1,000

Philadelphia Pretzel (thousands)

Current assets	$ 80	Current liabilities	$ 80
Other assets	40	Equity	120
Net fixed assets	80		
Total	$ 200	Total	$ 200

11. **Incorporating Goodwill**   In Problem 10, construct the new balance sheet for the new corporation assuming that the transaction is treated as a purchase. The market value of Philadelphia Pretzel's fixed assets is $120; the book values for current and other assets are the same as the market values. The balance sheet for Lager is still shown in book value terms. Lager issued $300,000 in new long-term debt to pay for the purchase.

12. **Cash versus Stock as Payment**   Fly-by-Night Couriers is analyzing the possible acquisition of Flash-in-the-Pan Restaurants. Both firms have no debt. The forecast of Fly-by-Night shows that the purchase would increase its annual total aftertax cash flow by $1,600,000 indefinitely. The current market value of Flash-in-the-Pan is $20 million, and that of Fly-by-Night is $35 million. The appropriate discount rate for the incremental cash flows is 7 percent.

Fly-by-Night is trying to decide whether it should offer 35 percent of its stock or $25 million in cash to Flash-in-the-Pan's shareholders.
a. What is the cost of each alternative?
b. What is the NPV of each alternative?
c. Which alternative should Fly-by-Night use?

13. **EPS, P/E, and Mergers**   Colorado Aviation has voted in favor of being bought out by Academy Financial Corporation. Information about each company is as shown:

	Academy Financial	Colorado Aviation
Price/earnings ratio	16	10.8
Number of shares	100,000	50,000
Earnings	$225,000	$100,000

Stockholders in Colorado Aviation will receive six tenths of a share of Academy for each share they hold in their company.

a. How will the EPS change for these two groups of shareholders?

b. What will the effect of changes in the EPS be on the original Academy stockholders?

14. **Calculating NPV**   Freeport Manufacturing is considering making an offer to purchase Portland Industries. The vice president of finance has collected the following information:

Challenge Problem

	Freeport	Portland
Price/earnings ratio	15	12
Number of shares	1,000,000	250,000
Earnings	$1,000,000	$750,000

She also knows that securities analysts expect the earnings and dividends (currently $1.80 per share) of Portland to grow at a constant rate of 5 percent each year. Her research tells her, however, that the acquisition would provide Portland with some economies of scale that would improve this growth rate to 7 percent per year.

a. What is the value of Portland to Freeport?

b. What would Freeport's gain be from this acquisition?

c. If Freeport offers $40 in cash for each outstanding share of Portland, what would the NPV of the acquisition be?

d. If, instead, Freeport were to offer 600,000 of its shares in exchange for the outstanding stock of Portland, what would the NPV be?

e. Should the acquisition be attempted, and, if so, should it be a cash or stock offer?

f. Freeport's management thinks that 7 percent growth is too optimistic and that 6 percent is more realistic. How does this change your previous answers?

15. **Merger NPV**   Show that the NPV of a merger can be expressed as the value of the synergistic benefits, ΔV, less the merger premium.

Challenge Question

Suggested Readings

A readable book on how to quantify the value from mergers and acquisitions is:

Rappaport, A. *Creating Shareholder Value: The New Standard for Business Performance.* New York: Free Press, 1986, Chapter 9.

Some good articles on mergers and acquisitions appear in:

Stern, J. M., and D. H. Chew, ed. *The Revolution in Corporate Finance.* New York: Basil Blackwell, 1986.

Chapter 22

International Corporate Finance

Corporations with significant foreign operations are often called *international corporations* or *multinationals*. Such corporations must consider many financial factors that do not directly affect purely domestic firms. These include foreign exchange rates, differing interest rates from country to country, complex accounting methods for foreign operations, foreign tax rates, and foreign government intervention.

The basic principles of corporate finance still apply to international corporations; like domestic companies, they seek to invest in projects that create more value for the shareholders than they cost and to arrange financing that raises cash at the lowest possible cost. In other words, the net present value principle holds for both foreign and domestic operations, but it is usually more complicated to apply the NPV rule to foreign investments.

One of the most significant complications of international finance is foreign exchange. The foreign exchange markets provide important information and opportunities for an international corporation when it undertakes capital budgeting and financing decisions. As we will discuss, international exchange rates, interest rates, and inflation rates are closely related. We will spend much of this chapter exploring the connection between these financial variables.

We won't have much to say here about the role of cultural and social differences in international business. We also will not be discussing the implications of differing political and economic systems. These factors are of great importance to international businesses, but it would take another book to do them justice. Consequently, we will focus only on some purely financial considerations in international finance and some key aspects of foreign exchange markets.

TERMINOLOGY | 22.1

A common buzzword for the student of business finance is *globalization*. The first step in learning about the globalization of financial markets is to conquer the new vocabulary. As with any specialty, international finance is rich in jargon. Accordingly, we get started on the subject with a highly eclectic vocabulary exercise.

The terms that follow are presented alphabetically, and they are not all of equal importance. We choose these particular ones because they appear frequently in the financial press or because they illustrate some of the colorful language of international finance.

1. An **American Depository Receipt (ADR)** is a security issued in the United States that represents shares of a foreign stock, allowing that stock to be traded in the United States. Foreign companies use ADRs, which are issued in U.S. dollars, to expand the pool of potential U.S. investors. ADRs are available in two forms for about 700 or so foreign companies: company sponsored, which are listed on an exchange, and unsponsored, which usually are held by the investment bank that makes a market in the ADR. Both forms are available to individual investors, but only company-sponsored issues are quoted daily in newspapers.

2. A **Belgian dentist** is a stereotype of the traditional Eurobond (see below) investor. This self-employed professional, a dentist, for instance, must report income, has a disdain for tax authorities, and likes to invest in foreign currencies. Anonymous-bearer Eurobonds fit the bill nicely for this type of investor because they are unregistered and therefore are untraceable. Such individual investors don't mind paying a premium for Eurobonds, because the bonds effectively are issued on a tax-free basis. The Belgian dentist may be an endangered species, however, and destined for replacement by the "Japanese butcher."

3. The **cross-rate** is the implicit exchange rate between two currencies (usually non-U.S.) when both are quoted in some third currency, usually the U.S. dollar.

4. A **European Currency Unit (ECU)** is a basket of 10 European currencies devised in 1979 and intended to serve as a monetary unit for the European Monetary System (EMS).

5. A **Eurobond** is a bond issued in multiple countries, but denominated in a single currency, usually the issuer's home currency. Such bonds have become an important way to raise capital for many international companies and governments. Eurobonds are issued outside the restrictions that apply to domestic offerings and are syndicated and traded mostly from London. Trading can and does take place anywhere there is a buyer and a seller.

6. **Eurocurrency** is money deposited in a financial center outside of the country whose currency is involved. For instance, Eurodollars—the most widely used Eurocurrency—are U.S. dollars deposited in banks outside the U.S. banking system.

American Depository Receipt (ADR)
A security issued in the United States representing shares of a foreign stock and allowing that stock to be traded in the United States.

Belgian dentist
Stereotype of the traditional Eurobond investor as a professional who must report income, has a disdain for tax authorities, and likes to invest in foreign currencies.

cross-rate
The implicit exchange rate between two currencies (usually non-U.S.) quoted in some third currency (usually the U.S. dollar).

European Currency Unit (ECU)
An index of 10 European currencies intended to serve as a monetary unit for the European Monetary System (EMS).

Eurobonds
International bonds issued in multiple countries but denominated in a single currency (usually the issuer's currency).

Eurocurrency
Money deposited in a financial center outside of the country whose currency is involved.

foreign bonds
International bonds issued in a single country, usually denominated in that country's currency.

7. **Foreign bonds,** unlike Eurobonds, are issued in a single country and are usually denominated in that country's currency. Often, the country in which these bonds are issued will draw distinctions between them and bonds issued by domestic issuers, including different tax laws, restrictions on the amount issued, or tougher disclosure rules.

   Foreign bonds often are nicknamed for the country where they are issued: Yankee bonds (United States), Samurai bonds (Japan), Rembrandt bonds (the Netherlands), and Bulldog bonds (Britain). Partly because of tougher regulations and disclosure requirements, the foreign-bond market hasn't grown in past years with the vigor of the Eurobond market. A substantial portion of all foreign bonds are issued in Switzerland.

gilts
British and Irish government securities, including issues of local British authorities and some overseas public-sector offerings.

8. **Gilts,** technically, are British and Irish government securities, although the term also includes issues of local British authorities and some overseas public-sector offerings.

London Interbank Offer Rate (LIBOR)
The rate most international banks charge one another for overnight Eurodollar loans.

9. The **London Interbank Offer Rate (LIBOR)** is the rate that most international banks charge one another for loans of Eurodollars overnight in the London market. LIBOR is a cornerstone in the pricing of money market issues and other short-term debt issues by both government and corporate borrowers. Interest rates are frequently quoted as some spread over LIBOR, and they then float with the LIBOR rate.

swaps
Agreements to exchange two securities or currencies.

10. There are two basic kinds of **swaps**: interest rate and currency. An interest rate swap occurs when two parties exchange a floating-rate payment for a fixed-rate payment or vice versa. Currency swaps are agreements to deliver one currency in exchange for another. Often both types of swaps are used in the same transaction when debt denominated in different currencies is swapped. Chapter 24 contains a more detailed discussion of swaps.

⌐CONCEPT QUESTIONS

22.1a What are the differences between a Eurobond and a foreign bond?

22.1b What are Eurodollars?

22.2 | FOREIGN EXCHANGE MARKETS AND EXCHANGE RATES

foreign exchange market
The market in which one country's currency is traded for another's.

The **foreign exchange market** is undoubtedly the world's largest financial market. It is the market where one country's currency is traded for another's. Most of the trading takes place in a few currencies: the U.S. dollar ($), the German deutsche mark (DM), the British pound sterling (£), the Japanese yen (¥), the Swiss franc (SF), and the French franc (FF). Table 22.1 lists some of the more common currencies and their symbols.

The foreign exchange market is an over-the-counter market, so there is no single location where traders get together. Instead, market participants are located in the major commercial and investment banks around the world. They communicate using computer terminals, telephones, and other telecommunications devices. For example, one communications network for foreign transactions is the Society for Worldwide Interbank Financial Telecommunications (SWIFT), a Belgian not-for-profit cooperative. Using data transmission lines, a bank in New York can send messages to a bank in London via SWIFT regional processing centers.

Country	Currency	Symbol
Australia	Dollar	A$
Austria	Schilling	Sch
Belgium	Franc	BF
Canada	Dollar	Can$
Denmark	Krone	DKr
Finland	Markka	FM
France	Franc	FF
Germany	Deutsche mark	DM
Greece	Drachma	Dr
India	Rupee	Rs
Iran	Rial	RI
Italy	Lira	Lit
Japan	Yen	¥
Kuwait	Dinar	KD
Mexico	Peso	Ps
Netherlands	Guilder	FL
Norway	Krone	NKr
Saudi Arabia	Riyal	SR
Singapore	Dollar	S$
South Africa	Rand	R
Spain	Peseta	Pta
Sweden	Kronar	Skr
Switzerland	Franc	SF
United Kingdom	Pound	£
United States	Dollar	$

Table 22.1

International currency symbols

The many different types of participants in the foreign exchange market include the following:

1. Importers who pay for goods involving foreign currencies.
2. Exporters who receive foreign currency and may want to convert to the domestic currency.
3. Portfolio managers who buy or sell foreign stocks and bonds.
4. Foreign exchange brokers who match buy and sell orders.
5. Traders who "make a market" in foreign currencies.
6. Speculators who try to profit from changes in exchange rates.

Exchange Rates

An **exchange rate** is simply the price of one country's currency expressed in terms of another country's currency. In practice, almost all trading of currencies takes place in terms of the U.S. dollar. For example, both the French franc and the German mark are traded with their prices quoted in U.S. dollars.

exchange rate

The price of one country's currency expressed in terms of another country's currency.

Table 22.2

Exchange rate quotations

EXCHANGE RATES

Tuesday, February 11, 1992

The New York foreign exchange selling rates below apply to trading among banks in amounts of $1 million and more, as quoted at 3 p.m. Eastern time by Bankers Trust Co., Telerate Systems Inc. and other sources. Retail transactions provide fewer units of foreign currency per dollar.

Country	U.S. $ equiv. Tues.	Currency per U.S. $ Tues.
Argentina (Peso)	1.02	.98
Australia (Dollar)	.7517	1.3303
Austria (Schilling)	.08913	11.22
Bahrain (Dinar).......	2.6525	.3770
Belgium (Franc).......	.03046	32.83
Brazil (Cruzeiro)	.00073	1363.88
Britain (Pound)	1.7995	.5557
30-Day Forward	1.7903	.5586
90-Day Forward	1.7719	.5644
180-Day Forward	1.7468	.5725
Canada (Dollar).......	.8462	1.1817
30-Day Forward	.8440	1.1848
90-Day Forward	.8398	1.1907
180-Day Forward	.8339	1.1992
Czechoslovakia (Koruna)		
Commercial rate.....	.0362450	27.5900
Chile (Peso)	.002943	339.83
China (Renminbi)	.183486	5.4500
Colombia (Peso)	.001745	573.00
Denmark (Krone)	.1617	6.1830
Ecuador (Sucre)		
Floating rate	.000763	1310.02
Finland (Markka)	.22989	4.3500
France (Franc)	.18415	5.4305
30-Day Forward	.18324	5.4572
90-Day Forward	.18142	5.5121
180-Day Forward	.17890	5.5897
Germany (Mark)	.6268	1.5955
30-Day Forward	.6240	1.6026
90-Day Forward	.6182	1.6175
180-Day Forward	.6102	1.6389
Greece (Drachma)	.005417	184.60
Hong Kong (Dollar)....	.12907	7.7480
Hungary (Forint)	.0132468	75.4900
India (Rupee).........	.03874	25.81
Indonesia (Rupiah)	.0004995	2002.00
Ireland (Punt)........	1.6720	.5981
Israel (Shekel)........	.4470	2.2373
Italy (Lira)	.0008333	1200.00

Table 22.2

(concluded)

Country	U.S. $ equiv. Tues.	Currency per U.S. $ Tues.
Japan (Yen)	.007843	127.50
30-Day Forward	.007834	127.65
90-Day Forward	.007819	127.90
180-Day Forward	.007805	128.13
Jordan (Dinar)	1.4738	.6785
Kuwait (Dinar)	3.4358	.2911
Lebanon (Pound)	.001138	879.00
Malaysia (Ringgit)	.3835	2.6075
Malta (Lira)	3.1949	.3130
Mexico (Peso)		
Floating rate	.0003267	3061.01
Netherland (Guilder)	.5563	1.7975
New Zealand (Dollar) . . .	.5405	1.8501
Norway (Krone)	.1597	6.2607
Pakistan (Rupee)	.0408	24.52
Peru (New Sol)	1.0466	.96
Philippines (Peso)	.03883	25.75
Poland (Zloty)	.00009634	10380.01
Portugal (Escudo)	.007346	136.12
Saudi Arabia (Riyal)	.26667	3.7500
Singapore (Dollar)	.6146	1.6270
South Africa (Rand)		
Commercial rate	.3595	2.7818
Financial rate	.2847	3.5120
South Korea (Won)	.0013072	765.00
Spain (Peseta)	.009953	100.47
Sweden (Krona)	.1724	5.7996
Switzerland (Franc)	.7003	1.4280
30-Day Forward	.6984	1.4318
90-Day Forward	.6945	1.4398
180-Day Forward	.6893	1.4507
Taiwan (Dollar)	.040404	24.75
Thailand (Baht)	.03951	25.31
Turkey (Lira)	.0001833	5455.00
United Arab (Dirham) . .	.2723	3.6725
Uruguay (New Peso)		
Financial	.000395	2530.01
Venezuela (Bolivar)		
Floating rate	.01586	63.04
SDR	1.40108	.71374
ECU	1.28100	. . . .

Special Drawing Rights (SDR) are based on exchange rates for the U.S., German, British, French and Japanese currencies. Source: International Monetary Fund.

European Currency Unit (ECU) is based on a basket of community currencies.

Reprinted by permission of *The Wall Street Journal,* © 1992 Dow Jones & Company, Inc., February 11, 1992. All Rights Reserved Worldwide.

Exchange Rate Quotations   Table 22.2 reproduces exchange rate quotations as they appear in *The Wall Street Journal*. The first column (labeled "U.S. $ equiv.") gives the number of dollars it takes to buy one unit of foreign currency. Since this is the price in dollars of a foreign currency, it is called a *direct* or *American quote* (remember that "Americans are direct"). For example, the Australian dollar is quoted at .7517, which means that you can buy one Australian dollar with U.S. $.7517.

The second column shows the *indirect* or *European exchange rate* (even though the currency may not be European). This is the amount of foreign currency per U.S. dollar. The Australian dollar is quoted here at 1.3303, so you can get 1.3303 Australian dollars for one U.S. dollar. Naturally, this second exchange rate is just the reciprocal of the first one, $1/.7517 = 1.3303$.

Example 22.1 On the Mark

Suppose you have $1,000. Based on the rates in Table 22.2, how many Japanese yen can you get? Alternatively, if a Porsche costs DM 200,000, how many dollars will you need to buy it (DM is the abbreviation for deutsche marks)?

The exchange rate in terms of yen per dollar (second column) is 127.50. Your $1,000 will thus get you:

$$\$1,000 \times 127.50 \text{ yen per } \$1 = 127,500 \text{ yen}$$

Since the exchange rate in terms of dollars per DM (first column) is .6268, you will need:

$$DM\ 200,000 \times .6268 \ \$ \text{ per DM} = \$125,360 \quad \blacksquare$$

Cross-Rates and Triangle Arbitrage   Using the U.S. dollar as the common denominator in quoting exchange rates greatly reduces the number of possible cross-currency quotes. For example, with five major currencies, there would potentially be 10 exchange rates instead of just 4.[1] Also, the fact that the dollar is used throughout cuts down on inconsistencies in the exchange rate quotations.

Earlier, we defined the cross-rate as the exchange rate for a non-U.S. currency expressed in terms of another non-U.S. currency. For example, suppose we observed the following:

$$FF \text{ per } \$1 = 10.00$$

$$DM \text{ per } \$1 = 2.00$$

---

[1]There are four exchange rates instead of five because one exchange rate would involve the exchange rate for a currency with itself. More generally, it might seem that there should be 25 exchange rates with five currencies. There are 25 different combinations, but, of these, 5 involve the exchange rate of a currency for itself. Of the remaining 20, half of them are redundant because they are just the reciprocals of another exchange rate. Of the remaining 10, 6 can be eliminated by using a common denominator.

Supose the cross-rate is quoted as:

FF per DM = 4.00

What do you think?

The cross-rate here is inconsistent with the exchange rates. To see this, suppose you have $100. If you convert this to deutsche marks, you will receive:

$100 × DM 2 per $1 = DM 200

If you convert this to francs at the cross-rate, you will have:

DM 200 × FF 4 per DM 1 = FF 800

However, if you just convert your dollars to francs without going through deutsche marks, you will have:

$100 × FF 10 per $1 = FF 1,000

What we see is that the franc has two prices, FF 10 per $1 and FF 8 per $1, depending on how we get them.

To make money, we want to buy low, sell high. The important thing to note is that francs are cheaper if you buy them with dollars because you get 10 francs instead of just 8. You should proceed as follows:

1. Buy 1,000 francs for $100.
2. Use the 1,000 francs to buy deutsche marks at the cross-rate. Since it takes four francs to buy a deutsche mark, you will receive FF 1000/4 = DM 250.
3. Use the DM 250 to buy dollars. Since the exchange rate is DM 2 per dollar, you receive DM 250/2 = $125, for a round-trip profit of $25.
4. Repeat steps 1 through 3.

This particular activity is called *triangle arbitrage* because the arbitrage involves moving through three different exchange rates:

$$\text{FF 10/\$1}$$

$$\text{DM 2/\$1} = \text{\$.50/DM 1} \longleftarrow \text{FF 4/DM 1} = \text{DM .25/FF 1}$$

To prevent such opportunities, it is not difficult to see that since a dollar will buy you either 10 francs or 2 deutsche marks, the cross-rate must be:

(FF 10/$1)/(DM 2/$1) = FF 5/DM 1

That is, five francs per deutsche mark. If it were anything else, there would be a triangle arbitrage opportunity.

Example 22.2 Shedding Some Pounds
Suppose the exchange rates for the British pound and German mark are:

Pounds per $1 = 0.60

DM per $1 = 2.00

The cross-rate is three marks per pound. Is this consistent? Explain how to go about making some money.

The cross-rate should be DM 2.00/£ .60 = DM 3.33 per pound. You can buy a pound for DM 3 in one market, and you can sell a pound for DM 3.33 in another. So we want to first get some marks, then use the marks to buy some pounds, and then sell the pounds. Assuming you have $100, you could:

1. Exchange dollars for marks: $100 × 2 = DM 200
2. Exchange marks for pounds: DM 200/3 = £66.67
3. Exchange pounds for dollars: £66.67/.60 = $111.12

This would result in an $11.12 round-trip profit. ∎

Types of Transactions

There are two basic types of trades in the foreign exchange market: spot trades and forward trades. A **spot trade** is an agreement to exchange currency "on the spot," which actually means that the transaction will be completed or settled within two business days. The exchange rate on a spot trade is called the **spot exchange rate.** Implicitly, all of the exchange rates and transactions we have discussed so far have referred to the spot market.

spot trade
An agreement to trade currencies based on the exchange rate today for settlement within two business days.

spot exchange rate
The exchange rate on a spot trade.

forward trade
Agreement to exchange currency at some time in the future.

forward exchange rate
The agreed-upon exchange rate to be used in a forward trade.

Forward Exchange Rates   A **forward trade** is an agreement to exchange currency at some time in the future. The exchange rate that will be used is agreed upon today and is called the **forward exchange rate.** A forward trade will normally be settled sometime in the next 12 months.

If you look back at Table 22.2, you will see forward exchange rates quoted for some of the major currencies. For example, the spot exchange rate for the Swiss franc is SF 1 = $.7003. The 180-day forward exchange rate is SF 1 = $.6893. This means that you can buy a Swiss franc today for $.7003, or you can agree to take delivery of a Swiss franc in 180 days and pay $.6893 at that time.

Notice that the Swiss franc is less expensive in the forward market ($.7003 versus $.6893). Since the Swiss franc is less expensive in the future than it is today, it is said to be selling at a *discount* relative to the dollar. For the same reason, the dollar is said to be selling at a *premium* relative to the Swiss franc.

Why does the forward market exist? One answer is that it allows businesses and individuals to lock in a future exchange rate today, thereby eliminating any risk from unfavorable shifts in the exchange rate.

Example 22.3 Looking Forward
Suppose you were expecting to receive a million British pounds in six months, and you agree to a forward trade to exchange your pounds for dollars. Based on Table 22.2, how many dollars will you get in six months? Is the pound selling at a discount or a premium relative to the dollar?

In Table 22.2, the spot exchange rate and the 180-day forward rate in terms of dollars per pound are $1.7995 = £1 and $1.7468 = £1, respectively. If you expect £1 million in 180 days, then you will get £1 million × $1.7468 per £ = $1.7468 million. Since it is cheaper to buy a pound in the forward market than in the spot market ($1.7468 versus $1.7995), the pound is selling at a discount relative to the dollar. ∎

As we mentioned earlier, it is standard practice around the world (with a few exceptions) to quote exchange rates in terms of the U.S. dollar. This means that rates are quoted as the amount of currency per U.S. dollar. For the remainder of this chapter, we will stick with this form. Things can get extremely confusing if you forget this. Thus, when we say things like "the exchange rate is expected to rise," it is important to remember that we are talking about the exchange rate quoted as units of foreign currency per dollar.

⌐CONCEPT QUESTIONS

22.2a What is triangle arbitrage?

22.2b What do we mean by the 90-day forward exchange rate?

22.2c If we say that the exchange rate is DM 1.90, what do we mean?

PURCHASING POWER PARITY | 22.3

Now that we have discussed what exchange rate quotations mean, we can address an obvious question: What determines the level of the spot exchange rate? In addition, we know that exchange rates change through time. A related question is thus: What determines the rate of change in exchange rates? At least part of the answer in both cases goes by the name of **purchasing power parity (PPP),** the idea that the exchange rate adjusts to keep purchasing power constant among currencies. As we discuss next, there are two forms of PPP, *absolute* and *relative.*

purchasing power parity (PPP)
The idea that the exchange rate adjusts to keep purchasing power constant among currencies.

Absolute Purchasing Power Parity

The basic idea behind *absolute purchasing power parity* is that a commodity costs the same regardless of what currency is used to purchase it or where it is selling. This is a very straightforward concept. If a beer costs £2 in London, and the exchange rate is £.60 per dollar, then a beer costs £2/.60 = $3.33 in New York. In other words, absolute PPP says that $1 will buy you the same number of, say, cheeseburgers, anywhere in the world.

More formally, let S_0 be the spot exchange rate between the British pound and the U.S. dollar today (Time 0), and remember that we are quoting exchange rates as the amount of foreign currency per dollar. Let P_{US} and P_{UK} be the current U.S. and British prices, respectively, on a particular commodity, say, apples. Absolute PPP simply says that:

$$P_{UK} = S_0 \times P_{US}$$

This tells us that the British price for something is equal to the U.S. price for that same something, multiplied by the exchange rate.

The rationale behind PPP is similar to that behind triangle arbitrage. If PPP did not hold, arbitrage would be possible (in principle) by moving apples from one country to another. For example, suppose that apples in New York are selling for $4 per bushel, while in London the price is £2.40 per bushel. Absolute PPP implies that:

$$P_{UK} = S_0 \times P_{US}$$
$$£2.40 = S_0 \times \$4$$
$$S_0 = £2.40/\$4 = £.60$$

That is, the implied spot exchange rate is £.60 per dollar. Equivalently, a pound is worth $1/£.60 = \$1.67$.

Suppose, instead, that the actual exchange rate is £.50. Starting with $4, a trader could buy a bushel of apples in New York, ship it to London, and sell it there for £2.40. Our trader then converts the £2.40 into dollars at the prevailing exchange rate, $S_0 = £.50$, yielding a total of £2.40/.50 = 4.80. The round-trip gain is 80 cents.

Because of this profit potential, forces are set in motion to change the exchange rate and/or the price of apples. In our example, apples would begin moving from New York to London. The reduced supply of apples in New York would raise the price of apples there, and the increased supply in Britain would lower the price of apples in London.

In addition to moving apples around, apple traders would be busily converting pounds back into dollars to buy more apples. This activity increases the supply of pounds and simultaneously increases the demand for dollars. We would expect the value of a pound to fall. This means that the dollar is getting more valuable, so it will take more pounds to buy one dollar. Since the exchange rate is quoted as pounds per dollar, we would expect the exchange rate to rise from £.50.

For absolute PPP to hold absolutely, several things must be true:

1. The transactions cost of trading apples—shipping, insurance, wastage, and so on—must be zero.
2. There are no barriers to trading apples, such as tariffs, taxes, or other political barriers such as VRAs (voluntary restraint agreements).
3. Finally, an apple in New York must be identical to an apple in London. It won't do for you to send red apples to London if the English eat only green apples.

Given the fact that the transactions costs are not zero and that the other conditions are rarely exactly met, it is not surprising that absolute PPP is really applicable only to traded goods, and then only to very uniform ones.

For this reason, absolute PPP does not imply that a Mercedes costs the same as a Ford or that a nuclear power plant in France costs the same as one in New York. In the case of the cars, they are not identical. In the case of the power plants, even if they were identical, they are expensive and very difficult to ship. On the other hand, we would be very surprised to see a significant violation of absolute PPP for gold.

Relative Purchasing Power Parity

As a practical matter, a relative version of purchasing power parity has evolved. *Relative purchasing power parity* does not tell us what determines the absolute level of the exchange rate. Instead, it tells what determines the *change* in the exchange rate over time.

The Basic Idea   Suppose again that the British pound/U.S. dollar exchange rate is currently $S_0 = £.50$. Further suppose that the inflation rate in Britain is predicted to be 10 percent over the coming year and (for the moment) the inflation rate in the United States is predicted to be zero. What do you think the exchange rate will be in a year?

   If you think about it, a dollar currently costs .50 pounds in Britain. With 10 percent inflation, we expect prices in Britain to generally rise by 10 percent. So we expect that the price of a dollar will go up by 10 percent and the exchange rate should rise to $£.50 \times 1.1 = £.55$.

   If the inflation rate in the United States is not zero, then we need to worry about the *relative* inflation rates in the two countries. For example, suppose the U.S. inflation rate is predicted to be 4 percent. Relative to prices in the United States, prices in Britain are rising at a rate of $10\% - 4\% = 6\%$ per year. So we expect the price of the dollar to rise by 6 percent, and the predicted exchange rate is $£.50 \times 1.06 = £.53$.

The Result   In general, relative PPP says that the change in the exchange rate is determined by the difference in the inflation rates between the two countries. To be more specific, we will use the following notation:

S_0 = Current (Time 0) spot exchange rate (foreign currency per dollar)

$E[S_t]$ = Expected exchange rate in t periods

h_{US} = Inflation rate in the United States

h_{FC} = Foreign country inflation rate

Based on our discussion just above, relative PPP says that the expected percentage change in the exchange rate over the next year, $(E[S_1] - S_0)/S_0$, is:

$$(E[S_1] - S_0)/S_0 = h_{FC} - h_{US} \qquad [22.1]$$

In words, relative PPP simply says that the expected percentage change in the exchange rate is equal to the difference in inflation rates. If we rearrange this slightly, we get:

$$E[S_1] = S_0 \times [1 + (h_{FC} - h_{US})] \qquad [22.2]$$

This result makes a certain amount of sense, but care must be used in quoting the exchange rate.

   In our example involving Britain and the United States, relative PPP tells us that the exchange rate will rise by $h_{FC} - h_{US} = 10\% - 4\% = 6\%$ per year.

Assuming the difference in inflation rates doesn't change, the expected exchange rate in two years, $E[S_2]$, will therefore be:

$$E[S_2] = E[S_1] \times (1 + .06)$$
$$= .53 \times 1.06$$
$$= .562$$

Notice that we could have written this as:

$$E[S_2] = .53 \times 1.06$$
$$= (.50 \times 1.06) \times 1.06$$
$$= .50 \times 1.06^2$$

In general, relative PPP, says that the expected exchange rate at sometime in the future, $E[S_t]$, is:

$$E[S_t] = S_0 \times [1 + (h_{FC} - h_{US})]^t \qquad [22.3]$$

As we will see, this is a very useful relationship.

Because we don't really expect absolute PPP to hold for most goods, we will focus on relative PPP in our discussion below. Henceforth, when we refer to PPP without further qualification, we mean relative PPP.

Example 22.4 It's All Relative
Suppose the Japanese exchange rate is currently 130 yen per dollar. The inflation rate in Japan over the next three years will run, say, 2 percent per year while the U.S. inflation rate will be 6 percent. Based on relative PPP, what will the exchange rate be in three years?

Since the U.S. inflation rate is higher, we expect that a dollar will become less valuable. The exchange rate change will be $2\% - 6\% = -4\%$ per year. Over three years, the exchange rate will fall to:

$$E[S_3] = S_0 \times [1 + (h_{FC} - h_{US})]^3$$
$$= 130 \times [1 + (-.04)]^3$$
$$= 115.02 \quad \blacksquare$$

Currency Appreciation and Depreciation   We frequently hear things like "the dollar strengthened (or weakened) in financial markets today" or "the dollar is expected to appreciate (or depreciate) relative to the pound." When we say the dollar strengthens or appreciates, we mean that the value of a dollar rises, so it takes more foreign currency to buy a dollar.

What happens to the exchange rates as currencies fluctuate in value depends on how exchange rates are quoted. Since we are quoting them as units of foreign currency per dollar, the exchange rate moves in the same direction as the value of the dollar: It rises as the dollar strengthens, and it falls as the dollar weakens.

Relative PPP tells us that the exchange rate will rise if the U.S. inflation rate is lower than the foreign country's. This happens because the foreign currency depreciates in value and therefore weakens relative to the dollar.

⌐ CONCEPT QUESTIONS

22.3a What does absolute PPP say? Why might it not hold for many types of goods?

22.3b According to relative PPP, what determines the change in exchange rates?

INTEREST RATE PARITY, UNBIASED FORWARD RATES, AND ⌐ 22.4
THE INTERNATIONAL FISHER EFFECT

The next issue we need to address is the relationship between the spot exchange rates, forward exchange rates, and interest rates. To get started, we need some additional notation:

F_t = Forward exchange rate for settlement at time t

R_{US} = U.S. nominal risk-free interest rate

R_{FC} = Foreign country nominal risk-free interest rate

As before, we will use S_0 to stand for the spot exchange rate. You can take the U.S. nominal risk-free rate, R_{US}, to be the T-bill rate.

Covered Interest Arbitrage

Suppose we observe the following information about U.S. and German currency in the market:

S_0 = DM 2.00 R_{US} = 10%

F_1 = DM 1.90 R_G = 5%

where R_G is the nominal risk-free rate in Germany. The period is one year, so F_1 is the 360-day forward rate.

Do you see an arbitrage opportunity here? There is one. Suppose you have $1 to invest, and you want a riskless investment. One option you have is to invest the $1 in a riskless U.S. investment such as a 360-day T-bill. If you do this, then, in one period, your $1 will be worth:

$ value in 1 period = $1 $\times$ (1 + R_{US})

= $1.10

Alternatively, you can invest in the German risk-free investment. To do this, you need to convert your $1 to deutsche marks and simultaneously execute a forward trade to convert marks back to dollars in one year. The necessary steps would be as follows:

1. Convert your $1 to $1 \times S_0 = $ DM 2.00
2. At the same time, enter into a forward agreement to convert marks back to dollars in one year. Since the forward rate is DM 1.90, you get $1 for every DM 1.90 that you have in one year.
3. Invest your DM 2.00 in Germany at R_G. In one year, you will have:

$$\text{DM value in 1 year} = \text{DM } 2.00 \times (1 + R_G)$$

$$= \text{DM } 2.00 \times 1.05$$

$$= \text{DM } 2.10$$

4. Convert your DM 2.10 back to dollars at the agreed upon rate of DM 1.90 = $1. You end up with:

$$\$ \text{ value in 1 year} = \text{DM } 2.10/1.90$$

$$= \$1.1053$$

Notice that the value in one year from this strategy can be written as:

$$\$ \text{ value in 1 year} = \$1 \times S_0 \times (1 + R_G)/F_1$$

$$= \$1 \times 2 \times (1.05)/1.90$$

$$= \$1.1053$$

The return on this investment is apparently 10.53 percent. This is higher than the 10 percent we get from investing in the United States. Since both investments are risk-free, there is an arbitrage opportunity.

To exploit the difference in interest rates, you need to borrow, say, $5 million at the lower U.S. rate and invest it at the higher German rate. What is the round-trip profit from doing this? To find out, we can work through the steps above:

1. Convert the $5 million at DM 2 = $1 to get DM 10 million.
2. Agree to exchange marks for dollars in one year at DM 1.90 to the dollar.
3. Invest the DM 10 million for one year at $R_G = 5\%$. You end up with DM 10.5 million.
4. Convert the DM 10.5 million back to dollars to fulfill the forward contract. You receive DM 10.5 million/1.90 = $5,526,316.
5. Repay the loan with interest. You owe $5 million plus 10 percent interest, for a total of $5.5 million. You have $5,526,316, so your round-trip profit is a risk-free $26,316.

The activity that we have illustrated here goes by the name of *covered interest arbitrage*. The term *covered* refers to the fact that we are covered in the event of a change in the exchange rate since we lock in the forward exchange rate today.

Interest Rate Parity (IRP)

If we assume that significant covered interest arbitrage opportunities do not exist, then there must be some relationship between spot exchange rates, forward exchange rates, and relative interest rates. To see what this relationship is, note that, in general, Strategy 1 above, investing in a riskless U.S. investment, gives us $(1 + R_{US})$ for every dollar we invest. Strategy 2, investing in a foreign risk-free investment, gives us $S_0 \times (1 + R_{FC})/F_1$ for every dollar we invest. Since these have to be equal to prevent arbitrage, it must be the case that:

$$(1 + R_{US}) = S_0 \times (1 + R_{FC})/F_1$$

Rearranging this a bit gets us the famous **interest rate parity (IRP)** condition:

$$F_1/S_0 = (1 + R_{FC})/(1 + R_{US}) \qquad\qquad [22.4]$$

There is a very useful approximation for IRP that illustrates very clearly what is going on and is not difficult to remember. If we define the percentage forward premium or discount as $(F_1 - S_0)/S_0$, then IRP says that this percent premium or discount is *approximately* equal to the difference in interest rates:

$$(F_1 - S_0)/S_0 = R_{FC} - R_{US} \qquad\qquad [22.5]$$

Very loosely, what IRP says is that any difference in interest rates between two countries for some period is just offset by the change in the relative value of the currencies, thereby eliminating any arbitrage possibilities. Notice that we could also write:

$$F_1 = S_0 \times [1 + (R_{FC} - R_{US})] \qquad\qquad [22.6]$$

In general, if we have t periods instead of just one, the IRP approximation would be written as:

$$F_t = S_0 \times [1 + (R_{FC} - R_{US})]^t \qquad\qquad [22.7]$$

interest rate parity (IRP)

The condition stating that the interest rate differential between two countries is equal to the percentage difference between the forward exchange rate and the spot exchange rate.

Example 22.5   Parity Check

Suppose the exchange rate for Japanese yen, S_0, is currently ¥120 = \$1. If the interest rate in the United States is $R_{US} = 10\%$ and the interest rate in Japan is $R_J = 5\%$, then what must the forward rate be to prevent covered interest arbitrage?

From IRP, we have:

$$
\begin{aligned}
F_1 &= S_0 \times [1 + (R_J - R_{US})] \\
&= ¥120 \times [1 + (.05 - .10)] \\
&= ¥120 \times .95 \\
&= ¥114
\end{aligned}
$$

Notice that the yen will sell at a premium relative to the dollar (why?). ∎

Forward Rates and Future Spot Rates

In addition to PPP and IRP, there is one more basic relationship we need to discuss. What is the connection between the forward rate and the expected future spot rate? The **unbiased forward rates (UFR)** condition says that the forward rate, F_1, is equal to the *expected* future spot rate, $E[S_1]$:

unbiased forward rates (UFR)

The condition stating that the current forward rate is an unbiased predictor of the future exchange rate.

$$F_1 = E[S_1]$$

With t periods, UFR would be written as:

$$F_t = E[S_t]$$

Loosely, the UFR condition says that, on average, the forward exchange rate is equal to the future spot exchange rate.

If we ignore risk, then the UFR condition should hold. Suppose the forward rate for the Japanese yen is consistently lower than the future spot rate by, say, 10 yen. This means that anyone who wanted to convert dollars to yen in the future would consistently get more yen by not agreeing to a forward exchange. The forward rate would have to rise to get anyone interested.

Similarly, if the forward rate were consistently higher than the future spot rate, then anyone who wanted to convert yen to dollars would get more dollars per yen by not agreeing to a forward trade. The forward exchange rate would have to fall to attract such traders.

For these reasons, the forward and actual future spot rates should be equal to each other on average. What the future spot rate will actually be is uncertain, of course. The UFR condition may not hold if traders are willing to pay a premium to avoid this uncertainty. If the condition does hold, then the 180-day forward rate that we see today should be an unbiased predictor of what the exchange rate will actually be in 180 days.

Putting It All Together

We have developed three relationships, PPP, IRP, and UFR, that describe the relationships between key financial variables such as interest rates, exchange rates, and inflation rates. We now explore the implications of these relationships as a group.

Uncovered Interest Parity   To start, it is useful to collect our international financial market relationships in one place:

PPP: $E[S_1] = S_0 \times [1 + (h_{FC} - h_{US})]$

IRP: $F_1 = S_0 \times [1 + (R_{FC} - R_{US})]$

UFR: $F_1 = E[S_1]$

We begin by combining UFR and IRP. Since $F_1 = E[S_1]$ from the UFR condition, we can substitute $E[S_1]$ for F_1 in IRP. The result is:

$$E[S_1] = S_0 \times [1 + (R_{FC} - R_{US})] \qquad [22.8]$$

This important relationship is called **uncovered interest parity (UIP)**, and it will play a key role in our international capital budgeting discussion below. With t periods, UIP becomes:

$$E[S_t] = S_0 \times [1 + (R_{FC} - R_{US})]^t \qquad [22.9]$$

uncovered interest parity (UIP)
The condition stating that the expected percentage change in the exchange rate is equal to the difference in interest rates.

The International Fisher Effect   Next, we compare PPP and UIP. Both of them have $E[S_1]$ on the left-hand side, so their right-hand sides must be equal. We thus have that:

$$S_0 \times [1 + (h_{FC} - h_{US})] = S_0 \times [1 + (R_{FC} - R_{US})]$$

$$h_{FC} - h_{US} = R_{FC} - R_{US}$$

This tells us that the difference in returns between the United States and a foreign country is just equal to the difference in inflation rates. Rearranging this slightly gives us the **international Fisher effect (IFE)**:

$$R_{US} - h_{US} = R_{FC} - h_{FC} \qquad [22.10]$$

international Fisher effect (IFE)
The theory that real interest rates are equal across countries.

The IFE says that *real* rates are equal across countries.[2]

The conclusion that real returns are equal across countries is really basic economics. If real returns were higher in, say, France than in the United States, money would flow out of U.S. financial markets and into French markets. Asset prices in France would rise and their returns would fall. At the same time, asset prices in the United States would fall and their returns would rise. This process acts to equalize real returns.

Having said all this, we need to note several things. First of all, we really haven't explicitly dealt with risk in our discussion. We might reach a different conclusion about real returns once we do, particularly if people in different countries have different tastes and attitudes toward risk. Second, there are many barriers to the movement of money and capital around the world. Real returns might be different between two countries for long periods of time if money can't move freely between them.

Despite these problems, we expect that capital markets will become increasingly internationalized. As this occurs, any differences in real rates that do exist will probably diminish. The laws of economics have very little respect for national boundaries.

⌐ **CONCEPT QUESTIONS**

22.4a What is covered interest arbitrage?

22.4b What is the international Fisher effect?

---

[2]Notice that our result here is in terms of the approximate real rate, $R - h$ (see Chapter 10), because we used approximations for PPP and IRP. For the exact result, see Problem 19 at the end of the chapter.

22.5 | INTERNATIONAL CAPITAL BUDGETING

Kihlstrom Equipment, a U.S.–based international company, is evaluating an overseas investment. Kihlstrom's exports of drill bits have increased to such a degree that it is considering building a plant in France. The project will cost FF 20 million to launch. The cash flows are expected to be FF 9 million a year for the next three years.

The current spot exchange rate for French francs is FF 5. Recall that this is francs per dollar, so a franc is worth $1/5 = $.20. The risk-free rate in the United States is 5 percent, and the risk-free rate in France is 7 percent. Notice that the exchange rate and the two interest rates are observed in financial markets, not estimated.[3] Kihlstrom's required return on dollar investments of this sort is 10 percent.

Should Kihlstrom take this investment? As always, the answer depends on the NPV, but how do we calculate the net present value of this project in U.S. dollars? There are two basic ways to go about doing this:

1. *The home currency approach.* Convert all the franc cash flows into dollars, and then discount at 10 percent to find the NPV in dollars. Notice for this approach, we have to come up with the future exchange rates in order to convert the future projected franc cash flows into dollars.

2. *The foreign currency approach.* Determine the required return on franc investments, and then discount the franc cash flows to find the NPV in francs. Then convert this franc NPV to a dollar NPV. This approach requires us to somehow convert the 10 percent dollar required return to the equivalent franc required return.

The difference between these two approaches is primarily a matter of when we convert from francs to dollars. In the first case, we convert before estimating the NPV. In the second case, we convert after estimating NPV.

It might appear that the second approach is superior because we only have to come up with one number, the franc discount rate. Furthermore, since the first approach requires us to forecast future exchange rates, it probably seems that there is greater room for error. As we illustrate next, however, based on our results above, the two approaches are really the same.

Method 1: The Home Currency Approach

To convert the project future cash flows into dollars, we will invoke the uncovered interest parity (UIP) relation to come up with the projected exchange rates. Based on our discussion above, the expected exchange rate at time t, $E[S_t]$ is:

$$E[S_t] = S_0 \times [1 + (R_{FR} - R_{US})]^t$$

---

[3]For example, the interest rates might be the short-term Eurodollar and Eurofranc deposit rates offered by large money center banks.

In Their Own Words . . .
Richard M. Levich on Forward Exchange Rates

What is the relationship between today's three-month forward exchange rate, which can be observed in the market, and the spot exchange rate of three months from today, which cannot be observed until the future? One popular answer is that there is no relationship. As every bank trader knows, the possibility of covered interest arbitrage between domestic and foreign securities establishes a close link between the forward premium and the interest rate differential. At any moment, a trader can check his screen and observe that the forward premium and the interest rate differentials are nearly identical, especially when Eurocurrency interest rates are used. Thus the trader might say, "The forward rate reflects today's interest differential. It has nothing to do with expectations."

To check the second popular belief, that the forward rate reflects exchange rate expectations, takes a bit more work. Take today's three-month forward rate as of January 15 and compare it to the spot exchange rate that actually exists three months later on April 15. This produces one observation on the forward rate as a forecaster — not enough to accept or reject a theory. The idea that the forward rate might be an unbiased predictor of the future spot rate suggests that, on average and looking at many observations, the prediction error is small. So collect more data using the forward rate of April 15 and match it with the spot rate of July 15, and then the forward rate of July 15 matched to the spot rate of October 15, and so on. Look at the data for 8–10 years to have a large sample of observations.

The data suggest [Levich (1989); for full citation see Suggested Readings] that in the early 1980s when the dollar was very strong, the forward rate significantly *under*estimated the strength of the dollar, and the forward rate was a biased predictor. But from 1985–1987 when the dollar depreciated sharply, the forward rate tended to *over*estimate the strength of the dollar, and the forward rate was again a biased predictor, but with the opposite sign as the earlier period. Looking at all of the 1980s — you guessed it — the forward rate was on average very close to the future spot exchange rate.

There are two messages here. First, even if there were "no relationship" between the forward rate and the future spot rate, the treasurer of General Motors would want to know exactly what that "nonrelationship" was. Because if the forward rate were *consistently* 3 percent higher than, or *consistently* 5 percent lower than, the future spot rate, the treasurer would be facing a tantalizing profit opportunity. A watch that is three minutes fast or five minutes slow is a very useful watch, as long as the bias is known and consistent. And finally, the data from the 1980s have revalidated Michael Mussa's [Mussa (1979); for full citation see Suggested Readings] interpretation of the 1970s. Mussa observed that "the forward rate is an unbiased predictor of the future spot rate, [it] is close to the best available predictor . . . but [it] is probably not a very good predictor. . . . "

Richard M. Levich is Professor of Finance and International Business at New York University. He has written extensively on exchange rates and other issues in international economics and finance.

---

where R_{FR} stands for the nominal risk-free rate in France. Since R_{FR} is 7 percent, R_{US} is 5 percent, and the current exchange rate (S_0) is FF 5:

$$E[S_t] = 5 \times [1 + (.07 - .05)]^t$$
$$= 5 \times 1.02^t$$

The projected exchange rates for the drill bit project are thus:

Year	Expected Exchange Rate
1	FF 5 $\times$ 1.02^1 = FF 5.100
2	FF 5 $\times$ 1.02^2 = FF 5.202
3	FF 5 $\times$ 1.02^3 = FF 5.306

Using these exchange rates, along with the current exchange rate, we can convert all of the franc cash flows to dollars:

Year	(1) Cash Flow in FF	(2) Expected Exchange Rate	(3) Cash Flow in $ (1)/(2)
0	−FF 20	FF 5.000	−$4.00
1	9	5.100	1.76
2	9	5.202	1.73
3	9	5.306	1.70

To finish off, we calculate the NPV in the ordinary way:

$$\text{NPV}_\$ = -\$4.00 + \$1.76/1.10 + \$1.73/1.10^2 + \$1.70/1.10^3$$

$$= \$.3 \text{ million}$$

So the project appears to be profitable.

Method 2: The Foreign Currency Approach

Kihlstrom requires a nominal return of 10 percent on the dollar-denominated cash flows. We need to convert this to a rate suitable for franc-denominated cash flows. Based on the international Fisher effect, we know that the difference in the nominal rates is:

$$R_{FR} - R_{US} = h_{FR} - h_{US}$$

$$= 7\% - 5\% = 2\%$$

The appropriate discount rate for estimating the franc cash flows from the drill bit project is approximately equal to 10 percent plus an extra 2 percent to compensate for the greater franc inflation rate.

If we calculate the NPV of the franc cash flows at this rate, we get:

$$\text{NPV}_{FF} = -FF\ 20 + FF\ 9/1.12 + FF\ 9/1.12^2 + FF\ 9/1.12^3$$

$$= FF\ 1.6 \text{ million}$$

The NPV of this project is FF 1.6 million. Taking this project makes us FF 1.6 million richer today. What is this in dollars? Since the exchange rate today is FF 5, the dollar NPV of the project is:

$$\text{NPV}_\$ = \text{NPV}_{FF}/S_0 = FF\ 1.6/5 = \$.3 \text{ million}$$

This is the same dollar NPV as we previously calculated.

The important thing to recognize from our example is that the two capital budgeting procedures are actually the same and will always give the same answer.[4] In this second approach, the fact that we are implicitly forecasting exchange rates is simply hidden. Even so, the foreign currency approach is computationally a little easier.

Unremitted Cash Flows

The previous example assumed that all aftertax cash flows from the foreign investment could be remitted to (paid out to) the parent firm. Actually, substantial differences can exist between the cash flows generated by a foreign project and the amount that can actually be remitted or "repatriated" to the parent firm.

A foreign subsidiary can remit funds to a parent in many ways, including the following:

1. Dividends
2. Management fees for central services
3. Royalties on the use of trade names and patents

However cash flows are repatriated, international firms must pay special attention to remittance for two reasons. First, there may be current and future controls on remittances. Many governments are sensitive to the charge of being exploited by foreign national firms. In such cases, governments are tempted to limit the ability of international firms to remit cash flows. Funds that cannot currently be remitted are sometimes said to be *blocked*.

⌐ CONCEPT QUESTIONS

22.5a What financial complications arise in international capital budgeting?
Describe two procedures for estimating NPV in this case.

22.5b What are blocked funds?

EXCHANGE RATE RISK | 22.6

Exchange rate risk is the natural consequence of international operations in a world where relative currency values move up and down. Managing exchange rate risk is an important part of international finance. As we discuss next, there are three different types of exchange rate risk or exposure: short-run exposure, long-run exposure, and translation exposure. Chapter 24 contains a more detailed discussion of the issues raised in this section.

exchange rate risk
The risk related to having international operations in a world where relative currency values vary.

Short-Run Exposure

The day-to-day fluctuations in exchange rates create short-run risks for international firms. Most such firms have contractual agreements to buy and sell

---

[4]Actually, there will be a slight difference because we are using the approximate relationships. If we calculate the required return as $(1.10) \times (1 + .02) - 1 = 12.2\%$, then we get exactly the same NPV. See Problem 19 for more detail.

goods in the near future at set prices. When different currencies are involved, such transactions have an extra element of risk.

For example, imagine that you are importing imitation pasta from Italy and reselling it in the United States under the Impasta brand name. Your largest customer has ordered 10,000 cases of Impasta. You place the order with your supplier today, but you won't pay until the goods arrive in 60 days. Your selling price is $6 per case. Your cost is 8,400 Italian lira per case, and the exchange rate is currently Lit 1,500, so it takes 1,500 lira to buy $1.

At the current exchange rate, your cost in dollars from filling the order is Lit 8,400/1,500 = $5.6 per case, so your pretax profit on the order is 10,000 × ($6 − $5.6) = $4,000. However, the exchange rate in 60 days will probably be different, so your profit will depend on what the future exchange rate turns out to be.

For example, if the rate goes to Lit 1,600, your cost is Lit 8,400/1,600 = $5.25 per case. Your profit goes to $7,500. If the exchange rate goes to, say, Lit 1,400, then your cost is Lit 8,400/1,400 = $6, and your profit is zero.

The short-run exposure in our example can be reduced or eliminated in several ways. The most obvious means of hedging is to enter into a forward exchange agreement to lock in an exchange rate. For example, suppose the 60-day forward rate is Lit 1,580. What will be your profit if you hedge? What profit should you expect if you don't?

If you hedge, you lock in an exchange rate of Lit 1,580. Your cost in dollars will thus be Lit 8,400/1,580 = $5.32 per case, so your profit will be 10,000 × ($6 − $5.32) = $6,800. If you don't hedge, then, assuming that the forward rate is an unbiased predictor (in other words, assuming the UFR condition holds), you should expect that the exchange rate will actually be Lit 1,580 in 60 days. You should expect to make $6,800.

Alternatively, if this is not feasible, you could simply borrow the dollars today, convert them into lira, and invest the lira for 60 days to earn some interest. From IRP, this amounts to entering into a forward contract.

Long-Run Exposure

In the long run, the value of a foreign operation can fluctuate because of unanticipated changes in relative economic conditions. For example, imagine that we own a labor-intensive assembly operation located in another country to take advantage of lower wages. Through time, unexpected changes in economic conditions can raise the foreign wage levels to the point where the cost advantage is eliminated or even becomes negative.

Hedging long-run exposure is more difficult than hedging short-term risks. For one thing, organized forward markets don't exist for such long-term needs. Instead, the primary option that firms have is to try and match up foreign currency inflows and outflows. The same thing goes for matching foreign currency–denominated assets and liabilities. For example, a firm that sells in a foreign country might try to concentrate its raw material purchases and labor expense in that country. That way, the dollar value of its revenues and costs will move up and down together.

Similarly, a firm can reduce its long-run exchange risk by borrowing in the foreign country. Fluctuations in the value of the foreign subsidiary's assets will then be at least partially offset by changes in the value of the liabilities.

Translation Exposure

When a U.S. company calculates its accounting net income and EPS for some period, it must "translate" everything into dollars. This can create some problems for the accountants when there are significant foreign operations. In particular, two issues arise:

1. What is the appropriate exchange rate to use for translating each balance sheet account?
2. How should balance sheet accounting gains and losses from foreign currency translation be handled?

To illustrate the accounting problem, suppose we started a small foreign subsidiary in Lilliputia a year ago. The local currency is the gulliver, abbreviated GL. At the beginning of the year, the exchange rate was GL 2 = $1, and the balance sheet in gullivers looked like this:

Assets	GL 1,000	Liabilities	GL 500
		Equity	500

At 2 gullivers to the dollar, the beginning balance sheet in dollars was:

Assets	$500	Liabilities	$250
		Equity	250

Lilliputia is a quiet place, and nothing at all actually happened during the year. As a result, net income was zero (before consideration of exchange rate changes). However, the exchange rate did change to 4 gullivers = $1 purely because the Lilliputian inflation rate is much higher than the U.S. inflation rate.

Since nothing happened, the accounting ending balance sheet in gullivers is the same as the beginning one. However, if we convert it to dollars at the new exchange rate, we get:

Assets	$250	Liabilities	$125
		Equity	125

Notice that the value of the equity has gone down by $125, even though net income was exactly zero. Despite the fact that absolutely nothing really happened, there is a $125 accounting loss. How to handle this $125 loss has been a controversial accounting question.

One obvious and consistent way to handle this loss is simply to report the loss on the parent's income statement. During periods of volatile exchange rates, this kind of treatment can dramatically impact an international company's reported EPS. This is purely an accounting phenomenon, but, even so, such fluctuations are disliked by some financial managers.

The current approach to translation gains and losses is based on rules set out in Financial Accounting Standards Boards (FASB) Statement Number 52, issued in December 1981. For the most part, FASB 52 requires that all assets and liabilities be translated from the subsidiary's currency into the parent's currency using the exchange rate that currently prevails.

Any translation gains and losses that occur are accumulated in a special account within the shareholder's equity section of the balance sheet. This account might be labeled something like "unrealized foreign exchange gains (losses)." These gains and losses are not reported on the income statement. As a result, the impact of translation gains and losses will not be recognized explicitly in net income until the underlying assets and liabilities are sold or otherwise liquidated.

Managing Exchange Rate Risk

For a large multinational firm, the management of exchange rate risk is complicated by the fact that there can be many different currencies involved in many different subsidiaries. It is very likely that a change in some exchange rate will benefit some subsidiaries and hurt others. The net effect on the overall firm depends on its net exposure.

For example, suppose a firm has two divisions. Division A buys goods in the United States for dollars and sells them in Britain for pounds. Division B buys goods in Britain for pounds and sells them in the United States for dollars. If these two divisions are of roughly equal size in terms of their inflows and outflows, then the overall firm obviously has little exchange rate risk.

In our example, the firm's net position in pounds (the amount coming in less the amount going out) is small, so the exchange rate risk is small. However, if one division, acting on its own, were to start hedging its exchange rate risk, then the overall firm's exchange rate risk would go up. The moral of the story is that multinational firms have to be conscious of the overall position that the firm has in a foreign currency. For this reason, management of exchange rate risk is probably best handled on a centralized basis.

> **CONCEPT QUESTIONS**
>
> 22.6a What are the different types of exchange rate risk?
> 22.6b How can a firm hedge short-run exchange rate risk? Long-run exchange rate risk?

22.7 | POLITICAL RISK

political risk

Risk related to changes in value that arise because of political actions.

One final element of risk in international investing concerns **political risk.** Political risk refers to changes in value that arise as a consequence of political actions. This is not purely a problem faced by international firms. For example, changes in U.S. tax laws and regulations may benefit some U.S. firms and hurt others, so political risk exists nationally as well as internationally.

Some countries do have more political risk than others, however. In such cases, the extra political risk may lead firms to require higher returns on overseas investments to compensate for the risk that funds will be blocked, critical operations interrupted, and contracts abrogated. In the most extreme case, the possibility of outright confiscation may be a concern in countries with relatively unstable political environments.

Political risk also depends on the nature of the business; some businesses are less likely to be confiscated because they are not particularly valuable in the hands of a different owner. An assembly operation supplying subcomponents that only the parent company uses would not an be attractive "takeover" target, for example. Similarly, a manufacturing operation that requires the use of specialized components from the parent is of little value without the parent company's cooperation.

Natural resource developments, such as copper mining or oil drilling, are just the opposite. Once the operation is in place, much of the value is in the commodity. The political risk for such investments is much higher for this reason. Also, the issue of exploitation is more pronounced with such investments, again increasing the political risk.

Political risk can be hedged in several ways, particularly when confiscation or nationalization is a concern. The use of local financing, perhaps from the government of the foreign country in question, reduces the possible loss because the company can refuse to pay on the debt in the event of unfavorable political activities. Based on our discussion above, structuring the operation such that it requires significant parent company involvement to function is another way to reduce political risk.

⌐ **CONCEPT QUESTIONS**

22.7a What is political risk?

22.7b What are some ways of hedging political risks?

SUMMARY AND CONCLUSIONS ⌐ 22.8

The international firm has a more complicated life than the purely domestic firm. Management must understand the connection between interest rates, foreign currency exchange rates, and inflation, and it must become aware of a large number of different financial market regulations and tax systems. This chapter is intended to be a concise introduction to some of the financial issues that come up in international investing.

Our coverage was necessarily brief. The main topics we discussed include:

1. Some basic vocabulary. We briefly defined some exotic terms such as LIBOR, Eurodollar, and Belgian dentist.
2. The basic mechanics of exchange rate quotations. We discussed the spot and forward markets and how exchange rates are interpreted.
3. The fundamental relationships between international financial variables:
   a. Absolute and relative purchasing power parity (PPP)
   b. Interest rate parity (IRP)
   c. Unbiased forward rates (UFR)

Absolute purchasing power parity states that $1 should have the same purchasing power in each country. This means that an orange costs the same whether you buy it in New York or in Tokyo.

Relative purchasing power parity means that the expected percentage change in exchange rates between the currencies of two countries is equal to the difference in their inflation rates.

Interest rate parity implies that the percentage difference between the forward exchange rate and the spot exchange rate is equal to the interest rate differential. We showed how covered interest arbitrage forces this relationship to hold.

The unbiased forward rates condition indicates that the current forward rate is a good predictor of the future spot exchange rate.

4. International capital budgeting. We showed that the basic foreign exchange relationships imply two other conditions:
   a. Uncovered interest parity
   b. International Fisher effect

By invoking these two conditions, we learned how to estimate NPVs in foreign currencies and how to convert foreign currencies into dollars to estimate NPV in the usual way.

5. Exchange rate and political risk. We described the various types of exchange rate risk and discussed some commonly used approaches to managing the effect of fluctuating exchange rates on the cash flows and value of the international firm. We also discussed political risk and some ways of managing exposure to it.

Key Terms

American Depository Receipt (ADR) 787
Belgian dentist 787
cross-rate 787
European Currency Unit (ECU) 787
Eurobond 787
Eurocurrency 788
foreign bonds 788
gilts 788
London Interbank Offer Rate (LIBOR) 788
swaps 788
foreign exchange market 788

exchange rate 789
spot trade 794
spot exchange rate 794
forward trade 794
forward exchange rate 794
purchasing power parity (PPP) 795
interest rate parity (IRP) 801
unbiased forward rates (UFR) 802
uncovered interest parity (UIP) 803
international Fisher effect (IFE) 803
exchange rate risk 807
political risk 810

Chapter Review Problems and Self-Test

22.1 Relative Purchasing Power Parity The inflation rate in the United States is projected at 6 percent per year for the next several years. The German inflation rate is projected to be 2 percent during that time. The exchange rate is currently DM 2.2. Based on relative PPP, what is the expected exchange rate in two years?

22.2   Covered Interest Arbitrage   The spot and 360-day forward rates on the Swiss franc are SF 1.8 and SF 1.7, respectively. The risk-free interest rate in the United States is 8 percent, and the risk-free rate in Switzerland is 5 percent. Is there an arbitrage opportunity here? How would you exploit it?

Answers to Self-Test Problems

22.1   From relative PPP, the expected exchange rate in two years, $E[S_2]$ is:

$$E[S_2] = S_0 \times [1 + (h_G - h_{US})]^2$$

where h_G is the German inflation rate. The current exchange rate is DM 2.2, so the expected exchange rate is:

$$E[S_2] = \text{DM } 2.2 \times [1 + (.02 - .06)]^2$$

$$= \text{DM } 2.2 \times .96^2$$

$$= \text{DM } 2.03$$

22.2   From interest rate parity, the forward rate should be (approximately):

$$F_1 = S_0 \times [1 + (R_{FC} - R_{US})]$$

$$= 1.8 \times [1 + .05 - .08]$$

$$= 1.75$$

Since the forward rate is actually SF 1.7, there is an arbitrage.

To exploit the arbitrage, we first note that dollars are selling for SF 1.7 each in the forward market. From IRP, this is too cheap because they should be selling for SF 1.75. So we want to arrange to buy dollars with Swiss francs in the forward market. To do this, we can:

1. Today: Borrow, say, $10 million for 360 days. Convert it to SF 18 million in the spot market, and forward contract at SF 1.7 to convert it back to dollars in 360 days. Invest the SF 18 million at 5 percent.

2. In one year: Your investment has grown to SF $18 \times 1.05 =$ SF 18.9 million. Convert this to dollars at the rate of SF 1.7 = $1. You will have SF 18.9 million/1.7 = $11,117,647. Pay off your loan with 8 percent interest at a cost of $10 million $\times$ 1.08 = $10,800,000 and pocket the difference of $317,647.

Questions and Problems

1.   Using Exchange Rates   Take a look back at Table 22.2 to answer the following questions:
     a. If you have $100, how many Mexican pesos can you get?
     b. How much is a peso worth?

c. If you have Ps 1 million (Ps stands for the Mexican peso), how many dollars do you have?

d. Which is worth more: an Italian lira or a Turkish lira?

e. Which is worth more: a Taiwan dollar or a Singapore dollar?

f. How many French francs can you get for a Belgian franc? What do you call this rate?

g. Per unit, what is the most valuable currency of the ones listed? The least valuable?

h. Can you think of a major world power that is not listed in Table 22.2? Why do you think there is no listing?

2. **Using the Cross-Rate**   Use the information in Table 22.2 to answer the following questions:

a. Which would you rather have, $100 or £100? Why?

b. Which would you rather have, DM 100 or £100? Why?

c. What is the cross-rate for deutsche marks in terms of pounds? For pounds in terms of deutsche marks?

3. **Forward Exchange Rates**   Again referring to Table 22.2:

a. What is the 180-day forward rate for the Japanese yen in yen per dollar? Is the yen selling at a premium or a discount? Explain.

b. What is the 90-day forward rate for the Swiss franc in dollars per franc? Is the dollar selling at a premium or a discount? Explain.

c. What do you think will happen to the value of the dollar relative to the yen and the Swiss franc? Explain.

4. **Using Spot and Forward Rates**   Suppose the spot exchange rate for the Canadian dollar is Can$ 1.2 and the 180-day forward rate is Can$ 1.25.

a. Which is worth more, a U.S. dollar or a Canadian dollar?

b. Assuming absolute PPP, what is the cost in the United States of an Elkhead beer if the price in Canada is Can$ 1.50? Why might it sell for a different price in the United States?

c. Is the Canadian dollar selling at a premium or a discount relative to the U.S. dollar?

d. Which currency is expected to appreciate in value?

e. What do you expect would be true concerning interest rates in the United States and Canada?

5. **Spot versus Forward Rates**   Suppose the exchange rate for the French franc is quoted as FF 5 on the spot market and FF 5.02 in the 90-day forward market.

a. Is the dollar selling at a premium or a discount relative to the franc?

b. Does the financial market expect the franc to strengthen relative to the dollar? Explain.

c. What do you suspect is true about relative economic conditions in the United States and France?

6. **Cross-Rates and Arbitrage**   Suppose the Canadian dollar exchange rate is Can$ 1 = U.S. $.80, and the French franc exchange rate is $1 = FF 5.

a. What is the cross-rate in terms of FF per Can$?

b. Suppose the cross-rate is FF 4.5 = Can$ 1. Is there an arbitrage? Explain how to exploit it.

7. **Inflation and Exchange Rates**   The rate of inflation in the United Kingdom will probably run about 2 percent higher than the U.S. inflation rate for the next several years. All other things being equal, what will happen to the exchange rate? What relationship are you relying on in answering?

8. **Changes in Interest Rates and Inflation**   The exchange rate for the Japanese yen is currently ¥ 120. This is expected to climb over the next year by 10 percent.
    a. Is the yen expected to get stronger or weaker?
    b. What do you think about the relative inflation rates in the United States and Japan?
    c. What do you think about the relative nominal interest rates in the United States and Japan? Relative real rates?

9. **Foreign Bonds**   Which of the following most accurately describes a "Samurai" bond?
    a. A bond issued by Toyota in the United States with the interest payable in yen.
    b. A bond issued by Toyota worldwide with the interest payable in yen.
    c. A bond issued by IBM in Japan with the interest payable in yen.
    d. A bond issued by IBM in Japan with the interest payable in dollars.
    e. An ancient ritual of the Secret Brotherhood of Ninja Warriors.

10. **Interest Rates and Arbitrage**   The treasurer of a major U.S. firm has $5 million to invest for three months. The annual interest rate in the United States is 1 percent per month. The interest rate in the United Kingdom is .75 percent. The spot rate of exchange is £.50, and the three-month forward rate is £.49. Ignoring transactions costs, in which country would the treasurer want to invest the company's funds? Why?

11. **Exchange Rate Risk**   Suppose you are importing coffee grinders from Spain. The exchange rate is given in Table 22.2. You have just placed an order for 50,000 grinders at a cost to you of 2,000 pesetas each. You will pay for them after they arrive in 90 days. You can sell the grinders for $25 apiece. Calculate your profits if the exchange rate goes up or down by 10 percent over the next 90 days. What is the break-even exchange rate?

12. **Inflation and Exchange Rates**   Suppose the current exchange rate for the deutsche mark is DM 3. The expected exchange rate in four years is DM 2.5. What is the difference in the annual inflation rates for the United States and Germany over this period? Assume that the anticipated rate is constant for both countries. What relationship are you relying on in answering?

13. **Exchange Rates and Arbitrage**   The spot and 180-day forward rates on the Canadian dollar are Can$ 1.1 and Can$ 1.15, respectively. The annual risk-free interest rate in the United States is 8 percent, and the risk-free rate in Canada is 9 percent.
    a. Is there an arbitrage here? How would you exploit it?
    b. What must the forward rate be to prevent arbitrage?

14. **Spot versus Forward Rates**   The spot and 90-day forward rates for the French franc are FF 6 and FF 6.02, respectively. In the United States, T-bills are yielding 9 percent annually.

   a. Is the franc expected to get stronger or weaker?

   b. What would you estimate is the difference between the inflation rates of the United States and France?

15. **Expected Spot Rates**   The spot exchange rate for the Greek drachma is Dr 200. Interest rates in the United States are 12 percent per year. They are double that in Greece. What do you predict the exchange rate will be in a year? In two years? What relationship are you using?

16. **Economic Conditions and Exchange Rates**   Are the following statements true or false? Explain why.

   a. If the general price index in Japan rises faster than that in the United States, we would expect the value of the yen to increase relative to the dollar.

   b. Suppose you are a French wine exporter who receives all payments in foreign currency and the French government begins to undertake an expansionary monetary policy. If it is certain that the result will be higher inflation in France compared to other countries, you would be wise to use forward markets to protect yourself against future losses resulting from the deterioration of the value of the French franc.

   c. If you could accurately estimate differences in relative inflation between two countries over a long period of time (and other participants in the markets were unable to do so), you could successfully speculate in spot currency markets.

17. **International Relationships**   We discussed five international capital market relationships: relative PPP, IRP, UFR, UIP, and the international Fisher effect. Which of these do you expect to hold most closely? Which do you think would be likely to be violated?

18. **Capital Budgeting**   You are evaluating a proposed expansion of an existing subsidiary located in Germany. The cost would be DM 9 million. The cash flows would be DM 4 million for the next three years. The dollar required return is 12 percent per year, and the current exchange rate is DM 2. The going rate on Eurodollars is 6 percent per year. It is 4 percent per year on Euromarks.

   a. What do you project will happen to exchange rates over the next three years?

   b. Based on your answer to part *a,* convert the projected deutsche mark flows into dollar flows and calculate the NPV.

   c. What is the required return on deutsche mark flows? Based on your answer, calculate the NPV in deutsche marks and then convert to dollars.

19. **Using the Exact International Fisher Effect**   This is a challenge question. From our discussion of the Fisher effect in Chapter 10, we know that the actual relationship between a nominal rate, R, a real rate, r, and an inflation rate, h, can be written as:

$$1 + r = (1 + R)/(1 + h)$$

This is the *domestic* Fisher effect.

    a. What is the nonapproximate form of the international Fisher effect?

    b. Based on your answer to *a*, what is the exact form for UIP? (Hint: recall the exact form of IRP and use UFR.)

    c. What is the exact form for relative PPP? (Hint: combine your previous two answers.)

    d. Recalculate the NPV for the Kihlstrom drill bit project (discussed in Section 22.5) using the exact forms for UIP and the international Fisher effect. Verify that you get precisely the same answer either way.

Suggested Readings

The following is a good book on the modern theory of international markets:

Grabbe, J. O. *International Financial Markets.* New York: Elsevier-North Holland Publishing, 1986.

These two articles describe budgeting for international projects:

Lessard, D. R. "Evaluating Foreign Projects: An Adjusted Present Value Approach." In *International Financial Management,* ed. D. R. Lessard. New York: Warren, Gorham & Lamont, 1979.

Shapiro, A. S. "Capital Budgeting for the Multinational Corporation." *Financial Management* 7, Spring 1978.

For more information on the relationship between the forward rate and the spot rate, see:

Levich, Richard M. "Is the Foreign Exchange Market Efficient?" *Oxford Review of Economic Policy* 5, no. 3, 1989, pp. 40–60.

Mussa, Michael. "Empirical Regularities in the Behavior of Exchange Rates and Theories of the Foreign Exchange Market." In *Policies for Employment, Prices and Exchange Rates,* ed. K. Bruner and A. Meltzer. Carnegie-Rochester Conference 11. Amsterdam: North-Holland, 1979.

Chapter 23

Leasing

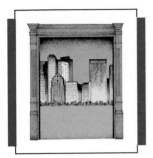

Leasing is a way businesses finance plant, property, and equipment.[1] Just about any asset that can be purchased can be leased, and as much equipment is financed today by leasing as by any other method of equipment financing.[2] There are many good reasons for leasing. For example, when we take vacations or business trips, renting a car for a few days is a convenient thing to do. After all, buying a car and selling it a week later would be a great nuisance. We discuss additional reasons for leasing in the sections that follow.

Although corporations engage in both short-term leasing and long-term leasing, this chapter is primarily concerned with long-term leasing, where long-term typically means more than five years. As we will discuss in greater detail shortly, leasing an asset on a long-term basis is much like borrowing the needed funds and simply buying the asset. Thus, long-term leasing is a form of financing much like long-term debt. When is leasing preferable to long-term borrowing? This is the question we seek to answer in this chapter.[3]

---

[1]We are indebted to James Johnson of Northern Illinois University for helpful comments and suggestions on this chapter.

[2]P. K. Nevitt and F. J. Fabozzi, *Equipment Leasing,* 2nd ed. (Homewood, Ill.: Dow-Jones Irwin, 1985).

[3]Our discussion of lease valuation is drawn, in part, from Chapter 23 of S. A. Ross, R.W. Westerfield, and J. F. Jaffe, *Corporate Finance,* 2nd ed. (Homewood, Ill. Richard D. Irwin, 1990), which contains a more comprehensive treatment and discusses some subtle, but important, issues that are not covered here.

LEASES AND LEASE TYPES | 23.1

A *lease* is a contractual agreement between two parties: the lessee and the lessor. The **lessee** is the user of the equipment; the **lessor** is the owner. Typically, a company first decides on the asset that it needs. It then negotiates a lease contract with a lessor for use of that asset. The lease agreement establishes that the lessee has the right to use the asset and, in return, must make periodic payments to the lessor, the owner of the asset. The lessor is usually either the asset's manufacturer or an independent leasing company. If the lessor is an independent leasing company, it must buy the asset from a manufacturer. The lessor then delivers the asset to the lessee, and the lease goes into effect.

There are some giant lessors in the United States. For example, AT&T Capital, General Electric Capital, and IBM Credit each lease more than $3 billion dollars in equipment annually. Large banks such as Chase Manhattan, Citicorp, and Bankers Trust also have large-scale leasing operations.

Leasing versus Buying

As far as the lessee is concerned, it is the use of the asset that is important, not necessarily who has title to it. One way to obtain the use of an asset is to lease it. Another way is to obtain outside financing and buy it. Thus, the decision to lease or buy amounts to a comparison of alternative financing arrangements for the use of an asset.

Figure 23.1 compares leasing and buying. The lessee, Sass Company, might be a hospital, a law firm, or any other firm that uses computers. The lessor is an independent leasing company that purchased the computer from a manufacturer such as Hewlett-Packard (HP). Leases of this type, in which the leas-

lessee

The user of an asset in a leasing agreement. The lessee makes payments to the lessor.

lessor

The owner of an asset in a leasing agreement. The lessor receives payments from the lessee.

Figure 23.1

Leasing versus buying

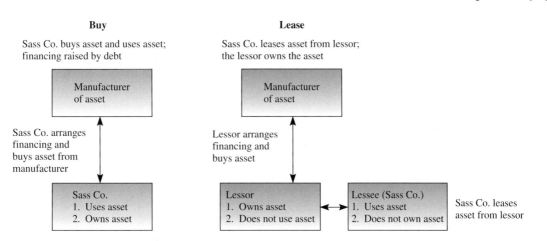

If Sass Co. buys the asset, then it will own the asset and use it. If Sass Co. leases the asset, the lessor will own it, but Sass Co. will still use it as the lessee.

ing company purchases the asset from the manufacturer, are called *direct leases*. Of course, HP might choose to lease its own computers, and many companies, including HP and some of the other companies mentioned above, have set up wholly owned subsidiaries called *captive finance companies* to lease out their products.[4]

As shown in Figure 23.1, Sass Company ends up using the asset either way. The key difference is that in one case (buy), Sass arranges the financing, purchases the asset, and holds title to the asset. In the other case (lease), the leasing company arranges the financing, purchases the asset, and holds title to it.

Operating Leases

operating lease

Usually a shorter-term lease under which the lessor is responsible for insurance, taxes, and upkeep. May be cancelable on short notice.

Years ago, a lease in which the lessee received an equipment operator along with the equipment was called an **operating lease.** Today, an operating lease (or *service lease*) is difficult to define precisely, but this form of leasing has several important characteristics.

First of all, with an operating lease, the payments received by the lessor are usually not enough to fully recover the cost of the asset. A primary reason is that operating leases are often relatively short-term. In such cases, the life of the lease may be much less than the economic life of the asset. For example, if you lease a car for two years, the car will have a substantial residual value at the end of the lease, and the lease payments you make would only pay off a fraction of the original cost of the car. The lessor in an operating lease either expects to lease the asset again or sell it when the lease terminates.

A second characteristic is that an operating lease frequently requires that the lessor maintain the asset. The lessor may also be responsible for any taxes or insurance. Of course, these costs would be passed on, at least in part, to the lessee in the form of higher lease payments.

The third, and perhaps most interesting, feature of an operating lease is the cancellation option. This option can give the lessee the right to cancel the lease before the expiration date. If the option to cancel is exercised, the lessee returns the equipment to the lessor and ceases to make payments. The value of a cancellation clause depends on whether technological and/or economic conditions are likely to make the value of the asset to the lessee less than the present value of the future lease payments under the lease.

To leasing practitioners, these three characteristics constitute an operating lease. However, as we will see shortly, accountants use the term in a somewhat different way.

Financial Leases

financial lease

Typically a longer-term, fully amortized lease under which the lessee is responsible for maintenance, taxes, and insurance. Usually not cancelable without penalty.

A **financial lease** is the other major type of lease. In contrast to an operating lease, the payments made under a financial lease (plus the anticipated residual

---

[4]In addition to arranging financing for asset users, captive finance companies (or subsidiaries) may purchase their parent company's accounts receivables. General Motors Acceptance Corporation (GMAC) and GE Capital are examples of captive finance companies.

or salvage value) are usually sufficient to fully cover the lessor's cost of purchasing the asset and pay the lessor a return on the investment. For this reason, a financial lease is sometimes said to be a fully amortized or full-payout lease whereas an operating lease is said to be partially amortized. Financial leases are often called *capital leases* by the accountants.

With a financial lease, the lessee (not the lessor) is usually responsible for insurance, maintenance, and taxes. Importantly, a financial lease generally cannot be canceled, at least not without a significant penalty. In other words, the lessee must make the lease payments or face possible legal action.

The characteristics of a financial lease, particularly the fact that it is fully amortized, make it very similar to debt financing, so the name is a sensible one. There are three types of financial leases that are of particular interest: *tax-oriented leases, leveraged leases,* and *sale and leaseback agreements.* We consider these next.

Tax-Oriented Leases
A lease in which the lessor is the owner of the leased asset for tax purposes is called a **tax-oriented lease.** Such leases are also called tax leases or true leases. In contrast, a *conditional sales agreement lease* is not a true lease. Here, the "lessee" is the owner for tax purposes. Conditional sales agreement leases are really just secured loans. The financial leases we discuss in this chapter are all tax leases.

Tax-oriented leases make the most sense when the lessee is not in a position to use tax credits or depreciation deductions that come with owning the asset. By arranging for someone else to hold title, a tax lease passes these benefits on. The lessee can benefit because the lessor may return a portion of the tax benefits to the lessee in the form of lower lease costs.

tax-oriented lease
A financial lease in which the lessor is the owner for tax purposes. Also called a true lease or a tax lease.

Leveraged Leases
A **leveraged lease** is a tax-oriented lease in which the lessor borrows a substantial portion of the purchase price of the leased asset on a *nonrecourse* basis. This means that if the lessee stops making the lease payments, the lessor does not have to keep making the loan payments. Instead, the lender must proceed against the lessee to recover its investment. In contrast, with a *single investor lease,* if the lessor borrows to purchase the asset, he or she remains responsible for the loan payments regardless of whether or not the lessee makes the lease payments.

leveraged lease
A financial lease in which the lessor borrows a substantial fraction of the cost of the leased asset on a nonrecourse basis.

Sale and Leaseback Agreements
A **sale and leaseback** occurs when a company sells an asset it owns to another party and immediately leases it back. In a sale and leaseback, two things happen:

1. The lessee receives cash from the sale of the asset.
2. The lessee continues to use the asset.

sale and leaseback
A financial lease in which the lessee sells an asset to the lessor and then leases it back.

An example of a sale and leaseback occurred in July 1985 when the city of Oakland, California, used the proceeds from the sale of its city hall and 23 other buildings to help meet the liabilities of its $150 million Police and Retirement System, which was underfunded by about $60 million. As part of the same transaction, Oakland leased back the buildings to provide for their continued use. With a sale and leaseback, the lessee may have the option to repurchase the leased assets at the end of the lease.

⌐ CONCEPT QUESTIONS

23.1a What are the differences between an operating lease and a financial lease?

23.1b What is a tax-oriented lease?

23.1c What is a sale and leaseback agreement?

23.2 | ACCOUNTING AND LEASING

Before November 1976, leasing was frequently called *off–balance sheet financing.* As the name implies, a firm could arrange to use an asset through a lease and not necessarily disclose the existence of the lease contract on the balance sheet. Lessees only had to report information on leasing activity in the footnotes of their financial statements.

In November 1976, the Financial Accounting Standards Board (FASB) issued its Statement of Financial Accounting Standards No. 13 (FASB 13), "Accounting for Leases." The basic idea is that certain financial leases must be "capitalized." Essentially, this requirement means that the present value of the lease payments must be calculated and reported along with debt and other liabilities on the right-hand side of the lessee's balance sheet. The same amount must be shown as the capitalized value of leased assets on the left-hand side of the balance sheet. Operating leases are not disclosed on the balance sheet. Exactly what constitutes a financial or operating lease for accounting purposes is discussed below.

The accounting implications of FASB 13 are illustrated in Table 23.1. Imagine a firm that has $100,000 in assets and no debt, implying that the equity is also $100,000. The firm needs a truck costing $100,000 (it's a big truck) that it can lease or buy. The top of the table shows the balance sheet assuming that the firm borrows the money and buys the truck.

If the firm leases the truck, then one of two things will happen. If the lease is an operating lease, then the balance sheet will look like the one in Part B of the table. In this case, neither the asset (the truck) nor the liability (the present value of the lease payments) appear. If the lease is a capital lease, then the balance sheet would look more like the one in Part C of the table, where the truck is shown as an asset and the present value of the lease payments is shown as a liability.[5]

As we discussed earlier, it is difficult, if not impossible, to give a precise definition of what constitutes a financial lease or an operating lease. For accounting purposes, a lease is declared to be a capital lease, and must therefore be disclosed on the balance sheet, if at least one of the following criteria is met:

1. The lease transfers ownership of the property to the lessee by the end of the term of the lease.

2. The lessee can purchase the asset at a price below fair market value (bargain purchase price option) when the lease expires.

---

[5]In Part C, we have made the simplifying assumption that the present value of the lease payments under the capital lease is equal to the cost of the truck. In general, it is the present value of the payments that must be reported, not the cost of the asset.

Table 23.1

Leasing and the balance sheet

A. *Balance Sheet with Purchase*

(the company buys a $100,000 truck with debt)

Truck	$100,000	Debt	$100,000
Other assets	100,000	Equity	100,000
Total assets	$200,000	Total debt plus equity	$200,000

B. *Balance Sheet with Operating Lease*

(the company finances the truck with an operating lease)

Truck	$ 0	Debt	$ 0
Other assets	100,000	Equity	100,000
Total assets	$100,000	Total debt plus equity	$100,000

C. *Balance Sheet with Capital Lease*

(the company finances the truck with a capital lease)

Assets under capital lease	$100,000	Obligations under capital lease	$100,000
Other assets	100,000	Equity	100,000
Total assets	$200,000	Total debt plus equity	$200,000

In the first case, a $100,000 truck is purchased with debt. In the second case, an operating lease is used; no balance sheet entries are created. In the third case, a capital (financial) lease is used; the lease payments are capitalized as a liability, and the leased truck appears as an asset.

3. The lease term is 75 percent or more of the estimated economic life of the asset.
4. The present value of the lease payments is at least 90 percent of the fair market value of the asset at the start of the lease.

If one or more of the four criteria is met, the lease is a capital lease; otherwise, it is an operating lease for accounting purposes.

A firm might be tempted to try and "cook the books" by taking advantage of the somewhat arbitrary distinction between operating leases and capital leases. Suppose a trucking firm wants to lease a $100,000 truck. The truck is expected to last for 15 years. A (perhaps unethical) financial manager could try to negotiate a lease contract for 10 years with lease payments having a present value of $89,000. These terms would get around criteria 3 and 4. If criteria 1 and 2 are similarly circumvented, the arrangement would be an operating lease and would not show up on the balance sheet.

There are several alleged benefits to "hiding" financial leases. One of the advantages to keeping leases off the balance sheet has to do with fooling financial analysts, creditors, and investors. The idea is that if leases are not on the balance sheet, they will not be noticed.

Financial managers who devote substantial effort to keeping leases off the balance sheet are probably wasting time. Of course, if leases are not on the balance sheet, traditional measures of financial leverage, such as the ratio of total debt to total assets, will understate the true degree of financial leverage.

As a consequence, the balance sheet will appear "stronger" than it really is, but it seems unlikely that this type of manipulation would mislead many people.

⌐ CONCEPT QUESTIONS

23.2a For accounting purposes, what constitutes a capital lease?

23.2b How are capital leases reported?

23.3 | TAXES, THE IRS, AND LEASES

The lessee can deduct lease payments for income tax purposes if the lease is deemed to be a true lease by the Internal Revenue Service. The tax shields associated with lease payments are critical to the economic viability of a lease, so IRS guidelines are an important consideration. Essentially, the IRS requires that a lease be primarily for business purposes and not merely for tax avoidance.

In broad terms, a valid lease from the IRS's perspective will meet the following standards:

1. The term of the lease must be less than 80 percent of the economic life of the asset. If the term is greater than this, the transaction will be regarded as a conditional sale.

2. The lease should not have an option to acquire the asset at the end of the lease term at a price below its then fair market value. This type of bargain option would give the lessee the asset's residual scrap value, implying an equity interest.

3. The lease should not have a schedule of payments that is very high at the start of the lease term and thereafter very low. If the lease requires early "balloon" payments, it would be evidence that the lease was being used to avoid taxes and not for a legitimate business purpose. The IRS may require an adjustment in the payments for tax purposes in such cases.

4. The lease payments must provide the lessor with a fair market rate of return. The profit potential of the lease to the lessor should be apart from the deal's tax benefits.

5. Renewal options must be reasonable and reflect the fair market value of the asset at the time of renewal. This requirement can be met by, for example, granting the lessee the first option to meet a competing outside offer.

The IRS is concerned about lease contracts because leases sometimes appear to be set up solely to defer taxes. To see how this could happen, suppose that a firm plans to purchase a $1 million bus that has a five-year life for depreciation purposes. Assume straight-line depreciation to a zero salvage value is used. The depreciation expense would be $200,000 per year. Now suppose that the firm can lease the bus for $500,000 per year for two years and buy the bus for $1 at the end of the two-year term. The present value of the tax benefits from acquiring the bus is clearly less than if the bus is leased. The speed-up of lease payments greatly benefits the firm and basically gives it a form of accelerated depreciation. In this case, the IRS might decide that the primary purpose of the lease was to defer taxes.

⌐ **CONCEPT QUESTIONS**

23.3a Why is the IRS concerned about leasing?

23.3b What are some of the standards the IRS uses in evaluating a lease?

THE CASH FLOWS FROM LEASING ⌐ **23.4**

To begin our analysis of the leasing decision, we need to identify the relevant cash flows. The first part of this section illustrates how this is done. A key point, and one to watch for, is that taxes are a very important consideration in a lease analysis.

The Incremental Cash Flows

Consider the decision confronting the Tasha Corporation, which manufactures pipe. Business has been expanding, and Tasha currently has a five-year backlog of pipe orders for the Trans-Missouri Pipeline.

The International Boring Machine Corporation (IBMC) makes a pipe-boring machine that can be purchased for $10,000. Tasha has determined that it needs a new machine, and the IBMC model will save Tasha $6,000 per year in reduced electricity bills for the next five years.

Tasha has a corporate tax rate of 34 percent. For simplicity, we assume five-year straight-line depreciation is used for the pipe-boring machine, and, after five years, the machine will be worthless. Johnson Leasing Corporation has offered to lease the same pipe-boring machine to Tasha for lease payments of $2,500 paid at the end of each of the next five years. With the lease, Tasha would remain responsible for maintenance, insurance, and operating expenses.[6]

Susan Smart has been asked to compare the direct incremental cash flows from leasing the IBMC machine to the cash flows associated with buying it. The first thing she realizes is that, because Tasha will get the machine either way, the $6,000 savings will be realized whether the machine is leased or purchased. Thus, this cost savings, and any other operating costs or revenues, can be ignored in the analysis.

Upon reflection, Ms. Smart concludes that there are only three important cash flow differences between leasing and buying:[7]

1. If the machine is leased, Tasha must make a lease payment of $2,500 each year. However, lease payments are fully tax deductible, so the aftertax lease payment would be $2,500 × (1 − 0.34) = $1,650. This is a cost of leasing instead of buying.

2. If the machine is leased, Tasha does not own it and cannot depreciate it for tax purposes. The depreciation would be $10,000/5 = $2,000 per year. A $2,000 depreciation deduction generates a tax shield of $2,000 ×

---

[6]We have assumed that all lease payments are made in arrears, that is, at the end of the year. Actually, many leases require payments to be made at the beginning of the year.

[7]There is a fourth consequence that we do not discuss here. If the machine has a nontrivial residual value, then, if we lease, we give up that residual value. This is another cost of leasing instead of buying.

Table 23.2	Lease versus Buy	Year 0	Year 1	Year 2	Year 3	Year 4	Year 5
Incremental cash flows for Tasha Corp. from leasing instead of buying	Aftertax lease payment		−$1,650	−$1,650	−$1,650	−$1,650	−$1,650
	Lost depreciation tax shield		− 680	− 680	− 680	− 680	− 680
	Cost of machine	+$10,000					
	Total cash flow	+$10,000	−$2,330	−$2,330	−$2,330	−$2,330	−$2,330

.34 = $680 per year. Tasha loses this valuable tax shield if it leases, so this a cost of leasing.

3. If the machine is leased, Tasha does not have to spend $10,000 today to buy it. This is a benefit to leasing.

The cash flows from leasing instead of buying are summarized in Table 23.2. Notice that the cost of the machine shows up with a positive sign in Year 0. This is a reflection of the fact that Tasha *saves* $10,000 by leasing instead of buying.

A Note on Taxes

Susan Smart has assumed that Tasha can use the tax benefits of the depreciation allowances and the lease payments. This may not always be the case. If Tasha were losing money, it would not pay taxes and the tax shelters would be worthless (unless they could be shifted to someone else). As we mentioned above, this is one circumstance under which leasing may make a great deal of sense. If this were the case, the relevant lines in Table 23.2 would have to be changed to reflect a zero tax rate. We will return to this point later.

⌐ CONCEPT QUESTIONS

23.4a What are the cash flow consequences of leasing instead of buying?

23.4b Explain why the $10,000 in Table 23.2 has a positive sign.

23.5 | LEASE OR BUY?

From our discussion thus far, Ms. Smart's analysis comes down to this: If Tasha Corp. leases instead of buys, it will save $10,000 today because it avoids having to pay for the machine, but it must give up $2,330 per year for the next five years in exchange. We now must decide whether getting $10,000 today and then paying back $2,330 per year is a good idea.

A Preliminary Analysis

Suppose Tasha were to borrow $10,000 today and promise to make aftertax payments of $2,330 per year for the next five years. This is essentially what Tasha will be doing if it leases instead of buys. What interest rate would Tasha be paying on this "loan"? Going back to Chapter 5, we need to find the unknown rate for a five-year annuity with payments of $2,330 per year and a present value of $10,000. It is easy to verify that the answer is 5.317 percent.

The cash flows on our hypothetical loan are identical to the cash flows from leasing instead of buying, and what we have illustrated is that when Tasha leases the machine, it effectively arranges financing at an aftertax rate of 5.317 percent. Whether this is a good deal or not depends on what rate Tasha would pay if it simply borrowed the money. For example, suppose Tasha can arrange a five-year loan with its bank at a rate of 7.57575 percent. Should Tasha sign the lease or should it go with the bank?

Because Tasha is in a 34 percent tax bracket, the aftertax interest rate would be 7.57575 × (1 − .34) = 5 percent. This is less than the 5.317 percent implicit aftertax rate on the lease. In this particular case, Tasha would be better off borrowing the money because it gets a better rate.

We have seen that Tasha should buy instead of lease. The steps in our analysis can be summarized as follows:

1. Calculate the incremental aftertax cash flows from leasing instead of buying.
2. Use these cash flows to calculate the implicit aftertax interest rate on the lease.
3. Compare this rate to the company's aftertax borrowing cost and choose the cheaper source of financing.

The most important thing about our discussion thus far is that in evaluating a lease, the relevant rate for the comparison is the company's *aftertax* borrowing rate. The fundamental reason is that the alternative to leasing is long-term borrowing, so the aftertax interest rate on such borrowing is the relevant benchmark.

Three Potential Pitfalls

There are three potential problems with the implicit rate on the lease that we calculated. First of all, this rate can be interpreted as the internal rate of return (IRR) on the decision to lease instead of buy, but doing so can be confusing. To see why, notice that the IRR from leasing is 5.317 percent, which is greater than Tasha's aftertax borrowing cost of 5 percent. Normally, the higher the IRR the better, but we decided that leasing was a bad idea here. The reason is that the cash flows are not conventional; the first cash flow is positive and the rest are negative, which is just the opposite of the conventional case (see Chapter 7 for a discussion). With this cash flow pattern, the IRR represents the rate we pay, not the rate we get, so the *lower* the IRR the better.

A second, and related, potential pitfall is that we calculated the advantage to leasing instead of buying. We could have done just the opposite and come up with the advantage to buying instead of leasing. If we did this, the cash flows would be same, but the signs would be reversed. The IRR would be the same. Now, however, the cash flows are conventional, so we interpret the 5.317 percent IRR as saying that borrowing and buying is better.

The third potential problem is that our implicit rate is based on the net cash flows of leasing instead of buying. There is another rate that is sometimes calculated, which is based solely on the lease payments. If we wanted to, we could note that the lease provides $10,000 in financing and requires five payments of $2,500 each. It is tempting to then determine an implicit rate based on these numbers, but the resulting rate is not meaningful for making lease versus buy decisions, and it should not be confused with the implicit return on leasing instead of borrowing and buying.

Perhaps because of these potential confusions, the IRR approach we have outlined thus far is not as widely used as the NPV-based approach that we describe next.

NPV Analysis

Now that we know that the relevant rate for evaluating a lease versus buy decision is the firm's aftertax borrowing cost, an NPV analysis is straightforward. We simply discount the cash flows back to the present at Tasha's aftertax borrowing rate of 5 percent as follows:

$$\text{NPV} = \$10,000 - 2,330 \times (1 - 1/1.05^5)/.05$$

$$= -\$87.68$$

net advantage to leasing (NAL)

The NPV of the decision to lease an asset instead of buying it.

The NPV from leasing instead of buying is $-\$87.68$, verifying our earlier conclusion that leasing is a bad idea. Once again, notice the signs of the cash flows; the first is positive, the rest are negative. The NPV that we have computed here is often called the **net advantage to leasing (NAL)**. Surveys indicate that the NAL approach is the most popular means of lease analysis in the real world.

A Misconception

In our lease versus buy analysis, it looks like we ignored the fact that if Tasha borrows the $10,000 to buy the machine, it will have to repay the money with interest. In fact, we reasoned that if Tasha leased the machine, it would be better off by $10,000 today because it wouldn't have to pay for the machine. It is tempting to argue that if Tasha borrowed the money, it wouldn't have to come up with the $10,000. Instead, Tasha would make a series of principal and interest payments over the next five years. This observation is true, but not particularly relevant. The reason is that if Tasha borrows $10,000 at an aftertax cost of 5 percent, the present value of the aftertax loan payments is simply $10,000, no matter what the repayment schedule is (assuming that the loan is fully amortized). Thus, we could write down the aftertax loan repayments and work with these, but it would just be extra work for no gain (see Problem 15 at the end of the chapter for an example).

Example 23.1 Lease Evaluation

In our Tasha Corp. example, suppose that Tasha is able to negotiate a lease payment of $2,000 per year. What would be the NPV of the lease in this case?

With this new lease payment, the aftertax lease payment would be $2,000 × (1 − .34) = $1,320, which is $1,650 − 1,320 = $330 less than before. Referring back to Table 23.2, the aftertax cash flows would be −$2,000 instead of −$2,330. At 5 percent, the NPV would be:

$$\text{NPV} = \$10,000 - 2,000 \times (1 - 1/1.05^5)/.05$$

$$= \$1,341.05$$

Thus, the lease is very attractive. ∎

CONCEPT QUESTIONS

23.5a What is the relevant discount rate for evaluating whether or not to lease an asset? Why?

23.5b Explain how to go about a lease versus buy analysis.

A LEASING PARADOX | 23.6

We previously looked at the lease versus buy decision from the perspective of the potential lessee, Tasha. We now turn things around and look at the lease from the perspective of the lessor, Johnson Leasing. The cash flows associated with the lease from Johnson's perspective are shown in Table 23.3. First, Johnson must buy the machine for $10,000, so there is a $10,000 outflow today. Next, Johnson depreciates the machine at a rate of $10,000/5 = $2,000 per year, so the depreciation tax shield is $2,000 × .34 = $680 each year. Finally, Johnson receives a lease payment of $2,500 each year on which it pays taxes. The aftertax lease payment received is $1,650, and the total cash flow to Johnson is $2,330 per year.

What we see is that the cash flows to Johnson are exactly the opposite of the cash flows to Tasha. This makes perfect sense because Johnson and Tasha

	Year 0	Year 1	Year 2	Year 3	Year 4	Year 5	**Table 23.3**
Aftertax lease payment		+$1,650	+$1,650	+$1,650	+$1,650	+$1,650	Incremental cash flows for Johnson Leasing
Depreciation tax shield		+ 680	+ 680	+ 680	+ 680	+ 680	
Cost of machine	−$10,000						
Total cash flow	−$10,000	+$2,330	+$2,330	+$2,330	+$2,330	+$2,330	

are the only parties to the transaction, and the lease is a zero-sum game. In other words, if the lease has a positive NPV to one party, it must have a negative NPV to the other. In our case, Johnson hopes that Tasha will do the deal because the NPV for Johnson would be +$87.68, the amount Tasha would lose.

We seem to have a paradox. In any leasing arrangement, one party must inevitably lose (or both parties exactly break even). Why would leasing take place? We know that leasing is very important in the real world, so the next section describes some factors that we have omitted from our analysis thus far. These factors can make a lease attractive to both parties.

Example 23.2 It's the Lease We Can Do
In our Tasha example, a lease payment of $2,500 makes the lease unattractive to Tasha, and a lease payment of $2,000 makes the lease very attractive. What payment would leave Tasha indifferent to leasing or not leasing?

Tasha will be indifferent when the NPV from leasing is zero. For this to happen, the present value of the cash flows from leasing instead of buying would have to be −$10,000. From our previous efforts, we know the lease payment must be somewhere between $2,500 and $2,000. To find the exact payment, we note that there are five payments and the relevant rate is 5 percent per year, so the cash flow from leasing instead of borrowing must be −$2,309.75 per year.

Now that we have the cash flow from leasing instead of borrowing, we have to work backwards to find the lease payment that produces this cash flow. Suppose we let LP stand for the lease payment. Referring back to Table 23.2, we must have that −LP × (1 − .34) − $680 = −$2,309.75. With a little algebra, we see that the zero NPV lease payment is $2,469.32. ∎

CONCEPT QUESTIONS

23.6a Why do we say that leasing is a zero-sum game?

23.6b What paradox does the above question create?

23.7 | REASONS FOR LEASING

Proponents of leasing make many claims about why firms should lease assets rather than buy them. Some of the reasons given to support leasing are good, and some are not. We discuss here the reasons for leasing we think are good and some of the ones that we think aren't so good.

Good Reasons for Leasing

If leasing is a good choice, it will probably be because one or more of the following is true:

1. Taxes may be reduced by leasing.
2. The lease contract may reduce certain types of uncertainty that might otherwise decrease the value of the firm.

3. Transactions costs can be lower for a lease contract than for buying the asset.

4. Leasing may require fewer (if any) restrictive covenants than secured borrowing.

5. Leasing may encumber fewer assets than secured borrowing.

Tax Advantages   As we have hinted in various places, by far the most important reason for long-term leasing is tax deferral. If the corporate income tax were repealed, long-term leasing would become much less important. The tax advantages of leasing exist because firms are in different tax positions. A potential tax shield that cannot be used as efficiently by one firm can be transferred to another by leasing.

Any tax benefits from leasing can be split between the two firms by setting the lease payments at the appropriate level, and the shareholders of both firms will benefit from this tax transfer arrangement. The loser will be the IRS. A firm in a high tax bracket will want to act as the lessor. Low tax bracket firms will be lessees, because they will not be able to use the tax advantages of ownership, such as depreciation and debt financing, as efficiently.

Recall the example of Section 23.6 and the situation of Johnson Leasing. The value of the lease it proposed to Tasha was $87.68. However, the value of the lease to Tasha was exactly the opposite (−$87.68). Since the lessor's gains came at the expense of the lessee, no mutually beneficial deal could be arranged. However, if Tasha pays no taxes and the lease payments are reduced to $2,475 from $2,500, both Johnson and Tasha will find there is positive NPV in leasing.

To see this, we can rework Table 23.2 with a zero tax rate and a $2,475 lease payment. In this case, notice that the cash flows from leasing are simply the lease payments of $2,475 because no depreciation tax shield is lost and the lease payment is not tax deductible. The cash flows from leasing are thus:

Lease versus Buy	Year 0	Year 1	Year 2	Year 3	Year 4	Year 5
Lease payment		−$2,475	−$2,475	−$2,475	−$2,475	−$2,475
Cost of Machine	$10,000					
Total cash flow	+$10,000	−$2,475	−$2,475	−$2,475	−$2,475	−$2,475

The value of the lease for Tasha is:

$$\text{NPV} = \$10,000 - 2,475 \times (1 - 1/1.0757575^5)/.0757575$$

$$= \$6.55$$

which is positive. Notice that the discount rate here is 7.5757 percent because Tasha pays no taxes; in other words, this is both the pretax and the aftertax rate.

From Table 23.3, the value of the lease to Johnson can be worked out. With a lease payment of $2,475, check that the cash flows to Johnson will be $2,313.50. The value of the lease to Johnson is therefore:

$$NPV = -\$10,000 + 2,313.50 \times (1 - 1/1.05^5)/.05$$

$$= \$16.24$$

which is also positive.

As a consequence of different tax rates, the lessee (Tasha) gains $6.55, and the lessor (Johnson) gains $16.24. The IRS loses. What this example shows is that the lessor and the lessee can gain if their tax rates are different. The lease contract allows the lessor to take advantage of the depreciation and interest tax shields that cannot be used by the lessee. The IRS will experience a net loss of tax revenue, and some of the tax gains to the lessor are passed on to the lessee in the form of lower lease payments.

A Reduction of Uncertainty   We have noted that the lessee does not own the property when the lease expires. The value of the property at this time is called the *residual value* (or *salvage value*). At the time the lease contract is signed, there may be substantial uncertainty as to what the residual value of the asset will be. A lease contract is a method of transferring this uncertainty from the lessee to the lessor.

Transferring the uncertainty about the residual value of an asset to the lessor makes sense when the lessor is better able to bear the risk. For example, if the lessor is the manufacturer, then the lessor may be better able to assess and manage the risk associated with the residual value. The transfer of uncertainty to the lessor amounts to a form of insurance for the lessee. A lease therefore provides something besides long-term financing. Of course the lessee pays for this insurance implicitly, but the lessee may view the insurance as a relative bargain.

Reduction of uncertainty is the motive for leasing most cited by corporations. For example, computers have a way of becoming technologically outdated very quickly, and computers are very commonly leased instead of purchased. In a recent survey, 82 percent of the responding firms cited the risk of obsolescence as an important reason for leasing, whereas only 57 percent cited the potential for cheaper financing.

Transactions Costs   The costs of changing ownership of an asset many times over its useful life will frequently be greater than the costs of writing a lease agreement. Consider the choice that confronts a person who lives in Los Angeles but must do business in New York for two days. It seems obvious that it will be cheaper to rent a hotel room for two nights than it would be to buy a condominium for two days and then sell it. Thus, transactions costs may be the major reason for short-term leases (operating leases). However, it is probably not the major reason for long-term leases.

Restrictions and Security   As we discussed in Chapter 12, with a secured loan, the borrower will generally agree to a set of restrictive covenants, spelled out in the indenture or loan agreement. Such restrictions are not generally found in lease agreements. Also, with a secured loan, the borrower may have to pledge other assets as security. With a lease, only the leased asset is so encumbered.

Bad Reasons for Leasing

Leasing and Accounting Income   Leasing can have a significant effect on the appearance of the firm's financial statements. If a firm is successful at keeping its leases off the books, the balance sheet and income statement can be made to look better. As a consequence, accounting-based performance measures such as return on assets (ROA) can appear to be higher.

For example, because an operating lease does not appear on the balance sheet, total assets (and total liabilities) will be lower than they would be if the firm borrowed the money and bought the asset. From Chapter 3, ROA is computed as net income divided by total assets. With an operating lease, the net income is usually bigger and total assets are smaller, so ROA will be larger.

As we have discussed, however, the impact that leasing has on a firm's accounting statements is not likely to fool anyone. As always, what matters are the cash flow consequences, and whether or not a lease has a positive NPV has little to do with its effect on a firm's financial statements. However, managerial compensation is sometimes based on accounting numbers, and this creates an incentive to lease assets. This may be an agency problem (see Chapter 1) if leasing is otherwise undesirable.

100 Percent Financing   It is often claimed that an advantage to leasing is that it provides 100 percent financing, whereas secured equipment loans require an initial down payment. Of course, a firm can simply borrow the down payment from another source that provides unsecured credit. Moreover, leases do usually involve a down payment in the form of an advance lease payment (or security deposit). Even when they do not, leases may implicitly be secured by assets of the firm other than those being leased (leasing may give the appearance of 100 percent financing, but not the substance).

Having said this, it may be the case that a firm (particularly a small one) simply cannot obtain debt financing because, for example, additional debt would violate a loan agreement. Operating leases frequently don't count as debt, so they may be the only source of financing available. In such cases, it isn't lease or buy—it's lease or die!

Low Cost   Unscrupulous lessors can encourage lessees to base leasing decisions on the "interest rate" implied by the lease payments. As we discussed above under potential pitfalls, this rate is not meaningful in leasing decisions.

Other Reasons for Leasing

There are, of course, many special reasons for some companies to find advantages in leasing. In one celebrated case, the U.S. Navy leased a fleet of tankers instead of asking Congress for appropriations. Thus, leasing may be used to circumvent capital expenditure control systems set up by bureaucratic firms. This is alleged to be a relatively common occurrence in hospitals, for example.

⌐CONCEPT QUESTIONS

23.7a Explain why differential tax rates may be a good reason for leasing.

23.7b If leasing is tax-motivated, who will have the higher tax bracket, lessee or lessor?

23.8 | SUMMARY AND CONCLUSIONS

A large fraction of America's equipment is leased rather than purchased. This chapter describes different lease types, accounting and tax implications of leasing, and how to evaluate financial leases.

1. Leases can be separated into two types, financial and operating. Financial leases are generally longer-term, fully amortized, and not cancelable without a hefty termination payment. Operating leases are usually shorter-term, partially amortized, and cancelable.

2. The distinction between financial and operating leases is important in financial accounting. Financial (capital) leases must be reported on a firm's balance sheet; operating leases are not. We discussed the specific accounting criteria for classifying leases as capital or operating.

3. Taxes are an important consideration in leasing, and the IRS has some specific rules about what constitutes a valid lease for tax purposes.

4. A long-term financial lease is a source of financing much like long-term borrowing. We showed how to go about an NPV analysis of leasing to decide whether leasing is cheaper than borrowing. A key insight was that the appropriate discount rate is the firm's aftertax borrowing rate.

5. We saw that differential tax rates can make leasing an attractive proposition to all parties. We also mentioned that a lease decreases the uncertainty surrounding the residual value of the leased asset. This is a primary reason cited by corporations for leasing.

Key Terms

lessee 819	tax-oriented lease 821
lessor 819	leveraged lease 821
operating lease 820	sale and leaseback 821
financial lease 820	net advantage to leasing (NAL) 828

Chapter Review Problems and Self-Test

23.1 **Lease or Buy**   Your company wants to purchase a new network file server for its wide-area computer network. The server costs $24,000. It will be completely obsolete in three years. Your options are to borrow the money at 10 percent or to lease the machine. If you lease it, the payments will be $9,000 per year, payable at the end of each of the next three years. If you buy the server, you can depreciate it straight-line to zero over three years. The tax rate is 34 percent. Should you lease or buy?

23.2 **NPV of Leasing**   In the previous question, what is the NPV of the lease to the lessor? At what lease payment will the lessee and the lessor both break even?

Answers to Self-Test Problems

23.1   If you buy the machine, the depreciation will be $8,000 per year. This generates a tax shield of $8,000 × .34 = $2,720 per year, which is lost if the machine is leased. The aftertax lease payment would be $9,000 × (1 − 0.34) = $5,940. Looking back at Table 23.2, the cash flows from leasing are thus:

Incremental cash flows from leasing instead of buying

Lease versus Buy	Year 0	Year 1	Year 2	Year 3
Aftertax lease payment		−$5,940	−$5,940	−$5,940
Lost depreciation tax shield		−2,720	−2,720	−2,720
Cost of machine	+$24,000			
Total cash flow	+$24,000	−$8,660	−$8,660	−$8,660

The appropriate discount rate is the aftertax borrowing rate of 0.10 × (1 − 0.34) = 6.6 percent. The NPV of leasing instead of borrowing and buying is:

$$NPV = \$24,000 - 8,660 \times (1 - 1/1.066^3)/.066$$

$$= \$1,106.31$$

so leasing is cheaper.

23.2   Assuming that the lessor is in the same tax situation as the lessee, the NPV to the lessor is −$1,106.31. In other words, the lessor loses precisely what the lessee makes.

For both parties to break even, the NPV of the lease must be zero. With a 6.6 percent rate for three years, a cash flow of −$9,078.48 per year has a present value of −$24,000. The lost depreciation tax shield is still −$2,720, so the aftertax lease payment must be $6,358.48. The lease payment that produces a zero NPV is therefore $6,358.48/0.66 = $9,634.06 per year.

Questions and Problems

1.   **Leasing Effects**   Comment on the following remarks:
    a. Leasing reduces risk and can reduce a firm's cost of capital.
    b. Leasing provides 100 percent financing.
    c. If the tax advantages of leasing were eliminated, leasing would disappear.

2.   **Accounting and Leasing**   Discuss the accounting criteria for determining whether or not a lease must be reported on the balance sheet. In each case, give a rationale for the criterion.

3.   **Taxes and Leasing**   Discuss the IRS criteria for determining whether or not a lease is valid. In each case, give a rationale for the criterion.

4.   **Off-Balance Sheet Financing**   What is meant by the term *off–balance sheet financing*? When do leases provide such financing, and what are the accounting and economic consequences of such activity?

5.   **Sale and Leaseback**   Why might a firm choose to engage in a sale and leaseback transaction? Give two reasons.

6.   **Leasing and the Discount Rate**   Explain why the aftertax borrowing rate is the appropriate discount rate to use in lease evaluation.

Use the following information to work Problems 7–12.

You work for a nuclear research laboratory that is contemplating leasing a diagnostic scanner (leasing is a very common practice with expensive, high-tech equipment). The scanner costs $540,000, and it would be depreciated straight-line to zero over four years. Because of radiation contamination, it will actually be completely valueless in four years. You can lease it for $160,000 per year for four years.

7.   **Lease or Buy**   Assume that the tax rate is 34 percent. You can borrow at 8 percent pretax. Should you lease or buy?

8.   **Leasing Cash Flows**   What are the cash flows from the lease from the lessor's viewpoint? Assume a 34 percent tax bracket.

9.   **Finding the Breakeven Payment**   What would the lease payment have to be for both lessor and lessee to be indifferent to the lease?

10.   **Taxes and Leasing Cash Flows**   Assume that your company does not contemplate paying taxes for the next several years. What are the cash flows from leasing in this case?

11.   **Setting the Lease Payment**   In the previous question, over what range of lease payments will the lease be profitable for both parties?

12.   **ACRS Depreciation and Leasing**   Rework Problem 7 assuming that the scanner is depreciated as three-year property under ACRS (see Chapter 8 for the depreciation allowances).

13.   **Lease or Buy**   Rework the first Self-Test question assuming that there are four lease payments of $6,961 each with the first payment made today instead of one year from now. How do you interpret the Year 0 cash flow?

Challenge Question

14.   **Leasing and Salvage Value**   In the first Self-Test question, suppose that the server had a projected salvage value of $2,000. How would you go about the lease-versus-buy analysis?

Challenge Problem

15.   **Lease versus Borrow and Buy**   In the first Self-Test question, suppose that the entire $24,000 is borrowed. The rate on the loan is 10 percent, and the loan will be repaid in equal installments. Create a lease-versus-buy analysis that explicitly incorporates the loan payments. Show that the NPV of leasing instead of buying is not changed. Why does this happen?

Suggested Readings

A classic article on lease valuation is:

Myers, S.; D. A. Dill; and A. J. Bautista. "Valuation of Financial Lease Contracts." *Journal of Finance*, June 1976.

A good review and discussion of leasing is contained in:

Smith, C.W., Jr., and L. M. Wakeman. "Determinants of Corporate Leasing Policy." *Journal of Finance,* July 1985.

The survey evidence mentioned in the chapter is from:

Mukherjee, Tarun K. "A Survey of Corporate Leasing Analysis." *Financial Management,* Autumn 1991.

For an explanation of how taxes can influence lease analysis, see:

Johnson, J. M. "Alternative Minimum Tax Implications for Lease/Buy Analysis." *Journal of Equipment Lease Financing,* Summer 1988.

Chapter 24

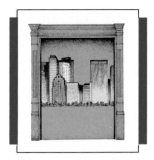

Risk Management

An Introduction to Financial Engineering

Since the early 1970s, prices for all types of goods and services have become increasingly volatile. This is a cause for concern because sudden and unexpected shifts in prices can create expensive disruptions in operating activities for even very well run firms. As a result, firms are increasingly taking steps to shield themselves from price volatility through the use of new and innovative financial arrangements.

The purpose of this last chapter is to introduce you to some of the basics of financial risk management. It is fitting that we end our study of corporate finance fundamentals with an introduction to risk management because the activities we discuss are on the frontier of modern, real-world financial management. By describing one of the rapidly developing areas in corporate finance, we hope to leave you with a sense of how the art and practice of financial management evolve in response to changes in the financial environment.

24.1 | HEDGING AND PRICE VOLATILITY

hedging

Reducing a firm's exposure to price or rate fluctuations. Also immunization.

In broad terms, reducing a firm's exposure to price or rate fluctuations is called **hedging**. The term *immunization* is sometimes used as well. As we will discuss, there are many different types of hedging and many different techniques. Frequently, when a firm desires to hedge a particular risk, there will be no direct way of doing so. The financial manager's job in such cases is to create a way by using available financial instruments to create new ones. This process has come to be called *financial engineering*.

derivative security

A financial asset that represents a claim to another financial asset.

Corporate risk management often involves the buying and selling of **derivative securities.** A derivative security is a financial asset that represents a claim to another financial asset. For example, a stock option gives the owner the right to buy or sell stock, a financial asset, so stock options are derivative securities.

Financial engineering frequently involves creating new derivative securities, or else combining existing derivatives to accomplish specific hedging goals. In a world where prices were very stable and only changed slowly, there would be very little demand for financial engineering. As this is written, however, financial engineering is very much a growth industry. As we illustrate next, the reason is that the financial world has become more risky.[1]

Price Volatility: A Historical Perspective

To understand why we claim that the financial world has become more risky, it is useful to look back at the history of prices. Figure 24.1 provides a very long-term view of price levels for England. The price-level series shown begins in 1666 and runs through the mid-1980s. The remarkable fact revealed by this series is that for the first 250 years, prices changed very little (except in wartime). In contrast, in the last 30 or 40 years, prices have increased dramatically. Figure 24.2 illustrates the same point with a somewhat shorter series from the United States.

One fact that gets obscured in the very long time series we have examined thus far is that the price increases have not been smooth and predictable. To see this, Figure 24.3 illustrates the annual rate of inflation in the United States from the early 1960s to the recent past. What is clear is that not only have prices been increasing, but the rate of increase has been very volatile from year to year.

Figure 24.3 also shows that the rate of change in prices has slowed in recent years. The important lesson, however, is that even though the inflation rate is now low, the uncertainty about the future rate of inflation remains. Beyond the unexpected changes in overall price levels, there are three specific areas of particular importance to businesses where volatility has also increased dramatically: interest rates, exchange rates, and commodity prices.

Interest Rate Volatility

We know that debt is a vital source of financing for corporations, and interest rates are a key component of a firm's cost of capital. Up until 1979, interest rates in the United States were relatively stable because the Federal Reserve actively managed rates to keep them that way. This goal has since been abandoned, and interest rate volatility has increased sharply. Figure 24.4 illustrates this increase by plotting the month-to-month changes in five-year Treasury bond rates. The increase in volatility following 1979 is readily apparent.

---

[1]This discussion is based on C.W. Smith, C.W. Smithson, and D. S. Wilford, *Managing Financial Risk,* Institutional Investor Series in Finance (New York: Harper & Row, 1990).

Figure 24.1

Price levels in England (1850 = 100)

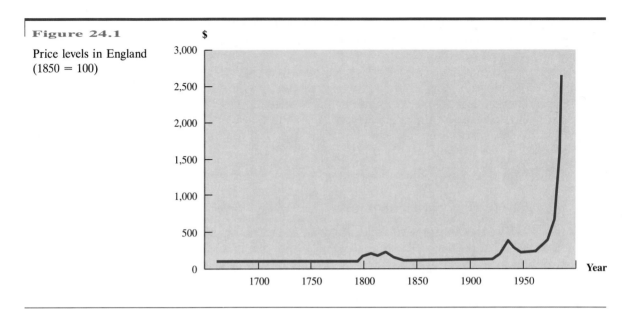

Source: C.W. Smith, C.W. Smithson, D. S. Wilford, *Managing Financial Risk,* Institutional Investor Series in Finance (New York: Harper & Row, 1990).

Figure 24.2

Price levels in the United States (1967 = 100)

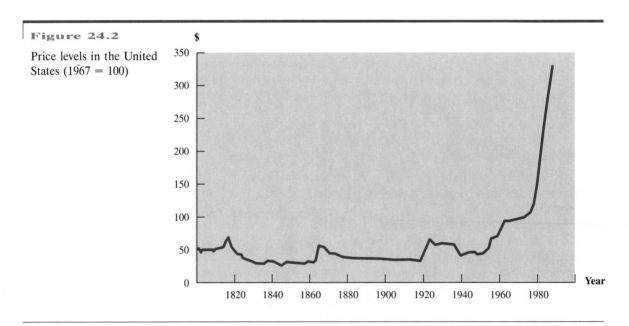

Source: C.W. Smith, C.W. Smithson, D. S. Wilford, *Managing Financial Risk,* Institutional Investor Series in Finance (New York: Harper & Row, 1990).

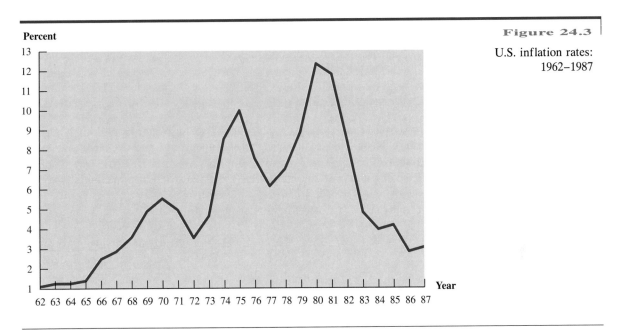

Figure 24.3

U.S. inflation rates: 1962–1987

Source: C.W. Smith, C.W. Smithson, and D.S. Wilford, *Managing Financial Risk,* Institutional Investor Series in Finance (New York: Harper & Row, 1990).

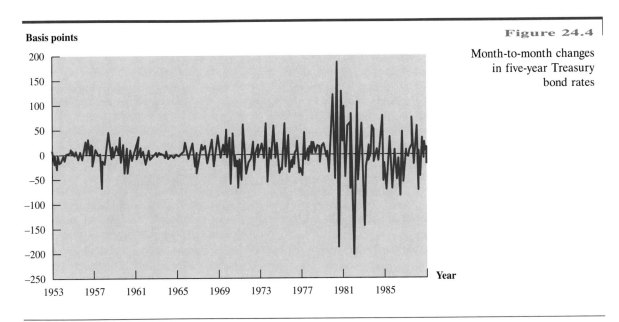

Figure 24.4

Month-to-month changes in five-year Treasury bond rates

The rate changes in this figure are measured in basis points, where 1 basis point is 1 percent of 1 percent, that is, 0.0001. Source: C.W. Smith, C.W. Smithson, D.S. Wilford, *Managing Financial Risk,* Institutional Investor Series in Finance (New York: Harper & Row, 1990).

Before 1979, U.S. firms were able to plan for and predict their future borrowing costs with some confidence. In today's financial world, because of the increased uncertainty surrounding interest rates, this is no longer the case.

Exchange Rate Volatility

As we discussed in Chapter 22, international operations are increasingly important to U.S. businesses. Consequently, exchange rates and exchange rate volatility have also become increasingly important. Figure 24.5 plots the monthly percentage changes in the Japanses yen/U.S dollar exchange rate and illustrates that exchange rate volatility increased enormously beginning in the early 1970s.

The reason for the increase in exchange rate volatility is the breakdown of the so-called Bretton Woods accord. Under the Bretton Woods system, exchange rates were fixed for the most part and significant changes occurred only rarely. As a result, importers and exporters could predict with relative certainty what exchange rates were likely to be in the future. In today's post–Bretton Woods era, exchange rates are set by market forces, and future exchange rates are very difficult to predict with precision.

Commodity Price Volatility

Commodity prices (the prices for basic goods and materials) are the third major area in which volatility has risen. Oil is one of the most important commodi-

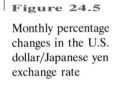

Figure 24.5

Monthly percentage changes in the U.S. dollar/Japanese yen exchange rate

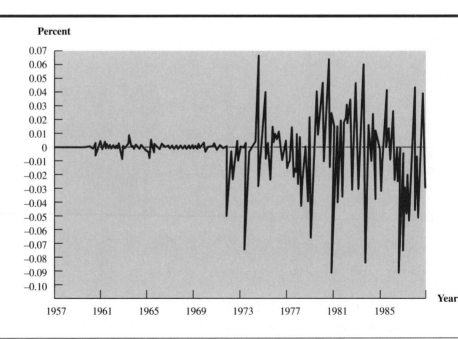

Source: C.W. Smith, C.W. Smithson, D.S. Wilford, *Managing Financial Risk,* Institutional Investor Series in Finance (New York: Harper & Row, 1990).

In Their Own Words...
Charles W. Smithson on
Financial Risk Management

Before risk management techniques and instruments were available, poor performance could be "explained away" by alluding to "adverse foreign exchange rate movements..." After all, the management of the company had no control over the yen/U.S. dollar exchange rate. Today, however, that explanation doesn't wash. The firm's management still has no control over the yen/U.S. dollar exchange rate, but the management team can insulate the firm from exchange rate movements.

Most of the commonly heard examples are Fortune 500 companies. For example, the pharmaceutical giant Merck has a significant exposure to foreign exchange since it has receipts in almost every currency in the world. With so much foreign exchange flowing through Merck in the course of day-to-day business, it was logical that Merck would perform a careful examination of its foreign exchange risk.

Likewise, it is easy to understand the importance of foreign exchange rates to a firm facing a competitor whose home currency is other than dollars — Kodak being the best-known example. In the absence of risk management, Kodak's ability to compete would be influenced by the yen/U.S. dollar exchange rate, that is, Kodak's sales and therefore net income would rise (fall) as the dollar weakened (strengthened) relative to the yen. Consequently, there was a strong business incentive to hedge.

However, foreign exchange risk is something that much smaller firms are now having to deal with. An example I encountered was a service company that had done well in the U.S. market and had expanded into England. It had never before had to worry about exchange rates...and it turned out that this experience was not a happy one.

- They found that the sterling/U.S. dollar exchange rate impacted on their balance sheet via receivables. There were instances where the firm performed £100 worth of service. Given the exchange rate that prevailed at the time the service was performed, they expected to receive $175 and booked the receivable accordingly. However, in the 90 days that passed until the payment was made and exchanged into U.S. dollars, the value of the U.S. dollars could rise to $1.50 per pound and the value of the receivable drops to $150.

- They found that the sterling/U.S. dollar exchange rate impacted on their income statement via the margin they received from the foreign operation. A strong dollar reduces the firm's margin. As illustrated in the simplified example below, if the dollar strengthened from $1.75 per pound to $1.50, the dollar value of the firm's margin declines.

	Sterling	U.S. Dollar Values	
		£1 = $1.75	£1 = $1.50
Revenues	£100	$175.0	$150
Expenses	50	87.5	75
Margin	£ 50	$ 87.5	$ 75

Furthermore, if the UK operation has costs in the United States, it could be the case that the viability of the foreign subsidiary would depend on the exchange rate.

The net result was that this company had no choice but to begin to manage foreign exchange rate risk. Without risk management, it had become too difficult to manage the business.

Charles W. Smithson is the managing director for research in the global risk management sector of Chase Manhattan Bank. He has been actively involved in the developing discipline of financial risk management. In addition to his articles in academic and professional journals, he is coauthor of *Managing Financial Risk* (with C.W. Smith and D.S. Wilford) and coeditor of *The Handbook of Financial Engineering* (with C.W. Smith). He is also coauthor of *Managerial Economics* (with S.C. Maurice and C.R. Thomas) and an economic perspective on commodity "crises," *The Doomsday Myth* (with S.C. Maurice).

ties, and, as Figure 24.6 shows, oil prices became increasingly uncertain beginning in the early 1970s.

The behavior of oil prices is not unique; many other key commodities have experienced increased volatility over the past two decades.

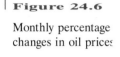

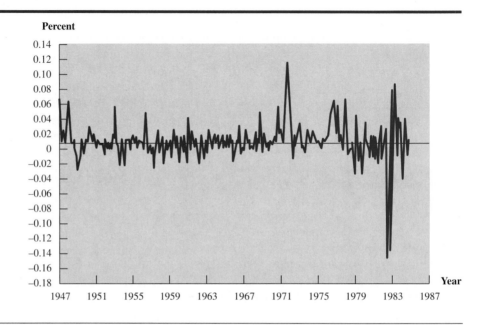

Monthly percentage changes in oil prices

Source: C.W. Smith, C.W. Smithson, and D. S. Wilford, *Managing Financial Risk,* Institutional Investor Series in Finance (New York: Harper & Row, 1990).

The Impact of Financial Risk: The U.S. Savings and Loan Industry

The best-known example of the effect of financial risk is the collapse of the once-thriving U.S. savings and loan (S&L) industry. At one time, the S&L industry was relatively simple. S&Ls accepted short-term deposits, and they made long-term, fixed-rate home mortgage loans. Before the increases in interest rate volatility came about, short-term interest rates were almost always lower than long-term rates, so the S&Ls simply profited from the spread.

When short-term interest rates became highly volatile, they exceeded long-term rates on various occasions, sometimes by substantial amounts. Suddenly, the S&L business got very complicated. Depositors removed their funds because higher rates were available elsewhere, but home owners held onto their low–interest rate mortgages. S&Ls were forced into borrowing short-term at very high rates. They began taking greater risks in lending in an attempt to earn higher returns, but this frequently resulted in much higher default rates, another problem with which the S&Ls were unfamiliar.

There were other economic and political factors that contributed to the astounding size of the S&L disaster, but the root cause was the increase in interest rate volatility. Today, surviving S&Ls and other financial institutions take specific steps to insulate themselves from interest rate volatility.

CONCEPT QUESTIONS

24.1a What is hedging?

24.1b Why do firms now place greater emphasis on hedging than in the past?

MANAGING FINANCIAL RISK | 24.2

We've seen that price and rate volatility have increased in recent decades. Whether or not this is a cause for concern for a particular firm depends on the nature of the firm's operations and its financing. For example, an all-equity firm would not be as concerned about interest rate fluctuations as a highly leveraged one. Similarly, a firm with little or no international activity would not be overly concerned about exchange rate fluctuations.

To effectively manage financial risk, financial managers need to identify the types of price fluctuations that have the greatest impact on the value of the firm. Sometimes these will be obvious, but sometimes they will not be. For example, consider a forest products company. If interest rates increase, then its borrowing costs will clearly rise. Beyond this, however, the demand for housing typically declines as interest rates rise. As housing demand falls, so does demand for lumber. An increase in interest rates thus leads to increased financing costs, and, at the same time, decreased revenues.

The Risk Profile

The basic tool for identifying and measuring a firm's exposure to financial risk is the **risk profile.** The risk profile is a plot showing the relationship between changes in the price of some good or service and changes in the value of the firm. Constructing a risk profile is conceptually very similar to performing a sensitivity analysis (described in Chapter 9).

risk profile
A plot showing how the value of the firm is affected by changes in prices or rates.

To illustrate, consider an agricultural products company that has a large-scale wheat farming operation. Because wheat prices can be very volatile, we might wish to investigate the firm's exposure to wheat price fluctuations, that is, its risk profile with regard to wheat prices. To do this, we plot changes in the value of the firm (ΔV) versus unexpected changes in wheat prices (ΔP_{wheat}). Figure 24.7 shows the result.

The risk profile in Figure 24.7 tells us two things. First, because the line slopes up, increases in wheat prices will increase the value of the firm. Because wheat is an output, this comes as no surprise. Second, because the line has a fairly steep slope, this firm has a significant exposure to wheat price fluctuations, and it may wish to take steps to reduce that exposure.

Reducing Risk Exposure

Fluctuations in the price of any particular good or service can have very different effects on different types of firms. Going back to wheat prices, we now consider the case of a food processing operation. The food processor buys large quantities of wheat and has a risk profile as illustrated in Figure 24.8. As with the agricultural products firm, the value of this firm is sensitive to wheat prices, but, because wheat is an input, increases in wheat prices lead to decreases in firm value.

Both the agricultural products firm and the food processor are exposed to wheat price fluctuations, but any fluctuations have opposite effects. If these two firms get together, then much of the risk can be eliminated. The grower

Figure 24.7

Risk profile for a wheat grower

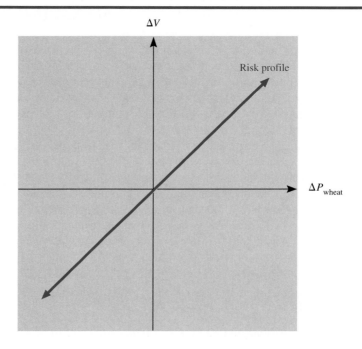

For a grower, unexpected increases in wheat prices increase the value of the firm.

and the processor can simply agree that, at set dates in the future, the grower will deliver a certain quantity of wheat, and the processor will pay a set price. Once the agreement is signed, both firms have locked in the price of wheat for as long as the contract is in effect, and both of their risk profiles with regard to wheat prices would be completely flat during that time.

We should note that, in reality, a firm that hedges financial risk usually won't be able to create a completely flat risk profile. For example, our wheat grower doesn't actually know what the size of the crop will be ahead of time. If the crop is larger than expected, then some portion of the crop will be unhedged. If the crop is small, then the grower will have to buy more to fulfill the contract and is thereby exposed to the risk of price changes. Either way, there is some exposure to wheat price fluctuations, but, by hedging, that exposure is sharply reduced.

There are a number of other reasons why perfect hedging is usually impossible, but this is not really a problem. With most financial risk management, the goal is to reduce the risk to more bearable levels and thereby flatten out the risk profile, not necessarily to eliminate the risk altogether.

In thinking about financial risk, there is an important distinction to be made. Price fluctuations have two components. Short-run, essentially temporary changes are the first component. The second component has to do with more long-run, essentially permanent changes. As we discuss next, these two types of changes have very different implications for the firm.

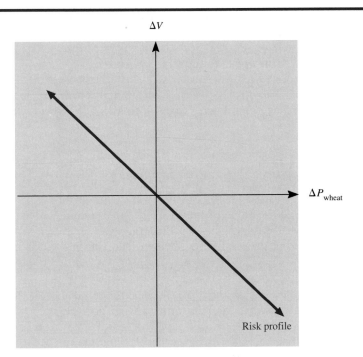

Figure 24.8

Risk profile for a wheat
buyer

ΔV

ΔP_{wheat}

Risk profile

For a buyer, unexpected increases in wheat prices decrease the value
of the firm.

Hedging Short-Run Exposure

Short-run, temporary changes in prices result from unforeseen events or
shocks. Some examples are sudden increases in orange juice prices because of
a late Florida freeze, increases in oil prices because of political turmoil, and
increases in lumber prices because available supplies are low following a hurri-
cane. Price fluctuations of this sort are often called *transitory* changes.

Short-run price changes can drive a business into financial distress even
though, in the long-run, the business is fundamentally sound. This happens
when a firm finds itself with sudden cost increases that it cannot pass on to its
customers immediately. A negative cash flow position is created, and the firm
may be unable to meet its financial obligations.

For example, wheat crops might be much larger than expected in a particular year because of unusually good growing conditions. At harvest time,
wheat prices would be unexpectedly low. By that time, a wheat farmer has
already incurred most of the costs of production. If prices drop too low, revenues from the crop would be insufficient to cover the costs, and financial distress may result.

Short-run financial exposure is often called **transactions exposure.** This
name stems from the fact that short-term financial exposure typically arises
because a firm must make transactions in the near future at uncertain prices

transactions exposure

Short-run financial exposure arising
from the need to buy or sell at
uncertain prices or rates in the
near future.

or rates. With our wheat farmer, for example, the crop must be sold at the end of the harvest, but the wheat price is uncertain. Alternatively, a firm may have a bond issue that will mature next year that it will need to replace, but the interest rate that the firm will have to pay is not known.

As we will see, short-run financial risk can be managed in a variety of ways. The opportunities for short-term hedging have grown tremendously in recent years, and firms in the United States increasingly hedge away transitory price changes.

Cash Flow Hedging: A Cautionary Note

One thing to notice is that, in our discussion thus far, we have talked conceptually about hedging the value of the firm. In our example concerning wheat prices, however, what is really hedged is the firm's near-term cash flow. In fact, at the risk of ignoring some subtleties, hedging short-term financial exposure, hedging transactions exposure, and hedging near-term cash flows amount to much the same thing.

It will usually be the case that directly hedging the value of the firm is not really feasible, and, instead, the firm will try to reduce the uncertainty of its near-term cash flows. If the firm is thereby able to avoid expensive disruptions, then cash flow hedging will act to hedge the value of the firm, but the linkage is indirect. In such cases, care must be taken to ensure that the cash flow hedging does have the desired effect.

For example, imagine a vertically integrated firm with an oil producing division and a gasoline retailing division. Both divisions are affected by fluctuations in oil prices. However, it may well be that the firm as a whole has very little transactions exposure because any transitory shifts in oil prices simply benefit one division and cost the other. The overall firm's risk profile with regard to oil prices is essentially flat. Put another way, the firm's *net* exposure is small. If one division, acting on its own, were to begin hedging its cash flows, then the firm as a whole would suddenly be exposed to financial risk. The point is that cash flow hedging should not be done in isolation. Instead, a firm needs to worry about its net exposure. As a result, any hedging activities should probably be done on a centralized, or at least cooperative, basis.

Hedging Long-Term Exposure

Price fluctuations also have longer-run, more permanent changes. These result from fundamental shifts in the underlying economics of a business. If improvements in agricultural technology come about, for example, then wheat prices will permanently decline (in the absence of agricultural price subsidies!). If a firm is unable to adapt to the new technology, then it will not be economically viable over the long run.

economic exposure
Long-term financial risk arising from permanent changes in prices or other economic fundamentals.

A firm's exposure to long-run financial risks is often called its **economic exposure.** Because long-term exposure is rooted in fundamental economic forces, it is much more difficult, if not impossible, to hedge on a permanent basis. For example, is it possible that a wheat farmer and a food processor could permanently eliminate exposure to wheat price fluctuations by agreeing on a fixed price forever?

The answer is no, and, in fact, such an agreement may even have the effect opposite of the one desired. The reason is that if, over the long run, wheat prices change on a permanent basis, one side of this agreement would ultimately not be able to keep it. Either the buyer would be paying too much, or the seller would be receiving too little. In either case, the loser would become uncompetitive and fail. Something of the sort happened in the 1970s when public utilities and other energy consumers entered into long-run contracts with natural gas producers. Natural gas prices plummeted in later years, and a great deal of turmoil followed.

In the long run, a business is either economically viable, or it will fail. No amount of hedging can change this simple fact. Nonetheless, by hedging over the near term, a firm gives itself time to adjust its operations and thereby adapt to new conditions without expensive disruptions. So, drawing our discussion in this section together, managing financial risks can accomplish two important things. The first is that the firm insulates itself from otherwise troublesome transitory price fluctuations. The second is that the firm gives itself a little breathing room to adapt to fundamental changes in market conditions.

⌐ **CONCEPT QUESTIONS**

24.2a What is a risk profile? Describe the risk profiles with regard to oil prices for an oil producer and a gasoline retailer.

24.2b What can a firm accomplish by hedging financial risk?

HEDGING WITH FORWARD CONTRACTS ⌐ 24.3

Forward contracts are among the oldest and most basic tools for managing financial risk. Our goal in this section is to describe forward contracts and discuss how they are used to hedge financial risk.

Forward Contracts: The Basics

A **forward contract** is a legally binding agreement between two parties calling for the sale of an asset or product in the future at a price agreed upon today. The terms of the contract call for one party to deliver the goods to the other on a certain date in the future, called the *settlement date*. The other party pays the previously agreed-upon *forward price* and takes the goods. Looking back, the agreement we discussed between the wheat grower and the food processor was, in fact, a forward contract.

Forward contracts can be bought and sold. The *buyer* of a forward contract has the obligation to take delivery and pay for the goods; the *seller* has the obligation to make delivery and accept payment. The buyer of a forward contract benefits if prices increase because the buyer will have locked in a lower price. Similarly, the seller wins if prices fall because a higher selling price has been locked in. Note that one party to a forward contract can only win at the expense of the other, so a forward contract is a zero-sum game.

forward contract

A legally binding agreement between two parties calling for the sale of an asset or product in the future at a price agreed upon today.

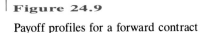

Figure 24.9

Payoff profiles for a forward contract

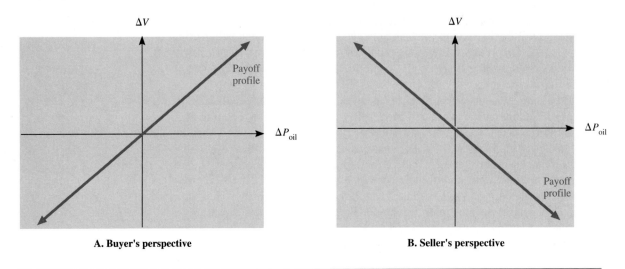

A. Buyer's perspective   B. Seller's perspective

The Payoff Profile

payoff profile

A plot showing the gains and losses that will occur on a contract as the result of unexpected price changes.

The **payoff profile** is the key to understanding how forward contracts and other contracts that we discuss later are used to hedge financial risks. In general, a payoff profile is a plot showing the gains and losses on a contract that result from unexpected price changes. For example, suppose we were examining a forward contract on oil. Based on our discussion, the buyer of the forward contract is obligated to accept delivery of a specified quantity of oil at a future date and pay a set price. Part A of Figure 24.9 shows the resulting payoff profile on the forward contract from the buyer's perspective.

What Figure 24.9 shows is that, as oil prices increase, the buyer of the forward contract benefits by having locked in a lower than market price. If oil prices decrease, then the buyer loses because he or she ends up paying a higher than market price. For the seller of the forward contract, things are simply reversed. The payoff profile of the seller is illustrated in Part B of Figure 24.9.

Hedging with Forward Contracts

To illustrate how forward contracts can be used to hedge, we consider the case of a public utility that uses oil to generate power. The prices that our utility can charge are regulated and cannot be changed rapidly. As a result, sudden increases in oil prices are a source of financial risk.[2] The utility's risk profile is illustrated in Figure 24.10.

_____

[2] Actually, many utilities are allowed to automatically pass on oil price increases.

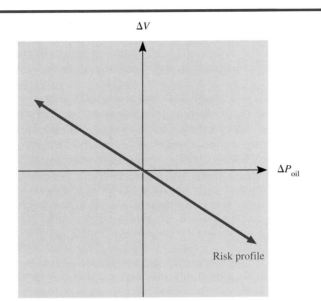

Figure 24.10

Risk profile for an oil buyer

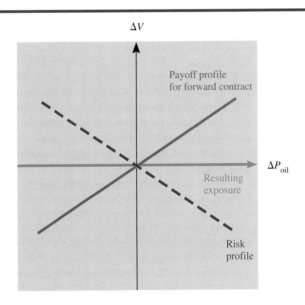

Figure 24.11

Hedging with forward contracts

If we compare the risk profile in Figure 24.10 to the buyer's payoff profile on a forward contract in Figure 24.9, we see what the utility needs to do. The payoff profile for the buyer of a forward contract on oil is exactly the opposite of the utility's risk profile with respect to oil. If the utility buys a forward contract, its exposure to unexpected changes in oil prices will be eliminated. This result is shown in Figure 24.11.

Our public utility example illustrates the fundamental approach to managing financial risk. We first identify the firm's exposure to financial risk using a risk profile. We then try to find a financial arrangement, such as a forward contract, that has an offsetting payoff profile.

A Caveat Figure 24.11 shows that the utility's net exposure to oil price fluctuations is zero. If oil prices rise, then the gains on the forward contract will offset the damage from increased costs. However, if oil prices decline, the benefit from lower costs will be offset by losses on the forward contract.

This illustrates an important thing to remember about hedging with forward contracts. Price fluctuations can be good or bad, depending on which way they go. If we hedge with forward contracts, we do eliminate the risk of an adverse price change. However, we also eliminate the potential gain from a favorable move. You might wonder if we couldn't somehow just hedge against unfavorable moves. We can, and we describe how in a subsequent section.

Credit Risk Another important thing to remember is that with a forward contract, no money changes hand when the contract is initiated. The contract is simply an agreement to transact in the future, so there is no upfront cost to the contract. However, because a forward contract is a financial obligation, there is credit risk. When the settlement date arrives, the party on the losing end of the contract has a significant incentive to default on the agreement. As we discuss in the next section, a variation on the forward contract exists that greatly diminishes this risk.

Forward Contracts in Practice Where are forward contracts commonly used to hedge? Because exchange rate fluctuations can have disastrous consequences for firms that have significant import or export operations, forward contracts are routinely used by such firms to hedge exchange rate risk. For example, Jaguar, the U.K. auto manufacturer (and subsidiary of Ford Motor Co.), historically hedged the U.S. dollar/British pound exchange rate for six months ahead. (The subject of exchange rate hedging with forward contracts is discussed in greater detail in Chapter 22.)

┌ CONCEPT QUESTIONS

24.3a What is a forward contract? Describe the payoff profiles for the buyer and the seller of a forward contract.

24.3b Explain how a firm can alter its risk profile using forward contracts.

24.4 | HEDGING WITH FUTURES CONTRACTS

futures contract
A forward contract with the feature that gains and losses are realized each day rather than only on the settlement date.

A **futures contract** is exactly the same as a forward contract with one exception. With a forward contract, the buyer and seller realize gains or losses only on the settlement date. With a futures contract, gains and losses are realized on a daily basis. If we buy a futures contract on oil, then, if oil prices rise today, we have a profit and the seller of the contract has a loss. The seller pays up, and we start again tomorrow with neither party owing the other.

The daily resettlement feature found in futures contracts is called *marking-to-market*. As we mentioned above, there is a significant risk of default with forward contracts. With daily marking-to-market, this risk is greatly reduced. This is probably why organized trading is much more common in futures contracts than in forward contracts (outside of international trade).

Trading in Futures

In the United States and elsewhere around the world, futures contracts for a remarkable variety of items are routinely bought and sold. The types of contracts available are traditionally divided into two groups, commodity futures and financial futures. With a financial future, the underlying goods are financial assets such as stocks, bonds, or currencies. With a commodity future, the underlying goods can be just about anything other than a financial asset.

There are commodity futures contracts on a wide variety of agricultural products such as corn, orange juice, and, yes, pork bellies. There is even a contract on fertilizer. There are commodity contracts on precious metals such as gold and silver, and there are contracts on basic goods such as copper and lumber. There are contracts on various petroleum products such as crude oil, heating oil, and gasoline.

Wherever there is price volatility, there may be a demand for a futures contract, and new futures contracts are introduced on a fairly regular basis. For example, a new contract has recently been proposed for computer DRAM memory chips. Many new contracts don't pan out because there is not enough volume; such contracts are simply discontinued.

Futures Exchanges

There are a number of futures exchanges in the United States and elsewhere, and more are being established. The Chicago Board of Trade (CBT) is among the largest. Other notable exchanges include the CME (Chicago Mercantile Exchange), the LIFFE (London International Financial Futures Exchange), and the NYFE (New York Futures Exchange, a part of NYSE).

Table 24.1 gives a partial *Wall Street Journal* listing for selected futures contracts. Taking a look at the corn contract in the upper left portion of the table, the contract trades on the CBT, one contract calls for the delivery of 5,000 bushels of corn, and prices are quoted in cents per bushel. The months in which the contracts mature are given in the first column.

For the corn contract with a May 1992 maturity, the first number in a row is the opening price (256 cents per bushel), the next number is the high price for the day (256½), and the following number is the low price for the day (252¾). The *settlement price* is the fourth number (253), and it is essentially the closing price for the day. For purposes of marking-to-market, this is the figure used. The change (−4¼), listed next, is the movement in the settlement price from the previous trading session. The highest (279¾) and lowest prices (234¾) over the life of the contract are shown next. Finally, the *open interest* (76,690), the number of contracts outstanding at the end of the day, is shown. At the end of a section, the volume of trading in all maturities is shown for that day (53,000) and the previous day (49,220) along with the total open interest for all maturities (272,428) and the change in the total open interest (+1,173).

Table 24.1

Sample *Wall Street Journal* futures price quotations

FUTURES PRICES

Wednesday, April 8, 1992.

Open Interest Reflects Previous Trading Day.

GRAINS AND OILSEEDS

CORN (CBT) 5,000 bu.; cents per bu.

	Open	High	Low	Settle	Change	Lifetime High	Low	Open Interest
May	256	256½	252¾	253	− 4¼	279¾	234⅜	76,690
July	260½	261¼	257¾	258	− 4¼	285	239½	106,285
Sept	256¼	256½	253½	253¾	− 3¼	279½	236½	16,458
Dec	253¾	254½	251¼	251½	− 3½	275¾	236½	65,675
Mr93	261½	261¾	258½	258¾	− 3¼	281¼	258	5,993
May	265½	266½	263	263	− 3	284¾	263	1,226

Est vol 53,000; vol Tues 49,220; open int 272,428, + 1,173.

LIVESTOCK AND MEAT

CATTLE−FEEDER (CME) 44,000 lbs.; cents per lb.

	Open	High	Low	Settle	Change	Lifetime High	Low	Open Interest
Apr	79.50	79.70	79.20	79.50	− .05	87.00	73.25	1,845
May	77.70	77.95	77.35	77.72	....	86.50	72.65	3,731
Aug	75.87	76.05	75.55	75.77	− .10	83.00	72.65	3,630
Sept	75.05	75.15	74.85	75.05	....	82.40	72.15	490
Oct	74.55	74.70	74.40	74.60	+ .07	79.50	72.10	837
Nov	75.00	75.17	74.95	75.05	....	77.50	72.30	191

Est vol 1,567; vol Tues 1,450; open int 10,724, + 159.

PORK BELLIES (CME) 40,000 lbs.; cents per lb.

	Open	High	Low	Settle	Change	Lifetime High	Low	Open Interest
May	34.60	35.25	34.20	35.07	+ .17	59.00	33.40	4,696
July	35.15	35.55	34.60	35.27	− .07	59.00	34.52	4,551
Aug	33.65	34.15	33.15	33.67	− .20	51.00	33.05	2,467
Feb	44.00	44.10	43.20	43.60	− .30	49.30	41.30	191

Est vol 2,907; vol Tues 2,055; open int 11,933, + 86.

FOOD AND FIBER

COCOA (CSCE)−10 metric tons; $ per ton.

	Open	High	Low	Settle	Change	Lifetime High	Low	Open Interest
May	945	952	937	943	− 7	1,388	937	12,445
July	988	990	983	986	− 7	1,410	983	17,374
Sept	1,028	1,030	1,021	1,024	− 10	1,427	1,021	8,141
Dec	1,080	1,082	1,075	1,076	− 6	1,460	1,075	6,678
Mr93	1,114	1,114	1,112	1,112	− 14	1,495	1,112	4,363
May	1,145	1,148	1,145	1,146	− 7	1,518	1,145	1,499
July	....	....	....	1,176	− 6	1,540	1,180	936
Sept	1,202	1,202	1,198	1,202	− 6	1,560	1,198	2,217
Dec	....	....	....	1,234	− 6	1,506	1,245	315

Est vol 6,342; vol Tues 6,033; open int 53,968, + 209.

EXCHANGE ABBREVIATIONS
(for commodity futures and futures options)

CBT-Chicago Board of Trade; CME-Chicago Mercantile Exchange; CMX-Commodity Exchange, New York; CRCE-Chicago Rice & Cotton Exchange; CTN-New York Cotton Exchange; CSCE-Coffee, Sugar & Cocoa Exchange, New York; FOX-London Futures and Options Exchange; IPE-International Petroleum Exchange; KC-Kansas City Board of Trade; MCE-Mid-America Commodity Exchange; MPLS-Minneapolis Grain Exchange; NYM-New York Mercantile Exchange; PBOT-Philadelphia Board of Trade; WPG-Winnipeg Commodity Exchange.

CURRENCY

JAPAN YEN (IMM)−12.5 million yen; $ per yen (.00)

	Open	High	Low	Settle	Change	Lifetime High	Low	Open Interest
June	.7586	.7516	.7527	+ .0015	.8125	.7015	58,986
Sept	.7564	.7582	.7510	.7523	+ .0014	.8080	.7265	2,323
Dec	.7562	.7568	.7525	.7525	+ .0013	.8045	.7410	1,631
Mr93	.7565	....	....	.7531	+ .0012	.8005	.7490	1,862

Est vol 27,967; vol Tues 22,335; open int 64,802, + 301.

INTEREST RATE

TREASURY BONDS (CBT)−$100,000; pts. 32nds of 100%

	Open	High	Low	Settle	Chg	Yield Settle	Chg	Open Interest
June	99-25	100-01	99-05	99-07	− 16	8.079	+ .051	283,445
Sept	98-25	98-30	98-03	98-05	− 16	8.189	+ .052	19,021
Dec	97-23	97-28	97-04	97-04	− 16	8.297	+ .053	5,774
Mr93	96-22	96-30	96-06	96-06	− 16	8.397	+ .054	1,943
June	96-02	96-02	95-11	95-11	− 16	8.488	+ .054	722
Sp94	92-26	92-26	92-05	92-05	− 21	8.843	+ .075	100

Est vol 335,000; vol Tues 205,259; op int 311,186, − 200.

METALS AND PETROLEUM

COPPER-HIGH (CMX)−25,000 lbs.; cents per lb.

	Open	High	Low	Settle	Change	Lifetime High	Low	Open Interest
Apr	101.60	101.70	100.10	100.10	− 2.05	103.70	93.50	1,025
May	101.90	102.00	100.20	100.35	− 2.05	106.20	93.30	24,959
June	100.70	100.70	100.40	100.40	− 1.85	103.10	94.80	876
July	101.65	101.75	100.20	100.40	− 1.75	103.80	92.80	11,469
Aug	....	....	....	100.45	− 1.60	102.00	95.70	671
Sept	101.70	101.70	100.30	100.40	− 1.40	103.45	92.80	4,299
Oct	....	....	....	100.50	− 1.35	102.20	95.90	415
Nov	....	....	....	100.50	− 1.25	102.00	96.00	306
Dec	101.40	101.40	100.00	100.50	− 1.15	102.15	91.60	3,980
Ja93	....	....	....	100.40	− 1.15	101.00	93.30	110
Mar	101.25	101.25	100.35	100.20	− 1.20	101.70	92.80	1,248
May	100.40	100.40	100.20	100.05	− 1.15	101.25	93.70	377
July	....	....	....	99.90	− 1.15	101.15	95.80	267
Sept	....	....	....	99.75	− 1.15	101.25	95.80	239
Dec	....	....	....	99.65	− 1.20	101.05	97.00	140

Est vol 15,000; vol Tues 3,017; open int 50,383, + 251.

CRUDE OIL, Light Sweet (NYM) 1,000 bbls.; $ per bbl.

	Open	High	Low	Settle	Change	Lifetime High	Low	Open Interest
May	20.40	20.67	20.40	20.62	+ .39	24.60	17.30	65,492
June	20.49	20.69	20.47	20.62	+ .31	24.50	17.70	72,092
July	20.45	20.63	20.43	20.57	+ .29	22.11	17.90	47,124
Aug	20.37	20.55	20.36	20.50	+ .28	21.80	17.75	23,841
Sept	20.31	20.47	20.29	20.42	+ .28	24.00	17.78	23,713
Oct	20.23	20.42	20.23	20.35	+ .27	21.56	18.42	15,562
Nov	20.18	20.35	20.18	20.29	+ .26	21.48	18.50	9,667
Dec	20.12	20.28	20.12	20.24	+ .25	24.00	18.25	19,508
Ja93	20.05	20.21	20.05	20.15	+ .24	21.35	18.62	9,394
Feb	20.05	20.14	20.04	20.07	+ .31	21.29	18.67	4,344
Mar	20.02	20.02	20.02	20.01	+ .22	21.26	18.75	4,202
Apr	20.00	20.00	19.94	19.98	+ .22	21.14	18.75	2,003
May	....	....	....	19.95	+ .21	21.10	18.93	2,243
June	....	....	....	19.93	+ .19	23.00	18.63	11,494
July	....	....	....	19.92	+ .18	19.65	18.97	5,519
Aug	....	....	....	19.92	+ .17	19.70	18.99	382
Sept	....	....	....	19.92	+ .16	21.13	18.90	4,624
Dec	19.99	19.99	19.99	19.95	+ .13	23.00	18.70	9,736
Mr94	19.98	19.98	19.98	19.97	+ .10	19.68	19.14	736
June	20.05	20.06	20.02	20.00	+ .07	21.35	19.25	9,683
Dec	....	....	....	20.10	+ .06	21.08	19.40	6,451

Est vol 111,319; vol Tues 61,186; open int 347,875, + 932.

To see how large futures trading can be, we take a look at the CBT Treasury bond contract (under the interest rate heading). One contract is for long-term Treasury bonds with a face or par value of $100,000. The total open interest for all months is about 300,000 contracts. The total face value outstanding is therefore $30 billion for this one contract!

Hedging with Futures

Hedging with futures contracts is conceptually identical to hedging with forward contracts, and the payoff profile on a futures contract is drawn just like the profile for a forward contract. The only difference in hedging with futures is that the firm will have to maintain an account with a broker so that gains and losses can be credited or debited each day as a part of the marking-to-market process.

Even though there are a large variety of futures contracts, it is unlikely that a particular firm will be able to find the precise hedging instrument it needs. For example, we might produce a particular grade or variety of oil, and no contract exists for exactly that grade. However, all oil prices tend to move together, so we could hedge our output using futures contracts on other grades of oil. Using a contract on a related, but not identical, asset as a means of hedging is called **cross-hedging**.

> **cross-hedging**
> Hedging an asset with contracts written on a closely related, but not identical, asset.

When a firm does cross-hedge, it does not actually want to buy or sell the underlying asset. This presents no problem because the firm can reverse its futures position at some point before maturity. This simply means that if the firm sells a futures contract to hedge something, it will buy the same contract at a later date, thereby eliminating its futures position. In fact, futures contracts are very rarely held to maturity by anyone (despite horror stories of individuals waking up to find mountains of soybeans in their front yards), and, as a result, actual physical delivery very rarely takes place.

⌐CONCEPT QUESTIONS

24.4a What is a futures contract? How does it differ from a forward contract?

24.4b What is cross-hedging? Why is it important?

HEDGING WITH SWAP CONTRACTS ⌐24.5

As the name suggests, a **swap contract** is an agreement by two parties to exchange or swap specified cash flows at specified intervals. Swaps are a recent innovation; they were first introduced to the public in 1981 when IBM and the World Bank entered into a swap agreement. The market for swaps has grown tremendously since that time.

> **swap contract**
> An agreement by two parties to exchange or swap specified cash flows at specified intervals in the future.

A swap contract is really just a portfolio or series of forward contracts. Recall that with a forward contract, one party promises to exchange an asset (e.g., bushels of wheat) for another asset (cash) on a specific future date. With a swap, the only difference is that there are multiple exchanges instead of just one. In principle, a swap contract could be tailored to exchange just about anything. In practice, most swap contracts fall into one of three basic categories:

currency swaps, interest rate swaps, and commodity swaps. Other types will surely develop, but we will concentrate on just these three.

Currency Swaps

With a *currency swap,* two companies agree to exchange a specific amount of one currency for a specific amount of another at specific dates in the future. For example, suppose a U.S. firm has a German subsidiary, and it wishes to obtain debt financing for an expansion of the subsidiary's operations. Because most of the subsidiary's cash flows are in deutsche marks, the company would like for the subsidiary to borrow and make payments in deutsche marks, thereby hedging against changes in the deutsche mark/dollar exchange rate. Unfortunately, the company has good access to U.S. debt markets, but not German debt markets.

At the same time, a German firm would like to obtain U.S. dollar financing. It can borrow cheaply in deutsche marks, but not in dollars. Both firms face a similar problem. They can borrow at favorable rates, but not in the desired currency. A currency swap is a solution. These two firms simply agree to exchange dollars for deutsche marks at a fixed rate at specific future dates (the payment dates on the loans). Each firm thus obtains the best possible rate and then arranges to eliminate exposure to exchange rate changes by agreeing to exchange currencies, a neat solution.

Interest Rate Swaps

Imagine a firm that wishes to obtain a fixed-rate loan, but can only get a good deal on a floating-rate loan, that is, a loan where the payments are adjusted periodically to reflect changes in interest rates. Another firm can obtain a fixed-rate loan, but wishes to obtain the lowest possible interest rate and is therefore willing to take a floating-rate loan. (Rates on floating-rate loans are generally lower than rates on fixed-rate loans; why?) Both firms could accomplish their objectives by agreeing to exchange loan payments; in other words, the two firms make each other's loan payments. This is an example of an *interest rate swap;* what is really being exchanged is a floating interest rate for a fixed one.

Interest rate swaps and currency swaps are often combined. One firm obtains floating-rate financing in a particular currency and swaps it for fixed-rate financing in another currency. Also, payments on floating-rate loans are always based on some index, such as the one-year Treasury rate. An interest rate swap might involve exchanging one floating-rate loan for another as a way of changing the underlying index.

Commodity Swaps

As the name suggests, a *commodity swap* is an agreement to exchange a fixed quantity of a commodity at fixed times in the future. Commodity swaps are the newest type of swap, and the market for them is small relative to other types. The potential for growth is enormous, however.

Swap contracts for oil have been engineered. For example, an oil user has a need for 20,000 barrels every quarter. The oil user could enter into a swap contract with an oil producer to supply the needed oil. What price would they agree on? As we mentioned above, they can't fix a price forever. Instead, they could agree that the price will be equal to the *average* daily oil price from the previous 90 days. By using an average price, the impact of the relatively large daily price fluctuations in the oil market will be reduced, and both firms benefit from a reduction in transactions exposure.

The Swap Dealer

Unlike futures contracts, swap contracts are not traded on organized exchanges. The main reason is that they are not sufficiently standardized. Instead, the *swap dealer* plays a key role in the swaps market. In the absence of a swap dealer, a firm that wished to enter into a swap would have to track down another firm that wanted the opposite end of the deal. This search would probably be expensive and time-consuming.

Instead, a firm wishing to enter into a swap agreement contacts a swap dealer, and the swap dealer takes the other side of the agreement. The swap dealer will then try to find an offsetting transaction with some other party or parties (perhaps another firm or another dealer). Failing this, a swap dealer will hedge its exposure using futures contracts.

Commercial banks are the dominant swap dealers in the United States. As a large swap dealer, a bank would be involved in a variety of contracts. It would be swapping fixed-rate loans for floating-rate loans with some parties and doing just the opposite with other participants. The total collection of contracts in which the dealer is involved is called the swap *book*. The dealer will try to keep a balanced book to limit its net exposure.

Interest Rate Swaps: An Example

To get a better understanding of swap contracts and the role of the swap dealer, we consider a floating-for-fixed interest rate swap. Suppose Company A can borrow at a floating rate equal to prime plus 1 percent or at a fixed rate of 10 percent. Company B can borrow at a floating rate of prime plus 2 percent or at a fixed rate of 9.5 percent. Company A desires a fixed-rate loan while Company B desires a floating-rate loan. Clearly, a swap is in order.

Company A contacts a swap dealer, and a deal is struck. Company A borrows the money at a rate of prime plus 1 percent. The swap dealer agrees to cover the loan payments, and, in exchange, the company agrees to make fixed-rate payments to the swap dealer at a rate of, say, 9.75 percent. Notice that the swap dealer is making floating-rate payments and receiving fixed-rate payments. The company is making fixed-rate payments, so it has swapped a floating payment for a fixed one.

Company B also contacts a swap dealer. The deal here calls for Company B to borrow the money at a fixed rate of 9.5 percent. The swap dealer agrees to cover the fixed loan payments, and the company agrees to make floating-rate payments to the swap dealer at a rate of prime plus, say, 1.5 percent. In this

Figure 24.12

Illustration of an interest rate swap

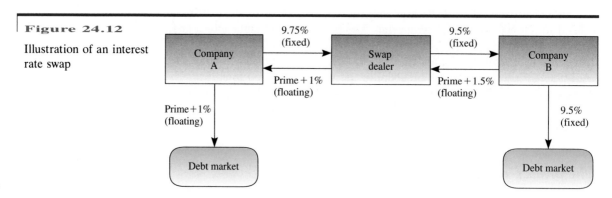

Company A borrows at prime plus 1% and swaps for a 9.75% fixed rate. Company B borrows at 9.5% fixed and swaps for a prime plus 1.5% floating rate.

second arrangement, the swap dealer is making fixed-rate payments and receiving floating-rate payments.

What's the net effect of these machinations? First, Company A gets a fixed-rate loan at 9.75 percent, which is cheaper than the 10 percent rate it can obtain on its own. Second, Company B gets a floating-rate loan at prime plus 1.5 instead of prime plus 2. The swap benefits both companies.

The swap dealer also wins. When all the dust settles, the swap dealer receives (from Company A) fixed-rate payments at a rate of 9.75 percent and makes fixed-rate payments (for Company B) at a rate of 9.5 percent. At the same time, it makes floating-rate payments (for Company A) at a rate of prime plus 1 percent and receives floating-rate payments at a rate of prime plus 1.5 percent (from Company B). Notice that the swap dealer's book is perfectly balanced, and it has no exposure to interest rate volatility.

Figure 24.12 illustrates the transactions in our interest rate swap. Notice that the essence of the swap transactions is that one company swaps a fixed payment for a floating payment, while the other exchanges a floating payment for a fixed one. The swap dealer acts as an intermediary and profits from the spread between the rates it charges and the rates it receives.

CONCEPT QUESTIONS

24.5a What is a swap contract? Describe three types.

24.5b Describe the role of the swap dealer.

24.5c Explain the cash flows in Figure 24.12.

24.6 | HEDGING WITH OPTION CONTRACTS

The contracts we have discussed thus far—forwards, futures, and swaps—are conceptually similar. In each case, two parties agree to transact on a future date or dates. The key is that both parties are *obligated* to complete the transaction.

In contrast, an **option contract** is an agreement that gives the owner the right, but not the obligation, to buy or sell (depending on the option type) some asset at a specified price for a specified time. We discussed the most common type of option, stock options, in Chapter 20. Here we will quickly review some option basics and then focus on using options to hedge volatility in commodity prices, interest rates, and exchange rates. In doing so, we will sidestep a wealth of detail concerning option terminology, option trading strategies, and option valuation.

option contract
An agreement that gives the owner the right, but not the obligation, to buy or sell a specific asset at a specific price for a set period of time.

Option Terminology

Options come in two flavors, puts and calls. The owner of a **call option** has the right, but not the obligation, to *buy* an underlying asset at a fixed price, called the *strike price* or *exercise price,* for a specified time. The owner of a **put option** has the right, but not the obligation, to *sell* an underlying asset at a fixed price for a specified time.

The act of buying or selling the underlying asset using the option contract is called *exercising* the option. Some options ("American" options) can be exercised anytime up to and including the *expiration date* (the last day); other options ("European" options) can only be exercised on the expiration date. Most options are American.

Because the buyer of a call option has the right to buy the underlying asset by paying the strike price, the seller of a call option is obligated to deliver the asset and accept the strike price if the option is exercised. Similarly, the buyer of the put option has the right to sell the underlying asset and receive the strike price. In this case, the seller of the put option must accept the asset and pay the strike price.

call option
An option that gives the owner the right, but not the obligation, to buy an asset.

put option
An option that gives the owner the right, but not the obligation, to sell an asset.

Options versus Forwards

There are two key differences between an option contract and a forward contract. The first is obvious. With a forward contract, both parties are obligated to transact; one party delivers the asset, and the other party pays for it. With an option, the transaction only occurs if the owner of the option chooses to exercise it.

The second difference between an option and a forward contract is that no money changes hand when a forward contract is created. However, the buyer of an option contract gains a valuable right and must pay the seller for that right. The price of the option is frequently called the *option premium.*

Option Payoff Profiles

Figure 24.13 shows the general payoff profile for a call option from the owner's viewpoint. The horizontal axis shows the difference between the asset's value and the strike price on the option. As illustrated, if the price of the underlying asset rises above the strike price, then the owner of the option will exercise it and enjoy a profit. If the value of the asset falls below the strike price, the

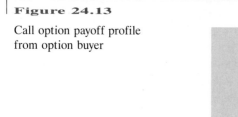

Figure 24.13

Call option payoff profile from option buyer

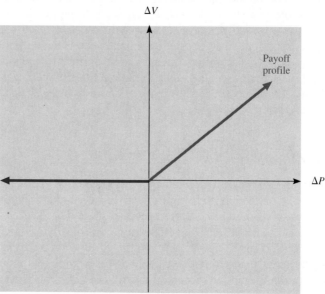

owner of the option will not exercise it. Notice that this payoff profile does not consider the premium that the buyer paid for the option.

The payoff profile that results from buying a call is repeated in Part A of Figure 24.14. Part B shows the payoff profile on a call option from the seller's side. A call option is a zero-sum game, so the seller's payoff profile is exactly the opposite of the buyer's.

Part C of Figure 24.14 shows the payoff profile for the buyer of a put option. In this case, if the asset's value falls below the strike price, then the buyer profits because the seller of the put must pay the strike price. Part D shows that the seller of the put option loses out when the price falls below the strike price.

Option Hedging

Suppose a firm has a risk profile that looks like the one in Part A of Figure 24.15. If the firm wishes to hedge against adverse price movements using options, what should it do? Examining the different payoff profiles in Figure 24.14, the one that has the desirable shape is C, buy a put. If the firm buys a put, then its net exposure is as illustrated in Part B of Figure 24.15.

In this case, by buying a put option, the firm has eliminated the "downside" risk, that is, the risk of an adverse price movement. However, the firm has retained the "upside" potential. In other words, the put option acts as a kind of insurance policy. Remember that this desirable insurance is not free; the firm pays for it when it buys the put option.

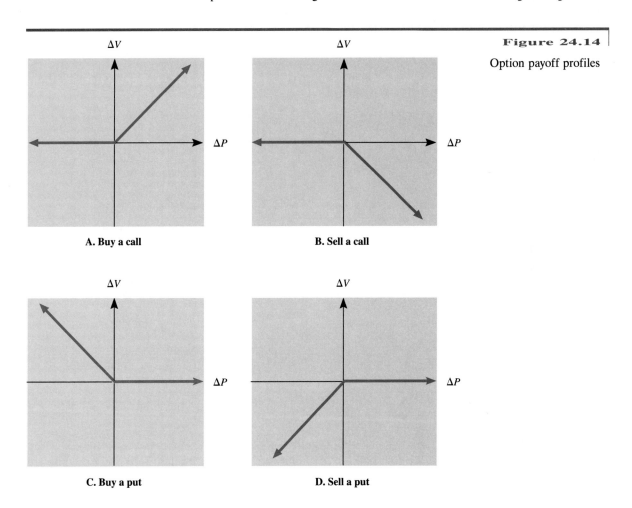

Figure 24.14

Option payoff profiles

A. Buy a call

B. Sell a call

C. Buy a put

D. Sell a put

Hedging Commodity Price Risk with Options

We saw earlier that there are futures contracts available for a variety of basic commodities. In addition, there are an increasing number of options available on these same commodities. In fact, the options that are typically traded on commodities are actually options on futures contracts, and, for this reason, they are called *futures options.*

The way these work is that when a futures call option on, for example, wheat is exercised, the owner of the option receives two things. The first is a futures contract on wheat at the current futures price. This contract can be immediately closed at no cost. The second thing the owner of the option receives is the difference between the strike price on the option and the current futures price. The difference is simply paid in cash.

Table 24.2 gives a few futures options quotations from *The Wall Street Journal.* These are quoted almost exactly like stock options (Chapter 20 con-

Figure 24.15

Hedging with options

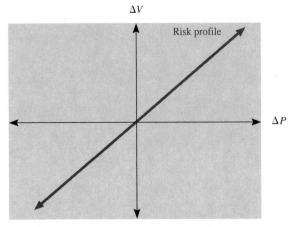

A. The unhedged risk profile

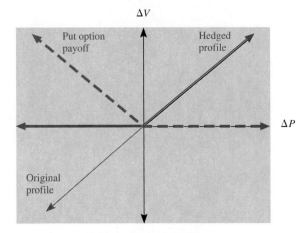

B. The hedged risk profile

The hedged profile is created by purchasing a put option, thereby eliminating the "downside" risk.

tains more detail about option quotes). Briefly, looking at the orange juice option, the first column of numbers tells us the different striking prices that are available. The next three columns are call option prices (or premiums) for three different months of expiration. The final three columns are put option prices for the same three months.

Suppose you buy the November 125 orange juice futures call option. You would pay $.049 per pound for the option (they're actually sold in multiples of 15,000, but we'll ignore this). If you exercise your option, you will receive a futures contract on orange juice and the difference between the current futures price and the strike price of 125 in cash.

Hedging Exchange Rate Risk with Options

Table 24.2 shows that there are futures options available on foreign currencies as well as commodities. These work exactly the same way as commodities futures options. In addition, there are other traded options where the underlying asset is just currency rather than a futures contract on a currency. Firms with significant exposure to exchange rate risk will frequently purchase put options to protect against adverse exchange rate changes.

Hedging Interest Rate Risk with Options

The use of options to hedge against interest rate risk is a very common practice, and there are a variety of options available. Some are futures options like

Table 24.2

Sample *Wall Street Journal* futures option price quotations

FUTURES OPTIONS PRICES

Wednesday, April 15, 1992.

AGRICULTURAL

ORANGE JUICE (CTN)
15,000 lbs.; cents per lb.

Strike Price	Calls—Settle Jly	Sep	Nov	Puts—Settle Jly	Sep	Nov
125	....	....	4.90	1.85	5.10	....
130	....	....	3.40	3.25	8.25	....
135	4.05	....	2.30	5.45	....	....
140	2.60	1.65	1.80	8.80	....	....
145	1.60	1.05	....	12.65	....	....
150	.95	....	....	17.30	....	....

Est. vol. 45;
Tues vol. 56 calls; 41 puts
Op. int. Tues 1,426 calls; 2,521 puts

CURRENCY

BRITISH POUND (IMM)
62,500 pounds; cents per pound

Strike Price	Calls—Settle May	Jun	Jly	Puts—Settle May	Jun	Jly
1675	6.50	7.06	5.78	0.24	0.82	1.98
1700	4.40	5.18	4.28	0.64	1.44	2.96
1725	2.68	3.62	3.06	1.40	2.34	4.22
1750	1.40	2.38	....	2.62	3.60	....
1775	0.66	1.50	....	4.36	5.20	....
1800	0.28	0.90	....	6.46	7.06	....

Est. vol. 2,112;
Tues vol. 869 calls; 584 puts
Op. int. Tues 11,732 calls; 11,822 puts

OIL

CRUDE OIL (NYM)
1,000 bbls.; $ per bbl.

Strike Price	Calls—Settle Jun	Jly	Aug	Puts—Settle Jun	Jly	Aug
18	2.01	2.13	....	.03	.11	.12
19	1.11	1.27	1.34	.13	.25	.32
20	.43	.64	.75	.45	.61	.72
21	.12	.28	.38	1.14	1.25	1.34
22	.04	.10	.18	2.06	2.06	....
23	.02	.05	.08	....	3.00	3.03

Est. vol. 31,712;
Tues vol. 16,754 calls; 13,698 puts
Op. int. Tues 131,561 calls; 98,772 puts

METALS

COPPER (CMX)
25,000 lbs.; cents per lb.

Strike Price	Calls—Settle Jly	Sep	Dec	Puts—Settle Jly	Sep	Dec
96	4.50	5.35	6.25	0.55	1.25	1.95
98	3.00	4.00	5.00	1.05	1.85	2.75
100	1.80	2.85	3.80	1.85	2.70	3.45
102	1.10	1.95	3.00	3.00	3.80	4.70
104	0.60	1.40	2.20	4.65	5.15	5.90
105	0.45	....	....	5.50	....	....

Est. vol. 100;
Tue vol. 230 calls; 312 puts
Op. int. Tue 4,096 calls; 2,451 puts

the ones we have been discussing, and these trade on organized exchanges. For example, we mentioned the Treasury bond contract in our discussion of futures. There are options available on this contract and a number of other financial futures as well. Beyond this, there is a thriving over-the-counter market in interest rate options. We will describe some of these in this section.

A Preliminary Note   Some interest rate options are actually options on interest-bearing assets such as bonds (or on futures contracts for bonds). Most of the options that are traded on exchanges fall into this category. As we discuss below, some others are actually options on interest rates. The distinction is important if we are thinking about using one type or the other to hedge. To illustrate, suppose we wanted to protect ourselves against an increase in interest rates using options; what should we do?

We need to buy an option that increases in value as interest rates go up. One thing we could do is buy a *put* option on a bond. Why a put? Remember that when interest rates go up, bond values go down, so one way to hedge against interest rate increases is to buy put options on bonds. The other way to hedge is to buy a *call* option on interest rates. We discuss this alternative in more detail below.

We actually saw interest rate options in Chapter 12 when we discussed the call feature on a bond. Remember that the call provision gives the issuer the right to buy back the bond at a set price, known as the *call price*. What happens is that if interest rates fall, the bond's price will rise. If it rises above the call price, the buyer will exercise its option and acquire the bonds at a bargain price. The call provision can thus be viewed as either a call option on a bond or a put option on interest rates.

Interest Rate Caps   An *interest rate cap* is a call option on an interest rate. Suppose a firm has a floating-rate loan. It is concerned that interest rates will rise sharply, and the firm will experience financial distress because of the increased loan payment. To guard against this, the firm can purchase an interest rate cap from a bank (there are banks that specialize in such products). What will happen is that if the loan payment ever rises above an agreed-upon limit (the "ceiling"), the bank will pay the difference between the actual payment and the ceiling to the firm in cash.

A *floor* is a put option on an interest rate. If a firm buys a cap and sells a floor, the result is a *collar*. The firm is protected against increases in interest rates beyond the ceiling by the cap. However, if interest rates drop below the floor, the put will be exercised against the firm. The result is that the rate the firm pays will not drop below the floor rate. In other words, the rate the firm will pay will always be between the floor and the ceiling.

Other Interest Rate Options   We will close out our chapter by briefly mentioning two relatively new types of interest rate options. Suppose a firm has a floating-rate loan. The firm is comfortable with its floating-rate loan, but it would like to have the right to convert it to a fixed-rate loan in the future.

What can the firm do? What it wants is the right, but not the obligation, to swap its floating-rate loan for a fixed-rate loan. In other words, the firm needs to buy an option on a swap. Swap options exist, and they have the charming name *swaptions*.

We've seen that there are options on futures contracts and options on swap contracts, what about options on options? Such options are called *compound* options. As we discussed just above, a cap is a call option on interest rates. Suppose a firm thinks that, depending on interest rates, it might like to buy a cap in the future. As you can probably guess, in this case, what the firm might want to do today is buy an option on a cap. Inevitably it seems, an option on a cap is called a *caption*, and there is a growing market for these instruments.

There are many other option types available, and more are created every day. One very important aspect of financial risk management that we have not discussed is that options, forwards, futures, and swaps can be combined in a wide variety of ways to create new instruments. These basic contract types are really just the building blocks used by financial engineers to create new and innovative products for corporate risk management.

⌐ CONCEPT QUESTIONS

24.6a Suppose that the unhedged risk profile in Figure 24.15 sloped down instead of up. What option-based hedging strategy would be suitable in this case?

24.6b What is a futures option?

24.6c What is a caption? Who might want to buy one?

SUMMARY AND CONCLUSIONS | 24.7

This chapter introduces some of the basic principles of financial risk management and financial engineering. The motivation for risk management and financial engineering is that a firm will frequently have an undesirable exposure to some type of risk. This is particularly true today because of the increased volatility in key financial variables such as interest rates, exchange rates, and commodity prices.

We describe a firm's exposure to a particular risk with a risk profile. The goal of financial risk management is to alter the firm's risk profile by buying and selling derivative assets such as futures contracts, swap contracts, and option contracts. By finding instruments with appropriate payoff profiles, a firm can reduce or even eliminate its exposure to many types of risk.

Hedging cannot change the fundamental economic reality of a business. What it can do is allow a firm to avoid otherwise expensive and troublesome disruptions that result from short-run, temporary price fluctuations. Hedging also gives a firm time to react and adapt to changing market conditions. Because of the price volatility and rapid economic change that characterize modern business, intelligently dealing with volatility has become an increasingly important task for financial managers.

Key Terms

hedging 838
derivative security 838
risk profile 845
transactions exposure 847
economic exposure 848
forward contract 849
payoff profile 850

futures contract 852
cross-hedging 855
swap contract 855
option contract 859
call option 859
put option 859

Chapter Review Problems and Self-Test

24.1 **Futures Contracts** Suppose Farmer Bob expects to harvest 100,000 bushels of corn in September. He is concerned about the possibility of price fluctuations between now and September. The futures price for September corn is $2.50 per bushel, and contract calls for 5,000 bushels. What action should Farmer Bob take to lock in the $2.50 price? Suppose the price of corn actually turns out to be $3.00. Evaluate Farmer Bob's gains and losses. Do the same for a price of $2.00. Ignore marking-to-market.

24.2 **Options Contracts** In the previous question, September futures put options with a strike price of $2.50 per bushel cost $.20 per bushel. Assuming that Farmer Bob hedges using put options, evaluate his gains and losses for corn prices of $2.00, $2.50, and $3.00.

Answers to Self-Test Questions

24.1 Farmer Bob wants to deliver corn and receive a fixed price, so he needs to *sell* futures contracts. Each contract calls for delivery of

5,000 bushels, so Bob needs to sell 20 contracts. No money changes hands today.

If corn prices actually turn out to be $3.00, then Bob will receive $300,000 for his crop, but he will have a loss of $50,000 on his futures position when he closes it because the contracts require him to sell 100,000 bushels of corn at $2.50, when the going price is $3.00. He thus nets $250,000 overall.

If corn prices turn out to be $2.00 per bushel, then the crop is only worth $200,000. However, Bob will have a profit of $50,000 on his futures position, so he again nets $250,000.

24.2   If Farmer Bob wants to insure against a price decline only, he can buy 20 put contracts. Each contract is for 5,000 bushels, so the cost per contract is 5,000 × $.20 = $1,000. For 20 contracts, the cost would be $20,000.

If corn prices turn out to be $3.00, then Bob will not exercise the put options (why not?). His crop is worth $300,000, but he is out the $20,000 cost of the options, so he nets $280,000.

If corn prices fall to $2.00, the crop is worth $200,000. Bob will exercise his puts, however, and thereby force the seller of the puts to pay $2.50 per bushel. He receives a total of $250,000. If we subtract the cost of the puts, his net is $230,000. In fact, check that his net at any price of $2.50 or lower is $230,000.

Questions and Problems

1. **Hedging with Futures**   If a firm is selling futures contracts on lumber as a hedging strategy, what must be true about the firm's exposure to lumber prices?

2. **Hedging with Options**   If a firm is buying call options on pork belly futures as a hedging strategy, what must be true about the firm's exposure to pork belly prices?

3. **Futures Contracts**   Look back at the cocoa futures contracts in Table 24.1. Suppose you had purchased a December 1992 contract. How much would you have made or lost if cocoa prices actually turned out to be $1,000 per ton at expiration?

4. **Futures Options**   Look back at the copper futures options in Table 24.2. Suppose you had purchased September 100 put options. How much did you pay per pound of copper? What would have been your gain or loss if copper prices ended up at $.80 per pound at expiration?

5. **Forwards versus Futures**   What is the difference between a forward contract and a futures contract? Why do you think that futures contracts are much more common?

6. **Hedging Interest Rates**   A company has a large bond issue maturing in a year. When it matures, the company will float a new issue. Current interest rates are attractive, and the company is concerned that rates next year will be higher. What are some strategies that the company might use in this case?

7.   Hedging with Futures   An oil producer would like to hedge its production by transacting in futures contracts. What should it do? Explain why it probably will not be able to achieve a completely flat risk profile with respect to oil prices. Give at least two reasons.

8.   Risk Analysis   A company produces an energy-intensive product and uses natural gas as the energy source. The competition primarily uses oil. Explain why this company is exposed to fluctuations in both oil and natural gas prices.

9.   Hedging with Futures   Take a look back at Table 24.1. A public utility knows that its need for oil will increase dramatically when cold weather begins, and it wants to lock in the price of oil for November 1992 delivery. What price can it lock in? If it estimates that it will need 20,000 barrels in November, what should the utility do? How much will your hedging strategy cost?

10.   Options versus Futures   If a textile manufacturer wanted to hedge against adverse cotton price movements, it could buy calls on cotton or it could buy futures on cotton. What are the pros and cons of the two approaches?

11.   Put and Call Payoffs   Suppose a financial manager buys call options on 40,000 barrels of oil with an exercise price of $20 per barrel. She simultaneously sells a put option on 40,000 barrels of oil with the same exercise price. Consider her gains and losses if oil prices are $10, $15, $20, $25, and $30. What do you notice about the payoff profile?

12.   Puts and Calls   Explain why a put option on a bond is conceptually the same as a call option on interest rates.

13.   Transactions versus Economic Exposure   What is the difference between transactions and economic exposure? Which can be hedged more easily? Why?

14.   Hedging Commodity Price Risks   For the following companies, describe some commodity price hedging strategies that might be considered.
      a. A public utility (e.g., Boston Edison).
      b. A candy manufacturer (e.g., Hershey).
      c. An airline (e.g., Delta).
      d. A manufacturer of photographic film (e.g., Kodak).

15.   Hedging Exchange Rate Risks   In Table 24.1, there is a futures contract for Japanese yen. If a U.S. company exports to Japan, how would it use this contract to hedge? Would it buy or sell? In answering, notice how the rate is quoted.

16.   Swaps   Suppose a firm enters into a fixed-for-floating interest rate swap with a swap dealer. Describe the cash flows that will occur as a result of the swap.

17.   Swaps   Explain why a swap is effectively a series of forward contracts. Suppose a firm enters into a swap with a swap dealer. Describe the nature of the default risk faced by both parties.

Challenge Question   18.   Financial Engineering   Suppose that there were call options and forward contracts available on coal, but no put options. Show how a financial engineer could synthesize a put option using the available contracts. What does your answer tell you about the general relationship between puts, calls, and forwards?

Suggested Readings

For an excellent treatment of the topics we have discussed, see:

Smith, C.W.; C.W. Smithson; and D.S. Wilford. *Managing Financial Risk*. Institutional Investor Series in Finance (New York: Harper & Row, 1990).

For more on financial engineering, see:

Marshall, J.F., and V.K. Bansal. *Financial Engineering* (Boston: Allyn & Bacon, 1992).

For more on options, futures, and derivative securities, see:

Hull, John. *Options, Futures, and Other Derivative Securities* (Englewood Cliffs, N.J.: Prentice-Hall, 1989).

Mathematical Tables

Table A.1

Future value of $1 at the end of t periods $= (1 + r)^t$

	Interest rate								
Period	1%	2%	3%	4%	5%	6%	7%	8%	9%
1	1.0100	1.0200	1.0300	1.0400	1.0500	1.0600	1.0700	1.0800	1.0900
2	1.0201	1.0404	1.0609	1.0816	1.1025	1.1236	1.1449	1.1664	1.1881
3	1.0303	1.0612	1.0927	1.1249	1.1576	1.1910	1.2250	1.2597	1.2950
4	1.0406	1.0824	1.1255	1.1699	1.2155	1.2625	1.3108	1.3605	1.4116
5	1.0510	1.1041	1.1593	1.2167	1.2763	1.3382	1.4026	1.4693	1.5386
6	1.0615	1.1262	1.1941	1.2653	1.3401	1.4185	1.5007	1.5869	1.6771
7	1.0721	1.1487	1.2299	1.3159	1.4071	1.5036	1.6058	1.7138	1.8280
8	1.0829	1.1717	1.2668	1.3686	1.4775	1.5938	1.7182	1.8509	1.9926
9	1.0937	1.1951	1.3048	1.4233	1.5513	1.6895	1.8385	1.9990	2.1719
10	1.1046	1.2190	1.3439	1.4802	1.6289	1.7908	1.9672	2.1589	2.3674
11	1.1157	1.2434	1.3842	1.5395	1.7103	1.8983	2.1049	2.3316	2.5804
12	1.1268	1.2682	1.4258	1.6010	1.7959	2.0122	2.2522	2.5182	2.8127
13	1.1381	1.2936	1.4685	1.6651	1.8856	2.1329	2.4098	2.7196	3.0658
14	1.1495	1.3195	1.5126	1.7317	1.9799	2.2609	2.5785	2.9372	3.3417
15	1.1610	1.3459	1.5580	1.8009	2.0789	2.3966	2.7590	3.1722	3.6425
16	1.1726	1.3728	1.6047	1.8730	2.1829	2.5404	2.9522	3.4259	3.9703
17	1.1843	1.4002	1.6528	1.9479	2.2920	2.6928	3.1588	3.7000	4.3276
18	1.1961	1.4282	1.7024	2.0258	2.4066	2.8543	3.3799	3.9960	4.7171
19	1.2081	1.4568	1.7535	2.1068	2.5270	3.0256	3.6165	4.3157	5.1417
20	1.2202	1.4859	1.8061	2.1911	2.6533	3.2071	3.8697	4.6610	5.6044
21	1.2324	1.5157	1.8603	2.2788	2.7860	3.3996	4.1406	5.0338	6.1088
22	1.2447	1.5460	1.9161	2.3699	2.9253	3.6035	4.4304	5.4365	6.6586
23	1.2572	1.5769	1.9736	2.4647	3.0715	3.8197	4.7405	5.8715	7.2579
24	1.2697	1.6084	2.0328	2.5633	3.2251	4.0489	5.0724	6.3412	7.9111
25	1.2824	1.6406	2.0938	2.6658	3.3864	4.2919	5.4274	6.8485	8.6231
30	1.3478	1.8114	2.4273	3.2434	4.3219	5.7435	7.6123	10.063	13.268
40	1.4889	2.2080	3.2620	4.8010	7.0400	10.286	14.974	21.725	31.409
50	1.6446	2.6916	4.3839	7.1067	11.467	18.420	29.457	46.902	74.358
60	1.8167	3.2810	5.8916	10.520	18.679	32.988	57.946	101.26	176.03

					Interest rate					
10%	12%	14%	15%	16%	18%	20%	24%	28%	32%	36%
1.1000	1.1200	1.1400	1.1500	1.1600	1.1800	1.2000	1.2400	1.2800	1.3200	1.3600
1.2100	1.2544	1.2996	1.3225	1.3456	1.3924	1.4400	1.5376	1.6384	1.7424	1.8496
1.3310	1.4049	1.4815	1.5209	1.5609	1.6430	1.7280	1.9066	2.0972	2.3000	2.5155
1.4641	1.5735	1.6890	1.7490	1.8106	1.9388	2.0736	2.3642	2.6844	3.0360	3.4210
1.6105	1.7623	1.9254	2.0114	2.1003	2.2878	2.4883	2.9316	3.4360	4.0075	4.6526
1.7716	1.9738	2.1950	2.3131	2.4364	2.6996	2.9860	3.6352	4.3980	5.2899	6.3275
1.9487	2.2107	2.5023	2.6600	2.8262	3.1855	3.5832	4.5077	5.6295	6.9826	8.6054
2.1436	2.4760	2.8526	3.0590	3.2784	3.7589	4.2998	5.5895	7.2058	9.2170	11.703
2.3579	2.7731	3.2519	3.5179	3.8030	4.4355	5.1598	6.9310	9.2234	12.166	15.917
2.5937	3.1058	3.7072	4.0456	4.4114	5.2338	6.1917	8.5944	11.806	16.060	21.647
2.8531	3.4785	4.2262	4.6524	5.1173	6.1759	7.4301	10.657	15.112	21.199	29.439
3.1384	3.8960	4.8179	5.3503	5.9360	7.2876	8.9161	13.215	19.343	27.983	40.037
3.4523	4.3635	5.4924	6.1528	6.8858	8.5994	10.699	16.386	24.759	36.937	54.451
3.7975	4.8871	6.2613	7.0757	7.9875	10.147	12.839	20.319	31.691	48.757	74.053
4.1772	5.4736	7.1379	8.1371	9.2655	11.974	15.407	25.196	40.565	64.359	100.71
4.5950	6.1304	8.1372	9.3576	10.748	14.129	18.488	31.243	51.923	84.954	136.97
5.0545	6.8660	9.2765	10.761	12.468	16.672	22.186	38.741	66.461	112.14	186.28
5.5599	7.6900	10.575	12.375	14.463	19.673	26.623	48.039	85.071	148.02	253.34
6.1159	8.6128	12.056	14.232	16.777	23.214	31.948	59.568	108.89	195.39	344.54
6.7275	9.6463	13.743	16.367	19.461	27.393	38.338	73.864	139.38	257.92	468.57
7.4002	10.804	15.668	18.822	22.574	32.324	46.005	91.592	178.41	340.45	637.26
8.1403	12.100	17.861	21.645	26.186	38.142	55.206	113.57	228.36	449.39	866.67
8.9543	13.552	20.362	24.891	30.376	45.008	66.247	140.83	292.30	593.20	1178.7
9.8497	15.179	23.212	28.625	35.236	53.109	79.497	174.63	374.14	783.02	1603.0
10.835	17.000	26.462	32.919	40.874	62.669	95.396	216.54	478.90	1033.6	2180.1
17.449	29.960	50.950	66.212	85.850	143.37	237.38	634.82	1645.5	4142.1	10143.
45.259	93.051	188.88	267.86	378.72	750.38	1469.8	5455.9	19427.	66521.	*
117.39	289.00	700.23	1083.7	1670.7	3927.4	9100.4	46890.	*	*	*
304.48	897.60	2595.9	4384.0	7370.2	20555.	56348.	*	*	*	*

*The factor is greater than 99,999.

Table A.2

Present value of $1 to be received after t periods $= 1/(1 + r)^t$

	Interest rate								
Period	1%	2%	3%	4%	5%	6%	7%	8%	9%
1	0.9901	0.9804	0.9709	0.9615	0.9524	0.9434	0.9346	0.9259	0.9174
2	0.9803	0.9612	0.9426	0.9246	0.9070	0.8900	0.8734	0.8573	0.8417
3	0.9706	0.9423	0.9151	0.8890	0.8638	0.8396	0.8163	0.7938	0.7722
4	0.9610	0.9238	0.8885	0.8548	0.8227	0.7921	0.7629	0.7350	0.7084
5	0.9515	0.9057	0.8626	0.8219	0.7835	0.7473	0.7130	0.6806	0.6499
6	0.9420	0.8880	0.8375	0.7903	0.7462	0.7050	0.6663	0.6302	0.5963
7	0.9327	0.8706	0.8131	0.7599	0.7107	0.6651	0.6227	0.5835	0.5470
8	0.9235	0.8535	0.7894	0.7307	0.6768	0.6274	0.5820	0.5403	0.5019
9	0.9143	0.8368	0.7664	0.7026	0.6446	0.5919	0.5439	0.5002	0.4604
10	0.9053	0.8203	0.7441	0.6756	0.6139	0.5584	0.5083	0.4632	0.4224
11	0.8963	0.8043	0.7224	0.6496	0.5847	0.5268	0.4751	0.4289	0.3875
12	0.8874	0.7885	0.7014	0.6246	0.5568	0.4970	0.4440	0.3971	0.3555
13	0.8787	0.7730	0.6810	0.6006	0.5303	0.4688	0.4150	0.3677	0.3262
14	0.8700	0.7579	0.6611	0.5775	0.5051	0.4423	0.3878	0.3405	0.2992
15	0.8613	0.7430	0.6419	0.5553	0.4810	0.4173	0.3624	0.3152	0.2745
16	0.8528	0.7284	0.6232	0.5339	0.4581	0.3936	0.3387	0.2919	0.2519
17	0.8444	0.7142	0.6050	0.5134	0.4363	0.3714	0.3166	0.2703	0.2311
18	0.8360	0.7002	0.5874	0.4936	0.4155	0.3503	0.2959	0.2502	0.2120
19	0.8277	0.6864	0.5703	0.4746	0.3957	0.3305	0.2765	0.2317	0.1945
20	0.8195	0.6730	0.5537	0.4564	0.3769	0.3118	0.2584	0.2145	0.1784
21	0.8114	0.6598	0.5375	0.4388	0.3589	0.2942	0.2415	0.1987	0.1637
22	0.8034	0.6468	0.5219	0.4220	0.3418	0.2775	0.2257	0.1839	0.1502
23	0.7954	0.6342	0.5067	0.4057	0.3256	0.2618	0.2109	0.1703	0.1378
24	0.7876	0.6217	0.4919	0.3901	0.3101	0.2470	0.1971	0.1577	0.1264
25	0.7798	0.6095	0.4776	0.3751	0.2953	0.2330	0.1842	0.1460	0.1160
30	0.7419	0.5521	0.4120	0.3083	0.2314	0.1741	0.1314	0.0994	0.0754
40	0.6717	0.4529	0.3066	0.2083	0.1420	0.0972	0.0668	0.0460	0.0318
50	0.6080	0.3715	0.2281	0.1407	0.0872	0.0543	0.0339	0.0213	0.0134

					Interest rate					
10%	12%	14%	15%	16%	18%	20%	24%	28%	32%	36%
0.9091	0.8929	0.8772	0.8696	0.8621	0.8475	0.8333	0.8065	0.7813	0.7576	0.7353
0.8264	0.7972	0.7695	0.7561	0.7432	0.7182	0.6944	0.6504	0.6104	0.5739	0.5407
0.7513	0.7118	0.6750	0.6575	0.6407	0.6086	0.5787	0.5245	0.4768	0.4348	0.3975
0.6830	0.6355	0.5921	0.5718	0.5523	0.5158	0.4823	0.4230	0.3725	0.3294	0.2923
0.6209	0.5674	0.5194	0.4972	0.4761	0.4371	0.4019	0.3411	0.2910	0.2495	0.2149
0.5645	0.5066	0.4556	0.4323	0.4104	0.3704	0.3349	0.2751	0.2274	0.1890	0.1580
0.5132	0.4523	0.3996	0.3759	0.3538	0.3139	0.2791	0.2218	0.1776	0.1432	0.1162
0.4665	0.4039	0.3506	0.3269	0.3050	0.2660	0.2326	0.1789	0.1388	0.1085	0.0854
0.4241	0.3606	0.3075	0.2843	0.2630	0.2255	0.1938	0.1443	0.1084	0.0822	0.0628
0.3855	0.3220	0.2697	0.2472	0.2267	0.1911	0.1615	0.1164	0.0847	0.0623	0.0462
0.3505	0.2875	0.2366	0.2149	0.1954	0.1619	0.1346	0.0938	0.0662	0.0472	0.0340
0.3186	0.2567	0.2076	0.1869	0.1685	0.1372	0.1122	0.0757	0.0517	0.0357	0.0250
0.2897	0.2292	0.1821	0.1625	0.1452	0.1163	0.0935	0.0610	0.0404	0.0271	0.0184
0.2633	0.2046	0.1597	0.1413	0.1252	0.0985	0.0779	0.0492	0.0316	0.0205	0.0135
0.2394	0.1827	0.1401	0.1229	0.1079	0.0835	0.0649	0.0397	0.0247	0.0155	0.0099
0.2176	0.1631	0.1229	0.1069	0.0930	0.0708	0.0541	0.0320	0.0193	0.0118	0.0073
0.1978	0.1456	0.1078	0.0929	0.0802	0.0600	0.0451	0.0258	0.0150	0.0089	0.0054
0.1799	0.1300	0.0946	0.0808	0.0691	0.0508	0.0376	0.0208	0.0118	0.0068	0.0039
0.1635	0.1161	0.0829	0.0703	0.0596	0.0431	0.0313	0.0168	0.0092	0.0051	0.0029
0.1486	0.1037	0.0728	0.0611	0.0514	0.0365	0.0261	0.0135	0.0072	0.0039	0.0021
0.1351	0.0926	0.0638	0.0531	0.0443	0.0309	0.0217	0.0109	0.0056	0.0029	0.0016
0.1228	0.0826	0.0560	0.0462	0.0382	0.0262	0.0181	0.0088	0.0044	0.0022	0.0012
0.1117	0.0738	0.0491	0.0402	0.0329	0.0222	0.0151	0.0071	0.0034	0.0017	0.0008
0.1015	0.0659	0.0431	0.0349	0.0284	0.0188	0.0126	0.0057	0.0027	0.0013	0.0006
0.0923	0.0588	0.0378	0.0304	0.0245	0.0160	0.0105	0.0046	0.0021	0.0010	0.0005
0.0573	0.0334	0.0196	0.0151	0.0116	0.0070	0.0042	0.0016	0.0006	0.0002	0.0001
0.0221	0.0107	0.0053	0.0037	0.0026	0.0013	0.0007	0.0002	0.0001	*	*
0.0085	0.0035	0.0014	0.0009	0.0006	0.0003	0.0001	*	*	*	*

*The factor is zero to four decimal places.

Table A.3

Present value of an annuity of $1 per period for t periods $= [1 - 1/(1 + r)^t]/r$

Number of periods	Interest rate								
	1%	2%	3%	4%	5%	6%	7%	8%	9%
1	0.9901	0.9804	0.9709	0.9615	0.9524	0.9434	0.9346	0.9259	0.9174
2	1.9704	1.9416	1.9135	1.8861	1.8594	1.8334	1.8080	1.7833	1.7591
3	2.9410	2.8839	2.8286	2.7751	2.7232	2.6730	2.6243	2.5771	2.5313
4	3.9020	3.8077	3.7171	3.6299	3.5460	3.4651	3.3872	3.3121	3.2397
5	4.8534	4.7135	4.5797	4.4518	4.3295	4.2124	4.1002	3.9927	3.8897
6	5.7955	5.6014	5.4172	5.2421	5.0757	4.9173	4.7665	4.6229	4.4859
7	6.7282	6.4720	6.2303	6.0021	5.7864	5.5824	5.3893	5.2064	5.0330
8	7.6517	7.3255	7.0197	6.7327	6.4632	6.2098	5.9713	5.7466	5.5348
9	8.5660	8.1622	7.7861	7.4353	7.1078	6.8017	6.5152	6.2469	5.9952
10	9.4713	8.9826	8.5302	8.1109	7.7217	7.3601	7.0236	6.7101	6.4177
11	10.3676	9.7868	9.2526	8.7605	8.3064	7.8869	7.4987	7.1390	6.8052
12	11.2551	10.5753	9.9540	9.3851	8.8633	8.3838	7.9427	7.5361	7.1607
13	12.1337	11.3484	10.6350	9.9856	9.3936	8.8527	8.3577	7.9038	7.4869
14	13.0037	12.1062	11.2961	10.5631	9.8986	9.2950	8.7455	8.2442	7.7862
15	13.8651	12.8493	11.9379	11.1184	10.3797	9.7122	9.1079	8.5595	8.0607
16	14.7179	13.5777	12.5611	11.6523	10.8378	10.1059	9.4466	8.8514	8.3126
17	15.5623	14.2919	13.1661	12.1657	11.2741	10.4773	9.7632	9.1216	8.5436
18	16.3983	14.9920	13.7535	12.6593	11.6896	10.8276	10.0591	9.3719	8.7556
19	17.2260	15.6785	14.3238	13.1339	12.0853	11.1581	10.3356	9.6036	8.9501
20	18.0456	16.3514	14.8775	13.5903	12.4622	11.4699	10.5940	9.8181	9.1285
21	18.8570	17.0112	15.4150	14.0292	12.8212	11.7641	10.8355	10.0168	9.2922
22	19.6604	17.6580	15.9369	14.4511	13.1630	12.0416	11.0612	10.2007	9.4424
23	20.4558	18.2922	16.4436	14.8568	13.4886	12.3034	11.2722	10.3741	9.5802
24	21.2434	18.9139	16.9355	15.2470	13.7986	12.5504	11.4693	10.5288	9.7066
25	22.0232	19.5235	17.4131	15.6221	14.0939	12.7834	11.6536	10.6748	9.8226
30	25.8077	22.3965	19.6004	17.2920	15.3725	13.7648	12.4090	11.2578	10.2737
40	32.8347	27.3555	23.1148	19.7928	17.1591	15.0463	13.3317	11.9246	10.7574
50	39.1961	31.4236	25.7298	21.4822	18.2559	15.7619	13.8007	12.2335	10.9617

					Interest rate				
10%	12%	14%	15%	16%	18%	20%	24%	28%	32%
0.9091	0.8929	0.8772	0.8696	0.8621	0.8475	0.8333	0.8065	0.7813	0.7576
1.7355	1.6901	1.6467	1.6257	1.6052	1.5656	1.5278	1.4568	1.3916	1.3315
2.4869	2.4018	2.3216	2.2832	2.2459	2.1743	2.1065	1.9813	1.8684	1.7663
3.1699	3.0373	2.9137	2.8550	2.7982	2.6901	2.5887	2.4043	2.2410	2.0957
3.7908	3.6048	3.4331	3.3522	3.2743	3.1272	2.9906	2.7454	2.5320	2.3452
4.3553	4.1114	3.8887	3.7845	3.6847	3.4976	3.3255	3.0205	2.7594	2.5342
4.8684	4.5638	4.2883	4.1604	4.0386	3.8115	3.6046	3.2423	2.9370	2.6775
5.3349	4.9676	4.6389	4.4873	4.3436	4.0776	3.8372	3.4212	3.0758	2.7860
5.7590	5.3282	4.9464	4.7716	4.6065	4.3030	4.0310	3.5655	3.1842	2.8681
6.1446	5.6502	5.2161	5.0188	4.8332	4.4941	4.1925	3.6819	3.2689	2.9304
6.4951	5.9377	5.4527	5.2337	5.0286	4.6560	4.3271	3.7757	3.3351	2.9776
6.8137	6.1944	5.6603	5.4206	5.1971	4.7932	4.4392	3.8514	3.3868	3.0133
7.1034	6.4235	5.8424	5.5831	5.3423	4.9095	4.5327	3.9124	3.4272	3.0404
7.3667	6.6282	6.0021	5.7245	5.4675	5.0081	4.6106	3.9616	3.4587	3.0609
7.6061	6.8109	6.1422	5.8474	5.5755	5.0916	4.6755	4.0013	3.4834	3.0764
7.8237	6.9740	6.2651	5.9542	5.6685	5.1624	4.7296	4.0333	3.5026	3.0882
8.0216	7.1196	6.3729	6.0472	5.7487	5.2223	4.7746	4.0591	3.5177	3.0971
8.2014	7.2497	6.4674	6.1280	5.8178	5.2732	4.8122	4.0799	3.5294	3.1039
8.3649	7.3658	6.5504	6.1982	5.8775	5.3162	4.8435	4.0967	3.5386	3.1090
8.5136	7.4694	6.6231	6.2593	5.9288	5.3527	4.8696	4.1103	3.5458	3.1129
8.6487	7.5620	6.6870	6.3125	5.9731	5.3837	4.8913	4.1212	3.5514	3.1158
8.7715	7.6446	6.7429	6.3587	6.0113	5.4099	4.9094	4.1300	3.5558	3.1180
8.8832	7.7184	6.7921	6.3988	6.0442	5.4321	4.9245	4.1371	3.5592	3.1197
8.9847	7.7843	6.8351	6.4338	6.0726	5.4509	4.9371	4.1428	3.5619	3.1210
9.0770	7.8431	6.8729	6.4641	6.0971	5.4669	4.9476	4.1474	3.5640	3.1220
9.4269	8.0552	7.0027	6.5660	6.1772	5.5168	4.9789	4.1601	3.5693	3.1242
9.7791	8.2438	7.1050	6.6418	6.2335	5.5482	4.9966	4.1659	3.5712	3.1250
9.9148	8.3045	7.1327	6.6605	6.2463	5.5541	4.9995	4.1666	3.5714	3.1250

Table A.4

Future value of an annuity of $1 per period for t periods $= [(1 + r)^t - 1]/r$

Number of periods	Interest rate								
	1%	2%	3%	4%	5%	6%	7%	8%	9%
1	1.0000	1.0000	1.0000	1.0000	1.0000	1.0000	1.0000	1.0000	1.0000
2	2.0100	2.0200	2.0300	2.0400	2.0500	2.0600	2.0700	2.0800	2.0900
3	3.0301	3.0604	3.0909	3.1216	3.1525	3.1836	3.2149	3.2464	3.2781
4	4.0604	4.1216	4.1836	4.2465	4.3101	4.3746	4.4399	4.5061	4.5731
5	5.1010	5.2040	5.3091	5.4163	5.5256	5.6371	5.7507	5.8666	5.9847
6	6.1520	6.3081	6.4684	6.6330	6.8019	6.9753	7.1533	7.3359	7.5233
7	7.2135	7.4343	7.6625	7.8983	8.1420	8.3938	8.6540	8.9228	9.2004
8	8.2857	8.5830	8.8932	9.2142	9.5491	9.8975	10.260	10.637	11.028
9	9.3685	9.7546	10.159	10.583	11.027	11.491	11.978	12.488	13.021
10	10.462	10.950	11.464	12.006	12.578	13.181	13.816	14.487	15.193
11	11.567	12.169	12.808	13.486	14.207	14.972	15.784	16.645	17.560
12	12.683	13.412	14.192	15.026	15.917	16.870	17.888	18.977	20.141
13	13.809	14.680	15.618	16.627	17.713	18.882	20.141	21.495	22.953
14	14.947	15.974	17.086	18.292	19.599	21.015	22.550	24.215	26.019
15	16.097	17.293	18.599	20.024	21.579	23.276	25.129	27.152	29.361
16	17.258	18.639	20.157	21.825	23.657	25.673	27.888	30.324	33.003
17	18.430	20.012	21.762	23.698	25.840	28.213	30.840	33.750	36.974
18	19.615	21.412	23.414	25.645	28.132	30.906	33.999	37.450	41.301
19	20.811	22.841	25.117	27.671	30.539	33.760	37.379	41.446	46.018
20	22.019	24.297	26.870	29.778	33.066	36.786	40.995	45.762	51.160
21	23.239	25.783	28.676	31.969	35.719	39.993	44.865	50.423	56.765
22	24.472	27.299	30.537	34.248	38.505	43.392	49.006	55.457	62.873
23	25.716	28.845	32.453	36.618	41.430	46.996	53.436	60.893	69.532
24	26.973	30.422	34.426	39.083	44.502	50.816	58.177	66.765	76.790
25	28.243	32.030	36.459	41.646	47.727	54.865	63.249	73.106	84.701
30	34.785	40.568	47.575	56.085	66.439	79.058	94.461	113.28	136.31
40	48.886	60.402	75.401	95.026	120.80	154.76	199.64	259.06	337.88
50	64.463	84.579	112.80	152.67	209.35	290.34	406.53	573.77	815.08
60	81.670	114.05	163.05	237.99	353.58	533.13	813.52	1253.2	1944.8

					Interest rate					
10%	12%	14%	15%	16%	18%	20%	24%	28%	32%	36%
1.0000	1.0000	1.0000	1.0000	1.0000	1.0000	1.0000	1.0000	1.0000	1.0000	1.0000
2.1000	2.1200	2.1400	2.1500	2.1600	2.1800	2.2000	2.2400	2.2800	2.3200	2.3600
3.3100	3.3744	3.4396	3.4725	3.5056	3.5724	3.6400	3.7776	3.9184	4.0624	4.2096
4.6410	4.7793	4.9211	4.9934	5.0665	5.2154	5.3680	5.6842	6.0156	6.3624	6.7251
6.1051	6.3528	6.6101	6.7424	6.8771	7.1542	7.4416	8.0484	8.6999	9.3983	10.146
7.7156	8.1152	8.5355	8.7537	8.9775	9.4420	9.9299	10.980	12.136	13.406	14.799
9.4872	10.089	10.730	11.067	11.414	12.142	12.916	14.615	16.534	18.696	21.126
11.436	12.300	13.233	13.727	14.240	15.327	16.499	19.123	22.163	25.678	29.732
13.579	14.776	16.085	16.786	17.519	19.086	20.799	24.712	29.369	34.895	41.435
15.937	17.549	19.337	20.304	21.321	23.521	25.959	31.643	38.593	47.062	57.352
18.531	20.655	23.045	24.349	25.733	28.755	32.150	40.238	50.398	63.122	78.998
21.384	24.133	27.271	29.002	30.850	34.931	39.581	50.895	65.510	84.320	108.44
24.523	28.029	32.089	34.352	36.786	42.219	48.497	64.110	84.853	112.30	148.47
27.975	32.393	37.581	40.505	43.672	50.818	59.196	80.496	109.61	149.24	202.93
31.772	37.280	43.842	47.580	51.660	60.965	72.035	100.82	141.30	198.00	276.98
35.950	42.753	50.980	55.717	60.925	72.939	87.442	126.01	181.87	262.36	377.69
40.545	48.884	59.118	65.075	71.673	87.068	105.93	157.25	233.79	347.31	514.66
45.599	55.750	68.394	75.836	84.141	103.74	128.12	195.99	300.25	459.45	700.94
51.159	63.440	78.969	88.212	98.603	123.41	154.74	244.03	385.32	607.47	954.28
57.275	72.052	91.025	102.44	115.38	146.63	186.69	303.60	494.21	802.86	1298.8
64.002	81.699	104.77	118.81	134.84	174.02	225.03	377.46	633.59	1060.8	1767.4
71.403	92.503	120.44	137.63	157.41	206.34	271.03	469.06	812.00	1401.2	2404.7
79.543	104.60	138.30	159.28	183.60	244.49	326.24	582.63	1040.4	1850.6	3271.3
88.497	118.16	158.66	184.17	213.98	289.49	392.48	723.46	1332.7	2443.8	4450.0
98.347	133.33	181.87	212.79	249.21	342.60	471.98	898.09	1706.8	3226.8	6053.0
164.49	241.33	356.79	434.75	530.31	790.95	1181.9	2640.9	5873.2	12941.	28172.3
442.59	767.09	1342.0	1779.1	2360.8	4163.2	7343.9	22729.	69377.	*	*
1163.9	2400.0	4994.5	7217.7	10436.	21813.	45497.	*	*	*	*
3034.8	7471.6	18535.	29220.	46058.	*	*	*	*	*	*

*The factor is greater than 99,999.

Table A.5

Cumulative normal distribution

d	N(d)	d	N(d)	d	N(d)	d	N(d)	d	N(d)	d	N(d)
−3.00	.0013	−1.58	.0571	−0.76	.2236	0.06	.5239	0.86	.8051	1.66	.9515
−2.95	.0016	−1.56	.0594	−0.74	.2297	0.08	.5319	0.88	.8106	1.68	.9535
−2.90	.0019	−1.54	.0618	−0.72	.2358	0.10	.5398	0.90	.8159	1.70	.9554
−2.85	.0022	−1.52	.0643	−0.70	.2420	0.12	.5478	0.92	.8212	1.72	.9573
−2.80	.0026	−1.50	.0668	−0.68	.2483	0.14	.5557	0.94	.8264	1.74	.9591
−2.75	.0030	−1.48	.0694	−0.66	.2546	0.16	.5636	0.96	.8315	1.76	.9608
−2.70	.0035	−1.46	.0721	−0.64	.2611	0.18	.5714	0.98	.8365	1.78	.9625
−2.65	.0040	−1.44	.0749	−0.62	.2676	0.20	.5793	1.00	.8414	1.80	.9641
−2.60	.0047	−1.42	.0778	−0.60	.2743	0.22	.5871	1.02	.8461	1.82	.9656
−2.55	.0054	−1.40	.0808	−0.58	.2810	0.24	.5948	1.04	.8508	1.84	.9671
−2.50	.0062	−1.38	.0838	−0.56	.2877	0.26	.6026	1.06	.8554	1.86	.9686
−2.45	.0071	−1.36	.0869	−0.54	.2946	0.28	.6103	1.08	.8599	1.88	.9699
−2.40	.0082	−1.34	.0901	−0.52	.3015	0.30	.6179	1.10	.8643	1.90	.9713
−2.35	.0094	−1.32	.0934	−0.50	.3085	0.32	.6255	1.12	.8686	1.92	.9726
−2.30	.0107	−1.30	.0968	−0.48	.3156	0.34	.6331	1.14	.8729	1.94	.9738
−2.25	.0122	−1.28	.1003	−0.46	.3228	0.36	.6406	1.16	.8770	1.96	.9750
−2.20	.0139	−1.26	.1038	−0.44	.3300	0.38	.6480	1.18	.8810	1.98	.9761
−2.15	.0158	−1.24	.1075	−0.42	.3373	0.40	.6554	1.20	.8849	2.00	.9772
−2.10	.0179	−1.22	.1112	−0.40	.3446	0.42	.6628	1.22	.8888	2.05	.9798
−2.05	.0202	−1.20	.1151	−0.38	.3520	0.44	.6700	1.24	.8925	2.10	.9821
−2.00	.0228	−1.18	.1190	−0.36	.3594	0.46	.6773	1.26	.8962	2.15	.9842
−1.98	.0239	−1.16	.1230	−0.34	.3669	0.48	.6844	1.28	.8997	2.20	.9861
−1.96	.0250	−1.14	.1271	−0.32	.3745	0.50	.6915	1.30	.9032	2.25	.9878
−1.94	.0262	−1.12	.1314	−0.30	.3821	0.52	.6985	1.32	.9066	2.30	.9893
−1.92	.0274	−1.10	.1357	−0.28	.3897	0.54	.7054	1.34	.9099	2.35	.9906
−1.90	.0287	−1.08	.1401	−0.26	.3974	0.56	.7123	1.36	.9131	2.40	.9918
−1.88	.0301	−1.06	.1446	−0.24	.4052	0.58	.7191	1.38	.9162	2.45	.9929
−1.86	.0314	−1.04	.1492	−0.22	.4129	0.60	.7258	1.40	.9192	2.50	.9938
−1.84	.0329	−1.02	.1539	−0.20	.4207	0.62	.7324	1.42	.9222	2.55	.9946
−1.82	.0344	−1.00	.1587	−0.18	.4286	0.64	.7389	1.44	.9251	2.60	.9953
−1.80	.0359	−0.98	.1635	−0.16	.4365	0.66	.7454	1.46	.9279	2.65	.9960
−1.78	.0375	−0.96	.1685	−0.14	.4443	0.68	.7518	1.48	.9306	2.70	.9965
−1.76	.0392	−0.94	.1736	−0.12	.4523	0.70	.7580	1.50	.9332	2.75	.9970
−1.74	.0409	−0.92	.1788	−0.10	.4602	0.72	.7642	1.52	.9357	2.80	.9974
−1.72	.0427	−0.90	.1841	−0.08	.4681	0.74	.7704	1.54	.9382	2.85	.9978
−1.70	.0446	−0.88	.1894	−0.06	.4761	0.76	.7764	1.56	.9406	2.90	.9981
−1.68	.0465	−0.86	.1949	−0.04	.4841	0.78	.7823	1.58	.9429	2.95	.9984
−1.66	.0485	−0.84	.2005	−0.02	.4920	0.80	.7882	1.60	.9452	3.00	.9986
−1.64	.0505	−0.82	.2061	0.00	.5000	0.82	.7939	1.62	.9474	3.05	.9989
−1.62	.0526	−0.80	.2119	0.02	.5080	0.84	.7996	1.64	.9495		
−1.60	.0548	−0.78	.2177	0.04	.5160						

This table shows the probability [N(d)] of observing a value less than or equal to d. For example, as illustrated, if d is −.24, then N(d) is .4052.

Key Equations

Chapter 2

1. The balance sheet identity or equation:
   Assets = Liabilities
   $\qquad$ + Shareholders' equity $\qquad$ [2.1]
2. The income statement equation:
   Revenues − Expenses = Income $\qquad$ [2.2]
3. The cash flow identity:
   Cash flow from assets
   = Cash flow to creditors
   + Cash flow to stockholders $\qquad$ [2.3]
   where

   a. Cash flow from assets = Operating cash flow (OCF) − Net capital spending − Additions to net working capital (NWC)

   (1) Operating cash flow = Earnings before interest and taxes (EBIT) + Depreciation − Taxes

   (2) Net capital spending = Ending net fixed assets − Beginning net fixed assets + Depreciation

   (3) Additions to net working capital = Ending NWC − Beginning NWC

   b. Cash flow to creditors = Interest paid − Net new borrowing

   c. Cash flow to stockholders = Dividends paid − Net new equity

Chapter 3

1. The current ratio:
   $$\text{Current ratio} = \frac{\text{Current assets}}{\text{Current liabilities}} \qquad [3.1]$$

2. The quick or acid-test ratio:
   Quick ratio
   $$= \frac{\text{Current assets} - \text{Inventory}}{\text{Current liabilities}} \qquad [3.2]$$

3. The cash ratio:
   $$\text{Cash ratio} = \frac{\text{Cash}}{\text{Current liabilities}} \qquad [3.3]$$

4. The ratio of net working capital to total assets:
   Net working capital to total assets
   $$= \frac{\text{Net working capital}}{\text{Total assets}} \qquad [3.4]$$

5. The interval measure:
   Interval measure
   $$= \frac{\text{Current assets}}{\text{Average daily operating costs}} \qquad [3.5]$$

6. The total debt ratio:
   Total debt ratio
   $$= \frac{\text{Total assets} - \text{Total equity}}{\text{Total assets}} \qquad [3.6]$$

7. The debt/equity ratio:
   Debt/equity ratio = Total debt/
   $\qquad$ Total equity $\qquad$ [3.7]

8. The equity multiplier:
   Equity multiplier = Total assets/
   $\qquad$ Total equity $\qquad$ [3.8]

9. The long-term debt ratio:
   Long-term debt ratio
   $$= \frac{\text{Long-term debt}}{\text{Long-term debt} + \text{Total equity}} \qquad [3.9]$$

10. The times interest earned (TIE) ratio:
    $$\text{Times interest earned ratio} = \frac{\text{EBIT}}{\text{Interest}} \qquad [3.10]$$

11. The cash coverage ratio:

Cash coverage ratio

$$= \frac{\text{EBIT} + \text{Depreciation}}{\text{Interest}} \quad [3.11]$$

12. The inventory turnover ratio:

Inventory turnover

$$= \frac{\text{Cost of goods sold}}{\text{Inventory}} \quad [3.12]$$

13. The average days' sales in inventory:

Days' sales in inventory

$$= \frac{365 \text{ days}}{\text{Inventory turnover}} \quad [3.13]$$

14. The receivables turnover ratio:

Receivables turnover

$$= \frac{\text{Sales}}{\text{Accounts receivable}} \quad [3.14]$$

15. The days' sales in receivables:

Days' sales in receivables

$$= \frac{365 \text{ days}}{\text{Receivables turnover}} \quad [3.15]$$

16. The net working capital turnover ratio:

$$\text{NWC turnover} = \frac{\text{Sales}}{\text{NWC}} \quad [3.16]$$

17. The fixed asset turnover ratio:

$$\text{Fixed asset turnover} = \frac{\text{Sales}}{\text{Net fixed assets}} \quad [3.17]$$

18. The total asset turnover ratio:

$$\text{Total asset turnover} = \frac{\text{Sales}}{\text{Total assets}} \quad [3.18]$$

19. Profit margin:

$$\text{Profit margin} = \frac{\text{Net income}}{\text{Sales}} \quad [3.19]$$

20. Return on assets (ROA):

$$\text{Return on assets} = \frac{\text{Net income}}{\text{Total assets}} \quad [3.20]$$

21. Return on equity (ROE):

$$\text{Return on equity} = \frac{\text{Net income}}{\text{Total equity}} \quad [3.21]$$

22. The price/earnings (P/E) ratio:

$$\text{P/E ratio} = \frac{\text{Price per share}}{\text{Earnings per share}} \quad [3.22]$$

23. The market-to-book ratio:

Market-to-book ratio

$$= \frac{\text{Market value per share}}{\text{Book value per share}} \quad [3.23]$$

24. The Du Pont identity:

$$\text{ROE} = \underbrace{\frac{\text{Net income}}{\text{Sales}} \times \frac{\text{Sales}}{\text{Assets}}}_{\text{Return on assets}} \times \frac{\text{Assets}}{\text{Equity}} \quad [3.24]$$

ROE = Profit margin

$\times$ Total asset turnover

$\times$ Equity multiplier

Chapter 4

1. The dividend payout ratio:

Dividend payout ratio = Cash dividends/
Net income $\quad [4.1]$

2. The internal growth rate:

$$\text{Internal growth rate} = \frac{\text{ROA} \times b}{1 - \text{ROA} \times b} \quad [4.2]$$

3. The sustainable growth rate:

$$\text{Sustainable growth rate} = \frac{\text{ROE} \times b}{1 - \text{ROE} \times b} \quad [4.3]$$

4. The capital intensity ratio:

Capital intensity ratio

$$= \frac{\text{Total assets}}{\text{Sales}} = \frac{1}{\text{Total asset turnover}} \quad [4.4]$$

Chapter 5

1. The future value of $1 invested for t periods at a rate of r per period:

Future value $= \$1 \times (1 + r)^t \quad [5.1]$

2. The present value of $1 to be received t periods in the future at a discount rate of r:

$$\text{PV} = \$1 \times [1/(1 + r)^t] = \$1/(1 + r)^t \quad [5.2]$$

3. The relationship between future value and present value (the basic present value equation):

$$\text{PV} \times (1 + r)^t = \text{FV}_t \quad [5.3]$$

$$\text{PV} = \text{FV}_t/(1 + r)^t = \text{FV}_t \times [1/(1 + r)^t]$$

4. The present value of an annuity of C dollars per period for t periods when the rate of return or interest rate is r:

Annuity present value

$$= C \times \left[\frac{1 - \text{Present value factor}}{r} \right] \quad [5.4]$$

$$= C \times \left[\frac{1 - \{1/(1 + r)^t\}}{r} \right]$$

5. The future value factor for an annuity:
Annuity FV factor
$$= \text{(Future value factor} - 1)/r \qquad [5.5]$$
$$= [\{(1 + r)^t\} - 1]/r$$

6. Present value for a perpetuity:
$$\text{PV for a perpetuity} = C/r = C \times (1/r) \qquad [5.6]$$

7. Effective annual rate (EAR), with m the number of times the interest is compounded:
$$\text{EAR} = [1 + \text{(Quoted rate)}/m]^m - 1 \qquad [5.7]$$

8. Effective annual rate (EAR), with q standing for the continuously compounded quoted rate:
$$\text{EAR} = e^q - 1 \qquad [5.8]$$

Chapter 6

1. Bond value if bond has (1) a face value of F paid at maturity, (2) a coupon of C paid per period, (3) t periods to maturity, and (4) a yield of r per period:

Bond value
$$= C \times [1 - 1/(1 + r)^t]/r + F/(1 + r)^t \qquad [6.1]$$

Bond value
$$= \begin{array}{c}\text{Present value} \\ \text{of the coupons}\end{array} + \begin{array}{c}\text{Present value} \\ \text{of the face amount}\end{array}$$

2. The dividend growth model:
$$P_0 = \frac{D_0 \times (1 + g)}{r - g} = \frac{D_1}{r - g} \qquad [6.4]$$

3. Required return:
$$r = D_1/P_0 + g \qquad [6.6]$$

Chapter 7

1. Net present value (NPV):
NPV = Present value of future cash flows − Investment cost

2. Payback period:
Payback period = Number of years that pass before the sum of an investment's cash flows equal the cost of the investment

3. Discounted payback period:
Discounted payback period = Number of years that pass before the sum of an investment's *discounted* cash flows equal the cost of the investment

4. The average accounting return (AAR):
$$\text{AAR} = \frac{\text{Average net income}}{\text{Average book value}}$$

5. Internal rate of return (IRR):
IRR = Discount rate of required return such that the net present value of an investment is zero

6. Profitability index:
$$\text{Profitability index} = \frac{\text{PV of cash flows}}{\text{Cost of investment}}$$

Chapter 8

1. Bottom-up approach to operating cash flow (OCF):
$$\text{OCF} = \text{Net income} + \text{Depreciation} \qquad [8.1]$$

2. Top-down approach to operating cash flow (OCF):
$$\text{OCF} = \text{Sales} - \text{Costs} - \text{Taxes} \qquad [8.2]$$

3. Tax shield approach to operating cash flow (OCF):
$$\text{OCF} = (\text{Sales} - \text{Costs}) \times (1 - T_c) + \text{Depreciation} \times T_c \qquad [8.3]$$

Chapter 9

1. Accounting break-even level:
$$Q = (\text{FC} + D)/(P - v) \qquad [9.1]$$

2. Relationship between operating cash flow and sales volume:
$$Q = (\text{FC} + \text{OCF})/(P - v) \qquad [9.3]$$

3. Cash break-even level:
$$Q = \text{FC}/(P - V)$$

4. Financial break-even level:
$$Q = (\text{FC} + \text{OCF}^*)/(P - V)$$
where
$$\text{OCF}^* = \text{Zero NPV cash flow}$$

5. Degree of operating leverage (DOL):
$$\text{DOL} = 1 + \text{FC}/\text{OCF} \qquad [9.4]$$

Chapter 10

1. Fisher effect:
$$(1 + R) = (1 + r) \times (1 + h) \qquad [10.3]$$

2. Variance of returns, VAR(R), or σ^2:
$$\text{Var}(R) = \frac{1}{T - 1}[(R_1 - \overline{R})^2 + \cdots + (R_T - \overline{R})^2] \qquad [10.6]$$

3. Standard deviation of returns, SD(R) or σ:
$$\text{SD}(R) = \sqrt{\text{Var}(R)}$$

Chapter 11

1. Risk premium:

   Risk premium = Expected return

   $\qquad$ − Risk-free rate [11.1]

2. Expected return:

   $E(R_P) = x_1 \times E(R_1) + x_2 \times E(R_2) + \cdots$

   $\qquad + x_n \times E(R_n)$ [11.2]

3. The reward-to-risk ratio:

   Reward-to-risk ratio $= \dfrac{E(R_i) - R_f}{\beta_i}$

4. The capital asset pricing model (CAPM):

   $E(R_i) = R_f + [E(R_M) - R_f] \times \beta_i$ [11.7]

Chapter 12

1. NPV of a bond refunding:

   $NPV = (c_0 - c_N)/c_N \times \$1,000 - CP$ [12A.1]

Chapter 13

1. Rights offerings:

   a. Numbers of new shares:

   Number of new shares $= \dfrac{\text{Funds to be raised}}{\text{Subscription price}}$

   $\qquad$ [13.1]

   b. Number of rights needed:

   $\dfrac{\text{Number of rights needed}}{\text{to buy a share of stock}} = \dfrac{\text{Old shares}}{\text{New shares}}$

   $\qquad$ [13.2]

   c. Value of a right:

   Value of a right = Rights-on price

   $\qquad$ − Ex-rights price

Chapter 14

1. Required return on equity, R_E (dividend growth model):

   $R_E = D_1/P_0 + g$ [14.1]

2. Required return on equity, R_E (CAPM):

   $R_E = R_f + \beta_E \times (R_M - R_f)$ [14.2]

3. Required return on preferred stock, R_P:

   $R_P = D/P_0$ [14.3]

4. The unadjusted weighted average cost of capital (WACC):

   WACC (unadjusted) $= (E/V) \times R_E$

   $\qquad + (D/V) \times R_D$ [14.6]

5. The weighted average cost of capital (WACC):

   WACC $= (E/V) \times R_E$

   $\qquad + (D/V) \times R_D \times (1 - T_C)$ [14.7]

6. Weighted average flotation cost, f_A:

   $f_A = \dfrac{E}{V} \times f_E + \dfrac{D}{V} \times f_D$ [14.8]

Chapter 15

1. Modigliani-Miller Propositions (no taxes):

   a. Proposition I:

   $V_L = V_U$

   b. Proposition II:

   $R_E = R_A + (R_A - R_D) \times (D/E)$ [15.1]

2. Modigliani-Miller Propositions (with taxes):

   a. Value of the interest tax shield:

   Value of the interest tax shield

   $\qquad = (T_C \times R_D \times D)/R_D$ [15.2]

   $\qquad = T_C \times D$

   b. Proposition I:

   $V_L = V_U + T_C \times D$ [15.3]

   c. Proposition II:

   $R_E = R_U + (R_U - R_D) \times (D/E)$

   $\qquad \times (1 - T_C)$ [15.4]

Chapter 17

1. The operating cycle:

   Operating cycle = Inventory period

   $\qquad$ + Accounts receivable

   $\qquad\qquad$ period [17.4]

2. The cash cycle:

   Cash cycle = Operating cycle

   $\qquad$ − Accounts payable period [17.5]

Chapter 18

1. Float measurement:

   a. Average daily float:

   Average daily float $= \dfrac{\text{Total float}}{\text{Total days}}$ [18.1]

   b. Average daily float:

   Average daily float

   $\qquad$ = Average daily receipts [18.2]

   $\qquad$ × Weighted average delay

2. The Baumol-Allais-Tobin (BAT) model:

   a. Opportunity costs:

   $$\text{Opportunity costs} = (C/2) \times R \qquad [18A.1]$$

   b. Trading costs:

   $$\text{Trading costs} = (T/C) \times F \qquad [18A.2]$$

   c. Total cost:

   $$\begin{aligned}\text{Total cost} &= \text{Opportunity costs} \\ &\quad + \text{Trading costs} \qquad [18A.3] \\ &= (C/2) \times R + (T/C) \times F\end{aligned}$$

   d. The optimal initial cash balance:

   $$C^* = \sqrt{(2T \times F)/R} \qquad [18A.4]$$

3. The Miller-Orr model:

   a. The optimal cash balance:

   $$C^* = L + (3/4 \times F \times \sigma^2/R)^{1/3} \qquad [18A.5]$$

   b. The upper limit:

   $$U^* = 3 \times C^* - 2 \times L \qquad [18A.6]$$

Chapter 19

1. The size of receivables:

   $$\begin{aligned}\text{Accounts receivable} &= \text{Average daily sales} \\ &\quad \times \text{ACP} \qquad [19.1]\end{aligned}$$

2. NPV of switching credit terms:

   a. Present value of switching:

   $$PV = [(P - v)(Q' - Q)]/R \qquad [19.4]$$

   b. Cost of switching:

   $$\begin{aligned}\text{Cost of switching} &= PQ \\ &\quad + v(Q' - Q) \qquad [19.5]\end{aligned}$$

   c. NPV of switching:

   $$\begin{aligned}\text{NPV of switching} &= -[PQ + v(Q' - Q)] \\ &\quad + (P - v) \\ &\quad \times (Q' - Q)/R \qquad [19.6]\end{aligned}$$

3. NPV of granting credit:

   a. With no repeat business:

   $$NPV = -v + (1 - \pi)P/(1 + R) \qquad [19.8]$$

   b. With repeat business:

   $$NPV = -v + (1 - \pi)(P - v)/R \qquad [19.9]$$

4. The economic order quantity (EOQ) model:

   a. Total carrying costs:

   $$\begin{aligned}\text{Total carrying costs} &= \text{Average inventory} \\ &\quad \times \text{Carrying costs} \\ &\quad\quad \text{per unit} \\ &= (Q/2) \times \text{CC} \qquad [19.10]\end{aligned}$$

   b. Total restocking costs:

   $$\begin{aligned}\text{Total restocking costs} \\ = \text{Fixed cost per order} \\ \times \text{Number of orders} = F \times (T/Q) \qquad [19.11]\end{aligned}$$

   c. Total costs:

   $$\begin{aligned}\text{Total costs} &= \text{Carrying costs} \\ &\quad + \text{Restocking costs} \\ &= (Q/2) \times \text{CC} + F \\ &\quad \times (T/Q) \qquad [19.12]\end{aligned}$$

   d. The optimal order size Q^*:

   $$Q^* = \sqrt{\frac{2T \times F}{\text{CC}}} \qquad [19.16]$$

Chapter 20

1. Value of a call option at maturity:

   a. $C_1 = 0 \quad \text{if} \quad (S_1 - E) \le 0 \qquad [20.1]$

   b. $C_1 = S_1 - E \quad \text{if} \quad (S_1 - E) > 0 \qquad [20.2]$

2. Bounds on the value of a call option:

   a. Upper bound:

   $$C_0 \le S_0 \qquad [20.3]$$

   b. Lower bound:

   $$C_0 \ge 0 \quad \text{if} \quad S_0 - E < 0 \qquad [20.4]$$
   $$C_0 \ge S_0 - E \quad \text{if} \quad S_0 - E \ge 0$$

3. Value of a call:

   $$\begin{aligned}\text{Call option value} \\ = \text{Stock value} \\ - \text{Present value of the exercise price} \\ C_0 = S_0 - E/(1 + R_f)^t \qquad [20.6]\end{aligned}$$

4. The Black-Scholes call option formula:

   $$\begin{aligned}C_0 &= S_0 \times N(d_1) - E/(1 + R_f)^t \\ &\quad \times N(d_2) \qquad [20A.1]\end{aligned}$$

   where

   $$\begin{aligned}d_1 &= [\ln(S_0/E) + (R_f + \tfrac{1}{2} \times \sigma^2) \times t]/ \\ &\quad (\sigma \times \sqrt{t}) \qquad [20A.2] \\ d_2 &= d_1 - \sigma \times \sqrt{t}\end{aligned}$$

Chapter 21

1. The NPV of a merger:

   $$\begin{aligned}NPV &= V_B^* - \text{Cost to Firm A of the} \\ &\quad \text{acquisition} \qquad [21.1]\end{aligned}$$

Chapter 22

1. Purchasing power parity (PPP):

$$E(S_t) = S_0 \times [1 + (h_{FC} - h_{US})]^t \qquad [22.3]$$

2. Interest Rate Parity (IRP):

   a. Exact:

$$F_1/S_0 = (1 + R_{FC})/(1 + R_{US}) \qquad [22.4]$$

   b. Approximate:

$$F_t = S_0 \times [1 + (R_{FC} - R_{US})]^t \qquad [22.7]$$

3. Uncovered interest parity (UIP):

$$E(S_t) = S_0 \times [1 + (R_{FC} - R_{US})]^t \qquad [22.9]$$

4. International Fisher effect (IFE):

$$R_{US} - h_{US} = R_{FC} - h_{FC} \qquad [22.10]$$

Answers to Selected End-of-Chapter Problems

Chapter 2

2.1 Net income = $99,000

2.3 Operating cash flow = $1,464

2.5 *a.* Net income (19X3) = $147.84
   b. Operating cash flow (19X2) = $342.9

2.9 Total = $182,000,000

2.11 Average tax
   rate = $217,600/640,000 = 34%

2.13 Addition to NWC = −$35

2.17 Net income (1992) = $225
   Owners' equity (1992) = $5,400

Chapter 3

3.1 *a.* No change (assuming a cash purchase)
   c. Increase
   e. No change

3.3 Debt/equity ratio = ⅔
   Equity multiplier = 1⅔

3.5 Quick ratio = 2.6

3.7 Long-term debt ratio (1992) = .08

3.9 *a.* Current ratio (1991) = .81
   c. NWC/Total assets (1992) = −.045
   e. Long-term debt ratio (1991) = .135

3.11 Days' sales in inventory = 53.52 days

3.13 Inventory turnover = 6.08
   Cost of goods sold = $30,417

3.15 Net *decrease* in cash = $900

3.17 ROE = 20%
   Equity multiplier = 2

3.20 .165 × .39 × 2.93 = .19

3.22 Interval measure = $\frac{1891}{1.92}$ = 984.9 days

3.24 Net income = $50

3.26 ROE = 19.6%

Chapter 4

4.1 Pro forma net income = $125
   Pro forma equity = $312.50
   Dividends (the plug) = $62.50

4.3 EFN = −$200 (a *surplus*)

4.5 EFN = $268.48

4.9 Addition to retained earnings
   (projected) = $605

4.11 EFN = −$255 (a *surplus*)

4.15 EFN = $445

4.17 g^* = 2.04%

4.21 g^* = 3.09%

4.23 p = 15.87%

4.25 $936

4.27 g^* = 1.52%
   New borrowing = $76
   With no outside financing, the maximum
   growth rate would be 1.01%.

Chapter 5

5.1 PV = $211.68
   PV = $484.31
   PV = $5,998.26
   PV = $304,976.65

5.3 5.95%

5.5 FV = $16,357.45

5.7 $40,000 per year: the PV is $67,327.44 (assuming the $40,000 per year is paid out at a rate of $10,000 per quarter)

5.9 APR = 5.91%
APR = 7.77%
APR = 11.33%
APR = 13.10%

5.11 At 10%, B has the higher PV ($253.59 vs. $248.69)
At 25%, A has the higher PV ($195.20 vs. $188.93)

5.13 PV = $43,264.53

5.15 r = 9.596%

5.17 t = 11.05 years
t = 7.48 years
t = 15 years
t = 16 years

5.19 PV = $3,072.28
PV = $4,713.46
PV = $4,957.41
PV = $5,000.00

5.21 r = 24.99%
r = 10.01%
r = 11.02%
r = 6%

5.23 There is an inverse relationship.
PV = $772.17
PV = $614.46
PV = $501.88

5.25 APR = 9.58%
EAR = 10.01%

5.27 In eight years, FV = $23,718.87
In ten years, FV = $29,224.02

5.29 78,588,423% (!)

5.31 EAR = 16.64%
EAR = 17.23%

5.33 PV = $246,978.55

5.35 *a.* Alternative 2 is better ($20,000 versus $10,000)
b. Alternative 2 is better ($12,418.43 vs. $9,090.91)
c. Alternative 1 is better ($8,333.33 vs. $8,037.55)

5.37 PV = $16,834.96

5.39 *a.* PV = $1,201,180.55
b. PV = $1,260,000.00

5.41 The EAR is $1,500/8,500 = 17.65%

5.43 EAR = 12.24%

5.45 APR = 23.56%
EAR = 26.27%

5.47 *a.* $592.33
b. $7,201.76

5.49 The future value of the payments is $297,310.25, which greatly exceeds the policy value.

5.51 PV = $335.65
PV = $289.35

Chapter 6

6.1 Bond price = $814.45

6.3 Bond price = $931.18

6.5 *a.* 12%
b. $779.20
c. $918.89

6.7 *a.* The bond sells for par.
b. The bond sells at a premium.
c. The bond sells at a discount.

6.9 7.435%

6.11 Current yield = 11.76%
Yield to maturity = 12.475% (with annual coupons)

6.13 P_0 = $19.80
P_4 = $26.94

6.15 6%; 8%

6.17 r = 14%

6.19 P_0 = $15.75

6.21 g = 5%

6.23 P_0 = $26.95

6.25 r = 17.1%

6.27 r = 16.17%

6.29 $1 million

Chapter 7

7.1 5 years; 7.5 years; never

7.3 NPV_A = $73.18; NPV_B = $83.96
Investment B is better.

7.5 6 years; 7.31 years; no payback at 20%.

7.7 The NPV is positive.

7.9 IRR = 10%

7.11 IRR_A = 80.19% (and −55.50%)
IRR_B = 52.14%

7.13 IRR_A = 0% (and 100%)
IRR_B = 27.08%

7.15 AAR = −5.16%

7.17 *a.* 3 years; 2.16 years
    b. 3 years
    c. $15.14
7.19 *c.* $IRR_A = 34.4\%$; $IRR_B = 36.3\%$
    d. 22.5% is the crossover rate
7.21 Project A is preferred (at a minimum) for all discount rates between 0% and 20%.
7.23 Payback = $1/IRR$
7.25 Worst case NPV = −$717.75

Chapter 8

8.1 Net income = $18,150
8.3 OCF = $3,436.38
8.5 Net proceeds = $18,393.60
8.7 NPV = $25,589.63
8.11 $440
8.13 IRR = 49.91%
8.15 $EAC_{jazz} = -\$14,979.80$
    $EAC_{disco} = -\$15,212.73$
8.17 No replacement: $NPV_1 = -\$949.74$;
    $NPV_2 = -\$1,053.59$
    With replacement: $EAC_1 = -\$381.90$;
    $EAC_2 = -\$332.38$
8.19 NPV = −$1,222,446
8.21 *a.* Savings = $17,023.86
    b. Savings = $15,222.09

Chapter 9

9.1 *a.* $3.75
    b. $1,370,000
    c. Accounting breakeven = 290,323 pints
9.3 *a.* DOL = 3.5
    c. Best case NPV = $78,036
        Worst case NPV = −$19,355
9.5 DOL = 2.67
9.11 $30.50
9.15 At 2,500 units, OCF = $6,750
     At 1,500 units, OCF = $2,250
9.17 *a.* Best case NPV = $42,476
        Best case NPV = $525,625
        Worst case NPV = −$391,958
    c. 38 units/year
9.19 *a.* NPV = −$13,075
    b. Abandon if Q ≤ 496 units
9.21 Option value = $25,194

Chapter 10

10.1 −20.48%
10.3 48.57%; 5.71%; 42.86%
10.5 15.36%
10.7 *a.* 12.1%
    b. 8.62%
10.9 The probability of a return less than −4% is approximately 1/6. The returns will lie in the range −12.1 to 21.9 about 95% of the time. The returns will lie in the range −20.6 to 30.4 about 99% of the time.
10.11 In the range .5%–2.5%
10.13 Average return on x = 5.4%
    Standard deviation of x = 8.96%

Chapter 11

11.1 15%
11.3 62.5% and 37.5%
11.5 $E(R_A) = 29.2\%$
    $\sigma_A = 13.12\%$
11.7 *a.* $E(R_A) = 8.8\%$
       $\sigma_A = .98\%$
    b. 8.4%
11.9 Yes, the standard deviation could be less, but the beta *cannot* be.
11.17 8.8%; 10.4%
11.19 If the risk-free rate is 6%, they are not correctly priced (Chen is undervalued). They are correctly priced if the risk-free rate is 2%.
11.21 5%; 5%
11.23 17%; 9%

Chapter 12

12.1 Total = $151,500
12.3 Total = $146,500
12.9 $PV_{dead} = \$50$ million
    $PV_{alive} = \$40$ million
    Liquidation is better.
12.11 *a.* Increase
     b. Decrease
     c. Decrease
     d. Probably decrease, but it depends on what the coupon rate is tied to.

Chapter 13

13.3 At $40: no effect
     At $20: new price will be $33.33
     At $10: new price will be $30

13.7 800,000

13.9 BV/share = $125
     MV/share = $31.25
     EPS = $6.25
     NPV = −$37,500

13.11 46.93%

13.13 *a.* Maximum = $25;
           minimum = anything > 0.
      b. 3 ⅓ million shares; 6.6 rights needed
      c. $23.684; $1.316

Chapter 14

14.1 14.38% (CAPM); 15.2% (Dividend growth model)

14.3 12.573%

14.5 WACC = 14.573%

14.9 Both should proceed. The appropriate discount rate does *not* depend on which company is involved; it depends on the risk of the investment. Superior is in the business, so it is closer to a "pure play." The NPV thus appears to be $1 million, regardless of who takes it.

14.11 *a.* 6.56%
      b. 20.65%

14.13 WACC = 18.69%

14.17 WACC = 15.56%

Chapter 15

15.1 *a.* EPS = $12; EPS = $10; EPS = $6
      b. EPS = $15; EPS = $11; EPS = $3

15.3 $50 (capital structure is irrelevant here)

15.9 *a.* 25.5%
      b. 31%
      c. 20%

15.11 $4,714.29; $5,394.29

15.13 $625,000

Chapter 16

16.1 *a.*

Common stock	$ 55
Capital surplus	745
Retained earnings	4,750
	$5,550

16.3 The ex-dividend date is Thursday, June 29 (because July 4 is a holiday!).

16.7 $1.58 per share

16.9 Price per share = $11.07
      To create an equal dividend each year, sell 52.87 shares in one year.

16.11 *a.* $20 million
      b. $4 per share
      c. $6 million
      d. $10 per share, no new borrowing

16.21 *a.* 35.7%
      b. $18.5 million
      c. 3.11

16.23 *a.* Price per share = $50 with dividend
                            = $100 with repurchase
           Shareholder wealth is not affected.
      b. With dividend: EPS = 5; P/E = 10
           With repurchase: EPS = 10; P/E = 10

Chapter 17

17.1 Cash = $250; Current assets = $1,500

17.7 Operating cycle: 84 days
      Cash cycle: −51 days

17.9 *a.*

Q1	Q2	Q3	Q4
$198.00	$157.80	$174.00	$248.40

17.11 *a.* 13.21%
      b. $3.21 million

17.17 Ending cash balance (June): $354,600

Chapter 18

18.3 Average daily float = $4,666.67

18.4 *a.*

Disbursement float:	$60,000
Collection float:	−$45,000
Net float:	$15,000

18.5 *a.* Total float = $36,000
      b. Average daily float = $1,200
      c. Average daily receipts = $233.33
           Weighted average delay = 5.14 days

18.7 *a.* $68,000
      b. 3.78 days; $68,000 ≈ 3.78 × $18,000
      c. $68,000
      d. $14.34
      e. Up to $36,000

18.9 *a.* $300,000
      b. $50,000
      c. $15/day; $.15/check

18.11 34/day

18.13 $6,240 (ignoring compounding)

Chapter 19

19.3   *a.*   120 days; $2,000
     b.   2%; 30 days; $1,960
     c. $40; 90 days

19.10 $7,397,260

19.11 *a.*   ACP = 30 days
     b.   Average balance = $280,000

19.13 EAR = 44.59%

19.16 *a.*   NPV = $63.41
     b.   Breakeven probability = 31.67%
     c.   NPV = $34 per unit
        Breakeven probability = 95%

19.19 $1,232,877

19.23 Carrying cost = $500
     Restocking cost = $62,400
     EOQ = 1,117.14 pots
     Orders per year = 4.65

19.24 NPV = $3.56 million

Chapter 20

20.7   *a.* $14,375
     b. $50,000
     c. $74,000; $15,000
     d. $1,000; $16,000; $74

20.11 *a.* $9.48
     b. $18.74
     c. $0

20.13 *a.* $13.60
     b. $6.69

20.15 *a.* $337.04
     b. $462.96; 8%

20.17 *a.* $0
     b.   Relative to the possible prices, the current stock price is too low; the *minimum* possible return is 10%. This exceeds the risk-free rate.

20.19 *a.* $1,040

20.21 *a.*   50; $20; 25%
     b. $797.88; $800
     c. $15.96
     d.   Market − Floor = $40
        Market − Straight bond = $42.12

20.23 $8.83

20.25 *a.* $96.67; $166.67
     c. $66.67

Chapter 21

21.1 $2 million

21.5   *a.* $9.09
     b. $181.82
     c.   P/E = 17.6

21.13 *a.*   New EPS = $2.50 versus $2.25 and $2.00.
     b.   Probably no effect.

Chapter 22

22.1   *a.*   306,101
     b.   .03267 cents
     c. $326.69
     d.   Italian lira
     e.   Singapore dollar
     f.   .1654; the cross rate

22.3   *a.*   ¥ 128.13; discount
     b.   SF .6945; discount
     c.   It will probably fall

22.11 Breakeven exchange rate; 80 pesetas = $1

22.13 *b.*   Can$ 1.105

22.15 Dr 224 in one year
     Dr 250.88 in two years
     UIP is the relationship.

Chapter 23

23.7   NAL = $6,264.28

23.9 $162,694.10

23.11 $162,694.10 to $163,037.23

23.13 NAL = $69.66; Year 0 cashflow is $24,000 − $6,961 × (1 − .34), which is the net savings in terms of initial cashflows.

Chapter 24

24.3   Loss = $760

24.4   Pay 2.70 cents per pound
     Gain $5,000 per contract
     Net gain = $4,325 per contract

24.9   Price $20.29 per barrel
     Buy 20 contracts. Zero initial investment.

24.11 Per barrel:

| | Gain | |
Price	Call	Put
$10	$ 0	−$10
$15	$ 0	−$ 5
$20	$ 0	$ 0
$25	$ 5	$ 0
$30	$10	$ 0

Name Index

Equation Index

Key Term Index

Subject Index

Functional Use of Color in the Second Edition

Throughout the second edition of *Fundamentals of Corporate Finance,* we make color a functional dimension of the discussion. In almost every chapter, color plays an extensive, nonschematic, and largely self-evident role. Color in these chapters alerts students to the relationship between the numbers in a discussion and an accompanying table or figure.

In several of the chapters, wherever appropriate, color is used *schematically,* to distinguish between items. For example, in Chapters 3 and 4, the colors green and blue represent the **income statement** and **balance sheet,** respectively. As the discussion progresses, numbers corresponding to each financial statement are highlighted in these same colors, helping students readily identify the origin of each. Below we list the chapters in which color is used schematically and briefly explain the underlying rationale.

In Section 2.4 of Chapter 2, green identifies **cash flow** numbers. This scheme is integrated throughout the two continuous examples in Chapter 2, Dole Cola and U.S. Corp.

In Chapters 3 and 4, blue indicates **balance sheet** numbers and green indicates **income statement** numbers. This scheme originates in the financial statement tables and is integrated throughout the accompanying text discussion. Note also that this same schematic use of color is followed in the presentation of all 23 ratios in Chapter 3.

In Section 6.1 of Chapter 6, green is used to identify the key numbers that combine to determine the value of a bond. The result, the **bond value,** is shown in blue.

In Section 7.5 in Chapter 7, green and blue represent two mutually exclusive investments—**Project A** and **Project B,** respectively.

In Section 10.5 of Chapter 10, green, blue, and brown indicate the three normal distribution ranges illustrated in Figure 10.11. These same colors are integrated into the accompanying text discussion to quickly illustrate from which range each number has been derived.

In Sections 11.1 and 11.2 of Chapter 11, green and blue represent **Stock L** and **Stock U.** This scheme is carried out in the tables and text discussion and culminates in the presentation of an equally weighted portfolio composed of these two stocks. Later, in Section 11.7, blue and green distinguish between **Asset A** and **Asset B** in the discussion of portfolio expected returns and betas.

In Section 12.3 in Chapter 12, green represents **implicit interest expense** and blue represents **straight-line interest expense** in both Table 12.1 and the accompanying text discussion.